Handbook of Research on Innovative Database Query Processing Techniques

Li Yan
Nanjing University of Aeronautics and Astronautics, China

A volume in the Advances in Data Mining and
Database Management (ADMDM) Book Series

Managing Director:	Lindsay Johnston
Managing Editor:	Keith Greenberg
Director of Intellectual Property & Contracts:	Jan Travers
Acquisitions Editor:	Kayla Wolfe
Production Editor:	Christina Henning
Development Editor:	Courtney Tychinski
Cover Design:	Jason Mull

Published in the United States of America by
Information Science Reference (an imprint of IGI Global)
701 E. Chocolate Avenue
Hershey PA, USA 17033
Tel: 717-533-8845
Fax: 717-533-8661
E-mail: cust@igi-global.com
Web site: http://www.igi-global.com

Library of Congress Cataloging-in-Publication Data

Handbook of research on innovative database query processing techniques / Li Yan, editor.
    pages cm
  Includes bibliographical references and index.
  ISBN 978-1-4666-8767-7 (hardcover) -- ISBN 978-1-4666-8768-4 (ebook) 1. Querying (Computer science)--Handbooks, manuals, etc. I. Yan, Li, 1964-
  QA76.9.D3H347328 2015
  005.74'1--dc23
                          2015019728

This book is published in the IGI Global book series Advances in Data Mining and Database Management (ADMDM) (ISSN: 2327-1981; eISSN: 2327-199X)

British Cataloguing in Publication Data
A Cataloguing in Publication record for this book is available from the British Library.

All work contributed to this book is new, previously-unpublished material. The views expressed in this book are those of the authors, but not necessarily of the publisher.

For electronic access to this publication, please contact: eresources@igi-global.com.

Advances in Data Mining and Database Management (ADMDM) Book Series

David Taniar
Monash University, Australia

ISSN: 2327-1981
EISSN: 2327-199X

MISSION

With the large amounts of information available to organizations in today's digital world, there is a need for continual research surrounding emerging methods and tools for collecting, analyzing, and storing data.

The **Advances in Data Mining & Database Management (ADMDM)** series aims to bring together research in information retrieval, data analysis, data warehousing, and related areas in order to become an ideal resource for those working and studying in these fields. IT professionals, software engineers, academicians and upper-level students will find titles within the ADMDM book series particularly useful for staying up-to-date on emerging research, theories, and applications in the fields of data mining and database management.

COVERAGE

- Predictive analysis
- Heterogeneous and Distributed Databases
- Profiling Practices
- Web-based information systems
- Database Security
- Enterprise systems
- Data Mining
- Association Rule Learning
- Neural Networks
- Decision Support Systems

IGI Global is currently accepting manuscripts for publication within this series. To submit a proposal for a volume in this series, please contact our Acquisition Editors at Acquisitions@igi-global.com or visit: http://www.igi-global.com/publish/.

Titles in this Series

For a list of additional titles in this series, please visit: www.igi-global.com

Handbook of Research on Trends and Future Directions in Big Data and Web Intelligence
Noor Zaman (King Faisal University, Saudi Arabia) Mohamed Elhassan Seliaman (King Faisal University, Saudi Arabia) Mohd Fadzil Hassan (Universiti Teknologi PETRONAS, Malaysia) and Fausto Pedro Garcia Marquez (Campus Universitario s/n ETSII of Ciudad Real, Spain)
Information Science Reference • copyright 2015 • 447pp • H/C (ISBN: 9781466685055) • US $285.00 (our price)

Improving Knowledge Discovery through the Integration of Data Mining Techniques
Muhammad Usman (Shaheed Zulfikar Ali Bhutto Institute of Science and Technology, Pakistan)
Information Science Reference • copyright 2015 • 392pp • H/C (ISBN: 9781466685130) • US $225.00 (our price)

Modern Computational Models of Semantic Discovery in Natural Language
Jan Žižka (Mendel University in Brno, Czech Republic) and František Dařena (Mendel University in Brno, Czech Republic)
Information Science Reference • copyright 2015 • 335pp • H/C (ISBN: 9781466686908) • US $215.00 (our price)

Mobile Technologies for Activity-Travel Data Collection and Analysis
Soora Rasouli (Eindhoven University of Technology, The Netherlands) and Harry Timmermans (Eindhoven University of Technology, The Netherlands)
Information Science Reference • copyright 2014 • 325pp • H/C (ISBN: 9781466661707) • US $225.00 (our price)

Biologically-Inspired Techniques for Knowledge Discovery and Data Mining
Shafiq Alam (University of Auckland, New Zealand) Gillian Dobbie (University of Auckland, New Zealand) Yun Sing Koh (University of Auckland, New Zealand) and Saeed ur Rehman (Unitec Institute of Technology, New Zealand)
Information Science Reference • copyright 2014 • 375pp • H/C (ISBN: 9781466660786) • US $265.00 (our price)

Data Mining and Analysis in the Engineering Field
Vishal Bhatnagar (Ambedkar Institute of Advanced Communication Technologies and Research, India)
Information Science Reference • copyright 2014 • 405pp • H/C (ISBN: 9781466660861) • US $225.00 (our price)

Handbook of Research on Cloud Infrastructures for Big Data Analytics
Pethuru Raj (IBM India Pvt Ltd, India) and Ganesh Chandra Deka (Ministry of Labour and Employment, India)
Information Science Reference • copyright 2014 • 570pp • H/C (ISBN: 9781466658646) • US $345.00 (our price)

www.igi-global.com

701 E. Chocolate Ave., Hershey, PA 17033
Order online at www.igi-global.com or call 717-533-8845 x100
To place a standing order for titles released in this series, contact: cust@igi-global.com
Mon-Fri 8:00 am - 5:00 pm (est) or fax 24 hours a day 717-533-8661

List of Contributors

Arcaini, Paolo / *Charles University in Prague, Czech Republic* 224
Badia, Antonio / *University of Louisville, USA* 25
Bai, Luyi / *Northeastern University, China* 275
Bi, Chongchun / *Liaoning Technical University, China* 1
Bordogna, Gloria / *CNR IREA, Italy* 224
Carrasquel, Soraya O. / *Universidad Simón Bolívar, Venezuela* 88
Chelmis, Charalampos / *University of Southern California, USA* 364
Cheng, Haitao / *Northeastern University, China* 479
Cheng, Jingwei / *Northeastern University, China* 439,460
Di Bartolo, Fabiola / *Universidad Simón Bolívar, Venezuela* 294
Gobbi, Alberto / *Universidad Simón Bolívar, Venezuela* 325
Goncalves, Marlene / *Universidad Simón Bolívar, Venezuela* 49,294,325
Holanda, Maristela / *University of Brasilia, Brazil* 415
Labbad, José Ángel / *Universidad Simón Bolívar, Venezuela* 158
Ma, Z. M. / *Northeastern University, China* 129,439,460,479
Meng, Xiangfu / *Liaoning Technical University, China* 1
Monascal, Ricardo R. / *Universidad Simón Bolívar, Venezuela* 88,158
Naidenova, Xenia / *Military Medical Academy, Russia* 522
Prasanna, Viktor K. / *University of Southern California, USA* 364
Reggio, Fabiana / *Universidad Simón Bolívar, Venezuela* 49
Rodríguez, Rosseline / *Universidad Simón Bolívar, Venezuela* 88
Sajja, Priti Srinivas / *Sardar Patel University, India* 500
Souza, Jane Adriana / *University of Brasilia, Brazil* 415
Sterlacchini, Simone / *CNR IDPA, Italy* 224
Tineo, Leonid / *Universidad Simón Bolívar, Venezuela* 88,158
Tong, Qiang / *Northeastern University, China* 460
Varela, Krisvely / *Universidad Simón Bolívar, Venezuela* 49
Vieira, Marcos R. / *IBM Research, Brazil* 250
Wang, Hairong / *Beifang University of Nationality, China* 439
Xu, Changming / *Northeastern University, China* 275
Yan, Li / *Nanjing University of Aeronautics and Astronautics, China* 129
Yan, Wei / *Liaoning University, China* 199,392
Zhang, Fu / *Northeastern University, China* 479
Zhang, Xiaoyan / *Liaoning Technical University, China* 1
Zois, Vasileios / *University of Southern California, USA* 364
Zviedris, Martins / *Institute of Mathematics and Computer Science, Latvia* 543

Table of Contents

Preface xix

Acknowledgment xxv

Section 1

Chapter 1
Top-k Relevant Term Suggestion Approach for Relational Keyword Search 1
    Xiangfu Meng, Liaoning Technical University, China
    Xiaoyan Zhang, Liaoning Technical University, China
    Chongchun Bi, Liaoning Technical University, China

Chapter 2
Set-Oriented Queries in SQL 25
    Antonio Badia, University of Louisville, USA

Chapter 3
Evaluating Top-k Skyline Queries on R-Trees 49
    Marlene Goncalves, Universidad Simón Bolívar, Venezuela
    Fabiana Reggio, Universidad Simón Bolívar, Venezuela
    Krisvely Varela, Universidad Simón Bolívar, Venezuela

Chapter 4
Processing of Queries with Fuzzy Similarity Domains 88
    Soraya O. Carrasquel, Universidad Simón Bolívar, Venezuela
    Ricardo R. Monascal, Universidad Simón Bolívar, Venezuela
    Rosseline Rodríguez, Universidad Simón Bolívar, Venezuela
    Leonid Tineo, Universidad Simón Bolívar, Venezuela

Chapter 5
Modeling and Querying Fuzzy Data: Current Approaches and Future Trends 129
    Li Yan, Nanjing University of Aeronautics and Astronautics, China
    Z. M. Ma, Northeastern University, China

Chapter 6

Fuzzy XQuery: A Real Implementation 158

    José Ángel Labbad, Universidad Simón Bolívar, Venezuela
    Ricardo R. Monascal, Universidad Simón Bolívar, Venezuela
    Leonid Tineo, Universidad Simón Bolívar, Venezuela

Chapter 7

Probabilistic Ranking Method of XML Fuzzy Query Results.. 199

    Wei Yan, Liaoning University, China

Section 2

Chapter 8

User Driven Query Framework of Social Networks for Geo-Temporal Analysis of Events of
Interest.. 224

    Gloria Bordogna, CNR IREA, Italy
    Simone Sterlacchini, CNR IDPA, Italy
    Paolo Arcaini, Charles University in Prague, Czech Republic

Chapter 9

Complex Motion Pattern Queries in Spatio-Temporal Databases 250

    Marcos R. Vieira, IBM Research, Brazil

Chapter 10

Spatiotemporal Query Algebra Based on Native XML 275

    Luyi Bai, Northeastern University, China
    Changming Xu, Northeastern University, China

Chapter 11

C2S: A Spatial Skyline Algorithm for Changing Data... 294

    Marlene Goncalves, Universidad Simón Bolívar, Venezuela
    Fabiola Di Bartolo, Universidad Simón Bolívar, Venezuela

Chapter 12

Supporting Position Change through On-Line Location-Based Skyline Queries 325

    Marlene Goncalves, Universidad Simón Bolívar, Venezuela
    Alberto Gobbi, Universidad Simón Bolívar, Venezuela

Section 3

Chapter 13

Querying of Time Series for Big Data Analytics.. 364

    Vasileios Zois, University of Southern California, USA
    Charalampos Chelmis, University of Southern California, USA
    Viktor K. Prasanna, University of Southern California, USA

Chapter 14

Parallel kNN Queries for Big Data Based on Voronoi Diagram Using MapReduce.........................392
  Wei Yan, Liaoning University, China

Chapter 15

Query Languages in NoSQL Databases 415
  Maristela Holanda, University of Brasilia, Brazil
  Jane Adriana Souza, University of Brasilia, Brazil

Section 4

Chapter 16

Fuzzy Querying of RDF with Bipolar Preference Conditions...439
  Hairong Wang, Beifang University of Nationality, China
  Jingwei Cheng, Northeastern University, China
  Z. M. Ma, Northeastern University, China

Chapter 17

RDF Storage and Querying: A Literature Review 460
  Jingwei Cheng, Northeastern University, China
  Z. M. Ma, Northeastern University, China
  Qiang Tong, Northeastern University, China

Chapter 18

A Review of Answering Queries over Ontologies Based on Databases..479
  Fu Zhang, Northeastern University, China
  Z. M. Ma, Northeastern University, China
  Haitao Cheng, Northeastern University, China

Section 5

Chapter 19

Application of Fuzzy User's Profile for Mining Reusable E-Learning Repositories on Web
through Lightweight Mobile Agent 500
  Priti Srinivas Sajja, Sardar Patel University, India

Chapter 20

Adding Context into Classification Reasoning Based on Good Classification Tests 522
  Xenia Naidenova, Military Medical Academy, Russia

Chapter 21
Readable Diagrammatic Query Language ViziQuer 543
    Martins Zviedris, Institute of Mathematics and Computer Science, Latvia

Compilation of References 563

About the Contributors 615

Index 622

Detailed Table of Contents

Preface xix

Acknowledgment xxv

Section 1

Chapter 1

Top-k Relevant Term Suggestion Approach for Relational Keyword Search 1

Xiangfu Meng, Liaoning Technical University, China
Xiaoyan Zhang, Liaoning Technical University, China
Chongchun Bi, Liaoning Technical University, China

This chapter proposes a novel approach, which can provide a list of keywords that both semantically related to the application domain and the given keywords by analyzing the correlations between query keywords and database terms. The database term is first modeled as <attribute, keyword> and suppose each query keyword can map into a database term. Then, a coupling relationship measuring method is proposed to measure both term intra- and inter-couplings, which can reflect the explicit and implicit relationships between terms in the database. Based on the coupling relationships between terms, for a given keyword query, an order of all terms in database is created for each query keyword and then the threshold algorithm (TA) is leveraged to expeditiously generate top-k ranked semantically related terms. The experiments demonstrate that our term coupling relationship measuring method can efficiently capture the semantic correlations between query keywords and terms in database.

Chapter 2

Set-Oriented Queries in SQL 25

Antonio Badia, University of Louisville, USA

Set-oriented queries are those that require a condition to hold of an arbitrary set of rows, either when comparing the set to a single row or to another set of rows. Examples of such queries are universally quantified queries and skyline queries. These queries, while important for data processing, are difficult to write and difficult to process. In this chapter we review research dealing with the specification and optimization of such queries. We present several approaches proposed to deal with universal quantification as well as with set predicates in general.

Chapter 3
Evaluating Top-k Skyline Queries on R-Trees..49
Marlene Goncalves, Universidad Simón Bolívar, Venezuela

Fabiana Reggio, Universidad Simón Bolívar, Venezuela

Krisvely Varela, Universidad Simón Bolívar, Venezuela

The Skyline queries retrieve a set of data whose elements are incomparable in terms of multiple user-defined criteria. In addition, Top-k Skyline queries filter the best k Skyline points where k is the number of answers desired by the user. Several index-based algorithms have been proposed for the evaluation of Top-k Skyline queries. These algorithms make use of indexes defined on a single attribute and they require an index for each user-defined criterion. In traditional databases, the use of multidimensional indices has shown that may improve the performance of database queries. In this chapter, three pruning criteria were defined and several algorithms were developed to evaluate Top-k Skyline queries. The proposed algorithms are based on a multidimensional index, pruning criteria and the strategies Depth First Search and Breadth First Search. Finally, an experimental study was conducted in this chapter to analyze the performance and answer quality of the proposed algorithms.

Chapter 4
Processing of Queries with Fuzzy Similarity Domains...88
Soraya O. Carrasquel, Universidad Simón Bolívar, Venezuela

Ricardo R. Monascal, Universidad Simón Bolívar, Venezuela

Rosseline Rodríguez, Universidad Simón Bolívar, Venezuela

Leonid Tineo, Universidad Simón Bolívar, Venezuela

There are some data models and query languages based on the application of fuzzy set theory. Their goal is to provide more flexible DBMS that allow the expression of user preferences in querying as well as imprecision in data. In this sense, the FuzzyEER data model proposes four kinds of fuzzy attributes. One of them, named Type 3, consists of a set of labels provided of a similarity relation. An extension of SQL, named FSQL, allows the expression and use of fuzzy attributes. Nevertheless, FSQL does not allow using fuzzy attributes in some clauses based on data ordering, due to semantics problem. This chapter presents a solution for this problem in case of Type 3 fuzzy attributes. Main contribution consists in how to process queries involving such attributes by means of an extension to an existing RDBMS. Formal semantics, grammar, catalogue definition and translation schemas are contained in this chapter.

Chapter 5
Modeling and Querying Fuzzy Data: Current Approaches and Future Trends...................................129
Li Yan, Nanjing University of Aeronautics and Astronautics, China

Z. M. Ma, Northeastern University, China

Imperfect information extensively exists in data and knowledge intensive applications, where fuzzy data play an import role in nature. Fuzzy set theory has been extensively applied to extend various database models and resulted in numerous contributions. The chapter concentrates on two main issues in fuzzy data management: fuzzy data models and fuzzy data querying based on the fuzzy data models. A full up-to-date overview of the current state of the art in fuzzy data modeling and querying is provided in the chapter. In addition, the relationships among various fuzzy data models are discussed in the chapter. The chapter serves as identifying possible research opportunities in the area of fuzzy data management in addition to providing a generic overview of the approaches to modeling and querying fuzzy data.

Chapter 6
Fuzzy XQuery: A Real Implementation 158
    José Ángel Labbad, Universidad Simón Bolívar, Venezuela
    Ricardo R. Monascal, Universidad Simón Bolívar, Venezuela
    Leonid Tineo, Universidad Simón Bolívar, Venezuela

Traditional database systems and languages are very rigid. XML data and query languages are not the exception. Fuzzy set theory is an appropriate tool for solving this problem. In this sense, Fuzzy XQuery was proposed as an extension of the XQUERY standard. This language defines the xs:truth datatype, the xml:truth attribute and allows the definition and use of fuzzy terms in queries. The main goal of this chapter is to show a high coupling implementation of Fuzzy XQuery within eXist-db, an open source XML DBMS. This extension strategy could also be used with other similar tools. This chapter also presents a statistical performance analysis of the extended fuzzy query engine using the XMark benchmark with user defined fuzzy terms. The study presents promising results.

Chapter 7
Probabilistic Ranking Method of XML Fuzzy Query Results.. 199
    Wei Yan, Liaoning University, China

Fuzzy query processing for XML database systems is an important issue. Based on the fuzzy set theory, XML fuzzy query can be expressed exploiting fuzzy predicates. To deal with the ranking problem of XML fuzzy query results, this chapter proposes a novel ranking approach. Firstly, according to the workload of XML documents, this chapter speculates how much the users care about each attribute node and assign a corresponding weight to it. Then, a membership degree ranking method, which ranks the fuzzy query results according to corresponding membership degree, is presented. Furthermore, this chapter proposes the probabilistic ranking method, which improves the PIR method. The improved probabilistic ranking method considers the relevance between the nodes specified by fuzzy query and the nodes unspecified by fuzzy query. Finally, top-k ranking algorithm of XML fuzzy query results is presented. The efficiency and effectiveness of the approach are also demonstrated by experimental results.

Section 2

Chapter 8
User Driven Query Framework of Social Networks for Geo-Temporal Analysis of Events of
Interest.. 224
    Gloria Bordogna, CNR IREA, Italy
    Simone Sterlacchini, CNR IDPA, Italy
    Paolo Arcaini, Charles University in Prague, Czech Republic

In this chapter we propose a framework for collecting, organizing into a database and querying information in social networks by the specification of content-based, geographic and temporal conditions to the aim of detecting periodic and aperiodic events. Our proposal could be a basis for developing context aware services. For example to identify the streets and their rush hours by analyzing the messages in social media periodically sent by queuing drivers and to report these critical spatio-temporal situations to help other drivers to plan alternative routes. Specifically, we rely on a focused crawler to periodically collect messages in social networks related with the contents of interest, and on an original geo-temporal clustering algorithm in order to explore the geo-temporal distribution of the messages. The clustering algorithm can be customized so as to identify aperiodic and periodic events at global or local scale based on the specification of geographic and temporal query conditions.

Chapter 9

Complex Motion Pattern Queries in Spatio-Temporal Databases 250
Marcos R. Vieira, IBM Research, Brazil

With the recent advancements and wide usage of location detection devices, very large quantities of data are collected by GPS and cellular technologies in the form of trajectories. The wide and increasing availability of such collected data has led to research advances in behavioral aspects of the monitored subjects (e.g., wild animals, people, and vehicles). Using trajectory data harvested by mobile devices, trajectories can be explored using motion pattern queries based on specific events of interest. While most research works on trajectory-based queries has focused on traditional range, nearest-neighbor, and similarity and join queries, there has been an increasing need to query trajectories using complex, yet more intuitive, motion patterns. In this chapter, we describe in detail complex motion pattern queries, which allow users to focus on trajectories that follow a specific sequence of spatio-temporal events. We demonstrate how these motion pattern queries can greatly help users to get insights from very large trajectory datasets.

Chapter 10

Spatiotemporal Query Algebra Based on Native XML 275
Luyi Bai, Northeastern University, China
Changming Xu, Northeastern University, China

A formal algebra is essential for applying standard database-style query optimization to XML queries. We propose a spatiotemporal XML data model and develop such an algebra based on Native XML, for manipulating spatiotemporal XML data. After studying NXD spatiotemporal database and query framework, formal representation of spatiotemporal query algebra is investigated, containing logical structure of spatiotemporal database, data type system, and querying operations. It shows that the model and algebra lay a firm foundation for managing spatiotemporal XML data.

Chapter 11

C2S: A Spatial Skyline Algorithm for Changing Data 294
Marlene Goncalves, Universidad Simón Bolívar, Venezuela
Fabiola Di Bartolo, Universidad Simón Bolívar, Venezuela

Skyline queries may be used to filter interesting data from a broad range of data. A Skyline query selects those data that are the best according to multiple user-defined criteria. A special case of Skyline queries are the Spatial Skyline Queries (SSQ). SSQ allow users to express preferences on the closeness between a set of data points and a set of query points. We study the problem of answering SSQ in presence of changing data, i.e., data whose values regularly change over a period of time. In this chapter, it is proposed an algorithm to evaluate SSQ on changing data. The proposed algorithm is able to avoid recomputation of the whole Skyline with each update on the data. Also, the performance of the proposed algorithm against state-of-the-art algorithms was empirically studied. The experimental study shows that the proposed algorithm may become 3 times faster than state-of-the-art algorithms.

Chapter 12
Supporting Position Change through On-Line Location-Based Skyline Queries 325
Marlene Goncalves, Universidad Simón Bolívar, Venezuela
Alberto Gobbi, Universidad Simón Bolívar, Venezuela

Location-based Skyline queries select the nearest objects to a point that best meet the user's preferences. Particularly, this chapter focuses on location-based Skyline queries over web-accessible data. Web-accessible may have geographical location and be geotagged with documents containing ratings by web users. Location-based Skyline queries may express preferences based on dynamic features such as distance and changeable ratings. In this context, distance must be recalculated when a user changes his position while the ratings must be extracted from external data sources which are updated each time a user scores an item in the Web. This chapter describes and empirically studies four solutions capable of answering location-based Skyline queries considering user's position change and information extraction from the Web inside an area search around the user. They are based on an M-Tree index and Divide & Conquer principle.

Section 3

Chapter 13
Querying of Time Series for Big Data Analytics... 364
Vasileios Zois, University of Southern California, USA
Charalampos Chelmis, University of Southern California, USA
Viktor K. Prasanna, University of Southern California, USA

Time series data emerge naturally in many fields of applied sciences and engineering including but not limited to statistics, signal processing, mathematical finance, weather and power consumption forecasting. Although time series data have been well studied in the past, they still present a challenge to the scientific community. Advanced operations such as classification, segmentation, prediction, anomaly detection and motif discovery are very useful especially for machine learning as well as other scientific fields. The advent of Big Data in almost every scientific domain motivates us to provide an in-depth study of the state of the art approaches associated with techniques for efficient querying of time series. This chapters aims at providing a comprehensive review of the existing solutions related to time series representation, processing, indexing and querying operations.

Chapter 14
Parallel kNN Queries for Big Data Based on Voronoi Diagram Using MapReduce.......................... 392
Wei Yan, Liaoning University, China

In cloud computing environments parallel kNN queries for big data is an important issue. The k nearest neighbor queries (kNN queries), designed to find k nearest neighbors from a dataset S for every object in another dataset R, is a primitive operator widely adopted by many applications including knowledge discovery, data mining, and spatial databases. This chapter proposes a parallel method of kNN queries for big data using MapReduce programming model. Firstly, this chapter proposes an approximate algorithm that is based on mapping multi-dimensional data sets into two-dimensional data sets, and transforming kNN queries into a sequence of two-dimensional point searches. Then, in two-dimensional space this chapter proposes a partitioning method using Voronoi diagram, which incorporates the Voronoi diagram into R-tree. Furthermore, this chapter proposes an efficient algorithm for processing kNN queries based on R-tree using MapReduce programming model. Finally, this chapter presents the results of extensive experimental evaluations which indicate efficiency of the proposed approach.

Chapter 15
Query Languages in NoSQL Databases 415
    Maristela Holanda, University of Brasilia, Brazil
    Jane Adriana Souza, University of Brasilia, Brazil

This chapter aims to investigate how NoSQL (Not Only SQL) databases provide query language and data retrieval mechanisms. Users attest to many advantages in using the NoSQL databases for specific applications, however, they also report that querying and retrieving data easily continues to be a problem. The NoSQL operations require that, during the project, the queries must be thought of as built-in application codes. The authors intend to contribute to the investigation of querying, considering different types of NoSQL databases.

Section 4

Chapter 16
Fuzzy Querying of RDF with Bipolar Preference Conditions 439
    Hairong Wang, Beifang University of Nationality, China
    Jingwei Cheng, Northeastern University, China
    Z. M. Ma, Northeastern University, China

To solve the problem of information bipolarity in fuzzy querying of RDF, we propose an approach of RDF fuzzy query with bipolar preference. We use linguistic variables to describe preference conditions, and realize an extended SPARQL syntax by adding bipolar preference conditions to FILTER clauses. We identify three types of bipolar information, dividing the bipolar preference query into univariate bipolarity and bivariate bipolarity, and provide a method for converting fuzzy SPARQL queries to standard SPARQL queries. For optimizing results, we use bipolar preference satisfaction degrees to calculate priority parameters of results for sequencing. Finally, the feasibility of the proposed approach is proved by the experimental system and results.

Chapter 17
RDF Storage and Querying: A Literature Review 460
    Jingwei Cheng, Northeastern University, China
    Z. M. Ma, Northeastern University, China
    Qiang Tong, Northeastern University, China

RDF plays an important role in representing Web resources in a natural and flexible way. As the amount of RDF datasets increasingly growing, storing and querying theses data have attracted the attention of more and more researchers. In this chapter, we first make a review of approaches for query processing of RDF datasets. We categorize existing methods as two classes, those making use of RDBMS to implement the storage and retrieval, and those devising their own native storage schemas. They are called Relational RDF Stores and Native Stores respectively. Secondly, we survey some important extensions of SPARQL, standard query language for RDF, which extend the expressing power of SPARQL to allow more sophisticated language constructs that meet the needs from various application scenarios.

Chapter 18

A Review of Answering Queries over Ontologies Based on Databases... 479
Fu Zhang, Northeastern University, China
Z. M. Ma, Northeastern University, China
Haitao Cheng, Northeastern University, China

Ontologies, as a standard (W3C recommendation) for representing knowledge in the Semantic Web, have been employed in many application domains. Currently, real ontologies tend to become very large to huge. Thus, one problem is considered that has arisen from practical needs: namely, efficient querying of ontologies. To this end, there are today many proposals for answering queries over ontologies, and until now the literature on querying of ontologies has been flourishing. In particular, on the basis of the efficient and mature techniques of databases, which are useful for querying ontologies. To investigate querying of ontologies and more importantly identifying the direction of querying of ontologies based on databases, in this chapter, we aim at providing a brief review of answering queries over ontologies based on databases. Some query techniques, their classifications and the directions for future research, are introduced. Other query formalisms over ontologies that are not related to databases are not covered here.

Section 5

Chapter 19

Application of Fuzzy User's Profile for Mining Reusable E-Learning Repositories on Web through Lightweight Mobile Agent 500
Priti Srinivas Sajja, Sardar Patel University, India

The creditability of an e-Learning system depends on its content, services and presentation of the material to the learners. Besides providing material on demand, an e-Learning system also manages knowledge for future use. It is observed that the learning material available on different locations may be reused in a proper way. The work presented here discusses generic design of an e-Learning system with various reusable learning material repositories. The architecture described here uses light weight mobile agents in order to access these repositories by taking help of fuzzy user profile. With notion of the fuzzy user profile, the system knows more about users' need and can present customized content to the users. Besides the architecture of the e-Learning system, the chapter also discusses the necessary concepts about the fuzzy logic and agent based systems, in depth literature survey, structure of the user profile, fuzzy membership function and design of the light weight mobile agent with necessary implementation details. At the end, the chapter concludes with the applications, advantages and future scope of the research work possible in the domain.

Chapter 20
Adding Context into Classification Reasoning Based on Good Classification Tests 522
Xenia Naidenova, Military Medical Academy, Russia

In this chapter, classification reasoning is considered. The concept of good classification test lies in the foundation of this reasoning. Inferring good classification tests from data sets is the inductive phase of reasoning resulted in generating implicative and functional dependencies supporting the deductive phase of reasoning. An algorithm of inferring good classification tests is given with the decomposition of it into subtasks allowing to choose sub-contexts for each obtained dependency and to control sub-contexts during both deductive and inductive phases of classification reasoning.

Chapter 21
Readable Diagrammatic Query Language ViziQuer 543
Martins Zviedris, Institute of Mathematics and Computer Science, Latvia

End-user interaction with data is one of key aspects in data processing. Nowadays a lot of information systems have a custom made user interface for data input and data querying. From 1970s it is envisioned that a generic, user-friendly approach for data querying could be built, but no wide spread solution has been developed. In the paper we present a diagrammatic query language. We have done an iterative approach to design and improve the diagrammatic query language to make it user readable. Readability is analyzed with questionnaires. Readable diagrammatic query language is the first step to create a more generic and user-friendly data querying.

Compilation of References 563

About the Contributors 615

Index 622

Preface

Databases are designed to support data storage, retrieval, and processing activities related to data management. The wide usage of databases in diverse application domains has resulted in an enormous wealth of data, which populate a great variety of databases around the worlds. Ones can find many categories of database systems, for example, relational databases, object-oriented databases, object-relational databases, deductive databases, parallel databases, distributed databases, multidatabase systems, Web databases, XML databases, multimedia databases, temporal/spatial databases, spatiotemporal databases, and uncertain databases. Recently some new databases are emerging, for example, NoSQL and NewSQL for big data management, RDF databases for metadata management, ontology bases for knowledge management in the Semantic Web, and so on. Various databases are being applied for managing different types of data in the context of concrete applications. Nowadays databases have become the repositories of large volumes of data.

Data management in databases is implemented with support of database management systems (DBMSs). Many categories of databases can be identified actually because they have different DBMSs typically provide data storage and querying for data management. Database query processing can be referred to such a procedure that DBMSs obtain the data needed by the users from the databases according to users' requirements and the answers are provided to users after these useful data are organized. It is very critical to deal with the enormity and retrieve the worth information for effective problem solving and decision making. Generally speaking, DBMSs provide users with querying languages, which can be used by users to describe their querying requirements. We can see, for example, SQL (Structured Query Language), a query language standard for relational databases, OQL (Object Query Language), a query language standard for object-oriented databases, and XQuery, a querying language designed by the World Wide Web Consortium (W3C) for XML. While the querying languages provide users with a primary means to represent users' querying requirements and DBMSs then return some answers accordingly, novel querying techniques and approaches are needed because of large volumes of data and a variety of data types as well as diverse users' requirements. The techniques of database query processing are challenging today's database systems and promote their evolvement. It is no doubt that database query systems play an important role in data management, and data management requires database query support.

The research and development of data queries over a great variety of databases are receiving increasing attention. By means of the query technology, large volumes of data in databases can be retrieved, and information systems are hereby built based on databases to support various problem solving and decision making. So database queries are the fields which must be investigated by academic researchers together with developers and users both from database and industry areas.

This book covers a fast-growing topic in great depth and focuses on the technologies of database query processing. Aiming at providing a single account of technologies and practices in advanced database query systems, the book investigates the issues of innovative database query processing techniques, including the technologies and methodologies of database and XML queries, spatiotemporal data queries, big data queries, metadata queries, and applications of database query systems. The objective of the book is to provide the state of the art information to academics, researchers and industry practitioners who are involved or interested in the study, use, design and development of advanced and emerging database queries with ultimate aim to empower individuals and organizations in building competencies for exploiting the opportunities of the data and knowledge society. This book presents the latest research and application results in database query systems. The different chapters in the book have been contributed by different authors and provide possible solutions for the different types of technological problems concerning database queries.

This book, which consists of twenty-one chapters, is organized into five major sections. The first section discusses the technologies and methodologies of database and XM queries in the first seven chapters. The next five chapters covering spatiotemporal data queries comprise the second section. The third section consists of the following three chapters after the second section, concentrating on big data querying. The next three chapters after the third section comprise the fourth section, discussing metadata RDF and Semantic Web ontology OWL querying. The fifth section containing the final three chapters focuses on other issues in database querying.

First, we take a look at the issues of the technologies and methodologies of database and XML queries.

Xiangfu Meng, Xiaoyan Zhang and Chongchun Bi propose a novel approach, which can provide a list of keywords that both semantically related to the application domain and the given keywords by analyzing the correlations between query keywords and database terms. The database term is first modeled as <attribute, keyword> and suppose each query keyword can map into a database term. Then, a coupling relationship measuring method is proposed to measure both term intra- and inter-couplings, which can reflect the explicit and implicit relationships between terms in the database. Based on the coupling relationships between terms, for a given keyword query, an order of all terms in database is created for each query keyword and then the threshold algorithm (TA) is leveraged to expeditiously generate top-k ranked semantically related terms. The experiments demonstrate that their term coupling relationship measuring method can efficiently capture the semantic correlations between query keywords and terms in database.

These are queries that use conditions on (non-fixed) set of tuples, and need to be expressed with negation and set difference in relational algebra (and with subqueries, negated conditions and set difference in SQL). Such queries are quite important, especially in Decision Support environments (for instance, skyline queries are a particular type of set-oriented queries), and that they are not well supported by current optimization approaches. Antonio Badia overviews research dealing with the query processing and optimization of set-oriented queries. He shows that set-oriented queries and queries with universal (and other types of non-existential) quantification are closely related.

The Skyline queries retrieve a set of data whose elements are incomparable in terms of multiple user-defined criteria. In addition, Top-k Skyline queries filter the best k Skyline points where k is the number of answers desired by the user. Several index-based algorithms have been proposed for the evaluation of Top-k Skyline queries. These algorithms make use of indexes defined on a single attribute and they require an index for each user-defined criterion. In traditional databases, the use of multidimensional indices has shown that may improve the performance of database queries. Marlene Goncalves, Fabiana

Reggio and Krisvely Varela define three pruning criteria and develop several algorithms to evaluate Top-k Skyline queries. The proposed algorithms are based on a multidimensional index, pruning criteria and the strategies Depth First Search and Breadth First Search. They finally conduct an experimental study to analyze the performance and answer quality of the proposed algorithms.

Chapter 4

There are some data models and query languages based on the application of fuzzy set theory. Their goal is to provide more flexible DBMSs that allow the expression of user preferences in querying as well as imprecision in data. In this sense, the FuzzyEER data model proposes four kinds of fuzzy attributes. One of them, named Type 3, consists of a set of labels provided of a similarity relation. An extension of SQL, named FSQL, allows the expression and use of fuzzy attributes. Nevertheless, FSQL does not allow using fuzzy attributes in some clauses based on data ordering, due to semantics problem. Soraya O. Carrasquel, Ricardo R. Monascal, Rosseline Rodríguez and Leonid Tineo present a solution for this problem in case of Type 3 fuzzy attributes. Their main contribution consists in how to process queries involving such attributes by means of an extension to an existing RDBMS. Formal semantics, grammar, catalogue definition and translation schemas are contained in this chapter.

Chapter 5

Imperfect information extensively exists in data and knowledge intensive applications, where fuzzy data play an import role in nature. Fuzzy set theory has been extensively applied to extend various database models and resulted in numerous contributions. Li Yan and Z. M. Ma concentrate on two main issues in fuzzy data management: fuzzy data models and fuzzy data querying based on the fuzzy data models. They provide a full up-to-date overview of the current state of the art in fuzzy data modeling and querying. In addition, they discuss the relationships among various fuzzy data models. They would like their work to serve as identifying possible research opportunities in the area of fuzzy data management in addition to providing a generic overview of the approaches t proposed to modeling and querying fuzzy data.

Traditional database systems and languages are very rigid. XML data and query languages are not the exception. Fuzzy set theory is an appropriate tool for solving this problem. In this sense, Fuzzy XQuery was proposed as an extension of the XQUERY standard. This language defines the xs:truth datatype, the xml:truth attribute and allows the definition and use of fuzzy terms in queries. José Ángel Labbad, Ricardo Monascal and Leonid Tineo show a high coupling implementation of Fuzzy XQuery within eXist-db, an open source XML DBMS. This extension strategy could also be used with other similar tools. They also present a statistical performance analysis of the extended fuzzy query engine using the XMark benchmark with user defined fuzzy terms. It is shown that extending XML with fuzzy logic does not affect its performance on classic queries (without fuzzy terms), and queries with fuzzy terms do not affect performance significantly in most cases.

XML fuzzy query can be expressed exploiting fuzzy predicates based on the fuzzy set theory. To deal with the ranking problem of XML fuzzy query results, Wei Yan proposes a novel ranking approach. He firstly, according to the workload of XML documents, speculates how much the users care about each attribute node and assign a corresponding weight to it. Then he presents a membership degree ranking method, which ranks the fuzzy query results according to corresponding membership degree. Furthermore, he proposes the probabilistic ranking method, which improves the PIR method. The improved probabilistic ranking method considers the relevance between the nodes specified by fuzzy query and the nodes unspecified by fuzzy query. Finally, he presents a top-k ranking algorithm of XML fuzzy query results. The efficiency and effectiveness of the approach are also demonstrated by experimental results.

The second section deals with the issues of spatiotemporal data queries.

Gloria Bordogna, Simone Sterlacchini and Paolo Arcaini propose a framework for collecting, organizing into a database and querying information in social networks by the specification of content-based, geographic and temporal conditions to the aim of detecting periodic and aperiodic events. Their proposal could be a basis for developing context aware services. Specifically, they rely on a focused crawler to periodically collect messages in social networks related with the contents of interest, and on an original geo-temporal clustering algorithm in order to explore the geo-temporal distribution of the messages. The clustering algorithm can be customized so as to identify aperiodic and periodic events at global or local scale based on the specification of geographic and temporal query conditions.

With the recent advancements and wide usage of location detection devices, very large quantities of data are collected by GPS and cellular technologies in the form of trajectories. The wide and increasing availability of such collected data has led to research advances in behavioral aspects of the monitored subjects (e.g., wild animals, people, and vehicles). Using trajectory data harvested by mobile devices, trajectories can be explored using motion pattern queries based on specific events of interest. While most research works on trajectory-based queries has focused on traditional range, nearest-neighbor, and similarity and join queries, there has been an increasing need to query trajectories using complex, yet more intuitive, motion patterns. Marcos R. Vieira describes in detail complex motion pattern queries, which allow users to focus on trajectories that follow a specific sequence of spatio-temporal events. He demonstrates how these motion pattern queries can greatly help users to get insights from very large trajectory datasets.

A formal algebra is essential for applying standard database-style query optimization to XML queries. Luyi Bai proposes a spatiotemporal XML data model and develop such an algebra based on Native XML, for manipulating spatiotemporal XML data. After studying NXD spatiotemporal database and query framework, he investigates the formal representation of spatiotemporal query algebra, containing logical structure of spatiotemporal database, data type system, and querying operations. He shows that the model and algebra lay a firm foundation for managing spatiotemporal XML data.

Skyline queries may be used to filter interesting data from a broad range of data. A Skyline query selects those data that are the best according to multiple user-defined criteria. A special case of Skyline queries is the Spatial Skyline Queries (SSQ). SSQ allow users to express preferences on the closeness between a set of data points and a set of query points. Marlene Goncalves and Fabiola Di Bartolo study the problem of answering SSQ in presence of changing data, i.e., data whose values regularly change over a period of time. They propose an algorithm to evaluate SSQ on changing data. The proposed algorithm is able to avoid re-computation of the whole Skyline with each update on the data. Also, the performance of the proposed algorithm against state-of-the-art algorithms is empirically study. Their experimental study shows that the proposed algorithm may become 3 times faster than state-of-the-art algorithms.

Chapter 12

Location-based Skyline queries select the nearest objects to a point that best meet the user's preferences. Marlene Goncalves and Alberto M. Gobbi particularly focus on location-based Skyline queries over web-accessible data. Web-accessible may have geographical location and be geotagged with documents containing ratings by web users. Location-based Skyline queries may express preferences based on dynamic features such as distance and changeable ratings. In this context, distance must be recalculated when a user changes his position while the ratings must be extracted from external data sources which are updated each time a user scores an item in the Web. They describes and empirically studies four solutions capable of answering location-based Skyline queries considering user's position change and information extraction from the Web inside an area search around the user, which are based on an M-Tree index and Divide & Conquer principle.

In the third section, we find the issues of big data queries.

Time series data emerge naturally in many fields of applied sciences and engineering including but not limited to statistics, signal processing, mathematical finance, weather and power consumption forecasting. Although time series data have been well studied in the past, they still present a challenge to the scientific community. Advanced operations such as classification, segmentation, prediction, anomaly detection and motif discovery are very useful especially for machine learning as well as other scientific fields. The advent of Big Data in almost every scientific domain motivates us to provide an in-depth study of the state of the art approaches associated with techniques for efficient querying of time series. Vasileios Zois, Charalampos Chelmis and Viktor Prasanna provide a comprehensive review of the existing solutions related to time series representation, processing, indexing and querying operations.

In cloud computing environments parallel kNN queries for big data is an important issue. The k nearest neighbor queries (kNN queries), designed to find k nearest neighbors from a dataset S for every object in another dataset R, is a primitive operator widely adopted by many applications including knowledge discovery, data mining, and spatial databases. This chapter proposes a parallel method of kNN queries for big data using MapReduce programming model. Wei Yan firstly proposes an approximate algorithm that is based on mapping multi-dimensional data sets into two-dimensional data sets, and transforming kNN queries into a sequence of two-dimensional point searches. Then, in two-dimensional space, he proposes a partitioning method using Voronoi diagram, which incorporates the Voronoi diagram into R-tree. Furthermore, he proposes an efficient algorithm for processing kNN queries based on R-tree using MapReduce programming model. Finally, He presents the results of extensive experimental evaluations which indicate efficiency of the proposed approach.

Maristela Holanda and Jane Adriana Souza investigate how NoSQL (Not Only SQL) databases provide query language and data retrieval mechanisms. Users attest to many advantages in using the NoSQL databases for specific applications, however, they also relate that querying and retrieving data in a simple way remains a difficult problem in NoSQL databases. The NoSQL operations require that, during the project, the queries must be thought of as built-in applications code.

The fourth section discusses the issues of RDF and OWL queries.

To solve the problem of information bipolarity in fuzzy querying of RDF, Hairong Wang, Jingwei Cheng and Z. M. Ma propose an approach of RDF fuzzy query with bipolar preference. They use linguistic variables to describe preference conditions, and realize an extended SPARQL syntax by adding bipolar preference conditions to FILTER clauses. They identify three types of bipolar information and divide the bipolar preference query into univariate bipolarity and bivariate bipolarity. They propose a method for converting fuzzy SPARQL queries to standard SPARQL queries. For optimizing results, they use bipolar preference satisfaction degrees to calculate priority parameters of results for sequencing. Finally, they show the feasibility of the proposed approach with the experimental results.

RDF plays an important role in representing Web resources in a natural and flexible way. As the amount of RDF datasets increasingly growing, storing and querying theses data haves attract the attention of more and more researchers. Jingwei Cheng, Z. M. Ma and Qiang Tong first make a review of approaches for query processing of RDF datasets. They categorize existing methods as two classes, those making use of relational database management system to implement the storage and retrieval, and those devising their only native storage schemas. Secondly, They survey some important extensions of SPARQL, standard query language for RDF, which extend the expressing power of SPARQL to allow more sophisticated language constructs that meet the needs from various application scenarios.

As a standard (W3C recommendation) for representing knowledge in the Semantic Web, Ontologies have been applied in many application domains. In many years, lots of ontologies have been created and real ontologies tend to become very large to huge. Thus, one problem is considered that has arisen from practical needs: namely, efficient querying of ontologies. To this end, there are today many proposals for answering queries over ontologies, and until now the literature on querying of ontologies has been flourishing. In particular, on the basis of the efficient and mature techniques of databases, which may be useful for querying ontologies. To investigate querying of ontologies and more importantly identifying the direction of querying of ontologies based on databases, Fu Zhang, Z. M. Ma and Haitao Cheng provide a brief review of answering queries over ontologies based on databases. Some query techniques, their classifications and the directions for future research, are introduced.

In the fifth section, we see several other issues in database querying.

The creditability of an e-Learning system depends on its content, services and presentation of its content. Besides providing material on demand, an e-Learning system also manages knowledge for future use. It is observed that the learning material available on different locations may be reused in a proper way. Priti Srinivas Sajja discusses generic design of an e-Learning system with various reusable learning material repositories. The architecture described here uses light weight mobile agents to access these repositories through fuzzy user profile. With notion of the fuzzy user profile, the system can present customized content to the users. Besides the architecture of the e-Learning system, he also discusses the necessary concepts about the fuzzy logic and agent based systems, in depth literature survey, structure of the user profile, fuzzy membership function and design of the light weight mobile agent with necessary implementation details.

Xenia Naidenova considers commonsense (plausible) reasoning. The concept of good classification test lies in the foundation of this reasoning. Inferring good classification tests from data sets is the inductive phase of reasoning resulted in generating implicative and functional dependencies supporting the deductive phase of reasoning. She gives an algorithm of inferring good classification tests with the decomposition of it into subtasks allowing to chose sub-contexts for each obtained dependency and to control sub-contexts during both deductive and inductive phases of classification reasoning.

End-user interaction with data is one of key aspects in data gathering process. Nowadays most information systems have a custom made user interface for data input and data querying. Still, this is costly and time-consuming process. From 1970s it is envisioned that there could be a generic user-friendly approach for data querying, but no suitable solution has been developed yet. Martins Zviedris presents a diagrammatic query language and does an iterative approach to design and improve the diagrammatic query language. Analytical questionnaires show that the diagrammatic query language is user readable. This is the first step to create a more generic and user friendly data querying.

Acknowledgment

The editor wishes to thank all of the authors for their insights and excellent contributions to this handbook and would like to acknowledge the help of all involved in the collation and review process of the handbook, without whose support the project could not have been satisfactorily completed. Most of the authors of chapters included in this handbook also served as referees for chapters written by other authors. Thanks go to all those who provided constructive and comprehensive reviews.

A further special note of thanks goes to all the staff at IGI Global, whose contributions throughout the whole process from inception of the initial idea to final publication have been invaluable. Special thanks also go to the publishing team at IGI Global. This book would not have been possible without the ongoing professional support from IGI Global.

The idea of editing this volume stems from the initial research work that the editor did in past several years. The research work of the editor was supported by the *National Natural Science Foundation of China* (61370075).

Li Yan
Nanjing University of Aeronautics and Astronautics, China
March 2015

Section 1

Chapter 1
Top-*k* Relevant Term Suggestion Approach for Relational Keyword Search

Xiangfu Meng
Liaoning Technical University, China

Xiaoyan Zhang
Liaoning Technical University, China

Chongchun Bi
Liaoning Technical University, China

ABSTRACT

This chapter proposes a novel approach, which can provide a list of keywords that both semantically related to the application domain and the given keywords by analyzing the correlations between query keywords and database terms. The database term is first modeled as <attribute, keyword> and suppose each query keyword can map into a database term. Then, a coupling relationship measuring method is proposed to measure both term intra- and inter-couplings, which can reflect the explicit and implicit relationships between terms in the database. Based on the coupling relationships between terms, for a given keyword query, an order of all terms in database is created for each query keyword and then the threshold algorithm (TA) is leveraged to expeditiously generate top-k ranked semantically related terms. The experiments demonstrate that our term coupling relationship measuring method can efficiently capture the semantic correlations between query keywords and terms in database.

1. INTRODUCTION

Keyword query is becoming a very popular way to obtain the information from the relational database along with its wide spread use on the Web. In real applications, however, most of common Web database users usually have insufficient knowledge about the database content and schema, and they are also lack of keywords related to the searching domain. Thus, it is not easy for them to find appropriate keywords

DOI: 10.4018/978-1-4666-8767-7.ch001

to express their query intentions. To explore the database, the user may issue a query with a few general keywords at first, and then gradually refines the query through observing the query results. In such an iteration, the user needs to check each result to identify whether it is related to his interest or not, which is a time-consuming and tedious work.

Consider a DBLP database consisting of 3 relations connected through primary-foreign-key relationships shown in Figure 1.

Suppose a master student who is a XML beginner just knows a few keywords about XML research field and wants to find chapters about the XML search techniques from DBLP website. Based on the DBLP database, he/she would issue a query Q containing keywords "XML, search". On receiving the query Q, the traditional keyword search approach will return a set of minimal total joint networks (MTJNTs), each of which

1. Is obtained from a single relation or by joining several relations, and
2. Contains all the query keywords.

Since there are too many chapters containing keywords "XML" and "search" in DBLP dataset, there are too many MTJNTs in the query results. In such a case, the user would like the system suggest a list of keywords that are semantically related to Q in order to reduce the searching scope. From Figure 1, it is clearly that the author "Jeffrey" and keywords "XPath", "XQuery", and "twig pattern" are very relevant to Q. That means these terms can refine Q to formulate a more selective query. As an example, the user would execute a query Q'=[Jeffrey, XML, search] to retrieve only the chapters of author Jeffrey on XML searching and the query results are "$a1 \bowtie w1 \bowtie p1$" and "$a1 \bowtie w2 \bowtie p4$". Additionally,

Figure 1. An example of DBLP database

	Aid	Name
u_1	a1	Jeffrey
u_2	a2	Charlie
u_3	a3	Michelle

	Pid	Title
u_4	p1	Enhancing XML search with XQuery and XPath
u_5	p2	XPath full-text query over semi-structured data
u_6	p3	Twig pattern searching in XML
u_7	p4	Full-text search using XQuery in XML

	Wid	Aid	Pid
u_8	w1	a1	p1
u_9	w2	a1	p4
u_{10}	w3	a2	p2
u_{11}	w4	a3	p3

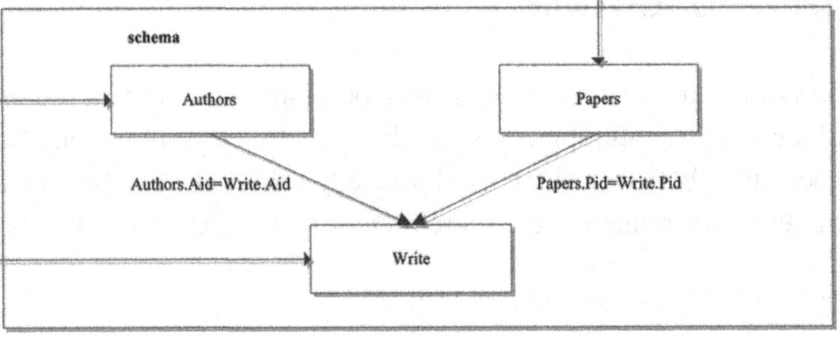

the tuples $p2$ and $p3$ containing "full-text", "semi-structured data", and "twig pattern" are also related to the query Q. While, these tuples would not be returned by the system due to the terms they contained are not specified explicitly by the user query. If the user is also interested in these topics, he/she can choose the keyword "full-text", "semi-structured data", and/or "twig pattern" to explore the database. Hence, it is necessary to provide a list of semantically related terms to the given query and then the user can refine or reformulate his/her query according to the terms in the list.

The challenge in selecting semantically related keywords is to understand the semantics of the original query and to measure the semantic relationships between query keywords and database terms. Several approaches have been proposed to deal with the issue of keyword search over relational databases (Aditya, Bhalotia, Chakrabarti, & Hulgeri, 2002; Agrawal, Chaudhuri, & Das, 2002; Hristidis & Papakonstantinou, 2002; Hristidis, Gravano, & Papakonstantinou, 2003; Tata, & Lohman, 2008). The basic idea of the approaches is to assume the query keywords are independent to each other and leverage full text matching to find all connected tuples explicitly contain all the query keywords. However, in real applications, there are various coupling relationships (Cao, Ou, & Yu, 2012) between objects, which have been shown valuable to be incorporated into analysis such as document term semantic analysis (Cheng, Miao, Wang, & Cao, 2013), clustering (Wang, Cao, Wang, Li, Wei, & Ou, 2011) and classification (Wang & Sukthankar, 2013; Wang, She, Cao, 2013). Similarly, terms contained in tuples are coupled in terms of co-occurrences and inter-related relationships. If the query keywords can be mapped into database terms, then the semantic relationships between query keywords and database terms can be estimated by the coupling relationships between database terms. The coupling relationship of terms is composed of *intra-coupling* and *inter-coupling*, where *intra-coupling* denotes the explicit relationship between terms (such as two terms co-occurred in same tuples) and *inter-coupling* represents the implicit relationship between terms (such as two terms occurred separately in different tuples are inter-related through at least one common term).On top of this idea, in this chapter, we propose a new approach which incorporates the term coupling relationships to provide a list of relevant terms rather than the MTJNTs. Given a set of keywords Q, and an integer k, our approach returns the k most semantically related terms from the database to Q.

The rest of this chapter is organized as follows. Section 2 reviews some related work. Section 3 gives a formal definition of the problem and outlines an overview of our solution framework. Section 4 proposes the term coupling relationship measuring method while Section 5 presents a top-k related term selection method. The experiment results are presented in Section 6. The chapter is concluded in Section 7.

2. RELATED WORK

Several methods have been proposed to handle keyword search on relational database, and the popularity of keyword search is ongoing (Yao, Cui, & Hua, 2012). The previous work can be classified into two main categories, depending on whether they retrieve MTJNTs based on candidate networks (CN) (Agrawal, Chaudhuri, & Das, 2002; Hristidis & Papakonstantinou, 2002; Luo, Lin, & Wang, 2007) or data graph (Aditya, Bhalotia, Chakrabarti, & Hulgeri, 2002; Tata & Lohman, 2008; Ding, Yu, & Wang, 2007). The CN-based approaches, such as DBXplorer (Agrawal, Chaudhuri, & Das, 2002), DISCOVER (Hristidis and Papakonstantinou, 2002), and SPARK (Luo, Lin, & Wang, 2007), generate all possible candidate networks following the database schema, and then identify the MTJNTs based on CNs. A CN is a joining network of tuples, in which the tuples are inter-connected through primary-foreign-key constraints. The data graph-based methods, such as BANKS (Aditya, Bhalotia, Chakrabarti, & Hulgeri, 2002) and its extensions (Tata & Lohman, 2008; Ding, Yu, & Wang, 2007), firstly model the database as a directed data graph, where nodes are tuples and the directed edges are foreign key references between tuples. A keyword query is then processed by traversing graph for searching MTJNTs containing the query keywords. In summary, the existing approaches mainly focus on searching MTJNTs explicitly containing the specified keywords and lack of considering the semantic relevance between answers and queries. As a result, they cannot identify the results from which some MTJNTs may also be very relevant to a query in semantic terms, even though they do not explicitly contain the query keywords.

This approach has a fundamental difference from the conventional keyword search (KS) approach: our approach extract terms, while KS approach fetches joint tree of tuples. More specifically, given a set of query keywords Q and an integer k, a top-k KS approach aims to find the k MTJNTs most relevant to Q and the MTJNTs are ranked according to their content relevance or tree size. In contrast, our approach selects the k terms most relevant to Q by measuring the coupling relationships between query keywords and database terms. Note that, the k terms produced by our approach do not necessarily appear in the k MTJNTs fetched by top-k KS approach. The reason is that, some of MTJNTs in results may not real relevant to the user intentions even it contains the query keywords, while some tuples do not contain the query keywords may very relevant to the user need in terms of semantic, these tuples would not be retrieved by the existing KS approach.

Recently, tentative work on keyword semantic understanding and approximate query has been undertaken. In (Sarkas, Bansal, & Das, 2009), the transformation rules are manually defined used for keyword query integration and the local results are analyzed used for finding relevant answers. In (Bergamaschi, Domnori, & Guerra, 2009), the metadata of database is used for translating keyword queries into meaningful SQL queries that describe the intended query semantics. In (Yao, Cui, & Hua, 2012), the data structural semantics are exploited and employed to reformulate the initial query. Although keyword/term semantics have been taken into consideration, most of the existing approaches usually assume that keywords in a query (resp. terms in database) are independent of one another, but in reality coupling relationships exist between objects such as keywords and terms as shown in (Wang, Cao, Wang, Li, Wei, & Ou, 2011; Cheng, Miao, Wang, & Cao, 2013).

3. PROBLEM DEFINITION AND SOLUTION

In this section, the problem definition is firstly presented and then the solution is introduced.

Problem Definition

Definition 1 (Schema Graph): Consider an relational database D *as* a collection of relations $D = \left(r\left(R_1\right), r\left(R_2\right), \ldots, r\left(R_n\right) \right)$, where each relation $r(R_i)$ in D contains n_i tuples with the schema R_i. A *schema graph* of relational database D is a directed graph $G_S(V, E)$, where V is the set of nodes and each of which represents a relation $r(R_i)$ in D, E is the set of edges and each of which represents a foreign key reference between a pair of relations in D. Given two relation schemas R_i

and R_j, there exists an edge in the schema graph G_S, from R_j to R_i, denoted $e(R_i{\rightarrow}R_j)$, if the foreign key defined on R_j references to the primary key defined on R_i. Figure 1 illustrates the schema graph of the sample DBLP database.

In this chapter, it supposed that any two relations are connected in the schema graph. If some relations are not connected, it should be decomposed into several groups of connected relations and apply our method on the decomposed groups. A relation R_i is called a *link relation* if there is no relation R_j, such that $R_j{\rightarrow}R_i$. That is, R_i only contains foreign keys to reference other relations but there is no primary key be defined on it. For example, the relation *Write* in DBLP is a link relation because relation *Write* has no primary key and there exists *Write→Authors* and *Write→Chapters* in the schema graph.

A relational database can be modeled as a database graph $G_D(V, E)$ on the schema graph G_S, where V represents the set of tuples in database, and E represents the set of connections between tuples. There is a connection between two tuples, t_i and t_j in G_D, if there exists at least on foreign key references from t_i to t_j (or t_j to t_i) in the database. Figure 2 illustrates the database graph G_D for the sample DBLP database showed in Figure 1.

Definition 2 (Minimal Total Joining Network of Tuples, MTJNT): Given a *l*-keyword query Q and a relational database D with schema graph G_S, a joining network of tuples (*JNT*) is a connected tree

Figure 2. Tuple connections of the sample DBLP database

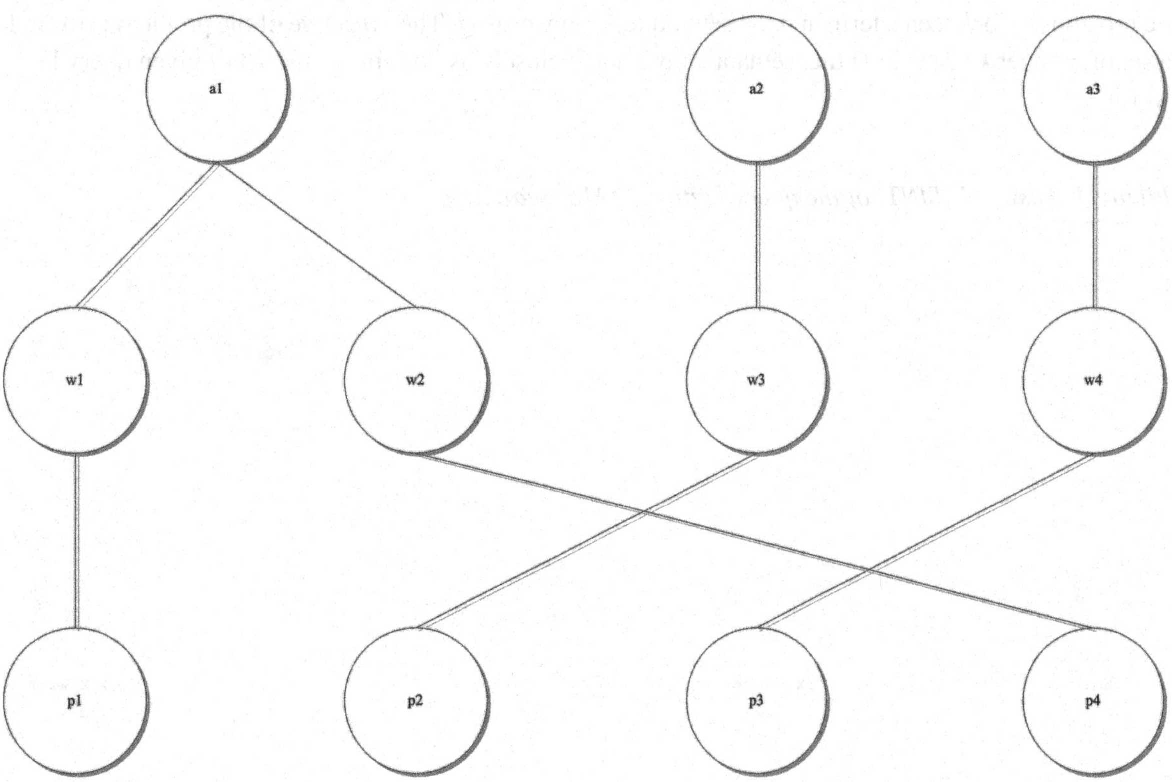

of tuples where two adjacent tuples, $t_i \in r(R_i)$ and $t_j \in r(R_j)$, can be joined according to the foreign key references defined on relational schema R_i and R_j in G_S. An MTJNT is a JNT that satisfy the following two conditions:

1. **Total:** Each keyword in query Q must be contained in at least one tuple of the JNT.
2. **Minimal:** No tuple of the JNT can be removed such that the remaining tuples is still a JNT contains all the keywords in Q. In other words, a JNT is not total if any tuple is removed.

Definition 3 (*l*-Keyword Query): A *l*-keyword query Q over database D is an ordered list of distinct keywords of size l, i.e., $Q = \{k_1, k_2, \ldots, k_l\}$, and searches inter-connected tuples that contain the given keywords in their text attributes. A *l*-keyword query returns a set of answers, each of them is a minimal total joining network of tuples (*MTJNT*).

For example, the T1 and T2 showed in Figure 3 is the answer for the query Q' mentioned in introduction.

Problem 1 (Top-*k* Semantically Related Term Selection): Let Q be a set of query keywords over a relational database D. The top-*k* semantically related term selection problem is defined as,

$$\Gamma_k = \arg\max\nolimits_{\Gamma'} \sum\nolimits_{i=1}^{k(k<n)} \delta_{SR}\left(t_i, Q\right) \tag{1}$$

where, Γ_k is a list of k terms, n is the number of all distinct terms in D, and δ_{SR} represents the semantic relationship between a term and the set of query keywords Q. The objective of the problem is to find a set of number k terms in D that semantically related closely as possible to the set of given query keywords.

Figure 3. Answer MTJNTs of the query [Jeffrey, XML, Search]

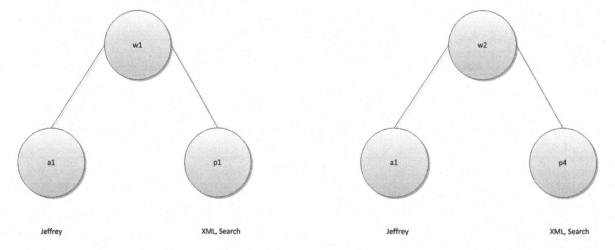

Solution

This chapter proposes a two-step processing solution to address this problem. The first step occurs offline. It firstly extracted all the distinct terms from the database, each of which takes the form of <attribute, keyword>, where *attribute* refers to the attribute name in the relation, *keyword* is a word or topical phrase in the values corresponding to the attribute. Here, we suppose the attributes belong to different relations have different names, so that each <attribute, keyword> is unique and would not be duplicated. In addition, the standard word-stemming technique should be applied, so that words like "obtain" and "obtaining" can be regarded as the same word. And then, a data view is generated by connecting all the relations in the database according to their primary-foreign-key references, following which the intra- and inter-couplings between different pairs of terms can be calculated by leveraging the correlation analysis method on data view. Consequently, the term intra- and inter-coupling can be combined into a coupling relationship to reflect the semantic relevance between terms.

The second step occurs online when a user makes a query. It first decomposes the input query into several distinct keywords. Based on coupling relationships between terms, it then creates orders of terms for each query keyword. Each order corresponds to a query keyword and the terms in each order are ranked according to their coupling relationships to that keyword. After this, the top-k related terms can be quickly captured by using Threshold Algorithm (TA) on the orders.

4. TERM COUPLING RELATIONSHIP ANALYSIS

This Section first generates the term relationship graph, and then describes how to measure the weights of nodes and edges in the term relationship graph.

Term Relationship Graph

The term relationship graph is used to model the relationships between terms in database. Figure 4 illustrates the relationships of the terms extracted from the example DBLP database in Figure 1. The set of nodes is the set of all terms. There is an edge between two nodes corresponding terms t_i and t_j, if

1. t_i and t_j are in the same tuple of a relation, or
2. t_i and t_j exist in tuples u_x and u_y from different relations that can be connected through a sequence of primary-foreign key references.

As showed in Figure 4, the relationships between terms can be divided into explicit and implicit relationships. Two nodes are explicitly related if there is an edge between them such as nodes *A* and *D*. Two nodes are implicitly related if they can be inter-connected through at least one link/common nodes but there is no edge between them. For example, the nodes *H* and *K* are inter-connected through the nodes *D* and *W*. To measure the relationships (including explicit and implicit relationships) between two terms in the graph, the weights for nodes and edges should be computed based on the database.

Figure 4. Term relationship graph for the DBLP database

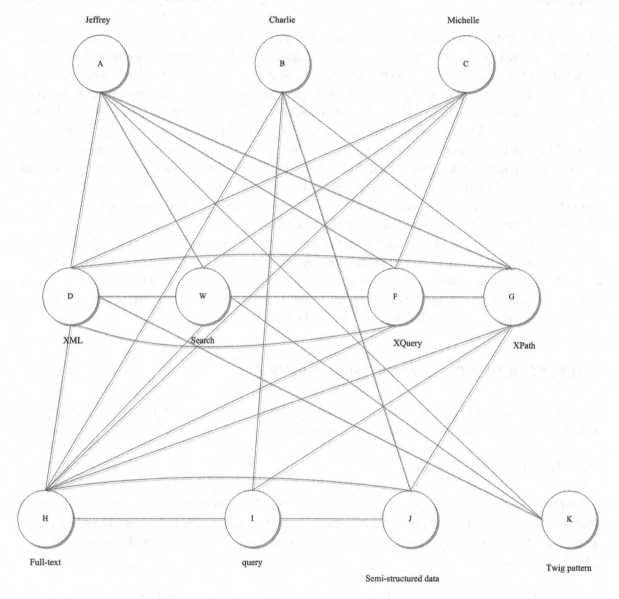

Weight of a Node

A straightforward way to weight the node of graph is to employ the TF·IDF-based method. Each tuple in the relation can be modeled as a document and the keywords in the tuple are treated as terms, and accordingly the technique of TF·IDF weighting function in IR and database literatures (Liu, Yu, & Meng, 2006; Li, Feng, & Zhou, 2008) can be borrowed and incorporated to weight the node in the graph.

Given a database D and a term t_i appearing in a tuple $u(u \in D)$, we use $f\left(t_i, u\right)$ to denote the number of occurrences of the term t_i in tuple u. N is the cardinality of tuples that include terms in database D (we do not count the number of tuples contained in link tables because of which containing no term), and N_i is the number of tuples containing term t_i in D. We then use the TF-IDF metric.

The normalized term frequency of term t_i in u, $ntf\left(t_i, u\right)$, can be defined as Equation (2),

$$ntf\left(t_i, u\right) = 1 + \ln\left(1 + f\left(t_i, u\right)\right) \tag{2}$$

The inverse tuple frequency $itf(t_i)$ is defined as Equation (3),

$$itf(t_i) = \ln\frac{N}{N_i + 1} \tag{3}$$

in which, the itf is normalized by dividing the total number of tuples in D over (N_i+1) and then applying the ln function.

Since the length of each tuple (i.e., the number of terms contained in a tuple) may different from each other, it needs to be normalized. The normalized tuple length (ntl), which is used to reduce the term weights in long tuples, is defined as Equation (4),

$$ntl(u) = (1 - s) + s * \frac{|u|}{\frac{\sum_{u' \in D} |u'|}{N}} \tag{4}$$

where, $|u|$ represents the number of terms in tuple u, and s is a constant that is usually set to 0.2. Normalized tuple length means the ratio of the number of terms in tuple u to the average of terms in the set of tuples in D.

After this, the weight of term t_i in tuple u can be defined as,

$$w(t_i, u) = \frac{ntf(t_i, u)}{ntl} * itf(t_i) \tag{5}$$

Since the term t_i may appear in several tuples, the weight of the node representing term t_i is normalized as follows,

$$w(t_i) = \frac{\sum_{u=1}^{N_i} w(t_i, u)}{N_i} \tag{6}$$

It is clearly that captures the importance of term t_i in a specific tuple u while $w(t_i)$ reflects the average importance of term t_i among all tuples containing it. For example, the sample DBLP database of Figure 1 contains N=7 tuples and $\sum_{u' \in D} |u'| = 18$ terms (here, we count the total number of terms showed in Figure 6 appearing in the tuples). The term "XML" appeared in N_i=3 tuples (u_4, u_6, u_7), and the times of term "XML" appeared in each of these tuples are both 1, i.e., $f\left(XML, u_4\right) = 1$, $f\left(XML, u_6\right) = 1$, and $f\left(XML, u_7\right) = 1$, respectively. Also, the length of these tuples are $|u_4| = 4$, $|u_6| = 3$, and $|u_7| = 4$, respectively. Consequently, the weight of the term "XML" in these tuples are,

$$w\left(XML, u_4\right) = \frac{1 + \ln\left(1+1\right)}{0.8 + 0.2 * 4 / \left(11/7\right)} * \ln\left(\frac{7}{4}\right) = 0.73,$$

$$w\left(XML, u_6\right) = \frac{1 + \ln\left(1+1\right)}{0.8 + 0.2 * 3 / \left(11/7\right)} * \ln\left(\frac{7}{4}\right) = 0.80,$$

and

$$w\left(XML, u_7\right) = \frac{1 + \ln\left(1+1\right)}{0.8 + 0.2 * 4 / \left(11/7\right)} * \ln\left(\frac{7}{4}\right) = 0.73,$$

respectively. As a result, the weight of node corresponding the term "XML" in graph is

$$w\left(XML\right) = average\left(0.73 + 0.80 + 0.73\right) = 0.75.$$

After this, all the nodes are finally normalized by dividing the maximum weight of the node in graph. The normalized weight of node t_i, $nw(t_i)$, is defined as,

$$nw(t_i) = \frac{w(t_i)}{MaxWeight} \tag{7}$$

Weight of Edges

To compute the weights of edges, this section first constructs a data view that is the collection of all connected tuples based on the database schema graph, and then captures the weight (composed of intra and inter coupling relationships) of edge between two connected nodes of term relationship graph based on data view.

Data View

Definition 4 (Data View): Given a database D with n connected relations, $r\left(R_1\right), r\left(R_2\right), \ldots, r\left(R_n\right)$, the data view V is formed by joining all connected relations in D through the primary-foreign-key relationships according to the schema graph, where each tuple u in V is a combination of connected tuples and represents a meaningful and integral unit.

For example, we can join the 3 relations in Figure 1 to create a data view as shown in Table 1.

The data view contains much richer structural information than the text document. Based on data view, we next present how to compute the term coupling relationship, which is inspired by the term coupled modeling in document analysis (Cheng, Miao, Wang, & Cao, 2013).

Table 1. An instance of data view for sample DBLP database

AID	PID	Name	Title
a1	p1	Jeffrey	Enhancing XML search with XQuery and XPath
a1	p4	Jeffrey	An efficient full-text search using XQuery in XML
a2	p2	Charlie	XPath full-text query over semi-structured data
a3	p3	Michelle	Twig pattern searching in XML

Term-Intra Couplings in the Tuples

In Information Retrieval, two terms are considered semantically related if they frequently co-occur in the same document. Similarly, each tuple in a data view is considered as a document so that this idea can be used to measure the intra-coupling between terms in database.

The frequency of co-occurrence of a pair of terms $\left(t_i, t_j\right)$ appearing in the same tuple can be measured by Jaccard coefficient as follows,

$$J(t_i, t_j) = \frac{|V(t_i) \cap V(t_j)|}{|V(t_i) \cup V(t_j)|} \tag{8}$$

in which, $V(t_i)$ and $V(t_j)$ represents the subset of tuples in view V containing terms t_i and t_j, respectively.

Given a term, such as <Author, Jeffrey>, it can be visualized as a selection query "Author=Jeffrey" that binds only a single attribute. By issuing a term query over the view, a set of tuples all containing the keyword of term can be identified.

It should be pointed out that, given a tuple u and any two terms in u, t_i and t_j, they can be classified into two cases according to their relationships in the tuple u as follows:

1. t_i and t_j bind the same attribute;
2. t_i and t_j correspond to different attribute.

It is clearly that t_i and t_j in case (1) are more relevant than those in case (2). Thus, we set the distance between two terms t_i and t_j in a tuple u, denoted as $d_r\left(t_i, t_j\right)$, as showed in Equation (9).

$$d(t_i, t_j) = \begin{cases} 0, & t_i \text{ and } t_j \text{ correspond to case (1)} \\ 1, & t_i \text{ and } t_j \text{ correspond to case (2)} \end{cases} \tag{9}$$

After this, we can define the *term intra-coupling* by considering both of the Jaccard coefficient and term distance.

Definition 5 (Intra-Coupling of Terms): Given a view V and any two terms t_i and t_j, there exists a intra-coupling relationship between t_i and t_j if they co-occur in at least one tuple u of V, the intra-coupling between t_i and t_j in V is defined as,

$$\delta_{IaR}(t_i, t_j \mid V) = \frac{J(t_i, t_j)}{d_r(t_i, t_j) + 1} \tag{10}$$

where, $J(t_i, t_j)$ is defined as Equation (8).

Since term t_i may also co-occur with other terms in the same tuple, it should be normalized by dividing the total number of intra-couplings between t_i and all other terms. Thus, the intra-coupling between t_i and t_j can be finally computed as follows,

$$\delta_{IaR}(t_i, t_j) = \begin{cases} 1, & i = j \\ \dfrac{\delta_{IaR}(t_i, t_j \mid V)}{\sum_{a=1, a \neq i}^{n} \delta_{IaR}(t_i, t_a \mid V)}, & i \neq j \end{cases} \tag{11}$$

in which, n is the number of all distinct terms extracted from database D.

For instance, given two terms "Jeffrey" and "XML" (for simple, we only use keyword to denote its corresponding term). The Jaccard coefficient of them in the view of Table 1 is $J(Jeffrey, XML) = \dfrac{2}{3}$ and the distance is $d(Jeffrey, XML) = 1$ respectively. Consequently, the intra-coupling between them is

$$\delta_{IaR}(Jeffrey, XML \mid V) = \frac{1}{3}.$$

Since the term "Jeffrey" also co-occurs with terms "search", "XQuery", "XPath", and "full-text" in the view and the intra-couplings between them are

$$\delta_{IaR}(Jeffrey, search \mid V) = \frac{1}{3},$$

$$\delta_{IaR}(Jeffrey, XQuery \mid V) = \frac{1}{2},$$

$$\delta_{IaR}(Jeffrey, XPath \mid V) = \frac{1}{6},$$

and

$$\delta_{IaR}\left(Jeffrey, full-text \mid V\right) = \frac{1}{6},$$

respectively. Finally, the normalized intra-coupling between "Jeffrey" and "XML" is

$$\delta_{IaR}\left(Jeffrey, XML\right) = \frac{1/3}{1/3 + 1/3 + 1/2 + 1/6 + 1/6} = \frac{2}{9}.$$

It is clearly to conclude that from the example above, for each pair of terms t_i and t_j, we have $\delta_{IaR}\left(t_i, t_j \mid V\right) \geq 0$ and $\sum_{j=1, j\neq i}^{n} \delta_{IaR}(t_i, t_j \mid V) = 1$. Note that, the values of $\delta_{IaR}\left(t_i, t_j\right)$ and $\delta_{IaR}\left(t_j, t_i\right)$ may not be equal to each other due to the different dominators. While, the matrix of $\delta_{IaR}\left(t_i, t_j\right) \mid V$ in Equation (10) is symmetric because of $J\left(t_i, t_j\right) = J\left(t_j, t_i\right)$, therefore we need to only compute the upper-half of the matrix of $\delta_{IaR}\left(t_i, t_j\right) \mid V$. The term intra-coupling relationship calculating algorithm is shown in Algorithm 1.

Using Algorithm 1, an intra-coupling matrix for each pair of terms can be obtained. Table 2 shows the intra-coupling matrix of terms extracted from the sample DBLP database. For simple, we use *A*, *B, C,D, E, F, G, H, I, J*, and *K* to denote the extracted terms *Jeffrey, Charlie, Michelle, XML, Search, XQuery, XPath, full-text, query, semi-structured data*, and *twig pattern*, respectively.

The intra-coupling reflects the explicit relationship between two co-occurred terms. Specifically, if there are two terms co-occur in the view, there must exist an edge between the two nodes in graph that the terms correspond to.

However, besides the intra-coupling, some co-occurred terms may also appear separately in different tuples and they are probably inter-related through their *common terms*. This chapter calls such implicit

Table 2. Example of intra-coupling matrix of terms

	A	B	C	D	E	F	G	H	I	J	K
A	1.00	0.00	0.00	0.22	0.22	0.33	0.11	0.11	0.00	0.00	0.00
B	0.00	1.00	0.00	0.00	0.00	0.00	0.17	0.17	0.33	0.33	0.00
C	0.00	0.00	1.00	0.20	0.20	0.00	0.00	0.00	0.00	0.00	0.60
D	0.11	0.00	0.06	1.00	0.33	0.22	0.08	0.08	0.00	0.00	0.11
E	0.11	0.00	0.06	0.33	1.00	0.22	0.08	0.08	0.00	0.00	0.11
F	0.20	0.00	0.00	0.27	0.27	1.00	0.13	0.13	0.00	0.00	0.00
G	0.06	0.10	0.00	0.10	0.10	0.13	1.00	0.13	0.19	0.19	0.00
H	0.06	0.10	0.00	0.10	0.10	0.13	0.13	1.00	0.19	0.19	0.00
I	0.00	0.20	0.00	0.00	0.00	0.00	0.20	0.20	1.00	0.40	0.00
J	0.00	0.20	0.00	0.00	0.00	0.00	0.20	0.20	0.40	1.00	0.00
K	0.00	0.00	0.43	0.29	0.29	0.00	0.00	0.00	0.00	0.00	1.00

correlation between terms is *inter-coupling relationship*, which would enhance the relationships between the co-occurred terms. For example, given two terms "XPath" and "XQuery", from the Table 1we can see that they co-occur in tuple 1 and appear separately in tuple 2 and tuple 3, respectively. Clearly, the common term between "XPath" and "XQuery" is "full-text", which appears together with "XPath" and "XQuery" in tuple2 and tuple3 of Table 1, respectively. Additionally, the terms have never co-occurred in the same tuples, may also inter-related via their common terms. For example, the terms "semi-structured data" and "XML" are inter related by their common terms "XPath" and "full-text". Next, it will propose the term inter-coupling measuring method below to capture the implicit relationships between inter-related terms.

The intra-coupling reflects the explicit relationship between two co-occurred terms. Specifically, if there are two terms co-occur in the view, there must exist an edge between the two nodes in graph that the terms correspond to.

However, besides the intra-coupling, some co-occurred terms may also appear separately in different tuples and they are probably inter-related through their *common terms*. In this chapter, we call such implicit correlation between terms is *inter-coupling relationship*, which would enhance the relationships between the co-occurred terms. For example, given two terms "XPath" and "XQuery", from the Table 1we can see that they co-occur in tuple 1 and appear separately in tuple 2 and tuple 3, respectively. Clearly, the common term between "XPath" and "XQuery" is "full-text", which appears together with "XPath" and "XQuery" in tuple 2 and tuple 3 of Table 1, respectively. Additionally, the terms have never co-occurred in the same tuples, may also inter-related via their common terms. For example, the terms "semi-structured data" and "XML" are inter related by their common terms "XPath" and "full-text". Next, we will propose the term inter-coupling measuring method below to capture the implicit relationships between inter-related terms.

Term Inter-Coupling across Tuples

Given a data view V and a term t_i, all the terms co-occurred with t_i in V can be seen as the relevant terms associated with t_i. For any two terms t_i and t_j that appear in different tuples, the inter-coupling between them can be estimated by the commonality in the relevant terms associated with them. For example, given a term<Title, XML> in Table 1,a set of terms <Author, Jeffrey >, <Author, Michelle>, <Title, search>, <Title, XQuery>, <Title, XPath>, <Title, twig pattern>, and <Title, full-text> is associated with it; while, a set of terms <Author, Charlie>, <Title, XPath>,<Title, full-text>, and <Title, query> is associated with the term <Title, semi-structured data>. Clearly, the overlapped terms between two sets are<Title, XPath> and <Title, full-text>. In this chapter, we call these terms are *common terms/common nodes* of the compared terms, which mean that two terms appearing in different tuples are inter-related through their common terms. According to this, the inter-coupling between terms t_i and t_j through their common term t_c can be defined as follows.

Definition 6 (Inter-Coupling of Terms): Given a data view V and any two terms t_i and t_j, they are inter-related if there is at least one common term t_c such that $\delta_{IaR}\left(t_i, t_c\right) > 0$ and $\delta_{IaR}\left(t_j, t_c\right) > 0$ hold but terms t_i and t_j appear in different tuples. The inter-coupling between term t_i and t_j via common term t_c is defined as follows,

$$\delta_{IeR}(t_i, t_j \mid t_c) = \min\{\delta_{IaR}(t_i, t_c), \delta_{IaR}(t_j, t_c)\} \tag{12}$$

where, $\delta_{IaR}(t_i, t_c)$ and $\delta_{IaR}(t_j, t_c)$ are the intra-coupling between terms t_i and t_c, t_j and t_c, respectively.

Since there may be more than one common term between t_i and t_j and each one have different weight in the term relationship graph, we use the following method to normalize the term inter-couplings. Suppose S be the set of common terms of t_i and t_j, that is,

$$S = \left\{ \left(t_c \middle| \delta_{IaR}(t_i, t_c) > 0 \wedge \delta_{IaR}(t_j, t_c) > 0 \right) \right\}.$$

Then, the inter-coupling between term t_i and t_j, inter-related by all the common terms in S, can be formalized as,

$$\delta_{IeR}(t_i, t_j) = \begin{cases} 1, & i = j \\ \dfrac{\sum_{\forall t_c \in S} nw(t_c) * \delta_{IeR}(t_i, t_j \mid t_c)}{|S|}, & i \neq j \end{cases} \tag{13}$$

where, $nw(t_c)$ represents the weight of term t_c which is computed by Equation (7), $|S|$ denotes the number of common terms in S, and $\delta_{IeR}(t_i, t_j \mid t_c)$ is the inter-coupling between t_i and t_j inter-connected via their common term t_c. Equation (13) means that the inter-coupling between term t_i and t_j is measured by the average strength of all the weights of edges between them. If $S=\Phi$, then $\delta_{IeR}(t_i, t_j)$ is zero. The term inter-coupling calculating algorithm is shown in Algorithm 2.

Using Algorithm 2, an inter-coupling matrix for each pair of terms can be obtained. Table 3 shows the inter-coupling matrix of terms extracted from the sample DBLP database showed in Figure 1.

Term Coupling Relationship

The coupling relationship between two terms t_i and t_j is composed of intra- and inter-coupling of them, which is defined as follows,

$$\delta_{SR}(t_i, t_j) = \begin{cases} 1, & i = j \\ (1 - \alpha) \cdot \delta_{IaR}(t_i, t_j) + \alpha \cdot \delta_{IeR}(t_i, t_j), & i \neq j \end{cases} \tag{14}$$

where, $\alpha \in [0, 1]$ is the parameter to determine the weight of intra- and inter-coupling. The Equation (14) would be intra-coupling if $\alpha=0$ while it would be inter-coupling if $\alpha=1$, which means the intra- and inter-coupling are the special cases of the term coupling relationship. Given two terms t_i and t_j, it is clearly that the higher the coupling relationship between t_i and t_j, the more the t_i semantically related to t_j, and the larger the weight of edge $w(t_i \rightarrow t_j)$ in graph; and vice versa. Note that there are two weights on the edge between any pair of connected nodes in the term relationship graph. More specifically,

Table 3. Example of inter-coupling matrix of terms

	A	B	C	D	E	F	G	H	I	J	K
A	1.00	0.05	0.07	0.07	0.07	0.06	0.04	0.04	0.05	0.05	0.07
B	0.05	1.00	0.00	0.04	0.04	0.06	0.11	0.11	0.13	0.13	0.00
C	0.07	0.00	1.00	0.08	0.08	0.07	0.03	0.03	0.00	0.00	0.07
D	0.07	0.04	0.08	1.00	0.07	0.07	0.05	0.05	0.04	0.04	0.07
E	0.07	0.04	0.08	0.07	1.00	0.07	0.05	0.05	0.04	0.04	0.07
F	0.06	0.06	0.07	0.07	0.07	1.00	0.05	0.05	0.06	0.06	0.09
G	0.04	0.11	0.03	0.05	0.05	0.05	1.00	0.08	0.10	0.10	0.03
H	0.04	0.11	0.03	0.05	0.05	0.05	0.08	1.00	0.10	0.10	0.03
I	0.05	0.13	0.00	0.04	0.04	0.06	0.10	0.10	1.00	0.13	0.00
J	0.05	0.13	0.00	0.04	0.04	0.06	0.10	0.10	0.13	1.00	0.00
K	0.07	0.00	0.07	0.07	0.07	0.09	0.03	0.03	0.00	0.00	1.00

given two connected nodes t_i and t_j in graph, the weights on the edge between t_i and t_j are, $w\left(t_i \rightarrow t_j\right)$ and $w\left(t_i \rightarrow t_j\right)$, which represent the coupling relationship from t_i to t_j, and t_j to t_i, respectively.

Table 4 shows the coupling relationship matrix of all terms extracted from sample DBLP database. Here, we set α to 0.5, which means the intra- and inter-coupling have the same ratio in measuring the term coupling relationship.

From Table 4, we can see that the coupling relationship between terms considering both of intra- and inter-coupling is more reasonable than that of only considering either intra-coupling or inter-coupling of terms. For example, we consider a pair of terms "<Title, XML>" (denoted by D) and "<Title, semi-structured data>" (denoted by J) in Table 4. If we only consider their intra-coupling, there is no relationship

Table 4. Example of coupling relationship matrix of terms

	A	B	C	D	E	F	G	H	I	J	K
A	1.00	0.03	0.03	0.14	0.14	0.20	0.08	0.08	0.03	0.03	0.04
B	0.03	1.00	0.00	0.02	0.02	0.03	0.14	0.14	0.23	0.23	0.00
C	0.03	0.00	1.00	0.14	0.14	0.03	0.02	0.02	0.00	0.00	0.33
D	0.09	0.02	0.07	1.00	0.20	0.14	0.06	0.06	0.02	0.02	0.09
E	0.09	0.02	0.07	0.20	1.00	0.14	0.06	0.06	0.02	0.02	0.09
F	0.13	0.03	0.03	0.17	0.17	1.00	0.09	0.09	0.03	0.03	0.04
G	0.05	0.10	0.02	0.07	0.07	0.09	1.00	0.11	0.14	0.14	0.02
H	0.05	0.10	0.02	0.07	0.07	0.09	0.10	1.00	0.15	0.15	0.02
I	0.03	0.17	0.00	0.02	0.02	0.03	0.15	0.15	1.00	0.27	0.00
J	0.03	0.17	0.00	0.02	0.02	0.03	0.15	0.15	0.27	1.00	0.00
K	0.04	0.00	0.25	0.18	0.18	0.04	0.02	0.02	0.00	0.00	1.00

between them as showed in Table 2. But in reality, "XML" and "semi-structured data" is related to each other in semantic and the relationship between them can be captured by our inter-coupling calculating algorithm. As a result, the coupling relationship between them would not be zero as showed in Table 4.

5. TOP-*k* SEMANTICALLY RELATED TERM SELECTION

Step 1: Create orders for terms.

For each query keyword k_i (suppose it corresponds to a database term t_i), create an order τ_i of all terms (except t_i) in database in descending order, according to their coupling relationships to t_i (i.e., k_i). The terms in order τ_i can be divided into two sets. The one is the relevant set, where the terms have coupling relationships to k_i. The other one is the irrelevant set, where the terms have no coupling relationship to k_i. Firstly, it is natural to assume that an irrelevant term is less important than a relevant one, thus the terms of irrelevant set should be ranked after the terms of relevant set in the order. Secondly, since there is no evidence to show that one of them in irrelevant set is more or less important than the other one, they are positioned randomly in the irrelevant set of the order.

Since there are totally l query keywords, the output of this procedure is a set of l orders. According to the output orders, each term t_j has a score that is associated with the position of t_j in order τ_i. The score of t_j in τ_i that corresponds to keyword k_i is:

$$s(t_j \mid k_i) = n - \tau_i(t_j) + 1 \tag{15}$$

in which, $\tau_i(t_j)$ represents the position of t_j in τ_i.

Step 2: Select top-*k* related terms.

For a set of query keywords Q, and the set of all distinct terms T in database D, using the output of Step 1, this step computes the set $Q_k(T) \subseteq T$ with $|Q_k(T)| = k$, such that $\forall t_j \in Q_k(T)$ and $t'_j \in \{T - Q_k(T)\}$ it holds that $score(t_j, Q) > score(t'_j, Q)$, with $score(t_j, Q) = \sum_{i=1}^{l} s(t_j \mid k_i)$, where $s(t_j \mid k_i)$ is computed by using the Equation (14).

The Threshold Algorithm (TA) (Fagin, Lotem, & Naor, 2001) is employed to find the top-*k* relevant terms for a set of given keywords. The TA uses *Sorted* and *Random* modes to access the terms in the orders. The *Sorted access* mode obtains the score of a term in an order by traversing the order of the terms sequentially from the top. The *Random access* mode obtains the score of a term in an order in one access. The *threshold* is set as the sum of the score of last visited term from each order for the current round-robin.

The top-*k* related term selection algorithm works as follows.

1. Accessing each one of the *l* orders of the terms in a round-robin. As a term *t* is seen in some order τ_i that corresponds to query keyword k_i, get the score of term *t* from every other orders $\{\tau_j \mid \tau_i \in Q_l$ and $j \neq i\}$ by using the random access. The final score of term *t* for the set of query keywords *Q* is computed as:

$$score(t_j, Q) = \sum_{i=1}^{l} s(t_j \mid k_i) \tag{16}$$

2. The threshold λ for the *j*-th round-robin cycle is defined as the sum of the score of last visited term from each order, that is,

$$\lambda = \sum_{i=1}^{l} s\left(\underline{t_j} \mid k_i\right) \tag{17}$$

where, $s\left(\underline{t_j} \mid k_i\right)$ denotes the score of last visited term of order $\tau_i \left(i \in \{1, \ldots, l\}\right)$ by the end of the *j*-the round-robin cycle. The algorithm terminates when *k* terms with score values greater or equal to the thresholdλ.

3. Output the *k* terms among the set of all found terms with the highest value for $score\left(t, Q\right)$.

Using the Algorithm above, a list of top-*k* related terms can be returned for a set of given query keywords. Then, user can choose term in the list to explore the database and view the results of the related terms in the list.

6. EXPERIMENTS

Experimental Settings

The experiments are conducted on a computer running Windows 2007 with Intel P4 3.2-GHz CPU, and 8 GB of RAM. All algorithms are developed in C# and SQL. We use the DBLP dataset to evaluate the performance of our methods. The download DBLP XML file is decomposed into several relations according to the schema showed in Figure 5.

Figure 5. The DBLP schema (PK refers to primary key and FK refers to foreign key)

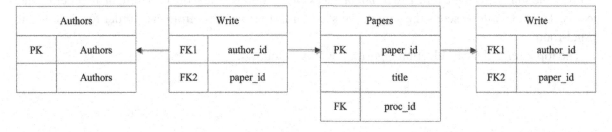

The 1000 tuples were selected from the four relations of the DBLP database as our testing dataset, and these tuples can be connected though primary-foreign-key references based on the database.

Precision of Term Coupling Relationships

This experiment aims to test the precision of term coupling relationship measuring method (short for TCR) that corresponds to different parameter value of α in Equation (14). To verify the accuracy of the TCR method, the strategy is adopted as follows. 10 people were invited, which are researchers and PhD students, to randomly choose 10 terms from the DBLP dataset. And then, for each term t_i, top5 terms were obtained by using our TCR method with respect to each value of parameter α in Equation (14) from 0 to 1 at the increments 0.1. After this, these terms are mixed together and a set K_i of 55 terms is generated consequently. Lastly, the terms with their corresponding K_i's were presented to each user in our study. The task of each user is to mark the top 5 terms that they considered semantically related to t_i. We then measured how closely the 5 terms marked as relevant by the user matched the 5 terms returned by each algorithm. The users were asked to describe whether they considered a term t' related to a given term t based on:

1. The terms t' and t are same or similar in semantic, such as the term "semi-structured data" and "XML data".
2. The terms t' and t are related in semantic, for example, the term "association rules" is usually associated with the term "apriori algorithm", hence they are considered to be related.

Figure 6 illustrates the *precision* in estimating the top 5 terms obtained by using our method with respect to different values of α. The precision is calculated as the number of terms retrieved among the top 5 terms that were marked as relevant, i.e.,

$$Precision = \frac{|\ relevant\ terms\ retrieved\ |}{5}.$$

Note that, the precision for each value of α is averaged over 10 selected terms.

It can be seen that the curve of precision reaches a peak at $\alpha=0.5$ for DBLP dataset, which demonstrates that our method performs best when α is set to 0.6 (the corresponding accuracy is 0.76). It also can be seen that, the precision raises as the parameter α increases from 0 to 0.6, which indicates the inter-coupling play a *positive* role on the coupling relationship measuring. While, the precision declines as the parameter α after 0.6, which means the inter-coupling brings negative impact into the coupling relationship measuring. It should be pointed out that the term coupling relationships depend on the dataset, and thus it is essential to optimize the setting of α to achieve the highest precision for different datasets.

The work that is most similar to ours is the FCT algorithm in (Tao & Yu, 2009), which finds the most frequent term co-occurring with the query keywords in the MTJNTs. In this experiment, the number of query keyword in the query is only one (each selected term is treated as a query), which makes the

Figure 6. Precision of relevant terms retrieved for different values of α *on DBLP dataset*

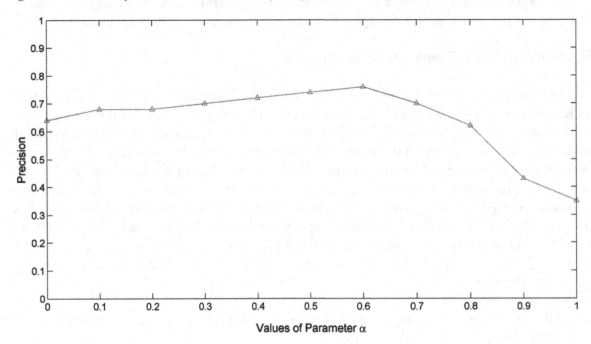

precision of FCT and TCR (when $\alpha=0$) equal, i.e., 0.64. It is clearly that the precision of TCR (when $\alpha=0.6$) is much higher than that of FCT over the DBLP dataset. This is because FCT only discover the relevant terms that frequently co-occur with the query keywords. In contrast, TCR considers both the term co-occurred and inter-related relationships, which can better reveal the explicit and implicit correlations between terms. Hence, the answers of TCR can meet the user's intentions more closely.

Execution Performance

This experiment aims to verify the execution time of the top-k related term selection algorithm. There are two parameters, l and k, in this algorithm, where l represents the number of query keywords and k denotes the number of terms needs to be selected. We fix the number of l to 2, 4, 6, 8, and 10, respectively and then test the execution time for different k values. Figure 7 illustrates the execution time on DBLP dataset for different k values when $l = \{2, 4, 6, 8, 10\}$.

From Figure 7, it can be seen that the performance of the algorithm decreases with the increasing of number l and k. This is because the top-k related term selection algorithm needs to deal with more terms in orders as the number l and k increased. We also computed the time consumption for computing the sum of coupling relationship between a term and each query keyword. It takes approximately 125 seconds for DBLP dataset. Our top-k related term selection algorithm clearly outperforms existing methods and demonstrates more efficient performance.

Figure 7. Execution time of top-k selection algorithm

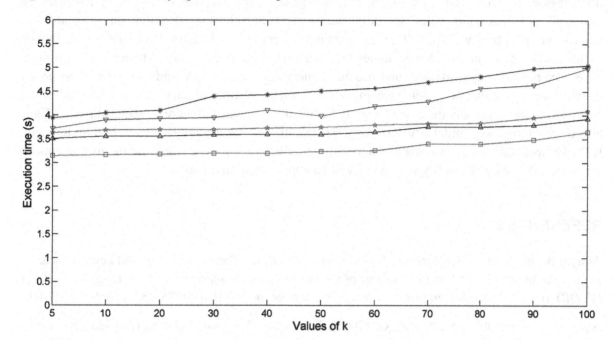

7. CONCLUSION AND FURTHER WORK

This chapter presented a novel approach, which leverages the coupling relationships between query keywords and terms in database, to find the top-*k* semantically related terms for a set of query keywords. Based on the database schema, a data view is first created by connected tuples of relations through primary-foreign-key constraints. The term coupling relationship is then estimated by considering both the intra- and inter-coupling between terms within and across the tuples of the view. For a set of given query keywords, the orders of all terms in database is generated for each query keyword according to the coupling relationships between terms and query keyword, and then TA algorithm is used to quickly find the top-*k* related terms based on these orders. The experiments on real dataset identified that the term coupling relationship method can capture the semantic relationships of terms more reasonable and the top-*k* related term selection algorithm also achieves high performance.

In the future, it would be interesting to investigate how to transform the keyword query to the structural query which can describe the user query intentions more efficiently. The traditional keyword query method is mainly based on data graph, where nodes are tuples and edges are foreign key references. For a given keyword query,a set of minimal connected tuple trees which cover all the query keywords in their leaf nodes will be found as the query results. This kind of method supposes each query keyword is independent to each other, and leverage full-text matching to find all tuples explicitly contain the query keywords. As a result, some result tuples are redundant if they are not real relevant to the user intentions even though they contain the query keywords. For example, given a keyword query Q: "agrawal, association rules" over DBLP, the mean of this query is most probably to find the chapter which is entitled "association rules" and proposed by author "agrawal", and thus the corresponding attributes for "agrawal" and "association rules" should be author_name and chapter_title. However, the traditional keywor query method will find all tuples containing "agrawal" and "association rules" even though "agrawal" contained in the other attributes (not contained in attribute "author_name"). The essential difference between keyword query and structural query (i.e. SQL) is keyword query does not specify the attributes in the database, that is we do not know which relations or attributes are specified by the query keywords, especially the case of a query keyword is contained in more than one attribute. Thus, how to transform a keyword query into an appropriate structural query is a challenge work in KS field. If the keyword query can be converted into a structural query which can describe the user intentions accurately, the efficiency of keyword query will be improved significantly.

REFERENCES

Aditya, B., Bhalotia, G., Chakrabarti, S., & Hulgeri, A. (2002). Banks: browsing and keyword searching in relational databases. In *Proceedings of the International Conference on Very Large Data Bases (VLDB)*. (pp 1083-1086). Hong Kong, China: Endowment. doi:10.1016/B978-155860869-6/50114-1

Agrawal, S., Chaudhuri, S., & Das, G. (2002). Dbxplorer: A system forkeyword-based search over relational databases. In *Proceedings of the International Conference on Data Engineering (ICDE)*. (pp 5-16). San Jose, CA: IEEE Computer Society. doi:10.1109/ICDE.2002.994693

Bergamaschi, S., Domnori, E., & Guerra, F. (2011). Keyword search over relational databases: a metadata approach. In *Proceedings of the ACM SIGMOD Conference on Data Management (SIGMOD)*. (pp 565-576). Athens, Greece: ACM. doi:10.1145/1989323.1989383

Cao, L. B., Ou, Y. M., & Yu, P. S. (2012). Coupled behavior analysis with applications. *IEEE Transactions on Knowledge and Data Engineering, 24*(8), 1378–1392. doi:10.1109/TKDE.2011.129

Cheng, X., Miao, D. Q., Wang, C., & Cao, L. B. (2013). Coupled term-term relation analysis for document clustering. In *Proceedings of the International Joint Conference on Neural Networks (IJCNN)*. (pp 1-8). Killarney, Ireland: IEEE Computer Society. doi:10.1109/IJCNN.2013.6706853

Ding, B., Yu, J. X., & Wang, S. (2007). Finding top-k min-cost connected trees in databases. In *Proceedings of the International Conference on Data Engineering (ICDE)*. (pp 468-477). Istanbul, Turkey: IEEE Computer Society. doi:10.1109/ICDE.2007.367929

Fagin, R., Lotem, A., & Naor, M. (2001). Optimal aggregation algorithms for middleware. In *Proceedings of the Internatioanl Conference on Principles of Database Systems (PODS)* (pp 102-113). Santa Barbara, CA: ACM.

Hristidis, V., Gravano, L., & Papakonstantinou, Y. (2003). Efficient IR-style keyword search over relational databases. In *Proceedings of the International Conference on Very Large Data Bases (VLDB)*. (pp 850-861). Berlin, Germany: Endowment. doi:10.1016/B978-012722442-8/50080-X

Hristidis, V., & Papakonstantinou, Y. (2002). Discover: keyword search in relational databases. In *Proceedings of the International Conference on Very Large Data Bases (VLDB)*. (pp 670-681). Hong Kong, China: Endowment. doi:10.1016/B978-155860869-6/50065-2

Li, G. L., Feng, J. Y., & Zhou, L. Z. (2008). Retune: retrieving and materializing tuple units for effective keyword search over relational databases. In *Proceedings of the International Conference on Conceptual Modeling (ER)*. (pp 469-483). Barcelona, Spain: Springer. doi:10.1007/978-3-540-87877-3_34

Liu, F., Yu, C., & Meng, W. Y. (2006). Effective keyword search in relational database. In *Proceedings of the ACM SIGMOD Conference on Data Management (SIGMOD)*. (pp 563-574). Chicago, IL: ACM.

Luo, Y., Lin, X. M., & Wang, W. (2007). SPARK: top-k keyword query in relational databases. In *Proceedings of the ACM SIGMOD Conference on Data Management (SIGMOD)*. (pp 305-316). Paris, France: ACM doi:10.1145/1247480.1247495

Tao, Y. F., & Yu, J. X. Finding frequent co-occurring terms in relational keyword search. (2009). In *Proceedings of the EDBT/ICDT Joint Conference (EDBT)*. (pp 839-850). Saint-Petersburg, Russia: ACM. doi:10.1145/1516360.1516456

Tata, S., & Lohman, G. M. (2008). SQAK: doing more with keywords. In *Proceedings of the ACM SIGMOD Conference on Data Management (SIGMOD)*. (pp 889-902). New York: ACM.

Wang, C., Cao, L. B., Wang, M. C., Li, J. J., Wei, W., & Ou, Y. M. (2011). Coupled nominal similarity in unsupervised learning. In *Proceedings of the ACM International Conference on Information & Knowledge Management (CIKM)*. (pp 973-978). New York: ACM.

Wang, C., She, Z., & Cao, L. B. (2013). Coupled clustering ensemble: incorporating coupling relationships both between base clusterings and objects. In *Proceedings of the International Conference on Data Engineering (ICDE)*. (pp 374-385). Brisbane, Australia: IEEE Computer Society. doi:10.1109/ICDE.2013.6544840

Wang, X., & Sukthankar, G. (2013). Multi-label relational neighbor classification using social context features. In *Proceedings of the ACM SIGKDD Conference on Knowledge Discovery and Data Mining (KDD)*. (pp 464-472). New York: ACM. doi:10.1145/2487575.2487610

Yao, J. J., Cui, B., & Hua, L. S. (2012). Keyword query reformulation on structured data. In *Proceedings of the International Conference on Data Engineering (ICDE)*. (pp 953-964). Washington, DC: IEEE Computer Society.

KEY TERMS AND DEFINITIONS

Coupling Relationship: There exists a coupling relationship between objects a and b if object a (or b) has an influence on object b (or a) or they interact with each other.

Precision: It is a measure that allows knowing how good or bad is an answer set in terms of effectiveness and completeness for a given keyword query.

Query Keyword: A term or phrase contained in a user query.

Term: It is a combination of the attribute and its corresponding value consisted in the database, such as <Author, Jeffrey> is a term extracted from the database.

Top-k Ranking: A set of k answer items with the highest ranking score according to the given scoring function.

Web Database: Web database is the online database that can be only accessed using the web form-based interface.

Chapter 2
Set–Oriented Queries in SQL

Antonio Badia
University of Louisville, USA

ABSTRACT

Set-oriented queries are those that require a condition to hold of an arbitrary set of rows, either when comparing the set to a single row or to another set of rows. Examples of such queries are universally quantified queries and skyline queries. These queries, while important for data processing, are difficult to write and difficult to process. In this chapter we review research dealing with the specification and optimization of such queries. We present several approaches proposed to deal with universal quantification as well as with set predicates in general.

1. INTRODUCTION

Over the years, the SQL standard has evolved to adapt to new challenges. The initial core of the language has been extended to deal with object-relational extensions, XML data, and text data ((Melton, 2001a)). Also, new operators (like CUBE and WINDOWS) have been added to deal with Decision-Support style queries ((Melton, 2001b)).

An issue already present at the birth of the language is that SQL, like Relational Algebra (henceforth RA), is biased towards *row-based* queries. These are queries defined by conditions that require the existence of a row or a *fixed* set of rows with some given constraints. Such queries correspond to the SPJ (Select-Project-Join) subset of RA and the SELECT ... FROM ... WHERE *simple* fragment of SQL (with no subqueries and no set operators). By contrast, *set-oriented* queries are those that require a condition to hold of an *arbitrary* set of rows, either when comparing the set to a single row or to another set of rows. Examples of such queries are *universally quantified* queries and *skyline* queries. Such queries are expressed in RA with negation and in SQL with subqueries (especially those using negated operators, like NOT IN and NOT EXISTS), or set difference (EXCEPT). In many cases, these queries can be paraphrased using grouping and counting.

In this chapter, we overview research dealing with the processing and optimization of set-oriented queries. In the next section, we provide a definition of the class and examples to show both the importance of such queries and the challenge that they present to traditional query optimization. In section 3,

DOI: 10.4018/978-1-4666-8767-7.ch002

we overview early attempts to deal with set-oriented queries and some of the solutions proposed. Then, in section 4 we introduce the framework of *Generalized Quantification*, used in (Badia, 2009) to give a unified solution to the problem. After an overview of the basic theory, we show in section 5 how it is applied to support quantification in SQL, and provide examples and a summary of the results of this research, as well as a comparison with other approaches in the literature. Finally, in section 6 we discuss open issues and future avenues of research. We close with a brief recapitulation of the main points of the chapter in section 7.

2. MOTIVATION

Tuple-based conditions, both in RA and SQL, involve the value of one or more attributes in a given tuple, but they apply to one tuple at a time only. For instance, in the TPCH benchmark[1], we can write a query to get the suppliers from Germany with a condition country_name='GERMANY' applied to each tuple in the join of SUPPLIER and NATION. To write more complex conditions involving several tuples, RA requires that we 'line up' all the tuples by using joins. For instance, to get the suppliers that supply two parts, we need to see two tuples with the same supplier id and different parts ids. To achieve this, we join the relation SUPPLIES with itself and use renaming (say, giving SUPPLIES the alias S2), and then apply the condition SUPPLIES.supkey = S2.supkey and SUPPLIES.partkey <>S2.partkey[2]. Such cases, however, require a *fixed* amount of joins (one, in the example); they can be seen as conditions over a fixed number of tuples (two, in the example). There are queries, though, that require an indeterminate number of tuples. One example is the query *select the orders where all suppliers are from Germany*, in which we do not know in advance how many suppliers there are in each order, or how many suppliers are from Germany (and both sets can change with the data). These and similar examples (for instance, *select the orders where at least half of the suppliers are from Germany*) cannot be expressed with a regular SPJ query; they require set difference (i.e. negation) or other set operations. Queries containing such conditions are called *set-oriented queries*. The case of universal quantification ("all") has been known for a long time as problematic for SQL, both to express and to optimize.

Set-oriented conditions come in three main types in SQL: one is a simple condition in a single set -for instance, existential quantification (checking whether the set is empty or not) is expressed with EXISTS or NOT EXISTS. An example would be a query like

```
QUERY 1
SELECT c_name
FROM Customer C1
WHERE NOT EXISTS (SELECT c_name
FROM Customer
WHERE c_acctbal > C1.c_acctbal
and c_nation = C1.c_nation)
```

which retrieves the names of customers who have the largest account balance among the suppliers of a given nation. Note that this query has exactly the structure of a skyline query (Borzsony, Kossmann, & Stocker, 2001)[3].

A second type of set query is the comparison of a single element to a set (usually expressed with IN or NOT IN, or simple comparisons modified with ALL or SOME). As an example of this type, consider the query

QUERY 2
```
SELECT c_name
FROM Customer C1
WHERE c_acctbal >= ALL
(SELECT c_acctbal
FROM Customer
WHERE c_nation = C1.c_nation)
```

Note that this query is equivalent to the previous example, that is, is a skyline query; this translation simply makes clear that skyline queries are an example of set queries. The typical strategy to deal with the subquery is to unnest by outerjoining table Customer with itself. This type of query can also be used with non-correlated subqueries; as an example,

QUERY 3
```
 SELECT c_name
FROM Customer C1
WHERE c_acctbal >= ALL
.(SELECT c_acctbal
FROM Customer)
```

simply retrieves the customers with the largest account (among all customers).

Finally, the third type of set query in SQL involves comparing two sets and checking some condition on them -typically, checking whether they intersect or not, or whether one is contained in the other. As an example, the following query retrieves the orders where all suppliers are from Germany:

QUERY 4
```
 Select O.o_orderkey
From Orders O, Lineitem L
Where O.o_orderkey = L.o_orderkey
and NOT EXISTS (Select S.supkey
From Supplier S
Where S.supkey = L.supkey and
S.nationkey NOT IN (Select N.n_nationkey
From Nation N
Where n_name = 'Germany'))
```

It should be noted that many SQL programmers have difficulty writing such queries; in general, the cognitive load of a query increases with the number and level of nesting of its subqueries. Most systems nowadays will try to unnest the query, using an antijoin for both the NOT EXISTS and NOT IN. However, this translation is only valid if there are no nulls in the attributes S.supkey and N.n_nationkey. Further, if antijoin is used, the optimizer cannot move such operators around in the query plan, since they do not commute with join or with each other -and the correlation of the first subquery introduces a join ((Galindo-Legaria & Rosenthal, 1997)). Thus, even the unnested plan may perform poorly.

We can see that set-oriented queries can be complicated to write and difficult to optimize. The problem can be traced to predicates with negation (those with NOT IN, NOT EXISTS or ALL), which are not well translated into RA. In effect, it is well known that RA is equivalent to a subset of First Order Logic (FOL). As such, RA can express the two quantifiers of FOL, existential and universal. There is, however, a deep lack of symmetry on how the quantifiers are expressed: the existential quantifier is represented directly, while the universal quantifier is represented indirectly, though the well known transformation

$$\forall x P(x) \equiv \neg \exists x \neg P(x)$$

This in turn has practical consequences when it comes to implementing RA queries, as the transformation above makes expressions containing universal quantification difficult to run in an efficient manner. Considerable research in the past (which we review in section 3) has been devoted to this problem.

It can be seen that set-oriented queries and quantification are intimately connected. In effect, in standard logic the most common use of the existential quantifier is as a prefix for a conjunctive formula, as in

$$\exists x (P(x) \wedge Q(x))$$

while the most common use of the universal quantifier is as a prefix for a conditional formulas, as in

$$\forall x (P(x) \rightarrow Q(x))$$

If we identify the predicates P and Q in the above formulas with the set of elements that satisfy them (so that $Pset=\{x \vee P(x)\}$ and $Qset=\{x \vee Q(x)\}$), we can see that the above formulas can be rewritten as set conditions, i.e.

$$Pset \cap Qset \neq \emptyset$$

and

$$Pset \subseteq Qset$$

The last expression gives rise to the keyword CONTAINS in SQL. Unfortunately, not all systems support CONTAINS[4].

While not easy to deal with, due to their convoluted translation, set-oriented queries in RA and SQL are, at the same time, very important in data analysis. Basically, all SQL complex predicates with subqueries, except those that use aggregation, can be considered as set-oriented. As we have seen, skyline queries are an example of set-oriented conditions[5]. Besides the examples shown here, there is also work that shows that quantifiers can be used to define some data mining tasks, like discovering association rules ((Hajeck, 1998)). And a recent report on the state of Database Research ((Abadi et al., 2014)) states: "... there is a growing recognition that more general, database-style query processing techniques are needed. These include cost-aware query optimizers and set-oriented query execution engines." Thus, data analysis requires set-oriented queries.

Finally, we point out that SQL (like RA and FOL) only uses the SOME and ALL quantifiers. However, there is an area of research in logic ((Lindstrom, 1966; Mostowski, 1957)) and formal semantics ((Westerstahl, 1989)) that argues that many other quantifiers can be defined: expressions like *half of*, *at least 3*, *10% of*... are considered examples of *generalized quantification*. Ideally, one would like to write an SQL query like

QUERY 5
```
SELECT c_name
FROM Customer C1
WHERE c_acctbal > HALF (SELECT c_acctbal
FROM Customer
WHERE c_nation = C1.c_nation)
```

with the intended meaning: retrieve the names of those customers whose account balance is greater than half of all customers from his/her nation. Note that this query can be written in SQL, as follows:

QUERY 6
```
SELECT C1.c_name
FROM Customer C1, Customer C2
WHERE C1.c_acctbal > C2.c_acctbal
GROUP BY C1.c_name
HAVING count(C1.c_acctbal) > (SELECT count(c_acctbal)
FROM Customer
WHERE c_nation = C1.c_nation)/ 2
```

However, this query requires a GROUP BY and a complex condition (and a subquery) in a HAVING clause. Such complex conditions are themselves difficult to optimize for traditional approaches.

To summarize, set-oriented predicates are important in many data-centric tasks. At the same time, such queries can be problematic for SQL programmers to write and for query optimizers to process. Thus, dealing with such queries constitutes an active area of research in query optimization.

3. EARLY PROPOSALS

The difficulty of dealing with universal quantification was noted early on; in this section, we review some of the early proposals to deal with this issue (and some more recent proposals that build on this past work).

One of the earliest proposals is that of (Demolombe, 1982), which proposes a generalization of the *division* operator in RA. The division operator is a direct counterpart to universal quantification, but is usually introduced as a syntactic shortcut. Given two relations R and S with sch(R)⊂sch(S) [6], the division of S by R is defined as follows: let us write sch(R)=X and sch(S)=X∪Y, where X,Y are sets of attributes. Then S divided by R is a relation with schema Y (that is, sch(S) – sch(R)), given by $\{y \in \pi_Y(S) \lor (y,x) \in S \forall x \in R\}$. That is, the values in $\pi_Y(S)$ are related in $\pi_X(S)$ to all the values present in R. As an example, Query 3 in section 2 can be written as the division of

$$\left(\pi_{orderkey,supkey} \left(ORDERS \bowtie LINEITEM \bowtie SUPPLIER \right) \right)$$

by $\pi_{supkey}(\sigma_{n\_name=Germany}(NATION))$. The first relation links each order with all its suppliers (and corresponds to the outer query block and the first subquery); the second one gives the set of all suppliers from Germany (and corresponds to the second subquery). The division yields the orders which are related to all suppliers from Germany, as intended. It is well known that the division operator can be defined using negation and Cartesian product; in this example, we have that the expression

$$\left(\pi_{orderkey} \left(ORDERS \right) \times \pi_{supkey} \left(SUPPLIERS \right) \right)$$
$$- \left(\pi_{orderkey,supkey} \left(ORDERS \bowtie LINEITEM \bowtie SUPPLIERS \right) \right)$$

will generate the orders which are *not* related to all suppliers in Germany (i.e. the opposite of what we want). Using negation on this set will provide the answer. However, it is easy to see that this translation is not an effective way to compute the results. To address this, (Demolombe, 1982) develops an extension of RA where division is treated as a first-class operator. The work of (Carlis, 1986) develops this idea further. In particular, this work argues for the design of algorithms to specifically support division. The basic intuition -that an algorithm that supports universal quantification directly may provide superior performance to the usual approach of translating and optimizing- will have considerable influence in later work. (Dadashzadeh, 1989) introduces another basic intuition: it points out the relationship between quantification and set operations (which we discussed in section 2). Thus, (Dadashzadeh, 1989) shows that quantification can be implemented also as an operation on sets: in the example above, consider, for a particular order $o \in \pi_{orderkey}(ORDERS)$, the set of associated suppliers

$$S_o = \pi_{supkey} \left(\sigma_{orderkey=o} \left(ORDERS \bowtie LINEITEM \bowtie SUPPLIER \right) \right)$$

and the set of all suppliers $Sup = \pi_{supkey}(SUPPLIERS)$. Then the division above can be seen as equivalent as asking whether $Sup \subseteq S_o$ (note that set containment is enough, since it is guaranteed that $S_o \subseteq Sup$, as Sup is the set of *all* suppliers in the database). (Fragatelli, 1991) proposes to add an operator for universal quantification to SQL: he points out that, if the universal operator (or an equivalent one) is available in the algebra, and direct support for it exists, then adding the universal operator in SQL would allow queries that use it to exploit such a direct support.

While all this past work focus exclusively on the universal quantifier, (Ozsoyogly & Wang, 1989) deals directly with set operations and expands the approach to include both existential and universal quantifiers, as well as other operations on sets (union, intersection, difference, and containment). However, the approach remains at the RA level, with no algorithms proposed to support the new operations. On the other hand, (Graefe & Cole, 1995) provides efficient algorithms for direct implementation of universal quantification. The idea is that, in order to check whether given sets A and B are such that $A \subseteq B$, one can use *hashing* to implement the test efficiently: one idea is to hash B with a given hash function h and thus build a hashing table, and then hash A with h too and probe the table: as we go hashing A values, we can check that each one of them corresponds to a B value by looking inside the corresponding bucket. If we hash all of A without a miss, then we know that A⊆B . Such algorithms are a precursor of modern day approaches to dealing with set-oriented computation ((Ramasamy, Patel, Naughton, & Kaushik, 2000; Mamoulis, 2003)). However, the modern approaches focuses on the cases where the sets involved are small, since it is assumed that the sets arise as a consequence of nesting a table or by allowing set-based attributes in a table, for instance text-based attributes which are used to represent small documents. Thus, in this case we have that A and B are assumed to be small enough to fit in memory, but there is a large collection of such sets, so the test must be repeated numerous times. Note that, in general, the set operation may have to be repeated multiple times (i.e. in our running example of orders with all suppliers from Germany, we need a check for each order) *and* the sets involved may be large; both conditions present a challenge for memory-based algorithms.

From a more recent perspective, (Rantzau & Mangold, 2006) focuses also on universal quantification, but delves deeply into *optimization*. This work gives several optimization choices for division, so that this operator can be considered on the basis of the whole query tree. For instance, division can interact with selection: it is possible to push down a selection past division in some cases. In the example above, suppose that after selecting the orders where all the suppliers are from Germany, a further selection filters out orders that do not fulfill another condition (for instance, the order was within the last 5 years). Then, it is clear that since the condition affects the order as a whole this filtering can be done *before* we check if all suppliers in the order are from Germany (presumably, the check on date is simpler and hence less costly than the set-based check). This kind of reasoning provides a new opportunity to reduce the cost of dealing with the universal quantifier, as most previous approaches considered the quantifier in isolation.

The idea of extending set-oriented queries to other data models besides relational was pioneered in (Sarathy, Van Gucht, & Badia, 1993), where a graphical interface for an object-oriented database is modified to express this type of queries. However, this approach does not consider implementation issues. More recently, (May, Helmer, & Moerkotte, 2004) studies subqueries and quantification but focusing on *ordered* structures. Incorporating order is an important idea in the context of SQL, since there are many SQL queries that require their result to be sorted. Also, in XML extensions of SQL, order is an inherent property of the data model, and therefore must be taken into account when studying query processing. In this respect, it is interesting to point out that languages like OQL and XQuery include syntax for universal quantification, a clear sign that modern language designs have learned of the importance of supporting such constructs directly.

The traditional approach to universal quantification in the context of SQL is to translate the quantification using correlated subqueries and negation (NOT EXISTS/NOT IN). Then such queries are unnested using traditional methods. However, this has the result of adding outerjoins and grouping to the query plan, which are difficult to deal with because they do not posses some properties of other relational operators (i.e. commuting). This has motivated research on dealing with such operators: (J. Rao, Pirahesh, & Zuzarte, 2004) provides several alternatives to dealing with outerjoins in the query tree, while (Galindo-Legaria & Rosenthal, 1997) gives conditions under which we can get rid of outerjoins (reducing them to joins), as well as a generalized outerjoin operator which has the advantage of commuting with joins -and hence can be moved around the query tree. (Cao & Badia, 2005) deals with complex subqueries in SQL by using nested algebra in the query tree. Complex conditions can be expressed then as simple selections with set predicates, instead of using outerjoins (negation, for instance, becomes set difference, or checking whether a given set is empty). For instance, in our recurring example the join of tables ORDER, LINEITEM, SUPPLIER and NATION can be nested by orderkey to associate the set of suppliers of each order (and their nationalities) directly to each order. Then a complex selection on the nested attribute supkey would demand that all supplier keys associated with an order have Germany as associated nationality. This can be expressed as a set condition or as a *Boolean* condition, supkey. nation=Germany (where the conjunction ranges over the set of suppliers for a given order). An advantage of this approach is that all types of conditions can be treated in a uniform manner: it can be shown that any SQL subquery predicate (predicates with IN, NOT IN, EXISTS, NOT EXISTS, and even comparisons and aggregations) can be processed with the same basic algorithm. This results in predictable query plans and costs for any SQL query. Even though this approach is shown to be superior to the traditional SQL approach in (Cao & Badia, 2005), there are also some drawbacks: specifically, both outerjoins and nested relations tend to create large intermediate tables, which negatively affects performance.

We summarize past contributions in Table 1. For each proposal, we identify the following characteristics:

- **Language:** In which high-level language, if any, is the proposal expressed? The most common choices are RA, SQL, or no language (when only an algorithm/implementation is proposed).
- **Coverage:** Which set operators/quantifiers are supported by the approach? The three levels are: universal/set inclusion (only the universal quantifier, or the set inclusion predicate, is supported), fixed (a fixed number of operators, including the universal quantifier/set inclusion, are supported), and extendible (an arbitrary number of operators is supported).
- **Implementation:** An implementation (algorithms) provided?
- **Data Model:** What data model does the proposal assume?

All the work cited is shown in chronological order, with earlier papers on top and later papers at the bottom. Table 1 allows us to make some general observations:

- Even though other cases are also covered, the universal quantifier has received more attention than any other quantifier.

Table 1. Comparison of approaches

Proposal	Language	Coverage	Implementation?	Data Model
Demolombe ((Demolombe, 1982))	RA	universal	No	Relational
Dadashzadeh ((Dadashzadeh, 1989))	RA	fixed	No	Relational
Ozsoyoglu and Want ((Ozsoyogly & Wang, 1989))	RA	fixed	No	Relational
Fragatelli (Fragatelli, 1991)	SQL	fixed	Yes	Relational
Graefe and Cole ((Graefe & Cole, 1995))	none	universal	Yes	Relational
Hsu and Parker ((Hsu & Parker, 1995))	SQL	fixed	No	Relational
Rao et al ((S. Rao, Van Gucht, & Badia, 1996))	SQL	fixed	Yes	Relational
May et al. (May et al., 2004)	XQuery	fixed	No	XML
Rantzau and Mangold ((Rantzau & Mangold, 2006))	SQL	universal	Yes	Relational
Cao et al. ((Cao & Badia, 2013))	SQL	extendible	Yes	Relational
Li et al. ((Li, He, Yan, & Safiullah, 2014))	SQL	universal	No	Relational

- Most of past work focused either on the language level or in the algorithmic level only, while most current work addresses both (proposals that extend the language without explaining how the extensions are to be incorporated into query processing will no longer do).
- Most work has focused on the relational model (likely a reflection that query optimization is more mature in this model). Only recently have other models been explored.
- Only the GQ (Generalized Quantifier) proposal supports an extendible set of operators.

Some further, more recent work is reviewed in Subsection 5.3.

4. GENERALIZED QUANTIFICATION

When giving the definition of the basic concept of this section, that of *Generalized Quantifier (GQ)*, it must be noted that GQs are extremely powerful; here we focus on a very narrow view that is enough for our purposes.

In general, a *type* is a finite sequence $[k_1 \dots k_n]$ of positive natural numbers, and a GQ of type $[k_1 \dots k_n]$ in domain D is a relation defined between subsets of $D^{k_1} \times \dots \times D^{k_n}$ (i.e. between elements of where P(A) denotes the *finite powerset* of A. Further, Q is closed under permutations: if $(A_1 \dots A_n)$ with $A_i \subseteq D^{k_i}$, $1 \leq i \leq n$ are in the extension of Q in D, and $f:D \rightarrow D$ is a permutation, then $(f[A_1] \dots f[A_n])$ is also in the extension of Q in D .

In this paper, we limit ourselves to types [1] (called *unary*) and [1,1] (called *binary*) GQs, and therefore adopt the following definitions.

Definition 4.1 *Given a domain* D,

- ○ *A generalized quantifier (GQ) of type* [1] *is a collection of finite subsets of* D *that is closed under permutations on* D .
- ○ *A generalized quantifier (GQ) of type* [1,1] *is a collections of pairs of finite subsets of* D *(equivalently, a binary relation on* P(D)×(D) *that is closed under permutations on* D .

The constraint to be closed under permutations makes GQs *generic* ((Abiteboul, Hull, & Vianu, 1995)), that is, it makes sure that they are not defined based on the particular data values of a database and hence are well defined across databases. Moreover, it can also be argued that the behavior of a quantifier should be independent of the context. Hence, it is sometimes assumed (and we will assume it here) that the definition is independent of D (formally, for all $D' \supseteq D$, $Q_D(A)$ iff $Q_{D'}(A)$ and $Q_D(A,B)$ iff $Q_{D'}(A,B)$). In the context of database query languages, independence from contexts ensures that GQs are *domain independent* ((Abiteboul et al., 1995)), that is, that their behavior in a database is solely determined by the elements in the domain of the database, and nothing outside such domain.

Some examples of type [1] GQs include (we assume from now on that a given set D, which can be identified with the *active domain* of the database, is given, and write Q(A) to indicate that set A belongs to the extension of Q in D):

$$
\begin{aligned}
\text{some}\!\left(A\right) &= \{A \subseteq D \mid A \neq \varnothing\} \\
\text{all}\!\left(A\right) &= \{A \subseteq D \mid A = D\} \\
\text{atleast3}\!\left(A\right) &= \{A \subseteq D \mid |A| \geq 3\} \\
\text{no}\!\left(A\right) &= \{A \subseteq D \mid |A| = \varnothing\} \\
\text{half}\!\left(A\right) &= \{A \subseteq D \mid |A| = \frac{|D|}{2}\} \\
\text{10\%of}\!\left(A\right) &= \{A \subseteq D \mid |A| = \frac{|D|}{10}\}
\end{aligned}
$$

Note that **some** corresponds to the existential quantifier of FOL (as used in $\exists x P(x)$), and **all** corresponds to the universal quantifier (as used in $\forall x P(x)$). Note also that the above examples can be easily generalized to include *at least* n, *at most* n, where n is any natural number, and to m%of, where n is any number between 1 and 100.

Similar GQs of type [1,1] are shown below.

all$(A,B) = \{A,B \subseteq D \mid A \subseteq B\}$

some$(A,B) = \{A,B \subseteq D \mid A \cap B \neq \varnothing\}$

no$(A,B) = \{A,B \subseteq D \mid A \cap B = \varnothing\}$

not all$(A,B) = \{A,B \subseteq D \mid \text{not } A \subseteq B\}$

all but n$(A,B) = \{A,B \subseteq D \mid |A - B| = n\}$

at least n$(A,B) = \{A,B \subseteq D \mid |A \cap B| \geq n\}$

half$(A,B) = \{A,B \subseteq D \mid |A| \times 2 = |A|\}$

I$(A,B) = \{A,B \subseteq D \mid |A| = |B|\}$

Note again that binary **some** corresponds to the existential quantifier of FOL (as used in $\exists x(P(x) \wedge Q(x))$), and binary **all** corresponds to the universal quantifier (as used in $\forall x(P(x) \rightarrow Q(x))$). That is, each type of quantifier reflects a certain typical use of that quantifier.

The following is a basic property of our definition of GQ that will be used in the following:

Lemma 4.2 *For any GQ* Q *on domain* D,
- *If* Q *is of type* [1], Q *can be defined by an arithmetic predicate with parameters* |A| *and* |D − A|.
- *If* Q *is of type* [1,1], Q *can be defined by an arithmetic predicate with parameters* |A − B|, |B − A|, |A∩B| *and* |D − (A∪B)|.

(This lemma is proved in (Westerstahl, 1989) and (Badia, 2009); the reader is referred to (Westerstahl, 1989) for more formal background on GQs). As an example, **all**(A) can be defined as |A|=|D|, or as |D − A|=0 ; **some**(A) can be defined by |A|>0, and so on. Likewise, **all**(A,B) can be defined as |A|=|A∩B|, or as |A − B|=0 ; **some**(A,B) can be defined by |A∩B|>0, and so on. This lemma explains why most subqueries in SQL can be rewritten using the aggregate COUNT. For instance, the predicate EXISTS (Select attr ...) can be considered equivalent to 0 < (Select count(attr) ...).

The above characterization can be simplified considerably by the following observations. First, as stated above most GQs are domain independent. Intuitively, a quantifier is *domain dependent* if D is used in its definition. Typical examples are **all**(A), **half**(A), **all − but − n**(A,B) [7]. A quantifier is *domain independent* if its definition depends only on A (for type [1]) or A and B (for type [1,1]). Typical examples are **some**(A) (and **some**(A,B)), **at least n, at most n** (both unary and binary). For the work developed here, the importance of this distinction is that domain independent type [1] quantifiers can be defined exclusively by |A|, while domain dependent quantifiers need |A| and |D − A| . But even for domain independent type [1] GQs, we have that for finite domains (the only ones we will consider here), |D - A| = |D| - |A|, which makes this parameter easier to compute. Finally, for GQs of type [1,1], is it extremely common that only domain independent examples are used; therefore they can be defined without regard for the parameter D − (A∪B) . Thus, in practice, most type [1] GQs can be defined by an arithmetic predicate on |A| or on |A| and |D| ; and most type [1,1] GQs can be defined by an arithmetic predicate on |A∩B|, |A - B| and |B − A| . Again, note that, on finite sets, |A − B|=|A| - |A∩B| and |B − A|=|B| - |A∩B| . Hence all we really need for binary GQs is |A|, |B| and |A∩B| . Moreover, for the most common cases, the arithmetic predicate involved is quite simple, as can be seen in the examples provided. As we will see, these simplifications are of considerable help in implementing the quantifiers as operators.

5. APPLICATION TO SQL

In this section we apply the theory to optimization of set-oriented SQL queries. In what follows, we call conditions in the WHERE clause that involve a subquery *linking conditions*. Most linking conditions in SQL involve the comparison of an attribute value with the result of a subquery, using a modifier. There are three such basic types of modifiers: IN (and its negation, NOT IN); comparisons with modifiers SOME and ALL; and direct comparisons with a subquery that computes an aggregate. A fourth type of linking condition just involves a subquery and the modifier EXISTS (or its negation, NOT EXISTS). For each linking condition, SQL subqueries can be classified as *non-correlated* and *correlated*. When a subquery is correlated, we call the predicate in the subquery that introduces the correlation *correlated predicate*. The comparison operator is the *correlated operator*, while the attribute from the outer query is the *correlated attribute*. As an example, in the queries of section 2, we have that in Query 1, NOT EXISTS c_name is the linking condition, and c_nation = C1.c_nation is the correlated predicate and C1.c_nation is the correlated attribute. In query 2, the linking condition here is C1.c_acctbal >= ALL c_acctbal, and the correlated condition is C1.c_nation = c_nation again (query 3 has the same linking condition but no correlation). In query 4, NOT EXISTS S.supkey and S.nationkey NOT IN N.n_nationkey are the linking conditions, and S.supkey = L.supkey is the correlated predicate, with L.supkey the correlated attribute.

As explained in section 2, we can divide set-oriented predicates in SQL in three main types: those involving a single set alone (EXISTS/NOT EXISTS), those involving a set and a tuple (IN/NOT IN, comparisons with SOME and ALL), and those involving a comparison between two sets. However, it is well known that queries with the EXISTS or NOT EXISTS predicate and a correlated subquery are equivalent to queries with the IN and NOT IN predicates (we saw an example in section 2, when Query 1 was rewritten as Query 2). Queries with the EXISTS or NOT EXISTS predicate and a non-correlated subquery are very rare, as they correspond to a condition which is either always true or always false, for all rows of a given relation. For instance, the query

QUERY 7
```
Select c_name
From Customer Where
EXISTS (Select *
            From Customer
            Where c_acctbal > 20,000)
```

will retrieve the names of all customers, if there exists at least one customer whose balance is higher than 20,000, or nobody at all (if there is no such customer). There is only one good way to execute such queries: to execute the subquery, check the result, and proceed with the outer query block in consequence (in this example, check if there is a customer whose balance is higher than 20,000; if this is so, scan Customer to retrieve all names; otherwise, don't do anything). Because they are quite unusual, and they don't lend themselves well to optimization, this type of queries are rarely studied. Thus, in practice, we can divide quantification in SQL into two main types: those comparing a tuple with a set, and those comparing two sets. The first type were called *semi-quantifiers* in (Wagner & Badia, 2014) since they can be seen as a predicate involving a quantifier of type [1] and a single row. The second type can be seen as using quantifiers of type [1,1] and were investigated in (Cao & Badia, 2013). We review each type in turn.

5.1 Semi-Quantifiers

Subqueries that compare a set with a single value can be formalized as follows:

Definition 5.1 *Given a set* A, *an element* e, *and a comparison operator* θ, *we define* $\Psi_{e,\theta}(A) = \{a \in A | (e \, \theta \, a)\}$.

As an example, let $A = \{1,2,3,4,5\}$. Then $\Psi_{3,<}(A) = \{4,5\}$, where $e=3$ and θ is $<$. Observe that $\Psi_{e,\theta}(A) \subseteq A$ for all e, θ . Observe also that this can be expressed in RA with   if we think of A as a table (a set of tuples) with schema $\{a\}$. The notation can be easily extended to arbitrary tuples by specifying which attribute within a tuple is to be used for the comparison, and we will do so later.

We can now use unary GQs to model linking conditions: a linking condition att θ MOD SUBQ, where att is an attribute name, θ a comparison operator, MOD one of ALL or SOME, and SUBQ an SQL subquery is true iff

$$MOD(\Psi_{attri,\theta}(A))$$

is true, where A is the result of evaluating the subquery SUBQ. As an example, att θ ALL SUBQ becomes $ALL_\theta(att,A)$; in a similar fashion, att θ SOME SUBQ becomes $SOME_\theta(att,A)$. For instance,

Queries 2 and 3 in Section 2 have as linking condition c_acctbal >= ALL c_acctbal which results in predicate $ALL(\Psi_{cacctbal,\geq}(A))$, where A represents the result of evaluating the subquery (so it contains a relation with schema (c_acctbal)).

This takes care of the linking condition. Call E the result of evaluating a query outer block *without the linking condition*. Then, evaluating the whole query comes down to evaluating the expression

$$\sigma_{MOD\left(\Psi_{att,\theta}(A)\right)}\left(E\right)$$

that is, the result of computing the linking predicate on the tuples of the outer query using the inner query as part of the predicate. In this notation, computing the linking predicate with quantifiers is naturally embedded within RA . As an example, Query 3 from Section 2 becomes

$$\pi_{c\_name}\left(\sigma_{ALL\left(\Phi_{c\_acctbal,\geq}\left(\pi_{c\_acctbal}(Cus)\right)\right)}\left(Cus\right)\right)$$

Correlated subqueries can be formalized with an extension of this approach. The basic difference between the non-correlated and the correlated case is that, in the correlated case, values from the outer block are not compared to a single, unchanged set A ; each value $e \in E$ is compared to a set A_e — one can think of the inner query as being divided into chunks or subset by the tuples in the outer query. For instance, in Query 2 in Section 2, A_e corresponds to dividing up table CUSTOMER by c_nation; here e is c_nation; thus, set A_e given by

$$A_e = \pi_{c\_name}(\sigma_{C1.c\_nation=c\_nation}(Customer))$$

(Recall that C1 is just an alias for table CUSTOMER).

Let E and A denote, as before, the result of evaluating the outer block (without the linking predicate) and the inner block (without the correlation). Then, for tuple $e \in E$, let A_e be the result of applying the correlation to A. Then, the linking predicate is true iff

$$MOD\left(\Psi_{attr_1,\theta}\left(A_e\right)\right)$$

is true. As before, we can compute the whole query by computing

$$\sigma_{MOD_{A_e}\left(\Psi_{attr_1,\theta}(A_e)\right)}\left(E\right)$$

As an example, Query 2 in Section 2 would result in expression

$$\pi_{c\_name}\left(\sigma_{ALL\left(\Phi_{c\_acctbal,\geq}(A_e)\right)}\left(Cus\right)\right)$$

where A_e is defined above.

As for other SQL predicates with subqueries, it is well known that IN is equivalent to = SOME, and is NOT IN equivalent to ≠ ALL. We can formalize this as:

$$IN(e,A) \equiv SOME(e,=,A) = \{a \in A | a = e)\} \neq \emptyset$$

Similarly,

$$NOT\text{–}IN(e,A) \equiv ALL(e,\neq,A) = \{a \in A | a \neq e) = A\}$$

Likewise, subqueries with EXISTS and a correlation predicate att θ att2 are equivalent to att θ SOME (SELECT att2...), while subqueries with NOT EXISTS have a similar translation using ALL and a negation of the θ operator (as we saw with Queries 1 and 2 in section 2). Therefore, all complex SQL predicates with (single) subqueries (except those that use aggregate functions) can be reduced to a semi-quantifier. As an example, the skyline query (Query 1) in section 2 gets translated as Query 2, as shown above.

This approach opens the door to an interesting possibility: as many more GQs are available than just **some** and **all**, one could conceive of SQL predicates corresponding to such other GQs. That is, other possibilities for MOD are possible, like 10%of, **half**, or **at most 5**. For instance, we have that

$$\textbf{at least } 3_\theta(e,A) = (|e,\theta,A|) \geq 3$$

$$\textbf{at most } 5_\theta(e,A) = (|e,\theta,A|) \leq 5$$

$$\textbf{10\%of}_\theta(e,A) = (|e,\theta,A|) = |A| \times .10$$

Thus, SQL could allow conditions like Query 5 of section 2, which in our approach becomes

$$\pi_{c\_name} \left(\sigma_{half\left(\Phi_{e,>}\left(\pi_{c\_acctbal}(Cus)\right)\right)_{c1.c\_nation}} (Cus) \right)$$

Note that this quantifier is treated similarly to others, without the need for any additional constructs. Finally, we note that in this approach there is even the possibility to allow users to define their own quantifiers ((Badia, 2009)) and hence their own semi-quantifiers. We will not explore this possibility here but will indicate how this approach can be efficiently supported.

When giving an implementation, one of the main challenges is to support a wide variety of GQs. To achieve this, we exploit the lemma 4.2 and provide a basic mechanism to evaluate |A| and |D| . We assume that for each quantifier Q, a predicate eval(Q,|A|,|D|) is given, and that such predicate is a simple arithmetic expression that depends only on Q -this is indeed the case for the more common quantifiers, see the examples above (and (Badia, 2009) for more details). We then translate set A into a Select-Project-Join query, then apply group by (if the subquery is correlated) and a count aggregate to get |A|. Then the arithmetic operator that defines Q can be seen as a simple selection, and therefore implementable in standard ways. As an example, the translation of query 3 is evaluated as follows: join CUSTOMER with itself on predicate CUSTOMER.c_acctbal >= C1.c_acctbal; apply group by c_name and the aggregate count to each group (yielding, for each customer c, the number of customers such that c has a larger or equal balance); separately, apply count to CUSTOMER (to find out the total number of customers). Finally, compare the number associated with each customer c with this value: if they coincide, c has an account balance larger or equal than all customers. Basically, we are checking **all** by computing $|A|=|D|$, where D here refers to the domain of reference for the query (the set of all customers).

As for correlated subqueries, we have the expression A_e, with the set A corresponding to the result of evaluating the inner query block of an SQL query, while the element e comes from the result of evaluating the outer query block of an SQL query, what we called E above. The approach here is to join A and E and split A into sets based on the e value, similarly to what is done in traditional unnesting. As an example, the translation of query 2 is evaluated as follows: join CUSTOMER with itself on predicate CUSTOMER.c_nation = C1.c_nation; apply group by c_name and the aggregate count to each group on condition CUSTOMER.c_acctbal >= C1.c_acctbal; (yielding, for each customer c, the number of customers from the same country as c such that c has a larger or equal balance); separately, apply count to the grouping of CUSTOMER by c_nation (to find out the total number of customers on each nation). Finally, compare the number associated with each customer c with the number of customers on c 's nation (a simple join): if they coincide, c has an account balance larger or equal than all customers on c 's nation. As before, we are checking **all** by computing $|A_e|=|D|$ [8].

This basic algorithm is completely general and it can be used to support any GQ, including **some, all**, or others like **half, 10%of**,…(note also the similarity of the correlated and non-correlated approaches.) At the same time, the algorithm can be optimized quite efficiently using general properties of GQs. For instance, the algorithm for ALL outlined above can be optimized by noting that the operator θ provides an *order* for the comparisons (as an example, in Queries 2 and 3 we compare account balances with $\geq$.) Thus, if we sort such balances from higher to lower, we can easily find out the account that is higher than all the others. Similarly, if we were asked to implement Query 5, we could scan down the ordered list of balances to find the ones which are higher than half of them quite easily. Similar optimizations are possible in other cases; these optimizations depends on θ (the particular comparison operator) and Q (the particular quantifier).

Even though this approach may seem simple, it has the advantage of being applicable to any GQ of type [1] considered here. In fact, it can be applied to any unary quantifier, including *user-defined* quantifiers: all a user has to do is to provide the arithmetic predicate that defines the quantifier. Then, the approach given above can incorporate such quantifier into query processing by using the given arithmetic predicate in a selection. This approach also takes maximum advantage of existing relational technology; in particular, it is amenable to relational optimization, since the quantified query is translated into a typical relational query. It can also be optimized using GQ properties. We do not discuss these details here due to lack of space; the interested reader can consult (Wagner & Badia, 2014), which includes experimental results showing that the approach is quite efficient. In particular, the GQ approach handles a large class of queries in a uniform manner. This has practical consequences for query optimization. In SQL, expression of different quantifiers requires different types of queries, some of them difficult to write and optimize. Some quantifiers (like **some, at least n**) are *monotonic* (Abiteboul et al., 1995) operators, and can be expressed easily in relational algebra/SQL (usually with join); on the other hand, some quantifiers (e.g., **all, no**) are *non-monotonic* operators, and are difficult to express in relational algebra/SQL. Usually, set difference or another set predicate is needed ((Leinders & den Bussche, 2005) provides theoretical justification for this distinction.) The experiments in (Wagner & Badia, 2014) show that the GQ approach outperforms the traditional SQL approach (using NOT IN/NOT EXISTS) in complex queries involving non-monotonic operators, while doing as well as SQL with monotonic operators[9]. Also, the GQ approach is shown to scale quite well, both in the complexity of the query and in size of data.

5.2 Full Quantifiers

Quantifiers of type [1,1] can be used to represent complex conditions that in SQL would require several subqueries (perhaps nested), or a rewrite using grouping, counting and (in many cases) subqueries in a HAVING clause. A typical example is the universal quantifier exhibited by Query 4 in section 2, which can be rewritten as

```
Select O.o_orderkey
From Orders O, Lineitem L
Where O.o_orderkey = L.o_orderkey
and ALL (Select S.supkey
From Supplier S
Where S.supkey = L.supkey)
(Select S.supkey
From Supplier S, Nation N
Where S.nationkey = N.n_nationkey
and n_name =      'Germany')
```

We have here a use of ALL(A,B) where A is the subquery denoting all suppliers for a given order, and B is the set of suppliers from Germany. If A is contained in B, this means that all suppliers for the order are from Germany, as the original query intended. Likewise, it would be very easy in this approach to retrieve the orders where some, half of, at least 10, etc. suppliers were from Germany: all we would need is to use the corresponding GQ instead of ALL.

The challenge of how to efficiently implement all such quantifiers can be answered in a manner similar to that used for semi-quantifiers. Again, lemma 4.2 tells us that if we can build the sets A and B, and determine the cardinalities of A, B and A∩B, we can decide whether Q(A,B) for any GQ Q by using the associated arithmetic predicate that defines it. A direct way to implement this approach is: first, compute A and B (note that we can assume that A and B correspond to simple SPJ queries since, if they are not, they can be expressed as a quantified query $Q''(A',B')$ which can be recursively processed); then, apply grouping (if the corresponding subquery is correlated) and the count aggregate, to obtain the cardinality (a join can be used to compute the cardinality of A∩B); finally, apply a selection where the condition is the arithmetic predicate defining the quantifier. If either A or B correspond to correlated subqueries, we have an expression A_e or B_e whose cardinality for each value of E can be calculated by using grouping. As an example, in query 4 we have that

$$A_e = \pi_{supkey}(Supplier)_{supkey=LINEITEM.supkey}$$

with the parameter e from LINEITEM.supkey, and

$$B = S\pi_{supkey} \left(\sigma_{S.nationkey=N.n\_nationkey \ and \ n\_name='Germany'}(Supplier \bowtie Nation) \right)$$

As stated, A_e corresponds to a correlated subquery, and B to a non-correlated subquery. We proceed as follows: once A_e and B are computed, we compute ALL(A_e,B) for each value e. This can be done, according to lemma 4.2, by computing $|A_e \cap B| = |A_e|$. This is implemented by joining A and B, grouping by e and applying a count aggregate to each group; for each e, the resulting count is compared to the result of applying the aggregate count to all of A_e. In the example above, we have the following: give A_e (the join of LINEITEM and ORDER) and B (a selection on the join of SUPPLIER and NATION, yielding the list of suppliers from Germany), we compute their join, group by orderkey and apply count(supkey), to get the number of suppliers from Germany for each order; likewise, we apply count(supkey) to B separately to get the number of suppliers from Germany. When the number of suppliers from Germany in a given order is equal to the total number of suppliers from Germany (which can now be checked with a simple condition), that order qualifies.

We point out that other evaluations are possible; for instance, we could compute $|A_e - B| = 0$ by using set difference (or antijoin): that is, we do a set difference (or antijoin) of A_e and B; as before, we group by orderkey and apply count(supkey) to the groups. When the count is zero, the order qualifies[10].

This approach was implemented and tested in (Cao & Badia, 2013); the results obtained there are very similar to the case of semi-quantification. In particular, the approach is very uniform and hence it shows very similar costs for all quantifiers, including the universal, existential and other quantifiers. Compared to a typical relational approach, monotonic GQs (which can be implemented in the SPJ framework) have similar costs on both the relational and quantification approaches. Where the latter shines is in the case of non-monotonic GQs, like the universal operator, where the quantification approach significantly outperforms the relational approach. As in the case of semi-quantifiers, there is also the possibility of optimizing quantified queries using GQ properties; these optimizations further increase the advantage of the quantification approach (see (Cao & Badia, 2013) for experimental results and details on GQ optimization).

5.3 Other Approaches

The approach proposed in the previous subsection has similarities with the SegmentApply operator of (Galindo-Legaria & Joshi, 2001) in the case of correlated subqueries. This is a *higher-level* relational operator, in that a given relation is partitioned with a grouping operator and then a complex condition is applied to each group -so SegmentApply deals with sets of relations, as each group is treated an an independent relation. For example, on our running example of the orders where all the suppliers are from Germany, SegmentApply would break the table ORDERS $\bowtie$ LINEITEM $\bowtie$ SUPPLIERS into groups for each order. Then a condition can be applied to each group. Note that each group represents the result of a correlated subquery, with each partition being the result of the subquery for a given value of the correlated parameter (in this example, each partition represents an order and its suppliers). Thus, the idea of applying the operations to each group is similar in both approaches, and the optimization proposed in (Galindo-Legaria & Joshi, 2001) and (Cao & Badia, 2013) overlap somewhat. The difference is that (Galindo-Legaria & Joshi, 2001) still has to deal with a set predicate on each group relying on (plain) relational algebra, while (Cao & Badia, 2013) can use Generalized Quantifiers and the approach explained in Subsection 5.2 to deal directly with it.

When dealing with the universal operator, the plans generated by the definition of ALL(A,B) as |A|=|A∩B| are very similar to those of (Chatziantoniou, Akinde, Johnson, & Kim, 2001). They implement their approach using a new operator called the Multidimensional join operator, which allows a relation to be joined with several others in parallel. The join is followed by a group by to compute several dimensions simultaneously. In our running example, only one join and one group by is required; but suppose that we wanted to check that all the suppliers in the order are from Germany and all items in the order cost more than $5; this would require two checks on different attributes. The work of (Chatziantoniou et al., 2001) is tailored for *Decision Support* queries over *data warehouses*; the relation to be joined is the *fact table*, which is matched to several *dimension tables*. The similarity of approaches shows how set-oriented queries are widely used in OLAP environments (albeit sometimes in a somewhat disguised form).

There are a few prior attempts to incorporate GQs in query languages ((Hsu & Parker, 1995; S. Rao et al., 1996)). (Hsu & Parker, 1995) argues for incorporating GQs into SQL in order to make queries easier to write. However, they only consider a finite, fixed set of GQ. The approach of (Hsu & Parker, 1995) is to write an SQL query with GQs, similarly to the rewriting of query 5 in subsection 5.2. Then, such queries are translated back into SQL without GQs by expanding the definition of the GQ into SQL, using subqueries and linking predicates as needed. For instance, GQ **all** is written using NOT EXISTS and NOT IN (see Query 4). However, it is acknowledged that the resulting query is quite inefficient; as a result, this approach may produce deficient performance. On the other hand, (S. Rao et al., 1996) provides tailored algorithms to compute the quantifiers **some, all, not some, not all** very efficiently. Relations are *encoded* using integers, so that the resulting representation can be efficiently stored in memory in many cases. Then, algorithms based on hashing are used, but the system picks a particular algorithm depending on the quantifier and applies it to the encoded data. For instance, for notall (A,B) the system would create a hash table on the encoding of B and prove it with the encoding of A, stopping as soon as some element of A fails to get into a bucket with a matching B element. The approach performs well and is highly scalable on the data; however, due to the encoding overhead, it does not do so well on complex queries that use several quantifiers. Moreover, the approach is only good for those four quantifiers, and could be very difficult to extend to arbitrary sets of quantifiers.

There has been more recent work on dealing with set predicates ((Li et al., 2014)). As in some past work, their idea is to make explicit the set manipulations required by a query instead of 'paraphrasing' them with relational operators. This makes it possible to implement set operators with dedicated algorithms. Two implementations are proposed: one that relies on grouping and counting, as in (Cao & Badia, 2013), and another one that relies on representing the set with bitmaps, and then using bit-wise operations to carry out comparisons. The bitmap approach is especially useful since compression can be used to represent large sets in memory. Moreover, histograms are used to provide useful estimates of the expected output size for each operator. The approach computes set inclusion on a collection of sets by using a hash table where each entry is a bitmap representing a set associated with a given value. Thus, in our ongoing example, a hash table for orders would be created, using a hash function on orderkey. Each entry would contain a bitmap, with a bit for each lineitem in the order. Each bitmap is compared to a bitmap for the set of German suppliers, and a bit is set to 1 if the supplier is found to be a German supplier. In the end, the hash table is scanned and an entry is chosen if the associated bitmap has n bits and represents (in binary) the number 2^n-1 (as this indicates that all bits are set to 1). This approach makes it very efficient to repeatedly check for set inclusion. Unfortunately, and also like most past work, only a fixed set of operations (CONTAINS, IS CONTAINED BY, and EQUAL) is supported by the given algorithms.

Beyond query processing and optimization research, generalized quantifiers were proposed as part of a natural language interface for databases ((Speelman, 1994)). A few years later, generalized quantifiers were also used to describe database contents in a formalization based on Description Logic ((Yi-Cheng Tu & Madnick, 1997)). However, none of these approaches considers practical aspects of implementation.

Finally, we mention that considerable work on GQs has been elaborated from a theoretical point of view (for instance, (Dawar & Hella, 1995)), as well as on applications to formal linguistics (for instance, (Westerstahl, 1995; van Benthem & Westerstahl, 1995; Keenan & Westerstahl, 1985)). The work presented here is much more pragmatic, focused on optimizing SQL. However, it is interesting to point out that the theoretical results of (Leinders & den Bussche, 2005) provide a justification for dealing with set-oriented computation at the algorithmic level, since it shows that there is no efficient way to express most set operations in the relational algebra.

6. OPEN ISSUES AND FURTHER AREAS OF RESEARCH

Even though research on processing and optimization of set-oriented queries has made tremendous progress in the last few years, there are still issues that deserve further consideration. Here we consider some of the most prominent ones; however, this list should not be regarded as neither complete nor particularly representative. Undoubtedly, in the future different researchers will focus their attention in different aspects of the problem as changes in available technology and needs make them more worthy of study.

One of the advantages of the Generalized Quantification framework is that it separates the logical issue of formalizing the semantics of operators in the language from the implementation issue of giving efficient algorithms for the operators. Thus, it is possible to implement GQs in several ways. We have already seen above that one possible implementation is through the use of grouping and counting. Another approach is the development of specific algorithms for each quantifier; in particular, algorithms based on hashing and on bitmaps have been proposed. Albeit such proposals can be difficult to develop for an unrestricted set of GQs, they can provide excellent performance for the most-commonly used GQs. To the best of our knowledge, there has been no attempt to compare all (or even some) of the available techniques to determine which approach is more efficient with large data sets. Such a comparison would allow a better understanding of the costs and resource needs of each approach, and would enable a system where all (or at least several) of those options are implemented to choose the one more appropriate to a given query and data load, just as it is done in the context of modern query optimization.

Even though we have focused on *set* oriented operations, in the context of SQL one must sometimes deal with *multisets* (that is, sets where elements may be repeated) and with *sequences* (that is, sets with an order relation among its elements). While conceptually it may not be difficult to extend GQs to deal with such cases and define a clear, formal semantics, the issue of how to optimize queries over multisets and sequences has not been studied in depth yet. There is, of course, much work in the context of XML, which is an inherently ordered data model, but such work has focused on more complex structures (usually, trees), and as not dealt with simple sets with order (see, for instance, (Chen et al., 2006; Han, Jiang, Ho, & Li, 2008)).

With the recent prominence of interest in Big Data and in tools like Hadoop ((Dean & Ghemawat, 2004)), it is natural to ask about extensions of the present issue to distributed environments. In particular, given a distributed (or parallel) database, what is the most efficient way to compute set-oriented queries? Much work has recently been devoted to SPJ queries in Hadoop and similar environments (see, for instance, (Afrati & Ullman, 2011)), but there is barely any work on queries that go beyond the SPJ framework in a distributed environment. A first attempt is presented in (Dobbs & Badia, 2014), where a *horizontally partitioned* database is queried with SQL extended with GQs, similar to the one introduced in subsection 5.2. An approach that extends the techniques of (Cao & Badia, 2013) to the distributed environment is given, as well as several optimizations specific to the distributed case. Even though the approach is experimentally shown to perform better than traditional distributed query processing, there is still much work to be done in this area.

7. CONCLUSION

We have introduced work in query processing and optimization of *set-oriented* queries. These are queries that use conditions on (non-fixed) set of tuples, and need to be expressed with negation and set difference in RA (and with subqueries, negated conditions and set difference in SQL). We have argued that such queries are quite important, especially in Decision Support environments (for instance, skyline queries are a particular type of set-oriented queries), and that they are not well supported by current optimization approaches. We have also shown that set-oriented queries and queries with universal (and other types of non-existential) quantification are closely related.

We have seen that the challenge these queries represent was recognized early on; in particular, the absence of a universal quantifier was noted and several attempts were made to incorporate it into RA (and later on, SQL). Also, several algorithms for its efficient computation have been proposed. Other recent work has also paid special attention to queries containing set-oriented predicates ((Melnik & Garcia-Molina, 2003; Mamoulis, 2003; Ramasamy et al., 2000)), showing their importance. The approach of (Badia, 2009) generalized past approaches by recognizing that not only the universal quantifier, but also other types of quantification, could be expressed as set predicates and incorporated into a query language. This approach is enough to cover all queries with subqueries in SQL ((Wagner & Badia, 2014; Cao & Badia, 2013)) except those that use aggregation.

While recent work has increased our understanding of set-oriented queries, there are still challenges to their processing and optimization, especially in the context of distributed systems for Big Data. Future research should pay attention to the special issues presented by this type of queries and address them directly, instead of relying on simply extending traditional approaches which may not be the best suited for the problem.

ACKNOWLEDGMENT

This material is based upon work supported by the National Science Foundation under Grant CAREER IIS-0347555. Any opinions, findings, and conclusions or recommendations expressed in this material are those of the author(s) and do not necessarily reflect the views of the National Science Foundation. The author wishes to thank Dr. Maria Zemankova for her patience and support.

REFERENCES

Abadi, D., Agrawal, R., Ailamaki, A., Balazinska, M., Bernstein, P. A., Carey, M. J., & Widom, J. et al. (2014). The Beckman Report on Database Research. *SIGMOD Record, 43*(3), 61–70. doi:10.1145/2694428.2694441

Abiteboul, S., Hull, R., & Vianu, V. (1995). *Foundations of databases*. Addison-Wesley.

Afrati, F., & Ullman, J. (2011). Optimizing joins in a map-reduce environment. *IEEE Transactions on Knowledge and Data Engineering, 23*(9), 1282–1298. doi:10.1109/TKDE.2011.47

Badia, A. (2009). *Quantifiers in action: Generalized quantifiers in logical, query and natural languages*. Springer.

Borzsony, S., Kossmann, D., & Stocker, K. (2001). The skyline operator. In *Proceedings of the IEEE international conference on data engineering (ICDE)* (p. 421-430). doi:10.1109/ICDE.2001.914855

Cao, B., & Badia, A. (2005). A nested relational approach to processing SQL subqueries. In *Proceedings of the ACM SIGMOD international conference on management of data* (p. 191-202). doi:10.1145/1066157.1066180

Cao, B., & Badia, A. (2013). Efficient implementation of generalized quantification in relational query languages. In *Proceedings of the very large database (vldb) endowment* (Vol. 6). Academic Press.

Carlis, J. (1986). HAS, a relational algebra operator or divide is not enough to conquer. In *Proceedings of the IEEE international conference on data engineering (ICDE)* (p. 254-261). IEEE.

Chatziantoniou, D., Akinde, M. O., Johnson, T., & Kim, S. (2001). MD-join: an operator for complex OLAP. In *Proceedings of the IEEE international conference on data engineering (ICDE)* (p. 524-533). doi:10.1109/ICDE.2001.914866

Chen, S., Li, H.-G., Tatemura, J., Hsiung, W.-P., Agrawal, D., & Candan, K. S. (2006). Twig. stack: Bottom-up processing of generalized-tree-pattern queries over xml documents. In *Proceedings of the very large database (vldb) endowment* (p. 283-294). Academic Press.

Dadashzadeh, M. (1989). An improved division operator for relational algebra. *Information Systems, 14*(5), 431–437. doi:10.1016/0306-4379(89)90007-0

Dawar, A., & Hella, L. (1995). The expressive power of finitely many generalized quantifiers. *Information and Computation, 123*(2), 172–184. doi:10.1006/inco.1995.1166

Dean, J., & Ghemawat, S. (2004). Mapreduce: Simplified data processing on large clusters. In *Proceedings of sixth symposium on operating system design and implementation*. Academic Press.

Demolombe, R. (1982). Generalized division for relational algebraic language. *Information Processing Letters, 14*(4), 174–178. doi:10.1016/0020-0190(82)90031-X

Dobbs, M., & Badia, A. (2014). Supporting quantified queries in distributed databases. *International Journal of Parallel. Emergent and Distributed Systems, 29*(5), 421–459. doi:10.1080/17445760.2014.894513

Fragatelli, C. (1991). Technique for universal quantification in SQL. *SIGMOD Record, 20*(3), 16–24. doi:10.1145/126482.126484

Galindo-Legaria, C. A., & Joshi, M. M. (2001). Orthogonal optimization of subqueries and aggregation. In *Proceedings of the ACM SIGMOD international conference on management of data* (p. 571-581). ACM.

Galindo-Legaria, C. A., & Rosenthal, A. (1997). Outerjoin simplification and reordering for query optimization. *ACM Transactions on Database Systems, 22*(1), 43–73. doi:10.1145/244810.244812

Graefe, G., & Cole, R. (1995). Fast algorithms for universal quantification in large databases. *ACM Transactions on Database Systems, 20*(2), 187–236. doi:10.1145/210197.210202

Hajeck, P. (1998). Logics for data mining. In ISAI workshop. ISAI.

Han, W.-S., Jiang, H., Ho, H., & Li, Q. (2008). Streamtx: extracting tuples from streaming xml data. *Proceedings of the Very Large Database (VLDB) Endowment, 1*(1), 289-300. doi:10.14778/1453856.1453891

Hsu, P. Y., & Parker, D. S. (1995). Improving SQL with generalized quantifiers. In *Proceedings of the IEEE international conference on data engineering (ICDE)* (p. 298-305). IEEE.

Keenan, E., & Westerstahl, D. (1985). Generalized quantifiers in linguistics and logic. In J. van Benthem & A. ter Meulen (Eds.), *Generalized quantifiers in natural language*. Foris Publications.

Leinders, D., & den Bussche, J. V. (2005). On the complexity of division and set joins in the relational algebra. In Proceedings of pods (p. 76-83). doi:10.1145/1065167.1065178

Li, C., He, B., Yan, N., & Safiullah, M. A. (2014). Set predicates in SQL: Enabling set-level comparisons for dynamically formed groups. *IEEE Transactions on Knowledge and Data Engineering, 26*(2), 438–452. doi:10.1109/TKDE.2012.156

Lindstrom, P. (1966). First order predicate logic with generalized quantifiers. *Theoria, 32*.

Mamoulis, N. (2003). Efficient processing of joins on set-valued attributes. In *Proceedings of the acm sigmod international conference on management of data* (p. 157-168). doi:10.1145/872757.872778

May, N., Helmer, S., & Moerkotte, G. (2004). Nested queries and quantifiers in an ordered context. In *Proceedings of the IEEE international conference on data engineering (ICDE)* (p. 239-249). doi:10.1109/ICDE.2004.1320001

Melnik, S., & Garcia-Molina, H. (2003). Adaptive algorithms for set containment joins. *ACM Transactions on Database Systems, 28*(1), 56–99. doi:10.1145/762471.762474

Melton, J. (2001a). *Advanced SQL: 1999: Understanding object-relational and other advanced features*. Morgan Kaufmann.

Melton, J. (2001b). *SQL: 1999: Understanding relational language components*. Morgan Kaufmann.

Mostowski, A. (1957). On a generalization of quantifiers. *Fundamenta Mathematica, 44*.

Ozsoyogly, G., & Wang, H. (1989). A relational calculus with set operators, its safety, and equivalent graphical languages. *IEEE Transactions on Software Engineering, 15*(9), 1038–1052. doi:10.1109/32.31363

Ramasamy, K., Patel, J., Naughton, J., & Kaushik, R. (2000). Set containment joins: The good, the bad and the ugly. In *Proceedings of the very large database (vldb) endowment* (p. 351-362). Academic Press.

Rantzau, R., & Mangold, C. (2006). Laws for rewriting queries containing division operators. In *Proceedings of the IEEE international conference on data engineering (ICDE)* (p. 21). IEEE. doi:10.1109/ICDE.2006.180

Rao, J., Pirahesh, H., & Zuzarte, C. (2004). Canonical abstraction for outerjoin optimization. In *Proceedings of the ACM SIGMOD international conference on management of data* (p. 671-682). ACM.

Rao, S., Van Gucht, D., & Badia, A. (1996). Providing better support for a class of decision support queries. In *Proceedings of the ACM SIGMOD international conference on management of data* (p. 217-227). doi:10.1145/233269.233334

Sarathy, V., Van Gucht, D., & Badia, A. (1993, May). Extended query graphs for declarative specification of set-oriented queries. In *Workshop on combining declarative and object-oriented databases (in conjunction with sigmod 93)*. Washington, DC: Academic Press.

Speelman, D. (1994). A natural language interface that uses generalized quantifiers. In *Lecture notes in computer science; lecture notes in artifical intelligence*. Academic Press.

van Benthem, J., & Westerstahl, D. (1995). Directions in generalized quantifier theory. *Studia Logica, 55*.

Wagner, A., & Badia, A. (2014). Complex SQL predicates as quantifiers. *IEEE Transactions on Knowledge and Data Engineering, 26*(7), 1617–1630. doi:10.1109/TKDE.2013.55

Westerstahl, D. (1989). Quantifiers in formal and natural languages. In D. Gabbay & F. Guenther (Eds.), *Handbook of philosophical logic* (Vol. IV). Reidel Publishing Company. doi:10.1007/978-94-009-1171-0_1

Westerstahl, D. (1995). Quantifiers: logics, models and computation. In M. Krynicki, M. Mostowski, & L. Szczerba (Eds.), *Quantifiers in Natural Language: A Survey of Some Recent Work*). Kluwer (Vol. I). Academic Press.

Yi-Cheng Tu, S., & Madnick, S. (1997). Incorporating generalized quantifiers into description logic for representing data source contents. In *Data mining and reverse engineering: Searching for semantics, ifip tc2/wg2.6 seventh conference on database semantics (ds-7)* (p. 329-335). Academic Press.

KEY TERMS AND DEFINITIONS

Generalized Quantifier: An extension of the concept of quantifier in first-order logic, a Generalized Quantifier (GQ) can be seen as an operation on sets. As a consequence, GQs can be used to capture properties of sets that sometimes are not expressible in a logic, thereby increasing its expressive power. In query processing, GQs are used to denote a desired condition on sets in a declarative way, leaving the query processor free to decide how to optimize its computation.

Query Optimization: The process whereby a query written in SQL (and, in general, in a declarative query language) is transformed into a query plan that will actually produce the results of running the query. Under the assumption that more than one query plan can be produced for a given query, the query optimizer chooses the plan that it deems better performing.

Set-Oriented Condition: A condition that involves a variable number of tuples. The precise tuples involved in the condition may have to be determined by another query (in SQL, a subquery).

Subquery: in SQL, it is possible to write complex conditions in the WHERE clause of a SELECT statement by using a whole query in the condition. Such a query is called a *nested query* or a *subquery*, and it can be correlated (some of its attributes depend on values of the query in which it is embedded) or non-correlated.

Tuple-Oriented Condition: A condition that involves only a single tuple in a relation, or a *fixed* number of tuples. A fixed number of tuples can be converted, within the relational algebra, to a single tuple, by using a fixed number of joins.

ENDNOTES

1   To provide examples, throughout this chapter we use the TPCH benchmark ((The TPCH Benchmark, www.tpc.org, n.d.)), a synthetic data warehousing environment used to test performance under Decision Support loads.

2   Note that this can also be done in SQL more efficiently with grouping and counting: that is, using GROUP BY supkey HAVING count(distinct partkey) = 2. However, this alternative approach is not possible when there are additional conditions; for instance, say that one part must cost over $5 and another must cost less than $5; then we need to go back to the self-join (or use the new CASE operator to get conditional counts; but this makes the query even more complex to write and optimize).

3   A skyline query typically compares tuples along several dimensions; for instance, customers would be compared not just on their account balance, but also on other attributes like their satisfaction rating, etc. But the logical structure of skyline queries is the one shown in the example.

4   Even the simpler usage of quantifiers in unanalyzed formulas ($\exists x P(x)$ and $\forall x P(x)$) correspond to set formulas (Pset$\neq\emptyset$ and Pset=D, where D is the whole universe).

5   In effect, the skyline operator is a prime example of an operator introduced into the language not because it is necessary, but because it expresses the solution to a certain class of problems in a direct manner, allowing the system to optimize such queries beyond what a traditional approach could do.

6   sch(R) denotes the schema of R, and likewise for sch(S).

7   Defined by **all-but**-n(A,B)={A,B$\subseteq$D||D-(A$\cup$B)|=n}.

8   Note that D here refers to the set of customers for a given country, i.e. it has changed to adjust to A_e.

9   In particular, after optimizations Query 5 is faster than Query 6.

10   Note that in the antijoin, tuples that do not match are kept, padded with nulls; hence the count will return zero. As for the set difference, instead of applying counting we modify it to keep the tuples that would *not* qualify for standard set difference, thus getting the result at once.

Chapter 3
Evaluating Top–k Skyline Queries on R–Trees

Marlene Goncalves
Universidad Simón Bolívar, Venezuela

Fabiana Reggio
Universidad Simón Bolívar, Venezuela

Krisvely Varela
Universidad Simón Bolívar, Venezuela

ABSTRACT

The Skyline queries retrieve a set of data whose elements are incomparable in terms of multiple user-defined criteria. In addition, Top-k Skyline queries filter the best k Skyline points where k is the number of answers desired by the user. Several index-based algorithms have been proposed for the evaluation of Top-k Skyline queries. These algorithms make use of indexes defined on a single attribute and they require an index for each user-defined criterion. In traditional databases, the use of multidimensional indices has shown that may improve the performance of database queries. In this chapter, three pruning criteria were defined and several algorithms were developed to evaluate Top-k Skyline queries. The proposed algorithms are based on a multidimensional index, pruning criteria and the strategies Depth First Search and Breadth First Search. Finally, an experimental study was conducted in this chapter to analyze the performance and answer quality of the proposed algorithms.

INTRODUCTION

In the last decade, many researchers have been interested in the problem of Skyline query evaluation because this kind of queries allows to filter relevant data from high volumes of data. A Skyline query selects those data that are non-dominated according to multiple user-defined criteria which induce a partial order over the data (Börzsönyi, Kossmann, & Stocker, 2001). It is said that one point a dominates another point b if a is as good or better than b for all criteria and strictly better than b in at least one cri-

DOI: 10.4018/978-1-4666-8767-7.ch003

terion. Skyline is also known as Pareto Curve or Maximal Vector Problem (Bentley, Kung, Schkolnick, & Thompson, 1978; Kung, Luccio & Preparata, 1975; Papadimitriou & Yannakakis, 2001; Preparata & Shamos, 1985).

However, the Skyline set may be huge because its size increases as the number of user-defined criteria augments (Bentley et al., 1978). The estimated Skyline size assuming independent dimensions is $O(\ln^{d-1}n)$ where n is the data size and d is the number of user-defined criteria (Bentley et al., 1978). Moreover, the user might require exactly k points on the result and, it is not possible for Skyline to discriminate among the answers because they are all optimal. To identify the best k Skyline points, Top-k Skyline has been proposed as a language that integrates Skyline and Top-k in order to retrieve exactly the best k points from the Skyline set based on a total order function (Goncalves & Vidal, 2009; Chan, Jagadish, Tan, Tung, & Zhang, 2006b; Lin, Yuan, Zhang, & Zhang, 2007). Particularly, Goncalves and Vidal (2012) define Top-k Skyline queries in terms of the Euclidean distance function with respect to a boundary condition defined by the user, i.e., a point belongs to the Top-k Skyline set if it is Skyline and it is one of the k nearest neighbors to the boundary condition. Also, k-Dominant Skyline (Chan, Jagadish, Tan, Tung, & Zhang, 2006a), Skyline Frequency (Chan et al., 2006b) and k Representative Skyline (Lin et al., 2007) are functions in order to measure the interestingness of each Skyline point. The Skyline Frequency ranks Skyline in terms of the number of times in which a Skyline point belongs to a non-empty subset or subspace of the multidimensional function; the user defined criteria is specified by a multidimensional function. The k-Dominant Skyline identifies Skyline points in k ≤ d dimensions of the multidimensional function. The k Representative Skyline produces the k Skyline points that have the maximal number of dominated points.

On the other hand, several existing algorithms make use of indexes defined on each user-defined criterion in order to evaluate a Top-k Skyline query (Goncalves & Vidal, 2012; Alvarado, Baldizan, Goncalves, & Vidal, 2013). In traditional databases, the use of multidimensional indexes has shown that can improve the query performance (Manolopoulos, Nanopoulos, Papadopoulos, & Theodoridis; 2013). In this chapter, R-tree based algorithms to evaluate Top-k Skyline queries are proposed where an R-tree is a multidimensional index structure that organizes the points by the closeness to each other and whose average-case search time is logarithmic (Göbel, 2007; Guttman, 1984). This index structure is a suitable to return points sorted by distance.

The proposed algorithms in this chapter apply two strategies for traversing the R-trees. These strategies are DFS (Depth First Search) and BFS (Breadth First Search) (Knuth, 1997). In addition, three pruning criteria are incorporated into the proposed algorithms in order to discard those R-tree regions in which there are not Skyline points. This way, if fewer regions are accessed because the R-tree is pruned using some pruning criterion, the algorithms will consume less time to return the response.

Finally, an experimental study on synthetic data applying our proposed algorithms was conducted in this chapter. Experimental results reveal that the BFS-based algorithms have better runtime than the DFS-based ones, except for the case with correlated data. Additionally, the pruning based algorithms typically require less time but can lose up to 18.9% of Skyline points. Therefore, the pruning criteria may reduce runtime of the algorithms although they may not produce complete answers.

This chapter is comprised of five sections in addition to section I that introduces the problem. Section II presents a motivating example and describes existing state-of-the-art approaches to compute Top-k Skyline queries. Section III defines the Top-k Skyline approach and the proposed algorithms that are able to identify the subset of the Skyline that will be required to produce the top-k objects. In Section IV, the quality and performance of the proposed techniques will be empirically evaluated. First, the execution time of the evaluation techniques will be analyzed. Second, the quality of the answer identified by the proposed techniques will be reported. Finally, the future research directions and conclusion of this chapter will be pointed out in the Sections V and VI, respectively.

BACKGROUND

This section presents a motivating example to illustrate the problem of computing Top-k Skyline queries and defines the Skyline approach and the R-tree structure. Also, several evaluation techniques are briefly described and then, it outlines the advantages and limitations of the existing solutions defined to calculate the Skyline or the Top-k Skyline set.

To motivate the problem of computing Top-k Skyline queries, suppose that a tourist needs to take a trip to the Bahamas from Venezuela. This tourist wants to choice a hotel with the lowest price and the shortest distance to the beach. A Skyline query (Börzsönyi et al., 2001) may be evaluated to suggest a set of hotels that meet the tourist's criteria, i.e., a good price and nearness to the beach. A hotel belongs to the Skyline set if and only if it is not dominated by any other hotel; a hotel dominates another one if it is better or equal in all criteria, and better in at least one criterion. However, the tourist's criteria are conflicting because the hotel closer to the beach is the most costly and the most economical hotel is far from the beach.

Table 1 shows a set of hotels with their respective distance to the beach and the average price per night. Also, on the left image of Figure 1, the hotels are represented as points on the Cartesian plane where the x-axis corresponds to the distance to the beach and the y-axis contains the price values. Additionally, a graphical representation of an R-tree structure is presented on the right image of Figure 1. An R-tree is a multidimensional index structure where the space is divided into MBR regions and the points are stored on the leaf levels. The regions of an R-tree enclose the points that are contained in a specific area and they are known as MBR (Minimum Bounding Rectangle). Thus, on the right image of Figure 1, the leaves of the R-tree includes from the hotel A to the hotel V, R_i is the region i, N_j is the node j and $Level_l$ is the level l of the tree.

This way, a hotel belongs to the Skyline set if there is no other hotel with better distance and price. In the Table 1, the hotels A, B and P are Skyline because there is not other hotel whose distance and

Figure 1. Hotels represented in the Cartesian plane and stored in an R-tree

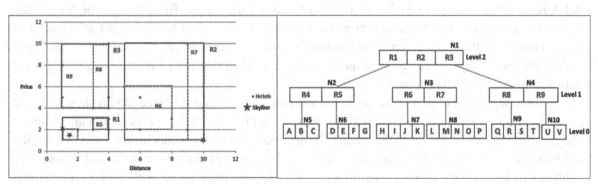

Table 1. Hotels

Id	Distance (Km)	Price (Dollars x 10²)
A	1	2
B	2	2
C	1.5	1.5
D	3	2
E	4	2
F	3	3
G	4	3
H	5	6
I	6	5
J	6	2
K	8	3
L	9	2
M	9	10
N	10	6
O	10	4
P	10	1
Q	3	4
R	4	4
S	4	5
T	4	10
U	1	5
V	1	8

price have better values than them. These hotels are represented as stars on the left image of Figure 1. Moreover, the other hotels are dominated and are not part of the Skyline set, e.g., the hotel B dominates the hotel E because it has an equal price and a better distance.

Intuitively, Skyline queries may help the tourist to make a decision when conflicting criteria are expressed. In this example, it is not possible to find a hotel closer to the beach with the lowest price. The hotel A is one of the closest to the beach, but its price is not the lowest. Even though, the hotel P has the lowest price but it is not the nearest hotel from the beach. Thus, it is hard to select an economical hotel that is close to the beach because the hotels near the beach are expensive. Therefore, economy and nearness are conflicting criteria. Skyline queries may be ideal in this situation because it may discard hotels that are worse on all criteria than some other.

Suppose now that the tourist needs to choose the best hotel among the three Skyline hotels. Top-k Skyline queries (Goncalves & Vidal, 2012) allow the tourist to filter the best k Skyline points where k is the number of answers desired by the tourist. To determine the k best points from the Skyline set, the Euclidean distance function with respect to a boundary condition for the tourist may be used. A boundary condition may be to get the points closest to the point (0,0), i.e., those hotels with the lowest price and the shortest distance from the beach. When the Euclidean distance is calculated by each Skyline hotel with respect to the boundary condition, the result is 2.23 for the hotel A, 2.23 for the hotel B and 10.05 for the hotel P. Therefore, the best hotel using the Euclidean distance or the Top-1 Skyline is the hotel A or B. Since there is a tie between A and B, either one is returned as Top-1 Skyline.

Skyline

A Skyline query selects interesting objects from a set of objects. An object is interesting if it is not dominated by any other object. It is said that an object o_i dominates another object o_j if it is equal to or better than o_j in all attributes and better in at least one attribute. Formally, let $DO = \{o_1, \ldots, o_n\}$ be a set of database objects, where each object o_i is characterized by p attributes $(a_1, \ldots, a_p)$; let m be a multidimensional function defined over a subspace S of the attributes $a_1, \ldots, a_q$ (with $q \leq p$) which induces a partial order of the objects in DO. For simplicity, we suppose that attributes related to the multidimensional function need to be minimized. The Skyline SKY_S on a space S according to a multidimensional function m is defined as follows:

$$SKY_S = \left\{ \begin{array}{l} o_i \in DO \\ | \neg \left(\exists o_j \in DO \middle| o_j.a_1 \leq o_i.a_1 \wedge \ldots \wedge o_j.aq \leq o_i.aq \wedge \left(\exists x \middle| 1 \leq x \leq q \wedge o_j.a_x < o_i.a_x \right) \right) \end{array} \right\} \quad (1)$$

In addition, (Börzsönyi et al., 2001) proposed to extend the SELECT statement of the SQL language with the SKYLINE OF clause in order to specify a Skyline query as following:

```
SELECT <attributes>
FROM <relations>
WHERE <conditions>
GROUP BY <attributes>
HAVING <conditions>
SKYLINE OF a_1 [MIN|MAX|DIFF],..., a_q [MIN|MAX|DIFF]
```

Syntactically, the SKYLINE OF clause is similar to the ORDER BY clause. $a_1, \ldots, a_q$, named dimensions, are the attributes. Domains of these attributes must have a natural ordering, such as integers, floats, and dates. MIN and MAX directives specify whether the user prefers low or high values, respectively. DIFF directive defines the interest in retaining best choices with respect to every distinct value of that attribute. The set of dimension-directive pairs comprises the multidimensional function that induces a partial order over the data.

Lastly, let

$$a_1 MIN, \ldots, a_k MIN, a_{k+1} MAX, \ldots, a_l MAX, a_{l+1} DIFF, \ldots, a_q DIFF$$

be the SKYLINE OF clause of a Skyline query, i.e., the attributes $a_1, \dots, a_k$ are maximized, the attributes $a_{k+1}, \dots, a_l$ are minimized, and the attributes $a_{l+1}, \dots, a_q$ are grouped by each distinct value. Then, an object

$$o_i = \left(v_{i1}, \dots, v_{ik}, v_{ik+1}, \dots, v_{il}, v_{il+1}, \dots, v_{iq}, v_{iq+1}, \dots, v_{in} \right)$$

dominates another object

$$o_j = \left(v_{j1}, \dots, v_{jk}, v_{jk+1}, \dots, v_{jl}, v_{jl+1}, \dots, v_{jq}, v_{jq+1}, \dots, v_{jn} \right)$$

if the following three conditions are true:

1. $v_{ir} \leq v_{jr}$ for all $r = 1, \dots, k$
2. $v_{ir} \geq v_{jr}$ for all $r = (k+1), \dots, l$
3. $v_{ir} = v_{jr}$ for all $r = (l+1), \dots, q$

where v_{il} represents the value for the attribute l of the object o_i.

If $v_{ir} = v_{jr}$ for all $r = 1, \dots, q$, then o_i and o_j are incomparable.

R-Tree

An R-tree is a multidimensional index able to organize the data according to a spatial relationship. Thus, a traditional tuple with d values may be stored in an R-tree as a d-dimensional point. These d-dimensional points are stored in regions of the R-tree in terms of the proximity between themselves. The elements of an R-tree are called nodes. Each R-tree has a root node which is a node that has no superior and the nodes without descendants are called leaf nodes. An ancestor node connects it to all lower-level or descendants nodes. Each node of the R-tree contains MBR (Minimum Bounding Rectangle) regions and has a maximum capacity to store the regions contained therein. MBRs are regions that enclose near points. Each MBR region contains in turn MBR regions in the next lower level. The MBR regions at leaves level may refer to regions or points located in the MBR region that contains them. The data entries are stored in leaf nodes. Each non-leaf node must contain the identifier of each descendant node and the information about all the regions within each descendant node. The non-leaf nodes contain index entries or pointer to descendant nodes. A MBR of a non-leaf node N is the smallest region that contains all MBRs associated with the descendant nodes; intuitively, it bounds the region containing all points stored in the sub tree connected to the node N. An example R-tree may be seen in Figure 1.

The R-trees are used to store data in pages and it is designed for the disk storage where each page has a maximum number of entries. Their indexing method is spatial because utilizes a kind of spatial relationship to organize data entries. In addition, an R-tree is a height-balanced index structure. It is said that a tree is height-balanced if the difference between heights of left subtree and right subtree is at most 1.

In this work, we develop algorithms based on R-tree indexes because they may improve the query performance on databases and they may avoid scanning the whole dataset. Using an R-tree can be known if a point dominates another point by means of its spatial location. For example, if a point "a" is above and to the right of another point "b" and the preference are maximizing criteria then the point "b" may be discarded because it is dominated by the point "a". Therefore, the spatial relationship can guide to discard dominated points or regions of the tree.

In contrast, in a B-tree index, the region associated with a node of the tree is a range of values. Suppose Figure 2, the points in the two-dimensional space of (price, distance) are totally ordered in a B-tree index. The dotted lines in Figure 2 indicate the order in which the points are stored in a B-tree; the points are sorting on price first and then on distance. Consider the point (10,1). In a B-tree, to determine if there is a point that dominates (10,1) in order to return the point (10,1) as Skyline point, all regions containing points whose distance is lower than 10 (range of values is between 1 and 9) must be accessed. Thus, for each value of distance lower than 10 and for each different value in price, it is required to verify if any point dominates (10,1). However, in an R-tree any region of the tree that is above and right will be discarded. The information area containing all points of a region is stored on each node of R-tree. Therefore, the spatial information about points and regions allow establishing conditions on regions and thus avoid accessing dominated points that will not be necessary for Skyline query processing. Although the structures of indices can avoid scanning the whole dataset, the R-tree structure allows to establish criteria on proximity in the *d*-dimensional space and therefore, some regions may be pruned. In this way, pruning criteria may be defined on MBR regions in order to discard regions without Skyline objects.

Our main goal is to avoid exploring many regions as possible because the points in those non-accessed regions will not be considered during the skyline processing. The cost of computing the skyline set will be higher as more data is accessed.

Figure 2. Total order of a B-tree

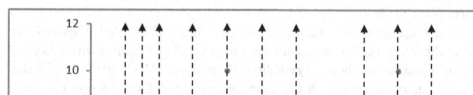

Related Work

The skyline approach has raised various research challenges. Initially, several algorithms have been developed for skyline computation on centralized databases. Initially, algorithms based on the strategies Block Nested Loops (BNL) and Divide and Conquer have been defined to evaluate Skyline queries on centralized databases (Börzsönyi et al., 2001). BNL scans the input table while it maintains a window of non-dominated tuples in main memory; tuples in the window can be replaced by any successive tuple. Later, (Chomicki, Godfrey, Gryz, & Liang, 2003) presented another algorithm called Sort-Filter-Skyline (SFS) which is a BNL variant that requires a previous topological sort compatible with the Skyline criteria and, unlike BNL, does not replace window tuples because of the initial sort phase. Finally, (Godfrey, Shipley, & Gryz, 2005) introduced Linear Elimination Sort for Skyline (LESS) that initially sorts the input like SFS does, but provides two improvements over it: the first sort phase uses an elimination-filter window to quickly discard dominated tuples and combines the last sort phase with the first Skyline filter to eliminate remaining dominated tuples.

Nonetheless, these algorithms must scan all the data to produce the Skyline set. Subsequently, progressive algorithms were developed in order to answer a Skyline query; an algorithm is progressive if may quickly return Skyline points without having to explore the whole data. By means of multidimensional structure indexes, progressive algorithms may discard regions avoiding the full reading of the data set. Some progressive algorithms based on R-trees are NN (Nearest Neighbor), which applies the Divide and Conquer principle (Kossmann, Ramsak, & Rost, 2002) and BBS (Branch and Bound Skyline) (Papadias, Tao, Fu, & Seeger, 2005). Similarly, some algorithms that use indexes defined on each Skyline criterion are RSJFH (RDF Join with Skyline Full Header) and its variants (Chen, Gao, & Anyanwu, 2011), and FOPA (Final Object Pruning Algorithm) (Alvarado et al., 2013). Nevertheless, none of these algorithms were designed to evaluate Top-k Skyline queries.

Alternatively, index-based algorithms have been proposed to evaluate Top-k Skyline queries. K-NNSkyline (K Nearest Neighbor Skyline) is an algorithm that searches the best k points from the Skyline set according to the minimum distance to a boundary condition (Goncalves & Vidal, 2012). To evaluate a Top-k Skyline query, these algorithms require a B-tree index for each user-defined criterion. However, in traditional databases, multidimensional indexes may improve the query performance on databases because they may avoid access some regions. Thus, the focus of this chapter is to develop algorithms for evaluating Top-k Skyline query in terms of R-tree indexes, the search strategies DFS and BFS, and pruning criteria.

On the other hand, with emerging trends in technologies, skyline queries have be applied to a variety of computing environments as distributed networks, real time systems, mobile devices, and Web. In distributed environment, a skyline query may be processed over distributed networks by evaluating skyline queries on different servers. The SkyPlan framework generates efficient execution plans for Skyline queries on different servers (Rocha-Junior, Vlachou, Doulkeridis, & Nørvåg 2011); an execution plan is the order in which a query will be processed. Each server stores a part of the data in distributed environments. Also, the problem of parallelizing skyline query execution over several computers has been addressed in (Wu, Zhang, Feng, Zhao, Agrawal, & El Abbadi, 2006; Cui, Lu, Xu, Chen, Dai, & Zhou, 2008; Valkanas, Apostolos, & Papadopoulos, 2010). Parallel algorithms for skyline queries on multi-core architectures are defined in (Im, Park, & Park, 2009; Cosgaya-Lozano, Rau-Chaplin, & Zeh, 2007). In addition, (Zhu, Zhou, Guanet, 2007) proposed an efficient skyline algorithm based on Chord which is a

Peer-to-peer (P2P) network infrastructure. The Skyline points are returned progressively in (Wu et al., 2006; Zhu et al., 2007). Additionally, (Cui, Chen, Xu, Lu, Song, & Xu, 2009; Chen, 2008) introduced a progressive skyline algorithm with adaptive filter technique in structured peer-to-peer networks.

In real time environment, the amount of available data may tend to be uncertain. (Kim, Im, & Park, 2011; Ding & Jin, 2011) proposed probabilistic algorithms in order to identify the skyline over an uncertain data set. Furthermore, the probabilistic contextual skyline query is defined in (Sacharidis, Arvanitis, & Sellis, 2010); it produces interesting points with high probability. Additionally, in many streaming applications, the data have a time interval in which they are valid. Thus, (Jiang, & Pei, 2009; Morse, & Patel, 2006; Hsueh, Zimmermann, Ku, & Jin, 2011) develop new algorithms in order to online answer skyline queries over a set of objects that are frequently updated.

Mobile devices are characterized by limited memory and hold a subset of the data. Thus, in mobile environment, techniques for answering skyline queries able of reducing the costs of communication among mobile devices, transferred data and execution time have been presented in (Shen, Chen, Deng, 2009; Huang, Jensen, Lu, Ooi, 2006). To handle a spatial range instead of a point or exact location, (Lin, Xu, & Hu, 2011; Qiao, Gu, Lin, & Jing Chen, 2010) proposed two algorithms in order to process the range-based skyline queries in mobile environment. Sensor applications may be supported with location based skyline queries including environment monitoring. A location based skyline query combines spatial and quality attributes simultaneously. Some works for evaluating location based skyline queries are (Reeba, & Kavitha, 2012; Xiao, Lü, Deng, 2010).

In the Web environment, to choose the best web service among similar Web services based on quality of service (QoS) parameters, efficient skyline algorithms over a set of QoS have been developed in (Alrifai, Skoutas, Risse, 2010; Benouaret, Benslimane, Hadjali, 2011). (Yu, & Bouguettaya, 2011) proposed an approach based on skyline for the problem of efficiently composing the best services in order to answer a query. Finally, skyline algorithms on service-oriented architecture (SOA) and cloud computing environments have been explored in (Huang, & Xiang, 2009; Huang, Xiang, 2010).

EVALUATING TOP-K SKYLINE QUERIES ON R-TREE

This section formalizes the Top-k Skyline definition and describes solutions to evaluate Top-k Skyline queries by traversing the R-tree structure and using pruning criteria to discard regions of the R-tree that do not contain Skyline objects.

TOP-k Skyline Queries

Let $DO = \{o_1, \ldots, o_n\}$ be a set of database objects, where each object o_i is characterized by p attributes $(a_1, \ldots, a_p)$; let d be the Euclidean distance function defined on some attributes a_p, which induces a total order of the objects in DO; let m be a multidimensional function defined over a subspace S of the attributes $a_1, \ldots, a_q$ (with $q \leq p$) which induces a partial order of the objects in DO; let SKY_S be the Skyline defined on a space S according to a multidimensional function m; let o be an object characterized by q values over a subspace S. The object o represents the boundary condition values. The conditions to be satisfied by the answers of a Top-k Skyline query with respect to the object o and the functions m and d, are described as follows:

$$\xi_{<dist,S,k>} = \left\{ o_i \in SKY_S \middle| \neg \left(\exists^{k-\left|SKY_S\right|} o_j \in SKY_S \land dist(o_j,o) \geq dist(o_i,o) \right) \right\}$$ (2)

where, $\exists^t$ means that exists at most t elements in the set and $dist\left(p,q\right)$ represents the Euclidean distance between the objects p and q.

TopKSkyDFS

In this section, we describe algorithms for computing Top-k Skyline queries when the data is indexed by an R-tree structure, using two basic strategies of tree-traversal: DFS and BFS. The meaning of the main methods invoked in each proposed algorithm is briefly defined in Table 2.

The first proposed algorithm is TopKSkyDFS which performs a depth-first search on an R-tree structure from the root node to each leaf node. Its selection criterion is based on the LIFO (Last In, First Out) principle and a stack is used to build the paths formed by each region of the R-tree.

TopKSkyDFS calculates the Top-k Skyline on the data stored in the leaves of the R-tree structure. The Skyline set for each leaf node is computed using BNL (Börzsönyi et al., 2001). BNL is used since its simplicity and it is expected that the leaves of the R-tree enclose few points. Then, the Skyline set of the first visited leaf is stored in a Global Window. Next, whenever the Skyline set is calculated on a leaf, it is compared against the Global Window. Thus, BNL is applied comparing Skylines of each leaf against data stored in the Global Window. When the R-tree is completely traversed, the Global Window contains the Skyline points. Finally, the top-k of the Global Window is calculated using the Euclidean distance function. In the Algorithm 1, the pseudocode of TopKSkyDFS is presented.

Table 2. Description of the main methods invoked in the proposed algorithms

Method	Definition
p.top()	Selects the top of a stack p.
a.pop()	Removes the first element of a stack or queue a.
a.push(r)	Inserts the element r in the structure a where r is a region and a is a queue or stack.
c.front()	Selects the first element of the queue c.
$v.BNL(pr)$	Executes BNL merging a window v and a list pr. This method is invoked for leaf nodes of an R-tree structure.
$rv.PruningBNL$ (rn)	Executes BNL merging a window rv and a list rn. This method is invoked for intermediate nodes of an R-tree structure in order to prune regions. It verifies the pruning criteria.
pr.insert(i)	Inserts the element i in the list pr, where i can be an integer, a list, a region or a point.
l.insert(p,o)	Inserts the point p and its distance from the point o into the list l.
p.dist(q)	Evaluates the Euclidean distance function between the points p and q.
s.sort()	Sorts elements of the list s.
s.TopK*Skyline*(k)	Returns the first k elements of the list s.
n.size()	Represents the capacity of the node n.

Algorithm 1. TopKSkyDFS

```
{Require: an R-tree a, a Point q, an Integer k}
1: Access to the root r of the R-tree a;
2: Create a stack p of nodes;
3: p.push (r);
4: Create a list tmp of points;
5: while p is not empty do
6:         n = p.top();
7:         p.pop();
8:          if n is a leaf node then
9:      /            Create a list pr of points;
10:                  for i = 0 to n.size() do
11:                         pr.insert (i); // Points contained in the current
                               node n are stored in pr
12:                  end for
13:                  tmp.BNL (pr);
14:         else // n is not a leaf node
15:                  for i = n.size() to 1 do
16:                         p.insert (i); // Regions contained in the current
                               node n are stored in p
17:                  end for
18:          end if
19: end while
20: Create a list s of Top-k Skyline points;
21: for each point pi into tmp do // Particularly, for each Skyline point
22:         d = pi.dist(q);
23:         s.insert (pi, d);
24: end for
25: s.sort ();
26: return s.TopKSkyline(k);
```

To illustrate the TopKSkyDFS execution, consider the R-tree structure in the Figure 3. First, TopK-SkyDFS accesses the root in line 1 of the Algorithm 1. In line 2, TopKSkyDFS creates a stack p which will store the nodes of the R-tree. In line 3, the root r of the R-tree is stored in the stack p. The MBR region associated to the root is $N1(1, 1, 10, 10)$. In line 4, the list *tmp* is created; *tmp* will contain Skyline points for apply BNL and represents the Global Window.

Since p is not empty (line 5), the top (1,1; 10,10) of p is stored in the variable n in line 6. Next, the top of p is popped in line 7. Due to the current region is not a leaf node (line 14), then the regions contained in n are inserted into the stack p from line 15 to line 17 and the stack state is $p=$ [(1,4; 4,10), (5,1; 10,10), (1,1; 4,3)], where the region (1,1; 4,3) is the stack top. In this case, the R-tree structure is traversed from left to right and therefore, the leftmost region of the node is on the stack top.

Figure 3. An R-tree for TopKSkyDFS

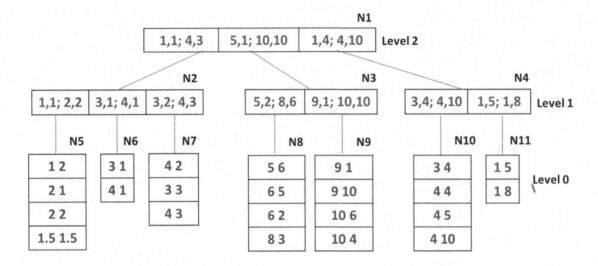

TopKSkyDFS continues iterating and (1,1; 4,3) is popped in line 7. In this moment, the stack state is p= [(1,4; 4,10), (5,1; 10,10), **(3,2; 4,3), (3,1; 4,1), (1,1; 2,2)**]. The region (1,1; 4,3) is replaced by its child nodes: (3,2; 4,3), (3,1; 4,1), and (1,1; 2,2).

When the stack state is p= [(1,4; 4,10), (5,1; 10,10), (3,2; 4,3), (3,1; 4,1), (1,1; 2,2)], the region $N5$(1,1; 2,2) is popped in line 7. Line 8 checks if $N5$ is a leaf node and thus, each point from $N5$ is inserted into the list pr from line 10 to line 12. The list pr contains [(1,2), (2,1), (2,2), (1.5, 1.5)] and the stack state is p= [(1,4; 4,10), (5,1; 10,10), (3,2; 4,3), (3,1; 4,1)]. In line 13, BNL is applied on the list pr and the Skyline set of the region (1,1; 2,2) is added to the Global Window tmp= [(1,2), (2,1), (1.5, 1.5)].

The above procedure is repeated, BNL is evaluated on $N6$, $N7$, and the remaining regions of the stack p = [(1,4; 4,10), (5,1; 10,10)]. Since these regions enclose dominated points, the Global Window tmp is equal to [(1,2), (2,1), (1.5, 1.5)]. Subsequently, the Top-k Skyline set is calculated in lines 20-26. In line 20, a list s of pairs is created. Each pair will contain the Skyline point and its distance to the point q. TopKSkyDFS accesses each Skyline point pi and calculates its distance d to the point q between the lines 21 and 24. After calculating the distance, the Skyline point pi and its distance d are inserted as a pair in the list s in line 23. Lastly, the line 25 sorts the list ascendly by distance and the first k points from the Skyline set are returned in line 26.

TopKSkyBFS

TopKSkyBFS is the second algorithm proposed in this chapter. It performs a breadth-first search on an R-tree structure and its selection criterion is based on the FIFO (First In, First Out) principle. A queue structure is used to store the visited regions.

TopKSkyBFS computes the Skyline set for all leaves of the R-tree and it stores the Skyline set for each leaf in Local Windows. The number of Local Windows is equal to the number of R-tree leaves. These Local Windows are merged using BNL by each level of the R-tree structure until obtaining a window at the level of the root node.

Intuitively, TopKSkyBFS traverses the R-tree by levels until the leaves are read and then, recursively merges regions by levels passing results up through ancestor nodes stopping when the root node is reached. In this step, the top-k of the root window is calculated in order to return the Top-k Skyline set. The Algorithm 2 introduces the TopKSkyBFS pseudocode.

Algorithm 2. TopKSkyBFS

```
{Require: an R-tree a, a Point q, an Integer k}
1: Access to the root r of the R-tree a;
2: Create a queue c of nodes;
3: c.push (r);
4: Create a list lv of local windows;
5: Create a list st2 of number of nodes per level;
6: Create a list st1 with the number of children per node;
7: while c is not empty do // First, the R-tree is traversed until the leaves
   are reached
8:          n = c.front ();
9:          c.pop ();
10:      if n is a leaf node then
11:              Create a list pr of points;
12:              Create a list tmp of points;
13:              for i = 0 to n.size() do
14:                      insert (i, pr); // Points contained in the
                         current node n are stored in pr
15:              end for
16:              tmp.BNL(pr);
17:          insert (tmp, lv); // The Skyline of the current node n is
                 stored in a list of local windows
18:       else // n is not a leaf node
19:              for i = 1 to n.size() do
20:                      c.push (i); // Regions contained in the current
                         node n are stored in c
21:               end for
22:            insert (n.num, st1); // The number of nodes referenced by
               the current node n is stored in st1
23:        end if
24: end while
25: for each level l of the R-tree
26:       insert (l.niv, st2); // The number of nodes in each level is stored
             st2
27: for each element e1 into st2 do // Second, the Skyline will be merged
28:       Create a list ve;
```

continued on following page

Algorithm 2. Continued

```
29:              for i = 1 to el do // Elements of st1 are grouped
30:                  Create a list tmp_p;
31:                  j = st1.get(i); // Get the number of elements to be grouped
32:                  List tmp_p = Get j elements from lv;
33:                   Create a list lv1 of points;
34:                   for all element e2 of tmp_p do
35:                          lv1.BNL(e2); //The Skyline is merged
36:                  ve.insert(lv1);
37:                  remove j elements from tmp;
38:          lv = ve;
39:          remove j elements from st1;
40: Create a list s of Top-k Skyline points;
41: for each point pi of lv do // Particularly, for each Skyline point
42:          d = dist (pi, q);
43:          insert (s, pi, d);
44: end for
45: s.sort ();
46: return s.TopKSkyline (k);
```

To exemplify the TopKSkyBFS execution, consider the R-tree in the Figure 4. Similar to TopKSkyDFS, TopKSkyBFS reads the root in line 1 of the Algorithm 2, it creates a queue c which will store the nodes of the R-tree in line 2, and the root r is inserted into the queue c in line 3. At this time, the queue state is $c = [(1,1; 10,10)]$. In line 4, a list lv of local windows is created; lv will contain the Skyline set of each node. In lines 5-6, two lists are created: the list $st2$ which contains the number of nodes per level and the list $st1$ which has the number of children for each node.

Since c is not empty (line 7), the front $(1,1; 10,10)$ of c is stored in the variable n in line 8. Then, the front of c is popped in line 9. Due to the current region is not a leaf node (line 18), then the regions contained in n are inserted into the queue c from line 19 to line 21 and the queue state is $c = [(1,4; 4,10), (5,1; 10,10), (1,1; 4,3)]$, where the region $(1,1; 4,3)$ is the queue front.

TopKSkyBFS continues iterating and the front $(1,1; 4,3)$ of c is popped in line 9. In this moment, the queue state is $c = [\mathbf{(3,2; 4,3), (3,1; 4,1), (1,1; 2,2)}, (1,4; 4,10), (5,1; 10,10)]$. The region $(1,1; 4,3)$ is replaced by its child nodes: $(3,2; 4,3), (3,1; 4,1)$ and $(1,1; 2,2)$.

When the queue state is $c = [(1,5;1,8), (3,4; 4,10), (9,1;10,10), (5,2; 8,6), (3,2; 4,3), (3,1; 4,1), \mathbf{(1,1; 2,2)}]$, the region $N5(1,1; 2,2)$ is popped in line 9. Line 10 checks if $N5$ is a leaf node and thus, lines 11-12 create the lists pr and tmp. Each point from $N5$ is inserted into the list pr in line 14. The list pr contains $[(1,2), (2,1), (2,2), (1.5, 1.5)]$ and the queue state is $c = [(1,5;1,8), (3,4; 4,10), (9,1;10,10), (5,2; 8,6), (3,2; 4,3), (3,1; 4,1)]$.

Line 16 invokes BNL for elements of pr merging with tmp. The window tmp contains $[(1,2), (2,1), (1.5, 1.5)]$ and represents the Skyline set of the region $(1,1; 2,2)$. This result is stored in the variable tmp and inserted into the list of local windows in lines 16-17. The current state of the queue is $c = [(1,5;1,8), (3,4; 4,10), (9,1;10,10), (5,2; 8,6), (3,2; 4,3), (3,1; 4,1)]$.

Figure 4. An R-tree for TopKSkyBFS

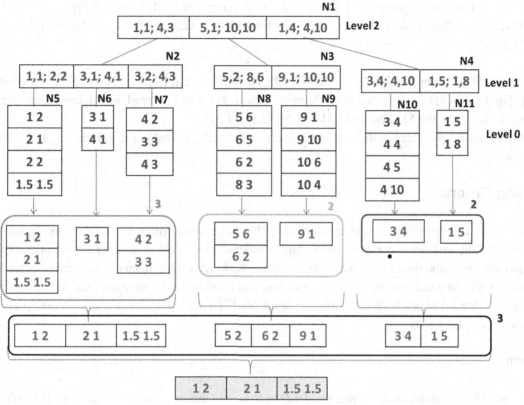

The above procedure is repeated, BNL is evaluated on *N6* and *N7*, *tmp* is updated for *N6* and *N7*, and then inserted into the list *lv*; *tmp*= [(3,1)] for *N6* and *tmp*= [(4,2),(3,3)] for *N7*.

While the R-tree structure is being traversed, two list *st1* and *st2* are created in lines 5-6; *st1* has the number of children for each node and *st2* has the number of nodes per level. The information contained in these lists during the R-tree traversal (lines 25-39) is the following:

st2= [3,1].

st1= [2,2,3,3].

lv= [[(1,5)], [(3,4)], [(9,1)], [(5,6), (6,2)], [(4,2), (3,3)], [(3,1)], [(1,2), (2,1), (1.5, 1.5)]].

The *st2* elements represent the number of *st1* elements to be grouped. Initially, the first element of *st2* is 3 which means that the first three elements [2,2,3] of *st1* will be grouped and the elements of *lv* will also grouped according to these values. Since the first element of *st1* is 2 (line 31), [(1,5)] and [(3,4)] are in the same group (line 32). Also, [(9,1)] and [(5,6), (6,2)] are part of another group (line 32) because the second element of *st1* is 2 (line 31). The third element is 3 (line 31) and represents the grouping of [(4,2), (3,3)] with [(3,1)] and [(1,2), (2,1), (1.5, 1.5)] (line 32). Subsequently, BNL is executed on each group in lines 34-35 and the result is as follows:

- BNL on the first group ([(1,5)] and [(3,4)]) returns: [(1,5), (3,4)].
- BNL on the second group ([(9,1)] and [(5,6), (6,2)]) returns: [(9,1), (5,6), (6,2)].
- BNL on the third group ([(4,2), (3,3)], [(3,1)] and [(1,2), (2,1), (1.5, 1.5)]) returns: [(1,2), (2,1), (1.5, 1.5)].

Next, the list *lv* is updated to [[(1,5), (3,4)], [(9,1), (5,6), (6,2)], [(1,2), (2,1), (1.5, 1.5)]] (line 38), *st2*= [1] and *st1*= [3] (line 39). When an element of the lists *st1* or *lv* is read, it is deleted from the lists. Finally, the last *lv* or the Skyline set is [(1.5, 1.5), (2,1), (1,2)].

Lastly, lines 40-46 calculate the Euclidean distance for each Skyline point and the Top-k Skyline set is returned.

Pruning Criteria

In this section, three pruning criteria are proposed. They are named Pruning, Pruning+ and Pruning++, respectively. The pruning criteria are conditions in order to reduce the number of dominance comparisons and the execution time of TopKSkyDFS and TopKSkyBFS. Dominance comparisons refer to the number of times in which the multidimensional function is evaluated by an algorithm. The idea of these criteria is to discard regions whose points are dominated. To achieve this goal, it is needed to verify if a region dominates another region.

Pruning

Let *r1* and *r2* be two *d*-dimensional regions; let *D* be the set of dimensions; let *r.high(x)* be the maximum value in the dimension *x* of the region *r*; and let *r.low(x)* be the minimum value in the dimension *x* of the region *r*. The first pruning criterion, named Pruning, verifies that the high values for each dimension of the region *r1* are less than or equal to the low values for each dimension of the region *r2*. Formally, the Pruning Criterion is defined as:

$$\left(\forall d \in D \mid r1.high\big[d\big] \leq r2.low\big[d\big] \right) \tag{3}$$

This is, any point of *r1* has better value than any point of *r2* and therefore, any point in *r1* dominates *r2*. To exemplify the Pruning criterion, consider the Figure 5. It can be noted that *r1*(1,1; 3,3) dominates *r2* (5,5; 7,7) because the high values (3,3) of the region *r1* are lower than the low values (5,5) of *r2*.

Pruning+

Let *r1* and *r2* be two *d*-dimensional regions; let *D* be the set of dimensions; let *r.high(x)* be the maximum value in the dimension *x* of the region *r*; and let *r.low(x)* be the minimum value in the dimension *x* of the region *r*. The second pruning criterion, named Pruning+, verifies that the high values for each dimension of the region *r1* are less than or equal to the high values for each dimension of the region *r2* and the low values for each dimension of the region *r1* are less than or equal to the low values for each dimension of the region *r2*. Formally, the Pruning+ Criterion is defined as:

Figure 5. An example of two-dimensional regions for the Pruning criterion

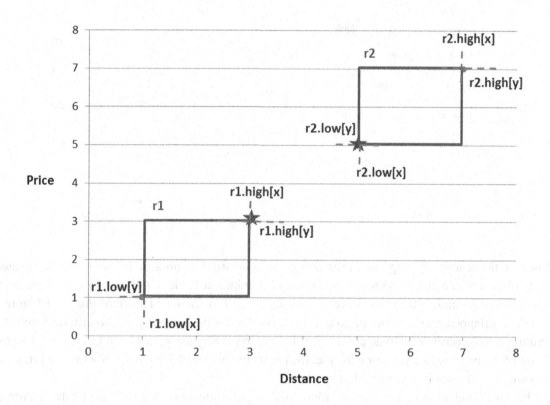

$$\left(\forall d \in D \mid r1.high\big[d\big] \leq r2.high\big[d\big] \land \mid r1.low\big[d\big] \leq r2.low\big[d\big] \right) \tag{4}$$

Pruning++

Let *r1* and *r2* be two *d*-dimensional regions; let *D* be the set of dimensions; let *r.high(x)* be the maximum value in the dimension *x* of the region *r*; and let *r.low(x)* be the minimum value in the dimension *x* of the region *r*. The third pruning criterion, named Pruning++, verifies that the low values for each dimension of the region *r1* are less than or equal to the low values for each dimension of the region *r2*. Therefore, Pruning++ is a criterion softer than Pruning+. Formally, the Pruning++ Criterion is defined as:

$$\left(\forall d \in D \mid r1.low\big[d\big] \leq r2.low\big[d\big] \right) \tag{5}$$

On the left image of Figure 6, *r1* dominates *r2*, *r3* and *r4* according to the criteria Pruning+ and Pruning ++. For example, *r1*(1,1; 3,3) dominates *r2*(5,5; 7,7) based on the Pruning+ Criterion because the low values (1,1) of *r1* are better than the low values (5,5) of *r2* and the high values (3,3) of *r1* are better than the high values (7,7) of *r2*.

Figure 6. Two examples of two-dimensional regions for the criteria Pruning+ and Pruning++

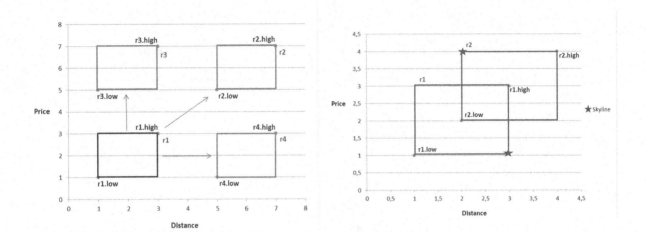

However, the criteria Pruning+ and Pruning++ verify a partial dominance between regions because they may not guarantee that all points in the region *r1* dominate all points in the region *r2*. Thus, some Skyline points may be lost using the criteria Pruning+ and Pruning++. The right image of Figure 6 shows two overlapped regions. The region *r2* is dominated by *r1* according to the criteria Pruning+ and Pruning++. Nevertheless, some points of *r2* belong to the Skyline set and will be discarded by the condition of the pruning criteria. For example, the points represented by a star are Skyline. In this case, every point of *r1* does not dominate all points of *r2*.

On the other hand, Pruning++ may lose more Skyline points than Pruning+. Consider the left image of Figure 7 in which the Skyline points are represented by stars and they are: (3,6), (6,3), (4.5,4.5). Since *r1*(1,1; 5,5) dominates *r2*(2,5; 4,7) using Pruning++, the Skyline point (3,6) is discarded. Nevertheless, *r1*(1,1; 5,5) does not dominate *r2*(2,5; 4,7) when the Pruning+ Criterion is checked and therefore, the Skyline point (3,6) is not lost. Similarly, when *r1* and *r3* are compared, the Skyline point (6,3) is discarded in terms of Pruning++ while it is not lost using the Pruning+ Criterion. Also, the right image of Figure 7 presents three 3-dimensional regions, where *r1* only discards *r3* if the Pruning Criterion is applied. According to the criteria Pruning+ y Pruning++, *r1* discards *r2* and *r3*. Nonetheless, *r1* may not dominate some points of *r2* because these regions overlap between themselves and therefore, it is possible that some points of *r2* belong to the Skyline set. Lastly, although some Skyline points may be lost if the pruning condition is soft, the experimental study shows that the pruning based algorithms reduce the execution time without losing many Skyline points.

Pruning Based Algorithms

TopKSkyDFS was extended with the three proposed pruning criteria. These extensions are named TopK-SkyDFSPru, TopKSkyDFSPru+, TopKSkyDFSPru++, respectively. For any extension of TopKSkyDFS, the lines 15-17 of the Algorithm 1 are replaced by the following lines:

```
15: Create a list tmp_r of regions;
16: tmp_r.PruningBNL(n.list());
```

Figure 7. Two examples of overlapped regions

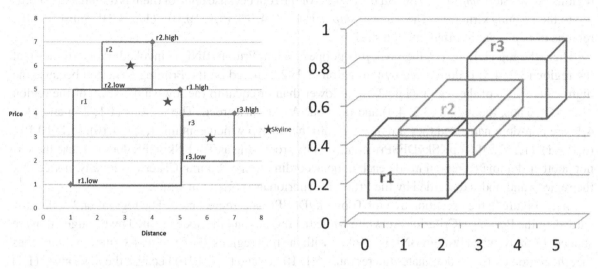

```
17: for each region reg in tmp_r do // Non-pruned regions are only considered
18:         insert(reg,p); // Non-pruned regions contained in the current node
            reg are stored in the stack p
19: end for
```

where PruningBNL discards dominated regions from the input parameter using a pruning criterion and returns non-dominated regions into *tmp_r*.

To illustrate the running of TopKSkyDFSPru consider the R-tree in the Figure 8. Similar to TopK-SkyDFS, the root is accessed. Since the root node is not a leaf, PruningBNL is invoked with the root

Figure 8. Execution tree for the TopKSkyDFSPru algorithm

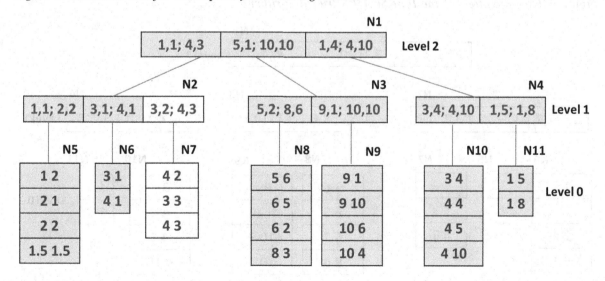

regions. In this step, *tmp_r* contains all the regions of the root because none of them is dominated according to the Pruning Criterion. The value of *tmp_r* is [(1,4; 4,10), (5,1; 10,10), (1,1; 4,3)]. Subsequently, regions of *tmp_r* are inserted into the stack *p*.

Then, the top (1,1; 4,3) of the stack *p* is popped. When PruningBNL is invoked, it determines that the region (3,2; 4,3) is dominated by the region (1,1; 2,2) based on the Pruning Criterion because the high values (2,2) of the region (1,1; 2,2) are lower than or equal to the low values (3,2) of the region (3,2; 4,3). Thus, the region (3,2; 4,3) and the node *N7* are discarded. The regions (1,1; 2,2) and (3,1; 4,1) are non-dominated and they are inserted into the stack *p* which contains [(1,4; 4,10), (5,1; 10,10), (3,1; 4,1), (1,1; 2,2)]. TopKSkyDFSPru continues its processing as TopKSkyDFS does because there is not another dominated region inside each node according to the Pruning Criterion. Finally, notice that the regions and nodes discarded by the Pruning Criterion are colored in white.

In the Figure 9, the execution tree for TopKSkyDFSPru+ is represented. The regions and nodes discarded by the Pruning+ Criterion are white while the regions and the nodes visited by the algorithm are shaded. Initially, when PruningBNL is invoked with the root regions, the Pruning+ Criterion establishes that the region (1,1; 4,3) dominates the regions (5,1; 10,10) and (1,4; 4,10) because the low values (1,1) of the region (1,1; 4,3) are lower than or equal to (5,1) and (1,4), and the high values (4,3) of the region (1,1; 4,3) are lower than or equal to (10,10) and (4,10). Thus, *p* has one region and this is [(1,1; 4,3)]. Next, the top of the stack *p* is popped and its regions are verified with the Pruning+ Criterion discarding the region (3,2; 4,3). It can be noted that the nodes *N3*, *N4*, and *N7-N11* are not read by TopKSkyDFS+ because they were discarded verifying the Pruning+ Criterion.

The Figure 10 shows the regions and nodes visited by TopKSkyDFS++; they are not colored in white. According to the Pruning++ Criterion, the regions (5,1; 10,10) and (1,4; 4,10) are dominated by the region (1,1; 4,3) since the low values (1,1) of the region (1,1; 4,3) are lower than or equal to (5,1) and (1,4). Analogously, the regions (3,1; 4,1) and (3,2; 4,3) of the node *N2* are dominated by the region (1,1; 2,2). Therefore, the nodes *N3*, *N4*, and *N6-N11* are not visited by the algorithm.

Figure 9. Execution tree for the TopKSkyDFSPru+ algorithm

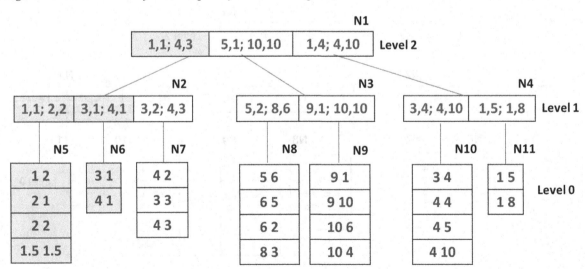

Figure 10. Execution tree for the TopKSkyDFSPru++ algorithm

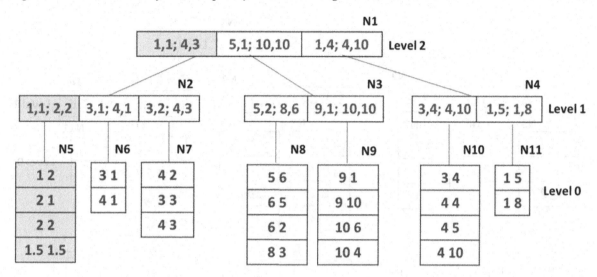

On the other hand, the algorithms TopKSkyBFSPru, TopKSkyBFSPru+ and TopKSkyBFSPru++ correspond to the TopKSkyBFS extension with the three proposed pruning criteria. For any extension of TopKSkyBFS, the lines 19-22 of the Algorithm 2 are replaced by the following lines:

```
19: Create a list tmp_r of regions;
20: tmp_r. PruningBNL(n.list()); // pruning is verified according to the
    pruning criteria
21: for each region reg in tmp_r do // Non-pruned regions are only considered
22:         insert (reg.num, st1); // The number of non-pruned nodes
            referenced by the current node is stored in st1
23: end for
```

To run the algorithms TopKSkyBFSPru, TopKSkyBFSPru+ and TopKSkyBFSPru++, consider the R-trees in the Figures 11-13. The root is accessed as TopKSkyBFS does. Then, PruningBNL is invoked with the root regions. TopKSkyBFSPru verifies the Pruning Criterion and no region is dominated on the root level. For TopKSkyBFSPru+ and TopKSkyBFSPru++, the region (1,1; 4,3) dominates the regions (5,1; 10,10) and (1,4; 4,10) according to the criteria Pruning+ and Pruning++, respectively.

On the level 1 of the R-tree, the region (3,2; 4,3) is dominated by the region (1,1; 2,2) in terms of the Pruning Criterion discarding the node N7. Thus, no other region or node is dominated using the Pruning Criterion and TopKSkyBFSPru continues traversing the R-tree as TopKSkyBFS does. However, the lists of TopKSkyBFSPru have different values:

st2= [3,1].

st1= [2,2,2,3].

lv= [[(1,5)], [(3,4)], [(9,1)], [(5,6), (6,2)], [(3,1)], [(1,2), (2,1), (1.5, 1.5)]].

Figure 11. Execution tree for the TopKSkyBFSPru algorithm

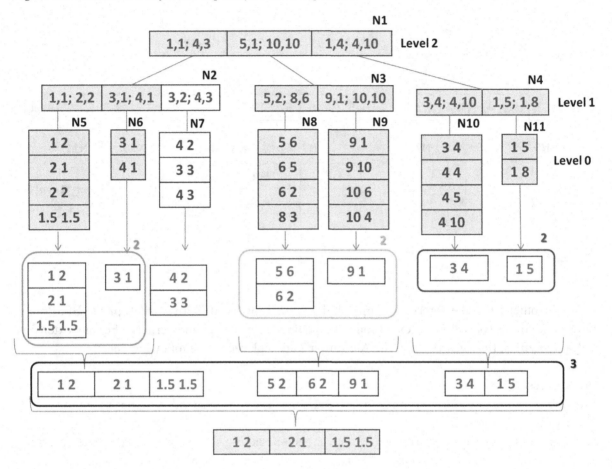

The BNL algorithm is executed on each group of pairs and the result is as follows:

- BNL on the first group ([(1,5)] and [(3,4)]) is: [(1,5), (3,4)].
- BNL on the second group ([(9,1)] and [(5,6), (6,2)]) is: [(9,1), (5,6), (6,2)].
- BNL on the third group ([(3,1)] and [(1,2), (2,1), (1.5, 1.5)]) is: [(1,2), (2,1), (1.5, 1.5)].

When the lists are updated, the Skyline set for each previous group is merged in order to produce the final Skyline. Thereafter, the k best points from the Skyline are calculated and returned.

In the Figure 12, the region (3,2; 4,3) is dominated by the region (1,1; 2,2) in terms of the Pruning+ Criterion discarding the node *N7*. Also, the nodes *N3* and *N4*, and their regions *N8-N11* were discarded by TopKSkyBFSPru+ when the root was visited. In this particular case, the lists of TopKSkyBFSPru+ contain the following values:

st2= [1,1].

st1= [2,1].

lv= [[(3,1)], [(1,2), (2,1), (1.5, 1.5)]].

Figure 12. Execution tree for the TopKSkyBFSPru+ algorithm

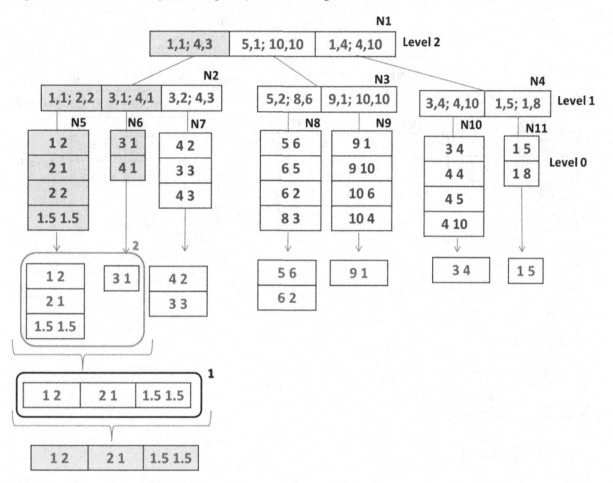

When BNL is executed on both group of *lv*, it produces the following Skyline: [(1,2), (2,1), (1.5, 1.5)]. Afterward, the Top-k Skyline set is returned.

Lastly, in the Figure 13, the regions (3,1; 4,1) and (3,2; 4,3) of the node *N2* are dominated by the region (1,1; 2,2) in terms of the Pruning++ Criterion discarding the nodes *N6* and *N7*. Also, the nodes *N3* and *N4*, and their regions *N8-N11* were discarded by TopKSkyBFSPru++ when the root was reached. Thus, the lists of TopKSkyBFSPru++ consist of the following values:

st2= [1,1].

st1= [1,1].

lv= [[(1,2), (2,1), (1.5, 1.5)]].

Finally, BNL is executed on *lv* and the Top-k is calculated on the Skyline set returning the final answer.

Figure 13. Execution tree for the TopKSkyBFSPru++ algorithm

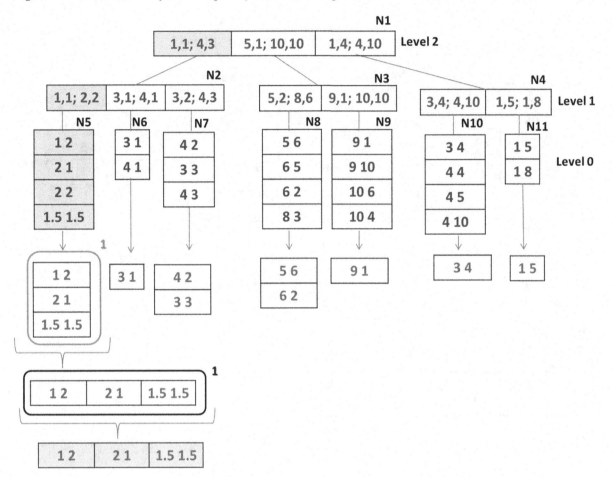

EXPERIMENTAL STUDY

In this section, we describe an experimental study to empirically analyze the quality and performance of the algorithms TopKSkyDFS and TopKSkyBFS with respect to their extensions with the three pruning criteria.

Datasets and Queries

This study was conducted on synthetic datasets. Synthetic datasets consist of a database populated from 1 to 4 million of objects. Each object contained an identifier and six columns; column values range from 0.0 to 1.0. A column may have duplicated values. Synthetic datasets were generated using the benchmark generator implemented by (Kossmann, 2009). Datasets with three different distributions were generated: correlated, anti-correlated and independent.

Additionally, five queries were randomly generated; the queries are characterized by the following properties:

1. The attributes in the multidimensional function were selected following a uniform distribution;
2. Directives for each attribute of the multidimensional function were selected considering maximizing or minimizing;
3. The number of attributes of the multidimensional function was from two to six; and
4. k was 3. These five queries were run over each dataset.

Metrics

To study the algorithm performance, the total number of comparisons, the total execution time, the memory usage, and throughput were reported. The total number of comparisons corresponds to the sum of comparisons performed to check if a point dominates another point. The total execution time and memory usage were measured by means of the time function of Linux. The total execution time represents the total number of CPU seconds required by the processor. Before running a query, we cleaned the indexes and reloaded their data to avoid keeping data in main memory that could benefit any of the algorithms. The memory usage is measured as the maximum size of the process during its lifetime in Kbytes. Throughput is the number of skyline tuples that an algorithm can produce per second.

Answer quality of the algorithms is measured in terms of response completeness. Response completeness corresponds to the percentage of Skyline points computed that are produced by the algorithm in terms of the whole Skyline; a value of 100% indicates that all the Skyline points are produced by the algorithm, while a value of 0%, says that no Skyline point is produced.

Implementations

The experimental study was conducted on a laptop Dell Inspiron 17R-5720 with an Intel Core i7-3632QM, a 2.2GHz processor, 1 TB hard drive, 8 GB DDR3 SDRAM, and 64 bits. The algorithms were executed on Linux Mint 14 Nadia version 3.5.0-17-generic (gcc version 4.7.2), and they were implemented in C++ using the SpatialIndex Library, version v.1.8.0 (Hadjieleftheriou, 2009). SpatialIndex Library is an open-source framework and provides the implementation of the R-tree structure. It supports robust methods for spatial indexing and spatial queries. In this work, new methods were incorporated to the SpatialIndex Library in order to evaluate Top-k Skyline queries.

Impact of the Data Distribution on the Algorithms with the First Pruning Criterion

This experiment was performed for three types of data considering TopKSkyDFS and TopKSkyBFS without pruning criteria and with the first pruning criterion. In this section, the study was conducted with the first pruning criterion because it allows to return the whole Skyline.

Figures 14-22 show the total number of comparisons, the total execution time and the memory usage by dataset size or number of dimensions. For independent and anticorrelated data, according to the right images of the Figures 14-17, the total execution time for the algorithms based on DFS is higher than for the algorithms based on BFS since the algorithms based on DFS accumulate points in a unique Global Window while traversing the R-tree structure. In consequence, more comparisons are performed over the Global Window impacting on the execution time (on the left images of the Figures 14-17). Furthermore, the anticorrelated data can be very good in one dimension but very bad in other dimensions.

Thus, more dominance comparison may be performed because the points which are part of the Skyline are distributed across all leaf nodes, even those that are in the rightest of the R-tree. Alternatively, the algorithms based on BFS make use of multiple Local Windows in order to progressively compute and merge the Skyline set over each R-tree region to finally calculate the Skyline at the last window of the R-tree root. Therefore, the algorithms based on BFS require less runtime because despite performing Skyline calculation through local windows, the comparisons performed in each local window are lower than those comparisons performed by the algorithms based on DFS in the Global Window.

Figure 14. Number of comparisons and execution time by dataset size – independent data

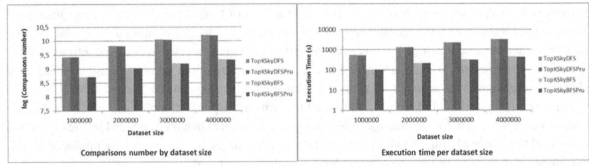

Figure 15. Number of comparisons and execution time by dimensions– independent data

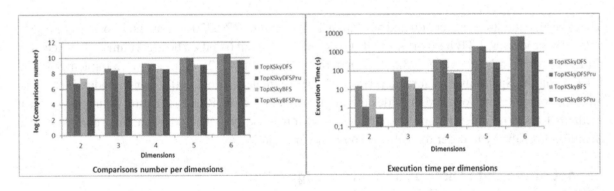

Figure 16. Number of comparisons and execution time by dataset size – anticorrelated data

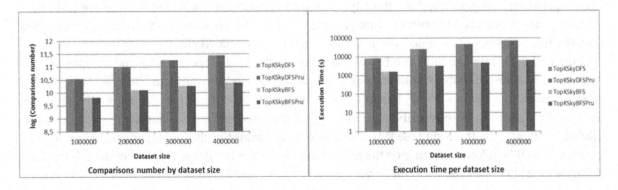

Figure 17. Number of comparisons and execution time by dimensions– anticorrelated data

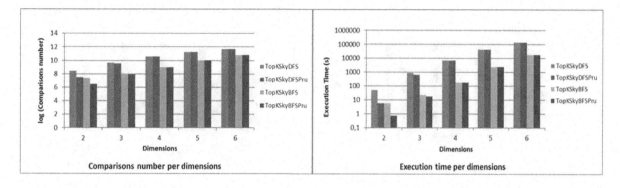

Figure 18. Number of comparisons and execution time by dataset size – correlated data

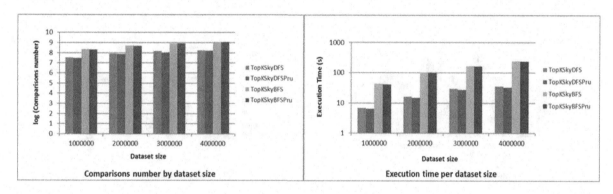

Figure 19. Number of comparisons and execution time by dimensions– correlated data

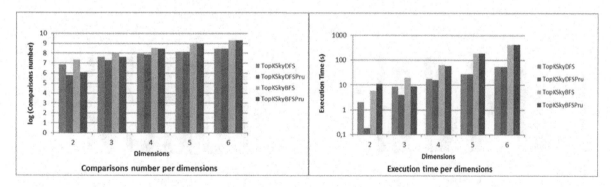

However, the total execution time and the total number of comparisons for the algorithms based on BFS are higher with respect to the algorithms based on DFS when data are correlated according to the Figures 18-19. This is because the algorithms based on DFS may quickly identify Skyline points which may be highly dominant, i.e., Skyline points that dominate many points. More specifically, this may be because a correlated datum is characterized by having good or bad values in all its dimensions. Assuming that attributes related to the multidimensional function need to be minimized, the points that are part of the Skyline are not distributed across all leaf nodes because these points will be in the leftest

Figure 20. Memory usage – independent data

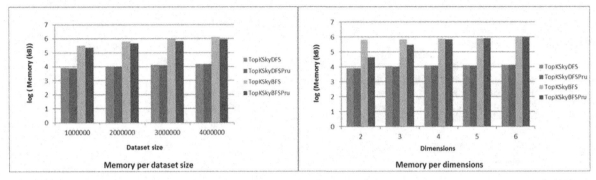

Memory per dataset size | Memory per dimensions

Figure 21. Memory usage – anticorrelated data

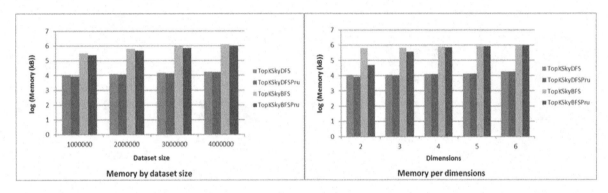

Memory by dataset size | Memory per dimensions

Figure 22. Memory usage – correlated data

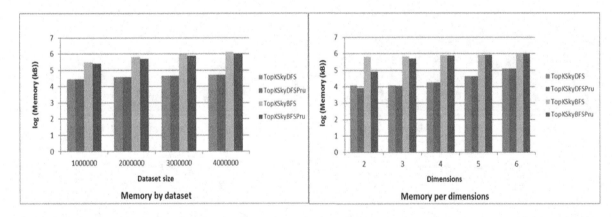

Memory by dataset | Memory per dimensions

nodes of the R-tree. Also, it is known that the size of the Skyline for correlated data is small in relation to independent and anti-correlated data. When data are correlated, most of the data are dominated by Skyline points. Furthermore, the algorithms based on BFS must traverse the R-tree by levels and then they calculate the Skyline set for each Local Window. Thus, algorithms based on BFS can make unnecessary comparisons since Local Windows can contain only dominated points. These dominated points will be discarded when they are compared against Skyline points during the merging phase. Additionally, it may also be noted that the number of comparisons and the execution time increase as dataset size or data dimensionality increases too.

On the other hand, Figures 20-22 show that the algorithms based on DFS require less memory than the algorithms based on BFS due to the number of windows; the algorithms based on BFS must preserve a local window for each node of the R-tree structure. It can also be seen that the memory usage increases as data size or dimensionality increases.

Lastly, TopKSkyDFS and TopKSkyBFS have a similar behavior than TopKSkyDFSPru and TopK-SkyBFSPru because the Pruning Criterion does not discard many regions in the R-tree structure.

When few regions are discarded by the pruning criterion, the number of comparisons performed by the algorithms based on pruning is quite similar to TopKSkyBFS and TopKSkyDFS and therefore, the execution time of the algorithms is similar. In the following section, the other two pruning criteria will be studied.

Impact of the Criteria Pruning+ and Pruning++ on Performance and Quality

The Figure 23 shows that the algorithms based on the criteria Pruning+ and Pruning++ take less time than those based on the Pruning Criterion. Using the criteria Pruning+ and Pruning++, the algorithms perform fewer comparisons (Figure 24) and moreover, they require less memory (Figure 25). The runtime of the algorithms based on Pruning++ is the best because few nodes are accessed.

Since algorithms based on the criteria Pruning+ and Pruning++ take less time and they may lose Skyline points, a completeness study was also performed. This study was conducted by calculating the percentage of Skyline points retrieved by the algorithms with respect to the whole Skyline set.

The left image of Figure 26 illustrates completeness by data size over independent data. It can be noted that the algorithms based on the Pruning+ Criterion retrieve 98.7% of the average Skyline while the algorithms based on the Pruning++ Criterion identify 81.05% of the average Skyline. On the other hand, the right image of Figure 26 shows completeness by dimensionality over independent data. It can be noted that the algorithms based on the Pruning+ Criterion produce 96.8% of the average Skyline while the algorithms based on the Pruning++ Criterion return 82.71% of the average Skyline.

In general, the algorithms based on the Pruning++ Criterion lose more Skyline points and therefore, the execution time of these algorithms is the lowest. In fact, the Skyline completeness with the Pruning

Figure 23. Execution time– independent data

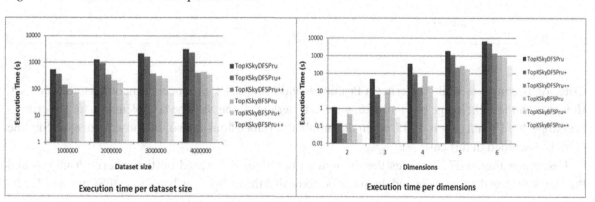

Figure 24. Number of comparisons – independent data

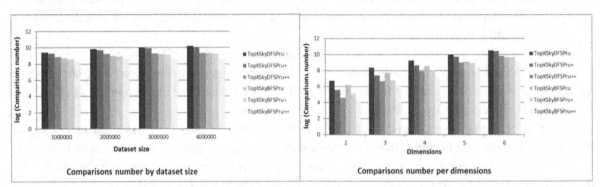

Figure 25. Memory usage – independent data

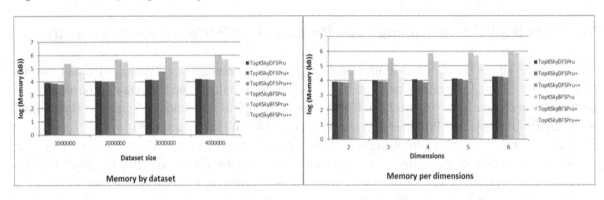

Figure 26. Completeness by data size and dimensionality

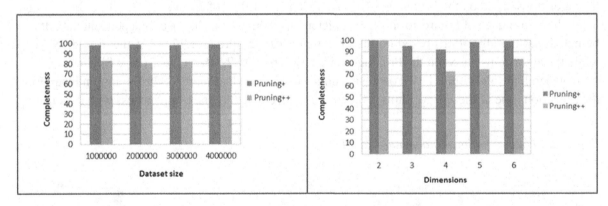

Criterion is complete while the criteria Pruning+ and Pruning++ produce an incomplete Skyline set. However on the right image of Figure 26, we can observe that the Skyline completeness for the criteria Pruning+ and Pruning++ is 100% when the number of dimensions is two; in consequence, no Skyline point is discarded in this case.

Lastly, the Figure 27 illustrates the throughput per algorithm based on the criteria Pruning+ and Pruning++ when data are independent. It can be noted that throughput for TopKSkyDFSPru+ and TopK-

Figure 27. Throughput

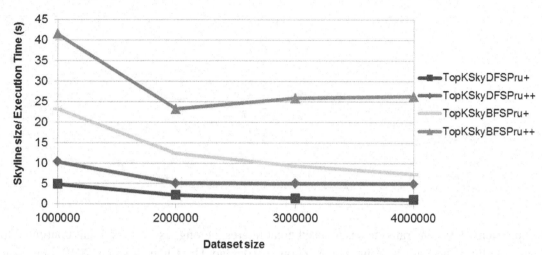

SkyDFSPru++ is lower than for TopKSkyBFSPru+ and TopKSkyBFSPru++ because the algorithms based on DFS require more time for computing the Top-k Skyline set. Additionally, the throughput is affected by the dataset size. Thus, we can observe that the throughput values decrease as the dataset size increases.

Furthermore, the left image of Figure 28 shows the throughput for TopKSkyDFS and its variants while the right image of Figure 28 illustrates the throughput for TopKSkyBFS and its variants. It can be noted that the throughput for TopKSkyDFS is very similar to TopKSkyDFSPru because it returns the whole Skyline while the throughput is higher for TopKSkyDFSPru+ and TopKSkyDFSPru++ because they discard more regions than TopKSkyDFSPru. In the same way, TopKSkyBFS and TopKSkyBFSPru have similar throughput and TopKSkyBFSPru+ and TopKSkyBFSPru++ have a better throughput.

Finally, the algorithms based on the criteria Pruning+ and Pruning++ produce a faster response than TopKSkyBFS and TopKSkyDFS because their throughputs are higher. However, these algorithms can lose up to nearly 20% of the whole Skyline set.

FUTURE RESEARCH DIRECTIONS

In the literature, no experimental studies on Top-k Skyline query evaluation algorithms that use different strategies of R-tree traversal were found. In this chapter, we have studied the behavior of the algorithms for calculating the Top-k Skyline using the Depth First Search and the Breadth First Search strategies. A future work is to study new strategies for the R-tree traversal. We plan to study several strategies such as BBS (Branch and Bound Search) in order to propose new Top-k Skyline algorithms capable of discarding regions based on a pruning criterion that simultaneously uses the multidimensional and Euclidean distance functions. Thus, the idea is to identify the Top-k Skyline set avoiding the complete calculation of the Skyline set. Also, we expect to complete our experimental study for automatic learning of some parameters by means of algorithms derived from machine learning techniques to tune the parameters and determine the best configuration of the algorithms.

Figure 28. Throughput for the algorithms TopKSkyDFS, TopKSkyBFS and their variants

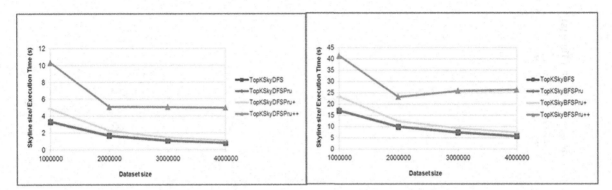

The problem of Skyline ranking has aroused great interest among researchers. It has continued to be widely studied in (Cheong, Lu, Yang, Du, & Zhou, 2010; Gao, Hu, Chen, & Chen, 2010; Lee, You, & Hwang, 2009; Loyer, Sadoun, & Zeitouni, 2013a; Loyer, Sadoun, & Zeitouni, 2013b; Kontaki, Papadopoulos, & Manolopoulos, 2008; Siddique & Morimoto, 2009;Vlachou, Doulkeridis, & Halkidi, 2012; Yang, Fung, Lu, Zhou, Chen, & Du, 2012). The authors propose solutions to discover the *k* skyline points that best describe all skyline points. However, determining the best *k* points of the Skyline set is a costly problem because the calculations are based on the multidimensional function. By means of the definition of multidimensional function, the interestingness of each Skyline point is calculated on the basis of the whole Skyline set. This chapter focuses on ranking the Skyline in terms of the Euclidean distance function over each point and not over the whole Skyline. In the future, it is expected to study the properties of the multidimensional and Euclidean distance functions in order to discard regions that do not contain a Top-k Skyline point.

Moreover, the Euclidean distance function may be very restrictive since it is equivalent to the length of the line segment between two points. For example, the roads in a city not correspond to straight lines and there are other distance functions more appropriate for this case. Thus, the Manhattan or orthodromic functions return the distance between two points in a city considering the design of the streets or the surface of the Earth, respectively. Then, the properties of these functions may be studied in order to discard points that are not Top-k Skyline. Additionally, we can also study the Skyline points returned by each distance function and compare their interestingness in order to the end user determines which point must have really returned for a Top-k Skyline query.

Additionally, the last two pruning criteria discard some Skyline points. We plan to empirically study the interestingness of the lost Skyline points into the Top-k Skyline set verifying if any of the lost Skyline points belong to the Top-k Skyline set. In the future, we also plan to study the quality of the answer making a study in a real scenario using real data gathered from real users. If Skyline points lost by the pruning criterion are not Top-k Skyline, they would not be losing answers. Therefore, we think also study the interestingness of the lost points to confirm that the response is complete. This way, a study of completeness of the algorithms will be performed to verify the answer to a Top-k Skyline query is complete.

Finally, the use of any algorithm depends on the user's decision. If the user needs a faster response, he can apply any of the algorithms based on pruning criteria. If the user wishes a complete answer, the algorithms TopkSkyDFS and TopkSkyBFS can be used.

On the other hand, Šumák and Gurský (2013) introduces an R++-tree which offers better search efficiency than an R-tree structure. As future work, the proposed algorithms could be implemented on an R++- tree to study the query performance between the two data structures. In addition, (Jang, Choi, Hyun, Jung, Jung, Jeong, & Chung, 2014) introduces the concept of closeness from a query to a collection of data; this study can be extended with the pruning criteria proposed in this chapter.

CONCLUSION

This chapter focused on the problem of evaluating Top-k Skyline queries on R-tree indexes. Top-k Skyline queries are used to specify user-defined preferences and they return the best k points from the Skyline set. The Skyline set is composed of points which are incomparable between themselves; these Skyline points are the best in terms of user-defined criteria. Since the Skyline size may be huge, Top-k Skyline queries allows to filter k points from the Skyline set. Thus, a smaller dataset may be analyzed by the users instead of examining the whole Skyline. Particularly, the k points are selected based on minimizing the Euclidean distance function, i.e., the Euclidean distance function allows to linearly sort the Skyline points and identify the top-k points from this ordering.

Firstly, two algorithms were proposed to evaluate Top-k Skyline queries traversing an R-tree index by means of the Depth First Search and Breadth First Search strategies. They are named TopKSkyDFS and TopKSkyBFS, respectively. Using these strategies allows to deal with the Top-k Skyline query evaluation as a Divide and Conquer problem because the data space is divided into smaller regions which correspond to MBR (Minimum Bounding Rectangles) of the R-tree index. Initially, the Skyline set is computed by each MBR and subsequently, each calculated skyline will be merged. This way, the merging goes on and on until there are no regions left.

Secondly, three criteria to prune the search space were introduced in this chapter. These criteria are named Pruning, Pruning+ and Pruning++. The algorithms TopKSkyDFS and TopKSkyBFS were extended with these three pruning criteria in order to decrease their number of dominance comparisons and reduce their execution time due to they explore a subset of the entire search space in order to build the Top-k Skyline set. These pruning criteria allow to guide the algorithms avoiding to explore all the R-tree index. Depending of the pruning criterion, the idea is to discard regions with dominated points because they do not belong to the query answer. Thus, some regions are not visited by the algorithms in order to verify if they have Skyline points. Between the proposed pruning criteria, the first criterion discards few regions in the R-tree index because its condition is the hardest. However, pruning criteria may lose some Skyline points when their condition is soften. Although the last two pruning criteria discard some Skyline points, the algorithms based on them require less execution time in order to produce the answer.

Thirdly, the algorithms TopKSkyDFS and TopKSkyBFS were empirically compared against their extensions with the first pruning criterion. In this empirical study, the performance was analyzed using synthetic data. Datasets were generated following three data distribution: Independent, anticorrelated and correlated. The algorithms extended with the first pruning criterion have a performance similar to TopKSkyDFS and TopKSkyBFS because they discard very few regions of the R-tree structure. In addition, the algorithms based on BFS require less time than the algorithms based on DFS for independent and anticorrelated data chiefly due to they compare against a window that progressively increases its size as the R-tree is traversed by the algorithm. Nevertheless, the performance for the algorithms based on BFS is worse than for the algorithms based on DFS if data are correlated since the Skyline size is small and most of the Local Windows contain dominated points performing unnecessary dominance comparisons; dominated points will be considered in future comparisons during the merging phase of the algorithms.

Fourthly, the impact of the last two pruning criteria on the performance and answer quality was empirically studied. The algorithms based on the last two pruning criteria take less runtime; however, they lose some Skyline points. Thus, a completeness study of algorithms based on the last two pruning criteria was performed to verify the percentage of Skyline points actually retrieved by each algorithm. Answer completeness measures how many Skyline points were actually produced by an algorithm. This study showed that the average percentage of answers was at least 80% of the whole Skyline set. Even, it was found that the last two criteria were complete for two dimensions data. In consequence, the algorithms based on the last two pruning criteria may quickly retrieve answers although discard some Skyline points.

REFERENCES

Alrifai, M., Skoutas, D., & Risse, T. (2010). Selecting Skyline Services for QoS based Web Service Composition. In *Proceedings of the 19th International Conference on World Wide Web (WWW)* (pp. 11-20). Raleigh, NC: ACM. doi:10.1145/1772690.1772693

Alvarado, A., Baldizan, O., Goncalves, M., & Vidal, M.-E. (2013). FOPA: A Final Object Pruning Algorithm to Efficiently Produce Skyline Points. In *Proceedings of the 24th International Conference on Database and Expert Systems Applications (DEXA)* (pp. 334-348). Prague, Czech Republic: Springer-Verlag. doi:10.1007/978-3-642-40173-2_27

Benouaret, K., Benslimane, D., & Hadjali, A. (2011). On the Use of Fuzzy Dominance for Computing Service Skyline Based on QoS. In *Proceedings of the International Conference on Web Services (ICWS)* (pp. 540-547). Washington, DC: IEEE. doi:10.1109/ICWS.2011.93

Bentley, J., Kung, H. T., Schkolnick, M., & Thompson, C. D. (1978). On the average number of maxima in a set of vectors and applications. *Journal of the ACM*, 25(4), 536–543. doi:10.1145/322092.322095

Börzsönyi, S., Kossmann, D., & Stocker, K. (2001). The skyline operator. In *Proceedings of the 17th International Conference on Data Engineering (ICDE)* (pp. 421–430). Washington, DC: IEEE Computer Society. doi:10.1109/ICDE.2001.914855

Chan, C.-Y., Jagadish, H. V., Tan, K.-L., Tung, A. K. H., & Zhang, Z. (2006a). Finding k-dominant skylines in high dimensional space. In *Proceedings of the 2006 ACM SIGMOD International Conference on Management of Data* (pp. 503-514). New York: ACM. doi:10.1145/1142473.1142530

Chan, C. Y., Jagadish, H. V., Tan, K.-L., Tung, A. K. H., & Zhang, Z. (2006b). On high dimensional Skylines. In *Proceedings of The International Conference on Extending Database Technology* (EDBT). (pp. 478-495). Munich, Germany: ACM

Chen, L., Cui, B., Lu, H., Xu, L., & Xu, Q. (2008). iSky: Efficient and Progressive Skyline Computing in a Structured P2P Network. In *Proceedings of the 28th International Conference on Distributed Computing Systems (ICDCS)* (pp. 160-167). Beijing, China: IEEE Computer Society.

Chen, L., Gao, S., & Anyanwu, K. (2011). Efficiently evaluating skyline queries on RDF databases. In *Proceedings of The Extended Semantic Web Conference (ESWC)* (pp. 123-138). Crete, Greece: Springer-Verlag. doi:10.1007/978-3-642-21064-8_9

Cheong, G. P., Lu, W., Yang, J., Du, X., & Zhou, X. (2010). Extract Interesting Skyline Points in High Dimension. In *Proceedings of the 15th International Conference on Database Systems for Advanced Applications (DASFAA)* (pp. 94-108). Tsukuba, Japan: Springer-Verlag. doi:10.1007/978-3-642-12098-5_7

Chomicki, J., Godfrey, P., Gryz, J., & Liang, D. (2003). Skyline with Presorting. In *Proceedings of The 19th International Conference on Data Engineering (ICDE)* (pp. 717–719). Bangalore, India: IEEE Computer Society.

Cosgaya-Lozano, A., Rau-Chaplin, A., & Zeh, N. (2007). Parallel Computation of Skyline Queries. In *Proceedings of 21st International Symposium on High Performance Computing Systems and Applications (HPCS'07)* (pp. 12). Saskatoon: IEEE Computer Society. doi:10.1109/HPCS.2007.25

Cui, B., Chen, L., Xu, L., Lu, H., Song, G., & Xu, Q. (2009). Efficient Skyline Computation in Structured Peer-to-Peer Systems. *IEEE Transactions on Knowledge and Data Engineering, 21*(7), 1059–1062. doi:10.1109/TKDE.2008.235

Cui, B., Lu, H., Xu, Q., Chen, L., Dai, Y., & Zhou, Y. (2008). Parallel Distributed Processing of Constrained Skyline Queries by Filtering. In *Proceedings of the International Conference on Data Engineering (ICDE)* (pp. 546-555). Cancun, Mexico: IEEE Computer Society. doi:10.1109/ICDE.2008.4497463

Ding, X., & Jin, H. (2011). Efficient and Progressive Algorithms for Distributed Skyline Queries over Uncertain Data. *IEEE Transactions on Knowledge and Data Engineering, 24*(8), 1448–1462. doi:10.1109/TKDE.2011.77

Gao, Y., Hu, J., Chen, G., & Chen, C. (2010). Finding the Most Desirable Skyline Objects. In *Proceedings of the 15th International Conference on Database Systems for Advanced Applications (DASFAA)* (pp. 116-122). Springer-Verlag: Tsukuba, Japan.

Göbel, R. (2007). Towards Logarithmic Search Time Complexity for R-trees. In *Proceedings of The Innovations and Advanced Techniques in Computer and Information Sciences and Engineering* (pp. 201-206). Dordrecht, The Netherland: Springer. doi:10.1007/978-1-4020-6268-1_37

Godfrey, P., Shipley, R., & Gryz, J. (2005). Maximal Vector Computation in Large Data Sets. In *Proceedings of The 31st International Conference on Very Large Databases (VLDB)* (pp. 229–240). Trondheim, Norway: ACM.

Goncalves, M., & Vidal, M.-E. (2009). Reaching the top of the Skyline: An efficient indexed algorithm for Top-k Skyline queries. In *Proceedings of The International Conference on Database and Expert Systems Applications* (DEXA) (pp. 471-485). Linz, Austria: Springer-Verlag. doi:10.1007/978-3-642-03573-9_41

Goncalves, M., & Vidal, M.-E. (2012). Efficiently Producing the K Nearest Neighbors in the Skyline for Multidimensional Datasets. In *Proceedings of the On The Move (OTM) Workshops* (pp. 673-676). Rome, Italy: Springer-Verlag. doi:10.1007/978-3-642-33618-8_92

Guttman, A. (1984). R-trees: A Dynamic Index Structure for Spatial Searching. In *Proceedings of The ACM SIGMOD International Conference on Management of Data* (pp. 47-57). Boston: ACM doi:10.1145/602259.602266

Hadjieleftheriou, M. (2009). *Libspatialindex*. Retrieved January 15, 2013, from http://libspatialindex. github.io

Hsueh, Y.-L., Zimmermann, R., Ku, W.-S., & Jin, Y. (2011). SkyEngine: Efficient Skyline Search Engine for Continuous Skyline Computations. In *Proceedings of the International Conference on Data Engineering (ICDE)* (pp. 1316-1319). Hannover, Germany: IEEE Computer Society. doi:10.1109/ICDE.2011.5767944

Huang, Z., Jensen, C. S., Lu, H., & Ooi, B. C. (2006). Skyline Queries against Mobile Lightweight Devices in MANET. In *Proceedings of the International Conference on Data Engineering (ICDE)* (pp. 66). Atlanta, GA: IEEE Computer Society. doi:10.1109/ICDE.2006.142

Huang, Z., & Xiang, Y. (2009). Improve the Usefulness of Skyline Analysis in Cloud Computing Environments. In *Proceedings of the 2nd International Symposium on Computational Intelligence and Design* (pp. 325-328). Changsha, China: IEEE. doi:10.1109/ISCID.2009.89

Huang, Z., & Xiang, Y. (2010). An Efficient Method for Diversifying Skylines in SOA Environment. In *Proceedings of the Conference on Intelligent Computing and Cognitive Informatics* (pp. 466-469). Kuala Lumpur, Malaysia: IEEE. doi:10.1109/ICICCI.2010.94

Im, H., Park, J., & Park, S. (2009). Parallel skyline computation on multi-core architectures. In *Proceedings of the 19th International Conference on Data Engineering (ICDE)* (pp. 808-823). Shanghai: IEEE Computer Society.

Jang, H.-J., Choi, W.-S., Hyun, K.-S., Jung, K.-H., Jung, S.-Y., Jeong, Y.-S., & Chung, J. (2014). Towards Nearest Collection Search on Spatial Databases. In *Proceedings of The International conference on Ubiquitous Information Technologies and Applications (CUTE)* (pp. 433-440). Berlin: Springer-Verlag. doi:10.1007/978-3-642-41671-2_55

Jiang, B., & Pei, J. (2009). Online Interval Skyline Queries on Time Series. In *Proceedings of the 25th International Conference on Data Engineering (ICDE)* (pp. 1036-1043). Shanghai: IEEE Computer Society. doi:10.1109/ICDE.2009.70

Kim, D., Im, H., & Park, S. (2011). Computing Exact Skyline Probabilities for Uncertain Databases. *IEEE Transactions on Knowledge and Data Engineering, 24*(12), 2113–2126. doi:10.1109/TKDE.2011.164

Knuth, D. (1997). *The Art Of Computer Programming* (3rd ed.; Vol. 1). Boston: Addison-Wesley.

Kontaki, M., Papadopoulos, A. N., & Manolopoulos, Y. (2008). Continuous K-dominant Skyline Computation on Multidimensional Data Streams. In *Proceedings of the 2008 ACM Symposium on Applied Computing* (pp. 956-960). New York: ACM. doi:10.1145/1363686.1363908

Kossmann, D., Ramsak, F., & Rost, S. (2002). Shooting stars in the sky: An online algorithm for skyline queries. In *Proceedings of The 28th International Conference on Very Large Data Bases (VLDB)* (pp. 275-286). Hong Kong, China: VLDB Endowment. doi:10.1016/B978-155860869-6/50032-9

Kossmann, M. (2009). *Skyline Data Generator*. Retrieved July 15, 2013, from http://www.pubzone. org/pages/publications/showWiki.do?deleteform=true&search=basic&pos=1&publicationId=298353

Kung, H. T., Luccio, F., & Preparata, F. P. (1975). On Finding the Maxima of a Set of Vectors. *Journal of the ACM, 22*(4), 469–476. doi:10.1145/321906.321910

Lee, J., You, G.-, & Hwang, S.-. (2009). Personalized Top-k Skyline Queries in High-dimensional Space. *Information Systems, 34*(1), 45–61. doi:10.1016/j.is.2008.04.004

Lin, X., Xu, J., & Hu, H. (2011). Range-based Skyline Queries in Mobile Environments. *IEEE Transactions on Knowledge and Data Engineering, 25*(4), 835–849. doi:10.1109/TKDE.2011.229

Lin, X., Yuan, Y., Zhang, Q., & Zhang, Y. (2007). Selecting Stars: The k Most Representative Skyline Operator. In *Proceedings of The International Conference on Database Theory (ICDE)* (pp. 86-95). Istanbul, Turkey: IEEE. doi:10.1109/ICDE.2007.367854

Loyer, Y., Sadoun, I., & Zeitouni, K. (2013a). Progressive Ranking Based on a Dominance List. In *Proceedings of the 7th International Workshop on Ranking in Databases (DBRank)* (pp. 6:1-6:3). ACM: Riva del Garda, Italy. doi:10.1145/2524828.2524834

Loyer, Y., Sadoun, I., & Zeitouni, K. (2013b). Personalized Progressive Filtering of Skyline Queries in High Dimensional Spaces. In *Proceedings of the 17th International Database Engineering & Applications Symposium (IDEAS)* (pp. 186-191). Barcelona, Spain: ACM. doi:10.1145/2513591.2513646

Manolopoulos, Y., Nanopoulos, A., Papadopoulos, A. N., & Theodoridis, Y. (2013). *R-trees: Theory and Applications*. Springer London.

Morse, M., & Patel, J. M. (2006). Efficient Continuous Skyline Computation. In *Proceedings of the International Conference on Data Engineering (ICDE)* (pp. 108). Atlanta, GA: IEEE Computer Society. doi:10.1109/ICDE.2006.56

Papadias, D., Tao, Y., Fu, G., & Seeger, B. (2005). Progressive skyline computation in database systems. *ACM Transactions on Database Systems, 30*(1), 41–82. doi:10.1145/1061318.1061320

Papadimitriou, C. H., & Yannakakis, M. (2001). Multiobjective Query Optimization. In *Proceedings of the ACM SIGMOD/SIGACT Conference on Principles of Database Systems (PODS)* (pp. 52–59). ACM.

Preparata, F. P., & Shamos, M. I. (1985). Computational Geometry: An Introduction. Springer-Verlag.

Qiao, Z., Gu, J., Lin, X., & Chen, J. (2010). Privacy-Preserving Skyline Queries in LBS. In *Proceedings of the International Conference on Machine Vision and Human-Machine Interface (MVHI)* (pp. 499-504). Kaifeng, China: IEEE. doi:10.1109/MVHI.2010.205

Reeba, R. S., & Kavitha, V. R. (2012). An Efficient Location Dependent System Based On Spatial Sky Line Queries. *International Journal of Soft Computing and Engineering, 1*(1), 27–29.

Rocha-Junior, J. B., Vlachou, A., Doulkeridis, C., & Nørvåg, K. (2011). Efficient Execution Plans for Distributed Skyline Query Processing. In *Proceedings of The International Conference on Extending Database Technology (EDBT)* (pp. 271-282). Uppsala, Sweden: Springer-Verlag. doi:10.1145/1951365.1951399

Sacharidis, D., Arvanitis, A., & Sellis, T. (2010). Probabilistic Contextual Skylines. In *Proceedings of The International Conference on Data Engineering (ICDE)* (pp. 273-284). Long Beach, CA: IEEE Computer Society.

Shen, H., Chen, Z., & Deng, X. (2009). Location-based Skyline Queries in Wireless Sensor Networks. In *Proceedings of The International Conference on Networks Security, Wireless Communications and Trusted Computing* (pp. 391-395). Wuhan, China: IEEE. doi:10.1109/NSWCTC.2009.314

Siddique, M. A. & Morimoto, Y. (2009). K-Dominant Skyline Computation by Using Sort-Filtering Method. In *Proceedings of the 13th Pacific-Asia Conference on Advances in Knowledge Discovery and Data Mining* (pp. 839-848). Berlin: Springer-Verlag. doi:10.1007/978-3-642-01307-2_87

Šumák, M., & Gurský, P. (2013). R++ -tree: An Efficient Spatial Access Method for Highly Redundant Point Data. In *Proceedings of the 17th East-European Conference on Advances in Databases and Information Systems*. Genoa, Italy: Springer.

Valkanas, G., & Papadopoulos, A. N. (2010). Efficient and Adaptive Distributed Skyline Computation. In *Proceedings of the 22nd International Conference on Scientific and Statistical Database Management (SSDBM)* (pp. 24-41). Heidelberg, Germany: Springer-Verlag.

Vlachou, A., Doulkeridis, C., & Halkidi, M. (2012). Discovering Representative Skyline Points over Distributed Data. *In Proceedings of the 24th International Conference on Scientific and Statistical Database Management* (pp. 141-158). Springer-Verlag. doi:10.1007/978-3-642-31235-9_9

Wu, P., Zhang, C., Feng, Y., Zhao, B., Agrawal, D., & El Abbadi, A. (2006). Parallelizing Skyline Queries for Scalable Distribution. In *Proceedings of The International Conference on Extending Database Technology (EDBT)* (pp. 112–130). Munich, Germany: Springer-Verlag

Yang, J., Fung, G., Lu, W., Zhou, X., Chen, H., & Du, X. (2012). Finding Superior Skyline Points for Multidimensional Recommendation Applications. *World Wide Web (Bussum)*, *15*(1), 33–60. doi:10.1007/s11280-011-0122-8

YingyuanXiao., Lü, K., Deng, H. (2010). Location-dependent Skyline Query Processing in Mobile Databases. In *Proceedings of the 7th Conference on Web Information Systems and Applications* (pp. 3-8). Hohhot, Mongolia: IEEE.

Yu, Q., & Bouguettaya, A. (2011). Efficient Service Skyline Computation for Composite Service Selection. *IEEE Transactions on Knowledge and Data Engineering*, *25*(4), 776–789. doi:10.1109/TKDE.2011.268

Zhu, L., Zhou, S., & Guan, J. (2007). *Efficient Skyline Retrieval on Peer-to-Peer Networks. Future Generation Communication and Networking (FGCN)*. Jeju, Korea: IEEE. doi:10.1109/FGCN.2007.115

ADDITIONAL READING

Bogh, K., Assent, I., & Magnani, M. (2013). Efficient GPU-based skyline computation. In *Proceedings of the Ninth International Workshop on Data Management on New Hardware*. (pp. 1-5). New York, USA: ACM. doi:10.1145/2485278.2485283

Chester, S., Mortensen, M. L., & Assent, I. (2014). On the Suitability of Skyline Queries for Data Exploration. In *Proceedings of the Workshops of the EDBT/ICDT 2014 Joint Conference*. (pp. 161-166). Athens, Greece: CEUR-WS.org.

Gupta, M., Gao, J., Yan, X., Cam, H., & Han, J. (2014). Top-K interesting subgraph discovery in information networks. In *Proceedings of The 30th International Conference on Data Engineering (ICDE)*. (pp. 820-831). Chicago, USA: IEEE. doi:10.1109/ICDE.2014.6816703

Khemmarat, S., & Gao, L. (2014). Fast top-k path-based relevance query on massive graphs. In *Proceedings of The 30th International Conference on Data Engineering (ICDE)*. (pp. 316-327). Chicago, USA: IEEE. doi:10.1109/ICDE.2014.6816661

Lofi, C., El Maarry, B., & Balke, W.-T. (2013). Skyline queries in crowd-enabled databases. In *Proceedings of The Joint 2013 EDBT/ICDT Conferences*. (pp. 465-476). Genoa, Italy: ACM. doi:10.1145/2452376.2452431

Magnani, M., & Assent, I. (2013). From stars to galaxies: skyline queries on aggregate data. In *Proceedings of the Joint 2013 EDBT/ICDT Conferences*. (pp. 477-488). Genoa, Italy: ACM. doi:10.1145/2452376.2452432

Olsen, P. W., Labouseur, A. G., & Hwang, J.-H. (2014). Efficient Top-k Closeness Centrality Search. In *Proceedings of The 30th International Conference on Data Engineering (ICDE)*. (pp. 196-207). Chicago, USA: IEEE.

Yiu, M., Lo, E., & Yung, D. (2012). Measuring the Sky: On Computing Data Cubes via Skylining the Measures. *IEEE Transactions on Knowledge and Data Engineering*, 24(3), 492–505. doi:10.1109/TKDE.2010.253

Yu, A., Agarwal, P. K., & Yang, J. (2014). Top-k preferences in high dimensions. In *Proceedings of The 30th International Conference on Data Engineering (ICDE)*. (pp. 748-759). Chicago, USA: IEEE.

KEY TERMS AND DEFINITIONS

Block Nested Loop: Its acronym is BNL. It is a traditional algorithm that computes the Skyline set scanning all the data.

Breadth First Search: Its acronym is BFS. It is an algorithm that searches elements traversing a graph by levels.

Depth First Search: Its acronym is DFS. It is a search algorithm that traverses a graph by paths.

Minimum Bounding Rectangle: Its acronym is MBR. It is the Minimum Bounding region that encloses a set of points. A MBR may contain other MBRs.

R-Tree: It is a multidimensional index structure which stores spatial data.

Skyline Techniques: Set of strategies for identifying incomparable elements that are characterized by multidimensional properties.

Top-k Skyline: Set of strategies for identifying the k non-dominated elements with the top values of a given metric or score function.

Chapter 4
Processing of Queries with Fuzzy Similarity Domains

Soraya O. Carrasquel
Universidad Simón Bolívar, Venezuela

Rosseline Rodríguez
Universidad Simón Bolívar, Venezuela

Ricardo R. Monascal
Universidad Simón Bolívar, Venezuela

Leonid Tineo
Universidad Simón Bolívar, Venezuela

ABSTRACT

There are some data models and query languages based on the application of fuzzy set theory. Their goal is to provide more flexible DBMS that allow the expression of user preferences in querying as well as imprecision in data. In this sense, the FuzzyEER data model proposes four kinds of fuzzy attributes. One of them, named Type 3, consists of a set of labels provided of a similarity relation. An extension of SQL, named FSQL, allows the expression and use of fuzzy attributes. Nevertheless, FSQL does not allow using fuzzy attributes in some clauses based on data ordering, due to semantics problem. This chapter presents a solution for this problem in case of Type 3 fuzzy attributes. Main contribution consists in how to process queries involving such attributes by means of an extension to an existing RDBMS. Formal semantics, grammar, catalogue definition and translation schemas are contained in this chapter.

INTRODUCTION

Traditional databases only handle precise data and conditions. In many scenarios this is not quite fit for representing the actual information needs of users. In the real world, there might be partial or imprecise information about the values of some data. The user may also have selection criteria that are not precise.

The incorporation of some of these concepts in the modeling and manipulation of databases gave birth to different fuzzy relational model proposals (Buckles & Petri, 1982; Fukami, Umano, Muzimoto & Tanaka, 1979). These were later generalized to an extended model for fuzzy relational databases, known as GEFRED (Generalized model of Fuzzy Relational Databases) (Medina, Pons, & Vila, 1994).

From the GEFRED model, the Enhanced Entity-Relationship model (EER) and the Structured Query Language (SQL) language were formally extended into the FuzzyEER model (*Encyclopedia of Information Science and Technology*, 2014) and the FSQL language (Galindo, Urrutia, & Piattini, 2006),

DOI: 10.4018/978-1-4666-8767-7.ch004

that is an extension of SQL that allows flexible conditions in queries. The EER is an ER model that allows for generalizations/specializations and categories. The FuzzyEER model is an extension of the EER model for the creation of conceptual schemas with fuzzy notation and semantics. This extension includes elements of different conceptual model proposals for fuzzy databases, such as fuzzy attributes, fuzzy entities, fuzzy relations, and fuzzy specializations, among others.

In order to incorporate concepts from the FuzzyEER model (Galindo et al., 2006) in a relational DMBS, previous work includes a relational implementation schema called FIRST (Fuzzy Interface for Relational SysTem) (Medina, Pons, & Vila, 1995). The most recent version of this schema is called FIRST-2. The metadata that defines the fuzzy elements of FuzzyEER in FIRST-2 are stored in a relational catalog called FMB (Fuzzy Metaknowledge Base).

For representing fuzzy data, FuzzyEER and FSQL (Galindo et al., 2006) define for types of fuzzy attributes:

Type 1: Attributes with precise data values, provided with linguistic labels, interpreted as fuzzy numbers with the purpose of being used in fuzzy conditionals.

Type 2: Attributes with fuzzy data values, represented as fuzzy numbers. These attributes are possibility distributions on an ordered domain.

Type 3: Attributes with values in a domain formed by labels provided with a similarity relations between such labels. It can additionally have possibility distributions.

Type 4: Similar to Type 3, without the similarity relationship.

FSQL forbids using fuzzy attributes in ordering and grouping criteria, except for Type 1, that are actually precise values. This is unsatisfying. The representation of fuzzy attributes is very limited and only allows a certain set of values. FSQL allows any fuzzy binary relationship in place of a similarity relationship, as it does not have a well-defined semantics for them. These deficiencies must be addressed and corrected. The focus of this chapter is in Type 3 fuzzy attributes, restricted to the case of a set of labels with a provided similarity relationship.

We extend SQL in order to integrate this attributes type in the database queries. The main contribution of this chapter is to describe the translation schemes that allow translate instructions of extended SQL to instructions of native SQL. Our proposal consists into implement a mildly coupled architecture where the translation schemes are incorporated into a mediator layer which extends a Relational Database Management System (RDBMS).

BACKGROUND

Fuzzy Set theory was proposed by Zadeh (1965) as a way of representing imprecision and uncertainty. His initial motivation was control system applications, but with time they were beginning to be used in prediction and optimization, pattern recognition and expert systems. This theory provides a mathematic on formal computational framework for representing the notions vague or imprecise nature.

In classical set theory the membership of an element to a set is rigid, given by an indicator function whose codomain is $\{0, 1\}$, where 0 represents exclusion and 1 inclusion. Fuzzy sets are characterized by a membership function (μ_F) whose codomain is in the real interval $[0, 1]$. As the membership degree of an element approaches 1, this element is possibly (or certainly) more included in the set. Thus, $\mu_F(x)=0$

is the measure of complete exclusion and $\mu_F(x)=1$ that of complete inclusion. The set formed by all elements that are partially included is known as the border of the fuzzy set. Formally, $border(F)=\{x \in X \mid 0<\mu_F(x)<1\}$. The set of all elements that are completely includes is called the kernel, $kernel(F)=\{x \in X \mid \mu_F(x)=1\}$. The elements that are not completely excluded are called the support, $support(F)=\{x \in X \mid \mu_F(x)>0\}$.

The membership function of a fuzzy set can be represented in different ways. In the case in which the fuzzy set is defined over an ordered universe, the simplest representation of the membership function is trapezoidal. This function is defined as a 4-tuple (x_1, x_2, x_3, x_4) of ordered elements $(x_1 \leq x_2 \leq x_3 \leq x_4)$ from the domain that define the vertices of the trapezium $\{(x_1, 0), (x_2, 1), (x_3, 1), (x_4, 0)\}$.

In databases, this concept allows assigning semantics to vague criteria (or fuzzy conditions) that express user preferences and particularities of the context of the data or application domain. Another application in databases is the representation and manipulation of attributes with imprecise data, called fuzzy data.

The FuzzyEER model and the FSQL language (Galindo et al., 2006) define four types of fuzzy attributes. One of them, called Type 3 fuzzy attributes, are based on the concept of similarity relations.

In 1971, Zadeh (1971) introduced the concept of fuzzy ordering as an extension to classical ordering. He also introduces the concept of a similarity relationship as a generalization of an equivalence relationship. According to Zadeh, a similarity relationship S in a universe X is a fuzzy subset of $X \times X$, with a reflexive and symmetric membership function that also fulfills the following transitivity property: $\mu_S(x,z)=max_y(min(\mu_S(x,y), \mu_S(y,z))), \forall x,y,z \in X$.

Following Zadeh's original definition, many authors have proposed different definitions for similarity relations, mainly differing in the form of the transitivity property.

Jacas (1990) studies similarity relations from the viewpoint of the representation theorem for T-indistinguishable operators, where T is a continuous t-norm. R is considered an T-undistinguishable operator if $\forall x,y,z \in X$ it is reflexive ($R(x,x)=1$), symmetric ($R(x,y)=R(y,x)$) and T-transitive ($T(R(x,y),R(y,z)) \leq R(x,z)$). This definition lays the foundation the construction of algorithms that handle similarity relations, for example finding a families minimal generator for a similarity relationship over a finite set X.

Calvo (1992) studies similarity relations in finite universes, based on the following definition: Given a fuzzy relationship $R: X \times X \rightarrow [0,1]$, R is identified with is associated matrix $A_R=(a_{ij})$ where $a_{ij}=\mu_R(x_i,x_j) \forall i,j \in \{1,...,n\}$. Reflexivity and symmetry of R have obvious interpretations in A_R. Transitivity is defined considering two binary operators $(\circ,*)$ in the interval $[0, 1]$. These operators are used in defining the $(\circ,*)$-product of two matrices $n \times n$, $B^\circ C=(d_{ij})$, where $d_{ij} = (b_{i1} * c_{1j})^\circ...^\circ(b_{in} * c_{nj})$ being $B=(b_{ij})$ and $C=(c_{ij})$. A relationship R is $(\circ,*)$-transitive if $A_R \circ A_R = A_R$. If R is reflexive, symmetric and $(\circ,*)$-transitive, then A_R is a similarity matrix. Usually, the pair of operators $(\circ,*)$ where $*$ is a t-norm and $\circ$ is its co-norm.

Ovchinnikov (1991) define similarity relations as a special class of proximity relations, also known as tolerance relations. A fuzzy binary relationship R is defined over families of fuzzy sets, where R is reflexive, symmetric and for each pair (x, y) in the proximity relationship, its membership function is lower than each of the reflexive pairs $R(x,x)$ and $R(y, y)$. According to Ovchinnikov, similarity relations are transitive proximity relations. He studies the equivalence among proximity relations, coverings and the fuzzy equivalent to equivalence relations and partitions. Given a finite set X and A, a finite set of its attributes such that each $\alpha \in X$ has at least one attribute $p \in A$, $X(p)$ is the set of every $\alpha \in X$ with attribute p.

A set $X(p)$, such that $X=\cup X(p)$ is called a covering of X. Then a relationship R is a proximity relationship when: aRb if there is $p \in A$ such that $a,b \in X(p)$. A similarity relationship is a transitive proximity relationship; that is: $\forall x,y,z \in X$ is reflexive ($R(x,x)=1$), symmetric ($R(x,y)=R(y,x)$) and transitive

$(R(x,y) \wedge R(y,z) \leq R(x,z))$, where $x \wedge y = min(x,y)$. Two classes of fuzzy relations are introduced according the preference level: Week preference and strict preference. According to its definition, a fuzzy binary relationship R is quasi-transitive if R is strongly complete and negatively transitive. That is, if R satisfies $(\forall x,y,z \in X) ((R(x,y) \vee R(y,x) = 1) \wedge (R(x,z) \leq R(x,y) \vee R(y,z)))$ then R is dual to a relationship R' such that $(\forall x,y,z \in X) ((R'(x,y) \wedge R'(y,x) = 0) \wedge (R'(x,y) \wedge R'(y,z) \leq R'(x,z)))$.

Faurous and Fillard (1993) reconsider the definition of reflexivity and transitivity of similarity relations, offering a novel intuitive base for the definition of fuzzy equivalence, such that the concept of a fuzzy partition is made more useful. They propose a new definition of transitivity that is consistent with the definition of a disjoint fuzzy partition. To ensure this, they propose the need for at least one element with total inclusion, or in other words, with a membership degree of 1. The transitive pair (x,z) of the relationship appears when one of them is an element y with total inclusion. The relationship μ is therefore reflexive if $(\forall x \in X)(\mu(x,x) > 0)$ and transitive if it fulfills the following conditions: $\{y \in X | \mu(y,y) = 1\} \neq \emptyset$ and $(\forall x,y,z \in X)(\mu(y,y) = 1 \Rightarrow \mu(x,z) \geq \mu(x,y) \ \mu(y,z))$. This definition is useful in the field of digital image processing.

Bèlohlávek (1999) studies similarities in conceptual structures: Object and Attribute Similarity; Concept Similarity; Concept Network Similarity. The first one proves that the similarity can be determined by the L-context, which is important from the computational perspective. The second one considers collections of similar elements, more than particular elements, using the abstraction process by factorization, where the original system is considered a "system modulo similarities". The third one defines the similarity degree of two concept networks B_1, B_2 in such a way that for each concept in B_1 there is a similar concept in B_2, and vice versa. This definition reduces the computation cost of calculating similarities of the corresponding contexts. It defines a similarity relationship as a fuzzy binary similarity $\otimes$−relationship R over a universe X such that R is reflexive $(\forall x,y,z \in X, R(x,x) = 1)$, symmetric $(R(x,y) = R(y,x))$ and transitive in the following manner: $R(x,y) \otimes R(y,z) \leq R(x,z)$.

The following simple example shows the application of the transitivity definitions mentioned.

Let X be the set of the following fields of study: $X = \{$Computer Science, Electronics, Electrical Engineering$\}$ and the similarity relationship S for such fields is defined, for each pair (x,y), in the interval $[0,1]$ as: μ_S(Computer Science, Electronics)$=0.82$, μ_S(Electronics, Electrical Engineering)$=0.85$, μ_S(Computer Science, Electrical Engineering)$=0.56$.

As can be observed, these values indicate that Electronics and Electrical Engineering are very similar fields, as are Computer Science and Electronics. However, Computer Science and Electrical Engineering are not so similar.

According to Zadeh (1971), applying transitivity should result in μ_S(Computer Science, Electrical Engineering) $= min(\mu_S$(Computer Science, Electronics), μ_S(Electronics, Electrical Engineering)). This does not allow representing the notions of Computer Science and Electrical Engineering not being so similar, despite Electronics and Electrical Engineering being very similar fields, as well as Electronics and Computer Science. Applying transitivity demands the similarity degree to be μ_S(Computer Science, Electronics)$=0.82$. However, the degree μ_S(Computer Science, Electrical Engineering)$=0.56$, proposed in the example would be more adequate.

According to Jacas (1990), calculating the t-norm of the minimum we obtain $min(\mu_S$(Computer Science, Electronics),μ_S(Computer Science, Electrical Engineering))$=0.82$ and as μ_S(Computer Science, Electrical Engineering)$=0.56$, it is not true that $T(\mu(x,y), \mu(y,z)) \leq \mu(x,z)$. If we use the product norm then $*(\mu_S$(Computer Science, Electronics),μ_S(Computer Science, Electrical Engineering))$=0.82*0.85=0.6804$, and once again the desired condition is not met. The pair does not fulfill transitivity.

Applying the transitivity proposed by Calvo (1992), the matrix $A_S = (a_{ij}) = S(x_i, x_j)$ is

$$A_S = \begin{vmatrix} 1 & 0.82 & 0.85 \\ 0.82 & 1 & 0.56 \\ 0.85 & 0.56 & 1 \end{vmatrix}$$

If we consider the pair (°, *) as (*max, min*) then, the product $A_S \circ A_S$ is the matrix

$$A_S = \begin{vmatrix} 1 & 0.82 & 0.85 \\ 0.82 & 1 & 0.82 \\ 0.85 & 0.82 & 1 \end{vmatrix}$$

It can be observed, that is differs from A_S.

According to Ochinnikov (1991), the relationship S is transitive if $\mu_S(x,y) \wedge \mu_S(y,z) \leq \mu_S(x,z)$. In the example, this condition is not satisfied, as μ_S(Computer Science, Electronics)=0.82, μ_S(Electronics, Electrical Engineering)=0.85 and μ_S(Computer Science, Electrical Engineering)=0.56. So $0.82 \wedge 0.85 = 0.82$, this value is not less than 0.56. On the other hand, S is not strongly complete, as μ_S(Computer Science, Electronics)$\wedge \mu_S$(Electronics, Electrical Engineering)=$0.82 \wedge 0.85 = min(0.82, 0.85) \neq 1$. Therefore it cannot be quasi-transitive (neither negatively transitive).

Applying the transitivity defined by Faurous and Fillard (1993), the condition $\{y \in X | \mu_S(y,y)=1\}$ is met for every element in the set X and it can be seen that μ_S(Electronics, Electrical Engineering)=1 $\Rightarrow \mu_S$(Computer Science, Electrical Engineering)$\geq \mu_S$(Computer Science, Electronics)$*\mu_S$(Electronics, Electrical Engineering).

We have shown that the definition of transitivity by Zadeh (1971), Jacas (1990), Ovchinnikov (1991) and Farous and Fillard (1993) do not always offer an "adequate" transitive pair. We then define a new reflexive and symmetric similarity relationship with a different transitivity condition, which allows the existence of transitive and non-transitive pairs.

In previous work (Carrasquel, Rodriguez, & Tineo), the authors proposed a new definition for a similarity relationship more appropriate for Type 3 attributes.

Let X be a classical set, S a fuzzy subset of $X \times X$ and $\mu_S : X \times X \rightarrow [0,1]$ the membership function that denotes the degree to which each pair (x, y) belongs to the fuzzy set S. S is a fuzzy set if it is:

Reflexive:

$(\mu_S(x,x)=1, \forall x \in X)$

Symmetric:

$(\mu_S(x,y)=\mu_S(y,x), \forall x,y \in X)$

Transitive:

$$((\forall x,z \in X, (\forall y(\mu_S(x,y)=1 \wedge \mu_S(y,z)=\beta) \Rightarrow \mu_S(x,z)=\beta)$$

$$\wedge$$

$$(\forall x,z \in X (\forall y(\mu_S(x,y)=\beta \wedge \mu_S(y,z)=1) \Rightarrow \mu_S(x,z)=\beta))$$

When the relationship is reflexive and symmetric, only one of the transitive conditions is necessary, as the other one follows immediately.

A fuzzy similarity relationship S induces a fuzzy partition over the set of values X. Each element of this fuzzy partition is called a *fuzzy similarity class* and is defined as follows: For a fixed element $x \in X$, the fuzzy similarity class of x is the fuzzy set of all values in X that are similar to x. That is, $S[x] = \{y/\mu_S(x,y) \mid y \in X\}$. A fuzzy similarity class can be simply called a *fuzzy class* or equivalently a *similarity class*.

As an example, consider the following fields of study: Electronics, Computer Science, Electrical Engineering, Mathematics, Physics, Chemistry and Material Science. It is possible to establish a similarity relationship that describes how similar these fields are. The similarity relationship can be defines as a fuzzy set where each pair (x, y) has a membership degree in the interval [0,1], as shown in the Table 1.

This relation establishes the fuzzy class of Electronics as:

Similar[*Electronics*] = { Chemistry, Computer Science, Material Science, Mathematics }

DATA DOMAINS WITH SIMILARITY RELATIONS

The standard language for databases, SQL, allows the definition of domains that describe new data types within a schema. In (Carrasquel et al., 2013) the SQL-DDL (SQL Data Definition Language) was extended with the possibility of creating Type 3 fuzzy data domains, This is a set of labels augmented with a similarity relation. The definition syntax in a Type 3 fuzzy domain is:

Table 1. Similarity relation for fields of study

Similar	Electronics	Computer Science	Electric Engineering	Mathematics	Physics	Chemistry	Material Science
Electronics	1	0.82	0.85	0.52	0.57	0.22	0.15
Computer Science	0.82	1	0.23	0.65	0.14	0.35	0.18
Electric Engineering	0.85	0.23	1		0.12		0.12
Mathematics	0.52	0.65		1		0.2	0.14
Physics	0.57	0.14	0.12		1		0.1
Chemistry		0.35		0.2		1	0.2
Material Science	0.15		0.12	0.14	0.1	0.2	1

```
CREATE FUZZY DOMAIN <name> AS
VALUES (<label >[,<label>,…,<label>])
[SIMILARITY { (<label>,<label>) / <value>
          [, (<label>,<label>) / <value>
        , …
        , (<label>,<label>) / <value> ] } ]
```

where <name> is the name of the new domain; (<label >[,<label>,…,<label>]) is the list of labels that define the domain; the expressions (<label>,<label>)/<value> corresponding to the pairs of the fuzzy similarity relation for that domain; being <value> the membership degree for that pair in the relation.

It is only necessary to specify the basic pairs of the relationship, for those corresponding to reflexivity, symmetry and transitivity can be easily inferred. The relationship formed by the basic pairs is known as the base relation. The membership degree is cero for any pair whose values are not specified in the instruction or attainable by means of reflexivity, symmetry and transitivity.

The SIMILARITY clause is optional. This would be a set of label for which at the time of their definition, the similarity is unknown. In (Carrasquel et al., 2013) a formalization of this sentence using fuzzy set theory is proposed as follows:

```
CREATE FUZZY DOMAIN fd AS
VALUES (l₁,l₂,…,lₖ)
[SIMILARITY { (l_{i1}, l_{j1}) / v₁
          , (l_{i2}, l_{j2}) / v₂
        , …
        , (l_{in}, l_{jn}) / vₙ } ]
```

This define a universe $fd=\{l_1,l_2,...,l_k\}$ augmented with a similarity relation S. Additionally, it specifies a fuzzy relation σ defined by $\forall r\in 1..n\ \mu_\sigma(l_{ir}, l_{jr}) = v_r$, that we will call base relation of the similarity relation S. This relation satisfies:

$$\forall x,y\in fd\ \mu_\sigma(x,y)\neq 0 \Rightarrow \mu_S(x,y)=\mu_\sigma(x,y)$$

$$\forall l\in fd\ \mu_S(l,l)=1 \text{ (reflexivity)}$$

$$\forall x,y\in fd\ \mu_S(x,y) = \mu_S(y,x) \text{ (symmetry)}$$

$$\forall x,z\in fd\ \forall y\in fd\ (\mu_S(x, y)=1 \wedge \mu_S(y,z)=v \Rightarrow \mu_S(x,z)=v) \text{ (transitivity)}$$

The membership degree to the similarity relation S is cero for any pair whose values are not specified in the instruction or attainable by means of reflexivity, symmetry and transitivity.

For example, for the relation Similar defined previously, the domain with fields of study (FieldStudy) is created, with a similarity relation as described in the following statement:

```
CREATE FUZZY DOMAIN FieldStudy AS
   VALUES (
```

```
      Electronics, Chemistry, Computer Science, Physics,
      Material Science, Mathematics, Electric Engineering,
 )
SIMILARITY {
    (Electronics, Chemistry)/0.12,
    (Electronics, Computer Science)/0.82,
    (Electronics, Physics)/0.57,
    (Electronics, Material Science)/0.15,
    (Electronics, Mathematics)/0.52,
    (Electronics, Electric Engineering)/0.85,
    (Chemistry, Computer Science)/0.35,
    (Chemistry, Material Science)/0.2,
    (Chemistry, Mathematics)/0.2,
    (Computer Science, Physics)/0.14,
    (Computer Science, Material Science)/0.18,
    (Computer Science, Mathematics)/0.65,
    (Computer Science, Electric Engineering)/0.23,
    (Physics, Material Science)/0.1,
    (Physics, Electric Engineering)/0.12,
    (Material Science, Mathematics)/0.14,
    (Material Science, Electric Engineering)/0.12
}
```

A statement is also provided that allows adding new values to the fuzzy domain with the following syntax:

```
ALTER FUZZY DOMAIN <name>
    ADD VALUES (<label>[,<label>,…,<label>])
```

Using the previously created domain *fd*, the formalization of the sentence would be expressed as:

```
ALTER FUZZY DOMAIN fd
    ADD VALUES (e₁, e₂, …, eₘ)
```

This statement must satisfy $e_i \neq l_j \; \forall i \neq j$. It's semantic is given by $fd = \{l_1, l_2, ..., l_k\} \cup \{e_1, e_2, ..., e_m\}$. For example, if new fields of study are to be added to FieldStudy, such as Informatics and Biology, the following statement could be used:

```
ALTER FUZZY DOMAIN FieldStudy
    ADD VALUES (Informatics, Biology)
```

Likewise, a statement is provided for adding new pared to the fuzzy similarity relation, using the following syntax:

```
ALTER FUZZY DOMAIN <name>
   ADD SIMILARITY { (<label>,<label>) / <value>)
                   [,(<label>,<label>) / <value>)
                   , ...
                   , (<label>,<label>) / <value>)]}
```

The formalization of this statement is given by:

```
ALTER FUZZY DOMAIN fd
   ADD SIMILARITY { (e_{i1}, e_{j1}) / w_1, (e_{i2}, e_{j2}) / w_2
                   , ...
                   , (e_{in}, e_{jp}) / w_p }
```

This statement must satisfy $\forall i,j\ e_{ij} \in fd$. This adds to the base relation σ, defined for the domain *fd*, the membership degrees specified by $\forall r \in 1..p\ \mu_\sigma(e_{ir}, e_{jr}) = w_r$.

For example, in order to add new pairs to the similarity relationship that indicates similarities between fields of study, the following statement could be used:

```
ALTER FUZZY DOMAIN FieldStudy
   ADD SIMILARITY { (Electronics, Informatics)/0.42
                   , (Electronics, Biology)/0.15 }
```

A statement for deleting labels from the fuzzy data domain, or pairs in the similarity relationship, is also provided, with the following syntax:

```
ALTER FUZZY DOMAIN fd
   DROP VALUES (e_1,e_2,...,e_m)
ALTER FUZZY DOMAIN fd
   DROP SIMILARITY { (e_{i1}, e_{j1})
                   , (e_{i2}, e_{j2})
                   , ...
                   , (e_{ip}, e_{jp}) }
```

In this case, the formalization of the first statement is given by:

```
ALTER FUZZY DOMAIN fd
   DROP VALUES (e_1, e_2, ..., e_m)
```

This statement must satisfy $\forall i \exists j (e_i = l_j)\ m < k$, with its semantic expressed as $fd = \{l_1, l_2, ..., l_k\} - \{e_1, e_2, ..., e_m\}$. The second statement is formalized as:

```
ALTER FUZZY DOMAIN fd
   DROP SIMILARITY { (e_{i1}, e_{j1})
```

$$, (e_{i2}, e_{j2})$$
$$, \ldots$$
$$, (e_{ip}, e_{jp}) \}$$

This alters the definition of the base relationship σ making $\forall r \in 1..p\ (\mu_\sigma(e_{ir}, e_{jr}) = 0)$.

For example, if Physics must be deleted from fields of study, along with every pair that corresponds to it in the similarity relationship, the following statement could be used:

```
ALTER FUZZY DOMAIN FieldStudy
   DROP VALUES (Physics)
```

If only the pair Electronics-Physics is to be deleted from the similarity relationship for the fields of study domain, the following statement could then be used:

```
ALTER FUZZY DOMAIN FieldStudy
  DROP SIMILARITY { (Electronics, Physics) }
```

Finally, a statement is provided that allows deleting an entire fuzzy data domain, which includes its similarity relationship if it exists. The following syntax should be used:

```
DROP FUZZY DOMAIN <name>
```

SIMILARITY RELATIONSHIP BASES ORDERING

The SQL standard allows ordering results in a query by means of an ORDER BY clause. In a Type 3 data domain, the similarity relationship induces order relationships among labels. It is therefore possible to extend the syntax and semantics of the ORDER BY clause.

As the similarity relationship is characterized by being reflexive, symmetric and transitive, it generates a fuzzy partition over the set of values of a given attribute. Each possible value has a fuzzy class associated with every value that is similar.

For example, in the similarity relationship for fields of study that we have been treating so far, the fields of study similar to *Electronics*, are those whose pair has a membership degree greater than zero in the similarity relationship. This degree can be observed in the similarity relationship given in the fuzzy domain. That is, *Chemistry*, *Computer Science*, *Material Science*, *Mathematics*, *Electrical Engineering* and *Physics*. These fields form a similarity class with *Electronics*. The pairs that correspond to fields that do not appear in the similarity relationship with *Electronics* have a default membership degree of zero. That is, they do not belong to the similarity class of *Electronics*.

The fuzzy classes allow extending the ORDER BY clause with a new semantics that allows ordering elements respect to the membership degree, in the similarity relationship, with respect to a fixed element. The syntax of the extended ORDER BY is:

```
ORDER BY    criterio₁
         , ...
         , criterioₒ
```

where each *criterio₁* take one of the following forms:

- $k_i d_i$, with k_i an attribute and d_i an order specifier among ASC or DESC.
- k_i START v_i, with k_i a Type 3 fuzzy attribute and v_i a label in the domain of that attribute.

The abbreviated form k_i can be used as a synonym for k_i ASC.

For k_i START v_i the following more verbose forms are also allowed:

- k_i STARTING FROM v_i
- SIMILARITY ON k_i START v_i
- SIMILARITY ON k_i STARTING FROM v_i

The use of an ordering criteria of the form k_i START v_i has the effect of ordering the set of resulting tuples in decreasing order by the membership degree $\mu_{S[vi]}$, with $S[v_i]$ the fuzzy class of v_i. Note that the ORDER BY clause does not have the semantics of a filter. No element from the fuzzy class will be suppressed, but instead will appear in the final result.

The formalization of this result for the new ORDER BY clause is presented next. Let C be the query:

```
SELECT c₁, c₂, ..., cₙ
FROM T
ORDER BY k₁ d₁, ..., kₒ dₒ
```

where $k_i \in \{ c_1, c_2, ..., c_n \}$ and $d_i \in \{$ ASC, DESC, START $v \}$.

Then, the result of C is the following sequence:

```
resultset (C) = ⟨ (tᵢ.c₁, tᵢ.c₂, ..., tᵢ.cₙ) | tᵢ∈ T⟩ i∈{1,...,m}
```

The order of the tuples in the sequence maintains the following restriction:

$\forall p,q \in \{1,...,m\}$ (

$\exists r \in \{1,...,o\}$ $(\rho(t_p.k_r, t_q.k_r) \land \forall j \in \{1,...,r\text{-}1\}\ \xi_j(t_p.k_j, t_q.k_j))$

$\Rightarrow (p \leq q)$

)

where, for each appropriate x,

$(d_x{=}\text{ASC} \Rightarrow \rho(t_p.k_x, t_q.k_x) \equiv (t_p.k_x < t_q.k_x) \land \xi_j(t_p.k_x, t_q.k_x) \equiv (t_p.k_x = t_q.k_x)) \land$

$$(d_x=\text{DESC} \Rightarrow \rho(t_p.k_x, t_q.k_x) \equiv (t_p.k_x > t_q.k_x) \wedge \xi_j(t_p.k_x, t_q.k_x) \equiv (t_p.k_x = t_q.k_x)) \wedge$$

$$(d_x = \text{START } v \Rightarrow \rho(t_p.k_x, t_q.k_x) \equiv (\mu_s(v, t_p.k_x) < \mu_s(v, t_q.k_x) \wedge$$

$$\xi_j(t_p.k_x, t_q.k_x) \equiv (\mu_s(v, t_p.k_x) = \mu_s(v, t_q.k_x)))$$

As an illustration of the use of this clause, consider the subjects that belong to the fields of study shown in Table 2.

And consider the following query:

```
SELECT Code, Name, Field
   FROM Subjects
   ORDER BY SIMILARITY ON Field STARTING FROM 'Electronics';
```

This query produces as a result, the tuples in Table 3. The results have been augmented with the μ value for clarity. This corresponds to the membership degree in the similarity relationship of the pair

Table 2. Subjects with their fields of study

Code	Name	Field
MA-1111	Calculus I	Mathematics
MA-3565	Statistics	Mathematics
FS-3111	Optics	Physics
CE-2341	Energy Conversion	Electrical Engineering
EE-3135	Digital Networks	Electronics
CI-3611	Databases	Computer Science
QP-2111	General Chemistry	Chemistry
MT-4123	Polymers	Material Science

Table 3. Result of the query with ordering

Code	Name	Field	μ
EE-3135	Digital Networks	Electronics	1
CE-2341	Energy Conversion	Electrical Engineering	0.85
CI-3611	Databases	Computer Science	0.81
FS-3111	Optics	Physics	0.57
MA-1111	Calculus I	Mathematics	0.52
MA-3565	Statistics	Mathematics	0.52
QP-2111	General Chemistry	Chemistry	0.22
MT-4123	Polymers	Material Science	0.15

formed by the value of column Field with the label: 'Electronics'. It is not part of the result, and has been added for reference. The result appears ordered by the membership degree (μ) of the similarity relationship. Therefore, fields closer to electronics will appear first.

ARCHITECTURE OF THE EXTENSION FOR A RDBMS

The implementation of Type 3 fuzzy attributes is made as an extension of a Relational Database Management System (RDBMS). Our proposal uses a *mildly coupled architecture* (Timarán, 2001). In this architecture, the logic of the extension is coded in the native language of the RDBMS. Additionally, there may be an external layer that implements a translation schema between the extended language and the native language. The architecture of the extension is show in Figure 1.

There are two other possible architecture types (Timarán, 2001): *loosely coupled*, where the extension in implemented as an external logical layer, that processes data extracted from a RDBMS; and *tightly coupled*, that consists in modifying the source code for the RDBMS itself. The first option has the advantage of portability, but can produce a significant overhead in the access to the external layer.

Figure 1. Architecture for the extended RDBMS

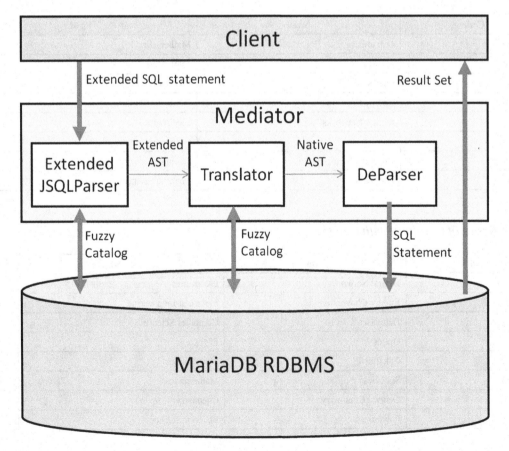

This layer can become a bottleneck, so it is best suited for small applications, with limited database access. The second option has no overhead issues, but requires a greater programming effort and can affect portability.

Fuzzy Catalog

In order to extend the RDBMS, the representation of fuzzy domains and their labels is needed, as well as the membership function of these domains and the column information of the database that are defined with fuzzy domains. This is modeled by means of a schema that represents such information in the catalog of the RDBMS that we shall call: *fuzzy catalog*.

The metadata corresponding to fuzzy domains for Type 3 attributes must be included in the relational catalog for objects in the database. For this, FUZZY_INFORMATION_SCHEMA was defined and it will be presented through a relational model. The primary keys are shown with a single underline; alternative keys are shown with double underline and foreign keys with the name of the table that they reference as a superscript.

```
DOMAIN(domainId, tableSchema, domainName)
LABEL(labelId, domainId DOMAIN, labelName)
SIMILARITY(label1Id LABEL, label2Id LABEL, value, derived)
COLUMN(tableSchema, tableName, columnName, domainId DOMAIN)
```

The relationship DOMAIN contains the different domains for Type 3 fuzzy attributes, identified by *domainName* within a database (*tableSchema*). A numeric key (*domainId*) is generated automatically in order to simplify its use. This table has a unique key the pair (*tableSchema, domainName*), so there can be no two domains with the same name in a given database.

The relationship LABEL stores the labels (*labelName*) of the fuzzy data domains, referenced by *domainId*. The key (*labelId*) is an automatically generated number. The different *labelName* correspond to the values that a Type 3 fuzzy attribute can have in that domain. However, instead of using these values in each data table, the key *labelId* shall be used. This table has as a unique key the pair (*domainId, labelName*), so there can be no two labels with the same name in the same domain.

The relationship SIMILARITY contains label pairs (*label1Id, label2Id*) that make a similarity relationship, indicating its associated membership degree (*value*). The *derived* attribute discriminates if the pair belongs to the base relationship or if it's derived from reflexivity, symmetry or transitivity.

The relationship COLUMN identifies Type 3 attribute columns, with a domain referenced by *domainId*. The identification of the column is composed with its name (*columnName*), the name of the table to which it belongs (*tableName*) and the name of the database in which the table is defined (*tableSchema*). Its purpose is to rapidly detect any SQL instruction that refers to columns that store Type 3 fuzzy attributes and the domain to which they correspond.

In this schema, every attribute is NOT NULL. Each foreign key, except *domainId* in table COLUMN, has a CASCADE effect in case of updates (ON UPDATE) or deletion (ON DELETE). This implies that the same action is made on the values of columns that reference these foreign keys. The *domainId* foreign key from table COLUMN has a CASCADE effect in case of update, but RESTRICT in case of deletions. This implies that deletion is not allowed in the referenced table.

Architecture Layers

In the selected architecture (mildly coupled), the external layer is a controller consisting of the modules: front-end, core and back-end. In the front-end module, a syntactic analyzer or parser for the extended SQL generates an abstract syntax tree (AST). The core module transforms the AST for the extended language into an equivalent AST for the native language. The back-end module takes the transformed AST and generates the SQL instruction that it represents.

During the syntactic analysis, the columns that correspond to Type 3 attributes are identified, as they require special treatment. For this, the expressions associated with the items in the SELECT, WHERE and ORDER BY clauses are inspected. In this process, each column is associated with its corresponding table. The fuzzy catalog is checked in order to determine the columns that store Type 3 fuzzy data, generating a list of columns that need translation. Although a column may appear in several sub-expressions of the query, it is inserted only once in the list.

Once the original sentence is validates, the translator is invoked. This translator uses the fuzzy catalo in order to generate an AST corresponding to the translated sentence into native SQL. In order to accomplish this task, translation schema were defined that allow transforming each extended SQL statement that involves Type 3 fuzzy attributes, into a SQL statement that only uses native constructions. These translation schemas are presented in the following section.

In the case of a SELECT statement, for instance, a list of references to table in the FROM clause is generated. During the translation, each table is replaced by its JOIN with the LABEL table from the fuzzy catalog in order to obtain the actual value. This value may be needed for comparisons with literal expressions or to be returned as an item for the SELECT statement. Additionally, in case of requiring fuzzy ordering or grouping, the values available in the SIMILARITY table will be used as the corresponding similarity relationship.

Afterwards, the AST is traversed in order to find expressions that involve columns with fuzzy data. These columns are replaced in the AST with the column from the LABEL table that contains the label known to the user. If this replacement is made in the SELECT clause, the translation guarantees that al names and aliases are preserved and usable in further statements.

The code generation takes the transformed AST and builds an SQL statement that is equivalent. This process is known as deparsing. Finally, the string with the translated SQL statement is sent to the RDBMS for its execution, thus obtaining the desired result.

Translation Schemes

The schemes allow translate the instructions of SQL extended to instructions of native SQL, using the fuzzy catalog. For this, we are specified each definition using first-order logic and notation of sets to represent tables and properties that appear in this definitions. These tables are the result of the different operations of extended SQL. The correction of translation schemes is done with formal tests that allow verify that the translation submitted is correct. Also, we show the use of these schemes with a case of study to visualize the usefulness and applicability of these.

The translation schemes include all use cases that involve Type 3 attributes, namely operations to defining and manipulating fuzzy data domains (CREATE, ALTER, and DROP DOMAIN FUZZY); operations DDL that involve Type 3 attributes (CREATE TABLE, ALTER TABLE and DROP TABLE);

operations DML that involve Type 3 attributes (INSERT, UPDATE and DELETE); operations of general queries that involve Type 3 attributes (SELECT and FROM clauses); finally, operations of queries that involve ordering (ORDER BY clause) on Type 3 attributes.

Create Fuzzy Domain

The CREATE FUZZY DOMAIN operation allows the insertion of a domain in the fuzzy catalog, their labels and their similarity relationship. The latter requires generate all pairs of complete similarity relationship from the base relation specified by the user. If the base relation is empty, i.e. not specified in the sentence, only the pairs that corresponding to the reflexive property, are generated. Furthermore, it is necessary validate non duplicity of labels within one domain and consistency of the similarity relationship generated from the properties of reflexivity, symmetry and transitivity.

The syntax of this statement is:

```
CREATE FUZZY DOMAIN domain_name AS
VALUES (label [, label,…])
[SIMILARITY {  (label, label) / value
          [, (label, label) / value
          , …] } ]
```

Recalling the example of the previous sections, to create a domain for Fields Study, we would use the statement

```
CREATE FUZZY DOMAIN FieldStudy AS
   VALUES (
      Electronics, Chemistry, Computer Science,
      Physics, Material Science, Mathematics,
      Electric Engineering, Informatics
   )
   SIMILARITY {
      (Electronics, Chemistry)/0.22,
      (Electronics, Computer Science)/0.81,
      (Electronics, Physics)/0.57,
      (Electronics, Material Science)/0.15,
      (Electronics, Mathematics)/0.52,
      (Electronics, Electric Engineering)/0.85,
      (Chemistry, Computer Science)/0.35,
      (Chemistry, Material Science)/0.2,
      (Chemistry, Mathematics)/0.2,
      (Computer Science, Physics)/0.14,
      (Computer Science, Mathematics)/0.65,
      (Computer Science, Electric Engineering)/0.23,
      (Computer Science, Material Science)/0.18,
      (Computer Science, Informatics)/1.0,
```

```
(Material Science, Mathematics)/0.14,
(Physics, Electric Engineering)/0.12,
(Mathematics, Electric Engineering)/0.12,
(Mathematics, Physics)/0.1,
}
```

The translation of this statement requires three steps. First, insert a new domain in the DOMAIN table of the fuzzy catalog. Second, the insertion of labels defined for this domain in the LABEL table. Third, calculate the similarity relationship and its insertion into the SIMILARITY table. The insertion of the new domain is done by the sentence

```
INSERT INTO FUZZY_INFORMATION_SCHEMA.DOMAIN
    VALUES (null, (select database()), domain_name)
```

In the example of fields study, this correspond to the statement

```
INSERT INTO FUZZY_INFORMATION_SCHEMA.DOMAIN
    VALUES (null, (select database()), 'FieldStudy')
```

The values of the inserted tuple correspond to the attributes of the DOMAIN table: domain identifier (domainId), name of current scheme (tableSchema) and domain name (domainName). The name of current scheme is obtained by invoking "select database ()", this may vary according to the particular dialect of RDBMS SQL used. When we insert a "null" value in the column domainId is necessary to indicate to the extended DBMS that automatically to generate a unique value. This must be specified in the definition of domainId column. This identifier is stored to be able generate the following statements.

```
SELECT domainId INTO auxDomainId
    FROM FUZZY_INFORMATION_SCHEMA.DOMAIN
    WHERE  tableSchema = select database()
        AND domainName = domain_name
```

The insertion of labels corresponding to the domain is performed with the sentence:

```
INSERT INTO FUZZY_INFORMATION_SCHEMA.LABEL
    VALUES    (null, auxDomainId, label_name)
          [, (null, domainId, label_name)
          , ... ];
```

For the example fields study, the sentence would be

```
INSERT INTO FUZZY_INFORMATION_SCHEMA.LABEL
    VALUES (null, auxDomainId, 'Electronics'),
           (null, auxDomainId, 'Chemistry'),
           (null, auxDomainId, 'Computer Science'),
```

```
(null, auxDomainId, 'Material Science'),
(null, auxDomainId, 'Mathematics'),
(null, auxDomainId, 'Electric Engineering'),
(null, auxDomainId, 'Physics'),
(null, auxDomainId, 'Informatics')
```

Analogously to domain insertion, each tuple stores a labelId automatically generated by the extended DBMS for each label. These identifiers will be used in the similarity relationship. In addition, the identifier generated for the domain (domainId) and the name of the label (labelName).

For calculating the similarity relationship complete, the base relationship specified by the user is taken. This latter can be empty because its specification is optional. In this case, the complete relationship will only contain the pairs that correspond to the reflexivity.

If the base relationship pairs are specified, the following algorithm is used to generate the similarity relationship complete:

1. If there has realized a previous calculation of the reflexive, symmetric or transitive pairs of the base relation, these pairs are eliminated. Only are left the base relation pairs. These pairs are identified through the *derived* attribute of the SIMILARITY table.
2. The reflexive closure is calculated. All labels are traversed and each reflective pair is generated.
3. The following cycle is executed:
    a. The symmetric closure is calculated. All relationship pairs are traversed and the symmetrical pairs that not exist are generated.
    b. The transitive closure is calculated. For this, the similarity relationship pairs with membership degree equal to 1, ie, of the form $(L_1, L_2, 1)$ are detected. For each pairs $(L_1, L_2, 1)$ is looked for a pair of the form (L_2, L_3, x). So, the transitive pair (L_1, L_3, x) is generated in the complete relationship.
    c. The cycle ends if another transitive pair is not discovered.

After calculating the pairs of similarity relationship complete, these are inserted in the fuzzy catalogue with the sentence:

```
INSERT INTO FUZZY_INFORMATION_SCHEMA.SIMILARITY
   VALUES    (label1Id, label2Id, value, derived)
         [, (label1Id, label2Id, value, derived)
      , … ];
```

where label1Id and label2Id are label identifiers, *value* is the membership degree of the pair; *derived* is true if the pair is obtained by applying the properties of reflexivity, symmetry and transitivity, or *derived* is false if the pair is part of the base relation.

For the example that is being developed, we called ElectronicsId, ChemistryId, ComputerScienceId, PhysicsId, MaterialScienceId, MathematicsId, ElectricEngineeringId, InformaticsId the automatically auto-generated identifiers for the labels "Electronics", "Chemistry", "Computer Science", "Physics", "Material Science", "Mathematics", "Electric Engineering", "Informatics", respectively.

The insertion of the similarity degrees in the fuzzy catalog would be as:

```
INSERT INTO FUZZY_INFORMATION_SCHEMA.SIMILARITY
    VALUES
        // base relationship pairs which were specified
        // in the creation of domain
        (ElectronicsId, ChemistryId,0.22,0), …,
        (ElectronicsId, PhysicsId,0.57,0),
        (ChemistryId, ComputerScienceId,0.35,0), …,
        (ChemistryId, MathematicsId,0.20,0), …,
        (ComputerScienceId, MaterialScienceId,0.18,0), …,
        (ComputerScienceId,InformaticsId,1.0,0), …,
        (MaterialScienceId, MathematicsId,0.14,0), …,
        (MathematicsId, ElectricEngineeringId,0.12,0), …,
        (MathematicsId, PhysicsId, 0.10,0), …,
        (ElectricEngineeringId, PhysicsId,0.12,0),

        // derived reflective pairs, one for each label
        // in the domain
        (ElectronicsId, ElectronicsId,1.0,1), …,
        (InformaticsId, InformaticsId, 1.0,1)

        // derived symmetric pairs that were specified
        // in creation of domain
        (ChemistryId, ElectronicsId, 0.22,1), …,
        (PhysicsId, ElectronicsId, 0.57,1),
        (ComputaciónId, ChemistryId,0.35,1), …,
        (MathematicsId, ChemistryId,0.20,1),
        (MaterialScienceId, ComputerScienceId,0.18,1), …,
        (InformáticaId, ComputerScienceId,1.0,1),
        (MathematicsId, MaterialScienceId,0.14,1),
        (ElectricEngineeringId, MathematicsId,0.12,1),
        (PhysicsId, MathematicsId, 0.10,1),
        (PhysicsId, ElectricEngineeringId,0.12,1),

        // derived transitive pairs induced by
        // not reflective pairs with similarity equal to 1
        (ElectronicsId, InformaticsId, 0.81,1),
        (InformaticsId, ElectronicsId,  0.81,1),
        (ChemistryId, InformaticsId,0.35,1),
        (InformaticsId, ChemistryId,0.35,1),
        (InformaticsId, MaterialScienceId,0.18,1),
        (MaterialScienceId, InformaticsId,0.18,1),
        (InformaticsId, MathematicsId,0.65,1),
        (MathematicsId, InformaticsId,0.65,1),
        (InformaticsId, ElectricEngineeringId,0.23,1),
```

```
(ElectricEngineeringId, InformaticsId,0.23,1),
(InformaticsId, PhysicsId,0.14,1),
(PhysicsId, InformaticsId,0.14,1)
```

```
// end of the insert statement
```

The translation of the **CREATE DOMAIN FUZZY** sentence require to validate that exists a connection to a database, that not exists a domain with same name in the current database and that not exists two labels with the same name in the domain. Also, it is necessary to verify the consistency of the properties of reflexivity, symmetry and transitivity in the complete similarity relationship generated from the base relation.

For this, the insertions are realized within a transaction, and they are validated through the constraints of foreign key, not nullity and uniqueness defined for the fuzzy catalog. This allows roll back the transaction and to produce a significant error message to the user.

In addition, an alternative syntax is provided that facilitates the creation of a fuzzy domain (domain_name) from labels taken as of a column (col_name) belonging to an existing table (table_name) of a database (schema).

```
CREATE FUZZY DOMAIN domain_name
    AS VALUES FROM [schema.]table_name.col_name
```

Using the example of fields study, if there is a table called DISCIPLINES that has a column named "area", we can create a fuzzy domain with the sentence

```
CREATE FUZZY DOMAIN FieldStudy
    AS VALUES FROM DISCIPLINES.area
```

The database of the current connection will be used by default when the schema is not specified. For this, it is necessary to validate that exist a connection to a database. Although the scheme is specified in the statement, the domain will be stored in the current database of the connection. Also, it is necessary to verify that not exists a domain with same name in the current scheme of the database, and, it must exist the schema, the table and the column that appear in the sentence. Also, there must be at least one non-null value in the column of the specified table.

The first two validations are made through the own restrictions of the fuzzy catalog. In order to verify the last two, the following query is executed:

```
SELECT COUNT(*)
    FROM schema.table_name
    WHERE col_name IS NOT NULL
```

For the case that have mentioned, the sentence would be

```
SELECT COUNT(*)
   FROM DISCIPLINES
   WHERE area IS NOT NULL
```

The execution should not produce error and its result should give a value greater than zero. Then, the domain is inserted in the DOMAIN table with the original syntax and the labels are inserted in the LABEL table, using the statement:

```
INSERT INTO FUZZY_INFORMATION_SCHEMA.LABEL
         (domainId, labelName)
   SELECT DISTINCT auxDomainId, table_name.col_name
      FROM [schema.]table_name
      WHERE col_name IS NOT NULL
```

where, auxDomainId contains the domain identifier that is being defined. This identifier was automatically generated when it was inserted in the fuzzy catalog.

In the example of the fields study, using the auxDomainId generated by the system to FieldStudy, the statement would be

```
INSERT INTO FUZZY_INFORMATION_SCHEMA.LABEL
         (domainId, labelName)
   SELECT DISTINCT auxDomainId, DISCIPLINES.area
      FROM DISCIPLINES
      WHERE area IS NOT NULL
```

An important aspect to note is that the values in the column col_name will be converted by default as VARCHAR. This may result in different labels to the originals in col_name. For example, if the original column was VARCHAR type and had a length greater than 64, its values will be truncated to 64 characters.

Finally, it must insert the domain similarity relation consisting only of reflective pairs, using the sentence:

```
INSERT INTO FUZZY_INFORMATION_SCHEMA.SIMILARITY
   SELECT labelId, labelId, 1.0, 1
      FROM FUZZY_INFORMATION_SCHEMA.LABEL
      WHERE domain_id = auxDomainId
```

Alter Fuzzy Domain

The ALTER FUZZY DOMAIN operation lets add and delete domain values (ADD VALUES and DROP VALUES), as well as, add and remove similarity relationship pairs (ADD SIMILARITY and DROP SIMILARITY).

Add Values

The syntax of this statement is as follows:

```
ALTER FUZZY DOMAIN domain_name
    ADD VALUES (label1 [, label2, …, labelN])
```

For example, in the case of fields study, if we want to add the areas of "Medicine" and "Anthropology", the statement would be used

```
ALTER FUZZY DOMAIN FieldStudy
    ADD VALUES (Medicine, Anthropology)
```

When values are aggregated is necessary to insert the reflective pairs of the similarity relationship in the fuzzy catalog and to verify the non-existence of these in the domain. Therefore, the translation would be the following sequence of SQL statements.

```
INSERT INTO FUZZY_INFORMATION_SCHEMA.LABEL
    VALUES  (null, auxDomainId, label1)
        , …
        , (null, auxDomainId, labelN)
INSERT INTO FUZZY_INFORMATION_SCHEMA.SIMILARITY
    VALUES  (null, label1Id, label1Id, 1.0, '1')
        , …
        , (null, labelNId, labelNId, 1.0, '1')
```

where, auxDomainId is the domain identifier in the fuzzy catalog; label1Id, …, labelNId are auto-generated identifiers in the fuzzy catalog for label1, …, labelN, respectively.

In addition, it is required to validate that the connection is using a database schema, because neither could have selected by the user. Also, it is necessary to verify that exist a domain in the scheme with the specified name and there are not labels in the domain with the same name specified in the statement.

Regarding similarity relationship, no validation is necessary since consistency is maintained because only reflexive pairs were inserted.

Drop Values

The syntax of this statement is as follows:

```
ALTER FUZZY DOMAIN domain_name
    DROP VALUES (value1 [, …, valueN])
```

For the example of fields study correspond to the sentence

```
ALTER FUZZY DOMAIN FieldStudy
    DROP VALUES (Anthropology, Medicine)
```

When values (or labels) are deleted from a domain, also, it must remove similarity relation pairs associated with these values. Furthermore, the complete similarity relationship must be recalculated to ensure properties. In addition, it must verify that exist the fuzzy values will be eliminated and they are not used in tables of other schemes. The translation of this sentence would be:

```
DELETE FROM FUZZY_INFORMATION_SCHEMA.LABEL
    WHERE domainId = auxDomainId
    AND labelName IN (value1, …, valueN)
```

where, auxDomainId is the domain identifier in the fuzzy catalog.

The execution of this statement removes similarity relationship pairs correspond with the deleted labels of the association with the foreign keys in the SIMILARITY table. Then, the complete similarity relationship is recalculated using the same algorithm explained in the previous section.

In addition, it is required to validate that the connection is using a database schema, because neither could have been selected by the user. Also, it is necessary to verify that exist a domain in the scheme with the specified name, that the specified labels exist in the databases and not exist columns in tables of other schemas that use the labels to be removed. These validations are performed by the DBMS through the foreign key constraints included in the fuzzy catalog definition.

Add Similarity

The syntax of this statement is as follows:

```
ALTER FUZZY DOMAIN domainName
    ADD SIMILARITY {  (label11, label12) / value1
                  [, …
                  , (labelN1, labelN2) / valueN]}
```

For the example of fields study correspond to the sentence

```
ALTER FUZZY DOMAIN FieldStudy
    ADD SIMILARITY {
        (Medicine, Electronics)/0.1,
        (Medicine, Chemistry)/0.6,
        (Medicine, Anthropology) / 0.5
    }
```

The base relation changes when new pairs are added in the similarity relationship. Therefore, it is necessary to insert new tuples in the base relation, as well as, all pairs generated by reflexivity and transitivity in the similarity relationship. For this, the same algorithm used for defining a domain is applied.

In addition, it is required to validate that the connection is using a database schema, because neither could have been selected by the user. Also, it is necessary to verify that exist a domain in the scheme with the specified name; that the specified labels belong to the domain; and that consistency is maintained with the properties of reflexivity, symmetry and transitivity in the complete similarity relationship generated from this new base relationship. The latter is ensured with the algorithm execution.

Drop Similarity

The syntax of this statement is as follows:

```
ALTER FUZZY DOMAIN domain_name
    DROP SIMILARITY {  (label11, label12)
                    [, …
                , (labelN1, labelN2)] }
```

For the example of fields study correspond to the sentence

```
ALTER FUZZY DOMAIN FieldStudy
    DROP SIMILARITY {(Medicine, Anthropology) }
```

When base relation pairs are deleted is necessary to recalculate the entire relationship using the algorithm specified in the previous sections. The translation would be

```
DELETE FROM FUZZY_INFORMATION_SCHEMA.SIMILARITY
    WHERE  domainId = auxDomainId
      AND (label1Id, label2Id)
        IN {  (label11Id, label12Id)
        , …
        , (labelN1Id, labeN12Id) }
```

Being auxDomainId the domain identifier in the fuzzy catalog, and label11Id, label12Id, ..., labelN1Id, labeN12Id, the identifiers in the fuzzy catalog for label11 labels, label12, ..., labelN1, labelN2 belonging to the specified domain.

In this translation scheme is required to validate that the connection is using a database schema, because neither could have been selected by the user. As well as, it is necessary to verify that there is a domain in the scheme with the specified name; that the specified labels belong to the domain; that the specified pairs belong to the base relation; and that consistency is maintained with the properties of reflexivity, symmetry and transitivity in the complete similarity relationship generated from base relation. The latter validations are guaranteed with the algorithm execution for calculating the complete similarity relationship presented in previous sections.

Drop Fuzzy Domain

The DROP FUZZY DOMAIN operation involves erasing the tuple associated to the domain from the fuzzy catalog. In addition, the values and pairs corresponding to the similarity relationship should be automatically deleted. The syntax of this statement is as follows:

```
DROP FUZZY DOMAIN domain_name
```

For the example of fields study correspond to the sentence

```
DROP FUZZY DOMAIN FieldStudy
```

Its translation consists in deleting from the DOMAIN table, the tuple corresponding to the specified domain. The labels and the pairs of the similarity relationship associated are automatically removed due to the foreign key constraints that are placed on each table definition.

The translation would be:

```
DELETE FROM FUZZY_INFORMATION_SCHEMA.DOMAIN
    WHERE  tableSchema = (SELECT database())
        AND domainName = 'domain_name'
```

For the above example corresponds to the sentence

```
DELETE FROM FUZZY_INFORMATION_SCHEMA.DOMAIN
    WHERE  tableSchema = (SELECT database())
        AND domainName = 'FieldStudy'
```

In this case, it is required to validate that the connection is using a database schema, because neither could have been selected by the user. In addition, the existence of the domain within the scheme should be verified and that there are not tables with columns associated with this domain.

In order to guarantee these validations, the DELETE operation is performed within a transaction, as well as, the constraints of foreign key, not null and uniqueness were defined in the fuzzy catalog. So, the transaction can be reverted and to produce a significant error message to the user. The eliminating is propagated in cascade toward LABEL and SIMILARITY tables.

Data Definition Operations

The translation schemes that are appertained to data definition language (CREATE TABLE, ALTER TABLE and DROP TABLE) require of multiple statements execution. For carry out these operations without the risk of an irreversible error during the execution, the translation is done by encapsulating these statements in a single operation. These operations are implemented as classes that execute a set of statements inside a transaction, which can be reversed.

Create Table

For the case of the CREATE TABLE operation, some attributes of the table to be created can be fuzzy, so that should add appropriate restrictions to validate that the columns reference to the fuzzy catalog.

The general syntax of this statement is as follows:

```
CREATE TABLE [schema_name.]table_name (
        col_name1 data_type1 options1
[, col_name2 data_type2 options2
, …
, col_nameN data_typeN optionsN]
)
```

In this syntax are omitted certain details as the definition options (NOT NULL, DEFAULT, UNIQUE, etc.), the foreign keys and the verification expressions (CHECK). This is necessary because the only information relevant for translation is the column name and its type.

During the translation is necessary examining each of the defined columns. If the column type is a fuzzy domain within the specified schema (or the used by the connection in the case that none is specified), then the type is changed to INTEGER. That is, the original expression "col_name data_type options" is translated in "col_name INTEGER options".

Before to create the table, it is necessary indicate in the fuzzy catalog that a new table is using a fuzzy domain. For that, a record is inserted into the COLUMN table with such information using the following statement.

```
INSERT INTO FUZZY_INFORMATION_SCHEMA.COLUMN
    VALUES  (schema_name, table_name, col_name1, domainId1)
        , …
        , (schema_name, table_name, col_nameN, domainIdN)
```

Note that each domainIdi corresponds to a fuzzy domain identifier, which is obtained from the DOMAIN table through the sentence.

```
SELECT domainName, domainIdi
   FROM FUZZY_INFORMATION_SCHEMA.DOMAIN
   WHERE  table_schema = 'schema_name'
      AND domainName
          IN (data_type1, data_type2, …, data_typeN)
```

This statement verifies that the types specified by the user are valid fuzzy domains.

For example, suppose that we want to create a SUBJECTS table with all courses of the Engineering Faculty, where it is indicated for each course: code, name and knowledge area. For this, it is required constructing the following statements:

```
CREATE TABLE ENGINIEERING.SUBJECTS (
   code VARCHAR(6),
   name VARCHAR(20),
   year NUMBER,
   area FieldStudy
)
```

The area column is inserted into the COLUMN table of the fuzzy catalog because of it has a fuzzy type. This is done using the sentence

```
INSERT INTO FUZZY_INFORMATION_SCHEMA.COLUMN
   VALUES (ENGINIEERING, SUBJECTS, area, FieldStudyId);
```

where, FieldStudyId is the fuzzy domain identifier (domainId) called 'FieldStudy', that is auto-generated by the system. This latter is obtained from the DOMAIN table through the sentence

```
SELECT domainName, domainId
   FROM FUZZY_INFORMATION_SCHEMA.DOMAIN
   WHERE  table_schema = 'ENGINEERING'
      AND domainName IN ('FieldStudy')
```

In addition, it is necessary add the constraints to maintain data consistency. One restriction validate that the fuzzy columns contain defined labels in the LABEL table of the fuzzy catalog. For each of the newly created fuzzy columns (column_name i) are added the following restrictions:

```
ALTER TABLE schema_name.table_name
   ADD CONSTRAINT
      FOREIGN KEY (col_name_i)
         REFERENCES FUZZY_INFORMATION_SCHEMA.LABEL (labelId)
   ON UPDATE CASCADE ON DELETE RESTRICT;
ALTER TABLE schema_name.table_name ADD CONSTRAINT CHECK (
   col_name_i IN (
      SELECT labelId
         FROM FUZZY_INFORMATION_SCHEMA.LABEL
         WHERE domainId = auxDomainId_i
   )
);
```

The first restriction ensures that you cannot remove a label from a domain if exists any row with that value in one of the fuzzy columns of the table. The second constraint verifies that only labels belonging to the domain where the column was defined are inserted. Note that this type of CHECK is not supported by all DBMS. So it must to adapt to the DBMS specific dialect.

The above statements are performed within a transaction so that the changes can revert if a mistake that puts at risk the consistency of the fuzzy catalog occurs.

Alter Table

The ALTER TABLE statement allows change aspects of a table: add, modify or delete columns; add, modify or delete primary key, unique key and foreign keys constraints; add, modify or delete indexes, etc. Despite the variety of forms that this statement can take, the translation scheme only considers the change of the column type to a fuzzy domain. This gives the user the possibility to change the columns types to fuzzy domains.

The statement syntax is as follow:

```
ALTER TABLE [schema_name.]table_name
    CHANGE COLUMN old_col_name new_col_name data_type options
```

where, schema_name is the database name where is located the table to be modified, table_name is the table name to be modified, old_col_name is the column name to be modified, new_col_name is the new name the modified column (can be the same), data_type is the new type of the column and options is a set of column configuration parameters as NOT NULL, DEFAULT, PRIMARY KEY, etc.

The translation of this sentence is performed when data_type is the name of a fuzzy domain defined in the schema where table_name is located. In this case, it is must make certain modifications to the statement and add other operations that will allow update the fuzzy catalog.

For example, if there is a SUBJECTS table where the type of "area" attribute is VARCHAR (15), we can transform the column type to fuzzy domain using the sentence

```
ALTER TABLE ENGINEERING.SUBJECTS
    CHANGE COLUMN area fuzzyArea FieldStudy
```

For this, it must validate that there is a connection to a database if the schema name is not specified in the statement. In addition, the table and column specified must exist. The current type of the column to modify must be VARCHAR to ensure that the values are labels. The new column type (data_type) must be the name of a fuzzy domain defined in the selected schema or in the current database if it is not specified. The values of the column to be modified must be labels of the specified fuzzy domain. Thus, it is ensured that the values in the column correspond to one label of the new domain.

For validate that the column is VARCHAR type, it is executed the following query:

```
SELECT data_type
    FROM FUZZY_INFORMATION_SCHEMA.COLUMN
    WHERE tableSchema = table_schema
        AND tableName = 'table_name'
        AND columnName = 'old_column_name'
```

For example, for the case of the SUBJECTS table, the following query would be realized

```
SELECT data_type
    FROM FUZZY_INFORMATION_SCHEMA.COLUMN
    WHERE tableSchema = ENGINEERING
```

```
            AND tableName = 'SUBJECTS'
            AND columnName = 'area'
```

If the query returns some result then it is validated that is VARCHAR type. If the query does not return any result, it could have happened that there is no scheme selected, or table_name not exist in the schema, or column_name not exist in table_name. In all these cases, the translation is not realized but the statement is executed directly on the DBMS.

Subsequently, it is checked if there is a value in the columns to modify that does not belong to the specified fuzzy domain (data_type) using the following query:

```
SELECT old_col_name
   FROM table_schema.table_name
      LEFT JOIN FUZZY_INFORMATION_SCHEMA.LABEL AS L
         ON (
            table_name.old_col_name = L.labelName
            AND L.domainId = (
               SELECT domain_id
                  FROM FUZZY_INFORMATION_SCHEMA.DOMAIN
                  WHERE  tableSchema = table_schema
                     AND domainName = data_type
            )
         )
   WHERE  table_name.old_col_name IS NOT NULL
      AND L.labelName IS NULL
   LIMIT 1 FOR UPDATE
```

For example, for the case of SUBJECTS table, the following query can be realized

```
SELECT area
   FROM ENGINEERING.SUBJECTS
      LEFT JOIN FUZZY_INFORMATION_SCHEMA.LABEL AS L
         ON (
            SUBJECTS.area = L.labelName
            AND L.domainId = (
               SELECT domain_id
                  FROM FUZZY_INFORMATION_SCHEMA.DOMAIN
                  WHERE  tableSchema = ENGINEERING
                     AND domainName = FieldStudy
            )
         )
   WHERE  SUBJECTS.area IS NOT NULL
      AND L.labelName IS NULL
   LIMIT 1 FOR UPDATE
```

If the result of this query is empty, all column values are fuzzy labels within the specified domain, then it is changed the column type. In case of a non-empty result, it is notified the error to the user.

First, it is necessary to change the column current values to the labels identifiers (labelId) of the domain that correspond to each value in the column. To make this change, the following statement is used:

```
UPDATE table_name
   SET old_col_name = (
      SELECT labelId
         FROM FUZZY_INFORMATION_SCHEMA.LABEL
         WHERE  labelName = old_col_name
            AND domainId = (
               SELECT domainId
                  FROM FUZZY_INFORMATION_SCHEMA.LABEL.DOMAIN
                  WHERE  domainName = data_type
                     AND tableSchema = table_schema
            )
   )
```

For example in the case of the SUBJECTS table, the following modification sentence must be made

```
UPDATE SUBJECTS
   SET area = (
      SELECT labelId
         FROM FUZZY_INFORMATION_SCHEMA.LABEL
         WHERE  labelName = area
            AND domainId = (
               SELECT domainId
                  FROM FUZZY_INFORMATION_SCHEMA.LABEL.DOMAIN
                  WHERE  domainName = FieldStudy
                     AND tableSchema = ENGINEERING
            )
   )
```

Then, the column type is changed to INTEGER with the sentence:

```
ALTER TABLE table_name
   CHANGE old_col_name new_col_name INTEGER options;
```

For the case of SUBJECTS table would be

```
ALTER TABLE SUBJECTS
   CHANGE area fuzzyArea INTEGER;
```

And foreign key constraint and check are added:

```
ALTER TABLE schema_name.table_name
   ADD CONSTRAINT
      FOREIGN KEY (col_name_i)
         REFERENCES FUZZY_INFORMATION_SCHEMA.LABEL (labelId)
   ON UPDATE CASCADE ON DELETE RESTRICT;
ALTER TABLE schema_name.table_name
   ADD CONSTRAINT CHECK (
      col_name_i IN (
         SELECT labelId
            FROM FUZZY_INFORMATION_SCHEMA.LABEL
            WHERE domainId = domain_id_i
      )
   );
```

In the example of SUBJECTS table would be the sentence:

```
ALTER TABLE ENGINEERING.SUBJECTS
   ADD CONSTRAINT
      FOREIGN KEY (fuzzyArea)
         REFERENCES FUZZY_INFORMATION_SCHEMA.LABEL (labelId)
   ON UPDATE CASCADE ON DELETE RESTRICT;
ALTER TABLE ENGINEERING.SUBJECTS
   ADD CONSTRAINT CHECK (
      fuzzyArea IN (
         SELECT labelId
            FROM FUZZY_INFORMATION_SCHEMA.LABEL
            WHERE domainId = FieldStudyId
      )
   );
```

Finally, the records of new columns associated with the fuzzy domain are inserted into the COLUMN table for the proper handling of queries, using the sentence

```
INSERT INTO FUZZY_INFORMATION_SCHEMA.COLUMN
   VALUES (table_schema, table_name, col_name, domain_id)
```

In our example of the SUBJECTS table would be

```
INSERT INTO FUZZY_INFORMATION_SCHEMA.COLUMN
   VALUES (ENGINEERING, SUBJECTS, fuzzyArea, FieldStudyId)
```

Drop Table

The syntax of the DROP TABLE statement is:

```
DROP TABLE table_name1 [, table_name2, …, table_nameN]
```

Although this statement does not require be translated, it is necessary to delete associations between columns of the dropped table and the fuzzy catalog. For this, the following statement is executed:

```
DELETE FROM FUZZY_INFORMATION_SCHEMA.COLUMN
    WHERE  tableSchema = 'schema_name'
      AND tableName IN (table_name1, …, table_nameN)
```

First, the DROP TABLE statement must be executed. If no error occurs (eg, nonexistent tables), it is proceeded to execute the DELETE statement. If the deleted table does not contain fuzzy columns, the second statement has no effect.

For example, if it is wanted to delete the SUBJECTS table would be necessary to make the following sentences

```
DROP TABLE SUBJECTS;
DELETE FROM FUZZY_INFORMATION_SCHEMA.COLUMN
    WHERE  tableSchema = 'ENGINEERING'
      AND 'SUBJECTS'
        IN ('SUBJECTS'
          , … the rest of the tables that
              appear in the schema)
```

Data Manipulation Operations

The presence of Type 3 attributes has effects on data manipulation operations (INSERT, UPDATE and DELETE). Whenever these operations affect some column whose type is a fuzzy domain, it is necessary to translate these operations using appropriate translation schemas to the representation of such values.

Insert

The translation schema of an INSERT is trivial. When it is wanted to insert a new record involving a Type 3 attribute, the label to be inserted is changed by its corresponding identifier in the LABEL table. If the label is not defined, the insertion fails, that is, the insertion cannot realized because a value for that identifier was not found. The syntax of this operation is

```
INSERT INTO table_schema.table_name
    VALUES (…, fuzzy_column, …)
```

An example, for the SUBJECTS table is the following sentence

```
INSERT INTO ENGINEERING.SUBJECTS
   VALUES ('MA1111', 'Mathematics I', '1', 'Mathematics')
```

Note that 'Mathematics' is the label for one fields of study that appear in the 'FieldStudy' fuzzy domain.

The translation schema consist in to change the fuzzy_column value by the corresponding labelId that is obtained by consulting to the fuzzy catalog

Update

The translation schema of the UPDATE operation is analogous to the INSERT operation. It is necessary to verify that the new label is defined in the fuzzy domain. If this label is not found, the UPDATE has not effect. The UPDATE syntax is

```
UPDATE table_schema.table_name
   SET fuzzy_column = label_expression
```

The label is changed by its identifier corresponding that is obtained of the fuzzy catalog.

If the UPDATE has a WHERE clause this latter have the same treatment as a WHERE clause of a SELECT. This will be explained in the next section.

Delete

For the DELETE operation is not necessary to make any translation. The record is deleted without problem and the constraints associated with the attributes of fuzzy catalog automatically update all that is necessary.

If the DELETE operation has a WHERE clause this latter have the same treatment as a WHERE clause of a SELECT. This will be explained in the next section.

Query Operation (Select)

The query operation or SELECT clause may have some output columns that involve fuzzy domains. In this case, the values produced belong to these domains. Additionally, the WHERE clause can contain an expression with Type 3 attributes.

The syntax of the SELECT statement that is considered here includes the extension to fuzzy system. Namely:

```
SELECT [DISTINCT] select_expr [, select_expr ...]
   FROM table_references
   WHERE where_condition
   ORDER BY   [col_name START label | expr]
            [, [col_name START label | expr] ...]
```

We have omitted for simplicity the additional verbose forms of the fuzzy ordering: STARTING FROM label, SIMILARITY ON ... START label, SIMILARITY ON ... STARTING FROM label.

The translation schemes suppose that the complete similarity relationship of the fuzzy domains associated to the query has already been calculated and stored in the fuzzy catalog. Furthermore, it is assumed that all pairs have nonzero similarity degree.

For final calculation of the response, the translation schemes include JOIN operations between the tables involved in the query (FROM clause) and the fuzzy catalog tables. That is, the translation process requires associating each column in select_expr, where_condition and col_name with the respective table in table_references where this column is obtained.

For each column (column_name) in a table (table_name) defined with a fuzzy domain, which is used in the expressions of SELECT, WHERE, GROUP BY, HAVING or ORDER BY (classic) clauses, the table_name must be replaced in the FROM clause by the following expression

```
table_name [AS alias]
    LEFT JOIN FUZZY_INFORMATION_SCHEMA.LABEL AS L
        ON col_name = L.labelId
```

This lets to create alias unique for FUZZY_INFORMATION_SCHEMA tables and to reference the fuzzy catalog attributes added by these JOINs anywhere of the statement.

For translation of the WHERE clause condition and the classical criteria of the ORDER BY clause, it is only necessary to replace each fuzzy attribute (col_name) by its corresponding L.labelName. L is the alias of the SIMILARITY table in the fuzzy catalog because the attribute is used as a label by the user. For the translation of the SELECT clause, in addition to the appropriate replacement, it is necessary renaming so that the result of the query will not have the attribute named labelName but with its real name (col_name).

This allows detecting which are the tables in table_references that require a JOIN and which columns in the expression "col_name START label" are fuzzy type. On this basis, it is proceed to explore the statement locating the different JOINs required between the fuzzy catalog and tables in the FROM clause, in order to get the label name, the similarity value with another label, and others.

Queries containing the ORDER BY clause on a Type 3 attribute allow ordering by membership degree in the similarity relationship for a given element (*value*). When this ordering is not specified the classic is assumed. The user specifies that wants a fuzzy ordering when in the ORDER BY clause appears a column whose domain is fuzzy. Furthermore, the "START *value*" expression (or STARTING FROM *value*, or SIMILARITY ON ... START *value*, or SIMILARITY ON ... STARTING FROM *value*, in its most verbose forms) appears corresponding to the fuzzy class of *value*. The translation scheme for this type of query is as follow.

For each expression "col_name START label" inside the ORDER BY clause, where col_name is defined with a fuzzy domain (domain_name) into table_name, the following expression is generated in the FROM clause instead of table_name

```
table_name [AS alias]
    LEFT JOIN FUZZY_INFORMATION_SCHEMA.SIMILARITY AS S
        ON (
            S.label1_id = (
                SELECT labelId
                    FROM FUZZY_INFORMATION_SCHEMA.LABEL
```

```
            WHERE   labelName = label
                AND domainId = (
                    SELECT domainId
                        FROM FUZZY_INFORMATION_SCHEMA.DOMAIN
                        WHERE domainName = domain_name
                )
        )
        AND S.label2_id = col_name
    )
```

In addition, the "col_name START label" expression and any of its verbose forms is replaced by "IFNULL (S.value, 0) DESC".

For example, if there is a query about the SUBJECTS table

```
SELECT Code, Name, FieldStudy
    FROM SUBJECTS
    ORDER BY fuzzyArea START 'Mathematics'
```

It is translated as

```
SELECT Code, Name, L.labelName AS fuzzyArea
    FROM SUBJECTS
        LEFT JOIN FUZZY_INFORMATION_SCHEMA.LABEL AS L
            ON fuzzyArea = L.labelId
        LEFT JOIN FUZZY_INFORMATION_SCHEMA.SIMILARITY AS S
            ON (
                S.label1_id = (
                    SELECT labelId
                        FROM FUZZY_INFORMATION_SCHEMA.LABEL
                        WHERE   labelName = 'Mathematics'
                            AND domainId = (
                                SELECT domainId
                                    FROM
                                        FUZZY_INFORMATION_SCHEMA.DOMAIN
                                    WHERE domainName = 'FieldStudy'
                            )
                )
                AND S.label2_id = FuzzyArea
            )
    ORDER BY IFNULL(S.value,0) DESC;
```

The following proof shows that presented translation schema, in case of queries with Type 3 fuzzy attributes in the ORDER BY clause, produce the expected ordering according to the proposed ordering definition.

Let C be a query, with possibly occurrences of Type 3 fuzzy attributes, and of the following form:

```
SELECT A FROM T ORDER BY K
```

A is an attribute list, T is a list of tables where the attributes can be found, and K is a list of pairs of the form $k_i d_i$, with $k_i \in A$ and $d_i \in \{ASC, DESC, START\ v\}$. It can also take the form k_i, with no specified d_i, in which case the default will be ASC.

The result of this query has the following form:

$$resultset(C) = <(t_i.c_1,\ t_i.c_2,\ ...,\ t_i.c_n)\ |\ t_i \in T>,\ with\ i \in \{1,\ ...,\ m\}$$

And it fulfills the following restriction:

$$\forall p,q \in \{1,...,m\}\ ($$

$$\exists r \in \{1,...,|T|\}\ (\rho(t_p.k_r,\ t_q.k_r) \wedge \forall j \in \{1,...,r\text{-}1\}\ \xi_j(t_p.k_j,\ t_q.k_j))$$

$$\Rightarrow (p \leq q)$$

$$)$$

where, for each appropriate x,

$$(d_x{=}ASC \Rightarrow \rho(t_p.k_x,\ t_q.k_x) \equiv (t_p.k_x < t_q.k_x) \wedge \xi_j(t_p.k_x,\ t_q.k_x) \equiv (t_p.k_x = t_q.k_x)) \wedge$$

$$(d_x{=}DESC \Rightarrow \rho(t_p.k_x,\ t_q.k_x) \equiv (t_p.k_x > t_q.k_x) \wedge \xi_j(t_p.k_x,\ t_q.k_x) \equiv (t_p.k_x = t_q.k_x)) \wedge$$

$$(d_x{=} START\ v \Rightarrow \rho(t_p.k_x,\ t_q.k_x) \equiv (\mu_s(v,\ t_p.k_x) < \mu_s(v,\ t_q.k_x) \wedge$$

$$\xi_j(t_p.k_x,\ t_q.k_x) \equiv (\mu_s(v,\ t_p.k_x) = \mu_s(v,\ t_q.k_x)))$$

Applying the translation schema, a new query C' is obtained, with the following form:

```
SELECT A FROM T' ORDER BY K'
```

T' is the table list and K' is the new list of pairs, both of them modified from T and K, respectively, by the translation schema. For a pair $k_i d_i \in K'$, now we have that $d_i \in \{ASC, DESC\}$. The second component of the pair, d_i, can once again be omitted and taken by default to be ASC.

The result of this query has the following form:

$$resultset(C') = <(t_i.c_1,\ t_i.c_2,\ ...,\ t_i.c_n)\ |\ t_i \in T'>,\ with\ i \in \{1,\ ...,\ m'\}$$

And it fulfills the following restriction:

$\forall p,q \in \{1,\dots,m'\}$ (

$\exists r \in \{1,\dots,|T'|\}$ $(\rho'(t_p.k_r, t_q.k_r) \land \forall j \in \{1,\dots,r-1\}\, t_p.k_j = t_q.k_j)$

$\Rightarrow (p \leq q)$

)

where, for each appropriate x,

$(d_x=\text{ASC} \Rightarrow \rho'(t_p.k_x, t_q.k_x) \equiv (t_p.k_x < t_q.k_x)) \land$

$(d_x=\text{DESC} \Rightarrow \rho'(t_p.k_x, t_q.k_x) \equiv (t_p.k_x > t_q.k_x))$

Note that there are no occurrences of "*START v*"

In order to prove the translation schema correct, two important properties must be verified:

1. The cardinalities of the result sets must be equal. That is, that $m = m'$.

Tables $t_i \in T$ that are not involved in the ordering of Type 3 fuzzy attributes, are not modified by the translation schema. Therefore, the results that depend only on these tables will be preserved in the result set of the translated query.

Tables $t_i \in T$ involved in the ordering of Type 3 fuzzy attributes are replaced by the translation schema with a LEFT JOIN of t_i with table LABEL of the fuzzy catalog. As it is a LEFT JOIN, every row of table t_i that would have been part of the result will be included, and no more. Therefore the number of results will not be affected.

As for any table $t_i \in T$ the results from t_i are conserved by the translation schema, the cardinality of the result set remains the same.

2. The order restriction is conserved by the translation. That is, if a pair of result is required to have a determined order in the original query, this order must be respected in the translated query.

Formally, the following condition must be true:

$\forall p,q \in \{1,\dots,m\}$ (

$\exists r \in \{1,\dots,|T|\}$ $(\rho(t_p.k_r, t_q.k_r) \land \forall j \in \{1,\dots,r-1\}\, \xi_j(t_p.k_j, t_q.k_j))$

$\Rightarrow (p \leq q)$

)

$\Rightarrow$

$\forall p,q \in \{1,\ldots,m'\}$ (

$\exists r \in \{1,\ldots,|T'|\}$ $(\rho'(t_p.k_r, t_q.k_r) \wedge \forall j \in \{1,\ldots,r\text{-}1\}$ $t_p.k_j = t_q.k_j)$

$\Rightarrow (p \leq q)$

)

If the premise of the application is assumed as *true*, then the conclusion must be shown to be true.

The translation schema does not alter the amount of tables over which the query is made. Each table that occurs in the FROM clause is translated in one of two fashions:

- If the table has Type 3 fuzzy attributes that are used in the query, it is replaced by a single LEFT JOIN with table LABEL from the fuzzy catalog.
- If the table has no Type 3 fuzzy attributes that are used in the query, then it is not modified by the translation schema.

Hence, although T may differ from T', the cardinality is preserved: $|T| = |T'|$.

Let $p, q \in \{1, \ldots, m'\}$, remembering that $m = m'$. Now the premise of the body in the universal quantifier is assumed to be true, replacing $|T|$ by $|T'|$. Then $p \leq q$ remains to be proven.

We have two hypotheses that concern p and q:

- H_0: $\exists r \in \{1,\ldots,|T|\}$ $(\rho(t_p.k_r, t_q.k_r) \wedge \forall j \in \{1,\ldots,r\text{-}1\}$ $\xi_j(t_p.k_j, t_q.k_j)) \Rightarrow (p \leq q)$
- H_1: $\exists r \in \{1,\ldots,|T'|\}$ $(\rho'(t_p.k_r, t_q.k_r) \wedge \forall j \in \{1,\ldots,r\text{-}1\}$ $t_p.k_j = t_q.k_j)$

Consider Hypothesis H_1, with r' as a witness for r:

$\rho'(t_p.k_r, t_q.k_r) \wedge \forall j \in \{1,\ldots,r\text{-}1\}$ $t_p.k_j = t_q.k_j$

As dj can only be ASC or DESC within H_1, then we can rewrite H_1 as:

$\rho'(t_p.k_r, t_q.k_r) \wedge \forall j \in \{1,\ldots,r\text{-}1\}$ $\xi_j(t_p.k_j, t_q.k_j)$

Note that p and p' have the same behavior for comparisons that do not involve Type 3 fuzzy attributes, for those that do, the translation schema replaces each *"col_name START label"* for *"IFNULL(S.value, 0) DESC"*.

The behavior of RO is a specialization of RO', that allows the ordering criteria to be "START v", for some v. In this case, the translation schema uses the value of the membership degree from the fuzzy catalog. A label w is considered more similar to v if this value, for w, is greater. This shows that ordering by similarity on v, is consistent with ordering from decreasingly respect to the membership degree. Therefore, $\rho'(t_p.k_r, t_q.k_r) \Rightarrow \rho(t_p.k_r, t_q.k_r)$, and thus, from this and H_1:

$\rho(t_p.k_r, t_q.k_r) \wedge \forall j \in \{1,\ldots,r\text{-}1\}$ $\xi_j(t_p.k_j, t_q.k_j)$

Now an existential quantifier can be introduced over r, in place of r'.

$$\exists r \in \{1,\ldots,|T|\}\ (\rho(t_p.k_r,\ t_q.k_r) \wedge \forall j \in \{1,\ldots,r\text{-}1\}\ \xi_j(t_p.k_j,\ t_q.k_j))$$

This has the form of the premise in hypothesis H_0. By performing this implication, the required $p \leq q$ is achieved. This shows that the order restriction is conserved after the translation process.

FUTURE RESEARCH DIRECTIONS

Despite several proposals for the extension of data models and languages with fuzzy logic, at present time there are not much real implementation and applications. It would be necessary to develop such tools and their applications. Nevertheless, there are still some semantics problems to deal with. One of these is the case of ordering for possibilistic data and their implications in query expressions. Other is the grouping of fuzzy data.

Also, it is necessary to do experimental proofs of the impact in the RDBMS performance of these type extensions. And, we should develop real applications for show the utility of the proposal.

CONCLUSION

In the last three decades, some data models and query languages based on the application of fuzzy set theory have been arisen. The goal in mind with that is to provide more flexible Database Management Systems that allow the expression of user preferences in querying as well as imprecision in data. Traditional DBMS do not allow that because they are based on classic sets and Boolean logic. Between those models we can mention the Generalized Fuzzy Relational Database model (GEFRED) and the Fuzzy Enhanced Entity Relationship Model (FuzzyEER). The relational database standard language SQL has been proposed to be extended as well. One of the proposals for extension is named FSQL, which is based on FuzzyEER and GEFRED as conceptual and logical models. The FuzzyEER is a data model that extends EER with concepts from fuzzy set theory. This model proposes four kinds of fuzzy attributes, supplely named Type 1, Type 2, Type 3 and Type 4 fuzzy attributes. Present chapter is focused on Type 3 fuzzy attributes. This kind of attributes is defined on a domain formed by a set of labels provided of a fuzzy similarity relation. FSQL allows the expression and use of fuzzy attributes. Nevertheless, FSQL does not allow using fuzzy attributes in some clauses based on data ordering, due to unsolved semantics problem. This chapter presents a solution for this problem in case of Type 3 fuzzy attributes. An accurate definition of fuzzy similarity relation is presented here. Also, the definition of SQL extension for Type 3 attributes definition and use is shown in this chapter. Main contribution of this chapter consists in how to process queries involving Type 3 fuzzy attributes by means of an extension to an existing RDBMS. Metadata for this kind of attributes is stored in a relational catalogue. In any SQL expression involving Type 3 attribute, this catalogue is consulted. In order to process these extended SQL expressions, they are translated into regular SQL. The chapter contains the needed translation schemas. They all can be formally proved to be correct. For the particular case of ORDER BY clause translation, the demonstration is done in the chapter. Feasibility of this processing mechanism has been proved by means the development of an extension for an existing RDBMS.

ACKNOWLEDGMENT

The work presented in this chapter is a result of the "Desafíos del Modelo Relacional Difuso" project. This project has the support of UNEXPO Vice-rectorship of Barquisimeto. Professor Carlos Lameda is thanked for coordinating this project. Thanks also to engineers Bishma Stornelli and Andras Gyomrey who participated in the development of this work. Finally *"And I thank Christ Jesus our Lord who has enabled me, because He counted me faithful, putting me into the ministry"* (1 Timothy 1:12, New King James Version).

REFERENCES

Belohlavek, R. (1999). Similarity Relations in Concept Lattices. Research Report. University of Ostrava, Czech Republic. 20, 1999.

Buckles, B. P., & Petry, F. E. (1982). A fuzzy representation of data for relational databases. *Fuzzy Sets and Systems*, *7*(3), 213–226. doi:10.1016/0165-0114(82)90052-5

Calvo, T. (1992). On fuzzy similarity relations. *Fuzzy Sets and Systems*, *47*(1), 121–123. doi:10.1016/0165-0114(92)90069-G

Carrasquel, S., Rodríguez, R., & Tineo, L. (2013). Consultas con Ordenamiento basado en Similitud. *Telematique*, *12*(1), 24–45.

Encyclopedia of Information Science and Technology. (2014, Aug 25). Retrieved from: http://www.books.google.co.ve/books?isbn=1466658894

Faurous, P., & Fillard, J. P. (1993). A New Approach to the Similarity Relations in the Fuzzy Set Theory. *Information Sciences*, *75*(3), 213–221. doi:10.1016/0020-0255(93)90055-Q

FSQL. (2014, Jun 20). Retrieved from: http://www.lcc.uma.es/~ppgg/FSQL/

Fukami, S., Umano, M., Muzimoto, M., & Tanaka, H. (1979). Fuzzy database retrieval and manipulation language. *IEICE Technical Reports*, *78*(233), 65–72.

Galindo, J., Urrutia, A., & Piattini, M. (2006). *Fuzzy Databases: Modeling, Design and Implementation*. Idea Group Publishing. doi:10.4018/978-1-59140-324-1

Jacas, J. (1990). Similarity Relations-The Calculation of Minimal Generating Families. *Fuzzy Sets and Systems*, *35*(2), 151–162. doi:10.1016/0165-0114(90)90190-H

Maria, D. B. Foundation. (2013). Retrieved from: https://mariadb.org/

Medina, J. M., Pons, O., & Vila, M. A. (1995). *FIRST: A Fuzzy Interface for Relational Systems VI IFSA World Congress, São Paulo, Brazil, II*. Academic Press.

Ovchinnikov, S. (1991). Similarity relations, fuzzy partitions, and fuzzy orderings. *Fuzzy Sets and Systems*, *40*(1), 107–126. doi:10.1016/0165-0114(91)90048-U

Timarán, R. (2001). Arquitecturas de Integración del Proceso de Descubrimiento de Conocimiento con Sistemas de Gestión de Bases de Datos: Un Estado del Arte. *Ingeniería y Competitividad.*, *3*(2), 45–55.

Zadeh, L. A. (1965). Fuzzy Sets. *Information and Control*, *8*(3), 338–353. doi:10.1016/S0019-9958(65)90241-X

Zadeh, L. A. (1971). Similarity Relations and Fuzzy Orderings. *Information Sciences*, *3*(2), 177–200. doi:10.1016/S0020-0255(71)80005-1

KEY TERMS AND DEFINITIONS

FSQL (Fuzzy SQL): An extension of the SQL language that allows some fuzzy data and conditions expression.

Fuzzy Catalog: Set of metadata tables that describe fuzzy domains as well as columns of these types that include labels and the definitions of similarity relationships.

Fuzzy Domain: User defined type for fuzzy data.

Fuzzy Set: Extended set where the belonging of an element is given by a membership function whose range is the [0, 1] interval.

FuzzyEER: An extension of the EER (Enhanced Entity Relationship) model for the creation of conceptual schemes with fuzzy semantic notation.

GEFRED (Generalized Model of Fuzzy Relational Databases): An extended model for fuzzy relational databases.

ORDER BY: Clause of SQL expression intended for ordering the list of retrieved tuples in a specific order, particularly, in this case the ordering is based in fuzzy similarity relationship.

Similarity Relationship: A fuzzy set in $X{\times}X$, whose membership function is reflexive, symmetric, and transitive. It is a generalization of the classical equivalence relationship.

Translation Scheme: A conversion pattern of an expression from a source language to an object language that preserves the semantics, particularly, in this case from a fuzzy extension of SQL to classic SQL.

Type 3 Attributes: Attributes with values in a fuzzy domain consisting of labels provided with a similarity relationship.

Chapter 5
Modeling and Querying Fuzzy Data:
Current Approaches and Future Trends

Li Yan
Nanjing University of Aeronautics and Astronautics, China

Z. M. Ma
Northeastern University, China

ABSTRACT

Imperfect information extensively exists in data and knowledge intensive applications, where fuzzy data play an import role in nature. Fuzzy set theory has been extensively applied to extend various database models and resulted in numerous contributions. The chapter concentrates on two main issues in fuzzy data management: fuzzy data models and fuzzy data querying based on the fuzzy data models. A full up-to-date overview of the current state of the art in fuzzy data modeling and querying is provided in the chapter. In addition, the relationships among various fuzzy data models are discussed in the chapter. The chapter serves as identifying possible research opportunities in the area of fuzzy data management in addition to providing a generic overview of the approaches to modeling and querying fuzzy data.

INTRODUCTION

One of the major areas of database research has been the continuous effort to enrich existing database models with a more extensive collection of semantic concepts. Database models have developed from hierarchical and network database models to the relational database model. As computer technology moves into non-traditional applications such as CAD/CAM, knowledge-based systems, multimedia, GIS and Internet systems and modeling and manipulation of complex objects and semantic relationships are required by such applications, many software engineers feel the limitations of relational databases in these data- and knowledge-intensive applications. Therefore, some non-traditional data models have been proposed for databases, such as the entity-relationship (ER) model (Chen, 1976), the enhanced (or extended) entity-relationship (EER) model (e.g., Embley and Ling, 1989), the object-oriented (OO) da-

DOI: 10.4018/978-1-4666-8767-7.ch005

tabase model, the object-relational database model and the logic database model. Among these database models, the object relational database model combines the robustness of the relational database model with the powerful modeling capabilities of the object-oriented paradigm (Stonebraker and Moore, 1996).

With the prompt development of the Internet, the requirement of managing information based on the Web has attracted much attention both from academia and industry. XML (eXtensible Markup Language) is widely regarded as the next step in the evolution of the World Wide Web, and has been the de-facto standard. It aims at enhancing content on the World Wide Web. XML and related standards are flexible that allow the easy development of applications which exchange data over the web such as e-commerce and supply chain management.

While traditional data models can provide efficient data management capabilities, they often suffer from some inadequacy of necessary semantics. One of these inadequacies can be generalized as the inability to handle imprecise and uncertain information (Sicilia and Mastorakis, 2004). In real-world applications, information is often imperfect. One of the semantic needs not adequately addressed by the traditional data models is that of uncertainty. Traditional data models assume that the models are a correct reflection of the world and further assume that the stored data is known, accurate and complete. It is rarely the case in real life that all or most of these assumptions are met. So fuzzy sets theory (Zadeh, 1965) and possibility theory (Zadeh, 1978) have been used to extend various data models in order to enhance the traditional data models such that fuzzy data can be represented and manipulated.

Management of fuzzy data typically involves two primary technical issues: storage and queries. In addition, to serve a given query more effectively, it is necessary to index fuzzy data. These three issues are actually closely related. Indexing of fuzzy data is enabled based on fuzzy data storage, and efficient querying of fuzzy data is supported by the storage and indexing structure. Among these three issues, fuzzy data modeling provides the infrastructure for fuzzy data management and fuzzy data querying is one major goal of fuzzy data management. Since fuzzy database approaches were first created in the late 1970s, much work has been done in the area of fuzzy databases and a number of research efforts have been undertaken to address these issues. This has resulted in numerous contributions, mainly with respect to the popular relational model or to some related form of it (Petry, 1996; Chen, 1999; Galindo, Urrutia and Piattini, 2006). Since classical relational database model and its extension of fuzziness do not satisfy the need of modeling complex objects with imprecision and uncertainty, currently many studies have been concentrated on fuzzy conceptual data models and fuzzy object-oriented database models in order to deal with complex objects and fuzzy data together (Yazici and George, 1999; Ma, 2005a). More recently, some work has been carried out in extending XML towards the representation of fuzzy concepts on the Web (Yan, Ma and Zhang, 2014b).

Although there have been a lot of fuzzy database papers published, ones only find few comprehensive review papers of fuzzy databases. Two early overview papers in this area are finished by Yazici, Buckles and Petry (1992) and Kerre and Chen (1995). In (Yazici, George, Buckles and Petry, 1992), conceptual and logical data models for uncertainty management are reviewed, in which the conceptual data model is the fuzzy IFO data model (IFO is a graph-based conceptual data model proposed in (Abiteboul and Hull, 1987)) and the logical data model is the fuzzy relational database model. In (Kerre and Chen, 1995), only the fuzzy ER (entity-relationship) model and the fuzzy relational databases (exactly data representation, queries, and design) are discussed. In (Urrutia and Galindo, 2010), an overview of different fuzzy database modeling definitions by different authors is presented, but they only highlight the fuzzy EER model, which is an extension of an EER model incorporating fuzzy semantics and notation.

In (Bosc, Kraft and Petry, 2005), a short summary about the applications of fuzzy sets in the database and information retrieval areas is presented. It mainly includes preferences for flexible queries and fuzzy functional dependencies and redundancy. Also fuzzy sets applications to areas such as data mining and geographical information systems are described. Two latest comprehensive overview papers have appeared in this area (Ma and Yan, 2008; Ma and Yan, 2010). After these two overview papers, some new research results in (e.g., fuzzy object-oriented databases, fuzzy conceptual data models and fuzzy XML models) come out. In (Ma and Yan, 2008), some fuzzy database models such as fuzzy relational databases and fuzzy object-oriented databases are reviewed, and some fuzzy conceptual data models such as fuzzy ER model, fuzzy EER model and fuzzy UML model are reviewed in (Ma and Yan, 2010). The issues of fuzzy XML and querying fuzzy data in fuzzy object-oriented databases are not included in (Ma and Yan, 2008) and (Ma and Yan 2010).

This chapter presents a full up-to-date overview of the current state of the art in fuzzy data modeling and querying. The various query approaches are classified according to the representation models of fuzzy data, including fuzzy relational databases, fuzzy object-oriented databases, fuzzy conceptual data models and fuzzy XML models. The objective of this chapter is two-fold. The first is to provide a generic literature overview of the approaches that have been proposed to modeling and querying fuzzy data. The second is to identify and analyze research opportunities in the area of fuzzy data management. Note that, due to the large number of fuzzy data management solutions, it was not feasible to include all of them in this chapter. Therefore, this chapter is not an exhaustive survey of this research area, but rather a selection of recent systems that illustrate the basic concepts of fuzzy data modeling and querying.

The rest of this chapter is organized as follows. Section 2 presents preliminaries of data models and query languages as well as fuzzy sets theory. Section 3 provides details of the different techniques in modeling fuzzy data. Section 4 provides details of different techniques in querying fuzzy data. Section 5 concludes the chapter and provides some suggestions for possible research directions.

PRELIMINARIES

Section 2 presents preliminaries of data models and query languages as well as fuzzy sets theory.

Data Models and Query Languages

Over the years, various data models, including conceptual data models (e.g., ER model, EER model, and UML data model) and logical database models (e.g., relational database model and object-oriented database model), are developed for data modeling and management. Moreover, with the popularity of Web-based applications, the requirement for data management has been put on the exchange and share of data over the Web. The XML provides a Web friendly and well-understood syntax for the exchange of data and impacts on data definition and share on Web. This is creating a new set of data management requirements involving XML. Corresponding to various data models, different query languages (e.g., SQL language for relational databases and XQuery for XML) and querying approaches are hereby developed for information retrieval. Currently, databases and XML play important roles for data management and have become the main means to realize the data management.

Relational Databases and Query Language

Relational database model introduced first by Codd (1970) has been extensively applied in most information systems. A relational database is a collection of relations. Each relation is a table, which rows are called *tuples* and columns are called *attributes*. For each *attribute*, there exists a range that the attribute takes values, called *domain* of the attribute. A domain is a finite set of values and every value is an atomic data, the minimum data unit with meanings. A relation has a relational schema. Formally let $A_1, A_2, ..., A_n$ be attribute names and the corresponding attribute domains be $D_1, D_2, ..., D_n (1 \leq i \leq n)$, respectively. Then relational schema R is represented as $R = (A_1, A_2, ..., A_n)$. The instances of R are the relation of R and are written by r or $r(R)$. So r is a set of n-tuples and can be represented as $r = \{t_1, t_2, ..., t_m\}$. A tuple t can be represented as $t = < v_1, v_2, ..., v_n >$, where $v_i \in D_i (1 \leq i \leq n)$, i.e., $t \in D_1 \times D_2 \times ... \times D_n$. The quantity r is therefore a subset of Cartesian product of attribute domains, i.e., $r \subseteq D_1 \times D_2 \times ... \times D_n$. If an attribute value or the values of an attribute group in a relation can solely identify a tuple from other tuples, the attribute or attribute group is called a *super key* of the relation. If any proper subsets of a super key are not a super key, such super key is called a *candidate key* or shortly *key*. For a relation, there may be several candidate keys. One chooses one candidate as the *primary key*, and other candidates are called *alternate key*.

Relational database model provides some operations, called the *relational algebra operations*. These operations can be subdivided into two classes:

- The operations for relations only (*select*, *project*, *join* and *division*);
- The set operations (*union*, *difference*, *intersection* and *Cartesian product*).

In addition, some new operations such as *outerjoin*, *outerunion* and *aggregate* operations are developed for database integration or statistics and decision support. By using these operations, one can query or update relations.

SQL (Structured Query Language) is a powerful, easy-to-use query language for relational databases (Eisenberg *et al.*, 2004). From a syntactic viewpoint, SQL is a block-structured language. Its basic structure is the base block whose general format is

select <attributes> *from* <relations> *where* <condition>.

Here, the clause of "*from*" specifies the relations of database that are concerned by the block. The clause of "*select*" describes the resulting relation made of attributes taken from the input relations. The clause of "*where*" gives the condition to be satisfied by the resulting relation. The condition is expressed as a logical expression where attribute values are compared to literals or to other attribute values. On other words, the condition is formed through combining the basic (simple) condition $A \theta Y$ as operands with operators *not*, *and*, and *or*, where A is an attribute of the relations, Y is either an attribute of the relations or a literal, and $\theta \in \{>, <, =, \neq, \geq, \leq, between, not between, in, not in, like, not like\}$. Note that if θ is the operator *between* (*not between*), $A \theta Y$ has the format of "*A between* (*not between*) Y_1 AND Y_2". On the basis of the basic structure of SQL, other blocks such as *order by*, *group by*, *having, distinct,* and *aggregate functions* (avg, max, min, and sum) as well as nested query can be used and the queries with complex condition can be conducted. Here a complex condition means an expression consisting of some basic conditions connected by logical operators *not*, *and*, and *or*.

Object-Oriented Databases and Query Language

Object-oriented database model is developed by adopting some concepts of semantic data models and knowledge expressing models, some ideas of object-oriented program language and abstract data type in data structure/programming. An object-oriented database is a collection of objects. Viewing from the structure, an object consists of *attributes*, *methods* and *constraints*. The attributes of an object can be simple data and other objects. The procedure that some objects constitute a new object is called *aggregation*. A method in an object contains two parts: signature of the method that illustrates the name of the method, parameter type, and result type; implementation of the method. The attributes, methods and constraints in an object are encapsulated as one unit. The state of an object is changed only by passing message between objects. Objects with the same attributes, methods and constraints can be incorporated into a *class*. In a class, attributes, methods and constraints must be declared. For a class, say *A*, its subset can be defined as a new class, say *B*. Then *B* is called a *subclass* and *A* is called *superclass*. A subclass can further be divided into new subclasses. A *class hierarchical structure* is hereby formed, in which it is possible that a subclass may have multiple direct or indirect superclasses. The relationship between superclass and subclass is called *IS-A relationship*, which represents a *specialization* from top to bottom and a *generalization* from bottom to top. Because one subclass can have several direct superclasses, a class hierarchical structure is not a tree but a class *lattice*. Because a subclass is a subset of its superclass, the subclass inherits the attributes and methods in its all superclasses. Besides inheritance, a subclass can define new attributes and methods or can modify the attributes and methods in the superclasses. If a subclass has several direct superclasses, the subclass inherits the attributes and methods from these direct superclasses. This is called *multiple inheritance*.

Unlike the relational databases which contain a standard set of algebraic operations, there is no widely accepted definition as to what constitutes a standard set of algebraic operations for the object-oriented databases although an object-oriented database standard has been released by the Object Data Management Group (ODMG) (Cattell *et al.*, 2000). In the context of object-oriented databases, some efforts refer to the algebraic operations in the relational databases and develop object algebra for object-oriented databases (Alhajj and Arkun, 1993; Zamulin, 2002). These algebraic operations of the object-oriented databases are basically classified into two types: algebraic operations for classes and algebraic operations for objects, and have similar semantics and processing with the relational algebraic operations.

Following the step of SQL, OQL (Object Query Language), a query language standard for object-oriented databases (Alashqur, Su and Lam, 1989; Cluet, 1998), is developed by ODMG. OQL is a SQL-like query language with special features dealing with complex objects, values and methods, and so its basic structure is the base block whose general format is ***select*** <attributes> ***from*** <classes> ***where*** <condition> also.

XML and Query Language

Being a data formatting recommendation proposed by the W3C (World Wide Web Consortium), XML supports user-defined tags, encourages the separation of document content from its presentation, and is able to automate web information processing. An XML document has a logical and a physical structure (Bray, Paoli and Sperberg-McQueen, 1998). The physical structure is consists of entities that are ordered hierarchically. The logical structure is explicitly described by markups that comprise declarations, elements, comments, character references, and processing instructions. Also XML documents can be associated with and validated against a schema specification in terms of a *document type definition* (DTD) (Bray, Paoli and Sperberg-McQueen, 1998) or by using the more powerful *XML Schema* language (Thompson, Beech, Maloney and Mendelsohn, 2001; Biron and Malhotra, 2001). Then XML document structure consists of an optional document type declaration containing the DTD/Schema and a document instance. The purpose of a DTD/Schema is to provide a grammar for a class of documents. DTDs, for example, consist of markup declarations, namely, element declarations, attribute-list declarations, entity declarations, notation declarations, processing instructions, and comments. As for these declarations, they are the elementary building blocks on which a DTD can be designed.

To manage XML data, it is necessary to integrate XML and databases (Bertino and Catania, 2001). Various databases, including relational, object-oriented, and object-relational databases, have been used for mapping to and from the XML document. Also reengineering relational databases into XML recently receives more attention (Wang, Lo, Alhajj and Barker, 2005; Lo, Özyer, Kianmehr and Alhajj, 2010).

XQuery (Chamberlin *et al.*, 2001) is a querying language designed by the W3C, which allows one to select the XML data elements of interest, reorganize and possibly transform them, and return the results in a structure of one's choosing. In the XQuery data model, the documents are represented as a tree of nodes; the nodes may be document, element, attribute, text, name-space, processing instruction, and comment. Additionally, the data model allows atomic values and literals, such as strings, Booleans, decimals, integers, floats and doubles, and dates. An XQuery query is made up of two parts: *a prolog* and *a body*. The query prolog is an optional section that appears at the beginning of a query. The prolog can contain various declarations that affect settings used in evaluating the query. This includes namespace declarations, imports of schemas, variable declarations, function declarations, and other setting values. In a query module of any size, the prolog is actually likely to be much larger than the body. The prolog consists of a series of declarations terminated by semicolon (;) characters. There are three distinct sections of the prolog. The first declaration to appear in the query prolog is a version declaration, if it exists. The second prolog section consists of setters, imports, and namespace declarations. The last section of the prolog consists of function, variable, and option declarations. They must appear after all the setters, imports, and namespace declarations. The query body is a single expression, but that expression can consist of a sequence of one or more expressions that are separated by commas.

Conceptual Data Models and Their Relationships with Database and XML Models

Generally the conceptual data models are used for data modeling at a high level of abstraction. The ER data model proposed by Chen (1976) can represent the real world semantics by using the notions of *entities*, *relationships*, and *attributes*. ER data schema described by the ER data model is generally represented by the *ER diagram*. In order to model complex semantics and relationships in many real-world applications, some new concepts have been introduced in the ER model and the enhanced (extended) entity-relationship (EER) data model is formed. These new notions introduced include *specialization and generalization, category, and aggregation*. The Unified Modeling Language (UML) (Booch, Rumbaugh and Jacobson, 1998; OMG, 2003) is a set of object-oriented modeling notations that has been standardized by the Object Management Group (OMG). The UML is based largely upon the ER notations, and includes the ability to capture all information that is captured in a traditional data model. From the database modeling point of view, the most relevant UML model is the UML class diagram model. The building blocks in this class model are those of *classes* and relationships between classes or class instances such as *aggregation and composition*, *generalization*, and *dependency*. Generally the conceptual data models are graphic data models, which are designed for data modeling at a high level of abstraction instead of data manipulation at a low level of abstraction. So, unlike the relational and object-oriented databases, little work has been done for algebraic operations and query processing in the conceptual data models.

Conceptual data models can capture and represent rich and complex semantics at a highly abstract level. The design of large and complex databases in applications generally starts with designing the conceptual data models, which are then mapped into the logical database models. Various conceptual data models have been used for the conceptual design of database schemas (Marcos, Vela and Cavero, 2001). For example, relational databases are designed by first developing a high-level conceptual data model, such as an ER model, and then an ER-diagram is mapped to a database schema (Teorey, Yang and Fry, 1986). In addition, XML lacks sufficient power in modeling real-world data and their complex inter-relationships in semantics. So it is necessary to use other methods to describe data paradigms and develop a true conceptual data model, and then transform this model into an XML encoded format. Conceptual data modeling of XML DTD (Conrad, Scheffner and Freytag, 2000; Elmasri etal., 2005; Mani, Lee and Muntz, 2001; Xiao, Dillon, Chang and Feng, 2001) and XML Schema (Bernauer, Kappel and Kramler, 2004) have been studied in the recent past. In (Conrad, Scheffner and Freytag, 2000), for example, UML was used for designing XML DTD.

Since the conceptual data models with powerful data abstraction contain clear and rich semantics and do not have data type limitation, the information integration based on conceptual data models is more advantageous than the information integration based on logical database models. It is necessary to reengineer databases for the purpose of reusing the information in databases. In (Alhajj, 2003) and (Yeh, Li and Chu, 2008), legacy relational databases are reengineered into the EER data model and the ER data model, respectively. Similarly, for the integration of XML data, first XML document can be transformed into conceptual models (dos Santos Mello and Heuser, 2001), and then the transformed conceptual models are integrated together.

Imperfect Data and Fuzzy Sets

Different models have been proposed to handle different categories of data quality (or the lack thereof). Five basic kinds of imperfection have been identified (Bosc and Prade, 1993), which are *inconsistency*, *imprecision*, *vagueness*, *uncertainty*, and *ambiguity*. Rather than providing the formal definitions of these types of imperfect information, we explain their meanings here.

Inconsistency is a type of semantic conflict, meaning that the same aspect of the real world is irreconcilably represented more than once in a database or in several different databases. For example, the *year of birth* of *George* is simultaneously stored as 1966 and 1967. Information inconsistency usually arises from information integration.

Intuitively, imprecision and vagueness are relevant to the content of an attribute value, which means that a choice must be made from a given range (interval or set) of values without knowing which one should be chosen. In general, vague information is represented by linguistic values. For example, assume that we do not know the exact year of birth of two persons named *Michael* and *John*, but we do know that the *year of birth* of *Michael* may be 1958, 1959, 1960, or 1961, and *John* is a baby. The information about *Michael*'s year of birth is imprecise, denoted by a set of values {1958, 1959, 1960, 1961}. The information about *John*'s year of birth is vague one, and can be denoted by the linguistic value, "*infant* ".

Uncertainty indicates that we can apportion some, but not all, of our belief to a given value or group of values. For example, the possibility that the *year of birth* of *Chris* is 1955 right now should be 98%. This paper does not consider random uncertainty, which can be described using probability theory. The ambiguity means that some elements of the model lack complete semantics, leading to several possible interpretations.

Generally, several different kinds of imperfection can co-exist with respect to the same piece of information. For example, the *year of birth* of *Michael* is a set of values {1958, 1959, 1960, 1961} with possibilities of 70%, 95%, 98%, and 85%, respectively. Imprecision, uncertainty, and vagueness are three major types of imperfect information and can be modeled with fuzzy sets (Zadeh, 1965) and possibility theory (Zadeh, 1978). Many current approaches to imprecision and uncertainty are based on the theory of fuzzy sets (Zadeh, 2005; Zadeh, 2008).

Let U be a universe of discourse and F be a fuzzy set in U. A membership function:

$$\mu_F: U \to [0, \hspace{8cm} 1]$$

is defined for F, where $\mu_F(u)$ for each $u \in U$ denotes the membership degree of u in the fuzzy set F. Thus, the fuzzy set F is described as follows:

$$F = \{(u_1, \mu_F(u_1)), (u_2, \mu_F(u_2)), ..., (u_n, \mu_F(u_n))\}.$$

When the membership degree $\mu_F(u)$ above is explained as a measure of the possibility that a variable X has the value u, where X takes on values in U, a fuzzy value is described by the possibility distribution π_X (Zadeh, 1978).

$$\pi_X = \{(u_1, \pi_X(u_1)), (u_2, \pi_X(u_2)), ..., (u_n, \pi_X(u_n))\}$$

Here, $\pi_X(u_i), u_i \in U$ denotes the possibility that u_i is true. Let π_X be the representation of the possibility distribution for the fuzzy value of a variable X. This means that the value of X is fuzzy, and X may take on one of the possible values $u_1, u_2, ..., and\ u_n$, with each possible value (say u_i) associated with a possibility degree (say $\pi_X(u_i)$).

Suppose F is a fuzzy set in universe of discourse U with the membership function $\mu_F : U \to [0,1]$. Then we have the following notions.

- **Support:** The support of F is a set of the elements that have non-zero degrees of membership in F, denoted by $supp\left(F'\right) = \left\{u \mid u \in U \text{ and } \mu_F\left(u\right) > 0\right\}$.
- **Kernel:** The kernel of F is a set of the elements that completely belong to F, denoted by $ker\left(F'\right) = \left\{u \mid u \in U \text{ and } \mu_F\left(u\right) = 1\right\}$.

- **α-Cut:** The strong (weak) α-cut of F is a set of the elements which degrees of membership in F are greater than (greater than or equal to) $\alpha, \textit{where } 0 \leq \alpha < 1 (0 < a \leq 1)$, denoted by

$$F_{\alpha+} = \left\{ u \mid u \in U \textit{ and } \mu_F \left(u \right) > \alpha \right\} \textit{ and } F_{\alpha} = \left\{ u \mid u \in U \textit{ and } \mu_F \left(u \right) \geq \alpha \right\}.$$

MODELING FUZZY DATA

Corresponding to the classical database models such as relational databases, object-oriented databases, conceptual data models (e.g., ER, EER and UML class diagram) and XML model, modeling fuzzy data can be carried in the fuzzy relational databases, fuzzy object-oriented databases, fuzzy conceptual data models and fuzzy XML model. This section reviews these fuzzy data models.

Fuzzy Relational Database Models

Fuzzy data management has been extensively investigated in the context of the relational databases and some questions have been discussed in the literature. Major issues in the studies of fuzzy relational databases (FRDBs) include *representations and models, semantic measures and data redundancies, query and data processing, data dependencies and normalizations*, and *implementation* (Ma and Yan, 2008). This chapter only focuses on the fuzzy relational database models.

Several approaches have been taken to incorporate fuzzy data into relational database models. One of the fuzzy relational data models is based on fuzzy relation (Raju and Majumdar, 1988) and similarity relation (Buckles and Petry, 1982). The other one is based on possibility distribution (Prade and Testemale, 1984), which can further be classified into two categories: tuples associated with possibilities and attribute values represented by possibility distributions.

The form of an n-tuple in each of the above-mentioned fuzzy relational models can be represented, respectively, as

$$t = <p_1, p_2, ..., p_i, ..., p_n>,$$

where $p_i \subseteq D_i$ with D_i being the domain of attribute A_i and $a_i \in D_i$. For each D_i, there exists a resemblance relation denoted Res_{Di}, and

$$t = <a_1, a_2, ..., a_i, ..., a_n, d> \text{ and } t = <\pi_{A1}, \pi_{A2}, ..., \pi_{Ai}, ..., \pi_{An}>,$$

where $d \in \left(0,1 \right], \pi_{Ai}$ is the possibility distribution of attribute A_i on its domain D_i, and $\pi_{Ai} \left(x \right), x \in D_i$, denotes the possibility that x is the actual value of $t[A_i]$.

Based on the above-mentioned basic fuzzy relational models, there are several extended fuzzy relational database models. First, one can combine two kinds of fuzziness in possibility-based fuzzy relational databases, where attribute values may be possibility distributions and tuples are connected with membership degrees (Takahashi, 1993). Such fuzzy relational databases are called *possibility-distribution-fuzzy relational models* in (Umano and Fukami, 1994). Second, it is possible to combine possibility distribution and similarity (proximity or resemblance) relation, and the *extended possibility-based fuzzy relational databases* are hereby proposed in (Chen, Vandenbulcke and Kerre, 1992; Ma, Zhang and Ma, 2000), where possibility distribution and resemblance relation arise in a relational database simultaneously. In (Medina, Pons, and Vila, 1994), a fuzzy database model, GEFRED (*Generalized Fuzzy Relational Database*), is proposed to integrate the advantages of both the possibilistic and similarity based models. In GEFRED, data are stored as *generalized fuzzy relations* that extend the relations of the relational model by allowing imprecise information and a compatibility degree associated with each attribute value.

Fuzzy Object-Oriented Database Models

The classical relational database model and its fuzzy extension do not satisfy the need to model complex objects with inherent imprecision and uncertainty. The requirements of modeling complex objects and information imprecision and uncertainty can be found in many application domains and have challenged the current database technology (Chamorro-Martínez *et al.*, 2007; Ozgur, Koyuncu and Yazici, 2009). Because the object-oriented database model can represent complex object structures without fragmenting the aggregate data and can also depict complex relationships among attributes, current efforts have concentrated on the fuzzy object-oriented databases and some related notions such as class, superclass/ subclass, and inheritance.

An initial way to manage fuzziness is on conventional object-oriented platforms. In (Berzal, Marín, Pons and Vila, 2007), a fuzzy object-oriented system is developed on top of an existing classical object-oriented system. In order to develop the fuzzy object-oriented database interface, fuzzy types (Marín, Vila and Pons, 2000; Marín, Pons and Vila, 2001) are added and applied. It is presented how the typical classes of an object-oriented database can be used to represent a fuzzy type and how the mechanisms of instantiation and inheritance can be modeled using this kind of new type on an object-oriented database.

In addition to the classical object-oriented databases, some new fuzzy object-oriented database models have been proposed for fuzzy data management. Basically we can identify two major kinds of fuzzy object-oriented database models such as *basic fuzzy object-oriented database models* and ODMG-based fuzzy object-oriented database models (Ma and Yan, 2010). For the latter, some efforts have been paid on the establishment of consistent framework for a fuzzy object-oriented model based on the standard for the ODMG object data model (Cross, de Caluwe and van Gyseghem, 1997). In (de Tré and de Caluwe, 2003), an object-oriented database modeling technique is presented based on the concept 'level-2 fuzzy set' to deals with a uniform and advantageous representation of both perfect and imperfect 'real world' information. It is illustrated and discussed how the ODMG data model can be generalized to handle 'real world' data in a more advantageous way.

For the basic fuzzy object-oriented database models, Umano, Imada, Hatono and Tamura (1998) define a fuzzy object-oriented database model that uses fuzzy attribute values with a certain factor. An UFO (uncertainty and fuzziness in an object-oriented) databases model is proposed in (van Gyseghem and de Caluwe, 1998) to model fuzziness and uncertainty by means of conjunctive fuzzy sets and generalized fuzzy sets, respectively. That the behaviors and structure of the object are incompletely defined results in a gradual nature for the instantiation of an object. The partial inheritance, conditional inheritance, and multiple inheritances are permitted in fuzzy hierarchies. Based on the extension of a graphs-based model object model, a fuzzy object-oriented data model is defined in (Bordogna, Pasi and Lucarella, 1999). The notion of strength expressed by linguistic qualifiers was proposed, which can be associated with the instance relationship as well as an object with a class. Fuzzy classes and fuzzy class hierarchies are thus modeled in the object-oriented databases. In addition, based on similarity relationship, in (George *et al.*, 1996), the range of attribute values is used to represent the set of allowed values for an attribute of a given class. Depending on the inclusion of the actual attribute values of the given object into the range of the attributes for the class, the membership degrees of an object to a class can be calculated. The weak and strong class hierarchies are defined based on monotone increase or decrease of the membership of a subclass in its superclass. Based on possibility theory, vagueness and uncertainty are represented in class hierarchies in (Dubois, Prade and Rossazza, 1991), where the fuzzy ranges of the subclass attributes defined restrictions on that of the superclass attributes and then the degree of inclusion of a subclass in the superclass is dependent on the inclusion between the fuzzy ranges of their attributes. Also, based possibility distribution theory, in (Ma, Zhang and Ma, 2004), some major notions in object-oriented databases such as objects, classes, objects–classes relationships, subclass/superclass, and multiple inheritances are extended under fuzzy information environment. A generic model for fuzzy object-oriented databases is hereby developed.

There are some studies of fuzzy object-oriented databases which pay more attention to investigate some special relationships. In (Cross, 2001 & 2003), for example, fuzzy relationships in object models are investigated. In (Ndouse, 1997), a fuzzy intelligent architecture based on the uncertain object-oriented data model is proposed. The classes include fuzzy *IF-THEN* rules to define knowledge and the possibility theory is used for representations of vagueness and uncertainty. In (Lee *et al.*, 1999), an approach to object-oriented modeling based on fuzzy logic is proposed to formulate imprecise requirements along four dimensions: *fuzzy class*, *fuzzy rules*, *fuzzy class relationships*, and *fuzzy associations between classes*. The fuzzy rules, i.e., the rules with linguistic terms are used to describe the relationships between attributes.

More recently, fuzzy object-relational databases have been proposed (Cuevas, Marín, Pons and Vila, 2008) that combine the characteristics of fuzzy relational databases and fuzzy object-oriented databases.

Fuzzy XML Data Models

Despite fuzzy values have been employed to model and handle imprecise information in databases since Zadeh introduced the theory of fuzzy sets (Zadeh, 1965), relative little work has been carried out in extending XML towards the representation of fuzzy concepts over the Web. Since XML is extendable and structured, it can represent fuzzy information naturally. An initial way to manage fuzziness in XML is on top of traditional XML databases. In (Jin and Veerappan, 2010), a fuzzy XML database system is developed on top of traditional XML databases. For this purpose, a critical architectural component, named fuzzy meta- knowledge base, is developed, which records different types of fuzzy distributions for database attributes. Also a query processor is built in the proposed system to allow the processing and execution of a fuzzy query over both fuzzy and crisp XML data.

Regarding directly modeling fuzzy information in XML, Turowski and Weng (2002) extended XML DTDs with fuzzy information to satisfy the need of information exchange. Lee and Fanjiang (2003) studied how to model imprecise requirements with XML DTDs and developed a fuzzy object-oriented modeling technique schema based on XML. Tseng, Khamisy and Vu (2005) presented an XML method to represent fuzzy systems for facilitating collaborations in fuzzy applications. Without presenting XML representation model, the data fuzziness in XML document was discussed directly according to the fuzzy relational databases in (Gaurav and Alhajj, 2006), and the simple mappings from the fuzzy relational databases to fuzzy XML document were provided also. A XML Schema definition is proposed in (Oliboni and Pozzani, 2008) for representing fuzzy information. The data type classification is adopted for the XML data context.

Two kinds of fuzziness in an XML document are identified in (Ma and Yan, 2007b), which are the fuzziness in elements and the fuzziness in attribute values of elements. Using the membership degrees associated with elements for the former one and the possibility distributions to represent values for the latter one, Ma and Yan (2007) introduce a possibility attribute, denoted *Poss*, to specify the possibility of a given element existing in the XML document, which is applied together with a fuzzy construct called *Val*. Based on pair *<Val Poss>* and *</Val>*, possibility distribution for an element can be expressed. Additionally, possibility distribution can be used to express fuzzy element values. For this purpose, Ma and Yan (2007) introduce another fuzzy construct called *Dist* to specify a possibility distribution. Typically, a *Dist* element has multiple *Val* elements as children, each with an associated possibility. Corresponding to the fuzziness in XML document, a fuzzy XML DTD data model is proposed in (Ma and Yan, 2007b) and furthermore a fuzzy XML data model based on XML Schema is developed in (Yan *et al*, 2009).

Fuzzy XML data models can be mapped into fuzzy database models so that fuzzy data can be managed with fuzzy databases. In (Ma and Yan, 2007b), the fuzzy XML DTD data model is mapped into the fuzzy relational databases. The fuzzy XML DTD data model is mapped into the fuzzy object-oriented databases in (Yan, Ma and Zhang, 2014b). Also in (Yan, Ma and Zhang, 2014b), the fuzzy object-oriented databases and the fuzzy object-oriented databases are mapped into the fuzzy XML DTD data model, respectively.

Fuzzy Conceptual Data Models

Fuzzy set theory was first applied to some of the basic ER concepts in (Zvieli and Chen, 1986). This work introduced the fuzzy entity type set, fuzzy relationship type set and fuzzy attribute set of entity types (or relationship types) in addition to fuzziness in entity occurrences, relationship occurrences and attribute values, constituting the following three levels of fuzziness in the ER model.

- At the first level, the entity type set, relationship type set and attribute set of entity (or relationship) types may be fuzzy.
- The second level is related to the fuzzy occurrences of entities and relationships.
- The third level concerns the fuzzy values of attributes in entities and relationships.

An ER model generally includes some entity types, which constitute a set of entity types and some relationship types, which constitute a set of relationship types. In addition, an entity type or a relationship type generally includes some attributes, which constitute a set of attributes. In the fuzzy ER model, the first level of fuzziness means that these three kinds of sets may be fuzzy sets. Let the entity type set be fuzzy. Then, an entity type belongs to the entity type set with a membership degree in [0, 1] that indicates the possibility that this entity type belongs to the entity type set. Similarly, if the relationship type set is a fuzzy set, a relationship type belongs to the relationship type set with a membership degree in [0, 1] that indicates the possibility that this relationship type belongs to the relationship type set; if the attribute set of an entity type or a relationship type is a fuzzy set, then an attribute belongs to the attribute set with a membership degree in [0, 1] that indicates the possibility that this attribute belongs to the attribute set. For example, consider the membership values for entity types, relationship types and attributes. Suppose that we have an ER model about a library that includes the two entity types *Book* and *Book Store*, and that there is a relationship *PurchasedFrom* between these two entity types. The model assumes that *Book Store* is a fuzzy entity type with a membership grade of 0.6. Then, *PurchasedFrom* is a fuzzy relationship type with a membership grade of 0.6. Also, *Book* may contain an attribute *Dimensions* in addition to the attributes *ID*, *Title*, *Authors*, *ISBN*, *Publisher*, etc., and *Dimensions* is a fuzzy attribute with a membership grade of 0.4.

Other efforts to extend the ER model can be found in (Ruspini, 1986; Vandenberghe, 1991; Vert, Morris, Stock and Jankowski, 2000). In (Ruspini, 1986), an extension of the ER model with fuzzy values in the attributes is proposed and a truth value can be associated with each relationship instance. In addition, some special relationships such as *same-object* and *subset-of*, member-of are also introduced. Vandenberghe (1991) applies Zadeh's extension principle to calculate the truth value of propositions. For each proposition, a possibility distribution was defined on the doubleton true, false of the classical truth values. Also some advanced ER concepts such as subclass/superclass, specialization/generalization, and category are discussed in (Vandenberghe, 1991). The proposal of (Vert, Morris, Stock and Jankowski, 2000) uses the fuzzy sets theory to treat data sets as a collection of fuzzy objects.

Without including graphical representations, the fuzzy extensions of several major EER concepts (including superclass/subclass, generalization/specialization, category and the subclass with multiple superclasses) are introduced in (Chen and Kerre, 1998). Three types of constraints with respect to fuzzy relationships are discussed, which are the inheritance constraint, the total participation constraint, and the cardinality constraint. But fuzzy constraints are not discussed. A full-fledged fuzzy extension to the EER model and the corresponding graphical representations are presented in (Ma, Zhang, Ma and Chen, 2001). Galindo, Urrutia, Carrasco and Piattini (2004) extend the EER models by relaxing some constraints with fuzzy quantifiers. Also they study several constraints that are not used in classic EER models but used in the FEER models. The fuzzy constraints studied in (Galindo, Urrutia, Carrasco and Piattini, 2004) include the fuzzy participation constraint, the fuzzy cardinality constraint, the fuzzy completeness constraint to represent classes and subclasses, the fuzzy cardinality constraint on overlapping specializations, fuzzy disjoint and fuzzy overlapping constraints on specializations, fuzzy attribute-defined specializations, fuzzy constraints in union types or categories, and fuzzy constraints in shared subclasses.

The IFO data model, a graph-based conceptual data model proposed in (Abiteboul and Hull, 1987), is also extended to deal with fuzzy information. In (Vila, Cubero, Medina and Pons, 1996), several types of imprecision and uncertainty are incorporated into the attribute domain of the object-based data model, such as the values without semantic representation, the values with semantic representation and disjunctive meaning, the values with semantic representation and conjunctive meaning, and the representation of uncertain information. However, some major concepts in object-based modeling (e.g., superclass/ subclass and class inheritance) are not discussed. In addition to the attribute-level uncertainty, Vila, Cubero, Medina and Pons (1996) consider the uncertainty to be at the level of object and class. In (Yazici, Buckles and Petry, 1999), two levels of uncertainty are considered based on similarity relations, namely the level of attribute values and the level of entity instances, giving rise to the ExIFO model. Based on fuzzy set and possibility theory, an extended fuzzy IFO model named IF_2O is proposed in (Ma, 2005c).

Although some studies perform fuzzy conceptual modeling, only a few incorporate fuzziness with the UML model. Sicilia and Mastorakis (2004) define several new fuzzy constructs for the extended UML model. The proposed model supports the representation of uncertainty at the attribute, object/ class and class/subclass levels. Initially UML model is fully extended in (Ma, 2005b) and the proposed fuzzy UML model can represent fuzziness at the levels of attribute, object/class and class/subclass as well as in the relationships of aggregation, association and dependency.

In addition to the ER/EER model, IFO data model and UML data model, a fuzzy semantic model (FSM) that draws on some constructs found in several fuzzy conceptual data models (e.g., fuzzy ER/EER, fuzzy IFO and fuzzy UML data models), is proposed in (Bouaziz *et al.*, 2007).

Based on the fuzzy ER model in (Zvieli and Chen, 1986), a methodology for the design and development of fuzzy relational databases is proposed in (Chaudhry, Moyne and Rundensteiner, 1999) through the rules developed for mapping the fuzzy ER schema to the fuzzy relational database schemas. The formal approaches to mapping a fuzzy EER model into a fuzzy object-oriented database schema and a fuzzy relational database schema are presented in (Ma, Zhang, Ma and Chen, 2001) and (Yan and Ma, 2014a), respectively. The mapping from the ExIFO model into the fuzzy nested relational database schemas is described in (Yazici, Buckles and Petry, 1999). The mappings from the IF_2O model, an extended fuzzy IFO model, into the fuzzy relational database schemas and the fuzzy object-oriented database schemas are described in (Ma, 2005c) and (Ma and Shen, 2006), respectively. Utilizing the fuzzy UML class diagrams, the fuzzy UML data model is mapped into the fuzzy relational database model in (Ma, Zhang and Yan, 2011) and the fuzzy object-oriented database model in (Ma, Yan and Zhang, 2012), respectively.

Fuzzy conceptual data models can also be applied to the conceptual design of fuzzy XML data model. In (Ma and Yan, 2007b), the fuzzy XML DTD data model is constructed by mapping the fuzzy UML data model. The fuzzy XML DTD data model is automatically constructed by translating the fuzzy EER model in (Yan and Ma, 2014b). Actually the fuzzy XML model can also be reengineered into the fuzzy conceptual data models. In (Yan and Ma, 2012b), the fuzzy XML model is mapped into the fuzzy EER model and the fuzzy XML model is mapped into the fuzzy UML data model in (Yan, Ma and Zhang, 2014b).

FUZZY QUERYING AND OPERATIONS

Classical databases suffer from a lack of flexibility in query because the given selection condition and the contents of the databases are all crisp. According to (Bosc and Pivert, 1992), a query is flexible if the following conditions can be satisfied:

- A qualitative distinction between the selected entities is allowed.
- Imprecise conditions inside queries are introduced when the user cannot define his/her needs in a definite way, or when a pre-specified number of responses are desired and therefore a margin is allowed to interpret the query.

Here typically, the former case occurs when the queried databases contain imperfect information and the query conditions are crisp and the latter case occurs when the query conditions are imprecise even if the queried databases do not contain imperfect information. Basically we can identify two kinds of fuzzy querying: the first one is fuzzy querying of traditional (crisp) databases and the second one is fuzzy querying of fuzzy databases. For the former, the databases (relational or object-oriented) do not contain any fuzzy data, but fuzzy terms which are typically for natural language, for example, *"tall"* and *"young"*, are applied in querying conditions. The semantics of these linguistic (fuzzy) terms is provided by appropriate fuzzy sets.

Fuzzy Queries and Operations in Relational Databases

Tahani (1977) is the first to propose the use of fuzzy logic to improve the flexibility of crisp database queries. A formal approach and architecture are proposed to deal with simple fuzzy queries. Since then, many works have been done to support fuzzy queries in the relational database context. In (Kacprzyk, Zadrozny and Ziokkowski, 1987), a "human-consistent" database querying system based on fuzzy logic with linguistic quantifiers is presented. Using clustering techniques, Kamel, Hadfield and Ismail (1990) present a fuzzy query processing method. Takahashi (1991) presents a fuzzy query language for relational databases. In (Bosc and Lietard, 1996), the concepts of fuzzy integrals and database flexible querying are presented.

More practical approaches to flexible fuzzy querying in crisp databases are well represented by SQLf (SQLfuzzy) (Bosc and Pivert, 1995), FQUERY (FuzzyQUERY) for Access (Kacprzyk and Zadrożny, 1995), FSQL (FuzzySQL) (Galindo, 2005) and SoftSQL (Bordogna and Psaila, 2008). FQUERY for Access is an example of the implementation of a specific "fuzzy extension" of SQL for Microsoft Access®, a popular desktop DBMS (database management system). Among these proposals, SQLf, which extends *selection*, *join* and *projection* operations to handle fuzzy conditions, is the most complete because it has more extended SQL statements and it is the unique solution updated on features SQL 2003 (Eisenberg *et al.*, 2004).

For the evaluation of fuzzy queries of traditional databases, FSQL and SoftSQL evaluate fuzzy queries by means of naïve mechanisms. In (Bosc and Pivert, 2000), an evaluation mechanism based on *α-cut* distribution on fuzzy query conditions is conceived. Then a fuzzy query is translated to a regular one. The translated query selects the desired subset of data without computing the satisfaction degree of fuzzy condition for the whole input data. This evaluation mechanism is known as Derivation Principle. The use of this principle has been a unified approach for fuzzy query evaluation on relational databases (Chen and Jong, 1997; Ma and Yan, 2007a).

For the querying of fuzzy relational databases, in (Zemankova and Kandel, 1985), the fuzzy relational data base (FRDB) model architecture and query language are presented and the possible applications of the FRDB in imprecise information processing are discussed. Based on matching strengths of answers in fuzzy relational databases, Chiang, Lin and Shis (1998) present a method for fuzzy query processing. The techniques of fuzzy query processing for fuzzy database systems are presented in (Chen and Chen, 2000). Yang *et al.* (2001) focus on nested fuzzy SQL queries in a fuzzy relational database.

Two fuzzy database query languages are proposed, which are a fuzzy calculus query language and a fuzzy algebra query language. In (Takahashi, 1993), the theoretical foundation of query languages to fuzzy databases is discussed. In this work, *a fuzzy calculus query language* is constructed based on the relational calculus, and *a fuzzy algebra query language* is also constructed based on the relational algebra. It is proved that the languages have equivalent expressive power. A complete relational calculus is introduced in (Buckles, Petry and Sachar, 1989) for similarity-based fuzzy relational databases. It is shown that the fuzzy relational algebra can be mapped into the calculus and the calculus can be implemented as a query language. Similarly, in (Galindo, Medina and Aranda, 1999), a domain relational calculus is proposed for the fuzzy database model GEFRED in (Medina, Pons and Vila, 1994), and its expressive power is demonstrated through the use of a method to translate any algebraic expression into an equivalent expression in fuzzy domain relational calculus. Compared with the fuzzy calculus query language, more attention has been paid on the fuzzy algebra query language based on the fuzzy relational algebra. In (Zhang and Wang, 2000), a type of fuzzy equi-join is defined using fuzzy equality indicators. The fuzzy relational algebra can be classified according to the fuzzy relational database models.

For the possibility-based fuzzy relational database model, Prade and Testemale (1984) propose an algebra for retrieving information from a fuzzy possibilistic relational database. In (Prade and Testemale, 1984), the basic operations of relational algebra, including *union, intersection, Cartesian product, projection* and *selection*, are extended to handle fuzzy queries. Approximate equalities and inequalities modeled by fuzzy relations are taken into account in the selection operation. Then, the main features of a query language based on the extended relational algebra are presented. In (Umano and Fukami, 1994), the set operations and relational operations in the fuzzy algebra for a possibility-distribution-fuzzy-relational model are classified into the primitive operations and the additional operations. The former contains *union, difference, extended Cartesian product, selection* and *projection*, and the latter contains *intersection, join* and *division*.

Based on the fuzzy database model GEFRED in (Medina, Pons and Vila, 1994), which integrates the advantages of both the possibilistic and similarity based models, an algebra called a *generalized fuzzy relational algebra* is defined in (Medina, Pons and Vila, 1994) to manipulate information stored in such a fuzzy database. The fuzzy relational algebra contains *generalized fuzzy union, generalized fuzzy difference, generalized fuzzy Cartesian product, generalized fuzzy projection, generalized fuzzy selection*, and *generalized fuzzy join*. In (Ma and Mili, 2002), a fuzzy relational algebra is defined for handling fuzzy information in the extended possibility-based fuzzy relational databases. The defined algebraic operations include *union, difference, Cartesian product, selection, projection, intersection, join* and *division* as well as rename and outerunion.

Fuzzy Queries and Operations in Fuzzy Object-Oriented Databases

In the fuzzy object-oriented databases, a foundational issue for fuzzy data processing is to compare fuzzy objects/classes to assess their semantic relationships. Without consideration of fuzzy data types, fuzzy object comparison is investigated in (Marín *et al.*, 2003) in the context of fuzzy object-oriented databases. The comparison of entity with fuzzy data types in fuzzy object-oriented databases in (Yan and Ma, 2012a). The entity with fuzzy data types may be fuzzy objects or fuzzy classes.

Based on the semantic measure of fuzzy objects, two kinds of fuzzy object redundancies (i.e., inclusion redundancy and equivalence redundancy) are classified and three kinds of merging operation for redundancy removal are defined in (Yan, Ma and Zhang, 2014a). On the basis, the fuzzy algebraic operations for fuzzy classes and fuzzy objects are developed in (Yan, Ma and Zhang, 2014a). Also, fuzzy querying strategies are discussed there, and the form of SQL-like fuzzy querying for the fuzzy object-oriented databases is presented. An SQL type data manipulation language is defined in (Umano, Imada, Hatono and Tamura, 1998) for a fuzzy object-oriented database model that uses fuzzy attribute values with a certain factor. Also in (Bordogna and Pasi, 2001), the definition of graph-based operations to select and browse a fuzzy object oriented database is proposed.

XML-Based Fuzzy Queries and Operations

Like fuzzy querying of databases, two kinds of fuzzy querying of XML can be identified: fuzzy querying of traditional (crisp) XML and (fuzzy) querying of fuzzy XML. For the former, few efforts have been done to incorporate fuzzy logic into XML query languages. XPath language is based on path expressions able to state the structure and the value of elements required by the user. In (Braga *et al.*, 2002), some ideas to extend XPath with fuzzy terms are introduced, which use fuzzy predicates and fuzzy quantifiers, and offer a set of few built-in predicates. Combination of fuzzy predicates is made by means of arithmetic operations on ranking variables instead of using fuzzy operators. But comparators and connectives as well quantified expressions and FLWOR expressions are not considered in this work. Also focusing on XPath, XPath selection queries are extended by using flexible constraints on structure and content of XML documents in (Damiani, Marrara and Pasi, 2008), and semantics of fuzzy XPath queries is introduced in (Fazzinga, Flesca and Pugliese, 2009), which rank the top-k answers in terms of their approximated degrees. In (Campi *et al.*, 2009), a XML querying framework FuzzyXPath is proposed, in which a function called "deep-similar" is introduced to replace XPath's typical "deep-equal" function. The main goal is to provide a degree of similarity between two XML trees, assessing whether they are similar both structure-wise and content-wise. In (Thomson, Fredrick and Radhamani, 2009), a fuzzy logic based XQuery language is proposed and some techniques to extract data from XML documents. In order to extend quantified and FLWOR expressions with fuzzy logic, Goncalves and Tineo (2010) extend the XQuery language to declare fuzzy terms and use them in querying expressions.

In order to explicitly process fuzzy data in XML, in (Yan, Ma and Zhang, 2014b), based on the fuzzy XML data model proposed in (Ma and Yan, 2007b), a set of fuzzy XML algebraic operations are defined for fuzzy XML tree(s), including *Union, Intersection, Difference, Cartesian product, Selection, Projection, Join, Grouping, Ordering*, and *Bind*. These algebraic operations serve as a target language for translation from declarative user oriented query language for fuzzy XML. Considering that the basic structure of XML is tree and an XML query is often formed as a twig pattern with predicates additionally imposed on the contents or attribute values of the tree nodes, also in (Ma, Yan and Zhang, 2014b), fuzzy XML queries with predicates, which are supported by fuzzy extended Dewey encoding, are investigated. Then three types of fuzzy XML twig query with predicates are proposed, which are the fuzzy XML twig query with AND-logic, fuzzy XML twig query with AND/OR-logic and NOT-logic. One can refer to (Yan, Ma and Zhang, 2014b) for more details.

Querying and Operations of Fuzzy Conceptual Data Models

The conceptual data models are mainly applied for conceptual design of logical databases. For this reason, few works have been done to discuss algebraic operations and query languages for the fuzzy conceptual data models. In (Zvieli and Chen, 1986), a fuzzy extension to the ER algebra (Chen, 1976) is sketched for the fuzzy ER model. Based on the fuzzy semantic model (FSM) proposed in (Bouaziz *et al.*, 2007), a query language adapted to FSM-based databases is introduced in (Bouaziz *et al.*, 2007).

SUMMARIES AND DISCUSSIONS

Incorporation of fuzzy information in data models has been an important topic of database research because such information extensively exists in data and knowledge intensive applications, where fuzzy data play an import role in nature. So research has been conducted into various approaches to represent and handle fuzzy data in the context of databases. This chapter has provided an up-to-date overview of the current state of the art in fuzzy data modeling and querying. The chapter presents the survey from two main perspectives: fuzzy data models and fuzzy data querying based on the fuzzy data models. The fuzzy data models discussed in the chapter include the fuzzy database models (e.g., the fuzzy relational databases, object-oriented databases and object-relational databases), fuzzy XML model, and fuzzy conceptual data models (e.g., the fuzzy ER, EER and UML data models). Also the relationships among these fuzzy data models are discussed in the chapter. Note that due to the chapter size limit, the chapter concentrates only on fuzzy data models and basic query techniques, and does not discuss the issue of indexing fuzzy data.

Two major directions for future research on fuzzy data modeling and querying are emphasized as follows. First, a major issue is to incorporate richer semantics into the fuzzy data models and develop related query-processing strategies. Some efforts have been made to enhance the expressive power of fuzzy data models. In (Yazici and Koyuncu, 1997; Koyuncu and Yazici, 2003 & 2005), for example, the fuzzy deductive object-oriented database model is proposed for knowledge-based complex fuzzy data processing. Incorporating probabilistic information into the fuzzy databases, the fuzzy and probabilistic object bases (Cao and Rossiter, 2003; Cao and Nguyen, 2011; Yan and Ma, 2014c) and the fuzzy and probabilistic relational databases (Yan and Ma, 2013) are proposed and their algebraic operations are developed. The fuzzy and probabilistic databases provide flexible database models to represent and process hybrid uncertain information. The advantages of such a hybrid system are that the strengths of its components are combined and the weaknesses of its components are complementary one to another.

Another major open issue is the uses of the fuzzy data models in some concrete domains to deal with special fuzzy data such as fuzzy temporal data, fuzzy spatial data, fuzzy spatio-temporal data, fuzzy multimedia data, and so on. In information management of a multimedia database, for example, the attributes of an image such as color, the description of an object and the spatial relations between objects may be imprecise (Aygun and Yazici, 2004; Chamorro-Martínez *et al.*, 2007), such as "*bright*" in color and "*near*" in spatial relation, which are highly useful in intelligent semantics-based image retrieval systems. Various fuzzy data models, including the fuzzy relational databases, fuzzy object-oriented databases, fuzzy object-relational databases and fuzzy conceptual data models, have been applied in multimedia data management (Majumdar, Bhattacharya and Saha, 2002; Chamorro-Martínez *et al.*, 2007; Ozgur, Koyuncu and Yazici, 2009; Aygun and Yazici, 2004; Kucuk, Burcuozgur, Yazici and Koyuncu, 2009; Yazici, Zhu and Sun, 2001). Also the fuzzy data models have been applied in some areas such as geospatial information systems (GISs) with fuzzy objects in (Cross and Firat, 2000) and fuzzy ER model in (Vert, Stock and Morris, 2002; Vert, Morris and Stock, 2003). In (Sözer, Yazici, Oğuztüzün and Tas, 2008), for example, a querying mechanism for fuzzy spatiotemporal data is proposed, which combines fuzzy object-oriented database model with a knowledgebase allowing a fuzzy deduction and querying capability to handle complex data and knowledge. Furthermore, the fuzzy XML model is applied to represent and query fuzzy spatiotemporal data in (Bai, Yan and Ma, 2013 & 2014).

ACKNOWLEDGMENT

This work was supported by the *National Natural Science Foundation of China* (61370075 and 61572118) and the *Program for New Century Excellent Talents in University* (NCET- 05-0288).

REFERENCES

Abiteboul, S., & Hull, R. (1987). IFO: A Formal Semantic Database Model. *ACM Transactions on Database Systems*, *12*(4), 525–565. doi:10.1145/32204.32205

Alashqur, A. M., Su, S. Y. W., & Lam, H. 1989, OQL: A Query Language for Manipulating Object-oriented Databases. In *Proceedings of the Fifteenth International Conference on Very Large Data Bases*. Academic Press.

Alhajj, R. (2003). Extracting the Extended Entity-Relationship Model from a Legacy Relational Database. *Information Systems*, *28*(6), 597–618. doi:10.1016/S0306-4379(02)00042-X

Alhajj, R., & Arkun, M. E. (1993). An Object Algebra for Object-Oriented Database Systems. *Database*, *24*(3), 13–22.

Aygun, R. S., & Yazici, A. (2004). Modeling and Management of Fuzzy Information in Multimedia Database Applications. *Multimedia Tools and Applications*, *24*(1), 29–56. doi:10.1023/B:MTAP.0000033982.50288.14

Bai, L., Yan, L., & Ma, Z. M. (2013). Determining Topological Relationship of Fuzzy Spatiotemporal Data Integrated with XML Twig Pattern. *Applied Intelligence*, *39*(1), 75-100.

Bai, L., Yan, L., & Ma, Z. M. (2014). Querying Fuzzy Spatiotemporal Data Using XQuery. *Integrated Computer-Aided Engineering*, *21*(2), 147-162.

Bernauer, M., Kappel, G., & Kramler, G. (2004). Representing XML Schema in UML – A Comparison of Approaches. In *Proceedings of the 4th International Conference on Web Engineering*. Academic Press.

Bertino, E., & Catania, B. (2001). Integrating XML and Databases. *IEEE Internet Computing*, *5*(July-August), 84–88. doi:10.1109/4236.939454

Berzal, F., Marín, N., Pons, O., & Vila, M. A. (2007). Managing Fuzziness on Conventional Object-Oriented Platforms. *International Journal of Intelligent Systems*, *22*(7), 781–803. doi:10.1002/int.20228

Biron, P. V., & Malhotra, A. (2001). *XML Schema Part 2: Datatypes, W3C Recommendation*. Retrieved from http://www.w3.org/TR/xmlschema-2/

Booch, G., Rumbaugh, J., & Jacobson, I. (1998). *The Unified Modeling Language User Guide*. Addison-Welsley Longman, Inc.

Bordogna, G., Pasi, G., & Lucarella, D. (1999). A Fuzzy Object-Oriented Data Model for Managing Vague and Uncertain Information. *International Journal of Intelligent Systems*, *14*(7), 623–651. doi:10.1002/(SICI)1098-111X(199907)14:7<623::AID-INT1>3.0.CO;2-G

Bordogna, G., & Psaila, G. (2008). *Customizable Flexible Querying Classic Relational Databases. In Handbook of Research on Fuzzy Information Processing in Databases* (pp. 191–215). Hershey, PA: Information Science. doi:10.4018/978-1-59904-853-6.ch008

Bosc, P., Kraft, D., & Petry, F. (2005). Fuzzy Sets in Database and Information Systems: Status and Opportunities. *Fuzzy Sets and Systems*, *156*(3), 418–426. doi:10.1016/j.fss.2005.05.039

Bosc, P., & Lietard, L. (1996), Fuzzy Integrals and Database Flexible Querying. In *Proceedings of the Fifth IEEE International Conference on Fuzzy Systems*. doi:10.1109/FUZZY.1996.551726

Bosc, P., & Pivert, O. (1992). Some Approaches for Relational Databases Flexible Querying. *Journal of Intelligent Information Systems*, *1*(3/4), 323–354. doi:10.1007/BF00962923

Bosc, P., & Pivert, O. (1995). SQLf: A Relational Database Language for Fuzzy Querying. *IEEE Transactions on Fuzzy Systems*, *3*(1), 1–17. doi:10.1109/91.366566

Bosc, P., & Pivert, O. (2000). *SQLf Query Functionality on Top of a Regular Relational Database Management System. In Knowledge Management in Fuzzy Databases* (pp. 171–190). Physica-Verlag.

Bosc, P., & Prade, H. (1993). An Introduction to Fuzzy Set and Possibility Theory Based Approaches to the Treatment of Uncertainty and Imprecision in Database Management systems. In *Proceedings of the Second Workshop on Uncertainty Management in Information Systems: From Needs to Solutions*. Academic Press.

Bouaziz, R., Chakhar, S., Mousseau, V., Ram, S., & Telmoudi, A. (2007). Database Design and Querying within the Fuzzy Semantic Model. *Information Sciences*, *177*(21), 4598–4620. doi:10.1016/j.ins.2007.05.013

Braga, D., Campi, A., Damiani, E., Pasi, G., & Lanzi, P. L. (2002). FXPath: Flexible Querying of XML Documents. In *Proceedings of the 2002 EUROFUSE Workshop on Information Systems*. Academic Press.

Bray, T., Paoli, J., & Sperberg-McQueen, C. M. (1998). *Extensible Markup Language (XML) 1.0, W3C Recommendation*. Retrieved from http://www.w3.org/TR/1998/REC-xml-19980210

Buckles, B. P., & Petry, F. E. (1982). A Fuzzy Representation of Data for Relational Database. *Fuzzy Sets and Systems*, *7*(3), 213–226. doi:10.1016/0165-0114(82)90052-5

Buckles, B. P., Petry, F. E., & Sachar, H. S. (1989). A Domain Calculus for Fuzzy Relational Databases. *Fuzzy Sets and Systems*, *29*(3), 327–340. doi:10.1016/0165-0114(89)90044-4

Campi, A., Damiani, E., Guinea, S., Marrara, S., Pasi, G., & Spoletini, P. (2009). A Fuzzy Extension of the XPath Query Language. *Journal of Intelligent Information Systems*, *33*(3), 285–305. doi:10.1007/s10844-008-0066-3

Cao, T. H., & Nguyen, H. (2011). Uncertain and Fuzzy Object Bases: A Data Model and Algebraic Operations. *International Journal of Uncertainty, Fuzziness and Knowledge-based Systems*, *19*(2), 275–305. doi:10.1142/S0218488511007003

Cao, T. H., & Rossiter, J. M. (2003). A Deductive Probabilistic and Fuzzy Object-Oriented Database Language. *Fuzzy Sets and Systems*, *140*(1), 129–150. doi:10.1016/S0165-0114(03)00031-9

Cattell, R. G. G., Barry, D. K., Berler, M., Eastman, J., Jordan, D., Russell, C., & Velez, F. et al. (2000). *The Object Data Management Standard: ODMG 3.0*. Morgan Kaufmann.

Chamberlin, D., Florescu, D., Robie, J., Simeon, J., & Stefanescu, M. (2001). *XQuery: A Query Language for XML, W3C Working Draft*. Retrieved from http://www.w3.org/TR/xquery

Chamorro-Martínez, J., Medina, J. M., Barranco, C. D., Galán-Perales, E., & Soto-Hidalgo, J. M. (2007). Retrieving Images in Fuzzy Object-Relational Databases Using Dominant Color Descriptors. *Fuzzy Sets and Systems*, *158*(3), 312–324. doi:10.1016/j.fss.2006.10.013

Chaudhry, N. A., Moyne, J. R., & Rundensteiner, E. A. (1999). An Extended Database Design Methodology for Uncertain Data Management. *Information Sciences*, *121*(1-2), 83–112. doi:10.1016/S0020-0255(99)00066-3

Chen, G. Q. (1999). *Fuzzy Logic in Data Modeling; Semantics, Constraints, and Database Design*. Kluwer Academic Publisher.

Chen, G. Q., & Kerre, E. E. (1998). Extending ER/EER Concepts towards Fuzzy Conceptual Data Modeling. In *Proceedings of the 1998 IEEE International Conference on Fuzzy Systems*. IEEE.

Chen, G. Q., Vandenbulcke, J., & Kerre, E. E. (1992). A General Treatment of Data Redundancy in a Fuzzy Relational Data Model. *Journal of the American Society for Information Science*, *43*(4), 304–311. doi:10.1002/(SICI)1097-4571(199205)43:4<304::AID-ASI6>3.0.CO;2-X

Chen, P. P. (1976). The entity-relationship model: Toward a unified view of data. *ACM Transactions on Database Systems*, *1*(1), 9–36. doi:10.1145/320434.320440

Chen, S. M., & Jong, W. T. (1997). Fuzzy Query Translation for Relational Database Systems. *IEEE Transactions on Systems, Man, and Cybernetics*, *27*(4), 714–721. doi:10.1109/3477.604117 PMID:18255911

Chen, Y. C., & Chen, S. M. (2000). Techniques of Fuzzy Query Processing for Fuzzy Database Systems. In *Proceedings of the Fifth Conference on Artificial Intelligence and Applications*. Academic Press.

Chiang, D. A., Lin, N. P., & Shis, C. C. (1998). Matching Strengths of Answers in Fuzzy Relational Databases. *IEEE Transactions on Systems, Man and Cybernetics. Part C, Applications and Reviews*, *28*(3), 476–481. doi:10.1109/5326.704592

Cluet, S. (1998). Designing OQL: Allowing Objects to be Queried. *Information Systems*, *23*(5), 279–305. doi:10.1016/S0306-4379(98)00013-1

Codd, E. F. (1970). A Relational Model of Data for Large Shared Data Banks. *Communications of the ACM*, *13*(6), 377–387. doi:10.1145/362384.362685

Conrad, R., Scheffner, D., & Freytag, J. C. (2000). XML Conceptual Modeling Using UML. In *Proceedings of the 19th International Conference on Conceptual Modeling*. Academic Press.

Cross, V. (2001). Fuzzy Extensions for Relationships in a Generalized Object Model. *International Journal of Intelligent Systems*, *16*(7), 843–861. doi:10.1002/int.1038

Cross, V. (2003). Defining Fuzzy Relationships in Object Models: Abstraction and Interpretation. *Fuzzy Sets and Systems*, *140*(1), 5–27. doi:10.1016/S0165-0114(03)00025-3

Cross, V., de Caluwe, R., & van Gyseghem, N. (1997). A Perspective from the Fuzzy Object Data Management Group (FODMG). In *Proceedings of the 1997 IEEE International Conference on Fuzzy Systems*. IEEE. doi:10.1109/FUZZY.1997.622800

Cross, V., & Firat, A. (2000). Fuzzy Objects for Geographical Information Systems. *Fuzzy Sets and Systems, 113*(1), 19–36. doi:10.1016/S0165-0114(99)00010-X

Cuevas, L., Marín, N., Pons, O., & Vila, M. A. (2008). pg4DB: A Fuzzy Object-Relational System. *Fuzzy Sets and Systems, 159*(12), 1500–1514. doi:10.1016/j.fss.2008.01.009

Damiani, E., Marrara, S., & Pasi, G. (2008). A Flexible Extension of XPath to Improve XML Querying. In *Proceedings of the 2008 International ACM SIGIR Conference on Research and Development in Information Retrieval*. ACM.

de Tré, G., & de Caluwe, R. (2003). Level-2 Fuzzy Sets and Their Usefulness in Object-Oriented Database Modelling. *Fuzzy Sets and Systems, 140*(1), 29–49. doi:10.1016/S0165-0114(03)00026-5

dos Santos Mello, R., & Heuser, C. A. (2001). A Rule-Based Conversion of a DTD to a Conceptual Schema. In *Proceedings of the 20th International Conference on Conceptual Modeling*. Academic Press.

Dubois, D., Prade, H., & Rossazza, J. P. (1991). Vagueness, Typicality, and Uncertainty in Class Hierarchies. *International Journal of Intelligent Systems, 6*(2), 167–183. doi:10.1002/int.4550060205

Eisenberg, A., Melton, J., Kulkarni, K., Michels, J.-E., & Zemke, F. (2004). SQL:2003 Has Been Published. *SIGMOD Record, 33*(1), 119–126. doi:10.1145/974121.974142

Elmasri, R., Li, Q., Fu, J., Wu, Y.-C., Hojabri, B., & Ande, S. (2005). Conceptual Modeling for Customized XML Schemas. *Data & Knowledge Engineering, 54*(1), 57–76. doi:10.1016/j.datak.2004.10.003

Embley, D. W., & Ling, T. W. (1989). Synergistic Database Design with an Extended Entity-Relationship Model. In *Proceedings of the Eight International Conference on Entity-Relationship Approach*. Academic Press.

Fazzinga, B., Flesca, S., & Pugliese, A. (2009). Top-k Answers to Fuzzy XPath Queries, In *Proceedings of the 2009 International Conference on Databases and Expert Systems Applications*. Academic Press.

Galindo, J. (2005). New Characteristics in FSQL, a Fuzzy SQL for Fuzzy Databases. *WSEAS Transactions on Information Science and Applications, 2*(2), 161–169.

Galindo, J., Medina, J. M., & Aranda, M. C. (1999). Querying Fuzzy Relational Databases through Fuzzy Domain Calculus. *International Journal of Intelligent Systems, 14*(4), 375–411. doi:10.1002/(SICI)1098-111X(199904)14:4<375::AID-INT3>3.0.CO;2-K

Galindo, J., Urrutia, A., Carrasco, R. A., & Piattini, M. (2004). Relaxing Constraints in Enhanced Entity-Relationship Models Using Fuzzy Quantifiers. *IEEE Transactions on Fuzzy Systems, 12*(6), 780–796. doi:10.1109/TFUZZ.2004.836088

Galindo, J., Urrutia, A., & Piattini, M. (2006). *Fuzzy Databases Modeling, Design and Implementation*. Idea Group Publishing. doi:10.4018/978-1-59140-324-1

Gaurav, A., & Alhajj, R. (2006). Incorporating Fuzziness in XML and Mapping Fuzzy Relational Data into Fuzzy XML. In *Proceedings of the 2006 ACM Symposium on Applied Computing*. doi:10.1145/1141277.1141386

George, R., Srikanth, R., Petry, F. E., & Buckles, B. P. (1996). Uncertainty Management Issues in the Object-Oriented Data Model. *IEEE Transactions on Fuzzy Systems, 4*(2), 179–192. doi:10.1109/91.493911

Goncalves, M., & Tineo, L. (2010). Fuzzy XQuery. In Soft Computing in XML Data Management. Springer.

Jin, Y., & Veerappan, S. (2010). A Fuzzy XML Database System: Data Storage and Query. In *Proceedings of 2010 IEEE International Conference on Information Reuse and Integration*. IEEE.

Kacprzyk, J., & Zadrożny, S. (1995). *FQUERY for Access: Fuzzy Querying for Windows-based DBMS. In Fuzziness in Database Management Systems* (pp. 415–433). Physica-Verlag. doi:10.1007/978-3-7908-1897-0_18

Kacprzyk, J., Zadrozny, S., & Ziokkowski, A. (1987). FQUERY III+: A "Human-consistent" Database Querying System Based on Fuzzy Logic with Linguistic Quantifiers. In *Proceedings of the Second International Fuzzy Systems Association Congress*. Academic Press.

Kamel, M., Hadfield, B., & Ismail, M. (1990). Fuzzy Query Processing Using Clustering Techniques. *Information Processing & Management, 26*(2), 279–293. doi:10.1016/0306-4573(90)90031-V

Kerre, E. E., & Chen, G. Q. (1995). *An Overview of Fuzzy Data Modeling. In Fuzziness in Database Management Systems* (pp. 23–41). Physica-Verlag. doi:10.1007/978-3-7908-1897-0_2

Koyuncu, M., & Yazici, A. (2003). IFOOD: An Intelligent Fuzzy Object-Oriented Database Architecture. *IEEE Transactions on Knowledge and Data Engineering, 15*(5), 1137–1154. doi:10.1109/TKDE.2003.1232269

Koyuncu, M., & Yazici, A. (2005). A Fuzzy Knowledge-Based System for Intelligent Retrieval. *IEEE Transactions on Fuzzy Sets and Systems, 13*(3), 317–330. doi:10.1109/TFUZZ.2004.839666

Kucuk, D., Burcuozgur, N., Yazici, A., & Koyuncu, M. (2009). A Fuzzy Conceptual Model for Multimedia Data with A Text-based Automatic Annotation Scheme. *International Journal of Uncertainty, Fuzziness and Knowledge-based Systems, 17*(Supplement), 135–152. doi:10.1142/S0218488509006066

Lee, J., & Fanjiang, Y. (2003). Modeling Imprecise Requirements with XML. *Information and Software Technology, 45*(7), 445–460. doi:10.1016/S0950-5849(03)00015-6

Lee, J., Xue, N. L., Hsu, K. H., & Yang, S. J. (1999). Modeling Imprecise Requirements with Fuzzy Objects. *Information Sciences, 118*(1-4), 101–119. doi:10.1016/S0020-0255(99)00042-0

Lo, A., Özyer, T., Kianmehr, K., & Alhajj, R. (2010). VIREX and VRXQuery: Interactive Approach for Visual Querying of Relational Databases to Produce XML. *Journal of Intelligent Information Systems, 35*(1), 21–49. doi:10.1007/s10844-009-0087-6

Ma, Z. M. (2005b). Extending UML for Fuzzy Information Modeling. In Advances in Object-Oriented Databases: Modeling and Applications. Idea Group Publishing.

Ma, Z. M. (2005a). *Fuzzy Database Modeling with XML*. Springer.

Ma, Z. M. (2005c). A Conceptual Design Methodology for Fuzzy Relational Databases. *Journal of Database Management, 16*(2), 66–83. doi:10.4018/jdm.2005040104

Ma, Z. M. and Shen, Derong. (2006). Modeling Fuzzy Information in the IF$_2$O and Object-Oriented Data Models. *Journal of Intelligent & Fuzzy Systems, 17*(6), 597–612.

Ma, Z. M. and Yan, Li. (2008). A Literature Overview of Fuzzy Database Models. *Journal of Information Science and Engineering, 24*(1), 189–202.

Ma, Z. M. and Yan, Li. (2010). A Literature Overview of Fuzzy Conceptual Data Modeling. *Journal of Information Science and Engineering, 26*(2), 427–441.

Ma, Z. M., & Mili, F. (2002). Handling Fuzzy Information in Extended Possibility-Based Fuzzy Relational Databases. *International Journal of Intelligent Systems, 17*(10), 925–942. doi:10.1002/int.10057

Ma, Z. M., & Yan, L. (2007a). Generalization of Strategies for Fuzzy Query Translation in Classical Relational Databases. *Information and Software Technology, 49*(2), 172–180. doi:10.1016/j.infsof.2006.05.002

Ma, Z. M., & Yan, L. (2007b). Fuzzy XML Data Modeling with the UML and Relational Data Models. *Data & Knowledge Engineering, 63*(3), 970–994. doi:10.1016/j.datak.2007.06.003

Ma, Z. M., Yan, L., & Zhang, F. (2012). Modeling Fuzzy Information in UML Class Diagrams and Object-Oriented Database Models. *Fuzzy Sets and Systems, 186*(1), 26–46. doi:10.1016/j.fss.2011.06.015

Ma, Z. M., Zhang, F., & Yan, L. (2011). Fuzzy Information Modeling in UML Class Diagram and Relational Database Models. *Applied Soft Computing, 11*(6), 4236–4245. doi:10.1016/j.asoc.2011.03.020

Ma, Z. M., Zhang, W. J., & Ma, W. Y. (2000). Semantic Measure of Fuzzy Data in Extended Possibility-based Fuzzy Relational Databases. *International Journal of Intelligent Systems, 15*(8), 705–716. doi:10.1002/1098-111X(200008)15:8<705::AID-INT2>3.0.CO;2-4

Ma, Z. M., Zhang, W. J., & Ma, W. Y. (2004). Extending Object-Oriented Databases for Fuzzy Information modeling. *Information Systems, 29*(5), 421–435. doi:10.1016/S0306-4379(03)00038-3

Ma, Z. M., Zhang, W. J., Ma, W. Y., & Chen, G. Q. (2001). Conceptual Design of Fuzzy Object-Oriented Databases Using Extended Entity-Relationship Model. *International Journal of Intelligent Systems, 16*(6), 697–711. doi:10.1002/int.1031

Majumdar, A. K., Bhattacharya, I., & Saha, A. K. (2002). An Object-Oriented Fuzzy Data Model for Similarity Detection in Image Databases. *IEEE Transactions on Knowledge and Data Engineering, 14*(5), 1186–1189. doi:10.1109/TKDE.2002.1033783

Mani, M., Lee, D. W., & Muntz, R. R. (2001). Semantic Data Modeling Using XML Schemas. In *Proceedings of the 20th International Conference on Conceptual Modeling*. Academic Press.

Marcos, E., Vela, B., & Cavero, J. M. (2001). Extending UML for Object-Relational Database Design. In *Proceedings of the 4th International Conference on the Unified Modeling Language, Modeling Languages, Concepts, and Tools*. Academic Press.

Marín, N., Medina, J. M., Pons, O., Sánchez, D., & Vila, M. A. (2003). Complex Object Comparison in A Fuzzy Context. *Information and Software Technology, 45*(7), 431–444. doi:10.1016/S0950-5849(03)00014-4

Marín, N., Pons, O., & Vila, M. A. (2001). A Strategy for Adding Fuzzy Types to an Object-Oriented Database System. *International Journal of Intelligent Systems*, *16*(7), 863–880. doi:10.1002/int.1039

Marín, N., Vila, M. A., & Pons, O. (2000). Fuzzy Types: A New Concept of Type for Managing Vague Structures. *International Journal of Intelligent Systems*, *15*(11), 1061–1085. doi:10.1002/1098-111X(200011)15:11<1061::AID-INT5>3.0.CO;2-A

Medina, J. M., Pons, O., & Vila, M. A. (1994). GEFRED: A Generalized Model of Fuzzy Relational Databases. *Information Sciences*, *76*(1-2), 87–109. doi:10.1016/0020-0255(94)90069-8

Ndouse, T. D. (1997). Intelligent Systems Modeling with Reusable Fuzzy Objects. *International Journal of Intelligent Systems*, *12*(2), 137–152. doi:10.1002/(SICI)1098-111X(199702)12:2<137::AID-INT2>3.0.CO;2-R

Object Management Group (OMG). (2003). *Unified Modeling Language (UML), version 1.5, Technical report*. OMG. Retrieved from www.omg.org

Oliboni, B., & Pozzani, G. (2008). Representing Fuzzy Information by Using XML Schema. In *Proceedings of the 2008 International Conference on Database and Expert Systems Applications*. doi:10.1109/DEXA.2008.44

Ozgur, N. B., Koyuncu, M., & Yazici, A. (2009). An Intelligent Fuzzy Object-Oriented Database Framework for Video Database Applications. *Fuzzy Sets and Systems*, *160*(15), 2253–2274. doi:10.1016/j.fss.2009.02.017

Petry, F. E. (1996). *Fuzzy Databases: Principles and Applications*. Kluwer Academic Publisher. doi:10.1007/978-1-4613-1319-9

Prade, H., & Testemale, C. (1984). Generalizing Database Relational Algebra for the Treatment of Incomplete or Uncertain Information and Vague Queries. *Information Sciences*, *34*(2), 115–143. doi:10.1016/0020-0255(84)90020-3

Raju, K. V. S. V. N., & Majumdar, K. (1988). Fuzzy Functional Dependencies and Lossless Join Decomposition of Fuzzy Relational Database Systems. *ACM Transactions on Database Systems*, *13*(2), 129–166. doi:10.1145/42338.42344

Ruspini, E. (1986). Imprecision and Uncertainty in the Entity-Relationship Model. In *Fuzzy Logic in Knowledge Engineering*. Verlag TUV Rheinland.

Sicilia, M. A., & Mastorakis, N. (2004). Extending UML 1.5 for Fuzzy Conceptual Modeling: A Strictly Additive Approach. *WSEAS Transactions on Systems*, *5*(3), 2234–2240.

Sözer, A., Yazici, A., Oğuztüzün, H., & Tas, O. (2008). Modeling and Querying Fuzzy Spatiotemporal Databases. *Information Sciences*, *178*(19), 3665–3682. doi:10.1016/j.ins.2008.05.034

Stonebraker, M., & Moore, D. (1996). *Object-Relational DBMSs: The Next Great Wave*. Morgan Kaufmann.

Tahani, V. (1977). A Conceptual Framework for Fuzzy Query Processing: A Step toward Very Intelligent Database Systems. *Information Processing & Management*, *13*(5), 289–303. doi:10.1016/0306-4573(77)90018-8

Takahashi, Y. (1991). A Fuzzy Query Language for Relational Databases. *IEEE Transactions on Systems, Man, and Cybernetics*, *21*(6), 1576–1579. doi:10.1109/21.135699

Takahashi, Y. (1993). Fuzzy Database Query Languages and Their Relational Completeness Theorem. *IEEE Transactions on Knowledge and Data Engineering*, *5*(1), 122–125. doi:10.1109/69.204096

Teorey, T. J., Yang, D. Q., & Fry, J. P. (1986). A Logical Design Methodology for Relational Databases Using the Extended Entity-Relationship Model. *ACM Computing Surveys*, *18*(2), 197–222. doi:10.1145/7474.7475

Thompson, H. S., Beech, D., Maloney, M., & Mendelsohn, N. (2001). *XML Schema Part 1: Structures, W3C Recommendation*. Retrieved from http://www.w3.org/TR/xmlschema-1/

Thomson, E., Fredrick, J., & Radhamani, G. (2009). Fuzzy Logic Based XQuery operations for Native XML Database Systems. *International Journal of Database Theory and Application*, *2*(3), 13–20.

Tseng, C., Khamisy, W., & Vu, T. (2005). Universal Fuzzy System Representation with XML. *Computer Standards & Interfaces*, *28*(2), 218–230. doi:10.1016/j.csi.2004.11.005

Turowski, K., & Weng, U. (2002). Representing and Processing Fuzzy Information: An XML-based Approach. *Knowledge-Based Systems*, *15*(1-2), 67–75. doi:10.1016/S0950-7051(01)00122-8

Umano, M., & Fukami, S. (1994). Fuzzy Relational Algebra for Possibility-Distribution-Fuzzy-Relational Model of Fuzzy Data. *Journal of Intelligent Information Systems*, *3*(1), 7–27. doi:10.1007/BF01014018

Umano, M., Imada, T., Hatono, I., & Tamura, H. (1998). Fuzzy Object-Oriented Databases and Implementation of Its SQL-Type Data Manipulation Language. In *Proceedings of the 1998 IEEE International Conference on Fuzzy Systems*. doi:10.1109/FUZZY.1998.686314

Urrutia, A., & Galindo, J. (2010). *Fuzzy Database Modeling: An Overview and New Definitions. In Soft Computing Applications for Database Technologies: Techniques and Issues* (pp. 1–21). IGI Global. doi:10.4018/978-1-60566-814-7.ch001

van Gyseghem, N., & de Caluwe, R. (1998). Imprecision and Uncertainty in UFO Database Model. *Journal of the American Society for Information Science*, *49*(3), 236–252. doi:10.1002/(SICI)1097-4571(199803)49:3<236::AID-ASI5>3.0.CO;2-B

Vandenberghe, R. M. (1991). An Extended Entity-Relationship Model for Fuzzy Databases Based on Fuzzy Truth Values. In *Proceedings of the 4th International Fuzzy Systems Association World Congress*. Academic Press.

Vert, G., Morris, A., & Stock, M. (2003). Converting a Fuzzy Data Model to an Object-Oriented Design for Managing GIS Data Files. *IEEE Transactions on Knowledge and Data Engineering*, *15*(2), 510–511. doi:10.1109/TKDE.2003.1185848

Vert, G., Morris, A., Stock, M., & Jankowski, P. (2000). Extending Entity-Relationship Modeling Notation to Manage Fuzzy Datasets. In *Proceedings of the 2000 International Conference on Information Processing and Management of Uncertainty in Knowledge-Based Systems*. Academic Press.

Vert, G., Stock, M., & Morris, A. (2002). Extending ERD Modeling Notation to Fuzzy Management of GIS Data Files. *Data & Knowledge Engineering, 40*(2), 163–179. doi:10.1016/S0169-023X(01)00049-0

Vila, M. A., Cubero, J. C., Medina, J. M., & Pons, O. (1996). A Conceptual Approach for Deal with Imprecision and Uncertainty in Object-Based Data Models. *International Journal of Intelligent Systems, 11*(10), 791–806. doi:10.1002/(SICI)1098-111X(199610)11:10<791::AID-INT6>3.0.CO;2-U

Wang, C. Y., Lo, A., Alhajj, R., & Barker, K. (2005). Novel Approach for Reengineering Relational Databases into XML. In *Proceedings of the 21st International Conference on Data Engineering Workshop.* doi:10.1109/ICDE.2005.249

Xiao, R. G., Dillon, T. S., Chang, E., & Feng, L. (2001). Modeling and Transformation of Object-Oriented Conceptual Models into XML Schema. In *Proceedings of the 12th International Conference on Database and Expert Systems Applications.* doi:10.1007/3-540-44759-8_77

Yan, L. (2009). Fuzzy Data Modeling Based on XML Schema. In *Proceedings of the 2009 ACM International Symposium on Applied Computing.* doi:10.1145/1529282.1529631

Yan, L., Ma, Z., & Zhang, F. (2014b). Fuzzy XML Data Management. Springer-Verlag. doi:10.1007/978-3-642-44899-7

Yan, L., & Ma, Z. M. (2012a). Comparison of Entity with Fuzzy Data Types in Fuzzy Object-Oriented Databases. *Integrated Computer-Aided Engineering, 19*(2), 199–212.

Yan, L., Ma, Z. M., & Zhang, F. (2014a). Algebraic Operations in Fuzzy Object-Oriented Databases. *Information Systems Frontiers, 16*(4), 543–556. doi:10.1007/s10796-012-9359-8

Yan, L., & Ma, Z. M., (2012b). Incorporating Fuzzy Information into the Formal Mapping from Web Data Model to Extended Entity-Relationship Model. *Integrated Computer-Aided Engineering, 19*(4), 313-330.

Yan, L., & Ma, Z. M. (2013). A Fuzzy Probabilistic Relational Database Model and Algebra. *International Journal of Fuzzy Systems, 15*(2), 244-253.

Yan, L., & Ma, Z. M. (2014a). Modeling Fuzzy Information in Fuzzy Extended Entity-Relationship Model and Fuzzy Relational Databases. *Journal of Intelligent and Fuzzy Systems, 27*(4), 1881-1896.

Yan, L., & Ma, Z. M. (2014b). Formal Translation from Fuzzy EER Model to Fuzzy XML Model. *Expert Systems with Applications, 41*(8), 3615-3627.

Yan, L., & Ma, Z. M. (2014c). A Probabilistic Object-Oriented Database Model with Fuzzy Measures and Its Algebraic Operations. *Journal of Intelligent & Fuzzy Systems.* DOI: 10.3233/IFS-141307

Yang, Q., Zhang, W. N., Liu, C. W., Wu, J., Yu, C. T., Nakajima, H., & Rishe, N. (2001). Efficient Processing of Nested Fuzzy SQL Queries in a Fuzzy Database. *IEEE Transactions on Knowledge and Data Engineering, 13*(6), 884–901. doi:10.1109/69.971185

Yazici, A., Buckles, B. P., & Petry, F. E. (1999). Handling Complex and Uncertain Information in the ExIFO and NF² Data Models. *IEEE Transactions on Fuzzy Systems, 7*(6), 659–676. doi:10.1109/91.811232

Yazici, A., & George, R. (1999). *Fuzzy Database Modeling.* Physica-Verlag. doi:10.1007/978-3-7908-1880-2

Yazici, A., George, R., Buckles, B. P., & Petry, F. E. (1992). *A Survey of Conceptual and Logical Data Models for Uncertainty Management. In Fuzzy Logic for Management of Uncertainty* (pp. 607–644). John Wiley and Sons Inc.

Yazici, A., & Koyuncu, M. (1997). Fuzzy Object-Oriented Database Modeling Coupled with Fuzzy Logic. *Fuzzy Sets and Systems*, *89*(1), 1–26. doi:10.1016/S0165-0114(96)00080-2

Yazici, A., Zhu, Q., & Sun, N. (2001). Semantic Data Modeling of Spatiotemporal Database Applications. *International Journal of Intelligent Systems*, *16*(7), 881–904. doi:10.1002/int.1040

Yeh, D. M., Li, Y. W., & Chu, W. (2008). Extracting Entity-Relationship Diagram from a Table-Based Legacy Database. *Journal of Systems and Software*, *81*(5), 764–771. doi:10.1016/j.jss.2007.07.005

Zadeh, L. A. (1965). Fuzzy Sets. *Information and Control*, *8*(3), 338–353. doi:10.1016/S0019-9958(65)90241-X

Zadeh, L. A. (1978). Fuzzy Sets as a Basis for a Theory of Possibility. *Fuzzy Sets and Systems*, *1*(1), 3–28. doi:10.1016/0165-0114(78)90029-5

Zamulin, A. V. (2002). An Object Algebra for the ODMG Standard. In *Proceedings of the 6th East European Conference on Advances in Databases and Information Systems*. doi:10.1007/3-540-45710-0_23

Zemankova, M., & Kandel, A. (1985). Implementing Imprecision in Information Systems. *Information Sciences*, *37*(1-3), 107–141. doi:10.1016/0020-0255(85)90008-8

Zhang, W. N., & Wang, K. (2000). An Efficient Evaluation of a Fuzzy Equi-Join Using Fuzzy Equality Indicators. *IEEE Transactions on Knowledge and Data Engineering*, *12*(2), 225–237. doi:10.1109/69.842264

Zvieli, A., & Chen, P. P. (1986). Entity-Relationship Modeling and Fuzzy Databases. In *Proceedings of the 1986 IEEE International Conference on Data Engineering*. IEEE.

KEY TERMS AND DEFINITIONS

Fuzzy Object-Oriented Database Model: Fuzzy object-oriented database model is an extended object-oriented database model, in which the attribute values of objects may be represented by fuzzy sets. As a result, the classes, the object-class relationships and the class-class relationships may be fuzzy also.

Fuzzy Query: Generally speaking, fuzzy query means the fuzzy querying of traditional database models and XML model as well as the querying of fuzzy database models and fuzzy XML model. The former is a kind of flexible query that a user can describe his/her demands with fuzzy query conditions.

Fuzzy Relational Database Model: Fuzzy relational database model is an extended relational database model, in which its tuples have membership degrees in [0, 1] and its attribute values may be represented by fuzzy sets.

Fuzzy Sets: Being an extension to the conventional sets, an element in a fuzzy set may or may not belongs to the corresponding fuzzy set and has a membership degree. Formally, let U be a universe of discourse and F be a fuzzy set in U. A membership function $\mu_F: U \to [0, 1]$ is defined for F, where μ_F (u) for each $u \in U$ denotes the membership degree of u in the fuzzy set F.

Fuzzy XML Model: Fuzzy XML model is an extended XML model, including fuzzy XML schema and fuzzy XML documents. In the fuzzy XML documents, two kinds of fuzziness can be identified, which are the fuzziness in elements and the fuzziness in attribute values of elements. Corresponding to the fuzzy XML documents, we have the fuzzy XML schema such as fuzzy DTD (Document Type Definition) or fuzzy XML Schema.

OQL: OQL (Object Query Language) developed by the Object Data Management Group (ODMG) is a query language standard for object-oriented databases.

SQL: SQL (Structured Query Language) is a powerful, easy-to-use query language for relational databases. SQL is originally based upon relational algebra and tuple relational calculus, which consists of a data definition language and a data manipulation language.

XPath: XPath (XML Path Language) defined by the World Wide Web Consortium (W3C) is a query language for selecting nodes from an XML document.

XQuery: XQuery is a querying language designed by the W3C, which allows one to select the XML data elements of interest, reorganize and possibly transform them, and return the results in a structure of one's choosing.

Chapter 6
Fuzzy XQuery:
A Real Implementation

José Ángel Labbad
Universidad Simón Bolívar, Venezuela

Ricardo R. Monascal
Universidad Simón Bolívar, Venezuela

Leonid Tineo
Universidad Simón Bolívar, Venezuela

ABSTRACT

Traditional database systems and languages are very rigid. XML data and query languages are not the exception. Fuzzy set theory is an appropriate tool for solving this problem. In this sense, Fuzzy XQuery was proposed as an extension of the XQUERY standard. This language defines the xs:truth datatype, the xml:truth attribute and allows the definition and use of fuzzy terms in queries. The main goal of this chapter is to show a high coupling implementation of Fuzzy XQuery within eXist-db, an open source XML DBMS. This extension strategy could also be used with other similar tools. This chapter also presents a statistical performance analysis of the extended fuzzy query engine using the XMark benchmark with user defined fuzzy terms. The study presents promising results.

INTRODUCTION

The Web has been become a popular tool for services such as travel agencies, shopping stores, car rental, encyclopedia, and so on. Thus, the Web plays an essential role in many online companies and it has made available an exorbitant amount of data from several websites. Many of these websites contain engines that query data from different existing sites. Most of these websites use XML (Extensible Markup Language) format (W3C, 2008) to interchange data, because it is the standard for this purpose.

XML documents may be queried through declarative query languages such as XPath (W3C, 2014) and XQuery (W3C, 2010). Both languages are XML-centric, i.e., their data model and type system are

DOI: 10.4018/978-1-4666-8767-7.ch006

based on XML. XQuery is an extension of XPath conceived to integrate multiple XML sources and it is the W3C standard language for XML data. Several database engines support XQuery either as native language or as an alternative language.

As several authors have adverted, XQuery is not accurate to handle search criteria based on user's preferences (Buche et al 2006) (Calmès et al 2007) (Goncalves and Tineo 2007) (Thomsom and Radhameni 2011) (Ueng 2012). XQuery is not able to discriminate query answers according to user's criteria. This weakness is often referred to as rigidity problem of query languages and it is due to query conditions are based on Boolean logic (Bordogna and Psaila, 2008).

As a motivating example, suppose researchers who want to attend a conference. They want to query a travel company website searching for the best flight trip according their own preferences. Someone would like a trip that were very cheap and made few connections. Another person might prefer a direct flight whose destination is a near city reaching the conference city by train.

Preference criteria in this example involve linguistic terms of vague nature. They are the natural language terms: very, cheap, few, and near. In general, semantics of such terms is context-dependent and may vary according to user's preference. For giving answers to user requests, in this case, many optional trips might exist, it would be helpful to discriminate them in terms of compatibility with user's criteria.

Fuzzy sets theory is a possible theoretical solution to this kind of needs. System might allow defining user's criteria and ranking query answers using a membership function; a membership function quantifies the satisfaction degree of each answer with respect to user's criteria and induces a total order of the dataset.

In order to give a solution to described problem, some proposals had arisen (Buche et al 2006) (Gaurav and Alhajj 2006) (Calmès et al 2007) (Goncalves and Tineo 2007) (Campi et al 2009) (Thomsom and Radhameni 2011) (Jin, Y. and Veerappan 2010) (Ma et al 2010) (Goncalves and Tineo 2010) (Ueng 2012) (Panic et al 2014). In particular, in a previous work Fuzzy XQuery has been defined (Goncalves and Tineo, 2010). At present time, fuzzy logic extensions introduced by Fuzzy XQuery are not included in the standard definition. Some efforts have been made in implementing such features, but resulting products are not wide available and there is still work to do.

This chapter shows the development of an implementation of Fuzzy XQuery, a language for fuzzy queries over XML. Fuzzy XQuery was proposed by Goncalves and Tineo (2010). Usual query languages fail at expressing user preferences and context sensitive search conditions. They are often very rigid because there based on Boolean logic. This implies that elements are either completely included or not included at all in a query's result set. This problem often keeps users from easily expressing their preferences in a natural language, which would help them obtain better results adapted to their needs. XQuery suffers of this problem as other query languages do. Fuzzy sets theory gives a mathematical and computational framework that allows the definition of fuzzy terms. This has been proposed as a solution for the rigidity of query languages.

This chapter addresses an implementation of Fuzzy XQuery, with three main objectives in mind. First, showing that the implementation is possible, such that running the queries in an appropriate way will produce the desired results. Second, checking if there is any mistake or inconsistency in the language definition. Third, conducting several performance analyses, checking that performance is not significantly affected by any additional computations needed for supporting fuzzy queries and to showing that, in the implemented extension, queries without fuzzy terms maintains the same performance as can be observed in the original DBMS.

This chapter describes how an existing XML DBMS was extended for supporting Fuzzy XQuery features. Some minor deficiencies were found on the Fuzzy XQuery definition. These deficiencies became evident during the implementation of Fuzzy XQuery. This chapter includes a description and proposed solution for each of these deficiencies. The performance analysis is described in detail, showing that extending the XML DBMS with fuzzy logic does not affect its performance on classic queries (without fuzzy terms), and queries with fuzzy terms do not affect performance significantly in most cases.

BACKGROUND

The idea of applying fuzzy set theory for extending XML and related query languages As XPath and XQuery has taken the attention of several researchers in the last ten years. Some of them focused their interest in imprecise semi structured data in XML. Others focused on the imprecise knowledge about data structure in XPath. In addition, some researchers focused on expression of queries involving user preferences in XQuery. As ever, there are also combinations of such interests.

Buche et al (2006) deal with XML data that may be imprecise and represented as possibility distributions. They propose to introduce flexibility into the query processing of the XML database, in order to take into account the imperfections due to the semantic enrichment of its data. This flexibility relies on fuzzy queries and query rewriting which consists in generating a set of approximate queries from an original query using three transformation techniques: deletion, renaming and insertion of query nodes.

Gaurav and Alhajj (2006) presented an approach for incorporating fuzzy and imprecise data in XML documents. They described the ways to introduce fuzziness using both possibility theory and similarity relations. They showed how to map the data from a fuzzy relational database into a fuzzy XML document, with the corresponding XML schema.

Calmès et al (2007) provided a general discussion about how flexible querying can be applied to semistructured data. They adapt flexible querying ideas, already used for classically structured databases, to XQuery like languages for managing users' priority and preferences, but also for tackling with the variability of underlying structures.

Goncalves and Tineo (2007) proposed an extension of path exp essions with fuzzy logic. It would be a new step towards a more flexible XQuery language for Web based non traditional information systems.

Campi et al (2009) described a XML querying framework, called FuzzyXPath, based on Fuzzy Set Theory, relying on fuzzy conditions for the definition of flexible constraints on stored data. They introduced a function called "deep-similar", which aims at substituting XPath's typical "deep-equal" function. Its goal is to provide a degree of similarity between two XML trees, assessing whether they are similar both structure-wise and content-wise.

Thomsom and Radhameni (2009) (2011) point out the rigidity problem of Boolean logic based queries and suggest the use of fuzzy logic in XQuery conditions. They propose to extract XML data form the DBMS and process fuzzy conditions in an external layer.

Jin, Y. and Veerappan (2010) described an approach to incorporate fuzzy logic into XML database systems. The system was built on top of traditional XML databases, while allows the storage of fuzzy data as well as crisp data. They described the structure of the system, starting with the critical architectural component named fuzzy metaknowledge base, which records different types of fuzzy distributions for database attributes. A fuzzy query language was presented that is based on the XQuery standard, while allowing fuzzy expressions in any condition in a query. A query processor was built to allow the processing and execution of a fuzzy query over both fuzzy and crisp XML data.

Ma et al (2010) proposed a new fuzzy XML data model based on XML Schema. With the model used, the fuzzy information in XML documents can be represented naturally. Along with the model, an associated algebra is presented formally. They also introduced how to use their algebra to capture queries expressed in XQuery. They showed that this model and algebra can establish a firm foundation for publishing and managing the histories of fuzzy data on the Web.

Goncalves and Tineo (2010) has extended XQuery in order to provide more flexibility in querying XML crisp data. They thus defined Fuzzy XQuery. They focused in propose fuzzy set based extensions to all different elements in the standard XQuery that are suitable of a treatment with fuzzy logic. They proposed an implementation mechanism based in translation form fuzzy queries to regular ones in XQuery and evaluation of fuzzy conditions over the result of such queries. This mechanism takes advantage of existing connections between fuzzy and classical sets. It is known as the derivation principle.

Ueng (2012) proposed a way to fuzzify XQuery language and implement an interpreter for a derivate using native XML database. Fuzzy logic extended XQuery queries are translated to standard XQuery queries and executed against an existing XML native database. Obtained results are then processed using fuzzy logic mechanisms in order to obtain the final results.

Panic et al (2014) developed XML extension which combines indefiniteness in the values of XML and indefiniteness in the structure of XML into a single fuzzy XML extension. They expanded XQuery syntax with fuzzy values and included priorities and thresholds in fuzzy XQuery extension. A tool for working with XML, XSD and DTD documents and prioritized fuzzy XQuery extension queries has been developed.

This chapter deals with the problem of how to realize Fuzzy XQuery of Goncalves and Tineo (2010) as an extension of an existing XML DBMS. The choice of this proposal obeys the fact that there is available a complete document of language definition. Such document comprises both syntax and semantics of Fuzzy XQuery language. According to research done, this proposal is the most complete in extending elements of the standard XQuery.

Fuzzy Set Theory

Zadeh (1965) proposed fuzzy set theory, where sets can contain elements partially. Fuzzy sets allow representing linguistic predicates in a natural way, by means of a numeric representation. These predicates can express gradual properties of elements in a universe of discourse.

Membership Functions

To represent gradual characteristics and define fuzzy sets, membership functions are used. The domain of these functions is a classic set. The range is the set of real numbers in the interval [0,1]. The application of a membership function for any element in a given universe renders a membership degree. This denotes the degree of inclusion of the element in the fuzzy set. The membership function of the fuzzy set A in a classic universe X is defined as follows:

$$\mu_A : X \rightarrow \left[0,1\right]$$

Fuzzy Sets Defined by Extension

A fuzzy set can be defined listing each one of the elements present in the fuzzy set, together with their associated degree, as follows:

$$\mu_A = \left\{ x_1 \big/ \mu_1, x_2 \big/ \mu_2, \ldots, x_n \big/ \mu_n \right\}$$

Any element in X, not included in this definition, has a membership degree of zero (0).

Fuzzy Sets Defined by Trapezium

A fuzzy set can be also defined specifying the four inflexion points of a trapezium, rendering a membership degree with the shape of this trapezium (see Figure 1). The inflexion points will be denoted by $\left(x_1, x_2, x_3, x_4 \right)$ where $x_1 \leq x_2 \leq x_3 \leq x_4$. The membership function is defined as follows:

$$\mu_A = \begin{cases} 0 & if \quad x < x_1 \\ \dfrac{x - x_1}{x_2 - x_1} & if \quad x_1 \leq x < x_2 \\ 1 & if \quad x_2 \leq x \leq x_3 \\ \dfrac{x_4 - x}{x_4 - x_3} & if \quad x_3 < x \leq x_4 \\ 0 & if \quad x_4 < x \end{cases}$$

Figure 1. Fuzzy set defined as a trapezium

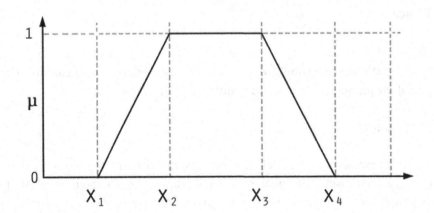

Fuzzy Set Support

The support of a fuzzy set is the classic set formed by every element from the fuzzy set that has a membership degree greater than zero, that is, those elements that are not fully excluded from the fuzzy set. Figure 2 illustrates the concept of support, using a trapezium defined fuzzy set. Formally, the support of a fuzzy set A is defined as follows:

$$support\left(A\right) = \left\{x \in X \middle| \mu_A\left(x\right) > 0\right\}$$

where A is a fuzzy set and μ_A is the membership function of the fuzzy set A.

Fuzzy Set Core

The core of a fuzzy set is the classic set formed by every element of the fuzzy set that has a membership degree equal to one, that is, that they are fully included in the fuzzy set. Figure 3 illustrates the concept of core, using a trapezium defined fuzzy set. Formally, the core of a fuzzy set A is defined as follows:

$$core\left(A\right) = \left\{x \in X \middle| \mu_A\left(x\right) = 0\right\}$$

Fuzzy Set Border

The border of a fuzzy set is the classic set formed by every element that is neither fully excluded nor fully included. Figure 4 illustrates the concept of border, using a trapezium defined fuzzy set. Formally, the border of a fuzzy set A is defined as follows:

Figure 2. Support of a fuzzy set

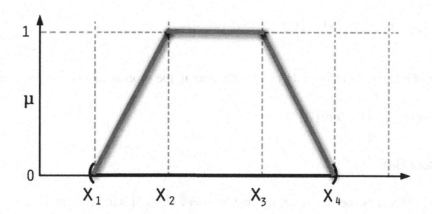

Figure 3. Core of a fuzzy set

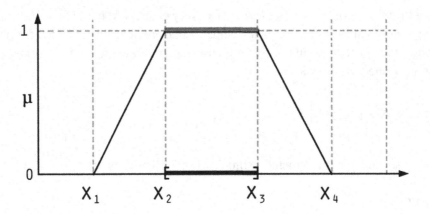

Figure 4. Border of a fuzzy set

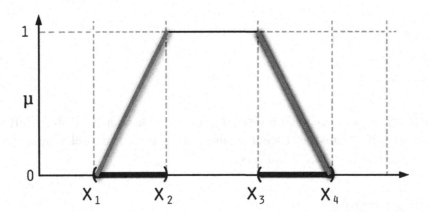

$$border\left(A\right) = \left\{x \in X \middle| 0 < \mu_A\left(x\right) < 1\right\}$$

The border of a fuzzy set is formed by every element in the support that is not in the core:

$$border\left(A\right) = support\left(A\right) - core\left(A\right)$$

Cut of a Fuzzy Set

The α_cut is defined as the classic set formed by every element with a degree greater or equal to a threshold $\alpha \in \left[0,1\right]$

$$\alpha\_cut(A) = \left\{ x \in X \middle| \mu_A(x) \geq \alpha \right\}$$

where A is a fuzzy set, μ_A is the membership function of the fuzzy set A, and $\alpha \in [0,1]$

If $\alpha = 1$ then the α_cut is equivalent to the core.

The Figure 5 is a graphic for an α_cut with $\alpha = 0.5$.

Strict Cut of a Fuzzy Set

The $\hat{\alpha}\_cut$ is defined as the classic set formed by all elements which degree is greater than a threshold $\alpha \in [0,1]$

$$\hat{\alpha}\_cut(A) = \left\{ x \in X \middle| \mu_A(x) > \alpha \right\}$$

where A is a fuzzy set, μ_A is the membership function of the fuzzy set A, and $\alpha \in [0,1]$

If $\alpha = 0$ then $\hat{\alpha}\_cut$ is equivalent to support

The Figure 6 shows a graphic for a strict $\hat{\alpha}\_cut$ with $\alpha = 0.5$.

Fuzzy Set Complement

The complement of a classic set is formed by those elements in the universe that are excluded in the set. Viewed as an indicatory function the complementation consists in changing 0 by 1 and vice versa. In the case of fuzzy sets, there are elements in the border. The idea of complements would be that as much as a border element is included in the fuzzy set, it must be near to be excluded from the complementary fuzzy set. Thus, the complement of a fuzzy set is defined by means of the membership function shown in Figure 7.

Figure 5. α_cut of a fuzzy set with α=0.5

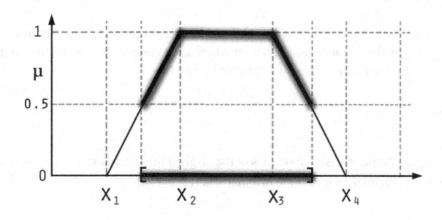

Figure 6. Strict cut of a fuzzy set

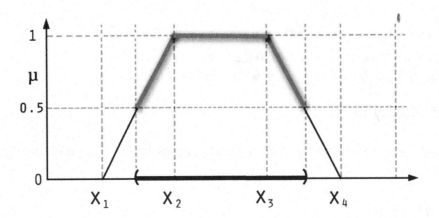

Figure 7. Complement of a fuzzy set

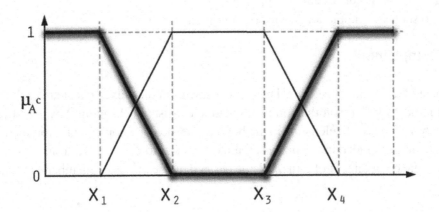

Fuzzy Sets Intersection

The idea of intersecting two sets is to obtain a set that contains elements that are in both sets. The intersection of fuzzy sets is thus defined as a fuzzy set where each element has the minimum membership degree between its membership degrees to intersected fuzzy sets.

$$\mu_{A \cap B}\left(x\right) = \min\left(\mu_{A}\left(x\right), \mu_{B}\left(x\right)\right)$$

where μ_A and μ_B are the membership functions of the original fuzzy sets and $\mu_{A \cap B}$ represents the result of apply the intersection operation over the original sets (Figure 8).

Figure 8. Fuzzy sets intersection

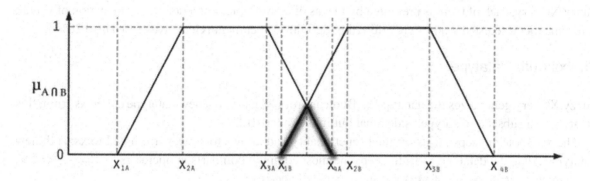

Fuzzy Sets Union

The union contains elements that are in at least one of its operands. In addition, the union is the dual of intersection. In this way, the maximum membership degree of an element in those fuzzy sets that are the operands of the union is taken as such element degree for the resulting fuzzy set.

$$\mu_{A \cup B}\left(x\right) = \max\left(\mu_A\left(x\right), \mu_B\left(x\right)\right)$$

where μ_A and μ_B are the membership functions of the original fuzzy sets and $\mu_{A \cup B}$ represents the result of apply the union operation over the original sets (Figure 9).

Fuzzy XQuery Language

XQuery (W3C, 2010) is a standard language for querying XML (W3C, 2098) data. The application of fuzzy sets theory for the extension of XQuery in order to allow flexible querying expressions has been

Figure 9. Fuzzy sets union

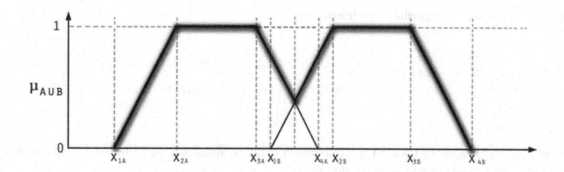

matter of a previous work (Goncalves and Tineo 2010). It has given birth to Fuzzy XQuery Language. Hereafter a brief summary of this language is presented. The summary comprises all new elements of Fuzzy XQuery, each of them is presented by means of an example. For a detailed explanation of syntax and semantic, interested readers are referred to definition document (Goncalves and Tineo 2010).

The xs:truth Datatype

Fuzzy XQuery generalizes the datatype xs:Boolean from XQuery to a new datatype called xs:truth, this datatype is a subset of datatype xs:decimal but in the range [0,1].

The xs:Boolean keeps all its original functionality and allows to convert from and to xs:truth new datatype. Also, the datatype xs:truth keeps the most common comparison operators (=, !=, <, <=, >, >=) which returns a value of xs:Boolean as originally occurred.

The xml:Truth Attribure

As Fuzzy XQuery applies fuzzy set theory in querying, the result of a query might be provided of a membership degree. Because this reason, the language defines an special attribute named xml:truth.

Fuzzy Terms

Fuzzy Predicates

Fuzzy XQuery allows the user to define fuzzy predicates in order to be used in queries. The predicates can represent adjectives in natural language. The meaning of these linguistic terms would be defined by fuzzy sets. The predicates can be specified by a trapezium or by extension membership function. When it's defined by a trapezium, the 4 trapezium points are specified, and when it's defined by extension all possible or desirable input values are specified with their respective truth degrees.

Example: Declaration of a predicate by extension.

```
declare fuzzy predicate
    dark ($color as xs:string)
    extension("false", "white", 0.3, "yellow",
              0.6, "brown", "true", "black")
```

Example: Declaration of a predicate by trapezium.

```
declare fuzzy predicate
    tall ($height as xs:int)
    trapezium(150, 180, xs:double("INF"), xs:double("INF"))
```

Fuzzy Modifiers

A fuzzy modifier is a unary operand that applies on fuzzy predicates to build new fuzzy predicates. Fuzzy modifiers can be defined in one of two ways.

The first form of defining a modifier is as a translation: the user indicates the number that will be added to the actual value of the predicate before its calculations.

The other way is as a power: applies the indicated power as argument when it declares at the resulting truth degree of the predicate.

Example: Declaration of a modifier by translation.

```
declare fuzzy modifier
   few translation (-100.0)
```

Example: Declaration of a modifier by power.

```
declare fuzzy modifier
   extremely power (+3.0)
```

Fuzzy Comparators

The user can specify the comparator name, it's two arguments and an expression that indicates how it's going to be calculated the result based on the parameters and using a trapezium, a definition by extension or a definition by similarity (the same that by extension but with symmetry and reflexivity properties)

Example: Declaration of a comparator by trapezium.

```
declare fuzzy comparator
   almostTheSame ($x as xs:int, $y as xs:int)
   ($x - $y) trapezium (-28, 0, 10, 35)
```

Example: Declaration of a comparator by similarity.

```
declare fuzzy comparator
   isClose ($x as xs:int, $y as xs:int)
   ($x,$y) similarity (true, "Venezuela", "Colombia",
                       0.5, "Argentina", "USA")
```

Fuzzy Connectives

A logical type operator defined by the user, it's result is always of type xs:truth

Example: Declaration of a connector.

```
declare fuzzy connective
   implication ($x, $y)
   {
      (not($x) or $y)
   }
```

Fuzzy Quantifiers

It is an operator type defined by the user, it represents quantitative adjectives, they can be of absolute type or proportional type to indicate its nature.

Example: Declaration of an absolute quantifier.

```
declare fuzzy quantifier
   nearTo300 absolute
   trapezium (250, 285, 315, 350)
```

Example: Declaration of a proportional quantifier.

```
declare fuzzy quantifier
   lessOrMore proportional
   trapezium (.30, .45, .55, .70)
```

Fuzzy Queries

The Fuzzy XQuery language extends the original XQuery expressions to fuzzy expressions, these expressions are of type:

Filter Expressions

Filter: Filters the obtained sequences with criteria of expression form.
Example: Get only the young people.

```
$people[young(age)]
```

Comparison Expressions

Comparison: They compare sequences with a comparative operator.
Example: Know if the value "quadruples the value" with which truth degree.

```
1000 quadruples 200
```

Logical Expressions

Logical: They allow using connectors of classic logic as well as the new fuzzy connectors defined by the user.
Example: Know if the white color is "dark" and if 175 feet is considered "tall".

```
dark("white") and tall(175)
```

Quantified Expressions

Quantified: Allows the users to use quantifiers of classical logic (universal and existential) and the fuzzy quantifiers defined by the user.

Example: Truth degree of numbers close to 300 that satisfies that they are almost equal.

```
closeTo300
    $num1 in 200 to 300,
    $num2 in 250 to 350
satisfies
    almostTheSame ($num1,$num2)
```

Conditional Expressions

Conditional: Allows the user to get different results based on the truth degree of a logical expression with classical or fuzzy logic.

Example: Check if a person is tall.

```
If (tall(185) threshold 0,75)
    then "Is tall"
    else "Is not tall"
```

FLWOR Expressions

FLWOR(For, Let, Where, Order, Return): Allows the construction of complex queries in XQuery iterating over variables, establish conditions, and other functions

Example: Get the best route with interconnection, with origin Caracas and destiny Beijing.

```
for $result in (
    for $v1 in $flights//flight
             [origin=Caracas][good(airline)],
        $v2 in $flights//flight
             [destiny=Beijing][good(airline)]
        let $v:= $opinions//opinion
                [airport = $v2/origin][age = middle]
        where $v1/destiny = $v2/origin
              and mostOf($x in $v) satisfies score = high
              and cheap ($v1/price + $v2/price)
        return <connection> $v1 $v2 </connection>
)
    order by $result.xml:truth descending
    return $result
```

ARCHITECTURE AND ENVIRONMENT

There are three types of architecture for adding a language extension to a DBMS, classified by its coupling to the system (Timarán 2001). These are low coupling, medium coupling and high coupling.

The low coupling architecture (Figure 10) refers to an extension made by a logical layer, and these extensions work by translating the new language queries into the original query language so they can be understood by the DBMS. This architecture allows freedom in choosing the programming language to realize the extension with and works even with proprietary DBMS. The extension would be stable through changes of DBMS versions, and in some cases can even work with multiple DMBS. However, this freedom comes with a price, and it is that making an extension in this manner could create additional overhead in the transactions, it could be difficult to integrate existing applications, and it could create scalability issues.

The medium coupling architecture (Figure 11) refers to an extension created directly on the DBMS using its own language. This also works with proprietary DBMS, in most cases would be stable through new versions of the DBMS, and is also easy to integrate with existing applications and tools. With this architecture, you cannot choose the programming language (it must be the one from the selected DBMS) and portability to another DBMS is more difficult.

The high coupling architecture (Figure 12) refers to an extension done with modifications to the DBMS source code itself. This is a good option if the integration with existing applications is a priority. It has better scalability possibilities compared to the other architectures discussed, does not add unnecessary computational overhead, but cannot be done with proprietary DBMS. The development process is significantly harder (it is necessary to understand the language and the source code), it is hard to maintain the extension with new DBMS versions, and it cannot be used in other DBMS.

The extension was made with a high coupling architecture. This would allow developing the complete selected subset of the new language without any disability. This also allowed getting the best possible performance in order to perform a just analysis, as described in this chapter.

Several DBMS implement XQuery. A list of them can be found in the W3C website. The idea here is to select one in order to implement Fuzzy XQuery. Some criteria to filter this list were defined. The

Figure 10. Low coupling architecture

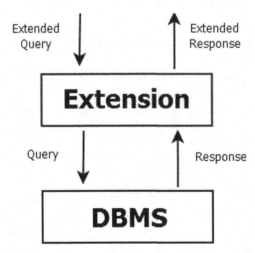

Figure 11. Medium coupling architecture

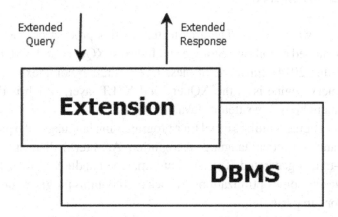

Figure 12. High coupling architecture

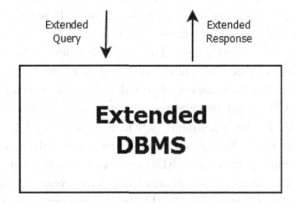

selected XQuery DBMS had to be open source. It had to implement the full XQuery language specification, not a reduced subset that could create problems in the development of the extension. It had to have available documentation. It must be recently updated, not an abandoned project. The first option in the list was BaseX, (2014), while the second was eXist-db (Siegel and Retter, 2014).

At first stage of the research work, BaseX was selected. BaseX is a light-weight, high-performance and scalable XML Database engine and XPath/XQuery 3.1 Processor, which includes full support for the W3C Update and Full Text extensions (BaseX, 2014). It is a great XML DBMS with a many advantages: the possibility of executing XQuery queries (in a fully implemented language), a good graphic interface, developed in the Java language, very frequent actualizations, available documentation and updated often.

The first try was to implement an extension to BaseX, but the architecture in which that system was implemented resulted very complex to understand. The processing techniques of its language differed in a significant way with many others at lexicographically, syntactically, and in tree creation.

A contact was made with the developers of this BaseX for help; they suggested not attempting modifying the DBMS, as it could be very complex. On the other hand, answer from eXist-db project developers' community was the opposite.

EXTENSION DEVELOPMENT

eXist-db is a complex software project. The architecture of this product comprises four layers. Form lower to higher they are named as follows: Storage and Indexes; XQuery and XSLT; Database Interface; and API (Siegel and Retter, 2014). Each one of these layers is rather complex due to different modules composing it. The XQuery engine is in the XQuery and XSLT layer, which is the central one in the architecture. eXist-db main body is written in Java.

The eXist-db XQuery engine is built as usual for a programming language interpreter. It has a front-end that deals with lexical and syntactical language recognition. An intermediate structure, named abstract syntactic tree or parse-tree is generated. This structure may be handled in order to perform semantics checks as well as rewrite and some optimizations. A back end contains program functions able to execute the corresponding actions in parse tree.

XQuery language interpreter in eXist-db is programmed using ANTLR with Java. ANTLR (ANother Tool for Language Recognition) is a parser generator for reading, processing, executing, or translating structured text or binary files (Parr, 2013). It is widely used to build languages, tools, and frameworks. From a grammar, ANTLR generates a parser that can build and walk parse trees.

As it has been stated in previous section, proposal here is to implement Fuzzy XQuery with a high coupling architecture. In this sense, source code of the eXist-db XQuery engine was intervened. At first, grammar was modified in order to recognize new lexical and syntactic elements of Fuzzy XQuery. The abstract syntactic tree or parse-tree structure was also modified in order to bring a representation of query expression in Fuzzy XQuery. The back end was also object of some modifications providing structures and functions that are needed for the execution of new features in Fuzzy XQuery.

A representative subset of Fuzzy XQuery has been implemented in the eXist-db extension described here. It comprises the following elements: xs:truth Datatype; xml:truth Attribute; Fuzzy Terms Predicates, Modifiers, Comparators & Connectors; Filter expressions; Comparison expressions; Logic expressions and Conditional expressions. Fuzzy quantifiers and FLOWR expressions were not included in this extension. Nevertheless, the same implementation mechanism may be used in order to complete the Fuzzy XQuery support in eXist-db.

In the document of Fuzzy XQuery definition, Goncalves and Tineo (2010) suggested the application of the derivation principle in order to process this language. This principle consists in deriving regular (crisp) queries from fuzzy ones, execute regular (derived) queries and after evaluate fuzzy conditions over the result of regular ones. This strategy had been conceived for low coupling implementation architecture. Therefore it could not be applied in the here presented extension.

The idea of taking advantage from existing connections between fuzzy sets and regular ones is the basis of the derivation principle. Someone can think that it would be possible to use these connections in order to make some optimization in a middle coupling architecture or a high coupling architecture. In eXist-db each filter expression is evaluated iteratively; therefore, unfortunately, no intermediate optimization can be performed in the corresponding queries.

Code Extensions

In order to support Fuzzy XQuery on an XML DMBS with a high coupling architecture extension, several modifications must be done in the source code of the XQuery engine. It is difficult to explain in a general way because it would be very dependent of source code. That is the problem with high coupling architecture: the portability. Some particular modifications were performed into eXist-db XQuery engine. Hereafter these modifications are briefly described. In order to understand it in detail, interested readers are aimed to explore eXist-db source code. Modifications are organized according to new features in Fuzzy XQuery.

xs:truth Datatype

This datatype is used to express fuzzy degrees, it's is contained in a Java class *"TruthValue"*, extension of *"DecimalValue" Java class, which represents the Decimal Datatpye defined in W3C standard but* restricted to the domain [0,0, 1.0] according to the *Fuzzy XQuery* specification. *True* and *False* constants are added to the definition as 1.0 and 0.0 respectively.

The "Type" Java class, which lists all types in XQuery and has a subtypes map, was modified in order to include *xs:truth* and to indicate that:

1.   xs:truth is a subset of numeric values.
2.   Booleans are a subset of xs:truth.

Each relevant *"convertTo"* method in other datatypes was modified in order to acknowledge the presence of *xs:truth*. These methods indicate for each datatype how it has to be converted to another one, and this can be specified one by one.

The Sequence Java interfacè was augmented with an *"effectiveTruthValue"* method with concrete definitions in each implementing class. This is an extension to the "effective booleanValue" defined in W3C.

A *FunTruth* class was also created corresponding to the implementation of *fn:truth* from the *Fuzzy XQuery* definition.

Fuzzy Predicates

In order to support fuzzy predicates, the grammar of the language had to be extended to include trapezium and extension definitions. Each of these fuzzy predicates is represented in Java classes *Predicate-FunctionTrapezium* and *PredicateFunctionExtension*, both subclasses of *PredicateFunction included in eXist-db original code,* moreover of *UserDefinedFunction class.*

The concrete syntax for evaluating these predicates is analogous to those of user-defined functions, with the difference that this evaluation is implemented in the corresponding classes for fuzzy predicates, with an additional case that manages thresholds as defined in *Fuzzy XQuery.*

Fuzzy Modifiers

The grammar was extended in order to support fuzzy modifiers, either by power or translation. These modifiers are represented in classes *ModifierFunctionPower* and *ModifierFunctionTranslation*, both subclasses of *ModifierFunction* and moreover of *UserDefinedFunction*

The evaluation of modifiers required an extension to general function evaluation. Originally, a function evaluation receives a *QName*, representing the function name, along with the arguments to the function. Now, the evaluation can receive one or two *QNames*. If the evaluation receives only one *QName*, then the traditional function evaluation is performed. Otherwise, modifier evaluation is performed as defined in *XQuery*.

Fuzzy Comparators and Connectors

The grammar was extended in order to support fuzzy comparators, defined either as a trapezium or by extension. These modifiers are represented in java classes *ComparatorFunctionTrapezium* and *ComparatorFunctionExtension*, both subclasses of *ComparatorFunction included in eXist-db* and moreover of *UserDefinedFunction*. The grammar was also extended in order to support fuzzy connectors, represented in a class *Connective Function*, also a subclass of *UserDefinedFunction*.

The evaluation of fuzzy comparators and connectors were extended from those for traditional comparators, by adding a case where the comparator can be a *QName as defined in XQuery standar* (representing the name of the desired comparator or connector).

Fuzzy Filter Expressions and the xml:truth Attribute

In order to support fuzzy filter expressions, the Predicate Java class was modified, where the following alternative evaluation techniques were added:

1. If a predicate is evaluated with a result of type xs:truth, the evalTruth method is invoked.
2. If a predicate corresponds to a threshold, as defined in Fuzzy XQuery, the evalThreshold is used.

Additionally, several methods were defined that allow adding, modifying and reading *xml:truth* attributes form XML elements. These methods are exclusively used within *evalTruth* and *evalThreshold*.

Logical and Conditional Expressions

The *OpAnd*, *OpOr* and *FunNot* Java classes corresponding to logical operations "And", "Or" and "Not" were modified in order to evaluate them in a fuzzy context. The *ConditionalExpression Java* class was modified as well in order to make Boolean evaluation be of type *xs:truth*. The grammar was slightly modified in order to allow specification of a threshold whenever necessary.

Compatibility Claims

While modifying eXists-db, some decisions were taken that makes the implemented Fuzzy XQuery little differs from its original definition by Goncalves and Tineo (2010):

1. In the original definition, translation modifiers are always defined with return type xs:truth. However, this is not always the case in practice. The returned value must have the same numeric type that the predicate need as an argument. This was changed, allowing different return types for this kind of modifiers.
2. The definition of connectors does not explicitly require that the effectiveTruthValue of each argument be calculated prior to the evaluation of the connector. In consequence, the connector will

have to receive xs:truth typed arguments. This definition can be refined in order to better specify this behavior.

3. The definition of comparators uses the "/" symbol as the division operator. However, this symbol is already used in XQuery for XPath type expressions. The decision to solve this was use "div" instead of "/".

4. In the definition of conditional expressions, it is not fully specified if the test-expression must be greater-or-equal or simply greater than the indicated threshold value in order to select the then-expression. The solution for this was to use the keyword "over" that is fuzzy with respect to this.

5. Implemented Fuzzy XQuery uses xs:double("INF") as indicated by the W3C recommendation, instead of xs:double(INF) as in Goncalves and Tineo (2010)

PERFORMANCE ANALYSIS

When an extension to a query engine is done, one think to take in mind is to do no degrade the performance of the system. The goal is to provide new features with a performance similar to that of original system. In order to see the practical accomplishment of this goal in the extension of eXists-db for Fuzzy XQuery, it has been made an experimental performance study using formal model statistic method. The idea of this method is to explain the influence of several considered factors in the observed values from experiments (Raj, 1991). The importance of a factor is measured by the proportion of the total variation in the response that is explained by the factor.

EXPERIMENTAL DESIGN

In order to measure the system's performance there have been applied a statistical analysis. The first step was to select all the factors to be considered relevant to the expected performance. After this, there will be test every combination of these factors, in order to determine the importance of each of them in the total performance.

The next is to get data for each one of these combinations in order to apply the desired studies and to define an answer variable, which represents the result for each combination of the selected factors.

One of the goals of implement Fuzzy XQuery was to analyze the performance of the new implementation compared to the original DMBS running classic queries (without fuzzy terms) as well as the performance of fuzzy queries compared to similar classic queries.

To achieve this goal, an experimental design was made based on the XMark benchmark (Schmidt et al 2002) (Schmidt 2003).

Factors and Data

The factors considered in this experiment were:

1. **Database Server:** It has two possible values. S1 is for the original database server (eXist Solutions, 2011) while S2 is for the modified server with the Fuzzy XQuery extension as described in this chapter.

2. **Type of Query:** It has two possible values. T1 means a classic query (without fuzzy terms) and T2 means a fuzzy query (a query with fuzzy terms). See APPENDIX: Fuzzy Queries used in experiments.

3. **Data Volume:** It has two possible values. It can be "Low"(V1) which is a database with 11 MB of size, or "High" (V2) which is a database with 111 MB of size, both of them included with XMark (CWI, 2009).

4. **Query:** It has twenty possible values, from Q1 to Q20. They refer to the 20 queries included with XMark. These queries were modified to include fuzzy terms, in order to test them. See APPENDIX: Fuzzy Queries used in experiments.

Observed Variable

The observed variable for these experiments was the total spent time in milliseconds for each query, using all different combinations for all the factors described previously.

Experimental Model

The proposed model is a 2^k. factorial model where the query is not taken as a factor, because the interest was mainly in the average response time. The experiment was designed in a way that once obtained the response time for every combination of factors, there could detected how each one of them affected the response variable. In addition, there were two replications for each query in order to get results that are more accurate.

Including Fuzzy Terms in Queries

In order to get fuzzy queries to compare with the queries included in XMark, the decision was to modify them to include fuzzy terms. These steps were followed to obtain the fuzzy queries:

1. Check each query searching for any expression that could be replaced for a fuzzy term, or any place of the query that could be used to add a fuzzy term.

2. After replacing or adding a fuzzy term, ran each query in order to check if the desired result in semantic terms were obtained, verifying that the number of elements in the result were similar to the original query.

3. The selection was made in a way such that, among all queries, had been used at least one fuzzy term of each kind implemented.

Programming the Experiment

Making use of Java, GNU/Linux scripts, and the useful help of eXist-db mailing list, there were developed programs that allowed the continuous execution of queries with each combination of the experimental factors described previously. The results were saved in text files for their subsequent analysis. In total were 240 queries: 160 classic queries and 80 fuzzy queries. To ensure a higher level of reliability each query was executed 2 times.

To run the queries there were used an Acer Aspire 5003WLMi laptop with an AMD Turion 1,8 ghz 64 bits processor. This laptop has 1,5 GB of 333 Mhz DDR memory and 80 GB hard drive capacity.

This computer only had installed the Ubuntu operating system, Java, and eXist-db. This laptop was used as dedicated server for running these experiments in order to minimize the influence of external factors that could affect the response time.

RESULT ANALYSIS

Experimental results were loaded into R Statistical Software (R Project 2014), in order to perform the corresponding analysis. In this tool were expressed the model that supposes to describe the results according to the considered factors. An ANOVA table is generated in order to know the significance of individual factors and their interactions. Then interactions that are more significant are plotted in order to make a descriptive analysis.

First Study

The first comparison attempts to show that the intervention of code that were performed did not affect the usual performance of the original DBMS. There were used just two factors: the database server system (original or modified) and the volume of data (low or high). There were run the same classic queries in both systems. Then the result is the ANOVA in Box 1.

In Box 1 it can be seen that the highest significance level is for data volume. In the same manner, can see that the used DBMS does not have a high significance level in the response times, which is the variable that is been studying in this experiment. In Figure 13 can see the graphic of the response times for high data volume and low data volume for the two DBMS (original and modified).

Second Study

The second comparison made was of response times when running classic queries of XMark in the modified eXist-db DBMS and the modified queries with fuzzy terms in the same DBMS. Here the considered factors where data volume (low or high) type of query (fuzzy or classic). With this could be checked in which sense the performance was or was not affected introducing fuzzy terms in the queries. The ANOVA table for this experiment is in Box 2.

Box 1. ANOVA table for first study

```
 Df Sum Sq Mean Sq F value Pr(>F)
SYSTEM 1 1.600e+10 1.600e+10 0.002 0.966
VOLUME 1 1.566e+14 1.566e+14 18.075 3.64e-05 ***
SYSTEM:VOLUME 1 1.530e+10 1.530e+10 0.002 0.967
Residuals 156 1.352e+15 8.666e+12
---
Signif. codes: 0 '***' 0.001 '**' 0.01 '*' 0.05 '.' 0.1 ' ' 1
```

Figure 13. Response times for high and low data volume in first study

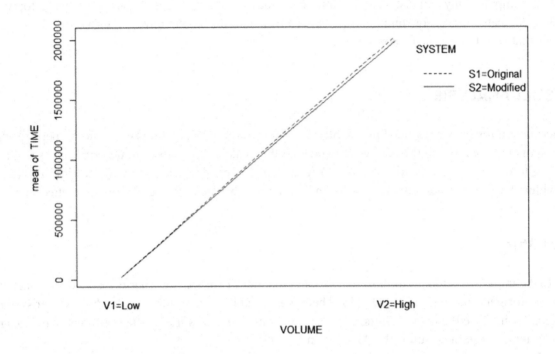

VOLUME

Box 2. ANOVA table for second study

```
Df Sum Sq Mean Sq F value Pr(>F)
VOLUME 1 2.092e+14 2.092e+14 15.897 0.000102 ***
TYPE 1 4.447e+12 4.447e+12 0.338 0.561837
VOLUME:TYPE 1 4.286e+12 4.286e+12 0.326 0.568977
Residuals 156 2.052e+15 1.316e+13
---
Signif. codes: 0 '***' 0.001 '**' 0.01 '*' 0.05 '.' 0.1 ' ' 1
```

In Box 2 it can be observed that the significance of the "Type of query" factor is low, while the "Volume" factor has a high significance value, then the later is the factor that affects the response times for each query. Next is the graphic generated by this experiment.

From Figure 14 it can be see that there is an increase of response times of about one third (1/3) in average, which doesn't represent a significant increase as the database size increased exponentially (from 11 MB of data to 111 MB of data). Given the fact that the data volume increased in exponentially, the ANOVA table considers the logarithm of response times. This is shown in Box 3.

In the ANOVA of Box 3 can be seen that the volume is still the factor with the highest significance value, and the query type has a very low significance value. This shows that the query type as a factor does not make a big difference in the response times.

Figure 14. Response times for fuzzy and classic queries in second study

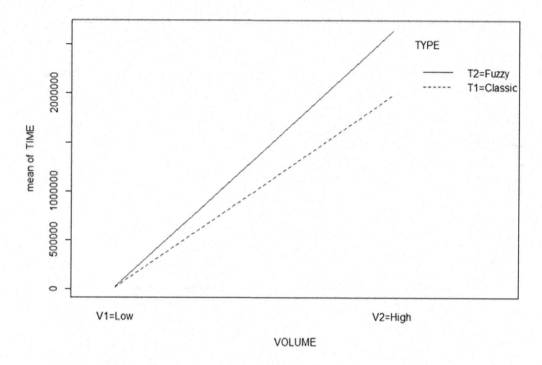

Box 3. ANOVA table for second study with logarithm of response times

```
 Df Sum Sq Mean Sq F value Pr(>F)
VOLUME 1 2.092e+14 2.092e+14 15.897 0.000102 ***
TYPE 1 4.447e+12 4.447e+12 0.338 0.561837
VOLUME:TYPE 1 4.286e+12 4.286e+12 0.326 0.568977
Residuals 156 2.052e+15 1.316e+13
---
Signif. codes: 0 '***' 0.001 '**' 0.01 '*' 0.05 '.' 0.1 ' ' 1
```

Now let analyze the graphic for this experiment that is shown in Figure 15.

In this new graphic can be seen that the fuzzy queries increase the response time for calculations starting from the low data volume. Even though the high data volume is 10 times bigger than the low data volume, can be observed that the difference in response times between classic and fuzzy queries for the high data volume doesn't increase in a significant way related to the increase in the volume data.

These results show that the performance is not affected in a significant way with the introduction of fuzzy terms in the queries, even without applying the derivation principle for the previously mentioned reasons.

In addition, it was decided to study which queries are affecting the average for each server. With this goal, it has been made a graphic with response times for each query with a low data volume, detailing the response time for each query being classic and with fuzzy terms included (Figure 16).

Figure 15. Logarithm response times for fuzzy and classic queries in second study

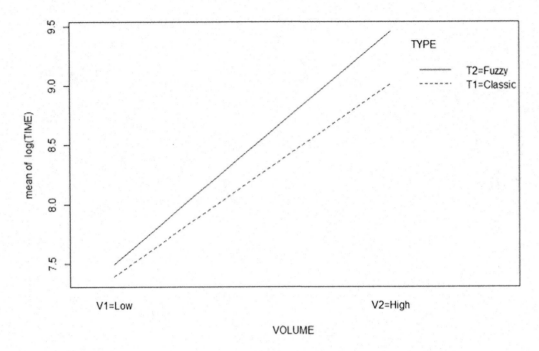

Figure 16. Detailed execution times for classic and fuzzy queries of second study, with low data volume

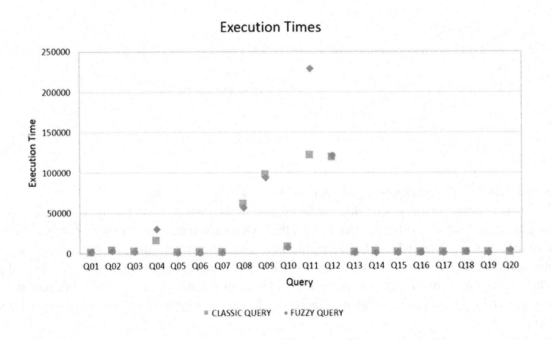

From this graphic can be seen that only Q04 and Q11 take additional response time for fuzzy queries. So, the decision was to analyze these two queries in order to understand this behavior.

The original Q4 query from XMark follows:

```
let $auction:= doc("auction.xml") return
    for $b in $auction/site/open_auctions/open_auction
        where
            some $pr1 in $b/bidder/personref
                        [@person = "person20"],
                $pr2 in $b/bidder/personref
                        [@person = "person51"]
            satisfies $pr1 << $pr2
        return <history>{$b/reserve/text()}</history>
```

The modified query (with fuzzy terms) is the following:

```
declare fuzzy predicate
 local:names($name as xs:string)
 extension (1.0, "person20");
declare fuzzy predicate
 local:names2($name as xs:string)
 extension (1.0, "person51");
let $auction:= doc("auction.xml") return
 for $b in $auction/site/open_auctions/open_auction
        where
            some $pr1 in $b/bidder/personref
                        [local:names(@person)],
                $pr2 in $b/bidder/personref
                        [local:names2(@person)]
        satisfies $pr1 << $pr2
        return <history>{$b/reserve/text()}</history>
```

In the original query the condition of the "where" clause tests equality over the attribute "person", while in the modified query it has to check two fuzzy predicates defined by extension for each datum that enters the clause. This generates additional calculation, which increases the response time for this query.

Now let analyze the Q11 query. The original Q11 query from XMark follows:

```
let $auction:= doc("auction.xml") return
    for $p in $auction/site/people/person
        let $l:=
            for $i in $auction/site/open_auctions
                    /open_auction/initial
                where $p/profile/@income
                    > 5000 * exactly-one($i/text())
```

```
        return $i
    return
        <items name="{$p/name/text()}">{count($l)}</items>
```

The modified query with Fuzzy Terms is:

```
declare fuzzy comparator
    local:muchGreater($x as xs:double, $y as xs:double)
    ($x - $y) trapezium(50, 100, "INF", "INF");
let $auction:= doc("auction.xml") return
    for $p in $auction/site/people/person
        let $l:=
            for $i in
                $auction/site/open_auctions/open_auction/initial
                where xs:truth(
                    (if (not(empty($p/profile/@income)))
                     then $p/profile/@income
                     else 0.0)
                        local:muchGreater
                        (5000 * exactly-one($i/text()))
                )
            return $i
    return
        <items name="{$p/name/text()}">{count($l)}</items>
```

In the "where" clause of the original query, a set of calculations and a simple "greater than" comparison is done. In the modified query the "where" clause uses a fuzzy comparison operator "muchGreather" instead of traditional ">". First argument of the comparison is a conditional expression used in order to avoid the empty, replacing it bay the value 0.0. The evaluation of the fuzzy comparators performs a subtraction of theirs arguments. A fuzzy trapezium function is applied to the result of the subtraction.

This explains the increase in the response times when the query was modified with fuzzy terms.

Now let's analyze what happens for a high data volume. Figure 17 is the detailed graphic for each query.

Once again, Q04 and Q11 are adding response time, just like in the low data volume case. In this case, also the Q12 query has some additional response time to be considered.

The original Q12 query from XMark follows:

```
let $auction:= doc("auction.xml") return
    for $p in $auction/site/people/person
        let $l:=
            for $i in $auction/site/open_auctions
                        /open_auction/initial
                where $p/profile/@income
                    > 5000 * exactly-one($i/text())
            return $i
```

Figure 17. Detailed execution times for classic and fuzzy queries of second study, with high data volume

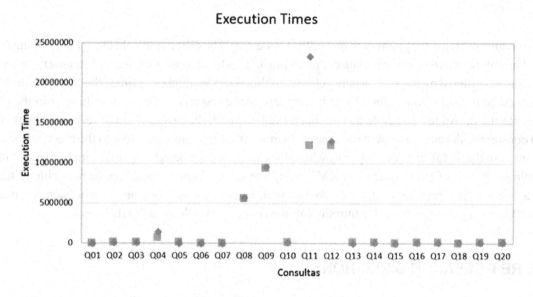

```
where $p/profile/@income > 50000
return <items person="{$p/profile/@income}">
        {count($l)}</items>
```

and the modified Q12 query with fuzzy terms:

```
declare fuzzy comparator
 local:muchGreater($x as xs:double, $y as xs:double)
 ($x - $y) trapezium(50, 100, "INF", "INF");
let $auction:= doc("auction.xml") return
 for $p in $auction/site/people/person
 let $l:=
 for $i in $auction/site/open_auctions
 /open_auction/initial
 where $p/profile/@income
 > 5000 * exactly-one($i/text())
 return $i
 where xs:truth(
 (if(not(empty($p/profile/@income)))
 then $p/profile/@income
 else 0.0)
 local:muchGreater
 (50000)
)
```

```
return <items person="{$p/profile/@income}">
{count($l)}</items>
```

The change in Q12 is very similar to that of the Q11 query. The difference is that in Q12 the change was applied in a more external "where" clause. Processing of this fuzzy condition analyzes a lower amount of results already filtered by the first "where" clause. In this way, the number of times that fuzzy terms have to be executed in Q12 is lower; therefore, the increase in the response time is not as high as in the Q11.

Despite the derivation principle has not been implemented, the increase in the response times is an added constant to the queries, and in most cases the response times are equivalent to the classic queries if there aren't multiple fuzzy terms in places where they must be calculated a significant number of times. This allows the use of fuzzy queries in XML using the Fuzzy XQuery language to be viable in terms of performance. This represents an acceptable computational cost for a business application and makes Fuzzy XQuery a good candidate for introducing the fuzzy terminology in XML Queries.

FUTURE RESEARCH DIRECTIONS

At present time, there are different existing XQuery engines. They might be extended for supporting fuzzy logic based features of Fuzzy XQuery in the same way that extension presented in this chapter. Here presented extension of XQuery engine was conceived with a high coupling architecture. It has the advantage of the best performance and scalability. Nevertheless, it has the difficult of source code intervention and lack of portability. It is a good idea to implement Fuzzy XQuery extension to existing query engines using a low coupling architecture. Since there are multiple benchmarks for XQuery, it is desirable to perform more experimentation with different benchmarks. Current definition of Fuzzy XQuery allows performing fuzzy queries on crisp data. In future works fuzzy data should be considered in order to provide more complete language. On the other hand, there are several query languages for XML data different to the standard XQuery. In near future it will be necessary to extend these languages in order to allow fuzzy querying.

CONCLUSION

Traditional database systems suffer of rigidity problem. They do not allow the expression of user preferences with linguistic natural terms whose boundaries are not perfectly defined. They assume data and queries to be perfect. XML documents databases and associated query languages are not the exception for this problem. According to several research works done in the frame of relational databases, fuzzy sets theory is the most accurate theoretical tool for solving this problem of database systems. In this sense, in a previous work, some authors defined Fuzzy XQuery. This query language for XML databases incorporates the application of fuzzy sets theory in querying. It is an extension of the W3C standard XQuery. Several XML native database systems implement XQuery. The idea in this chapter is to extend them in order to support Fuzzy XQuery. The main goal of this chapter was to show a high coupling implementation of Fuzzy XQuery. That is the development of an extension by means the intervention of source code. The extension was done into an open source XML DBMS name eXist-db. This extension technique could be used for other similar tools. This extended version supports the new xs:truth datatype that includes usual Boolean truth values true and false as well as numeric truth values in the real interval [0,1]. An automatic attribute named xml:truth is added to result of query expressions involving fuzzy terms, in order to store the corresponding satisfaction degree. Definition of those fuzzy terms is also supported by the presented extension, according to Fuzzy XQuery definition. Almost all XQuery querying expression were extended into eXist-db including the use of fuzzy logic based expressions that Fuzzy XQuery defines. Previous works had mainly focused in theoretical contributions to language definition, while work presented here deals with a real implementation. On the other hand, some researchers have reported also implementations of some fuzzy extensions to XML based systems. Main difference is the fact of using high coupling architecture in the solution presented here. Previous solutions involves reprocessing of results in order to evaluate fuzzy conditions, that is not necessary here. This chapter also presents a formal statistical performance analysis of extended fuzzy querying engine using the XMark benchmark and some user defined fuzzy term. The experimentation has shown that the extension of eXist-db preserves the usual performance for classic XQuery expressions evaluation. Also the evaluation of fuzzy queries gives a very reasonable behavior not much higher than regular query evaluation.

ACKNOWLEDGMENT

Thanks for renewing our strength: *"Have you not known? Have you not heard? The everlasting God, the Lord, The Creator of the ends of the earth, Neither faints nor is weary. His understanding is unsearchable. He gives power to the weak, And to those who have no might He increases strength. Even the youths shall faint and be weary, And the young men shall utterly fall, But those who wait on the Lord Shall renew their strength; They shall mount up with wings like eagles, They shall run and not be weary, They shall walk and not faint."* (Isaiah 40:28-31, New King James Version)

REFERENCES

Base X. Team. (2014). *BaseX. The XML Database: As flexible as your data*. Retrieved September 4, 2014, from http://basex.org/

Bordogna, G., & Psaila, G. (2008). Customizable Flexible Querying Classic Relational Databases. In J. Galindo (Ed.), *Handbook of Research on Fuzzy Information Processing in Databases* (pp. 189–215). Hershey, PA: Information Science. doi:10.4018/978-1-59904-853-6.ch008

Buche, P., Dibie-Barthèlemy, J., & Wattez, F. (2006). Approximate querying of XML fuzzy data. Flexible Query Answering Systems. *Lecture Notes in Computer Science*, *4027*, 26–38. doi:10.1007/11766254_3

Calmès, M., Prade, H., & Sedes, F. (2007, July). Flexible querying of semistructured data: A fuzzy-set based approach. *International Journal of Intelligent Systems*, *22*(7), 723–737. doi:10.1002/int.20225

Campi, A., Damiani, E., Guinea, S., Marrara, S., Pasi, G., & Spoletini, P. (2009). A Fuzzy Extension of the XPath Query Language. *Journal of Intelligent Information Systems*, *33*(3), 285–305. doi:10.1007/s10844-008-0066-3

CWI. (2009). *XMark - An XML benchmark project*. Retrieved October 22, 2014, from http://www.xml-benchmark.org/

eXist Solutions. (2011). *eXist-db (open source native XML database)*. Retrieved October 1, 2014, from http://exist.sourceforge.net/

Gaurav, A., & Alhajj, R. (2006). Incorporating fuzziness in XML and mapping fuzzy relational data into fuzzy XML. In *Proceedings of the 2006 ACM Symposium on Applied Computing*. doi:10.1145/1141277.1141386

Goncalves, M., & Tineo, L. (2007). A new step towards Flexible XQuery. *Revista Avances en Sistemas e Informática, 4*(3).

Goncalves, M., & Tineo, L. (2010). Fuzzy XQuery. In *Soft computing in XML data management: intelligent systems from decision to data mining, web intelligence and computer vision* (pp. 133–166). Springer. doi:10.1007/978-3-642-14010-5_6

Jin, Y., & Veerappan, S. (2010). A fuzzy XML database system: Data storage and query processing. In *Proceedings of International Conference on Information Reuse and Integration*. doi:10.1109/IRI.2010.5558919

Ma, Z. M., Liu, J., & Yan, L. (2010). Fuzzy data modeling and algebraic operations in XML. *International Journal of Intelligent Systems, 25*(9), 925–947.

Panic, G., Rackovic, M., & Škrbic, S. (2014). Fuzzy XML and prioritized fuzzy XQuery with implementation. *Journal of Intelligent & Fuzzy Systems, 26*, 303–316.

Parr, T. (2013). *The Definitive ANTLR 4 Reference* (2nd ed.). Pragmatic Bookshelf.

Project, R. (2014). *The R Project for Statistical Computing*. Retrieved October 15, 2014, from http://www.r-project.org/

Raj, J. (1991). *The art of computer systems performance*. Academic Press.

Schmidt, A. (2003). *XMark — An XML Benchmark Project*. Retrieved October 29, 2014, from http://www.ins.cwi.nl/projects/xmark/

Schmidt, A., Waas, F., Kersten, M., Carey, M. J., Manolescu, I., & Busse, R. (2002). XMark: a benchmark for XML data management. In *Proceedings of the 28th international conference on Very Large Data Bases* (VLDB '02). VLDB Endowment. doi:10.1016/B978-155860869-6/50096-2

Siegel, E., & Retter, A. (2014). eXist: A NoSQL Document Database and Application Platform. O'Reilly Media, Inc.

Thomsom, E. J., & Radhamani, G. (2009). *Fuzzy Logic based XQuery Operations for Native XML Database Systems*. International Journal Database Theory and Application.

Thomsom E.J. & Radhamani, G. (2011). Information retrieval using xquery processing techniques. *International Journal of Database Management Systems*.

Timarán, R. (2001). Arquitecturas de integración del proceso de descubrimiento de conocimiento con sistemas de gestión de bases de datos: un estado del arte. In *Ingeniería y competitividad, volumen 2.* Springer.

Ueng, P. S. (2012). Implementing XQuery fuzzy extensions using a native XML database. In *Proceedings of International Symposium on Computational Intelligence and Informatics*, (pp. 305-309). doi:10.1109/CINTI.2012.6496780

W3C. (2008). *Extensible Markup Language (XML) 1.0* (5th ed.). Retrieved January 26, 2015 from: http://www.w3.org/TR/REC-xml/

W3C. (2010). *XQuery 1.0: An XML Query Language* (2nd ed.). Retrieved January 26, 2015 from: http://www.w3.org/TR/xquery/

W3C. (2014). *XML Path Language (XPath) 3.0.* Retrieved January 26, 2015 from: http://www.w3.org/TR/xpath-30

Zadeh, L. A. (1965). Fuzzy sets. *Information and Control, 8*(3), 338–353. doi:10.1016/S0019-9958(65)90241-X

KEY TERMS AND DEFINITIONS

ANOVA: Analysis Of Variance. It is a collection of statistics models and their associated procedures.
Benchmark: technique used to measure the performance of a system or component of the system.
DBMS: Database Management System.
eXist-db: DataBase Management System in XML.
Fuzzy XQuery: XQuery Fuzzy Extension.
Java: Object Oriented Programming Language.
Parser: Tool for processing a string of symbols according to a formal grammar.
XML: Extensible Markup Language, it's a standard language proposed by W3C.
XQuery: Query Language over XML (XML Query Language).
XMark: XQuery's benchmark, which contents queries and a database generator with a desired size.

APPENDIX: FUZZY QUERIES USED IN EXPERIMENTS

The following queries were designed modifying XMark queries adding fuzzy terms in order to test several components of the proposed implementation, measuring response times in each case to analyze performance with multiple studies.

Q1: Return the name of the person with ID `person0`.

```
declare fuzzy predicate
 local:names($name as xs:string)
 extension (1.0, "person0");
let $auction:= doc("auction.xml") return
 for $b in $auction/site/people/person[local:names(@id)]
 return $b/name/text()
```

Q2: Return the truth degree about more or less for initial increases of all open auctions.

```
declare fuzzy predicate
 local:moreorless($mol as xs:double)
 trapezium (5.0,25.0,45.0,60.0);
let $auction:= doc("auction.xml") return
 for $b in $auction/site/open_auctions/open_auction
 return
 <increase>{
 if (xs:double($b/bidder[1]/increase/text())
 > 0.0)
 then
 local:moreorless
 (xs:double($b/bidder[1]/increase/text()))
 else
 local:moreorless(0.0)
 }</increase>
```

Q3: Return the IDs of all open auctions whose current increase is at least twice as high as the initial increase. And a truth degree about if the first increase is more or less than the second one.

```
declare fuzzy comparator
 local:mlt($x as xs:double, $y as xs:double)
 ($y - $x) trapezium(5, 15, 25, 30);
let $auction:= doc("auction.xml") return
 for $b in $auction/site/open_auctions/open_auction
```

```
where zero-or-one($b/bidder[1]/increase/text()) * 2
<= $b/bidder[last()]/increase/text()
return
<increase
first="{$b/bidder[1]/increase/text()}"
last="{$b/bidder[last()]/increase/text()}"
truth="{($b/bidder[1]/increase/text())
local:mlt
($b/bidder[last()]/increase/text())}"
/>
```

Q4: List the reserves of those open auctions where a certain person issued a bid before another person.

```
declare fuzzy predicate
 local:names($name as xs:string)
 extension (1.0, "person20");
declare fuzzy predicate
 local:names2($name as xs:string)
 extension (1.0, "person51");
let $auction:= doc("auction.xml") return
 for $b in $auction/site/open_auctions/open_auction
 where
 some $pr1 in
 $b/bidder/personref[local:names(@person)],
 $pr2 in
 $b/bidder/personref[local:names2(@person)]
 satisfies $pr1 << $pr2
 return <history>{$b/reserve/text()}</history>
```

Q5: How many sold items cost "much more" than 40?

```
declare fuzzy comparator
 local:muchMore($x as xs:double, $y as xs:double)
 ($x - $y) trapezium(0, 100, "INF", "INF");
let $auction:= doc("auction.xml") return
 count(
 for $i in
 $auction/site/closed_auctions/closed_auction
 where $i/price/text() local:muchMore 40
 return $i/price
 )
```

Q6: How many items are listed on all continents? And tells if it is a high quantity.

```
declare fuzzy predicate
 local:high($quantity as xs:double)
 trapezium (0,100,"INF","INF");
let $auction:= doc("auction.xml") return
 for $b in $auction//site/regions return
 local:high(count($b//item))
```

Q7: Tell us if a description, annotation or email address has a high count.

```
declare fuzzy predicate
 local:high($number as xs:decimal) as xs:truth
 trapezium (1000,6000,"INF","INF");
let $auction:= doc("auction.xml") return
 for $p in $auction/site
 return
 local:high(count($p//description)) or
 local:high(count($p//annotation)) or
 local:high(count($p//emailaddress))
```

Q8: List the names of persons and if they bought much items (joins person, closed_auction).

```
declare fuzzy predicate
 local:much($quantity as xs:int)
 extension (0.1, 0, 0.25, 1, 0.75, 2, 1.0, 3, 0.75, 4);
let $auction:= doc("auction.xml") return
 for $p in $auction/site/people/person
 let $a:=
 for $t in
 $auction/site/closed_auctions/closed_auction
 where $t/buyer/@person = $p/@id
 return $t
 return <item person="{$p/name/text()}">
 {local:much(count($a))}</item>
```

Q9: List how long is the name of each person and the names of the items they bought in Europe. (joins person, closed_auction, item)

```
declare fuzzy predicate
 local:large($legnth as xs:int) as xs:truth
 trapezium (1.0, 70.0, "INF", "INF");
let $auction:= doc("auction.xml") return
```

```
let $ca:= $auction/site/closed_auctions/closed_auction
return
let
$ei:= $auction/site/regions/europe/item
for $p in $auction/site/people/person
let $a:=
for $t in $ca
where $p/@id = $t/buyer/@person
return
let $n:= for $t2 in $ei
where $t/itemref/@item = $t2/@id return $t2
return <item>{$n/name/text()}</item>
return
<person truth="{local:large
(string-length($p/name/text()))}">{$a}</person>
```

Q10: List all persons according to their interest; use French markup in the result. And tells if their revenue is high

```
declare fuzzy predicate
 local:high($revenue as xs:double)
 trapezium (3000.0,90000.0,"INF","INF");
declare fuzzy modifier
 local:really($revenueTruth as xs:truth)
 power(2);
let $auction:= doc("auction.xml") return
 for $i in
 distinct-values
 ($auction/site/people/person
 /profile/interest/@category)
let $p:=
 for $t in $auction/site/people/person
 where $t/profile/interest/@category = $i
 return
 <personne>
 <statistiques>
 <sexe>{$t/profile/gender/text()}</sexe>
 <age>{$t/profile/age/text()}</age>
 <education>
 {$t/profile/education/text()}
 </education>
 <revenu>
 {fn:data($t/profile/@income)}
```

```
</revenu>
<revenu-high>
{local:really
local:high
(fn:data($t/profile/@income))}
</revenu-high>
</statistiques>
<coordonnees>
<nom>{$t/name/text()}</nom>
<rue>{$t/address/street/text()}</rue>
<ville>{$t/address/city/text()}</ville>
<pays>{$t/address/country/text()}</pays>
<reseau>
<courrier>
{$t/emailaddress/text()}
</courrier>
<pagePerso>
{$t/homepage/text()}</pagePerso>
</reseau>
</coordonnees>
<cartePaiement>
{$t/creditcard/text()}
</cartePaiement>
</personne>
return <categorie>{<id>{$i}</id>, $p}</categorie>
```

Q11: For each person, list the number of items currently on sale whose price does not exceed greatly 0.02% of the person's income.

```
declare fuzzy comparator
    local:muchGreater($x as xs:double, $y as xs:double)
    ($x - $y) trapezium(50, 100, "INF", "INF");
let $auction:= doc("auction.xml") return
    for $p in $auction/site/people/person
        let $l:=
          for $i in
              $auction/site/open_auctions/open_auction/initial
            where xs:truth(
                  (if (not(empty($p/profile/@income)))
                    then $p/profile/@income
                    else 0.0)
                local:muchGreater
                  (5000 * exactly-one($i/text()))
```

```
        )
          return $i
      return
        <items name="{$p/name/text()}">{count($l)}</items>
```

Q12: For each richer-than-average person, list the number of items currently on sale whose price does not exceed greatly 0.02% of the person's income.

```
declare fuzzy comparator
 local:muchGreater($x as xs:double, $y as xs:double)
 ($x - $y) trapezium(50, 100, "INF", "INF");
let $auction:= doc("auction.xml") return
 for $p in $auction/site/people/person
 let $l:=
 for $i in $auction/site/open_auctions
 /open_auction/initial
 where $p/profile/@income
 > 5000 * exactly-one($i/text())
 return $i
 where xs:truth(
 (if(not(empty($p/profile/@income)))
 then $p/profile/@income
 else 0.0)
 local:muchGreater
 (50000)
)
 return <items person="{$p/profile/@income}">
 {count($l)}</items>
```

Q13: List the name of all items in which a "large" name registered in Australia along with their descriptions.

```
declare fuzzy predicate
 local:nameSize($size as xs:int)
 extension (0.3, 5.0, 0.8, 6.0, 0.6, 7.0,
 0.95, 9.0, 1.0, 10.0, 1.0, 15.0);
let $auction:= doc("auction.xml") return
 for $i in $auction/site/regions/australia/item
 return
 $i/name[local:nameSize
 (string-length($i/name/text()))
 ][threshold 0.5][xs:truth(0.8)]
```

Q14: Return the names of certain items whose description contains the word `gold'.

```
declare fuzzy predicate
 local:names($name as xs:string)
 extension (0.5, "condemn ", 0.6, "shoot ",
 1.0, "murther ", 0.9, "whisper ",
 0.1, "gets ", 0.3, "sing ",
 0.7, "editions ", 1.0, "approves ");
let $auction:= doc("auction.xml") return
 for $i in $auction/site//item
 where contains(string(exactly-one($i/description)),
 "gold")
 return $i/name[local:names($i/name/text())]
```

Q15: Print the large keywords in emphasis in annotations of closed auctions. For short ones prints their length.

```
declare fuzzy predicate
 local:large($length as xs:int)
 trapezium (0.0, 50.0, 100.0, 300.0);
let $auction:= doc("auction.xml") return
 for $a in $auction/site/closed_auctions/closed_auction
 /annotation/description/parlist/listitem
 /parlist/listitem/text/emph/keyword/text()
 return
 if (local:large(string-length($a)) threshold 0.5)
 then <text>{$a}</text>
 else <largo>{string-length($a)}</largo>
```

Q16: Return the IDs of those auctions that have one or more keywords in emphasis. (cf. Q15) and indicates with truth attribute if the price of the auction is cheap

```
declare fuzzy predicate
 local:cheap($price as xs:double)
 trapezium ("-INF",50.0,70.0,200.0);
let $auction:= doc("auction.xml") return
 for $a in $auction/site/closed_auctions/closed_auction
 where not(empty($a/annotation/description/parlist
 /listitem/parlist/listitem/text
 /emph/keyword/text()))
 return <person id="{$a/seller/@person}"/>
 [local:cheap($a/price/text())]
```

Q17: Which persons have a short homepage or do not have a homepage?

```
declare fuzzy predicate
 local:short($length as xs:double)
 trapezium (0.0,0.0,1.0,5.0);
let $auction:= doc("auction.xml") return
 for $p in $auction/site/people/person
 where local:short(string-length($p/homepage/text()))
 return <person name="{$p/name/text()}"/>
```

Q18: Convert the currency of the reserve of all open auctions with "high quantity" to another currency.

```
declare namespace local = "http://www.foobar.org";
declare function
 local:convert($v as xs:decimal?) as xs:decimal?
 {
 2.20371 * $v (: convert Dfl to Euro:)
 };
declare fuzzy predicate
 local:high($quantity as xs:int)
 trapezium (0.0,3.0,"INF","INF");
let $auction:= doc("auction.xml") return
 for $i in $auction/site/open_auctions/open_auction
 [local:high(quantity)]
 return local:convert(zero-or-one($i/reserve))
```

Q19: Give an alphabetically ordered list of certain items according to their category along with their location.

```
declare fuzzy predicate
 local:category2($category as xs:string)
 extension (1.0, "category34", 0.6, "category26",
 0.25, "category51", 0.7, "category42");
let $auction:= doc("auction.xml") return
 for $b in $auction/site/regions//item
 let $k:= $b/name/text()
 order by zero-or-one($b/location)
 ascending empty greatest
 return <item name="{$k}">{$b/location/text()}</item>
 [local:category2($b/incategory[1]/@category)]
```

Q20: Group customers by their income and output the cardinality of each group defined in a fuzzy way.

```
declare fuzzy predicate
 local:category($x as xs:double) as xs:truth
 trapezium(10000, 150000, "INF","INF");
let $auction:= doc("auction.xml") return
 <result>
 <preferred>
 {count($auction/site/people/person/profile
 [local:category(xs:double(@income))]
 [threshold 0.75])}
 </preferred>
 <standard>
 {count($auction/site/people/person/profile
 [@income < 100000]
 [local:category(xs:double(@income))]
 [threshold 0.5])}
 </standard>
 <challenge>
 {count($auction/site/people/person/profile
 [@income < 30000]
 [local:category(xs:double(@income))]
 [threshold 0.1])}
 </challenge>
 <na>
 {count(
 for $p in $auction/site/people/person
 where empty($p/profile/@income)
 return $p
 )}
 </na>
</result>
```

Chapter 7
Probabilistic Ranking Method of XML Fuzzy Query Results

Wei Yan
Liaoning University, China

ABSTRACT

Fuzzy query processing for XML database systems is an important issue. Based on the fuzzy set theory, XML fuzzy query can be expressed exploiting fuzzy predicates. To deal with the ranking problem of XML fuzzy query results, this chapter proposes a novel ranking approach. Firstly, according to the workload of XML documents, this chapter speculates how much the users care about each attribute node and assign a corresponding weight to it. Then, a membership degree ranking method, which ranks the fuzzy query results according to corresponding membership degree, is presented. Furthermore, this chapter proposes the probabilistic ranking method, which improves the PIR method. The improved probabilistic ranking method considers the relevance between the nodes specified by fuzzy query and the nodes unspecified by fuzzy query. Finally, top-k ranking algorithm of XML fuzzy query results is presented. The efficiency and effectiveness of the approach are also demonstrated by experimental results.

INTRODUCTION

With the rapid development of the World Wide Web, the XML data has been recognized as a standard for data representation and transmission over the Internet. Many data have been produced and transformed into the XML data format, especially in scientific data and Web logs the information is kept in XML. Several query languages have been proposed until XPath and XQuery received a general consensus, becoming the standard query language. Traditional query processing method of XML data requires users to specify the precise queries, and the query processing systems return precise query results to the users. However, in many cases, the users can not express their query intentions accurately. Therefore, the traditional XML query processing systems lack flexibility to the users. The users would like to issue fuzzy query with fuzzy predicates, then XML database system is more convenient to the users.

DOI: 10.4018/978-1-4666-8767-7.ch007

For example, published information of the books is stored in an XML document. The user needs to search the books that were published in year around 2012 as well as the price is less than $60. In the XML document, the user may request the following fuzzy query:

```
//book[{@year close to 2012}][{@price at most 60}]
```

where, fuzzy predicates "close to" and "at most" express users' fuzzy query intension.

In the practical application, the users don't know exactly what they are looking for. When searching the XML document, the users often don't know the XML Schema in detail. The XML data format has the structure and content information. The same data sometimes can be described using different structure. Therefore, the users' query intensions are usually fuzzy or imprecise. How to extend XML query language as well as provide some flexibility to the users is an important issue. The XPath query language can select XML data nodes effectively through the expression of query traversal, then it able to formulate a query expression that accurately expresses users' query intensions. This chapter uses fuzzy predicates to expend XPath query language, to make the fuzzy query expression to express users' fuzzy query intension. Moreover, the users may propose the fuzzy query with fuzzy terms or fuzzy relations. Thus, the extensional fuzzy query expression can help users to improve their interaction with system in order to obtain more query results.

After fuzzy query of XML data, another problem faced by the users will be that how to use efficient ranking method to rank the fuzzy query results. This chapter uses the membership ranking method to rank the fuzzy query results according to their membership degree. For the nodes with the same membership degree, each node specified by fuzzy query is assigned a score according to its desirableness to the user. This chapter also considers the workload information of the XML documents, which is a log of past users' queries. Based on the workload, the chapter speculates how much the user cares about each node and assigns a corresponding weight to the attribute nodes according to their importance.

This chapter presents an automatic estimative approach via workload as well as data analysis to resolve above problem. Fuzzy query and probabilistic ranking (FQPR) method developed the ranking functions, which are based on probabilistic information retrieval (PIR) model (Chaudhuri *et al.* 2004, 2006). The architecture of FQPR ranking model has a pre-processing component that collects workload statistics to determine the appropriate ranking scores. The extracted ranking scores are materialized in an intermediate knowledge representation layer, to be used later by a query processing component for ranking the fuzzy query results. Although FQPR ranking approach derives these quantities automatically, the architecture allows users or domain experts to tune these quantities further. Therefore, FQPR ranking model may customize the ranking functions for different applications.

The objectives of the chapter are summarized as follows:

- This chapter proposes an XML fuzzy query method, and use fuzzy predicates to expand XPath query language.
- In order to resolve the raking problem of fuzzy query results, the chapter proposes a novel membership degree ranking method, which can rank the fuzzy query results according to their membership degree.
- Based on workload statistics, the chapter presents probabilistic ranking method, which considers the relevance between the nodes specified by fuzzy query and the nodes unspecified by fuzzy query.

BACKGROUND

Related Works

In the real world applications, user's query intension is often vague or ambiguous. Effects are mainly made in processing the XML fuzzy query. Campi *et al.* (2006) presented a fuzzy querying framework FXPath, which can use fuzzy predicates to express fuzzy query in XML. The authors also introduced the deep-similar function, which provided the similarity degree between two XML trees. Based on this research work, this chapter proposes a novel ranking approach which ranks the fuzzy query results according to corresponding membership degree. For the fuzzy query results with the same membership degree, this chapter proposes the FQPR method which improves the PIR method to rank fuzzy query results. Chan *et al.* (2008) described the design and implementation of a fuzzy nested querying system for XML data. This prototype system used graphical interface that allows the user to apply fuzziness to their XML searches. The authors of Buche (2006) and Damiani (2007) in their research introduced flexibility into the query processing of the XML data, where the flexibility relies on fuzzy queries and query rewriting which consist in generating a set of approximate queries from an original query. Approximate structure and content matching is supported via extension to standard XPath query syntax.

In recent years, the research of XML fuzzy query received extensive attention of academia. Seto *et al.* (2009) in their research discussed fuzzy query model for XML documents, presented a system with a query builder which generates XQuery statements that support for both strict and fuzzy qualifiers. Goncalves and Tineo (2010) showed in their previous work that a fuzzy set based extension to XQuery which allows user to express fuzzy query on XML documents. The fuzzy extension includes the built-in datatype xs:truth for representing truth degrees as well as the xml:truth attribute for handing satisfaction degrees in fuzzy query expressions of fuzzy XQuery. Alzebdi *et al.* (2011) proposed an approach of using intuitionistic fuzzy trees to achieve approximate XML query matching, making the query result include not just the XML data trees that exactly match the query, but also the ones that partially match it. Ma *et al.* (2011) introduced a novel fuzzy labeling scheme, which makes it possible to describe imprecise and uncertain data and to capture the structural information in fuzzy xml documents. Then, the authors introduced Einstein operator, which can evaluate membership information. Furthermore, the authors proposed an effective algorithm to match a twig pattern query with the AND/OR-logic in fuzzy XML. Liu *et al.* (2013) showed in their work that the methodology of storing and querying fuzzy XML data in relational databases. The authors presented a method of no schema information to shred fuzzy XML data into relational data. On this basis, the authors presented a generic approach to translate path expression queries into SQL for processing XML queries. Panic *et al.* (2014) expanded XQuery syntax with fuzzy values and included priorities and thresholds in fuzzy XQuery extension. The authors developed a tool for working with XML, XSD and DTD documents and prioritized fuzzy XQuery extension queries.

Another related area of work is ranking. In the database world, automatic ranking techniques for the results of structured queries have been recently proposed Su *et al.* (2006). In XML world, Schlieder *et al.* (2002) presented a retrieval technique that adopts the similarity measure of the vector space model, incorporates the document structure, and supports structured queries. Kotsakis *et al.* (2006) showed in their previous work that a method of ranking XML documents by employing proximity measures and the concept of editing distance between terms or XML paths. Fazzinga *et al.* (2009) investigated the problem of top-k fuzzy XPath querying, proposed a query language and its associated semantics, and discussed query evaluation.

There has been work on cooperative query answering which is related to this issue. Liu *et al.* (2007) presented a cooperative XML (CoXML) system that provides user-specific approximate query answering. The key features of the system include a query relaxation language that allows users to specify approximate search conditions, and a relaxation index structure for systematic query relaxation, and both content and structure similarity metrics for evaluating the relevancies of approximate answers. Halder *et al.* (2011) proposed a cooperative query answering scheme based on the abstract interpretation framework.

Fuzzy Set Theory

Fuzzy data is originally described as fuzzy set by Zadeh (1978). Let U be a universe of discourse. A fuzzy value on U is characterized by a fuzzy set F in U. A membership function $\mu_F: U \to [0, 1]$ is defined for the fuzzy set F, where $\mu_F(u)$, for each $u \in U$ denotes the membership degree of u in the fuzzy set F. Thus the fuzzy set F is described as follows: $F = \{\mu_F(u_1)/u_1, \mu_F(u_2)/u_2, ..., \mu_F(u_n)/u_n\}$. When U is an infinite set, then the fuzzy set F can be represented by $F = \int_{u \in U} \mu_F(u) / u$.

Let A and B be fuzzy set on the same universe of discourse U with the membership function μ_A and μ_B, respectively.

Definition 1 [Union]: The union of fuzzy set A and B, denoted $A \cup B$, is a fuzzy set on U with the membership function $\mu_{A \cup B}: U \to [0, 1]$, where $\forall u \in U, \mu_{A \cup B}(u) = \max(\mu_A(u), \mu_B(u))$.

Definition 2 [Intersection]: The intersection of fuzzy set A and B, denoted $A \cap B$, is a fuzzy set on U with the membership function $\mu_{A \cap B}: U \to [0, 1]$, where $\forall u \in U, \mu_{A \cap B}(u) = \min(\mu_A(u), \mu_B(u))$.

Definition 3 [Complementation]: The complementation of fuzzy set A, denoted by $\bar{A}$, is a fuzzy set on U with the membership function $\mu_{\bar{A}}: U \to [0, 1]$, where $\forall u \in U, \mu_{\bar{A}}(u) = 1 - \mu_A(u)$.

Definition 4: A fuzzy set F of the universe of discourse U is convex if and only if for all u_1, u_2 in $U, \mu_F(\lambda u_1 + (1-\lambda)u_2) \geq \min(\mu_F(u_1), \mu_F(u_2))$, where $\lambda \in [0, 1]$.

Definition 5: A fuzzy set F of the universe of discourse U is called a normal fuzzy set if $\exists u \in U, \mu_F(u) = 1$.

Definition 6: A fuzzy number is a fuzzy subset in the universe of discourse U that is both convex and normal.

Now several notions related to fuzzy number are discussed. Let U be a universe of discourse and F a fuzzy number in U with the membership function $\mu_F: U \to [0, 1]$.

Definition 7 [Support]: The set of the elements that have non-zero membership degree in F is called the support of F, denoted by $supp(F) = \{u | u \in U$ and $\mu_F(u) > 0\}$.

Definition 8 [Kernel]: The set of the elements that completely belong to F is called the kernel of F, denoted by $ker(F) = \{u | u \in U$ and $\mu_F(u) = 1\}$.

Definition 9 [α-Cut]: The set of the elements which membership degrees in F are greater than (greater than or equal to) α, where $0 \leq \alpha < 1$ $(0 < \alpha \leq 1)$, is called the strong (weak) α-cut of F, respectively, denoted by

$$F_{\alpha+} = \{u \mid u \in U \text{ and } \mu_F(u) > \alpha\}$$
$$F_{\alpha} = \{u \mid u \in U \text{ and } \mu_F(u) \geq \alpha\}$$

(1)

Fuzzy Basic Conditions

In the modern databases, the query processing relies on three-valued logic, which limits results to true, false and maybe, and hereby suffers from a lack of flexibility to query. A flexible query allows imprecise conditions inside queries when the user can not define his/her needs in a definite way, or when a number of responses are desired and therefore a margin is allowed to interpret the query.

The query condition is formed through combining the basic (simple) condition $A \theta Y$ as operands with operators *not*, *and*, and *or*, where A is an attribute of the relations, Y is either an attribute of the relations or a literal, and $\theta \in \{>, <, =, \neq, \geq, \leq, between, not between, in, not in, like, not like\}$. Note that if θ is the operator *between* (*not between*), $A \theta Y$ has the format of "*A between* (*not between*) Y_1 *AND* Y_2*". Since the select condition consists of the basic condition $A \theta Y$, this chapter only focuses on fuzzy basic condition in the following discussion.

Fuzzy Terms as Operands

Three kinds of fuzzy terms can be identified: simple fuzzy term, composite fuzzy term, and compound fuzzy term.

Definition 10 [Simple Fuzzy Term]: A simple fuzzy term such as "*young*" or "*tall*" is defined by a fuzzy number with membership function (Chen & Jong, 1997).

Definition 11 [Composite Fuzzy Term]: A composite fuzzy term such as "*very young*" or "*more or less tall*" is described by a fuzzy number with membership function (Zadeh, 1972). Note that is membership function is not defined but computed through the membership function of the corresponding simple fuzzy term. In order to compute the membership function of composite fuzzy term, some semantic rules should be used. Let F is a simple fuzzy term represented by a fuzzy number in the universe of discourse U and its membership function is $\mu_F: U \to [0, 1]$, then this section has the following rules.

Concentration rule:

$$\mu_{very\ F}(u) = (\mu_F(u))^2$$

More generally,

$$\mu_{very\ very...very\ F}(u) = (\mu_F(u))^{2\times(times\ of\ very)}$$

Dilation rule:

$$\mu_{\text{more or less F}}(u) = \left(\mu_F(u)\right)^{1/2}$$

Definition 12 [Compound Fuzzy Term]: A compound fuzzy term such as "*young* ∪ *very young*" is represented by simple fuzzy terms or composite fuzzy terms connected by union (∪), intersection (∩) or complementation connectors.

Using the fuzzy terms above and traditional operators such as >, <, ≠, ≥, ≤, *between*, and *not between*, the fuzzy query condition with fuzzy operands, which has the form $A \, \theta \, Y$, is formed. Here Y is a fuzzy terms given above as the operands.

Fuzzy Relations as Operators

Now consider fuzzy relations as operators and crisp values as operands. For $A \, \tilde{\theta} \, Y$, where A is an attribute, $\tilde{\theta}$ is a fuzzy relation, and Y is a crisp value, $\tilde{\theta} \, Y$ is a fuzzy number. There are many kinds of fuzzy relations as operators. This section will mainly discuss three types of fuzzy relations only in this chapter, which are "*close to (around)*", "*at least*", and "*at most*".

Firstly, let's focus on fuzzy relation "*close to (around)*". According to the work of Chen *et al.* (1997), the membership function of the fuzzy number "*close to Y (around Y)*" on the universe of discourse can be defined by

$$\mu_{close\ to\ Y}(u) = \frac{1}{1 + \left[\dfrac{u - Y}{\beta}\right]^2} \tag{2}$$

It should be noted that the fuzzy number above is a simple fuzzy term. Based on it, this chapter has the following composite fuzzy terms: "*very close to Y*", "*very very ... very close to Y*", and "*more or less close to Y*", which membership functions can be defined as

$$\mu_{very\ close\ to\ Y}(u) = \left(\mu_{close\ to\ Y}(u)\right)^2$$

$$\mu_{very\ very...very\ close\ to\ Y}(u) = \left(\mu_{close\ to\ Y}(u)\right)^{2\times(times\ of\ very)}$$

$$\mu_{more\ or\ less\ close\ to\ Y}(u) = \left(\mu_{close\ to\ Y}(u)\right)^{1/2}$$

In addition, based on fuzzy number "*close to Y*", a compound fuzzy term "*not close to Y*" can be defined. Its membership function is as follows:

$$\mu_{not\ close\ to\ Y}(u) = 1 - \mu_{close\ to\ Y}(u)$$

Second, let's focus on fuzzy relation "*at least*". The membership function of the fuzzy number "*at least Y*" on the universe of discourse can be defined by

$$\mu_{at\ least\ Y}(u) = \begin{cases} 0 & , \quad u \le \omega \\ \dfrac{u - \omega}{Y - \omega} & , \quad \omega < u < Y \\ 1 & , \quad u \ge Y \end{cases} \tag{3}$$

Based on fuzzy number "*at least Y*", a compound fuzzy term "*not at least Y*" can be defined. Its membership function is as follows:

$$\mu_{not\ at\ least\ Y}(u) = 1 - \mu_{at\ least\ Y}(u)$$

Finally, let's focus on fuzzy relation "*at most*". The membership function of the fuzzy number "*at most Y*" on the universe of discourse can be defined by

$$\mu_{at\ most\ Y}(u) = \begin{cases} 1 & , \quad u \le Y \\ \dfrac{\delta - u}{\delta - Y} & , \quad Y < u < \delta \\ 0 & , \quad u \ge \delta \end{cases} \tag{4}$$

Based on fuzzy number "*at most Y*", a compound fuzzy term "*not at most Y*" can be defined. Its membership function is as follows:

$$\mu_{not\ at\ most\ Y}(u) = 1 - \mu_{at\ most\ Y}(u)$$

The fuzzy relations "*close to*", "*not close to*", "*at least*", "*at most*", "*not at least*", and "*not at most*" can be viewed as "*fuzzy equal to*", "*fuzzy not equal to*", "*fuzzy greater than and equal to*", "*fuzzy less than and equal to*", "*fuzzy greater than*", and "*fuzzy less than*", respectively. Using these fuzzy relations and crisp values, the fuzzy query condition with fuzzy operators, is formed.

XML FUZZY QUERY MODEL

This chapter models an XML document as an ordered, labeled tree where each element (attribute) is represented as a node and each element-to-subelement (or element-to-attribute) relationship is represented as an edge between the corresponding nodes. This chapter represents each node as a triple <*id*, *label*, *text>*, where *id* uniquely identifies the node, *label* is the name of the corresponding element or attribute, and *text* is the corresponding element's textual content or attribute's value. The *text* is optional because not every element contains textual content.

In order to satisfy users' fuzzy query intension, this chapter uses fuzzy predicates (*close to, at most, at least*) to extend XPath query language. One of the typical features of XML data is the difference between content and structure. As an example, this section considers the two XML fragments.

```
<books>
  <book year = "2013" pages = "479">
    <author>Porter</author>
  </book>
  <book year = "2011" pages = "287">
    <author>James</author>
</book>
<book year = "2011" pages = "362">
    <author>Steve</author>
</book>
</books>
<books>
<year key = "2013">
    <book author = "Porter" pages = "479"/>
</year>
<year key = "2011">
    <book author = "James" pages = "287"/>
    <book author = "Steve" pages = "362"/>
</year>
</books>
```

These two XML fragments contain the same information of publication of the books. In the first fragment the information about the year of publication of the books is represented as an attribute within the content, however, in the second fragment it is represented as label within the structure.

When users have fuzzy query intension, the fuzzy predicates (*at most, at least, close to*) can be used in different contexts of query expression to express different conditions (on attribute element, label name, structure). Thus, this section proposes our XML fuzzy query model as follows:

Definition 13 [XML Fuzzy Query]: An XML document D with attributes $A = \{A_1, A_2, ..., A_m\}$ and a fuzzy query $Q = \{Q_1, Q_2, ..., Q_s\}$ over D, where each Q_i can be a precise condition (such as "$A_i \theta a_i$") or a fuzzy condition (such as "$A_i \theta \tilde{a_i}$" or "$A_i \tilde{\theta} a_i$"), but at least one is the fuzzy condition. Each A_i in the query condition is an attribute from A and a_i is a value in its domain. Here, θ is a regular operator such as "=, >, <, ≥, ≤, ≠, (*not*) *between*, (*not*) *in*, (*not*) *like*", $\tilde{\theta}$ is a fuzzy operator such as "(*not*) *close to /around*", "(*not*) *at least*" and "(*not*) *at most*", and $\tilde{a_i}$ is a fuzzy term.

This chapter adopts three fuzzy extended expressions:

1. When the fuzzy predicate is applied to an attribute value of XML document, the fuzzy query selects nodes in which the attribute has a value close to the value expressed in the fuzzy query. The syntax of the fuzzy extension is shown as follows:

```
path [{@attribute_name FuzzyPredicate compare_value}]
```

where, the path is a sequence of nodes connected by descendant axes ("//"). The FuzzyPredicate is composed of three kinds of fuzzy relations (at most, at least, close to). The symbol "{}" expresses users' fuzzy query intension.

For example, users wish to find books that were published as close to year 2013 as possible. This chapter uses a fuzzy predicate "*close to*" to express users' fuzzy query, which can be characterized as follows:

```
//books/book[{@year close to 2013}]
```

2. When the fuzzy predicate is applied to a label or to an attribute name, the query selects nodes with a name similar to the expressed in the fuzzy query, with the following syntax:

```
path[{/tagname() FuzzyPredicate compare_value}]
```

where, the expression /tagname() has the effect of extracting the name of element that contains each element, which is applied by fuzzy predicate.

For example, in second XML fragment users also wish to find books that were published as close to year 2011 as possible. The fuzzy query would be:

```
//books/[year{/tagname() close to 2011}]/book
```

3. When the fuzzy predicate is inserted into the axis of a path expression, the selection tries to extract elements, attributes or text that are successors of the current node. The following syntax is used:

```
path₁{FuzzyPredicate} // ... // pathₙ
```

For example, in second XML fragment users also wish to find the same books. The fuzzy query would be:

```
//books/ {close to} [year = "2011"]/book
```

ARCHITECTURE OF SYSTEM

The fuzzy query and probabilistic ranking method henceforth referred to as FQPR. The main idea of FQPR is to assign a ranking score to each XML attribute node, based on workload statistic of the fuzzy query results. The overall architecture of the FQPR system is shown in Figure 1.

Figure 1. Architecture of FQPR system

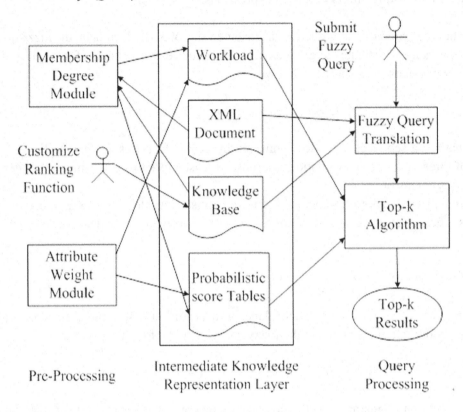

Such a system includes three components: pre-processing component, intermediate knowledge representation layer, and query processing component. The pre-processing component collects statistics about the workload. It computes the frequency of occurrence for all distinct value in the XML documents (resp. workload), and computes the weights as well as membership degree for each XML attribute. These quantities are stored as probabilistic score tables in the intermediate knowledge representation layer. The knowledge base (KB) stores information, such as membership function and the domain knowledge, which is needed to translate fuzzy query into precise query. The query processing component translates the fuzzy query and computes the ranking scores of the XML attribute by using the information from the intermediate knowledge representation layer.

After getting the information, each specified attribute value is assigned a score according to their membership degree to the fuzzy query, while each unspecified attribute value is assigned a score. The attribute weights and attribute value scores are combined to calculate the ranking score for each node in the answer. The query results are finally sorted by decreasing membership degree, for the fuzzy query results with the same membership degree, this chapter proposes the probabilistic ranking method. The probabilistic ranking method considers the relevance between the nodes specified by fuzzy query and the nodes unspecified by fuzzy query. The modular of our system allows customizing membership function as well as ranking function for different applications.

ATTRIBUTE WEIGHT ASSIGNMENT

In the real world, different users have different preferences. As a result, the importance of the same attribute node of XML document is usually different for users. This chapter needs to measure the attribute weight for the users. Hence, the chapter will assign the weight to each specified attribute by fuzzy query according to the distribution of its value in the workload.

Workload of XML Documents

Workload-log of past user queries, have been shown as being a good source for implicitly estimating the user interest. The workload information can help determine the frequency with which attribute is often specified by users and thus may be important to new users. Therefore, this section determines the attribute weight by the frequency of occurrence of the attribute specified by fuzzy query in the workload.

The intuition is that if certain pairs of values <u, v> often occur together in the workload, they are similar. Let $f(u, v)$ be the frequency of the values u and v of attribute A occurring together in the workload. Also let $f(u)$ be the frequency of occurrence of the value u of attribute A in the workload, and $f(v)$ be the frequency of occurrence of the value v of attribute A in the workload. Then, this section measures the similarity coefficient between u and v by using the following Equation.

$$Sim(u, v) = \frac{f(u, v)}{f(u) + f(v) - f(u, v)} \tag{5}$$

Evaluation of Attribute Weight

The well-known inverted element frequency (*IEF*) method has been used extensively in IR (Shaorong *et al*. 2004). The *IEF* suggests that commonly occurring words convey less information about user's needs than rarely occurring words, and thus should be weighted less. *IEF* (t) of a term t is defined as log ($n/F(t)$), where n is the number of elements and $F(t)$ is the number of elements containing t.

For evaluating the importance of attribute values, it is appropriate to adopt the definition of traditional *IEF* definition. Moreover, the frequency of attribute value should depend on nearby values. This chapter adopts the definition given in the work of Agrawal *et al*. (2003) to measure the similarity of attribute values. Let $\{t_1, t_2, ..., t_n\}$ be the values of attribute A that occur in expanded fuzzy query interval. For specified attribute value t in the fuzzy query, it defined *IEF* (t_i) as shown in Equation (6), where h is the bandwidth parameter.

$$IEF(t_i) = \log[\frac{n}{\sum_{i=1}^{n} e^{-\frac{1}{2}(\frac{t_i-t}{h})^2}}] \tag{6}$$

Here, a popular estimate for the bandwidth h is $h = 1.06\sigma n^{-1/5}$, where σ is the standard deviation of $\{t_1, t_2, ..., t_n\}$, and n is number of elements. Intuitively, the denominator in Equation (6) represents the sum of contributions to t from every the other point t_i. These contributions are modeled as Gaussion distributions, so that the further t is from t_i, the smaller is the contribution from t_i.

Moreover, if query condition is generalized as "t_i IN Q_i", where Q_i is a set of expanded interval of fuzzy query, the chapter defines the maximum log $(n/F(t))$ of each different value t in Q_i. The generalized importance measuring function is shown in Equation (7).

$$IEF(t) = \max_{t_i \in Q_i} IEF(t_i) \tag{7}$$

By normalized processing, the weight of attribute t specified by the query can be calculated by

$$W_{imp}(t) = \frac{IEF(t)}{\sum_{i=1}^{k} IEF(t_i)} \tag{8}$$

in which, k is the number of attributes specified by the fuzzy query. The denominator $\sum_{i=1}^{k} IEF(t_i)$ represents overall importance of the attribute nodes specified by the fuzzy query. The numerator $IEF(t)$ represents i-th importance of the attribute nodes specified by the fuzzy query.

MEMBERSHIP DEGREE RANKING

The main idea of membership degree ranking method is that the query results are ranked according to their membership degree to the fuzzy query. The larger the membership degree is answer, the higher the ranking score is result also.

Definition 14 [Membership Degree Ranking]: Let Q be a fuzzy query over the XML document D and T be an answer node for Q. Also let the set of attribute $X = \{X_1, X_2, ..., X_k\} \subseteq A$ be the set of attributes specified by the fuzzy conditions $<C_1, C_2, ..., C_k>$ in Q. Then, the membership degree of the answer T to the fuzzy query Q can be defined as

$$D(T,Q) = \sum_{i=1}^{k} W(X_i) \times \mu_{C_i}(t_i) \tag{9}$$

where, k is the number of fuzzy conditions in Q, X_i is the attribute specified by the fuzzy query condition C_i in Q, $W(X_i)$ is the weight of attribute X_i, $\mu_{C_i}(t_i)$ is the membership degree of the value t_i of attribute X_i to the fuzzy condition C_i.

However, for a large size XML document, it is insufficient by only using membership degree of the attributes to rank the fuzzy query results, this is because many nodes may tie for the same membership degree in the answer and thus get ordered arbitrarily. For example, consider a fuzzy query Q, several attribute nodes in the answer may have the same value and result in the membership degrees of these attributes are equivalence. In general, if only use the membership degree ranking method for ranking purposes, membership functions will partition the XML attribute nodes into several equivalence classes, where attributes within each class share the same membership degree. Thus, it is necessary to look the attributes unspecified by the fuzzy query and to estimate the attribute's relevance to the user's preferences for ranking.

PROBABILISTIC RANKING

This chapter adopts the improved PIR-based ranking function. It can be derived the strengths of correlations between the XML attribute nodes specified and unspecified by fuzzy query. This method based on workload statistics. Firstly, the chapter shows how PIR model can be adapted for semi-structured data. This chapter also shows the FQPR system can be estimated from variety of knowledge sources, such as semi-structured data and workload statistics.

Review of Probabilistic Information Retrieval

This section will need the following basic formulas from probability theory:

Bayes' Rule:

$$p(a \mid b) = \frac{p(b \mid a)p(a)}{p(b)}$$

Product Rule:

$$p(a, b \mid c) = p(a \mid c)p(b \mid a, c)$$

In the context of the information retrieval, this section considers a document collection D. For a fuzzy query Q, let R represent the set of relevant documents, and $\bar{R} = D - R$ be the set of irrelevant documents. In order to rank any attribute value t in D, the section needs to find the probability of the relevance of t. More formally, in probabilistic information retrieval, documents are ranked by decreasing order of their odds of relevance, defined as the following score:

$$Score(t) = \frac{p(R \mid t)}{p(\bar{R} \mid t)} = \frac{\frac{p(t \mid R)p(R)}{p(t)}}{\frac{p(t \mid \bar{R})p(\bar{R})}{p(t)}} \propto \frac{p(t \mid R)}{p(t \mid \bar{R})} \tag{10}$$

Adaptation of PIR Model for Semi-Structured Data

In the adaptation of PIR model (Chaudhuri, 2004, 2006) for semi-structured data in a single document D, where X is the set of attribute nodes specified by fuzzy query, and Y is the remaining set of unspecified by fuzzy query. So any attribute value t as partitioned into two parts, $t(X)$ and $t(Y)$, where $t(X)$ is the subset of values corresponding to the attributes in X, and $t(Y)$ is the remaining subset of values corresponding to the attributes in Y. Replacing t with X and Y, in this context X and Y are thus sets of values rather than sets of attributes, can get the Equation (11).

$$Score(t) \propto \frac{p(t \mid R)}{p(t \mid D)} = \frac{p(X,\ Y \mid R)}{p(X,\ Y \mid D)} = \frac{p(Y \mid R)}{p(Y \mid D)} \cdot \frac{p(X \mid Y, R)}{p(X \mid Y, D)}$$

$$Score(t) \propto \frac{p(Y \mid R)}{p(Y \mid D)} \cdot \frac{1}{p(X \mid Y,\ D)} \tag{11}$$

This section only makes limited forms of independence assumptions, given a fuzzy query Q and the X (and Y) values within themselves are assumed to be independent, though dependencies between the X and Y values are allowed. More precisely, the section assumes limited conditional independence, i.e., $p(X \mid C)$ (resp. $p(Y \mid C)$) may be written as $\prod_{x \in X} p(x \mid C)$ (resp. $\prod_{y \in Y} p(y \mid C)$), where C is any condition that only involves Y values (resp. X values), R, or D. By using the limited independence assumptions, the Equation (11) can be transformed as follows.

$$Score(t) \propto \frac{p(Y \mid R)}{p(Y \mid D)} \cdot \frac{1}{p(X \mid Y,\ D)} = \prod_{y \in Y} \frac{p(y \mid R)}{p(y \mid D)} \prod_{x \in X} \prod_{y \in Y} \frac{1}{p(x \mid y,\ D)} \tag{12}$$

The equation (12) represents a simplification of equation (11), but it can not compute directly, because R is unknown. The following section discusses how to estimate the quantities $p(y \mid R)$ next.

Workload-Based Estimation of Ranking Functions

Database workload is a log of past user's queries, have been shown as being a good source for implicitly estimating the user's interest. The workload information can help determine the frequency with which XML attribute nodes were often specified by users and thus may be important to new users. Therefore, the section determines the attribute weights by estimating the frequency of occurrence of the attribute specified by fuzzy query in the workload. In other words, the more frequency of the attribute specified by queries in the workload means it has been received more attention from users, so which should be weight higher.

Estimating the quantities $p(y \mid R)$ requires knowledge of R, which is unknown at query time. The usual technique for estimating R in information retrieval is through user feedback (relevance feedback) at query time, or through other forms of training. This section provides an automated approach that leverages available workload information for estimating $p(y \mid R)$.

As mentioned above, the workload W is represented as a set of tuples, where each record represents a user's fuzzy query and is a vector containing the corresponding attribute values. Consider an incoming fuzzy query Q which specifies a set X of attribute, suppose there are s attributes nodes in X, while the set Y are the unspecified attribute nodes. Thus $X = \{X_1, \dots, X_s\}$, $Y = \{Y_1, \dots, Y_{m-s}\}$. Suppose R as all query records in W that also request for X and then the user's preferences can be obtained by examining the subset of the workload that contains queries that also request for X. Therefore, for fuzzy query Q, with set X of attribute nodes specified by fuzzy query, $p(y|R)$ as $p(y|X, W)$. The $p(y|X, W)$ is prior probability, and a workload W is a dynamic entity. When the workload W updates, the relevant tuples R also update automatically. According to the work of Chaudhuri *et al.* (2004, 2006), making this substitution in Equation (12), this section gets:

$$Score(t) \propto \prod_{y \in Y} \frac{p(y \mid X, W)}{p(y \mid X, D)} \prod_{y \in Y} \prod_{x \in X} \frac{1}{p(x \mid y, D)} = \prod_{y \in Y} \frac{\dfrac{P(X, W \mid y)P(y)}{P(X, W)}}{P(y \mid D)} \prod_{y \in Y} \prod_{x \in X} \frac{1}{P(x \mid y, D)}$$

$$Score(t) \propto \prod_{y \in Y} \frac{P(X, W \mid y)P(y)}{P(y \mid D)} \prod_{y \in Y} \prod_{x \in X} \frac{1}{P(x \mid y, D)}$$

$$= \prod_{y \in Y} \frac{P(W \mid y)P(X \mid W, y)P(y)}{P(y \mid D)} \prod_{y \in Y} \prod_{x \in X} \frac{1}{P(x \mid y, D)}$$

$$Score(t) \propto \prod_{y \in Y} \frac{P(y \mid W) \prod\limits_{x \in X} P(x \mid y, W)}{P(y \mid D)} \prod_{y \in Y} \prod_{x \in X} \frac{1}{P(x \mid y, D)} \propto \prod_{y \in Y} \frac{P(y \mid W)}{P(y \mid D)} \prod_{y \in Y} \prod_{x \in X} \frac{P(x \mid y, W)}{P(x \mid y, D)}$$

This can be finally rewritten as:

$$Score(t) \propto \prod_{y \in Y} \frac{P(y \mid W)}{P(y \mid D)} \prod_{y \in Y} \prod_{x \in X} \frac{P(x \mid y, W)}{P(x \mid y, D)} \tag{13}$$

The equation (13) is the final ranking formula of PIR (probabilistic information retrieval) method. The equation (13) has effectively eliminated R from the formula, and is only left with quantities such as $p(y|W)$, $p(x|y, W)$, $p(y|D)$, and $p(x|y, D)$.

Improved PIR Model for Semi-Structured Data

This section improves the PIR model, and then proposes the improved ranking algorithm, the results of XML fuzzy query can be ranked in accordance with the users' needs and preferences.

By now, this section has only considered the case of membership degree ranking of fuzzy query results. Since many nodes have same membership degree in the answer, membership function will partition the XML attribute nodes into several equivalence classes, where attribute within each class share the same membership degree. Thus, the section adapts the PIR model, which considers the relevance between the nodes specified by fuzzy query and the nodes unspecified by fuzzy query. Therefore, this section should adapt the Equation (13) to make it suitable for measuring the relevance of fuzzy query results. This section can get the following formula.

$$Score(t) \propto \prod_{y \in Y} \frac{P(y \mid W)}{P(y \mid D)} \prod_{y \in Y} \prod_{x \in X} sim(x,y) \frac{P(x \mid y,W)}{P(x \mid y,D)} \tag{14}$$

where, $sim(x, y)$ is the relevance coefficient between the attribute x specified by the fuzzy query and the attribute y unspecified by the fuzzy query. The relevance coefficient $sim(x, y)$ can be calculated according to formula (5).

TOP-K RANKING ALGORITHM OF FUZZY QUERY RESULTS

This section describes a solution of ranking top-k answers problem, which employs the computations made in the offline steps, to provide ranked top-k answers for a user's fuzzy query. Then using the top-k ranking algorithm, this section can quickly retrieve the nodes with the highest k scores. This section adapts the Fagin's threshold ranking algorithm (Fagin *et al.* 2001), which can quickly provide best answers for the users.

The Algorithm 1 describes the Top-k ranking problem of fuzzy query results. From step 3 to step 12 the algorithm accesses the attribute node specified by fuzzy query. When the attribute node is found, the algorithm computes initial score of the node via a sequential access using formula (9), and according to equation (5) to compute the relevance coefficient $sim(x, y)$ between the attribute value x specified by fuzzy query and the attribute value y unspecified by fuzzy query. Then, the algorithm uses random access method to get the score of the attribute node t in the query history, and according to the equation (14) to calculate its overall score. Suppose t_j is last accessed score of the attribute node specified by the

Algorithm 1. Top-k ranking algorithm

Input: Fuzzy query q, XML document D, workload W.
Output: Top-k answers scoring table.
//Let B = (table_id, score) be a scoring table that can hold k scores.
//Let L be an array of size s storing the last scores.
Step 1: Repeat
Step 2: For all $i \in \{1, 2, ..., s\}$ do
Step 3: Retrieve next node from XML document D
Step 4: Compute initial score of the node via a sequential access using formula (9)
      Step 5: Compute the relevance coefficient $sim(x, y)$ between the attribute value x specified by fuzzy query and the attribute value y unspecified by fuzzy query.
Step 6: Update $L[i]$ with scores in workload W.
Step 7: If attribute value $t \in W$
Step 8: Get score of t from W via a random access.
Step 9: Calculate the scores of attribute value t.

$$Score(t) \propto \prod_{y \in Y} \frac{P(y \mid W)}{P(y \mid D)} \prod_{y \in Y} \prod_{x \in X} sim(x,y) \frac{P(x \mid y,W)}{P(x \mid y,D)}$$

Step 10: Insert $(t, score(t))$ into the correct position in B.
Step 11: End If
Step 12: End For

Step 13: Until $B[k].score \geq \prod_{i=1}^{s} L[i]$

Step 14: Return B

---

fuzzy query Q. The threshold is set to sum of the scores of the array L after j-th cycle. When k results exist in the scoring table B and their overall ranking score is not less than the threshold, the Top-k ranking algorithm stops. Finally, the algorithm outputs first k attribute node with the highest overall score in scoring table B.

EXPERIMENTS

Experimental Setup

To evaluate the effectiveness of the algorithms, this chapter used the DBLP and TreeBank dataset for an empirical evaluation of our method, and showed performance results for the fuzzy query and probabilistic ranking (FQPR) method. The DBLP dataset is an on-line resource providing bibliographic information on major computer science conference proceedings and journals. The DBLP dataset is highly structured. The TreeBank dataset is composed of English sentences, tagged with parts of speech. The text nodes have been encrypted because they are copywriting text from the Wall Street Journal. The TreeBank dataset is also structured with deep recursion. The deep recursive structure of this data makes it an interesting case for experiments. This chapter evaluated the results of experiments on DBLP dataset and TreeBank dataset, respectively 470 MB and 82 MB. All the experiments were implemented in JDK 6.0, and performed on a system with 2.8GHz Pentium D processor with 1GB of RAM, and running on windows XP system.

The results presented in this section were generated by averaging the results from running a workload of 5000 random queries on DBLP and TreeBank datasets. The fuzzy query template was chosen as Q_D = /dblp/article [{ @year *FuzzyPredicate* compare_value }]. The *FuzzyPredicate* is composed of three kinds of fuzzy relations (*at most, at least, close to*). The compare_value is users' expected query content.

The experiment aims at evaluating the efficiency of different ranking methods: (1) The fuzzy query and probabilistic ranking method, henceforth referred to as FQPR; (2) The probabilistic information retrieval approach described in the work of Chaudhuri *et al.* (2004, 2006), henceforth referred to as PIR, which applies principles of probabilistic models from information retrieval for structured data. Since PIR method can not handle the fuzzy conditions, thus the section uses precise query conditions, which were translated from the fuzzy query, as the input query conditions of PIR. Hence, the section can make sure that the same query results without the same order will be retrieved by using each ranking method.

Query Performance Experiment

This section evaluates query efficiency. Figure 2 and Figure 3 illustrate experimental execution time on the two datasets, respectively. In the experiment, the section compared FQPR method with PIR method on the two datasets. The experimental results show that FQPR performs better than PIR.

Precision and Recall of Different Ranking Method

This section uses the formal precision and recall metrics to measure the retrieval quality. Precision is the ratio of the number of relevant nodes retrieved to the total number of retrieved nodes:

Figure 2. Execution times of FQPR and PIR on DBLP

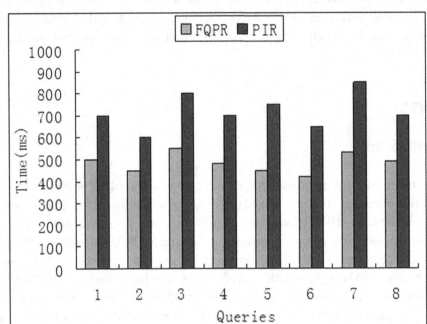

Figure 3. Execution times of FQPR and PIR on TreeBank

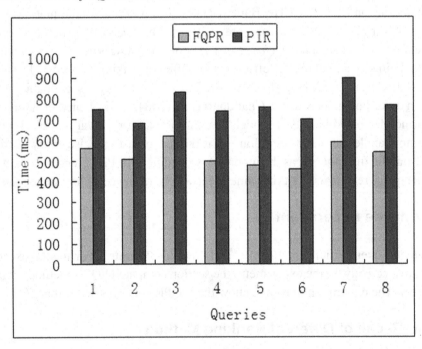

$$Precision = \frac{|\ relevant \cap retrieved\ |}{|\ retrieved\ |} \qquad (15)$$

Recall is the ratio of the number of relevant nodes retrieved to the total number of relevant nodes:

$$Recall = \frac{|\ relevant \cap retrieved\ |}{|\ relevant\ |} \qquad (16)$$

In order to get the precision and recall, the experiment compares two sets: the XML document set *retrieved* returned by the query; the XML document subset *relevant* related to query predicate. According to the two sets, this experiment calculates the precision and recall.

It can be seen that FQPR outperforms PIR, and FQPR always achieves higher precision than PIR on whatever values of recall. Moreover, the precision of PIR falls sharply with the increase of recall, while that of FQPR varies slightly. This is because PIR learns the attribute importance based on some pre-extracted data and the importance of attributes are invariant to the different user queries. It is also incapable of giving a specific weight to show how much important each attribute is. In contrast, FQPR speculates how much the user cares about each specified attribute according to the user's query and assigns a specific weight to each specified attribute. Thus, the attribute importance can be tailored to the user preferences. Additionally, the relevance between different attribute values is reasonable. Hence, the results for the fuzzy query can meet the user's needs and preferences more closely. This reflects that our method was superior to PIR method on various datasets.

Figure 4. Precision/recall curves of FQPR and PIR method (DBLP)

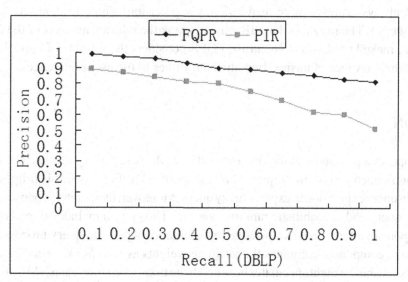

Figure 5. Precision/recall curves of FQPR and PIR method (TreeBank)

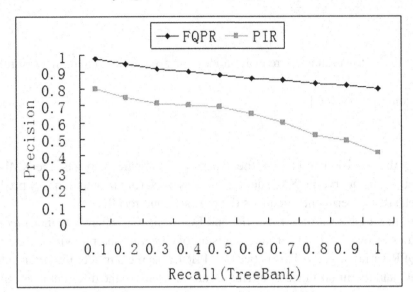

Top-k Precision of Different Ranking Method

To evaluate the query quality, this section employed another good metric, top-k precision, which measures the ratio of the number of accurate answers among the first k returned results with highest scores to k. As users are usually interested in the top-k answers, the section employed top-1, top-5, top-10, top-20, top-50 and top-100 precision to evaluate the query quality.

The obtained query result of the average top-k precision is illustrated in Figure 6 and Figure7. As expected, FQPR always achieves more than 90% top-k precision, which is about 20-30% higher than PIR on various queries. The reason is that PIR can only rank the relevant answers of the query while the exact answers are ranked randomly. In contrast, FQPR considers the weights of specified attributes by fuzzy query and the relevance of unspecified attribute values to the user preferences.

CONCLUSION

This chapter proposes a probabilistic ranking method of XML fuzzy query results. The users use fuzzy predicate to express intension of fuzzy query. The model of XML fuzzy query is proposed, which uses fuzzy predicate in query expression to express fuzzy query. Moreover, the chapter proposes the architecture of FQPR (fuzzy query and probabilistic ranking) system. The system includes three components: pre-processing component, intermediate knowledge representation layer, and query processing component. The pre-processing component computes the attribute weights as well as membership degree of fuzzy query results. The attribute weight speculates how much the users care about each XML attribute node and assign a corresponding weight to it. The intermediate knowledge representation layer includes workload,

Figure 6. Top-k precision of FQPR and PIR method on DBLP

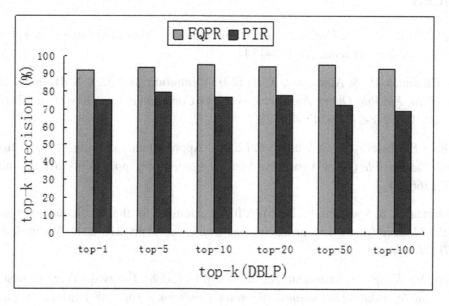

Figure 7. Top-k precision of FQPR and PIR method on TreeBank

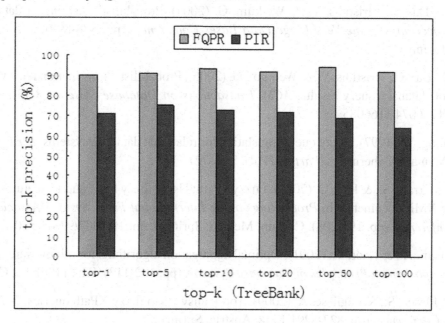

knowledge base and probabilistic score table. The query processing component uses probabilistic ranking method to rank the results of XML fuzzy query. Furthermore, this chapter presents the top-k ranking algorithm of XML fuzzy query results to get *k* results with highest scores. The extensive experimental results demonstrate that FQPR satisfies the user's needs and is better than existing works. The future research direction is the issue of fuzzy query for massive XML data and query optimization further.

REFERENCES

Agrawal, S., Chaudhuri, S., & Das, G. (2003). Automated ranking of database query results. *ACM Transactions on Database Systems, 28*, 140–174.

Alzebdi, M., Chountas, P., & Atanassov, K. T. (2011). Intuitionistic fuzzy XML query matching. *In Proceedings of the Flexible Query Answering Systems Conference*, (pp. 306-317). Ghent, Belgium: Springer. doi:10.1007/978-3-642-24764-4_27

Buche, P., Dibie-Barthelemy, J., & Wattez, F. (2006). Approximate querying of XML fuzzy data. In *Proceedings of the Flexible Query Answering Systems Conference*, (pp. 26-38). Milan, Italy: Springer. doi:10.1007/11766254_3

Campi, A., Guinea, S., & Spoletini, P. (2006). A fuzzy extension for the XPath query language. In *Proceedings of the Flexible Query Answering Systems Conference*, (pp. 210-221). Milan, Italy: Springer. doi:10.1007/11766254_18

Chan, A., Situ, N., Wong, K., Kianmehr, K., & Alhajj, R. (2008). Fuzzy querying of nested XML. In *Proceedings of the Information Reuse and Integration Conference*, (pp. 238-243). Las Vegas, NV: IEEE Systems, Man, & Cybernetics Society.

Chaudhuri, S., Das, G., Hristidis, V., & Weikum, G. (2004). Probabilistic ranking of database query results. In *Proceedings of the Very Large Data Bases Conference*, (pp. 888-899). Toronto, Canada: Morgan Kaufmann.

Chaudhuri, S., Das, G., Hristidis, V., & Weikum, G. (2006). Probabilistic information retrieval approach for ranking of database query results. *ACM Transactions on Database Systems, 31*(3), 1134–1168. doi:10.1145/1166074.1166085

Chen, S., & Jong, W. (1997). Fuzzy query translation for relational database systems. *IEEE Transaction on Systems*, Man and Cybernetics. *Part B, 27*(4), 714–721.

Damiani, E., Marrara, S., & Pasi, G. (2007). FuzzyXPath: Using fuzzy logic and IR features to approximately query XML documents. In *Proceedings of the International Fuzzy Systems Association World Congress Conference*, (pp. 199-208). Cancun, Mexico: Springer. doi:10.1007/978-3-540-72950-1_21

Fagin, R., Lotem, A., & Naor, M. (2001). Optimal aggregation algorithms for middleware. In *Proceedings of the Symposium on Principles of Database Systems*, (pp. 102-113). Santa Barbara, CA: ACM.

Fazzinga, B., Flesca, S., & Pugliese, A. (2009). Top-k answers to fuzzy XPath queries. In *Proceedings of the DEXA Conference*, (pp. 822-829). Linz, Austria: Springer.

Goncalves, M., & Tineo, L. (2010). Fuzzy XQuery. Soft Computing in XML Data Management. In Z. Ma & L. Yan (Ed.), Soft Computing in XML Data Management (pp. 133-163). Springer.

Halder, R., & Cortesi, A. (2011). Cooperative query answering by abstract interpretation. In *Proceedings of the Conference on Current Trends in Theory and Practice of Computer Science*, (pp. 284-296). Smokovec, Slovakia: Springer.

Kotsakis, E. (2006). XML fuzzy ranking. In *Proceedings of the Flexible Query Answering Systems Conference*, (pp. 159-169). Milan, Italy: Springer. doi:10.1007/11766254_14

Liu, J., Ma, Z. M., & Yan, L. (2013). Storing and querying fuzzy XML data in relational databases. *Applied Intelligence*, *39*(2), 386–396. doi:10.1007/s10489-012-0419-z

Liu, S., & Chu, W. W. (2007). CoXML: A cooperative XML query answering system. In *Proceedings of the 9th Asia-Pacific Web Conference, and 8th International Conference on Web-Age Information Management*, (pp. 614-621). Huang Shan, China: Springer. doi:10.1007/978-3-540-72524-4_63

Ma, Z. M., Liu, J., & Yan, L. (2011). Matching twigs in fuzzy XML. *Information Sciences*, *181*(1), 184–200. doi:10.1016/j.ins.2010.09.001

Panic, G., Rackovic, M., & Skrbic, S. (2014). Fuzzy XML and prioritized fuzzy XQuery with implementation. *Journal of Intelligent and Fuzzy Systems*, *26*(1), 303–316.

Schlieder, T., & Meuss, H. (2002). Querying and ranking XML documents. *Journal of the American Society for Information Science and Technology*, *53*(6), 489–503. doi:10.1002/asi.10060

Seto, J., Clement, S., Duong, D., Kianmehr, K., & Alhajj, R. (2009). Fuzzy Query Model for XML Documents. In *Proceedings of the Intelligent Data Engineering and Automated Learning Conference*, (pp. 333-340). Burgos, Spain: Springer.

Shaorong, L., Qinghua, Z., & Chu, W. (2004). Configurable Indexing and Ranking for XML Information Retrieval. In *Proceedings of the International Conference on Research and Development in Information Retrieval*, (pp. 88-95). Sheffield, UK: ACM.

Su, W., Wang, J., Huang, Q., & Lochovsky, F. H. (2006). Query result ranking over E-commerce web databases. In *Proceedings of the International Conference on Information and Knowledge Management*, (pp. 575-584). Arlington, VA: ACM. doi:10.1145/1183614.1183697

Zadeh, L. A. (1972). Fuzzy set theoretic interpretation of linguistic hedges. *Journal of Cybernetics*, *2*(3), 4–34. doi:10.1080/01969727208542910

Zadeh, L. A. (1978). Fuzzy sets as a basis for a theory of possibility. *Fuzzy Sets and Systems*, *1*(1), 3–28. doi:10.1016/0165-0114(78)90029-5

KEY TERMS AND DEFINITIONS

Composite Fuzzy Term: A composite fuzzy term such as *"very young"* or *"more or less tall"* is described by a fuzzy number with membership function.

Compound Fuzzy Term: A compound fuzzy term such as *"young ∪ very young"* is represented by simple fuzzy terms or composite fuzzy terms connected by union (∪), intersection (∩) or complementation connectors.

Fuzzy Relations: The fuzzy relations as operators and crisp values as operands. For $A\ \tilde{\theta}\ Y$, where A is an attribute, $\tilde{\theta}$ is a fuzzy relation, and Y is a crisp value, $\tilde{\theta}\ Y$ is a fuzzy number. In this chapter three types of fuzzy relations, which are *"close to (around)"*, *"at least"*, and *"at most"*.

Fuzzy Set: Fuzzy sets are sets whose elements have degrees of membership. Fuzzy sets were introduced by Lotfi A. Zadeh in 1965 as an extension of the classical notion of set.

PIR Model: The model is a probabilistic information retrieval method, which has probabilistic ranking functions to rank query results of databases.

Simple Fuzzy Term: A simple fuzzy term such as "*young*" or "*tall*" is defined by a fuzzy number with membership function.

XML Fuzzy Query: An XML document D with attributes $A = \{A_1, A_2, ..., A_m\}$ and a fuzzy query $Q = \{Q_1, Q_2, ..., Q_s\}$ over D, where each Q_i can be a precise condition (such as "$A_i \theta a_i$") or a fuzzy condition (such as "$A_i \theta \tilde{a_i}$" or "$A_i \tilde{\theta} a_i$"), but at least one is the fuzzy condition.

XML: Extensible Markup Language (XML) is a markup language. XML defines a set of rules for encoding documents in a format.

Section 2

Chapter 8

User Driven Query Framework of Social Networks for Geo–Temporal Analysis of Events of Interest

Gloria Bordogna
CNR IREA, Italy

Simone Sterlacchini
CNR IDPA, Italy

Paolo Arcaini
Charles University in Prague, Czech Republic

ABSTRACT

In this chapter we propose a framework for collecting, organizing into a database and querying information in social networks by the specification of content-based, geographic and temporal conditions to the aim of detecting periodic and aperiodic events. Our proposal could be a basis for developing context aware services. For example to identify the streets and their rush hours by analyzing the messages in social media periodically sent by queuing drivers and to report these critical spatio-temporal situations to help other drivers to plan alternative routes. Specifically, we rely on a focused crawler to periodically collect messages in social networks related with the contents of interest, and on an original geo-temporal clustering algorithm in order to explore the geo-temporal distribution of the messages. The clustering algorithm can be customized so as to identify aperiodic and periodic events at global or local scale based on the specification of geographic and temporal query conditions.

INTRODUCTION

The widespread use of social media by smartphones and other smart devices with GPS sensors is fostering a novel era of spatio-temporal computing applications.

The US red cross has reported that the US citizens are increasingly relying on social media and mobile devices to get information on ongoing critical situations, such as traffic jams, spread of pandemies,

DOI: 10.4018/978-1-4666-8767-7.ch008

and to seek assistance and safety information as well as to report their health and safety status during or after emergencies (Adam et al., 2012).

New location-based services and context-aware services can exploit social information sources for the most diverse applications in smart cities context, such as leisure recommendation, healthcare and safety, disaster management, critical periodic crisis identification, and so on.

Such services can exploit the information contents provided by users of social media, which can be in the form of free text, pictures and video, coupled with the timestamp and the geolocation as acquired by the GPS sensor of their device, to identify events occurred in specific regions at specific dates, and, depending on the kind of the event, to target either planning or alert responses.

In this chapter, we propose a framework for events' exploration based on querying a collection of social media messages collected by a focused crawler and organized into a database. The queries allow to specify spatio-temporal conditions to the aim of filtering and then analyzing periodic and aperiodic events at global or local scale. Our proposal could be a basis for developing context aware services. For example, to identify the streets and their rush hours by analyzing the messages in social media periodically sent by queuing drivers and to report these critical spatio-temporal situations to help other drivers to plan alternative routes.

Specifically, we rely on a focused crawler to periodically collect messages in social networks related to contents that may be of interest to categories of users, such as urban planners, who might need to know the streets in their city where most often traffic jams occur, territorial administrators and managers, who might need to identify in their territory of competence the periods when critical situation like floods usually occur, or cultural operators, who might be interested in planning the tour of musicians in specific regions and periods of the year more suitable to attract much audience.

In order to explore the collected messages, a query framework is proposed, consisting of two subsequent phases in order to allow the user to drive the exploration whose aim is to verify some "a priori" hypothesis he/she has on an event of interest.

In the first phase, the user can formulate queries specifying content, spatial and temporal conditions on the textual indexes and metadata parts of the messages, i.e., their geotags and timestamps, in order to filter out a subset of interesting messages from the collection. For example, an urban planner of "Bangkok" may want to select messages dealing with "traffic jams" in his/her city.

In the second phase, the user can specify some criteria in order to drive an original geo-temporal analysis of the selected messages to verify an "a priori" hypothesis. For example, the urban planner may hypothesize that traffic jams in "Bangkok" occur periodically in specific hours of the day, but may lack to know the streets and the hours of traffic jams. Thus, his/her criteria of analysis could be to consider a periodic geo-temporal distance so as to identify the most crowded hours of the day in each specific street.

An Italian cultural operator, in order to plan the tour of a musician, may be interested in selecting messages dealing with music events in Italy and in analyzing in which city in Italy and in which season the events had more resonance. In this case, he/she may formulate a query selecting messages dealing with entertainment events in Italy and then ask to group them in order to identify the cities and months where and when the most popular music events took place.

The grouping is performed by a geo-temporal clustering algorithm that can be flexibly customized to use a specific geo-temporal distance measure in order to identify aperiodic or periodic events at global or local scale.

A proof of concept framework has been implemented for Twitter social media and, through its usage, some examples of geo-temporal analysis are available.

First of all, the chapter introduces the context and the background of the approach; then, it outlines the schema of the proposed exploratory workflow. Subsequently, the three phases are formalized and, finally, examples of application of the exploratory workflow to the Twitter information source are illustrated. The conclusion summarizes the main achievements.

CONTEXT OF THE PROPOSAL: BACKGROUND AND FOREGROUND

The objective of the proposal in this chapter is to analyze events as reported in messages written in social contexts.

If we consider as background of our approach the set of messages publicly available in social contexts and written by many distinct authors, an event can be considered as a locally dense region in the multidimensional space defined by the (content, space, time) indexes representing the messages. The *content* indexes of the messages are the terms extracted from the messages text themselves through a full text analysis. The *spatial* indexes, i.e., the geographic coordinates from where the messages have been created by their authors, are generally available as metadata of the message when they are acquired by the GPS device incorporated into the author's mobile device. The *time* index, i.e., when the messages have been created, is generally associated with the message as metadata too.

The hypothesis behind this definition is that events have many active participants (i.e., the authors of messages) either close in space or in time (or even both in space and time), who deal in the message with the same contents by reporting their observations of events in social networks. In fact, events have a temporal reference (Raimond and Abdallah, 2007), and generally also have a spatial reference, so that also their location can be identified.

Thus, events can be identified by analyzing the geographic, temporal and content information of the messages. This analysis requires information retrieval functionalities to extract content indexes of messages and to query and retrieve messages about a content of interest, and spatio-temporal analysis (by means of unsupervised learning) to identify messages about the same contents close in time and possibly in space.

The events of potential interest include social events, such as economic crisis that may last for long periods of time, sports events, exhibitions, accidents, political campaigns, and also natural events, such as storms, hurricanes, and earthquakes.

Specifically, the objective of this chapter is defining a geographic and temporal exploratory framework to support a flexible geo-temporal analysis of the characteristics of messages dealing with a content of interest.

The foreground of the proposal is a framework in which the spatio-temporal analysis is driven by a user who formulates the query in order to verify some "a priori" hypothesis he/she has on the spatio-temporal characteristic of an event of interest. The user may have distinct roles and characteristics:

- An urban planner may be interested in identifying the hours of the day when the streets of a city are interested by traffic jams to support efficient mobility planning.
- An epidemiologist can be interested in identifying, at global scale, where are the localities more affected by the "Ebola" syndrome in a given period of time.

- A civil protection manager may be interested in verifying if there are specific localities in a region of interest most affected by recurrent seasonal floods in order to plan mitigation interventions.
- A cultural manager may be interested in verifying the cities where a specific music event has been most appreciated, in order to plan future similar events.

The originality of the proposal consists in the flexible user driven exploratory framework we define.

The query language allows the user to filter the messages created in desired periods of time and from specific regions and to deal with specific contents of interest. The subsequent phase allows the user to define the aim of the exploration, i.e., the geographic scale of analysis, that can be global or local, and the temporal analysis that can be periodic or aperiodic. The user specifications of the second phase allow to customize the behavior of a geo-temporal clustering algorithm, defined in (Arcaini et al., 2015), in order to perform the grouping of the messages, thus possibly highlighting where and when the event was reported by most people.

RELATED WORKS

The chapter deals with a problem of spatio-temporal mining in social networks, a topic that has been mainly addressed as either to identify groups of people whose activities on the social network co-occur in space and time or to identify frequent co-occurring tags in social media, like Flickr, in order to resolve co-referent objects, i.e., objects relative to the same real entity (Zhang et al., 2012).

Event detection in social networks has attracted many applications related to crisis management, as in (Sakaki et al., 2010), where detection of earthquakes is done considering Twitter as a social sensor: in fact the approach is based on the assumption that each Twitter user is regarded as a sensor and each tweet as sensory information affected by noise. Thus, event detection is reduced to the problem of object detection having spatial and temporal references and is tackled based on the application of an SVM classifier. Here the emphasis is on the identification of anomalous activities of a locally generated content to inform emergency services.

Other applications of geo-located analysis of Twitter messages have been used to inform urban managers, such as in (Frias-Martinez et al. 2012; Wakamiya et al., 2011), as well as in public health assessment (Ghosh and Guha, 2013).

A simplification of the problem of mining events in social media is the assumption that nowadays, in most of the social networks, the geo-location of the creators of the message is captured by the GPS device from which the message is sent and is encoded by a geotag in the message, and the time of the creation of the message from a mobile device is the time of observation of the event dealt with in the message. Although messages with explicit geotags are still a minority of the whole messages exchanged within social contexts, the growing diffusion of smart devices equipped with GPS sensors allows guessing that they will grow in the near future. For example, since 2009, Twitter released the location service that enables mobile users to publish their tweets with latitude and longitude. Our approach needs that messages have explicit geographic and temporal references, as in (Lee, 2012). Other approaches, like (Chandra, 2011), extract from the message the geographic reference.

A further distinction on event detection in social contexts can be made based on the fact that the detection must be made real time, as early as possible with respect to the event occurrence, or not. The first approach needs to filter a stream of messages (Watanabe, 2011; Thom et al., 2012), while the second one can rely on querying a repository of the messages, as in our case.

Currently, present methodologies to analyze events in Twitter choose a selection of words and hashtags and retrieve tweets containing the selected words being deemed relevant to the event. For example, recent papers monitor tweets containing the word "earthquake" and other related words (Sakaki et al., 2010).

Conversely, in a recent approach (Cheng and Wicks, 2014) the space-time scan statistics method is proposed to look for clusters within the dataset across both space and time, regardless of tweet content. By this approach, it is expected that clusters of tweets will emerge during spatio-temporally relevant events, as people will tweet more than expected in order to describe the event and spread information. The authors apply this approach to identify a disaster in London. Nevertheless, when distinct events occur in the same spatio-temporal region this approach cannot tell them apart and the previous one is preferable.

The originality of our proposal consists in the flexible user driven exploratory framework we define. The query language allows the user to filter the messages created in desired periods of time and from specific regions and to deal with specific contents of interest. The subsequent phase allows the user to define and customize the aim of the exploration. We did not find in the literature other approaches that flexibly combine these two subsequent phases for analyzing social media, nor we found any clustering algorithm that can be customized to use a desired distance measure as in our proposal, thus performing spatial, temporal or spatio-temporal analysis.

The approaches proposed in the literature for spatio-temporal analysis of events apply density based clustering algorithms, mainly DBSCAN algorithm as in (Lee, 2012), for its ability to detect clusters of any shape, which is one of the characteristics of the close geotags of messages whose geographic reference can even change over time.

As far as we know, no approach has been proposed for an integrated and user driven geographic-temporal analysis of messages in social contexts related to a specific topic, while most approaches mainly explore separately the geographic and the temporal relations among the messages. Moreover, no approach has been defined for identifying recurring periodic geographic events that are of interest for some application context, such as the identification of the streets and the hours of the day where "traffic jams" occur regularly.

We defined integrated spatio-temporal distance measures in a similar way as in (Oliveira et al., 2013). However in our proposal the geo-temporal distance measures are different and richer since we can identify geo-temporal clusters of periodically recurrent events.

USER DRIVEN EXPLORATION OF EVENTS IN SOCIAL MEDIA

The proposed framework allows a user to explore the spatio-temporal resonance, popularity or even consequences of events of interest as commented in messages of social information sources.

The schema of the workflow is shown in Figure 1. It can be seen that there are three main phases.

In the background collection phase, a focused crawler visits the social information sources to collect messages of potential interest, produces their representation, and organizes them into a NoSQL data structure. The other two foreground phases are activated by a user who first formulates a query to select

Figure 1. Flexible user driven exploratory framework of social media messages

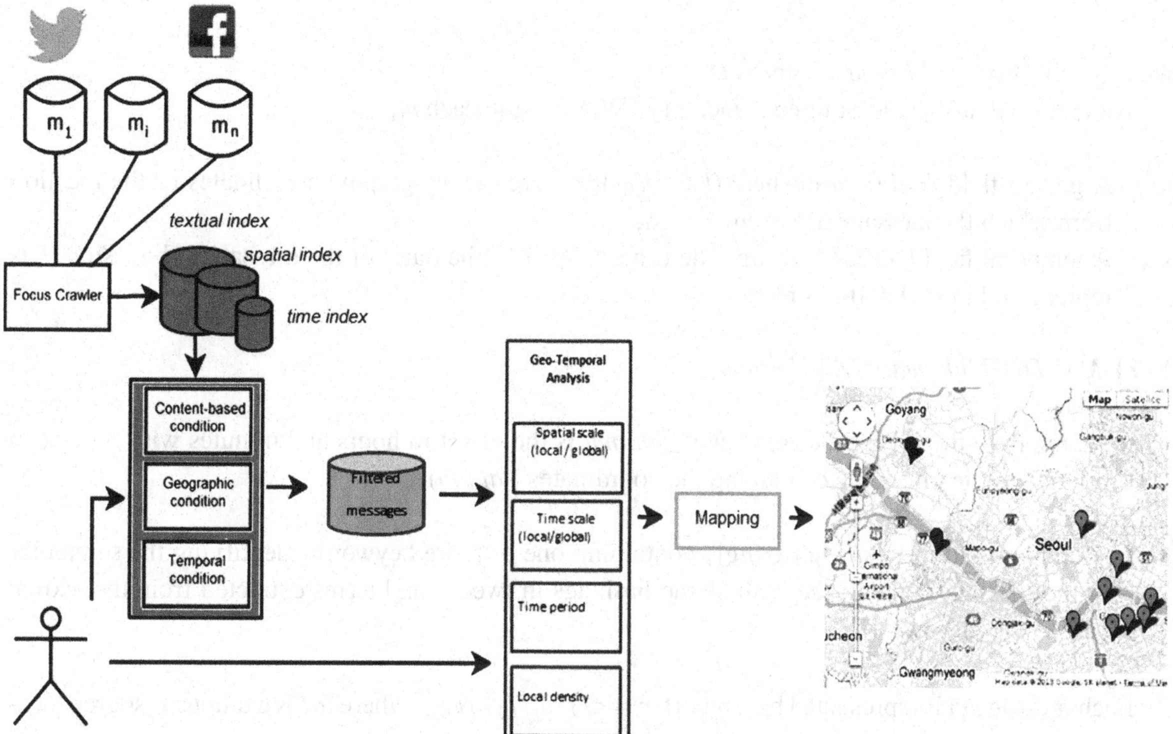

a set of reports to analyze, dealing with a specific event, and then he/she specifies the criteria of the geo-temporal analysis. A map with the results of the analysis is produced in which the distinct colored pins identify the reports with homogeneous characteristics with respect to the criteria of the analysis.

In the following sections, the three phases are detailed.

MESSAGES COLLECTION AND REPRESENTATION

The proposal needs that the social sources of information provide web services allowing a crawler to retrieve, from the social sources, the messages dealing with a given content of interest.

Let $S = \{s_1, \ldots, s_n\}$ be a set of (social) information sources (social platforms). Each $s_i \in S$ is represented as follows:

$$s_i = \{n_i, M_i, ws_i\}$$

where n_i is the name of the information source, M_i the set of stored messages, and ws_i a web service provided by the information source for querying and retrieving subsets of M_i. For the sake of simplicity, we assume that each message $m \in M_i$ is represented as a tuple of fields as follows:

$$m = \left\langle f_1, \ldots, f_f \right\rangle$$

where each f_i takes values on a domain D_i.

We require that $\forall s_i$ at least three mandatory fields exist in each m,

- A geotag field $f_s = (lat, lon)$, where $(lat, lon) \in R \times R$ are the geographic coordinates of the location from which the message has been created;

- A temporal field $f_t \in Date$ defining the timestamp (i.e., the date) of the message submission; f_t is represented in ISO 8601 format:

YYYY-MM-DD'T'hh:mm:ss'Z'[±hh:mm]   (1)

where Z refers to the UTC time zone, and $\pm hh:mm$ is the offset in hours and minutes with respect to UTC relative to the time zone containing the coordinates (*lat,lon*);

- A textual field $f_c \in \{string, [string]\}$ containing one or more keywords identifying the semantics of the message content; they can be the hashtags in tweets, and terms extracted from the textual part of the message.

Each message m is represented by a report $r = < f_s, f_t, f_c, url >$, where *url* is a unique resource location that uniquely identifies the report on its social platform. r is stored into a NoSQL data structure that is indexed with respect to the three fields, so as to ease the access and retrieval with respect to content conditions, spatial conditions and time conditions.

A content condition is generally specified by a set of terms, a simple spatial condition is specified by a pair of geographic coordinates (longitude, latitude) uniquely identifying a point on the Earth surface and a radius to delimit the interesting area around the point, while a time condition is a specific date with eventually hour, minutes and seconds indications too, and a time interval delimiting the time range around the date. Queries allowing content, spatial and time condition specifications are defined in the following.

In order to ease both the retrieval based on content keywords and the updating when new keywords must be added. the field f_c is indexed by a B-tree data structure f_c_index.

The spatial field f_s is indexed by an R-Tree data structure f_s_index, to easy the access when a spatial point query or a range query is formulated, such as when one asks to retrieve messages with geotag close to a given location.

The time field f_t is associated with its internal representation where each $t \in f_t$ is associated with a positive integer value. This value identifies a time point with a given time unit on the time line (see next section for the definition of time point and time unit). In this way, when one searches with a timestamp close to a date or within a time range, the matching is performed into the internal time representation.

The preliminary phase, which is asynchronously executed with respect to the user querying phase, is necessary to build and update the database of reports. This consists in extracting from the n monitored sources the messages that satisfy given requests representing the description of events of potential interest to the categories of users of the platform. To this end, first the categories are identified by specifying a set of keywords describing events the users may be interested in analyzing.

Then a crawler is run so as to periodically submit each request q_{ij} to the sources ($i=1,..n$), starting from a specified initial date $tstart_j$, with a given frequency δt_{ij} (for example, at each hour or each day) until an ending date $tend_j$ is reached. The interval $tstart_j$, $tend_j$ depends on the request's semantics, since one may be interested in retrieving messages dealing with an event that took place in a known range of time, such as July 2014 for the soccer world cup. On the other side the time frequency δt_{ij} by which the query is submitted to the information source also depends on the policy of the source itself that may impose limits:

$(q_{ij}, tstart_j, tend_j, \delta t_{ij})$

Each request q_{ij} is generated from a keyword c_j associated with each category of users in such a way to be interpreted by the sources' web services ws_i which are periodically invoked so as to retrieve only the messages whose content field f_c satisfies the request. This means that each keyword $c_j \in f_c$ must undergo a translation τ into the query language of the i-th information source: $\tau(c_j) = q_{ij}$ with $(i = 1, ..., n)$.

The retrieved messages are parsed to extract f_c, their geotag field f_s, and temporal field f_t, which are indexed and stored into the NoSQL database.

The collection R of all messages is then continuously updated and periodically indexed so as to be available to the user query phase.

USER QUERIES FORMULATION

Users queries formulated to retrieve messages in social networks that deal with events of interest may need to specify both content selection conditions, spatial and temporal conditions.

Queries containing spatial conditions are named *spatial queries*, while queries containing temporal conditions are *temporal queries*, and consequently *spatio-temporal queries* contain both spatial and temporal conditions. When more conditions are specified in the same query, one demands that they are possibly all satisfied.

Content selection conditions are conditions demanding the presence in the message of specific terms, keywords, characterizing the event of interest, for example, "*tennis cup*", "*live concert of Madonna*" etc.

Spatial selection conditions are specified when one is interested in events occurred in a specific location, for example, to know anything happened in a city, one can specify the city name or a pair of geographic coordinates and a distance.

Time selection conditions can be specified when one wants to retrieve all events happened anywhere in a specific span of time.

Obviously, when specifying content and spatio-temporal conditions in the same query, one is very specific in selecting messages: for example, the query "*live concert of Madonna*", "*Paris*", "*26-07-2012*" intends to collect messages commenting the live tour concert in *Paris* given by the pop singer *Madonna* on the *26 July 2012*.

A user can formulate queries by specifying a conjunction of a content based condition χ_c, a spatial condition χ_s, and a temporal condition χ_t:

$uq: = \chi_c \wedge \chi_s \wedge \chi_t$

The content condition is defined as

$\chi_c := \{c, [c]\}$

where $c \in$ *string* is a keyword specifying the topic of interest the message must deal with. If multiple keywords are specified, they are assumed in OR, i.e., it is sufficient that a message is indexed by one of the keywords to be selected by the user query.

The spatial condition is defined as

$$\chi_s := \{<(long, lat), \delta s>, [<(long, lat), \delta s>]\} \parallel <geoname, \delta s> \tag{2}$$

where:

- $<(long, lat), \delta s> \in R \times R \times R$ defines the area of interest. *(long, lat)* are the geographic coordinates of the desired location of the messages, i.e., of their geotag f_s, and δs the maximum acceptable distance from it in km. When more pairs $<(long, lat), \delta s>$ are specified, they are assumed in OR and, thus, a message is filtered if it satisfies at least one of them;
- $<geoname, \delta s> \in$ *string* $\times R$ where *geoname* identifies the geographic name of interest and δs the maximum acceptable distance from the geographic coordinates associated with *geoname*.

The temporal condition is defined as

$$\chi_t := \{<t, \delta t>, \parallel before\ t \parallel after\ t \parallel [t_{start}, t_{end}]\} \tag{3}$$

where:

- $<t, \delta t>$ where t is represented in ISO 8601 format and defines the date of the messages of interest; t is the perfect desired date, while δt is defined as a time range (see the definition in the following paragraph) and specifies the maximum distance in time granules from t for a message to be acceptable;
- *before t*, specifies the maximum acceptable date for a message to be filtered;
- *after t*, specifies the minimum acceptable date for a message to be filtered;
- $[t_{start}, t_{end}]$ specifies the time range including the dates for a message to be filtered.

Time Representation

In order to deal with time specifications and evaluation of time constraints, we adopt a homogenous representation of the temporal component (Bordogna et al., 2011) that permits to arrange *events* on a directed numeric time line with a given granularity, so that the computation of the time distance between two events is possible.

We assume as origin of the time line the Unix *epoch*, hereafter indicated by $d_0 = 1970\text{-}01\text{-}01\text{T}00\text{:}00Z$, and the finest granularity the *seconds*, so that the time distance between two events is expressed in seconds.

Therefore, when the time granularity in *seconds* is appropriate for the analyses we are carrying out, we have to convert each temporal field f_t of each report (given in ISO 8601 format) into a point of the time line, that is obtained by computing the distance in seconds of the date f_t from the time origin d_O.

Nevertheless, for some events and purposes, it may be irrelevant to evaluate their time distance from the origin in seconds. For example, in the case of messages about a sport match, it may be interesting to know if they are created when the match has been shown on TV: in this case the hour could be chosen as appropriate granularity, so that the messages sent during the match have the same time distance from the time origin of the match. To this end, we introduce the notion of time unit.

Time Unit

A time unit G is always multiple of the basic time unit (G_s, the time unit of seconds) and possibly also of another not basic time unit. For example, the time unit of minutes is $G_m = 60G_s$, and the time unit of hours is $G_h = 60G_m = 3600G_s$.

A time unit G determines a partitioning of the time line into consecutive *granules*; each granule contains events which are not discernible assuming G as time unit.

Time Point

Given a time unit G, we identify a *time point* with $[t, G]$, where t is the number of granules of unit G from the time origin (the Unix epoch). In order to compute a time point starting from a date in ISO 8601 format and a time unit G, we introduce two functions.

Function getTimePointUTC

Given a temporal field $c \in$ Date as defined in (1) and a time unit G, function *getTimePointUTC* computes the number of granules of type G contained between f_t and the time origin d_O, i.e.,

$$getTimePointUTC : \quad Date \times \{G_s, G_m, G_h, ...\} \rightarrow N \tag{4}$$

Notice that this function takes into account all the information in f_t (as defined in (1)) by transforming it in the equivalent date relative to the UTC timezone: so, given two *simultaneous* dates in different time zones, function *getTimePointUTC* returns the same result expressed in a desired time unit G.

For example, given the following dates:

```
2013-07-23T05:45:20Z (time zone UTC)
2013-07-23T14:45:20Z+09:00 (time zone Korea Standard Time)
2013-07-22T22:45:20Z-07:00 (time zone Pacific Daylight Time)
2013-07-22T22:45:25Z-07:00 (time zone Pacific Daylight Time)
```

by applying *getTimePointUTC* with time unit G_s (i.e., seconds), we obtain the same result 1374558320 for the first three dates, and the value 1374558325 for the last date. Instead, with the time unit G_y (i.e., year) we obtain the same result 43 for all the four dates. This exemplifies how we can perform temporal analyses by exploiting the information granule G in order to be more or less precise.

This transformation is used when one is interested in grouping simultaneous events, such as messages related to a live sport event at global scale.

Function getTimePointTZ

Function *getTimePointTZ* is defined as follows:

$$getTimePointTZ : Date \times \{G_s, G_m, G_h, ...\} \to N \tag{5}$$

Notice that this function, given a date f_t represented as in (1), disregards the offset information in f_t ([$\pm hh{:}mm$] after 'Z') and assumes the time zone UTC. Furthermore, it truncates the resulting date based on the specified information granule. For example, dates 2013-07-23T14:45:20Z+09:00 (time zone *Korea Standard Time*) and 2013-07-23T14:45:20Z (time zone *UTC*) are considered equivalent to 2013-07-23T14:45:20Z.

The application of *getTimePointTZ* to the four dates seen previously yields distinct results:

```
getTimePointTZ(2013-07-23T05:45:20Z, Gₛ) = 1374558320
getTimePointTZ(2013-07-23T14:45:20Z+09:00, Gₛ) = 1374590720
getTimePointTZ(2013-07-22T22:45:20Z-07:00, Gₛ) = 1374533120
getTimePointTZ(2013-07-22T22:45:25Z-07:00, Gₛ) = 1374533125
```

We can see that, for the dates not belonging to UTC, the computed value is different from the value computed by function *getTimePointUTC*.

Function *getTimePointTZ* is used when one wants to group events that are not necessarily simultaneous at global level, but that occur in close units of time (depending on the chosen granularity) relatively to their time zone. For example, if one wants to group events happening in close hours and minutes, he/she may use *getTimePointTZ* by specifying as time unit G_m, so that events occurring in the same hour of the same day and same minutes relatively to their time zone will get the same point on the time line, while events occurring in different hours of the day (e.g., one in the morning and one in the afternoon relatively to their time zone) or same hour but distinct minutes will appear in two distinct clusters of points on the time line.

Moreover, if one wants to identify periodically recurrent events occurring, for example, at the same hour of the day, irrespective of the day, month, and year, he/she has to use the functions defined in the following.

Time Interval

With [$\Delta n, G$] we identify a time interval of n granules of the time unit G. Note that the time interval is not related to the time origin. Moreover, notice that a time interval (as a time point) is a multiple of the basic time granule of seconds G_s (i.e., $[\Delta n, G] = [\Delta mn, G_s]$, with $m \in N$ and $G = m \cdot G_s$.

Period

Given a time line with time unit G, we can specify another time unit named *period,* indicated by $\tilde{G}$ with $\tilde{G} = n \cdot G(n \in N \; and \; n > 1)$, so that any time point $[t, G]$ of the time line can be mapped into $[t, G]$ $\tilde{G}$ by applying the modulo operation as follows:

$$\left[t, G\right]_{\tilde{G}} = \left[t \bmod n, G\right] = \left[r, G\right] with \; \tilde{G} = n \cdot G \, and \, r = t - n * trunc(t / n) \tag{6}$$

where *trunc*(.) removes the fractional part of its argument.

This transformation can be useful to identify events periodically recurring with a period $\tilde{G}$.

For example, if we were interested in social messages related to the *traffic jam* occurring daily, we should only consider the *hours, minutes,* and *seconds* of the message, but not the *year, month,* and *day*; in this case, the period of analysis would be the *day.*

The modulo operation can be applied also to time intervals in the following way:

$$\left[\Delta t, G\right]_{\tilde{G}} = \left[\Delta(t \bmod n), G\right] = \left[\Delta r, G\right] with \; \tilde{G} = n \cdot G \, and \, r = t - n * trunc(t / n) \tag{7}$$

RETRIEVAL MECHANISM

The retrieval mechanism applies an evaluation function μ of a user query *uq* to an archive of messages R and returns a subset of reports in R:

$$\mu(uq, R) := \mu_c (.) \cap \mu_s (.) \cap \mu_t (.) \rightarrow R_{uq} \subseteq R \tag{8}$$

in which $\mu_c (.)$, $\mu_s (.)$, $\mu_t (.)$ are the functions evaluating the content, spatial and temporal conditions respectively defined as follows:

$$\mu_c : \chi_c \times index\_f_c \rightarrow R_c \subseteq R$$

$$\mu_s : \chi_s \times index\_f_s \rightarrow R_s \subseteq R$$

$$\mu_t : \chi_t \times index\_f_t \rightarrow R_t \subseteq R$$

Given a content condition χ_c, μ_c searches in the textual index *index_f_c* each term in χ_c and then selects the set of reports R_c indexed by at least one of the terms.

Given a spatial condition χ_s, μ_s searches the single pairs *(lon, lat)* $\in \chi_s$ in *index_f_s* (by providing the maximum distance δs) and retrieves the set of reports R_s whose geotags are within a distance δs from *(lon, lat)*. In the case in which χ_s = <*geoname*, δs >, first *geoname* is geocoded by exploiting a geocoding service, such as the one provided by Google.

Given a time condition χ_t, μ_t evaluates the following relational operators:

- Given $<t, \delta t> \in \chi_t$, it retrieves the set of reports R_t whose timestamp f_t is within a date δt from t, i.e., $t - \delta t \leq f_t \leq t + \delta t$;
- Given *before* $t \in \chi_t$ (resp. *after* $t \in \chi_t$) it retrieves the set of reports R_t whose timestamp $f_t < t$ (resp. $f_t > t$);
- Given $[t_{start}, t_{end}] \in \chi_t$, it retrieves the set of reports R_t whose timestamp $t_{start} \leq f_t \leq t_{end}$.

In order to evaluate these relation operators, first the time values t (defined according to (1)) are converted by applying function *getTimePointUTC* into a point on the time line, assuming the basic time unit (*seconds*).

USER DRIVEN GEO-TEMPORAL ANALYSIS

Once the set of reports that satisfy the user query have been retrieved, the user can perform their geo-temporal analysis. The objective of this second phase is to generate groups of messages, by evaluating a geographic-temporal distance of their representation fields (f_s, f_t), so that the groups satisfy some criteria specified by the user.

When performing this analysis, the user must have in mind an hypothesis to test, i.e., an idea, although vague, of the duration and of the periodicity of an event he/she intend to analyze, and an idea of the spread of the event at local or global scale.

For example, in case the user has selected sport events, the meaningful granularity for the analysis could be hours and not the minutes, while, in case the user wants to study a pandemic event, the granularity of the analysis could be the day, since considering hours could be meaningless.

In the case the user is interested in analyzing the soccer world cup championship, he/she can assume that it is popular at global scale, while "a pop singer tour" can be object of a local analysis.

The approach relies on an unsupervised density based clustering algorithm defined in (Arcaini et al., 2015) that satisfies the following requirements:

- Each group might have a distinct unpredictable shape; some may have a round or oval shapes, while others may look like spiders;
- Each group might have a distinct cardinality; some groups may be big, while others may be small;
- The distribution of the groups can be heterogeneous in space and time;
- The number of the groups is not known in advance, since they may be many or a few.

The reason for defining a density-based clustering is the fact that many messages on the same topic, generated in a close area and/or sent simultaneously or at periodic timestamp, are indications of the resonance or popularity of some event.

Density-based clustering algorithms have a wide applicability in unsupervised spatial data mining. They apply a local criterion to group objects: clusters are regarded as regions in the data space where the objects are dense, and which are separated by regions of low object density (noise). Among the density based clustering algorithms, DBSCAN (Ester, 1996) is very popular due to both its low complexity and its ability to detect clusters of any shape, which is a desired characteristic when one does not have any knowledge of the possible clusters' shapes, or when the objects are distributed heterogeneously with distinct shapes, such as along paths of a graph or a road network. Furthermore, DBSCAN does not need as input the number of clusters to generate, which is indeed a requirement. Starting from DBSCAN, spatio-temporal density based clustering algorithms have been proposed such as ST-DBSCAN (Birant and Kut, 2007), where first the temporal neighbors are filtered and then the DBSCAN algorithm is applied to form the clusters. In this approach, space and time dimensions are not analyzed in an integrated manner, like it also happens with the STSNN spatio-temporal clustering (Liu et al., 2012). Conversely, 4D+SNN (Oliveira et al., 2013) is a spatio-temporal clustering algorithm that considers all dimensions simultaneously in the distance measure. The distances on each dimensions are aggregated in a compensative way (by a weighted sum) so that the spatio-temporal properties of the generated clusters may have different characteristics: one cluster might be generated because there are many reports that are very close either in space or in time or even averagely close both in space and time. Thus, it could be misleading presenting such grouped results to a user who might find difficulties in interpreting them. Taking ideas both from ST-DBSCAN and 4D+SNN, in (Arcaini et al, 2015) a Geo-Temporal DBSCAN (GT-DBSCAN) clustering algorithm has been proposed. The behavior of this algorithm can be customized by specifying the kind of distance to use and some parameters for the local density.

By customizing the behavior of the GT-DBSCAN clustering algorithm the user can drive distinct kinds of analyses; this is done by specifying the following criteria represented by a tuple:

$$(Distance, \varepsilon_s, \varepsilon_t, G, \tilde{G}, MinPts) \tag{9}$$

where:

- $Distance \in \{DistG, DistT, DistMT, DistGT, DistGMT\}$ is the name of a distance measure that the algorithm can use, namely: *Geographic distance (DistG), Temporal distance (DistT), Periodic-Temporal distance (DistMT)*, and, for analyzing periodic events, *Geo-Temporal distance (DistGT), Periodic Geo-Temporal distance (DistGMT)*;
- G and $\tilde{G} \in TimeGranules$ (an ascending ordered set *TimeGranules* = {*seconds, minutes, hours, day, week (7 days), month (30 days), season (4 months), year (12 months)*}) are time units, with $\tilde{G} = nG$ being a period of time;
- ε_s and ε_t, are numeric values whose domains depend on the parameter *Distance*, which define the reachability property between reports, i.e., the geographic local neighborhood limit of a report (in *kms*), and the temporal local neighborhood limit of a report (in a specific time unit);
- $MinPts \in N$ defines the minimum number of reports that must exists in the local neighborhood of a report to define a local dense area: the neighborhood can be either geographic, or temporal, or geo-temporal.

To group the retrieved messages sent by close geographic locations, i.e., with close geotag, neglecting their timestamps, so as to explore the resonance of events from long term, one has to specify the following criteria:

$$(DistG, \varepsilon_s, \propto, null, null, MinPts) \tag{10}$$

The greatest ε_s and *MinPts* are, the larger the clusters are. $\propto$ is an arbitrary large positive value. An example of such analysis is the exploration of geographic regions most interested by an economic, political or social crisis.

To group messages *simultaneously* sent, by neglecting their geotags, in order to analyze events at their global scale (e.g., the popularity of soccer matches of the world cup championship), one has to specify the following criteria:

$$(DistT, \propto, \varepsilon_t, G, null, MinPts) \tag{11}$$

where $\varepsilon_t \in N$ identifies the number of time granules of the adopted time unit G between two timestamps of two reports, $\propto$ is an arbitrary large positive value, G is a time granule selected in the ordered set *TimeGranules,* and *MinPts* is the minimum number of reports required in a local temporal neighborhood to form a cluster. The larger the value of G, the coarser distinction is made between the timestamps of the reports, since they become indistinguishable when their distance on the time line is smaller than G.

To group the retrieved messages sent at recurring timestamps with a given period, by neglecting their geotags, to analyze periodic events at global scale (e.g., to identify the hours of the day in which traffic jams are reported more often on Earth), one has to specify the following criteria:

$$(DistMT, \propto, \varepsilon_t, G, \tilde{G}, MinPts) \tag{12}$$

where $\varepsilon_t \in N$ identifies the number of time granules of the adopted time unit G between two timestamps of two reports, $\propto$ is an arbitrary large positive value, G is a time granule selected in the ordered set *TimeGranules* and $\tilde{G}$ a time granule multiple of G defining the time period of the analysis. Finally, *MinPts* is the minimum number of reports in a local temporal neighborhood. The larger is the period $\tilde{G}$, the greater is the distance between the timestamp of two reports that can be considered as belonging to the same cluster. In fact, in this case what matters is that the timestamps of the reports are close relatively to the beginning of a period and not in absolute on the timeline.

To group the retrieved messages *simultaneously* sent by *close* geographic locations on Earth, in order to analyze the local resonance of global events (e.g., the popularity of the soccer matches of the world cup championship in each region), one has to specify the following criteria:

$$(DistGT, \varepsilon_s, \varepsilon_t, G, null, MinPts) \tag{13}$$

The greater ε_s (ε_t) is, the wider is the geographic (temporal) local neighborhood is. For example, given (*DistGT*, 3 *km*, 15, *minutes*, *null*, 5) one demands that there exists at least 5 reports sent within 15 minutes and located within 3 *km* of a given report to start growing a cluster.

Finally, to group the retrieved messages *periodically* sent by *close* geographic locations on Earth (in order to analyze, for example, the hours of the day when most often traffic jams occur in each region), one has to specify the following criteria:

$$(DistGMT, \varepsilon_s, \varepsilon_{mt}, G, \tilde{G}, MinPts) \tag{14}$$

In this case $\tilde{G}$ specifies the period of the analysis and G the time granule of the analysis.

In the example of the traffic jam, one could set (*DistGMT*, 3 *km*, 15 *min*, *minutes*, *day*, 5) which demands to group reports starting from those having at least 5 reports sent within 15 *minutes* with respect to the beginning of the day (expressed in minutes time granules) and located within a distance of 3 *km*.

In the following section, we present a synthetic resume of the GT-DBSCAN clustering algorithm, referring to (Arcaini et al., 2015) for more details on the definitions of the distance measures.

GEO-TEMPORAL DENSITY BASED CLUSTERING

The Geo-Temporal DBSCAN algorithm (GT-DBSCAN) is defined by extending the classic DBSCAN to allow the evaluation of distinct distance measures.

The algorithm is defined as follows.

Given a set R_{uq} of n reports r_i, we represent each of them by a point p_i in a three dimensional geographic and temporal space so that $p_i = (x_{i1} ; x_{i2} ; x_{i3})$, with x_{i1} and x_{i2} corresponding to the geographic coordinates latitude and longitude, and being $x_{i3} = f_t$ the timestamp.

A point $p \in R \times R \times R^+$, associated with a report $r \in R_{uq}$, is a *core* point if at least a minimum number *minPts* of points p_j (associated with reports in $R(q)$ as well) exists such that the following function returns *True*:

$$Satisfy(Distance, p, p_j, \varepsilon_1, \varepsilon_2, G, \tilde{G}) = True \qquad (15)$$

where:

- *Distance*∈{*DistG, DistT, DistMT, DistGT, DistGMT*} is the name of a distance measure that the algorithm can use, namely: *Geographic distance* (*DistG*), *Temporal distance* (*DistT*), *Modulo-Temporal distance* (*DistMT*), *Geo-Temporal distance* (*DistGT*), *Geo-Modulo-Temporal distance* (*DistGMT*). These distance measures are defined in (Arcaini et al., 2015).
- G and $\tilde{G}$ are time units with $\tilde{G} = nG$ being a period of time.
- ε_1 and ε_2 are numeric values whose domains depend on the parameter *Distance*.

Satisfy(.) is a binary function that returns *True* when the points are within a geographic distance ε_1 and a (modulo)-temporal distance ε_2, while it returns *False* when at least one of the previous conditions is not satisfied.

Two core points p_i and p_j, with i ≠j and such that *Satisfy*(*Distance*, $p_i, p_j, \varepsilon_1, \varepsilon_2, G, \tilde{G}$) = *True*, define a cluster *cl* (i.e., $p_i, p_j \in cl$) and are core points of *cl*, i.e., $p_i, p_j \in$ core(*cl*).

A non-core point p is a *boundary* point of a cluster *cl* if $p \notin$ core(*cl*) and $\exists p_i \in$ core(*cl*) with

$$Satisfy(Distance, p, p_i, \varepsilon_1, \varepsilon_2, G, \tilde{G}) = True \qquad (16)$$

Finally, points that are not part of a cluster are considered as *noise*: p is a noise point if $\forall cl, p \notin$ core(*cl*) and $\neg \exists p_i \in$ core(*cl*) with *Satisfy*(*Distance*, $p, p_i, \varepsilon_1, \varepsilon_2, G, \tilde{G}$) = *True*.

A value *Distance*∈{*DistG, DistT, DistMT, DistGT, DistGMT*} can be used in an instantiation of the *GT-DBSCAN* algorithm as follows:

$$GT\text{-}DBSCAN(Distance, \varepsilon_1, \varepsilon_2, G, \tilde{G}, MinPts) \qquad (17)$$

with $MinPts \in N$. Note that the type of distance influences the kind of ε_1 and ε_2 that must be used.

EXAMPLES OF EVENTS ANALYSIS

In this section, we illustrate some examples of analysis performed by following the proposed exploratory workflow. For the sake of simplicity, we only consider one single information source $s=Twitter$ and perform several explorations of *tweets*. Specifically, we show the results of the application of our proposal for different purposes on a collection of tweets dealing with distinct topics.

Collection of Tweets

Several queries have been formulated related to the following events: traffic jam, the US OPEN 2013 tennis tournament, floods and storms, and the soccer world cup 2014. The queries were translated into hashtags and daily submitted to Twitter using the Twitter APIs by a focused crawler for a period of three months starting from July 2013 (except for the soccer world cup), and for two months starting from June 2014 (only for the soccer world cup). Totally, we collected 139.348 tweets.

As far as the traffic jam, distinct hashtags {*#trafficjam, #traffico, #stau, #engarrafamento, ...*} (i.e., the terms "traffic jam" was expressed in different languages: English, Italian, Dutch, Portuguese, Spanish, Turkish, French, German, Greek, Japanese, Korean, Russian, and Thai) were separately submitted as queries to Twitter APIs.

The tweets related to the US OPEN 2013 tennis tournament were collected by the hashtag *#usopen* submitted to Twitter APIs during the last week of the tournament, thus retrieving 5156 tweets.

Furthermore, messages related to floods and storms were collected by submitting the hashtags {*#flood, #inundation, #temporale, #storm, ...*}) to Twitter APIs for a period of two months starting in August 2013.

Finally, the tweets related to the soccer world cup 2014 were retrieved by the hashtags *#brasil2014* and *#worldcup*, submitted to Twitter APIs during June and July 2014, thus retrieving 60630 tweets.

Geographic Analysis

A first exploration was aimed at retrieving and analyzing the messages dealing with traffic congestions in Bangkok area. The following user query and analysis criteria were formulated:

uq: χ_c = " *traffic jam*" "รถติด" χ_s = *<Bangkok, 10 km >*

Analysis criteria: (*DistG*, 0.5 *km*, ∝, *null*, *null*, 4)

This means that first the subset of the reports of the whole collection that satisfy χ_c and χ_s were filtered and then they were analyzed by the following criterion: a geographic analysis (using distance *DistG*) is demanded with *MinPts* = 4 and the maximum geographic distance ε_s = 0.5 km. Being a geographic analysis, no constraint is defined for the temporal dimension.

Figure 2 shows the results of the exploration. Different colors identify different clusters that have been generated. We can see that there is an area with a big cluster in the middle of the city (plausibly, a traffic congested area) and small clusters on the streets entering this area.

Aperiodic Temporal Analysis

An example of temporal analysis can be performed to identify regions at global scale (Earth) in which people are more or less simultaneously testimonies of the same event. To this end, the following user query and analysis criteria were formulated:

uq: χ_c = "*US-Open 2013*" χ_t >2013-08-23T00:00:20Z (time zone *UTC*)

Analysis criteria: (*DistT,* $\propto$*, 10 min, min, null,* 90)

Figure 2. Results of the exploration using the Geographic distance on the tweets filtered by the user query – "traffic jam" "รถติด" in Bangkok

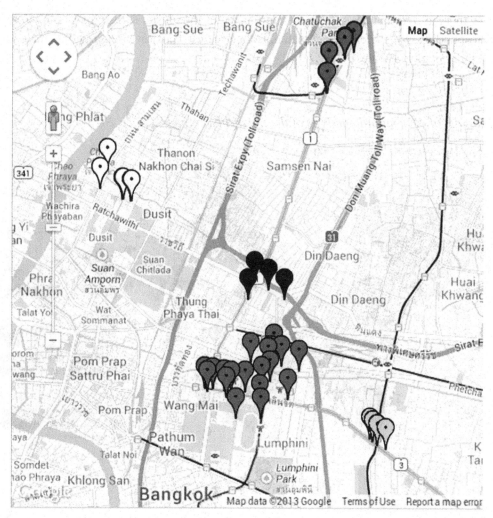

This means that first the subset of the reports of the whole collection that satisfy χ_c and χ_t were filtered and then they were temporarily analyzed (considering the temporal distance *DistT*) by requiring that *MinPts* = 90 exists within a time range ε_t = 10 min.

The idea is that people tend to send tweets about a sport event while the event is happening and is broadcasted on TV worldwide. Figure 3 shows the results of the temporal analysis about the US OPEN 2013 tennis tournament.

We have cross compared each cluster time range with the times of the main matches of the tournament and realized that each cluster is associated with a main event. In fact, it can be noticed that the 12 identified temporal clusters group tweets created during one of the last five matches of the tournament, specifically:

- 5 Sept 2013, 13:06 EDT - 23:56 EDT: Men's Quarterfinals;
- 6 Sept 2013, 13:52 EDT - 18:59 EDT: Women's Semifinals;
- 7 Sept 2013, 10:57 EDT - 19:24 EDT: Men's Semifinals;
- 8 Sept 2013, 11:47 EDT - 23:04 EDT: Women's Final;
- 9 Sept 2013, 15:05 EDT - 23:25 EDT: Men's Final.

We have also realized that the sum of the cardinality of the clusters with timestamp "9 September 2013", corresponding to the Men's Final match, is the greatest, thus revealing that this match has been the most popular at global scale.

Figure 3. Results of the temporal analysis of the tweets about the US Open 2013

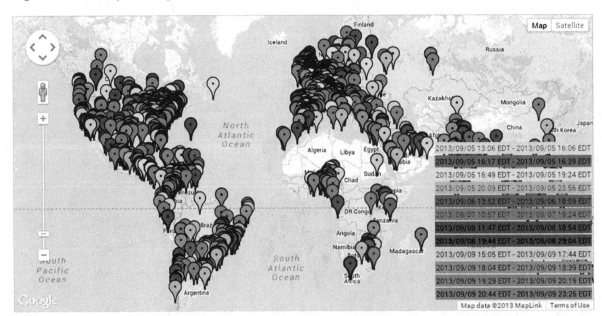

Periodic Temporal Analysis

An example of analysis of a periodically recurring event is related to traffic jam. To identify, at global scale, which are the time intervals of the day in which traffic jams occur more frequently on Earth, we submitted to following user query and analysis criteria:

uq: χ_c = "traffic jam" "traffic jam" "ingorgo stradale" "engarrafamento" "รถติด"

χ_t > 2013-01-23T00:00:20Z (time zone *UTC*)

Analysis criteria: (*DistMT*, ∝, *2 min, min, day*, 100)

This means that the subset of tweets about traffic jam were analyzed by considering the modulo temporal distance (*DistMT*) for grouping at least 100 reports sent within ε_{mt} = 2 min, every day (the period of analysis is $\tilde{G} = day$).

Figure 4 shows the results of the periodic temporal analysis of all the tweets about traffic jam, submitted all over the world.

Two temporal intervals of the day have been identified, one in the morning (7:41-9:35) and one in the late afternoon (16:24-20:13); as expected, these are the temporal intervals in which there are more traffic jams all over the world (when people go to or return from the work place). We can notice that there are much more tweets in the afternoon interval. This may be due to the fact that the temporal interval of the afternoon cluster is wider than the temporal interval of the morning cluster. However, we do not know if there is actually more congestion in the afternoon, or if people tend to complain more in the afternoon, maybe because they are tired of their working day and they want to reach home quickly. Notice that the unpredictability of human behavior is a bias of our approach (Kamath, 2013).

Figure 4. Results of the periodic daily analysis about Traffic jam all over the world

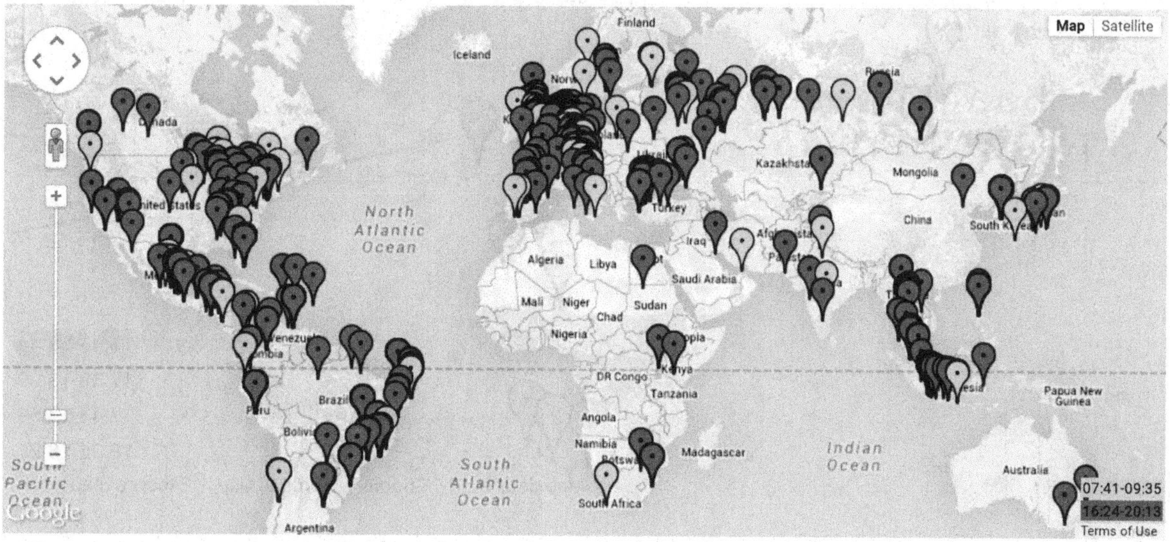

Periodic Geo-Temporal Analysis

Periodic geo-temporal analysis is useful for identifying the periods of time when events regularly occur in relation with the same area. We consider the tweets related to the traffic jams, which are events that may have a periodicity in specific regions: for example, it may happen that a particular road is always congested in a specific moment of the day. To this end we formulated the following user query and criteria of analysis:

uq: χ_c = *"traffic jam" "รถติด"* χ_s = *<Bangkok, 10 km>*

χ_t > 2013-01-23T00:00:20Z (time zone *UTC*)

Analysis criteria: (DistGMT, 1 km, 20 min, min, day, 3)

which means *MinPts* = 3, ε_s = 1 *km*, ε_{mt} = 20 *min*, *modulo* = G_d = *day*. This means that the tweets about traffic jams in Bangkok area are analyzed by considering their daily periodicity using the *DistGMT* distance. Three reports are needed within a distance of 1 km and sent within the same 20 minutes of the day. Figure 5 shows the results of this analysis.

We can see the congested areas in relation with the interval of time when the congestions occur. Some clusters slightly correspond to those discovered in the same area by the Geographic analysis (see Figure 2): nevertheless, in this analysis the clusters have been filtered by the time constraint, and thus they are smaller. For example, the big cluster shown in Figure 2 is reduced in size in Figure 5, since only tweets belonging to the temporal interval 15:08-15:44 have been kept. Some other clusters in Figure 2, instead, have not been identified when considering also the temporal constraint because they do not satisfy it.

Figure 5. Results of the periodic Geo-Temporal analysis of the Traffic jam in Bangkok

Validation

For the validation of the proposed exploratory framework we need to define an original evaluation procedure, since the approach consists of compound phases, a background and a foreground phase, the last one composed of two subsequent tasks, and thus the results are influenced by all these steps.

We decided to perform the evaluation of the foreground phase, assuming as true verity a collection of 139.348 tweets, related to four categories g1, ..., g4, retrieved by a background phase in which the crawler submitted to the Tweet source the four queries: g1="traffic jams", g2 ="US Open", g3 ="floods or storms or inundations" and g4 ="Brazil 2014 or soccer world cup". An evaluation of the partitions results obtained by applying distinct foreground exploratory objectives has been carried out by computing external measures of the clustering quality, i.e., recall and precision.

Given, as a result of the clustering process, k clusters C = {c1,...,ck} and considering that we have four categories that we assume are the reference truth, the Recall of a clustering partition is defined as the average of the recall of the partition for all the categories, i.e., the average of the greatest fraction of elements of a category assigned to a cluster. This measure indicates the average ability of a single cluster to collect all the messages of a category, and thus, its value is inversely proportional to the number of the clusters in the partition. Thus we can expect that the Recall values are small when we have many clusters. Precision of a clustering partition is defined as the average of the precision of the partition for all categories, i.e., the greatest fraction of elements of a category assigned to a cluster:

$$\text{Recall}(C) = \frac{\sum_{h=1}^{j} \text{recall}\left(g_h\right)}{j} \tag{18}$$

in which

$$\text{recall}(g_h) = \max_{i=1,\ldots,k} \frac{\left(\left|c_i \cap g_h\right|\right)}{\left|g_h\right|} \tag{19}$$

$$\text{Precision}(C) = \frac{\sum_{h=1}^{j} \text{precision}\left(g_h\right)}{j} \tag{20}$$

in which

$$\text{precision}(g_h) = \max_{i=1,\ldots,k} \frac{\left(\left|c_i \cap g_h\right|\right)}{\left|c_i\right|} \tag{21}$$

In order to evaluate the proposed foreground analysis, i.e., the process comprising the selection of tweets performed based on the evaluation of a user query and the following geo temporal exploration, we formulated two user queries "traffic jams", and "US Open" that selected 71696 and 5156 tweets respectively, and evaluated the average Recall and Precision of the obtained clustering partitions corresponding to several geo temporal explorations.

Additionally for each exploration we had to evaluate the variation of average Recall and average Precision by changing the parameters that define the minimal density of the clusters.

Firstly we performed a geographic exploration using *DistG* that produced, by varying the density parameters, ε_s=1 - 49, and *minPts*=2-67, the following average Recall of 0,08 and Precision of 0,98 respectively. The Recall was low because of the many clusters generated. Notice that with *minPts*< 17 the average Precision was 1, i.e., maximum, independently of the value of ε_s.

After that, we performed a temporal exploration of the messages obtaining an average Recall and Precision of 0,57 and 0,69 by varying in *DistT*, ε_t=30 – 172800 μsec, and *minPts*= 2-67. In this case, the average Recall was greater than in the previous case since a few clusters have been generated. Furthermore we observed that for *minPts* < 22 and ε_t < 21600 μsec the average Precision was 1.

Furthermore, we tried a periodic temporal exploration by varying in *DistMT*, ε_t=30 – 172800 μsec, *minPts*=2-67, with the time period *G*=86400 μsec (i.e., with the period of 1 day), and obtained an average Recall and Precision of 0,87 and 0,55 respectively. We noticed that for *minPts* < 17 and ε_t = 30 μsec the average Precision was above 0,94 while by increasing ε_t = 60 μsec the average Precision decreases to 0,85.

Finally, we performed a periodic geo-temporal exploration by using *DistGMT* and by varying ε_s=0.5 – 20, ε_t=30 – 172800 μsec, *minPts*= 2-67, and obtained, an average Recall of 0,04 while the average Precision was maximum 1. The low result of the average Recall is due to the many clusters in each partition and thus to the low proportion of messages in a category that a cluster can capture.

As a recap of these results we can state that the most appropriate exploration for the tweets about "*traffic jam*" and "*US open*" is a periodic geo-temporal exploration. This result is consistent with the fact that both events are likely to occur with a daily period: "*traffic jams*" generally happen during rush hours, and "*US Open*" messages are written during or just after the TV matches which are broadcasted daily during the tournament. Further evaluations are needed to finally assess the usefulness of the approach by extending the number of the categories.

CONCLUSION

In this chapter we proposed an original framework to perform a flexible geo-temporal analysis of information about events of interest in social network contexts.

The procedure is outlined as consisting of three subsequent phases: the first background phase that collects the messages from the social information sources that might be of interest for describing events; the second and the third foreground phases, activated by a user, firstly to filter by a query the messages regarding an event under study, and secondly to perform the geo-temporal analysis on the basis of specific criteria.

The first original aspect of the proposal is its flexibility, intended as both user driven analysis and kinds of geo-temporal analysis that can be performed of both aperiodic and periodic events, at global and local scale.

The second original aspect is the clustering algorithm that can be customized to use a desired distance measure, thus performing spatial, temporal or spatio-temporal analysis.

The procedure has been implemented for analyzing Twitter messages, collected by a focused crawler by querying the source of messages over a period of time, and subsequently by evaluating user requests to select messages about an event of interest and analyzing them based on their geotags and timestamps.

The approach can be applied to any message which contains metadata related to their geographic location and timestamp, so it is well suited to analyze geo-referenced messages.

In its current state, the approach does not allow to perform real time analysis of events reported in social contexts. In order to do this, we would need to further extend the algorithm performing the geo-temporal analysis, so as to incrementally generate and modify the clusters as new messages are retrieved by the crawler.

REFERENCES

Adam, N., Shafiq, B., & Staffin, R. (2012). Spatial computing and social media in the context of disaster management. *IEEE Intelligent Systems*, *12*, 1514–1672.

Arcaini, P., Bordogna, G., & Sterlacchini, S. (2015). Geo-temporal density based clustering for exploring periodic and aperiodic Events reported in Social networks, under review. *Information Science*.

Birant, D., & Kut, A. (2007). ST-DBSCAN: An algorithm for clustering spatial-temporal data. *Data & Knowledge Engineering*, *60*(1), 208–221. doi:10.1016/j.datak.2006.01.013

Bordogna, G., Bucci, F., Carrara, P., Pepe, M., & Rampini, A. (2011). *Flexible Querying of Imperfect Temporal Metadata in Spatial Data Infrastructures. In Advanced Database Query Systems: Techniques, Applications and Technologies* (pp. 140–159). IGI Global. doi:10.4018/978-1-60960-475-2.ch006

Chandra, S., Khan, L., & Muhaya, F. B. (2011). Estimating Twitter User Location Using Social Interactions – A Content Based Approac. In *Proceedings of 2011 IEEE International Conference on Privacy, Security, Risk, and Trust, and IEEE International Conference on Social Computing*, (pp. 838-843). doi:10.1109/PASSAT/SocialCom.2011.120

Cheng, T., & Wicks, T. (2014, March 6). Event Detection using Twitter: A Spatio-Temporal Approach. *PLOS One*.

Ester, M., Kriegel, H. P., Sander, J., & Xu, X. (1996). A density-based algorithm for discovering clusters in large spatial databases with noise. In *Proceedings of the 2nd International Conference on Knowledge Discovery and Data Mining (KDD-96)*, (pp. 226–231). AAAI Press.

Frias-Martinez, V., Soto, V., Hohwald, H., & Frias-Martinez, E. (2012). Characterizing Urban Landscapes Using Geolocated Tweets. In *Privacy, Security, Risk and Trust (PASSSAT), 2012 International Conference on Social Computing (SocialCom)*, (pp 239–248). Amsterdam: IEEE.

Ghosh, D., & Guha, R. (2013). What are we 'Tweeting' about Obesity? Mapping Tweets with Topic Modeling and Geographic Information System. *Cartography and Geographic Information Science*, *40*(2), 90–102. doi:10.1080/15230406.2013.776210 PMID:25126022

Kamath, K. Y., Caverlee, J., Lee, K., & Cheng, Z. (2013). Spatio-Temporal Dynamics of Online Memes: A Study of Geo-Tagged Tweets. In *Proceedings of the ACM WWW 2013*. Rio de Janeiro, Brazil: ACM.

Lee, C. H. (2012). Mining spatio-temporal information on microblogging streams using a density-based online clustering method. *Expert Systems with Applications*, *39*(10), 9623–9640. doi:10.1016/j.eswa.2012.02.136

Liu, Q., Deng, M., Bi, J., & Yang, W. (2012). A novel method for discovering spatio- temporal clusters of different sizes, shapes, and densities in the presence of noise. *International Journal of Digital Earth*, *12*, 1–20.

Oliveira, R., Santos, M. Y., & Pires, J. M. (2013). 4D+ SNN: A Spatio-Temporal Density-Based Clustering Approach with 4D Similarity. In *Proceedings of the IEEE 13th International Conference on Data Mining Workshops (ICDMW)*, (pp. 1045-1052). IEEE. doi:10.1109/ICDMW.2013.119

Raimond, Y., & Abdallah, S. (2007). *The event ontology*. Retrieved from http://motools.sourceforge.net/event/event.html

Sakaki, T., Okazaki, M., & Matsuo, Y. (2010). Earthquake Shakes Twitter Users: Real-time Event Detection by Social Sensors, Earthquake shakes twitter users: real-time event detection by social sensors. In *Proceedings of the 19th international conference on World Wide Web, WWW '10*, (pp. 851-860). New York: ACM. doi:10.1145/1772690.1772777

Thom, D., Bosch, H., Koch, S., Woerner, M., & Ertl, T. (2012). Spatio temporal anomaly detection through visual analysis of geolocated twitter messages. In *Proceedings of the IEEE Pacic Visualization Symposium (PacicVis)*. IEEE.

Wakamiya, S., Lee, R., & Sumiya, K. (2011). *Urban Area Characterization Based on Semantics of Crowd Activities in Twitter*. GeoSpatial Semantics; doi:10.1007/978-3-642-20630-6_7

Watanabe, K., Ochi, M., Okabe, M., & Onai, R. (2011). Jasmine: a real-time local-event detection system based on geolocation information propagated to microblogs. In *Proceedings of the 20th ACM international conference on Information and knowledge management, CIKM '11*, (pp. 2541-2544). doi:10.1145/2063576.2064014

Zhang, H., Korayem, M., You, E., & Crandall, D. J. (2012). Beyond co-occurrence: discovering and visualizing tag relationships from geo-spatial and temporal similarities. In *Proceedings of the fifth ACM international conference on Web search and data mining* (pp. 33-42). ACM. doi:10.1145/2124295.2124302

KEY TERMS AND DEFINITIONS

Cluster: It identifies a set of items sharing some common properties and identified based on an unsupervised algorithm; also known as: group, container.

Clustering: An unsupervised machine learning technique capable to automatically partition a set of items, described by a set of features, into disjoint groups, clusters. Also known as unsupervised learning mechanism, data mining technique.

Content, Spatial, and Temporal Query Conditions: Content conditions are generally specified by either terms in natural language or keyword categories and define the topics that the items of interest must deal with; spatial conditions, and geographic conditions, specify the (geographic) area of interest where the items must be located; temporal conditions specify the desired timestamp or time range of creation of the items of interest.

Focused Crawler: A web crawler that visits the Web pages on the Internet and fetches only those that deal with specific topics of interest.

Geo-Temporal Analysis: A process that allows to characterize subsets of items in a geographic database, for example events, with respect to the similarity of their location and timestamp.

Geo-Temporal Clustering: A clustering process that automatically partition a set of items based on the similarity of both their geographic attribute values and their timestamps.

Periodic and Aperiodic Event: An event is an something occurring in a specific time or spam of time, possibly in a given locality or geographic area, interesting or involving many people. A periodic event is characterized by a regular time occurrence, for example each day at the same hour, each month, season, every 10 years, and so on. An aperiodic event can happen just once or may occur several times without a specific time regularity.

Query: A request for information submitted by a user to a database in order to retrieve items of interest, i.e., records or documents. It consists of selection conditions that the items in the database must satisfy in order to be retrieved and judged relevant to the user request.

Social Media: A generic term identifying online applications and practices that people adopt to share text, images, video and audio on the Web.

Spatial Index: A type of extended index that allows to index a spatial attribute of an item in a spatial database so as to optimize the access by a spatial query.

Chapter 9
Complex Motion Pattern Queries in Spatio-Temporal Databases

Marcos R. Vieira
IBM Research, Brazil

ABSTRACT

With the recent advancements and wide usage of location detection devices, very large quantities of data are collected by GPS and cellular technologies in the form of trajectories. The wide and increasing availability of such collected data has led to research advances in behavioral aspects of the monitored subjects (e.g., wild animals, people, and vehicles). Using trajectory data harvested by mobile devices, trajectories can be explored using motion pattern queries based on specific events of interest. While most research works on trajectory-based queries has focused on traditional range, nearest-neighbor, and similarity and join queries, there has been an increasing need to query trajectories using complex, yet more intuitive, motion patterns. In this chapter, we describe in detail complex motion pattern queries, which allow users to focus on trajectories that follow a specific sequence of spatio-temporal events. We demonstrate how these motion pattern queries can greatly help users to get insights from very large trajectory datasets.

INTRODUCTION

The wide availability of location and mobile technologies (e.g., cheap GPS devices, ubiquitous cellular networks and Radio-Frequency Identification (RFID) tags), as well as the improved location accuracy has enabled a vast amount of new applications to collect and analyze data in the form of trajectories. For example, new generations of tracking systems have emerged, providing complex services to end users (e.g., detect when a truck deviate from its route, when two moving objects are closed together, when a bus will arrive at a certain bus stop). The accuracy of the generated spatio-temporal data has also improved: instead of the traditional cell phone tower triangulation method, assisted GPS (NAVCEN, 1996) was recently introduced to improve location accuracy, such as enhanced 911 services (Consumer & Governmental Affairs Bureau, 2013).

DOI: 10.4018/978-1-4666-8767-7.ch009

These advances have led to the generation of very large spatio-temporal datasets in the form of trajectories. A trajectory is a time- ordered sequence of spatial locations (e.g., latitude/longitude) for a moving object *id*. This sequence may also have some other reading, for instance, speed, outside temperature, and textual information. Figure 1 shows an example of a trajectory $T_{id} = \{mo_{id}, (l_1,t_1), (l_2,t_2), \dots (l_9,t_9)\}$ with 9 locations moving in the 2 dimensional space.

Given the huge volume of data generated in the form of trajectories, there is an increasing need to develop more effective and efficient techniques for data management and query evaluation over trajectories. Past research works on querying trajectory data have mainly concentrated on traditional spatio-temporal queries. Examples of such queries are:

1. Range and nearest neighbors queries, e.g., "find all trajectories that were in region q between 1pm and 3pm" (see Figure 2(a));
2. Similarity-based queries, e.g., "find the 2 *most similar* trajectories to trajectory q according to a predefined similarity measure" (see Figure 2(b)); and
3. Spatial-temporal join queries, e.g., "given two datasets S_1 and S_2, find *all pairs* of trajectories that are at most 10 miles distant from each other" (see Figure 2(c)).

A major problem with the above three approaches is that a range query may retrieve too many results, as exemplified in Figure 3(a). Since a spatio-temporal range query uses a single predicate to define the query condition, the returned answer may include a very large number of trajectories. On the other hand,

Figure 1. Example of a trajectory T_{id} with a sequence of 9 locations

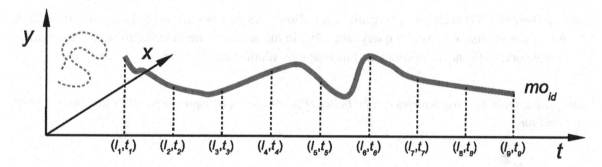

Figure 2. Examples of traditional spatio-temporal queries: (a) spatio-temporal range; (b) Spatio-temporal similarity; (c) spatial-temporal join

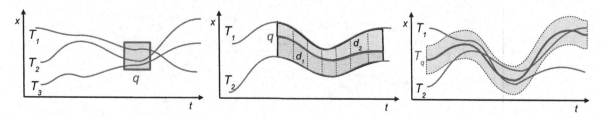

Figure 3. Limitations of traditional spatio-temporal queries: (a) traditional spatio-temporal range query; (b) similarity and join based queries

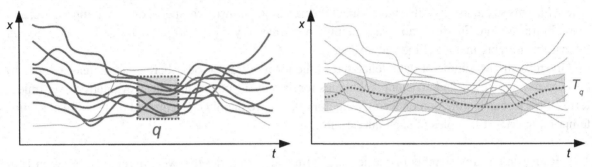

using a similarity-based and join queries may be too restrictive and, thus, return no result, as illustrated in Figure 3(b). Since the query is defined using a whole/part of trajectory, the qualified answers have to "follow" the same pattern in space and time, which may be too restrictive.

Nevertheless, trajectories are complex objects whose behavior over space and time can be better queried using a sequence of events defined by the user. Thus, in this chapter we describe "motion patterns" as a means to query trajectories in an efficient and effective way. For instance, as illustrated in Figure 4, a user may be interested in trajectories that passed by a spatio-temporal range predicate p_1, sometime later by another range predicate p_2, and later were as close as possible to the spatio-temporal nearest predicate p_3. This pattern query is expressed as a sequence of user defined events, where there is more flexibility than traditional spatio-temporal queries.

Chapter Overview: This chapter is organized as follows: we first provide some background; we then formalize the complex pattern query language; in the sequence we describe the query evaluation framework; in the next, we conclude this chapter with the final remarks.

Figure 4. Example how trajectories can be better captured using a sequence of interesting events over space and time

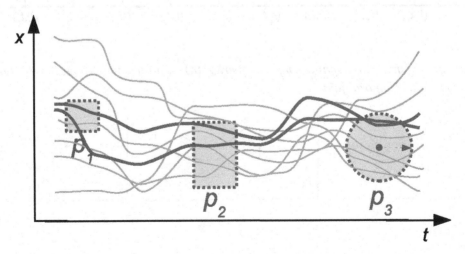

BACKGROUND

Complex Motion Pattern Queries (Vieira, Bakalov, & Tsotras, 2010, 2011) allow users to select trajectories based on a sequence of specific interesting events in space and time. Given the nature of trajectories as typically long sequences of events, a single range or nearest predicate may provide too many results (e.g., many trajectories passed through downtown Los Angeles), while a similarity-based query may be too restrictive (e.g., not many trajectories match the full extent of the query trajectory). Instead, we describe a framework for processing complex pattern queries over large repositories of trajectory data. Such pattern queries combine the ability of fixed and variable predicates, with explicit or implicit temporal constraints, and distance based constraints.

A complex pattern query specifies a sequence of spatio-temporal predicates that can thus capture only the parts of trajectories that are of interest to the user. For example: "find all trajectories that first visited downtown LA, then sometime later visited the Hollywood sign, and then went as close as possible to the LAX airport between 10pm and 11pm". This query, as illustrated in Figure 5, simply provides a collection of range and Nearest-Neighbor (NN) conditions, as well as an explicit time constraint that all have to be satisfied in the specified order (implicit temporal constraint). Another predicate that can also be used to build very complex patterns is "variables". For example, in the previous query, one may also add "..., and trajectories that started and ended up by the same area in an interval of 10 hours apart."). Conceptually, complex pattern queries cover the query choices between single spatio-temporal predicates and similarity queries.

Figure 5. Examples how trajectories can be better searched using complex pattern queries

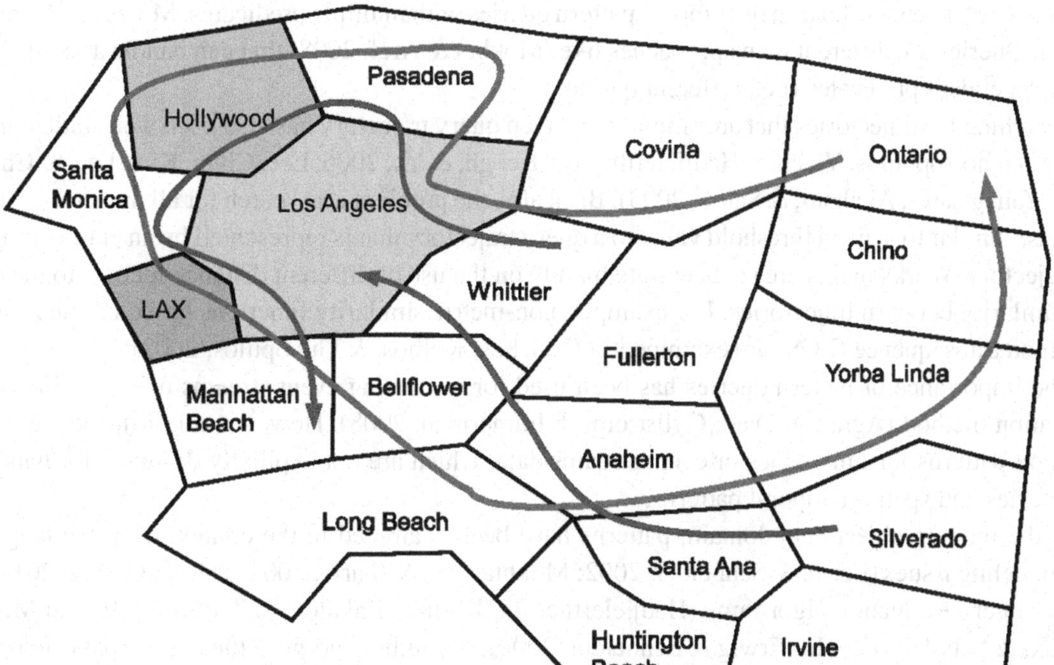

In this section, we describe complex pattern queries, which is a general and powerful framework that defines pattern queries as regular expressions over a finite spatial alphabet. Each letter in the alphabet corresponds to a non-overlapping region in the spatial domain; the union of all regions covers the entire space domain where the trajectories in the database lie. In the following we describe the language where users can build pattern queries. We then describe how pattern queries are evaluating using four different algorithms.

Overview of Previous Approaches

Previous works on evaluating spatio-temporal queries have mainly focused on either evaluation of a single spatio-temporal predicate (e.g., Range or Nearest Neighbor (NN) queries), or similarity/clustering queries where the entire (or a part of) trajectory is given as query and similar trajectories are sought.

Queries with a single spatio-temporal predicate for trajectory databases have been extensively studied in the past (Aggarwal & Agrawal, 2003; Benetis, Jensen, Karciauskas, & Saltenis, 2006; Ferhatosmanoglu, Stanoi, Agrawal, & Abbadi, 2001; Pfoser, Jensen, & Theodoridis, 2000; Tao, Papadias, & Shen, 2002). To make the evaluation process more efficient, the query predicates are typically evaluated utilizing hierarchical spatio-temporal indexing structures (Agarwal, Arge, & Erickson, 2000; M. Cai & Revesz, 2000; Elbassioni, Elmasry, & Kamel, 2003; Hadjieleftheriou, Kollios, Tsotras, & Gunopulos, 2006; Jensen, Lin, & Ooi, 2004; Patel, Chen, & Chakka, 2004; Prabhakar, Xia, Kalashnikov, Aref, & Hambrusch, 2002; Pelanis, Saltenis, & Jensen, 2006; Saltenis & Jensen, 2002). Most of these indexing structures use the concept of Minimum Bounding Regions (MBR) to approximate trajectories, which are then indexed using traditional spatial access methods, like MVR-tree (Tao & Papadias, 2001). These solutions, however, are focused only on single spatio-temporal predicate queries. Thus, none of them can be used for efficient evaluation of complex pattern queries with multiple predicates. Moreover, Complex Pattern Queries are different than approaches like (Mokbel & Aref, 2008) that can handle a set of single and independent predicates (i.e., different queries).

Searching for trajectories that are similar to a given query trajectory has also been well studied in the past (Anagnostopoulos, Vlachos, Hadjieleftheriou, Keogh, & Yu, 2006; Lee, Chun, Kim, Lee, & Chung, 2000; Yanagisawa, Akahani, & Satoh, 2003). Basically, the problem is to search for all trajectories in the database similar to a given threshold value to a query trajectory that is represented by an entire, or a part of, trajectory. Works in this area concentrate mainly on the use of different distance metrics to measure the similarity between trajectories. For example, non-metric similarity functions based on the Longest Common Subsequence (LCS) are examined in (Vlachos, Kollios, & Gunopulos, 2002).

The importance of pattern queries has been used for evaluating event streams using a NFA-based evaluation method (Agrawal, Diao, Gyllstrom, & Immerman, 2008). However, all of the above works focus on patterns for time-series or event streams data, which are not explicitly designed for handling trajectories and spatio- temporal patterns.

In the moving object data domain, patterns have been examined in the context of query language and modeling issues (Erwig & Schneider, 2002; Mokhtar, Su, & Ibarra, 2002; Sakr & Güting, 2011), as well as query evaluation algorithms (Hadjieleftheriou, Kollios, Bakalov, & Tsotras, 2005; du Mouza, Rigaux, & Scholl, 2005). In (Erwig & Schneider, 2002), the authors propose the use of spatio-temporal patterns as a systematic and scalable query mechanism to model complex object behavior in space and time. The work in (Mokhtar et al., 2002) presents a powerful query language able to model complex pattern queries using a combination of logical functions and quantifiers.

In (Hadjieleftheriou et al., 2005), it is examined incremental ranking algorithms for simple spatio-temporal pattern queries. Those queries consist of Range and NN predicates specified using only *fixed* regions. Complex Pattern Queries differ from (Hadjieleftheriou et al., 2005) since they provide a more general and powerful query framework where queries can involve both fixed and variable regions, as well as regular expression structures (repetitions, negations, optional structures, etc.) and explicit ordering of the predicates along the temporal axis. Moreover, Complex Pattern Query Language introduces explicit ordering of the predicates along the temporal axis, which allows the users to specify ordering constraints like "immediately after" or "immediately before" between predicates. In (du Mouza et al., 2005), a KMP-based algorithm (Knuth, Jr., & Pratt, 1977) is described to process motion patterns. This work, however, focuses only on range spatial predicates, and it cannot handle *explicit* and *implicit* temporal ordering of query predicates. Furthermore, the evaluation of pattern queries of this work is evaluated as a sequential scanning over the list of all trajectories stored in the database: each trajectory is checked individually, which becomes prohibitive for large trajectory databases.

While the use of variable predicates in specifying patterns greatly improves the expressive power, the query evaluation becomes more challenging. This is because variable spatio-temporal predicates provide many more opportunities for matching the pattern query to a specific trajectory in the repository, i.e., by simply changing the variable bindings in the pattern during the evaluation process.

SOLUTIONS AND RECOMMENDATIONS

We assume that a trajectory T_{id} of a moving object mo_{id} is stored in the database as an ordered sequence of w pairs $\{(l_1,t_1),\dots (l_w,t_w)\}$, where l_i is the moving object location recorded at timestamp t_i ($l_i \in \mathbb{R}^d$, $t_i \in \mathbb{N}$, $t_{i-1} < t_i$, and $0 < i \leq w$). Figure 1 illustrates an example of trajectory for moving object mo_{id} with a sequence of 9 locations, from (l_1,t_1) to (l_9,t_9).

Such trajectory data is generated from an assorted of different applications (e.g., GPS devices, cellular networks) and is stored in a database repository. Typically, monitored objects report their position using data packets containing a tuple (T_{id}, l_i, t_i). Depending on the application, objects may report continuously or simply when they change their location. For instance, if a trajectory is represented by a function f the (l_i, t_i) pairs can be created by sampling f at discrete timestamps (Y. Cai & Ng, 2004).

We assume that the spatial domain is partitioned to a fixed set Θ of non-overlapping regions. Figure 6 illustrates a hierarchical region alphabet with 3 layers, where the user has the ability to define queries with finer alphabet granularity (*zoom in*) for the portions of greater interest, and higher granularity (*zoom out*) elsewhere. Regions correspond to areas of interest (e.g., *airports*, *parks*, *city malls*) and form the alphabet used in our pattern query language. In the following we use capital letters to represent the region alphabet, $\Theta = \{A, B, C, D, \dots\}$.

A pattern query is defined as $Q = \{S \bigcup C\}$, where S corresponds to a sequence of spatio-temporal predicates and C represents a collection of distance functions (e.g., NN, top-k) or constrains (e.g., @ $x=\{A,C,B\}$, @$y!=$@z) a trajectory needs to satisfy. A trajectory matches the pattern query Q if it satisfies both S and C. In the following, we first describe how a pattern S is defined and then elaborate on the distance-based and other constraints C.

Figure 6. Region-based trajectory representation using 3 layers

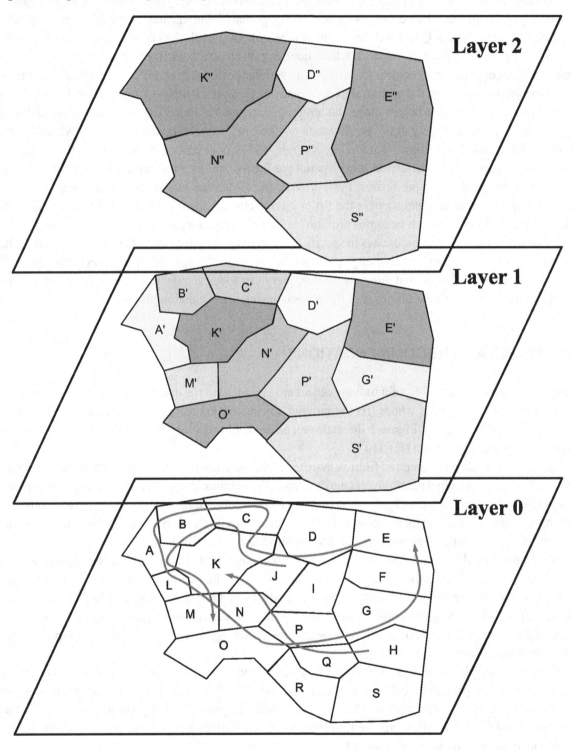

Spatio-Temporal Predicates

A sequence of spatio-temporal predicates S is defined as a path expression of an arbitrary number of spatio-temporal predicates P, as shown in Figure 7. The "$!$" unary operator defines a negation where a trajectory cannot match, "$\#$" defines the optional modifier, "$+$" defines the one or more repetition modifier, "$*$" defines the zero or more repetition modifier, and "$?$" defines the wild-card spatial predicate. Within the pattern S, the wild-card "$?$" predicate is used to specify parts in a trajectory's lifetime that are not important. This predicate can be of two types: "$?+$": one or more occurrences of any region predicate (e.g., $P_i.?^+.P_{i+1}$) implies that the predicate P_{i+1} appears "immediate after" P_i, with one or more regions visited between them); "$?^*$": zero or more occurrences of any region predicate (e.g., $P_i.?^*.P_{i+1}$ implies that the predicate P_{i+1} can be satisfied "any time after" P_i).

The sequence of predicates S is recursively defined by $S.S$, where the sequencer "$.$" appears between every two consecutive spatio-temporal predicates P. Each spatio-temporal predicate $P_i \in S$ is defined by a tuple $P_i = (op_i, R_i, int_i)$, where R_i corresponds to a predefined spatial region or a variable (i.e., $R_i \in \{\Theta \cup \Omega\}$, where Ω is the set of variables), op_i defines the topological relationship that a trajectory T_{id} and the spatial region R_i have to satisfy over the (optional) time interval int_i. In particular, we use the topological relationships described in (Erwig & Schneider, 2002); examples of such operators are the relations *Equal, Inside, Meet,* among others. Given a trajectory T_{id} and a region R_i, the operator op_i returns a Boolean value $\mathbf{B}=\{\mathbf{true}, \mathbf{false}\}$ whether the trajectory T_{id} and the region R_i satisfy the topological relationship op_i (e.g., an *Inside* operator will be **true** if the trajectory was sometime inside region R_i during time interval int_i). For simplicity, in the following we assume that the spatial operator is set to *Inside* and it is thus omitted from the query examples (Figure 7).

A predefined region $R_i \in \{\Theta \cup \Omega\}$ is specified by the user in the query predicate (e.g., "downtown Los Angeles"). On the other hand, a variable denotes an arbitrary region in the spatial domain and it is represented by a lowercase letter preceded by the "$@$" symbol (e.g., $@x$). A variable region is defined using symbols in $\Omega = \{@x, @y, @z, ...\}$, and it takes a single value (instance) from the regions in Θ (e.g., $@x=C$); however, one can also specify the possible values of a variable as a subset of Θ (e.g., $@x=\{A,B,C,D\}$). Conceptually, variables work as placeholders for spatial regions and can become instantiated during the query evaluation in a process similar to unification in logical programming.

A particular variable $@x$ can appear in several predicates of pattern S, referencing to the same region everywhere it occurs (i.e., bounding to the same region value in the pattern). This is useful for specifying complex queries that involve revisiting the same region many times. For example, a pattern $S=\{@x.?^*.B.@x\}$ finds trajectories that started from some region, specified by variable $@x$, then at

Figure 7. Specification of complex pattern query language

$$
\begin{aligned}
&Q \leftarrow (S \cup C) \\
&S \leftarrow S.\, S \mid P \mid !P \mid P^{\#} \mid ?^+ \mid ?^* \\
&P \leftarrow\, <op, R\,[,t]> \\
&op \leftarrow Disjoint \mid Meet \mid Overlap \mid Equal \mid Inside \mid Contains \mid Covers \mid CoveredBy \\
&R \in \{\Theta \cup \Omega\},\ \Theta = \{A, B, C, ...\},\ \Omega = \{@x, @y, @z, ...\} \\
&t \leftarrow (t_{from} : t_{to}) \mid t_s \mid t_r
\end{aligned}
$$

Table 1. Matrix M for trajectory T_2 and pattern S

	T_2		F	I	S	B	P	H	D	U	A	B	H	D	A
S	idx	i\j	1	2	3	4	5	6	7	8	9	10	11	12	13
?+	1	1	**-1**	**-1**	**-1**	**-1**	**-1**	**-1**	-1	-1	-1	-1	-1	-1	-1
@x	2	2	0	-2	-2	-2	-2	**-2**	**-2**	-2	-2	-2	-2	-2	-2
?*	2	3	0	2	-3	-3	-3	-3	**-3**	**-3**	-3	-3	-3	-3	-3
A	3	4	0	0	3	3	3	3	3	3	**-4**	4	4	4	-4
?*	3	5	0	0	3	-4	-4	-4	-4	-4	-4	-5	-5	-5	-5
B	4	6	0	0	0	-4	4	4	4	4	4	**-5**	5	5	5
?*	4	7	0	0	0	4	-5	-5	-5	-5	-5	-5	**-6**	-6	-6
@x	5	8	0	0	0	0	-5	-6	-6	-6	-6	-6	**-6**	**-7**	-7
?*	5	9	0	0	0	0	5	-6	-7	-7	-7	-7	-7	**-7**	-8
A	6	10	0	0	0	0	0	6	7	7	-8	8	8	8	**-8**

some point passed by region *B*, and immediately after they visited the same region they started from (defined by @x). Note that wild-card "?" is also considered a variable; however it refers to any region in the alphabet, and not necessarily the same region if it occurs multiple times within a pattern *S*.

Finally, a predicate P_i may include an explicit temporal constraint int_i in the form of an interval. This constraint implies that the spatial relationship op_i between a trajectory and region R_i should be satisfied in the time interval int_i (e.g., "passed by area *B* between 10am and 11am"). If the temporal constraint is missing, we assume that the spatial relationship can be satisfied any time in the duration of a trajectory lifespan. For simplicity we assume that if two predicates (P_i, P_j) occur within pattern *S* (where $i < j$) and have temporal constraints int_i, int_j, then these intervals do not overlap and int_i occurs before int_j on the time dimension.

Distance-Based and Other Constraints

Spatio-temporal predicates cannot answer queries with constraints (e.g., "best-fit" type of queries that find trajectories which best match a specified pattern), because topological predicates are binary and thus cannot capture distance based properties of trajectories. The Ω component is thus used to describe distance-based and other type of constraints among the variables used in Θ. A simple kind of constraint can involve comparisons among the used variables (e.g., @x!=@y) and distance-based constraint which has the form $AGG(d_1, ..., d_n); \theta)$.

For simplicity, we describe our examples using the Euclidean distance L_2, but other distances can also be used (e.g., Manhattan, Mahalanobis). For example, consider a pattern query *Q* whose pattern *S* contains three variables $\{@x, @y, @z\}$, S= $\{A.?*.B.@x.@y.C.?*.@z\}$. Among the trajectories that satisfy *S*, the user may specify that the sum of the distance between regions @x and @y $(d_1=d(@x, @y))$ and the distance between @z and the fixed region *E* $(d_2=d(@z, E))$ is less than 100 meters $(d_1 + d_2 < 100)$. Hence *C* contains a collection of distance terms $\{d_1, ..., d_n\}$ where term d_i represents the distance between two variable regions or between a variable region and a fixed one.

Distance terms need to be aggregated into a numerical value using an aggregation function (depicted as AGG in the definition of *C*). In the previous example, AGG=SUM, but other aggregators like AVG,

MIN, MAX, etc., can also be used. The aggregated numerical value for each trajectory needs to be mapped to a binary value so as to determine whether the trajectory satisfies C. This is done by the θ operator defined in C, which can be a simple check function (using $=$, $\leq$, and others). In our example, θ corresponds to "< 100 meters" and returns **true** for all trajectories whose aggregate distance is less than 100 meters. It is also possible to use other θ operators, e.g., MIN, MAX, TOP-k, etc. In the previous example, if the θ operator is changed to TOP-k, the query will return **true** only for the trajectories with the TOP-k aggregated distances. For simplicity of the description, in the remainder of this work we use AGG=SUM and θ=MIN, which corresponds to a NN query.

The use of variables in describing both the topological predicates and the numerical conditions provides a very powerful language to query very large trajectory repositories. To describe a query, the user can use fixed regions for the portions of the trajectory where the behavior should satisfy known (strict) requirements. The user can also employ variables for portions where the exact behavior is not known, but can be described by a sequence of variables and the constraints between them. The ability to use the same variable many times in the query allows for revisiting areas, while the ability to refer to these variables in the distance functions allows for easy description of NN and related queries.

EVALUATING COMPLEX PATTERN QUERIES

Index Framework

For simplicity we assume the spatial domain is partitioned into a set of non-overlapping regions, as illustrated in Figure 8(a). To efficiently evaluate complex pattern queries we use two index structures in the form of ordered lists (Figures 8(b)-(c)), which are stored in addition to the original trajectory data (Figure 8(d)). There is one region-list per region and one trajectory-list per trajectory. The region-list L_A of a given region A acts as an inverted index that contains **all** trajectories that passed by region A. Each entry in L_A contains a trajectory identifier T_{id}, the time interval (*t-entry*: *t-exit*) during which the moving object was inside region A, and a pointer to the trajectory-list of T_{id}. If a particular trajectory visits a given region A multiple times in different time intervals, we store an entry for each visit. Entries in a region-list are ordered first by the trajectory-id T_{id} and then by *t-entry*. For example, in Figure 8 the region-list entry for the region B is $\{T_2(7,9); T_2(21,23); T_3(5,10); ...\}$.

Figure 8. Example of a region-based trajectory representation with 3 trajectories T_1, T_2, T_3: (a) partitioned spatial domain; (b) region-list; (c) trajectory-list; (d) trajectory archive

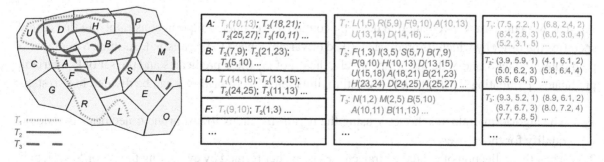

In order to fast prune trajectories that do not satisfy pattern S, each trajectory is approximated by the sequence of regions it visited. An entry of trajectory T_{id} in trajectory-list contains the region and the time interval (*t-entry*: *t-exit*), during which this region was visited by T_i, ordered by *t-entry*. In Figure 8(c) the trajectory-list entry for T_2 is $\{F(1,3); I(3,5); S(5,7); B(7,9); P(9,10); H(10,13); D(13,15); U(15,18); A(18,21); B(21,23); H(23,24); D(24,25); A(25,27)\}$. Entries from a region-list index point to the corresponding entries in a trajectory-list index. For example, entry $T_2(21,23)$ in region-list L_B contains a pointer to the page in the trajectory-list of T_2 that contains the corresponding entry $B(21,23)$.

Since variables in pattern S can be bounded to any values in the set Θ of regions, we need a representation of each trajectory using the alphabet elements in Θ. It is efficient to maintain a region representation of each trajectory to fast prune trajectories that do not satisfy the pattern S. That is, each trajectory is approximated by the sequence of regions it visited, where this compact representation is stored in the trajectory-list index. An entry of trajectory T_{id} in the trajectory-list contains the region and the time interval (*t-entry*: *t-exit*) during which this region was visited by T_i, ordered by *t-entry*. Figures 8(b-c) depict various region-lists and trajectory-lists. Note that entries from a region-list index point to the corresponding entries in a trajectory-list index. For example, consider the region-list L_B of region B and an entry in this list for trajectory T_2 with interval (t_1, t_2). The pointer included in this entry points to the page in the trajectory-list of T_2 that contains the corresponding entry $B(t_1, t_2)$.

There is a requirement for the regions in the partitioning to be non-overlapping. In practice, there may be a difference between the regions presented to the user and what region lists are created. Moreover, instead of a uniform grid, one could facilitate a dynamic space partitioning structure (e.g., adaptive grid files (Nievergelt, Hinterberger, & Sevcik, 1984), kdb-trees (Robinson, 1981)) that assigns grid cells sizes according to the data density. Then, dense areas will have finer cells which in return allow for better approximation of the regions, and thus fewer false positives are generated.

For evaluating pattern queries we propose two different strategies:

1. **Index Join Pattern (IJP) Algorithm:** Is based on a merge-join operation performed over the region-lists corresponding to every fixed predicate in the pattern S;
2. **Dynamic Programming Pattern (DPP) Algorithm:** Performs subsequence matching between the pattern S and the trajectory approximations stored as the trajectory-lists; All algorithms use the same two indexing structures for pruning purposes, but in different ways: IJP uses the region-lists for pruning and the trajectory-lists for the variable binding; all the other three algorithms use mainly the trajectory-lists for the subsequence matching and performs an intersection-based pruning on the region-lists.

Index-Join Pattern Algorithm (IJP)

We start with the case where pattern S does not contain any explicit temporal constraints. In this case, S specifies the order by which its predicates, fixed or variable, need to be satisfied. Assume S contains $|S|$ predicates and let S_f and S_v denote, respectively, the set of $|S_f|$ fixed predicates and the set of $|S_v|$ variable predicates. Evaluating S with the IJP Algorithm, illustrated in Algorithm 1 can be divided in two steps:

1. The algorithm evaluates the set S_f using the region-list index to fast prune trajectories that do not qualify for the answer;
2. Then the collection of candidate trajectories is further refined by evaluating the set of S_v variables.

Fixed Predicate Evaluation

All fixed predicates in S_f can be evaluated using an operation similar to a merge-join among their region-lists L_i, $i \in 1 \ldots |S_f|$. Entries from these $|S_f|$ lists are retrieved in sorted order of T_{id} and then joined by their T_{id} 's. Entries are pruned using the trajectory ids and the temporal intervals (*t-entry*: *t-exit*). In each list L_i a pointer p_i is used to track the entry currently considered for the join. This pointer p_i scans the list L_i starting from the first entry.

When the same region appears more than once in pattern S, a duplicate pointer traversing the region-list is used for each region appearance in S. For example, to process the pattern $S=\{?*.A.B.A\}$, the region-lists of A and B are accessed using: one pointer for region-list L_B (p_B) and; two pointers for traversing region-list L_A (p_{A1} and p_{A2}). A T_{id} is saved as a candidate solution if the T_{id} appears in all of the $|S_f|$ region-lists involved in Θ and their corresponding time intervals in all $|S_f|$ region-lists satisfy the ordering of the predicates.

There are cases during the merge-join operation where entries from a region-list can be skipped, thus resulting in faster processing. For example, assume that predicate $P_i \in S$ of region-list L_i is before predicate $P_j \in S$ of L_j. Also assume that the current entry considered in list L_i for the join has identifier T_r, while in list L_j the current entry has identifier T_s. If $T_s < T_r$, processing in list L_j can skip all its entries with $T_{id} < T_r$, that is, the pointer p_j in L_j can advance to the first entry with $T_{id} \geq T_r$. Essentially, predicate P_i cannot be satisfied by any of the trajectories in L_j with smaller T_{id} than T_r. Since entries in a region-list are sorted by T_{id}, L_i does not contain trajectories with smaller identifiers than $|S_v|$.

When an entry from the same trajectory T_s is found in two region-lists, L_i and L_j, the IJP algorithm checks whether the corresponding time intervals of entries match the order of predicates in S. Hence, a trajectory that satisfies S must visit the region of L_i before visiting L_j. If an entry of $T_s \in L_i$ has t-entry that falls after the corresponding *t-entry* of $T_s \in L_j$, then this entry can be skipped in L_i since it cannot satisfy the pattern query. Since region-lists are stored in ordered way, forwarding region-list to a specific location by $(T_{id}, t\text{-}entry)$ can be easily implemented using an index B$^+$-tree.

Example: The first step of IJP Algorithm is illustrated using the example in Figure 9. Assume the pattern S in the query Q contains three fixed (A, B, A) and three variable predicates ($?^+$, $@x$, $@x$), as in $S=\{?^+.@x.?*.A.?*.B.?*.@x.?*.A\}$. This pattern looks for trajectories that first visited an arbitrary region (denoted by $?^+$) one or more times, then visited some region denoted by variable $@x$, then (after visiting zero or more regions) it visited region A, then region B and then visited again the same region $@x$ before finally returning to A. The first step of the IJP Algorithm uses the region-list L_A and L_B for A and B, respectively. Figure 9 depicts two copies of list L_A, namely L_{A1} and L_{A2}, to represent two separate pointers in list L_A.

The IJP Algorithm begins with the first entry $T_1(10,13)$ in list L_{A1}. It then checks the first entry T_2 in list L_B. We can see that T_1 is not a candidate trajectory, since it does not appear in the list of L_B. Thus, we can skip T_1 from L_{A1} list and continue with the next entry $T_2(18,21)$. Since $T_2(7,9)$ in list L_B has interval before $(18,21)$, list L_B moves to its next entry $T_2(21:23)$. These two occurrences of T_2 coincide with the pattern $A.?*.B$ of S, thus we need to check whether T_2 passes again by region A. In this case, we consider the first entry $T_1(10:13)$ of list L_{A2}. Since it is not from T_2 it cannot be an answer, thus list L_{A2} advances to the next entry $T_2(18,21)$. Now every pointer in all lists has entries of T_2. However, $T_2(18,21)$ in L_{A2} does not satisfy the pattern because its time interval must be after the interval $(21,23)$ of T_2 in B. Hence

Figure 9. Trajectory examples T₁, T₂ and T₃ satisfying two spatial fixed predicates: A and B

Figure 9. Trajectory examples T_1, T_2 and T_3 satisfying two spatial fixed predicates: A and B

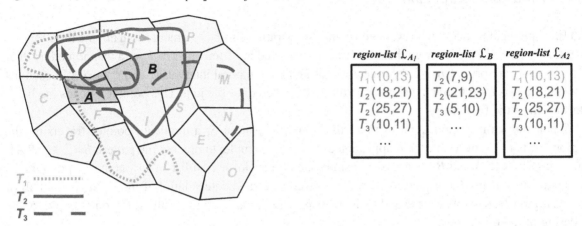

L_{A2} is advanced to the next entry, which happens to be $T_2(25,27)$. We now have an entry from the same trajectory T_2 in all lists and T_2 satisfies the temporal constraints. As a result, trajectory T_2 is kept as a candidate in U. In the next step it analyzes the following entry $T_2(25,27)$ in L_{A1}. However, this entry cannot satisfy the pattern S, thus it is skipped. Eventually L_{A1} will consider $T_3(10,11)$ which causes list L_B to move to $T_3(5,10)$. Trajectory T_3 cannot satisfy the temporal constraint, so it is skipped from list L_B and the algorithm terminates.

Algorithm 1. IJP: fixed spatial predicates

```
Input: Pattern S
Output: Trajectories satisfying S_f
        Candidate Set U ← ∅
        for (i ← 1 to |S_f|)
                Initialize L_i with the cell-list of P_i
        for (w ← 1 to |L_1|)
                p_1 ← w
                for (j ← 2 to |S_f|)
                        if (L_1[w].id ∉ L_j)
                                break
                        Let k be the first entry for L_1[w].id in L_j
                        while (L_1[w].id = L_j[k].id and L_{j-1}[p_{j-1}].t > L_j[k].t)
                                k ← k + 1
                        if (L_1[w].id ≠ L_j[k].id)
                                break
                        else
                                p_j = k
                if (L_1[w] qualifies)
                        U ← U ∪ L_1[w].id
        return U
```

Algorithm 1 can also be applied in case where the region partitioning is internally represented by a grid of smaller cells. In order to evaluate region of predicates, we need to first materialize a sorted list from all cell-lists involved in this region. However, since the individual cell-lists participating in the enclosure are already ordered by trajectory-id T_{id}, the sort order can be dynamically materialized by feeding the algorithm with the entry that has the smallest T_{id} among the heads of the participating cell-lists. Hence the algorithm proceeds without having to actually sort the participating region-lists. Additionally, the IJP Algorithm supports explicit temporal constraints assigned to the spatial predicates. These temporal conditions are evaluated during the join phase among the list entries.

Variable Predicate Evaluation

The second step evaluates the variable predicates S_v over the set of candidate trajectories U generated in the previous step. For a fixed predicate its corresponding region-list contains all trajectories that satisfy it. However, variable predicates can be bound to any region, so one would have to look at all region-lists in the spatial domain. Our approach is to use one list per each variable predicate, called variable-list. However, such variable-lists are not precomputed like the region-lists, but rather they are created during query execution time using the candidate trajectories filtered from the fixed predicate evaluation step.

To build a variable-list for a particular variable predicate $P_j \in S_v$, we compute the possible assignments for P_j by analyzing the trajectory-list for each candidate trajectory. We use the time intervals in a candidate trajectory to identify which portions of trajectory can be assigned to P_j. An example is shown in Figure 10, using the candidate trajectory T_2 from Figure 9. From the previous step we know that T_2 satisfies the fixed predicates at the following regions: $A(18,21)$, $B(21,23)$, $A(25,27)$. Using the pointers from the region-lists of the previous step, we know where the matching regions are in the trajectory-list of T_2. As a result, T_2 can be conceptually partitioned is three segments $\{Seq_1, Seq_2, Seq_3\}$, as shown in Figure 10. Note that Seq_2 is empty since there is no region between $A(18,21)$ and $B(21,23)$.

The trajectory segments are employed to create the variable-lists by identifying the possible assignments for variables in S_v. Each variable is restricted by the two fixed predicates that appear before and after the variable in the pattern. All variables between two fixed predicates are first grouped together. Then for every group of variables the corresponding trajectory segment, the segment between the fixed

Figure 10. Example on the IJP segmentation step for T_2 ($Seq_2=\varnothing$)

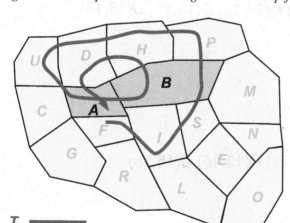

$$F(1,3)\ I(3,5)\ S(5,7)\ B(7,9)\ P(9,10)$$
$$H(10,13)\ D(13,15)\ U(15,18)\ A(18,21)$$
$$B(21,23)\ H(23,24)\ D(24,25)\ A(25,27)$$

S_1: $F(1,3)\ I(3,5)\ S(5,7)\ B(7,9)\ P(9,10)$
      $H(10,13)\ D(13,15)\ U(15,18)$

S_2: $\{\}$

S_3: $H(23,24)\ D(24,25)$

predicates, is used to generate the variable-lists for the group. Grouping is advantageous, since it can create variable lists for multiple variables through the same pass over the trajectory segments. Moreover, it ensures that the variables in the group maintain their order consistent with pattern S.

Assume that a group of variable predicates has w members. Each trajectory segment that affects the variables of this group is then "streamed" through a window of size w. The first w elements of the trajectory segment are placed in the corresponding predicate lists for the variables. The first element in the segment is then removed and the window shifts by one position. This proceeds until the end of the segment is reached. In the above example, there are two groups of variables: the first consists of variables $?^+$ and $@x$, while the second group has a single member $@x$. Figure 11 depicts the first three steps in the variable list generation for the group of variables $?^+$ and $@x$. This group streams through segment Seq_1, since it is restricted on the right by the fixed predicate A in pattern S. Each list is shown under the appropriate variable. A different variable list will be created for the second group with variable $@x$, since this group streams through segment Seq_3.

The generated variable-lists are then joined in a similar way for fixed predicates. Because the variable-lists are built by trajectory segments coming from the same trajectory, the join criteria checks only if the ordering of pattern S is satisfied. In addition, if the pattern contains variables with the same name, the join condition verifies that they are matched to the same region and time interval.

Figure 11. Example with 3 steps on how the IJP creates the variable list for T_2 and $?^+.@x$

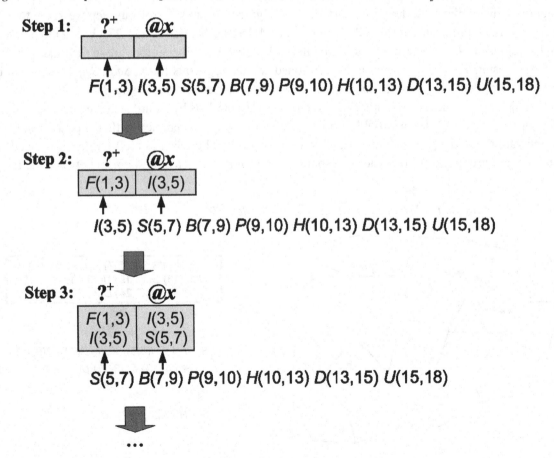

Distance-Based Constraints Evaluation

The evaluation of distance constraints C in pattern Q is performed as a post processing step. The intuition is that the spatial predicates in S will filter out a large number of candidate trajectories that need to be examined. Nevertheless, since the distance terms contain variables, there are still many possibilities to bind the values of these variables. The IJP algorithm has the advantage of re-using the variable lists created during the spatial predicate search. These lists effectively enumerate all possible value bindings. However, instead of using a *brute force* approach that will examine all possible bindings, the IJP approach uses a variation of the *Threshold Algorithm* (TA) (Fagin, Lotem, & Naor, 2001) to examine the possibilities in an incremental ordered fashion.

Regarding the IJP approach, assume that the S evaluation has returned a collection of trajectories T. For each variable in S one variable-list per trajectory in T is also created. All variable-lists for a given variable are concatenated and sorted, first by region id and then by trajectory id. Note that the same region may be associated with different trajectory ids. For simplicity, consider the scenario where the distance terms are combinations of a variable with a fixed region (i.e., $d(@x, A)$). The case where the distance term contains two variables is omitted for brevity.

For each distance term in C a separate list is created. As with the variable-lists, distance-lists are also dynamically computed. The idea is to incrementally examine the regions around the fixed variable of each distance term d_i. The distances between regions are calculated using the region boundaries. For example, given a term $d(@x, A)$, in the first iteration we examine the regions that are one grid cell away from the grid approximation of region A. The next iteration expands the vicinity by one cell, and so on. When we discover a region which appears also in the sorted concatenated list for $@x$, we load all the corresponding trajectory ids and place them in the list for this distance term. As the lists for all distance terms in C have been created incrementally, the TA algorithm finds the trajectory that appears in all distance-lists and minimizes the sum of the distances.

Dynamic Programming Pattern Algorithm (DPP)

The DPP algorithm is divided into two phases:

1. **Trajectory Selection:** Where the trajectory-lists are employed to select, using the fixed predicates in S, a candidate set of trajectories;
2. **Pattern Matching:** Where it performs a pattern matching to prune trajectories that do not match the correct sequence order of predicates in S, and also checks for appropriate variable bindings. The pseudo code for the DPP algorithm is described in Algorithm 2.

Trajectory Selection

For each region-list of a fixed region in S_f, we select the ids T_{id} for all trajectories that visited this region. Candidate set is computed by intersecting the collected set of T_{id}. That is, contains ids of the trajectories that have visited (independently of what order) all the regions in S. Nevertheless, since no order of these appearances has been verified, a further verification step must be performed on each $T' \in T$ to enforce the order of predicates in S. This verification step is performed using a dynamic programming approach.

Algorithm 2. DPP: fixed and variable spatial predicates

```
Input: Pattern S that consists of predicates P_i
Output: Trajectories satisfying S
Let T be the set of candidate trajectories from trajectory-list having all
fixed predicates in S
Answer ← { }
for (each trajectory T' ∈ T)
    Build(T', Θ)
        if (ABS(M[|S|][|T'|]) ≥ P_{|S|}.idx)
            Scan(|S|,|T'|)
Function: Build(T', S)
    for (i ← 0 to |S|)
        for (j ← 0 to |T'|)
            if (i=0 or j=0)
                M[i][j] ← 0
            else
                if (P_i.type is a fixed spatial predicate)
                    if (P_i.R = T.R_j)
                        M[i][j] ← -ABS(M[i-1][j-1]) + 1
                    else
                        M[i][j] ← MAX(ABS(M[i-1][j]), ABS(M[i][j-1]))
                else
                    if (P_i.type={?⁺, @})
                        M[i][j] ← -ABS(M[i-1][j-1]) + 1
                    else
                        if (i=P_i.idx)
                            M[i][j] ← ABS(M[i-1][j])
                        else
                            M[i][j] ← -ABS(M[i-1][j-1]) + 1
Function: Scan(i,j)
    if (i > 0)
        for (k ← j to k ≥ P_i.idx downto 1)
            if (ABS(M[i][k]) ≥ P_i.idx)
                if (M[i][k] ≤ 0)
                    if (P_i.type={@} and Match[P_i.link] ≠ T'.R_k)
                        continue
                    Match[i] ← T'.R_k
                    if (P_{i-1}.type={?*})
                        Scan(i-1, k)
                    else
                        Scan(i-1, k-1)
        else
            Answer ← Answer ∪ T'.id
```

Pattern Matching

For each candidate trajectory $T' \in T$ a dynamic programming matrix M is created. This matrix is later used to retrieve matches of S in T'. The matrix M records **all** occurrences of pattern S in T' in the specified order defined in S. Matrix M has a column j for each region visited by the trajectory T'. Multiple visits to the same region are represented with multiple columns in M, as it is stored the same way in the trajectory-list index. The rows i in the matrix correspond to the predicates $P_i \in S$. Thus, the size of M is $|S|.|T'|$. The value in each cell in $M[i][j]$ is computed based on the predicate P_i and the j-th element in the region approximation of the trajectory T' denoted as T'_j. When the pattern S contains only fixed spatial predicates, matrix M can be reduced by eliminating the regions in T' that are not present in S. This optimization does not compromise the sequence of patterns found, because for each R_j in T' the attribute $(t\text{-}entry_j;\ t\text{-}exit_j)$ is also kept.

Each M cell can have cells corresponds to the length of the longest match between S and T' discovered so far. A negative number in $M[i][j]$ denotes a match between P_i and trajectory region R_i, and its absolute value is the length of the longest match found so far. In this way M is employed to store both the match occurrences, represented with negative value, and the length of each match, represented with absolute values in $M[i][j]$.

Matrix M is computed cell-by-cell starting from $M[0][0]$ and ending with $M[|S|][|T'|]$ cell. At each step Build function compares the values of the current predicate P_i and the current region from the trajectory approximation T_j (the same as the T'_j). If there is no match between P_i and T_j, then the value of $M[i][j]$ is the highest absolute value among the neighbors $M[i-1][j]$ or $M[i][j-1]$. If there is a match between P_i and T_j, then $M[i][j]$ receives the value $|M[i-1][j-1]| + 1$, but it is stored as a negative number indicating that the current pair P_i, T_j participates in the match.

The above description applies only for fixed spatial predicates. As for wild-card (?+ and ?*) and variable predicates, the computation of $M[i][j]$ cell is done differently. Because such variables can be bound with any value of T_j, the value of $M[i][j]$ is always computed as a "match". Therefore, the cell receives the value of $-(|M[i-1][j-1]|+1)$. When a pattern S has variables that appear multiple times, the verification step is performed in the Scan function. Instances of the same variable are "linked" in a backward fashion with the following constraint: $P_i.\text{link} \leftarrow P_j$ if $P_i = P_j$ and $i < j$. Because M is verified for matching in a "backward" way (from $M[|S|][|T'|]$ to $M[1][1]$ cell), the pointers are associated to the next occurrence in the pattern S.

There is also a special case where predicate P_i is optional in the pattern S. In this case, the computation and further verification of matrix M has to consider the case where P_i does not match T_j. To deal with this case, another attribute $P_i.\text{idx}$ is associated with each predicate in S. Basically, this attribute stores the position of each predicate P_i in case the optional predicate does not match with any T_j. This idx attribute is defined in the following manner:

1. If $i=1$ then $P_i.\text{idx} = 1$;
2. If $P_i.\text{type} = \{?^*, ?^\#\}$ then $P_i.\text{idx} = P_{i-1}.\text{idx}$;
3. $P_i.\text{idx} = P_{i-1}.\text{idx} + 1$ all other cases.

After M is computed, all the matches have to be searched in the matrix using the Scan function. This function searches for negative numbers stored in M cells, where such numbers denote the occurrence of a match. The operation goes cell-by-bell starting with the bottom right cell. If ABS($M[|S|][|T'|]$) $\geq$ $P_{|S|}$.idx, then there is at least one match between S and T'. Otherwise we can safely prune the trajectory avoiding further processing. Because we are only interested in finding the longest match between S and T', we only look for entries that have values greater or equal than the S_i.idx index. If the cell value is less than the current pattern index S_i.idx, then the function Scan aborts the processing of the current row i.

If there is a match in $M[i][j]$, then the function Scan is called recursively to process the sub-matrix with bottom right corner $M[i-1][j-1]$. If the predicate P_i is optional (# and *) then the function is called for the $M[i-1][j]$ cell instead. The algorithm stops when all predicates in S are processed ($i=0$), thus finding all possible matches of S in T'.

Explicit Temporal Constraints

When pattern S contains as explicit temporal constrains int_i, the DPP algorithm only performs a check along with the match checks in order to satisfies int_i too (not shown in Algorithm 2). If both the above conditions are satisfied, then the value of $M[i][j]$ is computed as a match.

Example: To illustrate how the DPP algorithm works we use the same pattern S example in Figure 9.

Using *region-list* the trajectory identifiers that have all the grids A and B are in = $\{T_2, T_3\}$. For each trajectory T' in, the matrix M is computed using the function Build. The computation of matrix M for T_2 and S appears in Table 1. Since $P_{|S|}$.idx is 6, the Scan function looks for cell values equal to $M[10][j] \geq |-6|$ in the 10-*th* row of matrix M. In Scan, the $M[10][13]$ cell passes the checks of the algorithm and the $M[10][13]$ cell is stored as a match in *Match*[10] (A was found in the 13-*th* column of T_2) and then the function Scan is called for the $M[9][12]$ matrix. Again, $M[9][12]$ cell passes all the checks and it is called for $M[8][12]$. Because P_8 is a variable (i.e., variable @x) and it is the first variable encountered so far, it passes the bounded value check (*link* test) and then it is bounded to the grid B. Then the function Scan is called in the following sequence for entries in M: $M[7][11]$, $M[6][10]$, $M[5][10]$, $M[4][9]$, $M[3][8]$ and then for $M[2][8]$, but it fails for this last one because the *link* test does not pass ($M[2][8] \neq M[8][12]$). Then it is called for $M[2][7]$, and the *link* test satisfies because variable @x is bounded to grid B ($M[2][7]= M[8][12]$). Then Scan is called for $M[1][6]$ until j is 0. In the end, the pattern *?+.B.?*.M.?*.D.?*.B.?*.M* is found and added to *Answer*. The backtracking also evaluates the $M[8][11]$ cell and finds pattern *?+.H.?*.M.?*.D.?*.H.?*.M*. Other calls for other entries are called, e.g. $M[10][9]$ (-8), but they all fails to bound to other predicates in S. The 2 patterns found for the pattern S in trajectory T_2 are $M[1][1]$, $M[1][2]$, $M[1][3]$, $M[1][4]$, $M[1][5]$, $M[1][6]$, $M[2][7]$, $M[3][8]$, $M[4][9]$, $M[6][10]$, $M[7][11]$, $M[8][12]$, M}[10][13] and $M[1][1]$, $M[1][2]$, $M[1][3]$, $M[1][4]$, $M[1][5]$, $M[2][6]$, $M[3][7]$, $M[3][8]$, $M[4][9]$, $M[6][10]$, $M[8][11]$, $M[9][12]$, $M[10][13]$.

Adding Distance-Based Constraints

The evaluation of distance constraints Ω inside a pattern query Q is performed as a post filtering step after the pattern S evaluation. The DPP algorithm can only use a brute force approach since it maintains a trajectory as a sequence of regions but loses the spatial properties of these regions. Therefore, the DPP algorithm can only compute the distance for the constraint as a final step.

FUTURE RESEARCH DIRECTIONS

There are many interesting new research topics that could be explored in the area of complex pattern queries. These open research topics are:

1. To study cost models that could enable a query optimizer to pick the best technique based on the query parameters (e.g., size of the query pattern, number of variables, wild-cards);
2. To extend our complex pattern querying framework to support complex pattern trajectory joins (Bakalov, et al., 2005; Lu, Yang & Jensen, 2011), density-based pattern queries (Li, et al. 2013; Pelekis & Theodoridis, 2014; Tang, et al., 2014; Tripathi, Debnath & Elmasri, 2014; Vieira, Bakalov, & Tsotras, 2009; Zheng, et al., 2014), uncertain spatio-temporal data (Cheng, et al., 2014; Emrich, et al., 2012), and textual (Abdelhaq, Gertz, & Sengstock, 2013; Lappas, et al., 2012; Wang, et al., 2012);
3. To study how to evaluate continuous complex pattern queries in spatio-temporal data streams (Zou, et al., 2010);
4. To investigate how complex pattern queries can be integrated, evaluated and optimized into a commercial Relational Database Management System (RDBMS) (Damiani, et al., 2014);
5. To handle a dynamic region partition space where users could use any spatial region and the indexing structures would be optimized to such queries;
6. To study how the proposed querying framework could implemented using the MapReduce (Gupta & Lakshminarasimhan, 2014; Tan, Luo & Ni, 2012) framework to concurrently evaluate one or more complex pattern queries; and
7. To evaluate Complex Motion Pattern Queries using GPUs (Graphics Processing Units) and FPGAs (Field Programmable Gate Arrays) (Moussalli, et al., 2013; Moussalli, et al., 2014).

CONCLUSION

The wide availability of new applications that combine GPS and cellular technologies has created very large datasets of trajectories. Pattern queries provide a very intuitive way to search relevant data as they can select trajectories based on specific events of interest in space and time. However, as the complexity of pattern queries increases, so do the complexity of evaluating such queries.

In this chapter, we described Complex Motion Patterns for querying very large trajectory archives. Such pattern queries combine the ability of fixed and variable predicates, with explicit or implicit temporal constraints and distance-based constraints. Complex patterns are described as regular expressions over a spatial alphabet that can be implicitly or explicitly anchored to the time domain. More importantly, variables can be used to substantially enhance the flexibility and expressive power of pattern queries. Nevertheless, such flexibility of pattern queries imposes many challenges when evaluating such queries.

Previous works have considered only subsets of the described pattern queries. These previous works are either variations of the KMP algorithm or use finite automata to evaluate pattern queries. Nevertheless, our work proposed an index framework to efficiently and effectively evaluate complex pattern queries, which have more features than previous proposed approaches. We described two query processing techniques: one based on merge joins (IJP) and one based on subsequence matching (DPP). Among our approaches, *IJP* is more robust in that it can easily support *NN* queries, while *DPP* is more suitable for patterns with smaller number of predicates or wild-cards. Since however both approaches use the same indexing schemes, they can both be available to the query evaluation engine, which can call the appropriate algorithm based on query properties and available dataset statistics.

REFERENCES

Abdelhaq, H., Gertz, M., & Sengstock, C. (2013). Spatio-temporal characteristics of bursty words in Twitter streams. In *Proc. of the ACM International Conference on Advances in Geographic Information Systems (SIGSPATIAL)*, (pp. 194-203). doi:10.1145/2525314.2525354

Agarwal, P. K., Arge, L., & Erickson, J. (2000). Indexing moving points. In *Proc. of the ACM SIGMOD-SIGACT-SIGART Symp. on Principles of Database Systems (PODS)*, (pp. 175-186). ACM.

Aggarwal, C. C., & Agrawal, D. (2003). On nearest neighbor indexing of nonlinear trajectories. In *Proc. of the ACM SIGMOD-SIGACT-SIGART Symp. on Principles of Database Systems (PODS)*, (pp. 252-259). doi:10.1145/773153.773178

Agrawal, J., Diao, Y., Gyllstrom, D., & Immerman, N. (2008). Efficient pattern matching over event streams. In *Proc. of the ACM SIGMOD International Conference on Management of Data*, (pp. 147-160). ACM.

Anagnostopoulos, A., Vlachos, M., Hadjieleftheriou, M., Keogh, E. J., & Yu, P. S. (2006). Global distance-based segmentation of trajectories. In *Proc. of the ACM SIGKDD International Conference on Knowledge Discovery and Data Mining*, (pp. 34-43). ACM.

Bakalov, P., Hadjieleftheriou, M., Keogh, E., & Tsotras, V. (2005). Efficient trajectory joins using symbolic representations. In *Proc. of the International Conference on Mobile Data Management (MDM)*, (pp. 86-93). doi:10.1145/1071246.1071259

Benetis, R., Jensen, S., Karciauskas, G., & Saltenis, S. (2006, September). Nearest and reverse nearest neighbor queries for moving objects. *The VLDB Journal*, *15*(3), 229–249. doi:10.1007/s00778-005-0166-4

Cai, M., & Revesz, P. (2000). Parametric R-tree: An index structure for moving objects. In *International Conference on Management of Data (COMAD)*, (pp. 57-64). COMAD.

Cai, Y., & Ng, R. (2004). Indexing spatio-temporal trajectories with Chebyshev polynomials. In *Proc. of the ACM SIGMOD International Conference on Management of Data*, (pp. 599-610). ACM.

Cheng, R., Emrich, T., Kriegel, H.-P., Mamoulis, N., Renz, M., Trajcevski, G., & Züfle, A. (2014). Managing uncertainty in spatial and spatio-temporal data. In *Proc. of the IEEE International Conference on Data Engineering (ICDE)*, (pp. 1302-1305). doi:10.1109/ICDE.2014.6816766

Consumer & Governmental Affairs Bureau. (2013). *Wireless 911 services*. Retrieved from www.fcc.gov/guides/wireless-911-services

Damiani, M. L., Issa, H., Güting, R. H., & Valdes, F. (2014). Hybrid queries over symbolic and spatial trajectories: A usage scenario. In *IEEE International Conference on Mobile Data Management (MDM)*, (pp. 341-344). doi:10.1109/MDM.2014.49

du Mouza, C., Rigaux, P., & Scholl, M. (2005). Efficient evaluation of parameterized pattern queries. In *Proc. of the ACM International Conference on Information and Knowledge Management (CIKM)*, (pp. 728-735). ACM.

Elbassioni, K. M., Elmasry, A., & Kamel, I. (2003). An efficient indexing scheme for multidimensional moving objects. In *International Conference on Database Theory (ICDT)*, (pp. 425-439). ICDT.

Emrich, T., Kriegel, H.-P., Mamoulis, N., Renz, M., & Züfle, A. (2012). Indexing uncertain spatio-temporal data. In *Proc. of the ACM International Conference on Information and Knowledge Management (CIKM)*, (pp. 395-404). ACM.

Erwig, M., & Schneider, M. (2002, July). Spatio-temporal predicates. *IEEE Transactions on Knowledge and Data Engineering*, 14(4), 881–901. doi:10.1109/TKDE.2002.1019220

Fagin, R., Lotem, A., & Naor, M. (2001). Optimal aggregation algorithms for middleware. In *Proc. of the ACM SIGMOD-SIGACT-SIGART Symp. on Principles of Database Systems (PODS)*, (pp. 102-113). ACM.

Ferhatosmanoglu, H., Stanoi, I., Agrawal, D., & Abbadi, A. E. (2001). Constrained nearest neighbor queries. In *Proc. of the International Symp. on Advances in Spatial and Temporal Databases (SSTD)*, (vol.. 2121, pp. 257-278). doi:10.1007/3-540-47724-1_14

Gupta, H., & Lakshminarasimhan, S. (2014). Processing Spatio-temporal Data On Map-Reduce. In *Proc. of the International Conference on Big Data Analytics (BDA)*, (pp. 57-59). Academic Press.

Hadjieleftheriou, M., Kollios, G., Bakalov, P., & Tsotras, V. J. (2005). Complex spatio-temporal pattern queries. In *Proc. of the International Conference on Very Large Data Bases (VLDB)*, (pp. 877-888). VLDB.

Hadjieleftheriou, M., Kollios, G., Tsotras, V. J., & Gunopulos, D. (2006). Indexing spatiotemporal archives. *The VLDB Journal*, 15(2), 143–164. doi:10.1007/s00778-004-0151-3

Jensen, C. S., Lin, D., & Ooi, B. (2004). Query and update efficient B+-Tree based indexing of moving objects. In *Proc. of the International Conference on Very Large Data Bases (VLDB)*, (pp. 768-779). doi:10.1016/B978-012088469-8.50068-1

Knuth, D. E. Jr, Morris, J. H. Jr, & Pratt, V. R. (1977). Fast pattern matching in strings. *SIAM Journal on Computing*, 6(2), 323–350. doi:10.1137/0206024

Lappas, T., Vieira, M., Gunopulos, D., & Tsotras, V. (2012). On the spatiotemporal burstiness of terms. *Proceedings of the VLDB Endowment.*, 5(9), 836–847. doi:10.14778/2311906.2311911

Lee, S.-L., Chun, S.-J., Kim, D.-H., Lee, J.-H., & Chung, C.-W. (2000). Similarity search for multidimensional data sequences. In *Proc. of the IEEE International Conference on Data Engineering (ICDE)*, (pp. 599-608). IEEE.

Li, X., Ceikute, V., Jensen, C. S., & Tan, K.-L. (2013). Effective Online Group Discovery in Trajectory Databases. *IEEE Transactions on Knowledge and Data Engineering, 25*(12), 2752–2766. doi:10.1109/TKDE.2012.193

Lu, H., Yang, B., & Jensen, C. S. (2011). Spatio-temporal joins on symbolic indoor tracking data. In *Proc. of the IEEE International Conference on Data Engineering (ICDE)*, (pp. 816-827). doi:10.1109/ICDE.2011.5767902

Mokbel, M. F., & Aref, W. G. (2008, August). SOLE: Scalable on-line execution of continuous queries on spatio-temporal data streams. *The VLDB Journal, 17*(5), 971–995. doi:10.1007/s00778-007-0046-1

Mokhtar, H., Su, J., & Ibarra, O. (2002). On moving object queries. In *Proc. of the ACM SIGMOD-SIGACT-SIGART Symp. on Principles of Database Systems (PODS)*, (pp. 188-198). ACM.

Moussalli, R., Absalyamov, I., Vieira, M. R., Najjar, W. A., & Tsotras, V. J. (2014). High performance FPGA and GPU complex pattern matching over spatio-temporal streams. *GeoInformatica*, 1–30.

Moussalli, R., Vieira, M. R., Najjar, W. A., & Tsotras, V. J. (2013). Stream-mode FPGA acceleration of complex pattern trajectory querying. In *Proc. of the International Symp. on Advances in Spatial and Temporal Databases (SSTD)* (Vol. 8098, pp. 201-222). Springer. doi:10.1007/978-3-642-40235-7_12

NAVCEN. U. C. G. N. C. (1996, september). *Navstar GPS User Equipment Introduction.* Retrieved from www.navcen.uscg.gov/pubs/gps/gpsuser/gpsuser.pdf

Nievergelt, J., Hinterberger, H., & Sevcik, K. C. (1984, March). The grid file: An adaptable, symmetric multikey file structure. *ACM Transactions on Database Systems, 9*(1), 38–71. doi:10.1145/348.318586

Patel, J. M., Chen, Y., & Chakka, V. P. (2004). Stripes: an efficient index for predicted trajectories. In *Proc. of the ACM SIGMOD International Conference on Management of Data*, 635-646. doi:10.1145/1007568.1007639

Pelanis, M., Saltenis, S., & Jensen, C. S. (2006). Indexing the past, present, and anticipated future positions of moving objects. *ACM Transactions on Database Systems, 31*(1), 255–298. doi:10.1145/1132863.1132870

Pelekis, N., & Theodoridis, Y. (2014). *Mobility Data Management and Exploration.* New York: Springer. doi:10.1007/978-1-4939-0392-4

Pfoser, D., Jensen, C. S., & Theodoridis, Y. (2000). Novel approaches in query processing for moving object trajectories. In *Proc. of the International Conference on Very Large Data Bases (VLDB)*, (pp. 395-406). VLDB.

Prabhakar, S., Xia, Y., Kalashnikov, D. V., Aref, W. G., & Hambrusch, S. E. (2002). Query indexing and velocity constraint indexing: Scalable techniques for continuous queries on moving objects. *IEEE Transactions on Computers*, 1–17.

Robinson, J. T. (1981). The K-D-B-tree: a search structure for large multidimensional dynamic indexes. In *Proc. of the ACM SIGMOD International Conference on Management of Data*, (pp. 10-18). doi:10.1145/582318.582321

Sakr, M. A., & Güting, R. H. (2011). Spatiotemporal pattern queries. *GeoInformatica*, *15*(3), 497–540. doi:10.1007/s10707-010-0114-3

Saltenis, S., & Jensen, C. S. (2002). Indexing of moving objects for location-based services. In *Proc. of the IEEE International Conference on Data Engineering (ICDE)*, (pp. 463-472). doi:10.1109/ICDE.2002.994759

Tan, H., Luo, W., & Ni, L. M. (2012). CloST: a hadoop-based storage system for big spatio-temporal data analytics. In *Proc. of the ACM International Conference on Information and Knowledge Management (CIKM)*, (pp. 2139-2143). doi:10.1145/2396761.2398589

Tang, L.-A., Zheng, Y., Yuan, J., Han, J., Leung, A., Peng, W.-C., & La Porta, T. (2014). A framework of traveling companion discovery on trajectory data streams. ACM Trans. Intell. Syst. Technol. 5(1).

Tao, Y., & Papadias, D. (2001). MV3R-Tree: A spatio-temporal access method for timestamp and interval queries. In *Proc. of the International Conference on Very Large Data Bases (VLDB)*, (pp. 431-440). VLDB.

Tao, Y., Papadias, D., & Shen, Q. (2002). Continuous nearest neighbor search. In *Proc. of the International Conference on Very Large Data Bases (VLDB)*, (pp. 287-298). doi:10.1016/B978-155860869-6/50033-0

Tripathi, P. K., Debnath, M., & Elmasri, R. (2014). Extracting Dense Regions From Hurricane Trajectory Data. In *Proc. of the ACM Workshop on Managing and Mining Enriched Geo-Spatial Data (GeoRich'14)*. ACM.

Vieira, M., Bakalov, P., & Tsotras, V. (2009). On-line discovery of flock patterns in spatio-temporal data. In *Proc. of the ACM International Conference on Advances in Geographic Information Systems (SIGSPATIAL)*, (pp. 286-295). doi:10.1145/1653771.1653812

Vieira, M. R., Bakalov, P., & Tsotras, V. J. (2010). Querying trajectories using exible patterns. In *Proc. of the International Conference on Extending Database Technology (EDBT)*, (pp. 406-417). doi:10.1145/1739041.1739091

Vieira, M. R., Bakalov, P., & Tsotras, V. J. (2011). FlexTrack: A system for querying flexible patterns in trajectory databases. In *Proc. of the International Symp. on Advances in Spatial and Temporal Databases (SSTD)*, (pp. 475-480). doi:10.1007/978-3-642-22922-0_34

Vlachos, M., Kollios, G., & Gunopulos, D. (2002). Discovering similar multidimensional trajectories. In *Proc. of the IEEE International Conference on Data Engineering (ICDE)*, (pp. 673-684). IEEE.

Wang, B., Dong, H., Boedihardjo, A. P., Lu, C.-T., Yu, H., Chen, I.-R., & Dai, J. (2012). An integrated framework for spatio-temporal-textual search and mining. In *Proc. of the ACM International Conference on Advances in Geographic Information Systems (SIGSPATIAL)*, (pp. 570-573). doi:10.1145/2424321.2424418

Yanagisawa, Y., Akahani, J.-i., & Satoh, T. (2003). Shape-based similarity query for trajectory of mobile objects. In *Proc. of the IEEE International Conference on Mobile Data Management (MDM)*, (pp. 63-77.) doi:10.1007/3-540-36389-0_5

Zheng, K., Zheng, Y., Yuan, N. J., Shang, S., & Zhou, X. (2014). Online Discovery of Gathering Patterns over Trajectories. *IEEE Transactions on Knowledge and Data Engineering*, 26(8), 1974–1988. doi:10.1109/TKDE.2013.160

Zou, Q., Wang, H., Soulé, R., Hirzel, M., Andrade, H., Gedik, B., & Wu, K. L. (2010). From a stream of relational queries to distributed stream processing. *Proceedings of the VLDB Endowment*, 3(1-2), 1394–1405. doi:10.14778/1920841.1921012

KEY TERMS AND DEFINITIONS

Global Positioning System (GPS): A satellite navigation system that provides accurate location and time information anywhere on the Earth where there is an unobstructed sight to four or more GPS satellites.

Indexing Structure: A data structure that speed the search operations on a database. Creating and Maintaining an index structure has an associated cost of extra writes and storage space. This cost is amortized at the search phase, where querying using an index is faster than searching every row in a database.

Join Query: Given a distance threshold θ, a similarity function that returns how similar two objects are, and two datasets D_1 and D_2, a join query returns pair of objects from D_1 and D_2 that are at least θ similar to each other.

Moving Object: An object that has a set of associated locations indexed in the time dimension.

Query Predicate: A query predicate is a conditional expression that defines the filter condition in a query.

Radio-Frequency Identification (RFID): A system that uses wireless technology and two components: readers and tags. The reader device has antennas that emit radio waves and receive signals back from tag devices. Tags uses radio waves to communicate back to reader devices. Tag devices are used to automatically identify and track objects that are attached with the tags.

Similarity Query: Given a query object q, a dataset D, a distance threshold θ, and a similarity function that returns how similar two objects are, a similarity query returns a subset of objects from D that has at least θ similar to the query object q.

Spatial Index: A spatial index is a specialized indexing structure where the indexing key is the spatial location of objects indexed. The type of searches on an spatial index is the set of spatial queries, for example, range and overlapping queries.

Spatial k-Nearest Neighbor Query: Given a query object q and a dataset D, a k-nearest neighbor query returns the k closest spatial objects to query q.

Spatial Range Query: Given a query object q, a distance threshold θ and a dataset D, a spatial range query returns a set of objects in D that is at most θ distant from the query object q.

Spatial-Temporal Index: A spatial-temporal index is an advanced index structure where the indexing key is the location and timestamp of an object.

Spatio-Temporal Databases: a database that provides storage, management and query capabilities for spatio-temporal data.

Chapter 10
Spatiotemporal Query Algebra Based on Native XML

Luyi Bai
Northeastern University, China

Changming Xu
Northeastern University, China

ABSTRACT

A formal algebra is essential for applying standard database-style query optimization to XML queries. We propose a spatiotemporal XML data model and develop such an algebra based on Native XML, for manipulating spatiotemporal XML data. After studying NXD spatiotemporal database and query framework, formal representation of spatiotemporal query algebra is investigated, containing logical structure of spatiotemporal database, data type system, and querying operations. It shows that the model and algebra lay a firm foundation for managing spatiotemporal XML data.

INTRODUCTION

Since a considerable amount of spatiotemporal data emerges in spatiotemporal applications (Benferhat, Ben-Naim, Papini, 2010; Mehrotra, Sharma, 2009), the requirement of managing spatiotemporal data has attracted much attention both from academia and industry (Abiteboul, Quass, McHugh, et al., 1997a; Koyuncu, Yazici, 2003; Sözer, Yazici, Oğuztüzün, et al., 2008). As the next generation language of the Internet, XML is playing an increasingly important role. In addition, XML is gradually gaining acceptance as medium for integrating and exchanging data from different sources. In that case, the advent of XML seems to provide an opportunity for managing spatiotemporal data (Senellart, Abiteboul, 2007). Unfortunately, current efforts have mainly focused on the problems of modeling general data in XML (Ma, Liu, Yan, 2010) and modeling spatiotemporal data in XML (Huang, Yi, and Chan, 2004), and relative little work has been carried out in representing spatiotemporal data in XML.

As evidenced by the successful relational technology (Prade, Testemale, 1984), a formal algebra is absolutely essential for applying standard database-style query optimization to XML queries. Due to its significance, researches on this issue have been extensively proposed (Beeri, Tzaban, 1999; Buratti,

DOI: 10.4018/978-1-4666-8767-7.ch010

Montesi, 2006; Jagadish, Laks, Lakshmanan, et al., 2001; Magnani, Montesi, 2005). Beeri and Tzaban (Beeri, Tzaban, 1999) propose an algebra that can handle multi-valued attributes, has support for detection and handling of run-time errors, and most of its operations preserve order. Buratti and Montesi (Buratti, Montesi, 2006) address the import issue of establishing a formal background for the management of semi-structured data. They define a data model and propose an algebra which is able to represent most of XQuery expressions. Jagadish et al. (Jagadish, Laks, Lakshmanan, et al., 2001) present TAX, a Tree Algebra for XML, which extends relational algebra by considering collections of ordered labeled trees instead of relations as the basic unit of manipulation. Magnani and Montesi (Magnani, Montesi, 2005) present a model for the management of relational, XML, and mixed data. Their query algebra can represent queries not expressible by other proposals and by the current implementation of TAX. Moreover, they show that relational-like logical query rewriting can be extended to their algebraic expressions. However, they do not provide a formal algebra that can support the spatiotemporal XML queries. As a result, we need a valid formal algebra for the XML queries that can serve as a well understood and order-sensitive intermediate representation.

Accordingly, the motivation of the chapter is trying to build a spatiotemporal XML model for algebraic operations. The rest of the chapter is organized as follows. In Section 2, we introduce basic knowledge. A spatiotemporal data model is proposed in Section 3. After studying NXD spatiotemporal database and query framework in Section 4, formal representation of spatiotemporal query algebra based on Native XML is investigated in Section 5. Section 6 presents the related work, and Section 7 concludes the chapter.

SEMANTICS OF SPATIOTEMPORAL DATA

Spatiotemporal data have a set of characteristics that make them distinctly different from the more familiar lists and tables of alphanumeric data used in traditional business applications. In the case of spatiotemporal data, we measure it by five dimensions according to characteristics of spatiotemporal data (Bai, Yan, Ma, 2013). The dimensions of spatiotemporal data contain OID, ATTR, P, M, and T.

OID: It provides a means to refer to different spatiotemporal data, and describes changing history of the spatiotemporal data relating both its ancestor and descendant. The ancestor indicates where the object comes from and how it comes into being, and the descendant shows what the object finally changes into and why the change occurs. Moreover, changing types of spatiotemporal data typically include four types: create, split, merge, and eliminate.

1. **ATTR:** It is used to describe static properties of spatiotemporal data (e.g., land owner's name, area, typhoon intensity, air pressure, etc.). There may be one or more attributes in a spatiotemporal data. This dimension heavily depends on the application domain.
2. **P:** It describes position of the spatiotemporal data, which contains point, line, and region. From P, we can obtain: (a) position of spatiotemporal data; (b) relationship between two spatiotemporal data (topological, direction, and distance relationship).
3. **M:** It describes motion, which contains direction of movement and value of movement. The direction of movement denotes where the spatiotemporal data moves. The value of movement denotes the velocity of a spatiotemporal data.

4.   **T:** It describes time of the spatiotemporal data, which contains time point and time interval. Time describes:

   a.   Temporal behavior of changes in OID, ATTR, P, or M dimension;

   b.   Temporal relationships (temporal topology, etc.).

CLASSIFICATIONS OF SPATIOTEMPORAL QUERY

Concerning on spatiotemporal data queries, researches are made by extension of the traditional query language as follows.

Spatiotemporal database query language based on SQL: There are two approaches for extension of the traditional query language: extension that makes no extension to SQL and extension that makes extensions to SQL. STSQL can represent and query spatiotemporal data by extracting and operating spatiotemporal data classifications, which is compatible with SQL belonging to the former one. STQL makes extensions of WHEN clause and WHERE clause to SQL, which can support spatiotemporal data query by extending new clauses.

Spatiotemporal database query language based on OQL: Object-oriented database provides a high degree of data abstracting and modeling capabilities, which makes many benefits to complex spatiotemporal data management. Spatiotemporal query language is proposed based on ODMG model, which is the extension of OQL.

Spatiotemporal database query language based on XML: XQuery is a querying language designed by the W3C, which allows one to select the XML data elements of interest, reorganize and possibly transform them, and return the results in a structure of ones choosing. Despite expressive power of XQuery, this language is not compatible with spatiotemporal data. One can make spatiotemporal extensions to spatiotemporal database query language.

NATIVE XML DATA MANAGEMENT

XML data management system is called Native XML database system, which includes Lore (Abiteboul, Quass, McHugh, et al., 1997a) and Tamino (Schoning, 2001), etc. Lore (Lightweight Object Repository) is semi-structured database, which is built up for semi-structured data. It is compatible with XML document data after transformation. Lore is representative of data storage, querying language, and querying optimization for object database and semi-structured database.

Lore is initially used to manage semi-structured data, using OEM (Object Exchange Model) to describe data structure and DataGuides to index data and guide users to query. OEM is a self-descriptive and nested structural object model. The structure of OEM can be regarded as tagged directed graph. XML documents are mapped into OEM instances, which are directed or ordered graph. Node in the graph represents data element in XML documents. Edge in the graph represents relation between element and sub-element.

The query language Lorel offers a navigation mode called General Path Expressions, having richer path expression semantic. From the visual sense, users can define freely matching model of identifies in database, containing paths, identifies, and atomic objects. The querying process of Lore is listed as follows:

- Parse query sentences and obtain the query trees.
- Preprocess query trees and transfer to OQL queries.
- Construct query optimization.
- Optimize queries.
- Perform optimized queries.

The querying engine of Lorel is built up based on the standard querying processing operators such as Scan and Join, but have their own characteristics. Take Scan for example, it can perform complex searches in databases taking a path expression as reference. The operators in querying engine of Lore consist of physical querying operators and logical querying operators.

For querying process of path expressions in XML, three algorithms based on DataGuides (Goldman, Widom, 1997) are proposed (McHugh, Widom, 2003): top-down, bottom-up, and hybrid. The top-down approach traverses the XML document tree from the root node until the desired results. The bottom-up approach traverses the XML document tree from the bottom node to the root node until searching the desired results. The hybrid approach splits the long path expression into short sub-expressions, and then traverses the XML document tree using top-down approach or bottom-up approach. In addition, all results of sub-expressions are performed connecting operations based on parent-child relationship.

The Lore also implements several index to improve efficiency of queries, containing:

- **Value Index:** Operations on atomic objects of given predicates and names.
- **Identifier Index:** Operations on parent objects of objects given names.
- **Path Index:** Path instances operating on paths.

The architecture of Native XML database (Abiteboul, Quass, McHugh, et al., 1997b) is shown in Figure 1. XML data documents store in XML databases and XML query is directly processed by XML query processor. The XML query does not need any translation or transformation. The results are XML data so that they can be published directly.

Different from relational database and object-oriented database, although Native XML database is still developed in initial steps and several technologies is also still not mature, it is considered as the most promising solution. Classification of XML data management system is shown in Figure 2.

XBase is a Native XML data management system (Abiteboul, Quass, McHugh, et al., 1997b), shown in Figure 3. XBase contains XML loader, XML memory, and path querying processor. The function of XML loader is to parse XML documents, extract schema of XML documents, extract statistical data, and establish data index. Firstly, XML documents use XML document parser to parse, and store data information in XML memory. If XML documents do not contain DTD, XML loader will extract DTD from XML documents. Otherwise, DTD will be obtained directly. DTD of XML documents store in XML memory as internal system information. After parsing XML documents, XML statistical data will be extracted to query or querying optimization. XML statistical data contain data information and structural information. Index of XML data is established during the process of loading XML documents. The index data are stored in XML memory. XML memory use DOM as storage model of XML data, which is memory interface designed for XML schema information. XML statistical data and index data have their own storing structure. Queries of path expressions are performed by querying processor. Queries of path expressions consist of query preprocessing, simplifying path expressions, normalizing predicates,

Figure 1. The architecture of Native XML database

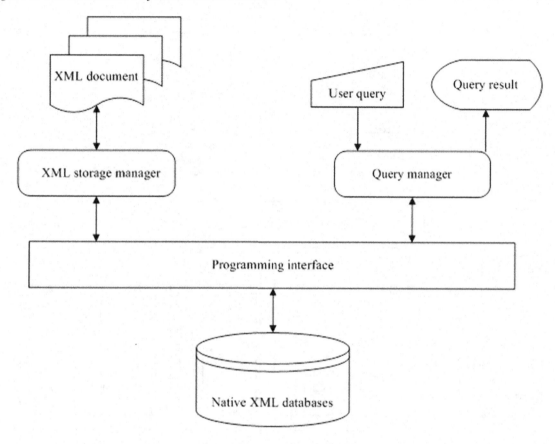

Figure 2. Classification of XML data management system

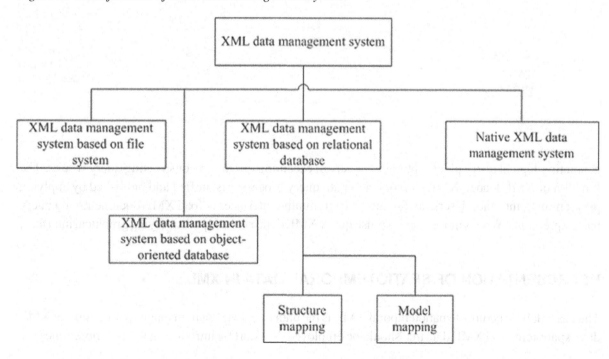

Figure 3. Architecture of XBase

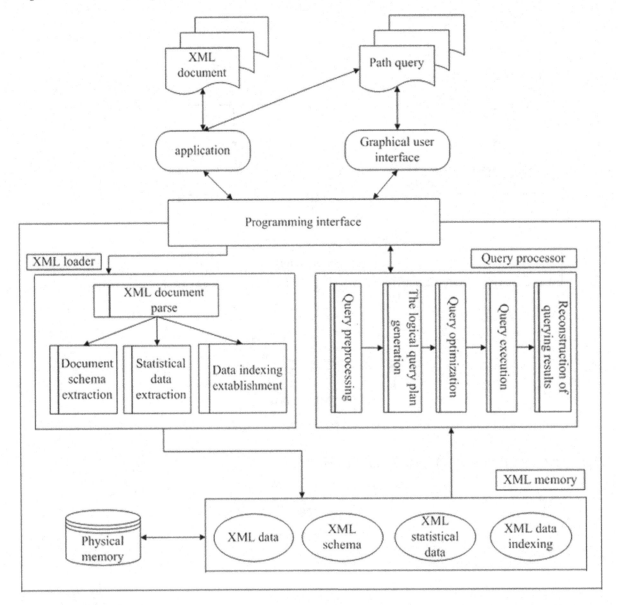

generating logical query plans, optimizing queries, executing queries, reconstructing query results. The function of XML loader, XML memory, and path query processor is unified and published by applying programming interface. Users can use these programming interfaces to load XML documents and query path expressions. What's more, users can also query XML data by visual path querying graphical interface.

REPRESENTATION OF SPATIOTEMPORAL DATA IN XML

The basic data structure of spatiotemporal XML is the data tree. In order to manage spatiotemporal XML data, spatiotemporal XML data tree should be employed. We start by introducing some simple concepts.

Definition 1: Let V be a finite set of vertices, $E \in V \times V$ be a set of edges, and $\ell: E \to \Gamma$ be a mapping from edges to a set Γ of strings called labels. The triple $G = (V, E, \ell)$ is an edge-labeled directed data tree.

Definition 1 is inspired by the tree patterns of XML but ignores a number of XML features such as data types, ordering, and the distinction between elements and attributes. Because ordering is one of the most import elements for managing spatiotemporal XML data, partial order is introduced to describe the ordering in XML.

Definition 2: A relation R is a partial order (denoted as "$\leq$") on a set S if it has the following properties:
- **Reflexivity:** $\forall \alpha \in S, (\alpha, \alpha) \in R$.
- **Antisymmetry:** If $(\alpha, \beta) \in R$ and $(\beta, \alpha) \in R$, then $\alpha = \beta$.
- **Transitivity:** If $(\alpha, \beta) \in R$ and $(\beta, \gamma) \in R$, then $(\alpha, \gamma) \in R$.

On the basis of the definitions above, we turn to develop the spatiotemporal XML data model. After defining spatiotemporal XML data and spatiotemporal XML data tree, correspondences between them are investigated. In addition, structure of the spatiotemporal XML data model is formally defined. According to the nature of spatiotemporal data, we firstly give the definition of spatiotemporal XML data as followings.

Definition 3 (Spatiotemporal XML Data): Spatiotemporal data SP is a 5-tuple, $SP = (OID, ATTR, P, M, T)$, where
- OID is the changing history of the spatiotemporal data.
- $ATTR$ is attributes of spatiotemporal data.
- P is position of spatiotemporal data.
- M is motion of spatiotemporal data.
- T is time of spatiotemporal data.

Since XML data are structured, XML can represent information naturally. In the case of XML document, we may have membership degrees associated with elements and possibility distributions associated with attribute values of elements. In succession, we investigate how to represent XML spatiotemporal data in the XML document.

Definition 4 (Spatiotemporal XML Data Tree): For the XML spatiotemporal document, we have $F = (V, \psi, T, \varpi, \wp, \tau, \xi)$, including:
- $V = \{V_1, V_2, ..., V_n\}$ is a finite set of vertices.
- $\psi \subset \{(V_i, V_j) \mid V_i, V_j \in V\}$, (V, ψ) is a directed tree.
- $T \in \psi \subset \{(V_i, V_j) \mid V_i, V_j \in V\}$ specifies time of V_j.
- ϖ is the nesting depth of V in the spatiotemporal data tree of the document. The ϖ of root node is 1, and the ϖ of each following level adds 1.
- $\wp$ preserves the order information in the spatiotemporal XML data tree. It can be generated by counting word numbers from root of the data tree until the start and end of the element, respectively. Here, we use preorder traversal.

○ τ is a set of labels.

○   For the node $v \in V$ and the label $\nabla \in \tau$, $\xi(v, \nabla)$ specifies v exists with label ∇.

As for the real life example, there are several illustrations: (a) elements of cloud are represented as vertices in its spatiotemporal XML document, such as identifiers, attributes, position, motion and so on; (b) edges connecting those vertices are directed trees; (c) time of those vertices are assigned to their edges; (d) the depth of cloud node is 1, and the depth of its child nodes adds 1. The rest can be done in the same manner; (e) cloud elements in the spatiotemporal XML document preserves the fixed order; (f) all cloud elements' name consist of a set of labels in the spatiotemporal XML document; (g) not all the elements of cloud have values in the spatiotemporal XML document. It is true that the identifier of the cloud should be represented in the spatiotemporal XML document. However, there may be no value in its predecessor or successor if the cloud remains constant.

Definition 5: Suppose $F = (V, \psi, T, \varpi, \wp, \tau, \xi)$ and $f = (V', \psi', T', \varpi', \wp', \tau', \xi')$ are two spatiotemporal XML data trees. f is a subtree of F, written $f \propto F$, when

○ $V' \subseteq V, \psi' = \psi \cap V' \times V'$.

○   if $(V_i, V_j) \in \psi$ and $V_i \in V'$, then $V_j \in V'$.

○ $T' \subseteq T$.

○   If $V_i \in V$, $V_i' \in V'$, and $\varpi(V_i) = \max\{\varpi_1, \varpi_2,..., \varpi_n\}$, $\varpi(V_i') = \max\{\varpi_1', \varpi_2',..., \varpi_n'\}$, then $\varpi(V_i') \leq \varpi(V_i)$.

○ $\wp'$, ξ' and τ' indicate the restriction of $\wp$, ξ and τ to the nodes in V', respectively.

According to the above definitions, a spatiotemporal XML data tree can be composed of multiple spatiotemporal XML data subtrees, and multiple spatiotemporal XML data trees can comprise a spatiotemporal XML data forest.

Theorem 1: Given any set of spatiotemporal XML data trees $F = \{f_1, f_2, ..., f_n\}$, there exists a corresponding spatiotemporal XML data forest matching with F.

Theorem 2: λ is a partial order relationship on a spatiotemporal XML data tree F, there exists a transitivity relationship λ' that satisfies

○ $\lambda \in \lambda'$.

○ λ' is a partial order relationship stems from λ, which keeps the reflexivity and antisymmetry of λ.

Proof. Firstly, we construct $\eta = \{\vartheta \mid \lambda \subseteq \vartheta\}$. It is obvious that $(\eta, \subseteq)$ is a partial order. Assuming $\vartheta = \bigcup_{i \in I} \vartheta_i$, and $\{\vartheta_i\}_{i \in I} \subseteq \eta$ are an ordering subtrees of F. For $\forall i \in I$, there is $\lambda \subseteq \vartheta_i$. According to the definition of partial order, $\vartheta_i (f, f) = 1$. For each $f \in F$, we have $\vartheta (f, f) = \bigvee_{i \in I} \vartheta_i (f, f) = 1$. Thus ϑ has reflexivity. Secondly, for every $\vartheta_i \subseteq \vartheta_j$, where $i, j \in I$, $\forall x, y \in F$, F has antisymmetry, denoted as ϖ. Then we have $\vartheta (x, y) \varpi \vartheta (y, x) = [\bigvee_{i \in I} \vartheta_i (x, y)] \varpi [\bigvee_{j \in I} \vartheta_j (y, x)] = \bigvee_{i, j \in I} [\vartheta_i (x, y) \varpi \vartheta_j (y, x)]$. On the other hand, $\vartheta_i (x, y) \varpi \vartheta_j (y, x) \leq \vartheta_j (x, y) \varpi \vartheta_j (y, x) = 0$. Accordingly, $\bigvee_{i, j \in I} [\vartheta_i (x, y) \varpi \vartheta_j (y, x)] =$

0. Thus $\vartheta (x, y) \varpi \vartheta (y, x) = 0$, ϑ has antisymmetry ϖ. Finally, we turn to the proof of transitivity. for every $\vartheta_i \subseteq \vartheta_j$, where $i, j \in I$, $\forall x, y, z \in F$, F has transitivity $\mathfrak{I}$. Then $\vartheta (x, y) \mathfrak{I} \vartheta (y, z) = [\underset{i \in I}{\vee} \vartheta_i$ $(x, y)] \mathfrak{I} [\underset{j \in I}{\vee} \vartheta_j (y, z)] = \underset{i, j \in I}{\vee} [\vartheta_i (x, y) \mathfrak{I} \vartheta_j (y, z)]$. $\vartheta_i (x, y) \mathfrak{I} \vartheta_j (y, z) \leq \vartheta_j (x, y) \mathfrak{I} \vartheta_j (y, z) \leq \vartheta_j (x, z)$ $\leq \vartheta (x, z)$. Thus $\vartheta (x, y) \mathfrak{I} \vartheta (y, z) \leq \vartheta (x, z)$, ϑ has transitivity $\mathfrak{I}$. Accordingly, there exists maximal element λ' in η that satisfies $\lambda \in \lambda'$. λ' is a partial order relationship that stems from λ, keeping the reflexivity and antisymmetry of λ. $\square$

As XML document is a labeled ordered rooted tree, we regard a spatiotemporal data as a structured tree for metadata. As a result, operations between spatiotemporal data are actually operations between trees. Consequently, spatiotemporal XML data trees should be considered as isomorphic.

Definition 6: Let spatiotemporal XML data trees $f_1 = (V_1, \psi_1, T_1, \varpi_1, \wp_1, \tau_1, \xi_1)$ and $f_2 = (V_2, \psi_2, T_2, \varpi_2, \wp_2, \tau_2, \xi_2)$ be the subtrees of $F = (V, \psi, T, \varpi, \wp, \tau, \xi)$. Then f_1 and f_2 are isomorphic (recorded $f_1 \cong f_2$), when

- $V_1 \cup V_2 \subseteq V$, $\psi_1 \cup \psi_2 \subseteq \psi$, $T_1 \cup T_2 \subseteq T$, $\tau_1 \cup \tau_2 \subseteq \tau$.
- $\varpi_1 = \varpi_2 \leq \varpi$.
- There is a one-to-one mapping, $I\xi: \xi_1 \rightarrow \xi_2$, which makes $\forall I\xi(\xi_1) = \xi_2$.

Theorem 3: Data tree F and its subtree f are isomorphic.

The proof of this theorem follows the analysis of spatiotemporal XML data tree and the corresponding definitions. It is quite straightforward.

After defining spatiotemporal XML data and spatiotemporal XML data tree, it is necessary to learn correspondences between them. In other words, we should know how elements in spatiotemporal XML data corresponding elements in spatiotemporal XML data tree.

Definition 7: For the spatiotemporal XML data $SP = (OID, ATTR, P, M, T)$ and the spatiotemporal XML data tree $F = (V, \psi, T, \varpi, \wp, \tau, \xi)$, we have:

- $OID \sim V, \psi, T, \varpi, \wp, \tau, \xi$.
- $ATTR \sim V, \psi, T, \varpi, \wp, \tau, \xi$.
- $FP \sim V, \psi, T, \varpi, \wp, \tau, \xi$.
- $FM \sim V, \psi, T, \varpi, \wp, \tau, \xi$.
- $FT \sim T, \tau, \xi$.

Here, "$\sim$" means refer to or have relationship with. Take the first one for example, it means OID in spatiotemporal XML data has relationship with $V, \psi, T, \varpi, \wp, \tau, \xi$ in spatiotemporal XML data tree. Others can be obtained in an analogous way.

Definition 8 (Structure of the Spatiotemporal Data Model): For the structure of the spatiotemporal data model, we have $S = (V, \psi, T, \varpi, \wp, \tau, \xi)$, including:

- $V = \{$*Spatiotemporal data, OID, ATTR, position, motion, type, predecessor, successor, $A_1,..., A_n$, x, y, κ, value, create|split|merge|eliminate, V_{A1}, V_{An}, V_x, V_y, xaxis, yaxis, xval, yval, $\rightarrow$|$\leftarrow$|$\leftrightarrow$, $\uparrow$|$\downarrow$|$\updownarrow$, $V_{xval}, V_{yval}\}$*.

- ○ $\psi \subset \{(V_i, V_j) \mid V_i, V_j \in V\}$, (V, ψ) is a directed tree.
- ○ $T \in \psi \subset \{(V_i, V_j) \mid V_i, V_j \in V\}$ specifies time of V_j.
- ○ ϖ *(Spatiotemporal data)* = 1, ϖ *(OID)* = ϖ *(ATTR)* = ϖ *(position)* = ϖ *(motion)* =2, ϖ *(type)* = ϖ *(predecessor)* = ϖ *(successor)* = ϖ *(A_1)* = ϖ *(A_n)* = ϖ *(x)* = ϖ *(y)* = ϖ *(κ)* = ϖ *(value)* =3, ϖ *(create|split|merge|eliminate)* = $\varpi(V_{A1})$ = ϖ *(V_{An})* = ϖ *(V_x)* = ϖ *(V_y)* = ϖ *(xaxis)* = ϖ *(yaxis)* = ϖ *(xval)* = ϖ *(yval)* = 4, ϖ *($\rightarrow$|$\leftarrow$|$\leftrightarrow$)* = ϖ *($\uparrow$|$\downarrow$|$\updownarrow$)* = ϖ *(V_{xval})* = ϖ *(V_{yval})* = 5.
- ○ *Spatiotemporal data $\wp$ OID $\wp$ type $\wp$ create|split|merge|eliminate $\wp$ predecessor $\wp$ successor $\wp$ ATTR $\wp$ A_1 $\wp$ V_{A1} $\wp$ A_n $\wp$ V_{An} $\wp$ position $\wp$ x $\wp$ V_x $\wp$ y $\wp$ V_y $\wp$ motion $\wp$ κ $\wp$ xaxis $\wp$ $\rightarrow$|$\leftarrow$|$\leftrightarrow$ $\wp$ yaxis $\wp$ $\uparrow$|$\downarrow$|$\updownarrow$ $\wp$ value $\wp$ xval $\wp$ V_{xval} $\wp$ yval $\wp$ V_{yval}.* Here, we use preorder traversal.
- ○ τ is a set of labels, and the name of $\tau \in V$.
- ○ For the node $v \in V$ and the label $\nabla \in \tau$, $\xi(v, \nabla)$ specifies v exists with label ∇.

For example: if there is a dark Mufia cloud numbered by 1 moves from {(100°E, 120°N), (120°E, 160°N)} to {(80°E, 100°N), (160°E, 140°N)} in one day and it comes from part of the cloud numbered by 2, we have the following values: OID is 1, type is split, predecessor is 2, A1 is cloud name, VA1 is Mufia, A2 is cloud color, VA2 is dark, Vx changes from 110°E to 120°E, Vy changes from 140°N to 120°N, xaxis is $\rightarrow$, yaxis is $\downarrow$, xval is 10°/day, yval is 20°/day.

NXD SPATIOTEMPORAL DATABASE SYSTEMS AND QUERY FRAMEWORK

NXD is designed for storing XML documents, which has ACID characteristics. The internal storage model of NXD is based on XML data tree, rather than relational model or object-oriented model. The semantic of querying in a NXD spatiotemporal database is to describe the indexing context as well as returning context. In this chapter, querying results consist of geographical elements having spatiotemporal semantics or spatiotemporal XML fragments containing geographical elements.

The NXD spatiotemporal database and query framework is shown in Figure 4. From the view of querying process, XML queries contain two stages. The first one is to transform the surface grammar of query languages to logic representation made up with meaningful mathematical symbols. The symbols make it easier to check syntax errors and variable static types. In this time, it does not depend on XML data, but is likely to import XML Schema. The second one is dynamic evaluation phase of querying. This stage is the deduction of querying results based on logic representation, and the querying optimization based on querying semantics. In this chapter, we mainly propose spatiotemporal query algebra, which focuses on logic operations of spatiotemporal database. It provides formal representations and operations for queries, containing series of judgments, operations, and functions from input of querying algorithms to the desired output.

FORMAL REPRESENTATIONS OF SPATIOTEMPORAL QUERY ALGEBRA

In 2001, W3C announced a standard XML query algebra called XQuery 1.0 Formal Semantics (XQuery-FS). The standard follows XDM data model and XQuery standard querying process recommended by

Figure 4. The NXD spatiotemporal database and query framework

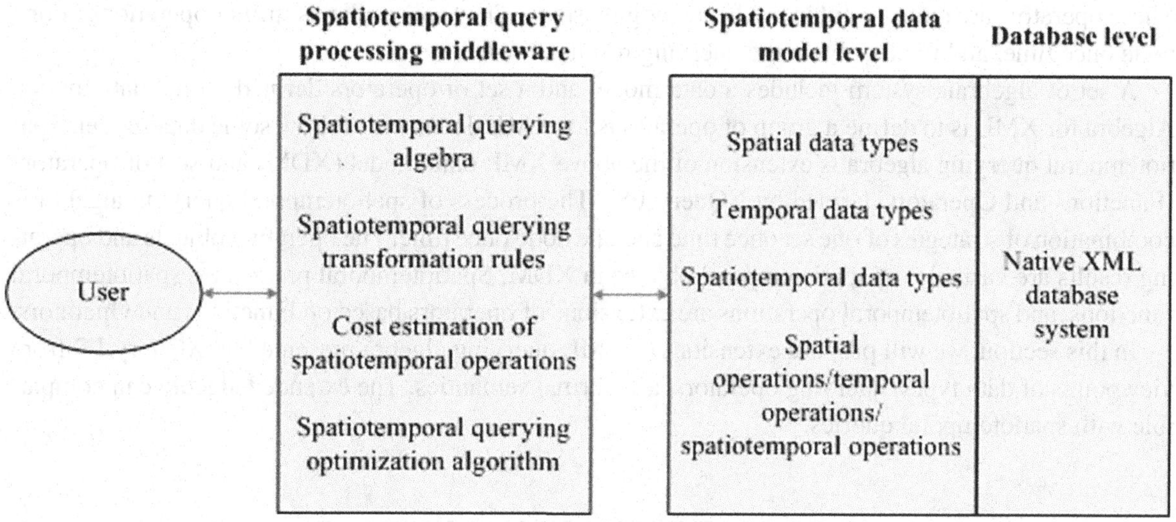

W3C. XQuery-FS strictly uses mathematic symbols to formally describe XQuery. The proposed formal spatiotemporal algebra will contribute to the algebra standardization of spatiotemporal querying, program reasoning, and improvement of software reliability.

There are two strategies of XQuery processing, which are approaches based on grammar and query algebra. The former is one node once time and the latter is one set once time. The latter is algebra architecture similar as relational algebra. The input of each algebraic operator is a set of XML data trees, and the output of each algebraic operator is also a set of XML data trees. The difference between input and output is that transformations are carried out from initial state to the desired state by operations on algebra. In general, in order to generate sets of XML data trees, one or more pattern trees are generated from XQuery. Pattern trees represent variable bindings with ancestor-descendant relationship, and then extract instance trees from the input XML data trees using pattern trees. For example:

Q1: FOR $b in (document ("bib.xml"))/bib/book

    WHERE $b/price<80
    RETURN <cheap-books>{$b/title}</cheap-books>

For Q1, it will extract the pattern tree *bib (book (price, title))*, and then get instance trees by matching the XML data tree using this pattern tree. Furthermore, predicate judgment (price<80) are carried out for this instance trees. Finally, the desired results are output. It can be observed that the biggest advantage of this querying process (one set once time) is to optimize the logical operating trees. The premise is that the XML data model can be able to participate in operations and the XML data model contains objects of nodes, types of nodes, document order of nodes, and the position of context (a/d, p/c) in XML documents or fragments.

The above data model only contain context of input XML documents or fragments, and do not study how to obtain a single document node, document order, and relationship. Defining a set of operators for operations on nodes can obtain node and structural information, and also construct querying results. These operators are quite useful in predicate judging stage. They are similar as further operations of one node once time, and finally obtain the querying results of Q1.

A set of algebraic system includes a data model and a set of operators defined on the data model. Algebra for XML is to define a group of operations for XML documents follow some data model. Spatiotemporal querying algebra is extension of the above XML data model (XDM) and sets of operators (Functions and Operators defined by XQuery-FS). The process of spatiotemporal querying algebra is combination of strategies of one set once time and one node once time. The operating objects and operating results are variables of spatiotemporal objects in XDM. Spatiotemporal predicates, spatiotemporal functions, and spatiotemporal operations are extensions of operators based on Functions and Operators.

In this section, we will propose extensions to XML querying algebra presented by XQuery-FS from viewpoints of data types, querying operators, and formal semantics. The extended algebra can compatible with spatiotemporal queries.

LOGICAL STRUCTURE OF SPATIOTEMPORAL DATABASE

A NXD spatiotemporal database is usually a forest constructed by rooted, ordered, labeled trees. Node represents element, attribute, or text. Directed edge represents relationship between two element nodes or between element node and value node.

Definition 1: An XML document is a rooted, ordered, labeled tree, which is represented by a tuple T = (N, E, R), where
- N represents nodes.
- E represents edges (pc or ad), while pc indicates parent-child relationship and ad indicates ancestor-descendant relationship.
- R represents root. When R is not a document node defined by INFOSET, the XML document is actually an XML fragment.

Definition 2: XML node is unit of XML document, which is represented by a tuple N = (L, T, V, C), where
- L represents labels used to describe meaning of nodes.
- T represents types of objects. There are several kinds of types, which are atomic type, complex type, and user-defined type. Each type is defined in XDM.
- V represents values of attributes or texts.
- C represents the extended prefix coding nodes used to indicate sequence of nodes in XML documents.

In Definition 2, there are several kinds of nodes such as document nodes, element nodes, attribute nodes, text nodes, CDATA nodes, comment nodes, processing instruction nodes, and document fragment nodes. In general, the first four kinds of nodes are commonly used. Document nodes stay in front of all nodes, which can be nested by single or multiple element nodes. Element nodes can be nested by zero or multiple attribute nodes or text nodes. These nested relationships are represented by edges of XML documents (pc or ad). Concerning on C in the tuple in Definition 2, relationship of two nodes can be judged by prefix codes of these two nodes (pc, ad, or sibling relationship). For each node, we can obtain a node sequence from the root node to this node.

Definition 3: Sequence is consist of zero or multiple items, while item is consist of zero or multiple XML nodes. Sequence is ordered, heterogeneous, repeated, and unnested. At the same time, sequence is value of XQuery expression, and can be used to reason as intermediate results of spatiotemporal operations or to return the results. The characteristics of sequence are as follows:

- $S \cong I$ if S contains only one I, where S indicates a sequence and I indicates an item.
- For two sequence S_i and S_j, $S_i \not\subset S_j$.
- For $i \in I$ in S, i is atomic value or XML node.

In Definition 3, a sequence contained only one item is equivalent to itself. For example, $S(1) \cong I(1)$ in W3C data model. A sequence is not contained by another sequence. For example, it does not exist the sequence in XQuery data model that $(1, (2, 3), 4, 5, 6)$.

Definition 4: Spatiotemporal database schema is STS = (T, E, R), where STS is a set of multiple spatiotemporal XML documents, and a labeled, ordered forest.

When a sequence contains spatiotemporal nodes, the sequence should be extended to spatiotemporal sequence. Similar as tuples and relations are basic unit in traditional relational database, XML documents/fragments and sets of XML documents are unit in NXD database.

Spatiotemporal element nodes are introduced, and can be represented spatiotemporal data and spatiotemporal changes. In addition, these nodes can be queried by specific spatiotemporal operations.

Data Type System

XQuery is not only a kind of functional language consisted of various of expressions but also a strongly typed language having strict data type system. The data type system is standard by XDM in XQuery specifications. XDM provides all the data types of input data and output data, and can be nested as well.

In the formal semantics and data model (XDM) of XQuery/XPath, a data model is composed of atomic values (boolean, double, etc.), XML nodes (document, element, attribute, etc.), and sequence. The item in sequence can be atomic type or node type. There are 25 basic data types or derived data types in XDM. In order to define spatiotemporal algebra, those data types should be extended when they are introduced.

Spatial data types, temporal data types, and geographical data types are formal defined in GML. Gml:Feature in geographical data types is a unit of time, space, and attribute, which is the core concept of spatiotemporal data model based on characteristics. In this chapter, we regard geographical elements as node type of sequence in XDM, shown in Figure 5.

In Figure 5, names of data types are the same as those defined in GML. However, the model is extended to express complex semantics of spatiotemporal changes (internal changes and external changes

Figure 5. Architecture of data types of spatiotemporal data model

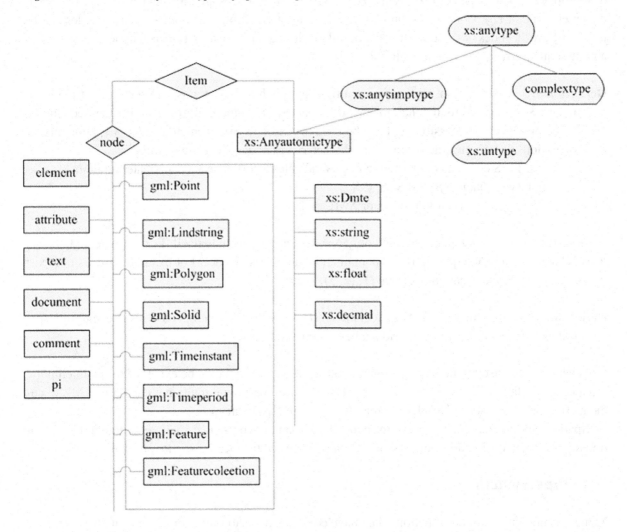

of spatiotemporal objects). On the other hand, Figure 5 only presents part of spatiotemporal data types from GML. In order to ensure closure and completeness of spatiotemporal algebra in the extended XDM, practical applications should import all the elements and attributes defined in GML. It can be observed that item in sequence can be atomic node, atomic data type defined in XML Schema, or complex type node extended from GML. The status of nodes defined in GML is equal to that in XDM.

In addition to define data types in Figure 5, XDM also define a series of access functions used during querying process. The querying engine can obtain semantics of sequence nodes quickly so that it will be matched according to type information or semantic rules rather than matched node by node according to grammar structure of XML. Spatiotemporal data types in GML are introduced in Figure 5. Accordingly, access functions of these new data types should also be defined, shown in Table 1.

Table 1. Access functions

Function Propotype	Input	Output	Description
Dm:st_type($n as node()) as xs:string	Node item in sequence	gml:Poing; gml:LineString; gml:Polygon; gml:solid; gml:TimeInstant; gml:Time Period; gml:_Feature; gml:_FeatureCollection; gml:nil	Judge whether or not nodes in sequence are spatiotemporal data types, and return names of types
Dm:srs_name($n as node()) as xs:string	Node item in sequence	uri or gml:nil (spatial reference)	Return spatial reference system names of spatiotemporal data types
Dm:tcs_name($n as node()) as xs:string	Node item in sequence	All names of types derived from Node type in XDM	Return temporal reference system names of spatiotemporal data types
Dm:node_type($n as node()) as xs:string	Node item in sequence	All names of types derived from Node type in XDM	Return types the input nodes
Dm:isdynamic($n as gml:_Feature) as xs:Boolean	Node item in sequence	Semantics of spatiotemporal changes (whether or not)	Return whether or not a dynamic geographic features

Querying Operations

XQuery-FS defines operations on projection, selection, and connection. In addition, XQuery-FS also introduce programming language such as structural recursion and condition judgment. These can be applied to the extended spatiotemporal types in XDM. However, spatiotemporal XML documents cannot be spatiotemporal queried since spatiotemporal XML documents are regarded as general documents. In order to reason and query spatiotemporal XML documents, we define a series of spatiotemporal predicates, spatiotemporal functions, and spatiotemporal operators concerning on spatiotemporal characteristics. The spatiotemporal predicates, spatiotemporal functions, and spatiotemporal operators have already been defined in traditional relational database. The difference is that the input and the output changes from tuples to sequences. In this chapter, we apply these to spatiotemporal queries in XDM.

In this subsection, we mainly study construct functions and constructors of gml:_Feature and gml:_FeatureCollection. Additionally, their internal changes and dynamic changes are studied as well. Constructions of data types based on XML Schema is more complex than that in relational database because the flexibility of XML data model. A geographic element may be a set of one element or a single element. The single element is combination of time, space, attribute, and their relations. The combination can form a tree structure, which can be constructed by an ordered sequence. Furthermore, the ordered sequence can be constructed by coding. As a result, we provide two kinds of constructors of spatiotemporal types, shown in Table 2.

Internal changes of spatiotemporal objects contain operations on obtaining spatiotemporal attributes of geographic elements and spatiotemporal operations, shown in Table 3.

Table 2. Constructors of spatiotemporal data

Constructors	Type
Fn:st_feature($n as gml:_Feature) as gml:_Feature	Geographic element
Fn:st_feature($n as dm:sequence) as gml:_Feature	Geographic element

Table 3. Acquiring spatiotemporal attributes

Function Propotype	Input	Output	Description
Fn:state($n as gml:_Feature) as gml:TimeSlice	Geographic element	Time instance	Acquiring current state of entity
Fn:prestate($n as gml:_Feature) as gml:TimeSlice	Geographic element	Time instance	Acquiring last state of entity
Fn:poststate($n as gml:_Feature) as gml:TimeSlice	Geographic element	Time instance	Acquiring next state of entity
Fn:duration($n1 as gml:TimeInstant, $n2 as gml:TimeInstant) as gml:History	Time instance	Set of time instance	Acquiring changing history of entity in the given time period

Spatiotemporal changes in spatiotemporal entities of spatiotemporal objects are useful for the process of spatiotemporal changes. In this chapter, we also present spatiotemporal changes in spatiotemporal entities of spatiotemporal objects, shown in Table 4.

RELATED WORK

Concerning on spatiotemporal data in XML, there are efforts to combine spatial and temporal properties into one framework, and analyze spatiotemporal data in XML. Huang et al. (Huang, Yi, and Chan, 2004) propose an approach to represent and query spatiotemporal data in XML. Liu and Wan (Liu, Wan, 2010) propose a feature-based spatiotemporal data model and use the Native XML Database to store the spatiotemporal data. The work of Franceschet et al. (Franceschet, Montanari, Gubiani, 2007) describe a translation algorithm that maps spatiotemporal conceptual schemas into XML schemas, and propose a framework that allows one to validate XML documents containing spatiotemporal information with respect to spatiotemporal conceptual schemas. Furthermore, concerning on fuzzy spatiotemporal data in XML, Bai et al. (Bai, Yan, Ma, 2013) propose a fuzzy spatiotemporal XML data model, but not support algebraic operations.

The algebraic approaches have been proven to be an effective way for queries in the XML database systems (Paparizos, Wu, Laks, et al., 2004). With the emergence of XQuery designed by the W3C as a standard query language for XML, efforts are made to apply algebra to XML queries. Fernandez et al. (Fernandez, Simeon, Wadler, 2000) propose an algebra for XML query using regular-expression types, which has been submitted to the W3C XML Query Working Group. Buratti and Montesi (Buratti, Montesi, 2006) propose a novel algebra for XML based on a simple data model in which trees and

Table 4. Basic operations on dynamic changes in spatiotemporal entities of spatiotemporal objects

Function Propotype	Input	Output	Description
Fn:lifespan($n gml:_Feature) as gml:TimePeriod	Geographic element	Time period	Acquiring lifespan of entity
Fn:was($n gml:_Feature) as gml:_Feature Collection	Geographic element	Geographic set of predecessor	Acquiring geographic set of predecessor
Fn:became($n gml:_Feature) as gml:_ Feature Collection	Geographic element	Geographic set of successor	Acquiring geographic set of successor

forests are the counterpart of the relational tuples and relations. The work of Che and Sojitrawala (Che, Sojitrawala, 2007) present a new algebra called DUMAX designed for XML and XML queries, which is introduced to help fuse node-based features and tree-based features (both are essential for XML) and to achieve accelerated execution of XML queries in large XML databases or repositories. Wang et al. (Wang, Murphy, et al., 2005) present a general approach for supporting order-sensitive XQuery-to-SQL translation that works irrespective of the chosen XML-to-relational data mapping and the selected order-encoding method. Unfortunately, the proposed algebraic approaches do not support spatiotemporal data, although there are other XML algebraic approaches, such as probabilistic XML algebra (Hung, Getoor, Subrahmanian, 2003) and fuzzy XML algebra (Ma, Liu, Yan, 2010).

Nevertheless, although the above researches do not straightforwardly deal with spatiotemporal data in XML, their efforts play a fundamental role in algebraic operations of spatiotemporal data in XML. Compared with their work, our model and algebra are well defined and powerful enough to support tree patterns, order-sensitive spatiotemporal XML queries.

CONCLUSION

We have proposed a spatiotemporal XML data model and presented an algebra based on Native XML for manipulating spatiotemporal XML data. In spite of the complex structure of the trees involved, the algebra has a couple of operators using the same basic structure for their parameters. In addition, the algebra is able to handle existence of order within a tree.

Furthermore, we also study NXD spatiotemporal database and query framework, and formal representation of spatiotemporal query algebra. The algebra studies on logical structure of spatiotemporal database, data type system, and querying operations. Our primary purpose in defining it is to use it as the basis for query evaluation and optimization, which are also our future work. In addition, we plan to extend our algebra to fuzzy spatiotemporal algebra and optimize them.

REFERENCES

Abiteboul, S., Quass, D., & McHugh, J. (1997a). The Lorel Query Language for Semistructured Data. *International Journal on Digital Libraries*, *1*, 68–88.

Abiteboul, S., Quass, D., & McHugh, J. (1997b). Lore: A Database Management System for Semistructured Data. *SIGMOD Record*, *26*(3), 54–66. doi:10.1145/262762.262770

Bai, L., Yan, L., & Ma, Z. M. (2013). Determining Topological Relationship of Fuzzy Spatiotemporal Data Integrated with XML Twig Pattern. *Applied Intelligence*, *39*(1), 75–100. doi:10.1007/s10489-012-0395-3

Beeri, C., & Tzaban, Y. (1999). SAL: An Algebra for Semistructured Data and XML. In *Proceedings of Workshop on Web Databases* (pp. 46-51). Academic Press.

Benferhat, S., Ben-Naim, J., Papini, O., & Würbel, E. (2010). An Answer Set Programming Encoding of Prioritized Removed Sets Revision: Application to GIS. *Applied Intelligence*, *32*(1), 60–87. doi:10.1007/s10489-008-0135-x

Buratti, G., & Montesi, D. (2006). A Data Model and An Algebra for Querying XML Documents. In *Proceedings of the 17th International Conference on Database and Expert Systems Applications*, (pp. 482-486). doi:10.1109/DEXA.2006.6

Che, D., & Sojitrawala, R. M. (2007). DUMAX: A Dual Mode Algebra for XML Queries. In *Proceedings of the 2nd International Conference on Scalable Information Systems*, (pp. 1-4). doi:10.4108/infoscale.2007.202

Fernandez, M., Simeon, J., & Wadler, P. (2000). An Algebra for XML Query. In *Proceedings of the 20th International Conference on Foundations of Software Technology and Theoretical Computer Science*, (pp. 11-45).

Franceschet, M., Montanari, A., & Gubiani, D. (2007). Modeling and Validating Spatio-Temporal Conceptual Schemas in XML Schema. In *Proceedings of the 18th International Conference on Database and Expert Systems Applications*, (pp. 25-29). doi:10.1109/DEXA.2007.106

Goldman, R., & Widom, J. (1997). DataGuides: Enabling Query Formulation and Optimization in Semistructured Databases. In *Proceedings of the 23rd International Conference on VLDB*, (pp. 436-445). VLDB.

Huang, B., Yi, S., & Chan, W. T. (2004). Spatio-Temporal Information Integration in XML. *Future Generation Computer Systems*, *20*(7), 1157–1170. doi:10.1016/j.future.2003.11.005

Hung, E., Getoor, L., & Subrahmanian, V. S. (2003). PXML: A Probabilistic Semi-Structured Data Model and Algebra. In *Proceedings of the 19th International Conference on Data Engineering*, (pp. 467-478). Academic Press.

Jagadish, H. V., Laks, V. S., & Lakshmanan, D. (2001). TAX: A Tree Algebra for XML. In *Proceedings of the International Workshop on Database Programming Languages*, (pp. 149-164). Academic Press.

Koyuncu, M., & Yazici, A. (2003). IFOOD: An Intelligent Fuzzy Object-Oriented Database Architecture. *IEEE Transactions on Knowledge and Data Engineering*, *15*(5), 1137–1154. doi:10.1109/TKDE.2003.1232269

Liu, X. H., & Wan, Y. C. (2010). Storing Spatio-Temporal Data in XML Native Database. In *Proceedings of the 2nd International Workshop on Database Technology and Applications*, (pp. 1-4). doi:10.1109/DBTA.2010.5659107

Ma, Z. M., Liu, J., & Yan, L. (2010). Fuzzy Data Modeling and Algebraic Operations in XML. *International Journal of Intelligent Systems*, *25*, 925–947.

Magnani, M., & Montesi, D. (2005). XML and Relational Data: Towards a Common Model and Algebra. In *Proceedings of the 9th International Database Engineering and Application Symposlum*, (pp. 96-101). doi:10.1109/IDEAS.2005.55

McHugh, J., & Widom, J. (2003). Query Optimization for XML. In *Proceedings of the 25th VLDB*, (pp. 898-909). VLDB.

Mehrotra, R., & Sharma, A. (2009). Evaluating Spatio-Temporal Representations in Daily Rainfall Sequences from Three Stochastic Multisite Weather Generation Approaches. *Advances in Water Resources*, *32*(6), 948–962. doi:10.1016/j.advwatres.2009.03.005

Paparizos, S., Wu, Y., & Laks, V. S. (2004). Tree Logical Classes for Efficient Evaluation of XQuery. In *Proceedings of the 2004 ACM SIGMOD International Conference on Management of Data*, (pp. 71-82). doi:10.1145/1007568.1007579

Prade, H., & Testemale, D. (1984). Generalizing Database Relational Algebra for the Treatment of Incomplete or Uncertain Information and Vague Queries. *Information Sciences*, *34*(2), 115–143. doi:10.1016/0020-0255(84)90020-3

Schoning, H. (2001). Tamino - A DBMS designed for XML. In *Proceedings of the ICDE Conference*. ICDE.

Senellart, P., & Abiteboul, S. (2007). On the Complexity of Managing Probabilistic XML Data. In *Proceedings of the 26th ACM SIGACT-SIGMOD-SIGART Symposium on Principles of Database Systems*, (pp. 283-292). doi:10.1145/1265530.1265570

Sözer, A., Yazici, A., Oğuztüzün, H., & Taş, O. (2008). Modeling and Querying Fuzzy Spatiotemporal Databases. *Information Science*, *178*(19), 3665–3682. doi:10.1016/j.ins.2008.05.034

Wang, L., Wang, S., & Murphy, B. (2005). Order-Sensitive XML Query Processing over Relational Sources: An Algebraic Approach. In *Proceedings of the 9th International Database Engineering and Application Symposium*, (pp. 175-184). doi:10.1109/IDEAS.2005.40

KEY TERMS AND DEFINITIONS

NXD: Native XML databases have an XML-based internal model and their fundamental unit of storage is XML.

TAX: A Tree Algebra for XML.

XBase: A Native XML data management system.

Chapter 11

C2S:
A Spatial Skyline Algorithm for Changing Data

Marlene Goncalves
Universidad Simón Bolívar, Venezuela

Fabiola Di Bartolo
Universidad Simón Bolívar, Venezuela

ABSTRACT

Skyline queries may be used to filter interesting data from a broad range of data. A Skyline query selects those data that are the best according to multiple user-defined criteria. A special case of Skyline queries are the Spatial Skyline Queries (SSQ). SSQ allow users to express preferences on the closeness between a set of data points and a set of query points. We study the problem of answering SSQ in presence of changing data, i.e., data whose values regularly change over a period of time. In this chapter, it is proposed an algorithm to evaluate SSQ on changing data. The proposed algorithm is able to avoid recomputation of the whole Skyline with each update on the data. Also, the performance of the proposed algorithm against state-of-the-art algorithms was empirically studied. The experimental study shows that the proposed algorithm may become 3 times faster than state-of-the-art algorithms.

INTRODUCTION

Skyline queries are particularly relevant in the area of decision support or data visualization. They may be used to filter interesting data from a broad range of data. Intuitively, a Skyline query selects those data that are the best according to multiple user's criteria; user's criteria consist of minimizing or maximizing the attributes of an input dataset simultaneously.

A special case of Skyline queries is the Spatial Skyline Queries (SSQ); SSQ focus on geometric or spatial data and they allow expressing preferences on the closeness between a set of data points and a set of query points (Sharifzadeh & Shahabi, 2006).

DOI: 10.4018/978-1-4666-8767-7.ch011

The Skyline query evaluation is a costly process for a large dataset. The worst case complexity is $O\left(|P|^2\right)$ where P is the dataset (Godfrey, Shipley, & Gryz, 2005). Clearly, the Spatial Skyline query evaluation is still more expensive because distance functions must be computed. In this sense, performing an exhaustive search increases the search space to $O\left(|P|^2|Q|\right)$ where Q is the set of query points (Sharifzadeh & Shahabi, 2006). Sharifzadeh and Shahabi (2006) exploit geometric properties in order to reduce the search space to $O\left(|S|^2|C|+\sqrt{|P|}\right)$, where S is the Skyline set and C is the vertex set belonging to the convex hull of the query points in Q. The convex hull of Q is the unique smallest convex polytope which contains all the points in Q (Sharifzadeh & Shahabi, 2006).

In this chapter, we study the problem of answering Spatial Skyline Queries (SSQ) in presence of both spatial and non-spatial changing data. Changing data are data whose values regularly change over a period of time. Suppose a recommendation system that is able to suggest the best parking spaces in a parking lot. A Spatial Skyline query may be evaluated to identify the best parking spaces. In this example, the data are changing, e.g., the driver's vehicle may move continuously or the availability of parking spaces may change frequently. Therefore, the Spatial Skyline set changes depending on the vehicle location and/ or the availability of spaces. Particularly, the availability of a parking space is a changing non-spatial datum and the location of the vehicle is a moving query point.

SSQ on changing data may have several applications. They may be used in logistics of services and parking lots of festivals and events such as Rock in Rio, Pinkpop Festival, Lollapalooza, Glastonbury Festival, Olympic Games, FIFA World Cup and Super Bowl to which attend thousands of citizens and tourists from different regions and countries (Lande & Lande, 2008). In these events the parking time could be critical if customers have to find a parking space by themselves without any help or suggestion.

In addition, SSQ on changing data may be applied in case of emergency or natural disaster to identify the highly vulnerable regions near the most endangered areas in order to plan and organize a rescue; the affected regions change their status among attended and urgent attention and have an impact level, so the most urgent and vulnerable regions are attended first. The SSQ on changing data may also be used in reservation systems able to recommend on the basis of criteria that meet the user's preferences. For example, a user may be interested in booking an event preferring a lower price seat which is close to the stage, to the exit and to the initial seat of any row; the seats availability may change because other customers canceled a reservation or made a new one. Another use could be in a mobile application to reserve a table for n people in a restaurant which is open, well rated and is on the way home, this means close to the user in motion and close to home. Lastly, the problem of answering SSQ on changing data is hard to solve because data is constantly changing while the Spatial Skyline set is been computed in polynomial time.

Additionally, the state-of-the-art algorithms may be adapted to evaluate SSQ on changing data. However, the Skyline set must be continuously refreshed according to data changes if these algorithms are executed. For example, the algorithms for SSQ introduced in (Sharifzadeh, Shahabi, & Kazemi, 2009) allow multiple query points, one of which is a moving query point. Using these algorithms, any change to non-spatial data will cause a recomputation of all the Skyline set.

Our contribution is to provide a solution to the problem of evaluating SSQ on changing data. We propose an algorithm to calculate the Spatial Skyline when data are changing. Our proposed algorithm is able to identify the Spatial Skyline based on changing characteristics of the data and prunes the search space using spatial properties, in order to avoid exhaustive searches. We have empirically studied the performance of our algorithm against state-of-the-art algorithms. Since our algorithm avoids recomputation of the whole Skyline set with each update on the data, its average running time is lower than the time of the state-of-the-art algorithms. In the best case, our experimental study shows that our algorithm may become 3 times faster than state-of-the-art algorithms.

The outline of this chapter is as follows. Section 2 describes existing state-of-the-art approaches to evaluate Skyline queries. Section 3 contains a motivation for this work and introduces basic definitions of Skyline. Section 4 describes two naive algorithms to evaluate SSQ on changing data and Section 5 defines our proposed solution. Section 6 reports the results of our experimental study. Finally, the future work and concluding remarks are pointed out in Sections 7 and 8, respectively.

BACKGROUND

Skyline queries have been extensively studied. The first algorithms to identify the Skyline over large databases were proposed by (Börzsönyi, Kossmann, & Stocker, 2001). BNL (Block Nested Loops) (Börzsönyi et al., 2001), SFS (Sort Filter Skyline) (Chomicki, Godfrey, Gryz, & Liang, 2003) and LESS (Linear Elimination Sort for Skyline) (Godfrey, Shipley, & Gryz, 2005) are algorithms that require scanning of the whole data in order to evaluate Skyline queries. BNL scans the entire table while maintains a window of non-dominated tuples, which could be replaced by any other tuple that is seen later. SFS begins sorting the table, after that it passes a cursor over the sorted rows and discards dominated rows. LESS initially sorts tuples as SFS does, but presents two improvements over it: in the first ordering phase, it uses an elimination-filter window to discard dominated tuples quickly and it combines the last phase of the sort algorithm with the Skyline filter phase of SFS to eliminate remaining dominated tuples. Additionally, properties of index structures are exploited in (Kossmann, Ramsak, & Rost, 2002; Papadias, Tao, Fu, & Seeger, 2005; Tan, Eng, & Ooi, 2001) to progressively return more and more results until the full Skyline is retrieved. (Kossmann, Ramsak, & Rost, 2002) defined the Nearest Neighbor (NN) algorithm which is based on an R-Tree index that recursively divides data in regions making use the nearest neighbor approach. In each recursion, the nearest neighbor is returned as part of the Skyline while discards those regions whose points are dominated by the nearest neighbor. The Branch & Bound Skyline (BBS) algorithm introduced by (Papadias et al., 2005) improves NN using a Branch & Bound approach. Tan, Eng and Ooi (2001) defined algorithms based on bitmaps and B-tree indexes. These algorithms use a vector of m bits or a B-tree index for each Skyline criterion. The bitmap based algorithm produces the whole Skyline by means of logical operations and the B-tree-based algorithm is able to discard objects checking a stop condition.

Solutions based on indices are highly costly to apply to the problem of evaluating SSQ on changing data because not only require pre-calculate distance functions belonging to each criterion of user's preferences but also need to build, load the index and update the distance functions and structures in each data change. In the worst case, if there was little evidence to satisfy the condition on the changing attribute, the use of any of these solutions will be highly costly because of the construction and loading of the index over the entire dataset.

Some works have focused on evaluating Skyline queries where criteria are defined on functions. This kind of Skyline is known as Dynamic Skyline (Papadias et al., 2005). Spatial Skyline Queries (SSQ) (Sharifzadeh & Shahabi, 2006) are a particular case of Dynamic Skyline Queries. Using Euclidean distance function, SSQ return those points such that there is no other point closer than them to a set of query points. Sharifzadeh and Shahabi (2006) proposed two algorithms to evaluate SSQ when the query points are not changing, i.e. static query points. A third algorithm, VCS^2 (Voronoi-based Continuous SSQ), is described in (Sharifzadeh & Shahabi, 2006) to answer SSQ with moving query points. Since two of the algorithms in (Sharifzadeh & Shahabi, 2006) fail to identify correct results, Sharifzadeh, Shahabi, and Kazemi (2009) introduced enhanced versions of their algorithms to compute all Spatial Skyline points.

Dynamic Skyline queries have aroused great interest in the database community. Some variants of Dynamic Skyline queries are Location-Dependent Skyline Queries (LDSQ) and Spatial Skylines based on direction vectors. LDSQ include one query point and multiple non-spatial dimensions as part of Skyline criteria (Huang, Chang, & Lee, 2012; Kodama, Iijima, Guo, & Ishikawa, 2009; Zheng, Lee, & Lee, 2008). In all these works, the spatial preferences are reduced to a single point and do not consider preferences over a changing non-spatial attribute.

The Spatial Skylines based on direction vectors returns the best objects around the user's location from different directions (Guo, Ishikawa, & Gao, 2010; Guo, Zheng, Ishikawa, & Gao, 2011). In addition, Dynamic Skylines have defined on road networks (Deng, Zhou, & Tao, 2007; Guo, Zheng, Ishikawa, & Gao, 2011; Iyer & Shanthi, 2012) and metric space (Chen, Lei, Lian, & Xiang, 2008; Skopal & Lokoc, 2010). Also, Direction-based Spatial Skyline is extended on road networks and is calculated within bounds of a maximum deviation angle in (El-Dawy, Mokhtar, & El-Bastawissy, 2011, 2012). Although there are several types of Dynamic Skyline queries, we focus on SSQ because they have been widely studied. Additionally, the geometric properties of the SSQ evaluation problem allow to devise algorithms for evaluating SSQ that are more efficient than algorithms for general Skyline queries. To the best our knowledge, algorithms for SSQ do not assume changing non-spatial data (Sharifzadeh et al., 2009) and Skyline algorithms for non-spatial data only allow one query point (Chen, Shou, Chen, Gao, & Dong, 2009, 2012; Huang, Chang, & Lee, 2012; Kodama, Iijima, Guo., & Ishikawa, 2009; Zheng, Lee, & Lee, 2008). The case of moving query points and static non-spatial dimensions has been considered in (Sharifzadeh et al., 2009), but there does not seem to be any work yet on both moving query points and changing non-spatial dimensions.

In this chapter, we extend the work presented in (Di Bartolo & Goncalves, 2013). In (Di Bartolo & Goncalves, 2013), the authors introduce the problem of evaluating SSQ on changing data and describe the ideas in which our algorithms are based. In this work, we formalize SSQ on changing data and we detail our algorithm named C2S. Additionally, we extend the experimental study done in (Di Bartolo & Goncalves, 2013) to analyze the impact of dimensionality, data updates, and dataset size in the SSQ performance.

Lastly, Skyline queries have received considerable attention with the continuous growth of the Web. The interested reader is referred to (Chen, Liang, & Yu, 2009; Chen, Cui, Lu, Xu, & Xu, 2008; Huang, Xin, Wang, & Li, 2009; Lee & Hwang, 2009; Liang, Chen, & Yu, 2008; Wang, Vu, Ooi, Tung, & Xu, 2009).

Skyline Queries

Börzsönyi et al., (2001) extended the SELECT command of the SQL language as following:

```
SELECT <attributes>
FROM <relations>
```

```
WHERE <conditions>
SKYLINE OF a₁ [MIN|MAX|DIFF],…,a_r [MIN|MAX|DIFF]
```

Syntactically, the SKYLINE OF clause is similar to the ORDER BY clause. a_1, …, a_r represents the attributes. Domains of these attributes must have a natural ordering, such as integers, floats, and dates. MIN and MAX directives specify whether the user prefers low or high values, respectively. DIFF directive defines the interest in retaining best choices with respect to every distinct value of that attribute.

Formally, let $T = \{t_1, t_2, …, t_n\}$ be a set of tuples and $A = \{a_1, a_2, …, a_r\}$ a set of attributes that characterizes the tuples belonging to T. For simplicity, we suppose that user's preference criteria correspond to minimization of dimensions. Then, the Skyline set, S, on A is defined as follows:

$$S = \left\{ t_i \in T \,\middle|\, \neg \left(\exists t_j \in T \,\middle|\, \left(\forall a_y \in A \,\middle|\, t_j.a_y \leq t_i.a_y \right) \wedge \left(\exists a_x \in A \,\middle|\, t_j.a_x < t_i.a_x \right) \right) \right\} \tag{1}$$

The Skyline set is a set of tuples where each tuple in the set is not dominated by other tuple; a tuple t_j dominates another tuple t_i if it is better or equal in all attributes, and is better in at least one attribute. This is, a tuple $t_j \in T$ dominates on A another tuple $t_i \in T$ if and only if:

$$\left(\forall a_y \in A \,\middle|\, t_j.a_y \leq t_i.a_y \right) \wedge \left(\exists a_x \in A \,\middle|\, t_j.a_x < t_i.a_x \right) \tag{2}$$

Spatial Skyline Queries

A Spatial Skyline query is an extension of Skyline query that uses Euclidean distance functions, dist(-,-), between d-dimensional points. On the other hand, a traditional tuple with d values may be seen as a d-dimensional point. Thus, the Spatial Skyline set may be defined on d-dimensional points. Given a set of points $P = \{p_1, p_2, …, p_n\}$ and a set of query points $Q = \{q_1, q_2, …, q_k\}$. (Sharifzadeh & Shahabi, 2006) define the Spatial Skyline set, SS, as follows:

$$SS = \left\{ p_i \in P \,\middle|\, \neg \left(\exists p_j \in P \,\middle|\, \left(\forall q_l \in Q \,\middle|\, d(p_j, ql) \leq d(p_i, q_l) \right) \wedge \left(\exists q_s \in Q \,\middle|\, d(p_j, qs) < d(p_i, q_s) \right) \right) \right\} \tag{3}$$

Consider a set P of points, say locations of parking spaces, and a set Q of query points, say locations of the vehicle and the exits. The goal of a Spatial Skyline Query is to find a set of points p in P that are the closest possible to each query point in Q, i.e., there is no other point p_i in P that spatially dominates p_j. In other words, p_j is at least as close as p_i to all the query points, and even closer to one of the query point. This is, a point $p_j \in P$ spatially dominates another point $p_i \in P$ with respect to Q if and only if:

$$\left(\forall q_l \in Q \,\middle|\, d(p_j, ql) \leq d(p_i, q_l) \right) \wedge \left(\exists q_s \in Q \,\middle|\, d(p_j, qs) < d(p_i, q_s) \right) \tag{4}$$

SPATIAL SKYLINE QUERIES OVER CHANGING DATA

Motivating Example

Suppose a recommendation system installed in any vehicle able to suggest available parking spaces in a parking lot. A customer may be interested in finding an available parking space close to a pedestrian exit gate, any of the parking exits, and his vehicle in movement. Additionally, the parking spaces may be characterized by non-spatial dimensions such as average exit time and its availability. Thus, an available parking space is preferred for the customer if it is close to the exits and his vehicle, and the average exit time is reduced at rush hours. In this example, availability and vehicle location are changing data, a space location is a spatial dimension, and locations of the exits and the vehicle correspond to the query points.

Figure 1 shows a parking lot. The table in Figure 1. presents the distance from the vehicle v to a parking space s, d(v,s), the distance from s to the pedestrian exit pe, d(s,pe), the distance from s to the parking exit pa, d(s,pa), and the average exit time in minutes for each parking space.

It can be noted that the space 4 at Sector 3, Row B (3B-4) is better than the space 2 at Sector 3, Row B (3B-2). Clearly, the space 3B-4 which is highlighted in dark gray, has the shortest distance to the vehicle since its value is d(v,s) = 0.4 meters (1.31 feet). Furthermore, the space 3B-4 is better than the space 3B-2 in all dimensions. Therefore, the space 3B-4 belongs to the system suggestions or the Skyline set because no one is better than it. Conversely, the space 3B-2 will be discarded from the suggestion because 3B-4 is better than 3B-2 in all dimensions.

Moreover, there may be spaces whose distance from the vehicle is not the smallest, but they satisfy other criteria. The spaces 3B-7 and 4B-1, highlighted in dark gray, are closer to the pedestrian exit

Figure 1. A parking lot

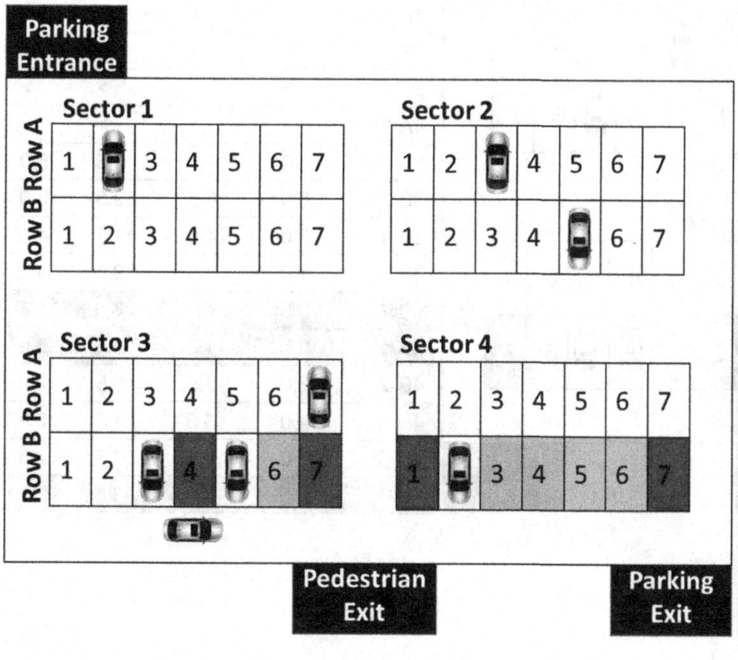

Space	d(v,s)	d(s,pe)	d(s,pa)	Time
1A-*	>	>	>	>
2A-*	>	>	>	>
1B-*	>	>	>	>
2B-*	>	>	>	>
3A-*	>	>	>	>
4A-*	>	>	>	>
3B-1	3.0	7.5	14.5	5.0
3B-2	2.0	6.5	13.5	5.0
3B-4	0.4	4.5	11.5	4.5
3B-6	2.0	2.5	9.5	4.0
3B-7	3.0	1.5	8.5	4.0
4B-1	5.0	1.5	6.5	3.0
4B-3	7.0	3.5	4.5	2.8
4B-4	8.0	4.5	3.5	2.8
4B-5	9.0	5.5	2.5	2.8
4B-6	10.0	6.5	1.5	2.5
4B-7	11.0	7.5	0.5	2.2

(minimum d(*s,pe*)); and the space 4B-7, highlighted in dark gray, has the lowest exit time and distance to the parking exit (minimum time and d(*s,pa*)). Notice that the spaces 3B-7 and 4B-1 are equal distance from the pedestrian exit, but one is closer to the vehicle and other is closer to the parking exit.

On the other hand, the spaces from 4B-3 to 4B-6, and 3B-6, highlighted in light gray, also belong to the best spaces or the Skyline set because no space is better than them in all the given criteria. All these spaces highlighted in gray, meet the customer's preferences because they minimize some criteria, but none satisfies all criteria simultaneously. Since no criterion is more important than the other, all these highlighted spaces will be suggested by the system and the driver's task will be choosing a parking space among the suggested parking spaces.

The non highlighted spaces in Figure 1, are discarded because they are worse than the highlighted spaces in all criteria. For example, 3A-6 is discarded by 3B-6 because it is farthest from the vehicle, the pedestrian exit and parking exit, as well as its exit time is higher. In table of Figure 1, those spaces whose values are greater than the rest are indicated as " > ".

In this example, the values of d(*s,pa*) and time are correlated, because usually the spaces closest to the exit are the ones with a lower exit time. However, a space may be very good in terms of non-spatial dimensions, but is away from the query points, e.g., a faraway space with time = 1.0.

Also, there may be spaces that could be Skyline such as 3B-3, 3B-5, and 4B-2, but they are unavailable. Once a customer decides to park his vehicle, the selected space is no longer available. Therefore, the system not only needs to adapt to changes in movement of the vehicle, but also to changes in the availability of spaces. We can observe a possible alteration of the initial environment of Figure 1 in Figure 2.

Figure 2. A state change of the parking lot

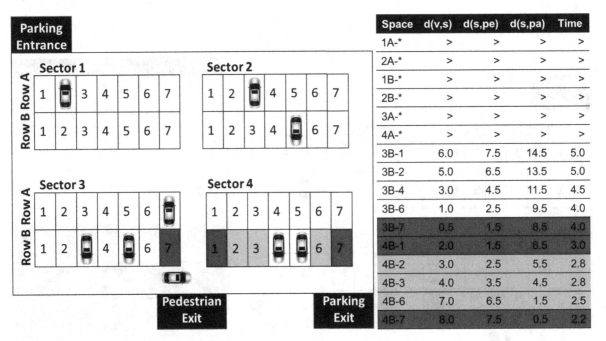

Space	d(v,s)	d(s,pe)	d(s,pa)	Time
1A-*	>	>	>	>
2A-*	>	>	>	>
1B-*	>	>	>	>
2B-*	>	>	>	>
3A-*	>	>	>	>
4A-*	>	>	>	>
3B-1	6.0	7.5	14.5	5.0
3B-2	5.0	6.5	13.5	5.0
3B-4	3.0	4.5	11.5	4.5
3B-6	1.0	2.5	9.5	4.0
3B-7	0.5	1.5	8.5	4.0
4B-1	2.0	1.5	6.5	3.0
4B-2	3.0	2.5	5.5	2.8
4B-3	4.0	3.5	4.5	2.8
4B-6	7.0	6.5	1.5	2.5
4B-7	8.0	7.5	0.5	2.2

Due to the changes, the spaces 4B-4 and 4B-5 are deleted from the suggestions because they are occupied and the space 4B-2 is included because it is available and it is close to the exits. Additionally, the set of suggested spaces changes because of the vehicle movement. Therefore, the distance d(v,s) has to be recalculated, and the spaces 3B-4 and 3B-6, which previously were good, now they have to be discarded because they are worse than the space 3B-7.

Intuitively, a Spatial Skyline query may be evaluated to identify the best spaces according to the characteristics desired by the customer. Spaces that are available in the parking lot not always are good options. Some spaces are away from the vehicle, the pedestrian exit and the parking exit. Therefore, the system must recognize which are the best spaces among all the available spaces. The spaces highlighted in Figures 1 and 2 are suggested by a Spatial Skyline query that simultaneously minimizes d(v,s), d(s,pe), d(s,pa) and time.

Initially, Skyline queries assume that dimensions or attributes are static (Börzsönyi et al., 2001; Tan et al., 2001; Kossmann et al., 2002; Papadias et al., 2005), i.e., d(v,s), d(s,pe), and d(s,pa) are precomputed. Nevertheless, d(v,s) is a dynamic function that varies with the position of the vehicle which it must be calculated during the movement of the vehicle.

Skyline queries have been extended as Spatial Skyline Queries (SSQ) in order to incorporate dynamic functions or Euclidean distance functions as part of preference criteria (Sharifzadeh & Shahabi, 2006). The SSQ criteria are defined by spatial and non-spatial dimensions. Spatial dimensions correspond to Euclidean distance functions from a set of data points to a set of query points, e.g., d(v,s) is calculated dynamically based on the location of the vehicle.

SSQ may not be suitable for changing data due to a new Spatial Skyline query must be evaluated for each change. Hence, new techniques to evaluate SSQ on changing data are required. A good technique should be able to provide the Skyline according to dynamic characteristics of the data and to prune the search space in order to avoid exhaustive searches.

Preliminaries

Given a set of points $P = \{p_1, p_2, ..., p_n\}$, a set of query points $Q = \{q_1, q_2, ..., q_k\}$, and a set of non-spatial dimensions $A = \{a_1, a_2, ..., a_r\} \cup \{a_{r+1}\}$ that characterizes the points belonging to P, where a_{r+1} is a changing non-spatial dimension. For simplicity, we suppose that user's preference criteria or multidimensional function correspond to minimization of dimensions. We introduce the Skyline set, S, on A -$\{a_{r+1}\}$ as follows:

$$S =$$
$$\left\{ p_i \in P \;\middle|\; \neg \left(\exists p_j \in P \;\middle|\; \left(\forall a_y \in A - \{a_{r+1}\} \middle| p_j.a_y \le p_i.a_y \right) \wedge \left(\exists a_x \in A - \{a_{r+1}\} \middle| p_j.a_x < p_i.a_x \right) \right) \right\}$$

$$(5)$$

where $p.a$ represents the value of the dimension $a \in A$ - $\{a_{r+1}\}$ on the point $p \in P$.

The Skyline set is a set of points where each point in the set is not dominated by some other point; a point p_j dominates another point p_i if p_j is better or equal in all dimensions, but better in at least one dimension. A Skyline query example is to find parking lots that have the best rating and price. The Skyline set consist of all parking lots such that there is no parking lot that is a better choice. A parking lot p_j dominates or is a better choice than the parking lot p_i, if p_j has equal or higher rating and price than p_i, but better in rating or price. A point $p_j \in P$ dominates on A - $\{a_{r+1}\}$ another point $p_i \in P$ if and only if:

$$\left(\forall a_y \in A - \left\{ a_{r+1} \right\} \middle| p_j . a_y \leq p_i . a_y \right) \wedge \left(\exists a_x \in A - \left\{ a_{r+1} \right\} \middle| p_j . a_x < p_i . a_x \right) \tag{6}$$

Nevertheless, the points belonging to P may be characterized with additional non-spatial dimensions. In our motivating example, a customer asks for parking spaces that are close to his vehicle and exits, which the exit time from these parking spaces is low. In this case, a point p_j in P will be in the Spatial Skyline set if there is no point p_i in P that is at least as close to all the query points in Q as p_j, whose exit time is at least as good as p_j's exit time, but better than p_j in the sense that it is either closer to some point in Q as p_j or has a better exit time than p_j.

We define the set of Spatial Skyline on non-spatial data, *SSS*, as follows:

$$SSS = \left\{ p_j \in P \middle| \neg \middle| \exists p_i \in P \middle| \begin{array}{l} \left(\forall a_y \in A - \left\{ a_{r+1} \right\} \middle| p_i . a_y \leq p_j . a_y \right) \wedge \left(\forall q_l \in Q \middle| d(p_i, ql) \leq d(p_j, q_l) \right) \\ \wedge \\ \left(\left(\exists a_x \in A - \left\{ a_{r+1} \right\} \middle| p_i . a_x < p_j . a_x \right) \vee \left(\exists q_s \in Q \middle| d(p_i, qs) < d(p_j, q_s) \right) \right) \end{array} \right\} \tag{7}$$

In this work, we propose the Spatial Skyline on changing data. Criteria of SSQ on changing data are spatial and non-spatial. Spatial criteria include preferences on the distances between a set of points and a set of query points. Non-spatial criteria may be defined on dimensions whose values are changing. SSQ on changing data return the Spatial Skyline set among those points whose value of a_{r+1} is equal to a given state or belongs to a domain V, e.g., parking spaces whose state is available. In this context, a point p_j dominates a point p_i ($p_i \prec p_j$) if and only if:

$$p_i \prec p_j = \begin{cases} p_i . a_{r+1} \in V \Rightarrow \left(\forall a_y \in A - \left\{ a_{r+1} \right\} \middle| p_j . a_y \leq p_i . a_y \right) \wedge \left(\forall q_l \in Q \middle| d(p_j, ql) \leq d(p_i, q_l) \right) \wedge \\ \qquad \left(\left(\exists a_x \in A - \left\{ a_{r+1} \right\} \middle| p_j . a_x < p_i . a_x \right) \vee \left(\exists q_s \in Q \middle| d(p_j, qs) < d(p_i, q_s) \right) \right) \\ \\ or \\ \\ p_i . a_{r+1} \notin V \Rightarrow True \end{cases} \tag{8}$$

where V is the set of desired values for a_{r+1}.

Finally, a point p_j is returned by SSQ on changing data if and only if:

$$\left(\neg \exists p_i \in P - \left\{ p_j \right\} \middle| p_j \prec p_i \right) \tag{9}$$

We study SSQ evaluation in a scenario where the query points may move and non-spatial dimensions may change over time. We only consider the case of one moving query point or one changing non-spatial dimension in each transformation of the input scenario. The algorithms process the updates on query points and non-spatial dimensions one at a time. The following data changes are allowed:

- **State Changes:** A non-spatial dimension changes its state on one or more objects.
- **Movement of a Query Point:** A moving query point changes its location following a straight line.

Therefore, the following algorithms receive these transformations or inputs which can be classified in:

- **Initial Configuration:** The original values of the data. There is no change in the data.
- **State Change Configuration:** New data state after a non-spatial dimension changes its value in one or more objects.
- **Position Change Configuration:** New data state after a moving query point has changed its position.

NAIVE ALGORITHMS

We devise two naive algorithms. The first algorithm, AB2S, is a naive solution which calculates the Spatial Skyline set using the BNL algorithm (Börzsönyi et al., 2001) at each change of the data. The second naive algorithm, VC2S+, is an adaptation of VCS2 (Sharifzadeh et al., 2009) that allows non-spatial changing data.

We chose BNL as baseline because it is a very simple algorithm and it is the most basic solution for identifying the skyline set. Also, we have studied different solutions looking for any algorithm that could be applied to the problem of evaluating SSQ on changing data. The solution that best relate to this problem was introduced by (Sharifzadeh, Shahabi, & Kazemi, 2009) because they receive a set of query points and the user's criteria include Euclidean distances on these query points. However, the authors did not implement a solution for non-spatial attributes and changing data. Thus, we adapted this solution to evaluate SSQ on changing data. Additionally, Sharifzadeh and Shahabi (2007) showed those algorithms that update the Skyline set behave better than those algorithms that recalculate the whole Skyline set, they consider SSQ over centralized environments with the presence of moving query points. The average response time decreases by 65%. Therefore, this kind of strategy in dynamic environments is necessary in order to avoid recurrent calculation of the Skyline set. The studied strategy is based on creating partitions for processing the Skyline and the use of filters to subsequently get candidate objects. In this way, the search space may be pruned while reducing the amount of data to be processed, therefore, the probability of the computation of the whole Skyline set decreases.

The Adapted BNL for Spatial Skyline (AB2S) algorithm does not have methods to update the Spatial Skyline according to changes of a moving query point. Hence, Spatial Skyline is built in any configuration to identify the correct points. Figure 3 shows the flowchart of AB2S.

In any configuration, AB2S performs BNL for finding candidates considering spatial and non-spatial dimensions to calculate the Spatial Skyline. An object will be a candidate if its changing non-spatial dimension has a desired value (an available parking space). Additionally, AB2S in the State Change Configuration maintains the previous Skyline set and updates it through dominance check. The dominance check is done by evaluating the objects that now have a desired value and the candidates of the previous configuration that are not yet in this set against the Skyline set. The update is done applying BNL with those objects over the previous Skyline set.

On the other hand, there are certain geometric properties that may be applied for minimizing dominance comparisons in order to identify the Spatial Skyline; dominance comparisons refer to the number of

Figure 3. Flowchart of AB2S

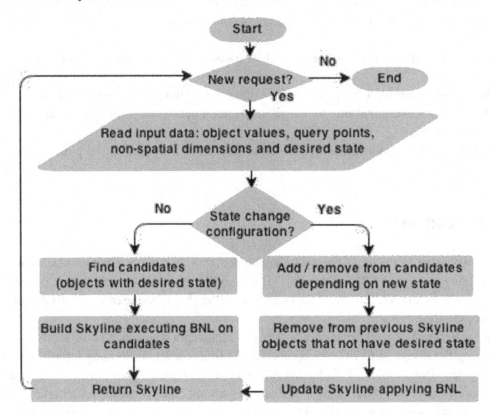

times in which the multidimensional function is evaluated by an algorithm. These properties are focused on the Convex Hull, i.e., the convex polygon formed by the set of query points. The query points may be vertices or be within the Convex Hull and each of them comprises a region of visibility that determines membership to the Skyline. Those query points that are not vertices of the Convex Hull does not affect the Skyline calculation because their region of visibility is contained in the region of visibility formed by the vertices. Moreover, any point that is within the Convex Hull or the Voronoi cells, which intersects the convex hull, are Skyline (Sharifzadeh & Shahabi, 2006).

These properties are the basis of VS2 and VCS2 proposed in (Sharifzadeh & Shahabi, 2006). VS2 by constructing a Voronoi diagram (Voronoi, 1908) uses the corresponding Delaunay graph (Delaunay, 1938) to explore the necessary objects and thus calculates the Spatial Skyline. Through Delaunay graph, it identifies the Spatial Skyline by means of those points whose Voronoi cells intersect with the Convex Hull or are within the Convex Hull. Intuitively, a Voronoi diagram is a way of partitioning space into regions and a Delaunay graph is the dual graph of a Voronoi diagram (Sharifzadeh et al., 2009).

This algorithm allows only static query points. To handle moving query points, the authors define VCS2 that continuously updates the Spatial Skyline based on the movement of a query point at a time. This algorithm allows the movement of a query point at a time, comparing if the previous position changes with respect to the current one. If VCS2 determines a change pattern in the query point location then it performs appropriate actions. (Sharifzadeh & Shahabi, 2006) identified six change patterns of the Convex Hull Q when a query point moves from q to q'.

Let Q be the set of query points; let Q' be a new set of locations; let q be the moving query point; and let q' be the new location of q. The pattern I corresponds to the case where the previous Convex Hull $CH(Q)$ and the current $CH(Q')$ are equal since q and q' are inside the Convex Hull. Since the Skyline does not change, it is not necessary to traverse the Delaunay graph.

For the patterns II-IV, the Delaunay graph is traversed. The regions outside visibility region of q and q' are not considered. According to the patterns II and IV, $CH(Q)$ is contained in $CH(Q')$, and therefore $CH(Q)$ is equal to $CH(Q) \cap CH(Q')$. In consequence, the objects from $CH(Q)$ that belongs to the Skyline are kept because they are inside $CH(Q')$. Thus, those objects belonging to $CH(Q') - CH(Q)$ are incorporated to the Skyline. Since the movement of the query point and the change of the dominance region, more candidates may belong to the Skyline and they are verified in order to decide whether they must be added to the Skyline.

In the pattern III, $CH(Q)$ contains $CH(Q')$, $CH(Q')$ is equal to $CH(Q) \cap CH(Q')$, and the objects of the intersection are maintained. Objects outside $CH(Q')$ are checked and they are removed from the Skyline if they are dominated. No object need to be added to the Skyline.

In the pattern V, those objects belonging to $CH(Q) \cap CH(Q')$ prevail in the Skyline. Those objects inside $CH(Q') - CH(Q)$ are incorporated into the Skyline and since the dominance region changed, it is necessary to check whether the objects outside $CH(Q')$ will be added or deleted from the Skyline.

For the pattern VI, the Skyline is not updated according to the change of position of the moving query point, so VS2 runs considering all query points as static. Hence, no optimization is performed on the Skyline calculation regarding to the occurred movement.

VCS2 has been adapted to the problem of evaluation of Spatial Skyline queries over changing data. This adapted algorithm is named VC2S+. Figure 4 illustrates the flowchart of VC2S+.

VC2S+ calculates the non-spatial Skyline or the Skyline on non-spatial dimensions, and builds a Voronoi diagram using the candidates or the available points; incorrect results may be produced if the undesired points (unavailable or occupied parking spaces) are included in the Voronoi diagram. The main disadvantage of this adaptation is that the Voronoi diagram and its Delaunay graph must be reconstructed in the State Change Configuration.

Originally, in presence of non-spatial dimensions, the search region in (Sharifzadeh et al., 2009) is composed of several circle areas. For each query point q, the middle point of each circle is q with radius equal to the distance from q to a Non-Spatial Skyline point p. The region outside the union of the circles, called dominance region, contains points dominated by the middle point p. The region inside the circles may have points that dominate the middle point p; these points inside a particular circle may dominate the middle point p due to their closeness to the regarding query point, but not necessarily dominate the middle point p in the other dimensions. The dominant region of a middle point p corresponds to the intersection of all the areas of the circles whose middle point is p. If the dominant region of a middle point p is not empty, then points belonging to this region spatially dominate p. We have adapted the search region for Spatial Skyline in presence of non-spatial dimensions. The search region for Spatial Skyline in presence of non-spatial dimensions corresponds to the minimum bounding rectangle of the union of the circle areas; the middle points of the circles are the Non-Spatial Skyline points. We assume that any Skyline point may not be further than any Non-Spatial Skyline point. The goal of our adaptation is to find the region in which a Skyline point may be. Thus, any point outside this search region is irrelevant.

VC2S+ starts on the Initial Configuration which finds the candidates or available points, constructs the Delaunay graph and proceeds to calculate the Non-Spatial Skyline on the candidates. Subsequently, VC2S+ computes the Spatial Skyline using the VS^2 algorithm (Sharifzadeh et al., 2009); VS^2 is an

Figure 4. Flowchart of VC2S+

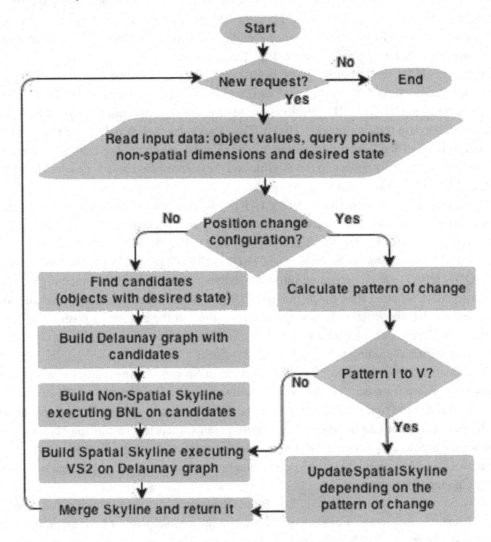

algorithm that produces the Spatial Skyline on static query points. Thus, the Delaunay graph scanning begins. Some dominance checks may be avoided, e.g., a point belonging to the convex hull formed by the query points is a Skyline point, and therefore, it is not necessary to check if is dominated.

In the State Change Configuration, VC2S+ re-initializes data structures for the Skyline, the Spatial Skyline, the Non-Spatial Skyline, and the Delaunay graph. Non available points are removed from candidates and new available points are inserted as candidates. The Non-Spatial Skyline is computed, and the search region and Delaunay graph are recalculated considering updated candidates. Using the Delaunay graph, the Spatial Skyline is identified using VS². Lastly, the final Skyline is built merging the Non-Spatial Skyline and the Spatial Skyline.

In the Position Change Configuration, due to the movement of the query point, VC2S+ stores the current convex hull as previous convex hull and creates a new one with the new position of the query point. Using these convex hulls, the algorithm identifies a movement pattern (Sharifzadeh et al., 2009) and updates the Skyline set in almost all the patterns. According to the movement patterns, the Skyline may maintain the same objects or it can change. The Skyline changes if new points have to be inserted or former points have to be deleted. The algorithm in pattern I (Sharifzadeh et al., 2009), returns the same Skyline. In patterns II and IV (Sharifzadeh et al., 2009), new points have to be added to the Skyline. In pattern III (Sharifzadeh et al., 2009), some former points have to be deleted from the Skyline. In pattern V (Sharifzadeh et al., 2009), some points have to be added to the Skyline set and others are deleted from it. In pattern VI (Sharifzadeh et al., 2009), there is no update, it applies VS^2. Also, the distances from each candidate to the moving query point are modified. The new search region is calculated. In this configuration the non-spatial Skyline remains without changes in all the patterns because it has not been a change of state. Finally, VC2S+ returns the final Skyline after updating and merging the Non-Spatial Skyline and the Spatial Skyline.

PROPOSED ALGORITHM

We propose an algorithm to evaluate SSQ on changing non-spatial data: The Changing Spatial Skyline (C2S) algorithm. This algorithm receives a Spatial Skyline query composed of multiple query points and non-spatial dimensions, one changing non-spatial dimension, and one moving query point. Also, it uses the Euclidean distance function to compute closeness between points.

C2S identifies the Spatial Skyline in terms of the changing features of the data. The Algorithm 1 shows the pseudocode of C2S for the Initial Configuration. At the beginning (line 1), it initializes a d-dimensional matrix with the state value of each point in P^d. If the non-spatial dimension is Boolean, its value may be saved in the matrix as a bit. Then, it fills the lists of query points and non-spatial dimensions with the spatial coordinates and values indicated by the user. Also, the search region and the two convex hulls are created. Initially, the search region is the minimum bounding rectangle that includes all the points in P. One of the convex hulls is formed by all the query points, and it is named Global Convex Hull. Another convex hull, the Static Convex Hull, is formed by the query points excluding the moving query point.

To explain the algorithm, we assume that the user preferences are expressed over points that have a particular Boolean state, for instance the value True or 1. Therefore, points whose state value is True are the candidates. To find these candidates in the matrix, the algorithm has to read each row value (or a piece of the row) as a number generated by the bits contained there. Only rows or row pieces that have

Algorithm 1. C2S: Initial configuration

```
Input: stateValues, qryPts, nonSpatialValues
1: init(stateV alues; qryPts; nonSpatialV alues)
2: findCandidates()                          // Only the available ones in the
   search region
3: if existsNonSpatialDims() then
4:         processNonSpatialSkyline() // using the static non-spatial criteria
5: end if
6: processRemainingSkyline()
7: return getSkyline()
```

a value greater than zero are will be verified to select the candidates. In the line 2, C2S looks for the candidates inside the search region and save them in a list. If the candidate is inside the Global Convex Hull, it is directly marked as Skyline. In this step, the Skyline is separated into two groups: Static Skyline and Dynamic Skyline. The first group is the set of candidates inside the Static Convex Hull, and the second group is the set of candidates between the Global Convex Hull and the Static Convex Hull. While each point is marked as Skyline, if there are not any preferences on non-spatial dimensions (only the preference over the changing non-spatial dimension), the search region is pruned by the intersection with the dominance region of each Skyline point. In presence of static non-spatial dimensions, similar to VC2S+, the Non-Spatial Skyline is calculated checking dominance between candidates considering only the non-spatial dimensions. In this case, the search region is formed by the union of the dominance regions of the Non-Spatial Skyline points (lines 3-5).

In the lines 6-7, the remaining Skyline (the Outer Skyline) is calculated verifying the dominance of the candidates which are between the search region and outside the bounds of the Global Convex Hull against the previous Skyline set. These candidates can be added or not to the Skyline set, but they do not eliminate the points already marked as Static Skyline, Dynamic Skyline or Non-Spatial Skyline. Finally, the Skyline set is returned in line 7.

When a change in the state of a non-spatial dimension occurs, C2S updates the Skyline set in the State Change Configuration (Algorithm 2). First, it stores the previous search region in a variable (line

Algorithm 2. C2S: State change configuration

```
Input: newValues
1:    Rectangle oldRegion← getSearchRegion()
2:    List<Point> oldCandidates ← ∅
3:    updatePlane(newV alues)
4:    Integer deleted← delPointsFromSkyline(newV alues)
5:    if deleted = 0 then                        // To only check new
      candidates
6:        oldCandidates ← getCandidateList()
7:        resetCandidateList()
8:    else
9:        updateSearchRegion()
10: end if
11: addPointsToSkyline(newV alues)               // New objects are added to
the candidate list and checked against the skyline
12: if deleted > 0 then                          // Search region has
    changed, find new candidates
13:        findMoreCandidates(oldRegion)
14:        processRemainingSkyline()                       // Excluding
           new candidates
15: else
16:        addToCandidateList(oldCandidates)
17: end if
18: return getSkyline()                          // Skyline updated
```

1). Then, the matrix is synchronized with the new state value of each point (line 3) and the points with a state value not required by the user (i.e. False or 0) are removed from the candidate and Skyline sets (line 4). If none of the points was deleted from the Skyline in the previous step, then the candidate set is temporarily stored in another variable and the current candidate set is reinitialized (lines 5 - 7). The reason is that old candidate points which were not in the Skyline set will still be dominated by the current Skyline, so there is no need to explore them in order to update the Skyline set. Nevertheless, if any Skyline point was deleted, then the candidate set is held because old candidates can now be Skyline points, because points dominated before by the deleted points can be not dominated by the current set. Thus, the new search region is created considering only the Skyline points that were not deleted (lines 8-10). The points whose state has changed to the value required and also are inside the search region, are added to the candidate set, each point is analyzed to determine its membership to the Skyline set (line 11). If a candidate is inside the Global Convex Hull, the point is directly added to the Skyline set, but some Skyline points outside the Global Convex Hull could be dominated by this new point; therefore, dominated points have to be deleted from the Skyline.

If some skyline point was deleted in the line 4, it is necessary to find the candidates between the old search region and the new one (lines 13-14). These points have to be added to the candidate set; also this set is revised to remove points that which not belong to the new search region. Through the candidate set, ignoring the objects already added in the line 11, the remaining Skyline set is obtained. On the contrary, (deleted = 0, line 4), old candidates are added to the current candidate set for the next execution. Lastly, the Skyline set is returned in line 18.

For each position change of the moving query point, in the Position Change Configuration, C2S updates the Skyline set (Algorithm 3). The algorithm applies the same pattern identification as VCS2 (Sharifzadeh et al., 2009) to evaluate the Skyline depending on the case (line 1). In this step, the new Global Convex Hull is calculated, but the Static Convex Hull remains without change, because always will be the same polygon. Also, the region where the Skyline is not affected by the movement is generated; this region is named the Invariant Sector.

For pattern I, the Skyline set is returned without changes (line 2). If there is any static non-spatial dimension, the distances of the Non-Spatial Skyline points to the moving query point are updated and the new search region is obtained (this Skyline does not change) (line 3). For pattern VI (lines 4-7), the distances of the Skyline points to the moving query point are updated (excluding the Non-Spatial Skyline) and if there is no static non-spatial dimension, the new search region is obtained. The Dynamic Skyline points which is formed by the points in the previous Global Convex Hull that are outside of the Static Convex Hull, combined with the Outer Skyline points are analyzed to delete dominated points; also, the non-skyline points in the candidate set inside the new search region are checked to add new points to the Dynamic Skyline and Outer Skyline. Before a point is compared, its distance to the moving query point has to be updated. For patterns II and IV (lines 8-9), it is necessary to analyze the candidate points outside the Invariant Sector in order to add new points to the Dynamic Skyline and Outer Skyline. For patterns III and V (lines 10-18), similar to pattern VI, the query point distances of the points belonging to the Skyline points and the new search region are updated. The Dynamic Skyline and Outer Skyline have to be checked in order to eliminate dominated points outside the Invariant Sector. Particularly for pattern III, distances of the non-skyline candidate points have to be updated for the next algorithm execution. For pattern V, the procedure is similar to the pattern VI, but the Invariant Sector is used to reduce points to be compared. Finally, the Skyline set is returned in line 19.

Algorithm 3. C2S: Position change configuration

```
Input: newPosition
1:    Polygon invariantSector ← processMovementPattern(newPosition)
2:    if getCase()= 1 then return getSkyline()              // Pattern I.
      Same Skyline
3:    if existsNonSpatialDims() then updateSearchRegion()
4:    if getCase()= 6 then                                  // Pattern VI.
      Add and remove points from Skyline
5:          updateSkylineDistancesAndSearchRegion(newPosition)
6:          delOldSkylinePoints()
7:          addNewSkylinePoints()
8:    else if getCase()= 2 or getCase()= 4 then             // Patterns II,
      IV. Add points only
9:          addNewSkylinePoints(invariantSector)
10: else                                                    //Patterns III,
      V
11:         updateSkylineDistancesAndSearchRegion(newPosition)
12:         delOldSkylinePoints(invariantSector)
13:         if getCase()= 3 then                            // Pattern III.
      Delete points only
14:               updateCandidateDistances(newPosition)
15:         else                                            // Pattern V.
      Add and delete points
16:               addNewSkylinePoints(invariantSector)
17:         end if
18: end if
19: return getSkyline()                                     // Skyline
      updated
```

Lastly, we illustrate the behavior of the C2S with a running example. For simplicity, we suppose in the query are not defined any static non-spatial dimension, only are given the query points and the changing non-spatial dimension. Consider the Figure 5 which are a representation of a parking lot, the green points correspond to available spaces, unavailable spaces are the red points, query points are the yellow circles, and the Skyline objects are the green circles.

In Initial Configuration, C2S determines the search region. Also, C2S creates the Global Convex Hull and the Static Convex Hull; the Non-Spatial Skyline is not built because there were no defined static non-spatial dimensions in this example. At this point, the Static and Dynamic Skyline can be retrieved. The search region is the gray area and the Global Convex Hull is represented as a polygon in Figure 5a. Then, C2S analyzes the points inside the search region but outside the Global Convex Hull in order to get the Outer Skyline. The Skyline set is composed of 14 parking spaces from which 5 spaces belong to Static Convex Hull and 9 spaces belong to the Outer Skyline.

Figure 5. C2S for the position change configuration

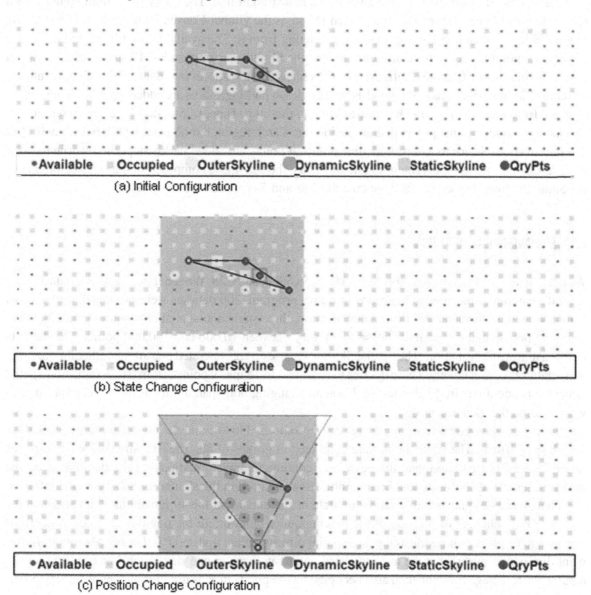

(a) Initial Configuration

(b) State Change Configuration

(c) Position Change Configuration

On the other hand, suppose a state change on availability of the spaces: 217 spaces change its status to occupied and 52 spaces change to available. In State Change Configuration, C2S deletes the new occupied spaces from the candidate and the Skyline sets. Since 11 unavailable spaces are deleted from the Skyline, the search region is slightly enlarged. If any new available space is inside the Global Convex Hull, then it is added to the Skyline. In this example, 2 spaces are inserted into the Skyline. The other new available spaces are compared against the current Skyline to return the new Skyline as is shown in Figure 5b where the cardinality of the Skyline set is 7, the Outer Skyline was reduced to 3 parking spaces and the Static Skyline has 4 parking spaces.

Finally, consider that the vehicle moves down in a straight line. The query point highlighted with a rectangle moved down generating the pattern IV, so as the Global Convex Hull increased its size, the Skyline is updated adding parking spaces not deleting from it. The available candidates and the Static Skyline are not updated in this configuration, and the Skyline is comprised of 17 spaces as is shown in Figure 5c. In Position Change Configuration, C2S scans the new spaces in order to insert directly into the Dynamic Skyline which are highlighted as blue circles, 5 parking spaces are added, and 3 parking spaces changed from Outer Skyline to Dynamic Skyline in this step. Then, C2S updates the search region and checks dominance against points that are inside the search region but outside the Global Convex Hull and the Invariant Sector to add new Skyline points, 4 points are added in this step; the Invariant Sector is represented as a green polygon in Figure 5c. Thus, the Skyline is composed of 4 spaces belonging to the Static Skyline, 8 spaces to the Dynamic Skyline and 5 spaces to the Outer Skyline.

EXPERIMENTAL STUDY

We empirically study the three algorithms: AB2S, VC2S+, and C2S. We generated synthetic datasets and several Spatial Skyline queries by means of a Java program. 200 datasets were produced; each dataset comprises points characterized by a spatial location, three static non-spatial dimensions, and a Boolean changing non-spatial dimension. Dataset sizes vary between 10,000 and 100,000 points. The datasets follow a uniform distribution. The Spatial Skyline Queries were generated one after another for querying these datasets consecutively. These queries vary from 3 to 18 query points, from 0 to 3 static non-spatial dimensions and a required value for the Boolean changing non-spatial dimension. In all experiments, we measured the total execution time.

Using these datasets and random change configurations, 340,000 simulations for the three algorithms have been fulfilled. The simulations were generated in groups of 50. The first simulation corresponds to the Initial Configuration, and the others are continuous transformations on the data based on the previous generated configuration. Four parameters were used in the simulations: *i)* Type of configuration change (mode) allows only changes of state of the data in all the 49 remaining simulations in the group, or only changes of position of the moving query point or, all the possible changes (mixed); *ii)* Percentage of points whose changing non-spatial dimension are updated (%stC); *iii)* Maximum movement distance in meters that the moving query point can reach in one simulation (maxD); *iv)* for each dataset, a percentage from the total area occupied by the points in P, is used for placing the query points in the Initial Configuration(%area).

The query points were chosen as follows: If %area $= 10\%$, then the convex hull formed by the query points occupies up to 10% from the area of the plane. Thus, the coordinates of the points are chosen under a discrete uniform distribution whose values are restricted by this area. Non-spatial dimensions were generated with a discrete uniform distribution. The initial states of the data were generated with a Bernoulli distribution; the state has a value of 1 or 0 with equal probability ($p = 0.5$). For the State Change Configuration, the points change their state to opposite value with a probability which depends on the %Change parameter, i.e., the probability of that the chosen point changes its state for %Change $=$ 10 is equal to 0.1. For the Position Change Configuration, the distance at which a query point moves is chosen between 1 and maxD with a uniform discrete distribution; the new position is within the boundaries of the area formed by the query data.

User preferences, such as query points, the non-spatial dimensions to be minimized and the desired state values are defined in a user profile and passed to algorithms together with current data at the begining of the execution. After that, any changes in data or the position of query points are given as an input to algorithms

Finally, the three algorithms were implemented in Java and were executed on an Intel Q6600 CPU with 4 GB RAM and disk of 100 GB.

Impact of the Number of Criteria in the Query Processing Performance

We have studied the performance of AB2S, VC2S+, and C2S in the evaluation of SSQ over 10,000 points, using multiple criteria, from 3 to 8 dimensions, from which 3 to 5 are query points and 0 to 3 are static non-spatial dimensions. The parameters are mode=All and %stC=random in two variants: #1 maxD=10 and #2 maxD=20.

Table 1 reports the average time μ_i in milliseconds for each algorithm, the ratio $\dfrac{\mu i}{\mu_3}$ with respect to C2S, and the standard deviation σ_i. We can observe in Table 1 that C2S has the best average execution time and the lowest standard deviation. C2S is 1.62 and 1.90 times faster than AB2S and VC2S+, respectively.

Figure 6 shows the average number of dominance comparisons and the average execution time taken by the three algorithms for 50 continuous simulations generated using the parameters mode, %stC and maxD. The horizontal axis of these figures corresponds to the number of criteria. We confirm C2S is the best algorithm in terms of execution time and number of comparisons while VC2S+ is the worst in terms of time. In fact the average execution time of C2S is almost the 60% and 50% of the time of AB2S and VC2S+ since C2S reduces the number of dominance comparisons performed to identify the Skyline. Although VC2S+ performs a lower number of comparisons than AB2S, VC2S+ must create the Delaunay graph in each status change configuration. In consequence, the building time of the Delaunay graph affects the evaluation time of VC2S+. Finally, we can observe that as the number of criteria increases, the execution time and the number of dominance comparisons also increase.

On the other hand, the Figure 7 depicts the Skyline cardinality for the same simulations. As the number of criteria increases, the skyline cardinality increases. Moreover, the Static Skyline cardinality (staS) is greater than the Dynamic Skyline cardinality (dynS), because there are more than one static query point and only one moving query point. Furthermore, the Static Skyline is greater than the Non-Spatial Skyline (nsS) and the Outer Skyline (outS). It is the reason why C2S performs fewer comparisons than the others algorithms. C2S takes advantage of the Static Skyline size because this Skyline is not updated.

Table 1. Average execution time

Algorithm	μ_i	$\dfrac{\mu i}{\mu_3}$	σ_i
(1) AB2S	636,707	1.62	591,983
(2) VC2S+	744,718	1.90	709,895
(3) C2S	392,334	1.0	380,064

Figure 6. Time and comparisons

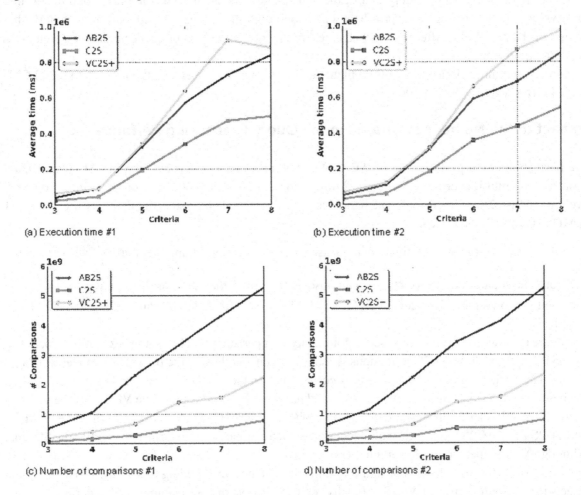

(a) Execution time #1

(b) Execution time #2

(c) Number of comparisons #1

d) Number of comparisons #2

Figure 7. Skyline Cardinality. Left image corresponds to Skyline composition #1. Right image corresponds to Skyline composition #2.

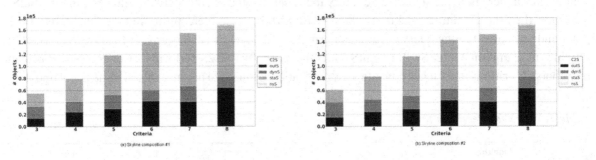

(a) Skyline composition #1

(b) Skyline composition #2

Impact of the Movement of the Query Point in the Query Processing Performance

We have evaluated the impact of moving one query point on the performance of AB2S, VC2S+, and C2S algorithms in the SSQ evaluation over 10,000 data. We consider mode= position changes only, %area=10 and vary maxD from 5 to 25.

Table 2 shows average, ratio and standard deviation in terms of execution time for each algorithm. As the distance maxD increases, the average time also increases. The average time for maxD = 25 outnumbers the average time for maxD = 5 at least three to one in the C2S and VC2S+ algorithms.

We can observe in Table 2 that C2S and VC2S+ require less execution time than AB2S to identify the Skyline when a query point is in movement, and C2S is at least 1.8 times faster than VC2S+. In this case, VC2S+ has better performance than AB2S because is able to prune the search space using spatial properties.

Impact of State Changes in the Query Processing Performance

We have studied the performance of AB2S, VC2S+, and C2S when the static non-spatial dimension changes its state on datasets of 10,000 points in the mode=status changes only, with %area=10 and varying %stC from 10 to 90.

Table 3 reports the average, ratio and standard deviation in terms of execution time for each algorithm. The results show that the execution time of C2S and AB2S is better than VC2S+ when a state change is produced. Since the Convex Hull formed by the query points is not modified, the algorithms require less time that the previous study because the query points remain in the 10% of the area occupied by all the dataset. Observe that the ratio $\dfrac{\mu i}{\mu_3}$ decreases as %Change increases because of the state updates done in the dataset. In consequence, the Skyline must be recalculated. We can notice that average time of AB2S for a high %Change is the best. This is due to the Skyline update performed by AB2S is simpler than C2S and the optimizations that C2S uses to prune the search space cease to be useful when 70% of the points or more have changed.

Lastly, we can notice that the average time in Table 3 of all the algorithms are significantly lower than results presented in Table 2.

Table 2. Average execution time when one query point moves

Algorithm	#1 maxD=5			#2 maxD=10			#3 maxD=15			#4 maxD=20			#5 maxD=25		
	μ_i	$\dfrac{\mu i}{\mu_3}$	σ_i	μ_i	$\dfrac{\mu i}{\mu_3}$	σ_i	μ_i	$\dfrac{\mu i}{\mu_3}$	σ_i	μ_i	$\dfrac{\mu i}{\mu_3}$	σ_i	μ_i	$\dfrac{\mu i}{\mu_3}$	σ_i
(1) AB2S	21,181	3.0	23,870	35,648	2.7	39,774	51,848	2.7	63,773	62,758	2.5	67,506	81,012	2.6	99,484
(2) VC2S+	19,936	2.8	15,720	30,080	2.2	24,935	38,775	2.0	33,474	46,899	1.8	36,185	56,920	1.8	50,419
(3) C2S	6,998	1.0	6,772	13,142	1.0	12,476	19,064	1.0	18,600	25,006	1.0	21,672	31,183	1.0	29,104

Table 3. Average execution time when state changes

Algorithm	#1%Change=10			#2%Change=30			#3%Change=70			#4%Change=90		
	μ_i	$\dfrac{\mu i}{\mu_3}$	σ_i	μ_i	$\dfrac{\mu i}{\mu_3}$	σ_i	μ_i	$\dfrac{\mu i}{\mu_3}$	σ_i	μ_i	$\dfrac{\mu i}{\mu_3}$	σ_i
(1) AB2S	2,667	1.43	2,081	3,100	1.08	2,049	4,145	1.00	2,487	4,343	1.00	2,643
(2) VC2S+	4,251	2.28	2,017	4,500	1.57	1,819	5,066	1.22	1,743	5,168	1.19	1,767
(3) C2S	1,868	1.00	1,338	2,875	1.00	2,008	4,162	1.00	2,828	4,347	1.00	3,032

Impact of % Area in the Query Processing Performance

We have evaluated the impact of a variation of %area for datasets of 50,000 points, mode=All in three variants: #1%area=10 - maxD=10; #2%area=25 - maxD=10 and #3%area=50 - maxD=10.

Table 4 shows that C2S has the best performance in all the variants. The results indicate that the execution time of VC2S+ is worse than C2S and AB2S. This is because of the number of dominance comparisons that VC2S+ have to perform and the construction of the Voronoi diagram. Also, we can observe that as %area increases, the time increases.

High Dimensional Skyline Query Processing Performance

In this section, we report the results for datasets of 100,000 points using queries from 12 to 18 query points and the parameter values mode=All, %stC=random, maxD=50 and %area=10. Two variants of simulations were generated: #1 zero static non-spatial dimensions and #2 one static non-spatial dimension.

In general terms, C2S has the lowest execution time. We can observe in Table 5 that C2S is at least 2.20 and 1.49 faster than VC2S+ and AB2S. The average execution time taken by C2S is 33% and 35% of the time of VC2S+ and AB2S. Additionally, SSQ evaluation with one static non-spatial dimension is costlier than SSQ with zero static non-spatial dimensions. This is because the Skyline set is less selective when there are more dimensions.

Table 4. Average execution time varying % area

Algorithm	#1%area=10%			#2%area=25%			#3%area=50%		
	μ_i	$\dfrac{\mu i}{\mu_3}$	σ_i	μ_i	$\dfrac{\mu i}{\mu_3}$	σ_i	μ_i	$\dfrac{\mu i}{\mu_3}$	σ_i
(1) AB2S	90,022	1.30	78,132	1,035,860	1.65	1,131,562	6,408,713	1.59	7,610,420
(2) VC2S+	112,067	1.62	76,400	1,211,269	1.93	1,353,082	6,749,080	1.67	8,278,597
(3) C2S	69,193	1.00	57,001	627,646	1.00	710,732	4,036,858	1.00	5,447,505

Table 5. Average execution time for highly dimensional Skyline queries

Algorithm	#1			#2		
	μ_i	$\dfrac{\mu i}{\mu_3}$	σ_i	μ_i	$\dfrac{\mu i}{\mu_3}$	σ_i
(1) AB2S	1,814,639	1.53	1,190,522	2,627,835	1.49	2,175,205
(2) VC2S+	2,598,829	2.20	1,766,741	3,094,533	1.75	2,655,859
(3) C2S	1,183,134	1.00	796,704	1,769,436	1.00	1,396,894

FUTURE RESEARCH DIRECTIONS

Firstly, a future work is to simplify or optimize the update mechanism of the Skyline for C2S in the presence of state changes. For this purpose, it is possible an extension of the algorithm, where after removing the skyline objects that are no longer Skyline candidates, the dominant region of each candidate object is calculated, and if it is not empty, C2S may check if an object is Skyline verifying against the Static Skyline and the Dynamic Skyline. In this case, the object will be spatially dominated, otherwise the object would already be in the skyline set, and so only the dominance check over its static non-spatial dimensions is needed. Thus, the number of dominance comparisons can be reduced. This dominant region may be calculated by forming circles centered on each point and with a radius equal to the distance to the coordinates of the candidate, and then these circles are intersected. Because of one query point is mobile, the algorithm may pre-compute the intersection of the circles corresponding to the static points and at the time of verification, the intersection is performed at the mobile point circle.

Secondly, in this chapter, only step wise data changes are allowed. As one of our future work, we plan to explore the issue of continuous changes on datasets and extend our algorithms when continuous change happens and not just moving from one configuration to the other. Another possible direction for future work is to adapt the algorithms to work for a mixed case of multiple moving query points and multiple changing non-spatial dimensions. We also plan to study theoretical the time complexity of the proposed algorithms and we will perform experiments using real-world datasets.

Thirdly, Spatial Skyline queries on changing data may be extended according to Directional Skyline queries and General Spatial Skyline. As Directional Skyline queries, the Spatial Skyline queries on changing data may be extended with movement directions. Directional Skyline queries (El-Dawy, Mokhtar & El-Bastawissy, 2012) supports movement direction of a query point on the Skyline in terms of a maximum deviation angle; those objects in another direction from the query point may be discarded. As General Spatial Skyline (Lin, Zhang, Zhang, & Li, 2012), query points may be differentiated in groups according to their type and return points near at least one point of each object type. For example, a query may be the available pharmacies nearest to the user's location and at least one query point of the kind ATM. Finally, the Skyline size rapidly increases as the number of dimensions increases. In consequence, users may have to discard irrelevant data manually and consider just a subset of the whole Skyline. To identify these points, the Top-k Skyline has been proposed (Goncalves & Vidal, 2009; Chan et al., 2006b; Lin et al., 2005). Top-k Skyline uses a score function to induce a total order of the Skyline points, and recognizes the top-k objects based on these criteria. Thus, ranking techniques applied to spatial objects such as top-k (Liu, Jing, Chen, & Sun, 2008) may be integrated in order to select those k-interesting objects from the Spatial Skyline on changing data.

CONCLUSION

This chapter discussed the applicability of the Skyline queries for specifying preferences on spatial objects. In this sense, the problem of evaluating Spatial Skyline queries over changing data was raised. Spatial Skyline queries over changing data include preferences on attributes spatial and non-spatial. Spatial preferences may be established on a set of query points in order to get closer objects while one of these points is in motion; non-spatial preferences are defined as traditional Skyline queries on numerical, qualitative or categorical attributes. Additionally, a condition over the objects to be eligible as candidates to the Skyline set must be met, a changing non-spatial preference; this condition is specified by the user.

In this chapter, several techniques for evaluating Spatial Skyline queries on changing data were studied. Techniques proposed in (Sharifzadeh & Shahabi, 2006; Chen et al., 2008; Guo, Ishikawa, & Gao, 2010; Soudani & Baraani-Dastgerdi, 2011; Lin et al., 2012) receive a set of query points without consider both non-spatial and changing preferences. Subsequently in (El-Dawy, Mokhtar & El-Bastawissy, 2011), the authors include non-spatial attributes in their techniques, but this attributes are not changing. Furthermore, there are some works about preferences on spatial objects (Kodama et al, 2009; Zheng, 2008; Huang, 2012; Chen et al., 2009), but the spatial preferences are reduced to a query point and do not consider preferences over a changing non-spatial attribute. Because of these limitations, three evaluation algorithms for Spatial Skyline queries on changing data were proposed: AB2S, VC2S+ and C2S. These algorithms continuously evaluate these queries from the environmental transformations generated by the movement of a query point or by new values of a non-spatial data.

This chapter also studies how to evaluate Spatial Skyline Queries on Changing Data. We have focused on the issue of computation of the SSQ on changing data, i.e., when the query points and the non-spatial data change. More specifically, three algorithms to identify Skyline objects were introduced. We propose to adapt two state-of-the-art algorithms and propose a new algorithm named C2S which is able to prune the search space in order to reduce dominance comparisons and decrease the execution time. C2S is guided by changing characteristics of the data and spatial properties in order to avoid exhaustive searches. In particular, we demonstrated the superior performance of C2S in our experimental study on synthetic data. Also, we empirically studied the impact of dimensionality, updates of query points and non-spatial data, and dataset size in the SSQ processing performance.

AB2S and VC2S+ are naive solutions which update the Skyline according to transformations generated by the new state of the objects. Particularly, VC2S+ is an adaptation of VCS2 (Sharifzadeh, Shahabi & Kazemi, 2009) that includes non-spatial and changing preferences. This algorithm updates the skyline (in most cases) during transformations produced by movement of a query point. VC2S+ supports a Voronoi diagram to store objects, forms a Convex Hull using the query points and updates the Skyline in five of six possible change patterns of the Convex Hull. It also computes the skyline progressively. If an object belongs to the Convex Hull, it is directly added to the Skyline without verification. The non-spatial

Skyline formed by the static non-spatial preferences is separately processed in each state change. When these changes occur, no previous Skyline is maintained; the algorithm must process the whole Skyline because its environment representation does not allow changing objects, only changing query points.

On the other hand, C2S is an improved solution which has a main Convex Hull formed by all query points and a Static convex hull comprised the static reference points. This algorithm progressively evaluates the skyline and updates it separating the Skyline into four sets: the non-Spatial Skyline from static non-spatial preferences; the Static Skyline formed by the objects within the Static Convex Hull; the Dynamic Skyline consisting of objects belonging to the main Convex Hull which are outside of the Static Convex Hull; and the Skyline outside the main Convex Hull.

C2S directly includes the objects within the Convex Hull in the skyline as VC2S+ does. Unlike VC2S +, C2S separates objects of the Convex Hull into two sets: the Static Skyline and the Dynamic Skyline. The Static Convex Hull does not change if a query point moves its location while the Dynamic Skyline may do it. Since the non-Spatial Skyline and the Static Skyline remain unchanged, they are not needed to be verified by the algorithm to confirm if they are Skyline. C2S as VC2S+ explore the entire search space in the presence of non-spatial dimensions in order to build the non-Spatial Skyline (only in the initial configuration for C2S).

The three proposed algorithms were empirically studied using simulations over synthetic data. Several parameters of the environment and simulations were varied. In this empirical study, the performance and answer quality of the algorithms were analyzed. Additionally, the impact of a query point movement and state change of the objects on the proposed algorithms was studied. Lastly, the impact of the area of the initial Convex Hull in the performance query and high-dimensional query were also considered in this empirical study.

Empirical study results show that the Skyline size increases as the number of query points and non-spatial dimensions increase. Also, the area of the Convex Hull affects the runtime of the algorithms and the Skyline size.

Concerning performance, the average time in the best case for C2S was 3.03 times lower than AB2S and 2.85 times lower than VC2S +. The average time in the worst case for C2S was 1.19 times lower than VC2S+ and was similar to the AB2S average time. Moreover, although it was not shown in the figures of experimental study, C2S had the best individual time at most of simulations. These results are due to the C2S separates the Skyline into four sets reducing the number of dominance comparisons at most cases; more than an order of magnitude with respect to the dominance comparisons of AB2S, and a less marked difference with respect to VC2S+ although C2S comparisons were six times lower than VC2S+ in some cases.

VC2S+ and C2S were better than AB2S when a query point moves because they update the Skyline in these circumstances. However, VC2S+ requires twice the time of AB2S when the objects change their states because it must rebuild their data structures with the objects to be eligible as Skyline candidates, generate a new non-spatial skyline (if static non-spatial preferences exist) and explore a greater number of objects to evaluate the Skyline.

Since the simplicity for updating the Skyline in the presence of state changes, AB2S had the best average evaluation time for the variants when the percentage of objects whose changing non-spatial dimension are updated is equal to 70% and 90% of the total objects, and the second best average at most experiments.

The lowest number of dominance comparisons was performed by C2S because it avoids some of them using the Static Convex Hull, because the Static Skyline remains the same when a change of position of the query point occurs.

REFERENCES

Börzsönyi, S., Kossmann, D., & Stocker, K. (2001). The skyline operator. In *Proceedings of the International Conference on Data Engineering (ICDE)* (pp. 421–430). Washington, DC: IEEE Computer Society. doi:10.1109/ICDE.2001.914855

Chen, B., Liang, W., & Yu, J. X. (2009). Progressive skyline query evaluation and maintenance in wireless sensor networks. In *Proceedings of the ACM Conference on Information and Knowledge Management (CIKM)* (pp. 1445-1448). New York, NY: ACM. doi:10.1145/1645953.1646141

Chen, L., Lian, & Xiang. (2008). Dynamic skyline queries in metric spaces. In *Proceedings of the International Conference On Extending Database Technology (EDBT)* (pp. 333-343). New York, NY: ACM.

Chen, L., Cui, B., Lu, H., Xu, L., & Xu, Q. (2008). isky: Efficient and progressive skyline computing in a structured p2p network. In *Proceedings of the International Conference on Distributed Computing Systems* (pp. 160-167). Los Alamitos, CA: IEEE Computer Society.

Chen, N., Shou, L., Chen, G., Gao, Y., & Dong, J. (2009). Predictive skyline queries for moving objects. In *Proceedings of the International Conference on Database Systems For Advanced Applications* (pp. 278-282). Berlin: Springer-Verlag. doi:10.1007/978-3-642-00887-0_23

Chen, N., Shou, L., Chen, G., Gao, Y, & Dong, J. (2012). Prismo: Predictive skyline query processing over moving objects. *Journal of Zhejiang University SCIENCE C, 1*(13), 99–117. doi:10.1631/jzus.C10a0728

Chomicki, J., Godfrey, P., Gryz, J., & Liang, D. (2003). Skyline with presorting. In *Proceedings of International Conference on Data Engineering (ICDE)* (pp.717-719). Bangalore, India: IEEE Computer Society.

Delaunay, B. (1934). Sur la sphère vide. A la mémoire de Georges Voronoï. *Bulletin de l'Académie des Sciences de l'URSS, 7*(1), 793–800.

Deng, K., Zhou, X., & Tao, H. (2007). Multi-source skyline query processing in road networks. In *Proceedings of the International Conference on Data Engineering (ICDE)* (pp. 796-805). Istanbul, Turkey: IEEE. doi:10.1109/ICDE.2007.367925

Di Bartolo, F., & Goncalves, M. (2013). Evaluating spatial skyline queries on changing data. In *Proceedings of the International conference on database and expert (DEXA)* (pp. 270-277). Prague, Czech Republic: Springer. doi:10.1007/978-3-642-40285-2_23

El-Dawy, E., Mokhtar, H., & El-Bastawissy, A. (2011). Multi-level continuous skyline queries (MCSQ). In *Proceedings of the International Conference on Data and Knowledge Engineering (ICDKE)* (pp. 36-40). Milano, Italy: IEEE.

El-Dawy, E., Mokhtar, H., & El-Bastawissy, A. (2012). Directional skyline queries. In *Proceedings of the International Conference on Data and Knowledge Engineering (ICDKE)* (pp. 15-28). Fujian, China: Springer.

Godfrey, P., Shipley, R., & Gryz, J. (2005). Maximal vector computation in large data sets. In *Proceedings of the International Conference on Very Large Data Bases (VLDB)* (pp. 229-240). Trondheim, Norway: ACM.

Guo, X., Ishikawa, Y., & Gao, Y. (2010). Direction-based spatial skylines. In *Proceedings of The ACM International Workshop on Data Engineering for Wireless and Mobile Access* (pp. 73-80). New York, NY: ACM.

Guo, X., Zheng, B., Ishikawa, Y., & Gao, Y. (2011, October). Direction-based surrounder queries for mobile recommendations. *The VLDB Journal, 20*(5), 743–766. doi:10.1007/s00778-011-0241-y

Huang, J., Xin, J., Wang, G., & Li, M. (2009). Efficient k-dominant skyline processing in wireless sensor networks. In *Proceedings of the International Conference on Hybrid Intelligent Systems (HIS)* (pp. 289-294). Shenyang, China: IEEE Computer Society. doi:10.1109/HIS.2009.273

Huang, Y.-K., Chang, C.-H., & Lee, C. (2012). Continuous distance-based skyline queries in road networks. *Information Systems, 37*(7), 611–633. doi:10.1016/j.is.2012.02.003

Iyer, K. B. P., & Shanthi, V. (2012). Goal Directed Relative Skyline Queries in Time Dependent Road Networks. *International Journal of Database Management Systems, 4*(2), 23–34. doi:10.5121/ijdms.2012.4202

Iyer, K. P., & Shanthi, V. (2012). Spatial boolean skyline boundary queries in road networks. In *Proceedings of the International Conference on Computing Communication Networking Technologies (ICCCNT)* (pp. 1 -6). Coimbatore, India: IEEE doi:10.1109/ICCCNT.2012.6396049

Kodama, K., Iijima, Y., Guo, X., & Ishikawa, Y. (2009). Skyline queries based on user locations and preferences for making location-based recommendations. In *Proceedings of the International Workshop on Location Based Social Networks* (pp. 9-16). New York, NY: ACM. doi:10.1145/1629890.1629893

Kossmann, D., Ramsak, F., & Rost, S. (2002). Shooting stars in the sky: An online algorithm for skyline queries. In *Proceedings of the International Conference on Very Large Data Bases (VLDB)* (pp. 275-286). Hong Kong, China: Endowment. doi:10.1016/B978-155860869-6/50032-9

Lande, N., & Lande, A. (2008). The 10 best of everything: An ultimate guide for travelers (2nd ed.). National Geographic Society.

Lee, J., & Hwang, S.-W. (2009). Skytree: scalable skyline computation for sensor data. In *Proceedings of the International Workshop on Knowledge Discovery from Sensor Data* (pp. 114-123). New York: ACM. doi:10.1145/1601966.1601985

Liang, W., Chen, B., & Yu, J. X. (2008). Energy-efficient skyline query processing and maintenance in sensor networks. In *Proceedings of the ACM Conference on Information and Knowledge Management* (pp. 1471-1472). New York, NY: ACM. doi:10.1145/1458082.1458339

Lin, Q., Zhang, Y., Zhang, W., & Li, A. (2012).General spatial skyline operator. In *Proceedings of the International Conference on Database Systems for Advanced Applications (DASFAA)* (pp. 494-508). Berlin: Springer-Verlag. doi:10.1007/978-3-642-29038-1_36

Liu, W., Jing, Y., Chen, K., & Sun, W. (2012). Combining top-k query in road networks. In *Proceedings of the International Conference on Web-Age Information Management (WAIM)* (pp. 63-75). Springer-Verlag. doi:10.1007/978-3-642-28635-3_6

Papadias, D., Tao, Y., Fu, G., & Seeger, B. (2005). Progressive skyline computation in database systems. *ACM Transactions on Database Systems, 30*(1), 41–82. doi:10.1145/1061318.1061320

Sharifzadeh, M., & Shahabi, C. (2006). The spatial skyline queries. In *Proceedings of the International Conference on Very Large Data Bases (VLDB)* (pp. 751-762). VLDB Endowment.

Sharifzadeh, M., Shahabi, C., & Kazemi, L. (2009). Processing spatial skyline queries in both vector spaces and spatial network databases. *ACM Transactions on Database Systems, 34*(3), 11–45. doi:10.1145/1567274.1567276

Skopal, T., & Lokoc, J. (2010). Answering metric skyline queries by pm-tree. In *Proceedings of the Annual International Workshop on DAtabases, TExts, Specifications and Objects (DATESO)* (pp. 22-37). Stedronin-Plazy, Czech Republic: CEUR-WS.org.

Soudani, N. M. & Baraani-Dastgerdi, A. (2011). The spatial nearest neighbor skyline queries. *The Computing Research Repository (CoRR)*, abs/1112.2336.

Tan, K., Eng, P., & Ooi, B. (2001). Efficient progressive skyline computation. In *Proceedings of the International Conference on Very Large Data Bases (VLDB)* (pp. 301-310). San Francisco, CA: Morgan Kaufmann Publishers Inc.

Voronoi, G. (1908). Nouvelles applications des parametres continus a la theorie des formes quadratiques, Rescherches sur les Parallelloedres Primitifs. *Journal fur die Reine und Angewandte Mathematik, 134*(1), 198–287.

Wang, S., Vu, Q. H., Ooi, B. C., Tung, A. K., & Xu, L. (2009). Skyframe: A framework for skyline query processing in peer-to-peer systems. *The VLDB Journal, 18*(1), 345–362. doi:10.1007/s00778-008-0104-3

Zheng, B., Lee, K., & Lee, W.-C. (2008). Location-dependent skyline query. In *Proceedings of the International Conference on Mobile Data Management (MDM)* (pp. 148 -155). Beijing, China: IEEE doi:10.1109/MDM.2008.14

ADDITIONAL READING

Afrati, F., Koutris, P., Suciu, D., & Ullman, J. (2012). Parallel skyline queries. In *Proceedings of the International Conference on Database Theory*. (pp. 274-284). Berlin, Germany: ACM.

Bai, M., Xin, J., & Wang, G. (2013). Subspace global skyline query processing. In *Proceedings of the Joint 2013 EDBT/ICDT Conferences*. (pp. 418-429). Genoa, Italy: ACM. doi:10.1145/2452376.2452425

Balke, W. T., Güntzer, U., & Zheng, J. X. (2004). Efficient distributed skylining for web information systems. In *Proceedings of the Extending Database Technology (EDBT)* (pp. 256-273). Heraklion, Crete, Greece: Springer-Verlag. doi:10.1007/978-3-540-24741-8_16

Bogh, K., Assent, I., & Magnani, M. (2013). Efficient GPU-based skyline computation. In *Proceedings of the International Workshop on Data Management on New Hardware*. New York, USA: ACM. doi:10.1145/2485278.2485283

Fan, W., Wang, X., & Wu, Y. (2012). Performance guarantees for distributed reachability queries. *VLDB Endowment, 5*(11), 1304–1316. doi:10.14778/2350229.2350248

Lin, X., Yuan, Y., Wang, W., & Lu, H. (2005). Stabbing the sky: Efficient skyline computation over sliding windows. In *Proceedings of the international Conference on Data Engineering (ICDE)*. (pp. 502-513). Washington, DC, USA: IEEE Computer Society.

Lofi, C., Balke, W.-T., & Guntzer, U. (2012). Equivalence Heuristics for Malleability-Aware Skylines. *Journal for Corrosion Science and Engineering, 6*(3), 207–218.

Lofi, C., El Maarry, B., & Balke, W.-T. (2013). Skyline queries in crowd-enabled databases. In *Proceedings of the Joint 2013 EDBT/ICDT Conferences*. (pp. 465-476). Genoa, Italy: ACM. doi:10.1145/2452376.2452431

Lofi, C., Guntzer, U., & Balke, W. T. (2012). Malleability-Aware Skyline Computation on Linked Open Data. In *Proceedings of the International Conference on Database Systems for Advanced Applications (DASFAA)*. (pp. 33-47). Busan, South Korea: Springer. doi:10.1007/978-3-642-29035-0_3

Magnani, M., & Assent, I. (2013). From stars to galaxies: skyline queries on aggregate data. In *Proceedings of the Joint 2013 EDBT/ICDT Conferences*. (pp. 477-488). Genoa, Italy: ACM. doi:10.1145/2452376.2452432

Selke, J., & Balke, W. T. (2011). SkyMap: A Trie-Based Index Structure for High-Performance Skyline Query Processing. In Proceedings of *the International Conference on Database and Expert Systems Applications (DEXA)*. (pp. 350-365). Toulouse, France: Springer. doi:10.1007/978-3-642-23091-2_30

Sheng, C., & Tao, Y. (2011). On finding skylines in external memory. In *Proceedings of the ACM SIGMOD-SIGACT-SIGART Symposium on Principles of Database Systems*. (pp. 107-116). Athens, Greece: ACM.

Son, W., Hwang, S.-w., & Ahn, H.-K. (2011). Mssq: Manhattan spatial skyline queries. In *Proceedings of the International Conference on Advances In Spatial and Temporal Databases (SSTD)*. (pp. 313-329). Minneapolis, MN, USA: Springer. doi:10.1007/978-3-642-22922-0_19

Valkanas, G., Papadopoulos, A., & Gunopulos, D. (2013). SkyDiver: a framework for skyline diversification. In *Proceedings of the Joint 2013 EDBT/ICDT Conferences*. (pp. 406-417). Genoa, Italy: ACM. doi:10.1145/2452376.2452424

Yiu, M., Lo, E., & Yung, D. (2012, March). Measuring the Sky: On Computing Data Cubes via Skylining the Measures. *IEEE Transactions on Knowledge and Data Engineering, 24*(3), 492–505. doi:10.1109/TKDE.2010.253

You, G.-W., Lee, M.-W., Im, H., & Hwang, S.-W. (2013). The Farthest Spatial Skyline Queries. *Information Systems, 38*(3), 286–301. doi:10.1016/j.is.2012.10.001

KEY TERMS AND DEFINITIONS

Convex Hull: It is the convex polygon formed by a given set of points in the Euclidean plane, whose vertices are some of these points; the remaining points are inside the polygon.

Delaunay Graph: Delaunay Triangulation which is the dual problem of a Voronoi diagram.

Dominance: An object a dominates another object b if and only if a is better than or equal to b on all dimensions of a multidimensional function and a is better than b on at least one dimension.

Non-Spatial Dimension: Characteristic of an object that is not related to spatial data. It is commonly static.

Progressive Skyline Algorithm: Algorithm that produces results over its execution, i.e., it returns initial results before identifying the whole skyline.

Skyline Techniques: Set of strategies for identifying incomparable elements that are characterized by multi-dimensional properties.

Skyline: Set of non-dominated objects.

Spatial Dimension: Corresponds to a spatial preference for a query point, i.e., the minimization of the distance from an object to a query point.

Voronoi Diagram: It is a geometric construction that divides the space into different regions of the Euclidean plane. It was studied by mathematician, Georgy Voronoi. Each point p has a corresponding region called Voronoi cell which consists of all points closer than any other point.

Chapter 12
Supporting Position Change through On-Line Location-Based Skyline Queries

Marlene Goncalves
Universidad Simón Bolívar, Venezuela

Alberto Gobbi
Universidad Simón Bolívar, Venezuela

ABSTRACT

Location-based Skyline queries select the nearest objects to a point that best meet the user's preferences. Particularly, this chapter focuses on location-based Skyline queries over web-accessible data. Web-accessible may have geographical location and be geotagged with documents containing ratings by web users. Location-based Skyline queries may express preferences based on dynamic features such as distance and changeable ratings. In this context, distance must be recalculated when a user changes his position while the ratings must be extracted from external data sources which are updated each time a user scores an item in the Web. This chapter describes and empirically studies four solutions capable of answering location-based Skyline queries considering user's position change and information extraction from the Web inside an area search around the user. They are based on an M-Tree index and Divide & Conquer principle.

INTRODUCTION

Skyline queries allow to filter large amounts of data returning a set of data that best meet the user's preferences. Initially, the problem of computing the Skyline was known as Pareto curve or maximal vector computation (Bentley, Kung, Schkolnick, & Thompson, 1978; Kung, Luccio, & Preparata, 1975). Given a set of vectors, the problem of the maximal vector computation consists in identifying the set of non-dominated vectors; a vector dominates another vector if is better or equal in all coordinates and better in at least one coordinate.

DOI: 10.4018/978-1-4666-8767-7.ch012

Subsequently, Spatial Skyline Queries (SSQ) and location-based Skyline queries were introduced in (Kodama, Lijima, Guo, & Ishikawa, 2009; Sharifzadeh & Shahabi, 2006). SSQ (Sharifzadeh & Shahabi, 2006) allow spatial data and the user's criteria are composed of the distances from spatial data (usually interesting places) to a set of points (usually users' locations). Location-based Skyline queries (Kodama et al., 2009) select the nearest objects to a point (usually a user's location) that best meet the user's criteria. Particularly, this chapter focuses on location-based Skyline queries over web-accessible data. Under this scenario, data may change their values through time.

To illustrate the problem presented in this chapter, consider a tourist in Barcelona, Spain. He goes throughout the city to find the restaurant that best meets his preferences. The tourist's preferred restaurants are those that have the shortest distance from his current location, and the best service quality, food and price; the restaurants must be within a range of 500 meters distance from his current position.

Location-based Skyline queries may be used to identify the restaurants preferred by the tourist. The Location-based Skyline is defined as the set of non-dominated points (restaurants); a point *A* dominates a point *B* based on a set of attributes *C* if *A* is better than *B* in all attributes of *C*, and is better in at least one attribute of the set *C*.

Figure 1 graphically shows the restaurants belonging to Location-based Skyline from the initial region *R1*. In Figure 1, the region inside the circle, *R1*, delimits an area of 500 meters established by the tourist; the location-based Skyline are highlighted inside the region *R1*. The middle point of *R1* represents the tourist's current location and the arrows indicate the direction in which the tourist will move.

Table 1 contains information on each restaurant. Each restaurant has an identifier (ID), the distance in meters (D) between the tourist's current location and the restaurants, the service quality (S) and the food quality in relation to price (P). The values of S and P are between 0 and 100, where 100 indicate the highest quality.

Figure 1. Location based-Skyline from the region R1

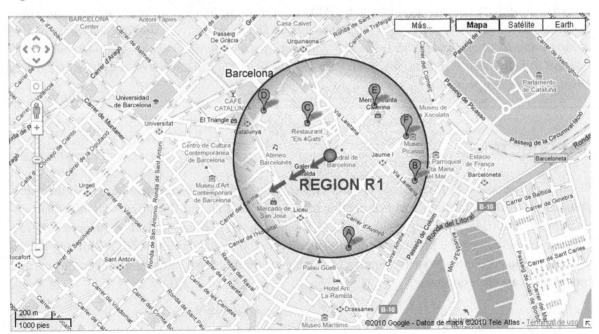

In Table 1, the restaurants A, B, C, D, E and F are location-based Skyline because doesn't exists others restaurants that dominates them. For example, A is a location-based Skyline Restaurant because there is not a restaurant that has the best value on the attributes D, S and P than the restaurant A.

Suppose now that the tourist has moved three blocks from the current position. Thus, the region R1 was transferred to the new region *R2*. Figure 2 shows the regions *R1* and *R2*, and their corresponding location-based Skyline.

Because of the tourist's displacement, the distance to the restaurants has changed respect to the information presented previously in Figure 1. It can be noted that although the restaurants *F* and *B* are location-based Skyline in the region *R1*, they are not part of the location-based Skyline in the region *R2* since they are outside the region. Also, the restaurant *E* is not location-based Skyline in the region *R2* because the restaurants *G* and *H* are better than it. Table 2 contains updated information on each restaurant.

Table 1. Hotels

ID	D	S	P
A	460.3	80	88
B	462.5	95	82
C	318.9	76	78
D	451.8	92	77
E	403.2	90	85
F	440.5	88	83

Figure 2. Location-based Skyline inside the regions R1 and R2

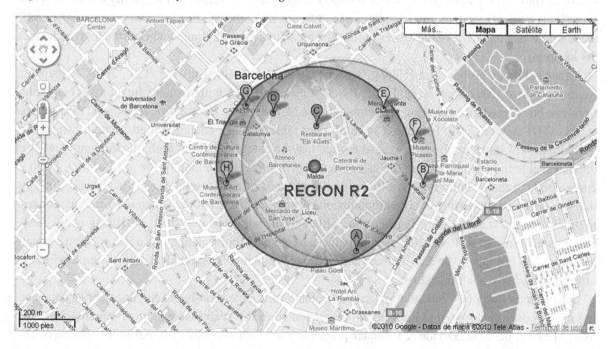

Table 2. Hotels inside the regionR2

ID	D	S	P
A	440.3	80	88
B	462.5	95	82
C	203.5	76	78
D	319.2	92	77
E	470.6	90	85
F	440.5	88	83
G	445.5	95	93
H	443.8	91	86

Moreover, applications such as Google Maps allow users to geotag objects on the map with documents containing comments and ratings. These comments and ratings are done by several users in the Web. These ratings are variable because users can score the restaurants at any time.

In this example, the tourist's query expresses his preferences based on dynamic features such as distance and changeable scores; the scores are found in documents stored in external data sources. In this context, distance must be recalculated because of the tourist's movement while the values for the scores of S and P must be extracted from external data sources because they are updated each time a user scores a restaurant in the Web.

Solutions presented in (Börzsönyi, Kossmann, & Stocker, 2001; Godfrey, Gryz, & Liang, 2003; Godfrey, Shipley, & Gryz, 2005; Tao, Fu, & Seeger, 2005; Tan, Eng, & Ooi, 2001) evaluate Skyline queries involve traditional attributes which are stored in databases. To evaluate the sample query, these solutions must pre-compute the distance function and extract the values of the quality attributes S and P, and subsequently store them in a database in order to return the Skyline set. Since data are dynamic, these solutions must retrieve the scores online and recalculate the Skyline whenever the tourist changes his locations.

Other solutions proposed in (Huang, Jensen, Lu, & Ooi, 2006; Kodama et al., 2009; Kossmann, Ramsak, & Rost, 2002) may be applied to the Skyline calculation with distance functions. These solutions can be adapted for answering the sample query. Nevertheless, the solution introduced in (Kodama et al., 2009) may be costly because it is based on a table for each categorical attribute; a categorical attribute groups its values by type, e.g., the price may be categorized into high, medium and low. It is unmanageable to keep and update the categorical tables since the domain of the attributes D, S and P corresponds to the real numbers. A differentiation of the solution presented in (Huang et al., 2006) is that was designed supporting data communication between ad hoc networks which is a different scenario in relation to the sample query. Furthermore, although the solutions described in (Huang et al., 2006; Kossmann, Ramsak, & Rost, 2002) support the nearest neighbor calculation, none of them extracts dynamic data through other data sources and both solutions involve a recalculation of the Skyline set after each tourist's position change.

This chapter describes four solutions capable of answering location-based Skyline queries considering user's position change and information extraction from the Web inside an area search around the user. They are based on Divide & Conquer principle and use a multidimensional index structure. The first solution is a naive one which performs an exhaustive search merging Skyline of each region in the multidimensional index structure. The second solution prunes the search space by mean of a pruning criterion. The third and fourth solutions take into consideration the previous state, i.e., the previous user's location and Skyline. The third solution avoids recalculate Skyline in those regions of the multidimensional index structure where were found Skyline points and the fourth solution prevents recomputed any region that was previously visited by the tourist.

This chapter is comprised of four sections in addition to Section I that introduce the problem by means of a motivating example. Section II describes the background on location-based Skyline queries. Section III introduces the problem statement, existing state-of-the-art approaches to compute location-based Skyline queries and the proposed algorithms. In Section IV, the quality and performance of the proposed techniques will be empirically evaluated. Finally, the conclusions of this work will be pointed out in Section V.

BACKGROUND

In this section, a review of related work is presented and some terms are formally defined in relation to location-based Skyline queries with user's position change and information extraction.

Börzsönyi et al. (2001) proposed the Block-Nested-Loops (BNL) algorithm, an extension of the Divide & Conquer algorithm presented by Kung, Luccio and Preparata (1975). BNL scans the entire table while maintaining a window of non-dominated tuples, which could be replaced by any other tuple later on. Successively, other algorithms such as SFS (Chomicki et al., 2003) and LESS (Godfrey, Shipley, & Gryz, 2005) emerged as solutions better than BNL. SFS algorithm begins sorting the table, after it passes a cursor over the sorted rows and it finally discards dominated rows. SFS improves the effectiveness of dominated objects discarding by means of an entropy function. LESS initially sorts tuples as SFS does, but presents two improvements over it: in the first ordering phase it uses an elimination-filter window to discard dominated tuples quickly and it combines the last phase of the sort algorithm with the Skyline filter phase of SFS to eliminate remaining dominated tuples.

However, all these algorithms require a complete scan of the input data. Subsequent works focused on processing the Skyline progressively, i.e., Skyline points are returned as they are obtained without scanning all the data. In this sense, Tan, Eng and Ooi (2001) defined algorithms based on bitmaps and B-tree indexes. The bitmap-based algorithm creates a vector of m bits for each Skyline criterion and then, produces the whole Skyline by logical operations. This solution implies that the data must be stored to calculate the vector size. Thus, each time the user changes his position, the vector of m bits must be created. On the other hand, the B-tree-based algorithm requires handling a B-tree index for each Skyline criterion. Therefore, a B-tree index must be updated by each user's movement. Afterward, Nearest Neighbor (NN) (Kossmann, Ramsak, & Rost, 2002) and Branch & Bound Skyline (BBS) (Papadias et al., 2005) were proposed. They return Skyline points progressively by means of an R-Tree index. NN recursively divides data in regions making use the nearest neighbor approach. In each recursion, the nearest neighbor is returned as part of the Skyline while discards those regions whose points are dominated by the nearest neighbor. Meanwhile, BBS improves NN using a Branch & Bound approach. Nevertheless, the disadvantage of applying these algorithms in the chapter problem is that they must recalculate the distance and the complete Skyline after each user's movement. The main limitation is data dynamic nature. The distance depends on a function for calculating it and attributes depends on information extraction of their values. In addition, BDS (Basic Distributed Skyline) proposed by Balke,

Güntzer and Zheng (2004) is a heuristic-based algorithm which identifies Skyline candidates in a first phase and then, in a second phase, it discards dominated candidates in order to return the Skyline. Next, Lo, Yip, Lin and Cheung (2006) presented the idea of progressive queries on the Web through the Distributed Progressive Skylining (PDS) algorithm. Although BDS and PDS consider data extraction from several Web sources, the indices must frequently be updated because of dynamic data. Additionally, BDS requires the creation of an index for each criterion.

On the other hand, Kodama et al. (2009) considered location-based Skyline queries. Their solution was designed to process data based on categorical tables; categories have small domains, e.g., a category for price is high, medium and low. Nevertheless, building and managing of the categorical table is not scalable for high volume of dynamic data. Also, Kossman, Ramsak, and Rost (2002) defined an algorithm for Skyline queries over mobile environments based on the nearest neighbor search. The disadvantage of this algorithm is that the Skyline must be recalculated if the user moves. (Zheng, Lee, & Lee, 2008) defined Location-Dependent Skyline Queries (LDSQ) as spatial queries with non-spatial attributes and a user's preference region named Valid Scope. This region allows to validate if the answer must be recalculated. However, the solutions presented in (Zheng, Lee & Lee, 2008) do not support dynamic data. In (Qiang, Lbath, & Daqing, 2012), LDSQ employs extraction methods to retrieve information of interest for the user and returns a recommendation based on gathered information. The gathered information is obtained by the application through historical access and queries performed by the user. Thus, the users can not explicitly indicate their preferences and the system returns answers as the user moves in the space. In this work, additional queries are performed to determine user's preferences and attributes are based on categories.

The sample query includes information extraction from several data sources in the Web. In this regard, many works have focused on retrieving Web documents by means of keyword relevance. Kushmerick Weld and Doorenbos (1997) presents the wrappers as a technique for extracting information in Web documents which return a data structure with information specific to a Web document. Information extraction is a subset of Information Retrieval. While the Information Retrieval consists of selecting documents related to a query, the Information Extraction retrieves a part of text from a document (Hobbs & Riloff, 2010).

Wrappers are procedures that extract information from a source using a word or regular expression (Kushmerick, Weld, & Doorenbos 1997). In this chapter, for each implemented solution, a wrapper was built in order to extract online a set of pairs (key, value) from a data source.

On one hand, the distance between the points (places) to be consulted and the user's location varies with the user's movement. On the other hand, the values of the attributes associated with each point (place) are often modified by users accessing Web pages. Additionally, when the user is in movement, the location-based Skyline may differ with respect to the previous user's location because of distance value and the search area change with the user's location. This chapter proposes algorithms for evaluating location-based Skyline queries considering user's position change and information extraction from data sources. These algorithms reduce re-computation after the user changes his location.

Skyline

Börzsönyi et al. (2001) introduced the Skyline operator in the context of relational databases. Skyline was proposed as a SQL extension in order to allow users to specify preference criteria. Thus, users define their criteria as a multi-criteria function into the SKYLINE OF clause. Syntactically, a Skyline query may be expressed as following:

SELECT <attributes> FROM <relations> WHERE <conditions> GROUP BY <attributes> HAVING <conditions>

SKYLINE OF a$_1$ [MIN|MAX|DIFF],...,a$_n$ [MIN|MAX|DIFF]

A SKYLINE OF clause body represents a list of attributes or dimensions used to rank the dataset. Each dimension can be an integer, float, or a date and may be annotated with the directives: MIN, MAX and DIFF. MIN and MAX indicate minimum or maximum values and the DIFF directive defines the interest in retaining the best choices with respect to every distinct value of the attribute.

The result of a Skyline query will be composed of all non-dominated tuples. A tuple is non-dominated if does not exist another tuple equally good or better in all dimensions and better in at least one.

Preliminaries

Firstly, a distance function $d(x, y)$ between two locations x and y is defined as a binary function whose domain is a real number, i.e., $d : R^n x R^n \rightarrow R^n$. In this chapter, the distance function meets the following properties (Burago, Burago, Ivanov, 2001):

- No negativity: $d(x, y) \geq 0, \forall x, y \in R^n$
- Symmetry: $d(x, y) = d(y, x), \forall x, y \in R^n$
- Triangle Inequality: $d(x, z) \leq d(x, y) + d(y, z), \forall x, y, z \in R^n$
- $d(x, x) = 0, \forall x \in R^n$
- If $x, y \in R^n$ and $d(x, y) = 0$, then $x = y$.

Let x and y be two locations; an object has moved from one location x to the location y if $d(x, y) \geq 0$.

Secondly, let $O = \{o_1, ..., o_n\}$ be a dataset of n objects and let $V = \{v_{i1}, ..., v_{im}\}$ be a set of attributes for each $o_i \in O$. The Skyline is a set S composed of all the objects $o_i \in O$ such that there is not a different object $oj \in O$ that dominates o_i in terms of V; the object o_i dominates the object o_j if and only if all the values v_{il} are better than or equal to the values v_{jl} for all l such that $1 \leq l \leq m$, and at least one value v_{iz} is better than v_{jz} for any z such that $1 \leq z \leq m$.

Thirdly, let Q be a location corresponding to user's location; let $O = \{o_1, ..., o_n\}$ be a dataset of n objects where each $o_i \in O$ has a location p_i and a set of attributes $V = \{v_{i1}, ..., v_{im}\}$. A location-based Skyline S is a set of objects $o_i \in O$ such that there is not a different object $oj \in O$ that dominates o_i in terms of $V \cup \{d_i\}$ with $d_i = d(p_i, Q)$.

Commonly, Web documents may be associated with a particular location. In this sense, the values for the attributes $V = \{v_{i1}, ..., v_{im}\}$ of each object $o_i \in O$ may be extracted from Web documents associated with its location. Thus, the problem to be addressed in this chapter is evaluating location-based Skyline queries with information extraction in a search area delimited by a user who is moving. In this case, the search area is an area enclosed by a circle with a fixed radius around the user's location.

PROPOSED ALGORITHMS

In this section, four algorithms for evaluating location-based skyline queries are described. All algorithms are based on Divide & Conquer principle and traverse an M-tree. An M-Tree (Ciaccia, Patella, & Zezula, 1997) is a data structure capable of dealing with dynamic data files and avoiding frequent reorganizations. An M-Tree index divides data according to their relative distances and employs a specific distance function. After applying the function, the data is stored in each node of the M-tree, where each node corresponds to a region of the considered space. Each node is delimited by the amount of data that it can store and the radius of the region. An M-tree was used because of its circular nature, i.e., regions have a circular shape which resembles the user's search area.

The first proposed algorithm calculates the Skyline in each M-Tree region within the search area and then, it merges the Skyline of each region until identify the whole skyline. The second algorithm uses a pruning criterion to prevent access to regions which have no skyline points. The third algorithm assumes regions with skyline points continuing having skyline points and therefore, it does not recalculate regions that contain skyline in the previous state. The fourth algorithm does not extract information for those points enclosed in regions previously visited by the algorithm. Notice that the latter two algorithms return an approximate set of the skyline because it works with the previous state to the user's position change.

All proposed algorithms receive as input an M-Tree, where each region of the index is composed of spatial data stored in a database (O). Each object $o_i \in O$ has a pair of coordinates (x, y) corresponding to its geographical location as well as an URL of the document that describes it. Additionally, the initial user's location, the search radius and the number of steps (states) to complete during the user's itinerary is established.

Naive Algorithm

The Algorithm 1 presents the pseudo-code of NA (Naive Algorithm).

Algorithm 1. NA

```
Input: a database O, a location loc, an integer rad, an integer steps, a query
q, and an M-Tree i
1: Create a list rl of regions;
2: for i = 1 to steps do
3:        rl = Get regions from the M-tree i inside the circle whose radius
          is rad and midpoint is loc;
4:        Get the values associated with each object in the regions rl;
5:        Calculate the Skyline of each region in rl;
6:        Create a list s for the Skyline
7:        for each region reg in rl do
8:              s = Calculate the Skyline between the points of s and reg;
                // Merge the Skylines
9:          print Skyline points from s;
10:         loc = Get new user's position;
```

The NA algorithm applies the Divide & Conquer principle accessing the regions that intersect the search area. In each region, all the points are compared against themselves to find the skyline for each region and subsequently, each skyline is merged to determine the final skyline. In the lines 3-5 of NA, the regions that intersect the circle associated to the search area are determined, the values of each point are extracted from the external data source, and subsequently the Skyline set is calculated by each region. Later, lines 6-8 of NA merging the Skyline of each region that intersects the search area in order to the current Skyline. To conclude, the current Skyline is printed and the current user's position is updated in lines 9-10 of NA. Thus, the algorithm continues iterating in the same way in each of the steps performed by the user until the user reaches the last position.

Lastly, NA is characterized by the following properties:

- At each user's step (state), only those objects that are within regions that intersect the search area are retrieved.
- The cost of calculating the whole Skyline at each user's step (state) is equal to identify and merge the Skyline from each region that intersects the search area.
- At each user's step (state), the wrapper is used to update the values associated with each of the objects in the regions that intersect the search area.

To illustrate the running of NA, consider Figure 3 which shows a subset of disjoints regions at a specific level of the M-tree. In other words, each circle (region) in the image of the Figure 3 represents an M-Tree node and contains a sub-tree where the points within each circle represent the objects inside each node. These regions are inside the search area.

Figure 3. Regions at a specific level of the M-tree

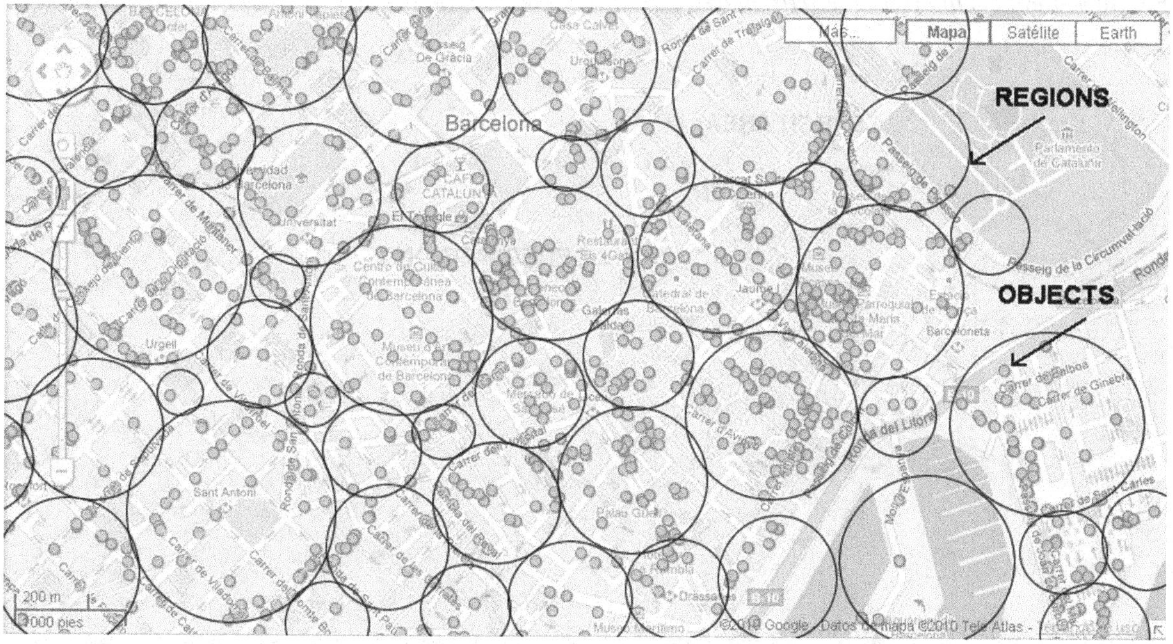

The M-Tree regions that intersect the search area are highlighted in the Figure 4 where the small blue circle represents the user's position, the larger blue circle corresponds to the search area and the remaining red circles around the user are the regions that intersect the search area.

In Figure 5, the Skyline objects obtained by each region are shown. It can be noted that not necessarily all Skyline objects are within the search area. Those objects surrounding at the boundary of the search area are also considered during the Skyline calculation.

Subsequently, NA merges the Skyline of each region that intersects the search area. For example, suppose the three regions R1, R2 and R3. First, NA merges Skyline objects of R1 with Skyline objects of R2, and then calculates the Skyline from the previous merging with the objects of R3. Figure 6 presents the Skyline set of the merging regions from the Figure 5.

Pruning Based Algorithm

The pseudo-code for PA is presented in Algorithm 2.

The PRUning Based Algorithm (PA) applies a pruning criterion to discard dominated regions of the M-tree index before merging the Skyline objects from two M-tree regions. The pruning criterion is based on the maximum and minimum values for each dimension from the Skyline of each region. Similar to NA, PA identifies the Skyline for each region that intersects the search area. However, it evaluates whether any object dominates a region before merging regions. It can be noted that the main changes with respect to NA are in lines 5-6 and 9-11, where the maximum and minimum values for each dimension of the Skyline objects inside a region are calculated and then the dominance between a Skyline point and a region is checked before merging regions. If a region *reg* is dominated by an object *x*, then *reg* is discarded and will not be merged.

Figure 4. Regions intersect the search area

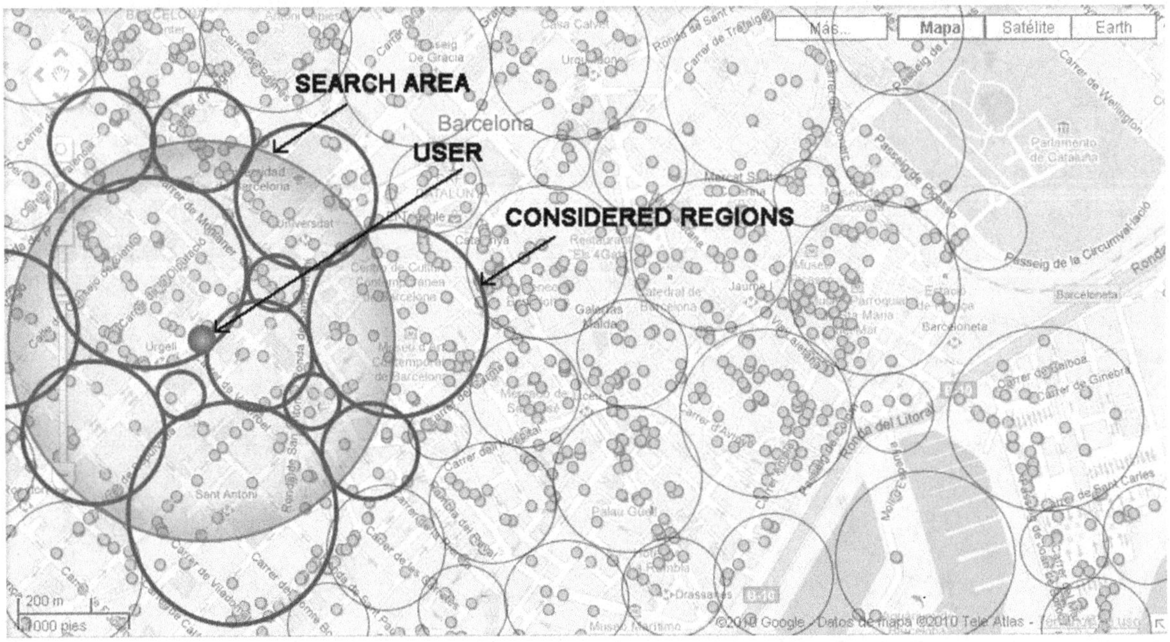

Figure 5. Skyline of each region intersects the search area

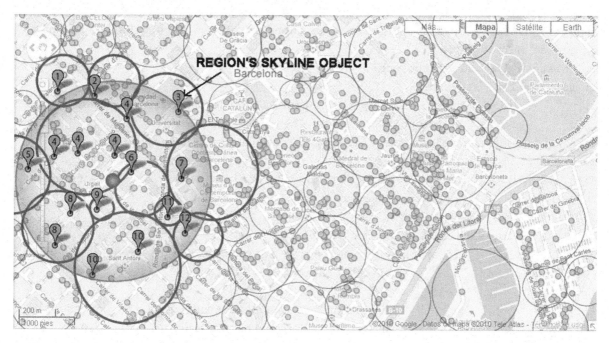

Figure 6. Current Skyline from regions intersect the search area

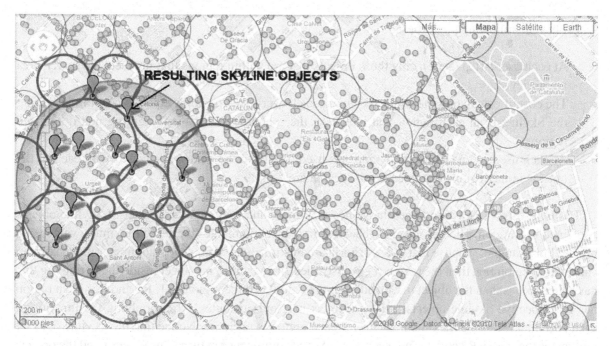

Algorithm 2. PA

Input: a database *O*, a location *loc,* an integer *rad*, an integer *steps*, a query
q, and an M-Tree *i*
1: Create a list *rl* of regions;
2: for *i* = 1 to *steps* do
3:        *rl* = Get regions from the M-tree *i* inside the circle whose radius
          is *rad* and midpoint is *loc*;
4:        Get the values associated with each object in the regions *rl*;
5:        While calculate the Skyline of each region in *rl* do
6;   Get the values minimum and maximum of Skyline objects in
                 each region of *rl*;
7:        Create a list *s* for the Skyline
8:         for each region *reg* in *rl* do
9:                if an object *x* belonging to *s* dominates the region *reg* then
10:                       Discard region *rgl*;
11:               else
12:                       *s* = Calculate the Skyline between the points of *s*
                          and *reg*; // Merge the Skylines
13:        print Skyline points from *s*;
14:         loc = Get new user's position;

PA has the following properties:

- At each user's step (state), only those objects that are within regions that intersect the search area are retrieved.
- The cost of calculating the whole Skyline at each user's step (state) is equal to cost of identifying the Skyline from each region that intersects the search area and then, merging non-dominated regions.
- At each user's step (state), the wrapper is used to update the values associated with each of the objects in the regions that intersect the search area.

Lastly, PA uses a function to get the values maximum and minimum from a set of Skyline objects contained in a region. The key idea is to check if any object dominates the set of maximum values of a region. For example, suppose that user's criteria are maximized. If an object *o* dominates the maximum values of a region *reg*, then the region *reg* is discarded since there is no object inside the region *reg* that has better values than the object *o*. Consider Figure 7 and its three regions R1, R2 and R3. Each region has its respective Skyline objects and each object has four attributes. After applying the function to each region, a list of the maximum values for each region is retrieved. Notice that the Skyline object *x* dominates the region R2 and it is not necessary to check dominance between the object *x* and the objects from the region R2. This way, some comparisons may be avoided and the execution time may be reduced.

Figure 7. An example for PA

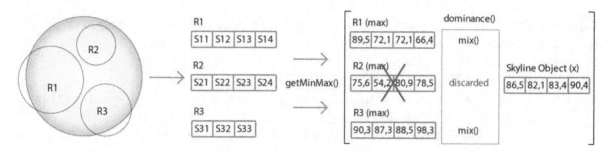

On contrary, the maximum values of a region cannot discard an object if is dominated. Figure 8 illustrates when an object x is dominated by the maximum values of the region R3; nevertheless, no object in R3 dominates x.

Approximate Pruning Based Algorithms

Algorithm 3 specifies the pseudo-code for APA.

The Approximate Pruning Based Algorithm (APA) applies the pruning criterion but it does not extract values from the data sources for those objects in the regions that enclose Skyline objects in the preceding state. In the initial user's position, APA behaves similarly to PA extracting the values associated with all objects inside regions that intersect the search region but the values are not updated for regions with Skyline objects when the user changes his position. In line 4, APA identifies which regions require their objects to be updated. Those regions with Skyline objects retain the same values previously extracted in the preceding state.

Since the time required for information extraction from data sources may be significant with respect to the total execution time of the algorithm, the heuristics consists in avoiding re-extracting values for those regions where were previously found Skyline objects. We suppose that those regions enclosing Skyline objects have at least one potential solution. In this sense, such solutions could maintain their values over time under a slightly changing scenario. However, those regions of previous states where no Skyline object was found may include Skyline objects in the new state whether the object values change.

Figure 8. A counterexample

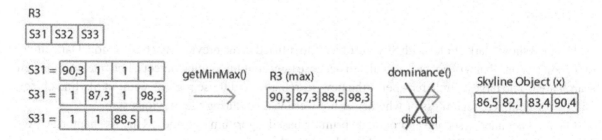

Algorithm 3. APA

Input: a database *O*, a location *loc,* an integer *rad*, an integer *steps*, a query *q*, and an M-Tree *i*

```
1: Create a list rl of regions;
2: for i = 1 to steps do
3:        rl = Get regions from the M-tree i inside the circle whose radius
          is rad and midpoint is loc;
4:        Get the values associated with each object in those regions from rl
          that do not contain Skyline objects;
5:        While calculate the Skyline of each region in rl do
6;              Get the values minimum and maximum of Skyline objects in
                each region of rl;
7:        Create a list s for the Skyline
8:        for each region reg in rl do
9:              if an object x belonging to s dominates the region reg then
10:                     Discard region rgl;
11:             else
12:                     s = Calculate the Skyline between the points of s
                        and reg; // Merge the Skylines
13:        print Skyline points from s;
14:         loc = Get new user's position;
```

The properties of APA are the following:

- At the user's initial step (state), only those objects that are within regions that intersect the search area are retrieved. Later, in the following user's steps (states), only those objects that are in regions that did not contain any skyline object in the preceding step (state) and intersect the search area are retrieved.
- The cost of calculating the whole Skyline at each user's step (state) is equal to cost of identifying the Skyline from each region that intersects the search area without Skyline objects in the preceding step and then, merging non-dominated regions.
- At each user's step (state), the wrapper is used to update the values associated with each of the objects in the regions that intersect the search area and do not have Skyline objects of the preceding step.

Figure 8 shows dark circles with Skyline objects identified in the previous user's location. Dark circles represent regions that will not be recalculated because they contain Skyline objects, and intersect the new search area. The largest circle represents the new search area and those regions without Skyline objects will be recalculated, regardless of whether or not were visited during the previous step.

On the other hand, a second approximate pruning based algorithm is proposed in this chapter: APA+. The pseudo-code for APA+ is presented in Algorithm 4.

Figure 9. Regions without information extraction

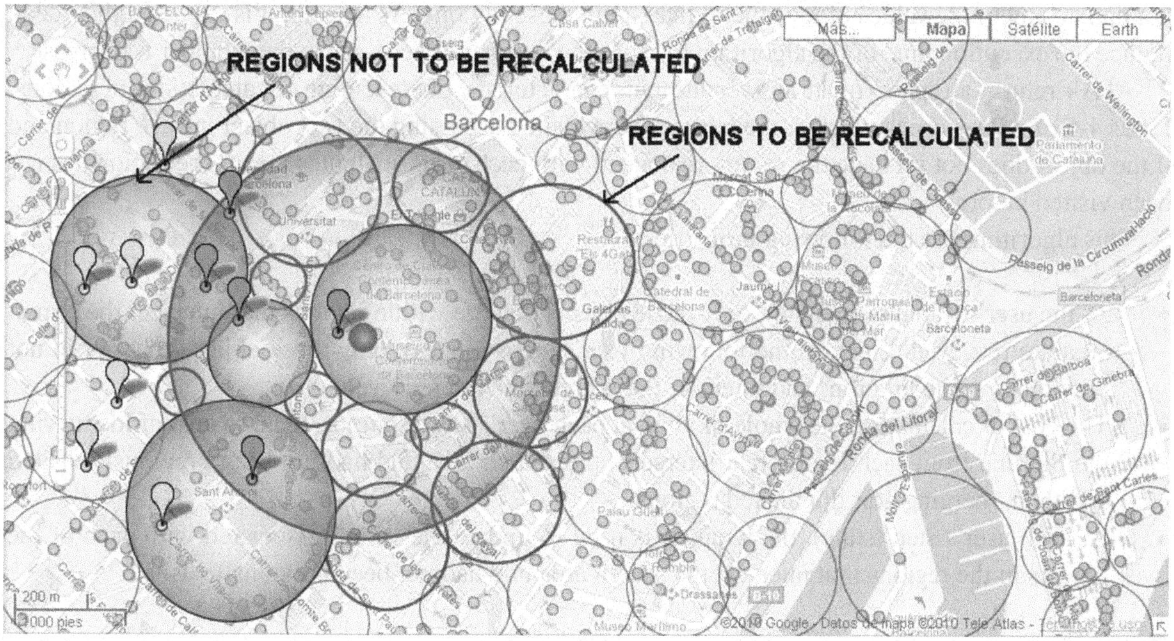

Algorithm 4. APA

Input: a database *O*, a location *loc,* an integer *rad*, an integer *steps*, a query *q*, and an M-Tree *i*

1: Create a list *rl* of regions;
2: for *i* = 1 to *steps* do
3:         *rl* = Get regions from the M-tree *i* inside the circle whose radius is *rad* and midpoint is *loc*;
4:         Get the values associated with each object in those regions from *rl* that were not visited in the previous step;
5:         While calculate the Skyline of each region in *rl* that were not visited in the previous step do
6;   Get the values minimum and maximum of Skyline objects in each region of *rl*;
7:         Create a list *s* for the Skyline
8:           for each region *reg* in *rl* do
9:                 if an object *x* belonging to *s* dominates the region *reg* then
10:                         Discard region *rgl*;
11:                 else
12:                         *s* = Calculate the Skyline between the points of *s* and *reg*; // Merge the Skylines
13:         print Skyline points from *s*;
14:          loc = Get new user's position;

APA+ does not re-calculate the Skyline in any region that was previously accessed and therefore, does not update any of the values of the objects that are in these regions. As a result, it is expected that it can reduce the execution time of the algorithm because the number of accesses to the wrapper is decreased.

APA+ returns an approximate answer due to its characteristic of preventing re-calculations of regions. Lines 4-5 of APA+ check whether the regions were visited accessing the first object in each region and if the object does not yet have the values associated with each of its attributes means the region has not been visited before.

This algorithm has the following properties:

- At the user's initial step (state), only those objects that are within regions that intersect the search area are retrieved. Later, in the following user's steps (states), only those objects that are in not previously visited regions and intersect the search area are retrieved.
- The cost of calculating the whole Skyline at each user's step (state) is equal to cost of identifying the Skyline from each region that intersects the search area and had not been previously visited and then, merging non-dominated regions.
- At each user's step (state), the wrapper is used to update the values associated with each of the objects in the regions that intersect the search area and had not been previously visited.

Summary

Table 3 summarizes the most important characteristics of each proposed algorithm in this chapter.

EXPERIMENTAL STUDY

This chapter describes the experimental study in order to evaluate performance and quality response of the four proposed algorithms. The experiments were performed on synthetic and real datasets. Syn-

Table 3. Summary of the algorithms

	Characteristics
NA	• At each step (state), NA considers only those regions that intersect the search area. • At each step (state), the wrapper retrieves values associated with each of the objects.
PA	• It is based on a pruning criterion. • At each step (state), PA considers only those regions that intersect the search area and have not been discarded by the pruning criterion. • At each step (state), the wrapper retrieves values associated with each of the objects.
APA	• It is based on a pruning criterion. • It does not recalculate the Skyline in those regions where Skyline objects were found in the previous step (state). • At each step (state), APA considers only those regions that intersect the search area and have not been discarded by the pruning criterion. • At initial step (state), the wrapper retrieves values associated with each of the objects. Subsequently, the wrapper is only used in those regions where have not found Skyline objects.
APA+	• It is based on a pruning criterion. • It does not recalculate the Skyline for those regions that have been previously visited in the preceding step (state). • At each step (state), APA+ considers only those regions that intersect the search area and have not been discarded by the pruning criterion. • At initial step (state), the wrapper retrieves values associated with each of the objects. Subsequently, the wrapper is only used in regions that have not been previously visited by the user.

thetic datasets are characterized by an identifier, a location attribute and eight scores; their size is ten thousand, one hundred thousand and one million registers. Web files with a similar structure to those found in real cases were generated in order to extract up to 8 scores. Data values vary from 0 to 100 and follow a uniform and correlated distribution. For correlated data, a correlation variable of 5% on the first generated data was established. Thus, the first generated data was chosen between 0 and 95 using the random function. Then, for each new generated value, the random function was invoked with values between 0 and 5, and the result was added to the first generated data. In this way, the set of correlated data for an object was obtained. The reason of choosing a 5% correlation variable is mainly because if the data are correlated, then the variation between their values must be low. To simulate the updates in the data presented on the web, after each change of user's position, values vary between 25% and 30% with respect to old values.

The data generator was developed in Perl using the random function and implements two modules to accomplish the task. A first module creates each of the Web pages associated with each location. Each Web file corresponds to an object in the dataset and contains twenty scores. The second module stores the locations of objects and web pages into the database.

Real dataset contains 10,587 objects with four scores. The location and scores are obtained from a web source. Real data are updated in every moment by the Web users, so they are dynamic over time. Each object corresponds to a restaurant for a particular zone. In this experimental study, the data were taken from the TripAdvisor page, which allows to query location in coordinates (latitude and longitude) and information about restaurants. TripAdvisor allows people to rate restaurants and hotels (mostly) and express their opinion. A restaurant may be scored in terms of food quality, service quality, decoration and price versus food quality. A set of 10587 restaurants from London was queried. We found restaurants with zero ratings to restaurants with ratings greater than 1500. Those restaurants with available ratings are not considered in this experimental study. From 10587 restaurants in London, 8783 were scored by users which represent about 83% of the dataset.

All experiments were performed under an AMD Phenom II x4 945 3.0GHz with 8 GB of RAM, a hard Drive WD Caviar Green 1TB SATA3 64MB, Windows XP Service Pack 3. Database was in a VMWare virtual machine with 1GB of RAM on Windows XP with 20GB disk. The database stores geographic coordinates (location) of each object and the URL of the associated document from which will be extracted the scores. In this experimental study, the algorithms were developed using a library named MESSIF revision svn 936 (Batko, Novak & Zezula, 2007; Edgewall Software, 2007; Sedmidubsky, Dohnal, & Zezula, 2008) which implements the M-Tree index.

On the other hand, we measured the following metrics:

- **Calculation Time of the Regions:** Time required to search each document associated with each object and extract its values from the Web document.
- **Skyline Time:** The time required to find the Skyline set at each user's step.
- **Run Time:** The total time consumed from the user's initial position to the end position.
- **Comparisons:** Number of times in which an object is verified if is dominated. Two types of comparisons are performed: i) Skyline comparisons are the number of comparisons performed between two objects in order to identify the Skyline set; and ii) Pruning comparisons are the number of comparisons using the pruning criterion to exclude one or more regions.
- **Intersected Regions:** Number of regions that intersect the search area.
- **Discarded Regions:** Number of regions pruned by the criterion.

- **No Recalculated Regions:** Number of regions whose objects are not updated.
- **D & NR (Discarded and No Recalculated) Regions:** Number of regions that were not recalculated and were discarded by the pruning criterion.
- **Evaluated Regions:** Number of regions that were not discarded and had to be recalculated.

Since two algorithms return an approximate response, precision and recall were reported to evaluate the answer quality. Precision and Recall are two values which validate how well or bad is a solution, or in other words, how relevant is the answer. Its use is very common in the area of Information Retrieval and pattern recognition (Powers, 2007/2011).

Precision indicates the relationship between the actually positive cases and predicted real cases that were obtained by the algorithm while Recall shows the relationship between the positive real cases that were obtained by the algorithm with the total real cases that should have been obtained (Powers, 2007/2011). In other words, Precision indicates how accurate is the response while Recall indicates how complete it is.

Skyline Size is the size of the solution set obtained in each user's state (step). In this experimental study, four states were considered.

Uniform Data

We first study the performance and quality response of each algorithm under a uniform data distribution. We report the time (ms), the number of comparisons, the number of regions, the answer quality and Skyline size.

In Figure 10a, we can observe the number total of comparisons performed by each algorithm varying the number of attributes. In this case, greater number of attributes, greater number of comparisons. Notice that for the algorithms APA and APA+, the number of comparisons needed to obtain the Skyline tends to be larger than the other algorithms. This condition is also reflected in the time required to calculate the Skyline presented in Figure 10b. Furthermore, the number of comparisons performed using the pruning criterion is very low with respect to the number of total comparisons. This can occur because the number of pruned regions is very small.

Subsequently, Figure 10b shows the total runtime consumed by the algorithms varying the number of attributes. In particular, we can distinguish three kinds of time: time consumed in calculating the Skyline set, time required on the selection of the regions that intersect the search area and the time spent on the rest of the run. It can be noted that while the remaining time is usually a constant for each of the algorithms, the computation time required to select regions occupies most of the execution time. On the other hand, we can also observe that as the number of attributes increases, also increases the time spent on calculating the Skyline.

Moreover, the APA+ algorithm effectively reduces the selection time of the regions which avoids recalculating certain regions; those regions that were visited in the previous state are not recalculated.

For PA, the execution time is slightly higher than NA. Basically, the idea of PA is to reduce the number of comparisons beyond decrease the execution time, but in the case of the uniform data, the number of discarded regions is very low.

Figure 11 illustrates the number detailed of regions varying the number of attributes. It reveals that few regions were discarded. Thus, the time consumed in applying the pruning criterion does not contribute in reducing the execution time.

Figure 10a. Comparisons and time over uniform data. From top to bottom: 10,000; 100,000 and 1,000,000 objects.

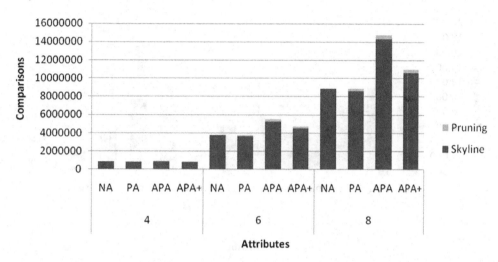

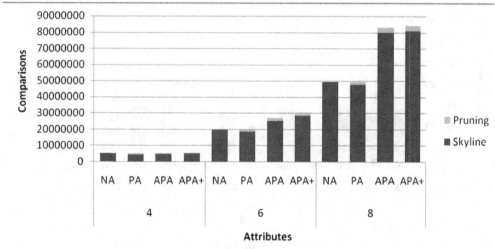

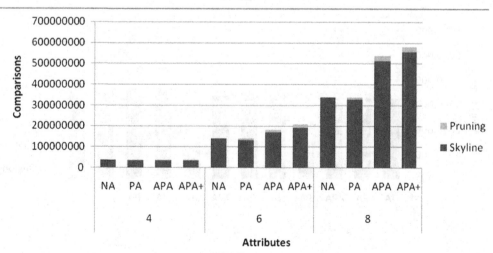

Figure 10b. Comparisons and time over uniform data. From top to bottom: 10,000; 100,000 and 1,000,000 objects.

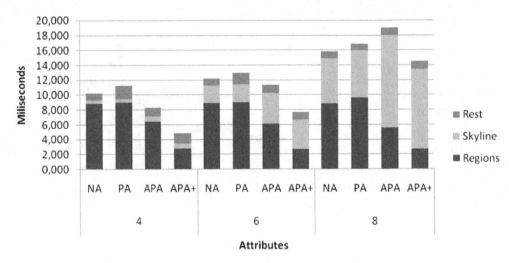

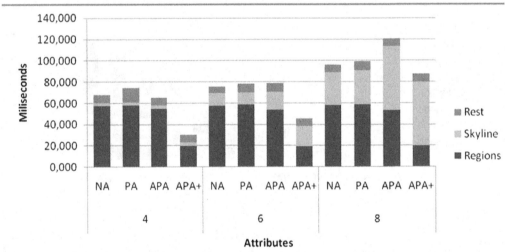

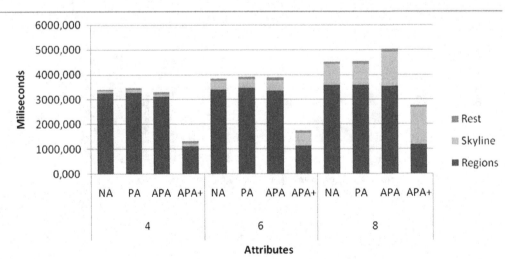

Figure 11. Distribution of regions over uniform data. From top to bottom: 10,000; 100,000 and 1,000,000 objects.

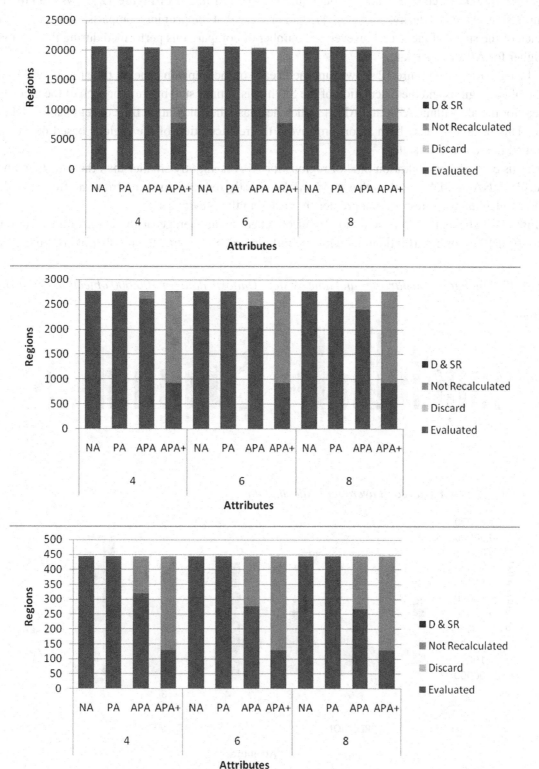

To show the performance of the algorithms at each user's step, we have selected three steps, a dataset of 100,000 objects and 8-dimensional queries. The left image of Figure 12 shows the number of comparisons evaluated during each step. We can observe that the pruning comparisons are very similar in each of the states of the user, however, the number of comparisons performed during the calculation is higher for APA and APA+.

The right image of Figure 12 shows runtime in each of the steps. In general, time taken for the calculation of the regions and the calculation of the Skyline is similar step by step for each of the algorithms, except for the algorithms APA and APA+ which decrease the calculation time of regions from the first state. This occurs because both algorithms avoid the recalculation of the regions based on the result obtained in the previous state.

In this case, the computation time of regions for APA is slightly smaller than the time taken by the algorithms NA and PA. On the other hand, APA+ greatly reduces this time from the first state due to avoid recalculate those regions not previously visited in the previous step.

Figure 13 shows the Precision and Recall obtained as an average of the algorithm executions on datasets of 10 thousand, 100 thousand and one million objects varying the number of attributes. Notice

Figure 12. Number of comparisons and time by step: Uniform data for 100,000 objects and 8 attributes

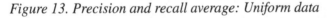

Figure 13. Precision and recall average: Uniform data

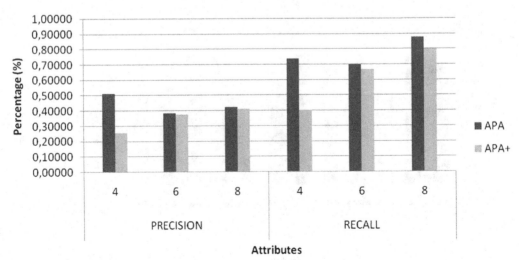

that APA is more complete than APA+ and its precision is between 40 and 50%. By keeping the recalculation of most of the regions, APA maintains a more complete solution, reaching almost 90% in the best case. APA+ is the less accurate solution (below 30%) basically because it avoids the recalculation of almost 90% of the regions.

Figure 14 presents the average size of the Skyline set by several datasets (10,000; 100,000 and 1,000,000) per number of attributes (4, 6 and 8). We can observe that the higher the number of attributes, the greater the Skyline size. On the other hand, it can be noted as the size of the Skyline varies only in approximate pruning based algorithms. Essentially, these algorithms are those in which a greater amount of Skyline points was obtained. This had an impact on the execution time of these algorithms.

Correlated Data

In this section, we study the performance and answer quality of each algorithm when the data are correlated. We report the execution time (milliseconds), the number of comparisons, the number of regions, the answer quality and the Skyline size.

Under a correlated scenario, the attribute values of an object are related, i.e., if an attribute has a high value, the other attributes will also possess a high value; likewise, if an attribute value is low, the other attributes also possess a low value. Due to the nature of the data, it is common to find regions whose maximum values are low and in consequence, these regions may be easily discarded. The same does not occur under a uniform distribution, where having an object with at least one attribute high value might involve compare all the objects in the region. Thus, PA discards more regions under a correlated distribution than under a uniform distribution of the data.

Furthermore, APA prevents recalculation in those regions where no Skyline objects were founded in the previous state while APA+ avoids recalculating all the regions previously visited. In this case, the number of visited regions will be greater than or equal to the number of regions with Skyline. In

Figure 14. Skyline average size: Uniform data

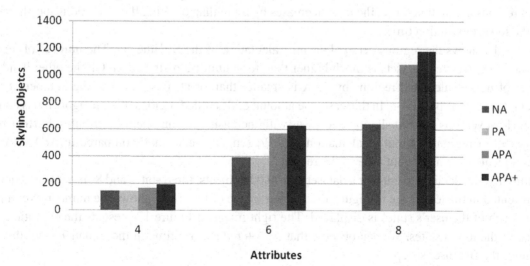

this sense, under a dynamic data scenario, where the attributes change value in each state of the user, it is supposed that the algorithm APA will be more precise and complete than APA+ basically because it updates more values than APA+.

Figure 15a introduces the number of comparisons because of comparisons between objects or the pruning criterion. In this case, a greater number of attributes, the greater number of comparisons, although the variation after increasing the number of attributes is not significant.

Note that in all cases presented in Figure 15a, NA has the highest number of comparisons to find the Skyline set while PA, APA and APA+ perform fewer comparisons. Thus, the number of comparisons performed by the algorithms based on pruning is less than or equal to the number of comparisons evaluated by NA since the algorithms based on pruning avoid increasing the number of comparisons when some regions are discarded. Particularly, there is a variation in the number of comparisons performed by APA and APA+. This variation is related to the fact that algorithms approximately calculate the answer. Due to some regions are not recalculated, new objects may be part of the solution set which translates to a greater or lesser number of comparisons.

According to Figure 15a, the number of attributes does not produce major changes in the number of comparisons when distribution data are correlated.

Figure 15b shows the execution time in milliseconds for the algorithms varying the number of attributes. It illustrates time required to calculate the Skyline set, time required on the computation of regions and time spent in the rest of execution. The execution time increases as the number of objects increases.

However, the time is maintained as the dimensionality increases due to the Skyline size is small. It may be noted as the computation time of Skyline unchanged after increasing the number of attributes. This is because the data are correlated and the Skyline size is considerably small compared to the size of the Skyline under a uniform distribution. In this sense, the Skyline set does not vary greatly by increasing the number of attributes.

On the other hand, it can be seen that APA and APA+ reduce the total execution time due to keep the computation time of the Skyline as the number of attributes increases.

In the case of APA, the computation time of the regions is similar to NA and PA since it depends on the number of regions where Skyline objects were identified. However, APA+ considers the previously visited regions and in this sense, the time decreases by more than 60% in all cases, and is the algorithm with the lowest execution time.

Figure 16 shows the regions detailed during calculation of the Skyline set. The number of regions discarded in correlated datasets is much higher than for a uniform distribution. On the other hand, the number of non-recalculated regions by APA is smaller than or at most equal to the number of non-recalculated regions by APA+. In this case, the amount of discarded regions in each algorithm is considerable. However, this amount slightly decreases with increasing the number of attributes. Furthermore, the number of regions without recalculation by APA remains very small compared to APA+. APA+ avoids a recalculation of about 60% of the regions.

Similarly, the detailed results for a dataset of 100,000 objects, three states and 8-dimensional queries are presented in the left image of Figure 17. The left image of Figure 17 shows the number of comparisons in each of the user's states is displayed. The right image of Figure 17 presents the execution time in each of the user's states. We can observe that APA+ reduces runtime in more than 70% of the total time after the first user's step.

Figure 15a. Comparisons and time over correlated data. From top to bottom: 10,000; 100,000 and 1,000,000 objects.

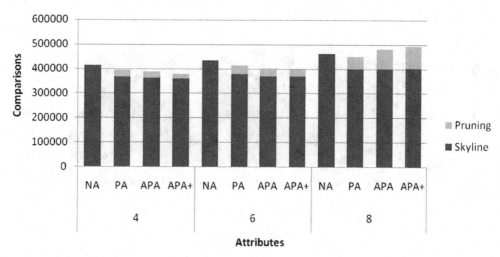

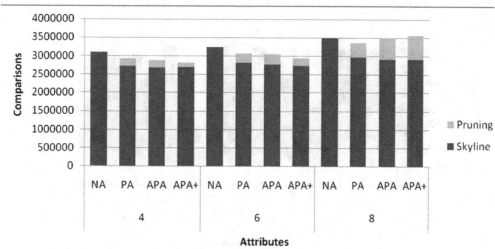

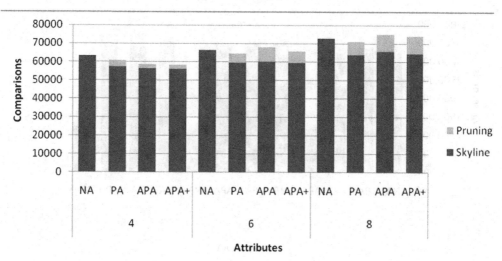

Figure 15b. Comparisons and time over correlated data. From top to bottom: 10,000; 100,000 and 1,000,000 objects.

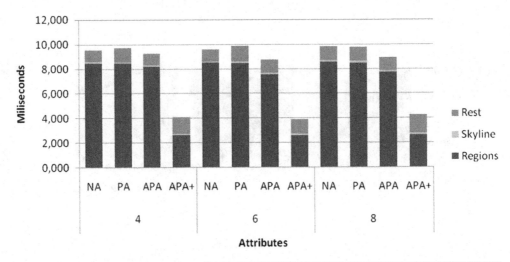

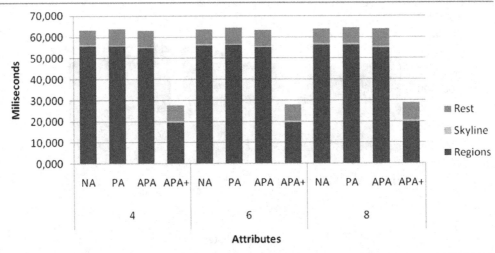

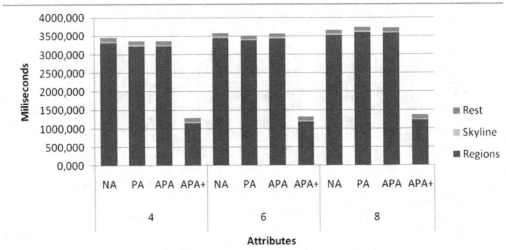

Figure 16. Distribution of regions over correlated data. From top to bottom: 10,000; 100,000 and 1,000,000 objects.

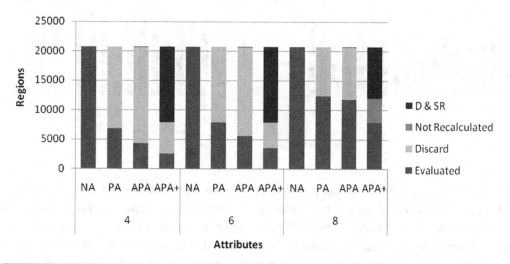

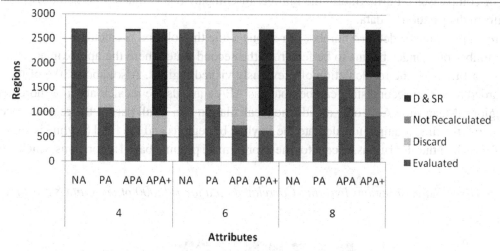

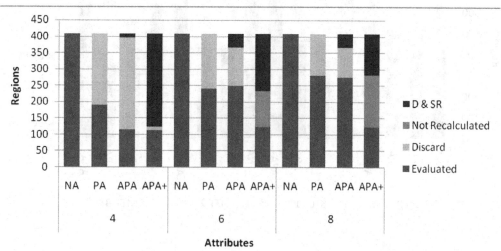

Figure 17. Number of comparisons and time by state: Correlated data for 100,000 objects and 8 attributes

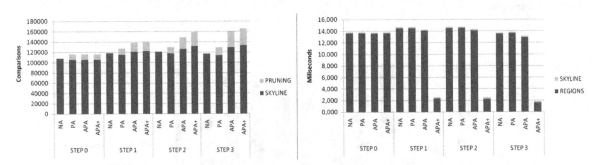

In the first state, the number of comparisons by the pruning based algorithms are similar than NA mainly because they do not avoid any recalculation. Nevertheless, from the second state it can be noted as increasing comparisons for APA and APA+. In the same way that under uniform distribution, the algorithms generate approximate solutions in order to avoid recalculations and this produces a greater number of comparisons. Furthermore, the number of comparisons is much less than those performed on a uniform distribution of data.

Figure 18 presents the detailed number of regions while the solution is calculated.

The number of changes begins to be felt from the second state where the approximate pruning algorithms start to avoid the recalculation of previously visited regions. Also, about 30% of the regions are discarded and from second state can be noted as APA+ avoids the recalculation of more than 85% of the regions. Meanwhile APA only avoids the recalculation of a small part of the regions concerned.

In general, the time required to calculate the Skyline by regions and the final Skyline is similar state by state for each of the algorithms, except for the approximate pruning based algorithms which decreases

Figure 18. Distribution of regions by state: Correlated data for 100,000 objects and 8 attributes

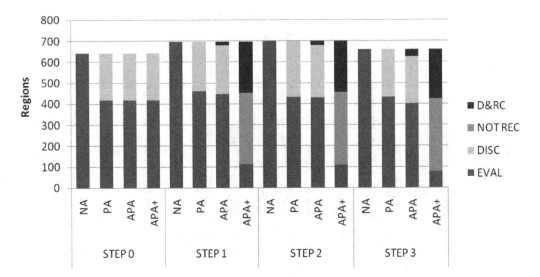

the time calculation of regions from the second state. However, the big difference can be seen in the time taken to calculate the Skyline, which is considerably lower compared to the time consumed on a uniform distribution.

Figure 19 presents the average precision and recall for each algorithm.

Similar to the uniform distribution, APA is the most complete and precise. APA maintains a completeness of at least 80% and at most 90%. APA+ returns a less complete solution. Since the number of non-recalculated regions by APA is smaller than or at most equal to the number of non-recalculated regions by APA+, APA is more precise and more complete than APA+. APA presented a precision of nearly 80% in the best case. Also, approximate pruning based algorithms lose precision as the number of attributes increases.

Although the algorithm APA has the best answer quality among the approximate based pruning algorithms, its execution time is very similar to NA. This presents a dilemma of deciding between answer quality and response time of the algorithm. Previously, it was observed that the faster algorithm was APA+ which reduces the running time to almost 50% but there is a cost to be paid at the level of precision and recall.

Lastly, Figure 20 shows the average Skyline size varying the number of attributes. Unlike a uniform distribution, the size of the Skyline on correlated data is very small. Also, the Skyline size increases as the number of attributes increases. In particular, the Skyline set is about 5% of the whole dataset when data is correlated.

Real Data

In this section, we study the performance and answer quality for each algorithm under a real data.

Figure 21 illustrates a possible user's trip through the restaurants where each circle encloses the search area at the user's step. Some regions are more populated than others. Initial and final positions were established such that the user goes through places not congested and very congested in order to analyze the behavior of the algorithms in the presence of many and few data.

Figure 19. Precision and recall average: Correlated data

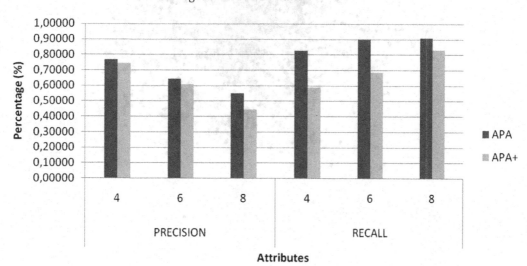

Figure 20. Skyline average size: Correlated data

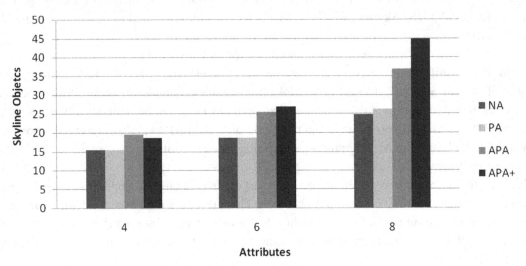

Figure 21. User path under a real data scenario

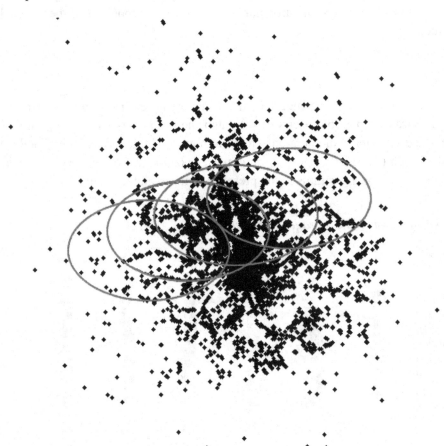

We report the number of comparisons and regions. The runtime was not reported due to the speed of bandwidth available for testing which was very low and greatly increased the run times.

Figure 22 shows the number of comparisons performed by each of the algorithms. Comparisons have been divided into two groups: number of comparisons between objects and pruning based comparisons. It can be noted as the pruning based algorithms perform fewer comparisons than NA to compute the Skyline set.

Particularly, approximate pruning based algorithms perform less number of comparisons since they avoid recalculations the Skyline in some regions.

In Figure 23, we can observe the detailed number of regions over real data. It may be noted as the number of discarded regions is more than 85% of the regions considered for the calculation of the Skyline set. With this information, we can say that the pruning criterion under this scenario is still effective and therefore the number of comparisons performed to calculate the Skyline tends to decrease.

Furthermore, it can be seen the number of no recalculated regions remains lower for APA and higher for APA+ which prevents recalculation of approximately 66% of the regions.

Figure 24 illustrates the number of comparisons for three user's states. The second and third states are the areas of highest number of restaurants. In this case, the number of comparisons is much higher than the rest.

Additionally, it can be noted as the number of pruning based comparisons also augments as increasing the number of restaurants in the area of user's search.

Figure 25 shows in more detail the behavior of the regions as the user is performing the route changing from one state to another.

In each user's step, the pruning criterion discards many regions. For steps 0 and 3 are discarded from 70% and 80% of the regions, whereas for steps 1 and 2, over 90%.

Figure 22. Number of comparisons: Real data

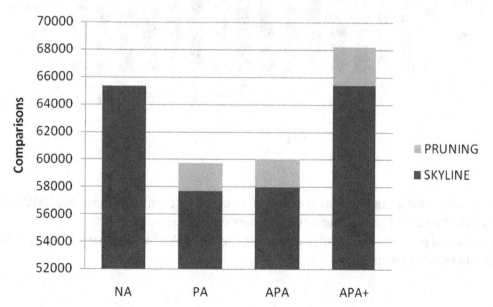

Figure 23. Distribution of regions: Real data

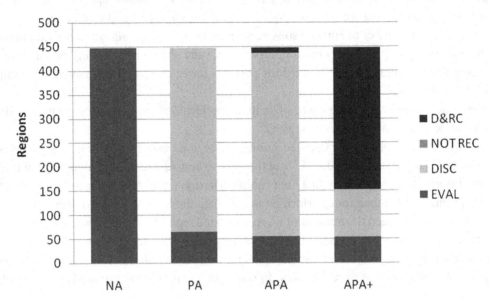

Figure 24. Number of comparisons by state: Real data

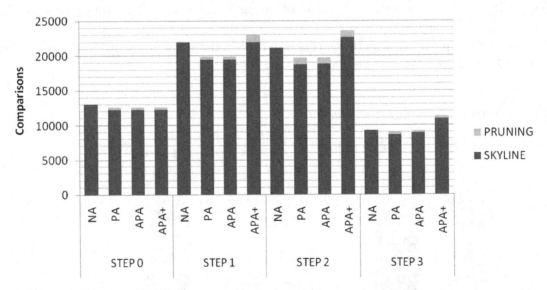

Figure 26 shows the average precision and recall obtained for each algorithm where APA tends to be higher than APA+ in both accuracy and completeness of the Skyline set.

APA maintains precision and recall at almost 90% while APA+ hardly passes 50% of precision and nearly 60% in terms of completeness.

Figure 25. Distribution of regions by state: Real data

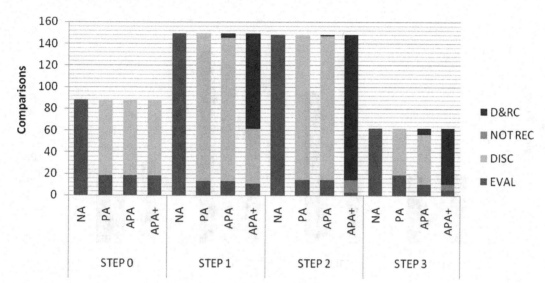

Figure 26. Precision and recall average: Real data

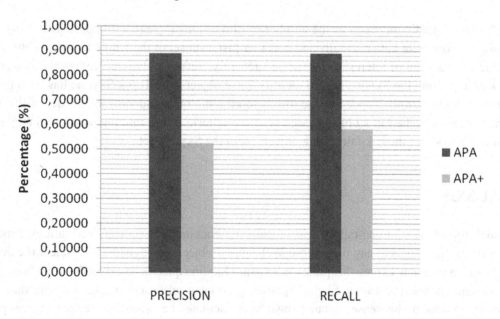

Figure 27 shows the Skyline size in the first three user's states. The third state where there are many restaurants contains the largest number of Skyline objects. On the other hand, it is interesting to note how APA still being an approximate pruning based algorithm return the same size of the Skyline set than NA. For this reason, the values of precision and recall are high for APA. However, the same number of objects in the Skyline set does not necessarily mean that the Skyline objects are the same, and that is why APA is not 100% complete.

Figure 27. Skyline average size: Real data

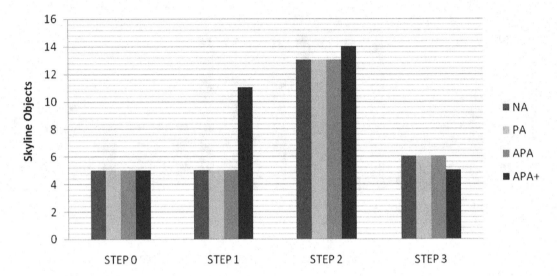

FUTURE RESEARCH DIRECTIONS

The Skyline size rapidly increases as the number of dimensions increases. In consequence, users may have to discard irrelevant data manually and consider just a subset of the whole Skyline. Thus, ranking the Skyline set has been of interest to researchers recently. Several solutions are based on discovering the best k objects from the Skyline set. To identify these objects, the Top-k Skyline has been proposed (Goncalves & Vidal, 2009). Top-k Skyline uses a score function to induce a total order of the Skyline points, and recognizes the top-k objects based on these criteria. Thus, ranking techniques may be integrated in order to select those k-interesting objects from the Skyline set.

CONCLUSION

Web spatial objects may be geo-tagged with documents containing comments and ratings. Since Web users can score the objects at any time, these Web spatial objects are dynamic. To select the best Web spatial objects, a user may express his preferences using Skyline queries based on dynamic features such as distance and changeable scores. Skyline queries have been proposed to filter relevant data from a great amount of data. In this sense, distance must be recalculated because of a user changes his position while the values for the scores must be extracted from external data sources because they are updated each time a user scores a restaurant in the Web.

When a Skyline query involves a distance function as part of its criteria, it is known as location-based Skyline. This chapter described algorithms to evaluate location-based Skyline queries delimited by a search area around the user with information extraction and user's position change. In such queries, it is considered that the data can be dynamic, i.e., change over time.

To answer this kind of queries, four algorithms were proposed which are based on an M-Tree index and the Divide & Conquer principle. The M-tree is a multidimensional index and it was selected because its representation in circular shape resembles the user's search area which encloses the regions that are within the search area.

The first solution is a naive one which performs an exhaustive search merging Skyline of each region in the M-tree index structure. The second solution prunes regions in the M-tree index by mean of a pruning criterion. This pruning criterion established a threshold which allows to discard regions in the M-tree index structure. The third and fourth solutions return approximate answers and take into consideration the previous state, i.e., the previous user's location and Skyline. The third solution avoids recalculate Skyline in those regions of the multidimensional index structure where were found Skyline points and the fourth solution prevents recomputed any region that was previously visited by the tourist.

Additionally, we have empirically studied the four solutions in terms of performance and response quality. According to the experimental study, APA+ had the best runtime. However, APA is the most precise and complete. Also, regarding the number of comparisons, the pruning based algorithms had a good behavior because the pruning criterion was able to reduce the number of comparisons performed during the calculation of the Skyline set. Moreover, in the experimental study, it was observed that an algorithm with the best answer quality is the lowest algorithm while the fastest algorithm has to be paid a high cost at the level of precision and recall. Therefore, the user must decide between answer quality and response time of the solutions. The user's decision is to choice between a solution faster and less precise against a solution slower, precise and complete.

REFERENCES

Balke, W. T., Güntzer, U., & Zheng, J. X. (2004). Efficient distributed skylining for web information systems. In *Proceedings of the Extending Database Technology (EDBT)* (pp. 256-273). Heraklion, Greece: Springer-Verlag. doi:10.1007/978-3-540-24741-8_16

Batko, M., Novak, D., & Zezula, P. (2007). MESSIF: Metric Similarity Search Implementation Framework. In *Proceedings of the 1st international conference on Digital libraries: research and development* (pp 1-10). Berlin: Springer-Verlag.

Bentley, J., Kung, H. T., Schkolnick, M., & Thompson, C. D. (1978). On the average number of maxima in a set of vectors and applications. *Journal of the ACM, 25*(4), 536–543. doi:10.1145/322092.322095

Börzsönyi, S., Kossmann, D., & Stocker, K. (2001). The skyline operator. In *Proceedings of the 17th International Conference on Data Engineering (ICDE)* (pp. 421–430). Washington, DC: IEEE Computer Society. doi:10.1109/ICDE.2001.914855

Burago, D., Burago, Y. D., & Ivanov, S. (2001). *A Course in Metric Geometry*. American Mathematical Society. doi:10.1090/gsm/033

Chomicki, J., Godfrey, P., Gryz, J., & Liang, D. (2003). Skyline with presorting. In *Proceedings of the 19th International Conference on Data Engineering (ICDE)* (pp.717-719). Bangalore, India: IEEE Computer Society.

Ciaccia, P., Patella, M., & Zezula, P. (1997). M-tree: An Efficient Access Method for Similarity Search in Metric Spaces. In *Proceeding of the 23rd International Conference on Very Large Data Bases (VLDB)* (pp. 426-435). San Francisco, CA: Morgan Kaufmann Publishers Inc.

Cong, G., Jensen, C. S., & Wu, D. (2009). Efficient Retrieval of the Top-k Most Relevant Spatial Web Objects. *PVLDB, 2*(1), 337–348.

Edgewall Software. (2007). *M-Tree Download*. Retrieved May 5, 2014, from http://mufin.fi.muni.cz/trac/mtree/wiki/download

Godfrey, P., Shipley, R., & Gryz, J. (2005). Maximal vector computation in large data sets. In *Proceedings of the 31st International Conference on Very Large Data Bases (VLDB)* (pp. 229-240). Trondheim, Norway: ACM.

Hobbs, J., & Riloff, E. (2010). Information Extraction. In Handbook of Natural Language Processing (2nd ed.). Chapman & Hall/CRC Press, Taylor & Francis Group.

Huang, Z., Jensen, C. S., Lu, H., & Ooi, B. C. H. (2006). Skyline Queries Against Mobile Lightweight Devices in MANETs. In *Proceeding of the International Conference on Data Engineering (ICDE)* (pp. 66-77). Atlanta, GA: IEEE Computer Society. doi:10.1109/ICDE.2006.142

Kodama, K., Iijima, Y., Guo, X., & Ishikawa, Y. (2009). Skyline queries based on user locations and preferences for making location-based recommendations. In *Proceedings of the International Workshop on Location Based Social Networks* (pp. 9-16). New York, NY: ACM. doi:10.1145/1629890.1629893

Kossmann, D., Ramsak, F., & Rost, S. (2002). Shooting stars in the sky: An online algorithm for skyline queries. In *Proceedings of the 28th International Conference on Very Large Data Bases (VLDB)* (pp. 275-286). Hong Kong, China: Endowment. doi:10.1016/B978-155860869-6/50032-9

Kung, H. T., Luccio, F., & Preparata, F. P. (1975). On Finding the Maxima of a Set of Vectors. *Journal of the ACM, 22*(4), 469–476. doi:10.1145/321906.321910

Kushmerick, N., Weld, D. S., & Doorenbos, R. (1997). Wrapper Induction for Information Extraction. In *Proceedings of the Fifteenth International Joint Conference on Artificial Intelligence (IJCAI)*. Nagoya, Japan: Morgan Kaufmann.

Lo, E., Yip, K., Lin, K.-I., & Cheung, D. (2006). Progressive Skylining over Web-Accessible Database. *Journal of Data and Knowledge Engineering, 7*(2), 122–147. doi:10.1016/j.datak.2005.04.003

Papadias, D., Tao, Y., Fu, G., & Seeger, B. (2005). Progressive skyline computation in database systems. *ACM Transactions on Database Systems, 30*(1), 41–82. doi:10.1145/1061318.1061320

Powers, D. M. W. (2007/2011). Evaluation: From Precision, Recall and F-Factor to ROC, Informedness, Markedness& Correlation. *Journal of Machine Learning Technologies, 2*(1), 37–63.

Qiang, P., Lbath, A., & Daqing, H. (2012). Location based recommendation for mobile users using language model and skyline query. The International Journal of Information Technology and Computer Science, 4(10), 19-28.

Sedmidubsky, J., Dohnal, V., & Zezula, P. (2008). *M-tree: Metric tree*. Retrieved May 5, 2014, from http://disa.fi.muni.cz/trac/mtree/

Sharifzadeh, M., & Shahabi, C. (2006). The spatial skyline queries. In *Proceedings of the 32nd International Conference on Very Large Data Bases (VLDB)* (pp. 751-762). VLDB Endowment.

Tan, K., Eng, P., & Ooi, B. (2001). Efficient progressive skyline computation. In *Proceedings of the 27th International Conference on Very Large Data Bases (VLDB)* (pp. 301-310). San Francisco, CA: Morgan Kaufmann Publishers Inc.

Zheng, B., Lee, K., & Lee, W.-C. (2008). Location-dependent skyline query. In *Proceedings of the 9th International Conference on Mobile Data Management (MDM)* (pp. 148 -155). Beijing, China: IEEE doi:10.1109/MDM.2008.14

ADDITIONAL READING

Bogh, K., Assent, I., & Magnani, M. (2013). Efficient GPU-based skyline computation. In *Proceedings of the Ninth International Workshop on Data Management on New Hardware*. (pp. 1-5). New York, USA: ACM. doi:10.1145/2485278.2485283

Chester, S., Mortensen, M. L., & Assent, I. (2014). On the Suitability of Skyline Queries for Data Exploration. In *Proceedings of the Workshops of the EDBT/ICDT 2014 Joint Conference*. (pp. 161-166). Athens, Greece: CEUR-WS.org.

El-Dawy, E., Mokhtar, H., & El-Bastawissy, A. (2012). Directional skyline queries. In *Proceedings of the Third International Conference on Data and Knowledge Engineering (ICDKE)*. (pp. 15-28). Fujian, China: Springer.

Gupta, M., Gao, J., Yan, X., Cam, H., & Han, J. (2014). Top-K interesting subgraph discovery in information networks. In *Proceedings of the 30th International Conference on Data Engineering (ICDE)*. (pp. 820-831). Chicago, USA: IEEE. doi:10.1109/ICDE.2014.6816703

Khemmarat, S., & Gao, L. (2014). Fast top-k path-based relevance query on massive graphs. In *Proceedings of the 30th International Conference on Data Engineering (ICDE)*. (pp. 316-327). Chicago, USA: IEEE. doi:10.1109/ICDE.2014.6816661

Lin, Q., Zhang, Y., Zhang, W., & Li, A. (2012).General spatial skyline operator. In *Proceedings of the 17th International Conference on Database Systems for Advanced Applications (DASFAA)*. (pp. 494-508). Berlin, Heidelberg: Springer-Verlag. doi:10.1007/978-3-642-29038-1_36

Lofi, C., El Maarry, B., & Balke, W.-T. (2013). Skyline queries in crowd-enabled databases. In *Proceedings of the Joint 2013 EDBT/ICDT Conferences*. (pp. 465-476). Genoa, Italy: ACM. doi:10.1145/2452376.2452431

Magnani, M., & Assent, I. (2013). From stars to galaxies: skyline queries on aggregate data. In *Proceedings of the Joint 2013 EDBT/ICDT Conferences*. (pp. 477-488). Genoa, Italy: ACM. doi:10.1145/2452376.2452432

Magnani, M., Assent, I., Hornbæk, K., Jakobsen, M., & Larsen, K. (2013). SkyView: A User Evaluation of the Skyline Operator. In *Proceedings of the 22Nd ACM International Conference on Information & Knowledge Management*. (pp. 2249-2254). New York, USA: ACM.

Sheng, C., & Tao, Y. (2011). On finding skylines in external memory. In *Proceedings of the Thirtieth ACM SIGMOD-SIGACT-SIGART Symposium on Principles of Database Systems*. (pp. 107-116). Athens, Greece: ACM.

Valkanas, G., Papadopoulos, A., & Gunopulos, D. (2013). SkyDiver: a framework for skyline diversification. In *Proceedings of the Joint 2013 EDBT/ICDT Conferences*. (pp. 406-417). Genoa, Italy: ACM. doi:10.1145/2452376.2452424

You, G.-W., Lee, M.-W., Im, H., & Hwang, S.-W. (2013). The Farthest Spatial Skyline Queries. *Information Systems*, *38*(3), 286–301. doi:10.1016/j.is.2012.10.001

Yu, A., Agarwal, P. K., & Yang, J. (2014). Top-k preferences in high dimensions. In *Proceedings of the 30th International Conference on Data Engineering (ICDE)*. (pp. 748-759). Chicago, USA: IEEE.

KEY TERMS AND DEFINITIONS

Divide and Conquer: It is an algorithm design paradigm that recursively breaks down a problem into simpler sub-problems. The original problem is solved as combination of these sub-problems.

Dominance: An object a dominates another object b if and only if a is better than or equal to b on all dimensions of a multidimensional function and a is better than b on at least onlock e dimension.

M-Tree: It is a multidimensional index structure which stores spatial data.

Precision and Recall (P&R): It is a measure that allows knowing how good or bad is a solution in terms of effectiveness and completeness for a given set.

Skyline Techniques: Set of strategies for identifying incomparable elements that are characterized by multi-dimensional properties.

Skyline: Set of non-dominated objects.

Web Wrapper: It is a part of the program that allows to a semi-structured web data source be consulted as if it was a common database.

Section 3

Chapter 13
Querying of Time Series for Big Data Analytics

Vasileios Zois
University of Southern California, USA

Charalampos Chelmis
University of Southern California, USA

Viktor K. Prasanna
University of Southern California, USA

ABSTRACT

Time series data emerge naturally in many fields of applied sciences and engineering including but not limited to statistics, signal processing, mathematical finance, weather and power consumption forecasting. Although time series data have been well studied in the past, they still present a challenge to the scientific community. Advanced operations such as classification, segmentation, prediction, anomaly detection and motif discovery are very useful especially for machine learning as well as other scientific fields. The advent of Big Data in almost every scientific domain motivates us to provide an in-depth study of the state of the art approaches associated with techniques for efficient querying of time series. This chapters aims at providing a comprehensive review of the existing solutions related to time series representation, processing, indexing and querying operations.

INTRODUCTION

Time series data refer to a collection of data points which represent the evolution or behavior of a specific entity in time. Examples include, but are not limited to consumption information from distinct customers on a power grid, stock price closing values (Bao, 2008), patient vital signs as monitored by special equipment and more recently tweets, blog posts. A time series is defined as a sequence of pair $\left[\left(s_1, t_1\right), \left(s_2, t_2\right) \ldots \left(s_k, t_k\right)\right]$ where s_i is a data point (value) and t_i is the timestamp at which s_i is recorded. Timestamps can be omitted for simplicity, in which case a time series object S is described by the vector $\left[s_1, s_2 \ldots s_k\right]$ where s_j is the observed value of the j-th time interval. Values are assumed to

DOI: 10.4018/978-1-4666-8767-7.ch013

be presented in the same order as they are observed, so for $i < j$, s_i appears before s_j in the corresponding vector. The length of the time interval between consecutive values can be fixed or variable. This definition refers to univariate time series (Chatfield, 2013). Multivariate time series (Box, Jenkins, & Reinsel, 2013), (Wang, Zhu, Li, Wan, & Zhang, 2014) refers to a sequence of observations with multiple value at every given point in time. Time series graphs refer to snapshots of evolving/temporal/dynamic graphs (Park, Priebe, & Youssef, 2013), (Wang, Tang, Park, & Priebe, 2014), (Yan & Eidenbenz, 2014). A collection of these snapshots are what constitute the time series object. This chapter focuses on univariate or multivariate time series and queries related to them. Graph time series are mentioned for completeness and will be mentioned only on a high level as part of the latter developments in the field. Difference in sampling rates can make it difficult for distinct time series objects to be compared. Interpolation is a standard preprocessing operation used to fill gaps between intervals induced either by incompatible sampling rates or missing values. Interpolation techniques are not discussed in this chapter but are mentioned for completeness as part of time series workflows. Other common preprocessing steps include time series normalization. Normalization is performed by eliminating the amplitude value through subtracting the mean and dividing with the standard deviation (Loh, Kim, & Whang, 2000).

Operations on time series data fall into two major categories: analysis and forecasting. Common operations include classification (Kamath, Lin, & De Jong, 2014), clustering (Euán, Ortega, & Alvarez-Esteban, 2014), motif discovery (Mueen, 2014), query by content (Esling & Agon, 2013). Efficient implementation of such operations presents a great challenge to researchers who need to ensure high throughput and consistent availability of data (Loboz, Smyl, & Nath, 2010). As time series data are inherently large to be processed entirely in memory there is a need for solutions that consider and minimize the effect of secondary memory access. Sliding window is commonly used to group fixed-size windows so that it can be processed in memory incrementally. However, this technique can increase the number of random I/Os if data are appropriately (Anderson, Arlitt, Morrey III, & Veitch, 2009), which affects the overall execution time which has been studied extensively over the years (Ding, Trajcevski, Scheuermann, Wang, & Keogh, 2008). Time series indexing can be effectively used for shape based matching operations which are common for many of the complex analytics operations that are mentioned above. Although indexing improves access to the underlying data it does not provide an easy to use management scheme. It is necessary for scientists to have an easy access to services that support real time querying and gathering of information from different sources. This can be achieved by a definition of some kind of a management system along with a query language suitable for the needs of a common user.

TIME SERIES AS BIG DATA

The advent of Big Data and the emergence of the Internet of Things, combined with the emerging applications on cyber-physical systems (Baheti & Gill, 2011) have resulted in an unprecedented volume of time series data, which is updated at staggering speeds. As a consequence, a dramatically increasing amount of interest in querying mining and analysis of time series data has resulted in a rich literature for indexing, search classification, clustering, predictive modeling, visualization, summarization and approximation. Time series data display all the characteristics that describe Big Data and are related to volume, velocity, variety, veracity and volatility of data (Russom, 2011). The large number of individual instances consisting of thousand data points each are what constitutes the volume of time series data (Ding, Wang, Dang, Fu, Zhang, & Zhang, 2015). It presents a major challenge to analytics techniques resulting from the inability of conventional systems to process them in real time. Specialized time series management systems have been proposed to overcome this challenge (Buevich, Wright, Sargent, & Rowe, 2013). Velocity refers to the speed at which new data is generated. There are numerous examples of time series data that present high changing rates including but not limited to data generated from sensors (Haber, Thomik, & Faisal, 2014), financial data (Bao, 2008) and times series graphs (Simmhan, Wickramaarachchi, Ravi, Raghavendra, & Prasanna, 2014). Variety refers to the structural heterogeneity of data. In the context of time series this appears in the form of different sampling rates, missing or incorrect values but also different types of data such as audio or video (Gandomi & Haider, 2015). This dimension induces an extra complexity to the analysis requiring often specialized algorithms to extract valuable information from the data. The veracity of data refers to the quality of the information which is usually tied to their implicit business value (Aman, Chelmis, & Prasanna, 2014). It is an important property which is usually overlooked based on the assumption that the gathered data are accurate. However, missing, incomplete or inaccurate data greatly affects the correctness of the analysis techniques (Aman, Chelmis, & Prasanna, 2014). Preprocessing of the data is used to tackle veracity before any analysis technique is applied. There are numerous ways to tackle veracity including simple methods such as interpolation and duplicate elimination or more complex methods such as data fusion (Lukoianova & Rubin, 2014) or use of an influence model (Aman, Chelmis, & Prasanna, 2014). Finally, Big Data volatility refers to how long the data are relevant to the current analysis (Normandeau, 2013). Time series are inherently time dependent data the period for which they are valid is often based on the application. For example consumption prediction often requires information that is gathered over a prolonged period of time referred to as historic data. In contrast, streaming applications that are used for event monitoring (Goldschmidt, Jansen, Koziolek, Doppelhamer, & Breivold, 2014) often utilize a window of fixed size for their analysis (O'Connor, Balasubramanyan, Routledge, & Smith, 2010). Data outside the specified window are considered to be irrelevant thus volatile for the current analysis.

For the above reasons, time series data is in fact Big Data. Specific algorithms to enable common analysis operations such as querying, classification, predictive modeling, visualization, summarization and approximation are required. This chapter covers in detail the different aspects of time series querying including transformation and indexing techniques, various distance functions and their usability, abstract languages for time series, types of queries that are useful to time series analysis and time series managements systems. In Table 1 an overview of the research work on the different components that are necessary for time series querying is depicted.

TIME SERIES REPRESENTATION

A major concern when managing time series data is the support of efficient storage and retrieval operations. A single time series object usually consists of several hundred to thousands of values (Chatfield, The analysis of time series: an introduction, 2013). This is a direct result of the sampling rate at which data are gathered, which overall increases the required storage space. Secondary memory is often used to retain the gathered data which need to be accessed directly for query answering. For complex analytics multiple passes over the data are necessary adding to the overall processing time making it highly inefficient to use the secondary memory directly. Motivated by this issue several representation

Table 1. Summarization of research work on the major research components as described in the following sections.[1]

Representation		Indexing	Distance Functions			Time Series Management	
Discrete Transformations	Data-Centric Transformations		Static	Elastic	Pattern Based	Query Languages	Storage
(Faloutsos, 1994)	(Yi, 2000), (Keogh, 2001)	(Guttman, 1984), (Sellis, 1987), (Beckmann, 1990)	(Yi & Faloutsos, 2000)	(Chen & Ng, 2004)	(Aßfalg, 2006)	(Psaila, 1995)	(Anderson, 2009)
(Korn, 1997)	(Golyandina, 2013)	(Lin, 1994)		(Chen, 2005)	(Chen, Nascimento, 2007)	(Motakis, 1997)	(Loboz, 2010)
(Chan, 2003)	(Lin, 2007), (Shieh, 2008), (Camerra, 2014)	(White D. A., 1996), (Kurniawati 1997)		(Müller, 2007)	(Ye & Keogh, 2009)	(Perng, 1999)	(Weigel, 2010)
(Cai, 2004)		(Li, Moon, 2004)			(Schäfer, 2014)	(Sadri, 2001)	(Melnik, 2010)
		(Assent, 2008)				(Bai, 2005)	(Deri, 2012), (Sigoure, 2012)
		(Li, 2014)				(Arasu, 2006)	(Lamb, 2012)
		(Liu, et al., 2014)				(Imamura, 2012)	(Buevich, 2013)

techniques have been proposed, aiming at minimizing the number of I/Os leveraging the main memory for processing thus reducing the overall execution time. Representation methods are often coupled with multidimensional data structures, which are being used to prune the search space for relevant objects thus minimizing the number of I/Os (Ding, Trajcevski, Scheuermann, Wang, & Keogh, 2008). Altering the representation of the original time series object is pivotal to efficient indexing (Ding, Trajcevski, Scheuermann, Wang, & Keogh, 2008). Multidimensional data structures often suffer from the so called dimensionality curse when attempting to manage high dimensional data such as time series data. Dimensionality curse refer to the series of phenomena arising from handling data of immense dimensions. In the context of data structures the dimensionality curse affects their performance resulting in access complexity which is equivalent to linear scan.

A common method to deal with dimensionality curse is to perform dimensionality reduction as in the case of General Multimedia Indexing algorithm (GEMINI). GEMINI relies on extracting a limited number of features from a time series object, aiming at preserving its general characteristics which are then used to identify similarities with a submitted query. Extracting features is achieved by a user defined function which corresponds to a transformation of the original object. The transformation coefficients are the derived features used to create an index in main memory. Time series objects resulting from this method can be seen as being defined in a new space referred to as feature space. The principle idea behind this procedure is that objects are represented in low dimensional space which can be efficiently indexed by existing data structures. The choice of transformation can greatly affect the performance of this method, as the approximation of the original object is correlated to the number of I/Os which are necessary for retrieval of relevant objects to the specified query.

A natural question arises that is related to the selection of a suitable transformation. The quality of a transformation is typically measured as a function of the reconstruction error (Keogh, Chakrabarti, Pazzani, & Mehrotra, 2001). A transformation is good, if it achieves a minimal reconstruction error of the original object retaining at most M features. This presents a good metric for comparing different transformation techniques as it can give an initial estimation of the pruning power of the transformation (Keogh, Chakrabarti, Pazzani, & Mehrotra, 2001). The most important property to which a transformation needs to adhere to is the so called lower bounding lemma (Faloutsos, Ranganathan, & Manolopoulos, 1994). This property states that the distance between two objects in the feature space needs to lower bound the distance of these objects in the original space (Faloutsos, Ranganathan, & Manolopoulos, 1994). For example, given two time series objects S and Q and their corresponding feature vectors $F(S), F(Q)$ that contain the coefficients of a transformation F, the following inequality must hold:

$$(1)\, D_F\big(F(S), F(Q)\big) \le D_T(S, Q).$$

Here D_F and D_T denote the distance metrics used in the feature and the original space respectively. Inequality (1) provides a framework for comparing transformations, as a tighter bound indicates a better approximation of the original object thus reducing the number of false positives (Keogh, Chakrabarti, Pazzani, & Mehrotra, 2001). An important implication of equation (1) is that transformations obeying this inequality do not produce any false negatives (Faloutsos, Ranganathan, & Manolopoulos, 1994). Specifically, given a query time series Q and a tolerance value ε, it can be ensured that all the time series with distance at most ε from Q are going to be retrieved, only by consulting the indexing structure that holds the transformed objects. False positives are a result of underestimating the true distance between any two time series objects since only their approximate form is considered. The number of false positives can be small for transformations that have a tight lower bound. In fact, the approximation accuracy increases with the number of retained features. However, it is usually the case to retain a small number of features, a practice which can be also used as a quality measure for different transformations that achieve a low reconstruction error with the minimal number of features retained. A tradeoff is usually observed between the number of retained features, resulting in increased dimensions, and the accuracy of the retrieval process where an overhead is induced by the post-processing step which is meant to discard false positives.

Some desirable properties of an efficient indexing schema based on the GEMINI algorithm are presented in (Faloutsos, Ranganathan, & Manolopoulos, 1994) and include efficient insertion and deletion of new data as well as support of various length queries. Support for multiple distance measures is also highlighted in (Keogh, Chakrabarti, Pazzani, & Mehrotra, 2001). In the following section some existing transformation techniques are reviewed, focusing on their ability to support the aforementioned properties. In Figure 1, the two major transformation categories are depicted.

Discrete Transformations

In this section, an in depth review of representation techniques that are classified under the category of discrete transformations are. Many of these techniques are inspired from the field of signal processing.

Figure 1. Categories of representation techniques for time series data

> - **Discrete Transformations**
>   - Discrete Fourier Transformation (DFT)
>   - Discrete Cosine Transformation (DCT)
>   - Chebysev Polynomials (CP)
>   - Discrete Wavelet Transformation (DWT)
> - **Data-Centric Transformations**
>   - Singular Value Decomposition (SVD)
>   - Principle Component Analysis (PCA)
>   - Piecewise Linear Approximation (PLA)
>   - Piecewise Aggregate Approximation (PAA)
>   - Adaptive Piecewise Constant Approximation (APCA)
>   - Symbolic Aggregate approXimation (SAX)

Discrete Fourier Transformation (DFT) used as a representation method for time series data, was introduced in (Faloutsos, Ranganathan, & Manolopoulos, 1994). The authors proposed using few DFT coefficients which were produced by the original time series object to create an index. Intuitively, the first few coefficients preserve well the characteristics of a signal, making this method ideal for dimensionality reduction. DTF can also be computed efficiently using the Fast Fourier Transformation (FFT), which requires $O\left(nlogn\right)$ steps, where n the number of observations in a time series object is. Finally, it can be proven that the transformation obeys the lower bounding lemma which is based on Parseval's theorem (Oppenheim & Schafer, 1975). DFT preserves the energy of a signal suggesting there is a 1-to-1 mapping of the generated coefficients to the original values of a time series object. Considering also that DFT is a linear transformation, the Euclidean Distance (ED) between two time series object is retained, i.e., $ED\left(x,y\right)=ED\left(X,Y\right)$, where x,y are two time series and X,Y their corresponding DFT. Retaining a larger number of Fourier coefficients results in a better approximation of the original object, however, retaining too much information has an inverse effect on the efficiency of indexing. Typically 2-3 coefficients are enough for indexing purposes (Agrawal, Faloutsos, & Swami, 1993). It should be noted that DFT works best for time series data that present some periodic behavior (Ding, Trajcevski, Scheuermann, Wang, & Keogh, 2008). Same is true for other spectral dimensionality reduction techniques, including Discrete Cosine Transformation (DCT) (Korn, Jagadish, & Faloutsos, 1997) and Chebysev Polynomials (CP) (Cai & Ng, 2004).

Discrete Wavelet Transformation (DWT) is another dimensionality reduction technique inspired from the field of signal processing. It was first proposed as an indexing schema in (Chan, Fu, & Yu, 2003). An important property of DWT is that it can create multi-resolution representations of a signal based on time frequency localization, a technique that leverages a signal's local characteristics in time. Specifically in contrast to DFT which retains information about the global shape of a time series object, DWT retains local information, which typically encodes a coarse approximation of the original sequence. Additionally the DWT can be computed in linear time as opposed to DFT which requires $O\left(nlogn\right)$ steps (Chan, Fu, & Yu, 2003).

Data-Centric Transformations

An important class of dimensionality reduction techniques focuses on adapting to data specific characteristics in order to provide a more accurate approximation of the original object. Aiming at minimizing the number of features retained, these techniques achieve a good performance when used to index non-periodic time series. In contrast, their efficiency drops for periodic data as the limited number of coefficients combined with the way they are extracted (e.g., sampling rate) result in an inaccurate approximation of the original series.

Singular Value Decomposition (SVD) (Korn, Jagadish, & Faloutsos, 1997) overcomes the limitations of spectral methods and can be applied to sequences of arbitrary size. Even though SVD can achieve optimal representation, it is computationally expensive and needs to be recomputed with the addition of new time series objects. However, there has been some work on approximately constructing the index to accommodate insertions more efficiently (Golyandina & Zhigljavsky, 2013).SVD along with Principle Component Analysis (PCA) can be used to achieve optimal representation, although their applicability is limited by their computational complexity and their inability to efficiently transform data in main memory.

Piecewise Aggregate Approximation (PAA) is a dimensionality reduction method introduced in (Yi & Faloutsos, 2000), (Keogh, Chakrabarti, Pazzani, & Mehrotra, 2001). PAA resembles a Haar transform in that it makes use of the average values among consecutive intervals. The main difference is that it uses a stable window that divides the time series in equal sized frames and retains the average value for each frame. PAA lower bounds the ED, it has linear complexity in the size of the input, and presents a good approximation for bursty data (Wang, Mueen, Ding, Trajcevski, Scheuermann, & Keogh, 2013). In contrast to other approaches, PAA can support queries of diverse lengths, leveraging a dedicated distance function defined over the feature space (Keogh, Chakrabarti, Pazzani, & Mehrotra, 2001).

An extension of PAA, called *Adaptive Piecewise Constant Approximation (APCA)* (Keogh, Chakrabarti, Pazzani, & Mehrotra, 2001), aimed at minimizing the reconstruction error of the original time series object. Similar to PAA, a time series object is divided into disjoint segments which can be of variable width. According to APCA, the highly variable parts of a time series should be described using more segments as opposed to parts of low variance. Specifically, APCA retains two quantities: the average value and the right endpoint of a segment. Optimal creation of segments is costly, requiring the use of dynamic programming (Pavlidis, 1973). When an optimal solution is not required, a heuristic can be used instead to determine the size and number of segments. Performing a wavelet compression first and then converting the solution back to the APCA representation results in an algorithm with only a fraction of the computation cost of the dynamic programming approach (Keogh, Chakrabarti, Pazzani, & Mehrotra, 2001).

Piecewise Linear Approximation (PLA) approximates a time series object with a set of straight lines while minimizing the overall reconstruction error (Chen Q., Chen, Lian, Liu, & Yu, 2007).The use of PLA as an indexing transformation requires the definition of a distance metric that obeys the lower bounding lemma (Chen Q., Chen, Lian, Liu, & Yu, 2007). PLA retains two coefficients for each line segment which are used to describe the equation of the corresponding line. Indexing with PLA is showed to achieve a higher pruning power than APCA and CP on real and synthetic data (Chen Q., Chen, Lian, Liu, & Yu, 2007).

Motivated by existing compression methods, a bitwise representation was proposed which is used to create clipped data from the original time series (Bagnall, 2006). This method supports efficient shape based similarity queries. Clipping or hard limiting is the process of transforming time series to a bitwise representation; 1 describes a point that is above average, 0 otherwise. This technique does not reduce the size of the time series object since it requires the same number of bits. However, it results in objects that can be highly compressed and managed easily using efficient bitwise matching operations. The advantage of using clipped data to represent time series is that there is no need for the definition of extra parameters, as opposed to techniques such as APCA, PAA, and IPLA.

Existing time series representation techniques focus mostly on providing an efficient indexing schema to support query by content. Higher level queries such as classification, summarization, anomaly detection and prediction can be coupled together with simple shape matching queries to provide an answer. However, extending simple matching queries to incorporate these operations is non-trivial. Transformations that discretize continuous values and convert them to alphanumeric characters were introduced to address such challenges.

In (Andre-Jonsson & Badal, 1997), signature files where used as means of representing time series data. There, time series are represented as a set of alphanumeric characters which describe the derivative between consecutive points. Characters are selected based on a predefined alphabet which maps a range of values to specific letters. The attainable space reduction results from the small number of bits that are required to encode the alphabet set. However, accessing the data requires a linear scan of the signature files which is computationally expensive. *Interactive Matching of Patterns with Advanced Constraints in Time-series* (IMPACTS) databases (Huang & Yu, 1999) also maps continues values into discrete symbols. Particularly, the change ratio between consecutive values is mapped to discrete symbols. The values being subjected to this transformation are the minimum and maximum values observed in the equal sized disjoint intervals to which the original time series object is divided. In this work, a suffix tree is utilized to retain the transformed objects. Discretization may affect the way matching is performed, resulting from symbols which are not comparable. Range queries are supported using the aforementioned transformation by relaxing the matching criteria to consider symbols as equals within a specific tolerance. This method can support multi-granular queries, biased similarity queries, vague trend queries, regular expression queries and maximum mismatch queries (Huang & Yu, 1999).

Symbolic Aggregate approXimation (SAX) is a transformation based on the symbolic representation of values in a specific (Lin, Keogh, Wei, & Lonardi, 2007). Symbolic representation coupled with indexing capabilities was achieved through dimensionality reduction on top of which discretization techniques are executed. Initially, PAA is used to extract a certain number of coefficients that describe the characteristics of a time series object. A symbol mapping phase follows, where symbols are assigned to a range of values using a set of breakpoints which are calculated utilizing a Gaussian curve. Two transformed time series can by comparing their symbols (consecutive symbols assigned to neighboring range intervals are considered equal) (Lin, Keogh, Wei, & Lonardi, 2007).

Several variations of SAX, aiming mostly at improving its indexing performance and expanding its use for billions of time series objects have been proposed. Examples include iSAX (Shieh & Keogh, 2008) and iSAX2+ (Camerra, Rakthanmanon, & Keogh, 2014). The resulting word strings are represented with iSAX as integers based on the binary representation of each character created from the breakpoints in regular SAX. Although there can be time series objects that map to words containing characters of different cardinality, the authors prove that it is possible to have a meaningful comparison between them (Shieh & Keogh, 2008). In fact, iSAX deals with this issue by lower bounding the distance between the time series of different cardinality. This is achieved through the expansion of characters with lower cardinality through addition of extra missing bits. Indexing the words resulting from iSAX requires a tree structure which similar to a prefix tree. This structure retains at each level the prefixes of increasing length, with nodes on the leaf level being iSAX words. The disadvantage of this structure is that it is not balanced. iSAX2+ improves on the indexing mechanism to support bulk loading, introducing in the process a balanced data structure that can index the words resulting from iSAX (Camerra, Rakthanmanon, & Keogh, 2014).

DATA STRUCTURES

Representation techniques are often used in combination with multi-dimensional data structures to support efficient querying of time series data. A significant amount of research has been performed on multi-dimensional data structures as well as on the adaptation of existing ones for emerging computational models (e.g., distributed computing, peer-to-peer systems). This section will section provides an overview of related work in this area.

A comprehensive survey of early data structures is presented in (Bentley & Friedman, 1979) as discussed in less detail as follows. Projection creates a sequence of records sorted by a specified attribute. Queries are executed based on a specific attribute which can be found by binary search followed by a brute force search on a smaller list to match the remaining attributes (Bentley & Friedman, 1979). Cells (Bentley & Friedman, 1979) are a technique that divides the space to multiple squares and retain indexes of different granularity (Bentley & Friedman, 1979). During query time each index needs to be referenced in a hierarchical way to detect relevant data. A natural generalization of binary trees is the so called k-d trees which have been used for indexing multidimensional data in main memory (Bentley & Friedman, 1979). Similar to binary trees, a key is used to discriminate between two nodes which are chosen from attributes that present the maximum spread of the sub-collection represented by the corresponding node. The median value of this attribute is used to partition between the left and right subtree. This technique is similar to projection as it utilizes one attribute from n available. Range trees (Bentley & Friedman, 1979) also use the binary tree as main building block. For the 2-dimensional case, range trees are created as a binary tree on a single dimension retaining a sorted array at each node of the second dimension. For more dimensions a multiple sorted lists are used.

The R-tree (Guttman, 1984) was motivated from the need to support efficient insert, delete and access operations. It groups objects using a minimum bounding rectangle (MBR). This procedure recursively creates several tree levels, each of a decreasing size MBR that contains the multidimensional objects. The idea is to retrieve relevant data that can be grouped together and fitted in a single block thus spending only one I/O operation. Intermediate nodes of the R-tree, retain rectangles containing several points grouped together and the leaf nodes contain pointers to specific blocks where objects are stored. Search time is reduced by to minimizing the overlap between MBRs of the same level. In this context, a single node needs to be expanded at each level of the tree in order for relevant objects to be retrieved at the leaf level. However, it is often too expensive to optimally split overflowing nodes in order to create non-overlapping MBRs. Heuristics have been proposed (Brakatsoulas, Pfoser, & Theodoridis, 2002), (Sleit, 2014) to make approximate grouping decisions which on average wield logarithmic search time. However, in the worst case search requires linear time (Srividhya & Lavanya, 2014). R+ trees, an extension to R-trees, were purposed to mend the problems induced from sub-optimally splitting nodes during the insertion of new data (Sellis, Roussopoulos, & Faloutsos, 1987). The main idea is to replicate the children of each node when an overlap is detected, requiring the expansion of a single node with replicated information. In the worst case this technique, can double the required space but search complexity is logarithmic with respect to the input size (Sellis, Roussopoulos, & Faloutsos, 1987). R*-tree, on the other hand aims at minimizing the area of overlapping rectangles while also increasing space coverage. However, the optimality of the grouping procedure is sensitive to the order in which points are inserted (Beckmann, Kriegel, Schneider, & Seeger, 1990). R*-tree enforces a reinsertion policy along with a revised splitting algorithm to achieve better grouping.

The importance of an effective splitting policy for overflowing nodes was recognized early (Kurniawati, Jin, & Shepard, 1997) and was correlated with the inherent performance of the R-tree and its variants. Specifically, the policy that produces the minimum overlap between rectangles while also maximizing their coverage in the multidimensional space can sustain a logarithmic access time independent from the number of insertions and deletions. Suitable splitting policies for R-tree optimizations include (White & Jain, 1996) and (Berchtold, Keim, & Kriegel, 2001). The former presents a method that assumes a global view of the dataset and partitions points recursively based on the dimension with the highest variance. The latter presents a method that attempts to minimize the overlap between rectangles by introducing supernodes. A supernode can sustain more elements than a simple node. It presents a better approach relative to overlapping directory node which would require expanding children nodes that are unrelated to the corresponding query.

The *TV-tree* (Lin, Jagadish, & Faloutsos, 1994) is related to dimensionality reduction and feature extraction techniques. The intuition behind the TV-tree is that data objects consist of discriminative features. Based on this observation objects are represented in a reduced space. The performance of TV-tree depends on the application; it is effective only when dimensions can be ordered by their significance and also if feature vectors exist that allow shifting (i.e., matching of coordinates on ordered feature vectors) of active dimensions (Lin, Jagadish, & Faloutsos, 1994).

Grouping of objects can be achieved by defining hyper-rectangles which are then represented by R-tree nodes. Shapes other than a rectangle can be used to achieve alternative groupings (White D. A., 1996). The SS-tree partitions multidimensional points into groups using hyper-spheres. The SS-tree structure has better performance on nearest neighbor queries (NN) since it divides the space into short diameter regions and it can more effectively support partial matching queries (White D. A., 1996). A variation of the SS-tree, the SR-tree (Katayama, 1997), aims at creating partitions of points utilizing the intersection between rectangles similar to those defined in R-trees, and spheres which are utilized by SS-trees. The performance of the SR-tree was evaluated in comparison with the SS-tree and showed greater pruning capabilities as well as a decreased complexity on the insertion operations (Katayama, 1997).

Recent advances on multi-dimensional data structures for time series data include (Li, Moon, & Lopez, 2004), (Assent, Krieger, Afschari, & Seidl, 2008). The former work introduces the concept of *Skyline Bounding Rectangles (SBR)* which are used similarly to MBRs to group multidimensional objects together. SBRs are free of internal overlap as they are defined using two skyline bounds (upper and lower bound) and two vertical lines between the skylines at the start and end time point. Since, defined skylines are as large as the indexed time series data, a dimensionality reduction technique is necessary to reduce the space requirements of the resulting data structure (Li, Moon, & Lopez, 2004). Consequently, the pruning power of the index is affected by the tightness of the lower bound introduced by the selected dimensionality reduction method. The TS-tree data structure (Assent, Krieger, Afschari, & Seidl, 2008) is a B-tree variant aiming at the reduction or even the elimination of the overlap between distinct subtrees. This is achieved using separators, which are similar to B-tree keys indicating the range of values residing in the children nodes. It further uses symbolic representation for dimensionality reduction. In this case, the leaves of the tree contain groups of time series with values less or more than the separator key respectively. This method is not very effective with continuous time series (Assent, Krieger, Afschari, & Seidl, 2008) therefore quantizing time series based on a fixed alphabet using existing dimensionality reduction techniques (e.g., SAX) can be beneficial in this case. As before the pruning power of the defined index is related to the representation technique being used.

As distributed systems are becoming more predominant in providing solutions for data intensive applications (Zhao, et al., 2014), there is an increasing need in successfully migrating existing data structures or inventing new ones to enable high throughput operations. Distributed systems owe their success to efficient data partitioning mechanisms that enable parallel read and write operations to reduce the latency of insert, update and retrieve operations. Solutions aiming at increasing the availability of data for concurrent complex queries have been proposed (Li, Ooi, Özsu, & Wu, 2014). Range-Queriable Data Structure (RAQ) (Nazerzadeh & Ghodsi, 2005) is an example of distributed data structure supporting range queries on multi-dimensional data. It utilizes a partition tree which divides the k-dimensional space into partitions retained in the nodes of the tree. Each leaf node contains a single data point, and internal nodes refer to the points contained by their children nodes. The partition tree is employed on top of network nodes, which are responsible for a certain group of data points. Each network node retains links to other nodes based on the structure of the partition tree. This enables forwarding of query requests to nodes that have the relevant data.

Recently, the *DGFIndex* (Liu, et al., 2014) was proposed. DGFIndex is motivated by Smart Grid, an emerging cyber-physical system. In Smart Grid, monitoring systems need to handle massive amounts of multi-dimensional data (e.g., time series of electricity consumption data) utilizing data warehousing systems such as Hive (Thusoo, et al., 2009). In the context of Smart Grid, it is imperative to create a multidimensional index structure that is at the same time small and provides fast access to the stored data (Liu, et al., 2014). DGFIndex was designed utilizes grid files to split the data space in Grid File Units (GFUs) which consist of a GFUKey and GFUValue. GFUkey is a concatenation of the left lower coordinates of each dimension for the specified region represented. GFUValue is a pointer in the split containing rows that fall into the given region as well as certain pre-computed aggregate functions (e.g., max, min, sum) which can be defined dynamically. Defined aggregate functions need to be additive in order for update operations to be fast (Liu, et al., 2014). Constructing the index requires the definition of certain parameters related to the splitting policy (interval size on every dimension) and the number of dimensions that constitute the given index. Although this is a static approach, it is adequate for monitoring operations that consist mostly of aggregation operations.

DISTANCE FUNCTIONS

In this section, the diverse distance functions that have been used extensively in the literature for comparing the similarity between two time series are presented. In Figure 2, an overview of all the distance functions discussed in this section is depicted.

Measuring similarity of time series objects is usually achieved using Lp-norm distances. Commonly used Lp-norms include the Euclidean Distance and Manhattan Distance (Yi & Faloutsos, 2000). They are mostly used for query by content operations but can also be used for complex operations such as motif discovery, classification and clustering operations. Lp-norms are classified as lock-step/static measures (Ding, Trajcevski, Scheuermann, Wang, & Keogh, 2008) because they statically match points of two

Figure 2. Categories of distance functions

- **Static Distance Function**
  - ○ Lp-Norms
- **Elastic Distance Function**
  - ○ Dynamic Time Warping (DTW)
  - ○ Edit Distance on Real Sequence (EDR)
  - ○ Edit Distance with Real Penalty (
- **Pattern Based Distance Function**
  - ○ Spatial Assembly Distance (SpADe)

---

sequences that have the same time index. Although these distance metrics are sufficient for certain applications such as exact matching, they are unable to handle operations like partial matching and phase shift matching (Ding, Trajcevski, Scheuermann, Wang, & Keogh, 2008).

Applications in signal processing and image recognition need to deal with phase shifting to make sense of content queries (Ghias, Logan, Chamberlin, & Smith, 1995). Consider for example applications for which there is no clear understanding of the shape to be matched or cannot be defined. Other situations arise when a query sequence does not match the size of sequences in our database. *Dynamic Time Warping (DTW)* is a distance measure designed to deal with such limitations. It is used to match out of phase sequences that are similar according to the application domain. Detecting movement using a camera or differentiating words in speech recognition, present some applications that can be favored by DTW (Müller, 2007). Given some restrictions such as the maximum size of the warping window, DTW manages to find the optimal warping path. The optimal warping path consists of sets of pairs of data points appearing in the sequences being compared, that are of distance in time less than the maximum warping window which result in the minimum distance value overall. Although DTW performs better than lock-step/static distance measures, it is computationally expensive to use. More importantly, DTW cannot be indexed with the indexing methods that were previously mentioned as it is not a metric[1] (Keogh & Ratanamahatana, 2005).

The popularity of DTW outweighs the difficulties of indexing its outputs. In (Yi, Jagadish, & Faloutsos, 1998) an indexing method was proposed based on the idea of projecting the original time series objects to a k-dimensional space while approximately preserving their distances. A multi-dimensional data structure is then used to prune the search space while retrieving relevant objects based on the DTW metric. Although this technique achieves significant speedup compared to sequential scanning, it can allow false dismissals with low probability (Yi, Jagadish, & Faloutsos, 1998). The first exact[2] indexing mechanism (Kim, Park, & Chu, 2001) retains 4 features (i.e., Fist, Last, Min, Max values of the time series) of the original time series object, which are used to create an index in main memory. The index is utilized to retrieve relevant objects that are of distance ε from a specified query sequence. A post-processing step discards false positives by computing the actual DTW distance. Because of the small number of features utilized, the number of false positives is greatly increased, significantly affecting the overall performance. An improved lower bounding technique was proposed in (Keogh & Ratanamahatana, 2005), inspired by the constraints often imposed on DTW. The warping window is used to define two time series that enclose the original time series object. The enclosing time series are defined as the maximum and minimum value respectively for consecutive values appearing in the warping window. Dimensionality reduction is then performed on the generated time series, which are then used to prune the search space and find suitable matches based on DTW. This method is an improvement over previous approaches as it ensures no false dismissals and provides a tighter bound than previous work, thus improving the overall pruning performance of the index.

DTW is classified as an elastic distance. Edit distance is a distance measure often used to partially match a pair of strings (Ooi, Hadjieleftheriou, Du, & Lu, 2014). It measures the minimum number of operations required to change one string into another. Applying an edit distance measure to time series data requires either representing the original object as a sequence of characters or perform some modification to the distance measure itself. *Edit distance on Real Sequence (EDR)* is a measure based on the latter approach. It was proposed along with several pruning strategies to speed up search on large time series databases (Chen, Ozsu, & Oria, 2005). The main idea behind EDR is relaxing the definition of equality by introducing a matching threshold, denoting the admissible maximum distance between two points in order to be considered equal. EDR is useful in that it can tolerate outliers produce by wrong measurements, missing data or noise by introducing gaps while considering the best candidates for matching subsequences between two objects. However, EDR has a significant drawback as it does not obey the triangular inequality which makes pruning through indexing approximate by allowing false dismissals (Chen, Ozsu, & Oria, 2005). An improvement of EDR is the *Edit distance with Real Penalty (ERP)* (Chen & Ng, 2004). Unlike EDR, ERP obeys the triangular inequality thus making it suitable for indexing ensuring the no-false dismissal property (Waterman, Smith, & Beyer, 1976). ERP evaluates gaps by measuring the distance of the non-gap element from a fixed point g. The L_1 - $norm$ is used to measure the effect of non-gaps on the overall measure. Although the latter requirement is similar to that of DTW, ERP includes the notion of gaps into its definition. ERP, in contrast to EDR, does not require the definition of a matching threshold and is concerned with penalizing appropriately the introduction of a gap.

A distance measure to answer efficiently the so called *threshold queries* was proposed in (Aßfalg, Kriegel, Kroger, Kunath, Pryakhin, & Renz, 2006). Threshold queries retrieve time series objects that consist of similar threshold crossing intervals: intervals in which the observed value crosses a specific threshold τ defined by the user. Applications dependent on threshold queries span fields of molecular biology, environmental analysis and pharmaceutical industry (Aßfalg, Kriegel, Kroger, Kunath, Pryakhin, & Renz, 2006). Finally, a pattern distance measure called *Spatial Assembling Distance (SpADe)* was proposed in (Chen, Nascimento, Ooi, & Tung, 2007). The goal of this distance measure was to allow matching of time series objects which are both shifted and scaled in time or amplitude respectively. It was also proposed as a distance metric tolerant to noise. SpADe detects segments of a time series object that are similar, using a sliding window to describe a local pattern (LP) based on certain features. These features are the position of the pattern in the time series object, the mean amplitude of the data in the LP, the shape signature and the temporal and amplitude scales of LP. The distance of two local patterns is measured using a weighted sum of the absolute differences for the amplitude and shape features. Although weights can be defined by the user fine tuning such parameters when switching domains may be undesirable. Experimental results indicate that the size of the LP is important. SpADe achieves a lower classification error on smooth shapes dataset (Chen, Nascimento, Ooi, & Tung, 2007) and experiments can outperform previous methods (e.g., ED, DTW, EDR) in terms of matching accuracy under time and amplitude shifting, time and amplitude scaling, while being more efficient in terms of computational complexity (Chen, Nascimento, Ooi, & Tung, 2007).

The *Shotgun Distance (SD)* (Schäfer, 2014) aims at aligning vertically and horizontally the time series segments of a query to a query time series. SD is calculated from the aggregation of the minimum ED between each disjoint query window and the sample time series. SD is not a metric because it does not satisfy the triangular inequality. Calculating SD requires the definition of two parameters; the window length and the mean normalization. The mean normalization is considered for the vertical alignment of the query and sample time series. The computational complexity of SD is quadratic in the length of the time series being compared.

Time series *shapelets* (Ye & Keogh, 2009), (Gordon, Hendler, Kontorovich, & Rokach, 2015), (He, Duan, Peng, Jing, Qian, & Wang, 2015), (Ulanova, Begum, & Keogh, 2015) constitute a method for classifying time series by identifying small segments that are particularly discriminative. Computing the shapelet of a time series dataset requires finding a subsequence that can function as an optimal splitting point that divides the time series into two classes (Ye & Keogh, 2009). The optimal splitting point is the distance threshold between a candidate shapelet and the time series in the dataset under examination that provides the maximum information gain (Ye & Keogh, 2009). The information gain for a splitting point is measured using entropy.

QUERY TYPES AND QUERY LANGUAGES

Time series data have been studied extensively in attempt to create abstractions that can be effectively used to enable efficient processing of diverse types of queries. Although the data structures are effective enough to handle different data and execution loads, there is an increasing need to create dedicated tools that are easy to use and have the ability to help users perform high level analytics on the underlying data. Successfully dealing with this issue requires formal query languages that include operators for complex analytics. Alternatively diverse set of distance measures that are capable of handling different types of queries can be utilized. Although the former approach is generic and domain independent it has a major drawback. It is difficult to provide a generic solution. The latter approach needs to retain information for every possible type of query and distinct data structures for different distance functions. In the following sections both of these approaches will be discussed and analyzed in depth. The different types of queries discussed in depth in the next section are sheen in Figure 3.

Figure 3. Different types of queries

- **Content Based Queries**
  - Nearest Neighbors Queries
  - Range Queries
  - Query by Humming
- **Pattern Based Queries**
  - Interval Skyline Queries
  - Threshold Crossing Queries

Types of Queries

K-Nearest Neighbor queries appear frequently in time series analysis. The distance measures discussed in the previous section are often used for such queries. Other important categories of time series queries include range queries (Li, Kim, Govindan, & Hong, 2003), queries by humming (Ghias, Logan, Chamberlin, & Smith, 1995) and interval skyline queries (Jiang, 2009). Range queries refer to operations which are used to retrieve all objects that are similar and within range ε from a query sequence. Queries often are used in sound signal IR application where a query tune is issued against a database of recordings. A query tune is a sound produced for example from a person in applications such as voice recognition and song matching (Ghias, Logan, Chamberlin, & Smith, 1995). The potential difference in frequency and amplitude between the query and time series in the database makes the problem challenging. DTW is often used to address this challenge (Kim & Park, 2013), (Park C. H., 2014). Interval skyline queries follow a similar idea to threshold crossing queries. Their main goal is to find a set of time series objects that are not being dominated by any other object in the database for a certain interval. Online skyline queries on time series data (Jiang, 2009) can be used for applications including finding webpages with the most hits for a given period of time or identifying users with the highest demand peak through consumption monitoring. A time series s is said to dominate another series q for an interval $[i : j]$ if and only if $\forall k \in [i : j], s[k] \geq q[k]$ and $\exists l \in [i : j], s[l] > q[l]$. Answering this type of query is computationally expensive and challenging given a very large database of time sequences. In fact applying skyline computations for online applications is impractical. (Jiang, 2009), proposed to extract the maximum and minimum values for fixed size intervals of each time series object and retain them in a radix tree, which is used during query time answer skyline queries.

Query Languages

A different approach of answering queries over time series data is based on the definition of dedicated query languages. This approach starts with the formal definition of a structured query language which is then utilized by users to provide a high level description of the matching content that needs to be retrieved. In contrast, distance measures have the disadvantage of requiring an explicit description of the corresponding query at fine granularity. Query languages allow users to partially match a high level description of an object which is not fully defined in terms of shape but in terms of behavior as it evolves over time (Psaila & Wimmers Mohamed & It, 1995). The query languages that have been proposed are summarized in Figure 4.

Shape Description Language (SDL), a unified query language model on time series data was proposed by (Psaila & Wimmers Mohamed & It, 1995). SDL consists of an alphabet that describes dedicated shapes and a set of operators that work with the specified alphabet. Alphabet symbols are defined by the user and have 4 properties describing the value of the upper bound, lower bound, as well as the initial value and final value of the shape described. A time sequence can be created by declaring a transition sequence composed of symbols of the specified alphabet. Individual shapes described from transition sequences can be stored and used with defined operators in a similar manner to that of regular expression matching on string objects. The expressive power of SDL lies in the fact that it can support blurry matching, natural language to express complex queries and can be implemented efficiently (Psaila & Wimmers Mohamed & It, 1995). Extending SQL to accommodate sequences of data was introduced in (Seshadri,

Figure 4. Different categories of query languages

- **Relational Query Languages**
  - ○ SEQ Model
- **Shape Description Languages**
  - ○ Shape Description Language (SDL)
- **Aggregation Query Languages**
  - ○ TREPL
- **Streaming Query Languages**
  - ○ SQL/LLP
  - ○ SQL-TS
  - ○ ESL-TS
- **Continuous Query Languages**
  - ○ Continuous Query Language (CQL)
  - ○ Trend Pattern Query Language (TPQL)

Livny, & Ramakrishnan, 1995) with SEQ model. The main advantage of this model is that it is based on the definition of SQL, which is extended for time series data. However, the model is comparatively weak in terms of expressing pattern queries (Seshadri, Livny, & Ramakrishnan, 1995). It relies on the regular definition of data in relational database and defines a set of operators dedicated to handle data sequences. Efficient evaluation of queries is based on the total ordering of records (Seshadri, Livny, & Ramakrishnan, 1995).

The *TREPL* language (Motakis & Zaniolo, 1997) supports aggregation queries. Aggregation queries differ from shape matching queries discussed above. Their usage is motivated from the need of complex event detection over sequences of data. Some examples of aggregation queries include counting aggregates, accumulation and running aggregates, moving window aggregates, temporal grouping aggregates and quantified temporal aggregates (Motakis & Zaniolo, 1997). Unlike Time Series Management Systems (TSMS) which assume a complete view of the data for processing, TREPL operates on active databases; reasoning on data is assumed to be on-line and a response must be available immediately. Important differences between the TSMS and TREPL are irregularity in the generation rate of observations/values/events that are monitored and the difference in response time and storage space needed to produce a decision. The language itself is an extension of EPL (Giuffrida & Zaniolo, 1994), a composite event language for relational databases to detect simple events. TREPL defines rules, i.e., events to be detected. Such rules can be used to define simple events and if combined can be used to detect complex events. Complex events include sequence, conjunction or disjunction of distinct events (Motakis & Zaniolo, 1997). Along with the definition of rules that denote specific events, the language provides a set of operators (e.g, star operator), to implement aggregation queries. TREPL allows users to define their own aggregation queries combining rules with the defined operators.

The *SQL/LPP* (Limited Patience Patterns) (Perng & Parker, 1999) language was developed to provide shape based matching capabilities over streaming data sequences. SQL/LPP, an extension of SQL can efficiently manage data sequences. It relies on incremental computation on individual segments of a sliding window using an attribute queue. Since pattern matching is often implemented utilizing a sliding window on the sequence under consideration, attribute queues can be used to incrementally compute the level of matching and emit an answer when the matching conditions are satisfied. The main building blocks of the SQL/LPP language are elementary pattern functions which can be used to define the pattern specifications or extended by users so as to define custom patterns. SQL/LPP's is clause "BY SEARCHING" enables searching the time series objects given a specific pattern. The "BY SEARCHING" clause can accommodate multiple patterns at a time which are treated as different streams and can be merged to one stream using the SYNC ON clause.

Other SQL extensions for streaming time series data include SQL-TS/ESL-TS (Sadri, 2001), (Bai, Luo, Thakkar, & Zaniolo, 2005) providing additional clauses to define streams and a way to be processed using the "PARTITION BY" clause. Such extensions also support aggregation queries which are either continuous or final, indicating the lifespan of the computation for an answer to be available. Users can define their own aggregates which computation can be blocking or non-blocking. Non-blocking aggregates can be used only on data streams as opposed to blocking which can be both employed over a stream or database table. Finally, other languages for streaming data include the Continuous Query Language (CQL) (Arasu, Babu, & Widom, 2006) and Trend Pattern Query Language (TPQL) (Imamura, Takayama, & Munaka, 2012). CQL is similar to SQL having the ability to support continuous queries over streaming data. TPQL is based on CQL and is mainly used for anomaly detection.

TIME SERIES MANAGEMENT SYSTEMS

A combination of indexing techniques, representation methods and query languages for time series data motivated the design of holistic systems capable of handling time series data. Time Series Management Systems (TSMS), have to provide a diverse set of domain independent operations to the user. However, such operations are inherently complex, computationally expensive and unique in nature to be supported by conventional database systems (i.e RDBMS). For this reason many attempts have been made in the past to formalize the design specifications and implement dedicated TSMSs.

Many of the approaches described can be incorporated into a formal database system. However it is not clear what types of conventional operation are needed since many scientific domains that utilize time series analysis techniques have different needs. A first attempt to formalize the requirements of a TSMS was made in (Dreyer, Dittrich, & Schmidt, 1994). The challenges related to creating a TSMS and the limitations of traditional database systems for time series data-centric applications were discussed in (Dreyer, Dittrich, & Schmidt, 1994). Necessary capabilities of a TSMS re better understood when realizing the different requirements it must fulfill, which are related to structural, functional, data exchange and synchronization requirements (Dreyer, Dittrich, & Schmidt, 1994). Structural requirements refer to the way time series data are maintained and utilized. In many cases a continuous representation is useful allowing primitive operations which involve periodicity transformation (e.g., weekly to daily values), derivation of new time series objects (e.g., data flow measured from stock price closing values) or filling missing values (e.g., interpolation). Also raw data can be grouped together as part of data analytics operations. Functional requirements refer to supported operations such as queries, aggregation function or general types of analytics (e.g., prediction, clustering, and classification). Many analytics tools have been part of specialized packages indicating that there is no need of re-implementing them a TSMS (Dreyer, Dittrich, & Schmidt, 1994). It makes sense for the developed system to play a supportive role providing preprocessing operations (e.g., moving average, transformation and streaming windows) before the final data analysis stage (Dreyer, Dittrich, & Schmidt, 1994). It is imperative to create an interface for updating and analyzing data (Dreyer, Dittrich, & Schmidt, 1994). Lastly, another important requirement is related to data synchronization. The inherit size of a time series objects as well as the rate at which new data are generated, does not only challenge their availability to the users but also complicates real-time decision making (Zois, Frincu, Chelmis, Saeed, & Prasanna, 2014).

Sensor networks are a predominant application domain where time series data are generated in bulk (Buevich, Wright, Sargent, & Rowe, 2013). Systems with the ability to robustly process information in parallel from multiple sources have been proposed in this context. Efficiently processing streaming data without information loss and dealing with the continuous increase of data size are challenges not only limited to the sensor network domain. In many cases time series data are generated from a diverse set of applications including resource monitoring in server farms, fraud detection through browsing history monitoring, user visitation of a webpage for advertisement purposes and similar operations observed from web data (Loboz, Smyl, & Nath, 2010). There is a broad spectrum of systems proposed for managing time series data which aim to tackle the aforementioned challenges. These include DataGarage (Loboz, Smyl, & Nath, 2010), TSDB (Deri, Mainardi, & Fusco, 2012), TSDS (Weigel, Lindholm, Wilson, & Faden, 2010), Dremel (Melnik, Shivakumar, Tolton, & Vassilakis, 2010), Vertica (Lamb, Fuller, Tran, Vandiver, Doshi, & Bear, 2012), Dataseries (Anderson, Arlitt, Morrey III, & Veitch, 2009) and Respawn (Buevich, Wright, Sargent, & Rowe, 2013), OpenTSDB (Sigoure, 2012), InfluxDB and RRDTool (Oetiker, 2005) which will be mentioned for the completeness although not discussed in detail since there is no published work for them.

It has been established that conventional DBMS systems are adequate to handle the sheer volume of time series data (Cattell, 2011). NoSQL systems and techniques have been introduced as a good alternative for managing massive amounts of data. Time series is a special case of data which rely on both efficient storage and complex operations. Hybrid solutions based on RDBMS and NoSQL systems, such as *DataGarage* have been used for resource monitoring in server farms. DataGarage benefits from the organization of data in tables which are subsequently stored to files on top of a distributed file-system (Loboz, Smyl, & Nath, 2010). This leverages the use of a complex querying interface available to SQL systems to the high throughput provided by parallel accessing of files using the Map-Reduce programming model. This hybrid architecture aims at storage efficiency, high query performance and a simple interface for query execution. It is based on the definition of *wide-tables* which are used to retain the corresponding time series data. The basic idea is to create a single table for each resource monitored by the system. As a consequence, the number of *wide-tables* is increases with the number of resources being monitored, making it difficult to handle them efficiently. Storing them as files in a distributed file-system helps alleviate the access overhead. Complex queries are processed in parallel on local instances of an embedded SQL database and results are aggregated.

TSDB (Deri, Mainardi, & Fusco, 2012) has been developed as an improvement of RRDTool (Oetiker, 2005). It organizes data per column in contrast to conventional DBMSs. This enables fast updating in order to consolidate data in the database, an operation which is restricted by the minimum sampling frequency over monitored sources. However, this complicates data retrieval. TSDB uses an indexing schema associating time series objects that are not stale with a unique identifier. The identifier can subsequently be used for efficient access of the whole object. Different compression techniques are utilized to reduce the data footprint in the database (Deri, Mainardi, & Fusco, 2012) to efficiently store, retrieve and update time series objects. Unlike TSDB, TSDS provides an API to easily operate over the time series data hiding any implementation details from the user.

Dremel is introduced as a column oriented database capable of handling trillions of aggregation queries (Melnik, Shivakumar, Tolton, & Vassilakis, 2010). It was developed by Google and works on top of the Google Filesystem (GFS). Similar to TSDB, Dremel organizes data into columns. Nested data are stored into multiple columns which are then traversed through a series of indices. Nested sequences are organized using a multi-level tree which processes queries in a hierarchical way (Melnik, Shivaku-mar, Tolton, & Vassilakis, 2010). Vertica is a similar system created on top of C-store (Stonebraker, et al., 2005) a column oriented datastore which is read rather than write optimized. Vertica considers two distinct workloads: (i) transactional workloads, which are characterized by many queries per second on a handful of tuples and (ii) analytic workloads, which are characterized by small number of requests referring to large portions of underlying data. Tables consisting of distinct columns hold the data, but are organized in *projections* (i.e., sorted groups of attribute subsets). Vertica's design tool called Database Designer (DBD) automatically creates the optimal projections based on a representative query workload that accounts for the load overhead and the space requirements. Lastly, *Dataseries* (Anderson, Arlitt, Morrey III, & Veitch, 2009), is a publicly available time series database. Dataseries assumes a set of records which contain multiple attributes and creates groups of records if they have the same attributes and attribute fields. The database is composed of Dataseries files which contain one or many extents (Melnik, Shivakumar, Tolton, & Vassilakis, 2010).

Respawn (Buevich, Wright, Sargent, & Rowe, 2013) is a time series datastore for event detection over streaming data on sensors networks. Respawn is designed to deal with challenges emerging in sensor networks which include real time updating of time series as well as real time query. It leverages these operations using edge nodes which are responsible for gathering sensor readings from remote sensors and communicating updated data to a cloud node (Buevich, Wright, Sargent, & Rowe, 2013). The cloud node is responsible for handling requests from clients wishing to get information on sensor readings. Data are managed from the Bodytrack Datastore (BTDS) which is a multi-resolution datastore for time series.

CONCLUSION

In this chapter, we reviewed the state of the art in time series analysis and we discussed various query types. We argued that altering the time series representation for the purpose of indexing is pivotal to fast query execution. We argued that complex analytics over time series data remains a major challenge. Time series querying, analysis and data mining is rapidly becoming a Big Data problem as cyber-physical systems and the Internet of Things are becoming the predominant contributors of data increase. The growing diversity of applications that utilize time series data supports the need for developing innovative technologies that will be able to support real time monitoring and decision making. This makes time series analysis and querying an interesting and extensive subject to discuss.

Our extensive literature review has uncovered the different components through which time series querying is made possible. Representation techniques, similarity measures and indexing methods are pivotal to the composition of time series systems that need to enable fast processing and real time decision making. However, the increasing volume and velocity of data from various sources make research in time series management systems of great importance. The contribution of time series management systems is accredited to the formalization of techniques that enable successful gathering, storing and retrieving data through the definition of comprehensive query languages. Although there is a vast amount of research covering both of the aforementioned aspects independently there is little to no work dealing with issues emerging from their combination. Time series management systems are largely based on distributed systems while most representation techniques, indexing methods and similarity measures are designed for centralized processing.

This chapter raises some implicit questions related to feature directions on time series research. We argued that there is no one solution for all problems. Instead we have found specialized solutions tailored to the needs of specific applications spanning various domains. With the advent of cyber-physical systems, we believe that even more specialized solutions will be required to address the need for time series analytics.

REFERENCES

Agrawal, R., Faloutsos, C., & Swami, A. (1993). *Efficient similarity search in sequence databases.* Springer. doi:10.1007/3-540-57301-1_5

Aman, S., Chelmis, C., & Prasanna, V. (2014). Addressing data veracity in big data applications. *Big Data (Big Data), 2014 IEEE International Conference on* (pp. 1--3). IEEE.

Anderson, E., Arlitt, M., Morrey, C. B. III, & Veitch, A. (2009). DataSeries: An efficient, flexible data format for structured serial data. *Operating Systems Review, 43*(1), 70–75. doi:10.1145/1496909.1496923

Andre-Jonsson, H., & Badal, D. Z. (1997). Using signature files for querying time-series data. In *Principles of Data Mining and Knowledge Discovery* (pp. 211–220). Springer. doi:10.1007/3-540-63223-9_120

Arasu, A., Babu, S., & Widom, J. (2006). The CQL continuous query language: semantic foundations and query execution. *The VLDB Journal—The International Journal on Very Large Data Bases, 15*(2), 121-142.

Arasu, A. A. (2002). *An abstract semantics and concrete language for continuous queries over streams and relations.* Academic Press.

Assent, I., Krieger, R., Afschari, F., & Seidl, T. (2008). The TS-tree: efficient time series search and retrieval. In *Proceedings of the 11th international conference on Extending database technology: Advances in database technology* (pp. 252--263). ACM. doi:10.1145/1353343.1353376

Aßfalg, J., Kriegel, H.-P., Kroger, P., Kunath, P., Pryakhin, A., & Renz, M. (2006). Similarity search on time series based on threshold queries. *Advances in Database Technology-EDBT, 2006*, 276–294.

Bagnall, A., Ratanamahatana, C. A., Keogh, E., Lonardi, S., & Janacek, G. (2006). A bit level representation for time series data mining with shape based similarity. *Data Mining and Knowledge Discovery, 13*(1), 11–40. doi:10.1007/s10618-005-0028-0

Baheti, R., & Gill, H. (2011). Cyber-physical systems. In The impact of control technology, (pp. 161-166). Academic Press.

Bai, Y., Luo, C. R., Thakkar, H., & Zaniolo, C. (2005). Efficient support for time series queries in data stream management systems. In *Stream Data Management* (pp. 113–132). Springer. doi:10.1007/0-387-25229-0_6

Bao, D. (2008). A generalized model for financial time series representation and prediction. *Applied Intelligence, 20*(1), 1–11. doi:10.1007/s10489-007-0063-1

Beckmann, N., Kriegel, H.-P., Schneider, R., & Seeger, B. (1990). *The R*-tree: an efficient and robust access method for points and rectangles*. Academic Press.

Bentley, J. L., & Friedman, J. H. (1979). Data structures for range searching. *ACM Computing Surveys, 11*(4), 397–409. doi:10.1145/356789.356797

Berchtold, S., Keim, D. A., & Kriegel, H.-P. (2001). The X-tree: An index structure for high-dimensional data. *Readings in multimedia computing and networking, 451.*

Box, G. E., Jenkins, G. M., & Reinsel, G. C. (2013). *Time series analysis: forecasting and control*. John Wiley & Sons.

Brakatsoulas, S., Pfoser, D., & Theodoridis, Y. (2002). Revisiting R-tree construction principles. In *Advances in Databases and Information Systems* (pp. 149–162). Springer.

Buevich, M., Wright, A., Sargent, R., & Rowe, A. (2013). Respawn: A Distributed Multi-Resolution Time-Series Datastore. *Real-Time Systems Symposium (RTSS), 2013 IEEE 34th* (pp. 288--297). IEEE. doi:10.1109/RTSS.2013.36

Cai, Y., & Ng, R. (2004). Indexing spatio-temporal trajectories with Chebyshev polynomials. *Proceedings of the 2004 ACM SIGMOD international conference on Management of data* (pp. 599--610). ACM. doi:10.1145/1007568.1007636

Camerra, A., Rakthanmanon, T., & Keogh, E. (2014). Beyond one billion time series: Indexing and mining very large time series collections with iSAX2+. *Knowledge and Information Systems, 39*(1), 123–151. doi:10.1007/s10115-012-0606-6

Cattell, R. (2011). Scalable SQL and NoSQL data stores. *SIGMOD Record, 39*(4), 12–27. doi:10.1145/1978915.1978919

Chan, F.-P., Fu, A.-C., & Yu, C. (2003). Haar wavelets for efficient similarity search of time-series: With and without time warping. *Knowledge and Data Engineering. IEEE Transactions on, 15*(3), 686–705.

Chatfield, C. (2013). *The analysis of time series: an introduction*. CRC Press.

Chen, L., & Ng, R. (2004). On the marriage of lp-norms and edit distance. In *Proceedings of the Thirtieth international conference on Very large data bases* (vol. 30, pp. 792--803). VLDB Endowment. doi:10.1016/B978-012088469-8.50070-X

Chen, L., Ozsu, M. T., & Oria, V. (2005). Robust and fast similarity search for moving object trajectories. In *Proceedings of the 2005 ACM SIGMOD international conference on Management of data* (pp. 491--502). ACM. doi:10.1145/1066157.1066213

Chen, Q., Chen, L., Lian, X., Liu, Y., & Yu, J. X. (2007). Indexable PLA for efficient similarity search. In *Proceedings of the 33rd international conference on Very large data bases* (pp. 435--446). VLDB Endowment.

Chen, Q., Chen, L. a., & Yu, J. X. (2007). Indexable PLA for efficient similarity search. In *Proceedings of the 33rd international conference on Very large data bases* (pp. 435--446). VLDB Endowment.

Chen, Y., Nascimento, M. A., Ooi, B. C., & Tung, A. (2007). Spade: On shape-based pattern detection in streaming time series. In *Data Engineering, 2007. ICDE 2007. IEEE 23rd International Conference on* (pp. 786--795). IEEE.

Chu, S., Keogh, E. J., Hart, D. M., & Pazzani, M. J. (2002). *Iterative deepening dynamic time warping for time series*. SIAM.

Deri, L., Mainardi, S., & Fusco, F. (2012). tsdb: A compressed database for time series. In Traffic Monitoring and Analysis. Springer.

Ding, H., Trajcevski, G., Scheuermann, P., Wang, X., & Keogh, E. (2008). Querying and mining of time series data: Experimental comparison of representations and distance measures. *Proceedings of the VLDB Endowment, 1*(2), 1542–1552. doi:10.14778/1454159.1454226

Ding, R., Wang, Q., Dang, Y., Fu, Q., Zhang, H., & Zhang, D. (2015). YADING: Fast Clustering of Large-Scale Time Series Data. *Proceedings of the VLDB Endowment, 8*(5), 473–484. doi:10.14778/2735479.2735481

Dreyer, W., Dittrich, A. K., & Schmidt, D. (1994). Research perspectives for time series management systems. *SIGMOD Record, 23*(1), 10–15. doi:10.1145/181550.181553

Esling, P., & Agon, C. (2013). Multiobjective time series matching for audio classification and retrieval. *Audio, Speech, and Language Processing. IEEE Transactions on, 21*(10), 2057–2072.

Euán, C., Ortega, J., & Alvarez-Esteban, P. C. (2014). Detecting Stationary Intervals for Random Waves Using Time Series Clustering. In *ASME 2014 33rd International Conference on Ocean, Offshore and Arctic Engineering* (pp. V04BT02A027--V04BT02A027). American Society of Mechanical Engineers. doi:10.1115/OMAE2014-24269

Faloutsos, C., Ranganathan, M., & Manolopoulos, Y. (1994). *Fast subsequence matching in time-series databases* (Vol. 23). ACM.

Fu, A. W.-C., Keogh, E., Lau, L. Y., Ratanamahatana, C. A., & Wong, R. C.-W. (2008). Scaling and time warping in time series querying. *The VLDB Journal—The International Journal on Very Large Data Bases, 17*(4), 899--921.

Gandomi, A., & Haider, M. (2015). Beyond the hype: Big data concepts, methods, and analytics. *International Journal of Information Management, 35*(2), 137–144. doi:10.1016/j.ijinfomgt.2014.10.007

Ghias, A., Logan, J., Chamberlin, D., & Smith, B. C. (1995). Query by humming: musical information retrieval in an audio database. In *Proceedings of the third ACM international conference on Multimedia* (pp. 231--236). ACM. doi:10.1145/217279.215273

Giuffrida, G., & Zaniolo, C. (1994). EPL: Event Pattern Language. In *Third CLIPS Conference*. NASA's Johnson Space Center.

Goldschmidt, T., Jansen, A., Koziolek, H., Doppelhamer, J., & Breivold, H. P. (2014). Scalability and Robustness of Time-Series Databases for Cloud-Native Monitoring of Industrial Processes. *Cloud Computing (CLOUD), 2014 IEEE 7th International Conference on* (pp. 602--609). IEEE.

Golyandina, N., & Zhigljavsky, A. (2013). *Singular Spectrum Analysis for time series*. Springer. doi:10.1007/978-3-642-34913-3

Gordon, D., Hendler, D., Kontorovich, A., & Rokach, L. (2015). Local-shapelets for fast classification of spectrographic measurements. *Expert Systems with Applications*, *42*(6), 3150–3158. doi:10.1016/j. eswa.2014.11.043

Guttman, A. (1984). *R-trees: a dynamic index structure for spatial searching*. Academic Press.

Haber, D., Thomik, A. A., & Faisal, A. A. (2014). Unsupervised time series segmentation for high-dimensional body sensor network data streams. *Wearable and Implantable Body Sensor Networks (BSN), 2014 11th International Conference on* (pp. 121--126). IEEE.

He, G., Duan, Y., Peng, R., Jing, X., Qian, T., & Wang, L. (2015). Early classification on multivariate time series. *Neurocomputing*, *149*, 777–787. doi:10.1016/j.neucom.2014.07.056

Huang, Y.-W., & Yu, P. S. (1999). Adaptive query processing for time-series data. In *Proceedings of the fifth ACM SIGKDD international conference on Knowledge discovery and data mining* (pp. 282--286). ACM. doi:10.1145/312129.318357

Imamura, M., Takayama, S., & Munaka, T. (2012). A stream query language TPQL for anomaly detection in facility management. In *Proceedings of the 16th International Database Engineering & Applications Sysmposium* (pp. 235--238). ACM. doi:10.1145/2351476.2351506

Jiang, B. a. (2009). Online interval skyline queries on time series. *Data Engineering, 2009. ICDE'09. IEEE 25th International Conference on* (pp. 1036--1047). IEEE.

Kamath, U., Lin, J., & De Jong, K. (2014). SAX-EFG: an evolutionary feature generation framework for time series classification. In *Proceedings of the 2014 conference on Genetic and evolutionary computation* (pp. 533--540). ACM. doi:10.1145/2576768.2598321

Katayama, N. a. (1997). *The SR-tree: An index structure for high-dimensional nearest neighbor queries*. Academic Press.

Keogh, E., Chakrabarti, K., Pazzani, M., & Mehrotra, S. (2001). Dimensionality reduction for fast similarity search in large time series databases. *Knowledge and Information Systems*, *3*(3), 263–286. doi:10.1007/PL00011669

Keogh, E., Chakrabarti, K., Pazzani, M., & Mehrotra, S. (2001). Locally adaptive dimensionality reduction for indexing large time series databases. *SIGMOD Record*, *30*(2), 151–162. doi:10.1145/376284.375680

Keogh, E., Lin, J., & Fu, A. (2005). Hot sax: Efficiently finding the most unusual time series subsequence. *Data mining, fifth IEEE international conference on* (pp. 8--pp). IEEE.

Keogh, E., & Ratanamahatana, C. A. (2005). Exact indexing of dynamic time warping. *Knowledge and Information Systems*, *7*(3), 358–386. doi:10.1007/s10115-004-0154-9

Keogh, E. J., & Pazzani, M. J. (2000). A simple dimensionality reduction technique for fast similarity search in large time series databases. In Knowledge Discovery and Data Mining. Current Issues and New Applications (pp. 122--133). Springer. doi:10.1007/3-540-45571-X_14

Kim, S.-W., Park, S., & Chu, W. W. (2001). An index-based approach for similarity search supporting time warping in large sequence databases. *Data Engineering, 2001. Proceedings. 17th International Conference on* (pp. 607--614). IEEE.

Kim, Y., & Park, C. H. (2013). Query by Humming by Using Scaled Dynamic Time Warping. *Signal-Image Technology & Internet-Based Systems (SITIS), 2013 International Conference on* (pp. 1--5). IEEE.

Korn, F., Jagadish, H. V., & Faloutsos, C. (1997). Efficiently supporting ad hoc queries in large datasets of time sequences. *SIGMOD Record, 26*(2), 289–300. doi:10.1145/253262.253332

Kurniawati, R., Jin, J. S., & Shepard, J. A. (1997). SS+ tree: an improved index structure for similarity searches in a high-dimensional feature space. In *Electronic Imaging'97* (pp. 110–120). International Society for Optics and Photonics.

Lamb, A., Fuller, M., Tran, N., Vandiver, B., Doshi, L., & Bear, C. (2012). The vertica analytic database: C-store 7 years later. *Proceedings of the VLDB Endowment, 5*(12), 1790–1801. doi:10.14778/2367502.2367518

Law, Y.-N., Wang, H., & Zaniolo, C. (2004). Query Languages and Data Models for Database Sequences and Data. In *Proceedings of the Thirtieth international conference on Very large data bases* (vol. 30, pp. 492--503). VLDB Endowment. doi:10.1016/B978-012088469-8.50045-0

Li, F., Ooi, B. C., Özsu, M. T., & Wu, S. (2014). Distributed data management using mapreduce. *ACM Computing Surveys, 46*(3), 31. doi:10.1145/2503009

Li, Q., Moon, B., & Lopez, I. (2004). Skyline index for time series data. *Knowledge and Data Engineering. IEEE Transactions on, 16*(6), 669–684.

Li, X., Kim, Y. J., Govindan, R., & Hong, W. (2003). Multi-dimensional range queries in sensor networks. In *Proceedings of the 1st international conference on Embedded networked sensor systems,* (pp. 63--75). doi:10.1145/958491.958500

Lin, J., Keogh, E., Lonardi, S., & Chiu, B. (2003). A symbolic representation of time series, with implications for streaming algorithms. In *Proceedings of the 8th ACM SIGMOD workshop on Research issues in data mining and knowledge discovery* (pp. 2--11). ACM. doi:10.1145/882082.882086

Lin, J., Keogh, E., Wei, L., & Lonardi, S. (2007). Experiencing SAX: A novel symbolic representation of time series. *Data Mining and Knowledge Discovery, 15*(2), 107–144. doi:10.1007/s10618-007-0064-z

Lin, K.-I., Jagadish, H. V., & Faloutsos, C. (1994). The TV-tree: An index structure for high-dimensional dat. *The VLDB Journal, 3*(4), 517–542. doi:10.1007/BF01231606

Liu, Y., Hu, S., Rabl, T., Liu, W., Jacobsen, H.-A., & Wu, K. (2014). DGFIndex for Smart Grid: Enhancing Hive with a Cost-Effective Multidimensional Range Index. *arXiv preprint arXiv:1404.5686.*

Loboz, C., Smyl, S., & Nath, S. (2010). DataGarage: Warehousing massive performance data on commodity servers. *Proceedings of the VLDB Endowment, 3*(1-2), 1447–1458. doi:10.14778/1920841.1921019

Loh, W.-K., Kim, S.-W., & Whang, K.-Y. (2000). Index interpolation: an approach to subsequence matching supporting normalization transform in time-series databases. In *Proceedings of the ninth international conference on Information and knowledge management* (pp. 480--487). ACM. doi:10.1145/354756.354856

Lukoianova, T., & Rubin, V. L. (2014). Veracity Roadmap: Is Big Data Objective, Truthful and Credible? *Advances in Classification Research Online*, *24*(1), 4–15. doi:10.7152/acro.v24i1.14671

Melnik, S., Shivakumar, S., Tolton, M., & Vassilakis, T. (2010). Dremel: Interactive analysis of web-scale datasets. *Proceedings of the VLDB Endowment*, *3*(1-2), 330–339. doi:10.14778/1920841.1920886

Mohsenian-Rad, A.-H., Wong, V. W., Jatskevich, J., Schober, R., & Leon-Garcia, A. (2010). Autonomous demand-side management based on game-theoretic energy consumption scheduling for the future smart grid. *Smart Grid. IEEE Transactions on.*, *1*, 320–331.

Motakis, I., & Zaniolo, C. (1997). Temporal aggregation in active database rules. *SIGMOD Record*, *26*(2), 440–451. doi:10.1145/253262.253359

Mueen, A. (2014). Time series motif discovery: Dimensions and applications. *Wiley Interdisciplinary Reviews: Data Mining and Knowledge Discovery*, *4*(2), 152–159.

Müller, M. (2007). Dynamic time warping. *Information retrieval for music and motion*, 69--84.

Nazerzadeh, H., & Ghodsi, M. (2005). RAQ: a range-queriable distributed data structure. In SOFSEM 2005: Theory and Practice of Computer Science (pp. 269--277). Springer. doi:10.1007/978-3-540-30577-4_30

Normandeau, K. (2013). *Beyond volume, variety and velocity is the issue of big data veracity*. Inside Big Data.

O'Connor, B., Balasubramanyan, R., Routledge, B. R., & Smith, N. A. (2010). From tweets to polls: Linking text sentiment to public opinion time series. *ICWSM*, *11*, 122–129.

Oetiker, T. (2005). *RRDtool*. Academic Press.

Ooi, B. C., Hadjieleftheriou, M., Du, X., & Lu, W. (2014). Efficiently Supporting Edit Distance based String Similarity Search Using B+-trees. *IEEE Transactions on Knowledge and Data Engineering*, 1.

Oppenheim, A. V., & Schafer, R. W. (1975). *Digital Signal Processing*. Englewood Cliffs, New York.

Park, C. H. (2014). *Query by humming based on multiple spectral hashing and scaled open-end dynamic time warping. Signal Processing*. Elsevier.

Park, Y., Priebe, C. E., & Youssef, A. (2013). Anomaly detection in time series of graphs using fusion of graph invariants. *Selected Topics in Signal Processing. IEEE Journal of*, *7*(1), 67–75.

Patri, O. P., Panangadan, A. V., Chelmis, C., McKee, R. G., & Prasanna, V. et al. (2014). Predicting Failures from Oilfield Sensor Data using Time Series Shapelets. *SPE Annual Technical Conference and Exhibition*. Society of Petroleum Engineers. doi:10.2118/170680-MS

Patri, O. P., Sharma, A. B., Chen, H. a., Panangadan, A. V., & Prasanna, V. K. (2014). Extracting discriminative shapelets from heterogeneous sensor data. *Big Data (Big Data), 2014 IEEE International Conference on* (pp. 1095--1104). IEEE.

Pavlidis, T. (1973). Waveform segmentation through functional approximation. *Computers. IEEE Transactions on, 100*(7), 689–697.

Perng, C.-S., & Parker, D. S. (1999). SQL/LPP: A time series extension of SQL based on limited patience patterns. In Database and Expert Systems Applications (pp. 218--227). Springer.

Psaila, R. A., Wimmers, M., & It, E. L. (1995). Querying shapes of histories. *Very Large Data Bases.* Zurich, Switzerland: IEEE.

Russom, P. a. (2011). *Big data analytics.* TDWI Best Practices Report, Fourth Quarter.

Sadri, R. a. (2001). A sequential pattern query language for supporting instant data mining for e-services. In *Proceedings of the 27th International Conference on Very Large Data Bases* (pp. 653--656). Morgan Kaufmann Publishers Inc.

Schäfer, P. (2014). *Experiencing the Shotgun Distance for Time Series Analysis.* Academic Press.

Sellis, T., Roussopoulos, N., & Faloutsos, C. (1987). *The R+--Tree: A Dynamic Index for Multi-Dimensional Objects.* VLDB Endowments.

Seshadri, P., Livny, M., & Ramakrishnan, R. (1995). SEQ: A model for sequence databases. In *Proceedings of the Eleventh International Conference on Data Engineering,* (pp. 232--239). IEEE. doi:10.1109/ICDE.1995.380388

Shieh, J., & Keogh, E. (2008). i SAX: indexing and mining terabyte sized time series. In *Proceedings of the 14th ACM SIGKDD international conference on Knowledge discovery and data mining* (pp. 623--631). ACM. doi:10.1145/1401890.1401966

Sigoure, B. (2012). *OpenTSDB scalable time series database (TSDB).* Stumble Upon. Retrieved from http://opentsdb. net

Simão, H. P., Jeong, H. a., Powell, W. B., Gagneja, A., Wu, L., & Anderson, R. (2013). *A Robust Solution to the Load Curtailment Problem.* IEEE.

Simmhan, Y., Wickramaarachchi, C. A., Ravi, S., Raghavendra, C., & Prasanna, V. (2014). Scalable analytics over distributed time-series graphs using goffish. *arXiv preprint arXiv:1406.5975.*

Sleit, A. N., & Al-Nsour, E. (2014). Corner-based splitting: An improved node splitting algorithm for R-tree. *Journal of Information Science, 40*(2), 222–236. doi:10.1177/0165551513516709

Srividhya, S., & Lavanya, S. (2014). Comparative Analysis of R-Tree and R-Tree in Spatial Database. *Intelligent Computing Applications (ICICA), 2014 International Conference on* (pp. 449--453). IEEE.

Stonebraker, M., Abadi, D. J., Batkin, A., Chen, X., Cherniack, M., Ferreira, M., ... (2005). C-store: a column-oriented DBMS. In *Proceedings of the 31st international conference on Very large data bases* (pp. 553--564). VLDB Endowment.

Thusoo, A., Sarma, J. S., Jain, N., Shao, Z., Chakka, P., & Liu, H. et al.. (2009). Hive: A warehousing solution over a map-reduce framework. *Proceedings of the VLDB Endowment, 2*(2), 1626–1629. doi:10.14778/1687553.1687609

Ulanova, L., Begum, N., & Keogh, E. (2015). *Scalable Clustering of Time Series with U-Shapelets*. SDM. doi:10.1137/1.9781611974010.101

Vlachos, M., Kollios, G., & Gunopulos, D. (2002). Discovering similar multidimensional trajectories. *Data Engineering, 2002. Proceedings. 18th International Conference on* (pp. 673--684). IEEE.

Wang, H., Tang, M., Park, Y., & Priebe, C. (2014). Locality statistics for anomaly detection in time series of graphs. *IEEE Transactions on Signal Processing, 62*(3), 703–717. doi:10.1109/TSP.2013.2294594

Wang, J., Zhu, Y., Li, S., Wan, D., & Zhang, P. (2014). *Multivariate Time Series Similarity Searching*. Hindawi Publishing Corporation.

Wang, X., Mueen, A., Ding, H., Trajcevski, G., Scheuermann, P., & Keogh, E. (2013). Experimental comparison of representation methods and distance measures for time series data. *Data Mining and Knowledge Discovery, 26*(2), 275–309. doi:10.1007/s10618-012-0250-5

Waterman, M. S., Smith, T. F., & Beyer, W. A. (1976). Some biological sequence metrics. *Advances in Mathematics, 20*(3), 367–387. doi:10.1016/0001-8708(76)90202-4

Weigel, R. S., Lindholm, D. M., Wilson, A., & Faden, J. (2010). TSDS: High-performance merge, subset, and filter software for time series-like data. *Earth Science Informatics, 3*(1-2), 29–40. doi:10.1007/s12145-010-0059-y

White, D. A. (1996). Similarity indexing with the SS-tree. *Data Engineering, 1996. Proceedings of the Twelfth International Conference on* (pp. 516--523). IEEE. doi:10.1109/ICDE.1996.492202

White, D. A., & Jain, R. (1996). *Similarity Indexing: Algorithms and Performance. In Storage and retrieval for image and video databases* (pp. 62–73). SPIE.

Yan, G., & Eidenbenz, S. (2014). Sim-Watchdog: Leveraging Temporal Similarity for Anomaly Detection in Dynamic Graphs. *Distributed Computing Systems (ICDCS), 2014 IEEE 34th International Conference on*, (pp. 154--165). IEEE.

Ye, L., & Keogh, E. (2009). Time series shapelets: a new primitive for data mining. In *Proceedings of the 15th ACM SIGKDD international conference on Knowledge discovery and data mining* (pp. 947--956). ACM. doi:10.1145/1557019.1557122

Yi, B.-K., & Faloutsos, C. (2000). *Fast time sequence indexing for arbitrary Lp norms*. VLDB.

Yi, B.-K., Jagadish, H., & Faloutsos, C. (1998). Efficient retrieval of similar time sequences under time warping. *Data Engineering, 1998. Proceedings., 14th International Conference on* (pp. 201--208). IEEE.

Zhao, D., Zhang, Z., Zhou, X., Li, T., Wang, K., & Kimpe, D. (2014). FusionFS: Toward supporting data-intensive scientific applications on extreme-scale distributed systems. In *Proceedings of IEEE International Conference on Big Data*. IEEE.

Zois, V., Frincu, M., Chelmis, C., Saeed, M. R., & Prasanna, V. (2014). Efficient Customer Selection for Sustainable Demand Response in Smart Grids. *Green Computing Conference (IGCC)*. doi:10.1109/IGCC.2014.7039149

Zois, V., Frincu, M., & Prasanna, V. (2014). Integrated platform for automated sustainable demand response in smart grids. *Intelligent Energy Systems (IWIES), 2014 IEEE International Workshop on* (pp. 64--69). IEEE.

KEY TERMS AND DEFINITIONS

Analytics: The discovery and transmission of patterns in data that are meaningful based on the context of data.

Big Data: Data that is collectively too large and complex to be analyzed with traditional data mining techniques.

Cyber-Physical System: A system consisting of computational components that are used to control and monitor physical entities.

Data Structure: A way of organizing data so that it can be efficiently accessed and updated.

Query Language: A computer language that aims at providing factual answers to questions or providing information that is relevant to the corresponding area of inquiry.

Relational Database Management Systems (RDBMS): A database management system that is based on the concept of tables and primary keys to organize data and relationships between them.

Time Series: A sequence of data points consisting of consecutive measurements that are made over a time interval.

ENDNOTES

[1]   It does not obey the triangular inequality, i.e., for objects $x, y, z \mid d\left(x, y\right) + d\left(y, z\right) \geq d\left(x, z\right)$.

[2]   Exact indexing as opposed to approximate indexing, refers to indexing methods that ensure no false negatives.

Chapter 14
Parallel kNN Queries for Big Data Based on Voronoi Diagram Using MapReduce

Wei Yan
Liaoning University, China

ABSTRACT

In cloud computing environments parallel kNN queries for big data is an important issue. The k nearest neighbor queries (kNN queries), designed to find k nearest neighbors from a dataset S for every object in another dataset R, is a primitive operator widely adopted by many applications including knowledge discovery, data mining, and spatial databases. This chapter proposes a parallel method of kNN queries for big data using MapReduce programming model. Firstly, this chapter proposes an approximate algorithm that is based on mapping multi-dimensional data sets into two-dimensional data sets, and transforming kNN queries into a sequence of two-dimensional point searches. Then, in two-dimensional space this chapter proposes a partitioning method using Voronoi diagram, which incorporates the Voronoi diagram into R-tree. Furthermore, this chapter proposes an efficient algorithm for processing kNN queries based on R-tree using MapReduce programming model. Finally, this chapter presents the results of extensive experimental evaluations which indicate efficiency of the proposed approach.

INTRODUCTION

With the development of the location-based services, the amount of geospatial data is rapidly growing. The nearest neighbor queries are important issue, especially the amount of data is huge with big datasets. In this way, the query requires a lot of time consuming. The Cloud computing enables a considerable reduction in operational expenses. Google's MapReduce programming model provides a cloud computing platform, which is parallel query processing for big datasets. Given the available cloud services and parallel geospatial queries, a variety of geospatial queries can be modeled using MapReduce programming model. This chapter proposes a method of parallel *k*NN queries for big dataset based on Voronoi diagram using MapReduce programming model.

DOI: 10.4018/978-1-4666-8767-7.ch014

The k-nearest neighbor query (kNN) is an important problem that has been frequently used, due to numerous applications including knowledge discovery, pattern recognition, and spatial databases. Given a data set S and a query set R, the kNN query is k nearest neighbors from points in S for each query point $r \in R$. Now, lots of researches (Yao *et al.* 2010) have been devoted to improve the performance of kNN query algorithms. However, all these approaches focus on methods that are to be executed on multi-dimensional data sets. In multi-dimensional data sets the kNN query is complex, and its efficiency is low. How to perform the kNN query on two-dimensional data sets is an important topic in cloud computing environments.

Previous work has concentrated on the spatial databases. In the solution methods the database engine is necessary. For example, new data index and query algorithms need to be incorporated into the database engine. This requirement poses the introduction of R-trees (Guttman 1984), which indexes multi-dimensional data and develops novel algorithms based on R-trees for various forms of Nearest Neighbor (NN) queries. All these approaches focus on methods that are to be executed in a single thread on a single machine. With the quick increase in the scale of the input datasets, processing big data in parallel and distributed database systems is becoming a popular practice.

Parallel spatial query processing has been studied in parallel database, cluster systems as well as cloud computing platform. In cloud computing environments, a large part of data-processing using MapReduce (Dean *et al.* 2004) programming model runs extensively on Hadoop. The MapReduce programming model provides a powerful parallel and distributed computing paradigm. A few recent studies construct R-tree index with MapReduce programming model (Cary *et al.* 2009), but these studies can not support any type of query. A data structure that is extremely efficient in exploring a local neighborhood in a geometric space is Voronoi diagram (Okabe *et al.* 2000). Given a set of points, a general Voronoi diagram uniquely partitions the space into disjoint regions. The region corresponding to a point p covers the points in space that are closer to p than to any other point.

This chapter presents an approximate algorithm using MapReduce programming model that is based on mapping multi-dimensional data sets into two-dimensional data sets, and transforming kNN query into a sequence of two-dimensional point searches. This chapter uses a small number of random vectors to shift the multi-dimensional data using space-filling z-curves. The z-curves can preserve the spatial locality, and map multi-dimensional data into two-dimensional data. Then, in two-dimensional space this chapter proposes a partitioning method using Voronoi diagram, which incorporates the resulting data into the R-tree index structure. Furthermore, this chapter proposes an efficient algorithm for processing kNN queries based on R-tree using MapReduce programming model.

The objectives of the chapter are summarized as follows:

- This chapter proposes an approximate algorithm using MapReduce programming model that is based on mapping multi-dimensional data sets into two-dimensional data sets.
- This chapter proposes a partitioning method using Voronoi diagram in two-dimensional space, which incorporates the resulting data into the R-tree index structure.
- This chapter proposes an efficient algorithm for processing kNN queries based on R-tree using MapReduce programming model.

BACKGROUND

Related Works

Performing kNN queries in spatial databases has been extensively studied in the research of Xia *et al.* (2004). Yao *et al.* (2010) proposed both the kNN query and the kNN join in the relational database, used the user-defined-function that a query optimizer cannot optimize. The authors designed algorithms that could be implemented by SQL operators using a small constant number of random shifts for databases, and guaranteed to find the approximate kNN. However, these works focus on the centralized, single-thread method that is not directly applicable in MapReduce programming model. Zhang *et al.* (2009) proposed a parallel spatial join algorithm in MapReduce, dealing with only spatial distance joins, which does not solve kNN joins. Zhang *et al.* (2012) proposed novel algorithms in MapReduce to perform efficient parallel kNN joins on large data. The authors proposed the exact H-BRJ algorithms and approximate H-zkNNJ algorithms, and the H-zkNNJ algorithms deliver performance which is orders of magnitude better than baseline methods, as evidenced from experiments on massive real datasets. Jiang *et al.* (2010) proposed the performance study of MapReduce (Hadoop) on a 100-node cluster of Amazon EC2 with various levels of parallelism. The authors identify five design factors that affect the performance of Hadoop, and investigate alternative but known methods for each factor. Their works show that by carefully tuning these factors, the overall performance of Hadoop can be improved by a factor of 2.5 to 3.5 for the same benchmark, and is thus more comparable to that of parallel database systems.

Kim *et al.* (2012) investigated how the top-k similarity join algorithms can get benefits from the popular MapReduce framework. The authors first developed the divide-and-conquer and branch-and-bound algorithms. Next, the authors proposed the all pair partitioning and essential pair partitioning methods to minimized the amount of data transfers between map and reduce functions. Finally, the authors performed the experiments with not only synthetic but also real-life data sets. Okcan *et al.* (2011) proposed join model simplifies creation and reasoning about joins in MapReduce. Using this model, the authors derive a surprisingly simple randomized algorithm, called 1-Bucket-Theta, for implementing arbitrary joins (theta-joins) in a single MapReduce job.

In the context of spatial databases, R-tree provides efficient algorithms using either the depth-first approach of Roussopoulos (1995) and the best-first approach of Hjaltason (1999). These algorithms utilize the simple rectangular grouping principle used by R-tree that represents close data points with their Minimum Bounding Rectangle (MBR). Yu *et al.* (2001) described how appropriate choices can effectively adapt the index structure to the data distribution. Yu *et al.* (2007) proposed IJoin, a B$^+$-tree based method to answer kNN join. The IJoin method employs a B$^+$-tree to maintain the objects of each dataset by splitting the two input datasets into respective set of partitions. MeanWhile, several approaches that use distributed hierarchical index structures such as R-tree based P2PR-tree of Mondal *et al.* (2004) and SD-Rtree of Mouza et al. (2007) have been proposed for parallel spatial query processing. But, theses researches do not scale due to the traditional top-down search that overloads the nodes near the tree root, and fail to provide full decentralization. Wang *et al.* (2010) proposed RT-CAN, a multi-dimensional indexing scheme in epiC. RT-CAN integrates CAN-based routing protocol and the R-tree based indexing scheme to support efficient multi-dimensional query processing in a Cloud system. Wu *et al.* (2010) presented a novel scalable B$^+$-tree based indexing scheme for efficient data processing in the Cloud. Akdogan *et al.* (2010) proposed the method of parallel geospatial query processing with the MapReduce programming model. The proposed approach creates a spatial index, Voronoi diagram, for given data points in two-dimensional space and enables efficient processing of a wide range of Geo-spatial queries. Vernica et al. (2010) proposed an efficient parallel set-similarity join in MapReduce. The authors propose a three-stage approach for end-to-end set-similarity joins, and take as input a set of records and output a set of joined records based on a set-similarity condition.

Z-Curve

The z-curve of a space point is calculated by z-function of point's coordinate values. The z-curve can be defined as follows:

Definition 1 [z-curve]: The z-curve can define as the one-to-one mapping between the d-dimension space R^d and the two-dimensional space R^2, and represent as $Z: R^d \rightarrow R^2$. If point $p \in R^d$, then $Z(p) \in R^2$, and the $Z(p)$ is z-function value of the point p.

For example, given a point (4, 9, 7) in a three-dimension space, the z-function value of the point is $Z(4, 9, 7)_3 = ((4, 9)_2, 7)_3$. Where, the 4 is the z_x value of the point, and the 9 is the z_y value of the point.

R-Tree

R-tree is proposed by the authors of Guttman et al. (1984), whcih is the index structure widely used for spacial query processing. R-tree groups the data points in d-dimensional space using d-dimensional rectangle, based on the closeness of the points. Fighre 1 shows the R-tree built using the set $P = \{p_1, p_2, ..., p_{14}\}$ of points in two-dimensional space.

Figure 1 shows the location of the point set $P = \{p_1, p_2, ..., p_{14}\}$. Figure 2 shows the R-tree index structure of the point set P in two-dimensional space. In the R-tree index, the capacity of each node is three entries. The leaf nodes $N_1, N_2, ..., N_5$ store the coordinates of the grouped points together with optional pointers to their corresponding records. Each intermediate node (e.g., N_6 and N_7) contains the Minimum Bounding Rectangle (MBR) of each of its child nodes (e.g. e1 for node N_1) and a pointer to the disk page storing the child. The same grouping criteria is used to group intermediate nodes into upper level nodes. Therefore, the MBRs stored in the single root of R-tree collectively cover the entire data set P.

In Figure 2, the root node R contains MBRs e_6 and e_7 enclosing the points in nodes N_6 and N_7, respectively. The algorithms based on R-tree utilize some metrics to bound their search space using the MBRs stored in the nodes. The widely used function is *mindist* (N_6, q) and *mindist* (N_7, q) for q.

kNN Queries

In n-dimensional space D, given two points r and s, $|r, s|$ represents the distance between point r and s in space D. In this chapter, the Euclidean distance is used as the distance.

$$|r, s| = (\sum_{i=1}^{n} (r[i] - s[i])^2)^{1/2}$$

(1)

where, $r[i]$ (resp. $s[i]$) denotes the value of r (resp. s) along the ith dimension in space D.

Figure 1. Location of the point in two-dimensional space

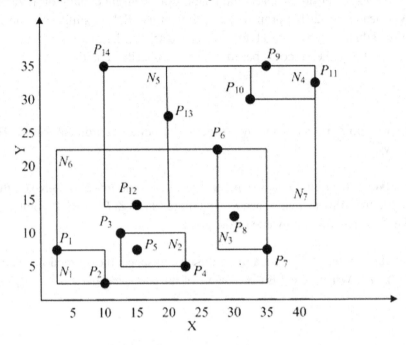

Figure 2. R-tree index structure

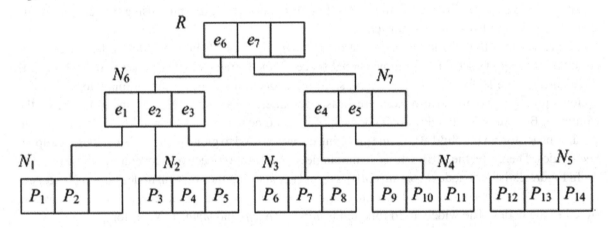

Definition 2 [*k* nearest neighbors]: Given a point *r*, a dataset *S* in space *D* and an integer *k*, the *k* nearest neighbors of *r* from *S*, denoted as $k\text{NN}(r, s)$, is a set of *k* point from *S* that $\forall p \in k\text{NN}(r, S)$, $\forall s \in S - k\text{NN}(r, S)$, $|p, r| \leq |s, r|$.

Definition 3 [*k*NN queries]: Given two dataset *R* and *S* in space *D*, and an integer *k*. *k*NN queries of *R* and *S* (denoted as *knnQ*), combine each point $r \in R$ with its *k* nearest neighbors from *S*.

$$knnQ(R, S) = \{(r, k\text{NN}(r, S)) \mid \text{for all } r \in R\} \tag{2}$$

Voronoi Diagram

The Voronoi diagram of a given set $P = \{p_1, p_2, ..., p_n\}$ of n points in R^d partitions the space of R^d into n regions. Each region includes all points in R^d with a common closest point in the given set P using the distance metric $Dist()$, which is proposed by the authors Okabe *et al.* (2000). The region corresponding to the point $p \in P$ contains all the points $q \in R^d$.

$$\forall p' \in P, p' \neq p, Dist(q, p) \leq Dist(q, p') \tag{3}$$

The equality holds for the points on the borders of p's regions.

Figure 3 shows the Voronoi diagram of five points in two-dimensional space, where the distance metric is Euclidean. This chapter represents the region $V(p)$ containing the point p as its Voronoi cell. Using Euclidean distance in two-dimensional space, $V(p)$ is a convex polygon. Each edge of the convex polygon is a segment of the perpendicular bisector of the line segment connecting p to another point of the set P. Each of these edges represents as Voronoi edge and each of its end-points as a Voronoi vertex of the point p. For each Voronoi edge of the point p, this chapter refers to the corresponding point in the set P as a Voronoi neighbor of p. This chapter uses $VN(p)$ to denote the set of all Voronoi neighbors of p. The point p represents as the generator of Voronoi cell $V(p)$. Finally, the set given by $VD(P) = \{V(p_1), V(p_2), ..., V(p_n)\}$ is called the Voronoi diagram generated by P with respect to the distance function $Dist()$. Throughout this chapter, the Euclidean distance function is used in two-dimensional space. Also, this chapter simply uses Voronoi diagram to denote ordinary Voronoi diagram of a set of points in two-dimensional space.

MapReduce Programming Model

MapReduce is a popular programming framework to support data-intensive applications using shared-nothing clusters (Dean, 2004). MapReduce programs typically consist of a pair of user-defined map and

Figure 3. Voronoi diagram

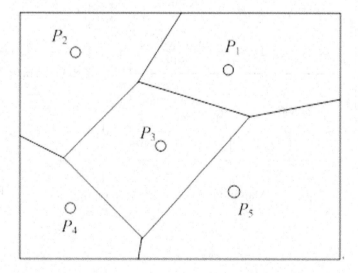

reduce functions. The map function takes an input key-value pair and produces a set of intermediate key-value pairs. MapReduce runtime system then groups and sorts all the intermediate values associated with the same intermediate key, and sends them to the reduce function. The reduce function accepts an intermediate key and its corresponding values, applies the processing logic, and produces the final result which is typically a list of values. The MapReduce programming model treats data as a list of (key, value) pairs and expresses a computation in terms of two functions: map and reduce.

$$\text{map } (k_1, v_1) \rightarrow \text{list } (k_2, v_2)$$

$$\text{reduce}(k_2, \text{list}(v_2)) \rightarrow \text{list } (k_3, v_3) \quad (4)$$

Figure 4 shows the framework of MapReduce programming model. Inputted data is loaded into HDFS (hadoop distributed file system), where each file is partitioned into smaller data blocks. A file's data blocks are then distributed, and possibly replicated, to different machines in the Mappers. A Map-Reduce computation begins with a Map phase where each inputted data block is processed in parallel by as many TaskTrackers. Each inputted data block is a list of key-value pairs (k_1, v_1). A TaskTracker applies the user-defined map function to each key-value pair to produce a list of outputted key-value pairs (k_2, v_2).

The outputted key-value pairs from a TaskTracker are partitioned on the basis of their key k_2. Each partition is then sent across the cluster to a remote node in the shuffle phase. Corresponding partitions from the TaskTrackers are merged and sorted to form the intermediate results. For each key k_2, the associated values are grouped together to form a list $\text{list}(v_2)$. The key and the corresponding list send to TaskTracker' of the Reducers. The Reducers can use the user-defined reduce function. The resulting key-value pairs list (k_3, v_3) are written back to the DFS and form the final output.

Figure 4. The framework of MapReduce programming model

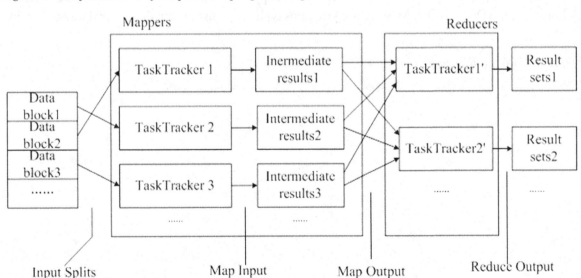

kNN QUERIES OF MULTI-DIMENSIONAL SPACE DATA

This section uses z-curves to map data point in multi-dimensional space into two-dimensional point, and then translates the *k*NN query for a query point *q* in multi-dimensional space into two-dimensional point search.

Mapping of Multi-dimensional Space Data

Generally, z-curves preserve the spatial locality and users can find *q*'s *k* nearest neighborhood. The z-curves use the z-functon z_x (resp. z_y) to map multi-dimensional point into two-dimensional point in x-axis (resp. y-axis).

Figure 5 shows the mapping of multi-dimensional data point into two-dimensional data point, which uses the z-function z_x and z_y. In order to get a theoretical guarantee, the chapter uses α, independent, randomly shifts the multi-dimensional data point *p* of the inputted data set *P*, and repeat the procedure for each randomly shifted version of *P*.

Specifically, this chapter proposes the random shift operation, as shifting all data points in *P* by a random vector $\vec{v} \in R^d$. This operation is simply $p + \vec{v}$ for all $p \in P$, and denoted as $P + \vec{v}$. This section independently at random generate α number of vectors $\{\vec{v_1}, \vec{v_2}, ..., \vec{v_\alpha}\}$, where $\forall i \in [1, \alpha]$, $\vec{v_i} \in R^d$. Let

Figure 5. Mapping of multi-dimensional data point

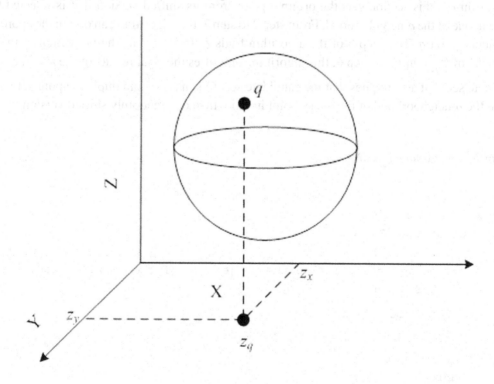

$P^i = P + \vec{v_i}$, $P^0 = P$ and $\vec{v_0} = \vec{0}$. The random shift is a linear shift. The linear shift can convert a vector to another vector, and give the corresponding relation of two vectors. In mathematics, the linear shift can maintain the characteristic of the vector. In the spatial database, the number of vector points is huge, and the space points are often sparse. The linear shift can convert the space point to a space area, and reduce the computational burden of the spatial query, and improve the query efficiency. For each P^i, its points are sorted by their z-function. Note that the random shift operation is executed only once for data set P and used for subsequent queries.

For a query point q and a data set P, let z_x (resp. z_y) be the projection of point q in x-axis (resp. y-axis) for points in P. The δ-neighborhood of query point q is defined as the δ points up and down next to z_q. For the special case, when z_q does not have δ points, this section simply takes enough points around z_q to make the total number of points in the δ-neighborhood to be $\pi\delta^2$.

The approximate kNN query algorithm maps multi-dimensional data sets into two-dimensional data sets, and transforms kNN queries into a sequence of two-dimensional point searches. The kNN query algorithm essentially finds the δ-neighborhood of the query point $q^i = q + \vec{v_i}$ in P^i for i $\in$ [1, α] and select the final top k from the points in the (α + 1) δ-neighborhood, with a maximum (α + 1) $\pi\delta^2$ number of distinct points.

Approximate kNN Queries Algorithm

This chapter denotes the approximate kNN query algorithm as the approximate z_q-kNN queries algorithm and it is shown in algorithm 1.

In algorithm 1, this section gets the original point from its shifted version if it is selected to be a candidate in one of the δ-neighborhood. From step 2 to step 7, this algorithm can obtain the approximate kNN of query point q. This step 3 of the algorithm finds z_x^i (resp. z_y^i) as the projection of the x-axis (resp. y-axis) of z_{q+v_i} in P^i. In step 6, this algorithm simplifies the final results of the kNN query from the candidate set C. It also implies that the candidate sets C^i's may contain duplicate points, i.e. a point may be in the δ-neighborhood of the query point in more than one randomly shifted version.

Algorithm 1. Approximate z_q-kNN

```
Input: query point q, point sets {P⁰, P¹, …, Pᵅ}
Output: k nearest neighborhood of query point q
1.        Candidates C = Ø
2.        for i = 0, 1, …, α do
3.            find zₓⁱ (resp. z_yⁱ) as the projection of the x-axis (resp. y-axis)
                 of z_{q+v̄ᵢ} in Pⁱ
4.            let Cⁱ be δ points around z_q in Pⁱ
5.            for each point p in Cⁱ, let p = p - v⃗ᵢ
6.            C = C ∪ Cⁱ
7.        endfor
8.        output kNN(q, C)
```

PARTITIONED METHOD BASED ON VORONOI DIAGRAM

After mapping multi-dimensional data sets into two-dimensional data sets, this section partitions the two-dimensional data sets using voronoi diagram.

Voronoi Diagram-Based Partitioned Method of Two-dimensional Space

The Voronoi diagram decomposes two-dimensional space into disjoint polygons. Given a set of point set S in two-dimensional space, the Voronoi diagram associates all point in the two-dimensional space to their closest point. Each point s has a Voronoi polygon consisting of all points closer to s than to any other point. Hence, the nearest neighbor of a query point q is closed Voronoi polygons. The set of Voronoi polygons associated with all the points is called the Voronoi diagram (VD). The polygons are mutually exclusive except for their boundaries.

Definition 4 [Voronoi Polygon]: Given set of points $P = \{p_1, p_2, ..., p_n\}$ where $2 < n < \infty$ and $p_i \neq p_j$ for $i \neq j$, i, j = 1, 2, ..., n, the Voronoi polygon of p_i is $VP(p_i) = \{p \mid d(p, p_i) \leq d(p, p_j)\}$ for $i \neq j$ and $p \in VP(p_i)$ where $d(p, p_i)$ specifies the minimum distance between p and p_i in Euclidean space.

Property 1: The Voronoi diagram for given set of points is unique.

Property 2: Let n and n_e be the number of points and Voronoi edges, respectively, then $n_e \leq 3n\text{-}6$.

Property 3: Every Voronoi edge is shared by two Voronoi polygons, the average number of Voronoi edges per Voronoi polygon is at most 6, i.e., $2*(3n\text{-}6)/n = 6n\text{-}12/n \leq 6$. This states that no average, each point has 6 adjacent points.

Property 4: The nearest points of p_i (e.g., p_j) is among the points whose Voronoi polygons share Voronoi edges with $VP(p_i)$.

Assume that the VD(P) is the Voronoi diagram of P. Figure 6 shows the Voronoi diagram of the same points shown in Figure 2. To bound the Voronoi polygons with infinite edges (e.g., $V(p_3)$), this section clips them using a large rectangle bounding the points in P (the dotted rectangle).

Constructing Voronoi Diagram with MapReduce

Construction of Voronoi diagram (VD) is suitable for MapReduce programming model, because Voronoi diagram can be obtained by merging multiple Voronoi polygons (VP). Specifically, each of Voronoi polygons (VP) can be created by the mappers using parallel method and the reducers using combining method in single Voronoi diagram (VD).

Given a set of data point $P = \{p_1, p_2, ..., p_n\}$ as input, firstly the point set is sorted in increasing order according to x coordinate. Secondly, the point set P is separated into several subsets of equal size. Finally, the Voronoi polygons (VP) are generated for the points of each subset, and then all of the Voronoi polygons (VP) are merged to obtain the final Voronoi diagram (VD) for the point set P.

Map phase of MapReduce programming model: Given a point set sorted by x coordinate, each mapper reads an input block using the format of <key, value>. Then each mapper generates a Voronoi polygons (VP) for the point set in its data block, marks the boundary polygons and emits the generated Voronoi

Figure 6. Voronoi diagram-based partition

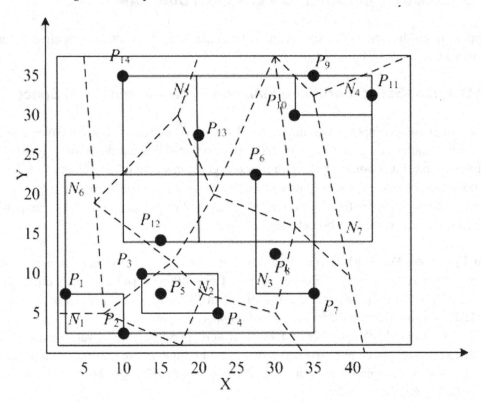

polygons (VP) in the form of <key', value$_i$'> where i denotes the number of data block. The key' is common to all Voronoi polygons (VP), so that all Voronoi polygons (VP) can be grouped together and merged in the subsequent reduce phase.

Reduce phase of MapReduce programming model: The reducers aggregates all Voronoi polygons (VP) in the same group and combines them into a single Voronoi diagram (VD). In the reduce phase, the boundary polygons are detected with a sequential scan, and then new Voronoi edges and vertices are generated by delecting superfluous boundary portions from Voronoi polygons (VP). As the final output, the reducers emit each point and its Voronoi neighbors.

INDEX THE VORONOI DIAGRAM USING R-TREE

This section depicts R-tree indexing method of the Voronoi diagram. The R-tree indexing of point set augmented with the points' Voronoi diagram. Suppose that this section stores all points set P in an R-tree, the pre-built Voronoi diagram of points set P is VD(P). Each leaf node of R-tree stores a subset of points of P. The leaves also include the data records containing extra information about the corresponding points. In the record of the point p, this section stores the pointer to the location of each Voronoi neighbor of p and also the vertices of the Voronoi polygons of p.

Figure 7 illustrates the R-tree indexing of the points of P. For simplicity, it shows only the contents of leaf node N_2 including points p_3, p_4, and p_5. The record associated with each point p in N_2 includes both

Voronoi neighbors and vertices of p in a common sequential order. This section represents the record as Voronoi record of p. Each Voronoi neighbor p' of p maintained in the record is actually a pointer to the disk page storing p's information.

Parallel kNN Queries Algorithm Using MapReduce

The MapReduce programming model processes data according to (key, value) pairs and it expresses computation model in terms of two functions: map and reduce. The map function produces key-value pairs based on the input data and outputs a list of intermediate key-value pairs. All intermediate values corresponding to the same intermediate key are grouped together and passed to a reduce function. The reduce function performs a specific task on a group of pairs with same key and produces a list of key-value pairs that form the final output. This section introduces parallel kNN queries algorithm using MapReduce programming model.

First MapReduce Phase

The first MapReduce phase constructs the projection in two-dimensional space of multi-dimensional point set R and S, R_i and S_i, also determines the partitioning value using Voronoi diagram for R_i and S_i. Firstly,

Figure 7. R-tree indexing of the points

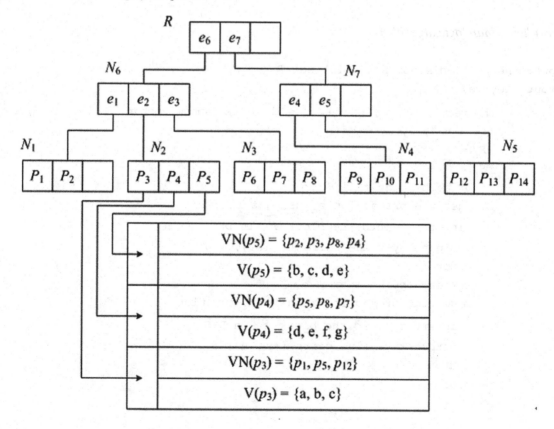

the master node generates the vectors $\{v_1, v_2, \ldots, v_\alpha\}$, saves these vectors to distributed file system (DFS), and adds the file to the distributed cache, which is communicated to all mappers during initialization.

Each mapper processes a split of R or S as a single point at a time. For each vector v_i, the mapper firstly computes $v_i + p$ of each point p and then computes the projection $z_{vi + p}$ in two-dimensional space of multi-dimensional point $v_i + p$ and writes an entry $(id, z_{vi + p})$ to a single-chunk file in distributed file system (DFS) identifiable by the source dataset R or S.

From step 5 to step 8, the Map logic algorithm gets the projection z_{ri} of each point r_i using z-function. Then, the algorithm 2 inserts z_{ri} into the block $\widetilde{R_i}$ in distributed file system (DFS). Furthermore, the algorithm 2 outputs key-value pairs. Meanwhile, the algorithm 2 gets the projection z_{si} of each point s_i using z-function. Then, the algorithm 2 inserts z_{si} into the block $\widetilde{S_i}$ in distributed file system (DFS). Finally, the algorithm 2 outputs key-value pairs.

In the reduce stage, a reduce task is started to handle each of the α partitions, consisting of points from $\widetilde{R_i}$ and $\widetilde{S_i}$. The algorithm uses a grouping comparator which groups by i to ensure each reducer task calls the reduce function only once, passing all points from $\widetilde{R_i}$ and $\widetilde{S_i}$ to the reduce function. The reduce function first iterates over each of the projection points in two-dimensional space and saves these points into an array. From lines 1 to lines 8 of the algorithm 3, the reducer computes each point z_{ri}. If the projection z_{ri} is same point, then the algorithm merges the same point z_{ri} as z_{ri}'. From lines 10 to lines 16 of the algorithm 3, the reducer computes each point z_{si}. If the projection z_{si} is same point, then the algorithm merges the same point z_{si} as z_{si}'.

Algorithm 2. Map logic algorithm

```
Input: the multi-dimensional point set R and S,
Output: key-value pairs

1.         the vector {v₂, v₃, …, vₐ}, v₁ = 0⃗, vᵢ is random vector in Rᵈ, i ∈ [1, α]
2.         for i = 1, 2, …, α do
3.             Rᵢ = vᵢ + R
4.             Sᵢ = vᵢ + S
5.             for each point rᵢ ∈ Rᵢ do
6.                 get the projection zᵣᵢ using z-function
7.                 insert zᵣᵢ into the block R̃ᵢ in DFS
8.                 output key-value pairs ((rᵢ, i), zᵣᵢ)
9.             endfor
10.            for each point sᵢ ∈ Sᵢ do
11.                get the projection zₛᵢ using z-function
12.                insert zₛᵢ into the block S̃ᵢ in DFS
13.                output key-value pairs ((sᵢ, i), zₛᵢ)
14.            endfor
15.        endfor
```

Algorithm 3. Reduce logic algorithm

```
Input: intermediate key-value pairs of Mappers
Output: key-value pairs of first MapReduce phase
1.        for each point z_ri do
2.           if the projection z_ri is same
3.              merge the same point z_ri as z_ri'
4.           else
5.              z_ri' = z_ri
6.           endif
7.              output key-value pairs  ((r_i, i), z_ri')
8.        endfor
9.        for each point z_ri do
10.          if the projection z_si is same
11.             merge the same point z_si as z_si'
12.          else
13.             z_si' = z_si
14.          endif
15.             output key-value pairs  ((s_i, i), z_si')
16.       endfor
```

Second MapReduce Phase

The second MapReduce phase partitions the points set $\widetilde{R}_i$ and $\widetilde{S}_i$ using Voronoi diagram, and uses the R-tree to index the points set in order to parallel kNN queries.

The second Map logic algorithm first places the file containing partition values for $\widetilde{R}_i$ and $\widetilde{S}_i$, which is the outputs of reducers in first MapReduce phase. Then, the master loads the file to the distributed cache, and starts mappers for each split of $\widetilde{R}_i$ and $\widetilde{S}_i$ files containing shifted points computed and written to distributed file system (DFS). The algorithm 4 sends points to one of the $\alpha*n$ total $(R_{i,j}, S_{i,j})$ partitions. Mappers read partition values for $\widetilde{R}_i$ and $\widetilde{S}_i$ from the distributed cache and store them in two arrays. From step 1 to step 6 of the algorithm 4, the algorithm partitions the two-dimensional space using the Voronoi diagram. The Voronoi polygons (VP$_j$) contains the point z_{ri}, and the algorithm inserts z_{ri} into the block $R_{i,j}$. Moreover, the algoritm 4 indexes z_{ri} using R-tree. Finally, the algorithm output key-value pairs $((index_j, r_i), z_{ri})$, where the $index_j$ is indexing of the R-tree. Meanwhile, the Voronoi polygons (VP$_j$) contains the point z_{si}, and the algorithm inserts z_{si} into the blok $S_{i,j}$. Finally, the algorithm outputs key-value pairs $((index_j, s_i), z_{si})$, where the $index_j$ is indexing of the R-tree.

The algorithm 5 computes $C_i(z_{ri})$ for each $z_{ri} \in R_{i,j}$ in partition $(R_{i,j}, S_{i,j})$, $\alpha*n$ reducers handle the $\alpha*n$ $(R_{i,j}, S_{i,j})$ partitions. A reducer first reads the vector file from the distributed cache. Each reduce task then calls the reduce function only once, passing in all points for its $(R_{i,j}, S_{i,j})$ partition. The reduce

Algorithm 4. Second Map logic algorithm

Input: the outputted key-value pairs of first Reduce logic algorithm
Output: key-value pairs

```
1.         for each point z_ri ∈ R̃_i do
2.             construct the Voronoi diagram to generate the Voronoi polygons
3.             find j ∈ [1, n] such that the Voronoi polygons (VP_j) contains
                the point z_ri
4.             insert z_ri into the block R_i, j
5.             index z_ri using R-tree
6.             output key-value pairs ((index_j, r_i), z_ri)
7.         endfor
8.         for each point z_si ∈ S̃_i do
9.             for j = 1, 2, …, n do
10.                if the Voronoi polygons (VP_j) can contain the point z_si
then
11.                    insert z_si into the blok S_i, j
12.                    index z_si using R-tree
13.                endif
14.            endfor
15.            output key-value pairs ((index_j, s_i), z_si)
16.        endfor
```

Algorithm 5. Second Reduce logic algorithm

Input: the outputted intermediate key-value pairs of second Map logic algorithm
Output: key-value pairs

```
1.         for i = 1, 2, …, α do
2.             find block R_i, j containing z_ri
3.             find C_i(z_ri) in S_i, j
4.             ∀ z_si ∈ C_i(z_ri)
5.             updates z_si = z_si - v_i
6.         endfor
```

7.   let $C(z_{ri}) = \cup_{i=1}^{\alpha} C_i(z_{ri})$

8.   output $(z_{ri}, kNN(z_{ri}, C(z_{ri})))$

function then iterates over all points by their *index* attributes, which is the R-tree index storing the points into two vectors: one containing points for $R_{i,j}$ and the other containing points from $S_{i,j}$. From line 1 to line 6 of the algorithm 5, the algorithm finds block $R_{i,j}$ containing z_{ri} and find $C_i(z_{ri})$ in $S_{i,j}$. Then, the algorithm updates $z_{si} = z_{si} - v_i$. Finally, the algorithm outputs the key-value pairs $(z_{ri}, kNN(z_{ri}, C(z_{ri})))$, and uses the inverse function of z-function to get the results of *k*NN queries.

EXPERIMENTS

Experimental Setup

To evaluate the effectiveness of the method, this chapter used the OpenStreet dataset from the OpenStreetMap project for an empirical evaluation, and showed performance results of the parallel kNN queries for big space data based on Voronoi diagram using MapReduce (PVDM) method. The Openstreet dataset represents the road networks for a US state. The entire dataset has the road networks for 50 states, containing more than 160 million records in 8GB. All the experiments were implemented in JDK 6.0, and performed on a heterogeneous cluster consisting of 17 nodes with 2.9GHz Intel Pentium G2020 processor and 4GB of RAM. Each node is connected to a Gigabit Ethernet switch and runs hadoop 2.2.0.

The default dimensionality is 2, and this chapter also uses the synthetic data sets to test all algorithms on the datasets of varying dimensionality 3. This chapter generates a number of different datasets as R and S from the complete OpenStreet dataset (50 states) by randomly selecting 10, 20, 40, 80, 100, 150 million records. This chapter uses $(M \times N)$ to denote a dataset configuration, where M and N are the number of records (in million) of R and S respectively, e.g., a (40×40) dataset has 40 million R and 40 million S records.

The experiment aims at evaluating the efficiency of different kNN queries methods: (1) The parallel kNN queries for big space data based on Voronoi diagram using MapReduce method, henceforth referred to as PVDM; (2) The Hadoop Block R-tree Join approach described in the work of Zhang *et al.* (2012), henceforth referred to as H-BRJ. The H-BRJ method is to build an index for the local S block in a bucket in the reducer, to help find kNNs of a record r from the local R block in the same bucket. For each block S_{bj} $(1 \leq j \leq n)$, the H-BRJ method builds a reducer-local spatial index over S_{bj}, in particular the H-BRJ method used the R-tree, before proceeding to find the local kNNs for every record from the local R block in the same bucket with S_{bj}. Then, the chapter uses kNN functionality from R-tree to answer $kNN(r, S_{bj})$ in every bucket in the reducer. Bulk-loading a R-tree for S_{bj} is very efficient, and kNN search in R-tree is also efficient, hence this overhead is compensated by savings from not running a local nested loop in each bucket.

Query Performance Experiment

This section evaluates the execution time of PVDM and H-BRJ method with different dataset configurations. The PVDM method delivers much better running time performance than H-BRJ method from Figure 8. The trends in Figure 8 also indicate PVDM becomes increasingly more efficient than H-BRJ as the dataset sizes increase.

Many factors contribute to the performance advantage of PVDM over H-BRJ. Firstly, H-BRJ needs to duplicate dataset blocks to achieve parallel processing, i.e. if the experiments construct n blocks, the experiments must duplicate each block n times for a total of n^2 partitions, while PVDM only has $\alpha*n$ partitions. Secondly, given the same number of block n in R and S, PVDM requires fewer machines to process all partitions for the kNN queries of R and S in parallel than H-BRJ does. The PVDM method needs $\alpha*n$ machines while H-BRJ needs n^2 machines to achieve the same level of parallelism.

Figure 8. Execution times of PVDM and H-BRJ method

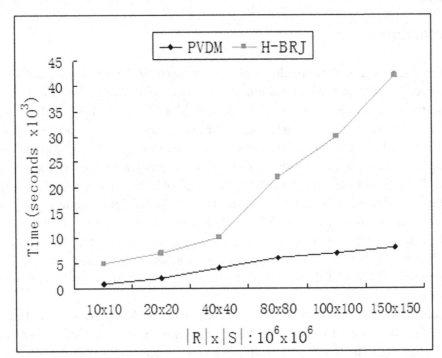

Precision and Recall of Different Queries Method

This section uses the formal precision and recall metrics to measure the retrieval quality. Precision is the ratio of the number of relevant query nodes retrieved to the total number of retrieved nodes:

$$Precision = \frac{|\, relevant \cap retrieved \,|}{|\, retrieved \,|} \tag{5}$$

Recall is the ratio of the number of relevant nodes retrieved to the total number of relevant nodes:

$$Recall = \frac{|\, relevant \cap retrieved \,|}{|\, relevant \,|} \tag{6}$$

This experiment measures the precision and recall of the results returned by PVDM and H-BRJ method. It can be seen that PVDM method outperforms H-BRJ method, and PVDM always achieves higher precision and recall than H-BRJ. The experiment uses the OpenStreet datasets and gradually increases datasets from (10x10) to (150x150). The average precision and recall of PVDM method are above 90% all the time. However, the average precision and recall of H-BRJ method are below 70%.

Figure 9. Precision of PVDM and H-BRJ method

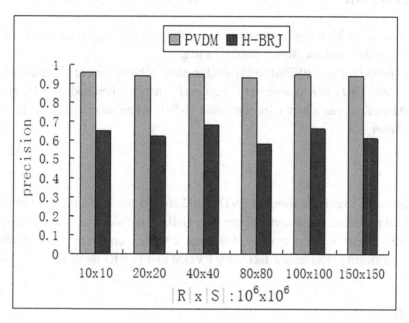

Figure 10. Recall of PVDM and H-BRJ method

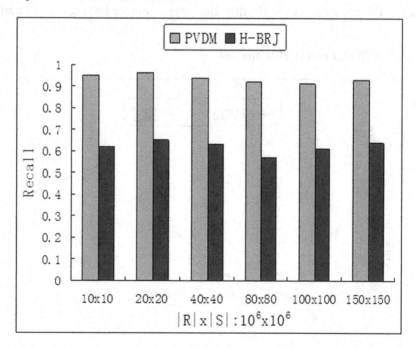

Speedup Experiment

The speedup for each algorithm is the ratio of the execution time on a given cluster configuration over the execution time on the smallest cluster configuration.

The Figure 11 shows that both PVDM and H-BRJ method achieve almost a linear speedup up to nodes 16. Both PVDM and H-BRJ method achieve the best performance when nodes n=16, and degrade when n>16. The PVDM method has a better speedup than H-BRJ when more physical slaves are becoming available in the cluster.

Effect of *k*

The Figure 12 shows the execution time for PVDM and H-BRJ method with different *k*. It can be seen that PVDM method performs consistently better than H-BRJ method. For small *k* values, *k*NN queries are the determining factors for performance. For large *k* values, communication overheads gradually become a more significant performance factor for PVDM and H-BRJ method.

CONCLUSION

This chapter proposes a method of parallel *k*NN queries for big space data based on Voronoi diagram using MapReduce programming model. Firstly, this chapter presents the *k*NN queries of multi-dimensional

Figure 11. Speedup of PVDM and H-BRJ method

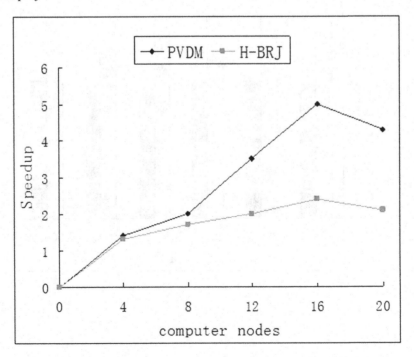

Figure 12. Execution time of PVDM and H-BRJ method with different k

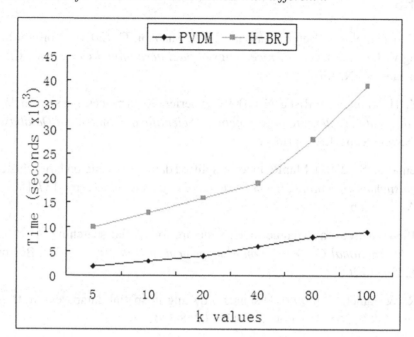

space data, and maps the multi-dimensional space data to two-dimensional space data using z-function and z-curves. In order to get a theoretical guarantee, this chapter uses the random shift to convert the space data point. In the spatial database, the number of vector points is huge. The random shift can convert the space point to a space area, and reduce the computational burden of the spatial query, and improve the query efficiency. Then, this chapter translates the kNN query for a query point q in multi-dimensional space into two-dimensional point search. Furthermore, this chapter proposes the approximate kNN queries algorithm, and the algorithm can obtain the approximate kNN of query point q.

Secondly, this chapter proposes the partitioned method based on Voronoi diagram in two-dimensional space. The Voronoi diagram decomposes two-dimensional space into disjoint polygons. This chapter constructs Voronoi diagram using MapReduce programming model, because Voronoi diagram can be obtained by merging multiple Voronoi polygons.

Thirdly, this chapter proposes the method of indexing the Voronoi diagram using R-tree. The R-tree indexing of point set augmented with the points' Voronoi diagram. Moreover, this chapter proposes the parallel kNN queries using MapReduce programming model, which consists of two MapReduce phase. Moreover, this chapter presents the algorithm of parallel query using MapReduce programming model.

Finally, the extensive experimental results demonstrate that proposed method is better than existing works. The future research direction is the issue of parallel query for big data using MapReduce programming model which is a well-accepted framework for data-intensive applications over clusters of computers, and studies the problem of parallel geospatial query processing with MapReduce programming model further.

REFERENCES

Akdogan, A., Demiryurek, U., Banaei-Kashani, F., & Shahabi, C. (2010). Voronoi-based geospatial query processing with mapreduce. In *Proceedings of the International Conference Cloud Computing*, (pp. 9-16). Indianapolis, IN: IEEE.

Cary, A., Sun, Z., Hristidis, V., & Rishe, N. (2009). Experiences on processing spacial data with MapReduce. In *Proceedings of the International Conference Scientific and Statistical Database Management*, (pp. 302-319). New Orleans, LA: Springer.

Dean, J., & Ghemawat, S. (2004). MapReduce: simplified data processing on large clusters. In *Proceedings of the Symposium on Operating System Design and Implementation*, (pp. 137-150). San Francisco, CA: USENIX Association.

Guttman, A. (1984). R-trees: a dynamic index structure for spatial searching. In *Proceedings of the ACM SIGMOD International Conference on Management of Data*, (pp. 47-57). Boston: ACM Press. doi:10.1145/602259.602266

Hjaltason, G. R., & Samet, H. (1999). Distance browsing in spatial databases. *ACM Transactions on Database Systems*, 24(2), 265–318. doi:10.1145/320248.320255

Jiang, D., Ooi, B. C., Shi, L., & Wu, S. (2010). The performance of MapReduce: An in-depth study. *Proceedings of the VLDB Endowment*, 3(1), 472–483. doi:10.14778/1920841.1920903

Kim, Y., & Shim, K. (2012). Parallel top-k similarity join algorithms using MapReduce. In *Proceedings of the International Conference on Data Engineering*, (pp. 510-521). Arlington, VA: IEEE Computer Society. doi:10.1109/ICDE.2012.87

Mondal, A., Lifu, Y., & Kitsuregawa, M. (2004). P2PR-Tree: An R-tree-based spacial index for peer-to-peer environments. In *Proceedings of the International Conference on Extending Database Technology Joint PhD Workshop*, (pp. 516-525). Heraklion, Greece: Springer. doi:10.1007/978-3-540-30192-9_51

Mouza, C., Litwin, W., & Rigaux, P. (2007). SD-Rtree: A scalable distributed Rtree. In *Proceedings of the International Conference on Data Engineering*, (pp. 296-305). Istanbul, Turkey: IEEE.

Okabe, A., Boots, B., Sugihara, K., & Chiu, S. N. (2000). *Spatial tessellations, concepts and applications of Voronoi diagrams* (2nd ed.). John Wiley and Sons Ltd. doi:10.1002/9780470317013

Okcan, A., & Riedewald, M. (2011). Processing theta-joins using MapReduce. In *Proceedings of the ACM SIGMOD International Conference on Management of Data*, (pp. 949-960). Athens, Greece: ACM.

Roussopoulos, N., Kelley, S., & Vincent, F. (1995). Nearest neighbor queries. In *Proceedings of the ACM SIGMOD International Conference on Management of Data*, (pp. 71-79). San Jose, CA: ACM Press.

Vernica, R., Carey, M. J., & Li, C. (2010). Efficient parallel set-similarity joins using mapreduce. In *Proceedings of the ACM SIGMOD International Conference on Management of Data*, (pp. 495-506). Indianapolis, IN: ACM.

Wang, J., Wu, S., Gao, H., Li, J., & Ooi, B. C. (2010). Indexing multi-dimensional data in a cloud system. In *Proceedings of the ACM SIGMOD International Conference on Management of Data*, (pp. 591-602). Indianapolis, IN: ACM. doi:10.1145/1807167.1807232

Wu, S., Jiang, D., Ooi, B. C., & Wu, K. L. (2010). Efficient b-tree based indexing for cloud data processing. *Proceedings of the VLDB Endowment*, *3*(1), 1207–1218. doi:10.14778/1920841.1920991

Xia, C., Lu, H., Ooi, B. C., & Hu, J. (2004). Gorder: an efficient method for knn join processing. In *Proceedings of the International Conference on Very Large Data Bases*, (pp. 756-767). Toronto, Canada: Morgan Kaufmann. doi:10.1016/B978-012088469-8.50067-X

Yao, B., Li, F., & Kumar, P. (2010). K nearest neighbor queries and kNN-joins in large relational databases (almost) for free. In *Proceedings of the International Conference on Data Engineering*, (pp. 4-15). Long Beach, CA: IEEE. doi:10.1109/ICDE.2010.5447837

Yu, C., Cui, B., Wang, S., & Su, J. (2007). Efficient index-based knn join processing for high-dimensional data. *Information and Software Technology*, *49*(4), 332–344. doi:10.1016/j.infsof.2006.05.006

Yu, C., Ooi, B. C., Tan, K. L., & Jagadish, H. V. (2001). Indexing the distance: an efficient method to knn processing. In *Proceedings of the International Conference on Very Large Data Bases*, (pp. 421-430). Roma, Italy: Morgan Kaufmann.

Zhang, C., Li, F., & Jestes, J. (2012). Efficient parallel kNN joins for large data in MapReduce. In *Proceedings of the International Conference on Extending Database Technology*, (pp. 38-49). Berlin, Germany: ACM. doi:10.1145/2247596.2247602

Zhang, S., Han, J., Liu, Z., Wang, K., & Xu, Z. (2009). SJMR: Parallelizing spacial join with MapReduce on clusters. In *Proceedings of the IEEE International Conference on Cluster Computing*, (pp. 1-8). New Orleans, LA: IEEE Computer Society. doi:10.1109/CLUSTR.2009.5289178

KEY TERMS AND DEFINITIONS

Distance between Points *r* and *s*: In *n*-dimensional space *D*, given two points *r* and *s*, |*r*, *s*| represents the distance between point *r* and *s* in space *D*. In this chapter, the Euclidean distance is used as the distance. $| r,s | = (\sum_{i=1}^{n} (r[i] - s[i])^2)^{1/2}$ where, $r[i]$ (resp. $s[i]$) denotes the value of *r* (resp. *s*) along the ith dimension in space *D*.

***k* Nearest Neighbors:** Given a point *r*, a dataset *S* in space *D* and an integer *k*, the *k* nearest neighbors of *r* from *S*, denoted as kNN(*r*, *s*), is a set of *k* point from *S* that $\forall p \in k$NN(*r*, *S*), $\forall s \in S - k$NN(*r*, *S*), |*p*, *r*|≤|*s*, *r*|.

***k*NN Queries:** Given two dataset *R* and *S* in space *D*, and an integer *k*. *k*NN queries of *R* and *S* (denoted as $k$nnQ), combine each point $r \in R$ with its *k* nearest neighbors from *S*. $k$nnQ(*R*, *S*) = {(*r*, kNN(*r*, *S*)) | for all $r \in R$}.

MapReduce Programming Model: MapReduce is a popular programming framework to support data-intensive applications using shared-nothing clusters.

R-Tree: R-tree is the index structure widely used for spacial query processing.

Voronoi Diagram: The Voronoi diagram of a given set $P = \{p_1, p_2, ..., p_n\}$ of n points in R^d partitions the space of R^d into n regions. Each region includes all points in R^d with a common closest point in the given set P using the distance metric $Dist()$. The region corresponding to the point $p \in P$ contains all the points $q \in R^d$. $\forall p' \in P, p' \neq p, Dist(q, p) \leq Dist(q, p')$.

Voronoi Polygon: Given set of points $P = \{p_1, p_2, ..., p_n\}$ where $2 < n < \infty$ and $p_i \neq p_j$ for $i \neq j$, i, $j = 1, 2, ..., n$, the Voronoi polygon of p_i is $VP(p_i) = \{p \mid d(p, p_i) \leq d(p, p_j)\}$ for $i \neq j$ and $p \in VP(p_i)$ where $d(p, p_i)$ specifies the minimum distance between p and p_i in Euclidean space.

Chapter 15
Query Languages in NoSQL Databases

Maristela Holanda
University of Brasilia, Brazil

Jane Adriana Souza
University of Brasilia, Brazil

ABSTRACT

This chapter aims to investigate how NoSQL (Not Only SQL) databases provide query language and data retrieval mechanisms. Users attest to many advantages in using the NoSQL databases for specific applications, however, they also report that querying and retrieving data easily continues to be a problem. The NoSQL operations require that, during the project, the queries must be thought of as built-in application codes. The authors intend to contribute to the investigation of querying, considering different types of NoSQL databases.

INTRODUCTION

Edgar Codd introduced the relational model in 1970, which had the main objective of providing support for data independence and integrity (Silva, 2011). As the relational model has a strong theoretical foundation, it has been fully accepted by the academia. In the past few decades, the relational database has become dominant database model.

Padhy et al. (2011) cite that from the time relational databases began, a few of model databases was introduced, such as object database (DB40, Velocity) and XML database (BaseX, Berkeley DB XML). Recently, a new database model known as NoSQL has emerged and promises to dominate the market, though the guaranteeing high performance, handle modern workloads, and ability to process large volumes of unstructured data.

Database systems must provide data structures and advanced techniques to improve access and retrieval activities for data management (Elmasri & Navathe, 2011). Traditional relational database systems usually have an interactive interface to run SQL (Structured Query Language) commands. The interactive interface is very convenient for *ad hoc* queries. It is also possible to interact with the database through

DOI: 10.4018/978-1-4666-8767-7.ch015

application programs using API (Application Programming Interface) or embedded SQL in applications. SQL language is useful in minimizing the impedance mismatch problem, which occurs due to differences between the model database and programming language.

The SQL language can be considered one of the most successful generators of relational database, because it is a widely used language with instructions for data definition, queries and updates. In addition, the SQL language provides a declarative language interface level so that users can easily declare what they wish.

The researches in cloud computing predict new architectures for data management, contributing to the rise in structured and unstructured data. The NoSQL databases are used in a cloud computing environment. The question is how to use the new database engine architectures, declarative programming languages, and the interplay of structured and unstructured data is a point to investigate (Elmasri & Navathe, 2011; Agrawal et al., 2009).

According to Hecht and Jablonski (2011), with the increasing amount of data generated by Web 2.0, the applications have storage requirements that exceed capacities and possibilities of traditional relational databases. The NoSQL databases come to store and process massive data, and the queries occur over huge amounts of data. The possibility of providing user-friendly query languages and exhibiting the results efficiently has been the object of academic study in NoSQL database. Recently, studies on data query language to unify NoSQL query interfaces appear as a possibility (Bach & Werner, 2014; Nasholm, 2012). One idea is to create a simple interface where users define the query for data independently of NoSQL databases. This is a challenge nowadays because there are many NoSQL databases with different data model. This chapter highlights the features of data query and retrieval mechanisms of some NoSQL databases and identify how the different NoSQL databases work with these operations.

The organization of this chapter is as follows. Section 2 presents background on NoSQL databases. NoSQL Query Languages are provided in Section 3. Section 4 presents Comparative Analysis of NoSQL languages, and the chapter closes with Recommendations plus Future Research Directions.

BACKGROUND

The need to manage big data encouraged the development of new database models. Some factors could be cited to demonstrate that the idea is inevitable, because of the limitations of traditional relational databases (Indrawan-Santiago, 2012):

- The advent of cloud computing with easy to access parallel computing;
- The proliferation of Web 2.0 applications and the interest of academia in e-science applications;
- The need to dealing with large amounts of data;
- The need to manage both structured and unstructured data.

Based on these factors, NoSQL databases were designed and developed.

With the requirements for big data applications, the use of NoSQL databases has become popular as suitable alternatives for data management. The NoSQL databases emerged as a leader in appropriately dealing with big data, because it has efficient big data storage and access requirements, easy and high scalability and availability, as well as providing low cost. The nomenclature NoSQL, is often understood as, "Not only SQL", which indicates that the dialect of SQL is unsupported (Nasholm, 2012; Porkorny, 2013). Some researchers find this nomenclature confusing, and suggest other terms such as, NoRel (Not RELational) or NoJoin (Not JOIN) (Bach & Werner, 2014). The main idea is that NoSQL differs from the traditional databases because it is a non-relational data model and lacks schema definitions (Nasholm, 2012).

Despite the advantages of using NoSQL databases, the ability to analyze and visualize data is still considered challenging for the database users compared to the use of traditional relational databases.

Researches have shown that NoSQL databases have mechanisms for data querying, and data retrieval, showing that a query language is necessary for these database models. Subsequently, the question arises: do those query languages contain common characteristics or are they similar to languages such as SQL language? Usually, each NoSQL database offers its own query interface.

The NoSQL operates requires that, during the project, it is necessary to consider whether the queries should be built-in application codes. In others words, the database should be defined by how applications use it, and if it is necessary to query and retrieve data.

SQL Query Language

The SQL language is one of the main languages used for database queries, data manipulation and data retrieval in Relational DataBase Management System (RDBMS). The SQL has statements for Data Definition Language (DDL) and a Data Manipulation Language (DML). The DDL commands for creating and modifying schemas, tables and constraints. The DML common commands are *select, insert, update* and *delete* for data manipulation.

The SQL provides a high-level declarative language so that users can easily declare what they wish (Elmasri & Navathe, 2011). Traditional relational database systems usually have an interactive interface to run SQL commands. The interactive interface is very convenient to facilitate the user/developer works. Also it is possible to interact with the database through application programs using APIs or embedded SQL.

In relational databases, the SQL language is considered valuable because it supports portability and expressiveness, and it is widely used by users (Porkony, 2013). The run queries on the RDBMS are considered essential, and query languages offer a high level abstraction in order to reduce complexity. So they are useful, mainly for users and database administrators, who need access data structures using friendly mechanisms.

NoSQL Databases

With the advances on the internet, the world is becoming increasingly connected and there is rapid growth in the volume of information. Tauro et al. (2012) showed, in a review of the International Data Corporation, an increase of nearly 25 times in the volume of data between 2007 to 2010. Additionally, according to Gartner statistics, 80% is unstructured data (Liu et al., 2011; Wei and Bo, 2010). The types of unstructured data include text, e-mail, multimedia, social media, graphics, images, audio and video.

New web 2.0 applications and big data requirements come to data management through the use of technologies for storing and processing massive data, encompassing elasticity properties, with provisions for computing resources, storage capacity, high availability, services on demand, and fast data access width bandwidth, and networking (Kllapi et al., 2013). The NoSQL database emerges as an appropriate model to lead with these types of data, as a solution to the issue of storage scalability, parallelism and processing large volumes of unstructured data, as well as big data storage and access requirements.

The relational databases are widely used in many applications for storing data. When the amount of information increases, and when handling large volumes of unstructured data, relational databases do not appear to be the best solution. Semi-structured or unstructured Information is difficulty to fit in the relational databases. The web applications players, Google and Amazon recognized that NoSQL databases are more appropriated to handle with unstructured data than traditional relational databases (Kaur & Rani, 2013).

The NoSQL databases should be used in situations where traditional relational databases are not appropriated (Mapanga & Kadebu, 2013). The NoSQL databases are specialized for particular use cases, so the "Use the right tool for the job" is motto of defenders (Hecht & Jablonski, 2011). Kaur and Rani (2013) consider traditional relational databases are focus on answers whereas NoSQL are focus on questions.

In general, the NoSQL databases have the following characteristics (Indrawan-Santiago, 2012; Muhammad, 2011; Tauro et al., 2012):

- Non relational;
- Distributed processing;
- High Availability;
- High scalability and reliability;
- Schemaless, usually, the NoSQL databases provide data models that do not have schema, and this results in a very simple data model, and faster run read and write data;
- Replication support;
- Ability to handle structured and unstructured data.
- Data access via API;
- Less strict adherence to consistency, which is done by relaxing ACID - atomicity, consistency, isolation, and durability – properties and building a protocol that eventually enables the establishment of a consistent state in the database;
- Improvements in performance.

NoSQL Database Models

There are 150 NoSQL databases cataloged according to electronic sources (NoSQL, 2015). Bach and Werner (2014), Indrawan-Santiago (2012), Hecht and Jablonski (2011) classified the NoSQL databases into four mainstream categories according to their data model: Key-Value, Document store, Column-Family and Graph database. Each model is described as follows.

- KEY-VALUE (KEY VALUE PAIR or KEY-VALUE STORES or BIG HASH TABLES)

In this database model, data is stored as key-value pairs. These systems are similar to dictionaries where the data are addressed by a single key. Values are isolated and independent from others, where the relationship is handled by the application logic.

Hecht and Jablonski (2011) present the Key-Value database as completely schema free, and the relationship between values and keys should be handled by an application. It is acceptable to have different data values at the time of reading relational databases. The application program or the client should be able to solve the problem of inconsistency.

The Key-Value database is a suitable solution for simple applications that work with a single kind of object, and the search for objects is based on a single attribute (Catell, 2010; Indrawan-Santiago, 2012). It has a simple structure, also known as distributed *hash* structures, which store objects indexed by keys. The search for these objects is from the keys (De Diana & Gerosa, 2010) and this result in a reduced query execution time. According Kaur and Rani (2013) this model is appropriate for applications where schema evolutions are constant. Usually these databases do not have ad-hoc querying features like join or aggregate operations.

Examples of Key-Value store database are Berkeley DB (BerkeleyDB, 2015), Tokyo Tyrant (FAL, 2015), Voldemort (Voldemort, 2015), Dynamo (Dynamo, 2015), Redis (Redis, 2015).

- Column-Family (column oriented stores, extensible record stores, WIDE-TABLE DATA STORE OR wide columnar stores)

The Column-Family database defines the structure of values as a predefined set of columns. The Column-Family store can be considered as a database schema, where the *super-columns* and *column-family* structures determine the schema of the database (Indrawan-Santiago, 2012).

The principal definitions are *column*, *super-columns* and *column-family*:

- A *column* is atomic information on the database. It is expressed by name and value.
- The *super-columns* associate columns to return together from the disk or have semantic association. It is useful for modeling complex types of data, such as addresses.
- A *column-family* joins *super-columns* and *columns*. The concept approaches a table in a relational model.

The Column-Family database is not a restrictive system: new columns or *super-columns* can be added easily to the production of environment databases. Each row in a Column-Family database may have different degrees, i.e. may have a variable number of *columns / super-columns*. Due to this characteristic, the Column-Family database supports spaced data. The columns of a table are divided over the nodes using *column groups*. These can be seen as a new complexity, but *column groups* are a simple way users can indicate which columns are best stored together (Catell, 2010).

According to De Diana and Gerosa (2010) the insertion of records is much more costly than those done in traditional databases. The relationships must be addressed by the application. *Sharding* the rows is done by the primary key. They are typically divided into intervals. The horizontal and vertical partitioning can be used simultaneously in the same table.

Hecht and Jablonski (2011) affirm that these databases are suitable for applications that deal with large data storage clusters and very large datasets, which have to be scaled to large sizes, so the data model can be efficiently partitioned. According to Catell (2010) for cases where you want to optimize the reading of structured data, column families are preferable because they keep the data contiguously by column. The authors Kaur and Rani (2013) consider these databases appropriate to analytical purposes because they deal with few specific columns.

Examples of Column-Family databases are Hbase (Hbase, 2015), PNUTS (Pnuts, 2015), Cassandra (Cassandra, 2015).

- DOCUMENT store (document database)

A Document store uses the concept of Key-Value store. The documents are collections of attributes and values, where an attribute can be multivalued. The keys inside documents must be unique. Each document contains an ID key, which is unique within a collection and identifies document. The data storage is an ISDN (Integrated Services Digital Network) document and has the additional advantage of supporting data types, which makes the Documents stores more developers/users friendly.

In general, Document store is schemaless: the document does not need to have a common structure. It is common for a Document database to store the values in a document-like structure such as JSON (JavaScript Object Notation) or XML (Extensible Markup Language). The JSON format is frequently used for such structures. JSON supports datatypes *list, map, date, boolean,* and also numbers with different accuracies (Indrawan-Santiago, 2012; Porkorny, 2013).

Catell (2010) points out that Document stores support more complex data than the Key-Value stores: a document in these systems can be any kind of "pointerless object". Unlike the Key-Value stores, it generally supports secondary indexes and multiple types of documents (objects) per database, and nested documents or lists. The documents are indexed and enable the run of a simple search engine.

Hecht and Jablonski (2011) affirm that these systems are easier to maintain and are therefore desirable for flexible web applications, with execution of dynamic queries, such as real time analytics, logging and the storage layer of small and flexible websites like blogs. An example of this is the management of different types of objects, where it is necessary to look for objects based on multiple fields.

Examples of Document stores are Mongo DB (Mongodb, 2015), Couch DB (CouchDB, 2015) and Riak (Riak, 2015).

- Graph database

A Graph database uses graphs to represent schema. Graph database works with three abstractions: Node, relationships between nodes and key-value pairs that can be attached to nodes and relationships (Tauro et al., 2012).

Unlike other types of NoSQL databases, this system is directly related to a model of established data, the graphs model. It supports the use of data integrity restrictions, such as restrictions identity and referential integrity. In other words, it ensures that relationships between elements remain consistent.

The Graph databases allow two strategies for queries and data retrieval: the first strategy call, Graph Patter Matching, tries to find parts of the original graph, which match the model graph defined. The second strategy, Graph Transversal, starts from the chosen node and transverses the graph according to the description (Hecht & Jablonski, 2011).

The Graph databases are specialized in managing large volumes of data, and used in domains where entities are as important as the relationships between them (Wei & Bo, 2010). These systems are desirable for applications based on data with many relationships within cost-intensive operations, such as *recursive joins,* which can be solved more easily (Hecht & Jablonski, 2011). The graph model is preferable to others when "information about the topology or interconnectivity of data is important, or as important as the data itself "(De Diana & Gerosa, 2010).

Due to Graph Theory, there are available query languages that can be used for databases of this model. Is possible cite like Cypher, Gremlin (Gremlin, 2015) and SPARQL (Kaur and Rani, 2013).

Examples of Graph databases are Neo4j (Neo4j, 2015), GraphDB (GrafphDB, 2015), InfoGrid (InfoGrid, 2015), Allegrograph (Allegrograph, 2015).

NOSQL QUERY LANGUAGES

Despite the advantages of NoSQL databases, each NoSQL model has owner query mechanisms or query language that are difficult for users to become acquainted with in a general way. It is necessary to understand and specialize in a particular NoSQL database type to be able to use its query mechanism. This condition differs from traditional databases, especially relational ones, which have the SQL language nomenclature as a standard maintained and adopted to various RDBMS.

Lawrence (2014) cited the primary reasons why the supporting SQL querying is interesting to NoSQL databases:

- SQL language allows descriptive queries while hiding implementation and query execution details;
- SQL allowing easy portability between database systems;
- SQL standards facilitate intercommunication;
- SQL is widely known by database developers and database administrators;
- Supporting SQL allows interact with other systems that use SQL and JDBC/ODBC;
- SQL allows isolate users and programmers from writing complicated data manipulation code, letting the database administrators with administrative database tasks.

Query and Retrieval Data Mechanisms in NoSQL Databases

The NoSQL databases differ from relational databases not only in their data model, but also in the richness of providing query and retrieval data mechanisms. Due to this, some aspects that are important for relational databases are not considered relevant in NoSQL databases such as data query language.

The database systems should provide the data structures and techniques suitable for easy data retrieval. The NoSQL databases demand a high level of expertise by users/developers to write complex queries. Usually the NoSQL databases have a very limited number of querying support and when there is one, no common query language is available in cases where every database differs in its supported query feature set. The query languages like Apache HIVE (hive, 2015) and Apache PIG (pig, 2015) and querying applications that run on a MapReduce framework have been used in NoSQL database. However, users consider the MapReduce framework difficult to use, and in many cases, the MapReduce (MapReduce, 2015) functions are too complicated to be expressed as easily as in a SQL query (Dean & Ghemawat, 2010).

NoSQL database queries occur over huge amounts of data. The ability to provide query languages for easy use and efficiently display outputs has been the subject of academic study. The query languages help to create an abstraction level that reduces complexity and are helpful when more complicated queries should be handled. The database users who frequently employ the SQL language in relational databases recognize that the low-level resources available by the NoSQL databases require sophisticated skills programming when compared with non-relational databases. Developers need to know data models to identify the query types that are supported by the database, because there is still no common query language – each NoSQL database differs in supported query characteristics. Thus, one of the challenges in getting users to accept this technology is accomplished by achieving a high-level query language for NoSQL databases (Catell, 2010).

Porkorny (2013) showed that a typical API for NoSQL databases contains operations such as:

- *get (key)*: extracts the value of a key;
- *put (key, value)*: creates or updates the value of a given key;
- *delete (key)*: deletes the key and its associated value;
- *execute (key, operations, parameters)*: invokes the operation for a given key value which is a special data structure, e.g. *list, set*.

ANALYSIS OF QUERY AND RETRIEVAL DATA IN NOSQL DATABASES

In this section, we will examine the query and retrieval data mechanisms of the NoSQL databases. If the focus of the query and retrieval mechanism occurs about database models, it is possible to identify some characteristics of the NoSQL databases.

The Key-Value NoSQL database has a simple structure, also known as, distributed hash structures, which store objects indexed by keys. The search for these objects occurs from the keys (De Diana & Gerosa, 2010). The Key-Value database supports query operations and modifications to data by primary keys, and the queries can be done easily using the Lucene (Lucene, 2015) or REST interfaces (Rest, 2015). Key-Value database usually provides commands such as *inserts, delete* and *index lookups* (Catell, 2010). The simplicity of the model allows the use of the operations *put, get,* and *delete* via API. Due the simplicity of the model, the importance for a query language for the Key-Value databases is questioned, because the implementation of complex queries could occur by application.

The Column-Family NoSQL database provides mechanisms for performing operations such as *in, and, or* and regular expressions, when it is applied in key rows or the indexed values (Hecht & Jablonski, 2011). The columns in the same *column-family* are stored on the same server to increase the performance of queries.

The Document database provides a query and retrieval data mechanism based on the restrictions of values of multiple attributes, which provide API for queries. Thus, queries containing intervals of values and nested documents can be carried out. They also permit operations such as *and, or, between* and support REST interfaces (Rest, 2015).

The Graph databases generally offer specific REST APIs for languages. Some query languages are supported by more than one type of Graph database. The SPARQL is a popular, declarative query language with a syntax provided by simple graph pattern matching. Ne04j supports it. Gremlin is an imperative programming language used to perform graph traversals. In addition to supporting Neo4j (Neo4j, 2015) and GraphDB (GraphDB, 2015), Sesame (Sesame, 2015) can also be found with Gremlin after a transformation in the graph.

The next section presents a descriptive summary of some characteristics of NoSQL database grouping by database models, focusing on methods of data querying and retrieval, and query languages, when they are present.

KEY-VALUE DATABASE MODEL

- Redis

Redis (Redis, 2015) is a Key-Value database. The project started with one person but with many contributors, being a BSD licensed open source. The development language is C.

Redis is executed when the data is loaded into memory, and performs all operations in memory, and then periodically the data is saved to disk asynchronously (Nasholm, 2012). Hecht and Jablonski (2011) showed that the characteristics of pure memory ensure good performance, and can treat more than 100,000 operations per second read and written. The disadvantage is that the ability of databases is limited by physical memory, such that Redis cannot be used as storage and big data scalability is poor.

The example below returns the element at index *index* in the list stored at key:

```
>LPUSH mylist "Chapter"
(integer) 1
 >LPUSH mylist "Title"
(integer) 2
 >LINDEX mylist 0
"Title"
 >LINDEX mylist -1
"Chapter"
```

Redis is desirable to provide high-performance computing for small amounts of data (Liu et al., 2011). The data access on Redis is done by implements operations *insert, delete and lookup operations*. It also includes operations *list and set*.

- Riak

Riak (Riak, 2015) is purely a distributed system, Open Source Apache2. It has been open source since 2009. Riak is described as Key-Value database and Document store.

The Riak supplier is Basho (Riak, 2015). The development language is Erlang, which is a general use programming language. Erlang was developed by Ericsson to support distributed and fault-tolerant applications to be performed in an uninterrupted, real-time environment.

Riak is recommended for applications that need to respond to many parallel read and write requests, and have to provide a certain level of consistency. For example with games, Riak is preferable.

Riak's data access provides a friendly query interface based on HTTP / JSON. It uses MapReduce Framework, and REST API to access objects from the cluster. Riak also uses *get, put* or *post* for storage operations and reading.

Riak uses Lucene Syntax as a query language. Lucene (Lucene, 2015) is a document and index software, written in the java. It is open source software from the Apache Software Foundation through the Apache license.

The next example calls the search_key function to return the chapter from a date:

Search_key (Chapter, date:[20150101 TO 20150201], Client)

COLUMN- FAMILY DATABASE MODEL

- Cassandra

Cassandra (Cassandra, 2015) is a Column-Family database, which was initially designed by the Facebook engineering team, in 2008. Nowadays, Cassandra has Apache licensing. Cassandra was developed based on Dynamo and BigTable (Catell, 2010).

Porkorny (2013) indicates that applications with real time transaction processing are commonly used. Facebook and other companies also use Cassandra, thus the code is reasonably mature.

Muhammad (2011) describes Cassandra as having high scalability, a decentralized nature, durability, fault-tolerance, and linear optimization in adding new machines.

Cassandra has a query language called CQL (Cassandra Query Language) similar to SQL. The data access uses the language as select commands. The following is an example to select author and chapter name from Chapter table:

```
SELECT chapter_author, chapter_name
FROM Chapter
WHERE chapter_writing_year = '1988'
```

In relation to data updates, Cassandra uses the general data access through the commands *get* and *put*. The update operations are placed in the memory and then released to the disk. In Cassandra there is no possibility of using joins and the indexes use the technique *ordered hash index*, which provides more benefits than both hash and B-tree indexes because is possible to identify which nodes could have a particular range instead searching all nodes (Catell, 2010).

- HBase

HBase (HBase, 2015) is a Column-Family database supplied by the Apache open source project, since 2007. The development language is Java, modeled based on BigTable, and using the HDFS (Hadoop Distributed File System).

HBase is commonly used for applications that need to respond to a large volume of parallel read and write requests, and has to provide a certain level of consistency (Hecht & Jablonski, 2011).

In relation to data access, HBase supports the MapReduce framework (MapReduce, 2015) and allows access via Java API, Thrift API (Thrift, 2015), REST API (Rest, 2015) and the support of JDBC / ODBC. For data updates, HBase puts the updates in memory and periodically writes in the files on disk. The updates operation goes to the end of the data file, to avoid search efforts (Catell, 2010).

The example below put and list data on 'Chapter' table:

```
> put 'Chapter', 'row1', 'cf:a', 'value1'
> put 'Chapter', 'row2', 'cf:b', 'value2'
> put 'Chapter, 'row3', 'cf:c', 'value3'
> list 'Chapter'
```

A SQL engine is integrated into HBase, which is based on *Apache Derby query engine* to process *joins* and other operations not supported by HBase (Lawrence, 2014).

- HyperTable

HyperTable (HyperTable, 2015) is a Column-Family database, which is very similar to HBase and BigTable. The development language is C++ and is supplied by Open-sourced by Zvents and Baidu has become a project sponsor.

Regarding data access, HyperTable provide programming language client interfaces and the updates operations are done in memory and then flushed to disk (Catell, 2010).

HyperTable uses a query language named HQL (Hypertable Query Language). The HQL is a declarative language similar to SQL. The logical grouping of tables is achieved by namespaces that can be compared with the hierarchy of folders in the file system. One example of using HQL:

```
SELECT chapter_name
FROM Chapter
WHERE chapter_author = "Souza "
```

Bach and Werner (2014) comment that HQL may define the conditions for rows, cells or timestamps. Despite the facilities there are many limitations in comparison with the SELECT statement in RDBMS, such as grouping and aggregate functions.

DOCUMENT STORE DATABASE MODEL

- MongoDB

The MongoDB (MongoDB, 2015) is a NoSQL database that supports the complex BJSON data structure for storing complex data types. Its development language is C++, and the supplier is 10gen.

Tauro et al. (2012) points out that due to its characteristics, many projects expected to increase data are considering using MongoDB instead of relational databases. They also present an interesting comparison: MongoDB provides high-speed access to mass data. When the data exceed 50GB, the access speed of Mongo DB is 10 times greater than in MySQL relational database. The horizontal scalability, high-availability and flexibility to handle unstructured data are MongoDB properties (Kaur & Rani, 2013). The simplicity and flexibility makes MongoDB use easier for many programmers without having to understand SQL. The authors Mapanga and Kadebu (2013) cite that MongoDB is used by Disney, SourceForge and The New York Times.

MongoDB stores data in a binary JSON-like format called BSON. BSON supports boolean, integer, float, date, string and binary types. MongoDB supports MapReduce framework and allows the JSON object stored to be easily converted into JavaScript code.

MongoDB has a powerful ad-hoc query language, called MQL (MongoDB query language). MQL allows functions such as the relational databases and support indexes. The select statement is writing as (Kaur & Rani, 2013):

db.collection.find({query}, {projection})

The find() method. has the arguments {query} and {projection}.
The {query} argument corresponds to where clause.
The {projection} corresponds to the list of select fields.
An example the listing the users posts is:

db.post.find({}, {_id:1, uid:1})

Queries can be extended with regular expressions. It provides additional operations such as *count* and *distinct*. It can perform queries based on a predicate, including range queries, but doesn't support joins (Tauro et al., 2012). The MongoDB supports dynamic queries with the automatic use of indices, like RDBMS.

According of Kaur and Rani (2013) MongoDB is suited for content management, mobiles, gaming and archiving applications.

- CouchDB

CouchDB (couchdb, 2015) is a NoSQL schemaless database. It is a Document store – data is stored and accessed from a Document database. The development language is Erlang, and the supplier is Apache. The CouchDB was created in 2008.

CouchDB is a flexible, fault tolerant database that supports the JSON data format. It provides a distributed P2P-based solution that supports bidirectional replication.

CouchDB is famous for its web applications, for being user friendly, and the nature of its distribution, as well as, for applications that must respond to many parallel read and write requests, and for providing a certain level of consistency.

With regard to data access, CouchDB provides an API-based HTTP REST-style interface. The queries can be distributed over the nodes in parallel using the mechanism of MapReduce. The queries can be made on what is called views that are defined in JavaScript to specify field constraints. The mechanism of the view places more responsibility for programmers than a declarative query language (Catell, 2010). The clients access the system through a RESTful interface. There are libraries in various languages such as Java, C, PHP, Python, LISP that convert the native API calls within the RESTful calls. For data updates, CouchDB does not notify an application if an update occurred in a document since the last search. The application can try to combine updates, or can only try upgrading and overwritting.

According to Catell (2010), CouchDB database supports procedural query language: it puts more work on the programmer and requires explicit utilization of indices. It includes a MapReduce mechanism for a more advanced selection and aggregation of data and it has basic database administration functionality. It uses B-tree to index the documents.

CouchDB uses views to query data from a collection. An example is:

```
Function(Chapter) {
If (Chapter.chapter_author=="Souza")
    emit(Chapter._id,Chapter);
}
```

- Tokyo Tyrant / Tokyo Cabinet

Tokyo Tyrant and Tokyo cabinet (FAL, 2015) are Document databases written in C language and the supplier is Sourcefourge.net, which was a project, but is now licensed and maintained by FAL (FAL, 2015).

Tauro et al. (2012) showed that Tokyo Cabinet (TC) is the multi-threaded high-concurrency servers and Tokyo Tyrant (TT) is the client library for remote access. TC provides high performance, while TT provides high services *muti-threaded* competition. It can treat 4-5 million read and write operations per second, while ensuring high competitive performance in reading and writing, using a reliable mechanism for data persistence. There are six different variations of Tokyo Cabinet: hash indexes in memory or the disk, disk BTree in memory or on disk, fixed-size record tables, and variable-length record tables. The mechanism differs clearly in performance characteristic, for example, fixed-length records allow fast lookups. There are slight variations in the API supported by mechanisms, but they all support the common operations to *get, set* and *update*. The search is made easily using a Lucene search engine.

To return a key or records use one of commands:

```
Chapter:get (key)
Chapter:getlist (key)
```

GRAPH DATABASE MODEL

- Neo4j

Neo4j (Neo4j, 2015) is a high performance Graph database with all of characteristics of a mature database and secure data. Neo4j was developed in Java. It provides *master-slave* replication and is supported by neo Technologies (Neo4j, 2015; Tauro et al., 2012).

Neo4j uses a declarative language called Cypher, and the script languages Gremlin (Gremlin, 2015) and JRuby (JRuby, 2015). Cypher (Cypher, 2015) is a declarative language for graph query that allows queries and updates graphs. It focuses on expression clarity for item recovery from the graph, in contrast to imperative languages as Java, and scripting languages like Gremlin and JRuby (Bach & Werner, 2014). The Cypher language syntax is similar to SQL, and was projected to be a humane query language suitable for developer community (Kaur & Rani, 2013). One example could be presented:

```
START
node = Chapter: Chapter (chapter_author = 'Souza')
RETURN Chapter
```

The START clause specifies the starting point in the graph, from where the query is executed. Cypher also allows insertion, modification and deletion commands.

The script language Gremlin (Gremlin, 2015) hosted in Groovy language – a superset of Java. It is a style of graph transversal that works over Graph databases with blueprint property graph data model (Mapanga & Kadebu, 2013).

- AllegroGraph

AllegroGraph (AllegroGraph, 2015) is a Graph database supplied by Franz Inc. Allegrograph. It provides an ad-hoc query language called SPARQL. The SPARQL (SPARQL Protocol And RDF Query Language) is a standard language for RDF files, designed by W3C RDF Group (Tauro et al., 2012). The SPARQL language syntax is similar to the classic SQL.

The SPARQL is considered a popular, declarative query language with a very simple syntax providing graph pattern matching, and is supported by most RDF stores, like sesame (Sesame, 2015). According of Mapanga and Kadebu (2013) SPARQL specifies four query variations: select, construct, ask and describe query.

An example of SPARQL code:

```
select * {
  ?Chapter fti:match ('Souza' 'Holanda') .
}
```

The W3C organization (W3C, 2015) was concerned with the need to develop a common query language for semantic web, thereby recommending the SPARQL product as a language and protocol standard for RDF files.

COMPARATIVE ANALYSIS OF NOSQL QUERY LANGUAGES

Of the 10 NoSQL databases studied in the previous section, the existence of some mechanism to access data in at least seven NoSQL databases that seem to have a query language that can be verified. Note that these search engines have information as characteristics, a restricted dialect, similar to commands SQL language, but mostly without providing, advanced commands such as *joins* or nested *selects*.

Table 1 associates NoSQL databases with the parameters: Data Model (M), Query Language, SQL similarity (S), Allow Join (J) and Allow Indexes (I). Note that null values indicate that no information was found about the parameter.

A query language that allow joins statements show a very powerful way of retrieving data of domain model through associations. However, how can observed in Table 1 the query languages described no announce these characteristics explicitly. The UnQL metalayer highlights that expressions could contain subqueries, but without presenting details.

The use of indexes to allow the database application to find data fast is a possibility in CQL, HQL, and MQL languages. However, the use of grouping or aggregate functions only is explicitly announced in Cypher and MQL languages.

The worried about similarity with SQL traditions is exhibit in the majority of query languages. Only Document stores are not concerned to follow this characteristic mainly because the document-like structure and JSON format to be often used to search such structures.

In Table 1 is possible to conclude that the majority NoSQL databases do not worry about high-friendly query languages and that:

Table 1. NoSQL database query languages

NoSQL	M	Query Language	S	J	I	Characteristics
CASSANDRA	C	CQL (Cassandra Query Language).	S	NJ	I	The Cassandra syntax is similar to SQL, however to data updates the commands *get* and *put* are used. In Cassandra is no possibility of using joins and the indexes uses the technique *ordered hash index*.
HyperTable	C	HQL	S		I	The HQL syntax is similar to SQL, however there is limitation on use of grouping or aggregate functions. HQL allows conditions for rows, cells or timestamps.
NEO4J	G	Cypher (Can also use SPARQL SPARQL Protocol And RDF Query Language)	S		NI	The Cypher syntax is similar to SQL. Cyper allows where and order by clauses and aggregate functions like count, min, max, avg, distinct, and predicates like all, none, single.
Allegrograph	G	SPARQL (SPARQL Protocol And RDF Query Language)	S			The SPARQL is similar to SQL, and specifies query variations: select, construct ask and describe.
Simpledb	D	Restricted query language without a defined name.	N	NJ		The traditional interface API developed with REST web services allows Select, Delete, GetAttributes, and PutAttributes operations, however the join, aggregation and subquery embedding operations are not supported. Calil, and Mello (2011) purpose a relational layer called SimpleSQL to facilitate query and retrieval data.
Riak	D	Apache Lucene	N		I	Riak acess data using Lucene Syntax by HTTP *get, put* or *post* operations.
Mongodb	D	MQL (MongoDB Query Language)	N	NJ	I	The MQL allows functions like relational databases, support indexes and count and distinct operators, but no joins. Queries can be extended with regular expressions, however there is no cache query. MQL provides a interactive javascript shell for database management, and uses db.collection.find() method to retrieve data from a collection.

According with the legend:
K – Key-value / G – Graph database / D - Document store / C - Column-Family
S - SQL Similarity
M - Database Model
J - Allow Join, NJ – No Join
I - Allow Indexes, NI – No Index

- The NoSQL query languages try to be similar to SQL RDBMS;
- The NoSQL query languages have a restricted dialect SQL commands;
- The NoSQL query functionality is not mature as RDBMS;
- The commands intend to be similar to SQL traditional syntax, however there is no a standard of the language between NoSQL families. Only SPARQL seems to be commonly used in Graph databases;
- The properties like support indexes or joins is heterogeneous to each NoSQL database;
- There are limitations with the use of grouping or aggregate functions for each query language.

In addition, the application developers that use NoSQL databases should additionally be concerned about the query optimization, integrity restrictions, rediscover indexing, concurrency control, locks and write code to complex operations like joins. In RDBMS, they did not need to treat these questions in application level, which would signify a change in culture.

Mainly, the study reveals a maturity of Graph databases for retrieval data because graph theory has a widely established theoretical foundation, which allows the use of research resources provided by the graph model.

Regarding the Key-Value database, due to the simplicity of the model, the search engine appears to be simple, as it is based only on the identification of the key. Also, some papers indicate that the simple structure implies a query speed higher than the relational database (Tauro et al., 2012). Hecht and Jablonski (2011) consider that a query language would be an unnecessary overhead for these stores. Thus, the use of REST interfaces is more adequate.

MongoDB's Document store has good data retrieval. This data store uses a query language, which allows functions of queries in simple tables of relational databases (Liu et al., 2011). According to Rith et. al. (2014), MongoDB has the capability to work with more complex queries. The other Document stores offer only APIs to access data. Even with this simplicity, no mechanism or unified language for queries that are friendly, appear, by users on these types of databases.

In a general, the level of programming expertise in writing queries in any NoSQL database is more advanced than that of RDBMS. Therefore, the interest in a query mechanism such as SQL appears to be desirable for NoSQL databases, mainly to garner user acceptance, which comes with restrictions and complexity in accessing data stored in these structures.

Another important question is that a properly query language make a task of administration a database easier. Migrate the RDBMS database to a NoSQL environment requires rewrite application code and architectural changes.

NoSQL Query Language Projects

There are some projects that address defining a query language, or user-friendly interface for queries and data retrieval in NoSQL databases. Some of them are listed as follows.

Damien Katz and Richard Hipp (UnQL, 2015), specified UnQL (*Unstructured Query Language*), a common query language for the adoption of NoSQL, as well as the SQL adoption in the relational database. The idea was to create a language that allows the manipulation of Document stores, like CouchDB and MongoDB. The syntax of the query language intended to be similar to hybrid SQL and include CRUD (create, update, delete) commands that work in collections of documents. It cannot change the schema database, and uses a JSON-like syntax to lead with documents.

Toad for Cloud Database (Toad, 2015) provides a SQL-based interface that makes it simple to migrate data between SQL and NoSQL data and also for consultations to various databases. The project cooperates with Apache HBase, Amazon SimpleDB, Azure Table, MongoDB, Apache Cassandra, Hadoop and all databases that use Open Database Connectivity (ODBC).

The project called Unity, that is a contribution by Lawrence (2014) aims to provide a single language that can be used by relational and non-relational systems. The intent is to allow queries to be automatically translated and performed using an API of *data sources* (Relational or NoSQL). The Unity intends to generalize the SQL query interface for both relational and NoSQL databases.

Jiang et al. (2013) considers an approach to store the unstructured data in relational databases, and rebuild the SQL statements to improve the ability to process unstructured data. The manner in which SQL language is widely used by relational databases, leads the authors to presume that the task of querying unstructured data into relational database will be easier.

Rith et al. (2014) presents a middleware that maps a restricted subset of SQL commands and translates them to Cassandra and MongoDB databases. The middleware provides a common interface where SQL statements and connectors are sent to translate to the NoSQL database that has been previously chosen.

Atzeni et al. (2012) proposes a common interface, called SOS (Save Our Systems) to Redis, Hbase and MongoDB databases. The tool enables creating and querying using a common set of simple operations.

These proposals, listed above, contribute to showing the benefits of using the common SQL language in the context of NoSQL databases. All of them are concerned with the development of an extensive mechanism, such as those that include interfaces and middleware to facilitate the access and retrieval of data from NoSQL databases. In cases where there is no common language, it is possible to simulate an environment where operations to translate SQL command dialects are transparent to users.

Therefore, the challenge of query languages for databases, such as the NoSQL databases, is an important subject of academic research and this emerging functionality is a way to expand and spread the use of NoSQL databases.

SOLUTIONS AND RECOMMENDATIONS

The users, mainly database administrators and programmers, are familiar with SQL language syntax, and consider that the use of SQL is simpler than the lower-level commands provided by NoSQL databases.

So the idea to migrate a project or create a new project in a NoSQL database should be carefully examined, and data must be evaluated in order to identify a suitable data model for the application's life cycle and requirements. Which queries the database should be supported by must also be considered, because these requirements influence the design of the data model (Wei & Bo, 2010).

Despite the advantages of NoSQL databases, after the database is created, and data is migrated, the work begins with the administration of the database environment through the use of command lines, tools and programming interfaces. The administration of the database environment should be able to rely on adequate tools to detect problems, improve performance, report generation, upgrade, and manipulate data. For those who will execute these tasks, it is fundamental that the appropriate tools should be available by the NoSQL databases. If there are no tools available, thereby compromising the database administration, this could cause problems in maintaining it.

Another consideration is whether the traditional database can be improved to guarantee availability, scalability and high processing, as is done in the NoSQL databases– migrating to a new type of database. The properties offered by databases should always be analyzed before migrating or working on a new project. Appropriately, considering the advantages offered by the new system, it is necessary to evaluate whether the advantages apply after the system is completed, within the administrative environment. In cases where the problems were not found at the start of the new project, they could appear when attempting to maintain the new system. In short, a query language is not a tool for data retrieval, but rather it should make data manipulation possible, facilitating the administration of the database system.

NoSQL databases were mainly designed to guarantee performance, optimizing the resource allocation, supporting distributed processing and the handling of large volumes of data, but it presents weaknesses when serving ad-hoc queries (Indrawan-Santiago, 2012). Note that aspects considered relevant in traditional databases are relaxed in NoSQL databases, such as the query language. As demonstrated in Table 1, there are few query languages catalogued in NoSQL databases, and when the query language exists it is specified for use in that database.

Without a high-level design for query languages with regards to data retrieval, it will be difficult for users, developers and database administrators to adopt NoSQL databases. It is also useless to try to make users understand that is necessary to think about what information is need early on in the development of database. During the operational use of a database, the users/developers may need to query data, and a high-level query language facilitates this task. For database administrators this is even more important, because some administrative data must access the dictionary of a database directly, using administrative tools and query language DDL syntax, and not directly via application.

FUTURE RESEARCH DIRECTIONS

This chapter has investigated how NoSQL databases provide querying and retrieval data mechanisms, such as languages and interfaces. There is consensus about the advantages of using NoSQL databases for specific applications, however querying and retrieving data in a simple way is a difficult problem reported by users, mainly those who need to manage administrative data.

In future researches, the authors intend to elaborate academic proposals to unify query languages to NoSQL databases. The academic research intends to culminate in a proposal for a query language of one NoSQL family.

Other questions addressed refer to the query languages handled, not only with DML commands, but also DDL commands, which are very useful, for example when migrating a traditional database to a different platform. The RDBMSs provide mechanisms that are usually based in DDL commands, to facilitate the necessary actions by a DBA (database administrator). A productive investigation is whether NoSQL databases are concerned with having similar mechanisms. The database administrator also needs to have autonomy to manipulate the querying and retrieval data mechanisms to be able to improve a particular query execution, for example, adding indexes or creating procedures or functions for a specific activity.

CONCLUSION

The use of NoSQL databases as an alternative for managing large volumes of data has become popular for web applications. The databases should provide the advanced data structures and techniques for improved access and recovery activities for data management. Despite the advantages of using NoSQL databases, the ability to recover data and data visualization is still considered unattractive to users and developers when compared to how easy it is to use the SQL language in relational DBMSs. Table 1 summarizes some NoSQL databases and their data retrieval mechanisms. Note that NoSQL databases are not concerned with establishing a query language.

This chapter has aimed at investigating how NoSQL databases provide mechanisms such as languages and interfaces for queries and data retrieval. Accessing data in a simple way is a problem frequently reported by users, especially those who need to manage DBMSs.

In the study conducted, we found the following characteristics with respect to mechanisms for consultations in NoSQL databases: they have a limited SQL dialect, with restrictions on the size of the output; generally operations *join*, aggregation and *subquery* are not supported; a typical API for NoSQL databases containing operations: *get (key), put (key, value), delete (key)* and *execute (key, operations, parameters)*; and the query is implicitly optimized during the database design, considering the type of distributed architecture and pattern available queries to be performed, i.e., even prior to the construction of the database, the types of queries the base will process and which best answer the query specification required, in order to build a project, are already considered.

NoSQL databases are continuously being developed, and additional query functionality is possible, eliminating the need to write applications for data management. NoSQL databases rely on heterogeneous query languages, but create a common query language or a common metalayer to translate commands. This appears to be a good option for improving the use of this type of database.

REFERENCES

Agrawal, R., Ailamaki, A., Philip, A., Bernstein, E., Michael, J., Carey, S., & Halevy, A. et al. (2009). The Claremont Report On Database Research. *Communications of the ACM, 52*(6), 56–65. doi:10.1145/1516046.1516062

Allegro InfoGrid Introduction. (2015, August 11). Retrieved August 20, 2015, from http://franz.com/agraph/support/documentation/current/agraph-introduction.html

Apache Software. (2014). *Apache Thrift Tutorial*. Retrieved August 21, 2015, from https://thrift.apache.org/docs

Atzeni, P., Bugiotti, F., & Rossi, L. (2012). SOS (Save Our Systems): A uniform programming interface for non-relational systems. In *Proceedings of the EDBT 2012*. Berlin, Germany: ACM. doi:10.1145/2247596.2247671

Avram, A. (2011, August 4). *Interview: Richard Hipp on UnQL, a New Query Language for Document Databases*. Retrieved August 20, 2015, from http://www.infoq.com/news/2011/08/UnQL

Bach, M., & Werner, A. (2014). Standardization Of Nosql Database Languages: Beyond Databases, Architectures, And Structure. In *Proceedings 10th International Conference (BDAS 2014)*. Ustron, Poland: Springer.

Banker, K. (2011). *MongoDB in Action* (2nd ed.). Greenwich: Manning Publications.

Britt, J. (2013, March 21). *The Pleasures of JRuby*. Retrieved August 20, 2015, from http://www.lea-phacking.com/posts/the-pleasures-of-jruby.html

Calil, A., & Mello, R. (2011). SimpleSQL: A Relational Layer for SimpleDB. In *Proceedings of the 16th East European conference on Advances in Databases and Information Systems Springer (ADBIS'12)*. Berlin, Heidelberg: Springer.

Capriolo, E., Wampler, D., & Rutherglen, J. (2012). *Programming Hive*. Sebastopol: O'Reilly Media.

Catell, R. (2010). Scalable SQL and NoSQL Data Stores. *Newsletter ACM SIGMOD Record, 39*(4), 12–27. doi:10.1145/1978915.1978919

Chris Anderson, J., Lehnardt, J., & Slater, N. (2010). *CouchDB: The Definitive Guide Time to Relax*. Sebastopol: O'Reilly Media.

Commons. (2015, August 18). *Getting Started with Sesame*. Retrieved August 20, 2015, from http://rdf4j.org/sesame/tutorials/getting-started.docbook?view

De Diana, M., & Gerosa, M. (2010). Um Estudo Comparativo de Bancos Não-Relacionais para Armazenamento de Dados na Web 2.0. In *Proceeding of the WTDBD IX Workshop de Teses e Dissertações em Banco de Dados*. Belo Horizonte, Brazil: WTDBD.

Dean, J., & Ghemawat, S. (2004, December). *MapReduce: Simplified Data Processing on Large Clusters*. Retrieved August 20, 2015, from http://research.google.com/archive/mapreduce.htm

Dean, J., & Ghemawat, S. (2010). MapReduce advantages over parallel databases include storage-system independence and fine-grain fault tolerance for large jobs. *Communications of the ACM, 53*(1), 72–77. doi:10.1145/1629175.1629198

Edlich, S. (2011). *NoSQL*. The Apache Software Foundation. Retrieved August 20, 2015, from http://nosql-databases.org/

Elmasri, R., & Navathe, S. (2011). *Sistemas De Banco De Dados*. São Paulo, Brazil: Pearson Addison Wesley Publisher.

Ferreira, G., Calil, A., & Mello, R. (2013). On Providing DDL Support for a Relational Layer over a Document NoSQL Database. In *Proceedings of the International Conference on Information Integration and Web-based Applications & Services (IIWAS '13)*. Vienna. Austria: ACM.

Fredrich, T. (2000). *Learn REST: A RESTful Tutorial*. Retrieved August 20, 2015, from http://www.restapitutorial.com/lessons/whatisrest.html

George, L. (2011). *HBase: The Definitive Guide*. Sebastopol: O'Reilly Media.

Han, J., Haihong, E., Guan, L., & Du, J. (2011). Survey on NoSQL Database. In *Proceedings of the 6th international conference on Pervasive computing and applications (ICPCA)*. Lanzhou, China: IEEE.

Hecht, R., & Jablonski, S. (2011). NoSQL Evaluation A Use Case Oriented Survey. In *Proceedings of the 2011 International Conference on Cloud and Service Computing (CSC '11)*. Hong Kong, China: IEEE. doi:10.1109/CSC.2011.6138544

Hirabayashi, M. (2010, August 5). *Introduction to Fal Tokyo Products*. Retrieved August 20, 2015, from http://fallabs.com/tokyocabinet/tokyoproducts.pdf

Hsieh, M., Chang, C., Ho, L., Wu, J., & Liu, P. (2011). SQLMR:A Scalable Database Management System for Cloud Computing. In *Proceedings of the International Conference on Parallel Processing (ICPP)*. Taipei, Taiwan: IEEE.

Indrawan-Santiago, M. (2012). Database Research: Are We At A Crossroad? In *Proceeding of the 2012 15th International Conference on Network-Based Information Systems (NBIS '12)*. Melbourne, Australia: ACM. doi:10.1109/NBiS.2012.95

Jiang, Z., Luo, Y., Wu, N., He, C., Yuan, P., & Jin, H. (2013). Managing Large Scale Unstructured Data with RDBMS. In *Proceedings of the 2013 IEEE 11th International Conference on Dependable, Autonomic and Secure Computing*. Jinan, China: IEEE. doi:10.1109/DASC.2013.135

Judd, D. (2014). *Hypertable User Guide*. Retrieved August 20, 2015, from http://hypertable.com/documentation/user_guide/

Kaur, K., & Rani, R. (2013). Modeling and Querying Data in NoSQL Databases. In *Proceedings of the IEEE International Conference on Big Data*. Silicon Valley, CA: IEEE. doi:10.1109/BigData.2013.6691765

Kllapi, H., Bilidas, D., Horrocks, I., Ioannidis, Y., Jiménez-Ruiz, E., Kharlamov, E., & Zheleznyakov, D. et al. (2013). Distributed Query Processing on the Cloud: the Optique Point of View (Short Paper). In *Proceedings of the Workshop on OWL: Experiences And Directions (OWLED)*. Montpellier, France: OWLED.

Lawrence, R. (2014). Integration and Virtualization of Relational SQL and NoSQL Systems including MySQL and MongoDB. In *Proceedings of the International Conference on Computational Science and Computational Intelligence (CSCI)*. Las Vegas, NV: IEEE. doi:10.1109/CSCI.2014.56

Leavitt, N. (2010). Technology News. Will NoSQL Databases Live Up to Their Promise? *Journal Computer*, *43*(2), 12–14. doi:10.1109/MC.2010.58

Liu, X., Lang, B., Yu, W., Luo, J., & Huang, L. (2011). AUDR: An Advanced Unstructured Data Repository. In *Proceedings 2011 6th International Conference on Pervasive Computing and Applications (ICPCA)*. IEEE.

Liu, Y., Dube, P., & Grayn, S. (2014). Run-Time Performance Optimization of a BigData Query Language. In *Proceedings of the 5th ACM/SPEC international conference on Performance engineering (ICPE '14)*. Dublin, Ireland: ACM. doi:10.1145/2568088.2576800

Mapanga, I., & Kadebu, P. (2013). Database Management Systems: A NoSQL Analysis. *Proceedings of the International Journal of Modern Communication Technologies & Research*, *1*(7).

McCandless, M., Hatcher, E., & Gospodnetić, O. (2010). *Lucene in Action* (2nd ed.). Manning.

Mohan, C. (2013). History Repeats Itself: Sensible and NonsenSQL Aspects of the NoSQL Hoopla. In *Proceedings of the 16th International Conference on Extending Database Technology (EDBT/ICDT '13)*. Genoa, Italy: ACM. doi:10.1145/2452376.2452378

Muhammad, Y. (2011). *Evaluation and Implementation of Distributed NoSQL Database for MMO Gaming Environment*. (Unpublished doctoral dissertation). Uppsala Universitety, Uppsala, Sweden.

Nasholm, P. (2012). *Extracting Data From Nosql Databases A Step Towards Interactive Visual Analysis Of Nosql data*. (Unpublished doctoral dissertation). Chalmers University of Technology. University of Gothenburg. Göteborg, Sweden.

Padhy, R., Patra, M., & Satapathy, S. (2011). RDBMS to NoSQL: Reviewing Some Next-Generation Non-Relational Database's. *International Journal of Advanced Engineering Science and Technologies*, *11*(1), 15-30.

Partner, J., Vukotic, A., Watt, N., Abedrabbo, T., & Fox, D. (2014). *Neo4j in Action*. New York: Manning Publication.

Porkorny, J. (2013). Nosql Databases: A Step To Database Scalability in Web enviromnent. In *Proceedings of the 13th International Conference on Information Integration and Web-based Applications and Services*. Bali, Indonesia: ACM.

Rith, J., Lehmayr, P., & Meyer-Wegener, K. (2014). Speaking in Tongues: SQL Access to NoSQL Systems. In *Proceedings of the 29th Annual ACM Symposium on Applied Computing (SAC '14)*. Gyeongju, Korea: ACM. doi:10.1145/2554850.2555099

Rodriguez, M. (2013, July 10). *Getting Started Gremlin*. Retrieved August 20, 2015, from https://github.com/tinkerpop/gremlin/wiki

Rouse, M. (2014, November 1). *Graph database*. Retrieved August 20, 2015, from http://whatis.techtarget.com/definition/graph-database

Sanfilippo, S. (2009). *An introduction to Redis data types and abstractions*. Retrieved August 20, 2015, from http://redis.io/topics/data-types-intro

Schumacher, R. (2015, January 2). *A Brief Introduction to Apache Cassandra*. Retrieved August 20, 2015, from https://academy.datastax.com/demos/brief-introduction-apache-cassandra

Silva, C. (2011). *Data Modeling with NoSQL: How, When and Why*. (Unpublished doctoral dissertation). Universidade do Porto, Porto, Portugal.

Slater, N. (2015, March 1). *Best Practices for Migrating from RDBMS to Amazon Dynamo DB*. Retrieved August 20, 2015, from http://aws.amazon.com/pt/dynamodb/

Software, S. (2001). *BekeleyDB*. Sams Publishing.

Tauro, C., Aravindh, S., & Shreeharsha, A.B. (2012). Comparative Study of the New Generation, Agile, Scalable, High Performance NOSQL Databases. *International Journal of Computer Applications, 48*(20).

The Neo4j Manual v2.2.4 Tutorials Cypher. (2015). Retrieved August 20, 2015, from http://neo4j.com/docs/stable/tutorials.htm

Toad for Cloud Databases. (2012, March 16). Retrieved August 20, 2015, from http://www.toadworld.com/products/toad-for-cloud-databases/w/wiki/10447.toad-for-cloud-databases-release-notes-eclipse-edition

Trencseni, M. (2009, February 15). *Thoughts on Yahoo's PNUTS distributed database*. Retrieved August 20, 2015, from http://highscalability.com/blog/2009/8/8/yahoos-pnuts-database-too-hot-too-cold-or-just-right.html

Voldemort. (n.d.). *GitHub*. Retrieved August 19, 2015, from http://www.project-voldemort.com/voldemort/

Wei, L. (2010). A tetrahedral data model for unstructured data management. *Science China Information Sciences, 53*(8), 1497–1510. doi:10.1007/s11432-010-4030-9

World Wide Web Consortium (W3C). (2015). Retrieved August 20, 2015, from http://www.w3.org/standards/

Zhao, J., Hu, X., & Meng, X. (2010). ESQP: An efficient SQL query processing for cloud data management. In *Proceedings of the second international workshop on Cloud data management (CloudDB '10)*. Toronto, Canada: ACM. doi:10.1145/1871929.1871931

KEY TERMS AND DEFINITIONS

BigData: Term that indicate a lot of data. An informal means indicate data that not could put fit in only a machine.

BigTable: Sparce multidimensional, distributed, and ordered map. Framework created by Google to management unstructured data.

CAP: Theorem created by Brewer teacher, indicate three properties Consistency, Availability and Partition Tolerance. The theorem implies that the database project should be choice two of three properties.

Erlang: Ericson programming language to be used in distributed and fault tolerant applications that need to be execute in real time environment. It is consider a nice programming language to distribute system.

JSON: The JavaScript Object Notation is the binary format to represent data like list, map, date, Boolean and different precision numbers.

Lucene: A search engine to search and API indexing of documents. It is written in the java and open source software from the Apache Software Foundation through the Apache license.

MapReduce: An engine which idea is divide a work in many tasks. With base in a table distribution, the algorithm divide a ad-hoc query in different sub-queries in the same time, with replicas, where one sub-query is mapped in k+1 sub-queries. Contains the map and reduce function to execute these tasks.

Sharding: The technique to divide a table in many nodes. The data are spread to nodes following arbitrary criteria.

SQL Language: Query Language to traditional databases. It contains instructions to data definition, data manipulation and query. Usually offers a high-level declarative interface to the end user could write his queries.

Section 4

Chapter 16
Fuzzy Querying of RDF with Bipolar Preference Conditions

Hairong Wang
Beifang University of Nationality, China

Jingwei Cheng
Northeastern University, China

Z. M. Ma
Northeastern University, China

ABSTRACT

To solve the problem of information bipolarity in fuzzy querying of RDF, we propose an approach of RDF fuzzy query with bipolar preference. We use linguistic variables to describe preference conditions, and realize an extended SPARQL syntax by adding bipolar preference conditions to FILTER clauses. We identify three types of bipolar information, dividing the bipolar preference query into univariate bipolarity and bivariate bipolarity, and provide a method for converting fuzzy SPARQL queries to standard SPARQL queries. For optimizing results, we use bipolar preference satisfaction degrees to calculate priority parameters of results for sequencing. Finally, the feasibility of the proposed approach is proved by the experimental system and results.

INTRODUCTION

Users are willing to describe negative and positive preferences in information retrieval. A Positive preference is a kind of expectation, which means that the expectation of an object property or value is greater than other properties. A negative preference is a kind of rejecting, denoting a mandatory condition. This kind of bipolarity is the inner subjective inclination of people, which evaluates an object from its positive and the negative aspects. When the positive and negative preferences coexist, it is called the bipolar preferences. The bipolar information and bipolar preferences are getting more and more attention as it can effectively express the varieties of user demands. The bipolar preference relation is firstly mentioned

DOI: 10.4018/978-1-4666-8767-7.ch016

in (Dubois and Prade, 2002), and a series of bipolar preference queries have been proposed. In particular, the bipolar preferences query with fuzzy winnow operator is introduced in (Zadrozny and Janusz, 2006). In (Ludovic, 2009; Tamani, Lietard and Rocacher, 2011), fuzzy set theory and relational algebra are used to describe bipolar preference conditions in SQL. The flexible bipolar query approach based on database is discussed in (Destercke, Buche and Guillard, 2011). The method in relational databases is based on the satisfaction degrees (Matthé, de Tré, Zadrozny, Kacprzyk and Bronselaer, 2011; Matthé and de Tré, 2009; de Tré, Zadrozny, Matthé, Kacprzyk and Bronselaer, 2009). The flexible method of fuzzy matching is to realize bipolar preference query (Zadrozny and Kacprzyk, 2009; Zadrozny and Kacprzyk, 2012; Zadrozny, Kacprzyk and de Tré, 2012).

With the development of the semantic Web, the RDF is sharply increasing, and this results in a large number of searching problems. So far, there have already been plenty of studies focusing on this field, such as the method of matching RDF graph model (Renzo, A. and Claudio, G., 2005; Stocker, Seaborne, Bernstein, Kiefer and Reynolds, 2008), the method based on SPARQL (Simple Protocol and RDF Query Language) (Unger, Bühmann, Lehmann, Ngomo, Gerber and Cimiano, 2012; Castillo, Rothe and Leser, 2010; Jarrar and Dikaiakos, 2012), and the method based on Zadeh's fuzzy set theory (Guéret, Oren, Schlobach and Schut, 2008; Hai, Liu and Zhou, 2012; Bahri, Bouaziz and Gargouri, 2009). Since natural language expression applied in real life has fuzziness and preferences, it is necessary to support fuzzy preference query for realizing RDF retrieval. Siberski, Pan and Thaden (2006) analyzed the disadvantages of expressing preference through sequencing. It added the qualifier (PREFERRING) in SPARQL to describe preference queries. Dolog, Stuckenschmidt, Wache and Diederich (2009) extended SPARQL language to describe preference conditions. It realizes a preference query through converting. Jin, Ning, Jia, Wu and Lu (2008) considered the preference problem of fuzzy and multiple conditions in practical query, and provided the relevancy computational formula, which realized preference query through sequencing. Halder and Cortesi (2011) provided a retrieval method, which is based on the preference satisfaction and structural similarity. User queries uses tape mark as annotated graphs and combine linguistic variables to express fuzzy preference conditions. It synthesized the weighted value of structural similarity and computational preference satisfaction for being sequencing parameters, and then realizing preference query through sequencing.

The existing fuzzy query methods supporting preference are focused on unipolarity preference model (only considering the preference of user's hope). In order to solve the coexist problem of positive and negative preferences in user retrieval demands, we propose an appoach to querying RDF with bipolar preference conditions. We identify three types of bipolar information. It permit user to use the natural language to express preference query request, extending SPAROL language to describe bipolar preference conditions, then removing fuzziness by calling linguistic variable. It defines a priority function to optimized results. The output is obtained by making the returned priority as the sequencing parameters, which is the sequence of users' satisfaction.

The rest of the chapter is organized as follows. The second section introduces the theory of bipolar information and preference query. The method of RDF fuzzy query with bipolar preference conditionis proposed in the third Section, which defines a priority function based on preference satisfaction and realizes result sequencing. The experimental system and results are built and analyzed in the fourth section, while the conclusions and further work are found in the final section.

BIPOLAR INFORMATION AND PREFERENCE QUERY

Bipolarity is the natural quality of information, which has the the positive aspect and the negative aspect. The positive information means its positive evaluation is same to the expectation. The negative information means that its negative evaluation excludes the expectation. The bipolar information simultaneously includes positive and negative evaluations. The bipolar information is divided into types I, II, and III (Dubois and Prade, 2008; Dubois and Prade, 2008).

Type I: Symmetric Univariabe Bipolarity. It divided the ordered set into two poles through a neutral value, which met the probability 0.5. The neutral value is the symmetry points, the message on the right is positive information, and the message on the left is negative information.

Type II: Symmetric Bivariate Unipolarity. This type of bipolarity focuses on one side of information (positive or negative). When the positive information is stronger, it uses two variables to evaluate positive information. When the negative information is stronger, it uses two variables to evaluate negative information.

Type III: Asymmetric Bipolarity. The positive and negative information evaluations are different in this type. It uses two bivariate unipolarities to describe. Because the positive and negative information evaluated the different objects, therefore, there is no symmetric relation.

Processing fuzzy query with complicated preference condition using bipolar information, such as "*to satisfy C, and possible to satisfy P*". The condition C must be satisfied and is called mandatory preference. In the precondition of satisfying C, the condition P may be also satisfied and is called optional preference. The bipolar preference query involved mandatory and optional preferences.

Definition 1 (bipolar preference query): A bipolar preference query is denoted as $Q_{cp} = \{(t, r_{cp}) | t \in T\}$, where T is domain, t is the results of satisfying conditions, and r_{cp} *is the bipolar conditions* with C and P. The expression of r_{cp} is defined as $r_{cp} = \{(A, \mu_{cp}(A|B), \neg\mu_{cp}(A|B) | A \in dom_A, B \in dom_B)\}$, in which A and B are preference properties, dom_A is the range of property A, and dom_B is the range of property B.

Two functions are used to evaluate the degrees of satisfying preference conditions: $\mu_{cp}(A|B)$, $\neg\mu_{cp}(A|B)$: $dom_A \to [0, 1]$, $dom_B \to [0, 1]$. Here $\mu_{cp}(A|B)$ is the satisfaction degree function for expressing the degree of satisfying preference condition from the positive aspect. $\neg\mu_{cp}(A|B)$ is the dissatisfaction degree function for expressing the degree of satisfying preference condition from the negative aspect.

Generally, the bipolar conditions have three forms:

1.   C and P in r_{cp} are the preferences of two properties within one thing and in opposition to each other. Their satisfaction degrees have complementary relation. If the degree of satisfying C is $\mu_c(A)$, then the degree of satisfying P is $\mu_p(B) = 1 - \mu_c(A)$. This type of bipolar condition is called univariate bipolar preference condition. The operation uses "logic or (*or*)" to link query condition.

2.   C and P in r_{cp} are the preferences of two properties within one thing and are irrelevant. Their satisfaction degrees are two independent values. If $\mu_c(A)$ is the satisfaction degree of C, $\mu_p(B)$ is the satisfaction degree of P, then $\mu_p(B) \neq 1 - \mu_c(A)$. This kind of bipolar condition is called bivariate bipolar preference condition. It cannot use one satisfaction degree to evaluate two independent preferences. Therefore, it defined two parameters to mark the satisfaction and dissatisfaction degrees

of every preference. If the satisfaction degree of C is $\mu_c(A)$, the dissatisfaction degree is $\neg\mu_c(A) = 1 - \mu_c(A)$. If the dissatisfaction degree of P is $\mu_p(B)$, the dissatisfaction degree is $\neg\mu_p(B) = 1 - \mu_p(B)$. The operation uses "logic and (and)" to link preference condition. If the preference condition includes negative preference, then "logic not (not)" is used to express negative relation.

3. If r_{cp} included many bipolar preference conditions, then it is called the complicated preference condition, which uses join operation to link multi-polar preference conditions.

The satisfaction degree is a very important parameter in bipolar preference query, which is used to measure the degrees of satisfying preference conditions. According to the difference of univariate and bivariate bipolar preference conditions, unipolarity and bipolarity satisfaction degrees are used to mark the degrees of positive and negative preferences, respectively.

Definition 2 (Bipolar preference satisfaction degree): Satisfaction degree is to evaluate the degree of fitting preference condition. If $\mu_c(A)$ is the satisfaction degree of C, $\mu_p(B)$ is the satisfaction degree of P, then $\mu_c(A) > \mu_p(B)$ and $0.5 < \mu_p(A) < 1, 0 < \mu_p(B) < 0.5$. If a preference condition includes negative words (such as "inexpensive"), then the satisfaction degree of preference condition is calculated through anti-operation, i.e., $\mu_{\neg x}(A) = 1 - \mu_x(A)$.

Definition 3 (Unipolarity Satisfaction Degree, USD): USD is used to express that each message in the result set fits with preference query conditions through the satisfaction degree parameters of positive or negative information. If $\mu_x(A)$ is the satisfaction degree of unipolarity preference, then it is defined by:

$$\forall A \in R_+ : \mu_x(A) = \frac{s}{\max(A)} \tag{1}$$

Here $\mu_x(A) \in [0, 1]$, s is the value of query propriety A, $max(A)$ is the maximum number of preference propriety interval.

Definition 4 (Bipolar Satisfaction Degree, BSD) (Matthe and de Tre, 2009): BSD is used to evaluate the satisfaction degree of preference condition from positive and negative aspects. BSD is a pair $(\mu_x(A), \neg\mu_x(A)) \in [0, 1]$, where $\mu_x(A)$ is the satisfaction degree, $\neg\mu_x(A)$ is the dissatisfaction degree. $\mu_x(A)$ and $\neg\mu_x(A)$ are independent with each other. The value 0 expresses fully satisfaction condition; the value 1 expresses fully dissatisfaction condition.

The satisfaction degree of bivariate bipolar preference condition $\mu_{cp}(A/B)$ is defined as

$$\mu_{cp}(A|B) = (\mu_c(A), \neg\mu_c(A)) \wedge (\mu_p(B), \neg\mu_p(B)) = (min(\mu_c(A), \mu_p(B)), max(\neg\mu_c(A), \neg\mu_p(B))) \tag{2}$$

Here $\mu_c(A)$ is mandatory preference satisfaction degree, $\neg\mu_c(A)$ is dissatisfaction degree, and $\neg\mu_c(A) = 1 - \mu_c(A)$; $\mu_p(B)$ is optional preferences satisfaction degree, $\neg\mu_p(B)$ is dissatisfaction degree, and $\neg\mu_p(B) = 1 - \mu_p(B)$.

Formula (2) expresses two kinds of preferences, which have two constrained relationships:

- The condition C and P in a query must be satisfactory. If the minimum of two conditions is satisfied, then two conditions are satisfied.
- One of conditions C and P in a query must be unsatisfactory. If the maximum of two conditions is dissatisfied, then two conditions are dissatisfied.

FUZZY QUERY WITH BIPOLAR PREFERENCES

According to the bipolar preferences conditions, we propose the processing method for fuzzy preference query. Fuzzy preference query permits user to use natural language expressions, which are fuzzy preference predicates. Fuzzy preference predicates consist of fuzzy numerical preference predicates (*about*, *between*, *max*, *min*, *lowest*, *Highest*) and fuzzy non-numerical preference predicates (*like*, *dislike*). We mainly discuss fuzzy numerical preference predicates in bipolar preference query. In order to recognize the requests of fuzzy query submitted by user, We extend SPARQL language by allowing fuzzy preference predicates in FILTER clauses. The extended fuzzy SPARQL has the ability to describe bipolar preference conditions. But the realization of a query needs to remove fuzziness, therefore, it needs to call the linguistic variable in RDF fuzzy query for removing fuzziness and getting approximate results. To evaluate degrees of how the results fit the bipolar preference conditions, we calculate the preferences satisfaction degree, and define a priority function for optimizing results through sequencing. Finally, the results are ranked based on the order of user satisfaction.

FUZZY SPARQL DESCRIPTION WITH BIPOLAR PREFERENCE CONDITIONS

SPARQL is the standard query language of RDF. A SPARQL Query is a triple (E, DS, QF), where E is an SPARQL algebra expression, DS is the RDF Dataset, and QF is the query form. A SPARQL algebra expression is a tree structure of the nested query, each layer is the sub-query of basic structure. Its syntactic structure is shown in Table 1.

The query forms of SPARQL determine the models of returned results. The query forms are as follows: the matching results and variable-bindings of SELECT will reverse back through the data sheet; the CONSTRUCT or DESCRIBE returns a matching subgraph; the ASK returns a Boolean value (T/F), which determine whether the query results match the conditions. Modifiers are the constraint condition of returned results: ORDER BY is the serialization query results; the OFFSET returns partial results,

Table 1. SPARQL syntax

Patterns	Modifiers	Query Forms	Other
RDF terms	*DISTINCT*	*SELECT*	*VALUES*
Property path expression	*REDUCED*	*CONSTRUCT*	*SERVEICE*
Property path patterns	*Projection*	*DESCRIBE*	
Groups	*ORDER BY*	*ASK*	
OPTIONAL	*LIMIT*		
UNION	*OFFSET*		
GRAPH	*Select expressions*		
BIND			
GROUP BY			
HAVING			
MINUS			
FILTER			

which start from the designated query results; the LIMIT restricts the returned number of query results. The FILTER clause in Patterns plays a very important role in SPARQL query, it filters the results of matching conditions in whole diagram.

The FILTER clause in SPARQL realize the filtering of query results. Generally, the preference query should define the preference condition through FILTER clause. At present, the FILTER has two kinds of preference expressions.

The first is numerical approach, which uses precise predicate to express query conditions. It added a real number in conditions to identify the user's desire degree of preference conditions (such as "*FILTER (? x ex: hasHeight ?Height) with* 0.8" (Cheng and Ma, 2010)).

The second is to use the fuzzy preference predicate for expressing query conditions (such as " *FILTER (?Price = about* 100000)"). It firstly considers the description of preference relation. To realize a SPARQL extension, the predicate of preference structure it added (such as "PREFERENCE") in Solution Modifiers (Siberski, Pan and Thaden, 2006; Dolog, Stuckenschmidt, Wache and Diederich, 2009). It has the ability to express the preference conditions, and results are optimized through sequencing. For example, the extended SPARQL description supporting preferences is shown as follows:

```
xsd:double fun:prefer (numeric r_i)
xsd:double fun:score (numeric ω_i)
SELECT ?object
WHERE {?object hasproperty ?property.
       FILTER (?property < comparison operator> typed-literal)}
       PREFERENCE
           ?object fun:prefer (r_i)
           ?object fun:score (?ω_i)
      ORDER BY DESC (?score)
      LIMIT n
```

The first method is difficult to use since using ration for describing the qualitative problems does not fit the user's needs. The second method is to express qualitative problems through the natural language, and it is same to the user's expression. Therefore, we combine the fuzzy preference predicates in this chapter with the linguistic variables in the second method to express preference conditions. The SPARQL language is thus extended by defining the fuzzy FILTER clause. This method linke the bipolar preference conditions through the logical operator, which is based on linguistic variables. It increase the call of "PREFERENCE" to realize the calculation of bipolar preference satisfaction degree and priority. The results can be ranked according to the priority. Users are also allowed to use "LIMIT" to controll the number of returned results. The returned results with traditional data sheet are more likely accepted by user, hence, the SELECT query form is still used in the extended fuzzy SPARQL.

The extended SPARQL supporting bipolar preference is described as follows:

```
xsd:double    fun:score (numeric μ_cp (A|B))
xsd:double fun:score (numeric γ_cp)
SELECT ('DISTINCT ' | ' REDUCED') ? (Var + | ' * ') DatasetClause *
WHERE GroupGraphPattern
FILTER ? (Var_c + ' = ' + C_p) θ (Var_p + ' = ' + P_p)
```

```
PREFERENCE
    ?object fun:score(?μ_cp (A|B))
     ?object fun:score (?γ_cp)
LIMIT INTEGER
ORDER BY (('ASC '|'DESC ') BrackettedExpression)|(?γ_cp)
```

The variable of Var_c in the FILTER clause is mandatory preference propriety. C_p is a mandatory preference fuzzy value with preference predicate, while the Var_p is optional preference propriety. P_p is an optional preference fuzzy value with preference predicate. θ is a bipolar preference logic operator ("*or*", "*and*", "*not*"). When the query requirement is bipolar single variate, the two preference proprieties keep the opposite relation, then it needs to use "Logic or *OR*" operator to link them. When the query requirement is dipole double variates, there will be no connection between mandatory and optional preference propriety. Then, the proper results should meet the two preferences. Here, we use the "logic '*AND*' " to link the preference condition. *fun:score*($?\mu_{cp}(A|B)$) *is* a preference satisfaction function, which returns a real number within the interval [0, 1] for checking whether the query result fits the preference condition, *fun:score*($?\gamma_{cp}$) is a priority function, which optimizes the query results of bipolar preference. The γ_{cp} is a priority parameter, which is a real number within the interval [0, 1]. It is the keyword in the sorted result.

Example 1: Suppose that we have a RDF data source of Car Sale. An user would like to search the cars which prices are about 100000 but not the brand X. Using the extended SPARQL, the user query can be described by the following form:

```
SELECT ?Price ? Brand ?Car
WHERE {?p ex: hasPrice ?Price.
       ?p ex: hasColor ?Brand.
FILTER (?Price = about 10000) and (not ?Brand = " X ") }
PREFERENCE
       ?p fun:score(?μ_about(Price), ?μ_not x (Brand))
       ?p fun:score(?γ_cp)
ORDER BY DESC(?γ_cp)
```

The extended fuzzy SPARQL can intuitively describe bipolar preference queries, but the fuzziness of query operations need to be removed. The query method of univariate and bivariate bipolar preference conditions is mainly studied in this chapter. These two queries will eventually convert the fuzzy FILTER to a precise filter condition. Because the complex bipolar preference conditions can be operated by connecting multiple bipolar preference conditions, such issues are not mentioned in the following methods.

UNIVARIATE BIPOLAR PREFERENCE QUERY

The univariate bipolar preference query realizes fuzzy condition conversion through a mapping function, called the univariate satisfaction degree function (see Formula 1). It calculate the preference satisfaction degree to evaluate the initial results, then optimizes and gets results through sequencing. This concrete process is as follows.

1. Defining a mapping function map_{cp} for realizing fuzzy conversion via linguistic variables of fuzzy queries. Based on type II fuzzy set theory, which uses trapezoid membership degree functions, ordered linguistic terms are divided into thirteen sub-. Fuzzy values in each sub-domain are described with a quaternary set $(a_i, b_i, \alpha_i, \beta_i)$. The a_i and b_i represent the lower and upper limit values in the sub-domain interval of membership degree. Here α_i and β_i indicate the fuzzy adjustment distance from each sub-domain to its upper and lower sub-domains. The ordered linguistic terms are shown in Table 2, where fuzzy preference predicates in FILTER clause are mapped to its values. Fuzzy condition conversion is realized according to the conversion rules shown in Table 3.
2. Calling the standard SPARQL implementation to execute query and return initial results;
3. Defining the preference satisfaction degree function to filter initial results: calculating the degree of preference satisfaction condition of each message in the result set. If the $\mu_c(A)$ and $\mu_p(B)$ dissatisfy the following conditions, which are "$\mu_c(A) > \mu_p(B)$ and $0.5 < \mu_c(A) < 1, 0 < \mu_p(B) < 0.5$", the message in result set will be deleted.
4. Calling the function $fun(\gamma_{cp})$ to calculate the priority of each mesage, and returning the final result in descending order.

The procedure of univariate bipolar query processing is showed in Algorithm 1.

The Q_{cp} in algorithm 1 is a bipolar preference query, C is mandatory preference condition, P is optional preference condition. The fuzzy condition conversion is realized by the mapping function map_{cp}. It calls the standard SPARQL language and executes query to get the result C(t), which satisfies C. Meanwhile, if it satisfies P as well, which will be marked with $C(t) \cup P(t)$. The preference query Q_{cp} is shown as follows:

$$Q_{cp} = \{t \in T: C(t) \cup P(t)\}$$

Table 2. Sub-domain of ordered linguistic values

Sub-Domain	Fuzzy Items	Fuzzy Values$(a_i, b_i, \alpha_i, \beta_i)$
S_{12}	Absolutely expensive, absolutely, etc. advanced, etc.	(1.0, 1.0, 0.0, 0.0)
S_{11}	Extremely expensive, extremely, etc. \advanced, etc.	(0.90, 1.0, 0.0, 0.5)
S_{10}	Very expensive, very advanced, very, etc. high, etc.	(0.81, 0.95, 0.05, 0.04)
S_9	Expensive, advanced, many, high, etc.	(0.71, 0.85, 0.04, 0.05)
S_8	Fairly expensive, fairly many, etc.	(0.62, 0.76, 0.05, 0.04)
S_7	Somewhat expensive, somewhat advanced, etc. etc.	(0.52, 0.66, 0.04, 0.05)
S_6	Neither expensive nor cheap, etc.	(0.43, 0.57, 0.05, 0.04)
S_5	Somewhat cheap, somewhat inferior, etc.	(0.33, 0.47, 0.04, 0.05)
S_4	Fairly cheap, fairly few, fairly low, etc.	(0.24, 0.38, 0.05, 0.04)
S_3	Cheap, inferior, few, low, etc.	(0.14, 0.28, 0.04, 0.05)
S_2	Very cheap, very inferior, very low, etc.	(0.05, 0.19, 0.05, 0.04)
S_1	Extremely cheap, extremely inferior, etc.	(0.0, 0.9, 0.04, 0.0)
S_0	Absolutely cheap, absolutely inferior, etc.	(0.0, 0.0, 0.0, 0.0)

Table 3. Transformation rules

Fuzzy Conditions	Sub-Domain	Precise Conditions
?x ="At least Y"	/	FILTER (?x $\geq$ Y)
?x ="Up to Y"	/	FILTER (?x $\leq$ Y)
?x ="Close to the Y"	S_6-S_{11}	FILTER (?x $\geq$ a &&? x $\leq$ b)
?x ="A bit closer to Y"	S_8-S_{11}	FILTER (?x $\geq$ a && ?x $\leq$ b)
?x ="About Y"	S_{10}-S_{11}	FILTER (?x $\geq$ a && ?x $\leq$ b)
?x ="Ordered linguistic values"	See table 2	/

Algorithm 1. The procedure of univariable bipolar preference query

```
Input: Q_cp = (C, P);
    T = {} is the result set of matching condition after removing fuzzy con-
version,
    T_cp = {} is the result set of satisfaction preference condition, C_p ∈ C,
P_p ∈ P,
    map_cpis is the mapping function of fuzzy preference condition.
Begin
    C_p, P_p→map_cp;
    //C_1, C_2, ..., C_i is the precise mandatory conditions after mapping, P_1,
P_2, ..., P_i is the precise optional conditions after mapping, opt is the rela-
tion operator.
    get (C_1, C_2, ..., C_i, P_1, P_2, ..., P_i);
    FITLER (Var_c opt C_1 ||...|| Var_c opt C_i) or (Var_p opt P_1||...|| Var_p opt P_i)
    get T = {t_1, t_2, ..., t_n};
    //i ∈ [1, n], t_i is the message in result set T, its mandatory preference
satisfaction degree is μ_c (t_i), and its optional preference satisfaction degree
is μ_p (t_i).
    μ_c (t_i)= fun (μ_x (A));
    μ_p (t_i) = fun (μ_x (B));
    for i = 1 to n do
        if (μ_c (t_i) > μ_p (t_i)) and (0.5 < μ_c (t_i) < 1) and (0 < μ_p (t_i) < 0.5)
        then T_cp = t_i ∪ T_cp;
    fun (γ_cp);
    ORDER BY DESC (γ_cp): T_cp ;
end.
    Output: T_cp
```

where the message t in discourse domain T satisfies bipolar preference condition. The satisfied relation is shown as follows, which reflects the mandatory preference constrains on the optional preference (Lacroix and Lavency, 1987).

$$C(t) \cup P(t) \equiv C(t) \wedge (\exists s(C(s) \wedge P(s)) \rightarrow P(t))$$

The structure "If" is used to restrict the query result of univariable bipolar preference. The result should firstly satisfy the mandatory preference, and then tries to satisfy the optional preference. Therefore, the mandatory preference satisfaction degree should be larger than optional preference satisfaction degree, that is $\mu_c(t_i) > \mu_p(t_i)$. In addition, these two preference conditions have the complementarity ($\mu_p(B) = 1 - \mu_c(A)$). The preference satisfaction degree in interval$(0.5,1]$ is of greater hope than that of in the interval $[0, 0.5]$. Therefore, setting the filter conditions as "$(0.5 < \mu_c(t_i) < 1)$ and $(0 < \mu_p(t_i) < 0.5)$" can meet different preference needs. We define a priority function "*fun* (γ_{cp})" for optimizing results, then calling the ORDER BY clause for realizing the priority sequencing.

Example 2: Here is the RDF data source of a real estate sales, user need to query houses that is cheap and with large area. The fuzzy SPARQL of bipolar preference conditions is as follows.

```
SELECT ?Hous ?Price ?Area
WHERE {?p ex: hasPrice ?Price.
          ?p ex: hasHous ?Area.
    FILTER (?Price = "cheap" or ?Area = "large") }
PREFERENCE
          ?p fun:score(?μ_cheap (Price), ?μ_large (Area))
```

In this example, the mandatory preference "Cheap price" and optional preference "Large area" have the opposite relation, their satisfaction degree keep complementary relationship. So using the "logical or OR" operator to link the preference condition. The mandatory preference "cheap" and optional preference "large" in the FILTER will be mapped to the corresponding membership degree interval $\mu_{cheap} (Price) \in [0.14, 0.28]$, $\mu_{large} (Area) \in [0.71, 0.85]$. If $Price \in [0, 2000000]$, $Area \in [0, 200]$, then call trapezoidal membership degree functions (see Formula 3). We get the cheap price within interval $[280000, 560000]$ and the large area within interval $[142, 170]$.

$$\mu_A(x) = \begin{cases} 0, x \leq a \\ \dfrac{x-a}{b-a}, a < x \leq b \\ 1, x > b \end{cases}$$

The interval of known query object will convert the fuzzy SPARQL with bipolar preferences to the standard SPARQL. The converted standard SPARQL expression forms are as follows:

```
SELECT ?Hous ?Price ?Area
WHERE {?p ex: hasPrice ?Price.
```

```
    ?p ex: hasHous ?Area.
  FILTER ((?Price >= 280000 && ?Price <= 560000) or (?Area >= 142 && ?Area
<= 170) }
```

Executing the query and calculating the preference satisfaction degree of each message, we get initial results. The results with preference satisfaction degree are shown in Table 4.

In this case, the mandatory condition "cheap" means inexpensive, therefore, its satisfaction degree can be calculated by $\mu_{cheap}(Price) = 1 - \mu_{expensive}(Price)$.

BIVARIATE BIPOLAR PREFERENCE QUERY

The bivariate bipolar preference has two irrelevant conditions. It needs to call bipolar satisfaction degree function to remove fuzziness in a query. It uses Formula 2 to calculate the satisfaction and dissatisfaction degrees of two preferences as the comprehensive evaluation parameters. According to the selected parameters, it calculates the priority. Finally, it returns the results in priority order. The procedure of bivariate bipolar query is as follows:

1. The mapping function map_{cp} calls the linguistic variable fuzzy query to realize the fuzzy conversion, then using the operator"logical & and" to link the preference condition.
2. Using the standard SPARQL to execute query and getting the initial results.
3. Defining preference satisfaction function and preference dissatisfaction function to evaluate the satisfaction degrees of initial results in querying. To filter out the message, which has satisfaction degree in interval (0.5, 1] and dissatisfaction degree in interval [0, 0.5).
4. Calling the function *fun* (γ_{cp}) to calculate the priority of filtered results and getting the final result with sequence.

The algorithm of bivariate bipolar query is shown in Algorithm 2.

Calling the satisfaction function *fun* ($\mu_x(A|B)$) and dissatisfaction function *fun* ($\neg\mu_x(A|B)$) in bivariate bipolar query procedure to calculate the result satisfaction degree $\mu_{cp}(A|B)$ via *t-norm*, and to calculate

Table 4. Basic data of fuzzy query results

#House	Price(yuan)	Area(m²)	$\mu_{cheap}(Price)$	$\mu_{large}(Area)$
1	283000	94	0.83	0.17
2	340000	112	0.8	0.2
3	480000	159	0.72	0.28
4	576000	191	0.66	0.34
5	427400	142	0.75	0.25
6	490000	163	0.72	0.28
7	511000	170	0.7	0.3

the result dissatisfaction degree $\neg\mu_{cp}$ $(A|B)$ through *t-conorm*. It restrains the satisfaction degree and dissatisfaction degree of initial results via the structure "if". Finally, realizing the filter of satisfied information, and sequencing the results.

Algorithm 2. Bivariate bipolar preference query procedure

```
Input: Q_cp = (C, P);
T={} is the result set after removing fuzzy
T_cp={} is the result set of satisfaction preference condition
C_p ∈ C, P_p ∈ P,
map_cp is the mapping function of fuzzy preference condition.
Begin
    C_p, P_p → map_cp;
        //C_1, C_2, ..., C_i is the precise mandatory condition after mapping, P_1,
P_2, ..., P_i is the precise optional condition after mapping, opt is the rela-
tion operator.
    get (C_1, C_2, ..., C_i, P_1, P_2, ..., P_i);
    FITLER (Var_c opt C_1 || ... || Var_c opt C_i) and(Var_p opt P_1||...|| Var_p opt P_i)
        get T = {t_1, t_2, ..., t_n};
    μ_cp (t_i) = fun (μ_x (A|B));
    ¬μ_cp (t_i) = fun (¬μ_x (A|B));
        //I ∈ [1, n], t_i is the message in result set T, its satisfaction degree
is μ_cp (t_i), and its dissatisfaction degree is ¬μ_cp (t_i).
        for i=1 to n do
    if (0.5 < μ_cp (t_i) < 1) and (0 < ¬μ_cp (t_i) < 0.5)
        then T_cp = t_i ∪ T_cp
    fun (γ_cp);
    ORDER BY DESC (γ_cp): T_cp ;
end.
        Output: T_cp
```

Example 3: There is a RDF data source of Car Sale. The user need to search the result, which is "the price of car about 100000 Yuan, the brand of car is not *X*", then the fuzzy SPARQL expression form with bipolar preference condition is shown as follows:

```
SELECT ?Price ? Brand ?Car
WHERE {?p ex:hasPrice ?Price.
        ?p ex:hasColor ?Brand.
    FILTER (?Price =" about 100000" and (not ?Brand ="X")) }
        ?p fun:score(?μ_about (Price), ?μ_{not X} (Brand))
```

In this example, the mandatory preference "The price about 100,000" and optional preference "Not X brand" are two irrelevant preferences on two natures but on same item, so their satisfaction degree don't exist complementary relationship. For the preferences are exclusive, here we use the "logical and AND" operator to link the preference conditions. Mapping the mandatory preference "about 100000" to the membership degree interval [0.81, 1.0], and calling the intermediate type membership degree function (formula 4) in *Cauchy* distribution for calculating the query object interval.

$$\mu_{aboutY}(x) = \frac{1}{1 + \left(\dfrac{x - y}{\beta}\right)^2} \tag{4}$$

If setting $\beta = 3000$ in this example, then getting the query interval [85500, 114500]. According to this interval, the fuzzy preference condition is converted into the precise condition. The converted standard *SPARQL* expression is as follows.

```
SELECT ?Car ?Price ?Brand
WHERE {?p ex:hasPrice ?Price.
          ?p ex:hasColor ?Brand.
    FILTER ((?Price >= 114500 and Price <= 85500) and (not ?Brand = "X brand"))
}
```

Executing the query and getting initial result set, then calculating the bipolar preference satisfaction degree of each message in result set. The results are shown in Table 5.

SEQUENCING METHOD OF OPTIMIZATION RESULTS

The fuzzy SPARQL with bipolar preferences can be converted to the precise conditions by using the mothod in the above section. It produces an unordered result set after querying. Although the result set includes satisfaction parameters, but two satisfaction parameters cannot sequence the results (see Table 4 and Table 5). Therefore, the returned results are not the permutation of user satisfaction degree, which leads to a trouble of quadratic sieve. For such issues, the bipolar preferences priority function "fun(y_{cp})" is defined. According to the features of univariate and bivariate bipolar preferences, it uses the different priority computing methods to optimize the initial result set, and then prioritizing the message that fit with the preferences.

Table 5. Initial results of fuzzy query

#Car	Price (Yuan)	Brand	$\mu_{about\,100000}$ (Price) $\wedge \mu_{not\,x}$(Brand)	$\neg\mu_{about\,100000}$ (Price) $\wedge\neg\mu_{not\,x}$ (Brand)
1	88900	A	0.78	0.17
2	99700	B	0.82	0.06
3	113800	C	0.91	0.09
4	102800	D	0.66	0.11
5	89700	E	0.78	0.15
6	108000	F	0.91	0.09
7	85800	G	0.74	0.23

The preference conditions in univariate bipolar preference query have the complementarity, which makes the satisfaction degrees of two conditions relevant. It has the same influence on the query results. Therefore, the priority is calculated by the difference value:

$$fun(y_{cp}) = u_c(A) - u_p(B), y_{cp} \in [0, 1] \tag{5}$$

The priority of Example 2 is calculated by the Formula 5 (Table 4), and the final results of priority are shown in Table 6.

The mandatory preference and optional preference are independent in bivariate bipolar preference query. Using the dissatisfaction degree to mark the message can easily fit the degree of user demands. In Example 3, it is more convenient to use "I don't like brand X" to replace "I like brand A or B or C". Therefore, the priority computing needs to consider the dissatisfaction and satisfaction preferences, and its computing method is shown as follows:

$$fun(\gamma_{cp}) = \frac{\mu_{cp}(A \mid B)}{\mu_{cp}(A \mid B) + \neg\mu_{cp}(A \mid B)} \bullet \frac{1 - \neg\mu_{cp}(A \mid B)}{(1 - \mu_{cp}(A \mid B)) + (1 - \neg\mu_{cp}(A \mid B))}, \gamma_{cp} \in [0, 1] \tag{6}$$

Here $(\mu_{cp}(A|B), \leftarrow\mu_{cp}(A|B)) \in [0, 1]$ that are the satisfaction and dissatisfaction degrees, e.g., "$\mu_{aroud100000}(Price) \wedge \mu_{not\,x}(Brand)$" and "$\leftarrow\mu_{about100000}(Price) \wedge \leftarrow\mu_{not\,x}(Brand)$". The priority of Example 3 is calculated by the Formula 6 (Table 5), and the optimal results are shown in Table 7.

Table 6. Sorted results

#House	Price (yuan)	Area (m²)	$\mu_{cheap}(Price)$	$\mu_{cheap}(Price) \wedge \mu_{large}(Area)$	γ_{cp}
1	283000	94	0.83	0.17	0.66
2	340000	112	0.8	0.2	0.6
5	427400	142	0.75	0.25	0.5
3	480000	159	0.72	0.28	0.44
6	490000	163	0.72	0.28	0.44
7	511000	170	0.7	0.3	0.4
4	576000	191	0.66	0.34	0.32

Table 7. Orderly results

#Car	Price(Yuan)	Brand	$\mu_{about\,100000}(Price) \wedge \mu_{not\,x}(Brand)$	$\neg\mu_{about\,100000}(Price) \wedge \neg\mu_{not\,x}(Brand)$	γ_{cp}
6	108000	F	0.91	0.09	0.83
3	113800	C	0.91	0.09	0.83
2	99700	B	0.82	0.06	0.78
1	88900	A	0.78	0.17	0.69
5	89700	E	0.78	0.15	0.67
4	102800	D	0.66	0.11	0.62
7	85800	G	0.74	0.23	0.57

By calculating the priority of bipolar preference query and sequencing results, the results is recommended by the satisfaction sequence of user, which reduces the repeated filtering results.

PERFORMANCE STUDIES

To validate our appraoch proposed in this chapter, an experimental system is developed with Eclipse. The system defines a public class to implement fuzzy conditions mapping. Also the satisfaction degree function is applied to calculate the satisfaction degree of bipolar preference query results. There are two kinds of bipolar preferences and the system has two majr interfaces shown in Figure 1 and Figure 2 for univariate bipolar fuzzy query and bivariate bipolar fuzzy query, respectively.

Figure 1. Interface of univariate bipolar preference query

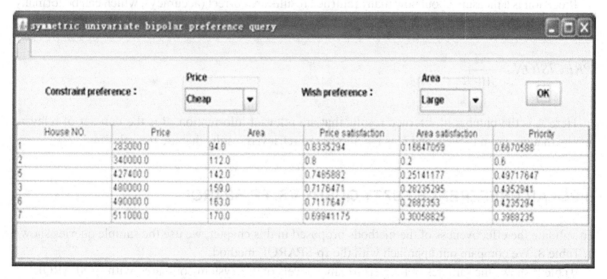

Figure 2. Interface of bivariate bipolar preference query

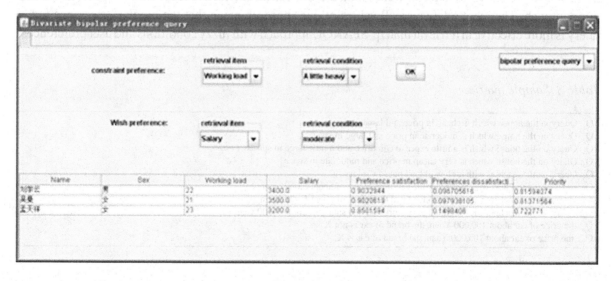

The Lehigh University Benchmark (LUBM) is one of the first RDF benchmarks (Guo, Pan and Heflin, 2004), which contains 6800,000 triples in the data set. We use LUBM as our testing framework.

MEASURES

To validate the effectiveness and performance of our approach, we use two measures, which are recall rate and precision. Recall is a measure about how many relevant results are obtained (coverage of system), which can be formally defined as follows.

$$RECALL = \frac{A}{A + C}$$

Precision is a measure about how many returned results are correct (accuracy), which can be formally defined as follows..

$$PRECISION = \frac{A}{A + B}$$

Here A is the number of returned results that are relevant information, B is the number of relevant results that are not retrieved, and C is the number of retrieved results that are not relevant.

BIPOLAR PREFERENCE FUZZY QUERY VS. FP-SPARQL

To validate the effectiveness of the methods proposed in this chapter, we use the sample queries shown in Table 8. We compare our approach with the fp-SPARQL method.

Table 9 shows the samples of the performance levels of our system compared with fp-SPARQL.

The above table depicts that the precision values of our approach are higher than the values obtained in fp-SPARQL. The relative recall values indicates the retrieval effectiveness between fp-SPARQL and our approach. The more relative recall values of our approach mean that the bipolar preference fuzzy query is more effective in retrieval than fp-SPARQL approach with fuzzy conditions and user preferences.

Table 8. Sample queries

Q_1: Queryon the house which is cheap in price and large in space
Q_2: Query on the house which is moderate in price and large in space
Q_3: Query on the house which is a little expensive in price and a little large in space
Q_4: Query on the house which is very cheap in price and moderate in space
Q_5: Query on the teachers with high workload but low salary
Q_6: Qery on the teachers with high work load and the salary of about 5,000 Yuan
Q_7: Query on the teachers with low workload and the salary of about 5,000 Yuan
Q_8: Query on the teachers with slightly heavy workload and salary of about 3,000 yuan
Q_9: the price of car about 100,000 Yuan, the brand of car is not X
Q_{10}: the price of car about 100,000 Yuan, the brand of car is X

Table 9. Precision and recall values of sample queries

SAMPLE QUERIES	fp-SPARQL		Our Approach	
	PRECISION	RECALL	PRECISION	RECALL
Q_1	0.45	0.38	0.54	0.40
Q_2	0.51	0.42	0.64	0.42
Q_3	0.38	0.51	0.78	0.56
Q_4	0.49	0.36	0.66	0.43
Q_5	0.33	0.17	0.61	0.40
Q_6	0.55	0.38	0.76	0.53
Q_7	0.46	0.30	0.65	0.58
Q_8	0.5	0.43	0.71	0.62
Q_9	0.58	0.41	0.77	0.55
Q_{10}	0.59	0.44	0.71	0.52

Figure 3 shows the precision vs recall graph for our approach and fp-SPARQL .

It can be seen in Figure 3 that the our approach achieves good performance. More results with higher accuracy can be returned, and it is especially ture when running bivariate bipolar preference query. The fp-SPARQL method requires users to propvide their preference conditions. Different user preferences will result in different query result order.

Figure 3. Precision and Recall of our approach and fp-SPARQL

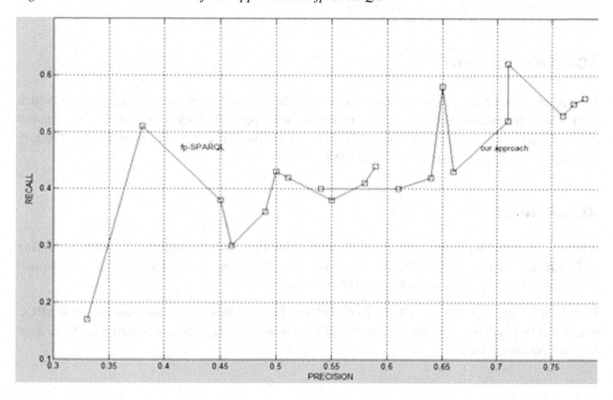

Fuzzy condition with univariate preference or bivariate bipolar preference is mapped to precise one through defining public class, expanding query conditions and setting the mandatory conditions of satisfaction degree. With the priority function, each message is computed sequentially with priority and the results will be recommended through the priority sequence. Our approach avoids to repeatedly filter the returned results.

CONCLUSION

Based on the features of three types of bipolar information, the chapter discussed the mandatory and optional preferences in RDF fuzzy query. If the properties of mandatory and optional preferences are complementary, the bipolar preference is an univariate one. Then an unipolarity satisfaction degree is applied to represent how preference conditions are satisfied. If the properties of mandatory and optional preferences are mutually independent, the bipolar preference is a bivariate one. Then a bipolar satisfaction degree from the positive and negative aspects are used to represent how preference conditions are satisfied.

To accomadate bipolar preferences in RDF fuzzy query, SPARQL was extended in the chapter. First, in order to represent the preference relations, fuzzy linguistic variables were added in FILTER clauses. Second, the query results are optimized by the priority sequence and then returned to the users. For validating the proposed method, an experimental system was developed. After using some query examples, it was shown that the proposed method can meet the daily fuzzy query requirements well because the positive and negative aspects of preferences are considered.

For future research work, more complex preferences should be considered in RDF queries to well satisfy diverse requirements in real applications. In addition, effective query approaches should be investigated in the context of massive RDF data.

ACKNOWLEDGMENT

The authors wish to thank the anonymous referees for their valuable comments and suggestions, which improved the technical content and the presentation of the chapter. The work is supported by the *National Natural Science Foundation of China* (61572118 and 61370075) and *the Program for New Century Excellent Talents in University* (NCET- 05-0288).

REFERENCES

Bahri, A., Bouaziz, R., & Gargouri, F. (2009). Fuzzy Ontology Implementation and Query Answering on Databases. In *Proceedings of the 28th North American Fuzzy Information Processing Society Annual Conference*. IEEE. doi:10.1109/NAFIPS.2009.5156413

Castillo, R., Rothe, C., & Leser, U. (2010). RDFMatView: Indexing RDF Data using Materialized SPARQL queries. In *Proceedings of the 2010 International Workshop on Scalable Semantic Web Knowledge Base Systems*. Academic Press.

Cheng, J. W., & Ma, Z. M. (2010). f-SPARQL: A Flexible Extension of SPARQL. In *Proceedings of the 21st International Conference on Database and Expert Systems Applications*. Bilbao, Spain: Springer.

de Tré, G., Zadrozny, S., Matthé, T., Kacprzyk, J., & Bronselaer, A. (2009). Dealing with Positive and Negative Query Criteria in Fuzzy Database Querying. In *Proceedings of the 8th International Conference on Flexible Query Answering Systems*. Roskilde, Denmark: Springer.

Destercke, S., Buche, P., & Guillard, V. (2011). A Flexible Bipolar Querying Approach with Imprecise Data and Guaranteed Results. *Fuzzy Sets and Systems, 169*(1), 51–64. doi:10.1016/j.fss.2010.12.014

Dolog, P., Stuckenschmidt, H., Wache, H., & Diederich, J. (2009). Relaxing RDF Queries Based on User and Domain Preferences. *Journal of Intelligent Information Systems, 33*(3), 239–260. doi:10.1007/s10844-008-0070-7

Dubois, D., & Prade, H. (2002). Bipolarity in Flexible Querying. In *Proceedings of the 5th International Conference on Flexible Query Answering Systems*. Copenhagen, Denmark: Springer. doi:10.1007/3-540-36109-X_14

Dubois, D., & Prade, H. (2008). An Introduction to Bipolar Representations of Information and Preference. *International Journal of Intelligent Systems, 23*(8), 866–877. doi:10.1002/int.20297

Dubois, D., & Prade, H. (2008). *Handling Bipolar Queries in Fuzzy Information Processing. In Handbook of Research on Fuzzy Information Processing in Databases* (pp. 97–114). IGI Global. doi:10.4018/978-1-59904-853-6.ch004

Guéret, C., Oren, E., Schlobach, S., & Schut, M. C. (2008). An Evolutionary Perspective on Approximate RDF Query Answering. In *Proceedings of the 2nd International Conference on Scalable Uncertainty Management*. Naples, Italy: Springer. doi:10.1007/978-3-540-87993-0_18

Guo, Y., Pan, Z., & Heflin, J. (2004). An Evaluation of Knowledge Base Systems for Large OWL Datasets. In *Proceedings of the 3th International Semantic Web Conference*. Hiroshima, Japan: Springer. doi:10.1007/978-3-540-30475-3_20

Hai, H., Liu, C. F., & Zhou, X. F. (2012). Approximating Query Answering on RDF Databases. *World Wide Web (Bussum), 15*(1), 89–114. doi:10.1007/s11280-011-0131-7

Halder, R., & Cortesi, A. (2011). Cooperative Query Answering by Abstract Interpretation. In *Proceedings of the 37th Conference on Current Trends in Theory and Practice of Informatics*. Nový Smokovec, Slovakia: Springer.

Jarrar, M., & Dikaiakos, M. D. (2012). A Query Formulation Language for the Data Web. *IEEE Transactions on Knowledge and Data Engineering, 24*(5), 783–798. doi:10.1109/TKDE.2011.41

Jin, H., Ning, X. M., Jia, W. J., Wu, H., & Lu, G. L. (2008). Combining Weights with Fuzziness for Intelligent Semantic Web Search. *Knowledge-Based Systems, 21*(7), 655–665. doi:10.1016/j.knosys.2008.03.040

Lacroix, M., & Lavency, P. (1987). Preferences: Putting more knowledge into Queries. In *Proceedings of the 13th International Conference on Very Large Databases*. Brighton, UK: Morgan Kaufmann.

Ludovic, L. (2009). On the Extension of SQL to Fuzzy Bipolar Conditions. In *Proceedings of the 28th North American Fuzzy Information Processing Society Annual Conference*. IEEE.

Matthe, T., & de Tre, G. (2009). Bipolar Query Satisfaction Using Satisfaction and Dissatisfaction Degrees: Bipolar Satisfaction Degrees. In *Proceedings of the 2009 ACM Symposium on Applied Computing*. Honolulu, HI: ACM. doi:10.1145/1529282.1529664

Matthe, T., & de Tre, G. (2012). Ranking of Bipolarity Satisfaction Degrees. In *Proceedings of the 14th International Conference on Information Processing and Management of Uncertainty in Knowledge-Based Systems*. Catania, Italy: Springer-Verlag.

Matthé, T., de Tré, G., Zadrozny, S., Kacprzyk, J., & Bronselaer, A. (2011). Bipolar Database Querying Using Bipolar Satisfaction Degrees. *International Journal of Intelligent Systems*, *26*(10), 890–910. doi:10.1002/int.20505

Renzo, A., & Claudio, G. (2005). Querying RDF Data from a Graph Database Perspective. In *Proceedings of the 2nd European Semantic Web Conference*. Heraklion, Greece: Springer.

Siberski, W., Pan, Z., & Thaden, U. (2006). Querying the Semantic Web with Preferences. In *Proceedings of the 5th International Semantic Web Conference*. Athens, GA: Springer.

Stocker, M., Seaborne, A., Bernstein, A., Kiefer, C., & Reynolds, D. (2008). SPARQL Basic Graph Pattern Optimization Using Selectivity Estimation. In *Proceedings of the 17th International Conference on World Wide Web*. Beijing, China: ACM. doi:10.1145/1367497.1367578

Tamani, N., Lietard, L., & Rocacher, D. (2011). Bipolar SQLf: A Flexible Querying Language for Relational Databases. In *Proceedings of the 9th International Conference on Flexible Query Answering Systems*. Ghent, Belgium: Springer.

Unger, C., Bühmann, L., Lehmann, J., Ngomo, A.-C. N., Gerber, D., & Cimiano, P. (2012). Template-based Question Answering over RDF Data. In *Proceedings of the 21st International Conference on World Wide Web*. Lyon, France: ACM. doi:10.1145/2187836.2187923

Zadrozny, S., & Janusz, K. (2006). Bipolar Queries and Queries with Preferences. In *Proceedings of the 17th International Workshop on Database and Expert Systems Applications*. Krakow, Poland: IEEE Computer Society.

Zadrozny, S., & Kacprzyk, J. (2009). *Bipolar Queries: A Way to Enhance the Flexibility of Database Queries. In Advances in Data Management* (pp. 49–66). Springer.

Zadrozny, S., & Kacprzyk, J. (2012). Bipolar Queries: An Aggregation Operator Focused Perspective. *Fuzzy Sets and Systems*, *196*, 69–81. doi:10.1016/j.fss.2011.10.013

Zadrozny, S., Kacprzyk, J., & de Tré, G. (2012). Bipolar Queries in Textual Information Retrieval: A New Perspective. *Information Processing & Management*, *48*(3), 390–398. doi:10.1016/j.ipm.2011.05.001

KEY TERMS AND DEFINITIONS

Bipolar Preferences: Users are willing to describe their negative and positive preferences in information retrieval. When the positive and negative preferences coexist, they are called the bipolar preferences.

Fuzzy Preferences Query: Fuzzy preference query permits user to use natural language to describe his/her preferences in query, which are fuzzy preference predicates. Two types of fuzzy preference predicates can be identified: fuzzy numerical preference predicates such as *about*, *between*, *max*, *min*, *lowest* and *Highest*, and fuzzy non-numerical preference predicates such as *like* and *dislike*.

Fuzzy Query: A fuzzy query is a kind of flexible query that a user can describe his/her demands with fuzzy query conditions.

Negative Preference: A negative preference is a kind of rejecting, denoting a mandatory condition.

Positive Preference: A Positive preference is a kind of expectation, which means that the expectation of an object property or value is greater than other properties.

Preference Query: A preference query is a kind of personalized query, which can return to a user a set of preferred answers from a large dataset.

RDF: Resource Description Framework (RDF) is a W3C (World Wide Web Consortium) recommendation which provides a generic mechanism for representing information about resources on the Web.

SPARQL: SPARQL (Simple Protocol and RDF Query Language) is an RDF query language which is a W3C recommendation. SPARQL contains capabilities for querying required and optional graph patterns along with their conjunctions and disjunctions.

Chapter 17
RDF Storage and Querying:
A Literature Review

Jingwei Cheng
Northeastern University, China

Z. M. Ma
Northeastern University, China

Qiang Tong
Northeastern University, China

ABSTRACT

RDF plays an important role in representing Web resources in a natural and flexible way. As the amount of RDF datasets increasingly growing, storing and querying theses data have attracted the attention of more and more researchers. In this chapter, we first make a review of approaches for query processing of RDF datasets. We categorize existing methods as two classes, those making use of RDBMS to imple-ment the storage and retrieval, and those devising their own native storage schemas. They are called Relational RDF Stores and Native Stores respectively. Secondly, we survey some important extensions of SPARQL, standard query language for RDF, which extend the expressing power of SPARQL to allow more sophisticated language constructs that meet the needs from various application scenarios.

INTRODUCTION

The Semantic Web (Berners-Lee, Hendler, & Lassila, 2001) is an extension of current Web, in which Web resources are given computer-understandable semantics, better enabling computers and people to work in cooperation. Resource Description Framework (RDF) (Manola, Miller, & McBride, 2004) pro-vides a natural and flexible way to describe resources in the Web and how they are related. RDF data is essentially a set of triples of the form (subject, predicate, object), each of which states that the subject is related to object through the predicate. As more and more information is characterized with RDF, storing huge amounts of RDF data and efficiently evaluating queries over these data plays a central role in achieving the Semantic Web vision. The vigorous development of RDF has attracted the attentions of

DOI: 10.4018/978-1-4666-8767-7.ch017

researchers from database and Web communities. Different solutions and practical systems for efficient and scalable management of RDF data are designed and implemented. SPARQL (Prud'Hommeaux, & Seaborne, 2008) is the standard query language of W3C, SPARQL 1.1 is its latest version (Harris, & Seaborne, 2010). SPARQL can be used to express queries across diverse data sources, whether the data is stored natively as RDF or viewed as RDF via middleware. SPARQL contains capabilities for querying required and optional graph patterns along with their conjunctions and disjunctions. SPARQL also supports aggregation, subqueries, negation, creating values by expressions, extensible value testing, and constraining queries by source RDF graph. The results of SPARQL queries can be result sets or RDF graphs.

We discuss in this chapter mainly query processing of RDF data. However, the efficient query processing heavily depends on the storage strategy of RDF data. The storage strategy, or how a RDF store internally represents RDF data, is a central topic which influences every aspect of the source, from indexing, to planning and evaluation. We use the term "RDF Store" to refer to any RDF management system to provide a mechanism for persistent storage and access of RDF data, usually provide an end-point for accepting queries and showing query results. We thus categorize these implementations around the storage strategies adopted by various RDF stores. They come in many different varieties. For small volume of RDF graphs, it is even possible to efficiently handle and manage data in computers' main memory. Larger RDF graphs render the deployment of persistent storage systems indispensable. RDF stores that make use of purpose-built databases for the storage and retrieval of any kind of data expressed in RDF are called "Relational RDF Stores" or "Relational Stores" in this chapter. In former literatures, the term "RDF Store" (Haslhofer et al., 2011) or "Triple Store" (Rohloff et al., 2007; Rusher, 2003) are frequently used to refer to this kind of systems. There are still other systems implementing their own native storage and indexing formats. We call these systems that do not make use of relational databases as "Native Stores" (Bizer & Schultz, 2009).

Currently, there have been lots of works concerning query processing of RDF datasets, but few comprehensive review papers can be found. Hertel, Broekstra, & Stuckenschmidt (2009) reviewed RDF storage and retrieval technologies as a common approach for accessing ontology-based data. Bizer, & Schultz (2008) introduced the Berlin SPARQL Benchmark (BSBM) for comparing the performance of these systems across architectures. They also presented the results of an experiment comparing the performance of D2R Server, a relational database to RDF wrapper, with the performance of Sesame, Virtuoso, and Jena SDB. Haslhofer et al. (2011) summarize the results of qualitative and quantitative study they carried out on existing RDF stores in the context of the European Digital Library project. The focus of these three works is to make a comparison of the performance of existing RDF storage and retrieval systems. Sakr, & Al-Naymat (2010) focuses on using relational query processors to store and query RDF data. They provided an overview of the different approaches and classify them according to their storage and query evaluation strategies. Kaoudi, & Kementsietsidis (2014) provided an overview of query processing techniques for the RDF data model using different system architectures. They focused on distributed RDF stores, including peer-to-peer, federated and cloud-based systems. This chapter reports the RDF storage and query processing of both RDBMS-based and native storage-based, i.e., Relational RDF Stores and Native Stores. We adapt the structure of (Sakr, & Al-Naymat, 2010) and (Kaoudi, & Kementsietsidis, 2014), with up-to-date literatures reflecting significant progresses in this area. Note that, however, it does not mean that this paper covers all publications in the research area and give complete descriptions.

In addition, we also survey some interesting extensions of SPARQL. Though SPARQL provides users with power of extracting information from RDF data (Arenas, & Pérez, 2011), there are still request for extensions from both theoretical and practical point of view. Recently, researchers have devoted to extend the expressing power of SPARQL to allow more sophisticated language constructs that meet the needs from various application scenarios. These extensions include SPARQL with Property Paths, continuous SPARQL, and SPARQL with fuzziness, etc.

The rest part of this chapter is organized as follows. Section PRELIMINARIES gives a brief introduction of RDF and SPARQL. Section RELATIONAL RDF STORES focuses on relational processing of RDF queries and Section NATIVE RDF STORE gives a brief skip of native stores. Section SPARQL EXTENSIONS presents the several important SPARQL extensions. Section CONCLUSION concludes this chapter along with a short discussion regarding future research directions on this field.

PRELIMINARIES

RDF

RDF is a W3C recommendation that provides a generic mechanism for giving machine readable semantics to resources. Resources can be anything we want to talk about on the Web, e.g., a single Web page, a person, a query, and so on. The semantics are given by adding annotations to resources. The semantic enrichment allows data to be shared, exchanged or integrated from different sources and enables applications to use data in different contexts, which converting the Web of document to a Web of data.

RDF provides a set of basic constructs to fulfill this task, including URIs, Literals, and Blank nodes. Universal Resource Identifiers (URIs) are superset of URLs, which are used to uniquely identify resources. Properties are special kinds of resources, which serve as attributes of resources or relations between resources. Literals are constant values of any property. Blank nodes are resources without URIs which are used to encode n-ary relationships that cannot be captured directly in RDF.

The basic building block in RDF is a subject-predicate-object triple, commonly written as a predicate logic formula of the form P(S, O), which means "a subject S has a predicate (or property) P with value O". More formally, let I, B, and L be pairwise disjointing infinite sets of IRIs (Internationalized URIs), blank nodes and RDF literals, respectively. A triple $(s,p,o) \in (I \cup B) \times I \times (I \cup B \cup L)$ is called an *RDF triple*. In such a triple, s is called the *subject*, p the *predicate* (or *property*), and o the *object*. An *RDF graph* is a set of RDF triples. An RDF dataset is a collection of RDF graphs. All but one of these graphs have an associated IRI or blank node. They are called *named graphs*, and the IRI or blank node is called the graph name. The remaining graph does not have an associated IRI, and is called the *default graph* of the RDF dataset.

SPARQL

SPARQL provides powerful facilities to extract information out of large sets of RDF data. SPARQL allows for a query to constitute of triple patterns, conjunctions, disjunctions and optional patterns. A SPARQL query is a quadruple $Q = (V, P, DS, SM)$, where V is a result form, P is a graph pattern, DS a data set and SM a set of solution modifiers. Among others, SPARQL allows for select *queries*, formed in a SELECT-FROM-WHERE manner. The result form represents the set of variables appearing in the

SELECT, the dataset forms the FROM part, constituted by a set of IRIs of RDF documents, while the graph pattern forms the WHERE part which is constituted by a set of RDF triples. The syntax of SPARQL (See (Prud'Hommeaux, & Seaborne, 2008) appendix for detail) is shown as follows.

```
Query::= Prologue (SelectQuery | ConstructQuery |
DescribeQuery | AskQuery)
SelectQuery::= 'SELECT' ('DISTINCT' | 'REDUCED')?(Var+ |'*')
DatasetClause* WhereClause SolutionModifier
WhereClause::= 'WHERE'? GroupGraphPattern
GroupGraphPattern::= ' {' TriplesBlock? ((GraphPatternNotTriples
| Filter) '.'? TriplesBlock?)*
Filter::= 'FILTER' Constraint ' }'
```

RELATIONAL RDF STORES

The majority of RDF data storage solutions use relational DBMSs. On the one hand, the efficient management of large data sets by leveraging existing mature storing technologies and query engines. On the other hand, providing users with a uniform accessing interface, just as suggested by OBDA (Ontology Based Data Accessing). In general, relational database management systems (RDBMSs) have repeatedly shown that they are very efficient, scalable and successful in hosting types of data which have formerly not been anticipated to be stored inside relational databases.

As is defined in Section 1 and in the following, we use "relational RDF stores" or "relational stores" referring to the RDF stores that make use of RDBMS to store and query RDF data. The relational RDF stores can be divided into four categories in accordance with previous works (Sakr, & Al-Naymat, 2010; Kaoudi, & Kementsietsidis, 2014):

- Vertical (Triple) store,
- Property table stores,
- Horizontal stores,
- Entity oriented stores.

Note that, some of the implementations support different storage scheme, such as Oracle and Sesame, we thus classify them as their primary storage scheme. According to the classification above, some important Relational RDF Stores are summarized in Table 1.

Vertical Triple Stores

The most naïve and simplest implementation of relational RDF stores is so-called vertical triple store or vertical store. In this method, the original structure of RDF data model, i.e. the triples, are preserve in the schema of the relational table. In a vertical relational store one whole RDF dataset is stored is a single relational table, containing one row for each statement.

In (Alexaki et al., 2001a), the vertical triple store is originally named the "Generic Representation", which has a single table where each record corresponds to a RDF triple.

Table 1. Relational RDF Stores

Store Types	Corresponding References
Vertical (Triple) store	(Beckett, 2002; Broekstra, Kampman, & Van Harmelen, 2002; McBride, 2002; Harris, & Gibbins, 2003; Harris, & Shadbolt, 2005; Ma et al., 2004; Chong et al., 2005; Neumann, & Weikum 2008, 2010; Weiss, Karras, & Bernstein, 2008)
Property table stores	(Wilkinson et al., 2003; Levandoski, & Mokbel, 2009)
Horizontal stores	(Abadi et al., 2009; Sidirourgos et al., 2008)
Entity oriented stores	(Bornea et al., 2013)

Redland (Beckett, 2002) is a flexible and efficient implementation of RDF that complements this power and provides high-level interfaces allowing instances of the model to be stored, queried and manipulated in C, Perl, Python, Tcl and other languages. Redland is implemented using an object-based API, providing several of the implementation classes as modules which can be added, removed or replaced to allow different functionality or application-specific optimizations. The framework provides the core technology for developing new RDF applications, experimenting with implementation techniques, APIs and representation issues.

Broekstra, Kampman, & Van Harmelen (2002) developed Sesame, an architecture for efficient storage and expressive querying of large quantities of meta-data in RDF and RDF Schema. As a storage facility, Sesame's design and implementation are independent from any specific storage device that will be used. Thus, Sesame can be implemented on top of a variety of storage devices, such as relational databases, triple stores, object-oriented databases etc., without having to change the query engine. Sesame's query engine implements RQL, the only query language at that time that offers native support for RDF Schema semantics. They discuss both the rationale and the design of Sesame, as well as its implementation and our first experiences with this implementation.

Jena of version 1 (McBride, 2002) (or Jena in short) is a free and open source Java framework for building semantic web and Linked Data applications. Jena provides two kinds of methods for storing and processing RDF data, Jena SDB and Jena TDB. Jena SDB uses a relational database as the backend for storing and querying RDF data. SDB supports many databases, whether Open Source, e.g. MySQL and PostgreSQL, or proprietary, e.g. Microsoft SQL Server and Oracle. The basic layout have a *Triples* table for the default graph, a *Quads* table for the named graphs. In the triples and quads tables, to save the storage space, the columns are not filled with entire string IRIs or literals, but integers serve as foreign keys referencing a *Nodes* table. In the hash form, the integers are 8-byte hashes of the node. In the index form, the integers are 4-byte sequence ids.

Jena SDB also comes along with an API including an RDF-abstraction for the access of the relational store. As for query evaluating, Jena provides supports of SPARQL queries by means of a sophisticated query engine ARQ. In ARQ, processing a SPARQL query involves the following steps: String to Query (parsing); Translation from Query to a SPARQL algebra expression (Cyganiak, 2005); Optimization of the algebra expression; Query plan determination and low-level optimization; Evaluation of the query plan. The definition of the SPARQL algebra is to be found in the SPARQL specification in section 12.

Though simple in design and easy in deployment, Jena SDB could not shows attractive performance. Jena development team thus strongly recommends the use of TDB instead of SDB for all new development due to TDBs substantially better performance and scalability. The Jena TDB is introduced in Section 4.

3store RDF (Harris, & Gibbins, 2003; Harris, & Shadbolt, 2005) is another representative vertical relational RDF storage system. In 3Store a similar idea is adopted as in Jena SDB. A central Triples table is used to hold the hash values of the subject, predicate, object and graph identifier. Two additional tables are adopted to store Resources and literals with a hash of their values used as the primary key. The same hashing function is used for both resources and for literals, so the Triples table contains a column named "literal" which serves as a flag to indicate whether the object of the triple is a literal or a resource. The arrangement ensures the reduction of storage and the records in the table are all of the same size. For evaluating SPARQL queries in 3store, the queries are transformed into relational algebras which are then executed over relational storage. First, the Triples table is joined once for each triple in the graph pattern and renamed to keep the source table from being modified. Then, by looking up the set of triples in the graph pattern, constant values in a triple are preserved and variable are bounded by resources or literals. The other occurrences of previously bounded variables in the graph pattern are used to constrain any appropriate joins with their initial binding.

Ma et al., (2004) presented an RDF storage and query system called RStar for enterprise resource management. RStar uses a relational database as the persistent data store and defines RStar Query Language (RSQL) for resource retrieval. In order to provide detailed performance analysis for several RDF systems, extensive experiments are conducted on a large scale data set to investigate the performance problem in RDF storage. Such analysis will be helpful for designing RDF storage and query systems as well as for understanding not well-solved issues in RDF based enterprise resource management. In addition, experiences and lessons learned in the implementation are presented for further research and development.

Chong et al. (2005) introduced a SQL table function RDF_MATCH to query RDF data. The syntax for RDF_MATCH is similar to SPARQL. The results of RDF_MATCH table function can be further processed by SQL's rich querying capabilities and seamlessly combined with queries on traditional relational data. Furthermore, the RDF_MATCH table function invocation is rewritten as a SQL query, thereby avoiding run-time table function procedural overheads. It also enables optimization of rewritten query in conjunction with the rest of the query. The resulting query is executed efficiently by making use of B-tree indexes as well as specialized subject-property materialized views. The paper describes the functionality of the RDF_MATCH table function for querying RDF data, which can optionally include user-defined rulebases, and discusses its implementation in Oracle RDBMS. It also presents an experimental study characterizing the overhead eliminated by avoiding procedural code at runtime, characterizing performance under various input conditions, and demonstrating scalability using 80 million RDF triples from UniProt protein and annotation data.

Neumann, & Weikum (2008, 2010) present the RDF-3X engine, an implementation of SPARQL that achieves excellent performance by pursuing a RISC-style architecture with a streamlined architecture and carefully designed, puristic data structures and operations. All triples are stored in a (compressed) clustered B+-tree. The triples are sorted lexicographically in the B+-tree, which allows the conversion of SPARQL patterns into range scans. As for query evaluation, SPARQL query is transformed into a tuple calculus representation, which is suitable for later optimizations. The salient points of RDF-3X are: 1) a generic solution for storing and indexing RDF triples that completely eliminates the need for physical-design tuning, 2) a powerful yet simple query processor that leverages fast merge joins to the largest possible extent, and 3) a query optimizer for choosing optimal join orders using a cost model based on statistical synopses for entire join paths. The performance of RDF-3X, in comparison to the previously best state-of-the-art systems, has been measured on several large-scale datasets with more than 50 million RDF triples and benchmark queries that include pattern matching and long join paths in the underlying data graphs.

Weiss, Karras, & Bernstein (2008) propose an RDF storage scheme that uses the triple nature of RDF as an asset. This scheme enhances the vertical partitioning idea and takes it to its logical conclusion. RDF data is indexed in six possible ways, one for each possible ordering of the three RDF elements. Each instance of an RDF element is associated with two vectors; each such vector gathers elements of one of the other types, along with lists of the third-type resources attached to each vector element. Hence, a sextuple indexing scheme emerges. This format allows for quick and scalable general-purpose query processing; it confers significant advantages (up to five orders of magnitude) compared to previous approaches for RDF data management, at the price of a worst-case five-fold increase in index space. The advantages of our approach on real-world and synthetic data sets with practical queries are experimentally documented.

Property Table Stores

The design of vertical table store means that any query has to search the whole database and queries that involve too many self-joins will be especially expensive. Oracle (Chong et al., 2005) also makes use of property tables as secondary structures, called materialized join views (MJVs).

Jena2 (Wilkinson et al., 2003) is the second generation of Jena, a leading semantic web programmers' toolkit. The persistence subsystem of Jena2 which is intended to support large datasets. Jena2 stores each triple either in a general purpose triple table or a property table, for a specific property (Carroll et al., 2004). The schema trades-off space for time. It uses a denormalized schema in which resource URIs and simple literal values are stored directly in the triple table. A separate literals table is used only to store literal values whose length exceeds a threshold or that are typed or have a language tag. This makes it possible to process a large class of queries without a join. However, a denormalized schema uses more database space because the same value (literal or URI) is stored repeatedly. The increase in database space consumption is addressed in several ways. First, common prefixes in URIs, such as namespaces, are stored in a separate table and the prefix in the URI is replaced by a reference. This prefix table will be cacheable in memory so expanding a prefix does not require a database join. Second, a literals table is used so that long literals are stored only once. Third, Jena2 supports property tables as described below. Property tables offer a modest reduction in space consumption in that the property URI is not stored. A property table (Wilkinson, 2006) (also known as attribute tables (Alexaki et al. 2001b)) holds statements for a specific property. They are stored as subject-value pairs in a separate table. Triple tables and property tables are disjoint - a statement is only stored once. For properties with a maximum cardinality of one, it is possible to cluster multiple properties together in a single table. A single row of the table stores property values for a common subject.

Levandoski, & Mokbel (2009) presented a data-centric approach for storage of RDF in relational databases. The intuition behind proposed approach is that each RDF dataset requires a tailored table schema that achieves efficient query processing by (1) reducing the need for joins in the query plan and (2) keeping null storage below a given threshold. Using a basic structure derived from the RDF data, they proposed a two-phase algorithm involving clustering and partitioning. The clustering phase aims to reduce the need for joins in a query. The partitioning phase aims to optimize storage of extra (i.e., null) data in the underlying relational database. Their approach does not assume a particular query workload, relevant for RDF knowledge bases with a large number of ad-hoc queries. Extensive experimental evidence using three publicly available real-world RDF data sets (i.e., DBLP, DBPedia, and Uniprot) shows that their schema creation technique provides superior query processing performance compared to state-of-the art storage approaches. Further, their approach is easily implemented, and complements existing RDF-specific databases.

Horizontal Stores

Abadi et al. (2009) examined the reasons why current data management solutions for RDF data scale poorly, and explore the fundamental scalability limitations of these approaches. They reviewed existing methods for improving performance of RDF databases and especially consider "property tables". They then discussed practically and empirically why this solution has undesirable features. As an improvement, they proposed an alternative solution: vertically partitioning the RDF data, and stored RDF using the decomposed storage model (Copeland, & Khoshafian, 1985). They made a comparison of the performance of vertical partitioning with prior art on queries generated by a Web-based RDF browser over a large-scale (more than 50 million triples) catalog of library data. The results show that a vertically partitioned schema achieves similar performance to the property table technique while being much simpler to design. Further, if a column-oriented DBMS (a database architected specially for the vertically partitioned case) is used instead of a row-oriented DBMS, another order of magnitude performance improvement is observed, with query times dropping from minutes to several seconds. Encouraged by these results, they described the architecture of SW-Store, a new DBMS that implements these techniques to achieve high performance RDF data management.

Sidirourgos et al. (2008) reported on the results of an independent evaluation of the techniques presented in (Abadi et al., 2009). They revisited the proposed benchmark and examine both the data and query space coverage. The benchmark is extended to cover a larger portion of the query space in a canonical way. Repeatability of the experiments is assessed using the code base obtained from the authors of (Neumann, & Weikum, 2008). Inspired by the proposed vertically-partitioned storage solution for RDF data and the performance figures using a column-store, they conducted a complementary analysis of state-of-the-art RDF storage solutions. To this end, they employed MonetDB/SQL, a fully-functional open source column-store, and a well-known – for its performance – commercial row-store DBMS. They implemented two relational RDF storage solutions – triple-store and vertically-partitioned – in both systems. This expands the scope of (Neumann, & Weikum, 2008) with the performance characterization along both dimensions – triple-store vs. vertically-partitioned and row-store vs. column-store – individually, before analyzing their combined effects. A detailed report of the experimental test-bed, as well as an in-depth analysis of the parameters involved, clarify the scope of the solution originally presented and position the results in a broader context by covering more systems.

Entity Oriented Stores

Bornea et al. (2013) described a novel storage and query mechanism for RDF which works on top of existing relational representations. Reliance on relational representations of RDF means that one can take advantage of 35+ years of research on efficient storage and querying, industrial-strength transaction support, locking, security, etc. However, there are significant challenges in storing RDF in relational, which include data sparsity and schema variability. They described novel mechanisms to shred RDF into relational, and novel query translation techniques to maximize the advantages of this shredded representation. They showed that these mechanisms result in consistently good performance across multiple RDF benchmarks, even when compared with current state-of-the-art stores. The work in (Bornea et al., 2013) provides the basis for RDF support in DB2 v.10.1.

NATIVE RDF STORES

Apart from the relational stores described in Section 3, there are still other systems implementing their own native storage and indexing formats, called native stores.

Jena TDB (Seaborne, 2011) is a component of Jena for RDF storage and query. TDB can be used as a high performance RDF store on a single machine. A TDB store can be accessed and managed with the provided command line scripts and via the Jena API. A dataset backed by TDB is stored in a single directory in the filing system. A dataset consists of the node table, Triple and Quad indexes, and the prefixes table. Here "table" and "index" don not directly correspond to concepts in SQL, but inner representations.

OWLIM is a high-performance Storage and Inference Layer (SAIL) for Sesame, which performs OWL DLP reasoning, based on forward-chaining of entailment rules. The reasoning and query evaluation are performed in memory, while in the same time OWLIM provides a reliable persistence, based on N-Triples files. Kiryakov, Ognyanov, & Manov (2005) presented OWLIM, together with an evaluation of its scalability over synthetic, but realistic, dataset encoded with respect to PROTON ontology. The experiment demonstrates that OWLIM can scale to millions of statements even on commodity desktop hardware. On an almost entry-level server, OWLIM can manage a knowledge base of 10 million explicit statements, which are extended to about 19 million after forward chaining. The upload and storage speed is about 3,000 statement/sec. at the maximal size of the repository, but it starts at more than 18,000 (for a small repository) and slows down smoothly. As it can be expected for such an inference strategy, delete operations are expensive, taking as much as few minutes. In the same time, a variety of queries can be evaluated within milliseconds. The experiment shows that such reasoners can be efficient for very big knowledge bases, in scenarios when delete operations should not be handled in real-time.

AllegroGraph (Aasman, 2006) is a modern, high-performance, persistent graph database. AllegroGraph uses efficient memory utilization in combination with disk-based storage, enabling it to scale to billions of quads while maintaining superior performance. AllegroGraph supports SPARQL, RDFS++, and Prolog reasoning from numerous client applications. AllegroGraph is designed for maximum loading speed and query speed. Loading of quads, through its highly optimized RDF/XML and N-Quads parsers, is best-of-breed, particularly with large files. The AllegroGraph product line has always pushed the performance envelope starting with version 1.0 in 2004, which was the first product to claim 1 billion triples loaded and indexed using standard x86 64-bit hardware. AllegroGraph, a purpose built (not a modified RDBMS), NoSQL Graph Database continued to drive innovation in the marketplace with the 2008 SemTech conference example of 10 billion quads loaded on Amazon's EC2 service. The new version 4 series continues to bring performance to the forefront of Franz's Semantic Technologies as the industry's first OLTP semantic web database. AllegroGraph's ability to automatically manage all available hardware resources to maximize loading, indexing and query capabilities once again raises the bar for RDF storage performance. The following table displays examples of AllegroGraph's performance in loading and indexing. Benchmark Results.

Harth et al. (2007) presented the architecture of an end-to-end semantic search engine that uses a graph data model to enable interactive query answering over structured and interlinked data collected from many disparate sources on the Web. In particular, they studied distributed indexing methods for graph-structured data and parallel query evaluation methods on a cluster of computers. They evaluated the system on a dataset with 430 million statements collected from the Web, and provide scale-up experiments on 7 billion synthetically generated statements.

Harris, Lamb, & Shadbolta (2009) described the design and implementation of the 4store RDF storage and SPARQL query system with respect to its cluster and query processing design. 4store was originally designed to meet the data needs of Garlik, a UK-based semantic web company. In 4store, RDF triples are represented as quads of (model, subject, predicate, object), as in 3Store (Harris, & Gibbins, 2003). In 4store, triples assigned to the default graph are placed in a particular model, which is used in query execution against the default graph – when the SPARQL default graph behavior is enabled. Although the quads are queried using a flat pattern structure, the internal structure more closely resembles property tables (Wilkinson, 2003).

SPARQL EXTENSIONS

After SPARQL was first released as a recommendation standard (Prud'Hommeaux, & Seaborne, 2008), there have been endeavors to extend SPARQL with new constructs to support user demands. Some of them, e.g. property paths, have been add to the latest version.

SPARQL with Property Paths

Versa (Olson, & Ogbuji, 2002) is, perhaps, the first attempt towards this direction. Versa is a specialized language for addressing and querying nodes and arcs in a Resource Description Framework (RDF) model. It uses a simple and expressive syntax, designed to be incorporated into other expression systems, including XML, where, for instance, Versa can be used in extension functions or attributes of extension elements that provide RDF-related capabilities. Versa operates on the abstract graph model of RDF, and not any particular serialization.

Kochut, & Janik (2007) present SPARQLeR, a novel extension of the SPARQL query language which allows path variables occurring in query graph patterns. The proposed extension fits seamlessly within the overall syntax and semantics of SPARQL and allows easy and natural formulation of queries involving a wide variety of regular path patterns in RDF graphs. SPARQLeR's path patterns can capture many low-level details of the queried associations. An implementation of SPARQLeR and its initial performance results are also presented.

Anyanwu, Maduko, & Sheth (2007) present an approach for supporting Path Extraction queries. This feature while crucial for many applications has limited support from most RDF querying systems. Their proposal comprises (*i*) a query language SPARQ2L which extends SPARQL with path variables and path variable constraint expressions, and (*ii*) a novel query evaluation framework based on efficient algebraic techniques for solving path problems which allows for path queries to be efficiently evaluated on disk resident RDF graphs. The effectiveness of their proposal is demonstrated by a performance evaluation of the proposed approach on both real world and synthetic datasets.

Alkhateeb, Baget, & Euzenat (2009) propose a method combining the features of SPARQL, which allows querying RDF through graph patterns, and regular path queries inspired by the work in databases, which use regular expressions for searching paths in RDF graphs. For this purpose, a kind of knowledge representation language called PRDF (for "Path RDF") is proposed. PRDF extends RDF such that the arcs of a graph can be labeled by regular expression patterns. PRDF is equipped with a semantics extending that of RDF. A correct and complete algorithm is proposed which, by computing a particular graph homomorphism, decides the consequence between an RDF graph and a PRDF graph. A PRDF query language called PSPARQL is defined, extending SPARQL with PRDF graph patterns and complying with RDF model theoretic semantics. PSPARQL is able to characterize paths of arbitrary length, e.g., "does there exist a trip from town A to town B?". PRDF thus offers both graph patterns and path expressions. This extension is proved not to increase the computational complexity of SPARQL and, based on the proposed algorithm, a correct and complete PSPARQL query engine is implemented.

To express constraints on internal nodes (e.g., "Moreover, one of the stops must provide a wireless connection.") of paths, Alkhateeb, Baget, & Euzenat (2008) present an extension of RDF, called CRDF (for Constrained paths RDF). For this extension of RDF, they provide an abstract syntax and an extension of RDF semantics. They characterize query answering (the query is a CRDF graph, the knowledge base is an RDF graph) as a case of CRDF entailment that can be computed using a particular of graph homomorphism. Finally, they use CRDF graphs to generalize SPARQL graph patterns, defining the CSPARQL extension of that query language, and prove that the problem of query answering using only CRDF graphs is an NP-hard problem.

The MapReduce programming model has gained traction in different application areas in recent years, ranging from the analysis of log files to the computation of the RDFS closure. Yet, for most users the MapReduce abstraction is too low-level since even simple computations have to be expressed as Map and Reduce phases. Przyjaciel-Zablocki et al. (2012) propose RDFPath, an expressive RDF path query language geared towards casual users that benefits from the scaling properties of the MapReduce framework by automatically transforming declarative path queries into MapReduce jobs. The evaluation on a real world data set shows that both large RDF graphs can be handled while scaling linear with the size of the graph and that RDFPath can be used to investigate graph properties such as a variant of the famous six degrees of separation paradigm typically encountered in social graphs.

Navigational features have been largely recognized as fundamental for graph database query languages. This fact has motivated several authors to propose RDF query languages with navigational capabilities. Pérez, Arenas, & Gutierrez (2010) propose the query language nSPARQL that uses nested regular expressions to navigate RDF data. They study some of the fundamental properties of nSPARQL and nested regular expressions concerning expressiveness and complexity of evaluation. Regarding expressiveness, they show that nSPARQL is expressive enough to answer queries considering the semantics of the RDFS vocabulary by directly traversing the input graph. They also show that nesting is necessary in nSPARQL to obtain this last result, and they study the expressiveness of the combination of nested regular expressions and SPARQL operators. Regarding complexity of evaluation, given an RDF graph G and a nested regular expression E, this problem can be solved in time $O(|G|*|E|)$.

The foregoing works finally led the W3C to include the property path feature in the new version of the standard SPARQL 1.1. Arenas, Conca, & Pérez (2012) tested several implementations of SPARQL 1.1 handling property path queries, and observed that existing evaluation methods for this class of queries have a poor performance even in some very simple scenarios. To formally explain this fact, they conduct a theoretical study of the computational complexity of property paths evaluation. The results imply that the poor performance of the tested implementations is not a problem of these particular systems, but of the specification itself. In fact, they show that any implementation that adheres to the SPARQL 1.1 specification (as of November 2011) is doomed to show the same behavior, the key issue being the need for counting solutions imposed by the current specification. They provide several intractability results, which together with their empirical results, provide strong evidence against the current semantics of SPARQL 1.1 property paths. Finally, they put the results in perspective, and propose a natural alternative semantics with tractable evaluation.

Though property paths allow SPARQL queries to evaluate regular expressions over graph data, they differ from standard regular expressions in several notable aspects. For example, they have a limited form of negation, they have numerical occurrence indicators as syntactic sugar, and their semantics on graphs is defined in a non-standard manner. Losemann, & Martens (2012) formalize the W3C semantics of property paths and investigate various query evaluation problems on graphs, which is conducted independently from (Arenas, Conca, & Pérez, 2012). More specifically, let x and y be two nodes in an edge-labeled graph and r be an expression. They study the complexities of (1) deciding whether there exists a path from x to y that matches r and (2) counting how many paths from x to y match r. The main results show that, compared to an alternative semantics of regular expressions on graphs, the complexity of (1) and (2) under W3C semantics is significantly higher. Whereas the alternative semantics remains in polynomial time for large fragments of expressions, the W3C semantics makes problems (1) and (2) intractable almost immediately. As a side-result, they prove that the membership problem for regular expressions with numerical occurrence indicators and negation is in polynomial time.

Querying RDF Streams

A lot of work has been done in the area of data stream processing. Most of the previous approaches regard only relational or XML based streams but do not cover semantically richer RDF based stream elements. Bolles, Grawunder, & Jacobi (2008) extend SPARQL, the W3C recommendation for an RDF query language, to process RDF data streams. To describe the semantics of the enhancement, they extended the logical SPARQL algebra for stream processing on the foundation of a temporal relational algebra based on multi-sets and provide an algorithm to transform SPARQL queries to the new extended algebra. For each logical algebra operator, they define executable physical counterparts. To show the feasibility of our approach, they implemented it within our ODYSSEUS framework in the context of wind power plant monitoring.

C-SPARQL (Barbieri et al., 2009a, 2010) is an extension of SPARQL whose distinguishing feature is the support of continuous queries, registered and continuously executed over RDF data streams, considering windows of such streams. Supporting streams in RDF format guarantees interoperability and opens up important applications, in which reasoners can deal with knowledge that evolves over time. C-SPARQL is presented by means of a full specification of the syntax, a formal semantics, and a comprehensive set of examples, relative to urban computing applications, that systematically cover the SPARQL extensions. The expression of meaningful queries over streaming data is strictly connected to the availability of aggregation primitives, thus C-SPARQL also includes extensions in this respect. In (Barbieri et al., 2009b), C-SPARQL is used for real-time analysis of social data.

Streams of events appear increasingly today in various Web applications such as blogs, feeds, sensor data streams, geospatial information, on-line financial data, etc. Event Processing (EP) is concerned with timely detection of compound events within streams of simple events. State-of-the-art EP provides on-the-fly analysis of event streams, but cannot combine streams with background knowledge and cannot perform reasoning tasks. On the other hand, semantic tools can effectively handle background knowledge and perform reasoning thereon, but cannot deal with rapidly changing data provided by event streams. To bridge the gap, Anicic et al. (2011) propose Event Processing SPARQL (EP-SPARQL) as a new language for complex events and Stream Reasoning. We provide syntax and formal semantics of the language and devise an effective execution model for the proposed formalism. The execution model is grounded on logic programming, and features effective event processing and inferencing capabilities over temporal and static knowledge. We provide an open-source prototype implementation and present a set of tests to show the usefulness and effectiveness of our approach.

Fuzzy Extensions

Until now, the standard SPARQL process information only in a crisp way. Therefore, existing SPARQL implementations, such as ARQ, and Sesame, do not allow users to form queries with preferences or vagueness, which could be desirable for the following reasons (Kraft & Petry, 1997):

- To express soft query conditions;
- To control the size of the answers;
- To produce a discriminated answer.

Example 1. An advertisement company requires 30 models who are *close to* 175cm and *not very young and not very old*.

Apparently, SPARQL cannot efficiently express and answer such a request. To address this problem, Cheng, Ma, & Yan (2010) proposed a flexible extension of SPARQL, called f-SPARQL. It allows, in FILTER constraint, the occurrence of fuzzy terms, e.g. *young* and *tall*, and fuzzy operators, e.g. *close to* and *at most*. The fuzzy terms and fuzzy operators along with the query variables form the so-called fuzzy constraints. Furthermore, membership degree thresholds are taken into account for every fuzzy constraint. The reason for this lies in the fact that each tuple satisfies a fuzzy constraint to a certain degree and hence if no threshold specified, all tuples are retrieved always.

The syntax of f-SPARQL, which extends two elements of SPARQL, i.e. the "Query" and the "Constrain", is shown as follows.

```
Query::= Prologue (QueryType SelectQuery | ConstructQuery |
DescribeQuery| AskQuery)
QueryType::= '#FQ#' | #top-k FQ# with k
Constraint::= BrackettedExpression | BuiltInCall | FunctionCall
| FlexibleExpression
FlexibleExpression::= FuzzyTermExpression | FuzzyOperatorExpression
FuzzyTermExpression::= (Var ['=','!=','>' '>=','<','<='] FuzzyTerm)? [with
threshold]
FuzzyOperatorExpression::= Var FuzzyOperator NumericLiteral
FuzzyOperator::= (Modifier)*FuzzyOperator
```

```
FuzzyTerm::= FuzzyTerm and FuzzyTerm | FuzzyTerm or FuzzyTerm
| not FuzzyTerm | ModifiedFuzzyTerm
ModifiedFuzzyTerm::= (Modifier)* ModifiedFuzzyTerm | (Modifier)* SimpleFuzzy-
Term
```

Each SELECT query is extended with the element QueryType, which can be further divide into #FQ# (flexible queries) and #top-k FQ# with k (top-k flexible queries). The "Constraint" element is extended with an additional "FlexibleExpression" element, as illustrated in the above subsections.

As for query processing, based on fuzzy set theory and α-cut of fuzzy number, a set of translation rules is developed, converting f-SPARQL into crisp ones, so as to take advantage of existing implementations of SPARQL. A scoring method is proposed for calculating the order of query results.

In (De Maio et al., 2012), f-SPARQL is used to perform both approximate querying and fuzzy clustering and classification of semantic sensor data. In order to enable logic inference, data are represented as RDF, OWL, etc. Additionally, soft computing techniques are introduced to approximate context recognition to enable a context aware computing. In particular, a Java implementation of f-SPARQL and the integrated support for fuzzy clustering and classification are discussed.

In order to realize a nature and visualized fuzzy retrieval operation, so as to achieve a user-centered interaction, Wang, Ma, & Cheng (2012) proposed a new fuzzy retrieval mechanism supporting user preference and a corresponding query language called fp-SPARQL (where fp stands for fuzzy and preference). Zadeh's type-II fuzzy set theory, as well as the concepts of α-cut set and linguistic variable is adopted to express user preference, which extends f-SPARQL for further realizing fuzzy and preferred expression. Moreover, ordered sub-domain table of linguistic values is constructed to realize the projection from the fuzzy values to related sub-domains in the table, so as to figure out the interval of membership. On this basis, fp-SPARQL queries are converted into standard SPARQL queries using defuzzification rules. According to the result of experiments, the method has improved the performance of RDF fuzzy retrieval, and correspondingly, users' satisfaction rate on the retrieval results is also enhanced. Besides, the retrieval method complies with users' habits, endowing the system with higher flexibility nature.

CONCLUSION

In this chapter, we review some interesting themes within the context of RDF query processing. We first introduce the methods for storage and retrieval of RDF datasets by using RDBMS or their own storage as backend, which are called Relational RDF Stores or Native Stores accordingly. We then report some extensions for W3C standard query language SPARQL. These extension may serve as instructive complements when there were first proposed, some of them finally are accepted as parts of newly released version of SPARQL.

There are still numerous interesting problems that can be tackled. SPARQL query containment under schema axioms is the problem of determining whether, for any RDF graph satisfying a given set of schema axioms, the answers to a query are contained in the answers of another query. This problem has major applications for verification and optimization of queries. Another important topic concerns query processing over distributed RDF Stores, from federated, peer-to-peer, to cloud systems. In addition to the factors need to be considered in query processing of centralized RDF Stores, data partitioning, metadata and source selection, and query planning and evaluation.

REFERENCES

Aasman, J. (2006). *Allegro graph: RDF triple database*. Technical report. Franz Incorporated. Retrieved from http://www.franz.com/agraph/allegrograph/

Abadi, D. J., Marcus, A., Madden, S. R., & Hollenbach, K. (2009). SW-Store: a vertically partitioned DBMS for Semantic Web data management. *The VLDB Journal—The International Journal on Very Large Data Bases*, *18*(2), 385-406.

Alexaki, S., Christophides, V., Karvounarakis, G., Plexousakis, D., & Tolle, K. (2001a). On Storing Voluminous RDF Descriptions: The Case of Web Portal Catalogs. In WebDB (pp. 43-48). WebDB.

Alexaki, S., Christophides, V., Karvounarakis, G., Plexousakis, D., & Tolle, K. (2001b). The ICS-FORTH RDFSuite: Managing Voluminous RDF Description Bases. In *Proc. of the 2nd Int'l Workshop on the Semantic Web* (SemWeb 2001). Hong Kong: CEUR-WS Press.

Alkhateeb, F., Baget, J. F., & Euzenat, J. (2008). Constrained regular expressions in SPARQL. In *Proceedings of the 2008 International Conference on Semantic Web and Web Services* (SWWS'08). Las Vegas, NV: SWWS.

Alkhateeb, F., Baget, J. F., & Euzenat, J. (2009). Extending SPARQL with regular expression patterns (for querying RDF). *Web Semantics: Science, Services, and Agents on the World Wide Web*, *7*(2), 57–73. doi:10.1016/j.websem.2009.02.002

Anicic, D., Fodor, P., Rudolph, S., & Stojanovic, N. (2011). EP-SPARQL: a unified language for event processing and stream reasoning. In *Proceedings of the 20th international conference on World Wide Web* (pp. 635-644). ACM. doi:10.1145/1963405.1963495

Anyanwu, K., Maduko, A., & Sheth, A. (2007). Sparq2l: towards support for subgraph extraction queries in rdf databases. In *Proceedings of the 16th international conference on World Wide Web* (pp. 797-806). ACM. doi:10.1145/1242572.1242680

Arenas, M., Conca, S., & Pérez, J. (2012). Counting beyond a Yottabyte, or how SPARQL 1.1 property paths will prevent adoption of the standard. In *Proceedings of the 21st international conference on World Wide Web* (pp. 629-638). ACM. doi:10.1145/2187836.2187922

Arenas, M., & Pérez, J. (2011). Querying semantic web data with SPARQL. In *Proceedings of the thirtieth ACM SIGMOD-SIGACT-SIGART symposium on Principles of database systems* (pp. 305-316). ACM.

Barbieri, D. F., Braga, D., Ceri, S., Della Valle, E., & Grossniklaus, M. (2009a). C-SPARQL: SPARQL for continuous querying. In *Proceedings of the 18th international conference on World Wide Web* (pp. 1061-1062). ACM. doi:10.1145/1526709.1526856

Barbieri, D. F., Braga, D., Ceri, S., Della Valle, E., & Grossniklaus, M. (2009b). Continuous queries and real-time analysis of social semantic data with c-sparql. In *Proceedings of Social Data on the Web Workshop at the 8th International Semantic Web Conference* (*Vol. 10*). Academic Press.

Barbieri, D. F., Braga, D., Ceri, S., Valle, E. D., & Grossniklaus, M. (2010). C-sparql: A continuous query language for rdf data streams. *International Journal of Semantic Computing*, *4*(01), 3–25. doi:10.1142/S1793351X10000936

Beckett, D. (2002). The design and implementation of the Redland RDF application framework. *Computer Networks*, *39*(5), 577–588. doi:10.1016/S1389-1286(02)00221-9

Berners-Lee, T., Hendler, J., & Lassila, O. (2001). The semantic web. *Scientific American*, *284*(5), 28–37. doi:10.1038/scientificamerican0501-34 PMID:11341160

Bizer, C., & Schultz, A. (2008). *Benchmarking the performance of storage systems that expose SPARQL endpoints*. World Wide Web Internet and Web Information Systems.

Bizer, C., & Schultz, A. (2009). The berlin sparql benchmark. *International Journal on Semantic Web and Information Systems*, *5*(2), 1–24. doi:10.4018/jswis.2009040101

Bolles, A., Grawunder, M., & Jacobi, J. (2008). Streaming SPARQL-Extending SPARQL to Process Data Streams. In *Proceeding of 5th European Semantic Web Conference, ESWC 2008* (pp 448-462). doi:10.1007/978-3-540-68234-9_34

Bornea, M. A., Dolby, J., Kementsietsidis, A., Srinivas, K., Dantressangle, P., Udrea, O., & Bhattacharjee, B. (2013). Building an efficient RDF store over a relational database. In *Proceedings of the 2013 international conference on Management of data* (pp. 121-132). ACM. doi:10.1145/2463676.2463718

Broekstra, J., Kampman, A., & Van Harmelen, F. (2002). Sesame: A generic architecture for storing and querying rdf and rdf schema. In *The Semantic Web—ISWC 2002* (pp. 54–68). Springer Berlin Heidelberg. doi:10.1007/3-540-48005-6_7

Carroll, J. J., Dickinson, I., Dollin, C., Reynolds, D., Seaborne, A., & Wilkinson, K. (2004). Jena: implementing the semantic web recommendations. In *Proceedings of the 13th international World Wide Web conference on Alternate track papers & posters* (pp. 74-83). ACM.

Cheng, J., Ma, Z. M., & Yan, L. (2010). f-SPARQL: a flexible extension of SPARQL. In Database and Expert Systems Applications (pp. 487-494). Springer Berlin Heidelberg.

Chong, E. I., Das, S., Eadon, G., & Srinivasan, J. (2005). An efficient SQL-based RDF querying scheme. In *Proceedings of the 31st international conference on Very large data bases* (pp. 1216-1227). VLDB Endowment.

Copeland, G. P., & Khoshafian, S. N. (1985). A decomposition storage model. *SIGMOD Record*, *14*(4), 268–279. doi:10.1145/971699.318923

Cyganiak, R. (2005). A relational algebra for SPARQL. *Digital Media Systems Laboratory HP Laboratories Bristol*. HPL-2005-170, 35.

De Maio, C., Fenza, G., Furno, D., & Loia, V. (2012). f-SPARQL extension and application to support context recognition. In *2012 IEEE International Conference on Fuzzy Systems (FUZZ-IEEE)*, (pp. 1-8). IEEE. doi:10.1109/FUZZ-IEEE.2012.6251224

Harris, S., & Gibbins, N. (2003). 3store: Efficient bulk RDF storage. In *Proceedings of the First International Workshop on Practical and Scalable Semantic Systems*. Sanibel Island, FL: Academic Press.

Harris, S., Lamb, N., & Shadbolt, N. (2009). 4store: The design and implementation of a clustered RDF store. In *5th International Workshop on Scalable Semantic Web Knowledge Base Systems* (SSWS2009) (pp. 94-109). SSWS.

Harris, S., & Seaborne, A. (2010). SPARQL 1.1 query language. *W3C recommendation*, 14.

Harris, S., & Shadbolt, N. (2005). SPARQL query processing with conventional relational database systems. In *Web Information Systems Engineering–WISE 2005 Workshops* (pp. 235–244). Springer Berlin Heidelberg. doi:10.1007/11581116_25

Harth, A., Umbrich, J., Hogan, A., & Decker, S. (2007). YARS2: A Federated Repository for Querying Graph Structured Data from the Web. In *proceedings of the Semantic Web: 6th International Semantic Web Conference, 2nd Asian Semantic Web Conference, ISWC 2007+ ASWC 2007*, (Vol. 4825, p. 211). Springer.

Haslhofer, B., Momeni Roochi, E., Schandl, B., & Zander, S. (2011). *Europeana rdf store report*. Academic Press.

Hertel, A., Broekstra, J., & Stuckenschmidt, H. (2009). RDF storage and retrieval systems. In *Handbook on ontologies* (pp. 489–508). Springer Berlin Heidelberg. doi:10.1007/978-3-540-92673-3_22

Kaoudi, Z., & Kementsietsidis, A. (2014). Query Processing for RDF Databases. In *Reasoning Web. Reasoning on the Web in the Big Data Era* (pp. 141–170). Springer International Publishing.

Kiryakov, A., Ognyanov, D., & Manov, D. (2005). OWLIM–a pragmatic semantic repository for OWL. In *Web Information Systems Engineering–WISE 2005 Workshops* (pp. 182–192). Springer Berlin Heidelberg.

Kochut, K. J., & Janik, M. (2007). SPARQLeR: Extended SPARQL for semantic association discovery. In *proceeding of 4th European Semantic Web Conference, ESWC 2007* (pp. 145-159). Springer Berlin Heidelberg. doi:10.1007/978-3-540-72667-8_12

Kraft, D. H., & Petry, F. E. (1997). Fuzzy information systems: Managing uncertainty in databases and information retrieval systems. *Fuzzy Sets and Systems*, *90*(2), 183–191. doi:10.1016/S0165-0114(97)00085-7

Levandoski, J. J., & Mokbel, M. F. (2009). RDF data-centric storage. In *IEEE International Conference on Web Services*. IEEE.

Losemann, K., & Martens, W. (2012). The complexity of evaluating path expressions in SPARQL. In *Proceedings of the 31st symposium on Principles of Database Systems* (pp. 101-112). ACM. doi:10.1145/2213556.2213573

Ma, L., Su, Z., Pan, Y., Zhang, L., & Liu, T. (2004). RStar: an RDF storage and query system for enterprise resource management. In *Proceedings of the thirteenth ACM international conference on Information and knowledge management* (pp. 484-491). ACM. doi:10.1145/1031171.1031264

Manola, F., Miller, E., & McBride, B. (2004). RDF primer. *W3C recommendation*, *10*(1-107), 6.

McBride, B. (2002). Jena: A semantic web toolkit. *IEEE Internet Computing, 6*(6), 55–59. doi:10.1109/MIC.2002.1067737

Neumann, T., & Weikum, G. (2008). RDF-3X: A RISC-style engine for RDF. *Proceedings of the VLDB Endowment, 1*(1), 647–659. doi:10.14778/1453856.1453927

Neumann, T., & Weikum, G. (2010). The RDF-3X engine for scalable management of RDF data. *The VLDB Journal, 19*(1), 91–113. doi:10.1007/s00778-009-0165-y

Olson, M., & Ogbuji, U. (2002). *The Versa Specification*. Retrieved from http://copia.ogbuji.net/files/Versa.html

Pérez, J., Arenas, M., & Gutierrez, C. (2010). nSPARQL: A navigational language for RDF. *Web Semantics: Science, Services, and Agents on the World Wide Web, 8*(4), 255–270. doi:10.1016/j.websem.2010.01.002

Prud'Hommeaux, E., & Seaborne, A. (2008). SPARQL query language for RDF. W3C recommendation, 15.

Przyjaciel-Zablocki, M., Schätzle, A., Hornung, T., & Lausen, G. (2012). Rdfpath: Path query processing on large rdf graphs with mapreduce. In *ESWC 2011 Workshops* (pp. 50–64). Springer Berlin Heidelberg. doi:10.1007/978-3-642-25953-1_5

Rohloff, K., Dean, M., Emmons, I., Ryder, D., & Sumner, J. (2007). An evaluation of triple-store technologies for large data stores. In *On the Move to Meaningful Internet Systems 2007: OTM 2007 Workshops* (pp. 1105–1114). Springer Berlin Heidelberg. doi:10.1007/978-3-540-76890-6_38

Rusher, J. (2003). Triple store. In *Workshop on Semantic Web Storage and Retrieval-Position Paper*. Academic Press.

Sakr, S., & Al-Naymat, G. (2010). Relational processing of RDF queries: A survey. *SIGMOD Record, 38*(4), 23–28. doi:10.1145/1815948.1815953

Seaborne, A. (2011). *Jena TDB*. Retrieved from http://jena.apache.org/documentation/tdb/index.html

Sidirourgos, L., Goncalves, R., Kersten, M., Nes, N., & Manegold, S. (2008). Column-store support for RDF data management: Not all swans are white. *Proceedings of the VLDB Endowment, 1*(2), 1553–1563. doi:10.14778/1454159.1454227

Wang, H., Ma, Z. M., & Cheng, J. (2012). fp-Sparql: an RDF fuzzy retrieval mechanism supporting user preference. In *9th International Conference on Fuzzy Systems and Knowledge Discovery* (FSKD 2012) (pp. 443-447). IEEE.

Weiss, C., Karras, P., & Bernstein, A. (2008). Hexastore: Sextuple indexing for semantic web data management. *Proceedings of the VLDB Endowment, 1*(1), 1008–1019. doi:10.14778/1453856.1453965

Wilkinson, K. (2006). Jena property table implementation. In *Second International Workshop on Scalable Semantic Web Knowledge Base Systems*. Athens, GA: Academic Press.

Wilkinson, K., Sayers, C., Kuno, H. A., & Reynolds, D. (2003). Efficient RDF Storage and Retrieval in Jena2. In SWDB (Vol. 3, pp. 131-150). SWDB.

KEY TERMS AND DEFINITIONS

ARQ: ARQ is a query engine for Jena that supports the SPARQL RDF Query language.

f-SPARQL: f-SPARQL is a fuzzy extension of SPARQL, which allows, in FILTER constraint, the occurrence of fuzzy terms, e.g. young and tall, and fuzzy operators, e.g. close to and at most. The fuzzy terms and fuzzy operators along with the query variables form the so-called fuzzy constraints.

Jena: Apache Jena (or Jena in short) is a free and open source Java framework for building semantic web and Linked Data applications. The framework is composed of different APIs interacting together to process RDF data.

RDF: Resource Description Framework (RDF) is a W3C recommendation that provides a generic mechanism for giving machine readable semantics to resources. Resources can be anything we want to talk about on the Web, e.g., a single Web page, a person, a query, and so on.

RDF Stream: An RDF stream S is a sequence of time-annotated graphs <g [t]> where g is an RDF graph and t is a timestamp.

RPQ: An RPQ (Regular Path Query) selects nodes connected by a path that belongs to a regular language over the labeling alphabet.

Semantic Web: is a term coined by World Wide Web Consortium (W3C) director Sir Tim Berners-Lee. It describes methods and technologies to allow machines to understand the meaning - or "semantics"- of information on the World Wide Web.

SPARQL: SPARQL can be used to express queries across diverse data sources, whether the data is stored natively as RDF or viewed as RDF via middleware. SPARQL contains capabilities for querying required and optional graph patterns along with their conjunctions and disjunctions.

Chapter 18
A Review of Answering Queries over Ontologies Based on Databases

Fu Zhang
Northeastern University, China

Z. M. Ma
Northeastern University, China

Haitao Cheng
Northeastern University, China

ABSTRACT

Ontologies, as a standard (W3C recommendation) for representing knowledge in the Semantic Web, have been employed in many application domains. Currently, real ontologies tend to become very large to huge. Thus, one problem is considered that has arisen from practical needs: namely, efficient querying of ontologies. To this end, there are today many proposals for answering queries over ontologies, and until now the literature on querying of ontologies has been flourishing. In particular, on the basis of the efficient and mature techniques of databases, which are useful for querying ontologies. To investigate querying of ontologies and more importantly identifying the direction of querying of ontologies based on databases, in this chapter, we aim at providing a brief review of answering queries over ontologies based on databases. Some query techniques, their classifications and the directions for future research, are introduced. Other query formalisms over ontologies that are not related to databases are not covered here.

INTRODUCTION

The integration of databases and ontology-based systems became an important research problem for the Semantic Web and database communities. On one hand, the databases may be enriched by an ontological theory that enforces expressive constraints over the databases. Such constraints go far beyond traditional integrity constraints and can be used to enable complex reasoning tasks over the database instances

DOI: 10.4018/978-1-4666-8767-7.ch018

(Gottlob, Orsi, & Pieris, 2011). On the other hand, the database research community has successfully developed a wide theory corpus and a mature and efficient technology to deal with large and persistent amounts of information. In this case, some mature database techniques (e.g., data management, maintenance, and query) may be employed to handle some issues of ontologies, such as storage and query of ontologies. To investigate these issues and more importantly serve as helping non-experts grasp the main ideas and results of querying ontologies with databases and identifying the direction of querying ontologies for the Semantic Web study, in this chapter, we aim at providing a review of answering queries over ontologies with databases.

In particular, one of the main tasks in databases and ontologies remains that of query answering. It is well-known that query is one of the things that make databases so powerful, and the related techniques of database queries have been investigated for many years. Also, querying is the fundamental mechanism for extracting information from a knowledge base. In the Semantic Web, the ontology layer is highly important, and has led to a vast corpus of literature. The ontology can provide a high-level conceptual view of the data repository, and specify implicit concepts and roles that extend the vocabulary of the database with terms that are relevant for specific applications (Ortiz & Simkus, 2012). When clients access the application ontology, the ontology can be exploited to access the data and to answer queries taking into account the knowledge that is implicit in the ontology. To this end, reasoning is of paramount importance when querying the implicit knowledge in the ontology. As we have known, description logics (DLs for short) (Baader, Calvanese, & McGuinness, 2003), as the logic foundation of the World Wide Web Consortium (W3C) recommendation Web Ontology Language (OWL), have a long tradition in knowledge representation and reasoning and play a central role in ontology reasoning. In these contexts, many works concerning query answering in ontologies refer in fact to DLs, which led to wide studies of answering queries over DL knowledge bases (KBs). Considering the different expressivity of the DLs and the trade-off between the expressivity of DLs and the complexity of their querying and reasoning problems, many query works focus on several different families of DLs, to name a few, the lightweight DLs of the DL-Lite (Calvanese et al., 2013, 2007) and $\mathcal{EL}$ (Baader, Brandt, & Lutz, 2005) families, and the families of expressive DLs (Ortiz, 2010). The references (Ortiz & Simkus, 2012) and (Ortiz, 2013) survey some query answering techniques for both lightweight and expressive DLs, and give an overview of the computational complexity landscape.

Being similar to the DLs, the basic query to be posed to ontologies or knowledge bases is instance checking, which determines whether a given individual is always an instance of a certain concept (i.e., whether this instance relationship is implied by the description of the individual and the definition of the concept). However, recently, the widening range of applications has led to extensive studies of answering queries over ontologies that require, beyond simple instance checking, to join pieces of information in finding the answer. In particular, a very well known query form is *Conjunctive Queries (CQs)*, which originated from research in relational databases (Chandra & Merlin, 1977). Moreover, disjunctions of these queries are known as *Unions of Conjunctive Queries (UCQs)*, and are also popular. These languages have been widely studied in the area of databases, and, more recently, there has been increasing interest in the problem of querying ontologies. Driven by this need, the problems related to the CQs and UCQs for ontologies have been studied in the literature (Lutz, Toman, & Wolter, 2009; Calvanese et al., 2006, 2013; Orsi & Pieris, 2011; Gottlob, Orsi, & Pieris, 2011; Ortiz, 2013; Lutz, 2008; Ortiz & Simkus, 2012; Baader et al., 2005). Moreover, as we have known, in the context of the Semantic Web, much information may be represented by the data format RDF and its vocabulary description language RDF Schema.

The main query languages adopted in Semantic Web consist of D2RQ, R2RML, RDQL, RQL, SeRQL, N3QL, Triple, and SPARQL (Prud'hommeaux & Seaborne, 2008). SPARQL is the W3C standard query language for RDF. Therefore, some SPARQL query answering techniques for RDF ontologies were proposed (Kollia & Glimm, 2013; Kollia, Glimm, & Horrocks, 2011). In addition, based on the mature database query techniques, some works are committed to establish correspondences between SPARQL and SQL. Both of these languages give the user access to create, combine, and consume structured data. In this case, some combination techniques of SQL and SPARQL are used to query ontologies (Vyšniauskas et al., 2010; Rodríguez-Muro, Hardi, & Calvanese, 2012; Cui et al., 2011; Kontchakov et al., 2014; Rodríguez-Muro & Rezk, 2014; Cyganiak, 2005; Elliott et al., 2009; Chebotko, Lu, & Fotouhi, 2009).

In our review, we will first introduce some basic similarities and differences between ontologies and databases. Then, some query answering techniques over ontologies based on databases will be introduced, including CQs, SPARQL, and other queries for ontologies based on databases. However, it does not mean that the chapter covers all publications in the area and gives complete descriptions.

The chapter is structured as follows. In Section 2, we provide a brief introduction about ontologies and databases; In Section 3, we survey some query answering techniques over ontologies based on databases; In Section 4, we conclude with a critical review of the state of the art and an analysis of directions for future research.

BACKGROUND

In this section, we introduce some basic similarities and differences between ontologies and databases, which are the basis for the issues discussed in the later section.

Ontologies

The vocabulary "ontology" has its roots in philosophy, the term ontology is today popular also in computer science. In general terms, ontologies are a *formal*, *explicit* specification of a *shared conceptualization* (Studer, Benjamins, & Fensel, 1998):

- *Conceptualization* refers to an abstract model of some part of the world which identifies the relevant concepts and relations between these concepts.
- *Explicit* means that the type of concepts, the relations between the concepts, and the constraints on their usage, are explicitly defined.
- *Formal* refers to the fact that the ontology should be machine readable.
- *Shared* means that the ontology should reflect the understanding of a community and should not be restricted to the comprehension of some individuals.

In specially, ontology allows the semantics of a domain to be expressed in a language understood by computers, enabling automatic processing of the meaning of shared information. Over the years, ontology often appears in various applications. Lots of ontology definitions have already been presented (Staab & Studer, 2009). From these definitions, we can identify some essential aspects of ontologies:

- Ontologies are used to describe a specific domain.
- The terms (including concepts, properties, individuals, and their relations) are clearly defined in that domain. Sometimes concepts, properties, and their relations are also called ontology axioms, and individuals are called facts.
- There is a mechanism to organize the terms commonly as a hierarchical structure.
- There is an agreement between users of an ontology in such a way the meaning of the terms is used consistently.

Ontologies can be defined by the languages such as RDF(S), OIL, DAML, DAML+OIL, OWL, etc (Horrocks, Patel-Schneider, & van Harmelen, 2003). Among them, created in 2004 and updated in 2009, the Web Ontology Language OWL is a prominent knowledge representation standard of the World Wide Web Consortium. OWL is based on Description Logics (DLs) that have a long tradition in knowledge representation and reasoning (Baader et al., 2003). In detail, two sub-languages of OWL, i.e., OWL Lite and OWL DL closely correspond to the DLs known as SHIF(D) and SHION(D), with some limitation on how datatypes are treated. The DL SROIQ(D) is underlying OWL 2, a new version of OWL.

With the development and appearance of ontologies in various applications, when clients access the application ontologies, it is very likely that one of the main services they need is the query answering. Despite the success of the Web Ontology Language OWL, the development of expressive means for querying ontologies is still an open issue.

Databases

A large number of data appears in various real-world application domains, and how to manage the data is particularly important. Databases are created to operate large quantities of data by inputting, storing, retrieving, and managing that data. The evolution of database systems was initially driven by the requirements of traditional data processing. The development of database technology can be divided into several eras: *navigational*, *relational*, and *post-relational* (Abiteboul, Hull, & Vianu, 1995; Elmasri & Navathe, 1994).

Hierarchical and network database models were adopted by (Database Management Systems) DBMSs as *navigational* database models in the 1960s and 1970s. The hierarchical and network database models have the drawbacks that they couple with the need for a formally based database model, which clearly separate the physical and logical model. Therefore, for enhancing the hierarchical and network database models, relational database model is hereby developed. The *relational* database model put forward by E. F. Codd in 1970s (Codd, 1970), has a simple structure and a solid mathematical foundation. It is made up of ledger-style tables, each used for a different type of entity. It rapidly replaced the hierarchical and network database models. Moreover, with the development of databases, several non-traditional database models were developed in succession to enlarge the application area of databases since the end of the 1970s, and they are called *post-relational database models*. Also, with the breadth and depth of database uses in many emerging areas as diverse as biology and genetics, artificial intelligence, computer aided design, and geographical information systems, it was realized that the relational database model as defined by Codd, had semantic and structured drawbacks when it came to modeling of such specialized applications. The next evolution of database models took the form of rich data models such as the *object-oriented data model*. In particular, object-oriented database model (Kim & Lochovsky, 1989) is a popular one of the post-relational database models. Relational database model and object-oriented database model are typical the representatives of the logical database models. Based on these two basic database models, there exists a kind of hybrid database model called object-relational database model. In addition, new developments in artificial intelligence and procedure control have resulted in the appearances of deductive databases, active databases, temporal databases, and spatial databases. These databases generally adopt either one of the above-mentioned two basic database models or a hybrid database model.

Among these databases, *relational databases* became the dominant database model for commercial database systems, and it is the most successful one and relational databases have been extensively applied in most information systems in spite of the increasing populations of object-oriented databases. In detail, a relational database is a digital database whose organization is based on the relational model of data. This model organizes data into one or more tables (or "relations") of rows and columns, with a unique key for each row. Generally, each entity type described in a database has its own table, the rows representing instances of that entity and the columns representing the attribute values describing each instance. Because each row in a table has its own unique key, rows in other tables that are related to it can be linked to it by storing the original row's unique key as an attribute of the secondary row (where it is known as a "foreign key"). Codd showed that data relationships of arbitrary complexity can be represented using this simple set of concepts. The various software systems used to maintain relational databases are known as Relational Database Management Systems (RDBMS). Virtually all relational database systems use SQL (Structured Query Language) as the language for querying and maintaining the database. In particular, one of the main tasks in database systems remains that of query answering. As we have known, SQL is designed to query relational data. Over the years, the database research community has successfully developed a wide theory corpus and a mature and efficient technology to deal with large and persistent amounts of information. Therefore, such mature database techniques may be used to query ontologies.

Ontologies vs. Databases

Based on the observations above, there are some similarities between ontologies and databases. For example, the axioms and facts in an ontology are analogous to the schema and data in a database, respectively. Moreover, most of the work concerning query answering in ontologies refers in fact to *Conjunctive Queries (CQs)*, which originated from research in relational databases (Chandra & Merlin, 1977). In addition, although SPARQL (Prud'hommeaux & Seaborne, 2008) can be used to query RDF ontology data while SQL is designed to query relational data, both languages are mature and rich with many similar capabilities as mentioned in (Polikoff, 2014; Kumar, Kumar, & Kumar, 2011), e.g., SQL and SPARQL have a similar set of aggregate functions used with a GROUP BY operator; To select data with values not matching some specified value, SQL uses NOT EQUAL and SPARQL uses the NOT EXISTS filter for similar purposes. Also, there is difference between SPARQL (RDF) and SQL in case of individual scope. In SQL individuals is unique in local table while in RDF they are globally unique.

However, as mentioned in (Godugula, 2008), an ontology differs from a database schema in that it provides more formal expression than a database schema. A schema is thus more restricted, it is generally used for a specific database (i.e., not reusable), does not provide explicit semantics for the data, whereas ontologies do. Often, they can be seen as formal descriptions at different levels of abstraction (where ontologies are the higher level). In more detail, there are some important differences as mentioned in (Horrocks, 2008). For example, ontology is based on the open world assumption (i.e., missing information is treated as unknown) while database is based on the closed world assumption (i.e., missing information is treated as false). Moreover, each individual in database has a unique name while individuals in ontology may have more than one name. In addition, in spite of the similarity between the axioms in ontology and the schema in database as mentioned above, the schema in database is used to define constraints on structure of data while the ontology axioms behave like implicit inference rules. These differences result in that query answering for ontology is also different from query answering for database, e.g., in database query answering the schema plays no role and the query may be implemented efficiently, while in ontology query answering the axioms (i.e., concepts and relations) play a important role and the query may have very high worst case complexity. More introductions about the relationships between ontologies and databases can be found in (Franconi, 2008).

On the basis of the similarities and differences between ontologies and databases, integrating existing databases with ontology-based systems is among the important research problems for the Semantic Web, and how to couple these two different types of query technologies smoothly and efficiently is becoming more and more important in the database and ontology areas and also is still an open issue.

ANSWERING QUERIES OVER ONTOLOGIES BASED ON DATABASES

Querying is the fundamental mechanism for accessing information from an ontology. In this section, we focus on the query answering techniques for ontologies based on databases, including conjunctive queries over ontologies based on databases, SPARQL-to-SQL query over ontologies, and query over ontologies with some special database techniques. In general, the literature on query answering techniques for ontologies based on databases can be summarized in Table 1.

Conjunctive Queries over Ontologies Based on Databases

The familiar and important queries to be posed to an ontology or a knowledge base is *instance checking*, which determines whether a given individual is always an instance of a certain concept. Some efficient

Table 1. Query answering techniques for ontologies based on databases

Conjunctive queries over ontologies based on databases	answer query over the DL-Lite ontologies	(Calvanese et al., 2006, 2013; Acciarri et al., 2005)
	answer query over the $\mathcal{EL}$ ontologies	(Lutz, Toman, & Wolter, 2009)
	bipolar conjunctive query evaluation for ontology based database querying	(Tamani, Lietard, & Rocacher, 2013)
SPARQL-to-SQL query over ontologies	(Vyšniauskas et al., 2010; Rodríguez-Muro, Hardi, & Calvanese, 2012; Cui et al., 2011; Kontchakov et al., 2014; Sakr & Al-Naymat, 2009; Cyganiak, 2005; Elliott et al., 2009; Chebotko, Lu, & Fotouhi, 2009; Sequeda, Arenas, & Miranker, 2012; Sequeda & Miranker, 2012; Rodríguez-Muro & Calvanese, 2012; Son, Jeong, & Baik, 2011; Son, Jeong, & Baik, 2008; Kumar, Kumar, & Kumar, 2011; Kashlev & Chebotko, 2011; Rachapalli et al., 2011; Newman, 2006; Chebotko & Lu, 2008)	
Query over ontologies with some special database techniques	(Rodríguez-Muro, Kontchakov, & Zakharyaschev, 2013; LePendu & Dou, 2011; Dehainsala, Pierra, & Bellatreche, 2007; Seylan, Franconi, & de Bruijn, 2009; Trißl & Leser, 2005; LePendu et al., 2008; Jean, Aït-Ameur, & Pierra, 2006; Delaitre & Kazakov, 2009; Calì, Gottlob, & Pieris, 2010, 2012; Peim et al., 2002; Zhao et al., 2008; Sören & Ives, 2007; Nolle & Nemirovski, 2013; Franconi, Kerhet, & Ngo, 2013; Vyšniauskas, Nemuraite, & Paradauskas, 2011; Tzacheva et al., 2013)	

algorithms have been developed and implemented, and existing reasoners are highly optimized and can handle large ontology knowledge bases. For example, FaCT++ (Tsarkov & Horrocks, 2006), Racer (Haarslev & Möller, 2003), Pellet (Sirin & Parsia, 2006), HermiT (Shearer, Motik, & Horrocks, 2008), and KAON2 (Hustadt, Motik, & Sattler, 2007).

With the development of ontologies, the widening range of applications has led to extensive studies of answering queries over ontologies that require, beyond simple instance checking, to join pieces of information in finding the answer. In this case, *Conjunctive Queries (CQs)* originated from research in relational databases (Chandra & Merlin, 1977), and, more recently, have also been identified as a desirable form of answering complex queries over ontologies. In brief, as defined in (Orsi & Pieris, 2011), in ontological database management systems, an extensional relational database D (also called ABox in the description logic community) is combined with an *ontological theory* Σ (also called TBox) describing rules and constraints which derive new intensional data from the extensional data. A *query* is answered against the logical theory $D \cup \Sigma$, and not just against D. Formally, if $Q: q(X) \leftarrow \varphi(X,Y)$ is a CQ with output variables X, then its answer in the ontological database consists of all the tuples t of constants such that $D \cup \Sigma \models \exists u\, \varphi(t, u)$, or, equivalently, t belongs to the answer of Q over I, for each instance I that contains D and satisfies Σ. The detailed form of CQs can be found in (Calvanese et al., 2006, 2013; Bienvenu et al., 2013; Orsi & Pieris, 2011; Gottlob, Orsi, & Pieris, 2011; Ortiz, 2013). Moreover, disjunctions of these queries are known as *Unions of Conjunctive Queries (UCQs)*, and are also popular in recent years.

A prominent approach to conjunctive query answering over ontologies is via rewriting the given input into formalisms for which efficient data retrieval systems exist. An up-to-date survey of rewriting approaches for ontological query answering can be found in (Gottlob, Orsi, & Pieris, 2011). As mentioned in (Calvanese et al., 2013; Orsi & Pieris, 2011; Gottlob, Orsi, & Pieris, 2011; Ortiz, 2013), such idea here is to get rid of the ontological knowledge first, and then use existing database technologies. That is, one reduces query answering in the presence of an ontology to answering another query, possibly in a different language, but over a single relational structure (a plain database). In more detail, given a CQ and an ontology, the query is compiled into a first-order query, called the perfect rewriting, that embeds the intensional knowledge (i.e., axioms in ontology) implied by the ontology. Then, for every database D (i.e., facts in ontology), the answer is obtained by directly evaluating the perfect rewriting over D. Since first-order queries can be easily translated into SQL, ontological query answering can be delegated to traditional database management systems (DBMSs). This allows to utilize all the query optimization techniques available in the underlying DBMSs.

However, comparing to databases, the use of an ontology typically leads to an increase in the complexity of CQ answering. For example, all hitherto known algorithms for CQ answering in the basic propositionally closed DL $\mathcal{ALC}$ and its extensions require double exponential time (Lutz, 2008; Ortiz & Simkus, 2012). In this case, identifying expressive fragments of ontological theories under which query answering is decidable is a challenging new problem for database and ontology researches (Gottlob, Orsi, & Pieris, 2011). To this end, many researches focus on ontologies formulated in lightweight DLs of the DL-Lite (Calvanese et al 2006, 2013) and $\mathcal{EL}$ (Baader et al., 2005) families, which enjoy better computational properties. As mentioned in (Bienvenu et al., 2013), CQ answering for DL-Lite knowledge bases has the same data and combined complexity as for plain databases, whereas for $\mathcal{EL}$, CQ answering is P-complete in data complexity, but remains NP-complete in combined complexity (Here, the data complexity denotes that when the ontology and query are considered fixed, and the complexity is measured in the size of the data only; the combined complexity denotes that when the complexity is measured in terms of the combined sizes of the query, ontology, and data). A classic result in database theory states that *CQ* answering becomes feasible in polynomial time when restricted to the class of *acyclic CQs* (Yannakakis, 1981). it seems natural to ask whether these tractability results also transfer to the DL setting.

Based on the techniques of databases, in (Calvanese et al., 2006, 2013), the database technology is used to answer query over the DL-Lite ontologies, and their query-answering algorithms are based on the idea of expanding the original query into SQL according to TBox (i.e., ontology axioms) that can be directly evaluated by an SQL engine over the ABox (i.e., ontology facts), thus taking advantage of well-established query optimization strategies supported by current industrial-strength relational technology. In the approach, the ABox is represented as relations managed in secondary storage by a database management system. The query was implemented in the QuOnto system (Acciarri et al., 2005). In QuOnto, the information regarding the instances of ontologies are stored in a relational database.

Moreover, in (Lutz, Toman, & Wolter, 2009), the authors also proposed a novel approach to *CQ* answering using relational database management systems (RDBMSs), and paves the way to using RDBMSs for *CQ* answering in the $\mathcal{EL}$ family of DLs. But the approach is different from the standard query rewriting approach since their algorithm rewrites both the query and the ABox w.r.t. the TBox. Their central idea is to incorporate the consequences of the TBox *T* into the relational instance corresponding to the given ABox *A*. Moreover, a notion of combined first-order (FO) rewritability is introduced. They pointed out a DL enjoys combined FO rewritability if it is possible to effectively rewrite (*i*) *A* and *T* into an FO structure (independently of a query *q*) and (*ii*) *q* and (possibly) *T* into an FO query *q** (independently of *A*) such that query answers are preserved, i.e, the answer to *q** over the FO structure is the same as the answer to *q* over *A* and *T*. The connection to RDBMSs then relies on the well-known equivalence between FO structures and relational databases, and FO queries and SQL queries.

In addition, the bipolar conjunctive query evaluation for ontology based database querying is discussed in (Tamani, Lietard, & Rocacher, 2013), and they developed a three-step algorithm which is the basis of the proposed bipolar conjunctive query evaluation approach. The first step details the rules to apply to substitute atoms of a given query based on the applicable subsumption axioms. The second one shows the way in which substitutions are applied on a query to derive the set of its complementary queries. The third one is aimed at translating a conjunctive query into bipolar SQLf statements. This evaluation process is developed under a bipolar knowledge base relying on bipolar conditions of both types "and if possible" and "or else", implemented as a standalone application and saved in a relational database managed by PostgreSQLf DBMS extended to the aforementioned framework of bipolarity.

SPARQL-to-SQL Queries over Ontologies

The well-known query language SPARQL, the W3C standard query language for RDF (Resource Description Framework, the data format of the Semantic Web), has been attracting significant attention in the context of the Semantic Web. The data model RDF and its vocabulary description language RDF Schema can describe the Web resource information and their semantics as the lightweight ontologies. Therefore, some SPARQL query answering techniques for ontologies were proposed (Kollia & Glimm, 2013; Kollia, Glimm, & Horrocks, 2011). In addition, based on the mature database query techniques, some works are committed to establish correspondences between SPARQL and SQL. Both of these languages give the user access to create, combine, and consume structured data.

An approach for query ontology stored in relational database was presented in (Vyšniauskas et al., 2010), where SPARQL is used to querying ontology structures in a main memory and SQL (obtained by converting fragments of SPARQL to SQL) is used for querying instances in the database. Moreover, efficient SPARQL-to-SQL query for RDF and OWL was investigated in (Rodríguez-Muro, Hardi, & Calvanese, 2012). The authors introduce Quest, a new system that provides SPARQL query answering with support for OWL 2 QL and RDFS. Quest allows to link the vocabulary of an ontology to the content of a relational database through mapping axioms. These are used together with the ontology to answer a SPARQL query by means of a single SQL query that is then executed over the database. Quest uses highly-optimized query rewriting techniques to generate the SQL query which not only takes into account the entailments of the ontology and data, but is also 'lean' and simple so that it can be executed efficiently by any SQL engine.

Moreover, in (Cui et al., 2011), the authors gave a storage method to store the ontology with integrity constraints in relational database, and then presented the corresponding translation of SPARQL to SQL for querying the stored ontology. In (Kontchakov et al., 2014), the authors gave both a theoretical background and a practical implementation of a procedure for answering SPARQL 1.1 queries under the OWL2 QL direct semantics entailment regime in the scenario where data instances are stored in a relational database whose schema is connected to the language of the given OWL 2 QL ontology via an R2RML mapping. Also, the SPARQL queries are transformed into equivalent SQL queries. In (Sequeda, Arenas, & Miranker, 2012), an approach for ontology-based data access using views was developed. In more detail, they proposed a new approach to answering SPARQL queries on OWL 2 QL ontologies over existing relationally stored data. Their proposal is to replace answering queries via query rewriting with answering queries using views, and the SQL infrastructure can be leveraged in order to support effective SPARQL query answering on OWL 2 QL ontologies over existing relationally stored data. In (Sequeda & Miranker, 2012), a system that can execute SPARQL queries at almost equivalent execution speed as its semantically equivalent SQL queries. The experimental studies demonstrated that existing approaches were several magnitudes slower. Their main insight was to represent the relational data as RDF triples using views. SPARQL queries are syntactically translated to SQL queries which operate on the views. They observed that two relational optimizations are needed in order for relational database to effectively execute SPARQL queries: detection of unsatisfiable conditions and self-join elimination.

In addition, the report in (Cyganiak, 2005) describes a transformation from SPARQL into the relational algebra, an abstract intermediate language for the expression and analysis of queries. This makes existing work on query planning and optimization available to SPARQL implementors. A further translation into SQL is outlined, and mismatches between SPARQL semantics and the relational approach are discussed. The work in (Elliott et al., 2009) presents a feature-complete translation from SPARQL into efficient SQL. They propose "SQL model"-based algorithms that implement each SPARQL algebra operator via SQL query augmentation, and generate a flat SQL statement for efficient processing by relational database query engines. SPARQL-to-SQL translation presented is feature-complete, since it applies to all SPARQL language features. They also demonstrate the performance and scalability of our method by an extensive evaluation using recent SPARQL benchmark queries, and a benchmark dataset, as well as a real-world photo dataset. The work in (Chebotko, Lu, & Fotouhi, 2009) also discusses the semantics preserving SPARQL-to-SQL translation. They formalize a relational algebra based semantics of SPARQL, which bridges an important gap between the Semantic Web and relational databases, and prove that the semantics is equivalent to the mapping-based semantics of SPARQL. Based on this semantics, they propose the provably semantics preserving SPARQL-to-SQL translation for SPARQL triple patterns, basic graph patterns, optional graph patterns, union graph patterns, and value constraints. The translation algorithm is generic and can be directly applied to existing RDBMS-based RDF stores.

Finally, they extend the defined semantics and translation to support the bag semantics of a SPARQL query solution and outline a number of simplifications for the SPARQL-to-SQL translation to generate simpler and more efficient SQL queries.

In recently, in (Rodríguez-Muro & Calvanese, 2012), the authors introduce Quest, a system that provides SPARQL query answering with support for OWL 2 QL and RDFS. Quest allows to link the vocabulary of an ontology to the content of a relational database through mapping axioms. These are used together with the ontology to answer a SPARQL query by means of a single SQL query that is then executed over the database. Quest uses highly-optimised query rewriting techniques to generate the SQL query which not only takes into account the entailments of the ontology and data, but is also 'lean' and simple so that it can be executed efficiently by any SQL engine. Quest supports commercial and open source databases, including database federation tools like Teiid to allow for Ontology Based Data Integration of relational and other sources (e.g., CSV, Excel, XML).

Also, the work in (Kashlev & Chebotko, 2011) studies bottom-up and top-down translations of SPARQL queries with complex nested optional graph patterns that yield SQL queries with left outer joins whose reordering is not always possible. They report their on-going research and performance study featuring SPARQL queries with nested optional graph patterns over semantic data repositories instantiated in Oracle, DB2, and PostgreSQL. The work in (Rachapalli et al., 2011) present a framework called RETRO, which investigates the reverse direction i.e. to look at RDF through Relational lenses. RETRO generates a relational schema from an RDF store, enabling a user to query RDF data using SQL. A significant advantage of this direction in-addition to interoperability is that it makes numerous relational tools developed over past several decades, available to the RDF stores. RETRO's schema mapping derives a domain specific relational schema from RDF data and its query mapping transforms an SQL query over the schema into a provably equivalent SPARQL query, which in-turn is executed upon the RDF store. In (Newman, 2006), a formal model is proposed for querying the Semantic Web using a relational based SPARQL. It is shown that using the relational model as a basis for SPARQL provides an easier to implement, more efficient, more consistent and extensible query language than is currently provided. This approach allows the reuse of existing relational optimisation techniques and can be used as a basis to extend SPARQL functionality.

In the dissertation (Chebotko & Lu, 2008), the authors propose the first provably semantics-preserving SPARQL-to-SQL translation algorithm and develop RDFPROV, a relational RDF store for querying and managing Semantic Web data and scientific workflow provenance. Their main research contributions are: (i) formalizing a relational algebra based semantics of SPARQL and proving its equivalence to the mapping-based semantics of SPARQL; (ii) defining the provably semantics preserving and generic SPARQL-to-SQL translation in the literature with support of SPARQL triple patterns, basic graph patterns, optional graph patterns, alternative graph patterns, and value constraints; (iii) proposing a novel relational join, nested optional join, to efficiently evaluate SPARQL queries with well-designed graph patterns and nested optional patterns; and (iv) designing the relational RDF store RDFProv that is optimized for storing and querying scientific workflow provenance as part of the Semantic Web of Scientific Workflow Provenance.

In special, many translation algorithms from SPARQL-to-SQL are dependent on a specific storage model. If the storage structure is changed, the corresponding translation algorithm should be modified accordingly. In this case, the work in (Son, Jeong, & Baik, 2008) developed a system model to overcome this difficulty. The proposed system model enables independent usage of a SPARQL-to-SQL translation algorithm on storages structure. Furthermore, with this model, the usability and practicality of translation algorithms can be increased and the development cost is lesser than that incurred with the storage-dependent model. Further, in (Son, Jeong, & Baik, 2011), the authors describe different evaluation models and compare the performance efficiency of the proposed storage-independent model with that of the storage-dependent model. In addition, they give a clear account of the performance evaluation results to prove the efficiency of the system model proposed in their previous work (Son, Jeong, & Baik, 2008).

A brief survey on SPARQL-to-SQL can be found in (Rodríguez-Muro & Rezk, 2014; Sakr & Al-Naymat, 2009).

Queries over Ontologies with Some Special Database Techniques

Besides the approaches mentioned above, other approaches for querying ontologies based on databases were developed.

In (Rodríguez-Muro, Kontchakov, & Zakharyaschev, 2013), the authors present the architecture and technologies underpinning the OBDA (Ontology-Based Data Access) system Ontop and taking full advantage of storing data in relational databases. Also, they analyze the performance of Ontop in a series of experiments and demonstrate that, for standard ontologies, queries and data stored in relational databases, Ontop is fast, efficient and produces SQL rewritings of high quality.

In (LePendu & Dou, 2011), an ontology database, which takes a Semantic Web ontology as input and generates a database schema based on it, was proposed. When individuals in the ontology are asserted in the input, the database tables are populated with corresponding records. Internally, the database management systems processes the data and the ontology in a way that maintains the knowledge model, much like a basic knowledge base would. As a result, after the database is bootstrapped in this way, users may pose SQL queries to the system declaratively, based on terms from the ontology, and they get answers in return that incorporate the term hierarchy or other logical features of the ontology. Also, an ontology-based database architecture, called OntoDB for storing ontology instance data was developed in (Dehainsala, Pierra, & Bellatreche, 2007), and then several queries can be done in the database architecture.

The authors in (Seylan, Franconi, & de Bruijn, 2009) introduced the notion of DBoxes as a faithful encoding of databases, and they also find an equivalent rewriting of the query in terms of the DBox predicates to allow the use of standard database technology for answering the query. The queries considered in their work are concept expressions (and the answers are their instances), and the ontologies are general $\mathcal{ALC}$ TBoxes. In (Nolle & Nemirovski, 2013), the federated query engine ELITE that facilitates a complete and transparent integration and querying of distributed autonomous data sources was presented. To achieve this aim a combination of existing approaches for Ontology-based Data Access (OBDA) and federated query processing on Linked Open Data (LOD) are applied. Consolidating technologies like entailment regimes, the DL-Lite formalism, query rewriting, mapping relational data to RDF and an improved implementation of R-Tree based indexing contributes to the unique features of this federation engine. ELITE thereby enables the integration of various kinds of data sources, for example as relational databases or triple stores, simplicity of query design, guaranteed completeness of query results and highly efficient query processing. The federation engine has been developed and evaluated in the domain of carbon reduction in urban planning.

In (Franconi, Kerhet, & Ngo, 2013), the authors study a general framework for query rewriting in the presence of an arbitrary first-order logic ontology over a database signature. They have found the exact conditions which guarantee that a safe-range reformulation exists, and show that it can be evaluated as a relational algebra query over the database to give the same answer as the original query under the ontology. A non-trivial case study has been presented in the field of description logics. In (Vyšniauskas, Nemuraite, & Paradauskas, 2011), the authors present a method based on reversible, information preserving transformations and transformation algorithms between OWL 2 ontology and relational database (OWL2ToRDB). The advantages of such transformation are twofold. From the one side, it is desirable to store large ontologies in relational databases as these have ensured the best facilities for storing, updating and querying the information of problem domain. From the other side, the massive amounts of relational data need for exposing them on the Semantic Web along with mapping these data structures to an existing ontology or extracting the corresponding ontology from relational database.

The work in (Tzacheva et al., 2013) present an easy method for users to manage an ontology plus its instances with an off-the-shelf database management system like MySQL, through triggers. These sorts of databases are called ontology databases in their work. An ontology database system takes a Semantic Web ontology as input, and generates a database schema based on it. When individuals in the ontology are asserted in the input, the database tables are populated with corresponding records. Internally, the database management system processes the data and the ontology in a way that maintains the knowledge model, in the same way as a basic knowledge-base system. After the database is bootstrapped in this way, users may pose SQL queries to the system declaratively, i.e. based on terms from the ontology, and they get answers in return that incorporate the term hierarchy or other logical features of the ontology. In this way, the proposed system is useful for handling ontology-based queries. That is, users get answers to queries that take the ontological subsumption hierarchy into account.

Moreover, a method for querying ontologies in relational database systems was proposed in (Trißl & Leser, 2005), and they developed a new method for querying directed acyclic graphs (DAGs) of an ontology using a pre-computed index structure. In (LePendu et al., 2008), the authors proposed an automatic method for modeling a relational database that uses SQL triggers and foreign-keys to efficiently answer positive semantic queries about ground instances for a Semantic Web ontology. In (Jean, Aït-Ameur, & Pierra, 2006), the authors presented OntoQL, an exploitation ontology query language for an OBDB (ontology-based database) data model designed by a layered approach on top of a relational database model, and they further proposed a formal algebra of operators together with the definition of the OntoQL database exploitation language for managing OBDBs.

In (Delaitre & Kazakov, 2009), the authors described a secondary memory implementation of a classification procedure for $\mathcal{ELH}$ ontologies using an SQL relational database management system, and performed a series of query and reason experiments. The authors in (Sören & Ives, 2007) suggested the strategies to push as many inference tasks as possible into standard relational database systems are a feasible way to reason about large ontologies, as DBMS query processing is designed to handle large data volumes, where they developed such an approach, and in the approach SQL queries are used to query ontologies stored in databases. The authors in (Calì, Gottlob, & Pieris, 2010, 2012) addressed the problem of answering conjunctive queries under constraints representing schemata expressed in an extended version of the Entity–Relationship model. The authors in (Zhao et al., 2008) presented a method to enable ontology query on spatial data available from WFS services and on data stored in databases, where ontology queries are rewrote to getFeature requests to WFS services and SQL queries to relational databases to obtain answers.

In addition, an approach for querying ontologies based on oriented-object databases was proposed in (Peim et al., 2002). The approach takes a query and translates it into a calculus expression over an oriented-object model (not represented as relation model, as in most other proposals) derived from an ontology by Ontology-to-Object-Model mapping approach, and shows how queries over an *ALCIQ* ontology can be mapped to the monoid calculus for evaluation.

FUTURE RESEARCH DIRECTIONS

After reviewing some proposals of answering queries over ontologies based on databases, it has been approved that such query techniques could play an important role in the context of the Semantic Web and other application domains by serving as a framework for access information. However, query of ontologies is of interest in its own right; it is still a young research topic, and there are many challenging research problems to be tackled. Currently, the researches on ontology query are still in a developing stage and still the full potential has not been exhaustively explored. Also, some issues still may be important in order for ontology query to be more widely adoptable in the Semantic Web and other application domains:

1. Although many approaches have been developed to *query over lightweight DL ontologies*, answering queries over expressive ontologies is still a young research topic. Some techniques and complexity results on query answering in expressive description logics can be found in (Ortiz, 2010). Investigating this trade-off between the expressivity of DL ontologies and the complexity of their query problems has been one of the most important issues in DL and ontology query research. In particular, on the basis of the mature and efficient query technologies in databases, answering queries over expressive ontologies based on some database techniques may be very interesting topics for future research.
2. Currently, it can be found that some databases techniques, e.g., index and sort, are not fully employed for answering queries over ontologies. Therefore, how to couple these technologies with the ontology query techniques smoothly and efficiently still expects to be addressed in more research works.
3. As we have known, SPARQL is designed to query RDF data while SQL is designed to query relational data. As such, both languages and their respective advantages closely reflect the data models they work with. Therefore, how to establish correspondences between them for efficiently querying ontologies become the important research lines.
4. With the emergence of fuzzy information in many applications and tasks both of the Semantic Web as well as of applications using OWL, DLs, and ontologies, answering queries over fuzzy ontologies increasingly receive attention, and some efforts have been made in fuzzy ontology queries (Pan et al., 2008; Straccia, 2006; Cheng et al., 2009a, 2009b). Also, in (Bahri, Bouaziz, & Gargouri, 2009; Buche et al., 2005), the problems of implementation and query answering of fuzzy ontologies on databases were addressed. Based on the rapid development and the relatively mature techniques of fuzzy databases, research on answering queries over fuzzy ontologies based on database techniques may be an interesting topic for future research.
5. In more recently, the important issue of data quality in ontology-based data access is discussed in (Console & Lenzerini, 2014). Quality of data is characterized by different dimensions, such as completeness, consistency, accuracy, and currency. In (Console & Lenzerini, 2014), they concentrate

on one of the most important dimensions considered both in the literature and in the practice of data quality, namely consistency. And a formal framework for data consistency in ontology-based data access was proposed. More researches about the quality of data in ontology-based data access still expect to be addressed in more research works.

6. A typical problem that end-users face when dealing with Big Data is the data access problem, the work in (Calvaneseet et al., 2013) discussed the rewriting and answering queries in ontology-based data access systems for Big Data. With the popular of the term "Big Data", research on answering queries in the context of Big Data may be an interesting topic for future research.

CONCLUSION

Based on the introduction in the previous sections, it is shown that answering queries over ontologies based on databases increasingly receives attention in order to access information in the context of the Semantic Web and other real-world applications. In the brief review of this chapter, we focus our attention on the research achievements on answering queries over ontologies based on databases. Other query formalisms over ontologies that are not related to databases are not covered here. In our review, we provide a brief review on answering queries over ontologies based on databases, which can contribute to investigating ontology query and more importantly serving as helping non-experts grasp the main ideas and results of querying ontologies and identifying the direction for the Semantic Web study.

ACKNOWLEDGMENT

The work is supported by the *National Natural Science Foundation of China* (61202260, 61370075) and *Fundamental Research Funds for the Central Universities* (N140404005, N140404010).

REFERENCES

Abiteboul, S., Hull, R., & Vianu, V. (1995). *Foundations of Databases*. Boston, MA: Addison Wesley.

Acciarri, A., Calvanese, D., De Giacomo, G., Lembo, D., Lenzerini, M., Palmieri, M., & Rosati, R. (2005). QuOnto: Querying Ontologies. In *Proceedings of the 20th National Conference on Artificial Intelligence* (pp. 1670-1671). Pittsburgh, PA: AAAI Press.

Baader, F., Brandt, S., & Lutz, C. (2005). Pushing the $\mathcal{EL}$ envelope. In *Proceedings of the IJCAI* (pp. 364-369). Edinburgh, UK: Morgan Kaufmann Publishers.

Baader, F., Calvanese, D., & McGuinness, D. (Eds.). (2003). *The Description Logic Handbook: Theory, Implementation and Applications*. New York, NY: Cambridge University Press.

Bahri, A., Bouaziz, R., & Gargouri, F. (2009). Fuzzy ontology implementation and query answering on databases. In *Proceedings of the 28th North American Fuzzy Information Processing Society Annual Conference*. Cincinnati, OH: OmniPress/IEEE. doi:10.1109/NAFIPS.2009.5156413

Bienvenu, M., Ortiz, M., Simkus, M., & Xiao, G. (2013). Tractable Queries for Lightweight Description Logics. In *Proceedings of the IJCAI* (pp. 768-774). Beijing, China: AAAI Press.

Buche, P., Dervin, C., Haemmerle, O., & Thomopoulos, R. (2005). Fuzzy Querying of Incomplete, Imprecise, and Heterogeneously Structured Data in the Relational Model Using Ontologies and Rules. *IEEE Transactions on Fuzzy Systems, 13*(3), 373–383. doi:10.1109/TFUZZ.2004.841736

Calì, A., Gottlob, G., & Pieris, A. (2010). Advanced processing for ontological queries. *PVLDB, 3*(1), 554–565.

Calì, A., Gottlob, G., & Pieris, A. (2012). Ontological query answering under expressive Entity-Relationship schemata. *Information Systems, 37*(4), 320–335. doi:10.1016/j.is.2011.09.006

Calvanese, D., De Giacomo, G., Lembo, D., Lenzerini, M., & Rosati, R. (2006). Data complexity of query answering in description logics. In *Proceedings of the 10th Int. Conf. on the Principles of Knowledge Representation and Reasoning* (pp. 260-270). The Lake District, UK: AAAI Press.

Calvanese, D., De Giacomo, G., Lembo, D., Lenzerini, M., & Rosati, R. (2007). Tractable reasoning and efficient query answering in description logics: The DL-Lite family. *Journal of Automated Reasoning, 39*(3), 385–429. doi:10.1007/s10817-007-9078-x

Calvanese, D., Horrocks, I., Jiménez-Ruiz, E., Kharlamov, E., Meier, M., Rodríguez-Muro, M., & Zheleznyakov, D. (2013). On Rewriting and Answering Queries in OBDA Systems for Big Data. In *Proceedings of OWLED*. Montpellier, France: CEUR-WS.org.

Chandra, A. K., & Merlin, P. M. (1977). Optimal implementation of conjunctive queries in relational data bases. In *Proceedings of the 9th annual ACM Symposium on Theory of Computing* (pp. 77-90). New York, NY: ACM Press. doi:10.1145/800105.803397

Chebotko, A., & Lu, S. (2008). *Querying and managing semantic web data and scientific workflow provenance using relational databases*. (Doctoral Dissertation). Detroit, MI: Wayne State University.

Chebotko, A., Lu, S., & Fotouhi, F. (2009). Semantic preserving SPARQL-to-SQL translation. *Data & Knowledge Engineering, 68*(10), 973–1000. doi:10.1016/j.datak.2009.04.001

Cheng, J., Ma, Z. M., Zhang, F., & Wang, X. (2009a). Deciding Query Entailment in Fuzzy Description Logic Knowledge Bases. In *Proceedings of the 20th International Conference on Database and Expert Systems* (pp. 830-837). Linz, Austria: Springer. doi:10.1007/978-3-642-03573-9_70

Cheng, J., Ma, Z. M., Zhang, F., & Wang, X. (2009b). Deciding Query Entailment for Fuzzy SHIN Ontologies. In *Proceedings of the 4th Annual Asian Semantic Web Conference* (pp. 120-134). Linz, Austria: Springer. doi:10.1007/978-3-642-10871-6_9

Codd, E. F. (1970). A relational model of data for large shared data banks. *Communications of the ACM, 13*(6), 377–387. doi:10.1145/362384.362685

Console, M., & Lenzerini, M. (2014). Data Quality in Ontology-Based Data Access: The Case of Consistency. In *Proceedings of the Twenty-Eighth AAAI Conference on Artificial Intelligence* (pp. 1020-1026). Québec, Canada: AAAI Press.

Cui, X., Ouyang, D., Ye, Y., & Wang, X. (2011). Translation of Sparql to SQL Based on Integrity Constraint. *Journal of Computer Information Systems*, 7(2), 394–402.

Cyganiak, R. (2005). A relational algebra for SPARQL. *HP-Labs Technical Report*.

Dehainsala, H., Pierra, G., & Bellatreche, L. (2007). OntoDB: An Ontology-Based Database for Data Intensive Applications. In *Proceedings of Database Systems for Advanced Applications* (pp. 497–508). Bangkok, Thailand: Springer Berlin Heidelberg. doi:10.1007/978-3-540-71703-4_43

Delaitre, V., & Kazakov, Y. (2009). Classifying ELH Ontologies In SQL Databases. In *Proceedings of the 6th International Workshop on OWL: Experiences and Directions*. Chantilly, VA: CEUR.

Elliott, B., Cheng, E., Ogbuji, C. T., & Meral Ozsoyoglu, Z. (2009). A complete Translation from SPARQL into Efficient SQL. In *Proceedings of the International Database Engineering and Application Symposium* (pp. 31-42). Calabria, Italy: ACM. doi:10.1145/1620432.1620437

Elmasri, R., & Navathe, S. B. (1994). *Fundamentals of Database Systems* (2nd ed.). Redwood, CA: Benjamin/Cummings.

Franconi, E. (2008). Ontologies and Databases: myths and challenges. In *Proceedings of the VLDB Endowment* (pp. 1518-1519). Auckland, New Zealand: ACM.

Franconi, E., Kerhet, V., & Ngo, N. (2013). Exact Query Reformulation over Databases with First-order and Description Logics Ontologies. *Journal of Artificial Intelligence Research*, *48*, 885–922.

Godugula, S. (2008). *Survey of Ontology Mapping Techniques*. Retrieved from http://www.cs.uni-paderborn.de/fileadmin/Informatik/AG-Engels/Lehre/SS08/Seminar_Software-Qualit%C3%A4tssicherung/Seminararbeiten/Vers._1.0/ontology_seminar_report_august1.pdf

Gottlob, G., Orsi, G., & Pieris, A. (2011). Ontological query answering via rewriting. In *Proceedings of ADBIS* (pp. 1-18). Vienna, Austria: Springer.

Haarslev, V., & Möller, R. (2003). Racer: an OWL reasoning agent for the Semantic Web. In *Proceedings of Web Intelligence Workshops* (pp. 91–95). Halifax, Canada: IEEE.

Horrocks, I. (2008). *Ontologies and Databases*. Stavanger, Norway: Semantic Days.

Horrocks, I., Patel-Schneider, P. F., & van Harmelen, F. (2003). From SHIQ and RDF to OWL: The Making of a Web Ontology Language. *Journal of Web Semantics*, *1*(1), 7–26. doi:10.1016/j.websem.2003.07.001

Hustadt, U., Motik, B., & Sattler, U. (2007). Reasoning in description logics by a reduction to disjunctive datalog. *Journal of Automated Reasoning*, *39*(3), 351–384. doi:10.1007/s10817-007-9080-3

Jean, S., Aït-Ameur, Y., & Pierra, G. (2006). Querying Ontology Based Database Using OntoQL (An Ontology Query Language). In *Proceedings of OTM* (pp. 704-721). Montpellier, France: Springer. doi:10.1007/11914853_43

Kashlev, A., & Chebotko, A. (2011). SPARQL-to-SQL Query Translation: Bottom-Up or Top-Down? In *Proceedings of IEEE International Conference on Services Computing*. Washington, DC: IEEE.

Kim, W., & Lochovsky, F. H. (1989). *Object-Oriented Concepts, Databases and Applications*. Addison Wesley.

Kollia, I., & Glimm, B. (2013). Optimizing SPARQL Query Answering over OWL Ontologies. *Journal of Artificial Intelligence Research, 48*, 253–303.

Kollia, I., Glimm, B., & Horrocks, I. (2011). SPARQL Query Answering over OWL Ontologies. In *Proceedings of ESWC* (pp. 382-396). Heraklion, Crete: CEUR-WS.org.

Kontchakov, R., Rezk, M., Rodriguez-Muro, M., Xiao, G., & Zakharyaschev, M. (2014). Answering SPARQL Queries over Databases under OWL 2 QL Entailment Regime. In *Proceedings of Semantic Web Conference* (pp. 552-567). Riva Del Garda, Italy: CEUR-WS.org. doi:10.1007/978-3-319-11964-9_35

Kumar, A. P., Kumar, A., & Kumar, V. N. (2011). A Comprehensive Comparative study of SPARQL and SQL. *International Journal of Computer Science and Information Technologies, 2*(4), 1706–1710.

LePendu, P., & Dou, D. (2011). Using ontology databases for scalable query answering, inconsistency detection, and data integration. *Journal of Intelligent Information Systems, 37*(2), 217–244. doi:10.1007/s10844-010-0133-4 PMID:22163378

LePendu, P., Dou, D., Frishkoff, G. A., & Rong, J. (2008). Ontology Database: A New Method for Semantic Modeling and an Application to Brainwave Data. In *Proceedings of SSDBM* (pp. 313-330). Hong Kong, China: Springer. doi:10.1007/978-3-540-69497-7_21

Lutz, C. (2008). The complexity of conjunctive query answering in expressive description logics. In *Proceedings of the 4th International Joint Conference Automated Reasoning* (pp. 179-193). Sydney, Australia: Springer. doi:10.1007/978-3-540-71070-7_16

Lutz, C., Toman, D., & Wolter, F. (2009). Conjunctive query answering in the description logic EL using a relational database system. In *Proceedings of IJCAI* (pp. 2070-2075). Pasadena, CA: AAAI.

Newman, A. (2006). *Querying the Semantic Web using a Relational Based SPARQL*. The University of Queensland. Submitted for the degree of Bachelor of Information Technology.

Nolle, A., & Nemirovski, G. (2013). ELITE: An Entailment-Based Federated Query Engine for Complete and Transparent Semantic Data Integration. In *Proceedings of Description Logics* (pp. 854–867). Ulm, Germany: CEUR.

Orsi, G., & Pieris, A. (2011). Optimizing query answering under ontological constraints. *PVLDB, 4*(11), 1004–1015.

Ortiz, M. (2010). *Query Answering in Expressive Description Logics: Techniques and Complexity Results*. (Doctoral dissertation). Vienna University of Technology.

Ortiz, M. (2013). Ontology Based Query Answering: The Story So Far. In *Proceedings of AMW*. Puebla/Cholula, Mexico: CEUR.

Ortiz, M., & Simkus, M. (2012). Reasoning and query answering in description logics. In *Proceedings of Reasoning Web* (pp. 1–53). Tallinn, Estonia: Springer. doi:10.1007/978-3-642-33158-9_1

Pan, J. Z., Stamou, G., Stoilos, G., Taylor, S., & Thomas, E. (2008). Scalable Querying Service over Fuzzy Ontologies. In *Proceedings of International World Wide Web Conference* (pp. 575-584). Beijing, China: ACM.

Peim, M., Franconi, E., Paton, N. W., & Goble, C. A. (2002). Query processing with description logic ontologies over object-wrapped databases. In *Proceedings of SSDBM* (pp. 27-36). Edinburgh, UK: IEEE. doi:10.1109/SSDM.2002.1029703

Polikoff, I. (2014). *Comparing SPARQL with SQL*. Retrieved from http://www.topquadrant.com/2014/05/05/comparing-sparql-with-sql/

Prud'hommeaux, E., & Seaborne, A. (2008). *SPARQL query language for RDF*. W3C Recommendation. Retrieved from http://www.w3.org/TR/rdf-sparql-query/

Rachapalli, J., Khadilkar, V., Kantarcioglu, M., & Thuraisingham, B. (2011). RETRO: A Framework for Semantics Preserving SQL-to-SPARQL Translation. In *Proceedings of the Joint Workshop on Knowledge Evolution and Ontology Dynamics, Co-located with the 10th International Semantic Web Conference.* Bonn, Germany: Springer.

Rodrıguez-Muro, M., & Calvanese, D. (2012). Quest, an OWL 2 QL reasoner for ontology-based data access. In *Proceedings of the 9th int. workshop on owl: experiences and directions*. Crete, Greece: Springer.

Rodríguez-Muro, M., Hardi, J., & Calvanese, D. (2012). Quest: Effcient SPARQL-to-SQL for RDF and OWL. In *Proceedings of International Semantic Web Conference*. Boston, MA: Springer.

Rodriguez-Muro, M., Kontchakov, R., & Zakharyaschev, M. (2013). Ontology-Based Data Access: Ontop of Databases. In *Proceedings of International Semantic Web Conference* (pp. 558-573). Sydney, Australia: Springer.

Rodriguez-Muro, M., & Rezk, M. (2014). Efficient SPARQL-to-SQL with R2RML mappings. *Journal of Web Semantics*.

Sakr, S., & Al-Naymat, G. (2009). Relational Processing of RDF Queries: A Survey. *SIGMOD Record*, *38*(4), 23–28. doi:10.1145/1815948.1815953

Sequeda, J. F., & Arenas, M., & Miranker, Daniel P. (2012). Ontology-Based Data Access Using Views. In *Proceedings of RR* (pp. 262-265). Vienna, Austria: Springer.

Sequeda, J. F., & Miranker, D. P. (2012). *Ultrawrap: Sparql execution on relational data*. Technical Report TR-12-10. The University of Texas at Austin, Department of Computer Sciences.

Seylan, I., Franconi, E., & de Bruijn, J. (2009). Effective Query Rewriting with Ontologies over DBoxes. In *Proceedings of IJCAI* (pp. 923-925). Pasadena, CA: AAAI.

Shearer, R., Motik, B., & Horrocks, I. (2008). HermiT: A highly-efficient OWL reasoner. In *Proceedings of the 5th Int. Workshop on OWL: Experiences and Directions*. Karlsruhe, Germany: CEUR.

Sirin, E., & Parsia, B. (2006). Pellet system description. In *Proceedings of the 19th Int. Workshop on Description Logic*. Lake District, UK: CEUR.

Son, J., Jeong, D., & Baik, D. (2008). Practical Approach: Independently Using SPARQL-to-SQL Translation Algorithms on Storage. In *Proceedings of the 4th International Conference on Networked Computing and Advanced Information Management*. Gyeongju, Korea: IEEE. doi:10.1109/NCM.2008.151

Son, J., Jeong, D., & Baik, D. (2011). Performance Evaluation of Storage-Independent Model for SPARQL-to-SQL Translation Algorithms. In *Proceedings of the 4th IFIP International Conference on New Technologies, Mobility and Security* (pp. 1-4). Paris, France: IEEE.

Sören, A., & Ives, Z. G. (2007). *Integrating Ontologies and Relational Data. Technical Reports*. CIS.

Staab, S., & Studer, R. (Eds.). (2009). *Handbook on Ontologies* (2nd ed.). Springer. doi:10.1007/978-3-540-92673-3

Straccia, U. (2006). Answering Vague Queries in Fuzzy DL-LITE. In *Proceedings of the 11th International Conference on Information Processing and Management of Uncertainty in Knowledge-Based Systems* (pp. 2238-2245). Paris, France: Springer.

Studer, R., Benjamins, R., & Fensel, D. (1998). Knowledge engineering: Principles and methods. *Data & Knowledge Engineering, 25*(1-2), 161–198. doi:10.1016/S0169-023X(97)00056-6

Tamani, N., Lietard, L., & Rocacher, D. (2013). Bipolar Conjunctive Query Evaluation for Ontology Based Database Querying. In *Proceedings of FQAS* (pp. 389-400). Granada, Spain: Springer. doi:10.1007/978-3-642-40769-7_34

Trißl, S., & Leser, U. (2005). Querying Ontologies in Relational Database Systems. In *Proceedings of DILS* (pp. 63-79). San Diego, CA: Springer.

Tsarkov, D., & Horrocks, I. (2006). FaCT++ description logic reasoner: System description. In *Proceedings of the 3rd Int. Joint Conf. on Automated Reasoning* (pp. 292-297). Seattle, WA: AAAI. doi:10.1007/11814771_26

Tzacheva, A. A., Toland, T. S., Poole, P. H., & Barnes, D. J. (2013). Ontology Database System and Triggers. In *Proceedings of The Twelfth International Symposium on Intelligent Data Analysis* (pp. 416-426). London, UK: Springer.

Vysniauskas, E., Nemuraite, L., & Paradauskas, B. (2011). Hybrid Method for Storing and Querying Ontologies in Databases. *Electronics and Electrical Engineering, 9*(115), 67–72.

Vyšniauskas, E., Nemuraite, L., Sukys, A., & Paradauskas, B. (2010). Enhancing connection between ontologies and databases with OWL 2 concepts and SPARQL. In *Proceedings of the 16th International Conference on Information and Software Technologies* (pp. 350-357). Kaunas, Lithuania: IEEE.

Yannakakis, M. (1981). Algorithms for acyclic database schemes. In *Proceedings of VLDB* (pp. 82-94). Cannes, France: IEEE Computer Society.

Zhao, T., Zhang, C., Wei, M., & Peng, Z. R. (2008). Ontology-based geospatial data query and integration. In *Proceedings of Geographic Information Science* (pp. 370–392). Park City, UT: Springer. doi:10.1007/978-3-540-87473-7_24

KEY TERMS AND DEFINITIONS

Conjunctive Queries: The conjunctive queries are simply the fragment of (domain independent) first-order logic given by the set of formulae that can be constructed from atomic formulae using conjunction $\land$ and existential quantification $\exists$, but not using disjunction $\lor$, negation $\neg$, or universal quantification $\forall$.

DBMS: Database Management System.

Description Logics: Is the most recent name for a family of knowledge representation (KR) formalisms that represent the knowledge of an application domain (the "world") by first defining the relevant concepts of the domain (its terminology), and then using these concepts to specify properties of objects and individuals occurring in the domain (the world description).

Ontology: An ontology is a formal, explicit specification of a shared conceptualization.

RDF: Resource Description Framework (RDF) is a framework for expressing information about resources. Resources can be anything, including documents, people, physical objects, and abstract concepts.

SPARQL: Is an RDF query language, that is, a semantic query language for databases, able to retrieve and manipulate data stored in Resource Description Framework format.

SQL: Structured Query Language (SQL) is a query language used for accessing and modifying information in a database.

UCQs: The disjunctions of the conjunctive queries are known as *Unions of Conjunctive Queries (UCQs)*.

Section 5

Chapter 19

Application of Fuzzy User's Profile for Mining Reusable E-Learning Repositories on Web through Lightweight Mobile Agent

Priti Srinivas Sajja
Sardar Patel University, India

ABSTRACT

The creditability of an e-Learning system depends on its content, services and presentation of the material to the learners. Besides providing material on demand, an e-Learning system also manages knowledge for future use. It is observed that the learning material available on different locations may be reused in a proper way. The work presented here discusses generic design of an e-Learning system with various reusable learning material repositories. The architecture described here uses light weight mobile agents in order to access these repositories by taking help of fuzzy user profile. With notion of the fuzzy user profile, the system knows more about users' need and can present customized content to the users. Besides the architecture of the e-Learning system, the chapter also discusses the necessary concepts about the fuzzy logic and agent based systems, in depth literature survey, structure of the user profile, fuzzy membership function and design of the light weight mobile agent with necessary implementation details. At the end, the chapter concludes with the applications, advantages and future scope of the research work possible in the domain.

INTRODUCTION

Advances of Information and Communication Technology (ICT) such as internet and the Web have accelerated scope and usability of the system to a high extent. It can be stated that majority of the modern information systems are distributed systems. Web enable e-Learning system is also an example of such distributed system. Primary goal of any e-Learning system is to provide learning material and enable

DOI: 10.4018/978-1-4666-8767-7.ch019

users to learn anytime, anywhere. Secondary goal of such systems is knowledge management by documenting knowledge and reusing the knowledge in future for problem solving and training.

Following are the crucial aspects that must be taken care while developing any e-Learning system in general.

- Quality and amount of material.
- User interface, access and choices through efficient learning processes and flexible content delivery.
- Technical infrastructures.
- Cost effectiveness.
- Meeting the existing standards of the content and technology.

Since most of the repositories storing e-Learning material are stored on distributed platform, it becomes trivial to efficiently retrieve learning material to the intended user. Lightweight mobile agents are good alternative for required content retrieval.

An agent is a software program or entity that acts on behalf of its users in co-operative, autonomous and pro-active manner. Agents are categorized according to their nature and application into various classes such as query agent, information agent, interface agent, mobile agent, and intelligent agent. An agent may combine philosophy and structure of two or more agents; in this case the agent is called hybrid agents. Agents offer advantages of robustness, improve cost-effectiveness of the solution and increases overall efficiency of the business. A mobile agent is an agent that moves between given list of location with necessary permission as well as supporting information and remotely executes various tasks.

This chapter discusses design of lightweight mobile agent for an e-Learning system. This type of agents travel within the specified territories or websites to extract required learning material for users. Mobile agent designed in this system use minimal code to accomplish its task. A mobile agent has to be smaller, simpler and faster as it needs frequent movement to remote locations. Writing minimum code within mobile agents makes them 'lightweight' and mobility of the agent is accelerated. The mobile agent described in this work uses some vague meta-knowledge about users and learners in form of fuzzy user profile.

Besides requirement of the Web enable distributed platform for e-Learning system along with lightweight mobile agent, the e-Learning content stored in various repositories (or databases) must be reusable. It is observed that there are so many common topics in various courses at different levels. Content within the repository must be reusable to design various courses to avoid conflict and redundancy while presenting material to the users.

This chapter illustrates generic design of multi layer structure of e-Learning system along with reusable content repositories and design of a lightweight mobile agent. The chapter organization is as follows. Section 2 presents a brief conceptual background for fuzzy logic and agents. Section 3 presents a literature survey and justifies the need of the proposed work by highlighting observations from the study and enlisting limitations of the existing solutions. Section 4 discusses generic structure of multi layer structure of web based e-Learning system with reusable repositories and structure of fuzzy user profile with membership functions. Section 5 discusses the design of lightweight mobile agent. Section 6 presents results, discussion on experiment and benefits of the research work and concludes the work presented with limitations and possible future extension.

FUZZY LOGIC AND AGENTS AS FACILITATORS

Typically logic is defined as a systematic set of principles meant for correct reasoning and decision making. It is science of identifying and evaluating parameters and arguments for reasoning. The term "logic" has come from the Greek word "logos", which is sometimes translated as "sentence", "discourse", "reason", "rule", and "ratio". There are various types of logic; one of them is computational logic. Most of the typical logics are bi-valued logic, also called "bivalent". Such bivalent logic describes only two traditional values called "true" and "false". These values are often represented as '0' and '1'. Fuzzy logic is a multi-valued logic which can take multiple values between "true" and "false" including these two ("true" and "false"). The fuzzy logic is used to provide reasoning in an approximate manner. In contrast to the typical bivalent logic, the fuzzy logic variable takes any value between "true" and "false" (or 0 and 1). By doing so, the fuzzy logic facilitates handling of partial truth. The degree of the partial truth is managed by linguistic variables. Such linguistic variable take adjective values such as high, low, very low, moderate, slightly, fairly, etc. with the use of such linguistic variables, vague representation of a situation can be handled. The term "fuzzy logic" was introduced by Prof. Lotfi A. Zadeh (1965) in his proposal of fuzzy set theory in 1965. Fuzzy logic is based on fuzzy set concept which is described below.

Fuzzy Sets and Fuzzy Logic

Set is defined as a collection of things that is bounded by some definition. Any given item may belong to the set or may not belong to the set, which is determined by the definition of the set. The fuzzy set deals with partial belongingness of an item into the set. Here is an example. Consider a set of tall people. As per the crisp (non-fuzzy) set definition, any person having height greater or equal to 5 feet and 6 inches are considered as member of tall people and they belongs to the set of tall people. Here the membership definition is very strict and allows only two possibilities: either total belongingness into the set or not. That is, boundaries of the set are very sharp and strict, which is good for typical logic and mathematics; however, it will not be much effective in reality. According to the definition of the set of tall people, person having height 4 feet and 6 inches feed does not belong to the set of tall people and person with 6 feet 2 inches belongs to the set of tall people.

The very first thing you notice in the definition is this. A person with 5 feet and 6 inches height is equally (and simply) tall in comparison with person with 6 feet and 6 inches height. In reality the second person is much taller than the first one! The difference in height is significant; even though they both fall into the tall category. On other side, person having 5 feet and 5 inches does not fit into the set as definition says the minimum height must be 5 feet and 6 inches. The difference between the permissible heights is 1 inch only, though the person with an extra inch falls under the tall category and another with just an inch less falls into the short people category.

Concept of the fuzzy set provides better representation of situation. Instead of providing rigid straight boundary, the fuzzy set provides you inclining smooth function as shown in Figure 1.

In the first situation (upper half) shown in Figure 1 there is a straight line showing boundaries between two distinct sets (tall and short people). In the second half of the figure, there is a curve showing smooth progress from one category to another category. The mathematical function presented by the curve gives definition of a membership functions. The vertical axis, on a scale of 0 to 1, provides the

Figure 1. A fuzzy membership function for tall people

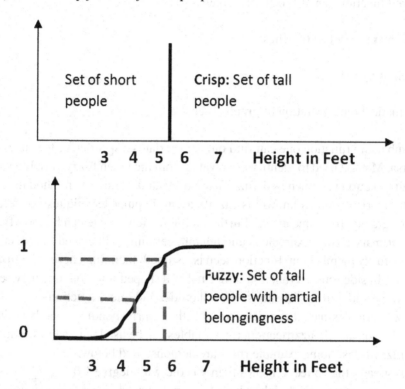

membership value (value of belongingness) of the height in the fuzzy set. On horizontal axis, units of height are shown. According to the function, the person with height 5 feet 6 inch belongs to the set of tall person with degree 0.9. Similarly, person with the height 4 feet 5 inches also belongs to the set of tall people with degree 0.45.

The definition of the fuzzy set can be given as follows.

For any fuzzy set A, the function μA represents the membership function for which μA(x, where each x belongs to X) indicates the degree of membership that x, of the universal set X, belongs to set A and is, usually, expressed as a number between 0 and 1. That is:

$$\mu A(x): X \rightarrow [0,1]$$

Following data collected from domain experts can be used to create the fuzzy membership for set of tall people discussed above.

Table 1. Data to create fuzzy membership function

Height in feet	4.0	4.5	5.0	5.2	5.4	5.6	6.0	6.5	7.0
Fuzzy degree	0	0.25	0.45	0.65	0.85	1.0	1.0	1.0	1.0

The generalized function can also be represented as

Tall (x) =1 if height(x) >=5 feet 6 inches

Tall (x) = 0 if height(x) < 4 feet

Tall (x) = mathematical representation of graph otherwise

From the membership function one can find out appropriate crisp value of the fuzzy linguistic variable and vice versa. Method used to identify crisp value from the given fuzzy variable value through the fuzzy membership function is known as defuzzification method. Similarly, method used for identifying fuzzy values from a crisp value is known as fuzzification. Popular techniques for defuzzification are centroid, center of gravity, fuzzy mean, etc. Further, a linguistic variable can be modified via linguistic hedge applied to primary terms. Example is enough tall, certainly tall, closed to tall, etc.

In Figure 1, the fuzzy membership function seen is a smooth inclining curve. The fuzzy membership functions may vary. Besides curved function or normal bell shaped function, one may see the triangular fuzzy functions, trapezoidal fuzzy functions, right shoulder and linear functions.

Once the fuzzy variables have been defined with their corresponding membership functions and methods of fuzzification and defuzzification, the variables can be used with a knowledge representation scheme such as fuzzy rules. Some example rules are demonstrated below.

If height (x) is greater than 5 feet 5 inches then x is old with degree 1.0.

If x is tall then assign category_A_job; where x is a member of people class denoted by X.

If x is short then assign category_B_job; where x is a member of people class denoted by X.

A fuzzy rule may contain more than one fuzzy variables. One can define integrated set of fuzzy function at once as shown in Figure 2.

Multiple rules related to the area are collected from various resources such as domain experts, senior researchers, academicians and users, media, and the Internet. Determination of the fuzzy variable and corresponding fuzzy membership functions along with fuzzification and defuizzification methods

Figure 2. Integrated fuzzy membership functions for the height parameter

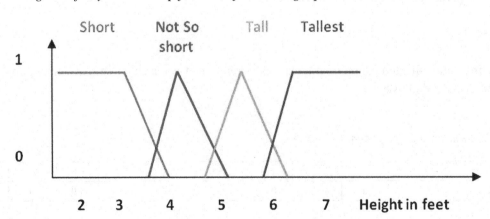

is one of the key tasks here. These fuzzy variables can be accommodated in various decision making situations and fuzzy rules are formed. These fuzzy rules are kept into the rule base (or knowledge base) of the system. That is why, the system is identified as fuzzy rule based system. Besides the rule base, there must be some other component in the system, which can be named as inference engine, conflict resolution strategy, meta knowledge (knowledge about knowledge) and action interface. Optionally local database support and readymade web services from the Internet platform can also be used as supporting components.

Figure 3 describes the typical structure of fuzzy logic based system. As discussed earlier, the prime component of the system is rule base. Users interact with the system in their natural way using vague and fuzzy information. That is, users may interact with the system using linguistic (native) and vague instructions through fuzzy interface. Utility of the inference engine facilitates reasoning and deduction of decision. For this purpose the inference mechanism uses either forward chaining or backward chaining. If any conflict exists, then the system applies conflict resolution strategy defined by the developer and domain expert together. Once rules are selected, appropriate action would be fired. For selecting an action to be performed, it is necessary to identify the valid rules and then to identify and understand the linguistic variable (fuzzy variable) they use. The meaning of the linguistic variable is derived from the membership function definitions. However, from users fuzzy input, appropriate fuzzy rule and its

Figure 3. General architecture of typical fuzzy logic based system

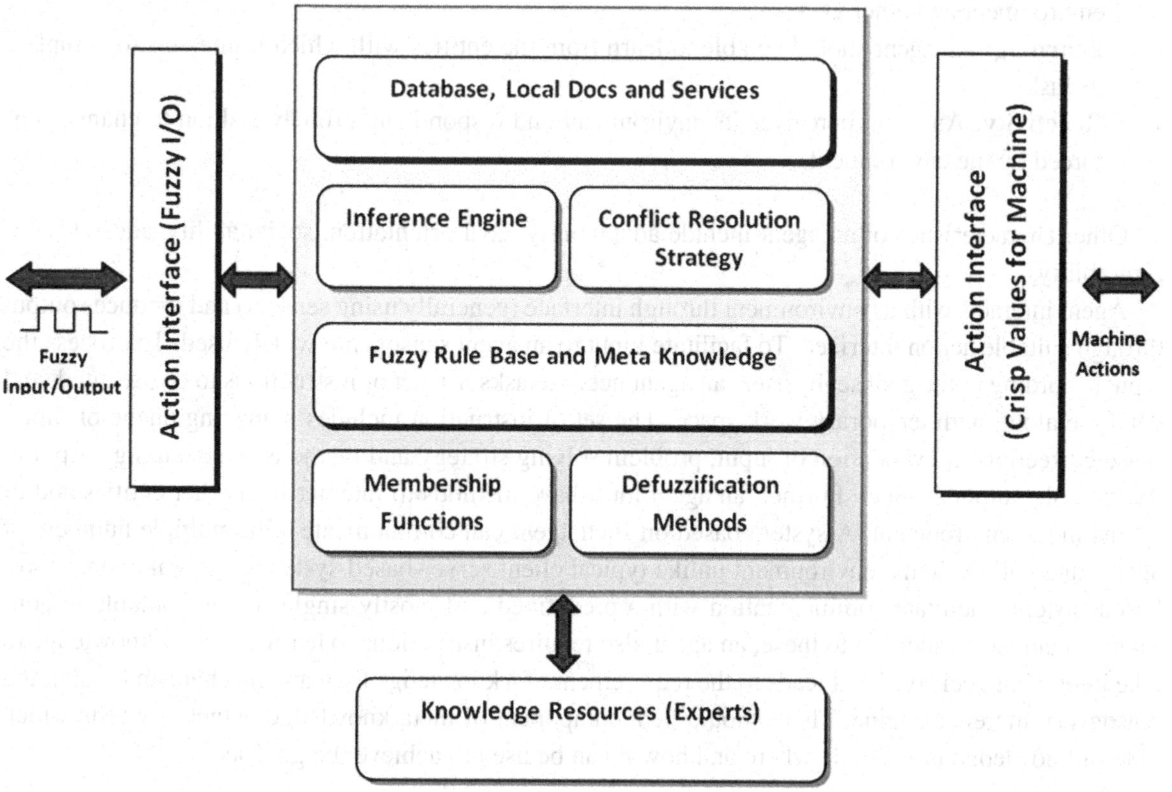

understanding is found out. It is necessary to convert the fuzzy values into their equivalent crisp values. The corresponding crisp values can be obtained by the defuzzification methods defined for the system. Once the crisp values are available, machine can perform the required actions through its action interface and generates output. The output may further be converted into equivalent fuzzy form again and send it to the users making them happy with output in native form. All the process remains transparent from the user and user can interact friendly with the system with ease. This is the way how a typical fuzzy logic based system handles imprecision and vagueness and offers benefit of ease of use and increase degree of the acceptability of the system.

Agent Based Systems

An agent is any device, technique, person or procedure to perform an intended task on behalf of its users. The agents can be hardware, software or combination of most of the cases in reality. Agents are capable to sense the environment, identify requirements of the user, and meet the goals set by the system and act in proactive manner in order to solve the problem. To do so, the agent must have an ability to learn, be co-operative with other entities and agents in the environment and independent enough to make some decision and perform necessary actions. These characteristics are described below.

- **Autonomous:** An agent must be able to work without human intervention with help of required skills and resources.
- **Co-Operation:** In order to complete the assigned tasks, an agent must interact with users, the environment and other agents.
- **Learning:** An agent should be able to learn from the entities with which it interacts to complete its task.
- **Reactivity:** An agent perceives its environment and responds in a timely fashion to changes enforced by the environment.

Other characteristics of an agent include adaptability, goal orientation, social ability, and self configurability.

Agent interacts with its environment through interface (generally using sensors) and produces output through suitable action interface. To facilitate input to an agent sensors are widely used. To process the input according to the goal set by users an agent needs a tasks list, set of instructions to be executed, and database along with temporary work space. The set of instruction includes managing queue of input, noise correction and validation of input, problem solving strategy and methods of streaming output to the suitable output channel. Further, an agent must have methods to interact with other entities and/or agents in the environment. A system based on such agent can communicate with multiple numbers of agents and entities in the environment unlike typical client server-based systems. Typical client server based systems facilitate communication with a predefined and mostly single server available in continuous manner. In addition to these, an agent also requires instructions to learn and infer knowledge to take intelligent decision. That leads to the requirement of a knowledge base and mechanism to infer and reason via inference engine. There should be a component of meta knowledge, which suggests which kind of knowledge is available where and how it can be used to achieve the goal set.

The agents are used to solve problems in three basic categories of situations as follows.

1. When resources are not available;
2. When expertise is not available; and
3. When there is lack of time and effort.

Agents are used to solve large and complex problems in efficient ways. The agent designed allows interconnection and interoperation of multiple existing legacy systems. Agents are well suitable in situation when resources, expertise or the problem itself is/are distributed in nature. Agent enhances modularity, speed by facilitating autonomous and distributed problem solving, reliability by providing professional approach to meet the goal set, flexibility, and reusability in problem solving.

Typology of Agents

There are various types of agents, which can be categorized according to its nature and characteristics. One broad categorization is proactive agents and reactive agents. Agents may be classified according to the role played by them. Here are some popular categories based on the working of agents.

The very first agent category is *Collaborative Agent*. Collaborative agents interconnect different stand-alone legacy system and agents to get problem definition, resources, and expertise from distributed resources. A classical example of a collaborative agent is a tour guide expert system. The system takes support from typical ticket reservation system, site seeing programmes, accommodation, temple visit, weather forecasting and news services. These components can be independent utilities or readymade (third party) services. The main task of the collaborative agent is to interact with these components and to provide a feasible plan for the tour.

Another type of agent is an *Interface Agent*. The interface agent is the most suitable mean to arrange user-friendly environment to work with a highly technical application. An interface agent is considered as an assistant helping users to interact with the system. With the capability of learning, such interface agent can act as a customized mechanism to identify user's level and interact according to the need and style of users in the user's native language.

An agent with the capability of mobility is classified into a *Mobile Agent* category. Mobility of an agent refers to the ability of the agent to move around in one or more given networks. To achieve such mobility, such agents are encompassed with techniques to interact with the wide area network such as World Wide Web (WWW). The typical tasks that they can perform are searching, collecting, executing and verifying information and/or programs on remote locations on behalf of their owners. The ability to interact with the remote systems save time and effort as well as provide better access and control to the systems within a given network. Mobile agents also exhibit sophisticated social ability, proactiveness, and autonomy (Moraitakis, 1997).

Information may be available from variety of sources. The information kept on collaborative resources platform such as the Web has no common and well defined ontology or structure. An Information Agent helps in searching, extracting and managing information from various heterogeneous platforms on behalf of its users. These agents are enriched with techniques for information searching, ranking, extracting, and filtering according to the need. Information agents working in distributed network area like the Internet are specifically known *as Internet Agents*.

An agent is supposed to be autonomous, proactive and capable to learn in order to take right decisions. *Intelligent agent* is type of agent which uses artificial intelligence technique in order to perform the job of taking effective decisions. Michael Wooldridge (2002) and Ira Rudowsky (2004) defined intelligent agents as agents that are capable of exhibiting flexible and autonomous actions to meet their design objectives. Such intelligent agent learns multiple objectives, creates plan for acting, process information received, and performs reasoning (through inference, synthesis, and analysis) with the help of AI techniques. Since AI techniques are used, complete information will not be compulsory for an intelligent agent for its working. To work with partial information, an intelligent agent uses its own internal knowledge architecture, inference mechanisms, and user interface providing explanation and reasoning. An agent is encompassed with a control function to manage all these activities. The controller controls interaction with the environment and selects task to be performed according to the goal and capability of the agent. Other main components of a typical intelligent agent besides controller are interface mechanism, I/O queue management, knowledge-base, executable tasks' list, and goals & objectives.

Any agent, according to need may follow topology of more than one agent. Such agent is called a *Hybrid Agent*. Such hybrid agents can be placed at upper level of hierarchy of the agents and hence become application specific. For example, an information agent can adopt philosophy and working style of mobile agent along with its main job. In this case, the main task of the agent remains extraction of information from various resources accessible through a network; however, to access the remote location or a server on a remote location, the interface agent has to be mobile.

Multi Agent System and Communication between Agents

A system comprising of multiple agents working independently but in co-operation with each other is generally called multi agent system. It is a king of loosely coupled network of problem solving components. Such multi agent system is useful especially when complex problems require the services of multiple agents with diverse capabilities and needs. Researchers have discovered that multi agent systems can accomplish tasks as well as or even better than their centralized single program counterparts (Ferber, 1999). MAS can manifest self-organization and complex behaviors even when the individual strategies of all their agents are simple (Bobek & Perko, 2006).

Multi agent systems (MAS) are capable to solve complex real life problem by implementing parallelism in its working through multiple agents. Each agent is capable to solve a specific problem professionally and effectively. This is the situation where standard legacy systems are not much powerful. A multi agent system allows many different independent systems to work interconnected manner and facilitates cooperation among them. Such multi agent systems are able to provide efficient solutions where information, resource or even problem is distributed among different places as stated earlier. Further, agents in the multi agent systems are independent commodities in a loosely coupled framework. The agents may be used in other system as per the requirement and need. The multi agent systems offer software reusability and flexibility to adopt different agent capabilities to solve problems in one or more application domains.

Besides multiple agents related to the domain, a multi agent system (MAS) provides an environment for the agents, establishes relationships between the entities and provides a platform for a set of operations that can be performed by the agents. The multi agent system may use middle agent services and agent meeting place. The agents' meeting place can facilitate communication between agents and provides temporary workspace for different agents. The services may be ready made third party web services, which can be dynamically collected from the Web. Besides services, one can take help of protocols, standards and other existing models of services on demand. There may be a control or a master agent in order to manage activities and communication between components of the multi agent system. The agents of the system may communicate using the following three major utilities.

- **An inner language such as Knowledge Interchange Format (KIF):** The knowledge interchange format allows manipulation and management of knowledge from permissible knowledge representation structures using first order predictive calculus. It is similar to the knowledge presentation structure such as frames. However, its main objective is not to represent knowledge, but to facilitate interchange of valid knowledge between the components such as agents.
- **An outer language known as Knowledge Query and Manipulation Language (KQML):** The knowledge query and manipulation language is also considered as a protocol for communication between agents and intelligent systems. The basic objective of the KQML is sharing of knowledge from various valid resources in order to reuse the knowledge and minimize effort of managing the knowledge from various distributed resources. Inspite of its basic purpose of sharing of knowledge between various knowledge based systems, the system is mostly used as agents' communication language. KQML allows setting of performative operations on candidate agent's knowledge base and goal lists. KQML has special utility called communication facilitator, which co-ordinates the communication between agents. KQML was one of the earliest attempts to construct an agent communication language based on speech act theory. Some communicative actions are most fundamental and common regardless of the agent's type and application. Some of the action examples are inform, request, query-reference, etc. The KQML is superseded by Agent Communication Language (ACL), proposed by the Foundation for Intelligent Physical Agents (FIPA).
- **Common vocabularies such as ontologies:** Use of common vocabularies make the interaction between agents easy. They help in integrating, organizing and managing content in a better way and data integration. W3C provides a large set of readymade vocabularies in a standard format. Some of them are RDF and RDF Schemas, Simple Knowledge Organization System (SKOS), Web Ontology Language (OWL), and the Rule Interchange Format (RIF).

WORK DONE SO FAR

e-Learning is defined as electronic learning, supporting learning through all forms of electronically supported devices and tools. ICT infrastructure has been serving as an efficient platform to enable e-Learning system. Many researchers and academician did significant work in the domain of e-Learning system.

An e-Learning system is typically thought as computer managed material presentation or instruction system. Basic information about e-Learning goal, methods and limitations are presented in work of Devajit Mahanta & Majidul Ahmed (2012). Based on the concept of e-Learning, one of the initial efforts towards e-Learning design and implementation was made in the year 1960 at the University of Illinois with a few users (Srivastava & Agarwal, 2013). Computer Managed Instructional (CMI) systems offer facilities to identify learning needs of users and suggest suitable instructional activities (Park & Lee, 2003). Soon, multimedia support is added to the CMI systems. Many researchers have considered Intelligent Tutoring Systems (ITS) as enhanced e-Learning systems. Shute & Psotka (1996) discussed ITS as one-on-one learning process between the teacher and a student. This leads to the development of Adaptive Hypermedia Systems (AHS). Eklund & Sinclair (2000) suggested combination of adaptive instructional systems and hypermedia-based systems. Gradually these systems have evolved as learning management systems (LMSs). A typical LMS generally provides online course materials, assignments, quizzes and tests, forums for interaction and links to other resources on the Web. According to Lokken & Womer (2007), majority of two- and four-year colleges in the USA had an LMS system. Then comes era of virtual world, digital educational games and mobile environment to attract special target users such as young learners. Work presented by Teall, Wang, Callaghan & Ng (2014) discusses mobile learning framework to support e-Learning. Nilay Vaidya & Priti Sajja (2014) designed virtual collaborative learning environment to learn from various distributed resources. Standards and quality parameters related to e-Learning based systems were also analyzed and presented by Priti Sajja (2008).

Agents are also being utilized in the field of e-Learning. Kunjal Mankad & Priti Sajja (2008) have used agents in a dedicated learning environment. For regional language learning for adult education an agent based system is also developed by Priti Sajja (2006). Some adaptive conversation tutors to enhance learners' autonomy are designed by Abu-Shawar & Atwell (2007). To enhance the interaction between the system and users a multi expert model is proposed by Nakano et al. (2011) which presents a multi expert model for dialogue and behavior control between robots and agents. David Griol and Zoraida Callejas (2012) have also proposed an architecture to develop multi model educative applications support through a chatboot application. To improve instructional design in e-Learning Kathleen Scalise & Leanne Ketterlin-Geller (2012) designed and developed innovative instruction design models introduces quality e-Learning designs (Ghislandi, 2012).

All these solutions discussed above are using Information and Communication Technology infrastructure and try to meet the basic goals of e-Learning system. However, major limitations observed from the existing solution can be summarized as follows.

- Lack of reusability and efficient design of course: For most of the e-Learning application, there is a course specific and dedicated content repository. Many existing components (topics) in different courses are redundant in an e-Learning system and there may be conflict too.
- Lack of suitability of presented content: the content presented to the users may not be much useful and users may be frustrated when content appeared has nothing to do with their interests.
- Efficient searching of material: Searching for suitable material must be fast and concurrent from various suggested resources or locations.
- Identification of learner level: Each learner's need is special and unique. The search keyword may be same; however, depending on context the user may want different things. Further, many learners are slow learners in a given topic, many needs just a hint!
- Flexibility: There should be enough scope to add topic, courses, users and other resources on need. As most of the system has perspired courses, no dynamic or on demand courses can be generated.
- Need of a generic architecture: The system components must be loosely bounded and the system should be based on a genetic multi-purpose framework to support development of variety of e-Learning solution.
- Use of lightweight mobile agent: To mine e-Learning content repositories on remote locations there is a requirement of mobile agent which is fast, simple and easy to move. Most of the e-Learning solutions support dedicated rigid agents.

Considering the aforementioned requirements, generic multi layer architecture to support e-Learning system is designed. Section 3 discusses the generic architecture.

ARCHITECTURE OF THE SYSTEM

To achieve benefit of structuredness and modularity, architecture of the proposed system is designed in different layers. These layers are illustrated graphically in form of Figure 4. The creditability of an e-Learning system depends on its quality content besides services to its user. Hence, the very first layer of the architecture is a *resource layer*. The resource layer consists of resources from various locations. The popular resources include general resources on the Web, databases of the institutes on the Web and other local resources. The resource layer is also known as a repository layer. Besides these resources, the main resource is the various e-Learning repositories containing quality material in form of small, independent and reusable course components. These learning objects follow a common representation strategy to enable the reusability of the learning objects. The IEEE (Institute of Electrical and Electronics Engineers Standards Association, New York) Standard for Learning Object Metadata is considered as an internationally recognized open standard for the description of such learning objects. The standard was reaffirmed in the year 2009. According to this standard defined by IEEE, commonly included major information components are as given below.

- Identifier for the learning component,
- Title of the learning object,
- Language used to describe the learning component,
- Learning outcomes,
- Prerequisites for learners, if any,
- Catalog scheme and standards,
- Description of the learning component,
- Keywords and synonyms,
- Area or Coverage and applications of the learning component,
- Structure of the learning component,
- Aggregation Level,
- Life cycle and version information,
- Status,
- Role,
- Last update information and last used dates,
- Technical information such as size and location,
- Type such as interactivity and learning resource,
- Target users and type of users,
- Age group,
- Difficulty level,
- Typical learning time,
- Exception,
- Description and any other detail, if any,
- Type of information.

Immediately above the resource layer, there is a service layer. Some services that are common and available in a readymade manner on platform like the Web, can be searched (either dynamically or from the repositories of the developed services) are collected used through the service layer. The basic task

Figure 4. Generic multi layer architecture of the e-learning system using multiple agents

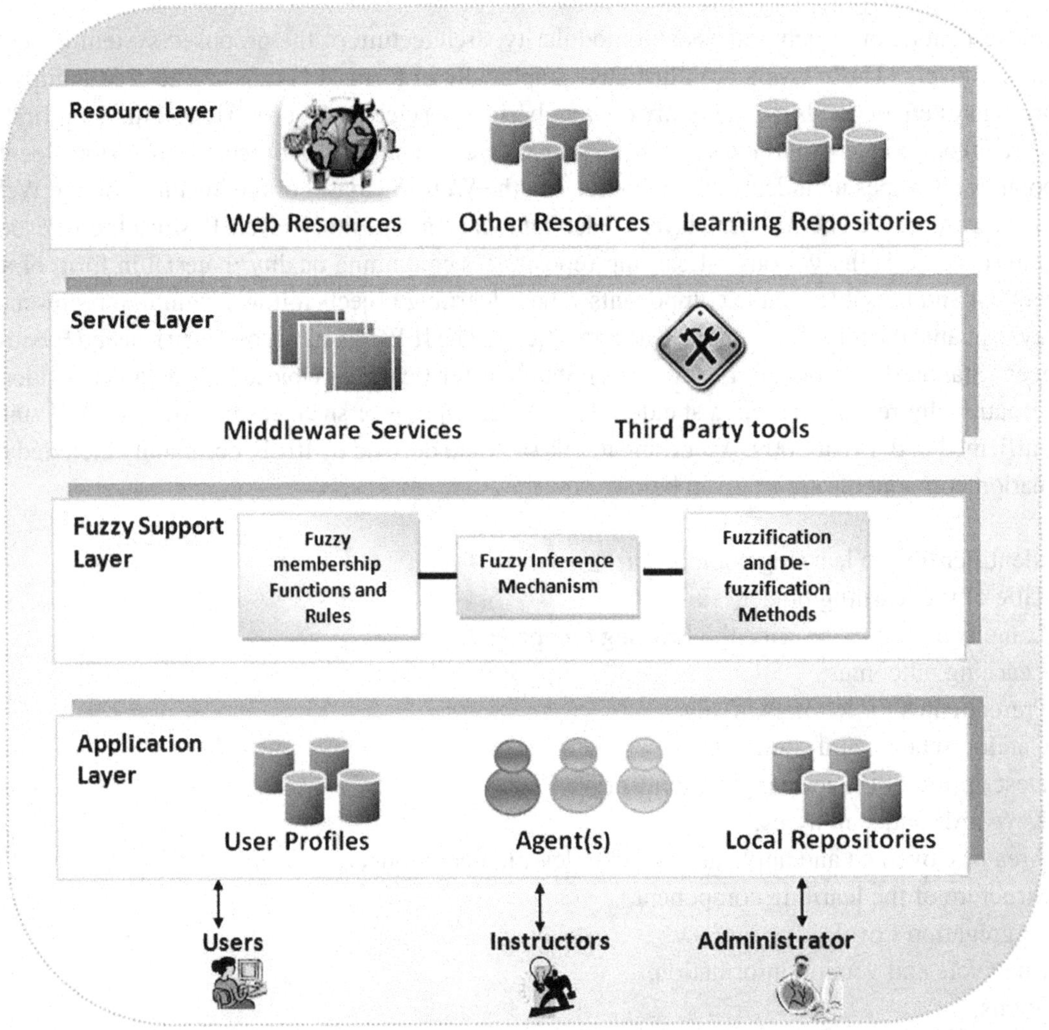

of the service layer is to provide permissible and valid services to one or more agents of the system on request depending on the access rights. Such services are from a third party or provided through a middleware. Most of the services are well tested, professional and many of them are freely available on the Web platform. Further, most of the middleware services run on multiple platforms. These characteristics make them interoperable between agents of the system. These services are transparent in nature and hide the unnecessary complexity from the developers and users of the system. Following are the examples where middleware services or third party services can be used.

- For searching, extracting, and data conversion;
- Managing presentations, generating reports as well as formatting the existing content;

- Computations such as typical mathematical processes, sorting and string operations;
- Controlling threads and flow of control and request scheduler;
- Auditing and authentication services.

The next layer supports working with fuzzy and vague information. The layer is known as is the *fuzzy support layer*. This layer contains fuzzy membership functions to understand the fuzzy variables and vague information provided by the users. Once understanding of the fuzzy variable is understood by the system, fuzzy rules can be interpreted and executed. Result will be in machine generated form, which can be again reconverted into natural like language using the fuzzy membership functions. To do so, the layer accommodates and uses the fuzzification and defuzzification methods.

The last layer is an *application layer*. The application layer facilitates the applications of the system. It typically consists of light weight mobile agents, local repositories and user profiles. Here a user profile contains some basic information and some vague information about the users. The basic purpose to encompass users' information in a form of fuzzy user profile is to get the maximum knowledge about the users and their goals. If system knows its users, the system interaction with users will be more effective and system can serve in a better way to the users. Figure 4 illustrates pictorial representation of the multi layer architecture discussed here.

The user profile generally contains basic information about the users such as their identification, name, educational information and other fuzzy information such as ability of learning termed as 'High', 'Medium, 'Low' and 'Poor'. Such categories of the learner with different learning abilities are initially taken from the users themselves and then get update from the user's response. To automatically calculate the learning ability of a user, parameters such as user's response time and correct answers to the questions fired from sample drill/quizzes are considered. These parameters are used to generate the speed correctness ration of the user, which is one of the mean to identify a learner's level. This is generally known as speed correctness ration. An appropriate learning material will be fetched by the mobile agent and presented to the user. To identify suitable material for a user, learning object description help is taken. For example, the learning object difficulty level must be matched with the users learning ability calculated. That means the learning repository may have different version of learning materials for various types of users. For learners with the poor ability of learning, material with more explanation and examples is presented and for learners with high ability to learn, some brainstorming debatable questions can also be placed to force them think out of box.

As stated earlier, to distinguish different types of learners, notion of speed correctness ration is used. A sample (practice) round of question is fired to the user and correct answers and time taken to provide correct answers are taken into consideration. Additionally, difficulty level of questions may also be considered, if questions are of different capacity and difficulty level. From such speed correctness ration the learning ability of the user is identified, based on which, types of users can be categorised into a few categories such as learners with high ability to learn (also called fast learners), learners with medium ability to learn and learners who have poor ability to learn. The fuzzy membership function for determining the learning ability is defined as below.

Users learning ability = High if S/C >=0.70

= Medium if 0.70< S/C >= 0.55

= Low if 0.55< S/C >= 0.30

= Poor if 0.30< S/C

where S/C is the speed correctness ration. Depending on the fuzzy membership function described above, a graph can be prepared as shown in Figure 5.

Along with the learning ability of the user, there is a requirement of other basic information such as personal information of users, identification or registration number, educational background and courses opted for e-Learning. The outline of a user's profile consists of following information.

- Identification, name, gender etc.,
- Accessibility type,
- Basic contact information such as mail, cell number, website etc.,
- Languages known to the learners and main language / medium of the course,
- Guardian and/or sponsors,
- Experiences,
- Educational information such as school and graduation details with marks earned,
- Current course,
- Learning ability,
- Preferences and priorities,
- Hobbies,
- Goal,
- Status,
- Path to sequence of material used,
- Etc.

More information about users as per the need can be added into the profile of users.

Figure 5. An integrated fuzzy membership function for types of learners

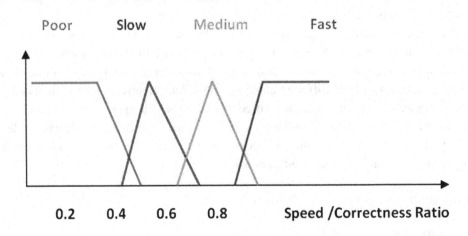

LIGHTWEIGHT MOBILE AGENT

Mobile agent has virtue of mobility to move around various locations in a predefined environment in order to perform the intended tasks. Moreover, mobile agent can operate asynchronously and autonomously of the process that created them. A mobile agent is often described as "an executing program that can migrate from machine to machine in a heterogeneous network to perform a job" (Gray, Cybenko, Kotz & Rus, 2001; Xu, Yin, Deng & Ding, 2003). Tasks that involve visiting various remote locations and performing tasks such as executing something on each location, collecting information from each location, etc. are well suited jobs for a mobile agent. According to Danny Lange & Mitsuru Oshima (1998) a mobile agent reduces network traffic, overcomes network latency, and offers robust as well as fault tolerant systems. Typically, most of the agents posses characteristics such as autonomy, co-operation, learning and pro-activeness. Along with these typical characteristics, the mobile agents offer mobility on distributed platform. The virtue of mobility of such agents is desirable for many specific applications on web platform for current business scenario.

Since the mobile agent has to travel and explore many remote locations in efficient manner, it is desired to carry minimal load and content in it. The content within the mobile agent must be light in terms of line of code and data associated with it. However, a mobile agent must carry some data regarding remote location information and permissions to access these locations. Further, the complexity of the content within the agent must be low. That is, the mobile object must be fast, simple and easy to move. In comparison with non-mobile (stationary) agents, the mobile agents need to be smaller, simpler and faster to transport themselves.

Structure of Mobile Agent and Ticket

Mobile agents are initially defined in a domain called host domain and afterwards they travel in other remote locations. Mobile agents facilitate users to control selected distributed information resources from host domain and gain access to other shared information resources through the relevant resource agents. Mobile agents are equipped with a set of goal specific instructions to the user's application that describe the nature and limits of their functionality. The mobile agents are equipped with methods of security, authentication, validation, and other restrictions that exist within domains.

Mobile agents are also demanded on need by other location besides the host network possessing the agent. On such valid request from any remote location or any network, a ticket is generated and copy of an agent with ticket would be sent to the guest network. A mobile agent stipulates its travel plan through tickets/itinerary. The ticket may consider a fix list of valid agents to visit. Alternatively, the list of agents can be determined dynamically. The guest network authenticates the data and allows agent to work in its environment. The network connectivity is required only to pass the request for an agent, to pass a copy of agent and appropriate ticket. After that the connectivity can be broken. There may be multiple requests from different networks for a common facility or an agent. In this case priority can also be set. Figure 6 describes mobility of mobile agents in two different networks.

The mobile agent can be imported from agent class designed and developed by IBM's Aglets Workbench. To create customised mobile agent based on the programming language java, this abstract class can be used. Typically the Aglet class is a hybridization of Agent and typical java Applet (browser enable executable java applications mechanism. It is also considered as an applet enable agent in the java.

Figure 6. Mobility of an agent in networks

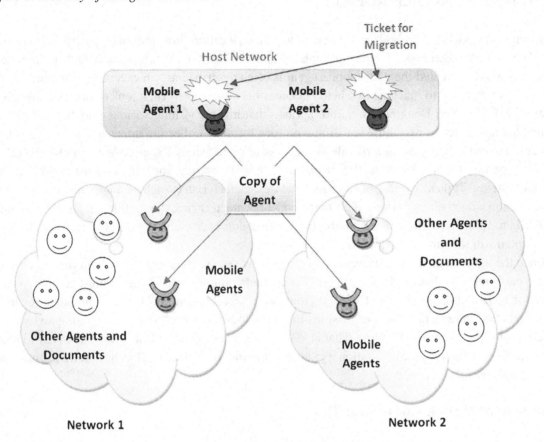

It is a mobile agent platform by the java programming language, which provides library that aids the development of mobile based applications. It is available as open source project at sourceforge.net and distributed under IBM Public License. An Aglet object can have various status such as Created, Cloned, Dispatched, Retracted, Activated, Deactivated, and Disposed.

To use the java Aglet class, one has to import and initialise at least one user defined class from the Aglet class as follows.

```
import aglet.*;
public class UserAgent extends Aglet { ... }
public void onCreation(Object init) {
    // initialization code...
    ...... ....... ...... ......... .......... .......... .........
    ...... ...... ........ . ... .... .. .
    }
```

To dispatch the agent on different networks following code segment can be used (Listing 1).

Ticket verification is done at receiving stage. It is the receiving network's responsibility to determine whether to trust the agent or not.

Listing 1.

```
boolean _flag = false;
public void onCreation(Object o) {
    addMobilityListener(
        new MobilityAdapter() {
    public void onDispatching(MobilityEvent e) {
    //... .... ...... ...... ....

    ...... ..... ......... ...... ...... ...... ......
        }
    public void onArrival(MobilityEvent e) {
        flag = true;
        //... ... ...... ......
    }
  }
 }
}
public void run() {
if (!_flag) {
    // native code ....
    ..... ..... ...... ......
    try {
    dispatch(destination);
        // ...
        } catch (Exception e) {
    System.out.println(e.getMessage());
    }
} else {
    // The remote aglet runs here...
    ... ...... ..... .. .. .... ....
    }
 }
 }
```

CONCLUSION AND FUTURE ENHANCEMENT

The chapter discusses the generic structure of the e-learning system using multiple agents. The basic objective of the structure is to access various resources containing e-Learning material. The majority of the agents employed in the system are light weight mobile agents, which can identify the suitable material according to the level of users using parameters such as identifier, keywords, description, difficulty level, etc. as discussed earlier. The material need not have to be stored in a rigid course-wise format at one particular location, but can be stored at various remote locations. However, the learning components must follow the common standard (such as IEEE) defined and described in this chapter. For application point of view, such standards can also be defined in tailor made way by the implementing agency or e-Learning solution providing agency itself. One or more mobile agents in the system explore the permissible network and search for the resources as per the requirements of users. The fuzzy user profiles stored at application layer helps in identifying the material.

The work described in this chapter has many advantages as described below.

The architecture designed in this work uses multiple agents. Since agents are used in the system, it provides all the benefits of using agents in a system such as:

- Modularity,
- Working in Parallel, independent and efficient fashion,
- Manages the distributed resources in a flexible manner,
- Enable co-operation with other agents and components of the system,
- Enhances reusability as the agents may be reused on need.

Another benefit of the proposed work is its generic nature. It can be applicable not only to e-Learning application. The generic structure can be applied to any suitable domain concerns with mining distributed resources such as the Web for knowledge acquisition and text extraction. Web content mining, web log mining and web structure mining can be done with similar architecture by just changing mobile agent mechanism. Another possible application that may employ the proposed architecture is customized search engine based on profile of users. Depending on user's need, content on the Web or the semantic web can be explored and ranked in customized manner according to the user's requirements. By implementing such architecture at client side, typical search engine results are managed. After such implementation, using a typical search engine, if 'Mirror' key word is fired by user with the profile describing a house wife, content related to simple mirrors will be presented with priority managed by the system implemented at the client. For writer and critics, review about the film "Mirror Mirror" will be given higher rank for same keyword and presented to them. If a software engineer or a programmer searches the same word 'Mirror', he will be provided content related to software mirrors. This is possible due to the system based on the architecture proposed is installed at client, where through user's profile, the machine knows its user. The system will modify the result of search engine at the client side only.

Besides the agent related benefits and applications in variety of domains, there are other benefits of the proposed work. Prominent of them are personalization, user friendliness and ease of using the system. Such advantages increase the acceptability and usability of the system. Now a days, when most of the resources are on distributed platform such as the Web or the Intranet server of an institution, there is no need to create a big and local repository or database of resources; rather it will be more effective to handle such content through one or more mobile agents. However, the content which is to be utilized should be created using a common vocabulary (ontology) or homogeneous structure (e.g. following a common representation strategy such as relational database), then only the proposed architecture works well. In future, a dedicated agent can be created that converts the fetched material into a common ontology before presenting the material against the users of the system.

Further, one may define various protocols for communication and co-operation between the agents of the system. This is also a possible future enhancement having research scope in it. An intelligent algorithm to identify proper web services from the Web is also a small but innovative extension of the work.

The proposed architecture uses mobile agents and it is the receiving network's duty to determine that the mobile agent travel from a remote host is to be trusted or not. Finding validation and security techniques for the mobile agent from a remote host can be other challenging future enhancement. At this stage the mobile agent defined in this system has a valid ticket containing IP (Internet Protocol) addresses with the prior permission. However, on need the ticket may experience dynamic update of IP addresses as the network evolved by time.

REFERENCES

Abu-Shawar, B., & Atwell, E. (2007). Fostering Language Learner Autonomy Through Adaptive Conversation Tutors. In Proceedings of Corpus Linguistics. Birmingham, UK: Academic Press.

Bobek, S., & Perko, I. (2006). Intelligent Agent Based Business Intelligence. In *Proceedings of 4th International Conference on Multimedia and Information and Communication Technologies in Education*. Academic Press.

Eklund, J., & Sinclair, K. (2000). An Empirical Appraisal of Adaptive Interfaces for Instructional Systems. *Educational Technology and Society Journal, 3*, 165–177.

Ferber, J. (1999). *Multi-Agent Systems: An Introduction to Distributed Artificial Intelligence*. Boston, MA: Addison-Wesley.

Gislandi, P. (2012). adAstra: A Rubrics' Set for Quality eLearning Design. In P. Ghislandi (Ed.), eLearning - Theories, Design, Software and Applications (pp. 91-106). InTech - Open Access Publisher.

Gray, R., Cybenko, G., Kotz, D., & Rus, D. (2001). Mobile Agents: Motivations and State of the Art. In J. Bradshaw (Ed.), *Handbook of Agent Technology*. Cambridge, MA: AAAI/MIT Press.

Griol, D., & Callejas, Z. (2013). An Architecture to Develop Multimodal Educative Applications with Chatbots. *International Journal of Advanced Robotic Systems, 10*, 1–15. doi:10.5772/55791

Lange, B. D., & Oshima, M. (1998). Mobile Agents with Java: The Aglet API. *World Wide Web (Bussum), 1*(3), 111–121. doi:10.1023/A:1019267832048

Lokken, F., & Womer, L. (2007). *Trends in E-Learning: Tracking the Impact of E-Learning in Higher Education. 2006 Distance Education Survey Results*. Washington, DC: Instructional Technology Council.

Mahanta, D., & Ahmed, M. (2012). E-Learning Objectives, Methodologies, Tools and its Limitations. *International Journal of Innovative Technology and Exploring Engineering, 2*(1), 46–61.

Mankad, K. B., & Sajja, P. S. (2008). Applying Multi-Agent Approach for Comparative Studies of Intelligence Among Students. *ADIT Journal of Engineering, 5*(1), 25–28.

Moraitakis, N. (1997). *Intelligent Software Agents: Application and Classification*. Retrieved October 10, 2014 from http://www.doc.ic.ac.uk/~nd/surprise_97/journal/vol1/nm1/

Nakano, M., Hasegawa, Y., Funakoshi, K., Takeuchi, J., Torii, T., Nakadai, K., & Tsujino, H. et al. (2011). A Multi-Expert Model for Dialogue and Behaviour Control of Conversational Robots and Agents. *Knowledge-Based Systems, 24*(2), 248–256. doi:10.1016/j.knosys.2010.08.004

Park, O., & Lee, J. (2003). Adaptive Instructional Systems. *Educational Technology Research and Development*, *25*, 651–684.

Rudowsky, I. (2004). Intelligent Agents. *Communications of the Association for Information Systems*, *14*, 275–290.

Sajja, P. S. (2006). Parichay: An Agent for Adult Literacy. *Prajna*, *14*, 17–24.

Sajja, P.S. (2008). Enhancing Quality in E-learning by Knowledge-Based IT Support. *International Journal of Education and Development using Information and Communication Technology, 4*(1), 109-119.

Scalise, K., & Ketterlin-Geller, L. (2012). Reciprocal Leading: Improving Instructional Designs in E-Learning. In P. Ghislandi (Ed.), eLearning - Theories, Design, Software and Applications (pp. 73-90). InTech - Open Access Publisher.

Shute, V. J., & Psotka, J. (1996). Intelligent Tutoring Systems: Past, Present, and Future. In D. Jonassen (Ed.), *Handbook of Research for Educational Communications and Technology* (pp. 570–600). New York, NY: Macmillan.

Srivastava, E., & Agarwal, N. (2013). E-Learning: New Trend in Education and Training. *International Journal of Advanced Research, 1*(8), 797–810.

Teall, E., Wang, M., Callaghan, V., & Ng, J. W. P. (2014). An Exposition of Current Mobile Learning Design Guidelines and Frameworks. *International Journal on E-Learning, 13*(1), 79–99.

Vaidya, N. M., & Sajja, P. S. (2014). Intelligent Virtual Collaborative Learning Environment. *International Journal of Research in Computer Science and Information Technology, 2*(2), 116–118.

Wooldridge, M. (2002). *An Introduction to Multi Agent Systems*. Chichester, UK: John Wiley & Sons.

Xu, D., Yin, J., Deng, Y., & Ding, J. (2003). A Formal Architectural Model for Logical Agent Mobility. *IEEE Transactions on Software Engineering, 29*(1), 31–45. doi:10.1109/TSE.2003.1166587

Zadeh, L. A. (1965). Fuzzy Sets. *Journal of Information and Control, 8*(3), 338–353. doi:10.1016/S0019-9958(65)90241-X

ADDITIONAL READING

Akerkar, R. A., & Sajja, P. S. (2009). *Knowledge-Based Systems*. Sudbury, MA, USA: Jones & Bartlett Publishers.

Dagger, D., O'Connor, A., Lawless, S., Walsh, E., & Wade, V. P. (2007). Service-Oriented E-Learning Platforms: From Monolithic Systems to Flexible Services. *IEEE Internet Computing, 11*(3), 28–35. doi:10.1109/MIC.2007.70

Dong, B., Zheng, Q., Yang, J., Li, H., & Qiao, M. (2009). An E-Learning Ecosystem Based on Cloud Computing Infrastructure. In *Proceedings of International Conference on Advanced Learning Technologies*. Riga, 125-127. doi:10.1109/ICALT.2009.21

Hawalah, A., & Fasli, M. (2011). A Multi-Agent System Using Ontological User Profiles for Dynamic User Modelling. In *Proceeding of International Conference on Web Intelligence and Intelligent Agent Technology*. Lyon, France, 430-437. doi:10.1109/WI-IAT.2011.76

Liaw, S. S., Huang, H. M., & Chen, G. D. (2007). Surveying Instructor and Learner Attitudes Towards E-learning. *Computers & Education, 49*(4), 1066–1080. doi:10.1016/j.compedu.2006.01.001

Macwan, N. A., & Sajja, P. S. (2014). Fuzzy Logic: An Effective User Interface Tool for Decision Support System. *International Journal of Engineering Science and Innovative Technology., 3*(3), 278–283.

Mahdizadeh, H., Biemans, H., & Mulder, M. (2007). Determining Factors of the Use of E-Learning Environments by University Teachers. *Computers & Education, 51*(1), 142–154. doi:10.1016/j.compedu.2007.04.004

Regli, W. C., Mayk, I., Dugan, C. J., Kopena, J. B., Lass, R. N., Modi, P. J., & Sultanik, E. A. et al. (2009). Development and Specification of a Reference Model for Agent-Based Systems. *IEEE Transactions on Systems, Man, and Cybernetics, 39*(5), 572–596. doi:10.1109/TSMCC.2009.2020507

Sajja, P. S., & Akerkar, R. A. (2012). *Intelligent Technologies for Web Applications. CRC Press*. Boka Raton, FL, USA: Taylor & Francis Group. doi:10.1201/b12118

KEY TERMS AND DEFINITIONS

Agent: An Agent is a computational entity that acts on behalf of other entities in an autonomous fashion; and exhibits properties like learning, cooperation, and mobility to a certain extent.

Agent Mobility: A mobile agent used to travel in heterogeneous environment by passing code or passing itself with proper validation and authentication process. This feature is known as mobility of agents.

Aglet: An agent is a mobile agent platform by the programming language java, which provides library that aids the development of mobile based applications. It is an open source project available at sourceforge.net.

E-Learning: e-Learning is defined as electronic learning, supporting learning through all forms of electronically supported devices and tools. Information and Communication Technology infrastructure has been serving as an efficient platform to enable e-Learning system.

Fuzzy Logic: Fuzzy logic is a multi valued logic based on fuzzy sets. This type of logic is very nearer to the way how humans identify and categorize things into the classes whose boundaries are not fixed.

Fuzzy Membership Functions: The function which maps fuzzy linguistic value to an appropriate crisp value between the interval [0, 1] is called a fuzzy membership function. Usage of such membership functions facilitate fuzzy logic based systems to represent and reason with linguistic and vague type of knowledge.

Light Weight Agent: An agent with minimum code and simple in nature so that it is less complex and occupies less memory. It should carry less data in order to move efficiently in the given network. This is one of the desirable characteristics for a mobile agent; as a mobile agent has to be light enough to travel in its network.

Multi-Agent Systems: A multi-agent system is comprised of several agents working together towards a goal or completion of a task. It is a loosely coupled network of problem-solving entities that work together to find answers to problems that are beyond the capacity of any individual problem-solving entity.

Chapter 20
Adding Context into Classification Reasoning Based on Good Classification Tests

Xenia Naidenova
Military Medical Academy, Russia

ABSTRACT

In this chapter, classification reasoning is considered. The concept of good classification test lies in the foundation of this reasoning. Inferring good classification tests from data sets is the inductive phase of reasoning resulted in generating implicative and functional dependencies supporting the deductive phase of reasoning. An algorithm of inferring good classification tests is given with the decomposition of it into subtasks allowing to choose sub-contexts for each obtained dependency and to control sub-contexts during both deductive and inductive phases of classification reasoning.

INTRODUCTION

The symbolic methods of machine learning work on objects with symbolic, Boolean, integer, and categorical attributes. With this point of view, these methods can be considered as ones of mining conceptual knowledge. We concentrate on the supervised conceptual learning. Now, the theory of conceptual learning does not include classification reasoning as its inalienable component, although precisely this reasoning constitutes an integral part of any mode of reasoning (Mill, 1872; Michalski & Kaufman, 1998; Spencer, 1898; Piaget & Inelder, 1954; Sechenov, 2001). Furthermore, current models of commonsense reasoning do not include classification too (Russel & Norvig, 2010). However, classification, as a process of thinking, performs the following operations (Polia, 1954; Bynum, 1972, Mill, 1872; Quinlan, 1989):

- Generalizing or specifying object descriptions;
- Interpreting logical expressions on a set of all thinkable objects;
- Learning concepts from examples;
- Decision tree construction;

DOI: 10.4018/978-1-4666-8767-7.ch020

- Extracting hierarchical object classifications from examples;
- Forming knowledge and data contexts adequate to a current situation of reasoning;
- Reducing the domain of searching for a solution of some problem;
- Revealing essential elements of reasoning (objects, attributes, values of attributes etc);
- Revealing the links of object sets and their descriptions with external contexts interrelated with them.

This list can be continued.

We believe that conceptual learning is a special class of methods based on mining and using conceptual knowledge the elements of which are objects, attributes (values of attributes), classifications (partitions of objects into disjoint blocks), and links between them. These links are expressed by the use of implications: "object ↔ class", "object ↔ property", "values of attributes ↔ class", and "subclass ↔ class".

We understand classification reasoning as a process of thinking based on which the causal connections between objects, their properties and classes of objects are revealed. In fact, this reasoning is critical for the formation of conceptual knowledge or ontology in the contemporary terminology.

Studying the processes of classification within the framework of machine learning and knowledge discovery led to the necessity of reformulating the entire class of symbolic machine learning problems as the problems of finding approximations of a given classification of objects (Naidenova, 1996). This reformulation is based on the concept of a good diagnostic (or classification) test (GDT) for the given classification of objects (Naidenova & Polegaeva, 1986; Naidenova, 2006). A GDT has a dual nature. On the one hand, it is a logical expression in the form of implication or functional dependency; on the other hand, it generates the partition of a set of objects equivalent to a given classification of this set or partition that is nearest to the given classification with respect to the inclusion relation between partitions.

If we take into account that implications express relations between concepts (the object ↔ the class, the object ↔ the property, the property ↔ the class), we can assume that schemes of extracting and applying implications (rules of the "if–then" type) form the core of classification processes. Deductive steps of reasoning imply using known facts and statements of the "if–then" type to infer consequences from them. Inductive steps imply applying data and existing knowledge to infer new implicative assertions and correct those that turned out to be in contradiction with the existing knowledge. Inductive rules of reasoning are the inductive canons stated by British logician John Stuart Mill: the Methods of Agreement, the Method of Difference, the Joint Method of Agreement and Difference, the Method of Concomitant Variations and the Method of Residues (Mill, 1872).

The analysis of algorithms of searching for all GDTs in terms of constructing Galois lattice (Naidenova, 2011) allowed us to decompose this problem into sub-problems and operations that represent known deductive and inductive modes (modus operandi) of classification reasoning. Each step of constructing a classification lattice can be interpreted as a mental act (Naidenova, 2006). These acts can be found in any reasoning: stating new propositions, choosing the relevant part of knowledge and/or data for further steps of reasoning, involving a new rule of reasoning. Lattice construction engages both inductive and deductive reasoning rules. The implicative dependencies (implications, interdictions, rules of compatibility) generated in a process of GDTs are used immediately in this process for pruning the search space with the aid of deduction.

Classification reasoning requires a lot of techniques related to increasing its efficiency. One of the important techniques is decomposition of the main problem into sub-problems. As a whole, reasoning can be considered as gradually extending and narrowing the context of reasoning.

CLASSIFICATION REASONING AND SEARCHING FOR IMPLICATIVE AND FUNCTIONAL DEPENDENCIES

We assume that objects are described by a set U of symbolic or numeric attributes. To give a target classification of objects, we use an additional attribute KL not belonging to U. A target attribute partitions a given set of objects into disjoint classes the number of which is equal to the number of values of this attribute. In Table 1, we have two classes: 1) the objects in description of which the target value k appears (positive examples); 2) all the other objects (negative examples).

One of the tasks to infer GDTs is the formation of the best descriptions of a given object class (class of positive objects) against the objects not belonging to this class (i.e. class of negative objects). We assume that objects are described in terms of values of a given set U of attributes (see, please, Table 1).

Let $M = \{\cup \, dom(attr), attr \in U\}$, where $dom(attr)$ is the set of all values of $attr$. Let $X \subseteq M$. Let G be the set of objects considered, $G = G_+ \cup G_-$, where G_+ and G_- the sets of positive and negative objects, respectively; let $P(X) = \{$all the objects in description of which X appears$\}$. We call $P(X)$ the interpretation of X in the power set 2^G. If $P(X)$ contains only positive objects and the number of these objects more than 2, then we call X a description of some positive objects and $(P(X), X)$ a test for positive objects.

We define a good test or good description of a subset of positive objects as follows.

Definition 1: A set $X \subseteq M$ of attribute values is a good description of a subset of positive objects if and only if it is a description of this subset and no such subset $Y \subseteq M$ exists, such that $P(X) \subset P(Y) \subseteq G_+$.

This problem is reduced to searching for causal dependencies in the form $X \to v$, $X \subseteq M$, v is value of an attribute (Naidenova, 1992; Kuznetsov, 2005, Ob'jedkov, 2007).

If we have a partition of objects into several disjoint blocks (classes), then we define the classification test as an approximation of this partition as follows. Let $I(B)$, $B \subseteq U$ be the partition of G generated by attributes of set B. We call $I(B)$ the interpretation of B in the set of all possible partitions of G into disjoint blocks. If $I(B) \subseteq I(KL)$, then $(I(B), B)$ is a test for classification KL and the functional dependency $B \to KL$ holds (Naidenova, 1982; Baixeries et al., 2012).

Definition 2: The set of attributes $B \subseteq U$ is a good test for classification KL if and only if no such subset $Z \subseteq U$, $Z \neq B$ exists that $I(B) \subset I(Z) \subseteq I(KL)$.

Table 1. Example of data classification

Index of Object	Height	Color of Hair	Color of Eyes	KL (Target Classification)
1	Low	Blond	Blue	k (+)
2	Low	Brown	Blue	not k (−)
3	Tall	Brown	Hazel	not k (−)
4	Tall	Blond	Hazel	not k (−)
5	Tall	Brown	Blue	not k (−)
6	Low	Blond	Hazel	not k (−)
7	Tall	Red	Blue	k (+)
8	Tall	Blond	Blue	k (+)

It has been shown (Naidenova, 1992; Baixeries et al., 2012) that searching for functional dependencies is reduced to searching for implicative ones (i.e. to object class description).

In what follows, we shall deal with searching for and using good descriptions of positive or negative classes of objects. We consider the set of object descriptions with its partition into positive and negative classes as an initial classification context for the task of GDTs.

CLASSIFICATION REASONING BASED ON GOOD CLASSIFICATION TESTS

The GDTs generate implicative dependencies. Practically without loss of knowledge, different logical assertions can be represented with the use of only one class of logical rules, namely, implicative dependencies between names. The following types of rules realize classification reasoning:

INSTANCES or relationships between objects or facts really observed. Instance can be considered as a logical rule with the least degree of generalization.

RULES OF THE FIRST TYPE or logical assertions. They describe regular relationships between objects and their properties, between properties of different objects, between objects and their classes. The rules of the first type can be given explicitly by an expert or derived automatically from instances via some learning process.

RULES OF THE SECOND TYPE or classification reasoning rules are ones with the help of which rules of the first type are used, updated, and inferred from data. These rules embrace both inductive and deductive reasoning rules.

The rules of the first type can be represented with the use of only one class of logical statements, namely, implicative dependencies between names. Names are used for designating concepts, things, events, situations, or any evidences. They can be considered as attributes and attributes' values in the formal representations of logical rules. Consider the rules of the first type.

Implication: $a, b, c \rightarrow d$. This rule means that if the values standing on the left side of the rule are simultaneously true, then the value on the right side of the rule is always true.

Interdiction or forbidden rule: $a, b, c \rightarrow false$ (never). This rule interdicts a combination of values enumerated on the left side of the rule. This rule can be transformed into several implications such as $a, b \rightarrow$ not c; $a, c \rightarrow$ not b; $b, c \rightarrow$ not a.

Compatibility: $a, b, c \rightarrow VA$, where *VA* is the frequency of occurrence of the rule. The compatibility is equivalent to several implications as follows:

$a, b \rightarrow c, VA$; $a, c \rightarrow b, VA$; $b, c \rightarrow b, VA$.

Generally, the compatibility rule represents the most common combination of values characterized by an insignificant number of exceptions from the regularity.

Diagnostic rule: $x, d \rightarrow a$; $x, b \rightarrow$ not a; $d, b \rightarrow false$. For example, d and b can be two values of the same attribute. This rule works when the truth of 'x' has been proven and it is necessary to determine whether 'a' is true or not. If '$x \& d$' is true, then 'a' is true, but if '$x \& b$' is true, then 'a' is false.

Rule of alternatives: a or $b \rightarrow true$ (always); $a, b \rightarrow false$. This rule says that a and b cannot be simultaneously true, either a or b can be true but not both.

Deductive steps of reasoning consist of inferring consequences from observed facts with the use of implications. For this goal, deductive rules of reasoning are applied the main forms of which are modus ponens, modus tollens, modus ponendo tollens, and modus tollendo ponens.

Let x be a set of true values of some attributes observed simultaneously.

Using implication: Let r be an implication, left(r) and right(r) be the left and right parts of r, respectively. If left(r) $\subseteq x$, then x can be extended by right(r): $x \leftarrow x \cup$ right(r). Using implication is based on modus ponens: if A, then B; A; hence B.

Using interdiction: Let r be an implication $y \rightarrow$ not k. If left(r) $\subseteq x$, then k is the forbidden value for all extensions of x. Using interdiction is based on modus ponendo tollens: either A or B (A, B – alternatives); A; hence not B; either A or B; B; hence not A.

Using compatibility: Let $r =$ '$a, b, c \rightarrow k, VA$', where VA is the value of special attribute that characterizes the frequency of occurrence of the rule. If left(r) $\subseteq x$, then k can be used to extend x along with the calculated value VA for this extension (calculating the estimate VA requires special consideration).

Using diagnostic rules: Let r be a diagnostic rule such as '$x, d \rightarrow a$; $x, b \rightarrow$ not a', where 'x' is true, and 'a', 'not a' are hypotheses or possible values of some attribute. Using the diagnostic rule is based on modus ponens and modus ponendo tollens.

There are several ways for refuting one of the hypotheses:

- To infer either d or b using existing knowledge;
- To involve new known facts (extended context) and/or propositions for inferring (with the use of inductive reasoning rules of the second type) new rules of the first type for distinguishing between the hypotheses 'a' and 'not a'; to apply the newly obtained rules;
- To get the direct answer of an expert on whether d or b is true.

Using rule of alternatives: Let 'a' and 'b' be two alternative hypotheses about the value of some attribute, and the truth of one of hypotheses has been established, then the second hypothesis is rejected. Using the rule of alternatives is based on modus tollendo ponens: either A or B (A, B – alternatives); not A; hence B; either A or B; not B; hence A.

The rules listed above are ones of "forward inference". In natural classification reasoning, so called "backward inference" is used.

Generating hypothesis or abduction rule. Let r be an implication $y \rightarrow k$. Then the following hypothesis is generated "if k is true, then y may be true".

Using modus tollens. Let r be an implication $y \rightarrow k$. If 'not k' is inferred, then 'not y' is also inferred.

When applied, the above given rules generate the reasoning, which is not demonstrative. The purpose of the reasoning is to infer all possible hypotheses on the value of some objective attribute. It is essential that hypotheses do not contradict with knowledge (first-type rules) and the observable real situation, where the reasoning takes place (or contextual knowledge). Inference of hypotheses is constructing all maximal intrinsically consistent extensions of the set of values x.

We describe a very simple structure of a knowledge base (KB). The KB consists of two parts: the Attribute Base (*AtB*), containing the relations between problem domain concepts, and the Assertion Base (*AsB*), containing implications formulated in terms of the concepts.

The domain concepts are represented by the use of names. With respect to its role in the KB, a name can be one of two kinds: name of attribute and name of attribute value. However, with respect to its role in the problem domain, a name can be the name of an object, the name of a class of objects and the name of a classification of objects. A class of objects can contain only one object hence the name of an object is a particular case of the name of a class. In the KB, names of objects and classes of objects become names of attribute values, and names of classifications become names of attributes.

The link between the name of an attribute and the names of its values is implicative. It can be expressed by the following way: (<name of value$_1$>, <name of value$_2$>, ..., <name of value$_k$>) → <name of attribute>, where the sign "→" denotes the relation "is a".

For example, (*asp, oak, fir-tree, cedar, pine-tree, birch*) → *kind of trees*, and, for each value of '*kind of trees*', the assertion of the following type can be created: "*asp* is a *kind of trees*".

The set of all attributes' names and the set of all values' names must not intersect. This means that the name of a classification cannot simultaneously be the name of a class. However, this is not the case in natural languages: the name of a class can be used for some classification and vice versa. For example, one can say that '*pine-tree*', '*fir-tree*', '*cedar*' are '*conifers*'. But one may also say that '*conifers*', '*leaf-bearing*' are '*kinds of trees*'. Here the word '*conifers*' serves both as the name of a classification and as the name of a class. In this setting, class is a particular case of classification.

For using names in the way we do in real life we permit the introduction of auxiliary names for the subsets of the set of an attribute's values. The name of a subset of values of attribute *A* will be used as the name of a new attribute which, in its turn, will serve as the name of a value with respect to *A*.

The *AsB* (Assertion Base) contains the expert's implications. Each assertion links a collection of values of different attributes with a certain value of a special attribute (*SA*) that evaluates how often this collection of values appears in practice. The values of a special attribute are: *always, never, rarely*, and *frequently*. Assertions have the following form: (<name of value>, <name of value>, ..., <value of SA>) = *true*.

For simplicity, we omit the word '*true*', because it appears in any assertion. For example, the assertion "pine-tree and cedar can be found frequently in the meadow type of forest" will be expressed in the following way: (*meadow, pine-tree, cedar, frequently*). We also omit the sign of conjunction between values of different attributes and the sign of disjunction (separating disjunction) between values of the same attribute. For example, the assertion in the form (*meadow, pine-tree, cedar, often*) is equivalent to the following expression of formal logic: P((type of forest = *meadow*) & ((kind of trees = *pine-tree*) V (kind of trees = *cedar*)) & (*SA* = *frequently*)) = *true*.

The following kind of requests to the KB is used: SEARCHING VALUE OF <name of attribute> [, <name of attribute>,...] IF (<name of value>, <name of value>, ...), where "name of value" is the known value of an attribute, "name of attribute" means that the value of this attribute is unknown. For example, the request "to find the type of forest for a region with plateau, without watercourse, with the prevalence of pine-tree" will be represented as follows: SEARCHING VALUE OF the type of forest IF (*plateau, without watercourse, pine-tree*).

An Example of Inferring All Possible Hypotheses about the Type of Woodland from an Incomplete Description of Some Evidences

Let *x* be a request to the KB equal to:

SEARCHING VALUE OF type of woodland IF (*plateau, without watercourse, pine-tree*). Let the content of the KB be the following collection of assertions (Naidenova & Polegaeva, 1985; Kropov, 1995):

AtB:

1. (meadow, bilberry wood, red bilberry wood ....) → types of woodland;
2. (pine-tree, spruce, cypress, cedars, birch, larch, asp, fir-tree) → dominating kinds of trees;
3. (plateau, without plateau) → presence of plateau;
4. (top of slope, middle part of slope, ...) → parts of slope;
5. (peak of hill, foot of hill) → parts of hill;
6. (height on plateau, without height on plateau) → presence of a height on plateau;
7. (head of watercourse, low part of watercourse, ...) → parts of water course;
8. (steepness ≥ 4°, steepness ≤ 3°, steepness < 3°, ...) → features of slope;
9. (north, south, west, east) → the four cardinal points;
10. (watercourse, without watercourse) → presence of a watercourse.

   AsB:

1. (meadow, pine-tree, larch, frequently);
2. (meadow, pine-tree, steepness ≤ 4°, never);
3. (meadow, larch, steepness ≥ 4°, never);
4. (meadow, north, west, south, frequently);
5. (meadow, east, rarely);
6. (meadow, fir-tree, birch, asp, rarely);
7. (meadow, plateau, middle part of slope, frequently);
8. (meadow, peak of hill, watercourse heads, rarely);
9. (plateau, steepness ≤ 3°, always);
10. (plateau, watercourse, rarely);
11. (red bilberry wood, pine-tree, frequently);
12. (red bilberry wood, larch, rarely);
13. (red bilberry wood, peak of hill, frequently);
14. (red bilberry wood, height on plateau, rarely);
15. (meadow, steepness < 3°, frequently).

The process of reasoning evolves according to the following sequence of steps:

Step 1: Take out all the assertions t in AsB containing at least one value from the request, i.e., $t \in$ AsB and $t \cap x \neq \emptyset$, where x is the request. These are assertions 1, 2, 7, 9, 10, 11, and 14.

Step 2: Delete (from the set of selected assertions) all the assertions that contradict with the request. Delete assertion 10 because it contains the value of attribute 'presence of water course' which is different from the value of this attribute in the request. The remaining assertions are 1, 2, 7, 9, 11, and 14.

Step 3: Take out the values of attribute '*type of woodland*' appearing in assertions 1, 2, 7, 9, 11, and 14. We have two hypotheses: '*meadow*' and '*red bilberry*'.

Step 4: An attempt is made to refute one of the hypotheses. For this goal, it is necessary to find an assertion that has the value of *SA* equal to '*never*' and contains one of the hypotheses, some subset of values from the request and does not contain any other value. There is only one assertion with the value of *SA* equal to '*never*'. This is assertion 2: (*meadow, pine-tree, steepness ≤ 4°, never*). However, we cannot use this assertion because it contains the value '*steepness ≤ 4°*' which is not in the request.

Step 5: An attempt is made to find a value of some attribute that is not in the request (in order to extend the request). For this goal, it is necessary to find an assertion with the value of *SA* equal to '*always*' that contains a subset of values from the request and one and only one value of some new attribute the values of which are not in the request. Only one assertion satisfies this condition. This is assertion 9: (*plateau, steepness* ≤ 3°, *always*).

Step 6: Forming the extended request:

SEARCHING VALUE OF *the type of woodland* IF (*plateau, without watercourse, pine-tree, steepness* ≤ 3°).

Steps 1, 2, and 3 are repeated. Assertion 15 is involved in the reasoning.

Step 4 is repeated. Now assertion 2 is used because the value '*steepness* ≤ 4° is in accordance with the values of '*feature of slope*' in the request. We conclude that the type of woodland cannot be '*meadow*'. The non-refuted hypothesis is "*the type of woodland = red bilberry*".

The process of deductive reasoning can require inferring new rules of the first type from data when

- The result of reasoning contains several hypotheses and it is impossible to choose one and only one of them (uncertainty);
- There does not exist any hypothesis.

The Interaction of Deductive and Inductive Reasoning Rules in Classification Reasoning

It is not difficult to see that the steps of reasoning described above use the deductive reasoning rules of the second types.

Step 1 performs *Introducing Assertions* into the reasoning process. This step aims at drawing knowledge into reasoning. The selected assertions form the meaningful context of reasoning.

Step 2 performs *Deleting Assertions* from the reasoning process. This step *uses Rule of Alternative*. Consequently, step 2 narrows the context of reasoning.

Step 3 performs *Introducing Hypotheses* of the goal attribute values. The source of hypotheses is the context of reasoning.

Step 4 performs *Deleting Hypotheses* via using *Interdiction (Forbidden) Rules*. Let H be a hypothesis and FR be a forbidden rule '$H, \{Y\} \rightarrow never$', and X be a request, where X, Y – the sets of attributes values. If $Y \subseteq X$, then hypothesis H is disproved.

Step 5 performs *Introducing Assumptions* of values of attributes. Let A be the value of an attribute not contained in the request, IR be the rule '$A, Y \rightarrow always$', and X be a request, where X, Y – the sets of attributes values. If $Y \subseteq X$, then the request can be extended as follows: $X' = X \cup A$.

Step 6 performs *Forming the Extended Request* in accordance with every not disproved hypothesis.

With the extended requests, the steps 1 – 6 are performed untill only one hypothesis remains.

The compatibility rule can be used for extending the request with some limitations: value $v(A)$ of an attribute A can be determined by a compatibility rule R with *VA* equal to *Z*, if value $v(A)$ is also inferred independently, with the same or higher value of *VA*, by means of a rule different from R.

If the number of hypotheses is more than 1 and no one of them can be disproved, then we deal with a situation requiring the aid of diagnostic rules and extending context of reasoning.

If the set of hypotheses is empty, then it is natural to extend the request by the use of Introducing Assumptions (Step 5) taking as a goal any attribute with unknown value from the reasoning context. The absence of hypotheses indicates the need of expanding the KB by using an extended context of reasoning.

Inductive Extension of Incomplete Knowledge with the Use of Rules of the Second Type

It is indispensable to draw into reasoning the steps of inductive inference in two variants:

- Using a part of existing KB not included in the context of reasoning if this part contains a set of observations potentially applicable as the source of new assertions related to the difficult situations of reasoning;
- Initiating a new investigation of the forest region for collecting observations to enrich the KB.

In the first variant, we do the purpose-directed steps of inductive reasoning. Let A, B be the hypotheses or phenomena under investigations. The purpose-directed steps of inductive reasoning means that we must choose in KB the instances containing a set of attributes' values of the request, say X, then, among these instances, we must select the instances in which phenomenon A occurs but phenomenon B does not occur and the instances in which phenomenon B occurs but phenomenon A does not occur.

Inductive reasoning rules of the second type serve for obtaining the rules of the first type. In this chapter, we propose a new algorithm of inferring contextual GDTs from a given data set one of the peculiarities of which consists in decomposing the main context of inference into sub-contexts associated with objects (concept), attributes or values of attributes. Therefore, we obtain context-dependent logical rules.

THE CONCEPT OF GOOD CLASSIFICATION TEST

To define good classification tests, we assume that $G = \{1, 2,..., N\}$ is the set of objects' indices (objects, for short) and $M = \{m_1, m_2, ..., m_j, ...m_m\}$ is the set of attributes' values (values, for short). Each object is described by a set of values from M. The object descriptions are represented by rows of a table the columns of which are associated with the attributes taking their values in M (see, please, Table 1).

Let $A \subseteq G$, $B \subseteq M$. Denote by B_i, $B_i \subseteq M$, $i = 1,..., N$ the description of object with index i. The Galois connection (Ore, 1944) between the ordered sets $(2^G, \subseteq)$ and $(2^M, \subseteq)$ is defined by the following mappings called derivation operators: for $A \subseteq G$ and $B \subseteq M$, $A' = \text{val}(A) = \{$intersection of all $B_i: B_i \subseteq M, i \in A\}$ and $B' = \text{obj}(B) = \{i: i \in G, B \subseteq B_i\}$. Of course, we have $\text{obj}(B) = \{$intersection of all $\text{obj}(m)$: $\text{obj}(m) \subseteq G, m \in B\}$.

We introduce two closure operators: generalization_of$(B) = B'' = \text{val}(\text{obj}(B))$; generalization_of$(A)$ $=A'' = \text{obj}(\text{val}(A))$. A set A is closed if $A = \text{obj}(\text{val}(A))$. A set B is closed if $B = \text{val}(\text{obj}(B))$.

For $g \in G$ and $m \in M$, $\{g\}'$ is denoted by g' and called *object intent*, and $\{m\}'$ is denoted by m' and called *value extent* (Ganter and Wille, 1999; Kuznetsov, 2011).

Let $K = (G, M, I)$ be a given classification context and $K = K_+ \cup K_-$, where $K_+ = (G_+, M, I_+)$, $K_- = (G_-, M, I_-)$, $G = G_+ \cup G_-$ $(G_- = G \backslash G_+)$. Diagnostic test is defined as follows.

Definition 3: *A diagnostic test* for G_+ is a pair (A, B) such that $B \subseteq M$ $(A = \text{obj}(B) \neq \varnothing)$, $A \subseteq G_+$ and $B \not\subseteq \text{val}(g)$ & $B \neq \text{val}(g)$, $\forall g, g \in G_-$. Equivalently, $\text{obj}(B) \cap G_- = \varnothing$.

In general case, a set B is not closed for diagnostic test (A, B), i. e., a diagnostic test is not obligatory a concept of FCA (Ganter and Wille, 1999). This condition is true only for the special class of tests called 'maximally redundant ones'.

Definition 4: A diagnostic test (A, B), $B \subseteq M$ $(A = \text{obj}(B) \neq \varnothing)$ for G_+ is *maximally redundant* if $\text{obj}(B \cup m) \subset A$, for all $m \notin B$ and $m \in M$.

Definition 5: A diagnostic test (A, B), $B \subseteq M$ $(A = \text{obj}(B) \neq \varnothing)$ for G_+ is *good* if and only if any extension $A^* = A \cup i$, $i \notin A$, $i \in G_+$ implies that $(A^*, \text{val}(A^*))$ is *not a test* for G_+.

In this paper, we deal with GMRTs. If a good test (A, B), $B \subseteq M$ $(A = \text{obj}(B) \neq \varnothing)$ for G_+ is maximally redundant, then any extension $B^* = B \cup m$, $m \notin B$, $m \in M$ implies that $(\text{obj}(B^* \cup m), (B^* \cup m))$ is *not a good test* for G_+.

Any object description $D(o^*)$ in a given classification context is a maximally redundant set of values because for any value $m \notin D(o^*)$, $m \in M$, $\text{obj}(D(o^*) \cup m)$ is equal to $\varnothing$.

In Table 1, $((1, 8), \text{‘}Blond Blue\text{’})$ is a GMRT for Class(+) but it is irredundant one, simultaneously; $((4, 6), \text{‘}Blond Hazel\text{’})$ is a GMRT for Class(−) but it is not a good one; and $((3,4,6), \text{‘}Hazel\text{’})$ is a good irredundant test for Class(−).

The Decomposition of GMRT Inferring into Subtasks

We introduce two kinds of subtasks (Naidenova & Ermakov, 2001) as follows. For a given set of positive objects:

1. Given a set of values $B \subseteq M$, $\text{obj}(B) \neq \varnothing$, B is not included in any description of negative object, find all GMRTs $(\text{obj}(B^*), B^*)$ such that $B^* \subset B$;
2. Given a non-empty set of values $X \subseteq M$ such that $(\text{obj}(X), X)$ is not a test for positive objects, find all GMRTs $(\text{obj}(Y), Y)$ such that $X \subset Y$, $Y \subseteq M$.

To solve the subtasks we form sub-contexts of a given classification context K. These subtasks are associated with the following projections corresponding with two kinds of sub-contexts.

Object projection of a positive object description t on the set $D(+)$ (descriptions of all positive objects) is $\text{proj}[t] = \{z: (z \text{ is non empty intersection of } t \text{ and } t^*), (t^* \in D(+)), ((\text{obj}(z), z) \text{ is a test for } D(+))\}$. ($t$ is included in the projection).

Value projection of a given value m on a given set $D(+)$ of positive objects is $\text{proj}[m] = \{t: (t \in D(+)), (m \text{ appears in } t)\}$. Another way to define this projection is: $\text{proj}[m] = \{t_i: i \in (\text{obj}(m) \cap G_+)\}$.

Algorithm ASTRA, based on value projections and algorithm DIAGaRa, based on object projections, have been given in (Naidenova, 2006).

The following theorem gives the foundation of reducing sub-contexts (Naidenova 2006).

Theorem 1: Let $m \in M$, $X \subseteq M$, $(\text{obj}(X), X)$ be a maximally redundant test for positive objects and $\text{obj}(m) \subseteq \text{obj}(X)$. Then m can not belong to any GMRT for positive objects different from $(\text{obj}(X), X)$.

Consider some example of reducing sub-context (see, please, Table 1).

Let splus(*m*) be obj(*m*) ∩ G$_+$ (obj(*m*) ∩ G$_-$) and SPLUS be {splus(*m*): *m* ∈ *M*}. In Table 1, we have for values *Hazel*, *Brown*, *Tall*, *Blue*, *Blond*, and *Low*, SPLUS = {obj(*m*) ∩ G$_-$} = {{3, 4, 6}, {2, 3, 5}, {3, 4, 5}, {2, 5}, {4, 6}, {2, 6}}.

We have val(obj(*Hazel*)) = *Hazel*, hence ((3,4,6), *Hazel*) is a test for G$_-$. Then value *Blond* can be deleted from consideration, because splus(*Blond*) ⊂ splus(*Hazel*). Delete values *Blond* and *Hazel* from consideration. After that, the description of object 4 is included in the description of object 8 of G$_+$ and the description of object 6 is included in the description of object 1 of G$_+$. Delete objects 4 and 6. Then for values *Brown*, *Tall*, *Blue*, and *Low*, SPLUS = {{2, 3, 5}, {3, 5}, {2, 5}, {2}}. Now we have val(obj(*Brown*)) = *Brown* and ((2,3,5), *Brown*) is a test for G$_-$. All values are deleted and all GMRTs for G$_-$ have been obtained.

The projection is a subset of object descriptions defined on a restricted subset *t** of values. Let *s** be the subset of indices of objects the descriptions of which produce the projection. In the projection, splus(*m*) = obj(*m*) ∩ *s**, *m* ∈ *t**.

It is useful to introduce the characteristic W(*t*) of any collection *t* of values named by the weight of *t* in the projection: W(*t*) = ‖obj(*t*) ∩ *s**‖ = ‖splus(*t*)‖ is the number of positive objects of the projection containing *t*. Let WMIN be the minimal permissible value of weight. We assume that WMIN = 1.

Let *STGOOD* be the partially ordered set of elements *s* satisfying the condition that (*s*, val(*s*)) is a good test for *D*(+).

The basic recursive procedure for solving any kind of subtask consists of applying the sequence of the following steps:

Step 1: Check whether (*s**, val(*s**)) is a test and if so, then *s** is stored in *STGOOD* if *s** corresponds to a good test at the current step; in this case, the subtask is over. Otherwise the next step is performed.

Step 2: For each value *m* in the projection, the weight W(*m*) is determined and if the weight is less than WMIN, then the value *m* is deleted from the projection. We can also delete the value *m* if W(*m*) is equal to WMIN and (splus (*m*), val(splus(*m*)) is not a test – in this case *m* cannot appear in any GMRT satisfying WMIN (we use the function to_be_test(*t*): if obj(*t*) ∩ splus (*t*) = obj(*t*) (obj(*t*) ⊆ *s**) then *true* else *false*).

Step 3: The value *m* can be deleted from the projection if splus(*m*) ⊆ *s* for some *s* ∈ *STGOOD*.

Step 4: For each value *m* in the projection, check whether (splus(*m*), val(splus(*m*))) is a test and if so, then value *m* is deleted from the projection and splus(*m*) is stored in *STGOOD* if it corresponds to a good test at the current step.

Step 5: If at least one value has been deleted, then the reduction of the projection is necessary. The reduction consists in checking, for each element *t* of the projection, whether (obj(*t*), *t*) is not a test (as a result of previous eliminating values) and if so, this element is deleted from the projection. If, under reduction, at least one element has been deleted, then Step 2, Step 3, Step 4, and Step 5 are repeated.

Step 6: Check whether the subtask is over or not. The subtask is over when either the projection is empty or the intersection of all elements of the projection corresponds to a test (see, please, Step 1). If the subtask is not over, then the choice of an object (value) in this projection is selected and the new subtask is formed. The new subsets *s** and *t** are constructed and the basic algorithm runs recursively.

Forming the Set *STGOOD*

Let $L(S)$ be the set of all subsets of the set S. $L(S)$ is the set lattice (Rasiova, 1974). The ordering determined in the set lattice coincides with the set-theoretical inclusion. It will be said that subset s_1 is absorbed by subset s_2, that is $s_1 \leq s_2$, if and only if the inclusion relation is hold between them, that is $s_1 \subseteq s_2$. Under formation of *STGOOD*, a collection s of object indices is stored in *STGOOD* if and only if it is not absorbed by any element of this set. It is necessary also to delete from *STGOOD* all the elements that are absorbed by s if s is stored in *STGOOD*. Thus, when the algorithm is over, the set *STGOOD* contains all the collections of objects that correspond to GMRTs and only such collections.

The set *TGOOD* of all the GMRTs is obtained as follows: $TGOOD = \{tg: tg = (s, \text{val}(s)), s \in STGOOD\}$.

Selecting and Ordering Sub-Contexts in Inferring GMRTs

Inferring GMRTs is constructed by the rules of selecting and ordering sub-contexts of the main context. Before entering into the details, we give some new definitions.

Definition 6: Let t be a set of values such that $(\text{obj}(t), t)$ is a test for G_+. We say that the value $m \in M$, $m \in t$ is essential in t if $(\text{obj}(t\backslash m), (t\backslash m))$ is not a test for a given set of object.

Generally, we are interested in finding the maximal subset $\text{sbmax}(t) \subset t$ such that $(\text{obj}(t), t)$ is a test but $(\text{obj}(\text{sbmax}(t)), \text{sbmax}(t))$ is not a test for a given set of positive objects. Then $\text{sbmin}(t) = t\backslash\text{sbmax}(t)$ is a minimal set of essential values in t.

Definition 7: Let $s \subseteq G_+$; assume also that $(s, \text{val}(s))$ is not a test. The object $t_j, j \in s$ is said to be an essential in s if $(s\backslash j, \text{val}(s\backslash j))$ proves to be a test for a given set of positive objects.

Generally, we are interested in finding the maximal subset $\text{sbmax}(s) \subset s$ such that $(s, \text{val}(s))$ is not a test but $(\text{sbmax}(s), \text{val}(\text{sbmax}(s)))$ is a test for a given set of positive objects. Then $\text{sbmin}(s) = s\backslash\text{sbmax}(s)$ is a minimal set of essential objects in s.

Finding quasi-maximal (minimal) subsets of objects and values is the key procedure behind searching for initial content of STGOOD and determining the number of subtasks to be solved.

An Approach for Searching for Initial Content of *STGOOD*

In the beginning of inferring GMRTs, the set *STGOOD* is empty. Next, we describe a procedure to obtain the initial content of it. This procedure extracts a quasi-maximal subset $s^* \subseteq G_+$ which is the extent of a test for G_+ (maybe not good).

We begin with the first index i_1 of s^*, then we take the next index i_2 of s^* and evaluate the function to_be_test $(\{i_1, i_2\}, \text{val}(\{i_1, i_2\}))$. If the value of the function is *true*, then we take the next index i_3 of s^* and evaluate the function to_be_test $(\{i_1, i_2, i_3\}, \text{val}(\{i_1, i_2, i_3\}))$. If the value of the function to_be_test $(\{i_1, i_2\}, \text{val}(\{i_1, i_2\}))$ is *false*, then the index i_2 of s^* is skipped and the function to_be_test $(\{i_1, i_3\}, \text{val}(\{i_1, i_3\})))$ is evaluated. We continue this process until we achieve the last index of s^*.

To obtain the initial content of *STGOOD*, we use the set SPLUS = $\{\text{splus}(m): m \in M\}$ and apply the procedure described above to each element of SPLUS.

Table 2. The set D(+) of positive object descriptions

Index of Object	D(+)
1	$m_1\ m_2\ m_5\ m_6\ m_{21}\ m_{23}\ m_{24}\ m_{26}$
2	$m_4\ m_7\ m_8\ m_9\ m_{12}\ m_{14}\ m_{15}\ m_{22}\ m_{23}\ m_{24}\ m_{26}$
3	$m_3\ m_4\ m_7\ m_{12}\ m_{13}\ m_{14}\ m_{15}\ m_{18}\ m_{19}\ m_{24}\ m_{26}$
4	$m_1\ m_4\ m_5\ m_6\ m_7\ m_{12}\ m_{14}\ m_{15}\ m_{16}\ m_{20}\ m_{21}\ m_{24}\ m_{26}$
5	$m_2\ m_6\ m_{23}\ m_{24}$
6	$m_7\ m_{20}\ m_{21}\ m_{26}$
7	$m_3\ m_4\ m_5\ m_6\ m_{12}\ m_{14}\ m_{15}\ m_{20}\ m_{22}\ m_{24}\ m_{26}$
8	$m_3\ m_6\ m_7\ m_8\ m_9\ m_{13}\ m_{14}\ m_{15}\ m_{19}\ m_{20}\ m_{21}\ m_{22}$
9	$m_{16}\ m_{18}\ m_{19}\ m_{20}\ m_{21}\ m_{22}\ m_{26}$
10	$m_2\ m_3\ m_4\ m_5\ m_6\ m_8\ m_9\ m_{13}\ m_{18}\ m_{20}\ m_{21}\ m_{26}$
11	$m_1\ m_2\ m_3\ m_7\ m_{19}\ m_{20}\ m_{21}\ m_{22}\ m_{26}$
12	$m_2\ m_3\ m_{16}\ m_{20}\ m_{21}\ m_{23}\ m_{24}\ m_{26}$
13	$m_1\ m_4\ m_{18}\ m_{19}\ m_{23}\ m_{26}$
14	$m_{23}\ m_{24}\ m_{26}$

Table 3. The set D(−) of negative object descriptions

Index of Object	D(−)	Index of Object	D(−)
15	$m_3\ m_8\ m_{16}\ m_{23}\ m_{24}$	32	$m_1\ m_2\ m_3\ m_7\ m_9\ m_{13}\ m_{18}$
16	$m_7\ m_8\ m_9\ m_{16}\ m_{18}$	33	$m_1\ m_5\ m_6\ m_8\ m_9\ m_{19}\ m_{20}\ m_{22}$
17	$m_1\ m_{21}\ m_{22}\ m_{24}\ m_{26}$	34	$m_2\ m_8\ m_9\ m_{18}\ m_{20}\ m_{21}\ m_{22}\ m_{23}\ m_{26}$
18	$m_1\ m_7\ m_8\ m_9\ m_{13}\ m_{16}$	35	$m_1\ m_2\ m_4\ m_5\ m_6\ m_7\ m_9\ m_{13}\ m_{16}$
19	$m_2\ m_6\ m_7\ m_9\ m_{21}\ m_{23}$	36	$m_1\ m_2\ m_6\ m_7\ m_8\ m_{13}\ m_{16}\ m_{18}$
20	$m_{19}\ m_{20}\ m_{21}\ m_{22}\ m_{24}$	37	$m_1\ m_2\ m_3\ m_4\ m_5\ m_6\ m_7\ m_{12}\ m_{14}\ m_{15}\ m_{16}$
21	$m_1\ m_{20}\ m_{21}\ m_{22}\ m_{23}\ m_{24}$	38	$m_1\ m_2\ m_3\ m_4\ m_5\ m_6\ m_9\ m_{12}\ m_{13}\ m_{16}$
22	$m_1\ m_3\ m_6\ m_7\ m_9\ m_{16}$	39	$m_1\ m_2\ m_3\ m_4\ m_5\ m_6\ m_{14}\ m_{15}\ m_{19}\ m_{20}\ m_{23}\ m_{26}$
23	$m_2\ m_6\ m_8\ m_9\ m_{14}\ m_{15}\ m_{16}$	40	$m_2\ m_3\ m_4\ m_5\ m_6\ m_7\ m_{12}\ m_{13}\ m_{14}\ m_{15}\ m_{16}$
24	$m_1\ m_4\ m_5\ m_6\ m_7\ m_8\ m_{16}$	41	$m_2\ m_3\ m_4\ m_5\ m_6\ m_7\ m_9\ m_{12}\ m_{13}\ m_{14}\ m_{15}\ m_{19}$
25	$m_7\ m_{13}\ m_{19}\ m_{20}\ m_{22}\ m_{26}$	42	$m_1\ m_2\ m_3\ m_4\ m_5\ m_6\ m_{12}\ m_{16}\ m_{18}\ m_{19}\ m_{20}\ m_{21}\ m_{26}$
26	$m_1\ m_2\ m_3\ m_5\ m_6\ m_7\ m_{16}$	43	$m_4\ m_5\ m_6\ m_7\ m_8\ m_9\ m_{12}\ m_{13}\ m_{14}\ m_{15}\ m_{16}$
27	$m_1\ m_2\ m_3\ m_5\ m_6\ m_{13}\ m_{18}$	44	$m_3\ m_4\ m_5\ m_6\ m_8\ m_9\ m_{12}\ m_{13}\ m_{14}\ m_{15}\ m_{18}\ m_{19}$
28	$m_1\ m_3\ m_7\ m_{13}\ m_{19}\ m_{21}$	45	$m_1\ m_2\ m_3\ m_4\ m_5\ m_6\ m_7\ m_8\ m_9\ m_{12}\ m_{13}\ m_{14}\ m_{15}$
29	$m_1\ m_4\ m_5\ m_6\ m_7\ m_8\ m_{13}\ m_{16}$	46	$m_1\ m_3\ m_4\ m_5\ m_6\ m_7\ m_{12}\ m_{13}\ m_{14}\ m_{15}\ m_{16}\ m_{23}\ m_{24}$
30	$m_1\ m_2\ m_3\ m_6\ m_{12}\ m_{14}\ m_{15}\ m_{16}$	47	$m_1\ m_2\ m_3\ m_4\ m_5\ m_6\ m_8\ m_9\ m_{12}\ m_{14}\ m_{16}\ m_{18}\ m_{22}$
31	$m_1\ m_2\ m_5\ m_6\ m_{14}\ m_{15}\ m_{16}\ m_{26}$	48	$m_2\ m_8\ m_9\ m_{12}\ m_{14}\ m_{15}\ m_{16}$

To illustrate this procedure, we use the sets $D(+)$ and $D(-)$ represented in Tables 2 and 3. In these tables, $M = \{m_1, \ldots, m_{26}\}$.

The set SPLUS for positive class of examples is in Table 4. The initial content of $STGOOD = \{(2,10), (3, 10), (3, 8), (4, 12), (1, 4, 7), (1, 5,12\}, (2, 7, 8), (3, 7, 12), (1, 2, 12, 14), (2, 3, 4, 7), (4, 6, 8, 11)\}$. In this table and in what follows, we denote subsets of values $(m_8\, m_9)$, $(m_{14}\, m_{15})$ by m_* and m_+, respectively. Applying operation generalization_of$(s) = s'' = obj(val(s))$ to $s \in STGOOD$, we obtain:

$STGOOD = \{(2,10), (3, 10), (3, 8), (4, 7, 12), (1, 4, 7), (1, 5,12\}, (2, 7, 8), (3, 7, 12), (1, 2, 12, 14), (2, 3, 4, 7), (4, 6, 8, 11)\}$.

By Theorem 1, we can delete value m_{12} from consideration (see, please, splus(m_{12}) in Table 4).

The initial content of *STGOOD* allows to decrease the number of using the procedure to_be_test() and the number of putting extents of tests into *STGOOD*. Apart from this, it helps to find essential objects in sub-contexts (projections).

The number of subtasks to be solved. This number is determined by the number of essential values in the set M. The quasi-minimal subset of essential values in M we can find by a procedure analogous to the procedure applicable to search for the initial content of *STGOOD*.

We begin with the first value m_1 of M, then we take the next value m_2 of M and evaluate the function to_be_test $(obj(\{m_1, m_2\}), \{m_1, m_2\})$. If the value of the function is *false*, then we take the next value m_3 of M and evaluate the function to_be_test $(obj(\{m_1, m_2, m_3\}), \{m_1, m_2, m_3\})$. If the value of the function to_be_test $(obj(\{m_1, m_2\}), \{m_1, m_2\})$ is *true*, then value m_2 of M is skipped and the function to_be_test $(obj(\{m_1, m_3\}), \{m_1, m_3\})$ is evaluated. We continue this process until we achieve the last value of M.

As a result of this procedure, we have quasi-maximal subset sbmax(M), such that $(obj(sbmax(M)), sbmax(M))$ is not a test for positive examples. Then subset LEV = M\sbmax(M) is quasi-minimal subset of essential values in M.

For our example, we have list LEV = $(m_{16}, m_{18}, m_{19}, m_{20}, m_{21}, m_{22}, m_{23}, m_{24}, m_{26})$.

Proposition 1: Each essential value is included at least in one positive object description.

Proof of Proposition 1. Assume that for an object description t_i, $i \in G_+$, we have $t_i \cap$ LEV $= \varnothing$. Then $t_i \subseteq$ M\LEV. But M\LEV is included at least in one of negative object descriptions and, consequently, t_i also possesses of this property. But it contradicts to the fact that t_i is a description of positive object.

Table 4. The set SPLUS

SPLUS = {splus(m_i): $m_i \in M$}	
splus(m_*) → {2,8,10}	splus(m_{22}) → {2,7,8,9,11}
splus(m_{13}) → {3,8,10}	splus(m_{23}) → {1,2,5,12,13,14}
splus(m_{16}) → {4,9,12}	splus(m_3) → {3,7,8,10,11,12}
splus(m_1) → {1,4,11,13}	splus(m_4) → {2,3,4,7,10,13}
splus(m_5) → {1,4,7,10}	splus(m_6) → {1,4,5,7,8,10}
splus(m_{12}) → {2,3, 4,7}	splus(m_7) → {2,3,4,6,8,11}
splus(m_{18}) → {3,9,10,13}	splus(m_{24}) → {1,2,3,4,5,7,12,14}
splus(m_2) → {1,5,10,11,12}	splus(m_{20}) → {4,6,7,8,9,10,11,12}
splus(m_+) → {2,3,4,7,8}	splus(m_{21}) → {1,4,6,8,9,10,11,12}
splus(m_{19}) → {3,8,9,11,13}	splus(m_{26}) → {1,2,3,4,6,7,9,10,11,12,13,14}

Proposition 2: Assume that $X \subseteq M$. If $X \cap LEV = \varnothing$, then to_be_test(obj(X), X)) = *false*.

This proposition is the consequence of Proposition 1.

Proposition 3: For finding all GRMTs containing in a given classification context, it is sufficient to solve this problem only for sub-contexts associated with essential values.

Note that the description of $t_{14} = \{m_{23}, m_{24}, m_{26}\}$ is closed because of obj($\{m_{23}, m_{24}, m_{26}\} = \{1, 2, 12, 14\}$ and val($\{1, 2, 12, 14\} = \{m_{23}, m_{24}, m_{26}\}$. We have obtained this result during generalization of elements of *STGOOD*. So (obj($\{m_{23}, m_{24}, m_{26}\}$)), $\{m_{23}, m_{24}, m_{26}\}$) is a maximally redundant test for positive objects and we can, consequently, delete t_{14} from consideration.

As a result of deleting m_{12} and t_{14}, we have the modified set SPLUS (Table 5).

Table 5. The modified set SPLUS

SPLUS = {splus(m_i): $m_i \in M$}	
splus(m_8) → {2,8,10}	splus(m_{22}) → {2,7,8,9,11}
splus(m_{13}) → {3,8,10}	splus(m_{23}) → {1,2,5,12,13}
splus(m_{16}) → {4,9,12}	splus(m_3) → {3,7,8,10,11,12}
splus(m_1) → {1,4,11,13}	splus(m_4) → {2,3,4,7,10,13}
splus(m_5) → {1,4,7,10}	splus(m_6) → {1,4,5,7,8,10}
splus(m_{18}) → {3,9,10,13}	splus(m_7) → {2,3,4,6,8,11}
splus(m_2) → {1,5,10,11,12}	splus(m_{24}) → {1,2,3,4,5,7,12}
splus(m_4) → {2,3,4,7,8}	splus(m_{20}) → {4,6,7,8,9,10,11,12}
splus(m_{19}) → {3,8,9,11,13}	splus(m_{21}) → {1,4,6,8,9,10,11,12}
	splus(m_{26}) → {1,2,3,4,6,7,9,10,11,12,13}

Table 6. Auxiliary information

Index of Object	m_{16}	m_{18}	m_{19}	m_{20}	m_{21}	m_{22}	m_{23}	m_{24}	m_{26}	$\sum(m_{ij})$
1					1		1	1	1	4
2						1	1	1	1	4
3		1	1					1	1	4
5							1	1		2
7				1		1		1	1	4
9	1	1	1	1	1	1			1	7
10		1		1	1				1	4
12	1			1	1		1	1	1	6
13		1	1				1		1	4
4	1				1	1		1	1	
6					1	1			1	
8			1	1	1	1			1	
11			1	1	1	1			1	
$\sum$(ti)	2	4	3	4	4	3	5	6	8	39

The main question is how we should approach the problem of selecting and ordering subtasks (sub-contexts). Consider Table 6 with auxiliary information. The columns of it correspond to the essential values, the lines of it correspond to the objects of the main classification context.

It is clear that if we shall have all the intents of GMRTs entering into descriptions of objects 1, 2, 3, 5, 7, 9, 10, 12, and 13, then the main task will be over because the remaining object descriptions (objects 4, 6, 8, 11) give, in their intersection, the intent of already known test (see, please, the initial content of *STGOOD*). Thus, we have to consider only the sub-contexts of essential values associated with object descriptions 1, 2, 3, 5, 7, 9, 10, 12, 13. The number of such sub-contexts is 39. However, this estimation is not realistic.

We begin with ordering indices of objects by the number of their entering into elements of STGOOD (Table 7).

Now we shall select sub-contexts (subtasks), based on proj$[t \times m]$, where t is object description whose index enters into smallest number of elements of STGOOD and m is an essential value in t, entering in the smallest number of object descriptions in proj (t) (we do not consider objects 4, 6, 8, 11). After solving each subtask, we have to correct the sets *SPLUS*, *STGOOD*, and Auxiliary information. So, the first sub-task is $t_9 \times m_{16}$. Solving this sub-task, we have not any new test, but we can delete m_{16} from t_9 and then we solve the sub-task $t_9 \times m_{19}$. As a result, we introduce $s = \{9, 11\}$ in *STGOOD* and delete t_9 from consideration because of m_{16}, m_{19} are the only essential values in this object description (each object description has several individual minimal subset of essential values).

Then we solve subtasks $t_{13} \times m_{19}$ and $t_{13} \times m_{18}$. The result is introducing $s = \{13\}$ in *STGOOD* and deleting t_{13} because m_{18} is the only essential value in this object description. After deleting t_9, $t_{13,}$ we can modify *SPLUS* and delete from it $splus(m_{16}) = \{4, 12\}$ and $splus(m_{18}) = \{3,10\}$. This means that we delete from consideration values m_{16}, m_{18}.

Table 8 and 9 contain the modified set *SPLUS* and Auxiliary information.

In this example, we have the following sequence of subtasks (Table 10).

Table 7. Ordering indices of objects

Index of object	9	13	5	10	1	2	3	12	7
The number of entering into elements of STGOOD	0	0	1	2	3	4	4	4	5

Table 8. The modified set SPLUS(2)

SPLUS = {splus(m_i): $m_i \in M$}	
$splus(m_*) \rightarrow \{2,8,10\}$ $splus(m_{13}) \rightarrow \{3,8,10\}$ $splus(m_1) \rightarrow \{1,4,11\}$ $splus(m_5) \rightarrow \{1,4,7,10\}$ $splus(m_2) \rightarrow \{1,5,10,11,12\}$ $splus(m_+) \rightarrow \{2,3,4,7,8\}$ $splus(m_{19}) \rightarrow \{3,8,11\}$	$splus(m_{22}) \rightarrow \{2,7,8,11\}$ $splus(m_{23}) \rightarrow \{1,2,5,12\}$ $splus(m_3) \rightarrow \{3,7,8,10,11,12\}$ $splus(m_4) \rightarrow \{2,3,4,7,10\}$ $splus(m_6) \rightarrow \{1,4,5,7,8,10\}$ $splus(m_7) \rightarrow \{2,3,4,6,8,11\}$ $splus(m_{24}) \rightarrow \{1,2,3,4,5,7,12\}$ $splus(m_{20}) \rightarrow \{4,6,7,8,10,11,12\}$ $splus(m_{21}) \rightarrow \{1,4,6,8,10,11,12\}$ $splus(m_{26}) \rightarrow \{1,2,3,4,6,7,10,11,12\}$

Table 9. Auxiliary information (2)

Index of Object	m_{19}	m_{20}	m_{21}	m_{22}	m_{23}	m_{24}	m_{26}	$\sum(m_{ij})$
1			1		1	1	1	4
2				1	1	1	1	4
3	1					1	1	3
5					1	1		2
7		1		1		1	1	4
10		1	1				1	3
12		1	1		1	1	1	5
4		1	1			1	1	
6		1	1				1	
8	1	1	1	1			1	
11	1	1	1	1			1	
$\sum(t_i)$	1	3	3	2	4	6	6	25

Table 10. The sequence of subtasks

N	Sub-Context	Extent of New Test	Deleted Values	Deleted Objects
1	$t_9 \times m_{16}$			
2	$t_9 \times m_{19}$	(9, 11)		t_9
3	$t_{13} \times m_{18}$			
4	$t_{13} \times m_{19}$	(13)	m_{16}, m_{18}	t_{13}
5	$t_5 \times m_{23}$	-	m_{23}	
6	$t_5 \times m_{24}$			t_5
7	$t_{10} \times m_{20}$	(8,10)		
8	$t_{10} \times m_{21}$			
9	$t_{10} \times m_{26}$		m_{*}, m_{13}, m_4, m_5	t_{10}
10	$t_1 \times m_{21}$			
11	$t_1 \times m_{24}$		m_1, m_2	t_1
12	$t_2 \times m_{22}$	(7,8,11)	m_{22}	
13	$t_2 \times m_{24}$			
14	$t_2 \times m_{26}$			t_2
15	$t_3 \times m_{19}$	(3,11)	m_{19}	
16	$t_3 \times m_{24}$		m_{24}	t_{12}, t_7
17	$t_3 \times m_{26}$			t_3

The final content of STGOOD ={(13), (2,10), (3, 10), (3, 8), (3,11), (8,10), (9,11), (4, 7, 12), (1, 4, 7), (1, 5,12}, (2, 7, 8), (3, 7, 12), (7,8,11), (1, 2, 12, 14), (2, 3, 4, 7), (4, 6, 8, 11)}. Table 11 shows the sets *STGOOD* and *TGOOD*.

All subtasks did not require recursion.

Table 11. The final sets STGOOD and TGOOD

STGOOD	TGOOD	Nº	STGOOD	TGOOD
13	$m_1\, m_4\, m_{18}\, m_{19}\, m_{23}\, m_{26}$	9	2,7,8	$m_+\, m_{22}$
2,10	$m_4\, m_*\, m_{26}$	10	1,5,12	$m_2\, m_{23}\, m_{24}$
3,10	$m_3\, m_4\, m_{13}\, m_{18}\, m_{26}$	11	4,7,12	$m_{20}\, m_{24}\, m_{26}$
8,10	$m_3\, m_6\, m_*\, m_{13}\, m_{20}\, m_{21}$	12	3,7,12	$m_3\, m_{24}\, m_{26}$
9,11	$m_{19}\, m_{20}\, m_{21}\, m_{22}\, m_{26}$	13	7,8,11	$m_3\, m_{20}\, m_{22}$
3,11	$m_3\, m_7\, m_{19}\, m_{26}$	14	2,3,4,7	$m_4\, m_{12}\, m_+\, m_{24}\, m_{26}$
3,8	$m_3\, m_7\, m_{13}\, m_+\, m_{19}$	15	4,6,8,11	$m_7\, m_{20}\, m_{21}$
1,4,7	$m_5\, m_6\, m_{24}\, m_{26}$	16	1,2,12,14	$m_{23}\, m_{24}\, m_{26}$

Some modification of this algorithm are given in (Naidenova &Parkchomenko, 2014).

There are various ways of using the proposed decomposition and extracted initial information about GMRTs, but we confine ourselves to the most important ideas allowing to obtain not only classification tests but also, simultaneously, contexts inside of which these tests have been inferred. The contexts can be used during deductive phases of classification reasoning. But applying context for pattern recognition is a problem for future research.

The most efficient program for GDTs inferring and their using for pattern recognition is the Diagnostic Test Machine (DTM) (Naidenova & Shagalov, 2009). This program is based on the subtask of the second kind. The experiment conducted with publicly available dataset of 8124 mushrooms have showed that the result of the DTM turned out to be better with respect to classification accuracy (97,5%) than the result (95%) informed in (Schlimmer, 1987.) for the same dataset.

CONCLUSION

In this chapter, a sketch of classification reasoning system is given. The key concepts of this system are concepts of classification and its good approximations based on GDTs. The good tests have the dual nature: they generate functional and implicative dependencies and, in the same time, sets of objects satisfying these dependencies. The dependencies are logical assertions on the base of which deductive phase of classification reasoning is realized. Inductive classification reasoning consists in inferring GDTs for a given context in the form of attributive object descriptions. We have given an algorithm for inferring GMRTs from a set of data. We have introduced a decomposition of the main task of inferring GMRTs into subtasks associated with the certain types of sub-contexts. There are various ways of using the proposed decomposition and extracted initial information about GMRTs, but we confine ourselves to the most important ideas allowing to obtain not only classification tests but also, simultaneously, contexts inside of which these tests have been inferred. The contexts obtained can be used during deductive phases of classification reasoning.

REFERENCES

Baixeries, J., Kaytoue, M., & Napoli, A. (2012). Computing Functional Dependencies with Pattern Structures. In *Proceedings of the 11ᵗʰ International Conference on "Concept lattices and their applications"* (vol. 972, pp. 175-186). CEUR WS.

Bynum, T. (Ed.). (1972). *Conceptual notation and related articles*. Oxford, UK: Clarendon Press.

Ganter, B., & Wille, R. (1992). *Formal Concept Analysis: Mathematical foundations*. Berlin: Springer.

Kropov, P. A. (1995). *Interpretation of forest types in the mountain forests of Siberia and Mongolia for Aerospace imagery mapping*. (Unpublished doctoral dissertation). Forest Technical Academy, SPB (in Russian).

Kuznetsov, S. O. (2005). Galois connections in data analysis: contributions from the Soviet Era and modern Russian research. In *Formal Concept Analysis, LNAI 3626* (pp. 196–226). Berlin: Springer-Verlag.

Kuznetsov, S. O., Kundu, M. K., Mandal, D. P., & Pal, S. K. (Eds.). (2011). *Proceedings of the 4th International Conference "Pattern Recognition and Machine Intelligence"* (LNCS), (vol. 6744). Springer.

Michalski, R., & Kaufman, K. (1998). Data Mining and Knowledge Discovery: A review of Issues and a Multi-strategy Approach. In R. S. Michalski, I. Bratko, & M. Kubat (Eds.), *Machine learning and Data Mining: Methods and Applications* (pp. 71–112). London: John Wiley & Sons.

Mill, J. S. (1872). *The System of Logic Ratiocinative and Inductive Being a Connected View of the Principles of Evidence, and the Methods of Scientific Investigation* (Vol. 1). London: West Strand.

Naidenova, X. (2011). Constructing Galois lattice in good classification tests mining. In Dmitry I. Ignatov, Sergei O. Kuznetsov, Jonas Poelmans (Eds), *International Workshop on concept discovery in unstructured data* (pp. 43-48). Moscow: The National Research University High School of Economics.

Naidenova, X., & Ermakov, A. E. (2001). The decomposition of good diagnostic test inferring algorithms. In *Proceedings of the 4-th International Conference «Computer-Aided Design of Discrete Devices" (CAD DD'2001)* (*vol. 3*, pp. 61-68). Belarus, Minsk: Institute of Technical Cybernetics.

Naidenova, X. A. (1982). Relational model for analyzing experimental data. *The Transaction of Acad. Sci. of USSR. Series Technical Cybernetics, 4*, 103–119.

Naidenova, X. A. (1992). Machine learning as a diagnostic task. In I. Arefiev (Ed.), *Knowledge-Dialogue-Solution, Materials of the Short-Term Scientific Seminar*, (pp. 26-36). Saint-Petersburg, Russia: State North-West Technical University. doi:10.4018/978-1-60566-810-9.ch006

Naidenova, X. A. (1996). Reducing machine learning tasks to the approximation of a given classification on a given set of examples. In *Proceedings of the 5-th National Conference at Artificial Intelligence* (vol. 1, pp. 275-279). Academic Press.

Naidenova, X. A. (2006). An Incremental Learning Algorithm for Inferring Logical Rules from Exampled in the Framework of the Common Reasoning Process. In E. Triantaphyllou & G. Felici (Eds.), *Data Mining and Knowledge Discovery Approaches Based on Rule Induction Techniques* (pp. 89–147). Heidelberg, Germany: Springer. doi:10.1007/0-387-34296-6_3

Naidenova, X. A. (2012). Good Classification Tests as Formal Concepts. In F. Domenach, D. I. Ignatov, & J. Poelmans (Eds.), ICFCA 2012, LNAI 7278 (pp. 211–226). Springer.

Naidenova, X. A., & Parkchomenko, V. L. (2014). Attributive and object sub-contexts in inferring good maximally redundant tests. In *Proceedings of the 11ᵗʰ International Conference on "Concept lattices and their applications"* (pp. 181-193). Pavol Jozef Šafárik Univercity in Košice: SAIS.

Naidenova, X. A., & Polegaeva, J. G. (1985). Model of human reasoning for deciphering forest's images and its implementation on computer. In *Semiotic aspects of the intellectual activity formalization, Theses of Papers and Reports of School-Seminar* (pp. 49–52). Kutaisy, Georgia Soviet Socialist Republic. (in Russian)

Naidenova, X. A., & Polegaeva, J. G. (1986). An algorithm of finding the best diagnostic tests. In G. E. Mintz & P. P. Lorents (Eds.), *The application of mathematical logic methods* (pp. 63–67). Tallinn, Estonia: Institute of Cybernetics, National Acad. of Sciences of Estonia. (in Russian)

Naidenova, X. A., & Shagalov, V. L. (2009). Diagnostic Test Machine. In: M. Auer (Ed.), *Proceedings of the Interactive Computer Aided Learning Conference* (pp. 505-507). Austria: Kassel University Press.

Ob'iedkov, S., & Duquenne, V. (2007). Attribute-incremental construction of the canonical implication basis. *Annals of Mathematics and Artificial Intelligence Archive*, 49(1-4), 77–99. doi:10.1007/s10472-007-9057-2

Ore, O. (1944). Galois Connexions. *Transactions of the American Mathematical Society*, 55(1), 493–513. doi:10.1090/S0002-9947-1944-0010555-7

Piaget, J., & Inhelder, B. (1959). *La Genèse des Structures Logiques Elémentaires Classifications et Sériations*. Neuchâtel: Delachaux & Niestlé.

Poya, G. (1954). *Mathematics and plausible reasoning*. Princeton, NJ: Princeton Univrsity Press.

Quinlan, J. R., & Rivest, R. L. (1989). Inferring Decision Trees Using the Minimum Description Length Principle. *Information and Computation*, 80(3), 227–248. doi:10.1016/0890-5401(89)90010-2

Rasiowa, H. (1974). An algebraic Approach to Non-classical Logics. PWN, Polish Scientific Publishers: Warszawa and North-Holland Publishing Company.

Russel, S., & Norvig, P. (2010). *Artificial Intelligence. A Modern approach*. Prentice Hall.

Sechenov, I. M. (2001). Elements of Thoughts. Saint-Petersburg, Russia: Publishing House "Piter".

Slimmer, J. S. (1987). *Concept acquisition through representational adjustment*. Technical report 87-19. Department of Information and Computer Science, University of California, Irvine.

Spencer, H. (1898). *Principles of Psychology*. Academic Press.

KEY TERMS AND DEFINITIONS

Classification Reasoning: Reasoning based on classification operations (generalization and specification).

Conceptual Learning: Extracting concepts from observations and examples.

Deductive Reasoning Rule: A rule with the help of which good classification tests are used for pattern recognition.

Good Classification Test: A set of attributes' values distinguishes between a maximally possible number of objects of a given class and objects of alternative class (classes).

Inductive Reasoning Rule: A rule with the use of which good classification tests are inferred from a data set.

Task of the First Kind: Inferring good tests restricted by a set of attributes' values.

Task of the Second Kind: Inferring good tests restricted by a set of object descriptions.

Chapter 21
Readable Diagrammatic Query Language ViziQuer

Martins Zviedris
Institute of Mathematics and Computer Science, Latvia

ABSTRACT

End-user interaction with data is one of key aspects in data processing. Nowadays a lot of information systems have a custom made user interface for data input and data querying. From 1970s it is envisioned that a generic, user-friendly approach for data querying could be built, but no wide spread solution has been developed. In the paper we present a diagrammatic query language. We have done an iterative approach to design and improve the diagrammatic query language to make it user readable. Readability is analyzed with questionnaires. Readable diagrammatic query language is the first step to create a more generic and user-friendly data querying.

INTRODUCTION

Databases are keystone in modern data storage. Databases comes hand in hand with data access via query language or user-friendly interfaces that uses predefined queries. Data access and analytics is vital part of data processing. Still, there is ongoing research how to develop more users-friendly and easier-to-use data interface for domain specialist users.

Graphical query languages as an interaction level between databases and end-users have been developed from late 1970s. One of the first proposed solution was Query-by-example that was developed at the IBM (Zloof 1975). Similar approach with table-based interfaces is used other existing solutions, for example, Microsoft Access query designer.

A wide survey (Catarci, Costabile, Levialdi & Batini 1997) gives an overview of different query languages designed for SQL. The survey divides languages into three paradigms – diagrammatic, iconic and form-based. It is also possible to combine two of named paradigms together. The survey does not separate a query language syntax from the tool that supports the query formulation process for an end-users[1]. Four different approaches for query formulation in a tool are named – by schema navigation, by sub-queries[2], by matching and by range selection[3].

DOI: 10.4018/978-1-4666-8767-7.ch021

In a paper (Catarci & Santucci 1995) is given an example analysis that compares how well an end-user can write a query in a diagrammatic language QBD[4] compared to the SQL. One of main conclusions state that naïve and intermediate end-users writes queries faster and more precise in QBD rather than in the SQL. Expert users have similar results in both languages. Similar comparison of visual and textual query languages is given in (Catarci T. & Santucci G. 1995-1).

By emergence of the Semantic Web (Berners-Lee, Hendler & Lassila 2001) scientists refocused on new visual query language designs. Main feature that enable visual language redesign is that data in the Semantic Web is stored in a more semantically understandable way for end-users as the data has less technical details compared to data in relational databases.

First of all, primary and foreign keys in the Semantic Web are omitted. In our opinion, this is vital gain as in relational databases these technical terms is presented with additional column that is not easy explainable to domain end-users.

Other features includes – objects that can be contained in more than just one class, while in relational databases each object is contained in exactly one class (relation). This gives ability to define object class hierarchies in explicit manner rather than implicit via attribute values that are commonly used in relational databases design. Secondly, in the Semantic Web is no need to implement additional tables for n-to-n relations as relations. More detailed explanation between relational databases and the Semantic Web approach is available at (Barzdins, Barzdins & Cerans 2008).

As in relational databases is developed the formal query language SQL then in the Semantic Web is developed query language SPARQL (Harris & Seaborne 2013). We will not cover SPARQL in more details in this paper as there is a lot of different sources that explain SPARQL, for example, beginners tutorial (Baskauf 2014).

There are different solutions that propose a graphical notation rather than textual syntax for a query composition. For example, GRQL (Athanasis, Christophides & Kotzinos 2004), ViziQuer (Zviedris & Barzdins 2011), Tabulator (Berners-Lee et al. 2006), gFacet (Heim, Ertl & Ziegler 2010), NiteLight (Russell & Smart 2008), Gruff (Franz 2015), SPARQLgraph (Schweiger et al. 2014), OptiqueVQS (Soylu et al. 2013) or VisiNav (Harth 2010). Different approach try to utilize in the Semantic Web included semantics and generate SPARQL queries from keywords. The approach is called SPARK (Zhou, Wang, Xiong, Wang & Yu 2007).

In our opinion, one of the main drawbacks of existing approaches is that developers do not study how well end-users perceive developed query language. Languages are developed more from a viewpoint of researchers rather than end-users.

It is well known that "one picture represents 1000 words", but it is also true that a picture can be read in 1000 different ways. Thus, it is important that picture is précises and easy to read for end-users to incorporate these 1000 words in a pinpoint manner. In this paper we give a solution that shows how diagrammatic query language is developed that it can be read in a pinpoint manner by an end-user.

In our opinion, more careful studies should be done regarding to a designed graphical query language readability. A study (Juel 1988) found that there is correlation that children, who are bad readers, tend to become bad writers. We think that this is true also in a graphical query language as it is important to grasp at first language concepts by reading them, thus becoming better writers later, as the acknowledged concepts are used to write new queries. Without good concept understanding, it is hard to use these concepts later on.

Therefore, we make an assumption that – if an end-user cannot read a query in the developed language syntax then he/she will have problems later on with query composition. Thus, each graphical language syntax at first should be tested for readability by end-users. For example, at least 75% of cases the language elements are readable by test subjects. Only then a tool for query composition should be developed.

Remaining work will be structured as following: in the section 2 will be given a short description of a diagrammatic query language that is designed in a scientific way to cover SPARQL semantics and overview of a questionnaire about language readability. In the section 3 will be given an overview of an improved diagrammatic query language where readability is considerably improved. In the section 4 will be discussed readability results of the improved diagrammatic query language. In section 5 will be presented conclusions about iterative approach to design user readable query languages.

DESIGNED DIAGRAMMATIC QUERY LANGUAGE: VIZIQUER FULL

We have developed a diagrammatic query language to represent queries for semantic databases that uses the SPARQL query language for data retrieval. The ViziQuer query notation is based on UML (OMG 2003) style diagrammatic notation. UML is used for knowledge and systems description, for example, to describe real-time systems (Selic & Rumbaugh1998).

We selected UML style design, as it is possible to represent concept classes and relations between classes in this style. Also it includes object class attributes. Thus, it covers basic elements of a data query language.

Secondly, computer scientists and IT specialists have validated the designed UML language in different use-cases (Eriksso & Magnus 1999). Overview of practical UML usage (Dobing & Parsons 2006) states that clients understand system specification and use some parts of it. Still, the overview states that full UML language complexity is a concern for its usage.

Thus, we omitted complex parts of the UML and adapted it for a diagrammatic query language. As clients sometimes use at least part of UML language to understand a systems specification (Dobing & Parsons 2006) then we thought that it is possible to adapt basic elements for query construction.

The created diagrammatic language is composed of few main elements – object class selection, restrictions on object's class attributes, relationships between classes, negation and optional relationships. More detailed language specification is described in Barzdins, Rikacovs & Zviedris (2009).

First prototype was implemented and applied in a field of medical science area (Barzdins, Liepins, Veilande & Zviedris (2008); Barzdins, Rikacovs, Veilande & Zviedris 2009). It was an experimental project that involved part of Latvian medical statistic data that was translated to the RDF and made available via a SPARQL endpoint. From the medical side there was involved around 10 end-users that queried the data for statistical analysis to verify proposed hypothesis. The users were already familiar with database data retrieval, as they had previously used SQL in some cases for data retrieval and would be categorized as intermediate end-users.

The initial results were satisfactory as in interviews with medical scientists a positive feedback about the designed query language was received. The language and the supporting tool was easy-to-use to gather initial data. The users liked that they could produce data queries faster and more convenient than they did in the SQL.

SPARQL syntax:

```
?X1 RDF:type Onto:Person
```

We should stress that medical researchers had previous experience with SQL. They also have had a formal training in data analysis, thus they should be qualified as intermediate end-users.

An early version of the designed language is described in a paper (Barzdins, Rikacovs & Zviedris (2009), but we will give a brief overview of main language elements and their translation to the SPARQL query language.

In Figure 1 is depicted a central element of the diagrammatic query language. It represents a set of objects. In the depicted case a set of all persons is presented.

In Figure 2 is depicted an expanded central element. It represents all persons that is older that 20 and has income less that 2000. We go further and define a set of attributes that will be visible in the query's answer. In this case, we want to see person's name and if a person has a nickname then also display a nickname.

In a database there is two different cases how an attributes is displayed in an answer. In the first case, all attributes must have a value. If there is an object that does not have an attributes value then it is omitted from the answer. In the second case, if there is no value for an attribute then leave a blank space for this value or display value if it has one.

The second is default practice in a relational database query languages while the first is default practice in the SPARQL as it matches all pattern including attribute. Still, we need a way to separate both cases.

SPARQL syntax:

```
SELECT ?name ?nickname WHERE {
?X1 RDF:type Onto:Person.
?X1 Onto:name ?name.
OPTIONAL {?X1 Onto:nickname ?nickname.}
?X1 Onto:age ?age.
?X1 Onto:income ?income.
FILTER (?age > XSD:integer("20") &&
?income < XSD:integer("2000")) }
```

The third building block of the query language is a relation between two objects. In Figure 3 is depicted a query that selects all persons and display all papers that a person has authored.

Figure 1. Set of objects

Figure 2. Set of object with restriction and attributes

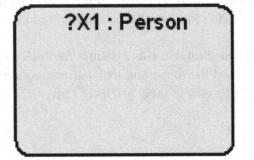

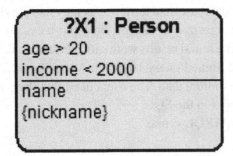

Figure 3. Object sets with a relation

Via relationship we introduce a concept of optional and negation groups. As it was possible to define an attribute in a set to be non-obligatory it is also possible to define a part of a designed query to be non-obligatory (optional). It is equivalent to left outer join in the SQL.

The optional group concept is displayed in Figure 4. It displays all persons and if a person has authored a system's description then also display a title of this description.

SPARQL syntax:

```
SELECT ?name ?surname ?title ?abstract WHERE {
?X1 RDF:type Onto:Person.
?X1 Onto:name ?name.
?X1 Onto:surname ?surname.
?X2 RDF:type Onto:Paper.
?X1 Onto:author ?X2.
?X2 Onto:title ?title.
?X2 Onto:abstract ?abstract.}
```

Similar to non-obligatory group is a negation group. With the negation group it is possible to set that a concept does not have a specific relationship. In Figure 5 we display all those persons that have not authored a system's description.

Figure 4. Non-obligatory group inside a query

Figure 5. Negation group inside a query

More elaborate elements of the diagrammatic query language is out of scope of this paper and one can find more detailed description in (Zviedris 2014). Presented elements cover the basic of the diagrammatic query language that was used to assess a readability of the designed diagrammatic query language.

SPARQL syntax:

```
SELECT ?name ?surname ?title WHERE {
?X1 RDF:type Onto:Person.
?X1 Onto:name ?name.
?X1 Onto:surname ?surname.
OPTIONAL {?X2 RDF:type Onto:SystemDescription.
?X1 ?link ?X2.
?X2 Onto:title ?title.}}
```

We use partly proposed test queries from a paper (Catarci & Santucci 1995) to verify designed query language readability. Additionally we added queries that includes optional and negation groups as in the paper (Catarci & Santucci 1995) proposed queries did not covered this aspect.

SPARQL syntax:

```
SELECT ?name ?surname ?title WHERE {
?X1 RDF:type Onto:Person.
?X1 Onto:name ?name.
?X1 Onto:surname ?surname.
OPTIONAL {?X2 RDF:type Onto:SystemDescription.
?X1 ?link ?X2.}
FILTER (!bound(?X2))}
```

An initial questionnaire included total 18 queries and covered all the basic concepts of the designed diagrammatic query language. Our approach to test the syntax readability was to present a responded with a diagrammatic query and ask him or her to explain the query in natural language.

Initial study included total 10 participants. We used crowdsourcing approach to gather answers from participants. Participants did not receive any tutorial or training in the designed query language, as we wanted to test how intuitively it was for common end-user to read presented diagrammatic concepts.

The study's main task was to assess if we are on the right track and whether or not we think alike with common end-users for whom the diagrammatic query language is intended to. The initial results was a bit shocking as only 2 out of 10 participants could explain queries correctly that included more than one object set with attributes. In total we identified four main problems in queries understanding and explanation.

First of all, end-users lacked ability to explain join operation of two object's sets. Each person that has received a formal course or lecture about databases will know one of basic operation that joins data from two object sets together. Still, this is not easy to grasp for a person that has not received a formal IT education or training.

Participants could explain examples where was joined two object sets together, but attributes to answer was taken just from one object set. The second object set was joined as condition. It is somehow possible to explain as in natural language is no concept that deals with data join from two different object sets that is used in everyday communication.

Second, users had difficulties reading queries in a *correct* order. They either started with more familiar concept class or the one that was in up left corner. It is easy to explain this error as in the existing diagrammatic query language is no hints where to start to read a query.

Third, users had difficulties to explain used variables besides object set's names. As it is normal for mathematicians and computer scientists to work with variables, but it is not well known for end-users to have day-to-day situations, where one would need to analyze expression with variables.

Fourth, participants had problems with non-obligatory groups. This concept is even harder to explain in natural language compared to the join operation.

The initial study's readability was below 50%. We understand that initial questionnaire included small group of participants, but poor results and discovered problems in the diagrammatic language design indicated that the language need a redesign to have better readability.

IMPROVED DIAGRAMMATIC QUERY LANGUAGE: VIZIQUER LITE

We redesigned the diagrammatic query language to mitigate problems that was achieved in the first version. Main improvement was to introduce a central objects set.

The central object set was designed to solve two problems that were encountered in the initial evaluation. First of all, users had problems finding right direction how to read the designed query. With the central object set it is more obvious that reading should start at the central object set. The central object set would use color, size and shape differences to make it more visible and noticeable compared to other graphical elements.

Second problem that we plan to partly solve with the central object set introduction is join operation understanding. It is hard to grasp how to equivalent terms can be linked together. But it is more normal to understand how prioritized elements are joined together. For example, it is just normal to name person and all cars that he owns.

By introducing central object set we also introduce a prioritizing between object links. Thus, objects relates in sequence to more important object set. We should refer to a data warehouse, where a star schema is used (Chaudhuri & Dayal 1997) that utilizes the same object sets prioritizing.

The third problem that users have hard time grasping formal variable we mitigate by leaving just a name of variable in a diagrammed query language element.

In everyday communication we do not use formal variables like x or y, but we use more semantic variables, for example, an African country or John's dogs. Often we use just a name of the set as a variable name, for example, persons that are younger than 25 years. For these reasons it would be sufficient enough to display semantic variable name in the diagrammatic query element. Object's set name is omitted and will be available only via a tool that supports the language input.

For the fourth problem with non-obligatory groups we do not have a clear solution how to improve users understanding. This is more advanced feature that needs at least small user education.

We also tested a possible improvement that negation and non-obligatory groups can be displayed via special links rather than boxes. We ran simple parallel experiments, where users were presented with non-obligatory and negation groups via special link, box that includes elements or combination of both. The best results were achieved in a questionnaire with the special link example.

Other feature to improve understandability and readability was to introduce a small hint names inside the diagrammatic language elements. For example, central object set selection has a prefix "*What are*". Such a prefix gives an emphasis that we search elements from the central object selection. Other improvement was adding prefixes for links between object selection sets.

For example, connecting two sets via standard link then there is prefix in form "*the object sets variable*" that follows by link name (for example, the Person owns). Negation links also has "*not*" after a variable name and non-obligatory group has "*optionally*" after a variable name.

The added hints actually makes language expressions more explicit and harder to interpret in different ways. It is one of key elements to develop as explicit and precise visual communication as possible.

Someone could argue that it is not a visual query language anymore. But we have introduced visual grouping of object sets. All information and constraints inside an object sets already is written in textual form, thus such a small textual addition would not diminish meaning of visual concepts.

Further we will present an improved version of the diagrammatic query language. We will start with the central object set selection. In Figure 6 we select all doctor names that is younger than 35 years. Compared to the initial version we also introduce two colors inside the element to separate answer attributes from condition attributes.

SPARQL syntax:

```
?Doctor a Onto:Doctor.
?Doctor Onto:name ?doctorName.
?Doctor Onto:age ?age_condition.
FILTER (?age_condition < XSD:integer("35"))
```

Second element is object set selection that is linked to the central object set selection. It is similar in form to central set, but it differs in color and compartment order. Answers sections color is changed to central object set color to indicate that these are similar. An example is depicted in Figure 7, where we select appointments longer than 30 minutes and want to see time when they start.

Figure 6. Central object set selection

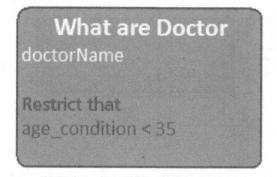

Figure 7. Object set selection

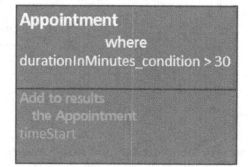

SPARQL syntax:

```
?Appointment a Onto: Appointment.
? Appointment Onto: timeStart?timeStart.
? Appointment Onto:durationInMinutes
? durationInMinutes _condition.
FILTER
(?durationInMinutes_condition > XSD:integer("30"))
```

Next is connection between objects set selection. As we mentioned earlier, there is three possible ways to interlink objects sets together. One possibility is normal link (join) between two sets. Other two are more advanced to set that there is no link or it has non-obligatory link (left outer join). We will display all three cases with doctor and connection with an appointment. In Figure 8 is displayed normal link where we want to see all doctor's names older than 35 years and show start time of appointments that has duration longer than 30 minutes.

In Figure 9 we display the same link, but now we want to see doctors that do not have appointments longer than 30 minutes. In the last example in Figure 10 we display doctors and if they have appointment longer than 30 minutes then also the start time of the appointment. Actually the last case is union of both previous examples in terms of query logic.

Figure 8. Link between object sets

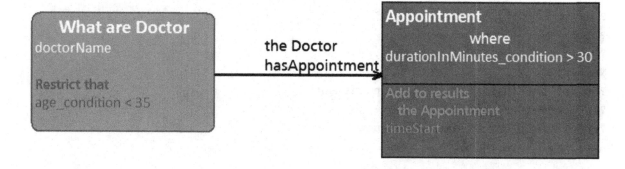

Figure 9. Negation link between object sets

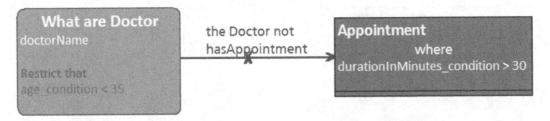

Figure 10. Non-obligatory link between object sets

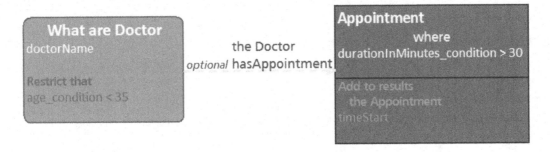

SPARQL syntax:

```
?Doctor a Onto:Doctor.
?Doctor Onto:name ?doctorName.
?Doctor Onto:age ?age_condition.
?Doctor onto:hasAppointment ?Appointment.
?Appointment a Onto:Appointment.
?Appointment Onto:durationInMinutes
?durationInMinutes_conditions.
?Appointment Onto:timeStart ?timeStart.
FILTER (?age_condition < XSD:integer("35"))
FILTER (?durationInMinutes_condition > XSD:integer("30"))
```

SPARQL syntax:

```
?Doctor a Onto:Doctor.
?Doctor Onto:name ?doctorName.
?Doctor Onto:age ?age_condition.
NOT EXIST {
?Doctor onto:hasAppointment ?Appointment.
?Appointment a Onto:Appointment.
?Appointment Onto:durationInMinutes
```

```
?durationInMinutes_conditions.
FILTER (
?durationInMinutes_condition > XSD:integer("30"))}
FILTER (?age_condition < XSD:integer("35"))
```

SPARQL syntax:

```
?Doctor a Onto:Doctor.
?Doctor Onto:name ?doctorName.
?Doctor Onto:age ?age_condition.
Optional {
?Doctor onto:hasAppointment ?Appointment.
?Appointment a Onto:Appointment.
?Appointment Onto:durationInMinutes
?durationInMinutes_conditions.
?Appointment Onto:timeStart ?timeStart.
FILTER(
?durationInMinutes_condition >  XSD:integer("30"))}
FILTER (?age_condition < XSD:integer("35"))
```

We have also added two additional graphical elements. First is a comment element, where end-users can write free text comments. It main purpose is to make diagrammatic query more understandable, readable in future by commenting the query.

Second element's purpose is to allow advanced users combine graphical elements with advanced textual SPARQL expressions. As one can write some SPARQL query parts that will be added to generated the SPARQL query from diagrammatic syntax.

The second element is "Full SPARQL" and it is implemented as a hack for advanced users. In the ViziQuer full we tried to introduce complex graphical elements for different complex SPARQL constructions, for example, UNION or HAVING clause. But these elements require more formal knowledge in data querying, thus mostly advanced users will use it.

The full specification of diagrammatic query language ViziQuer is displayed in Figure 11. It also has abstract element *box* to display that links can be made between both object set selections.

As was found in (Catarci & Santucci 1995) then advanced query composition precision and time is similar in textual form as in visual form. Thus, there is no need to make a diagrammatic syntax more complex to cover part that will mostly be used only by advanced users that has minimal or no advantaged using a diagrammatic language.

Main lacking element in the designed query language is sub-query. In (Zviedris, Romane, Barzdins & Cerans 2014) was argued that at least part of queries could be stored in an ontology. This approach would be limited to add new queries.

We think that sub-queries could be introduced via groups that were presented in ViziQuer full for negation and optional grouping. Still, it needs further research and analysis how main element in a sub-query would differ from other elements in the sub-query.

Figure 11. ViziQuer lite specification

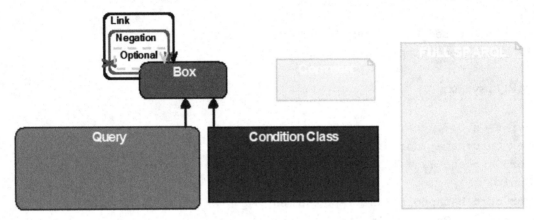

READABILITY ANALYSIS

We argued in the introduction that at first a visual language syntax should be test for a readability to conclude where the language is readable enough to continue with its implementation.

We concluded two questionnaires where we determined how well responded could read presented queries depicted in the ViziQuer lite diagrammatic query language. The questionnaires were different in an aspect if responders had a basic introduction into diagrammatic query elements.

First questionnaire had a brief tutorial with 6 different queries depicted in diagrammatic form, explained in natural language and displayed few rows of matching answers. One of tutorial pages is displayed in Figure 12. The second questionnaire asked responders to explain displayed diagrammatic queries without any tutorial.

To gather answers we used crowdsourcing approach. It was done via CrowdFlower platform (Crowd-Flower 2014). Each of questionnaires had in total 26 respondents. The responders also answered about they proficiency in IT (in scale of 1 to 7) and proficiency with databases (in scale of 1 to 6). We divided them into two groups – experts in databases (proficiency level 4 to 6) and beginner level (proficiency level 1 to 3).

In Figure 13 and Figure 14 are depicted respondents proficiency levels with databases. Average proficiency for users with tutorial is 3.27 and for users without tutorial it is 3.42.

It is easy to verify end-user answers, when they create a query, because it either selects desired data or not. With asking them to explain answers in natural language it is harder to check if the meaning of respondents answer match meaning of displayed query as natural language can be interpreted in different ways.

A query that achieved largest error rate is depicted in Figure 15. It asked to select all departments' name and are and to display division name, where it belongs. In both questionnaires there were 23.1% error rate. Mostly users selected division just as condition that department should also belong to a division rather that added also divisions' name to the answer. Partly this error could be explained with semantic overlapping as the term "*name*" is used twice.

Figure 12. Example of tutorial page

Query language tutorial (3 of 6)
Additional class restriction

Objects are joined to other objects by relationships. Thus, we want to include these relationships into our queries. Query can contain other object clases (puprple) and if they are connected by arrow to central class then it adds relationship restriction.

The example says - select and display student's name and age of those who take course with name "Algebra"

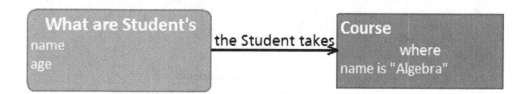

Example answer:

name	age
John	23
Casper	42
Bill	22

In contrast we can present a query depicted in Figure 16, where only 7.7% error rate in case with tutorial and 11.5% error rate was in case without tutorial. It shows that basic elements of the developed language are understandable by most of the users.

Error count without tutorial can be seen in Figure 17 and error rate with tutorial can be seen in Figure 18. Average error rate without tutorial is 2.46 (13.7%) and error rate with tutorial is 2.16 (12%). It shows that small tutorial can improve query readability. Beginner users made 3.91 errors in questionnaire without tutorial compared to 2.77 errors with tutorial. Expert users had 1.4 errors in case without tutorial and 1.5 errors in case with tutorial. This shows that expert users actually are already familiar with given concepts.

Also reading tutorial took only 3 minutes of user time. On average responders spent 23 minutes without tutorial and 26 minutes with tutorial. It was interesting that expert users devoted on average 3 more minutes in both cases compared to beginner users. Thus, for novice users short tutorial can be useful for improvement.

Figure 13. Respondend database proficiency without tutorial

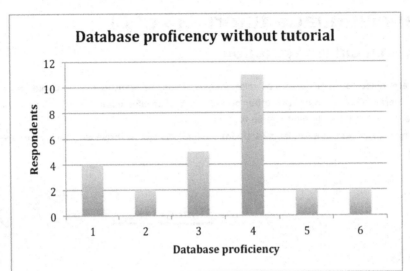

Figure 14. Respondend database proficiency with tutorial

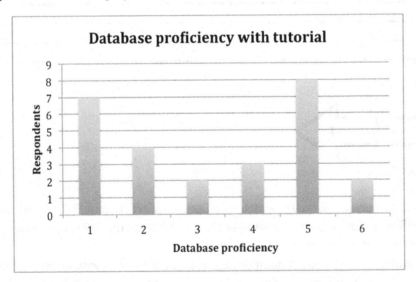

Figure 15. Query with worst case percentage

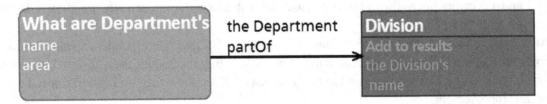

Figure 16. Query with above average percentage

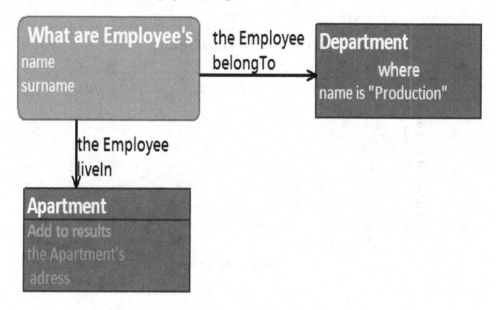

Figure 17. Error rate without tutorial

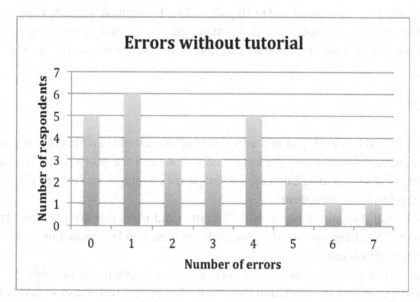

Making some tweaks in the graphical language, where end-users had difficulties explaining, made significant improvement comparing to the initial language version. Readability rate was improved from below 50% to acceptable 85%. Also users could achieve good results either with or without simple language tutorial.

Improvements made diagrammatic language more explicit and it eased the language readability for end-user. We think that this will be sufficient enough for query writing process as users will be able to understand and comprehend what they have written in the diagrammatic form and, in case of error, will tweak a query in right direction.

Figure 18. Error rate with tutorial

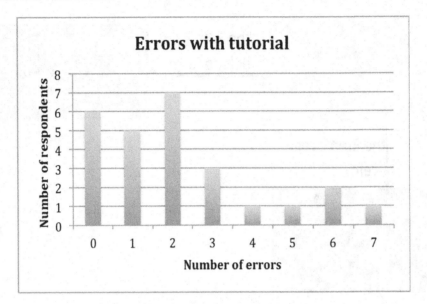

We have developed a technical implementation for the developed language ViziQuer lite. The supporting tool is available for download and testing (Zviedris, Barzdins & Rikacovs 2013).

Interviews with the ViziQuer tool users have gained insights that the language is usable in real case query composition. Still, we see that sub-query formulation would improve the language.

CONCLUSION

Visual languages should be developed in a way that they are tested if end-users can actually read and understand them. Readability is one of the key preconditions that the query language is usable.

Initial readability studies in diagrammatic and graphical languages can give new insights about the design flaws and possible improvements.

This process is vital if intended user group is common end-users that does not have specific knowledge. Often we develop a language based on our knowledge and understanding rather than that of users for whom the language is intended.

One of key aspect in a language development is to make it as explicit as possible. More explicit design leaves less space for free interpretation that can lead to errors. But it also should balance between explicit design and too much mathematic or formal design. To achieve an explicit design, one must use a combination of graphics and text as each concept should be presented in a manner where it adds less complexity to the resulting language.

Scientists prefer to communicate in a rather formal way that is not often viable in real life situations. If a developed language is intended for end-users that does not have a formal education then a formal presentation should be omitted as much as possible.

We have also received positive insights from respondents that participated in questionnaires. For example, "I haven't looked at database queries in a long time, this was fun!" or "I like the graphical query. It is short and precious enough." or "queries are good". These comments show that diagrammed query langue can be useful for at least some of end-users.

Most attention was based on the diagrammed query representation, but we gained an insight of methodology how data queries should be presented and taught to end-users.

For end-users it is vital to have a top-down approach in query composition. It is represented with central object set selection. It could be helpful to introduce even more specific order of a query readability and composition.

Still, some of language elements are hard to represent, as they do not have good explanation in natural language. It would be useful to understand subset of graphical query language that actually could be developed for broad usage via graphical elements and part that should be left as add-on for expert users. This is not a mathematical problem how to cover all textual elements in a visual form, but rather how to achieve least complexity of the developed language.

We think that we have made a good progress towards user approachable diagrammatic query language. The language is developed for the Semantic Web domain where SPARQL query language is used. But principles of a readable query language can be adopted also in domain of the relation databases and SQL.

The support tool is developed that shows that users can create diagrammatic queries in approachable way. We have received positive feedback from a few of the tool users.

ACKNOWLEDGMENT

Partially supported by Latvian State Research program "NexIT" project No.1.

REFERENCES

Athanasis, N., Christophides, V., & Kotzinos, D. (2004). Generating On the Fly Queries for the Semantic Web: The ICS-FORTH Graphical RQL Interface (GRQL). In *Proceedings of the 3rd International Semantic Web Conference (ISWC2004)*. ISWC.

Barzdins, G., Barzdins, J., & Cerans, K. (2008). *From Databases to Ontologies. In Semantic Web Engineering in the Knowledge Society* (pp. 242–266). IGI Global.

Barzdins, G., Liepins, E., Veilande, M., & Zviedris, M. (2008) Semantic Latvia approach in the medical domain. In *Proc. 8th International Baltic Conference on Databases and Information Systems*. Tallinn University of Technology Press.

Barzdins, G., Rikacovs, S., Veilande, M., & Zviedris, M. (2009). Ontological Re-Engineering of Medical Databases/ *Proceedings of the Latvian Academy of Sciences, Section B, 63*(4/5), 153–155.

Barzdins, G., Rikacovs, S., & Zviedris, M. (2009). Graphical query language as SPARQL frontend. In *Local Proceedings of 13th East-European Conference (ADBIS 2009)*. ADBIS.

Baskauf, S. (2014). *Beginner's Guide to RDF*. Retrieved from https://code.google.com/p/tdwg-rdf/wiki/Beginners

Berners-Lee, T., Chen, Y., Chilton, L., Connolly, D., Dhanaraj, R., Hollenbach, J., & Sheets, D. (2006). Tabulator: Exploring and analyzing linked data on the semantic web. In *Proceedings of the 3rd International Semantic Web User Interaction Workshop. Academic Press.*

Berners-Lee, T., Hendler, J., & Lassila, O. (2001). The Semantic Web. *Scientific American, 284*(5), 34–43. doi:10.1038/scientificamerican0501-34 PMID:11396337

Catarci, T., Costabile, M. F., Levialdi, S., & Batini, C. (1997). Visual Query Systems for Databases: A Survey. *Journal of Visual Languages and Computing, 8*(2), 215–260. doi:10.1006/jvlc.1997.0037

Catarci, T., & Santucci, G. (1995a) Are Visual Query Languages Easier to Use then Traditional Ones? An Experimental Proof. In *Proceedings of the tenth Conference of the British Computer Society Human Computer Interaction Specialists Group-People and Computers X*, (pp. 323-338). Academic Press.

Catarci, T., & Santucci, G. (1995b). Diagrammatic vs Textual Query Languages: A Comparative Experiment. In *Proc. of the IFIP W.G. 2.6 Working Conference on Visual Databases*. IFIP.

Chaudhuri, S., & Dayal, U. (1997). An Overview of Data Warehousing and OLAP Technology. *SIGMOD Record, 26*(1), 65–74. doi:10.1145/248603.248616

CrowdFlower. (2014). Available from http://www.crowdflower.com

Dobing, B., & Parsons, J. (2006). How UML is used. *Communications of the ACM, 49*(5), 109–113. doi:10.1145/1125944.1125949

Eriksso, H., & Magnus, P. (1999). *Business Modeling with UML: Business Patterns at work*. Wiley & Sons.

Franz. (2015). *Gruff (Version 5.9.0)* [Software]. Available from http://franz.com/agraph/gruff/

Harris, S., & Seaborne, A. (2013). *SPARQL 1.1 Query Language*. W3C Recommendation. Retrieved from http://www.w3.org/TR/sparql11-query/

Harth, A. (2010). Visinav: A system for visual search and navigation on web data. *Web Semantics: Science, Services, and Agents on the World Wide Web, 8*(4), 348–354. doi:10.1016/j.websem.2010.08.001

Heim, P., Ertl, T., & Ziegler, J. (2010). Facet graphs: Complex semantic querying made easy. In *The Semantic Web: Research and Applications* (pp. 288–302). Springer Berlin Heidelberg. doi:10.1007/978-3-642-13486-9_20

Juel, C. (1988). Learning to read and write: A longitudinal study of 54 children from first through fourth grades. *Journal of Educational Psychology, 80*(4), 437–447. doi:10.1037/0022-0663.80.4.437

OMG. (2003). UML 2.0 Superstructure Specification. *OMG document ptc/03-08-02*.

Russell, A., & Smart, P. R. (2008). NITELIGHT: A graphical editor for SPARQL queries. In *International Semantic Web Conference (Posters & Demos)*. Academic Press.

Schweiger, , Trajanoski, Z., & Pabinger, S. (2014). SPARQLGraph: A web-based platform for graphically querying biological Semantic Web databases. *BMC Bioinformatics, 15*(1), 279. doi:10.1186/1471-2105-15-279 PMID:25127889

Selic, B., & Rumbaugh, J. (1998). *Using UML for Modeling Complex Real-Time Systems.* ObjecTime. doi:10.1007/BFb0057795

Soylu, A., Giese, M., Jimenez-Ruiz, E., Kharlamov, E., Zheleznyakov, D., & Horrocks, I. (2013) OptiqueVQS: towards an ontology-based visual query system for big data. In *Proceedings of the Fifth International Conference on Management of Emergent Digital EcoSystems.* ACM. doi:10.1145/2536146.2536149

Zhou, Q., Wang, C., Xiong, M., Wang, H., & Yu, Y. (2007). SPARK: adapting keyword query to semantic search. In *The Semantic Web Conference.* Springer Berlin Heidelberg. doi:10.1007/978-3-540-76298-0_50

Zloof, M. M. (1975) Query by Example. In *Proc. AFIPS 1975 NCC,* (Vol. 44). AFIPS Press.

Zviedris, M. (2014). *Data as ontology – storage, query and visualization.* (PhD thesis). University of Latvia.

Zviedris, M., & Barzdins, G. (2011). ViziQuer: a tool to explore and query SPARQL endpoints, *In The Semantic Web: Research and Applications. Springer Berlin Heidelberg, 6643,* 441–445.

Zviedris, M., Barzdins, G., & Rikacovs, S. (2013), *ViziQuer* (Version 11.26.2013) [Software]. Available from http://viziquer.lumii.lv/

Zviedris, M., Romane, A., Barzdins, G., & Cerans, K. (2014). Ontology-Based Information System. In *Proceedings of the 3rd Joint International Semantic Technology Conference, Revised Selected Papers,* (LNCS), (vol. 8388, pp. 33-47). Springer.

KEY TERMS AND DEFINITIONS

Diagrammatic Query Language: It is a query language where a query is built with boxes and lines. Diagrammatic elements are added with text structures that represent basic key terms that cannot be represented with generic diagrammatic constructions.

Query Readability: Each data query can be interpreted by an end-user. It is done in natural language, thus measurement is not précises, but approximate.

Semantic Data: Data in the Semantic Web that is represented in user-friendlier manner that contains less technical data and more data itself. It is stored in form subject, predicate, object.

ENDNOTES

[1]   In usability tests one needs a suitable query language tool support that end-users can write queries. The difference lies in aspect that query's language syntax is defined that it should be readable and easy to understand, while the tool is responsible for the part where an end-user can easily compose queries in designed query language. The query language syntax is not separated from the tool that supports query language input, but, in our opinion, it should be separated as for each syntax it is possible to design more than one tool that supports the input in a different way.

[2] In the survey (Catarci, Costabile, Levialdi & Batini 1997) presented examples is more similar to navigation, but not through a database schema, but predefined or stored data queries.

[3] Range selection is based on a predefined query where one can select ranges of attributes to get preferred results.

[4] QBD – query-by-design is described in the same paper.

Compilation of References

Aasman, J. (2006). *Allegro graph: RDF triple database*. Technical report. Franz Incorporated. Retrieved from http://www.franz.com/agraph/allegrograph/

Abadi, D. J., Marcus, A., Madden, S. R., & Hollenbach, K. (2009). SW-Store: a vertically partitioned DBMS for Semantic Web data management. *The VLDB Journal—The International Journal on Very Large Data Bases, 18*(2), 385-406.

Abadi, D., Agrawal, R., Ailamaki, A., Balazinska, M., Bernstein, P. A., Carey, M. J., & Widom, J. et al. (2014). The Beckman Report on Database Research. *SIGMOD Record, 43*(3), 61–70. doi:10.1145/2694428.2694441

Abdelhaq, H., Gertz, M., & Sengstock, C. (2013). Spatio-temporal characteristics of bursty words in Twitter streams. In *Proc. of the ACM International Conference on Advances in Geographic Information Systems (SIGSPATIAL)*, (pp. 194-203). doi:10.1145/2525314.2525354

Abiteboul, S., & Hull, R. (1987). IFO: A Formal Semantic Database Model. *ACM Transactions on Database Systems, 12*(4), 525–565. doi:10.1145/32204.32205

Abiteboul, S., Hull, R., & Vianu, V. (1995). *Foundations of databases*. Addison-Wesley.

Abiteboul, S., Hull, R., & Vianu, V. (1995). *Foundations of Databases*. Boston, MA: Addison Wesley.

Abiteboul, S., Quass, D., & McHugh, J. (1997a). The Lorel Query Language for Semistructured Data. *International Journal on Digital Libraries, 1*, 68–88.

Abiteboul, S., Quass, D., & McHugh, J. (1997b). Lore: A Database Management System for Semistructured Data. *SIGMOD Record, 26*(3), 54–66. doi:10.1145/262762.262770

Abu-Shawar, B., & Atwell, E. (2007). Fostering Language Learner Autonomy Through Adaptive Conversation Tutors. In Proceedings of Corpus Linguistics. Birmingham, UK: Academic Press.

Acciarri, A., Calvanese, D., De Giacomo, G., Lembo, D., Lenzerini, M., Palmieri, M., & Rosati, R. (2005). QuOnto: Querying Ontologies. In *Proceedings of the 20th National Conference on Artificial Intelligence* (pp. 1670-1671). Pittsburgh, PA: AAAI Press.

Adam, N., Shafiq, B., & Staffin, R. (2012). Spatial computing and social media in the context of disaster management. *IEEE Intelligent Systems, 12*, 1514–1672.

Aditya, B., Bhalotia, G., Chakrabarti, S., & Hulgeri, A. (2002). Banks: browsing and keyword searching in relational databases. In *Proceedings of the International Conference on Very Large Data Bases (VLDB)*. (pp 1083-1086). Hong Kong, China: Endowment. doi:10.1016/B978-155860869-6/50114-1

Afrati, F., & Ullman, J. (2011). Optimizing joins in a map-reduce environment. *IEEE Transactions on Knowledge and Data Engineering, 23*(9), 1282–1298. doi:10.1109/TKDE.2011.47

Agarwal, P. K., Arge, L., & Erickson, J. (2000). Indexing moving points. In *Proc. of the ACM SIGMOD-SIGACT-SIGART Symp. on Principles of Database Systems (PODS)*, (pp. 175-186). ACM.

Aggarwal, C. C., & Agrawal, D. (2003). On nearest neighbor indexing of nonlinear trajectories. In *Proc. of the ACM SIGMOD-SIGACT-SIGART Symp. on Principles of Database Systems (PODS)*, (pp. 252-259). doi:10.1145/773153.773178

Agrawal, J., Diao, Y., Gyllstrom, D., & Immerman, N. (2008). Efficient pattern matching over event streams. In *Proc. of the ACM SIGMOD International Conference on Management of Data*, (pp. 147-160). ACM.

Agrawal, R., Ailamaki, A., Philip, A., Bernstein, E., Michael, J., Carey, S., & Halevy, A. et al. (2009). The Claremont Report On Database Research. *Communications of the ACM*, *52*(6), 56–65. doi:10.1145/1516046.1516062

Agrawal, R., Faloutsos, C., & Swami, A. (1993). *Efficient similarity search in sequence databases*. Springer. doi:10.1007/3-540-57301-1_5

Agrawal, S., Chaudhuri, S., & Das, G. (2002). Dbxplorer: A system for keyword-based search over relational databases. In *Proceedings of the International Conference on Data Engineering (ICDE)*. (pp 5-16). San Jose, CA: IEEE Computer Society. doi:10.1109/ICDE.2002.994693

Agrawal, S., Chaudhuri, S., & Das, G. (2003). Automated ranking of database query results. *ACM Transactions on Database Systems*, *28*, 140–174.

Akdogan, A., Demiryurek, U., Banaei-Kashani, F., & Shahabi, C. (2010). Voronoi-based geospatial query processing with mapreduce. In *Proceedings of the International Conference Cloud Computing*, (pp. 9-16). Indianapolis, IN: IEEE.

Alashqur, A. M., Su, S. Y. W., & Lam, H. 1989, OQL: A Query Language for Manipulating Object-oriented Databases. In *Proceedings of the Fifteenth International Conference on Very Large Data Bases*. Academic Press.

Alexaki, S., Christophides, V., Karvounarakis, G., Plexousakis, D., & Tolle, K. (2001a). On Storing Voluminous RDF Descriptions: The Case of Web Portal Catalogs. In WebDB (pp. 43-48). WebDB.

Alexaki, S., Christophides, V., Karvounarakis, G., Plexousakis, D., & Tolle, K. (2001b). The ICS-FORTH RDFSuite: Managing Voluminous RDF Description Bases. In *Proc. of the 2nd Int'l Workshop on the Semantic Web* (SemWeb 2001). Hong Kong: CEUR-WS Press.

Alhajj, R. (2003). Extracting the Extended Entity-Relationship Model from a Legacy Relational Database. *Information Systems*, *28*(6), 597–618. doi:10.1016/S0306-4379(02)00042-X

Alhajj, R., & Arkun, M. E. (1993). An Object Algebra for Object-Oriented Database Systems. *Database*, *24*(3), 13–22.

Alkhateeb, F., Baget, J. F., & Euzenat, J. (2008). Constrained regular expressions in SPARQL. In *Proceedings of the 2008 International Conference on Semantic Web and Web Services* (SWWS'08). Las Vegas, NV: SWWS.

Alkhateeb, F., Baget, J. F., & Euzenat, J. (2009). Extending SPARQL with regular expression patterns (for querying RDF). *Web Semantics: Science, Services, and Agents on the World Wide Web*, *7*(2), 57–73. doi:10.1016/j.websem.2009.02.002

Allegro InfoGrid Introduction. (2015, August 11). Retrieved August 20, 2015, from http://franz.com/agraph/support/documentation/current/agraph-introduction.html

Alrifai, M., Skoutas, D., & Risse, T. (2010). Selecting Skyline Services for QoS based Web Service Composition. In *Proceedings of the 19th International Conference on World Wide Web (WWW)* (pp. 11-20). Raleigh, NC: ACM. doi:10.1145/1772690.1772693

Alvarado, A., Baldizan, O., Goncalves, M., & Vidal, M.-E. (2013). FOPA: A Final Object Pruning Algorithm to Efficiently Produce Skyline Points. In *Proceedings of the 24th International Conference on Database and Expert Systems Applications (DEXA)* (pp. 334-348). Prague, Czech Republic: Springer-Verlag. doi:10.1007/978-3-642-40173-2_27

Alzebdi, M., Chountas, P., & Atanassov, K. T. (2011). Intuitionistic fuzzy XML query matching.*InProceedings of the Flexible Query Answering Systems Conference*, (pp. 306-317). Ghent, Belgium: Springer. doi:10.1007/978-3-642-24764-4_27

Aman, S., Chelmis, C., & Prasanna, V. (2014). Addressing data veracity in big data applications. *Big Data (Big Data), 2014 IEEE International Conference on* (pp. 1--3). IEEE.

Anagnostopoulos, A., Vlachos, M., Hadjieleftheriou, M., Keogh, E. J., & Yu, P. S. (2006). Global distance-based segmentation of trajectories. In *Proc. of the ACM SIGKDD International Conference on Knowledge Discovery and Data Mining*, (pp. 34-43). ACM.

Anderson, E., Arlitt, M., Morrey, C. B. III, & Veitch, A. (2009). DataSeries: An efficient, flexible data format for structured serial data. *Operating Systems Review*, *43*(1), 70–75. doi:10.1145/1496909.1496923

Andre-Jonsson, H., & Badal, D. Z. (1997). Using signature files for querying time-series data. In *Principles of Data Mining and Knowledge Discovery* (pp. 211–220). Springer. doi:10.1007/3-540-63223-9_120

Anicic, D., Fodor, P., Rudolph, S., & Stojanovic, N. (2011). EP-SPARQL: a unified language for event processing and stream reasoning. In *Proceedings of the 20th international conference on World Wide Web* (pp. 635-644). ACM. doi:10.1145/1963405.1963495

Anyanwu, K., Maduko, A., & Sheth, A. (2007). Sparq2l: towards support for subgraph extraction queries in rdf databases. In *Proceedings of the 16th international conference on World Wide Web* (pp. 797-806). ACM. doi:10.1145/1242572.1242680

Apache Software. (2014). *Apache Thrift Tutorial*. Retrieved August 21, 2015, from https://thrift.apache.org/docs

Arasu, A. A. (2002). *An abstract semantics and concrete language for continuous queries over streams and relations*. Academic Press.

Arasu, A., Babu, S., & Widom, J. (2006). The CQL continuous query language: semantic foundations and query execution. *The VLDB Journal—The International Journal on Very Large Data Bases, 15*(2), 121-142.

Arcaini, P., Bordogna, G., & Sterlacchini, S. (2015). Geo-temporal density based clustering for exploring periodic and aperiodic Events reported in Social networks, under review. *Information Science*.

Arenas, M., Conca, S., & Pérez, J. (2012). Counting beyond a Yottabyte, or how SPARQL 1.1 property paths will prevent adoption of the standard. In *Proceedings of the 21st international conference on World Wide Web* (pp. 629-638). ACM. doi:10.1145/2187836.2187922

Arenas, M., & Pérez, J. (2011). Querying semantic web data with SPARQL. In *Proceedings of the thirtieth ACM SIGMOD-SIGACT-SIGART symposium on Principles of database systems* (pp. 305-316). ACM.

Assent, I., Krieger, R., Afschari, F., & Seidl, T. (2008). The TS-tree: efficient time series search and retrieval. In *Proceedings of the 11th international conference on Extending database technology: Advances in database technology* (pp. 252--263). ACM. doi:10.1145/1353343.1353376

Aßfalg, J., Kriegel, H.-P., Kroger, P., Kunath, P., Pryakhin, A., & Renz, M. (2006). Similarity search on time series based on threshold queries. *Advances in Database Technology-EDBT, 2006*, 276–294.

Athanasis, N., Christophides, V., & Kotzinos, D. (2004). Generating On the Fly Queries for the Semantic Web: The ICS-FORTH Graphical RQL Interface (GRQL). In *Proceedings of the 3rd International Semantic Web Conference (ISWC2004)*. ISWC.

Atzeni, P., Bugiotti, F., & Rossi, L. (2012). SOS (Save Our Systems): A uniform programming interface for non-relational systems. In *Proceedings of the EDBT 2012*. Berlin, Germany: ACM. doi:10.1145/2247596.2247671

Avram, A. (2011, August 4). *Interview: Richard Hipp on UnQL, a New Query Language for Document Databases.* Retrieved August 20, 2015, from http://www.infoq.com/news/2011/08/UnQL

Aygun, R. S., & Yazici, A. (2004). Modeling and Management of Fuzzy Information in Multimedia Database Applications. *Multimedia Tools and Applications*, *24*(1), 29–56. doi:10.1023/B:MTAP.0000033982.50288.14

Baader, F., Brandt, S., & Lutz, C. (2005). Pushing the $\mathcal{EL}$ envelope. In *Proceedings of the IJCAI* (pp. 364-369). Edinburgh, UK: Morgan Kaufmann Publishers.

Baader, F., Calvanese, D., & McGuinness, D. (Eds.). (2003). *The Description Logic Handbook: Theory, Implementation and Applications*. New York, NY: Cambridge University Press.

Bach, M., & Werner, A. (2014). Standardization Of Nosql Database Languages: Beyond Databases, Architectures, And Structure. In *Proceedings 10th International Conference (BDAS 2014)*. Ustron, Poland: Springer.

Badia, A. (2009). *Quantifiers in action: Generalized quantifiers in logical, query and natural languages*. Springer.

Bagnall, A., Ratanamahatana, C. A., Keogh, E., Lonardi, S., & Janacek, G. (2006). A bit level representation for time series data mining with shape based similarity. *Data Mining and Knowledge Discovery*, *13*(1), 11–40. doi:10.1007/s10618-005-0028-0

Baheti, R., & Gill, H. (2011). Cyber-physical systems. In The impact of control technology, (pp. 161-166). Academic Press.

Bahri, A., Bouaziz, R., & Gargouri, F. (2009). Fuzzy Ontology Implementation and Query Answering on Databases. In *Proceedings of the 28th North American Fuzzy Information Processing Society Annual Conference*.IEEE. doi:10.1109/NAFIPS.2009.5156413

Bai, L., Yan, L., & Ma, Z. M. (2013). Determining Topological Relationship of Fuzzy Spatiotemporal Data Integrated with XML Twig Pattern. *Applied Intelligence*, *39*(1), 75-100.

Bai, L., Yan, L., & Ma, Z. M. (2014). Querying Fuzzy Spatiotemporal Data Using XQuery. *Integrated Computer-Aided Engineering*, *21*(2), 147-162.

Bai, L., Yan, L., & Ma, Z. M. (2013). Determining Topological Relationship of Fuzzy Spatiotemporal Data Integrated with XML Twig Pattern. *Applied Intelligence*, *39*(1), 75–100. doi:10.1007/s10489-012-0395-3

Baixeries, J., Kaytoue, M., & Napoli, A. (2012). Computing Functional Dependencies with Pattern Structures. In *Proceedings of the 11th International Conference on "Concept lattices and their applications"* (vol. 972, pp. 175-186). CEUR WS.

Bai, Y., Luo, C. R., Thakkar, H., & Zaniolo, C. (2005). Efficient support for time series queries in data stream management systems. In *Stream Data Management* (pp. 113–132). Springer. doi:10.1007/0-387-25229-0_6

Bakalov, P., Hadjieleftheriou, M., Keogh, E., & Tsotras, V. (2005). Efficient trajectory joins using symbolic representations. In *Proc. of the International Conference on Mobile Data Management (MDM)*, (pp. 86-93). doi:10.1145/1071246.1071259

Balke, W. T., Güntzer, U., & Zheng, J. X. (2004). Efficient distributed skylining for web information systems. In *Proceedings of the Extending Database Technology (EDBT)* (pp. 256-273). Heraklion, Greece: Springer-Verlag. doi:10.1007/978-3-540-24741-8_16

Banker, K. (2011). *MongoDB in Action* (2nd ed.). Greenwich: Manning Publications.

Bao, D. (2008). A generalized model for financial time series representation and prediction. *Applied Intelligence, 20*(1), 1–11. doi:10.1007/s10489-007-0063-1

Barbieri, D. F., Braga, D., Ceri, S., Della Valle, E., & Grossniklaus, M. (2009b). Continuous queries and real-time analysis of social semantic data with c-sparql. In *Proceedings of Social Data on the Web Workshop at the 8th International Semantic Web Conference (Vol. 10)*. Academic Press.

Barbieri, D. F., Braga, D., Ceri, S., Della Valle, E., & Grossniklaus, M. (2009a). C-SPARQL: SPARQL for continuous querying. In *Proceedings of the 18th international conference on World Wide Web* (pp. 1061-1062). ACM. doi:10.1145/1526709.1526856

Barbieri, D. F., Braga, D., Ceri, S., Valle, E. D., & Grossniklaus, M. (2010). C-sparql: A continuous query language for rdf data streams. *International Journal of Semantic Computing, 4*(01), 3–25. doi:10.1142/S1793351X10000936

Barzdins, G., Rikacovs, S., & Zviedris, M. (2009). Graphical query language as SPARQL frontend. In *Local Proceedings of 13th East-European Conference (ADBIS 2009)*. ADBIS.

Barzdins, G., Rikacovs, S., Veilande, M., & Zviedris, M. (2009). Ontological Re-Engineering of Medical Databases/ *Proceedings of the Latvian Academy of Sciences, Section B, 63*(4/5), 153–155.

Barzdins, G., Barzdins, J., & Cerans, K. (2008). *From Databases to Ontologies. In Semantic Web Engineering in the Knowledge Society* (pp. 242–266). IGI Global.

Barzdins, G., Liepins, E., Veilande, M., & Zviedris, M. (2008) Semantic Latvia approach in the medical domain. In *Proc. 8th International Baltic Conference on Databases and Information Systems*. TallinnUniversity of Technology Press.

Base X. Team. (2014). *BaseX. The XML Database: As flexible as your data*. Retrieved September 4, 2014, from http://basex.org/

Baskauf, S. (2014). *Beginner's Guide to RDF*. Retrieved from https://code.google.com/p/tdwg-rdf/wiki/Beginners

Batko, M., Novak, D., & Zezula, P. (2007). MESSIF: Metric Similarity Search Implementation Framework. In *Proceedings of the 1st international conference on Digital libraries: research and development* (pp 1-10). Berlin: Springer-Verlag.

Beckett, D. (2002). The design and implementation of the Redland RDF application framework. *Computer Networks, 39*(5), 577–588. doi:10.1016/S1389-1286(02)00221-9

Beckmann, N., Kriegel, H.-P., Schneider, R., & Seeger, B. (1990). *The R*-tree: an efficient and robust access method for points and rectangles*. Academic Press.

Beeri, C., & Tzaban, Y. (1999). SAL: An Algebra for Semistructured Data and XML. In *Proceedings of Workshop on Web Databases* (pp. 46-51). Academic Press.

Belohlavek, R. (1999). Similarity Relations in Concept Lattices. Research Report. University of Ostrava, Czech Republic. 20, 1999.

Benetis, R., Jensen, S., Karciauskas, G., & Saltenis, S. (2006, September). Nearest and reverse nearest neighbor queries for moving objects. *The VLDB Journal, 15*(3), 229–249. doi:10.1007/s00778-005-0166-4

Benferhat, S., Ben-Naim, J., Papini, O., & Würbel, E. (2010). An Answer Set Programming Encoding of Prioritized Removed Sets Revision: Application to GIS. *Applied Intelligence, 32*(1), 60–87. doi:10.1007/s10489-008-0135-x

Benouaret, K., Benslimane, D., & Hadjali, A. (2011). On the Use of Fuzzy Dominance for Computing Service Skyline Based on QoS. In *Proceedings of the International Conference on Web Services (ICWS)* (pp. 540-547). Washington, DC: IEEE. doi:10.1109/ICWS.2011.93

Bentley, J. L., & Friedman, J. H. (1979). Data structures for range searching. *ACM Computing Surveys, 11*(4), 397–409. doi:10.1145/356789.356797

Bentley, J., Kung, H. T., Schkolnick, M., & Thompson, C. D. (1978). On the average number of maxima in a set of vectors and applications. *Journal of the ACM, 25*(4), 536–543. doi:10.1145/322092.322095

Berchtold, S., Keim, D. A., & Kriegel, H.-P. (2001). The X-tree: An index structure for high-dimensional data. *Readings in multimedia computing and networking, 451.*

Bergamaschi, S., Domnori, E., & Guerra, F. (2011). Keyword search over relational databases: a metadata approach. In *Proceedings of the ACM SIGMOD Conference on Data Management (SIGMOD)*. (pp 565-576). Athens, Greece: ACM. doi:10.1145/1989323.1989383

Bernauer, M., Kappel, G., & Kramler, G. (2004). Representing XML Schema in UML−A Comparison of Approaches. In *Proceedings of the 4th International Conference on Web Engineering*. Academic Press.

Berners-Lee, T., Chen, Y., Chilton, L., Connolly, D., Dhanaraj, R., Hollenbach, J., & Sheets, D. (2006). Tabulator: Exploring and analyzing linked data on the semantic web. In *Proceedings of the 3rd International Semantic Web User Interaction Workshop. Academic Press.*

Berners-Lee, T., Hendler, J., & Lassila, O. (2001). The semantic web. *Scientific American, 284*(5), 28–37. doi:10.1038/scientificamerican0501-34 PMID:11341160

Bertino, E., & Catania, B. (2001). Integrating XML and Databases. *IEEE Internet Computing, 5*(July-August), 84–88. doi:10.1109/4236.939454

Berzal, F., Marín, N., Pons, O., & Vila, M. A. (2007). Managing Fuzziness on Conventional Object-Oriented Platforms. *International Journal of Intelligent Systems, 22*(7), 781–803. doi:10.1002/int.20228

Bienvenu, M., Ortiz, M., Simkus, M., & Xiao, G. (2013). Tractable Queries for Lightweight Description Logics. In *Proceedings of the IJCAI* (pp. 768-774). Beijing, China: AAAI Press.

Birant, D., & Kut, A. (2007). ST-DBSCAN: An algorithm for clustering spatial-temporal data. *Data & Knowledge Engineering, 60*(1), 208–221. doi:10.1016/j.datak.2006.01.013

Biron, P. V., & Malhotra, A. (2001). *XML Schema Part 2: Datatypes, W3C Recommendation.* Retrieved from http://www.w3.org/TR/xmlschema-2/

Bizer, C., & Schultz, A. (2008). *Benchmarking the performance of storage systems that expose SPARQL endpoints.* World Wide Web Internet and Web Information Systems.

Bizer, C., & Schultz, A. (2009). The berlin sparql benchmark. *International Journal on Semantic Web and Information Systems, 5*(2), 1–24. doi:10.4018/jswis.2009040101

Bobek, S., & Perko, I. (2006). Intelligent Agent Based Business Intelligence. In *Proceedings of 4th International Conference on Multimedia and Information and Communication Technologies in Education*. Academic Press.

Bolles, A., Grawunder, M., & Jacobi, J. (2008). Streaming SPARQL-Extending SPARQL to Process Data Streams. In *Proceeding of 5th European Semantic Web Conference, ESWC 2008*(pp 448-462). doi:10.1007/978-3-540-68234-9_34

Booch, G., Rumbaugh, J., & Jacobson, I. (1998). *The Unified Modeling Language User Guide.* Addison-Welsley Longman, Inc.

Bordogna, G., Bucci, F., Carrara, P., Pepe, M., & Rampini, A. (2011). *Flexible Querying of Imperfect Temporal Metadata in Spatial Data Infrastructures. In Advanced Database Query Systems: Techniques, Applications and Technologies* (pp. 140–159). IGI Global. doi:10.4018/978-1-60960-475-2.ch006

Bordogna, G., Pasi, G., & Lucarella, D. (1999). A Fuzzy Object-Oriented Data Model for Managing Vague and Uncertain Information. *International Journal of Intelligent Systems*, *14*(7), 623–651. doi:10.1002/(SICI)1098-111X(199907)14:7<623::AID-INT1>3.0.CO;2-G

Bordogna, G., & Psaila, G. (2008). *Customizable Flexible Querying Classic Relational Databases. In Handbook of Research on Fuzzy Information Processing in Databases* (pp. 191–215). Hershey, PA: Information Science. doi:10.4018/978-1-59904-853-6.ch008

Bornea, M. A., Dolby, J., Kementsietsidis, A., Srinivas, K., Dantressangle, P., Udrea, O., & Bhattacharjee, B. (2013). Building an efficient RDF store over a relational database. In *Proceedings of the 2013 international conference on Management of data* (pp. 121-132). ACM. doi:10.1145/2463676.2463718

Borzsony, S., Kossmann, D., & Stocker, K. (2001). The skyline operator. In *Proceedings of the IEEE international conference on data engineering (ICDE)* (p. 421-430). doi:10.1109/ICDE.2001.914855

Bosc, P., & Prade, H. (1993). An Introduction to Fuzzy Set and Possibility Theory Based Approaches to the Treatment of Uncertainty and Imprecision in Database Management systems. In *Proceedings of the Second Workshop on Uncertainty Management in Information Systems: From Needs to Solutions*. Academic Press.

Bosc, P., Kraft, D., & Petry, F. (2005). Fuzzy Sets in Database and Information Systems: Status and Opportunities. *Fuzzy Sets and Systems*, *156*(3), 418–426. doi:10.1016/j.fss.2005.05.039

Bosc, P., & Lietard, L. (1996), Fuzzy Integrals and Database Flexible Querying. In *Proceedings of the Fifth IEEE International Conference on Fuzzy Systems*. doi:10.1109/FUZZY.1996.551726

Bosc, P., & Pivert, O. (1992). Some Approaches for Relational Databases Flexible Querying. *Journal of Intelligent Information Systems*, *1*(3/4), 323–354. doi:10.1007/BF00962923

Bosc, P., & Pivert, O. (1995). SQLf: A Relational Database Language for Fuzzy Querying. *IEEE Transactions on Fuzzy Systems*, *3*(1), 1–17. doi:10.1109/91.366566

Bosc, P., & Pivert, O. (2000). *SQLf Query Functionality on Top of a Regular Relational Database Management System. In Knowledge Management in Fuzzy Databases* (pp. 171–190). Physica-Verlag.

Bouaziz, R., Chakhar, S., Mousseau, V., Ram, S., & Telmoudi, A. (2007). Database Design and Querying within the Fuzzy Semantic Model. *Information Sciences*, *177*(21), 4598–4620. doi:10.1016/j.ins.2007.05.013

Box, G. E., Jenkins, G. M., & Reinsel, G. C. (2013). *Time series analysis: forecasting and control*. John Wiley & Sons.

Braga, D., Campi, A., Damiani, E., Pasi, G., & Lanzi, P. L. (2002). FXPath: Flexible Querying of XML Documents. In *Proceedings of the 2002 EUROFUSE Workshop on Information Systems*. Academic Press.

Brakatsoulas, S., Pfoser, D., & Theodoridis, Y. (2002). Revisiting R-tree construction principles. In *Advances in Databases and Information Systems* (pp. 149–162). Springer.

Bray, T., Paoli, J., & Sperberg-McQueen, C. M. (1998). *Extensible Markup Language (XML) 1.0, W3C Recommendation*. Retrieved from http://www.w3.org/TR/1998/REC-xml-19980210

Britt, J. (2013, March 21). *The Pleasures of JRuby*. Retrieved August 20, 2015, from http://www.leaphacking.com/posts/the-pleasures-of-jruby.html

Broekstra, J., Kampman, A., & Van Harmelen, F. (2002). Sesame: A generic architecture for storing and querying rdf and rdf schema. In *The Semantic Web—ISWC 2002* (pp. 54–68). Springer Berlin Heidelberg. doi:10.1007/3-540-48005-6_7

Buche, P., Dervin, C., Haemmerle, O., & Thomopoulos, R. (2005). Fuzzy Querying of Incomplete, Imprecise, and Heterogeneously Structured Data in the Relational Model Using Ontologies and Rules. *IEEE Transactions on Fuzzy Systems*, *13*(3), 373–383. doi:10.1109/TFUZZ.2004.841736

Buche, P., Dibie-Barthèlemy, J., & Wattez, F. (2006). Approximate querying of XML fuzzy data. Flexible Query Answering Systems. *Lecture Notes in Computer Science*, *4027*, 26–38. doi:10.1007/11766254_3

Buckles, B. P., & Petry, F. E. (1982). A fuzzy representation of data for relational databases. *Fuzzy Sets and Systems*, *7*(3), 213–226. doi:10.1016/0165-0114(82)90052-5

Buckles, B. P., Petry, F. E., & Sachar, H. S. (1989). A Domain Calculus for Fuzzy Relational Databases. *Fuzzy Sets and Systems*, *29*(3), 327–340. doi:10.1016/0165-0114(89)90044-4

Buevich, M., Wright, A., Sargent, R., & Rowe, A. (2013). Respawn: A Distributed Multi-Resolution Time-Series Datastore.*Real-Time Systems Symposium (RTSS), 2013 IEEE 34th* (pp. 288--297). IEEE. doi:10.1109/RTSS.2013.36

Burago, D., Burago, Y. D., & Ivanov, S. (2001). *A Course in Metric Geometry*. American Mathematical Society. doi:10.1090/gsm/033

Buratti, G., & Montesi, D. (2006). A Data Model and An Algebra for Querying XML Documents. In *Proceedings of the 17th International Conference on Database and Expert Systems Applications*, (pp. 482-486). doi:10.1109/DEXA.2006.6

Bynum, T. (Ed.). (1972). *Conceptual notation and related articles*. Oxford, UK: Clarendon Press.

Cai, M., & Revesz, P. (2000). Parametric R-tree: An index structure for moving objects. In *International Conference on Management of Data (COMAD)*, (pp. 57-64). COMAD.

Cai, Y., & Ng, R. (2004). Indexing spatio-temporal trajectories with Chebyshev polynomials. In *Proc. of the ACM SIGMOD International Conference on Management of Data*, (pp. 599-610). ACM.

Cai, Y., & Ng, R. (2004). Indexing spatio-temporal trajectories with Chebyshev polynomials.*Proceedings of the 2004 ACM SIGMOD international conference on Management of data* (pp. 599--610). ACM. doi:10.1145/1007568.1007636

Calì, A., Gottlob, G., & Pieris, A. (2010). Advanced processing for ontological queries. *PVLDB*, *3*(1), 554–565.

Calì, A., Gottlob, G., & Pieris, A. (2012). Ontological query answering under expressive Entity-Relationship schemata. *Information Systems*, *37*(4), 320–335. doi:10.1016/j.is.2011.09.006

Calil, A., & Mello, R. (2011). SimpleSQL: A Relational Layer for SimpleDB. In *Proceedings of the 16th East European conference on Advances in Databases and Information Systems Springer (ADBIS'12)*. Berlin, Heidelberg: Springer.

Calmès, M., Prade, H., & Sedes, F. (2007, July). Flexible querying of semistructured data: A fuzzy-set based approach. *International Journal of Intelligent Systems*, *22*(7), 723–737. doi:10.1002/int.20225

Calvanese, D., Horrocks, I., Jiménez-Ruiz, E., Kharlamov, E., Meier, M., Rodríguez-Muro, M., & Zheleznyakov, D. (2013). On Rewriting and Answering Queries in OBDA Systems for Big Data. In *Proceedings of OWLED*. Montpellier, France: CEUR-WS.org.

Calvanese, D., De Giacomo, G., Lembo, D., Lenzerini, M., & Rosati, R. (2006). Data complexity of query answering in description logics. In *Proceedings of the 10th Int. Conf. on the Principles of Knowledge Representation and Reasoning* (pp. 260-270). The Lake District, UK: AAAI Press.

Calvanese, D., De Giacomo, G., Lembo, D., Lenzerini, M., & Rosati, R. (2007). Tractable reasoning and efficient query answering in description logics: The DL-Lite family. *Journal of Automated Reasoning, 39*(3), 385–429. doi:10.1007/s10817-007-9078-x

Calvo, T. (1992). On fuzzy similarity relations. *Fuzzy Sets and Systems, 47*(1), 121–123. doi:10.1016/0165-0114(92)90069-G

Camerra, A., Rakthanmanon, T., & Keogh, E. (2014). Beyond one billion time series: Indexing and mining very large time series collections with iSAX2+. *Knowledge and Information Systems, 39*(1), 123–151. doi:10.1007/s10115-012-0606-6

Campi, A., Damiani, E., Guinea, S., Marrara, S., Pasi, G., & Spoletini, P. (2009). A Fuzzy Extension of the XPath Query Language. *Journal of Intelligent Information Systems, 33*(3), 285–305. doi:10.1007/s10844-008-0066-3

Campi, A., Guinea, S., & Spoletini, P. (2006). A fuzzy extension for the XPath query language. In *Proceedings of the Flexible Query Answering Systems Conference*, (pp. 210-221). Milan, Italy: Springer. doi:10.1007/11766254_18

Cao, B., & Badia, A. (2013). Efficient implementation of generalized quantification in relational query languages. In *Proceedings of the very large database (vldb) endowment* (Vol. 6). Academic Press.

Cao, B., & Badia, A. (2005). A nested relational approach to processing SQL subqueries. In *Proceedings of the ACM SIGMOD international conference on management of data* (p. 191-202). doi:10.1145/1066157.1066180

Cao, L. B., Ou, Y. M., & Yu, P. S. (2012). Coupled behavior analysis with applications. *IEEE Transactions on Knowledge and Data Engineering, 24*(8), 1378–1392. doi:10.1109/TKDE.2011.129

Cao, T. H., & Nguyen, H. (2011). Uncertain and Fuzzy Object Bases: A Data Model and Algebraic Operations. *International Journal of Uncertainty, Fuzziness and Knowledge-based Systems, 19*(2), 275–305. doi:10.1142/S0218488511007003

Cao, T. H., & Rossiter, J. M. (2003). A Deductive Probabilistic and Fuzzy Object-Oriented Database Language. *Fuzzy Sets and Systems, 140*(1), 129–150. doi:10.1016/S0165-0114(03)00031-9

Capriolo, E., Wampler, D., & Rutherglen, J. (2012). *Programming Hive*. Sebastopol: O'Reilly Media.

Carlis, J. (1986). HAS, a relational algebra operator or divide is not enough to conquer. In *Proceedings of the IEEE international conference on data engineering (ICDE)* (p. 254-261). IEEE.

Carrasquel, S., Rodríguez, R., & Tineo, L. (2013). Consultas con Ordenamiento basado en Similitud. *Telematique, 12*(1), 24–45.

Carroll, J. J., Dickinson, I., Dollin, C., Reynolds, D., Seaborne, A., & Wilkinson, K. (2004). Jena: implementing the semantic web recommendations. In *Proceedings of the 13th international World Wide Web conference on Alternate track papers & posters* (pp. 74-83). ACM.

Cary, A., Sun, Z., Hristidis, V., & Rishe, N. (2009). Experiences on processing spacial data with MapReduce. In *Proceedings of the International Conference Scientific and Statistical Database Management*, (pp. 302-319). New Orleans, LA: Springer.

Castillo, R., Rothe, C., & Leser, U. (2010). RDFMatView: Indexing RDF Data using Materialized SPARQL queries. In *Proceedings of the 2010 International Workshop on Scalable Semantic Web Knowledge Base Systems*. Academic Press.

Catarci, T., & Santucci, G. (1995a) Are Visual Query Languages Easier to Use then Traditional Ones? An Experimental Proof. In *Proceedings of the tenth Conference of the British Computer Society Human Computer Interaction Specialists Group-People and Computers X*, (pp. 323-338). Academic Press.

Catarci, T., Costabile, M. F., Levialdi, S., & Batini, C. (1997). Visual Query Systems for Databases: A Survey. *Journal of Visual Languages and Computing, 8*(2), 215–260. doi:10.1006/jvlc.1997.0037

Catarci, T., & Santucci, G. (1995b). Diagrammatic vs Textual Query Languages: A Comparative Experiment. In *Proc. of the IFIP W.G. 2.6 Working Conference on Visual Databases*. IFIP.

Cattell, R. (2011). Scalable SQL and NoSQL data stores. *SIGMOD Record, 39*(4), 12–27. doi:10.1145/1978915.1978919

Cattell, R. G. G., Barry, D. K., Berler, M., Eastman, J., Jordan, D., Russell, C., & Velez, F. et al. (2000). *The Object Data Management Standard: ODMG 3.0*. Morgan Kaufmann.

Chamberlin, D., Florescu, D., Robie, J., Simeon, J., & Stefanescu, M. (2001). *XQuery: A Query Language for XML, W3C Working Draft*. Retrieved from http://www.w3.org/TR/xquery

Chamorro-Martínez, J., Medina, J. M., Barranco, C. D., Galán-Perales, E., & Soto-Hidalgo, J. M. (2007). Retrieving Images in Fuzzy Object-Relational Databases Using Dominant Color Descriptors. *Fuzzy Sets and Systems, 158*(3), 312–324. doi:10.1016/j.fss.2006.10.013

Chan, A., Situ, N., Wong, K., Kianmehr, K., & Alhajj, R. (2008). Fuzzy querying of nested XML. In *Proceedings of the Information Reuse and Integration Conference*, (pp. 238-243). Las Vegas, NV: IEEE Systems, Man, & Cybernetics Society.

Chan, C. Y., Jagadish, H. V., Tan, K.-L., Tung, A. K. H., & Zhang, Z. (2006b). On high dimensional Skylines. In *Proceedings of The International Conference on Extending Database Technology* (EDBT). (pp. 478-495). Munich, Germany: ACM

Chan, C.-Y., Jagadish, H. V., Tan, K.-L., Tung, A. K. H., & Zhang, Z. (2006a). Finding k-dominant skylines in high dimensional space. In *Proceedings of the 2006 ACM SIGMOD International Conference on Management of Data* (pp. 503-514). New York: ACM. doi:10.1145/1142473.1142530

Chandra, A. K., & Merlin, P. M. (1977). Optimal implementation of conjunctive queries in relational data bases. In *Proceedings of the 9th annual ACM Symposium on Theory of Computing* (pp. 77-90). New York, NY: ACM Press. doi:10.1145/800105.803397

Chandra, S., Khan, L., & Muhaya, F. B. (2011). Estimating Twitter User Location Using Social Interactions – A Content Based Approac. In *Proceedings of 2011 IEEE International Conference on Privacy, Security, Risk, and Trust, and IEEE International Conference on Social Computing*, (pp. 838-843). doi:10.1109/PASSAT/SocialCom.2011.120

Chan, F.-P., Fu, A.-C., & Yu, C. (2003). Haar wavelets for efficient similarity search of time-series: With and without time warping. *Knowledge and Data Engineering. IEEE Transactions on, 15*(3), 686–705.

Chatfield, C. (2013). *The analysis of time series: an introduction*. CRC Press.

Chatziantoniou, D., Akinde, M. O., Johnson, T., & Kim, S. (2001). MD-join: an operator for complex OLAP. In *Proceedings of the IEEE international conference on data engineering (ICDE)* (p. 524-533). doi:10.1109/ICDE.2001.914866

Chaudhry, N. A., Moyne, J. R., & Rundensteiner, E. A. (1999). An Extended Database Design Methodology for Uncertain Data Management. *Information Sciences, 121*(1-2), 83–112. doi:10.1016/S0020-0255(99)00066-3

Chaudhuri, S., Das, G., Hristidis, V., & Weikum, G. (2004). Probabilistic ranking of database query results. In *Proceedings of the Very Large Data Bases Conference*, (pp. 888-899). Toronto, Canada: Morgan Kaufmann.

Chaudhuri, S., Das, G., Hristidis, V., & Weikum, G. (2006). Probabilistic information retrieval approach for ranking of database query results. *ACM Transactions on Database Systems, 31*(3), 1134–1168. doi:10.1145/1166074.1166085

Chaudhuri, S., & Dayal, U. (1997). An Overview of Data Warehousing and OLAP Technology. *SIGMOD Record, 26*(1), 65–74. doi:10.1145/248603.248616

Chebotko, A., & Lu, S. (2008). *Querying and managing semantic web data and scientific workflow provenance using relational databases*. (Doctoral Dissertation). Detroit, MI: Wayne State University.

Chebotko, A., Lu, S., & Fotouhi, F. (2009). Semantic preserving SPARQL-to-SQL translation. *Data & Knowledge Engineering, 68*(10), 973–1000. doi:10.1016/j.datak.2009.04.001

Che, D., & Sojitrawala, R. M. (2007). DUMAX: A Dual Mode Algebra for XML Queries. In *Proceedings of the 2nd International Conference on Scalable Information Systems*, (pp. 1-4). doi:10.4108/infoscale.2007.202

Chen, L., & Ng, R. (2004). On the marriage of lp-norms and edit distance. In *Proceedings of the Thirtieth international conference on Very large data bases* (vol. 30, pp. 792--803). VLDB Endowment. doi:10.1016/B978-012088469-8.50070-X

Chen, L., Cui, B., Lu, H., Xu, L., & Xu, Q. (2008). iSky: Efficient and Progressive Skyline Computing in a Structured P2P Network. In *Proceedings of the 28th International Conference on Distributed Computing Systems (ICDCS)* (pp. 160-167). Beijing, China: IEEE Computer Society.

Chen, L., Cui, B., Lu, H., Xu, L., & Xu, Q. (2008). isky: Efficient and progressive skyline computing in a structured p2p network. In *Proceedings of the International Conference on Distributed Computing Systems* (pp. 160-167). Los Alamitos, CA: IEEE Computer Society.

Chen, L., Lian, & Xiang. (2008). Dynamic skyline queries in metric spaces. In *Proceedings of the International Conference On Extending Database Technology (EDBT)* (pp. 333-343). New York, NY: ACM.

Chen, Q., Chen, L. a., & Yu, J. X. (2007). Indexable PLA for efficient similarity search. In *Proceedings of the 33rd international conference on Very large data bases* (pp. 435--446). VLDB Endowment.

Chen, Q., Chen, L., Lian, X., Liu, Y., & Yu, J. X. (2007). Indexable PLA for efficient similarity search. In *Proceedings of the 33rd international conference on Very large data bases* (pp. 435--446). VLDB Endowment.

Chen, S., Li, H.-G., Tatemura, J., Hsiung, W.-P., Agrawal, D., & Candan, K. S. (2006). Twig. stack: Bottom-up processing of generalized-tree-pattern queries over xml documents. In *Proceedings of the very large database (vldb) endowment* (p. 283-294). Academic Press.

Chen, Y. C., & Chen, S. M. (2000). Techniques of Fuzzy Query Processing for Fuzzy Database Systems. In *Proceedings of the Fifth Conference on Artificial Intelligence and Applications*. Academic Press.

Chen, Y., Nascimento, M. A., Ooi, B. C., & Tung, A. (2007). Spade: On shape-based pattern detection in streaming time series. In *Data Engineering, 2007. ICDE 2007. IEEE 23rd International Conference on* (pp. 786--795). IEEE.

Chen, B., Liang, W., & Yu, J. X. (2009). Progressive skyline query evaluation and maintenance in wireless sensor networks. In *Proceedings of the ACM Conference on Information and Knowledge Management (CIKM)* (pp. 1445-1448). New York, NY: ACM. doi:10.1145/1645953.1646141

Cheng, J., Ma, Z. M., & Yan, L. (2010). f-SPARQL: a flexible extension of SPARQL. In Database and Expert Systems Applications (pp. 487-494). Springer Berlin Heidelberg.

Cheng, T., & Wicks, T. (2014, March 6). Event Detection using Twitter: A Spatio-Temporal Approach. *PLOS One.*

Chen, G. Q. (1999). *Fuzzy Logic in Data Modeling; Semantics, Constraints, and Database Design.* Kluwer Academic Publisher.

Chen, G. Q., & Kerre, E. E. (1998). Extending ER/EER Concepts towards Fuzzy Conceptual Data Modeling. In *Proceedings of the 1998 IEEE International Conference on Fuzzy Systems*. IEEE.

Chen, G. Q., Vandenbulcke, J., & Kerre, E. E. (1992). A General Treatment of Data Redundancy in a Fuzzy Relational Data Model. *Journal of the American Society for Information Science, 43*(4), 304–311. doi:10.1002/(SICI)1097-4571(199205)43:4<304::AID-ASI6>3.0.CO;2-X

Cheng, J. W., & Ma, Z. M. (2010). f-SPARQL: A Flexible Extension of SPARQL. In *Proceedings of the 21st International Conference on Database and Expert Systems Applications.* Bilbao, Spain:Springer.

Cheng, J., Ma, Z. M., Zhang, F., & Wang, X. (2009a). Deciding Query Entailment in Fuzzy Description Logic Knowledge Bases. In *Proceedings of the 20th International Conference on Database and Expert Systems* (pp. 830-837). Linz, Austria: Springer. doi:10.1007/978-3-642-03573-9_70

Cheng, J., Ma, Z. M., Zhang, F., & Wang, X. (2009b). Deciding Query Entailment for Fuzzy SHIN Ontologies. In *Proceedings of the 4th Annual Asian Semantic Web Conference* (pp. 120-134). Linz, Austria: Springer. doi:10.1007/978-3-642-10871-6_9

Cheng, R., Emrich, T., Kriegel, H.-P., Mamoulis, N., Renz, M., Trajcevski, G., & Züfle, A. (2014). Managing uncertainty in spatial and spatio-temporal data. In *Proc. of the IEEE International Conference on Data Engineering (ICDE)*, (pp. 1302-1305). doi:10.1109/ICDE.2014.6816766

Cheng, X., Miao, D. Q., Wang, C., & Cao, L. B. (2013). Coupled term-term relation analysis for document clustering. In *Proceedings of the International Joint Conference on Neural Networks (IJCNN).* (pp 1-8). Killarney, Ireland: IEEE Computer Society. doi:10.1109/IJCNN.2013.6706853

Chen, L., Gao, S., & Anyanwu, K. (2011). Efficiently evaluating skyline queries on RDF databases. In *Proceedings of The Extended Semantic Web Conference (ESWC)* (pp. 123-138). Crete, Greece: Springer-Verlag. doi:10.1007/978-3-642-21064-8_9

Chen, L., Ozsu, M. T., & Oria, V. (2005). Robust and fast similarity search for moving object trajectories. In *Proceedings of the 2005 ACM SIGMOD international conference on Management of data* (pp. 491--502). ACM. doi:10.1145/1066157.1066213

Chen, N., Shou, L., Chen, G., Gao, Y., & Dong, J. (2009). Predictive skyline queries for moving objects. In *Proceedings of the International Conference on Database Systems For Advanced Applications* (pp. 278-282). Berlin: Springer-Verlag. doi:10.1007/978-3-642-00887-0_23

Chen, N., Shou, L., Chen, G., Gao, Y, & Dong, J. (2012). Prismo: Predictive skyline query processing over moving objects. *Journal of Zhejiang University SCIENCE C, 1*(13), 99–117. doi:10.1631/jzus.C10a0728

Chen, P. P. (1976). The entity-relationship model: Toward a unified view of data. *ACM Transactions on Database Systems, 1*(1), 9–36. doi:10.1145/320434.320440

Chen, S. M., & Jong, W. T. (1997). Fuzzy Query Translation for Relational Database Systems. *IEEE Transactions on Systems, Man, and Cybernetics, 27*(4), 714–721. doi:10.1109/3477.604117 PMID:18255911

Chen, S., & Jong, W. (1997). Fuzzy query translation for relational database systems. *IEEE Transaction on Systems*, Man and Cybernetics. *Part B, 27*(4), 714–721.

Cheong, G. P., Lu, W., Yang, J., Du, X., & Zhou, X. (2010). Extract Interesting Skyline Points in High Dimension. In *Proceedings of the 15th International Conference on Database Systems for Advanced Applications (DASFAA)* (pp. 94-108). Tsukuba, Japan: Springer-Verlag. doi:10.1007/978-3-642-12098-5_7

Chiang, D. A., Lin, N. P., & Shis, C. C. (1998). Matching Strengths of Answers in Fuzzy Relational Databases. *IEEE Transactions on Systems, Man and Cybernetics. Part C, Applications and Reviews, 28*(3), 476–481. doi:10.1109/5326.704592

Chomicki, J., Godfrey, P., Gryz, J., & Liang, D. (2003). Skyline with presorting. In *Proceedings of International Conference on Data Engineering (ICDE)* (pp.717-719). Bangalore, India: IEEE Computer Society.

Chomicki, J., Godfrey, P., Gryz, J., & Liang, D. (2003). Skyline with Presorting. In *Proceedings of The 19th International Conference on Data Engineering (ICDE)* (pp. 717–719). Bangalore, India: IEEE Computer Society.

Chomicki, J., Godfrey, P., Gryz, J., & Liang, D. (2003). Skyline with presorting. In *Proceedings of the 19th International Conference on Data Engineering (ICDE)* (pp.717-719). Bangalore, India: IEEE Computer Society.

Chong, E. I., Das, S., Eadon, G., & Srinivasan, J. (2005). An efficient SQL-based RDF querying scheme. In *Proceedings of the 31st international conference on Very large data bases* (pp. 1216-1227). VLDB Endowment.

Chris Anderson, J., Lehnardt, J., & Slater, N. (2010). *CouchDB: The Definitive Guide Time to Relax*. Sebastopol: O'Reilly Media.

Chu, S., Keogh, E. J., Hart, D. M., & Pazzani, M. J. (2002). *Iterative deepening dynamic time warping for time series*. SIAM.

Ciaccia, P., Patella, M., & Zezula, P. (1997). M-tree: An Efficient Access Method for Similarity Search in Metric Spaces. In *Proceeding of the 23rd International Conference on Very Large Data Bases (VLDB)* (pp. 426-435). San Francisco, CA: Morgan Kaufmann Publishers Inc.

Cluet, S. (1998). Designing OQL: Allowing Objects to be Queried. *Information Systems*, 23(5), 279–305. doi:10.1016/S0306-4379(98)00013-1

Codd, E. F. (1970). A Relational Model of Data for Large Shared Data Banks. *Communications of the ACM*, 13(6), 377–387. doi:10.1145/362384.362685

Commons. (2015, August 18). *Getting Started with Sesame*. Retrieved August 20, 2015, from http://rdf4j.org/sesame/tutorials/getting-started.docbook?view

Cong, G., Jensen, C. S., & Wu, D. (2009). Efficient Retrieval of the Top-k Most Relevant Spatial Web Objects. *PVLDB*, 2(1), 337–348.

Conrad, R., Scheffner, D., & Freytag, J. C. (2000). XML Conceptual Modeling Using UML. In *Proceedings of the 19th International Conference on Conceptual Modeling*. Academic Press.

Console, M., & Lenzerini, M. (2014). Data Quality in Ontology-Based Data Access: The Case of Consistency. In *Proceedings of the Twenty-Eighth AAAI Conference on Artificial Intelligence* (pp. 1020-1026). Québec, Canada: AAAI Press.

Consumer & Governmental Affairs Bureau. (2013). *Wireless 911 services*. Retrieved from www.fcc.gov/guides/wireless-911-services

Copeland, G. P., & Khoshafian, S. N. (1985). A decomposition storage model. *SIGMOD Record*, 14(4), 268–279. doi:10.1145/971699.318923

Cosgaya-Lozano, A., Rau-Chaplin, A., & Zeh, N. (2007). Parallel Computation of Skyline Queries. In *Proceedings of 21st International Symposium on High Performance Computing Systems and Applications (HPCS'07)* (pp. 12). Saskatoon: IEEE Computer Society. doi:10.1109/HPCS.2007.25

Cross, V. (2001). Fuzzy Extensions for Relationships in a Generalized Object Model. *International Journal of Intelligent Systems*, 16(7), 843–861. doi:10.1002/int.1038

Cross, V. (2003). Defining Fuzzy Relationships in Object Models: Abstraction and Interpretation. *Fuzzy Sets and Systems*, 140(1), 5–27. doi:10.1016/S0165-0114(03)00025-3

Cross, V., de Caluwe, R., & van Gyseghem, N. (1997). A Perspective from the Fuzzy Object Data Management Group (FODMG). In *Proceedings of the 1997 IEEE International Conference on Fuzzy Systems*. IEEE. doi:10.1109/FUZZY.1997.622800

Cross, V., & Firat, A. (2000). Fuzzy Objects for Geographical Information Systems. *Fuzzy Sets and Systems, 113*(1), 19–36. doi:10.1016/S0165-0114(99)00010-X

CrowdFlower. (2014). Available from http://www.crowdflower.com

Cuevas, L., Marín, N., Pons, O., & Vila, M. A. (2008). pg4DB: A Fuzzy Object-Relational System. *Fuzzy Sets and Systems, 159*(12), 1500–1514. doi:10.1016/j.fss.2008.01.009

Cui, B., Chen, L., Xu, L., Lu, H., Song, G., & Xu, Q. (2009). Efficient Skyline Computation in Structured Peer-to-Peer Systems. *IEEE Transactions on Knowledge and Data Engineering, 21*(7), 1059–1062. doi:10.1109/TKDE.2008.235

Cui, B., Lu, H., Xu, Q., Chen, L., Dai, Y., & Zhou, Y. (2008). Parallel Distributed Processing of Constrained Skyline Queries by Filtering. In *Proceedings of the International Conference on Data Engineering (ICDE)* (pp. 546-555). Cancun, Mexico: IEEE Computer Society. doi:10.1109/ICDE.2008.4497463

Cui, X., Ouyang, D., Ye, Y., & Wang, X. (2011). Translation of Sparql to SQL Based on Integrity Constraint. *Journal of Computer Information Systems, 7*(2), 394–402.

CWI. (2009). *XMark - An XML benchmark project*. Retrieved October 22, 2014, from http://www.xml-benchmark.org/

Cyganiak, R. (2005). A relational algebra for SPARQL. *Digital Media Systems Laboratory HP Laboratories Bristol.* HPL-2005-170, 35.

Cyganiak, R. (2005). A relational algebra for SPARQL. *HP-Labs Technical Report.*

Dadashzadeh, M. (1989). An improved division operator for relational algebra. *Information Systems, 14*(5), 431–437. doi:10.1016/0306-4379(89)90007-0

Damiani, E., Marrara, S., & Pasi, G. (2007). FuzzyXPath: Using fuzzy logic and IR features to approximately query XML documents. In *Proceedings of the International Fuzzy Systems Association World Congress Conference*, (pp. 199-208). Cancun, Mexico: Springer. doi:10.1007/978-3-540-72950-1_21

Damiani, E., Marrara, S., & Pasi, G. (2008). A Flexible Extension of XPath to Improve XML Querying. In *Proceedings of the 2008 International ACM SIGIR Conference on Research and Development in Information Retrieval*. ACM.

Damiani, M. L., Issa, H., Güting, R. H., & Valdes, F. (2014). Hybrid queries over symbolic and spatial trajectories: A usage scenario. In *IEEE International Conference on Mobile Data Management (MDM)*, (pp. 341-344). doi:10.1109/MDM.2014.49

Dawar, A., & Hella, L. (1995). The expressive power of finitely many generalized quantifiers. *Information and Computation, 123*(2), 172–184. doi:10.1006/inco.1995.1166

De Diana, M., & Gerosa, M. (2010). Um Estudo Comparativo de Bancos Não-Relacionais para Armazenamento de Dados na Web 2.0. In *Proceeding of the WTDBD IX Workshop de Teses e Dissertações em Banco de Dados*. Belo Horizonte, Brazil: WTDBD.

De Maio, C., Fenza, G., Furno, D., & Loia, V. (2012). f-SPARQL extension and application to support context recognition. In *2012 IEEE International Conference on Fuzzy Systems (FUZZ-IEEE)*, (pp. 1-8). IEEE. doi:10.1109/FUZZ-IEEE.2012.6251224

de Tré, G., & de Caluwe, R. (2003). Level-2 Fuzzy Sets and Their Usefulness in Object-Oriented Database Modelling. *Fuzzy Sets and Systems, 140*(1), 29–49. doi:10.1016/S0165-0114(03)00026-5 de Tré, G., Zadrozny, S., Matthé, T., Kacprzyk, J., & Bronselaer, A. (2009). Dealing with Positive and Negative Query Criteria in Fuzzy Database Querying. In *Proceedings of the 8th International Conference on Flexible Query Answering Systems*. Roskilde, Denmark: Springer.

Dean, J., & Ghemawat, S. (2004). Mapreduce: Simplified data processing on large clusters. In *Proceedings of sixth symposium on operating system design and implementation*. Academic Press.

Dean, J., & Ghemawat, S. (2004, December). *MapReduce: Simplified Data Processing on Large Clusters*. Retrieved August 20, 2015, from http://research.google.com/archive/mapreduce.htm

Dean, J., & Ghemawat, S. (2004). MapReduce: simplified data processing on large clusters. In *Proceedings of the Symposium on Operating System Design and Implementation*, (pp. 137-150). San Francisco, CA: USENIX Association.

Dean, J., & Ghemawat, S. (2010). MapReduce advantages over parallel databases include storage-system independence and fine-grain fault tolerance for large jobs. *Communications of the ACM*, *53*(1), 72–77. doi:10.1145/1629175.1629198

Dehainsala, H., Pierra, G., & Bellatreche, L. (2007). OntoDB: An Ontology-Based Database for Data Intensive Applications. In *Proceedings of Database Systems for Advanced Applications* (pp. 497–508). Bangkok, Thailand: Springer Berlin Heidelberg. doi:10.1007/978-3-540-71703-4_43

Delaitre, V., & Kazakov, Y. (2009). Classifying ELH Ontologies In SQL Databases. In *Proceedings of the 6th International Workshop on OWL: Experiences and Directions*. Chantilly, VA: CEUR.

Delaunay, B. (1934). Sur la sphère vide. A la mémoire de Georges Voronoï. *Bulletin de l'Académie des Sciences de l'URSS*, *7*(1), 793–800.

Demolombe, R. (1982). Generalized division for relational algebraic language. *Information Processing Letters*, *14*(4), 174–178. doi:10.1016/0020-0190(82)90031-X

Deng, K., Zhou, X., & Tao, H. (2007). Multi-source skyline query processing in road networks. In *Proceedings of the International Conference on Data Engineering (ICDE)* (pp. 796-805). Istanbul, Turkey: IEEE. doi:10.1109/ICDE.2007.367925

Deri, L., Mainardi, S., & Fusco, F. (2012). tsdb: A compressed database for time series. In Traffic Monitoring and Analysis. Springer.

Destercke, S., Buche, P., & Guillard, V. (2011). A Flexible Bipolar Querying Approach with Imprecise Data and Guaranteed Results. *Fuzzy Sets and Systems*, *169*(1), 51–64. doi:10.1016/j.fss.2010.12.014

Di Bartolo, F., & Goncalves, M. (2013). Evaluating spatial skyline queries on changing data. In *Proceedings of the International conference on database and expert (DEXA)* (pp. 270-277). Prague, Czech Republic: Springer. doi:10.1007/978-3-642-40285-2_23

Ding, B., Yu, J. X., & Wang, S. (2007). Finding top-k min-cost connected trees in databases. In *Proceedings of the International Conference on Data Engineering (ICDE)*. (pp 468-477). Istanbul, Turkey: IEEE Computer Society. doi:10.1109/ICDE.2007.367929

Ding, H., Trajcevski, G., Scheuermann, P., Wang, X., & Keogh, E. (2008). Querying and mining of time series data: Experimental comparison of representations and distance measures. *Proceedings of the VLDB Endowment*, *1*(2), 1542–1552. doi:10.14778/1454159.1454226

Ding, R., Wang, Q., Dang, Y., Fu, Q., Zhang, H., & Zhang, D. (2015). YADING: Fast Clustering of Large-Scale Time Series Data. *Proceedings of the VLDB Endowment*, *8*(5), 473–484. doi:10.14778/2735479.2735481

Ding, X., & Jin, H. (2011). Efficient and Progressive Algorithms for Distributed Skyline Queries over Uncertain Data. *IEEE Transactions on Knowledge and Data Engineering*, *24*(8), 1448–1462. doi:10.1109/TKDE.2011.77

Dobbs, M., & Badia, A. (2014). Supporting quantified queries in distributed databases. *International Journal of Parallel. Emergent and Distributed Systems*, *29*(5), 421–459. doi:10.1080/17445760.2014.894513

Dobing, B., & Parsons, J. (2006). How UML is used. *Communications of the ACM*, *49*(5), 109–113. doi:10.1145/1125944.1125949

Dolog, P., Stuckenschmidt, H., Wache, H., & Diederich, J. (2009). Relaxing RDF Queries Based on User and Domain Preferences. *Journal of Intelligent Information Systems*, *33*(3), 239–260. doi:10.1007/s10844-008-0070-7

dos Santos Mello, R., & Heuser, C. A. (2001). A Rule-Based Conversion of a DTD to a Conceptual Schema. In *Proceedings of the 20th International Conference on Conceptual Modeling*. Academic Press.

Dreyer, W., Dittrich, A. K., & Schmidt, D. (1994). Research perspectives for time series management systems. *SIGMOD Record*, *23*(1), 10–15. doi:10.1145/181550.181553

du Mouza, C., Rigaux, P., & Scholl, M. (2005). Efficient evaluation of parameterized pattern queries. In *Proc. of the ACM International Conference on Information and Knowledge Management (CIKM)*, (pp. 728-735). ACM.

Dubois, D., & Prade, H. (2002). Bipolarity in Flexible Querying. In *Proceedings of the 5th International Conference on Flexible Query Answering Systems*. Copenhagen, Denmark:Springer. doi:10.1007/3-540-36109-X_14

Dubois, D., & Prade, H. (2008). An Introduction to Bipolar Representations of Information and Preference. *International Journal of Intelligent Systems*, *23*(8), 866–877. doi:10.1002/int.20297

Dubois, D., & Prade, H. (2008). *Handling Bipolar Queries in Fuzzy Information Processing. In Handbook of Research on Fuzzy Information Processing in Databases* (pp. 97–114). IGI Global. doi:10.4018/978-1-59904-853-6.ch004

Dubois, D., Prade, H., & Rossazza, J. P. (1991). Vagueness, Typicality, and Uncertainty in Class Hierarchies. *International Journal of Intelligent Systems*, *6*(2), 167–183. doi:10.1002/int.4550060205

Edgewall Software. (2007). *M-Tree Download*. Retrieved May 5, 2014, from http://mufin.fi.muni.cz/trac/mtree/wiki/download

Edlich, S. (2011). *NoSQL*. The Apache Software Foundation. Retrieved August 20, 2015, from http://nosql-databases.org/

Eisenberg, A., Melton, J., Kulkarni, K., Michels, J.-E., & Zemke, F. (2004). SQL:2003 Has Been Published. *SIGMOD Record*, *33*(1), 119–126. doi:10.1145/974121.974142

Eklund, J., & Sinclair, K. (2000). An Empirical Appraisal of Adaptive Interfaces for Instructional Systems. *Educational Technology and Society Journal*, *3*, 165–177.

Elbassioni, K. M., Elmasry, A., & Kamel, I. (2003). An efficient indexing scheme for multidimensional moving objects. In *International Conference on Database Theory (ICDT)*, (pp. 425-439). ICDT.

El-Dawy, E., Mokhtar, H., & El-Bastawissy, A. (2011). Multi-level continuous skyline queries (MCSQ). In *Proceedings of the International Conference on Data and Knowledge Engineering (ICDKE)* (pp. 36 -40). Milano, Italy: IEEE.

El-Dawy, E., Mokhtar, H., & El-Bastawissy, A. (2012). Directional skyline queries. In *Proceedings of the International Conference on Data and Knowledge Engineering (ICDKE)* (pp. 15-28). Fujian, China: Springer.

Elliott, B., Cheng, E., Ogbuji, C. T., & Meral Ozsoyoglu, Z. (2009). A complete Translation from SPARQL into Efficient SQL. In *Proceedings of the International Database Engineering and Application Symposium* (pp. 31-42). Calabria, Italy: ACM. doi:10.1145/1620432.1620437

Elmasri, R., Li, Q., Fu, J., Wu, Y.-C., Hojabri, B., & Ande, S. (2005). Conceptual Modeling for Customized XML Schemas. *Data & Knowledge Engineering*, *54*(1), 57–76. doi:10.1016/j.datak.2004.10.003

Elmasri, R., & Navathe, S. (2011). *Sistemas De Banco De Dados*. São Paulo, Brazil: Pearson Addison Wesley Publisher.

Elmasri, R., & Navathe, S. B. (1994). *Fundamentals of Database Systems* (2nd ed.). Redwood, CA: Benjamin/Cummings.

Embley, D. W., & Ling, T. W. (1989). Synergistic Database Design with an Extended Entity-Relationship Model. In *Proceedings of the Eight International Conference on Entity-Relationship Approach*. Academic Press.

Emrich, T., Kriegel, H.-P., Mamoulis, N., Renz, M., & Züfle, A. (2012). Indexing uncertain spatio-temporal data. In *Proc. of the ACM International Conference on Information and Knowledge Management (CIKM)*, (pp. 395-404). ACM.

Encyclopedia of Information Science and Technology. (2014, Aug 25). Retrieved from: http://www.books.google.co.ve/books?isbn=1466658894

Eriksso, H., & Magnus, P. (1999). *Business Modeling with UML: Business Patterns at work*. Wiley & Sons.

Erwig, M., & Schneider, M. (2002, July). Spatio-temporal predicates. *IEEE Transactions on Knowledge and Data Engineering*, *14*(4), 881–901. doi:10.1109/TKDE.2002.1019220

Esling, P., & Agon, C. (2013). Multiobjective time series matching for audio classification and retrieval. *Audio, Speech, and Language Processing. IEEE Transactions on*, *21*(10), 2057–2072.

Ester, M., Kriegel, H. P., Sander, J., & Xu, X. (1996). A density-based algorithm for discovering clusters in large spatial databases with noise. In *Proceedings of the 2nd International Conference on Knowledge Discovery and Data Mining (KDD-96)*, (pp. 226–231). AAAI Press.

Euán, C., Ortega, J., & Alvarez-Esteban, P. C. (2014). Detecting Stationary Intervals for Random Waves Using Time Series Clustering. In *ASME 2014 33rd International Conference on Ocean, Offshore and Arctic Engineering* (pp. V04BT02A027--V04BT02A027). American Society of Mechanical Engineers. doi:10.1115/OMAE2014-24269

eXist Solutions. (2011). *eXist-db (open source native XML database)*. Retrieved October 1, 2014, from http://exist.sourceforge.net/

Fagin, R., Lotem, A., & Naor, M. (2001). Optimal aggregation algorithms for middleware. In *Proc. of the ACM SIGMOD-SIGACT-SIGART Symp. on Principles of Database Systems (PODS)*, (pp. 102-113). ACM.

Fagin, R., Lotem, A., & Naor, M. (2001). Optimal aggregation algorithms for middleware. In *Proceedings of the Internatioanl Conference on Principles of Database Systems (PODS)* (pp 102-113). Santa Barbara, CA: ACM.

Fagin, R., Lotem, A., & Naor, M. (2001). Optimal aggregation algorithms for middleware. In *Proceedings of the Symposium on Principles of Database Systems*, (pp. 102-113). Santa Barbara, CA: ACM.

Faloutsos, C., Ranganathan, M., & Manolopoulos, Y. (1994). *Fast subsequence matching in time-series databases* (Vol. 23). ACM.

Faurous, P., & Fillard, J. P. (1993). A New Approach to the Similarity Relations in the Fuzzy Set Theory. *Information Sciences*, *75*(3), 213–221. doi:10.1016/0020-0255(93)90055-Q

Fazzinga, B., Flesca, S., & Pugliese, A. (2009). Top-k Answers to Fuzzy XPath Queries, In *Proceedings of the 2009 International Conference on Databases and Expert Systems Applications*. Academic Press.

Fazzinga, B., Flesca, S., & Pugliese, A. (2009). Top-k answers to fuzzy XPath queries. In *Proceedings of the DEXA Conference*, (pp. 822-829). Linz, Austria: Springer.

Ferber, J. (1999). *Multi-Agent Systems: An Introduction to Distributed Artificial Intelligence*. Boston, MA: Addison-Wesley.

Ferhatosmanoglu, H., Stanoi, I., Agrawal, D., & Abbadi, A. E. (2001). Constrained nearest neighbor queries. In *Proc. of the International Symp. on Advances in Spatial and Temporal Databases (SSTD)*, (vol.. 2121, pp. 257-278). doi:10.1007/3-540-47724-1_14

Fernandez, M., Simeon, J., & Wadler, P. (2000). An Algebra for XML Query. In *Proceedings of the 20th International Conference on Foundations of Software Technology and Theoretical Computer Science*, (pp. 11-45).

Ferreira, G., Calil, A., & Mello, R. (2013). On Providing DDL Support for a Relational Layer over a Document NoSQL Database. In *Proceedings of the International Conference on Information Integration and Web-based Applications & Services (IIWAS '13)*. Vienna. Austria: ACM.

Fragatelli, C. (1991). Technique for universal quantification in SQL. *SIGMOD Record*, *20*(3), 16–24. doi:10.1145/126482.126484

Franceschet, M., Montanari, A., & Gubiani, D. (2007). Modeling and Validating Spatio-Temporal Conceptual Schemas in XML Schema. In *Proceedings of the 18th International Conference on Database and Expert Systems Applications*, (pp. 25-29). doi:10.1109/DEXA.2007.106

Franconi, E. (2008). Ontologies and Databases: myths and challenges. In *Proceedings of the VLDB Endowment* (pp. 1518-1519). Auckland, New Zealand: ACM.

Franconi, E., Kerhet, V., & Ngo, N. (2013). Exact Query Reformulation over Databases with First-order and Description Logics Ontologies. *Journal of Artificial Intelligence Research*, *48*, 885–922.

Franz. (2015). *Gruff (Version 5.9.0)* [Software]. Available from http://franz.com/agraph/gruff/

Fredrich, T. (2000). *Learn REST: A RESTful Tutorial*. Retrieved August 20, 2015, from http://www.restapitutorial.com/lessons/whatisrest.html

Frias-Martinez, V., Soto, V., Hohwald, H., & Frias-Martinez, E. (2012). Characterizing Urban Landscapes Using Geo-located Tweets. In *Privacy, Security, Risk and Trust (PASSSAT),2012 International Conference on Social Computing (SocialCom)*, (pp 239–248). Amsterdam: IEEE.

FSQL. (2014, Jun 20). Retrieved from: http://www.lcc.uma.es/~ppgg/FSQL/

Fu, A. W.-C., Keogh, E., Lau, L. Y., Ratanamahatana, C. A., & Wong, R. C.-W. (2008). Scaling and time warping in time series querying. *The VLDB Journal—The International Journal on Very Large Data Bases, 17*(4), 899--921.

Fukami, S., Umano, M., Muzimoto, M., & Tanaka, H. (1979). Fuzzy database retrieval and manipulation language. *IEICE Technical Reports*, *78*(233), 65–72.

Galindo, J. (2005). New Characteristics in FSQL, a Fuzzy SQL for Fuzzy Databases. *WSEAS Transactions on Information Science and Applications*, *2*(2), 161–169.

Galindo, J., Medina, J. M., & Aranda, M. C. (1999). Querying Fuzzy Relational Databases through Fuzzy Domain Calculus. *International Journal of Intelligent Systems*, *14*(4), 375–411. doi:10.1002/(SICI)1098-111X(199904)14:4<375::AID-INT3>3.0.CO;2-K

Galindo, J., Urrutia, A., Carrasco, R. A., & Piattini, M. (2004). Relaxing Constraints in Enhanced Entity-Relationship Models Using Fuzzy Quantifiers. *IEEE Transactions on Fuzzy Systems*, *12*(6), 780–796. doi:10.1109/TFUZZ.2004.836088

Galindo, J., Urrutia, A., & Piattini, M. (2006). *Fuzzy Databases: Modeling, Design and Implementation*. Idea Group Publishing. doi:10.4018/978-1-59140-324-1

Galindo-Legaria, C. A., & Joshi, M. M. (2001). Orthogonal optimization of subqueries and aggregation. In *Proceedings of the ACM SIGMOD international conference on management of data* (p. 571-581). ACM.

Galindo-Legaria, C. A., & Rosenthal, A. (1997). Outerjoin simplification and reordering for query optimization. *ACM Transactions on Database Systems*, *22*(1), 43–73. doi:10.1145/244810.244812

Gandomi, A., & Haider, M. (2015). Beyond the hype: Big data concepts, methods, and analytics. *International Journal of Information Management*, *35*(2), 137–144. doi:10.1016/j.ijinfomgt.2014.10.007

Ganter, B., & Wille, R. (1992). *Formal Concept Analysis: Mathematical foundations*. Berlin: Springer.

Gao, Y., Hu, J., Chen, G., & Chen, C. (2010). Finding the Most Desirable Skyline Objects. In *Proceedings of the 15th International Conference on Database Systems for Advanced Applications (DASFAA)* (pp. 116-122). Springer-Verlag: Tsukuba, Japan.

Gaurav, A., & Alhajj, R. (2006). Incorporating Fuzziness in XML and Mapping Fuzzy Relational Data into Fuzzy XML. In *Proceedings of the 2006 ACM Symposium on Applied Computing*. doi:10.1145/1141277.1141386

George, L. (2011). *HBase: The Definitive Guide*. Sebastopol: O'Reilly Media.

George, R., Srikanth, R., Petry, F. E., & Buckles, B. P. (1996). Uncertainty Management Issues in the Object-Oriented Data Model. *IEEE Transactions on Fuzzy Systems*, *4*(2), 179–192. doi:10.1109/91.493911

Ghias, A., Logan, J., Chamberlin, D., & Smith, B. C. (1995). Query by humming: musical information retrieval in an audio database. In *Proceedings of the third ACM international conference on Multimedia* (pp. 231--236). ACM. doi:10.1145/217279.215273

Ghosh, D., & Guha, R. (2013). What are we 'Tweeting' about Obesity? Mapping Tweets with Topic Modeling and Geographic Information System. *Cartography and Geographic Information Science*, *40*(2), 90–102. doi:10.1080/1523 0406.2013.776210 PMID:25126022

Gislandi, P. (2012). adAstra: A Rubrics' Set for Quality eLearning Design. In P. Ghislandi (Ed.), eLearning - Theories, Design, Software and Applications (pp. 91-106). InTech - Open Access Publisher.

Giuffrida, G., & Zaniolo, C. (1994). EPL: Event Pattern Language. In *Third CLIPS Conference*. NASA's Johnson Space Center.

Göbel, R. (2007). Towards Logarithmic Search Time Complexity for R-trees. In *Proceedings of The Innovations and Advanced Techniques in Computer and Information Sciences and Engineering* (pp. 201-206). Dordrecht, The Netherland: Springer. doi:10.1007/978-1-4020-6268-1_37

Godfrey, P., Shipley, R., & Gryz, J. (2005). Maximal vector computation in large data sets. In *Proceedings of the 31st International Conference on Very Large Data Bases (VLDB)* (pp. 229-240). Trondheim, Norway: ACM.

Godfrey, P., Shipley, R., & Gryz, J. (2005). Maximal Vector Computation in Large Data Sets. In *Proceedings of The 31st International Conference on Very Large Databases (VLDB)* (pp. 229–240). Trondheim, Norway: ACM.

Godfrey, P., Shipley, R., & Gryz, J. (2005). Maximal vector computation in large data sets. In *Proceedings of the International Conference on Very Large Data Bases (VLDB)* (pp. 229-240). Trondheim, Norway: ACM.

Godugula, S. (2008). *Survey of Ontology Mapping Techniques*. Retrieved from http://www.cs.uni-paderborn.de/fileadmin/Informatik/AG-Engels/Lehre/SS08/Seminar_Software-Qualit%C3%A4tssicherung/Seminararbeiten/Vers._1.0/ontology_seminar_report_august1.pdf

Goldman, R., & Widom, J. (1997). DataGuides: Enabling Query Formulation and Optimization in Semistructured Databases. In *Proceedings of the 23rd International Conference on VLDB*, (pp. 436-445). VLDB.

Goldschmidt, T., Jansen, A., Koziolek, H., Doppelhamer, J., & Breivold, H. P. (2014). Scalability and Robustness of Time-Series Databases for Cloud-Native Monitoring of Industrial Processes. *Cloud Computing (CLOUD), 2014 IEEE 7th International Conference on* (pp. 602--609). IEEE.

Golyandina, N., & Zhigljavsky, A. (2013). *Singular Spectrum Analysis for time series*. Springer. doi:10.1007/978-3-642-34913-3

Goncalves, M., & Tineo, L. (2007). A new step towards Flexible XQuery. *Revista Avances en Sistemas e Informática, 4*(3).

Goncalves, M., & Tineo, L. (2010). Fuzzy XQuery. In Soft Computing in XML Data Management. Springer.

Goncalves, M., & Tineo, L. (2010). Fuzzy XQuery. Soft Computing in XML Data Management. In Z. Ma & L. Yan (Ed.), Soft Computing in XML Data Management (pp. 133-163). Springer.

Goncalves, M., & Vidal, M.-E. (2012). Efficiently Producing the K Nearest Neighbors in the Skyline for Multidimensional Datasets. In *Proceedings of the On The Move (OTM) Workshops* (pp. 673-676). Rome, Italy: Springer-Verlag. doi:10.1007/978-3-642-33618-8_92

Goncalves, M., & Tineo, L. (2010). Fuzzy XQuery. In *Soft computing in XML data management: intelligent systems from decision to data mining, web intelligence and computer vision* (pp. 133–166). Springer. doi:10.1007/978-3-642-14010-5_6

Goncalves, M., & Vidal, M.-E. (2009). Reaching the top of the Skyline: An efficient indexed algorithm for Top-k Skyline queries. In *Proceedings of The International Conference on Database and Expert Systems Applications* (DEXA) (pp. 471-485). Linz, Austria: Springer-Verlag. doi:10.1007/978-3-642-03573-9_41

Gordon, D., Hendler, D., Kontorovich, A., & Rokach, L. (2015). Local-shapelets for fast classification of spectrographic measurements. *Expert Systems with Applications, 42*(6), 3150–3158. doi:10.1016/j.eswa.2014.11.043

Gottlob, G., Orsi, G., & Pieris, A. (2011). Ontological query answering via rewriting. In *Proceedings of ADBIS* (pp. 1-18). Vienna, Austria: Springer.

Graefe, G., & Cole, R. (1995). Fast algorithms for universal quantification in large databases. *ACM Transactions on Database Systems, 20*(2), 187–236. doi:10.1145/210197.210202

Gray, R., Cybenko, G., Kotz, D., & Rus, D. (2001). Mobile Agents: Motivations and State of the Art. In J. Bradshaw (Ed.), *Handbook of Agent Technology*. Cambridge, MA: AAAI/MIT Press.

Griol, D., & Callejas, Z. (2013). An Architecture to Develop Multimodal Educative Applications with Chatbots. *International Journal of Advanced Robotic Systems, 10*, 1–15. doi:10.5772/55791

Guéret, C., Oren, E., Schlobach, S., & Schut, M. C. (2008). An Evolutionary Perspective on Approximate RDF Query Answering. In *Proceedings of the 2nd International Conference on Scalable Uncertainty Management*. Naples, Italy: Springer. doi:10.1007/978-3-540-87993-0_18

Guo, X., Ishikawa, Y., & Gao, Y. (2010). Direction-based spatial skylines. In *Proceedings of The ACM International Workshop on Data Engineering for Wireless and Mobile Access* (pp. 73-80). New York, NY: ACM.

Guo, X., Zheng, B., Ishikawa, Y., & Gao, Y. (2011, October). Direction-based surrounder queries for mobile recommendations. *The VLDB Journal, 20*(5), 743–766. doi:10.1007/s00778-011-0241-y

Guo, Y., Pan, Z., & Heflin, J. (2004). An Evaluation of Knowledge Base Systems for Large OWL Datasets. In *Proceedings of the 3th International Semantic Web Conference*. Hiroshima, Japan:Springer. doi:10.1007/978-3-540-30475-3_20

Gupta, H., & Lakshminarasimhan, S. (2014). Processing Spatio-temporal Data On Map-Reduce. In *Proc. of the International Conference on Big Data Analytics (BDA)*, (pp. 57-59). Academic Press.

Guttman, A. (1984). *R-trees: a dynamic index structure for spatial searching*. Academic Press.

Guttman, A. (1984). R-trees: A Dynamic Index Structure for Spatial Searching. In *Proceedings of The ACM SIGMOD International Conference on Management of Data* (pp. 47-57). Boston: ACM doi:10.1145/602259.602266

Haarslev, V., & Möller, R. (2003). Racer: an OWL reasoning agent for the Semantic Web. In *Proceedings of Web Intelligence Workshops* (pp. 91–95). Halifax, Canada: IEEE.

Haber, D., Thomik, A. A., & Faisal, A. A. (2014). Unsupervised time series segmentation for high-dimensional body sensor network data streams. *Wearable and Implantable Body Sensor Networks (BSN), 2014 11th International Conference on* (pp. 121--126). IEEE.

Hadjieleftheriou, M. (2009). *Libspatialindex*. Retrieved January 15, 2013, from http://libspatialindex.github.io

Hadjieleftheriou, M., Kollios, G., Bakalov, P., & Tsotras, V. J. (2005). Complex spatio-temporal pattern queries. In *Proc. of the International Conference on Very Large Data Bases (VLDB)*, (pp. 877-888). VLDB.

Hadjieleftheriou, M., Kollios, G., Tsotras, V. J., & Gunopulos, D. (2006). Indexing spatiotemporal archives. *The VLDB Journal, 15*(2), 143–164. doi:10.1007/s00778-004-0151-3

Hai, H., Liu, C. F., & Zhou, X. F. (2012). Approximating Query Answering on RDF Databases. *World Wide Web (Bussum), 15*(1), 89–114. doi:10.1007/s11280-011-0131-7

Hajeck, P. (1998). Logics for data mining. In ISAI workshop. ISAI.

Halder, R., & Cortesi, A. (2011). Cooperative query answering by abstract interpretation. In *Proceedings of the Conference on Current Trends in Theory and Practice of Computer Science*, (pp. 284-296). Smokovec, Slovakia: Springer.

Halder, R., & Cortesi, A. (2011). Cooperative Query Answering by Abstract Interpretation. In *Proceedings of the 37th Conference on Current Trends in Theory and Practice of Informatics*. Nový Smokovec, Slovakia: Springer.

Han, W.-S., Jiang, H., Ho, H., & Li, Q. (2008). Streamtx: extracting tuples from streaming xml data. *Proceedings of the Very Large Database (VLDB) Endowment, 1*(1), 289-300. doi:10.14778/1453856.1453891

Han, J., Haihong, E., Guan, L., & Du, J. (2011). Survey on NoSQL Database. In *Proceedings of the 6th international conference on Pervasive computing and applications (ICPCA)*. Lanzhou, China: IEEE.

Harris, S., & Seaborne, A. (2010). SPARQL 1.1 query language. *W3C recommendation*, 14.

Harris, S., & Seaborne, A. (2013). *SPARQL 1.1 Query Language*. W3C Recommendation. Retrieved from http://www.w3.org/TR/sparql11-query/

Harris, S., Lamb, N., & Shadbolt, N. (2009). 4store: The design and implementation of a clustered RDF store. In *5th International Workshop on Scalable Semantic Web Knowledge Base Systems* (SSWS2009) (pp. 94-109). SSWS.

Harris, S., & Gibbins, N. (2003). 3store: Efficient bulk RDF storage. In *Proceedings of the First International Workshop on Practical and Scalable Semantic Systems*. Sanibel Island, FL: Academic Press.

Harris, S., & Shadbolt, N. (2005). SPARQL query processing with conventional relational database systems. In *Web Information Systems Engineering–WISE 2005 Workshops* (pp. 235–244). Springer Berlin Heidelberg. doi:10.1007/11581116_25

Harth, A., Umbrich, J., Hogan, A., & Decker, S. (2007). YARS2: A Federated Repository for Querying Graph Structured Data from the Web. In *proceedings of the Semantic Web: 6th International Semantic Web Conference, 2nd Asian Semantic Web Conference, ISWC 2007+ ASWC 2007,* (Vol. 4825, p. 211). Springer.

Harth, A. (2010). Visinav: A system for visual search and navigation on web data. *Web Semantics: Science, Services, and Agents on the World Wide Web, 8*(4), 348–354. doi:10.1016/j.websem.2010.08.001

Haslhofer, B., Momeni Roochi, E., Schandl, B., & Zander, S. (2011). *Europeana rdf store report*. Academic Press.

Hecht, R., & Jablonski, S. (2011). NoSQL Evaluation A Use Case Oriented Survey. In *Proceedings of the 2011 International Conference on Cloud and Service Computing (CSC '11)*. Hong Kong, China: IEEE. doi:10.1109/CSC.2011.6138544

He, G., Duan, Y., Peng, R., Jing, X., Qian, T., & Wang, L. (2015). Early classification on multivariate time series. *Neurocomputing, 149*, 777–787. doi:10.1016/j.neucom.2014.07.056

Heim, P., Ertl, T., & Ziegler, J. (2010). Facet graphs: Complex semantic querying made easy. In *The Semantic Web: Research and Applications* (pp. 288–302). Springer Berlin Heidelberg. doi:10.1007/978-3-642-13486-9_20

Hertel, A., Broekstra, J., & Stuckenschmidt, H. (2009). RDF storage and retrieval systems. In *Handbook on ontologies* (pp. 489–508). Springer Berlin Heidelberg. doi:10.1007/978-3-540-92673-3_22

Hirabayashi, M. (2010, August 5). *Introduction to Fal Tokyo Products*. Retrieved August 20, 2015, from http://fallabs. com/tokyocabinet/tokyoproducts.pdf

Hjaltason, G. R., & Samet, H. (1999). Distance browsing in spatial databases. *ACM Transactions on Database Systems, 24*(2), 265–318. doi:10.1145/320248.320255

Hobbs, J., & Riloff, E. (2010). Information Extraction. In Handbook of Natural Language Processing (2nd ed.). Chapman & Hall/CRC Press, Taylor & Francis Group.

Horrocks, I. (2008). *Ontologies and Databases*. Stavanger, Norway: Semantic Days.

Horrocks, I., Patel-Schneider, P. F., & van Harmelen, F. (2003). From SHIQ and RDF to OWL: The Making of a Web Ontology Language. *Journal of Web Semantics, 1*(1), 7–26. doi:10.1016/j.websem.2003.07.001

Hristidis, V., & Papakonstantinou, Y. (2002). Discover: keyword search in relational databases. In *Proceedings of the International Conference on Very Large Data Bases (VLDB)*. (pp 670-681). Hong Kong, China: Endowment. doi:10.1016/B978-155860869-6/50065-2

Hristidis, V., Gravano, L., & Papakonstantinou, Y. (2003). Efficient IR-style keyword search over relational databases. In *Proceedings of the International Conference on Very Large Data Bases (VLDB)*. (pp 850-861). Berlin, Germany: Endowment. doi:10.1016/B978-012722442-8/50080-X

Hsieh, M., Chang, C., Ho, L., Wu, J., & Liu, P. (2011). SQLMR:A Scalable Database Management System for Cloud Computing. In *Proceedings of the International Conference on Parallel Processing (ICPP)*. Taipei, Taiwan: IEEE.

Hsu, P. Y., & Parker, D. S. (1995). Improving SQL with generalized quantifiers. In *Proceedings of the IEEE international conference on data engineering (ICDE)* (p. 298-305). IEEE.

Hsueh, Y.-L., Zimmermann, R., Ku, W.-S., & Jin, Y. (2011). SkyEngine: Efficient Skyline Search Engine for Continuous Skyline Computations. In *Proceedings of the International Conference on Data Engineering (ICDE)* (pp.1316-1319). Hannover, Germany: IEEE Computer Society. doi:10.1109/ICDE.2011.5767944

Huang, B., Yi, S., & Chan, W. T. (2004). Spatio-Temporal Information Integration in XML. *Future Generation Computer Systems, 20*(7), 1157–1170. doi:10.1016/j.future.2003.11.005

Huang, J., Xin, J., Wang, G., & Li, M. (2009). Efficient k-dominant skyline processing in wireless sensor networks. In *Proceedings of the International Conference on Hybrid Intelligent Systems (HIS)* (pp. 289-294). Shenyang, China: IEEE Computer Society. doi:10.1109/HIS.2009.273

Huang, Y.-K., Chang, C.-H., & Lee, C. (2012). Continuous distance-based skyline queries in road networks. *Information Systems, 37*(7), 611–633. doi:10.1016/j.is.2012.02.003

Huang, Y.-W., & Yu, P. S. (1999). Adaptive query processing for time-series data. In *Proceedings of the fifth ACM SIGKDD international conference on Knowledge discovery and data mining* (pp. 282--286). ACM. doi:10.1145/312129.318357

Huang, Z., Jensen, C. S., Lu, H., & Ooi, B. C. (2006). Skyline Queries against Mobile Lightweight Devices in MANET. In *Proceedings of the International Conference on Data Engineering (ICDE)* (pp. 66). Atlanta, GA: IEEE Computer Society. doi:10.1109/ICDE.2006.142

Huang, Z., & Xiang, Y. (2009). Improve the Usefulness of Skyline Analysis in Cloud Computing Environments. In *Proceedings of the 2nd International Symposium on Computational Intelligence and Design* (pp. 325-328). Changsha, China: IEEE. doi:10.1109/ISCID.2009.89

Huang, Z., & Xiang, Y. (2010). An Efficient Method for Diversifying Skylines in SOA Environment. In *Proceedings of the Conference on Intelligent Computing and Cognitive Informatics* (pp. 466-469). Kuala Lumpur, Malaysia: IEEE. doi:10.1109/ICICCI.2010.94

Hung, E., Getoor, L., & Subrahmanian, V. S. (2003). PXML: A Probabilistic Semi-Structured Data Model and Algebra. In *Proceedings of the 19th International Conference on Data Engineering*, (pp. 467-478). Academic Press.

Hustadt, U., Motik, B., & Sattler, U. (2007). Reasoning in description logics by a reduction to disjunctive datalog. *Journal of Automated Reasoning, 39*(3), 351–384. doi:10.1007/s10817-007-9080-3

Imamura, M., Takayama, S., & Munaka, T. (2012). A stream query language TPQL for anomaly detection in facility management. In *Proceedings of the 16th International Database Engineering & Applications Sysmposium* (pp. 235--238). ACM. doi:10.1145/2351476.2351506

Im, H., Park, J., & Park, S. (2009). Parallel skyline computation on multi-core architectures. In *Proceedings of the 19th International Conference on Data Engineering (ICDE)* (pp. 808-823). Shanghai: IEEE Computer Society.

Indrawan-Santiago, M. (2012). Database Research: Are We At A Crossroad? In *Proceeding of the 2012 15th International Conference on Network-Based Information Systems (NBIS '12)*. Melbourne, Australia: ACM. doi:10.1109/NBiS.2012.95

Iyer, K. B. P., & Shanthi, V. (2012). Goal Directed Relative Skyline Queries in Time Dependent Road Networks. *International Journal of Database Management Systems, 4*(2), 23–34. doi:10.5121/ijdms.2012.4202

Iyer, K. P., & Shanthi, V. (2012). Spatial boolean skyline boundary queries in road networks. In *Proceedings of the International Conference on Computing Communication Networking Technologies (ICCCNT)* (pp. 1 -6). Coimbatore, India: IEEE doi:10.1109/ICCCNT.2012.6396049

Jacas, J. (1990). Similarity Relations-The Calculation of Minimal Generating Families. *Fuzzy Sets and Systems, 35*(2), 151–162. doi:10.1016/0165-0114(90)90190-H

Jagadish, H. V., Laks, V. S., & Lakshmanan, D. (2001). TAX: A Tree Algebra for XML. In *Proceedings of the International Workshop on Database Programming Languages*, (pp. 149-164). Academic Press.

Jang, H.-J., Choi, W.-S., Hyun, K.-S., Jung, K.-H., Jung, S.-Y., Jeong, Y.-S., & Chung, J. (2014). Towards Nearest Collection Search on Spatial Databases. In *Proceedings of The International conference on Ubiquitous Information Technologies and Applications (CUTE)* (pp. 433-440). Berlin: Springer-Verlag. doi:10.1007/978-3-642-41671-2_55

Jarrar, M., & Dikaiakos, M. D. (2012). A Query Formulation Language for the Data Web. *IEEE Transactions on Knowledge and Data Engineering, 24*(5), 783–798. doi:10.1109/TKDE.2011.41

Jean, S., Aït-Ameur, Y., & Pierra, G. (2006). Querying Ontology Based Database Using OntoQL (An Ontology Query Language). In *Proceedings of OTM* (pp. 704-721). Montpellier, France: Springer. doi:10.1007/11914853_43

Jensen, C. S., Lin, D., & Ooi, B. (2004). Query and update efficient B+-Tree based indexing of moving objects. In *Proc. of the International Conference on Very Large Data Bases (VLDB)*, (pp. 768-779). doi:10.1016/B978-012088469-8.50068-1

Jiang, B. a. (2009). Online interval skyline queries on time series. *Data Engineering, 2009. ICDE'09. IEEE 25th International Conference on* (pp. 1036--1047). IEEE.

Jiang, B., & Pei, J. (2009). Online Interval Skyline Queries on Time Series. In *Proceedings of the 25th International Conference on Data Engineering (ICDE)* (pp. 1036-1043). Shanghai: IEEE Computer Society. doi:10.1109/ICDE.2009.70

Jiang, D., Ooi, B. C., Shi, L., & Wu, S. (2010). The performance of MapReduce: An in-depth study. *Proceedings of the VLDB Endowment, 3*(1), 472–483. doi:10.14778/1920841.1920903

Jiang, Z., Luo, Y., Wu, N., He, C., Yuan, P., & Jin, H. (2013). Managing Large Scale Unstructured Data with RDBMS. In *Proceedings of the 2013 IEEE 11th International Conference on Dependable, Autonomic and Secure Computing*. Jinan, China: IEEE. doi:10.1109/DASC.2013.135

Jin, Y., & Veerappan, S. (2010). A fuzzy XML database system: Data storage and query processing. In *Proceedings of International Conference on Information Reuse and Integration*. doi:10.1109/IRI.2010.5558919

Jin, Y., & Veerappan, S. (2010). A Fuzzy XML Database System: Data Storage and Query. In *Proceedings of 2010 IEEE International Conference on Information Reuse and Integration*. IEEE.

Jin, H., Ning, X. M., Jia, W. J., Wu, H., & Lu, G. L. (2008). Combining Weights with Fuzziness for Intelligent Semantic Web Search. *Knowledge-Based Systems, 21*(7), 655–665. doi:10.1016/j.knosys.2008.03.040

Judd, D. (2014). *Hypertable User Guide*. Retrieved August 20, 2015, from http://hypertable.com/documentation/user_guide/

Juel, C. (1988). Learning to read and write: A longitudinal study of 54 children from first through fourth grades. *Journal of Educational Psychology, 80*(4), 437–447. doi:10.1037/0022-0663.80.4.437

Kacprzyk, J., Zadrozny, S., & Ziokkowski, A. (1987). FQUERY III+: A "Human-consistent" Database Querying System Based on Fuzzy Logic with Linguistic Quantifiers. In *Proceedings of the Second International Fuzzy Systems Association Congress*. Academic Press.

Kacprzyk, J., & Zadrożny, S. (1995). *FQUERY for Access: Fuzzy Querying for Windows-based DBMS. In Fuzziness in Database Management Systems* (pp. 415–433). Physica-Verlag. doi:10.1007/978-3-7908-1897-0_18

Kamath, K. Y., Caverlee, J., Lee, K., & Cheng, Z. (2013). Spatio-Temporal Dynamics of Online Memes: A Study of Geo-Tagged Tweets. In *Proceedings of the ACM WWW 2013*. Rio de Janeiro, Brazil: ACM.

Kamath, U., Lin, J., & De Jong, K. (2014). SAX-EFG: an evolutionary feature generation framework for time series classification. In *Proceedings of the 2014 conference on Genetic and evolutionary computation* (pp. 533--540). ACM. doi:10.1145/2576768.2598321

Kamel, M., Hadfield, B., & Ismail, M. (1990). Fuzzy Query Processing Using Clustering Techniques. *Information Processing & Management, 26*(2), 279–293. doi:10.1016/0306-4573(90)90031-V

Kaoudi, Z., & Kementsietsidis, A. (2014). Query Processing for RDF Databases. In *Reasoning Web. Reasoning on the Web in the Big Data Era* (pp. 141–170). Springer International Publishing.

Kashlev, A., & Chebotko, A. (2011). SPARQL-to-SQL Query Translation: Bottom-Up or Top-Down? In *Proceedings of IEEE International Conference on Services Computing*. Washington, DC: IEEE.

Katayama, N. a. (1997). *The SR-tree: An index structure for high-dimensional nearest neighbor queries*. Academic Press.

Kaur, K., & Rani, R. (2013). Modeling and Querying Data in NoSQL Databases. In *Proceedings of the IEEE International Conference on Big Data*. Silicon Valley, CA: IEEE. doi:10.1109/BigData.2013.6691765

Keenan, E., & Westerstahl, D. (1985). Generalized quantifiers in linguistics and logic. In J. van Benthem & A. ter Meulen (Eds.), *Generalized quantifiers in natural language*. Foris Publications.

Keogh, E. J., & Pazzani, M. J. (2000). A simple dimensionality reduction technique for fast similarity search in large time series databases. In Knowledge Discovery and Data Mining. Current Issues and New Applications (pp. 122--133). Springer. doi:10.1007/3-540-45571-X_14

Keogh, E., Lin, J., & Fu, A. (2005). Hot sax: Efficiently finding the most unusual time series subsequence. *Data mining, fifth IEEE international conference on* (pp. 8--pp). IEEE.

Keogh, E., Chakrabarti, K., Pazzani, M., & Mehrotra, S. (2001). Dimensionality reduction for fast similarity search in large time series databases. *Knowledge and Information Systems, 3*(3), 263–286. doi:10.1007/PL00011669

Keogh, E., Chakrabarti, K., Pazzani, M., & Mehrotra, S. (2001). Locally adaptive dimensionality reduction for indexing large time series databases. *SIGMOD Record, 30*(2), 151–162. doi:10.1145/376284.375680

Keogh, E., & Ratanamahatana, C. A. (2005). Exact indexing of dynamic time warping. *Knowledge and Information Systems, 7*(3), 358–386. doi:10.1007/s10115-004-0154-9

Kerre, E. E., & Chen, G. Q. (1995). *An Overview of Fuzzy Data Modeling. In Fuzziness in Database Management Systems* (pp. 23–41). Physica-Verlag. doi:10.1007/978-3-7908-1897-0_2

Kim, S.-W., Park, S., & Chu, W. W. (2001). An index-based approach for similarity search supporting time warping in large sequence databases. *Data Engineering, 2001. Proceedings. 17th International Conference on* (pp. 607--614). IEEE.

Kim, Y., & Park, C. H. (2013). Query by Humming by Using Scaled Dynamic Time Warping. *Signal-Image Technology & Internet-Based Systems (SITIS), 2013 International Conference on* (pp. 1--5). IEEE.

Kim, D., Im, H., & Park, S. (2011). Computing Exact Skyline Probabilities for Uncertain Databases. *IEEE Transactions on Knowledge and Data Engineering, 24*(12), 2113–2126. doi:10.1109/TKDE.2011.164

Kim, W., & Lochovsky, F. H. (1989). *Object-Oriented Concepts, Databases and Applications*. Addison Wesley.

Kim, Y., & Shim, K. (2012). Parallel top-k similarity join algorithms using MapReduce. In *Proceedings of the International Conference on Data Engineering*, (pp. 510-521). Arlington, VA: IEEE Computer Society. doi:10.1109/ICDE.2012.87

Kiryakov, A., Ognyanov, D., & Manov, D. (2005). OWLIM–a pragmatic semantic repository for OWL. In *Web Information Systems Engineering–WISE 2005 Workshops* (pp. 182–192). Springer Berlin Heidelberg.

Kllapi, H., Bilidas, D., Horrocks, I., Ioannidis, Y., Jiménez-Ruiz, E., Kharlamov, E., & Zheleznyakov, D. et al. (2013). Distributed Query Processing on the Cloud: the Optique Point of View (Short Paper). In *Proceedings of the Workshop on OWL: Experiences And Directions (OWLED)*. Montpellier, France: OWLED.

Knuth, D. (1997). *The Art Of Computer Programming* (3rd ed.; Vol. 1). Boston: Addison-Wesley.

Knuth, D. E. Jr, Morris, J. H. Jr, & Pratt, V. R. (1977). Fast pattern matching in strings. *SIAM Journal on Computing*, *6*(2), 323–350. doi:10.1137/0206024

Kochut, K. J., & Janik, M. (2007). SPARQLeR: Extended SPARQL for semantic association discovery. In *proceeding of 4th European Semantic Web Conference, ESWC 2007* (pp. 145-159). Springer Berlin Heidelberg. doi:10.1007/978-3-540-72667-8_12

Kodama, K., Iijima, Y., Guo, X., & Ishikawa, Y. (2009). Skyline queries based on user locations and preferences for making location-based recommendations. In *Proceedings of the International Workshop on Location Based Social Networks* (pp. 9-16). New York, NY: ACM. doi:10.1145/1629890.1629893

Kollia, I., Glimm, B., & Horrocks, I. (2011). SPARQL Query Answering over OWL Ontologies. In *Proceedings of ESWC* (pp. 382-396). Heraklion, Crete: CEUR-WS.org.

Kollia, I., & Glimm, B. (2013). Optimizing SPARQL Query Answering over OWL Ontologies. *Journal of Artificial Intelligence Research*, *48*, 253–303.

Kontaki, M., Papadopoulos, A. N., & Manolopoulos, Y. (2008). Continuous K-dominant Skyline Computation on Multidimensional Data Streams. In *Proceedings of the 2008 ACM Symposium on Applied Computing* (pp. 956-960). New York: ACM. doi:10.1145/1363686.1363908

Kontchakov, R., Rezk, M., Rodriguez-Muro, M., Xiao, G., & Zakharyaschev, M. (2014). Answering SPARQL Queries over Databases under OWL 2 QL Entailment Regime. In *Proceedings of Semantic Web Conference* (pp. 552-567). Riva Del Garda, Italy: CEUR-WS.org. doi:10.1007/978-3-319-11964-9_35

Korn, F., Jagadish, H. V., & Faloutsos, C. (1997). Efficiently supporting ad hoc queries in large datasets of time sequences. *SIGMOD Record*, *26*(2), 289–300. doi:10.1145/253262.253332

Kossmann, D., Ramsak, F., & Rost, S. (2002). Shooting stars in the sky: An online algorithm for skyline queries. In *Proceedings of The 28th International Conference on Very Large Data Bases (VLDB)* (pp. 275-286). Hong Kong, China: VLDB Endowment. doi:10.1016/B978-155860869-6/50032-9

Kossmann, M. (2009). *Skyline Data Generator*. Retrieved July 15, 2013, from http://www.pubzone.org/pages/publications/showWiki.do?deleteform=true&search=basic&pos=1&publicationId=298353

Kotsakis, E. (2006). XML fuzzy ranking. In *Proceedings of the Flexible Query Answering Systems Conference*, (pp. 159-169). Milan, Italy: Springer. doi:10.1007/11766254_14

Koyuncu, M., & Yazici, A. (2003). IFOOD: An Intelligent Fuzzy Object-Oriented Database Architecture. *IEEE Transactions on Knowledge and Data Engineering*, *15*(5), 1137–1154. doi:10.1109/TKDE.2003.1232269

Koyuncu, M., & Yazici, A. (2005). A Fuzzy Knowledge-Based System for Intelligent Retrieval. *IEEE Transactions on Fuzzy Sets and Systems*, *13*(3), 317–330. doi:10.1109/TFUZZ.2004.839666

Kraft, D. H., & Petry, F. E. (1997). Fuzzy information systems: Managing uncertainty in databases and information retrieval systems. *Fuzzy Sets and Systems*, *90*(2), 183–191. doi:10.1016/S0165-0114(97)00085-7

Kropov, P. A. (1995). *Interpretation of forest types in the mountain forests of Siberia and Mongolia for Aerospace imagery mapping.* (Unpublished doctoral dissertation). Forest Technical Academy, SPB (in Russian).

Kucuk, D., Burcuozgur, N., Yazici, A., & Koyuncu, M. (2009). A Fuzzy Conceptual Model for Multimedia Data with A Text-based Automatic Annotation Scheme. *International Journal of Uncertainty, Fuzziness and Knowledge-based Systems, 17*(Supplement), 135–152. doi:10.1142/S0218488509006066

Kumar, A. P., Kumar, A., & Kumar, V. N. (2011). A Comprehensive Comparative study of SPARQL and SQL. *International Journal of Computer Science and Information Technologies, 2*(4), 1706–1710.

Kung, H. T., Luccio, F., & Preparata, F. P. (1975). On Finding the Maxima of a Set of Vectors. *Journal of the ACM, 22*(4), 469–476. doi:10.1145/321906.321910

Kurniawati, R., Jin, J. S., & Shepard, J. A. (1997). SS+ tree: an improved index structure for similarity searches in a high-dimensional feature space. In *Electronic Imaging '97* (pp. 110–120). International Society for Optics and Photonics.

Kushmerick, N., Weld, D. S., & Doorenbos, R. (1997). Wrapper Induction for Information Extraction. In *Proceedings of the Fifteenth International Joint Conference on Artificial Intelligence (IJCAI)*. Nagoya, Japan: Morgan Kaufmann.

Kuznetsov, S. O., Kundu, M. K., Mandal, D. P., & Pal, S. K. (Eds.). (2011). *Proceedings of the 4th International Conference "Pattern Recognition and Machine Intelligence"* (LNCS), (vol. 6744). Springer.

Kuznetsov, S. O. (2005). Galois connections in data analysis: contributions from the Soviet Era and modern Russian research. In *Formal Concept Analysis, LNAI 3626* (pp. 196–226). Berlin: Springer-Verlag.

Lacroix, M., & Lavency, P. (1987). Preferences: Putting more knowledge into Queries. In *Proceedings of the 13th International Conference on Very Large Databases*. Brighton, UK:Morgan Kaufmann.

Lamb, A., Fuller, M., Tran, N., Vandiver, B., Doshi, L., & Bear, C. (2012). The vertica analytic database: C-store 7 years later. *Proceedings of the VLDB Endowment, 5*(12), 1790–1801. doi:10.14778/2367502.2367518

Lande, N., & Lande, A. (2008). The 10 best of everything: An ultimate guide for travelers (2nd ed.). National Geographic Society.

Lange, B. D., & Oshima, M. (1998). Mobile Agents with Java: The Aglet API. *World Wide Web (Bussum), 1*(3), 111–121. doi:10.1023/A:1019267832048

Lappas, T., Vieira, M., Gunopulos, D., & Tsotras, V. (2012). On the spatiotemporal burstiness of terms. *Proceedings of the VLDB Endowment., 5*(9), 836–847. doi:10.14778/2311906.2311911

Law, Y.-N., Wang, H., & Zaniolo, C. (2004). Query Languages and Data Models for Database Sequences and Data. In *Proceedings of the Thirtieth international conference on Very large data bases* (vol. 30, pp. 492--503). VLDB Endowment. doi:10.1016/B978-012088469-8.50045-0

Lawrence, R. (2014). Integration and Virtualization of Relational SQL and NoSQL Systems including MySQL and MongoDB. In *Proceedings of the International Conference on Computational Science and Computational Intelligence (CSCI)*. Las Vegas, NV: IEEE. doi:10.1109/CSCI.2014.56

Leavitt, N. (2010). Technology News. Will NoSQL Databases Live Up to Their Promise? *Journal Computer, 43*(2), 12–14. doi:10.1109/MC.2010.58

Lee, C. H. (2012). Mining spatio-temporal information on microblogging streams using a density-based online clustering method. *Expert Systems with Applications, 39*(10), 9623–9640. doi:10.1016/j.eswa.2012.02.136

Lee, J., & Fanjiang, Y. (2003). Modeling Imprecise Requirements with XML. *Information and Software Technology*, *45*(7), 445–460. doi:10.1016/S0950-5849(03)00015-6

Lee, J., & Hwang, S.-W. (2009). Skytree: scalable skyline computation for sensor data. In *Proceedings of the International Workshop on Knowledge Discovery from Sensor Data* (pp. 114-123). New York: ACM. doi:10.1145/1601966.1601985

Lee, J., Xue, N. L., Hsu, K. H., & Yang, S. J. (1999). Modeling Imprecise Requirements with Fuzzy Objects. *Information Sciences*, *118*(1-4), 101–119. doi:10.1016/S0020-0255(99)00042-0

Lee, J., You, G.-, & Hwang, S.-. (2009). Personalized Top-k Skyline Queries in High-dimensional Space. *Information Systems*, *34*(1), 45–61. doi:10.1016/j.is.2008.04.004

Lee, S.-L., Chun, S.-J., Kim, D.-H., Lee, J.-H., & Chung, C.-W. (2000). Similarity search for multidimensional data sequences. In *Proc. of the IEEE International Conference on Data Engineering (ICDE)*, (pp. 599-608). IEEE.

Leinders, D., & den Bussche, J. V. (2005). On the complexity of division and set joins in the relational algebra. In Proceedings of pods (p. 76-83). doi:10.1145/1065167.1065178

LePendu, P., & Dou, D. (2011). Using ontology databases for scalable query answering, inconsistency detection, and data integration. *Journal of Intelligent Information Systems*, *37*(2), 217–244. doi:10.1007/s10844-010-0133-4 PMID:22163378

LePendu, P., Dou, D., Frishkoff, G. A., & Rong, J. (2008). Ontology Database: A New Method for Semantic Modeling and an Application to Brainwave Data. In *Proceedings of SSDBM* (pp. 313-330). Hong Kong, China: Springer. doi:10.1007/978-3-540-69497-7_21

Levandoski, J. J., & Mokbel, M. F. (2009). RDF data-centric storage. In *IEEE International Conference on Web Services*. IEEE.

Liang, W., Chen, B., & Yu, J. X. (2008). Energy-efficient skyline query processing and maintenance in sensor networks. In *Proceedings of the ACM Conference on Information and Knowledge Management* (pp. 1471-1472). New York, NY: ACM. doi:10.1145/1458082.1458339

Li, C., He, B., Yan, N., & Safiullah, M. A. (2014). Set predicates in SQL: Enabling set-level comparisons for dynamically formed groups. *IEEE Transactions on Knowledge and Data Engineering*, *26*(2), 438–452. doi:10.1109/TKDE.2012.156

Li, F., Ooi, B. C., Özsu, M. T., & Wu, S. (2014). Distributed data management using mapreduce. *ACM Computing Surveys*, *46*(3), 31. doi:10.1145/2503009

Li, G. L., Feng, J. Y., & Zhou, L. Z. (2008). Retune: retrieving and materializing tuple units for effective keyword search over relational databases. In *Proceedings of the International Conference on Conceptual Modeling (ER)*. (pp 469-483). Barcelona, Spain: Springer. doi:10.1007/978-3-540-87877-3_34

Lindstrom, P. (1966). First order predicate logic with generalized quantifiers. *Theoria*, 32.

Lin, J., Keogh, E., Lonardi, S., & Chiu, B. (2003). A symbolic representation of time series, with implications for streaming algorithms. In *Proceedings of the 8th ACM SIGMOD workshop on Research issues in data mining and knowledge discovery* (pp. 2--11). ACM. doi:10.1145/882082.882086

Lin, J., Keogh, E., Wei, L., & Lonardi, S. (2007). Experiencing SAX: A novel symbolic representation of time series. *Data Mining and Knowledge Discovery*, *15*(2), 107–144. doi:10.1007/s10618-007-0064-z

Lin, K.-I., Jagadish, H. V., & Faloutsos, C. (1994). The TV-tree: An index structure for high-dimensional dat. *The VLDB Journal*, *3*(4), 517–542. doi:10.1007/BF01231606

Lin, Q., Zhang, Y., Zhang, W., & Li, A. (2012).General spatial skyline operator. In *Proceedings of the International Conference on Database Systems for Advanced Applications (DASFAA)* (pp. 494-508). Berlin: Springer-Verlag. doi:10.1007/978-3-642-29038-1_36

Lin, X., Xu, J., & Hu, H. (2011). Range-based Skyline Queries in Mobile Environments. *IEEE Transactions on Knowledge and Data Engineering, 25*(4), 835–849. doi:10.1109/TKDE.2011.229

Lin, X., Yuan, Y., Zhang, Q., & Zhang, Y. (2007). Selecting Stars: The k Most Representative Skyline Operator. In *Proceedings of The International Conference on Database Theory (ICDE)* (pp. 86-95). Istanbul, Turkey: IEEE. doi:10.1109/ICDE.2007.367854

Li, Q., Moon, B., & Lopez, I. (2004). Skyline index for time series data. *Knowledge and Data Engineering. IEEE Transactions on, 16*(6), 669–684.

Liu, X., Lang, B., Yu, W., Luo, J., & Huang, L. (2011). AUDR: An Advanced Unstructured Data Repository. In *Proceedings 2011 6th International Conference on Pervasive Computing and Applications (ICPCA)*. IEEE.

Liu, Y., Hu, S., Rabl, T., Liu, W., Jacobsen, H.-A., & Wu, K. (2014). DGFIndex for Smart Grid: Enhancing Hive with a Cost-Effective Multidimensional Range Index. *arXiv preprint arXiv:1404.5686.*

Liu, F., Yu, C., & Meng, W. Y. (2006). Effective keyword search in relational database. In *Proceedings of the ACM SIGMOD Conference on Data Management (SIGMOD)*. (pp 563-574). Chicago, IL: ACM.

Liu, J., Ma, Z. M., & Yan, L. (2013). Storing and querying fuzzy XML data in relational databases. *Applied Intelligence, 39*(2), 386–396. doi:10.1007/s10489-012-0419-z

Liu, Q., Deng, M., Bi, J., & Yang, W. (2012). A novel method for discovering spatio- temporal clusters of different sizes, shapes, and densities in the presence of noise. *International Journal of Digital Earth, 12*, 1–20.

Liu, S., & Chu, W. W. (2007). CoXML: A cooperative XML query answering system. In *Proceedings of the 9th Asia-Pacific Web Conference, and 8th International Conference on Web-Age Information Management*, (pp. 614-621). Huang Shan, China: Springer. doi:10.1007/978-3-540-72524-4_63

Liu, W., Jing, Y., Chen, K., & Sun, W. (2012). Combining top-k query in road networks. In *Proceedings of the International Conference on Web-Age Information Management (WAIM)* (pp. 63-75). Springer-Verlag. doi:10.1007/978-3-642-28635-3_6

Liu, X. H., & Wan, Y. C. (2010). Storing Spatio-Temporal Data in XML Native Database. In *Proceedings of the 2nd International Workshop on Database Technology and Applications*, (pp. 1-4). doi:10.1109/DBTA.2010.5659107

Liu, Y., Dube, P., & Grayn, S. (2014). Run-Time Performance Optimization of a BigData Query Language. In *Proceedings of the 5th ACM/SPEC international conference on Performance engineering (ICPE '14)*. Dublin, Ireland: ACM. doi:10.1145/2568088.2576800

Li, X., Ceikute, V., Jensen, C. S., & Tan, K.-L. (2013). Effective Online Group Discovery in Trajectory Databases. *IEEE Transactions on Knowledge and Data Engineering, 25*(12), 2752–2766. doi:10.1109/TKDE.2012.193

Li, X., Kim, Y. J., Govindan, R., & Hong, W. (2003). Multi-dimensional range queries in sensor networks. In *Proceedings of the 1st international conference on Embedded networked sensor systems*, (pp. 63--75). doi:10.1145/958491.958500

Lo, A., Özyer, T., Kianmehr, K., & Alhajj, R. (2010). VIREX and VRXQuery: Interactive Approach for Visual Querying of Relational Databases to Produce XML. *Journal of Intelligent Information Systems, 35*(1), 21–49. doi:10.1007/s10844-009-0087-6

Loboz, C., Smyl, S., & Nath, S. (2010). DataGarage: Warehousing massive performance data on commodity servers. *Proceedings of the VLDB Endowment, 3*(1-2), 1447–1458. doi:10.14778/1920841.1921019

Lo, E., Yip, K., Lin, K.-I., & Cheung, D. (2006). Progressive Skylining over Web-Accessible Database. *Journal of Data and Knowledge Engineering, 7*(2), 122–147. doi:10.1016/j.datak.2005.04.003

Loh, W.-K., Kim, S.-W., & Whang, K.-Y. (2000). Index interpolation: an approach to subsequence matching supporting normalization transform in time-series databases. In *Proceedings of the ninth international conference on Information and knowledge management* (pp. 480--487). ACM. doi:10.1145/354756.354856

Lokken, F., & Womer, L. (2007). *Trends in E-Learning: Tracking the Impact of E-Learning in Higher Education. 2006 Distance Education Survey Results*. Washington, DC: Instructional Technology Council.

Losemann, K., & Martens, W. (2012). The complexity of evaluating path expressions in SPARQL. In *Proceedings of the 31st symposium on Principles of Database Systems* (pp. 101-112). ACM. doi:10.1145/2213556.2213573

Loyer, Y., Sadoun, I., & Zeitouni, K. (2013a). Progressive Ranking Based on a Dominance List. In *Proceedings of the 7th International Workshop on Ranking in Databases (DBRank)* (pp. 6:1-6:3). ACM: Riva del Garda, Italy. doi:10.1145/2524828.2524834

Loyer, Y., Sadoun, I., & Zeitouni, K. (2013b). Personalized Progressive Filtering of Skyline Queries in High Dimensional Spaces. In *Proceedings of the 17th International Database Engineering & Applications Symposium (IDEAS)* (pp. 186-191). Barcelona, Spain: ACM. doi:10.1145/2513591.2513646

Ludovic, L. (2009). On the Extension of SQL to Fuzzy Bipolar Conditions. In *Proceedings of the 28th North American Fuzzy Information Processing Society Annual Conference.* IEEE.

Lu, H., Yang, B., & Jensen, C. S. (2011). Spatio-temporal joins on symbolic indoor tracking data. In *Proc. of the IEEE International Conference on Data Engineering (ICDE)*, (pp. 816-827). doi:10.1109/ICDE.2011.5767902

Lukoianova, T., & Rubin, V. L. (2014). Veracity Roadmap: Is Big Data Objective, Truthful and Credible? *Advances in Classification Research Online, 24*(1), 4–15. doi:10.7152/acro.v24i1.14671

Luo, Y., Lin, X. M., & Wang, W. (2007). SPARK: top-k keyword query in relational databases. In *Proceedings of the ACM SIGMOD Conference on Data Management (SIGMOD).* (pp 305-316). Paris, France: ACM doi:10.1145/1247480.1247495

Lutz, C. (2008). The complexity of conjunctive query answering in expressive description logics. In *Proceedings of the 4th International Joint Conference Automated Reasoning* (pp. 179-193). Sydney, Australia: Springer. doi:10.1007/978-3-540-71070-7_16

Lutz, C., Toman, D., & Wolter, F. (2009). Conjunctive query answering in the description logic EL using a relational database system. In *Proceedings of IJCAI* (pp. 2070-2075). Pasadena, CA: AAAI.

Ma, Z. M. (2005b). Extending UML for Fuzzy Information Modeling. In Advances in Object-Oriented Databases: Modeling and Applications. Idea Group Publishing.

Magnani, M., & Montesi, D. (2005). XML and Relational Data: Towards a Common Model and Algebra. In *Proceedings of the 9th International Database Engineering and Application Symposlum*, (pp. 96-101). doi:10.1109/IDEAS.2005.55

Mahanta, D., & Ahmed, M. (2012). E-Learning Objectives, Methodologies, Tools and its Limitations. *International Journal of Innovative Technology and Exploring Engineering, 2*(1), 46–61.

Majumdar, A. K., Bhattacharya, I., & Saha, A. K. (2002). An Object-Oriented Fuzzy Data Model for Similarity Detection in Image Databases. *IEEE Transactions on Knowledge and Data Engineering*, *14*(5), 1186–1189. doi:10.1109/TKDE.2002.1033783

Ma, L., Su, Z., Pan, Y., Zhang, L., & Liu, T. (2004). RStar: an RDF storage and query system for enterprise resource management. In *Proceedings of the thirteenth ACM international conference on Information and knowledge management* (pp. 484-491). ACM. doi:10.1145/1031171.1031264

Mamoulis, N. (2003). Efficient processing of joins on set-valued attributes. In *Proceedings of the acm sigmod international conference on management of data* (p. 157-168). doi:10.1145/872757.872778

Mani, M., Lee, D. W., & Muntz, R. R. (2001). Semantic Data Modeling Using XML Schemas. In *Proceedings of the 20th International Conference on Conceptual Modeling*. Academic Press.

Mankad, K. B., & Sajja, P. S. (2008). Applying Multi-Agent Approach for Comparative Studies of Intelligence Among Students. *ADIT Journal of Engineering*, *5*(1), 25–28.

Manola, F., Miller, E., & McBride, B. (2004). RDF primer. *W3C recommendation*, *10*(1-107), 6.

Manolopoulos, Y., Nanopoulos, A., Papadopoulos, A. N., & Theodoridis, Y. (2013). *R-trees: Theory and Applications*. Springer London.

Mapanga, I., & Kadebu, P. (2013). Database Management Systems: A NoSQL Analysis. *Proceedings of the International Journal of Modern Communication Technologies & Research*, *1*(7).

Marcos, E., Vela, B., & Cavero, J. M. (2001). Extending UML for Object-Relational Database Design. In *Proceedings of the 4th International Conference on the Unified Modeling Language, Modeling Languages, Concepts, and Tools*. Academic Press.

Maria, D. B.Foundation. (2013). Retrieved from: https://mariadb.org/

Marín, N., Medina, J. M., Pons, O., Sánchez, D., & Vila, M. A. (2003). Complex Object Comparison in A Fuzzy Context. *Information and Software Technology*, *45*(7), 431–444. doi:10.1016/S0950-5849(03)00014-4

Marín, N., Pons, O., & Vila, M. A. (2001). A Strategy for Adding Fuzzy Types to an Object-Oriented Database System. *International Journal of Intelligent Systems*, *16*(7), 863–880. doi:10.1002/int.1039

Marín, N., Vila, M. A., & Pons, O. (2000). Fuzzy Types: A New Concept of Type for Managing Vague Structures. *International Journal of Intelligent Systems*, *15*(11), 1061–1085. doi:10.1002/1098-111X(200011)15:11<1061::AID-INT5>3.0.CO;2-A

Matthe, T., & de Tre, G. (2009). Bipolar Query Satisfaction Using Satisfaction and Dissatisfaction Degrees: Bipolar Satisfaction Degrees. In *Proceedings of the 2009 ACM Symposium on Applied Computing*. Honolulu, HI: ACM. doi:10.1145/1529282.1529664

Matthe, T., & de Tre, G. (2012). Ranking of Bipolarity Satisfaction Degrees. In *Proceedings of the 14th International Conference on Information Processing and Management of Uncertainty in Knowledge-Based Systems*.Catania, Italy: Springer-Verlag.

Matthé, T., de Tré, G., Zadrozny, S., Kacprzyk, J., & Bronselaer, A. (2011). Bipolar Database Querying Using Bipolar Satisfaction Degrees. *International Journal of Intelligent Systems*, *26*(10), 890–910. doi:10.1002/int.20505

May, N., Helmer, S., & Moerkotte, G. (2004). Nested queries and quantifiers in an ordered context. In *Proceedings of the IEEE international conference on data engineering (ICDE)* (p. 239-249). doi:10.1109/ICDE.2004.1320001

Ma, Z. M. (2005a). *Fuzzy Database Modeling with XML*. Springer.

Ma, Z. M. (2005c). A Conceptual Design Methodology for Fuzzy Relational Databases. *Journal of Database Management*, *16*(2), 66–83. doi:10.4018/jdm.2005040104

Ma, Z. M. and Shen, Derong. (2006). Modeling Fuzzy Information in the IF$_2$O and Object-Oriented Data Models. *Journal of Intelligent & Fuzzy Systems*, *17*(6), 597–612.

Ma, Z. M. and Yan, Li. (2008). A Literature Overview of Fuzzy Database Models. *Journal of Information Science and Engineering*, *24*(1), 189–202.

Ma, Z. M. and Yan, Li. (2010). A Literature Overview of Fuzzy Conceptual Data Modeling. *Journal of Information Science and Engineering*, *26*(2), 427–441.

Ma, Z. M., Liu, J., & Yan, L. (2010). Fuzzy data modeling and algebraic operations in XML. *International Journal of Intelligent Systems*, *25*(9), 925–947.

Ma, Z. M., Liu, J., & Yan, L. (2010). Fuzzy Data Modeling and Algebraic Operations in XML. *International Journal of Intelligent Systems*, *25*, 925–947.

Ma, Z. M., Liu, J., & Yan, L. (2011). Matching twigs in fuzzy XML. *Information Sciences*, *181*(1), 184–200. doi:10.1016/j.ins.2010.09.001

Ma, Z. M., & Mili, F. (2002). Handling Fuzzy Information in Extended Possibility-Based Fuzzy Relational Databases. *International Journal of Intelligent Systems*, *17*(10), 925–942. doi:10.1002/int.10057

Ma, Z. M., & Yan, L. (2007a). Generalization of Strategies for Fuzzy Query Translation in Classical Relational Databases. *Information and Software Technology*, *49*(2), 172–180. doi:10.1016/j.infsof.2006.05.002

Ma, Z. M., & Yan, L. (2007b). Fuzzy XML Data Modeling with the UML and Relational Data Models. *Data & Knowledge Engineering*, *63*(3), 970–994. doi:10.1016/j.datak.2007.06.003

Ma, Z. M., Yan, L., & Zhang, F. (2012). Modeling Fuzzy Information in UML Class Diagrams and Object-Oriented Database Models. *Fuzzy Sets and Systems*, *186*(1), 26–46. doi:10.1016/j.fss.2011.06.015

Ma, Z. M., Zhang, F., & Yan, L. (2011). Fuzzy Information Modeling in UML Class Diagram and Relational Database Models. *Applied Soft Computing*, *11*(6), 4236–4245. doi:10.1016/j.asoc.2011.03.020

Ma, Z. M., Zhang, W. J., & Ma, W. Y. (2000). Semantic Measure of Fuzzy Data in Extended Possibility-based Fuzzy Relational Databases. *International Journal of Intelligent Systems*, *15*(8), 705–716. doi:10.1002/1098-111X(200008)15:8<705::AID-INT2>3.0.CO;2-4

Ma, Z. M., Zhang, W. J., & Ma, W. Y. (2004). Extending Object-Oriented Databases for Fuzzy Information modeling. *Information Systems*, *29*(5), 421–435. doi:10.1016/S0306-4379(03)00038-3

Ma, Z. M., Zhang, W. J., Ma, W. Y., & Chen, G. Q. (2001). Conceptual Design of Fuzzy Object-Oriented Databases Using Extended Entity-Relationship Model. *International Journal of Intelligent Systems*, *16*(6), 697–711. doi:10.1002/int.1031

McBride, B. (2002). Jena: A semantic web toolkit. *IEEE Internet Computing*, *6*(6), 55–59. doi:10.1109/MIC.2002.1067737

McCandless, M., Hatcher, E., & Gospodnetić, O. (2010). *Lucene in Action* (2nd ed.). Manning.

McHugh, J., & Widom, J. (2003). Query Optimization for XML. In *Proceedings of the 25th VLDB*, (pp. 898-909). VLDB.

Medina, J. M., Pons, O., & Vila, M. A. (1995). *FIRST: A Fuzzy Interface for Relational Systems VI IFSA World Congress, São Paulo, Brazil, II*. Academic Press.

Medina, J. M., Pons, O., & Vila, M. A. (1994). GEFRED: A Generalized Model of Fuzzy Relational Databases. *Information Sciences, 76*(1-2), 87–109. doi:10.1016/0020-0255(94)90069-8

Mehrotra, R., & Sharma, A. (2009). Evaluating Spatio-Temporal Representations in Daily Rainfall Sequences from Three Stochastic Multisite Weather Generation Approaches. *Advances in Water Resources, 32*(6), 948–962. doi:10.1016/j.advwatres.2009.03.005

Melnik, S., & Garcia-Molina, H. (2003). Adaptive algorithms for set containment joins. *ACM Transactions on Database Systems, 28*(1), 56–99. doi:10.1145/762471.762474

Melnik, S., Shivakumar, S., Tolton, M., & Vassilakis, T. (2010). Dremel: Interactive analysis of web-scale datasets. *Proceedings of the VLDB Endowment, 3*(1-2), 330–339. doi:10.14778/1920841.1920886

Melton, J. (2001a). *Advanced SQL: 1999: Understanding object-relational and other advanced features.* Morgan Kaufmann.

Melton, J. (2001b). *SQL: 1999: Understanding relational language components.* Morgan Kaufmann.

Michalski, R., & Kaufman, K. (1998). Data Mining and Knowledge Discovery: A review of Issues and a Multi-strategy Approach. In R. S. Michalski, I. Bratko, & M. Kubat (Eds.), *Machine learning and Data Mining: Methods and Applications* (pp. 71–112). London: John Wiley & Sons.

Mill, J. S. (1872). *The System of Logic Ratiocinative and Inductive Being a Connected View of the Principles of Evidence, and the Methods of Scientific Investigation* (Vol. 1). London: West Strand.

Mohan, C. (2013). History Repeats Itself: Sensible and NonsenSQL Aspects of the NoSQL Hoopla. In *Proceedings of the 16th International Conference on Extending Database Technology (EDBT/ICDT '13).* Genoa, Italy: ACM. doi:10.1145/2452376.2452378

Mohsenian-Rad, A.-H., Wong, V. W., Jatskevich, J., Schober, R., & Leon-Garcia, A. (2010). Autonomous demand-side management based on game-theoretic energy consumption scheduling for the future smart grid. *Smart Grid. IEEE Transactions on., 1,* 320–331.

Mokbel, M. F., & Aref, W. G. (2008, August). SOLE: Scalable on-line execution of continuous queries on spatio-temporal data streams. *The VLDB Journal, 17*(5), 971–995. doi:10.1007/s00778-007-0046-1

Mokhtar, H., Su, J., & Ibarra, O. (2002). On moving object queries. In *Proc. of the ACM SIGMOD-SIGACT-SIGART Symp. on Principles of Database Systems (PODS),* (pp. 188-198). ACM.

Mondal, A., Lifu, Y., & Kitsuregawa, M. (2004). P2PR-Tree: An R-tree-based spacial index for peer-to-peer environments. In *Proceedings of the International Conference on Extending Database Technology Joint PhD Workshop,* (pp. 516-525). Heraklion, Greece: Springer. doi:10.1007/978-3-540-30192-9_51

Moraitakis, N. (1997). *Intelligent Software Agents: Application and Classification.* Retrieved October 10, 2014 from http://www.doc.ic.ac.uk/~nd/surprise_97/journal/vol1/nm1/

Morse, M., & Patel, J. M. (2006). Efficient Continuous Skyline Computation. In *Proceedings of the International Conference on Data Engineering (ICDE)* (pp. 108). Atlanta, GA: IEEE Computer Society. doi:10.1109/ICDE.2006.56

Mostowski, A. (1957). On a generalization of quantifiers. *Fundamenta Mathematica, 44.*

Motakis, I., & Zaniolo, C. (1997). Temporal aggregation in active database rules. *SIGMOD Record, 26*(2), 440–451. doi:10.1145/253262.253359

Moussalli, R., Absalyamov, I., Vieira, M. R., Najjar, W. A., & Tsotras, V. J. (2014). High performance FPGA and GPU complex pattern matching over spatio-temporal streams. *GeoInformatica,* 1–30.

Moussalli, R., Vieira, M. R., Najjar, W. A., & Tsotras, V. J. (2013). Stream-mode FPGA acceleration of complex pattern trajectory querying. In *Proc. of the International Symp. on Advances in Spatial and Temporal Databases (SSTD)* (Vol. 8098, pp. 201-222). Springer. doi:10.1007/978-3-642-40235-7_12

Mouza, C., Litwin, W., & Rigaux, P. (2007). SD-Rtree: A scalable distributed Rtree. In *Proceedings of the International Conference on Data Engineering*, (pp. 296-305). Istanbul, Turkey: IEEE.

Mueen, A. (2014). Time series motif discovery: Dimensions and applications. *Wiley Interdisciplinary Reviews: Data Mining and Knowledge Discovery, 4*(2), 152–159.

Muhammad, Y. (2011). *Evaluation and Implementation of Distributed NoSQL Database for MMO Gaming Environment.* (Unpublished doctoral dissertation). Uppsala Universitety, Uppsala, Sweden.

Müller, M. (2007). Dynamic time warping. *Information retrieval for music and motion*, 69--84.

Naidenova, X. (2011). Constructing Galois lattice in good classification tests mining. In Dmitry I. Ignatov, Sergei O. Kuznetsov, Jonas Poelmans (Eds), *International Workshop on concept discovery in unstructured data* (pp. 43-48). Moscow: The National Research University High School of Economics.

Naidenova, X. A. (1992). Machine learning as a diagnostic task. In I. Arefiev (Ed.), *Knowledge-Dialogue-Solution, Materials of the Short-Term Scientific Seminar*, (pp. 26-36). Saint-Petersburg, Russia: State North-West Technical University. doi:10.4018/978-1-60566-810-9.ch006

Naidenova, X. A. (2012). Good Classification Tests as Formal Concepts. In F. Domenach, D. I. Ignatov, & J. Poelmans (Eds.), ICFCA 2012, LNAI 7278 (pp. 211–226). Springer.

Naidenova, X. A., & Parkchomenko, V. L. (2014). Attributive and object sub-contexts in inferring good maximally redundant tests. In *Proceedings of the 11th International Conference on "Concept lattices and their applications"* (pp. 181-193). Pavol Jozef Šafárik Univercity in Košice: SAIS.

Naidenova, X., & Ermakov, A. E. (2001). The decomposition of good diagnostic test inferring algorithms. In *Proceedings of the 4-th International Conference «Computer-Aided Design of Discrete Devices" (CAD DD'2001) (vol. 3,* pp. 61-68). Belarus, Minsk: Institute of Technical Cybernetics.

Naidenova, X. A. (1982). Relational model for analyzing experimental data. *The Transaction of Acad. Sci. of USSR. Series Technical Cybernetics, 4,* 103–119.

Naidenova, X. A. (1996). Reducing machine learning tasks to the approximation of a given classification on a given set of examples. In *Proceedings of the 5-th National Conference at Artificial Intelligence* (vol. 1, pp. 275-279). Academic Press.

Naidenova, X. A. (2006). An Incremental Learning Algorithm for Inferring Logical Rules from Exampled in the Framework of the Common Reasoning Process. In E. Triantaphyllou & G. Felici (Eds.), *Data Mining and Knowledge Discovery Approaches Based on Rule Induction Techniques* (pp. 89–147). Heidelberg, Germany: Springer. doi:10.1007/0-387-34296-6_3

Naidenova, X. A., & Polegaeva, J. G. (1985). Model of human reasoning for deciphering forest's images and its implementation on computer. In *Semiotic aspects of the intellectual activity formalization, Theses of Papers and Reports of School-Seminar* (pp. 49–52). Kutaisy, Georgia Soviet Socialist Republic. (in Russian)

Naidenova, X. A., & Polegaeva, J. G. (1986). An algorithm of finding the best diagnostic tests. In G. E. Mintz & P. P. Lorents (Eds.), *The application of mathematical logic methods* (pp. 63–67). Tallinn, Estonia: Institute of Cybernetics, National Acad. of Sciences of Estonia. (in Russian)

Naidenova, X. A., & Shagalov, V. L. (2009). Diagnostic Test Machine. In: M. Auer (Ed.), *Proceedings of the Interactive Computer Aided Learning Conference* (pp. 505-507). Austria: Kassel University Press.

Nakano, M., Hasegawa, Y., Funakoshi, K., Takeuchi, J., Torii, T., Nakadai, K., & Tsujino, H. et al. (2011). A Multi-Expert Model for Dialogue and Behaviour Control of Conversational Robots and Agents. *Knowledge-Based Systems, 24*(2), 248–256. doi:10.1016/j.knosys.2010.08.004

Nasholm, P. (2012). *Extracting Data From Nosql Databases A Step Towards Interactive Visual Analysis Of Nosql data.* (Unpublished doctoral dissertation). Chalmers University of Technology. University of Gothenburg. Göteborg, Sweden.

NAVCEN. U. C. G. N. C. (1996, september). *Navstar GPS User Equipment Introduction.* Retrieved from www.navcen.uscg.gov/pubs/gps/gpsuser/gpsuser.pdf

Nazerzadeh, H., & Ghodsi, M. (2005). RAQ: a range-queriable distributed data structure. In SOFSEM 2005: Theory and Practice of Computer Science (pp. 269--277). Springer. doi:10.1007/978-3-540-30577-4_30

Ndouse, T. D. (1997). Intelligent Systems Modeling with Reusable Fuzzy Objects. *International Journal of Intelligent Systems, 12*(2), 137–152. doi:10.1002/(SICI)1098-111X(199702)12:2<137::AID-INT2>3.0.CO;2-R

Neumann, T., & Weikum, G. (2008). RDF-3X: A RISC-style engine for RDF. *Proceedings of the VLDB Endowment, 1*(1), 647–659. doi:10.14778/1453856.1453927

Neumann, T., & Weikum, G. (2010). The RDF-3X engine for scalable management of RDF data. *The VLDB Journal, 19*(1), 91–113. doi:10.1007/s00778-009-0165-y

Newman, A. (2006). *Querying the Semantic Web using a Relational Based SPARQL.* The University of Queensland. Submitted for the degree of Bachelor of Information Technology.

Nievergelt, J., Hinterberger, H., & Sevcik, K. C. (1984, March). The grid file: An adaptable, symmetric multikey file structure. *ACM Transactions on Database Systems, 9*(1), 38–71. doi:10.1145/348.318586

Nolle, A., & Nemirovski, G. (2013). ELITE: An Entailment-Based Federated Query Engine for Complete and Transparent Semantic Data Integration. In *Proceedings of Description Logics* (pp. 854–867). Ulm, Germany: CEUR.

Normandeau, K. (2013). *Beyond volume, variety and velocity is the issue of big data veracity.* Inside Big Data.

Ob'iedkov, S., & Duquenne, V. (2007). Attribute-incremental construction of the canonical implication basis. *Annals of Mathematics and Artificial Intelligence Archive, 49*(1-4), 77–99. doi:10.1007/s10472-007-9057-2

Object Management Group (OMG). (2003). *Unified Modeling Language (UML), version 1.5, Technical report.* OMG. Retrieved from www.omg.org

O'Connor, B., Balasubramanyan, R., Routledge, B. R., & Smith, N. A. (2010). From tweets to polls: Linking text sentiment to public opinion time series. *ICWSM, 11*, 122–129.

Oetiker, T. (2005). *RRDtool.* Academic Press.

Okabe, A., Boots, B., Sugihara, K., & Chiu, S. N. (2000). *Spatial tessellations, concepts and applications of Voronoi diagrams* (2nd ed.). John Wiley and Sons Ltd. doi:10.1002/9780470317013

Okcan, A., & Riedewald, M. (2011). Processing theta-joins using MapReduce. In *Proceedings of the ACM SIGMOD International Conference on Management of Data*, (pp. 949-960). Athens, Greece: ACM.

Oliboni, B., & Pozzani, G. (2008). Representing Fuzzy Information by Using XML Schema. In *Proceedings of the 2008 International Conference on Database and Expert Systems Applications.* doi:10.1109/DEXA.2008.44

Oliveira, R., Santos, M. Y., & Pires, J. M. (2013). 4D+ SNN: A Spatio-Temporal Density-Based Clustering Approach with 4D Similarity. In *Proceedings of the IEEE 13th International Conference on Data Mining Workshops (ICDMW)*, (pp. 1045-1052). IEEE. doi:10.1109/ICDMW.2013.119

Olson, M., & Ogbuji, U. (2002). *The Versa Specification*. Retrieved from http://copia.ogbuji.net/files/Versa.html

OMG. (2003). UML 2.0 Superstructure Specification. *OMG document ptc/03-08-02*.

Ooi, B. C., Hadjieleftheriou, M., Du, X., & Lu, W. (2014). Efficiently Supporting Edit Distance based String Similarity Search Using B+-trees. *IEEE Transactions on Knowledge and Data Engineering*, 1.

Oppenheim, A. V., & Schafer, R. W. (1975). *Digital Signal Processing*. Englewood Cliffs, New York.

Ore, O. (1944). Galois Connexions. *Transactions of the American Mathematical Society, 55*(1), 493–513. doi:10.1090/S0002-9947-1944-0010555-7

Orsi, G., & Pieris, A. (2011). Optimizing query answering under ontological constraints. *PVLDB, 4*(11), 1004–1015.

Ortiz, M. (2010). *Query Answering in Expressive Description Logics: Techniques and Complexity Results*. (Doctoral dissertation). Vienna University of Technology.

Ortiz, M. (2013). Ontology Based Query Answering: The Story So Far. In *Proceedings of AMW*. Puebla/Cholula, Mexico: CEUR.

Ortiz, M., & Simkus, M. (2012). Reasoning and query answering in description logics. In *Proceedings of Reasoning Web* (pp. 1–53). Tallinn, Estonia: Springer. doi:10.1007/978-3-642-33158-9_1

Ovchinnikov, S. (1991). Similarity relations, fuzzy partitions, and fuzzy orderings. *Fuzzy Sets and Systems, 40*(1), 107–126. doi:10.1016/0165-0114(91)90048-U

Ozgur, N. B., Koyuncu, M., & Yazici, A. (2009). An Intelligent Fuzzy Object-Oriented Database Framework for Video Database Applications. *Fuzzy Sets and Systems, 160*(15), 2253–2274. doi:10.1016/j.fss.2009.02.017

Ozsoyogly, G., & Wang, H. (1989). A relational calculus with set operators, its safety, and equivalent graphical languages. *IEEE Transactions on Software Engineering, 15*(9), 1038–1052. doi:10.1109/32.31363

Padhy, R., Patra, M., & Satapathy, S. (2011). RDBMS to NoSQL: Reviewing Some Next-Generation Non-Relational Database's. *International Journal of Advanced Engineering Science and Technologies, 11*(1), 15-30.

Panic, G., Rackovic, M., & Škrbic, S. (2014). Fuzzy XML and prioritized fuzzy XQuery with implementation. *Journal of Intelligent & Fuzzy Systems, 26*, 303–316.

Panic, G., Rackovic, M., & Skrbic, S. (2014). Fuzzy XML and prioritized fuzzy XQuery with implementation. *Journal of Intelligent and Fuzzy Systems, 26*(1), 303–316.

Pan, J. Z., Stamou, G., Stoilos, G., Taylor, S., & Thomas, E. (2008). Scalable Querying Service over Fuzzy Ontologies. In *Proceedings of International World Wide Web Conference* (pp. 575-584). Beijing, China: ACM.

Papadias, D., Tao, Y., Fu, G., & Seeger, B. (2005). Progressive skyline computation in database systems. *ACM Transactions on Database Systems, 30*(1), 41–82. doi:10.1145/1061318.1061320

Papadimitriou, C. H., & Yannakakis, M. (2001). Multiobjective Query Optimization. In *Proceedings of the ACM SIGMOD/SIGACT Conference on Principles of Database Systems (PODS)* (pp. 52–59). ACM.

Paparizos, S., Wu, Y., & Laks, V. S. (2004). Tree Logical Classes for Efficient Evaluation of XQuery. In *Proceedings of the 2004 ACM SIGMOD International Conference on Management of Data*, (pp. 71-82). doi:10.1145/1007568.1007579

Park, C. H. (2014). *Query by humming based on multiple spectral hashing and scaled open-end dynamic time warping. Signal Processing*. Elsevier.

Park, O., & Lee, J. (2003). Adaptive Instructional Systems. *Educational Technology Research and Development, 25,* 651–684.

Park, Y., Priebe, C. E., & Youssef, A. (2013). Anomaly detection in time series of graphs using fusion of graph invariants. *Selected Topics in Signal Processing. IEEE Journal of, 7*(1), 67–75.

Parr, T. (2013). *The Definitive ANTLR 4 Reference* (2nd ed.). Pragmatic Bookshelf.

Partner, J., Vukotic, A., Watt, N., Abedrabbo, T., & Fox, D. (2014). *Neo4j in Action.* New York: Manning Publication.

Patel, J. M., Chen, Y., & Chakka, V. P. (2004). Stripes: an efficient index for predicted trajectories. In *Proc. of the ACM SIGMOD International Conference on Management of Data,* 635-646. doi:10.1145/1007568.1007639

Patri, O. P., Sharma, A. B., Chen, H. a., Panangadan, A. V., & Prasanna, V. K. (2014). Extracting discriminative shapelets from heterogeneous sensor data. *Big Data (Big Data), 2014 IEEE International Conference on* (pp. 1095--1104). IEEE.

Patri, O. P., Panangadan, A. V., Chelmis, C., McKee, R. G., & Prasanna, V. et al. (2014). Predicting Failures from Oilfield Sensor Data using Time Series Shapelets.*SPE Annual Technical Conference and Exhibition.* Society of Petroleum Engineers. doi:10.2118/170680-MS

Pavlidis, T. (1973). Waveform segmentation through functional approximation. *Computers. IEEE Transactions on, 100*(7), 689–697.

Peim, M., Franconi, E., Paton, N. W., & Goble, C. A. (2002). Query processing with description logic ontologies over object-wrapped databases. In*Proceedings of SSDBM* (pp. 27-36). Edinburgh, UK: IEEE. doi:10.1109/SSDM.2002.1029703

Pelanis, M., Saltenis, S., & Jensen, C. S. (2006). Indexing the past, present, and anticipated future positions of moving objects. *ACM Transactions on Database Systems, 31*(1), 255–298. doi:10.1145/1132863.1132870

Pelekis, N., & Theodoridis, Y. (2014).*Mobility Data Management and Exploration.* New York: Springer. doi:10.1007/978-1-4939-0392-4

Pérez, J., Arenas, M., & Gutierrez, C. (2010). nSPARQL: A navigational language for RDF. *Web Semantics: Science, Services, and Agents on the World Wide Web, 8*(4), 255–270. doi:10.1016/j.websem.2010.01.002

Perng, C.-S., & Parker, D. S. (1999). SQL/LPP: A time series extension of SQL based on limited patience patterns. In Database and Expert Systems Applications (pp. 218--227). Springer.

Petry, F. E. (1996). *Fuzzy Databases: Principles and Applications.* Kluwer Academic Publisher. doi:10.1007/978-1-4613-1319-9

Pfoser, D., Jensen, C. S., & Theodoridis, Y. (2000). Novel approaches in query processing for moving object trajectories. In *Proc. of the International Conference on Very Large Data Bases (VLDB),* (pp. 395-406). VLDB.

Piaget, J., & Inhelder, B. (1959). *La Genèse des Structures Logiques Elémentaires Classifications et Sériations.* Neuchâtel: Delachaux & Niestlé.

Polikoff, I. (2014). *Comparing SPARQL with SQL.* Retrieved from http://www.topquadrant.com/2014/05/05/comparing-sparql-with-sql/

Porkorny, J. (2013). Nosql Databases: A Step To Database Scalability in Web enviromnent. In *Proceedings of the 13th International Conference on Information Integration and Web-based Applications and Services.* Bali, Indonesia: ACM.

Powers, D. M. W. (2007/2011). Evaluation: From Precision, Recall and F-Factor to ROC, Informedness, Markedness& Correlation. *Journal of Machine Learning Technologies*, *2*(1), 37–63.

Poya, G. (1954). *Mathematics and plausible reasoning*. Princeton, NJ: Princeton Univrsity Press.

Prabhakar, S., Xia, Y., Kalashnikov, D. V., Aref, W. G., & Hambrusch, S. E. (2002). Query indexing and velocity constraint indexing: Scalable techniques for continuous queries on moving objects. *IEEE Transactions on Computers*, 1–17.

Prade, H., & Testemale, C. (1984). Generalizing Database Relational Algebra for the Treatment of Incomplete or Uncertain Information and Vague Queries. *Information Sciences*, *34*(2), 115–143. doi:10.1016/0020-0255(84)90020-3

Preparata, F. P., & Shamos, M. I. (1985). Computational Geometry: An Introduction. Springer-Verlag.

Project, R. (2014). *The R Project for Statistical Computing*. Retrieved October 15, 2014, from http://www.r-project.org/

Prud'Hommeaux, E., & Seaborne, A. (2008). SPARQL query language for RDF. W3C recommendation, 15.

Prud'hommeaux, E., & Seaborne, A. (2008). *SPARQL query language for RDF*. W3C Recommendation. Retrieved from http://www.w3.org/TR/rdf-sparql-query/

Przyjaciel-Zablocki, M., Schätzle, A., Hornung, T., & Lausen, G. (2012). Rdfpath: Path query processing on large rdf graphs with mapreduce. In *ESWC 2011 Workshops* (pp. 50–64). Springer Berlin Heidelberg. doi:10.1007/978-3-642-25953-1_5

Psaila, R. A., Wimmers, M., & It, E. L. (1995). Querying shapes of histories. *Very Large Data Bases*. Zurich, Switzerland: IEEE.

Qiang, P., Lbath, A., & Daqing, H. (2012). Location based recommendation for mobile users using language model and skyline query. The International Journal of Information Technology and Computer Science, 4(10), 19-28.

Qiao, Z., Gu, J., Lin, X., & Chen, J. (2010). Privacy-Preserving Skyline Queries in LBS. In *Proceedings of the International Conference on Machine Vision and Human-Machine Interface (MVHI)* (pp. 499-504). Kaifeng, China: IEEE. doi:10.1109/MVHI.2010.205

Quinlan, J. R., & Rivest, R. L. (1989). Inferring Decision Trees Using the Minimum Description Length Principle. *Information and Computation*, *80*(3), 227–248. doi:10.1016/0890-5401(89)90010-2

Rachapalli, J., Khadilkar, V., Kantarcioglu, M., & Thuraisingham, B. (2011). RETRO: A Framework for Semantics Preserving SQL-to-SPARQL Translation. In *Proceedings of the Joint Workshop on Knowledge Evolution and Ontology Dynamics, Co-located with the 10th International Semantic Web Conference*. Bonn, Germany: Springer.

Raimond, Y., & Abdallah, S. (2007). *The event ontology*. Retrieved from http://motools.sourceforge.net/event/event.html

Raj, J. (1991). *The art of computer systems performance*. Academic Press.

Raju, K. V. S. V. N., & Majumdar, K. (1988). Fuzzy Functional Dependencies and Lossless Join Decomposition of Fuzzy Relational Database Systems. *ACM Transactions on Database Systems*, *13*(2), 129–166. doi:10.1145/42338.42344

Ramasamy, K., Patel, J., Naughton, J., & Kaushik, R. (2000). Set containment joins: The good, the bad and the ugly. In *Proceedings of the very large database (vldb) endowment* (p. 351-362). Academic Press.

Rantzau, R., & Mangold, C. (2006). Laws for rewriting queries containing division operators. In *Proceedings of the IEEE international conference on data engineering (ICDE)* (p. 21). IEEE. doi:10.1109/ICDE.2006.180

Rao, J., Pirahesh, H., & Zuzarte, C. (2004). Canonical abstraction for outerjoin optimization. In *Proceedings of the ACM SIGMOD international conference on management of data* (p. 671-682). ACM.

Rao, S., Van Gucht, D., & Badia, A. (1996). Providing better support for a class of decision support queries. In *Proceedings of the ACM SIGMOD international conference on management of data* (p. 217-227). doi:10.1145/233269.233334

Rasiowa, H. (1974). An algebraic Approach to Non-classical Logics. PWN, Polish Scientific Publishers: Warszawa and North-Holland Publishing Company.

Reeba, R. S., & Kavitha, V. R. (2012). An Efficient Location Dependent System Based On Spatial Sky Line Queries. *International Journal of Soft Computing and Engineering, 1*(1), 27–29.

Renzo, A., & Claudio, G. (2005). Querying RDF Data from a Graph Database Perspective. In *Proceedings of the 2nd European Semantic Web Conference*. Heraklion, Greece: Springer.

Rith, J., Lehmayr, P., & Meyer-Wegener, K. (2014). Speaking in Tongues: SQL Access to NoSQL Systems. In *Proceedings of the 29th Annual ACM Symposium on Applied Computing (SAC '14)*. Gyeongju, Korea: ACM. doi:10.1145/2554850.2555099

Robinson, J. T. (1981). The K-D-B-tree: a search structure for large multidimensional dynamic indexes. In *Proc. of the ACM SIGMOD International Conference on Management of Data*, (pp. 10-18). doi:10.1145/582318.582321

Rocha-Junior, J. B., Vlachou, A., Doulkeridis, C., & Nørvåg, K. (2011). Efficient Execution Plans for Distributed Skyline Query Processing. In *Proceedings of The International Conference on Extending Database Technology (EDBT)* (pp. 271-282). Uppsala, Sweden: Springer-Verlag. doi:10.1145/1951365.1951399

Rodriguez, M. (2013, July 10). *Getting Started Gremlin*. Retrieved August 20, 2015, from https://github.com/tinkerpop/gremlin/wiki

Rodriguez-Muro, M., & Calvanese, D. (2012). Quest, an OWL 2 QL reasoner for ontology-based data access. In *Proceedings of the 9th int. workshop on owl: experiences and directions*. Crete, Greece: Springer.

Rodríguez-Muro, M., Hardi, J., & Calvanese, D. (2012). Quest: Effcient SPARQL-to-SQL for RDF and OWL. In *Proceedings of International Semantic Web Conference*. Boston, MA: Springer.

Rodriguez-Muro, M., Kontchakov, R., & Zakharyaschev, M. (2013). Ontology-Based Data Access: Ontop of Databases. In *Proceedings of International Semantic Web Conference* (pp. 558-573). Sydney, Australia: Springer.

Rodriguez-Muro, M., & Rezk, M. (2014). Efficient SPARQL-to-SQL with R2RML mappings. *Journal of Web Semantics*.

Rohloff, K., Dean, M., Emmons, I., Ryder, D., & Sumner, J. (2007). An evaluation of triple-store technologies for large data stores. In *On the Move to Meaningful Internet Systems 2007: OTM 2007 Workshops* (pp. 1105–1114). Springer Berlin Heidelberg. doi:10.1007/978-3-540-76890-6_38

Rouse, M. (2014, November 1). *Graph database*. Retrieved August 20, 2015, from http://whatis.techtarget.com/definition/graph-database

Roussopoulos, N., Kelley, S., & Vincent, F. (1995). Nearest neighbor queries. In *Proceedings of the ACM SIGMOD International Conference on Management of Data*, (pp. 71-79). San Jose, CA: ACM Press.

Rudowsky, I. (2004). Intelligent Agents. *Communications of the Association for Information Systems, 14*, 275–290.

Rusher, J. (2003). Triple store. In *Workshop on Semantic Web Storage and Retrieval-Position Paper*. Academic Press.

Ruspini, E. (1986). Imprecision and Uncertainty in the Entity-Relationship Model. In *Fuzzy Logic in Knowledge Engineering*. Verlag TUV Rheinland.

Russell, A., & Smart, P. R. (2008). NITELIGHT: A graphical editor for SPARQL queries. In *International Semantic Web Conference (Posters & Demos)*. Academic Press.

Russel, S., & Norvig, P. (2010). *Artificial Intelligence. A Modern approach*. Prentice Hall.

Russom, P. a. (2011). *Big data analytics*. TDWI Best Practices Report, Fourth Quarter.

Sacharidis, D., Arvanitis, A., & Sellis, T. (2010). Probabilistic Contextual Skylines. In *Proceedings of The International Conference on Data Engineering (ICDE)* (pp. 273-284). Long Beach, CA: IEEE Computer Society.

Sadri, R. a. (2001). A sequential pattern query language for supporting instant data mining for e-services. In *Proceedings of the 27th International Conference on Very Large Data Bases* (pp. 653--656). Morgan Kaufmann Publishers Inc.

Sajja, P.S. (2008). Enhancing Quality in E-learning by Knowledge-Based IT Support. *International Journal of Education and Development using Information and Communication Technology, 4*(1), 109-119.

Sajja, P. S. (2006). Parichay: An Agent for Adult Literacy. *Prajna, 14*, 17–24.

Sakaki, T., Okazaki, M., & Matsuo, Y. (2010). Earthquake Shakes Twitter Users: Real-time Event Detection by Social Sensors, Earthquake shakes twitter users: real-time event detection by social sensors. In *Proceedings of the 19th international conference on World Wide Web, WWW '10*, (pp. 851-860). New York:ACM. doi:10.1145/1772690.1772777

Sakr, M. A., & Güting, R. H. (2011). Spatiotemporal pattern queries. *GeoInformatica, 15*(3), 497–540. doi:10.1007/s10707-010-0114-3

Sakr, S., & Al-Naymat, G. (2010). Relational processing of RDF queries: A survey. *SIGMOD Record, 38*(4), 23–28. doi:10.1145/1815948.1815953

Saltenis, S., & Jensen, C. S. (2002). Indexing of moving objects for location-based services. In *Proc. of the IEEE International Conference on Data Engineering (ICDE)*, (pp. 463-472). doi:10.1109/ICDE.2002.994759

Sanfilippo, S. (2009). *An introduction to Redis data types and abstractions*. Retrieved August 20, 2015, from http://redis.io/topics/data-types-intro

Sarathy, V., Van Gucht, D., & Badia, A. (1993, May). Extended query graphs for declarative specification of set-oriented queries. In *Workshop on combining declarative and object-oriented databases (in conjunction with sigmod 93)*.Washington, DC: Academic Press.

Scalise, K., & Ketterlin-Geller, L. (2012). Reciprocal Leading: Improving Instructional Designs in E-Learning. In P. Ghislandi (Ed.), eLearning - Theories, Design, Software and Applications (pp. 73-90). InTech - Open Access Publisher.

Schäfer, P. (2014). *Experiencing the Shotgun Distance for Time Series Analysis*. Academic Press.

Schlieder, T., & Meuss, H. (2002). Querying and ranking XML documents. *Journal of the American Society for Information Science and Technology, 53*(6), 489–503. doi:10.1002/asi.10060

Schmidt, A. (2003). *XMark — An XML Benchmark Project*. Retrieved October 29, 2014, from http://www.ins.cwi.nl/projects/xmark/

Schmidt, A., Waas, F., Kersten, M., Carey, M. J., Manolescu, I., & Busse, R. (2002). XMark: a benchmark for XML data management. In *Proceedings of the 28th international conference on Very Large Data Bases* (VLDB '02). VLDB Endowment. doi:10.1016/B978-155860869-6/50096-2

Schoning, H. (2001). Tamino - A DBMS designed for XML. In *Proceedings of the ICDE Conference*. ICDE.

Schumacher, R. (2015, January 2). *A Brief Introduction to Apache Cassandra*. Retrieved August 20, 2015, from https://academy.datastax.com/demos/brief-introduction-apache-cassandra

Schweiger, , Trajanoski, Z., & Pabinger, S. (2014). SPARQLGraph: A web-based platform for graphically querying biological Semantic Web databases. *BMC Bioinformatics, 15*(1), 279. doi:10.1186/1471-2105-15-279 PMID:25127889

Seaborne, A. (2011). *Jena TDB*. Retrieved from http://jena.apache.org/documentation/tdb/index.html

Sechenov, I. M. (2001). Elements of Thoughts. Saint-Petersburg, Russia: Publishing House "Piter".

Sedmidubsky, J., Dohnal, V., & Zezula, P. (2008). *M-tree: Metric tree*. Retrieved May 5, 2014, from http://disa.fi.muni.cz/trac/mtree/

Selic, B., & Rumbaugh, J. (1998). *Using UML for Modeling Complex Real-Time Systems*. ObjecTime. doi:10.1007/BFb0057795

Sellis, T., Roussopoulos, N., & Faloutsos, C. (1987). *The R+--Tree: A Dynamic Index for Multi-Dimensional Objects*. VLDB Endowments.

Senellart, P., & Abiteboul, S. (2007). On the Complexity of Managing Probabilistic XML Data. In *Proceedings of the 26th ACM SIGACT-SIGMOD-SIGART Symposium on Principles of Database Systems*, (pp. 283-292). doi:10.1145/1265530.1265570

Sequeda, J. F., & Arenas, M., & Miranker, Daniel P. (2012). Ontology-Based Data Access Using Views. In *Proceedings of RR* (pp. 262-265). Vienna, Austria: Springer.

Sequeda, J. F., & Miranker, D. P. (2012). *Ultrawrap: Sparql execution on relational data*. Technical Report TR-12-10. The University of Texas at Austin, Department of Computer Sciences.

Seshadri, P., Livny, M., & Ramakrishnan, R. (1995). SEQ: A model for sequence databases. In *Proceedings of the Eleventh International Conference on Data Engineering*, (pp. 232--239). IEEE. doi:10.1109/ICDE.1995.380388

Seto, J., Clement, S., Duong, D., Kianmehr, K., & Alhajj, R. (2009). Fuzzy Query Model for XML Documents. In *Proceedings of the Intelligent Data Engineering and Automated Learning Conference*, (pp. 333-340). Burgos, Spain: Springer.

Seylan, I., Franconi, E., & de Bruijn, J. (2009). Effective Query Rewriting with Ontologies over DBoxes. In *Proceedings of IJCAI* (pp. 923-925). Pasadena, CA: AAAI.

Shaorong, L., Qinghua, Z., & Chu, W. (2004). Configurable Indexing and Ranking for XML Information Retrieval. In *Proceedings of the International Conference on Research and Development in Information Retrieval*, (pp. 88-95). Sheffield, UK: ACM.

Sharifzadeh, M., & Shahabi, C. (2006). The spatial skyline queries. In *Proceedings of the 32nd International Conference on Very Large Data Bases (VLDB)* (pp. 751-762). VLDB Endowment.

Sharifzadeh, M., & Shahabi, C. (2006). The spatial skyline queries. In *Proceedings of the International Conference on Very Large Data Bases (VLDB)* (pp. 751-762). VLDB Endowment.

Sharifzadeh, M., Shahabi, C., & Kazemi, L. (2009). Processing spatial skyline queries in both vector spaces and spatial network databases. *ACM Transactions on Database Systems, 34*(3), 11–45. doi:10.1145/1567274.1567276

Shearer, R., Motik, B., & Horrocks, I. (2008). HermiT: A highly-efficient OWL reasoner. In *Proceedings of the 5th Int. Workshop on OWL: Experiences and Directions*. Karlsruhe, Germany: CEUR.

Shen, H., Chen, Z., & Deng, X. (2009). Location-based Skyline Queries in Wireless Sensor Networks. In *Proceedings of The International Conference on Networks Security, Wireless Communications and Trusted Computing* (pp. 391-395). Wuhan, China: IEEE. doi:10.1109/NSWCTC.2009.314

Shieh, J., & Keogh, E. (2008). i SAX: indexing and mining terabyte sized time series. In *Proceedings of the 14th ACM SIGKDD international conference on Knowledge discovery and data mining* (pp. 623--631). ACM. doi:10.1145/1401890.1401966

Shute, V. J., & Psotka, J. (1996). Intelligent Tutoring Systems: Past, Present, and Future. In D. Jonassen (Ed.), *Handbook of Research for Educational Communications and Technology* (pp. 570–600). New York, NY: Macmillan.

Siberski, W., Pan, Z., & Thaden, U. (2006). Querying the Semantic Web with Preferences. In *Proceedings of the 5th International Semantic Web Conference*. Athens, GA: Springer.

Sicilia, M. A., & Mastorakis, N. (2004). Extending UML 1.5 for Fuzzy Conceptual Modeling: A Strictly Additive Approach. *WSEAS Transactions on Systems, 5*(3), 2234–2240.

Siddique, M. A. & Morimoto, Y. (2009). K-Dominant Skyline Computation by Using Sort-Filtering Method. In *Proceedings of the 13th Pacific-Asia Conference on Advances in Knowledge Discovery and Data Mining* (pp. 839-848). Berlin: Springer-Verlag. doi:10.1007/978-3-642-01307-2_87

Sidirourgos, L., Goncalves, R., Kersten, M., Nes, N., & Manegold, S. (2008). Column-store support for RDF data management: Not all swans are white. *Proceedings of the VLDB Endowment, 1*(2), 1553–1563. doi:10.14778/1454159.1454227

Siegel, E., & Retter, A. (2014). eXist: A NoSQL Document Database and Application Platform. O'Reilly Media, Inc.

Sigoure, B. (2012). *OpenTSDB scalable time series database (TSDB)*. Stumble Upon. Retrieved from http://opentsdb. net

Silva, C. (2011). *Data Modeling with NoSQL: How, When and Why*. (Unpublished doctoral dissertation). Universidade do Porto, Porto, Portugal.

Simão, H. P., Jeong, H. a., Powell, W. B., Gagneja, A., Wu, L., & Anderson, R. (2013). *A Robust Solution to the Load Curtailment Problem*. IEEE.

Simmhan, Y., Wickramaarachchi, C. A., Ravi, S., Raghavendra, C., & Prasanna, V. (2014). Scalable analytics over distributed time-series graphs using goffish. *arXiv preprint arXiv:1406.5975*.

Sirin, E., & Parsia, B. (2006). Pellet system description. In *Proceedings of the 19th Int. Workshop on Description Logic*. Lake District, UK: CEUR.

Skopal, T., & Lokoc, J. (2010). Answering metric skyline queries by pm-tree. In *Proceedings of the Annual International Workshop on DAtabases, TExts, Specifications and Objects (DATESO)* (pp. 22-37). Stedronin-Plazy, Czech Republic: CEUR-WS.org.

Slater, N. (2015, March 1). *Best Practices for Migrating from RDBMS to Amazon Dynamo DB*. Retrieved August 20, 2015, from http://aws.amazon.com/pt/dynamodb/

Sleit, A. N., & Al-Nsour, E. (2014). Corner-based splitting: An improved node splitting algorithm for R-tree. *Journal of Information Science, 40*(2), 222–236. doi:10.1177/0165551513516709

Slimmer, J. S. (1987). *Concept acquisition through representational adjustment*. Technical report 87-19. Department of Information and Computer Science, University of California, Irvine.

Software, S. (2001). *BekeleyDB*. Sams Publishing.

Son, J., Jeong, D., & Baik, D. (2008). Practical Approach: Independently Using SPARQL-to-SQL Translation Algorithms on Storage. In *Proceedings of the 4th International Conference on Networked Computing and Advanced Information Management*. Gyeongju, Korea: IEEE. doi:10.1109/NCM.2008.151

Son, J., Jeong, D., & Baik, D. (2011). Performance Evaluation of Storage-Independent Model for SPARQL-to-SQL Translation Algorithms. In *Proceedings of the 4th IFIP International Conference on New Technologies, Mobility and Security* (pp. 1-4). Paris, France: IEEE.

Sören, A., & Ives, Z. G. (2007). *Integrating Ontologies and Relational Data. Technical Reports*. CIS.

Soudani, N. M. & Baraani-Dastgerdi, A. (2011). The spatial nearest neighbor skyline queries. *The Computing Research Repository (CoRR)*, abs/1112.2336.

Soylu, A., Giese, M., Jimenez-Ruiz, E., Kharlamov, E., Zheleznyakov, D., & Horrocks, I. (2013) OptiqueVQS: towards an ontology-based visual query system for big data. In *Proceedings of the Fifth International Conference on Management of Emergent Digital EcoSystems*. ACM. doi:10.1145/2536146.2536149

Sözer, A., Yazici, A., Oğuztüzün, H., & Tas, O. (2008). Modeling and Querying Fuzzy Spatiotemporal Databases. *Information Sciences, 178*(19), 3665–3682. doi:10.1016/j.ins.2008.05.034

Speelman, D. (1994). A natural language interface that uses generalized quantifiers. In *Lecture notes in computer science; lecture notes in artifical intelligence*. Academic Press.

Spencer, H. (1898). *Principles of Psychology*. Academic Press.

Srivastava, E., & Agarwal, N. (2013). E-Learning: New Trend in Education and Training. *International Journal of Advanced Research, 1*(8), 797–810.

Srividhya, S., & Lavanya, S. (2014). Comparative Analysis of R-Tree and R-Tree in Spatial Database. *Intelligent Computing Applications (ICICA), 2014 International Conference on* (pp. 449--453). IEEE.

Staab, S., & Studer, R. (Eds.). (2009). *Handbook on Ontologies* (2nd ed.). Springer. doi:10.1007/978-3-540-92673-3

Stocker, M., Seaborne, A., Bernstein, A., Kiefer, C., & Reynolds, D. (2008). SPARQL Basic Graph Pattern Optimization Using Selectivity Estimation. In *Proceedings of the 17th International Conference on World Wide Web*. Beijing, China: ACM. doi:10.1145/1367497.1367578

Stonebraker, M., Abadi, D. J., Batkin, A., Chen, X., Cherniack, M., Ferreira, M., ... (2005). C-store: a column-oriented DBMS. In *Proceedings of the 31st international conference on Very large data bases* (pp. 553--564). VLDB Endowment.

Stonebraker, M., & Moore, D. (1996). *Object-Relational DBMSs: The Next Great Wave*. Morgan Kaufmann.

Straccia, U. (2006). Answering Vague Queries in Fuzzy DL-LITE. In *Proceedings of the 11th International Conference on Information Processing and Management of Uncertainty in Knowledge-Based Systems* (pp. 2238-2245). Paris, France: Springer.

Studer, R., Benjamins, R., & Fensel, D. (1998). Knowledge engineering: Principles and methods. *Data & Knowledge Engineering, 25*(1-2), 161–198. doi:10.1016/S0169-023X(97)00056-6

Šumák, M., & Gurský, P. (2013). R++ -tree: An Efficient Spatial Access Method for Highly Redundant Point Data. In *Proceedings of the 17th East-European Conference on Advances in Databases and Information Systems*. Genoa, Italy: Springer.

Su, W., Wang, J., Huang, Q., & Lochovsky, F. H. (2006). Query result ranking over E-commerce web databases. In *Proceedings of the International Conference on Information and Knowledge Management*, (pp. 575-584). Arlington, VA: ACM. doi:10.1145/1183614.1183697

Tahani, V. (1977). A Conceptual Framework for Fuzzy Query Processing: A Step toward Very Intelligent Database Systems. *Information Processing & Management, 13*(5), 289–303. doi:10.1016/0306-4573(77)90018-8

Takahashi, Y. (1991). A Fuzzy Query Language for Relational Databases. *IEEE Transactions on Systems, Man, and Cybernetics, 21*(6), 1576–1579. doi:10.1109/21.135699

Takahashi, Y. (1993). Fuzzy Database Query Languages and Their Relational Completeness Theorem. *IEEE Transactions on Knowledge and Data Engineering, 5*(1), 122–125. doi:10.1109/69.204096

Tamani, N., Lietard, L., & Rocacher, D. (2011). Bipolar SQLf: A Flexible Querying Language for Relational Databases. In *Proceedings of the 9th International Conference on Flexible Query Answering Systems*. Ghent, Belgium: Springer.

Tamani, N., Lietard, L., & Rocacher, D. (2013). Bipolar Conjunctive Query Evaluation for Ontology Based Database Querying. In *Proceedings of FQAS* (pp. 389-400). Granada, Spain: Springer. doi:10.1007/978-3-642-40769-7_34

Tang, L.-A., Zheng, Y., Yuan, J., Han, J., Leung, A., Peng, W.-C., & La Porta, T. (2014). A framework of traveling companion discovery on trajectory data streams. ACM Trans. Intell. Syst. Technol. 5(1).

Tan, H., Luo, W., & Ni, L. M. (2012). CloST: a hadoop-based storage system for big spatio-temporal data analytics. In *Proc. of the ACM International Conference on Information and Knowledge Management (CIKM)*, (pp. 2139-2143). doi:10.1145/2396761.2398589

Tan, K., Eng, P., & Ooi, B. (2001). Efficient progressive skyline computation. In *Proceedings of the 27th International Conference on Very Large Data Bases (VLDB)* (pp. 301-310). San Francisco, CA: Morgan Kaufmann Publishers Inc.

Tan, K., Eng, P., & Ooi, B. (2001). Efficient progressive skyline computation. In *Proceedings of the International Conference on Very Large Data Bases (VLDB)* (pp. 301-310). San Francisco, CA: Morgan Kaufmann Publishers Inc.

Tao, Y. F., & Yu, J. X. Finding frequent co-occurring terms in relational keyword search. (2009). In *Proceedings of the EDBT/ICDT Joint Conference (EDBT)*. (pp 839-850). Saint-Petersburg, Russia: ACM. doi:10.1145/1516360.1516456

Tao, Y., & Papadias, D. (2001). MV3R-Tree: A spatio-temporal access method for timestamp and interval queries. In *Proc. of the International Conference on Very Large Data Bases (VLDB)*, (pp. 431-440). VLDB.

Tao, Y., Papadias, D., & Shen, Q. (2002). Continuous nearest neighbor search. In *Proc. of the International Conference on Very Large Data Bases (VLDB)*, (pp. 287-298). doi:10.1016/B978-155860869-6/50033-0

Tata, S., & Lohman, G. M. (2008). SQAK: doing more with keywords. In *Proceedings of the ACM SIGMOD Conference on Data Management (SIGMOD)*. (pp 889-902). New York: ACM.

Tauro, C., Aravindh, S., & Shreeharsha, A.B. (2012). Comparative Study of the New Generation, Agile, Scalable, High Performance NOSQL Databases. *International Journal of Computer Applications, 48*(20).

Teall, E., Wang, M., Callaghan, V., & Ng, J. W. P. (2014). An Exposition of Current Mobile Learning Design Guidelines and Frameworks. *International Journal on E-Learning, 13*(1), 79–99.

Teorey, T. J., Yang, D. Q., & Fry, J. P. (1986). A Logical Design Methodology for Relational Databases Using the Extended Entity-Relationship Model. *ACM Computing Surveys, 18*(2), 197–222. doi:10.1145/7474.7475

The Neo4j Manual v2.2.4 Tutorials Cypher. (2015). Retrieved August 20, 2015, from http://neo4j.com/docs/stable/tutorials.htm

Thom, D., Bosch, H., Koch, S., Woerner, M., & Ertl, T. (2012). Spatio temporal anomaly detection through visual analysis of geolocated twitter messages. In *Proceedings of the IEEE Pacic Visualization Symposium (PacicVis)*. IEEE.

Thompson, H. S., Beech, D., Maloney, M., & Mendelsohn, N. (2001). *XML Schema Part 1: Structures, W3C Recommendation*. Retrieved from http://www.w3.org/TR/xmlschema-1/

Thomsom E.J. & Radhamani, G. (2011). Information retrieval using xquery processing techniques. *International Journal of Database Management Systems.*

Thomsom, E. J., & Radhamani, G. (2009). *Fuzzy Logic based XQuery Operations for Native XML Database Systems.* International Journal Database Theory and Application.

Thomson, E., Fredrick, J., & Radhamani, G. (2009). Fuzzy Logic Based XQuery operations for Native XML Database Systems. *International Journal of Database Theory and Application, 2*(3), 13–20.

Thusoo, A., Sarma, J. S., Jain, N., Shao, Z., Chakka, P., & Liu, H. et al.. (2009). Hive: A warehousing solution over a map-reduce framework. *Proceedings of the VLDB Endowment, 2*(2), 1626–1629. doi:10.14778/1687553.1687609

Timarán, R. (2001). Arquitecturas de integración del proceso de descubrimiento de conocimiento con sistemas de gestión de bases de datos: un estado del arte. In *Ingeniería y competitividad, volumen 2.* Springer.

Timarán, R. (2001). Arquitecturas de Integración del Proceso de Descubrimiento de Conocimiento con Sistemas de Gestión de Bases de Datos: Un Estado del Arte. *Ingeniería y Competitividad., 3*(2), 45–55.

Toad for Cloud Databases. (2012, March 16). Retrieved August 20, 2015, from http://www.toadworld.com/products/toad-for-cloud-databases/w/wiki/10447.toad-for-cloud-databases-release-notes-eclipse-edition

Trencseni, M. (2009, February 15). *Thoughts on Yahoo's PNUTS distributed database.* Retrieved August 20, 2015, from http://highscalability.com/blog/2009/8/8/yahoos-pnuts-database-too-hot-too-cold-or-just-right.html

Tripathi, P. K., Debnath, M., & Elmasri, R. (2014). Extracting Dense Regions From Hurricane Trajectory Data. In *Proc. of the ACM Workshop on Managing and Mining Enriched Geo-Spatial Data (GeoRich'14).* ACM.

Trißl, S., & Leser, U. (2005). Querying Ontologies in Relational Database Systems. In *Proceedings of DILS* (pp. 63-79). San Diego, CA: Springer.

Tsarkov, D., & Horrocks, I. (2006). FaCT++ description logic reasoner: System description. In *Proceedings of the 3rd Int. Joint Conf. on Automated Reasoning* (pp. 292-297). Seattle, WA: AAAI. doi:10.1007/11814771_26

Tseng, C., Khamisy, W., & Vu, T. (2005). Universal Fuzzy System Representation with XML. *Computer Standards & Interfaces, 28*(2), 218–230. doi:10.1016/j.csi.2004.11.005

Turowski, K., & Weng, U. (2002). Representing and Processing Fuzzy Information: An XML-based Approach. *Knowledge-Based Systems, 15*(1-2), 67–75. doi:10.1016/S0950-7051(01)00122-8

Tzacheva, A. A., Toland, T. S., Poole, P. H., & Barnes, D. J. (2013). Ontology Database System and Triggers. In *Proceedings of The Twelfth International Symposium on Intelligent Data Analysis* (pp. 416-426). London, UK: Springer.

Ueng, P. S. (2012). Implementing XQuery fuzzy extensions using a native XML database. In *Proceedings of International Symposium on Computational Intelligence and Informatics,* (pp. 305-309). doi:10.1109/CINTI.2012.6496780

Ulanova, L., Begum, N., & Keogh, E. (2015). *Scalable Clustering of Time Series with U-Shapelets.* SDM. doi:10.1137/1.9781611974010.101

Umano, M., & Fukami, S. (1994). Fuzzy Relational Algebra for Possibility-Distribution-Fuzzy-Relational Model of Fuzzy Data. *Journal of Intelligent Information Systems, 3*(1), 7–27. doi:10.1007/BF01014018

Umano, M., Imada, T., Hatono, I., & Tamura, H. (1998). Fuzzy Object-Oriented Databases and Implementation of Its SQL-Type Data Manipulation Language. In *Proceedings of the 1998 IEEE International Conference on Fuzzy Systems.* doi:10.1109/FUZZY.1998.686314

Unger, C., Bühmann, L., Lehmann, J., Ngomo, A.-C. N., Gerber, D., & Cimiano, P. (2012). Template-based Question Answering over RDF Data. In *Proceedings of the 21st International Conference on World Wide Web*. Lyon, France: ACM. doi:10.1145/2187836.2187923

Urrutia, A., & Galindo, J. (2010). *Fuzzy Database Modeling: An Overview and New Definitions. In Soft Computing Applications for Database Technologies: Techniques and Issues* (pp. 1–21). IGI Global. doi:10.4018/978-1-60566-814-7.ch001

Vaidya, N. M., & Sajja, P. S. (2014). Intelligent Virtual Collaborative Learning Environment. *International Journal of Research in Computer Science and Information Technology, 2*(2), 116–118.

Valkanas, G., & Papadopoulos, A. N. (2010). Efficient and Adaptive Distributed Skyline Computation. In *Proceedings of the 22nd International Conference on Scientific and Statistical Database Management (SSDBM)* (pp. 24-41). Heidelberg, Germany: Springer-Verlag.

van Benthem, J., & Westerstahl, D. (1995). Directions in generalized quantifier theory. *Studia Logica, 55*.

van Gyseghem, N., & de Caluwe, R. (1998). Imprecision and Uncertainty in UFO Database Model. *Journal of the American Society for Information Science, 49*(3), 236–252. doi:10.1002/(SICI)1097-4571(199803)49:3<236::AID-ASI5>3.0.CO;2-B

Vandenberghe, R. M. (1991). An Extended Entity-Relationship Model for Fuzzy Databases Based on Fuzzy Truth Values. In *Proceedings of the 4th International Fuzzy Systems Association World Congress*. Academic Press.

Vernica, R., Carey, M. J., & Li, C. (2010). Efficient parallel set-similarity joins using mapreduce. In *Proceedings of the ACM SIGMOD International Conference on Management of Data*, (pp. 495-506). Indianapolis, IN: ACM.

Vert, G., Morris, A., Stock, M., & Jankowski, P. (2000). Extending Entity-Relationship Modeling Notation to Manage Fuzzy Datasets. In *Proceedings of the 2000 International Conference on Information Processing and Management of Uncertainty in Knowledge-Based Systems*. Academic Press.

Vert, G., Morris, A., & Stock, M. (2003). Converting a Fuzzy Data Model to an Object-Oriented Design for Managing GIS Data Files. *IEEE Transactions on Knowledge and Data Engineering, 15*(2), 510–511. doi:10.1109/TKDE.2003.1185848

Vert, G., Stock, M., & Morris, A. (2002). Extending ERD Modeling Notation to Fuzzy Management of GIS Data Files. *Data & Knowledge Engineering, 40*(2), 163–179. doi:10.1016/S0169-023X(01)00049-0

Vieira, M. R., Bakalov, P., & Tsotras, V. J. (2010). Querying trajectories using exible patterns. In *Proc. of the International Conference on Extending Database Technology (EDBT)*, (pp. 406-417). doi:10.1145/1739041.1739091

Vieira, M. R., Bakalov, P., & Tsotras, V. J. (2011). FlexTrack: A system for querying flexible patterns in trajectory databases. In *Proc. of the International Symp. on Advances in Spatial and Temporal Databases (SSTD)*, (pp. 475-480). doi:10.1007/978-3-642-22922-0_34

Vieira, M., Bakalov, P., & Tsotras, V. (2009). On-line discovery of flock patterns in spatio-temporal data. In *Proc. of the ACM International Conference on Advances in Geographic Information Systems (SIGSPATIAL)*, (pp. 286-295). doi:10.1145/1653771.1653812

Vila, M. A., Cubero, J. C., Medina, J. M., & Pons, O. (1996). A Conceptual Approach for Deal with Imprecision and Uncertainty in Object-Based Data Models. *International Journal of Intelligent Systems, 11*(10), 791–806. doi:10.1002/(SICI)1098-111X(199610)11:10<791::AID-INT6>3.0.CO;2-U

Vlachos, M., Kollios, G., & Gunopulos, D. (2002). Discovering similar multidimensional trajectories. *Data Engineering, 2002. Proceedings. 18th International Conference on* (pp. 673--684). IEEE.

Vlachos, M., Kollios, G., & Gunopulos, D. (2002). Discovering similar multidimensional trajectories. In *Proc. of the IEEE International Conference on Data Engineering (ICDE)*, (pp. 673-684). IEEE.

Vlachou, A., Doulkeridis, C., & Halkidi, M. (2012). Discovering Representative Skyline Points over Distributed Data. *InProceedings of the 24th International Conference on Scientific and Statistical Database Management* (pp. 141-158). Springer-Verlag. doi:10.1007/978-3-642-31235-9_9

Voldemort. (n.d.). *GitHub*. Retrieved August 19, 2015, from http://www.project-voldemort.com/voldemort/

Voronoi, G. (1908). Nouvelles applications des parametres continus a la theorie des formes quadratiques, Rescherches sur les Parallelloedres Primitifs. *Journal fur die Reine und Angewandte Mathematik, 134*(1), 198–287.

Vysniauskas, E., Nemuraite, L., & Paradauskas, B. (2011). Hybrid Method for Storing and Querying Ontologies in Databases. *Electronics and Electrical Engineering, 9*(115), 67–72.

Vyšniauskas, E., Nemuraite, L., Sukys, A., & Paradauskas, B. (2010). Enhancing connection between ontologies and databases with OWL 2 concepts and SPARQL. In *Proceedings of the 16th International Conference on Information and Software Technologies* (pp. 350-357). Kaunas, Lithuania: IEEE.

W3C. (2008). *Extensible Markup Language (XML) 1.0* (5ᵗʰ ed.). Retrieved January 26, 2015 from: http://www.w3.org/TR/REC-xml/

W3C. (2010). *XQuery 1.0: An XML Query Language* (2ⁿᵈ ed.). Retrieved January 26, 2015 from: http://www.w3.org/TR/xquery/

W3C. (2014). *XML Path Language (XPath) 3.0*. Retrieved January 26, 2015 from: http://www.w3.org/TR/xpath-30

Wagner, A., & Badia, A. (2014). Complex SQL predicates as quantifiers. *IEEE Transactions on Knowledge and Data Engineering, 26*(7), 1617–1630. doi:10.1109/TKDE.2013.55

Wakamiya, S., Lee, R., & Sumiya, K. (2011). *Urban Area Characterization Based on Semantics of Crowd Activities in Twitter*. GeoSpatial Semantics; doi:10.1007/978-3-642-20630-6_7

Wang, H., Ma, Z. M., & Cheng, J. (2012). fp-Sparql: an RDF fuzzy retrieval mechanism supporting user preference. In *9th International Conference on Fuzzy Systems and Knowledge Discovery* (FSKD 2012) (pp. 443-447). IEEE.

Wang, B., Dong, H., Boedihardjo, A. P., Lu, C.-T., Yu, H., Chen, I.-R., & Dai, J. (2012). An integrated framework for spatio-temporal-textual search and mining. In *Proc. of the ACM International Conference on Advances in Geographic Information Systems (SIGSPATIAL)*, (pp. 570-573). doi:10.1145/2424321.2424418

Wang, C. Y., Lo, A., Alhajj, R., & Barker, K. (2005). Novel Approach for Reengineering Relational Databases into XML. In *Proceedings of the 21st International Conference on Data Engineering Workshop*. doi:10.1109/ICDE.2005.249

Wang, C., Cao, L. B., Wang, M. C., Li, J. J., Wei, W., & Ou, Y. M. (2011). Coupled nominal similarity in unsupervised learning. In *Proceedings of the ACM International Conference on Information & Knowledge Management (CIKM)*. (pp 973-978). New York: ACM.

Wang, C., She, Z., & Cao, L. B. (2013). Coupled clustering ensemble: incorporating coupling relationships both between base clusterings and objects. In *Proceedings of the International Conference on Data Engineering (ICDE)*. (pp 374-385). Brisbane, Australia: IEEE Computer Society. doi:10.1109/ICDE.2013.6544840

Wang, H., Tang, M., Park, Y., & Priebe, C. (2014). Locality statistics for anomaly detection in time series of graphs. *IEEE Transactions on Signal Processing, 62*(3), 703–717. doi:10.1109/TSP.2013.2294594

Wang, J., Wu, S., Gao, H., Li, J., & Ooi, B. C. (2010). Indexing multi-dimensional data in a cloud system. In *Proceedings of the ACM SIGMOD International Conference on Management of Data*, (pp. 591-602). Indianapolis, IN: ACM. doi:10.1145/1807167.1807232

Wang, J., Zhu, Y., Li, S., Wan, D., & Zhang, P. (2014). *Multivariate Time Series Similarity Searching*. Hindawi Publishing Corporation.

Wang, L., Wang, S., & Murphy, B. (2005). Order-Sensitive XML Query Processing over Relational Sources: An Algebraic Approach. In *Proceedings of the 9th International Database Engineering and Application Symposium*, (pp. 175-184). doi:10.1109/IDEAS.2005.40

Wang, S., Vu, Q. H., Ooi, B. C., Tung, A. K., & Xu, L. (2009). Skyframe: A framework for skyline query processing in peer-to-peer systems. *The VLDB Journal*, *18*(1), 345–362. doi:10.1007/s00778-008-0104-3

Wang, X., Mueen, A., Ding, H., Trajcevski, G., Scheuermann, P., & Keogh, E. (2013). Experimental comparison of representation methods and distance measures for time series data. *Data Mining and Knowledge Discovery*, *26*(2), 275–309. doi:10.1007/s10618-012-0250-5

Wang, X., & Sukthankar, G. (2013). Multi-label relational neighbor classification using social context features. In *Proceedings of the ACM SIGKDD Conference on Knowledge Discovery and Data Mining (KDD)*. (pp 464-472). New York: ACM. doi:10.1145/2487575.2487610

Watanabe, K., Ochi, M., Okabe, M., & Onai, R. (2011). Jasmine: a real-time local-event detection system based on geo-location information propagated to microblogs. In *Proceedings of the 20th ACM international conference on Information and knowledge management, CIKM '11*, (pp. 2541-2544). doi:10.1145/2063576.2064014

Waterman, M. S., Smith, T. F., & Beyer, W. A. (1976). Some biological sequence metrics. *Advances in Mathematics*, *20*(3), 367–387. doi:10.1016/0001-8708(76)90202-4

Weigel, R. S., Lindholm, D. M., Wilson, A., & Faden, J. (2010). TSDS: High-performance merge, subset, and filter software for time series-like data. *Earth Science Informatics*, *3*(1-2), 29–40. doi:10.1007/s12145-010-0059-y

Wei, L. (2010). A tetrahedral data model for unstructured data management. *Science China Information Sciences*, *53*(8), 1497–1510. doi:10.1007/s11432-010-4030-9

Weiss, C., Karras, P., & Bernstein, A. (2008). Hexastore: Sextuple indexing for semantic web data management. *Proceedings of the VLDB Endowment*, *1*(1), 1008–1019. doi:10.14778/1453856.1453965

Westerstahl, D. (1995). Quantifiers: logics, models and computation. In M. Krynicki, M. Mostowski, & L. Szczerba (Eds.), *Quantifiers in Natural Language: A Survey of Some Recent Work*). Kluwer (Vol. I). Academic Press.

Westerstahl, D. (1989). Quantifiers in formal and natural languages. In D. Gabbay & F. Guenther (Eds.), *Handbook of philosophical logic* (Vol. IV). Reidel Publishing Company. doi:10.1007/978-94-009-1171-0_1

White, D. A. (1996). Similarity indexing with the SS-tree. *Data Engineering, 1996.Proceedings of the Twelfth International Conference on* (pp. 516--523). IEEE. doi:10.1109/ICDE.1996.492202

White, D. A., & Jain, R. (1996). *Similarity Indexing: Algorithms and Performance. In Storage and retrieval for image and video databases* (pp. 62–73). SPIE.

Wilkinson, K. (2006). Jena property table implementation. In *Second International Workshop on Scalable Semantic Web Knowledge Base Systems*. Athens, GA: Academic Press.

Wilkinson, K., Sayers, C., Kuno, H. A., & Reynolds, D. (2003). Efficient RDF Storage and Retrieval in Jena2. In SWDB (Vol. 3, pp. 131-150). SWDB.

Wooldridge, M. (2002). *An Introduction to Multi Agent Systems*. Chichester, UK: John Wiley & Sons.

World Wide Web Consortium (W3C). (2015). Retrieved August 20, 2015, from http://www.w3.org/standards/

Wu, P., Zhang, C., Feng, Y., Zhao, B., Agrawal, D., & El Abbadi, A. (2006). Parallelizing Skyline Queries for Scalable Distribution. In *Proceedings of The International Conference on Extending Database Technology (EDBT)* (pp. 112–130). Munich, Germany: Springer-Verlag

Wu, S., Jiang, D., Ooi, B. C., & Wu, K. L. (2010). Efficient b-tree based indexing for cloud data processing. *Proceedings of the VLDB Endowment, 3*(1), 1207–1218. doi:10.14778/1920841.1920991

Xia, C., Lu, H., Ooi, B. C., & Hu, J. (2004). Gorder: an efficient method for knn join processing. In *Proceedings of the International Conference on Very Large Data Bases*, (pp. 756-767). Toronto, Canada: Morgan Kaufmann. doi:10.1016/B978-012088469-8.50067-X

Xiao, R. G., Dillon, T. S., Chang, E., & Feng, L. (2001). Modeling and Transformation of Object-Oriented Conceptual Models into XML Schema. In *Proceedings of the 12th International Conference on Database and Expert Systems Applications*. doi:10.1007/3-540-44759-8_77

Xu, D., Yin, J., Deng, Y., & Ding, J. (2003). A Formal Architectural Model for Logical Agent Mobility. *IEEE Transactions on Software Engineering, 29*(1), 31–45. doi:10.1109/TSE.2003.1166587

Yan, G., & Eidenbenz, S. (2014). Sim-Watchdog: Leveraging Temporal Similarity for Anomaly Detection in Dynamic Graphs. *Distributed Computing Systems (ICDCS), 2014 IEEE 34th International Conference on*, (pp. 154--165). IEEE.

Yan, L., & Ma, Z. M. (2013). A Fuzzy Probabilistic Relational Database Model and Algebra. *International Journal of Fuzzy Systems, 15*(2), 244-253.

Yan, L., & Ma, Z. M. (2014a). Modeling Fuzzy Information in Fuzzy Extended Entity-Relationship Model and Fuzzy Relational Databases. *Journal of Intelligent and Fuzzy Systems, 27*(4), 1881-1896.

Yan, L., & Ma, Z. M. (2014b). Formal Translation from Fuzzy EER Model to Fuzzy XML Model. *Expert Systems with Applications, 41*(8), 3615-3627.

Yan, L., & Ma, Z. M. (2014c). A Probabilistic Object-Oriented Database Model with Fuzzy Measures and Its Algebraic Operations. *Journal of Intelligent & Fuzzy Systems*. DOI: 10.3233/IFS-141307

Yan, L., & Ma, Z. M., (2012b). Incorporating Fuzzy Information into the Formal Mapping from Web Data Model to Extended Entity-Relationship Model. *Integrated Computer-Aided Engineering, 19*(4), 313-330.

Yan, L., Ma, Z., & Zhang, F. (2014b). Fuzzy XML Data Management. Springer-Verlag. doi:10.1007/978-3-642-44899-7

Yanagisawa, Y., Akahani, J.-i., & Satoh, T. (2003). Shape-based similarity query for trajectory of mobile objects. In *Proc. of the IEEE International Conference on Mobile Data Management (MDM)*, (pp. 63-77.) doi:10.1007/3-540-36389-0_5

Yang, J., Fung, G., Lu, W., Zhou, X., Chen, H., & Du, X. (2012). Finding Superior Skyline Points for Multidimensional Recommendation Applications. *World Wide Web (Bussum), 15*(1), 33–60. doi:10.1007/s11280-011-0122-8

Yang, Q., Zhang, W. N., Liu, C. W., Wu, J., Yu, C. T., Nakajima, H., & Rishe, N. (2001). Efficient Processing of Nested Fuzzy SQL Queries in a Fuzzy Database. *IEEE Transactions on Knowledge and Data Engineering, 13*(6), 884–901. doi:10.1109/69.971185

Yan, L. (2009). Fuzzy Data Modeling Based on XML Schema. In *Proceedings of the 2009 ACM International Symposium on Applied Computing*. doi:10.1145/1529282.1529631

Yan, L., & Ma, Z. M. (2012a). Comparison of Entity with Fuzzy Data Types in Fuzzy Object-Oriented Databases. *Integrated Computer-Aided Engineering*, *19*(2), 199–212.

Yan, L., Ma, Z. M., & Zhang, F. (2014a). Algebraic Operations in Fuzzy Object-Oriented Databases. *Information Systems Frontiers*, *16*(4), 543–556. doi:10.1007/s10796-012-9359-8

Yannakakis, M. (1981). Algorithms for acyclic database schemes. In *Proceedings of VLDB* (pp. 82-94). Cannes, France: IEEE Computer Society.

Yao, B., Li, F., & Kumar, P. (2010). K nearest neighbor queries and kNN-joins in large relational databases (almost) for free. In *Proceedings of the International Conference on Data Engineering*, (pp. 4-15). Long Beach, CA: IEEE. doi:10.1109/ICDE.2010.5447837

Yao, J. J., Cui, B., & Hua, L. S. (2012). Keyword query reformulation on structured data. In *Proceedings of the International Conference on Data Engineering (ICDE)*. (pp 953-964). Washington, DC: IEEE Computer Society.

Yazici, A., Buckles, B. P., & Petry, F. E. (1999). Handling Complex and Uncertain Information in the ExIFO and NF^2 Data Models. *IEEE Transactions on Fuzzy Systems*, *7*(6), 659–676. doi:10.1109/91.811232

Yazici, A., & George, R. (1999). *Fuzzy Database Modeling*. Physica-Verlag. doi:10.1007/978-3-7908-1880-2

Yazici, A., George, R., Buckles, B. P., & Petry, F. E. (1992). *A Survey of Conceptual and Logical Data Models for Uncertainty Management*. *In Fuzzy Logic for Management of Uncertainty* (pp. 607–644). John Wiley and Sons Inc.

Yazici, A., & Koyuncu, M. (1997). Fuzzy Object-Oriented Database Modeling Coupled with Fuzzy Logic. *Fuzzy Sets and Systems*, *89*(1), 1–26. doi:10.1016/S0165-0114(96)00080-2

Yazici, A., Zhu, Q., & Sun, N. (2001). Semantic Data Modeling of Spatiotemporal Database Applications. *International Journal of Intelligent Systems*, *16*(7), 881–904. doi:10.1002/int.1040

Yeh, D. M., Li, Y. W., & Chu, W. (2008). Extracting Entity-Relationship Diagram from a Table-Based Legacy Database. *Journal of Systems and Software*, *81*(5), 764–771. doi:10.1016/j.jss.2007.07.005

Ye, L., & Keogh, E. (2009). Time series shapelets: a new primitive for data mining. In *Proceedings of the 15th ACM SIGKDD international conference on Knowledge discovery and data mining* (pp. 947--956). ACM. doi:10.1145/1557019.1557122

Yi, B.-K., Jagadish, H., & Faloutsos, C. (1998). Efficient retrieval of similar time sequences under time warping. *Data Engineering, 1998. Proceedings., 14th International Conference on* (pp. 201--208). IEEE.

Yi, B.-K., & Faloutsos, C. (2000). *Fast time sequence indexing for arbitrary Lp norms*. VLDB.

Yi-Cheng Tu, S., & Madnick, S. (1997). Incorporating generalized quantifiers into description logic for representing data source contents. In *Data mining and reverse engineering: Searching for semantics, ifip tc2/wg2.6 seventh conference on database semantics (ds-7)* (p. 329-335). Academic Press.

YingyuanXiao., Lü, K., Deng, H. (2010). Location-dependent Skyline Query Processing in Mobile Databases. In *Proceedings of the 7th Conference on Web Information Systems and Applications* (pp. 3-8). Hohhot, Mongolia: IEEE.

Yu, C., Cui, B., Wang, S., & Su, J. (2007). Efficient index-based knn join processing for high-dimensional data. *Information and Software Technology*, *49*(4), 332–344. doi:10.1016/j.infsof.2006.05.006

Yu, C., Ooi, B. C., Tan, K. L., & Jagadish, H. V. (2001). Indexing the distance: an efficient method to knn processing. In *Proceedings of the International Conference on Very Large Data Bases*, (pp. 421-430). Roma, Italy: Morgan Kaufmann.

Yu, Q., & Bouguettaya, A. (2011). Efficient Service Skyline Computation for Composite Service Selection. *IEEE Transactions on Knowledge and Data Engineering*, 25(4), 776–789. doi:10.1109/TKDE.2011.268

Zadeh, L. A. (1965). Fuzzy Sets. *Information and Control*, 8(3), 338–353. doi:10.1016/S0019-9958(65)90241-X

Zadeh, L. A. (1971). Similarity Relations and Fuzzy Orderings. *Information Sciences*, 3(2), 177–200. doi:10.1016/S0020-0255(71)80005-1

Zadeh, L. A. (1972). Fuzzy set theoretic interpretation of linguistic hedges. *Journal of Cybernetics*, 2(3), 4–34. doi:10.1080/01969727208542910

Zadeh, L. A. (1978). Fuzzy Sets as a Basis for a Theory of Possibility. *Fuzzy Sets and Systems*, 1(1), 3–28. doi:10.1016/0165-0114(78)90029-5

Zadrozny, S., & Janusz, K. (2006). Bipolar Queries and Queries with Preferences. In *Proceedings of the 17th International Workshop on Database and Expert Systems Applications*. Krakow, Poland: IEEE Computer Society.

Zadrozny, S., & Kacprzyk, J. (2009). *Bipolar Queries: A Way to Enhance the Flexibility of Database Queries. In Advances in Data Management* (pp. 49–66). Springer.

Zadrozny, S., & Kacprzyk, J. (2012). Bipolar Queries: An Aggregation Operator Focused Perspective. *Fuzzy Sets and Systems*, 196, 69–81. doi:10.1016/j.fss.2011.10.013

Zadrozny, S., Kacprzyk, J., & de Tré, G. (2012). Bipolar Queries in Textual Information Retrieval: A New Perspective. *Information Processing & Management*, 48(3), 390–398. doi:10.1016/j.ipm.2011.05.001

Zamulin, A. V. (2002). An Object Algebra for the ODMG Standard. In *Proceedings of the 6th East European Conference on Advances in Databases and Information Systems*. doi:10.1007/3-540-45710-0_23

Zemankova, M., & Kandel, A. (1985). Implementing Imprecision in Information Systems. *Information Sciences*, 37(1-3), 107–141. doi:10.1016/0020-0255(85)90008-8

Zhang, C., Li, F., & Jestes, J. (2012). Efficient parallel kNN joins for large data in MapReduce. In *Proceedings of the International Conference on Extending Database Technology*, (pp. 38-49). Berlin, Germany: ACM. doi:10.1145/2247596.2247602

Zhang, H., Korayem, M., You, E., & Crandall, D. J. (2012). Beyond co-occurrence: discovering and visualizing tag relationships from geo-spatial and temporal similarities. In *Proceedings of the fifth ACM international conference on Web search and data mining* (pp. 33-42). ACM. doi:10.1145/2124295.2124302

Zhang, S., Han, J., Liu, Z., Wang, K., & Xu, Z. (2009). SJMR: Parallelizing spacial join with MapReduce on clusters. In *Proceedings of the IEEE International Conference on Cluster Computing*, (pp. 1-8). New Orleans, LA: IEEE Computer Society. doi:10.1109/CLUSTR.2009.5289178

Zhang, W. N., & Wang, K. (2000). An Efficient Evaluation of a Fuzzy Equi-Join Using Fuzzy Equality Indicators. *IEEE Transactions on Knowledge and Data Engineering*, 12(2), 225–237. doi:10.1109/69.842264

Zhao, D., Zhang, Z., Zhou, X., Li, T., Wang, K., & Kimpe, D. (2014). FusionFS: Toward supporting data-intensive scientific applications on extreme-scale distributed systems. In *Proceedings of IEEE International Conference on Big Data*. IEEE.

Zhao, J., Hu, X., & Meng, X. (2010). ESQP: An efficient SQL query processing for cloud data management. In *Proceedings of the second international workshop on Cloud data management (CloudDB '10)*. Toronto, Canada: ACM. doi:10.1145/1871929.1871931

Zhao, T., Zhang, C., Wei, M., & Peng, Z. R. (2008). Ontology-based geospatial data query and integration. In *Proceedings of Geographic Information Science* (pp. 370–392). Park City, UT: Springer. doi:10.1007/978-3-540-87473-7_24

Zheng, B., Lee, K., & Lee, W.-C. (2008). Location-dependent skyline query. In *Proceedings of the International Conference on Mobile Data Management (MDM)* (pp. 148 -155). Beijing, China: IEEE doi:10.1109/MDM.2008.14

Zheng, K., Zheng, Y., Yuan, N. J., Shang, S., & Zhou, X. (2014). Online Discovery of Gathering Patterns over Trajectories. *IEEE Transactions on Knowledge and Data Engineering, 26*(8), 1974–1988. doi:10.1109/TKDE.2013.160

Zhou, Q., Wang, C., Xiong, M., Wang, H., & Yu, Y. (2007). SPARK: adapting keyword query to semantic search. In *The Semantic Web Conference*. Springer Berlin Heidelberg. doi:10.1007/978-3-540-76298-0_50

Zhu, L., Zhou, S., & Guan, J. (2007). *Efficient Skyline Retrieval on Peer-to-Peer Networks. Future Generation Communication and Networking (FGCN)*. Jeju, Korea: IEEE. doi:10.1109/FGCN.2007.115

Zloof, M. M. (1975) Query by Example. In *Proc. AFIPS 1975 NCC, (*Vol. 44). AFIPS Press.

Zois, V., Frincu, M., & Prasanna, V. (2014). Integrated platform for automated sustainable demand response in smart grids. *Intelligent Energy Systems (IWIES), 2014 IEEE International Workshop on* (pp. 64--69). IEEE.

Zois, V., Frincu, M., Chelmis, C., Saeed, M. R., & Prasanna, V. (2014). Efficient Customer Selection for Sustainable Demand Response in Smart Grids.*Green Computing Conference (IGCC)*. doi:10.1109/IGCC.2014.7039149

Zou, Q., Wang, H., Soulé, R., Hirzel, M., Andrade, H., Gedik, B., & Wu, K. L. (2010). From a stream of relational queries to distributed stream processing. *Proceedings of the VLDB Endowment, 3*(1-2), 1394–1405. doi:10.14778/1920841.1921012

Zviedris, M. (2014). *Data as ontology – storage, query and visualization.* (PhD thesis). University of Latvia.

Zviedris, M., Barzdins, G., & Rikacovs, S. (2013), *ViziQuer* (Version 11.26.2013) [Software]. Available from http://viziquer.lumii.lv/

Zviedris, M., Romane, A., Barzdins, G., & Cerans, K. (2014). Ontology-Based Information System. In *Proceedings of the 3rd Joint International Semantic Technology Conference, Revised Selected Papers*, (LNCS), (vol. 8388, pp. 33-47). Springer.

Zviedris, M., & Barzdins, G. (2011). ViziQuer: a tool to explore and query SPARQL endpoints, *In The Semantic Web: Research and Applications. Springer Berlin Heidelberg, 6643*, 441–445.

Zvieli, A., & Chen, P. P. (1986). Entity-Relationship Modeling and Fuzzy Databases. In *Proceedings of the 1986 IEEE International Conference on Data Engineering*. IEEE.

About the Contributors

Li Yan received her Ph.D. degree from Northeastern University, China. She is currently a Full Professor of College of Computer Science & Technology at Nanjing University of Aeronautics and Astronautics, China. Her research interests include database modeling, XML data management, as well as imprecise and uncertain data processing. She has published over 50 papers in international journals, conferences and books in these areas since 2008. She also authored and edited several scholarly books published by Springer-Verlag and IGI Global, respectively.

* * *

Paolo Arcaini is assistant professor at the Faculty of Mathematics and Physics, Charles University in Prague (Czech Republic). He is member of the Formal Methods Group of the Department of Distributed and Dependable Systems. He graduated and received a PhD in Computer Science at the University of Milan, Italy. His research topics include specification, verification and runtime verification using Abstract State Machines, and model-based testing. He serves as member of the program committee of international conferences. He published papers in international journals and in proceedings of international conferences.

Antonio Badia is an associate professor in the Computer Engineering and Computer Science department at the University of Louisivlle in KY, USA. He received a PhD in Computer Science from Indiana University. He has received, among other funding, the U.S. National Science Foundation CAREER Award, and has authored over 50 publications, including some in the top journals and conferences in database research. His interests include data analytics, data integration, and intelligent database querying.

Luyi Bai received his Ph.D. degree from Northeastern University, China. He is currently a lecturer at Northeastern University at Qinhuangdao, China. His current research interests include uncertain databases and fuzzy spatiotemporal XML data management. He has published papers in several journals such as Integrated Computer-Aided Engineering and Applied Intelligence.

Chongchun Bi is a Master student in Liaoning Technical University. His research interests include machine learning and recommender system.

Gloria Bordogna received the Laurea degree in Physics from the University of Milano in 1984. In 1986 she joined CNR where she currently holds the position of senior researcher. Since 09-2013 she is temporarily affiliated to IREA CNR in Milano. In 2013 she obtained the Italian National Scientific Qualification to function as full professor for the information systems scientific area. From 2003 to 2010, she was adjunct professor of Information Retrieval and Geographic Information Systems at Bergamo University. Her research interests focus on fuzzy logic and soft computing for the management of imprecision and uncertainty of textual and geographic information, Volunteered Geographic Information quality assessment, information retrieval and Flexible Query Languages, Decision support for Environmental applications. Since 2008 she co-organizes the special track on "Information Access and Retrieval" at the ACM Symposium on Applied Computing. She is in the editorial board of the international journals ACM SIGAPP – Applied Computing Review and of the Scientific World Journal, "Intelligent Decision Technologies", IOS Press. She participated in the European funded projects e-.court, Peng, Ide-Univers, and Italian projects among which the current ones RITMARE, SISTEMATI, SPACE4AGRI, CARE-G and SIMULATOR. She was a project reviewer of national agencies such as the Research Foundation of Flanders (FWO), the French National Research Agency (ANR), ERCEA peer reviewer for the "Ideas Specific Program, PE5 and PE7 - ICT, ERC Council Starting Grants". She co-edited 4 volumes and one special issue of the JASIST on the themes of her research activity and published over 40 paper in ISI Journals.

Soraya O. Carrasquel, Assistant Professor at Simon Bolivar University working in the Department of Computer Information Technology. MSc in Mathematics. Áreas of interest: Fuzzy Logic Context Awareness, Combinatorics, Ramsey theory and Zero Sum, Gender Studies.

Charalampos Chelmis is Research Associate at the University of Southern California Viterbi School of Engineering. He received his Ph.D. and M.Sc. in Computer Science from the University of Southern California and the B.Eng. in Computer Engineering and Informatics from the University of Patras, Greece. His research interests include big data analytics and mining, modelling and analysis of composite networks, and social computing, scalable machine learning, and information integration. He has over 25 publications in these areas in competitive international conferences and journals. He has served and is serving as a member of the program committee or reviewer for numerous international conferences and workshops. These include serving as PC member of the IEEE International Conference on Social Computing and as co-chair of the International Workshop on Scalable Computing for Real-Time Big Data Applications (SCRAMBL), which is held in conjunction with CCGrid. More information about Dr. Chelmis is available at http://www-scf.usc.edu/~chelmis/index.php.

Haitao Cheng was born in 1986. Since 2013, he has been a Ph.D. candidate at Northeastern University, China. His current research interests include fuzzy spatio-temporal description, fuzzy spatio-temporal ontology and fuzzy spatio-temporal knowledge management.

Jingwei Cheng is now a lecturer at the College of Information Science and Engineering, Northeastern University. He received his PhD degree from Northeastern University in January, 2011. His current research interests include Description Logics, RDF, SPARQL and Semantic Web. He has published in conference proceedings of DEXA, WI/IAT, ASWC and FuzzIEEE.

Fabiola Di Bartolo got her MSc in Computer Science degree from the Simón Bolívar University in Venezuela in 2013. She is a Computer Engineer graduated from the Simón Bolívar University in 2007. During her university period, she worked as a Research Assistant in Graph Databases and Semantic Web, and she was member of the Artificial Intelligence and Database research groups. Her main areas of specialization are Preference Databases, Query Optimization, Semantic Web, Artificial Intelligence, Data Mining and Software Engineering. She has over 7 years of experience working in service-oriented companies, as a developer, consultant and team leader. Currently, she is working at Inter-American Development Bank as Senior Analyst in the fields of Data Visualization and Analytics.

Alberto M. Gobbi is a Computer Science Engineer with a Master Degree in Computer Science, both titles from the Universidad Simón Bolívar.

Marlene Goncalves, PhD in Computer Science, Universidad Simón Bolívar, Caracas, Venezuela, 2009. MsC in Computer Science, Universidad Simón Bolívar, Caracas, Venezuela, 2002. Lic. in Computing, Universidad Central de Venezuela, Caracas, Venezuela, 1998. Titular Professor (since 2013), Staff Member of Universidad Simón Bolivar (since 2001). In the area of Preference Databases, she has 4 book chapters, more than thirty articles in extenso in arbitrated Proceedings, more than ten articles in indexed journals and more than forty advisories of works conducing to academic titles.

Maristela Holanda received her B.S. Electronic Engineering from the Federal University of Rio Grande do Norte – UFRN, Brazil, in 1996. She completed her M.S. degree from the University of Brasilia, Brazil, in 1999. She received a PhD degree from the University of Rio Grande do Norte – UFRN, Brazil, in 2007. Since 2009 she has been working for the University of Brasilia – UnB, at the Department of Computer Science. Her current research interests include noSQL databases, transaction concurrency control systems, geographical database and biological databases. Currently, she coordinates a project at the Brazilian Ministry of Planning, Budget and Management for developing the new management system for public employees from Brazil.

José Ángel Labbad is a Computer Engineer from Simón Bolívar University.

Zongmin Ma received the Ph. D. degree from the City University of Hong Kong and is currently a Full Professor of College of Information Science and Engineering at Northeastern University, China. His current research interests include intelligent database systems, knowledge representation and reasoning, the Semantic Web and XML, knowledge-bases systems, and big data processing. He has published over 100 papers in international journals, conferences and books in these areas since 1999. He also authored and edited several scholarly books published by Springer-Verlag and IGI Global, respectively.

Xiangfu Meng received his PhD degree from Northeastern university of China at 2010. His research interests include web database query and data analysis.

Ricardo R. Monascal is a computer scientist, specialized in programming languages, algorithms and logic. He earned his "Computer Engineer" degree from Universidad Simón Bolivar (Venezuela) in 2009, and his "Master in Computer Science" from the same alma mater in 2014.

Viktor K. Prasanna (V. K. Prasanna Kumar) is Charles Lee Powell Chair in Engineering and is Professor of Electrical Engineering and Professor of Computer Science at the University of Southern California (USC) and serves as the director of the Center for Energy Informatics (CEI). He is the executive director of the USC-Infosys Center for Advanced Software Technologies (CAST). He is an associate member of the Center for Applied Mathematical Sciences (CAMS). He leads the Integrated Optimizations (IO) efforts at the USC-Chevron Center of Excellence for Research and Academic Training on Interactive Smart Oilfield Technologies (CiSoft) at USC USC and the demand response optimizations in the LA Smartgrid project. His research interests include High Performance Computing, Parallel and Distributed Systems, Reconfigurable Computing, Cloud Computing and Embedded Systems. He received his BS in Electronics Engineering from the Bangalore University, MS from the School of Automation, Indian Institute of Science and Ph.D in Computer Science from the Pennsylvania State University. Prasanna has published extensively and consulted for industries in the above areas. He is the Steering Committee Co-Chair of the International Parallel & Distributed Processing Symposium (IPDPS) [merged IEEE International Parallel Processing Symposium (IPPS) and Symposium on Parallel and Distributed Processing (SPDP)]. He is the Steering Committee Chair of the International Conference on High Performance Computing (HiPC). In the past, he has served on the editorial boards of the IEEE Transactions on Very Large Scale Integration (VLSI) Systems, IEEE Transactions on Parallel and Distributed Systems (TPDS), Journal of Pervasive and Mobile Computing, and the Proceedings of the IEEE. He serves on the editorial boards of the Journal of Parallel and Distributed Computing and the ACM Transactions on Reconfigurable Technology and Systems. During 2003-'06, he was the Editor-in-Chief of the IEEE Transactions on Computers. He was the founding chair of the IEEE Computer Society Technical Committee on Parallel Processing. He is a Fellow of the IEEE, the Association for Computing Machinery (ACM) and the American Association for Advancement of Science (AAAS). He is a recipient of the 2005 Okawa Foundation Grant. He received an Outstanding Engineering Alumnus Award from the Pennsylvania State University in 2009. He has received best paper awards at several international forums including ACM Computing Frontiers (CF), IEEE International Parallel and Distributed Processing Symposium (IPDPS), International Conference on Parallel and Distributed Systems (ICPADS), International Symposium on Computer Architecture and High Performance Computing (SBAC-PAD), International Conference on Parallel and Distributed Computing and Systems (PDCS), IEEE International Conference on High Performance Switches and Routers (HPSR), among others. He currently serves as the Editor-in-Chief of the Journal of Parallel and Distributed Computing (JPDC).

Fabiana Reggio is a Computer Engineer from Simón Bolívar University (USB), Caracas, Venezuela, 2014. Her interest area is in database design and administration. She was Assistant Professor on databases laboratory in Simón Bolívar University (2014-2015). Big Data Diploma (2015). Currently she is working at Predictvia, doing researching on graph databases.

Rosseline Rodriguez. Master of Computer Science, Simón Bolívar University (USB), Caracas, Venezuela, 1995. Engineer in Computation, USB, 1991. She is member of the academic staff of the USB (since 1991). He is currently Associate Professor (since 2013). Currently, she is accredited in the Program of Stimulus for Research and Innovation as Researcher Level A (since 2011). She is currently Head of the Teaching Section of Algorithms and Programming Languages and Member of the Advisory Board of the Department of Computing and Information Technology, USB. In the last five years, she has eleven contributions in refereed Conference Proceedings, ten short notes published, thirteen articles in Journals Indexed, and more than twelve tutorials of degree works. Her research areas are Fuzzy Databases, Formal Specification and Software Development Methodologies. She was member of the Organizing Committee of the XXXIX Latin American Conference on Informatics (CLEI 2013) and the Second National Conference on Computing, Information and Systems (CONCISA 2014). She is a founding member of the Venezuelan Society of Computing (SVC).

Priti Srinivas Sajja (b.1970) joined the faculty of the Department of Computer Science, Sardar Patel University, India in 1994 and presently working as a Professor. She received her M.S. (1993) and Ph.D (2000) in Computer Science from the Sardar Patel University. Her research interests include knowledge-based systems, soft computing, multiagent systems, and software engineering. She has more than 160 publications in books, book chapters, journals, and in the proceedings of national and international conferences. Her four publications have won best research paper awards. She is co-author of 'Knowledge-Based Systems' and 'Intelligent Technologies for Web Applications'. She is supervising work of a few doctoral research students. She was Principal Investigator of a major research project funded by UGC, India. She is serving as a member in editorial board of many international science journals and served as program committee member for various international conferences.

Jane Adriana Souza is a Bachelor in Computer Science. She graduated with a specialization in Strategic Information Management from Federal University of Minas Gerais, UFMG, Brazil, in 2004. Her academic interests include database querying, cloud databases and NoSQL databases. She is currently a Post-Graduate Student at the University of Brasilia, and is working in a developer a middleware that maps a subset of DDL SQL commands and translates them to NoSQL databases.

Simone Sterlacchini obtained his Ph.D. in Geomorphology and Engineering Geology with a thesis on "Geographical Information Systems in Landslide Hazard Zonation" at the University of Ferrara (Italy). He joined CNR IDPA in December 2001 where he currently leads the scientific group on Multi-Risk Scenarios for Emergency Planning and Disaster Management. He is assistant Professor in GIS and natural hazard and risk assessment and management courses for BSc, MSc and PhD. He is Work Package co-leader within EU and international projects and scientific responsible of several national funded projects.

Leonid Tineo. PhD in Computer Science, Universidad Simón Bolívar (USB), Caracas, Venezuela (2006). MSc in Computer Science, USB (1992). Computer Engineering (Cum Laude), USB (1990). Member of the academic staff of the USB (since 1991). He is currently Full Professor (since 2007). He was visiting professor at the Université de Rennes 1 ENSSAT, Lannion, France (2009). Accreditation Program for Promotion of Venezuela Researcher Level 1 (2003-2010). Currently accredited in Program encouragement for Research and Innovation PEII Researcher Level B (since 2011). He held the position of Coordinator of Information and Integration of the Dean of Research and Development in the USB (2002-2007). He was Head of the Department of Computing and Information Technology USB (2011-2012). Currently Director of Development Professorial USB (since 2013). Head of the postraduade "Specialization in Game Design and Programming" USB (since May 2014). In the Database area, it has over sixty refereed contributions in memory of congress, about twenty articles in refereed journals, three book chapters, more than fifty short notes on conventions and over thirty AsoVAC tutoring work leading to a degree.

Qiang Tong is now a lecturer at the Software College, Northeastern University. His current research interests include RDF, SPARQL and Semantic Web.

Krisvely Varela is a Computer Engineer graduated from Simón Bolívar University in Venezuela. She is specialized in Database Design and Administration, also in Operations Research. She has over 4 years experience in Unix / Linux Systems Administration. During her university period, she worked in areas like Discrete mathematics. Now, she is working at Mageretailer LLC as a web Developer on an e-commerce system.

Marcos R. Vieira is a Research Staff Member with the Natural Resources Analytics Group at IBM Research - Brazil, since April 2012. His research interests include spatio-temporal databases, indexing and query optimization techniques, and big data analytics. Prior to joining IBM Research, Marcos received his Ph.D. in Computer Science (2011) from the University of California, Riverside, M.Sc. in Computer Science (2004) from the University of Sao Paulo at Sao Carlos, Brazil, and B.E. in Computer Engineering (2001) from Federal University of Sao Carlos, Brazil.

Hairong Wang received her Ph.D. degree from Northeastern University, China. She is currently a lecture at Ningxia Institute of Science and Technology, China. Her research interests include RDF data management and fuzzy querying. She have published several papers in national journals and international conferences.

Naidenova Xenia was born at Leningrad (Saint-Petersburg, the Russian Federation) in 1940. She graduated from Lenin Electro-Technical Institute of Leningrad (now Saint-Petersburg Electro-Technical University) in 1963 and received the Diploma on computer engineering. From this institute, she received her doctor's degree (Ph.D.) in Technical Sciences in 1979. She had been an invited professor at the University of Paris-Sud, ORSAY, FRANCE, Research Laboratory of Information Sciences under the head of Dr. N. Spyratos, March, 1991. In 1995, she started to work as senior researcher at the Research Centre of Saint-Petersburg Military Medical Academy where she is engaged in developing knowledge discovery and data mining program systems to support solving medicine and psychological diagnostic tasks. Under Xenia Naidenova, some advanced knowledge acquisition systems based on machine learning original algorithms have been developed including a tool for adaptive programming applied diagnostic medical systems. She received the Diploma of Senior Researcher from the Military Medical Academy in 1999. In 2010, she received the Award of the Russian Association for Artificial Intelligence for the best fundamental work in Artificial Intelligence. She has published over 200 papers on a wide range of topics in computer science; she is also the editor (together with Ignatov, D.) of the monograph "Diagnostic Test Approaches to Machine Learning and Commonsense Reasoning Systems" (IGI Global, 2013). She is a Fellow of the Russian Association for Artificial Intelligence founded in 1989. She works as a constant member of the Organizing Committee of the International Conference "Knowledge-Dialog-Solution". In 2011, she has been a member of the Program Committee of the Workshop "Soft Computing Applications and Knowledge Discovery" co-located with the 13th International Conference on Rough Sets, Fuzzy Sets, Data Mining, and Granular Computing (RSFDGrC-2011) June 2011, Moscow, Russia.

Changming Xu is currently a lecturer at Northeastern University of China. He has completed his Ph.D. in Computer Science from Northeastern University of China. His research focuses on machine learning and data mining.

Wei Yan's research interest includes XML flexible query and XML data management.

Fu Zhang received a PhD from the Northeastern University (China) in 2011, and is currently working as an associate professor in the College of Information Science and Engineering at Northeastern University, China. His current research interests include XML, description logics, and ontology in the Semantic Web.

Xiaoyan Zhang received MS degree at 2008 from Northeastern University, China. Her research interests include data mining.

Vasileios Zois got his Diploma in Computer Engineering and Informatics from the University of Patras, Greece. He's currrently a PhD student at the University of Southern California, pursuing a degree in Computer Science.

Martins Zviedris is interested in the Semantic Web, SPARQL, modelling, domain specific modelling, user centric queries, visual languages.

Index

A

Agent 500-501, 506-510, 513, 515-516, 518-519, 521
Agent Mobility 521
Aglet 515-516, 521
Algebra 25, 30-31, 39, 41, 43, 48, 132-133, 143-145, 157, 161, 275-276, 284-288, 290-291, 293, 440, 443, 464, 471, 487-488, 490
Analytics 364-366, 377, 380, 382-383, 391, 420, 543

B

Benchmark 26, 72, 158, 177, 187, 189, 394, 454, 461, 466-468, 487
Big Data 43-44, 364-366, 382, 391-393, 411, 416-418, 423, 437
BigTable 424-425, 437
Bipolar Preferences 439-446, 448-456, 459
bivariate bipolarity 439
Block Nested Loop 87
Breadth First Search 49-50, 79, 81, 87

C

Classification Reasoning 522-526, 529, 539, 542
Cluster 237-239, 241-246, 248, 393-394, 398, 407, 410, 423, 466, 469
Clustering 3, 143, 224-225, 227-228, 236-237, 239, 245-249, 254, 365, 374, 380, 466, 473
Composite Fuzzy Term 203, 221
Compound Fuzzy Term 203-205, 221
Conceptual Learning 522-523, 542
Conjunctive Queries 480, 483-485, 490, 498
Content Queries 375
Content, Spatial, and Temporal Query Conditions 249
Convex Hull 295, 304-312, 315, 318-320, 324

Coupling

Coupling Relationship 1, 3, 7, 10, 15-17, 19-21, 23
Cyber-Physical System 374, 391

D

Database model 126, 129-133, 138, 142-144, 146, 156, 415, 418, 423-425, 427, 483, 490
Data Structure 133, 160, 228, 230, 274, 277, 280, 330, 332, 372-375, 391, 393, 425
Deduction 146, 284, 505, 523
Deductive Reasoning Rule 542
Delaunay Graph 304-306, 313, 324
Depth First Search 49-50, 79, 81, 87
Description Logics 480, 482, 490, 498
Design 30, 80, 130, 135, 142, 145, 177, 201, 362, 380, 382, 394, 431-433, 464, 466-467, 469, 482, 489, 500-501, 508-510, 543-545, 549, 558
Diagrammatic 543-546, 548-550, 553-554, 557-559, 561
Diagrammatic Query Language 543-546, 548-550, 553-554, 559, 561
Divide and Conquer 56, 81, 362
document database 420, 422, 426
Dominance 64, 66, 74, 81-82, 303, 305-306, 308, 312-313, 316-320, 324, 334, 336, 362

E

E-Learning 500-501, 509-512, 514, 517-518, 521
Erlang 423, 426, 437
Euclidean distance 50, 52-53, 57-58, 64, 79-81, 258, 296, 298, 301, 307, 369, 374, 395, 397, 413

F

Focused Crawler 224-225, 228, 240, 247, 249
FSQL (Fuzzy SQL) 128
Fuzzy Catalog 101-105, 107-115, 119-121, 124-125, 128

fuzzy databases 89, 130, 140, 142-143, 146

Fuzzy Domain 93, 95, 97, 103, 107-108, 112-116, 118-121, 128, 143

FuzzyEER 88-90, 126, 128

Fuzzy Extension 128, 138, 141, 143, 145, 189, 201, 478

Fuzzy Logic 126, 139, 143, 145, 159-161, 186-187, 500-502, 505-506, 521

Fuzzy Membership Functions 504, 513, 521

Fuzzy Object-Oriented Database Model 138, 142, 144, 146, 156

Fuzzy Preferences Query 459

Fuzzy Query 139, 143, 156, 158, 161, 199-201, 204-213, 215, 217-219, 222, 439-441, 443, 453-454, 456, 459

Fuzzy Relational Database Model 126, 130, 142, 144, 156

Fuzzy Relations 89, 91, 138, 144, 200, 204-205, 207, 215, 221

Fuzzy Sets 88-90, 92-94, 126, 128-131, 135-136, 138-142, 156, 158-168, 174, 186, 199, 201-202, 222, 440, 473, 502-503, 521

Fuzzy Similarity Relation 94-95, 126

Fuzzy Terms 142, 145, 158-160, 168, 174, 177-179, 181, 183-187, 190, 200, 203-204, 221, 472, 478

Fuzzy XML Model 137, 142, 146, 156-157

Fuzzy XQuery 158-161, 167-168, 170, 172, 174-177, 186-187, 189, 201

G

GEFRED (Generalized Model of Fuzzy Relational Databases) 88, 128

Generalized Quantifier 33, 47

generalized quantifiers 41, 43

Geo-Temporal Analysis 224-226, 229, 236, 244, 246-247, 249

Geo-Temporal Clustering 224-225, 227, 249

Global Positioning System (GPS) 274

Good Classification Test 522, 530, 542

graph database 418, 420, 422, 427-428, 468, 470

H

High Coupling Architecture 172-174, 186-187

I

Indexing Structure 130, 274, 368

Inductive Reasoning Rule 542

Information Extraction 325, 328-331, 337, 339, 358

J

Java 173-176, 178-179, 189, 312-313, 423-424, 426-427, 437, 464, 473, 478, 515-516, 521

Jena 461, 464-466, 468, 478

John Stuart Mill 523

Join Query 274

JSON 420, 423, 425-426, 428, 437

K

Key-Value database 419, 422-423, 430

Keyword Query 1, 4, 21-23

k Nearest Neighbors 50, 392-393, 413

kNN Queries 392-395, 399-400, 403, 405-407, 410-411, 413

L

Light Weight Agent 521

Logical assertions 525, 539

Lucene 422-423, 427, 437

M

Machine Learning 79, 248, 364, 522-523

MapReduce 392-395, 397-398, 401-403, 405, 407, 410-411, 413, 421, 423-426, 437, 470

MapReduce Programming Model 392-394, 397-398, 401-403, 410-411, 413, 470

membership degree ranking 199, 210, 213

Minimum Bounding Rectangle 51, 54, 87, 305, 307, 372, 394-395

Moving Object 251, 254-255, 259, 274

M-Tree 325, 332-334, 341, 359, 362

Multi-Agent Systems 521

Multidimensional Index 49-51, 54, 87, 328-329, 359, 362, 374

Multidimensional Indexes 50, 56

N

Negative Preference 439, 459

Non-Spatial Dimension 301-303, 307-310, 312, 315-316, 319, 324

noSQL database 231, 416-418, 421-422, 425, 430-431

O

Ontologies 479-487, 489-492

Ontology 463, 468, 480-492, 498, 507, 518, 523, 553

Open Source 158, 173, 186, 423-424, 437, 464, 467, 478, 488, 516, 521

ORDER BY clause 53, 97-98, 103, 121-122, 126, 298, 448

Overview 3, 26, 129-131, 145, 254, 366, 372, 374, 461, 480, 543, 545-546

P

parallel query 392, 411, 469

Parser 102, 174, 189, 278

Pattern Queries 250, 253-255, 259-260, 269, 379

Pattern recognition 89, 342, 393, 539, 542

Performance Analysis 158, 160, 177, 187, 465

Periodic and Aperiodic Event 249

Positive Preference 439, 459

Precision and Recall (P&R) 362

Preference Queries 439-446, 449-450, 452-453, 455, 459

probabilistic ranking 199-200, 207-208, 211, 215, 218-219, 222

Progressive Skyline Algorithm 57, 324

Property Path 470

Pruning Criteria 49-50, 55-57, 64, 66, 69, 72-73, 77, 80-82

Q

Query Evaluation 49, 79, 81, 143, 187, 201, 251, 254-255, 257, 270, 291, 295, 461, 465, 468-469, 471, 486

querying 88, 126, 129-131, 134, 142-146, 156-157, 160-161, 167-168, 186-187, 201, 224-225, 228-230, 247, 251, 269, 274-275, 277-278, 280, 284-286, 288-289, 291, 312, 364-366, 372, 381-382, 415, 417, 419, 421-422, 430-432, 439-440, 451, 459-461, 464-465, 467, 469-471, 473, 478-480, 482-484, 486-490, 492, 543, 553

Query Keyword 1, 7, 17, 19-22, 24

Query Language 44, 48, 88, 132-133, 143-145, 157, 161, 172, 186, 189, 199-201, 206, 227-228, 231, 254-255, 257, 277, 290, 365, 378, 380, 391, 415-417, 421-428, 430-433, 437, 440, 443, 459-461, 464-465, 469-471, 473, 478, 481, 483, 486, 488, 490, 498, 543-546, 548-550, 553-554, 558-559, 561

Query Optimization 25, 29, 39, 43, 48, 219, 275, 429, 485-486

Query Predicate 217, 257, 274

Query Processing 29, 31, 39, 43-44, 47, 55, 135, 143, 160, 199-201, 203, 208, 218-219, 269, 313, 315-316, 392-395, 411, 414, 446, 460-461, 466-467, 469, 473, 489-490

Query Processing Techniques 29, 269, 461

Query Readability 555, 559, 561

R

Radio-Frequency Identification (RFID) 250, 274

Ranking Techniques 201, 318, 358

RDF Store 461-462, 468, 488

RDF Stream 478

Readability 543-545, 548-550, 554-555, 557-559, 561

Relational Database 1, 3, 5, 89, 100, 126, 129-132, 137-138, 142-144, 156, 160, 278, 287, 289, 379, 391, 394, 415-417, 425, 430, 461, 463-466, 482-483, 485-488, 490, 518, 546

Relational Database Management Systems (RD-BMS) 391, 483

R-Tree 50-51, 54-63, 67, 69, 73-74, 76-77, 79, 81, 87, 230, 296, 329, 372-373, 392-396, 402-403, 405-407, 411, 414, 489

S

satisfaction degree 143, 159, 187, 441-445, 448-451, 453, 456

Semantic Data 133, 488, 561

Semantic Web 428, 440, 460, 464, 466, 468-469, 478-481, 484, 486-492, 518, 544, 559, 561

set-oriented 25-26, 28-29, 31, 35, 42-44, 48

Set-Oriented Condition 48

Shape Based Matching 365, 379

Sharding 419, 437

Similarity Query 274

Similarity Relationship 89-93, 96-97, 99-105, 107-112, 121, 128, 138

Simple Fuzzy Term 203-204, 222

Skyline 25-28, 38, 44, 50-62, 64, 66, 70-71, 73-82, 87, 294-317, 319-320, 324-338, 340, 342, 346-348, 352-359, 362, 373, 378

Skyline Techniques 87, 324, 362

Social Media 224-229, 249, 417

social networks 224-227, 231

Spatial Dimension 299, 324

Spatial Index 249, 274, 394, 407

Spatial k-Nearest Neighbor Query 274

Spatial Range Query 274
Spatial-Temporal Index 274
Spatiotemporal data 146, 275-277, 280-281, 283, 287-288, 290-291
Spatio-Temporal Databases 250, 274
SQL Language 53, 128, 131, 297, 416-417, 421, 428, 430-432, 437
Stream 228, 380, 471-472, 478
Subquery 27-30, 32, 35-38, 40-41, 48, 432

T

Task of the First Kind 542
Task of the Second Kind 542
Time Series 364-383, 391
Time Series Management Systems 366, 379-380, 382-383
Top-k Ranking 24, 199, 214-215, 219
Top-k Skyline 49-52, 56-58, 60-61, 64, 71, 73, 79-81, 87, 317-318, 358
Trajectories 250-255, 257-261, 263, 265, 269
Translation Schema 100, 102, 111, 115, 119-125, 128
Triple Store 461, 463
Truth Degree 169
Tuple-Oriented Condition 48
Type 3 Attributes 92, 101-103, 119-120, 126, 128

U

univariate bipolarity 439

V

Visual 277, 280, 544, 550, 553-554, 558-559
Voronoi Diagram 304-305, 316, 318, 324, 392-394, 397, 401-403, 405, 407, 410-411, 414
Voronoi Polygon 401, 414

W

Web Database 1, 24, 468
Web Wrapper 362
Wrappers 330

X

XBase 278, 280, 293
XMark 158, 177-179, 183-184, 187, 189-190
XML 2, 6, 9-10, 12-14, 16-18, 25, 31, 43, 130-131, 133-135, 137, 139-140, 142, 144-146, 156-157, 159-161, 167-168, 173-174, 176, 186-187, 189, 199-202, 205-213, 217-219, 222, 275-291, 293, 415, 420, 468-469, 471, 488
XML Fuzzy Query 199, 201, 205-206, 213, 218-219, 222
xml:truth attribute 158, 174, 176, 201
XPath 2, 12-14, 145, 157-160, 173, 199-201, 206, 287
XQuery 2, 12-14, 31, 131, 134, 145, 157-161, 167-168, 170-171, 173-177, 186-187, 189, 199, 201, 276-277, 284-285, 287, 290
xs:truth datatype 158, 168, 174-175, 187

Printed in the United States
By Bookmasters